EMBATTLED FARMERS

EMBATTLED FARMERS

*Campaigns and Profiles
of Revolutionary Soldiers
from Lincoln, Massachusetts,
1775–1783*

Richard C. Wiggin

LINCOLN
MASSACHUSETTS
HISTORICAL
SOCIETY

©2013 by Richard C. Wiggin.

All rights reserved. No part of this publication may be reproduced, stored in a retrieval system, or transmitted in any form or by any means, electronic, mechanical, photocopying, recording, or otherwise, without the prior permission of the Author.

ISBN:
hardbound edition   978-0-944856-10-9
paperback edition   978-0-944856-11-6

Book and cover design by Erica Schultz: www.erica-schultz.com/design

Cover image: Moving quickly into the fields, the British flankers traded musket fire with the growing army of Provincials. Past the Mason house, the Hartwells', and the Smith farm, the battle raged. Past the Foster farm and the Nelson farm, the Redcoats retreated through Lincoln in growing disarray. The home of Josiah Nelson bears witness, in this 1998 painting by John Rush, to the running battle as it sweeps through Lincoln. (Courtesy of Minute Man National Historical Park)

Printed in the United States of America.

Second printing, 2013

Published by:
Lincoln Historical Society
P.O. Box 6084
Lincoln, MA 01773
www.lincolnhistoricalsociety.org

For further information, contact the publisher.

Contents

	Preface	vii
	Introduction: Notes on the Research	xi

PART I: IN DEFENSE OF OUR CHARTER RIGHTS AND PRIVILEGES

Chapter 1	Embattled Farmers and Tradesmen	3
Chapter 2	Incentives and Enlistment	21
Chapter 3	The War in Massachusetts Bay, 1775–1776	43
Chapter 4	Service to the Northward and Southward, 1775–1776	67
Chapter 5	Fighting for Survival, 1776–1777	91
Chapter 6	A Renewed Spirit and Renewed Dangers, 1777–1780	111
Chapter 7	The War Turns South, 1780–1781	137
Chapter 8	"To make a good peace…" 1781–1783	153
Chapter 9	Honoring the Legacy	157

PART II: MUSTER ROLLS

Chapter 10	The Army of the Revolution	173
Chapter 11	The Army of the King	449
Chapter 12	The "Detachment" of Unsubstantiated Claimants	457

APPENDICES: ORDER OF BATTLE

Appendix A	Units & Commanding Officers	473
Appendix B	Ages	505
Appendix C	Rank and Non-infantry Roles	512
Appendix D	Length of Service	514
Appendix E	Lincoln Residency	518
Appendix F	Identified Patriots of Color	521
Appendix G	Deserted, Captured, Wounded, or Died in Service	522
Appendix H	Pension Recipients	524
Appendix I	Burial Location	526

	Bibliography	533
	Index	551

In the early hours of April 19, 1775, an estimated 105 to 116 men from Lincoln were the first to arrive in Concord to assist in its defense. Hours later, they made up approximately 20 to 25 percent of the colonial force that engaged the Regulars at the North Bridge. These engravings, which were made by Connecticut militia volunteer, Amos Doolittle, following his visit to the site just weeks later, depict the arrival of the British in Concord, and the subsequent fight at the North Bridge. *In the upper drawing*, the British officers are shown atop Hill Cemetery, watching the Provincials, who have withdrawn across the river. A detachment of Regulars (*background left*) is at work destroying Provincial stores. *In the lower scene*, the Provincials are shown marching down the hill, taking fire from the patrol of Regulars assigned to guard the bridge, and returning the British fire. The Doolittle engravings are the only contemporary pictorial record of the events of April 19, 1775, and for the authentic, unembroidered detail with which the scenes are rendered, they are considered of inestimable value to historians.

Preface

It was a simple task that turned out to be not so simple: as captain of the modern company of Lincoln Minute Men, I had a list of Revolutionary War soldiers buried in Lincoln cemeteries that needed verification. The list was of unknown provenance and accuracy, but the Lincoln Minute Men had been using it ceremonially for forty years. Had these individuals really served in the Revolution? If so, where? Were they really buried here? And of equal importance, were there other deserving patriots who had not made it onto the list and were thus going unrecognized in our April ceremonies?

To my surprise, I found that reliable data about service by Lincoln residents in the American Revolution was scattered and not easily accessible. I had assumed (naively, as it turned out) that this information would be readily available, having been carefully compiled and chronicled by preceding generations of historians.

Lincoln, after all, is justifiably proud of its rich April 19, 1775, history. The minute men and militia companies from Lincoln had been the first to arrive to the assistance of Concord. Lincoln men had participated in the fight at the North Bridge, shoulder to shoulder with their neighbors from Concord, Acton, and Bedford. The fighting along Battle Road had boiled over, through Lincoln, leaving more casualties at the Bloody Angles and the Hartwell, Smith, and Nelson farms in Lincoln than had occurred at Lexington's Green and Concord's bridge combined. I was eventually to discover that in the eight years following the explosive outbreak of the American Revolution at Lexington, Concord, *and* Lincoln, Lincoln sons had served at nearly every major engagement and iconic venue of the war. But despite this proud heritage, compiled information about Lincoln's Revolutionary soldiers seemed to end with sundown on April 19, 1775.

So this work began quite by accident. In time, I found a couple of old compilations of Revolutionary soldiers from Lincoln. But material differences between these lists and the data I was generating from the records drove me to dig deeper. I found 52 new individuals missed in the previous lists, and in the end, I had to "de-list" 21 who had previously been credited with service, but for whom I could find no corroborating record. The picture that emerges is, I believe, a more complete close-up of the sons—and fathers—of Lincoln who became soldiers of the Revolution.

The composite picture is an interesting one. Among the myriad cousins, brothers, father-and-son combinations, in-laws, and extended family connections, an estimated 75 to 80 percent of Lincoln's service-age male population served during the war. Comparable data has been hard to find, but this appears to rank among the highest participation rates to be found anywhere in the 13 rebellious colonies.[1] More than a dozen slaves and free-blacks

---

[1] Most other estimates (typically derived using aggregate data) fall in the 20 percent to low 30 percent range. Differences in methodology may account for some of the difference in the magnitude of the estimates, but certainly not all.

provided service. In addition to the 62 members of the minute company, an estimated 43 to 53 others marched on the Alarm of April 19th as members of the militia company, as part of the command structure, and as volunteers. Another 22 to 26 Lincoln-connected individuals marched on the Alarm of April 19th as members of various other units from other towns. In all, at least 255 Lincoln boys and men, ages 11 to 68, participated in the war. And lest the modern reader assume that they all served as patriots, four of them—remaining loyal to their King—served on the opposite side of the conflict.

As my investigation progressed, additional questions began to present themselves. Who were these people, and how did they fit into the local community? Why and where did they serve? What were their experiences? What were their backgrounds? And what became of them after their war service? I have tried to preserve individual stories, and to present this information within the contexts both of the progress of the war and of the real-life circumstances that motivated individual behavior. However, all too often, the individual stories have been lost with the passing generations, and my focus in this work has always been first and foremost to identify and document those who served, and where they served.

Unfortunately, the reality is that some of the individuals in the picture remain out of focus. Others may yet be discovered in the mists of history by future researchers. My hope is that this work will inspire further investigation, and trigger further discoveries to the delight and respect of future generations.

Eighteenth-century records presented some interesting challenges. I quickly discovered a number of idiosyncrasies of eighteenth-century recordkeeping which generate some curious interpretive pitfalls for the researcher. To get the story right, I occasionally had to strip away errors or misinterpretations of previous researchers. These, along with the judgments I had to make in defining the scope and parameters of the work, are discussed in general terms in the Introduction. Many of the specific instances are explained in individual footnotes. Such is the nature of historical investigation that future historians may find errors or problems with my interpretations. I welcome any future efforts that collectively lead us closer to an accurate understanding of the historical record.

I have been most fortunate throughout this work in having invaluable guidance and encouragement from a number of very able professionals. Local historians Jack MacLean, Don Hafner, Mike Ryan, and George Quintal have been wonderful sources of leads for digging deeper and deeper into the historical record. In addition, they have served yeoman duty as sounding boards with which to discuss data, test hypotheses, and explore entirely new interpretations of the available evidence. I have appreciated their seemingly endless enthusiasm and enjoyed the many sessions during which, eyes sparkling, we pondered and debated differences in how to read various records.

Jack MacLean, in particular, deserves special recognition. No one knows Lincoln history better, and no one is a more competent and careful researcher. In editing my manuscript and assisting with illustrations, he tirelessly kept me on my toes, questioning my interpretations, challenging me to dig deeper into the historical record, and in many cases prompting me to rewrite whole sections of the manuscript. If the additional expenditure of time was sometimes frustrating, the result is a vastly superior product.

With similar dedication to historical accuracy, Lincoln historian Peg Martin also provided valuable guidance. Minute man Alex Hoar guided me enthusiastically through his family history. Jeanne Bracken, Barbara Miles, and Marie Wasnock at the Lincoln Public Library kept me enthusiastically supplied with archival materials from the town's vault.

Kathy Ludwig, at the David Library in Washington's Crossing, PA, John Hannigan at the Massachusetts Archives, and Leslie Wilson in Special Collections at the Concord Public Library helped source valuable records that I had not been able to find elsewhere.

Gail Hamel, Steve Humphrey, Ruth Hodges, Jim Hogan, Don Hafner, and Mike Ryan, who as fellow re-enactors, friends, and colleagues in the modern company of the Lincoln Minute Men, gave their valuable time to read and comment on my draft. From the Lincoln Historical Society, Connie Lewis, Mary Ann Hales, Palmer Faran, and Harry Hoover provided valuable advice about how to present and package my findings for publication. My nephew Ted Wiggin enthusiastically provided expertise to complete the collection of maps.

All of this came together through the patient professionalism of layout designer Erica Schultz, whose masterful work turned the manuscript into the book you are now reading.

I had no idea when I stumbled into this project that it would be quite the marathon that it became. The seemingly endless hours over many years spent researching, compiling, and fact-checking took much time that rightfully belonged to my family. I thank my wife Agnes and my daughter Allison for their encouragement, constructive suggestions, and proofreading, as well as for their understanding, forbearance, and love.

Finally, I thank generations of future readers, the anticipation of which drove me onward. My sincere hope is that future readers will honor the legacy of these Lincoln soldiers of the American Revolution; that they will continue to derive inspiration from the spirit of these men, and that they will rededicate themselves to the principles of Liberty and self-government for which these Lincoln men put their lives on the line.

Richard C. Wiggin
Lincoln, Massachusetts

Rarely is artwork considered reliable as historical evidence, which typically consists of written records of various sorts. But the literal rendering and precise—if crude—detail of Doolittle's contemporary engravings bestows on them the quality of authenticity which makes them invaluable as historical documentation. *In the top image,* the British troops are shown opening fire, at dawn, on the Lexington militia as the out-numbered locals were dispersing from their show of defiance on the Lexington Green. *In the lower engraving,* the timely arrival of Earl Percy's reinforcements on the outskirts of Lexington rescues the beleaguered Regulars on their return march to Boston, from the "galling fire" of the growing ranks of Provincials. As militia volunteers from Connecticut, Doolittle and his artist companion visited the sites within a few weeks of the events, collecting information, talking with eyewitnesses, making sketches, and posing as models, from which Doolittle created the engravings during the following months.

Introduction

Notes about the Research

The Army of the Revolution was a home-grown army, encompassing an ever-changing array of different types of units. Among these were the local minute men, and the provincial militia organized typically by town and county; volunteers, often in loosely organized "militia" bands in southern and mid-Atlantic provinces; the hastily assembled and short-lived Massachusetts Provincial Army; the Continental Army; state troops raised for Continental service; and state troops assigned to guard the coast. Privateers were also commissioned to prey on enemy shipping, supplemental to a fledgling navy.

Sources of Information

It should be of no surprise, therefore, that evidence of Revolutionary War participation takes many forms—from recruitment records, muster rolls, and payment records, to depositions, personal correspondence, and pension declarations; and from petitions for reimbursement for losses, to receipts for travel expenses to and from places of deployment. These records are found variously in Federal, state, and local archives, as well as in various published sources, historical societies, university libraries, private collections, and online.

The unfortunate reality is that many of the records and compilations of records are incomplete. Significant numbers of records from the revolutionary period have simply disappeared. Many were considered unimportant and discarded at the time, the pragmatic consequence of day-to-day life. Others, particularly official state and Continental documents, either never made it into the state and Federal archives, or disappeared during nineteenth-century housecleaning. Many of these—particularly those involving important historical figures—have found their way into private collections and subsequent publication. Others have simply been lost, probably for all time.

Similar holes exist in Vital Records as well: substantial numbers of eighteenth-century births, marriages, and deaths simply went unrecorded. The available Vital Records are generally fairly accurate as far as they go (subject to the care of the recording clerk), but they, too, are not comprehensive. Subsequent genealogical work and family histories can fill some of the holes, but many gaps remain.

Vital Records also contain occasional information that was added years after the fact by spouses or parents or other family members in their town of residence, rather than in the town of occurrence. These can create interpretive errors that can be difficult to sort out. As a rule, however, I have taken Vital Records at face value.

My work began with the "go to" source for information about Revolutionary soldiers from Massachusetts: *Massachusetts Soldiers and Sailors of the Revolutionary War*, a nineteenth-century compilation of Revolutionary War service records in the Massachusetts State Archives. However, while this is an indispensable source of data as far as it goes, it cannot in any way be considered comprehensive. The original source data it contains can certainly identify or confirm service by a given individual, but the reverse is not true: the absence of an individual listing or record in *Massachusetts Soldiers and Sailors of the Revolutionary War* is not evidence that the individual did not serve.

Accordingly, I augmented this source and found further elaboration and specific detail in the official records of the town of Lincoln (Town Meeting records, Treasurer's accounts, and Vital Records), in Federal Pension records, in the depositions taken in the aftermath of April 19, 1775, and in various other letters, journals, affidavits, memoirs, and accounts recorded by participants either at the time or in later years.

In the Lincoln Public Library, I eventually found three separate lists which purport to identify Lincoln individuals who served in the Revolutionary War. The first, compiled in 1890 by William Wheeler, appears in Hurd's *History of Middlesex County* (Vol. II, pp. 620–624). Another listing appeared in 1905 in *An Account of the Celebration*, the official 150th Anniversary history of the town. A third list from 1960 appears in wonderful calligraphy in the *War Memorial Book*, kept in the Historical Room under lock and key.[1] Each list contains approximately 168 names, but beyond that the dis-similarities are many. Errors, omissions, and misinterpretations make each list different and—unfortunately—unreliable. Further, the absence of source citations makes the information impossible to trace. In each case, I found it necessary to locate reliable primary-source confirmation before accepting the validity of any name on any of these lists.

Many of the primary-source records fail to provide identifying details or to list the individual's town of residence, often making attribution of a particular service record to a Lincoln person difficult. Spelling variations further complicate identifications, and I found myself frequently forced to rely on subtle clues or reasoned judgment to determine whether or not the service record belonged to a Lincoln person, or whether the soldier in one record is the same individual as the soldier in another record. Is the Phineas Alin, for example, who appears on a muster roll as a minute man from Concord the same individual as *Phineas Allen* who was living in Lincoln at the time, and who was later paid by the town of Lincoln for guard duty in Cambridge in 1778? I am inclined to think so, but I am less certain if this is the same Phineas Allen who appears on a pay warrant in Capt. John Robinson's Company in 1783. In such instances where uncertainty remains, I have generally included the service record in the individual profiles in Part II, but noted that the attribution remains uncertain.

Scope of the Work

As my work progressed, I discovered that it was necessary to define what constitutes a "Lincoln person." Could I justify excluding *Ephraim Hartwell, Jr.*, for example, a Lincoln son who had moved away from Lincoln a year or two before the war began, while including his four brothers who were still in town? What if, like *Amos Jones*, the individual had moved into Lincoln *after* the war, but had been unconnected to Lincoln at the time of his service? Should I include the individuals who were recruited from out of town to fulfill Lincoln's service quota, but who apparently had no other Lincoln connection? *Eden London* was very

---

[1] As this book was going to press, the *War Memorial Book* was being updated to reflect the results of the author's research, as contained in the pages herein.

Introduction: Notes about the Research xiii

briefly a Lincoln slave, but he had been sold out of town some years before the start of the war. Was his very tenuous connection to Lincoln sufficient to call him a Lincoln person? And if not, then how could I justify including *James Nichols*, a temporary Lincoln resident whose second thoughts at the North Bridge personify the human drama of April 19th, and whose real story I have finally teased from the record, but whose Lincoln tenure may have been equally truncated? There could be only one solution, of course, and that was to include anyone whom the record indicated had lived in Lincoln before, during, or after the war, or whose service had been credited to Lincoln.

Similar judgments had to be made to define what constitutes service. Obviously, the essence of this work was military service. But should this include carting provisions, or blankets, or clothing to the army camped at Cambridge? What if the individual went to Concord as an un-enlisted volunteer? Or is recorded as providing a man for service? What about un-enlisted medical personnel? A line had to be drawn. For this work, service is defined to include volunteers who served in the field during a campaign or battle. This allows me to include *Charles Russell*, the Lincoln doctor and prominent Tory, who tended British casualties at Bunker Hill. And it allows me to exclude an individual who sent another person to serve in his place, or who carted wood or hay from Lincoln into the army at Cambridge, as that could hardly be considered military service. On the other hand, the record of the eight Lincoln men who conducted a supply expedition to Worthington is strongly suggestive of a military operation (even without evidence of formal enlistment). As indicated by its inclusion on a 1778 report to Town Meeting of war-service expenditures, the Worthington expedition is included within the scope of this work.

Eighteenth-Century Names

The reader may observe that the spellings of many of the names in this work differ from spellings found elsewhere. Such is the nature of eighteenth-century records that spelling variations are many. In each case, I have tried to show the range of spellings that I have found in the historical records. My choice of a preferred spelling, in general, follows either the most common usage from the records, or if it can be determined, the spelling which seems to have been preferred by the particular individual.

In this, however, there is less science than judgment. It is apparent from the records that name variations bespeak not just of imprecise spelling, but also of transition. Clearly, *Gearfield, Wesson, Willington,* and *Peirce,* for example, were on their way to becoming *Garfield, Weston, Wellington,* and *Pierce*. Even among siblings, *Zechariah, Nathan,* and *Jonathan* seem to have preferred *"Weston,"* whereas their brothers *Daniel* and *John* seem to have been content with *"Wesson."* Accordingly, the reader will find the names *Wesson* and *Weston* listed together in Part II, as he will also find *Garfield* and *Gearfield*. While I have tried to be faithful to the spellings of the time, this work is not primarily about spelling. I have no expectation of being taken as the final word on whether *Abbot* should be spelled with one or two "t"s, for example, or on whether there should be an "s" on the name *Billing* or *Child,* or on a preferred form of any particular name.

Many eighteenth-century practices differ from those of the modern age, and these represent significant potential pitfalls in interpreting the records within the context in which they were created. Chief among these is the pragmatic use of the identifiers "Jr." and "Sr." in eighteenth-century names. While any record that does not identify an individual as a "Jr." or "Sr." can lead to imprecise identification, eighteenth-century practice frequently applied the designations "Jr.," "Sr.," and "III" pragmatically to refer only to living individuals; upon the death of one, the designations would slide to the next generation. When, for example, Nathan Brown, Jr., died (Nathan Sr. was still living at the time), *Nathan III* became known as *Nathan Jr.* Thus, records identifying Nathan Brown, Nathan Brown, Jr., and *Nathan Brown III* may all refer to the same person, or they may refer to separate individuals. The potential quagmire is apparent, and the appropriate context is easily mistaken.

In addition, the designation "Jr." was also used pragmatically to distinguish between unrelated individuals with the same name, the younger of the two being referred to as "Jr." Thus, when two individuals named *John Wesson* served together as minute men, the record identifies one of them as *John Jr.,* even though no record has been found of a father/son combination with this name.

Identifications are further complicated by the eighteenth-century practice of giving a newborn the same name as that of a previous child who had died. When attempting to identify individuals and their ages, I had to be especially careful to ensure that a record matched discernible details in the Vital Records.

Slave records pose other interpretive problems. While slavery as practiced in New England is still an emerging field of study, it is apparent that slavery in colonial New England was a very different institution from more popular conceptions of slavery in the antebellum south. It became necessary to acquaint myself with the works of Lorenzo Greene, William Piersen, Edgar McManus, and other scholars of slavery in the north. To correct popular misconceptions, I evaluated critically the evidence in the historical record and questioned unsupported suppositions or summary conclusions.

Slave records, unfortunately, are sparse. Accurate interpretation of the records that do exist is further hindered by the widespread (but certainly not universal) practice of slaves changing their names upon manumission. A few cases of this are explicitly demonstrated in the record. *Jack Hatch*, for example, is positively identifiable as the former *Jack Farrar*. In other cases, the preponderance of evidence and logic can provide reasonable confidence to connect two individuals with different names. Although lacking a "proof" document, per se, there can be little doubt that *Peter Brooks* is the same individual as *Peter Bowes*.

On the other hand, linking names can be fraught with error. More often than not, *Sippio Brister* is confused with Brister Freeman, even by otherwise careful researchers. The record identifies them unmistakably, however, as distinct and unconnected individuals: Lincoln's *Sippio Brister* was the former *Brister Hoar*, a former slave of *John Hoar*; Brister Freeman was the former Brister Cuming, a former slave of John Cuming of Concord. In general, I found it necessary to avoid supposing that records for individuals with different names could apply to a single person, at least without a compelling evidence-based argument consistent with appropriate scholarship.

Eighteenth-Century Military Practices

Service records, themselves, pose their own contextual issues. Recruiting bounties, payments for service, and substitution practices were vastly different in the eighteenth century than in the modern era. In addition, different rules applied to militia service and Continental Army enlistments, and the rules changed regularly during the course of the war.

Revolutionary soldiers were paid for their service variously by town, state, and Continental authorities. The applicable rules remain somewhat obscure, but I found that deciphering them was not germane to this study. Apart from a continuing curiosity about the subject, my concern was less the source of the payment than it was the payment as evidence of service.

Understanding what the payment was for, however, was material. The Treasurer's accounts of the town record payments to Lincoln individuals both for service and "for providing a man for service." These are separate designations, and must not be confused with each other. Providing a man for service was, in fact, the antithesis of providing service. It was recognized as an acceptable means of fulfilling one's military obligation without actually serving.

In a number of cases, and in combination with other records, it can be determined that the town's payment for service was made to a different individual than the one who actually served. In such cases, invariably the payment was made to a parent (or next of kin) for the service of a son, or to a slaveholder for the service of a slave, or to a person drafted for service who hired a "substitute" to serve in his place.

The town paid Widow Rebeckah Brown, for example, for service at Cambridge in 1775 and Canada in 1776. Obviously, the Widow Rebeckah Brown did not provide this service. Through a careful analysis of Vital Records, service records, pension records, and other transactions in the Treasurer's accounts, we can identify the Widow Rebeckah Brown as the mother of *George Brown,* who logically provided the service, and who was away in Continental service when the payment was made. Deacon Samuel Farrar, age 67-plus, was paid for service at Ticonderoga and with the Continental Army, which service appears to have been provided by his orphaned grandson, *Jonas Bond.* In another example, *John Hoar* was paid for service at Ticonderoga in 1776, Dorchester in 1776, Saratoga in 1777, and Cambridge in 1778, but at age 69 to 71, logically he did not provide that service himself. We can reasonably attribute the Dorchester, Saratoga, and Cambridge payments to matching service records of his son, *Leonard Hoar,* who was away in other service when the payment was made. The Ticonderoga payment, however, does not logically apply to service by either of his sons. We can only guess, consistent with other data points and with the mode of record keeping in the Treasurer's accounts, that this service may have been provided by his slave, *Brister.*

Later in the war, recruitment quotas were apportioned according to a system of economic classification, and some town payment records explicitly state that they were for service by a different individual from the payee (who appears usually to be a representative of the economic class).

Substitution was an interesting eighteenth-century practice that has disappeared in the modern era. Evidence indicates that this practice was fairly commonplace as a means both for individuals to avoid having to serve, and for soldiers having to leave the service before the expiration of their enlistments. Records of this, however, are anecdotal. We know that *Joshua Child, Jr.,* hired the slave *Brister Hoar* to serve for him at Saratoga because his name is listed on the muster roll, below which was added in a separate hand, "Brister Hoar appears in the room of Joshua Child Junr." Other substitutes, as well, appear to have gone to Saratoga in lieu of those drafted, but the record of this is less clear. *Edward Adams* tells us in his pension declaration that he served in Cambridge for a month as a substitute for

Joseph Peirce, then another three months for *Elijah Willington*. *John Barrett* says he found a substitute so he could return home to his sick mother. How many others found substitutes or served as substitutes, we can only imagine.

Historical Bias

Much quality history has been written about the Revolutionary War, and about the specific battles, campaigns, and events that occurred during the war. Many genealogical tracts (including family histories preserved in the Lincoln Public Library) identify individual participants and trace the family histories that give life to the story. The New England Historic Genealogical Society houses a preeminent collection of such works, as well. And as a compendium of Lincoln history, nothing surpasses Jack MacLean's *A Rich Harvest*. I have been happy to rely on many quality secondary sources to provide context and to fill in the details of various campaigns.

On the other hand, the quality of any historical material, including primary-source data, is dependent upon the care and circumstances under which it was recorded, collected, and interpreted. Even first-hand accounts must be viewed within this context. The depositions taken after April 19th, for example, were taken for propaganda purposes, not for historical recordkeeping. As historical records, they must be understood as being somewhat tainted. Similarly, Col. John Haslet's account of the action at White Plains and his disparagement of *Col. Eleazer Brooks's* militia regiment must be viewed through the lens of his insistent propensity to blame others in order to claim credit for his own command, more than for any objective clarity in the relating of events. As well, allowances must be made for information contained within the pension declarations. These were the product of 40, 50 and 60-year-old memories. They were often related by widows, second or third-hand, from stories overheard in the reminiscences of old soldiers. And of course, they were shaped by the need to conform to the eligibility and benefit requirements of the particular Pension Act under which they were filed.[1]

Such factors lead to much uncertainty and occasional mismatch and conflict in the historical evidence. In each case, particularly where the facts appear to be in conflict, my challenge was to balance discernible evidence with logic, historical circumstance, and context to arrive at a faithful recounting of the historical record.

---

1 The 1818 Act granted half-pay to all Continental officers and enlisted men, marines, and those in the naval service of the United States, if they were in need of financial assistance. A needs test was implemented in 1820, but neither the 1818 Act nor the 1820 Act extended eligibility to state troops or those in militia service. In 1832, eligibility was extended to cover anyone who could show at least six months of service, and any military unit qualified. Widows also qualified if they had been married to the soldier at the time of the war. Financial need was no longer a requirement. The longer the service, the greater the pension benefits, up to full pay for those who could show two or more years of service. The bias this introduced in length-of-service claims is observable in some of the pension declarations. *Abijah Munroe*, for example, omitted 17 months of militia service from his pension declaration because it did not qualify under the act of 1818. *Edward Adams*, on the other hand, strung together 14½ months of service (including 11 months consecutively) in his pension claim under the act of 1832, whereas the service records suggest the probability of somewhat less service with intervening gaps between the supposedly consecutive stints.

In 1838, widows who had been married to the veteran by 1795 were included. The 1848 Act included widows who had been married to the veteran before 1800. By 1855, all widows were eligible, regardless of when they had married the veteran (see Dann, *The Revolution Remembered*, pp. xv–xvi).

Introduction: Notes about the Research

Jeduthan Bemis is an interesting case in point. His pension declaration states that he served at the Battle of White Plains in October 1776, and that he was discharged at "the Cedars of Canada" in December 1776. Because the Canadian campaign and the New York campaign were conducted concurrently, this would not logically have been possible. Even the Commissioner of Pensions noted this incongruity. However, Bemis would not likely have been discharged in Canada in December 1776, as the army had retreated from Canada months before and was serving through November in the defense of Ticonderoga. If he was discharged at "the Cedars of Canada," it must have been before the retreat. But why? My investigation discovered a prisoner exchange at the end of May 1776, following a series of engagements at The Cedars. Suddenly, everything fit into place, historical logic matching the surviving service records. Exchanged prisoners were typically not allowed to return to the ranks. Allowing for a slight memory lapse in his pension declaration, we can reasonably conclude that Bemis must have been captured and exchanged at The Cedars, then discharged to return home. This explains how he was able, as the record tells us, to enlist in Colonel Brooks's Militia Regiment when it was called to the New York area in September.

Unfortunately, many other cases remain indeterminate. I suspect that *John Barter*, reported in one record to have enlisted in Col. John Greaton's Regiment to the credit of Lincoln, and John Bortor, reported in a 1778 record to have mustered into Col. John Greaton's Regiment, and *John Porter* of Lincoln, reported to have served in the Continental Army, may all be the same individual, for example, but the connective tissue is not quite strong enough to make that determination. Invariably, questions remain.

In short, this research has been much like doing an old jigsaw puzzle; the specific records being the individual pieces of the puzzle. Only by locating individual records among vast quantities of other records, then interpreting their shapes and colors, finding the proper orientations and placements, and fitting the pieces accurately into the puzzle, can the historical picture take shape. Often, the pieces did not fit together the way it first appeared that they should, and missing pieces invariably left frustrating holes in the overall picture. But piece by piece, through sometimes untold numbers of hours, a comprehensive image slowly emerged. And the remaining holes notwithstanding, I found considerable satisfaction in assembling the diverse pieces into a coherent group portrait of the fathers and sons of Lincoln who became soldiers of the American Revolution.

My hope is that this work will rekindle interest and pride in the 252 identified Lincoln men and boys who served in the Revolutionary Army (along with four others who served for the Crown) during the eight years of war that began with the bloodshed on the Lexington Green, the North Bridge in Concord, and the Bloody Angles in Lincoln, and ended only after the Treaty of Paris was signed in 1783.

PART I

In Defense of Our Charter Rights and Privileges

"...we are ready...to face the sword, the bayonet, or the mouth of a cannon rather than to be the slaves, dupes and fools...." The colorful language in this draft letter from Lincoln's Committee of Correspondence, in response to the Boston Tea Party, was reworked before it was approved by Town Meeting on December 27, 1773. Compare it with the final wording *(right)*, *"...we are ready...to face the formidable forces, rather than tamely to surrender up our rights and privileges...."* The militancy of this letter contrasts with a similar but much milder letter approved by Town Meeting eleven months earlier, on January 25, 1773. The earlier letter emphasized lawful means of redress: "...we hereby assure, that we will not be wanting in our assistance according to our ability, in the prosecuting [of] *all Lawful and Constitutional measures* as shall be thought proper for the continuance of all our Rights Priviledges & Liberties, both civil and Religious, being of opinion that a Steady united persevering Conduct, *in a Constitutional way*, is the best means under God for obtaining the redress of all our Grievances" ("Lincoln First Book of Records," January 25, 1773; italics added). While the acceptable means of redress seems to have become more militant by the time of the December 27, 1773, letter, the commitment to defend their rights and privileges, both civil and religious, was a constant. (Courtesy of Lincoln Town Archives, Lincoln, MA)

Chapter 1

Embattled Farmers and Tradesmen

Charter Rights and Privileges

"We trust we have courage and resolution," wrote Lincoln's Committee of Correspondence in the wake of the Boston Tea Party, *"sufficient to encounter all the horrors of war in the defense of those rights and privileges, civil and religious, which we esteem more valuable than our lives. And we do hereby assure, not only the town of Boston, but the world, that…we are ready to join with our brethren to face the formidable forces, rather than tamely to surrender up our rights and privileges into the hands of any of our own species, not distinguished from ourselves except to be in disposition to enslave us. At the same time, we have the highest esteem for all lawful authority; and rejoice in our connection with Great Britain, so long as we can enjoy our charter rights and privileges."*[1]

This extraordinary passage, contained in a letter approved by Town Meeting on December 27, 1773, leaves little doubt about where the town stood in the simmering conflict with the Crown, and it demonstrates that the principles at stake in the conflict with Great Britain were clear to the inhabitants of Lincoln long before the hostilities actually broke out. The importance the inhabitants placed on these principles is underscored by the fact that when the time came on April 19, 1775, more than half of Lincoln's households responded, many with multiple family members. In one exceptional case, seven members of the Baker family (five brothers, a brother-in-law, and their father) were all in arms at Concord.[2]

As patriot leader Joseph Warren wrote to a friend at the time the foregoing passage was written, there were probably not fifty men in the colony who expected that it would actually come to a fight.[3] However, by the spring of 1775, "numberless… instances… wherein small differences have been blown up to murder and death by the parties leaving the merits of the dispute and calling each other villains, rogues, scoundrels, cowards, and a thousand like

---

1 Letter from the Lincoln Committee of Correspondence to the Boston Committee of Correspondence, approved by the Town Meeting on December 27, 1773 (spelling and punctuation cleaned up as per Brooks, *Trial by Fire*, p. 6). The Committee consisted of Deacon Samuel Farrar, *Abijah Peirce,* and *Eleazer Brooks*; it is generally believed that the letter was largely the work of *Eleazer Brooks* (for individuals whose names are italicized in Part I of this work, the reader will find a service record in Part II).

2 Shattuck, *History of the Town of Concord* (p. 300), says there were 88 dwelling houses in town in 1784. He also gives the overall population as 639 in 1764, and 740 in 1790. The general stability in these numbers during this period is reflected in his comment that (over the ensuing fifty years) the demographic estimates "would not essentially vary from the above" (see Shattuck, *History of the Town of Concord*, pp. 309–310). Two of the *Baker* brothers were married (*Jacob Jr.,* and *James*), as was the brother-in-law (*Daniel Hosmer*). Whether the Baker clan is counted as one or four households, it does not change the observation that more than half the Lincoln households responded to the Alarm.

3 Brooks, *Trial by Fire*, p. 6.

> In y name of god Amen. we whose names are underwriten, the loyall subjects of our dread soueraigne Lord King James by y grace of god, of great Britaine, franc, & Ireland king defendor of y faith, &c
>
> Haueing vndertaken, for y glorie of god, and aduancemente of y christian faith and honour of our king & countrie, a voyage to plant y first colonie in y Northerne parts of Virginia. doe by these presents solemnly & mutualy in y presence of god, and one of another, Couenant, & combine our selues togeather into a Ciuill body politick, for y our better ordering, & preseruation & furtherance of y ends aforsaid; and by vertue hearof to Enacte, Constitute, and frame shuch just & equall Lawes, ordinances, Acts, constitutions, & offices, from time to time, as shall be thought most meete & conuenient for y generall good of y Colonie: vnto which we promise all due submission and obedience. In witnes wherof we haue here vnder subscribed our names at Cap-Codd y 11 of Nouember, in y year of y raigne of our soueraigne Lord king James of England, francs, & Ireland y eighteenth and of Scotland y fiftie fourth. An°: dom· 1620·|

The Mayflower Compact, drawn up on November 11, 1620—shown here as transcribed in 1646 by Gov. William Bradford in *Of Plimoth Plantation*—established the tradition of community-based self-government that still persists in much of New England to this day.

words…" had so polarized the dispute between the colonies and the mother country that peaceful resolution had become a fruitless dream.[1]

Actually, the fighting that broke out in Lexington and Concord on April 19, 1775, then intensified in Lincoln and raged into Menotomy[2] and Cambridge, was the inevitable clash of two systems with deep-rooted differences. Notwithstanding the common tradition embedded in 150 years of intertwined English history, fealty, and family connections—including cultural, linguistic, and economic ties—a fundamental difference existed between England and English America. For years, those differences had been sublimated to an ever-present threat to the security of the colonies—first by indigenous Americans, and then by the French. But the problems with the indigenous populations had been largely confined to the perimeter settlements by the early 1700s; and by 1763 the French threat to English America was eliminated by the defeat of the French in the Seven Years' War, the American portion of which we now call the French and Indian War. With security no longer an issue, the fundamental differences moved onto center stage.

Sprouting from the earliest seed of the Mayflower Compact, English America had developed a grassroots tradition of participatory government. England, despite the growth of the parliamentary system, was still tied to the medieval system of Royal authority, hierarchical class-privilege, and feudal structure.

---

1 *Eleazer Brooks* speech to the General Court, quoted in Brooks, *Trial by Fire*, p. 47.

2 Now the town of Arlington.

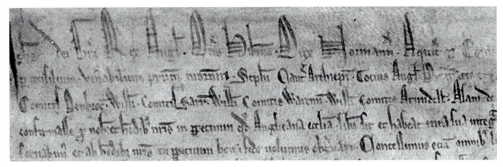

Written in medieval Latin in 1215, the Magna Carta is the cornerstone of the English legal system. Its provisions protect the rights and property of freemen from the arbitrary authority of the Crown, establishing the principle of due process of law. Shown here is a detail from one of the four surviving original copies. (The British Library)

True, English America had prospered under the hierarchical English system of colonial administration. But the fact is that within that framework, New England and much of the rest of colonial America was self-governing. The fundamental difference was irreconcilable: in America, governmental authority lay primarily with the people of each local community, and government was built from the bottom up; whereas, in England, it still flowed from the top down.

In New England, Town Meeting was the essential manifestation of self government (and it still is today in Lincoln and many other communities). There were other manifestations, as well. For the most part, in America judges were appointed locally, and locally-elected colonial assemblies had primary legislative responsibility over the affairs of each colony. Although administrative authority was exercised through an appointed Royal Governor, his authority over the internal affairs of the colony was in most cases subject to legislative review by a locally-elected assembly, which held the purse strings of the colonial administration.

Furthermore, since the Magna Carta in 1215, the 550-year march of English rights and privileges had long since solidified into a set of common-law guarantees against the usurpation of those rights. In addition to an independent judiciary, it was an article of faith that as British subjects, their right to a fair trial by a jury of one's peers was inviolable.

The Massachusetts Charter provided for local, provincial government in Massachusetts, and it guaranteed its people the same rights and privileges as if they had been born in England. But the locals were also aware of the limitation of such guarantees, as when just a few generations before, in 1684, King Charles II had revoked the original Massachusetts Charter. The issues had been multiple and complex, but in the process their forebears had lost their colonial assembly, the rights and privileges of land ownership, and their all-important right to determine their own taxes. And a number of local officials had been jailed for objecting to this Royal usurpation. Eventually, William and Mary had issued a new Charter in 1691, but now, 80 years later, the colonists still understood the essential lessons: not only that the Charter itself was inadequate protection against a despotic king, but also that there would be no one but themselves to defend these rights if they were again threatened. The importance of the Charter and its relevance to the local mindset in

The Massachusetts Bay Colony had been self-governing since the original Royal Charter of 1629 was carried to America in 1630. The original charter was revoked in 1684, but it was replaced with this new charter in 1691, which granted to all inhabitants of Massachusetts "all Libertyes and Immunities of Free and naturall Subjects…as if they and every of them were borne within this Our Realme of England." (Massachusetts Archives; transcription from The Avalon Project)

pre-Revolutionary Lincoln is demonstrated in the passage from the town's December 27, 1773, letter, which specifically mentions "our *charter* rights and privileges."[1]

Sure enough, shortly after this passage was penned by Lincoln's Committee of Correspondence, these Charter rights and privileges were, again, effectively revoked. In the early months of 1774, in the aftermath of the Boston Tea Party, Parliament enacted the set of laws that collectively came to be known by the colonists as the "Coercive" or "Intolerable" Acts, which effectively wiped out the 150-year tradition of self-government in Massachusetts. Town Meeting was severely curtailed and subjected to the Governor's approval. The General Court became subject to dissolution at the whim of the Governor. Judges were to be appointed from London. And colonists could now be sent to London for trial without the benefit of a jury of their peers. General Gage, the new governor, arrived in Boston with 3,000 troops, a show of force designed to restore law and order, and to maintain Royal authority.

Gage met with instant resistance when he tried to implement the Coercive Acts. These measures proved to the colonists beyond any further doubt that their charter rights and privileges as Englishmen were no longer safe, and that those rights would be lost unless they were willing to defend them by force of arms, if necessary. The principles at stake already had been clearly laid out and understood by 1773, even if few were really ready

---

1 Morison, *Oxford History*, pp. 116–120, 123.

to embrace the prospect of war. The Coercive Acts demonstrated the reality of what was at stake, and they pushed the colonists into active preparation for the probable reality of having to fight, even though there were few who wished it. This is not to suggest that everyone was in lockstep on these issues, or that there were no Tories in Lincoln. Of course, neither of these would be true. But the dynamic reality (at least in Lincoln) is that during 1773, 1774, and the spring of 1775, the sentiment of the town swung decidedly away from those having faith in reconciliation, and towards those preparing to defend their rights by force of arms, if necessary.[1]

So it was not surprising, when the dispute turned hot on April 19, 1775, that by and large, the residents of Lincoln and neighboring towns responded with a principled conviction in the justice of their cause and with a determination not to be denied their constitutional rights as Englishmen. Defending their charter rights as Englishmen was essential to protecting their homes, their families, and their way of life. The alternative was seen as effective slavery. The large Lincoln turnout on April 19, 1775, and for subsequent military service during the war, leaves little doubt as to their clear understanding and support of the principles at stake. These were principles so dear that they were willing to risk everything in their defense.[2]

The Alarm

As an agricultural community, Lincoln was no stranger to early morning activity. But in the early hours of April 19, 1775, the level of activity was unusual even by Lincoln standards. In the waning hours of the night before, ten British officers had hidden themselves in a pasture just off the Bay Road in the northern part of town, and their trap had already snared a trio of Lexington men sent to find out just what the officers were up to. Then, shortly after midnight, Paul Revere, in the company of William Dawes and Samuel Prescott, came riding down the road, spreading the Alarm on their way to Concord. In a flurry of activity, Revere was captured and dismounted. Dawes wheeled about and outran his pursuers back toward Lexington. Catching his captors by surprise, Prescott jumped his horse over a stone wall and escaped down a connecting farm road. The officers interrogated Revere, and realizing how exposed they were with the countryside arming around them, they purposefully escorted their prey back toward the safety of the advancing British column.

The morning quiet had been shattered. Having been warned of the British march by Revere and Prescott, 28-year-old *Nathaniel Baker,* who had been courting his fiancé in Lexington, sped home to west Lincoln, probably awakening townspeople along the way. From his home on the Bay Road, *Josiah Nelson* rode the Alarm into Bedford. Meanwhile, after regaining the Bay Road, Prescott stopped to warn the *Hartwells,* then he made haste to Concord. Mary Hartwell, in her turn, carried the Alarm to her neighbor, *Captain William*

---

1 See Raphael, *The First American Revolution* (pp. 59–168), for an excellent recounting of the almost instant transformation of what had been to this point largely a trade and tariff related dispute centered in the port towns into a populist uprising across all of Massachusetts.

2 Although there were certainly other factors to encourage enlistment as the war dragged on, those other factors played out largely within a widespread understanding about what was at stake. Historian David Hackett Fischer's description of the character of New Englanders is appropriate: "Once committed to what they regarded as a just and necessary war, these sons of Puritans hardened their hearts and became the most implacable of foes" (Fischer, *Paul Revere's Ride,* p. 155).

"God damn you stop," demanded the British officer. "If you go an inch further, you are a dead Man." The capture of Paul Revere along the Bay Road (modern-day Route 2A) in Lincoln shattered the early morning quiet on April 19, 1775. Aiden Lassell Ripley depicts the scene in this sketch for a painting that he never completed. (Courtesy of Unum Group)

Smith of the minute men. A hurry of hoofs passed the news from awakened household to awakening neighbor, and soon the Meeting House bell pealed the night air. Intermittent musket fire told those beyond earshot of the bell that the long anticipated—but dreaded—Alarm was afoot. In short order, the whole town was mobilizing.

From the Bay Road, three *Hartwell* brothers were joined by three *Mason* brothers. From the eastern edge of town, came the *Thorning* brothers, saw mill operator *Daniel Harrington,* and *Nathaniel Gove.* On their way to muster on the Town Common, one or another doubtlessly stopped briefly to await nineteen-year-old *Abijah Munroe* and his fifty–two-year-old father, *Benjamin,* or to link up with the *Peirce* brothers. From the southern part of town, *William Hosmer, Jr.* and *Sr., Abraham Gearfield, David Fisk,* and a whole platoon of *Parks* kinfolk clamored into action. *James Adams* and *Humphrey Farrar* sprang to ready themselves in the southwest corner of town. There too, Humphrey's cousin, *Samuel Farrar, Jr.,* having already begun his morning chores by moonlight and departed for the mill when the news overtook him, immediately altered his course to address the new imperative.

Closer to the center of town, *Nathan Brown* reached for his musket; his brother *Daniel* reached for his drum. *Jonathan Smith, Ephraim Flint,* brothers *Joshua* and *Daniel Child,* and the younger *John Wesson,* muskets in hand, ran out among friends and neighbors on their way to the Common. Within a couple of hours, following an equipment check, attendance taking, last minute instructions, perhaps some final drill, and certainly some anxious leave-taking, Lincoln's men-in-arms were on their way to Concord. After a short distance, near the outflow of Flint's Pond, they were joined by another group coming in from the western part of town: *Nathaniel Baker*, with six other members of the *Baker* clan, and probably three *Billings* as well.

The Lincoln men marched as two distinct units: a company of minute men and a company of militia. Minute men were fast-response troops, detached from militia companies during times of impending danger and organized into separate companies with separate command structures. This had been established practice since the earliest colonial period, although the term "minute men" was first used in 1756 during the French and Indian War. In October 1774, the Massachusetts Provincial Congress, meeting in defiance of General Gage, had directed the towns to begin forming minute companies. Lincoln's minute men appear to have been organizing and drilling as early as January 1775, although Town Meeting did not approve funding until March 1775.

Now, leaving their homes and families exposed, the two Lincoln companies marched together toward Concord before the eastern sky began to brighten. They would be the first troops from neighboring towns to arrive in Concord.[1]

Meanwhile, *Joseph Abbot, Sr.*, who ran a grist mill on the northeast edge of town, headed east into Lexington, possibly dispatched to gather the latest intelligence. He would witness the British musket fire on the Lexington Green.[2] Shortly thereafter, the "victorious" Redcoats, their column stretching a quarter of a mile in length, their bayonets "glistening" in the rising sun, kicked up the Bay Road dust on their march through Lincoln on their way to Concord.[3]

More than half of Lincoln's 88 households were represented in Concord that morning. Of the balance, there could scarcely have been a household that had not been awakened by the general commotion. And it is doubtful if there were any individuals left in town who did not undertake at once to hide their valuables and secure their families and property against the uncertainties inherent in the approach of unwanted and potentially hostile troops.

For three families in particular, the news must have been met with a quite different foreboding. *Dr. Charles Russell*, Lincoln's highly respected and most prominent citizen, must quickly have realized that this would necessarily be his last day in Lincoln. As an outspoken Tory, he had watched his standing in town diminish over the past year to the point that his carriage had been shot at. Before the day was over, he would move his family to the protective custody of the British garrison in Boston. His Lincoln estate (today known as the

---

1 That the militia company responded as expeditiously as the minute company probably had much to do with the immediacy and proximity of the threat. It should also be noted that compared with other towns, a somewhat higher percentage of Lincoln's militia company had joined the minute company. Further, the separate command structures appear not to have fully sorted themselves out by April 19, *Abijah Peirce* had just been appointed colonel of the regiment of minute companies (he had not yet even received his commission), but he appears also to have still been captain of the militia company. *Samuel Farrar, Jr.*, was lieutenant of the minute company, but he appears also to have still been lieutenant of the militia company.

2 Whether or not he reported what he had seen to Concord is a matter of speculation. *Abbot's* account, given under oath, leaves us hanging: "Our horses immediately started and we rode off. And further saith not" (Deposition of Joseph Abbot).

3 The image of glistening bayonets is attributed to Mary Hartwell, who is reported to have told her grandchildren, "The army of the King marched up in fine order, and their bayonets glistened in the sunlight like a field of waving grain. If it hadn't been for the purpose they came for, I should say it was the handsomest sight I ever saw in my life" (see Hersey, *Heroes*, p. 23). It is uncertain whether Mary stayed at home to witness the afternoon battle rage through her yard, or perhaps more probably she may have packed her young family into safer quarters elsewhere in town.

In Short Order, the Whole Town was Mobilizing.

Residence Locations of many of Lincoln's men-in-arms on April 19th

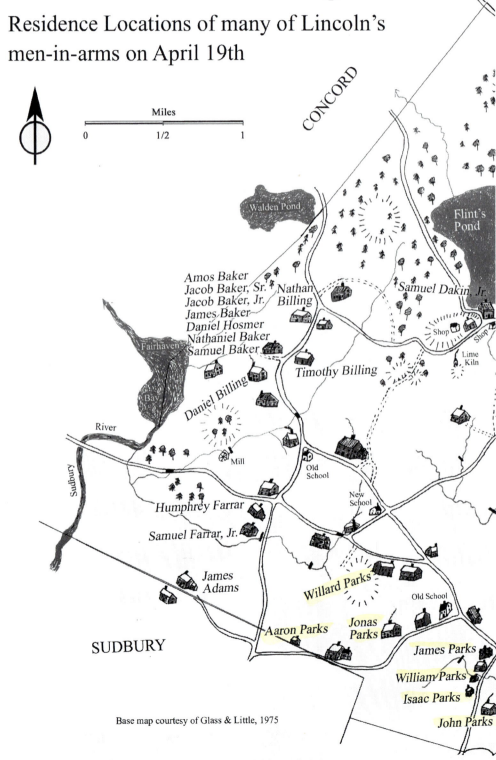

Base map courtesy of Glass & Little, 1975

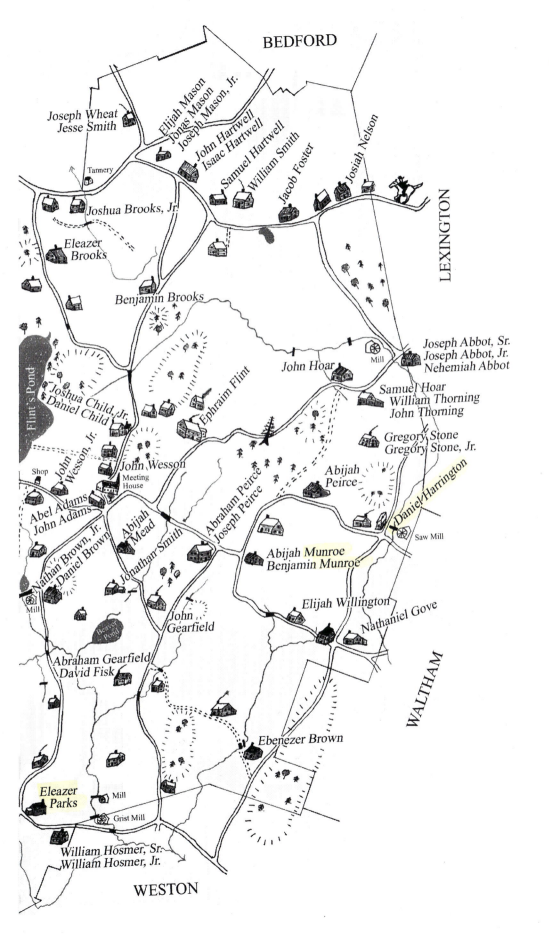

> **Accounting for Lincoln's Men-in-Arms on April 19th**
>
> Unfortunately, the exact count of Lincoln's men-in-arms at Concord on April 19, 1775, will never be known for certain, as the muster roll for the militia company has never been found.
>
> There were 62 minute men under the command of Lincoln's *Capt. William Smith*. In addition, *Phineas Allen*, from north Lincoln, served as a minute man in Capt. David Brown's Company from Concord. *Ephraim Brooks* and *Stephen Brooks* served as minute men in Capt. Charles Miles's Company from Concord. *Samuel Bacon* went to Concord in Capt. John Moore's Militia Company from Bedford. *Eleazer Brooks* (perhaps informally) and *Col. Abijah Peirce* were part of the regimental command structure. Another 14 Lincoln men show up in depositions and affidavits testifying to their presence at Concord. Other undocumented claims of having been at Concord have been handed down through various traditions.
>
> It is presumed that most of the others were members of the militia company, with the probable exception of *John Hoar*, who at age 68 was beyond service age and probably there on his own volition, either to support younger family members (a son and two sons-in-law) or to demonstrate solidarity with the Provincial cause.
>
> Ten months later, the militia company was called out again, to reinforce the Continental Army during the fortification of Dorchester Heights. This is the only other time that the militia went into service as an intact unit, but too many unknown variables thwart the effort to estimate the size of the Lincoln militia company on April 19th from the 59 names on the Dorchester Heights muster roll.
>
> It may be possible to come at it from a different direction, by bracketing a probable size of Lincoln's overall turnout on April 19th. By matching what appear to be intact April 19th muster rolls from 17 other towns with population data from those towns, ▶

Codman House) would later be confiscated and sold. Near the Russell estate, Capt. Joseph Adams shared a fearsome burden with the town's pastor, the Rev. William Lawrence, in the center of town. Their newlywed son and daughter (respectively), *Joseph Adams, Jr.*, and Lovey (Lawrence) Adams, were no longer living in Lincoln. But *Joseph Jr.* was known to have been passing intelligence to crown authorities in Boston. By the end of the day, he would be placed under house arrest for six months; later, after repeated additional arrests, he would escape in the night to the protection of the British forces occupying New York. He would eventually go to England, where Lovey joined him after the war.

Altogether, there are 82 men from Lincoln known to have been in arms that morning at Concord's North Bridge. Probably, the number may have been closer to 105 or 115. They were members of the two Lincoln companies, two Concord companies, and a Bedford company, as well as part of the regimental command structure. Another twenty-plus Lincoln men (mostly living outside of Lincoln at the time) mobilized on the Alarm as members of other companies, which were not at the bridge.

As the morning dawned, it was already clear that this would be a day like no other before or since in Lincoln.

it can be shown that an average of about 12% of the populations of these towns responded to the April 19th Alarm. There is, of course, some variation from town to town, but the numbers cluster between 10% and 15%. Without extensive study, it would be difficult to fully explain the town-to-town differences, but the towns geographically closest to Lincoln tend toward the higher end of the range (Bedford, 16.4%; Sudbury, 11.5%; Lexington, 15.9%; data is unavailable for Concord, Weston, Waltham). This higher average (14.6%) accords, as well, with other towns reputed for a strong April 19th response (Reading, 14.7%; Woburn, 15.1%; Danvers, 14.5%), and suggests a probable range of around 105 to 116 (13.5% to 15%) Lincoln men in-arms on April 19, 1775. This would yield a militia company at Concord (exclusive of those serving as minute men) of around 43 to 53 men (2 to 2½ dozen of whom remain unknown).

Of the twenty-two to twenty-four individuals who mobilized and marched on the Alarm of April 19th, but were not at Concord's North Bridge, most were Lincoln sons living in other towns at the time; some were not yet Lincoln connected. *Joseph Abbot, Sr.*, was at the Lexington Green. Three were members of two Sudbury companies; another was with a company from Framingham. They entered the fray near the Concord/Lincoln town line. Four more, serving in two Weston companies, caught up with the action in Lincoln or Lexington. *Samuel Hastings, Jr.*, with the Lexington Company, laid-in-wait for the return of the enemy at the Lincoln/Lexington town line. *Moses Brown*, with a Beverly company, would arrive to join the fight in Menotomy. And another eleven to thirteen mobilized and marched on the Alarm of April 19th with companies from Waltham, Watertown, Westford, Westminster, Princeton, possibly Medfield, possibly Townsend, New Ipswich (New Hampshire), and Mason (New Hampshire), but they would not arrive in time to participate in the action along the Battle Road.

[See Coburn, *Muster Rolls*, pp. 5–7, 11–13, 15–34, 36–45, 54–76. Population data is from the 1776 Massachusetts census (in Vital Records of the various towns). See also, Hudson, *History of the Town of Lexington (revised)*, Vol. 1, p. 477; Clarke, *History of Needham*, p. 532; Worthington, *History of Dedham*, p. 128.]

A Reflection of the Community

The Alarm that mobilized Lincoln that morning signaled the commencement of an eight-year struggle, during which a vast majority of Lincoln men of service age enlisted at least briefly in the Army of the Revolution. Not all who served, however, were of service age. *John Hoar*, who was age 68 at Concord, had long since aged off the service lists. There were also a number of individuals who participated before they reached service age. *Asa Adams* served at Cambridge as a fifer, and probably participated in the Battle of Bunker Hill—at age 15. Similarly, *Leonard Parks* was a fifer at Bunker Hill at age 14. *Peter Nelson* was at Saratoga at age 14, and he served again in the Hudson Valley before turning 16. *Joseph Nixon* fifed camp routines at Cambridge and battle commands on Bunker Hill as an 11-year old.

Lincoln's rural character is reflected in this undated view of Elisha Gearfield's farm. It was one of three Gearfield homes that stood in Lincoln during the Revolution. Like other Lincoln extended families, the Gearfields worked the land. Elisha also operated a saw mill near the Weston town line. In 1776, at age 48, he answered the call for service at Ticonderoga. Three other Gearfields and two Gearfield in-laws served on the April 19th Alarm and at other venues of the war. The family also spawned a future descendent who became the 20th President of the United States, James A. Garfield. (Courtesy of Lincoln Town Archives, Lincoln, MA)

Brothers *Aaron* and *Joseph Parker* were of impressionable ages (seven and nine) when the war broke out. No doubt they watched wistfully as their neighbors went off to fight. One can imagine their fascination with the stories told by returning soldiers, and one can almost picture their wide-eyed dreams of adventure and glory. Their father was a cooper, and quite possibly the family income may have suffered from the economic depredations of the war. *Joseph* must have been green with envy when his brother *Aaron* seized an opportunity to enlist in the Continental Army in 1781 at age 15 (still eight months shy of his 16th birthday). Three months later, *Joseph* seized his opportunity and also enlisted in the Continental Army. The enlistment record lists his age as 16; in fact he was only 13. Instinctively, one presumes that to pass for a 16-year old, he must have been a strapping boy, big for his age. But it is hard to imagine that he fooled very many people. He measured in at only 4 feet, 10 inches high.

Nor should it be assumed that everyone from Lincoln served on the patriot side. After fleeing Lincoln for the safety of the British garrison in Boston, *Dr. Charles Russell* tended the British casualties at the Battle of Bunker Hill. *Joseph Adams, Jr.*, escaped repeated arrests in Townsend where he had settled, went to New York, and there joined a loyalist militia regiment. Later, he served in the Royal Navy as a surgeon and surgeon's mate. Neither ever set foot in Lincoln again.

Nor did the *Cutler* brothers, *Ebenezer Jr.*, and *Zaccheus*. *Ebenezer Cutler, Jr.*, was arrested in Northborough as "an avowed enemy of his country," but he was allowed to go to Boston without his effects. There he joined a loyalist regiment and served with the British army in New York, New Jersey, and South Carolina. *Zaccheus Cutler*, having "proved himself inimical to his country," fled to Boston, where he served garrison duty as a lieutenant. Later, he served with the British army at New York before being lost at sea in 1780.

Lincoln's Army of the Revolution reflected the makeup of the community: farmers, housewrights, coopers, and cordwainers. There were tanners, mill operators, woodworkers, and innkeepers; also merchants, blacksmiths, laborers, stonemasons, and carpenters. They cut across social, economic, and racial lines to the extent that it would be utterly impossible to identify or profile a "typical" Lincoln soldier of the Revolution.

For example:

- *Moses Brown*, who had grown up in Lincoln, was a former Lincoln school teacher turned merchant in Beverly who was well on his way to economic and social prominence.
- *Benjamin Cleaveland* was a native of southeastern Massachusetts, living in Boston when he enlisted in the Continental Army to the credit of Lincoln. He enlisted in another Continental unit at the same time (a common scam to collect the enlistment bounty twice), then he fathered a child out of wedlock. He did eventually marry the mother, six months after the child was born.
- *Peter Brooks* was a slave, trained as a cordwainer, who gained his freedom through his war service.
- *William Lawrence, Jr.*, the son of the town's minister and brother-in-law of Loyalist *Joseph Adams, Jr.*, was a storekeeper who reportedly developed a serious drinking problem.
- *Artemas Reed* was a stonemason and farmer, a relative newcomer to Lincoln, who moved his family out of Lincoln during the war between stints in his otherwise almost continuous service throughout the war.

Many were town fathers and members of Lincoln's leading families. *Deacon Joshua Brooks, Abijah Peirce, Edmond Wheeler*, and *Aaron Brooks* were among those who had served as Selectmen. Many others had served terms in a variety of other official town positions. *William Smith, Timothy Brooks, John Hoar, Samuel Farrar, Jr.*, and perhaps *John Adams* were among the town's largest landowners.[1] At the other end of the spectrum were the "Negro servants" and free African-Americans: *Salem Middlesex, Cuff Hoar, Peter Oliver*, and others. *Brister Hoar* was hired out by his owner, *John Hoar*, to serve at Saratoga for *Joshua Child*.

---

1 MacLean, *A Rich Harvest*, pp. 134, 154.

Peter Nelson served at Saratoga and in the Hudson Valley by the time he turned age 16; his owner, 49-year-old *Josiah Nelson,* served at Cambridge and possibly at Ticonderoga.

Five sons of wealthy farmer and tavern-keeper Ephraim Hartwell served repeated stints during the war. So too did *Phineas Allen,* a landless farmer, and *Solomon Whitney,* who appears with his family to have been perpetually supported by the town. *Abner Mathis* and *Noah Parkhurst* had been "warned out" by town officials (commonly indicating no reliable means of support) when they had moved to Lincoln. *James Nichols* was an itinerant. All provided substantial service for the patriot cause.

There were at least a dozen father and son combinations among those who served in the war. More often than not, they served separate stints, but at Concord alone, *John* and *Samuel Hoar, William Hosmer* and *William Hosmer, Jr., Benjamin* and *Abijah Munroe, Gregory Stone* and *Gregory Stone, Jr.,* and *Jacob Baker* with his five sons and son-in-law were all in-arms together. A few months later, we find *Ephraim Brooks* and *Ephraim Brooks, Jr.,* shoulder to shoulder at Dorchester Heights.

On the other hand, this was the war that split apart Lincoln families. Two of Capt. Joseph Adams's sons were Tories who went to England and Canada, while a third son, *Nathan,* may have served faithfully at Ticonderoga and in the Continental Army. *Daniel Brown* served at Concord, Dorchester Heights, New York, and Saratoga, mostly alongside his brother *Nathan,* after which it appears that he may have changed loyalties and been prevented from returning home. *Joseph Wheat* served at Concord, Cambridge, and Dorchester Heights before enlisting in the Continental Army, while two of his sisters remained loyal to the Crown and left the country as "friend[s] to the Enemies of this Continent." Rev. William Lawrence's loyalties, already sufficiently suspect for him to have been prevented from preaching one Sunday, must certainly have been further questioned by the marriage of his daughter, Lovey, to an outspoken Tory. After the war broke out, one of his sons served three years in the Continental Army, while another son fled the country as a loyalist. His son-in-law also fled, and after the war, when Lovey left Lincoln to join her exiled husband, a third son accompanied her to England, also never to return.[1]

Individual Stories

Not surprisingly, the individual stories are as varied as the DNA and the personal experiences of the individuals themselves. *Joshua Child* served as a minute man on April 19, 1775, along with his brother, Daniel. Ten months later, he marched with the militia company to Dorchester Heights. After digging themselves in, they waited five days for the British to attack, in what would almost certainly have been a reprise of the battle on Bunker Hill. When the attack never came, the men from Lincoln were released to return home. Perhaps this had been enough excitement for Joshua, because after being drafted for service 18 months later, to help check Burgoyne's advance down the Upper Hudson Valley from Canada, he thought better of it, and arranged at the last minute for *Brister Hoar* to serve in his place. Brister was a slave belonging to *John Hoar,* who is known to have hired

---

[1] Lovey's husband *Joseph Adams, Jr.,* was already living in Townsend when they were married in September 1774. After he fled to New York in 1777, she had no means of supporting herself, and was reported as being "destitute of the necessities of life." She is presumed to have moved back to live with her parents in Lincoln, before eventually sailing for England with her younger brother in 1784.

Chapter 1: Embattled Farmers and Tradesmen

William Smith acquired his Lincoln home through his wife, Catherine Louisa. Smith was new to town, but when his neighbors elected him captain of the minute company, they may have been influenced by his previous involvement with the Sons of Liberty in Boston and the fact that he was the brother-in-law of provincial leader John Adams. He also appeared to be fairly prosperous, having a substantial Lincoln farmstead. However, because of his drinking and spendthrift ways, he actually did not own it. Even before he settled in town, William mortgaged the property to his father to pay off his debts, and the following year his father acquired title to the property. After William abandoned his family in the early 1780s, his father provided for Catherine Louisa and the children to remain on the farm. (Hersey, *Heroes*)

out his slaves from time to time. We can only wonder how much Joshua paid John Hoar for Brister's service. For his part, Brister had already served at least one previous stint, and may subsequently have served again the following year. He eventually secured his freedom, changed his name to *Sippio Brister,* and remained in Lincoln until he died in 1820. His grave is the only marked grave in town for a former slave, and the modern Lincoln Minute Men honor his service by decorating the grave each April.

Minute man *Capt. William Smith* was appointed captain of a company in the Massachusetts Provincial Army after April 19th, but after failing to take the field with his company at Bunker Hill, his military career stagnated. Unable to obtain a commission as a captain in the Continental Army (despite the appeals made on his behalf by his politically powerful relatives), he became a privateer in 1777, going to sea as a captain of marines. After a lucrative season preying on British shipping, his luck ran out. He was captured by a British warship and imprisoned at Halifax before being repatriated in a prisoner exchange. He never held another command. His debts and drinking problem eventually overwhelmed him and, his life spinning out of control, he abandoned his family. He eventually ended up and died on skid row either in New York or in Philadelphia.

His neighbor, *Jonas Hartwell,* had four brothers who were in arms on April 19th, and possibly he may also have been at Concord himself. He entered Harvard a year later, but appears to have taken repeated leaves of absence from his studies for "nervous disorders." He probably used the time for military service, instead, as he served both at Dorchester and in the Continental Army during this time. Despite his multiple leaves of absence, he obtained both an undergraduate degree and a graduate degree by the war's end. A few years later, visiting Bilbao, Spain, as a merchant, he was imprisoned and poisoned to death at the hands of the Spanish Inquisition.

According to tradition, *Leonard Parks* was a fifer at Concord at age 14. Subsequently, he is reputed to have participated in the battles of Bunker Hill, Trenton, Princeton, Brandywine, and Saratoga, all before he turned age 18. After the war, it is reported that he loved to entertain his Cambridgeport neighbors with his fifing, which he did until he died many years later. However, it is difficult to reconcile his having been at several of the battles so claimed. One suspects that he may have enjoyed entertaining his neighbors with stories of his war service as much as with his fifing, and that he may also have been quite adept at embellishing his stories for maximum entertainment value.

After incidental service around Boston, *Edward Adams* went to sea as a privateer. He had been at sea for a while, when their 14-gun brigantine encountered the British frigate *Milford,* which carried twice as many guns as they had. The *Milford* gave chase. For four hours they tried to escape, getting pretty badly beaten up. Several were killed in the action; others drowned. Toward evening and in flames, they were run onto the beach at Chatham, the survivors scattering in barges, by swimming, and across the sand. A couple of weeks later, he was back in service—this time remaining on terra-firma.

Daniel Brooks was age 10 on April 19, 1775, when the fighting broke out and raged through Lincoln, not far from his home. One can imagine excitement and curiosity getting the better of him, and imagine him sneaking through the woods or running across the field to get as close as he dared, perhaps peering over a stone wall to witness the action and experience the danger. According to family tradition, he defied his mother's insistent command to stay away, and he became a spectator of the fight. Six years later, at age 17, he enlisted in the Continental Army and served in the Hudson Valley. After three months, the war winding down in the aftermath of Yorktown, he was discharged. According to family tradition, he began walking home, penniless because he had not been paid. It was a difficult journey, and without money for food, he became hungry and sick. Finally, exhausted, starving, and ready to die, he sat down on a doorstep, unable to go any further. Inside was a kindly family who came to his rescue. They took him in, fed and nursed him back to health, and he was able to continue his journey home.

James Nichols, evidently a young itinerant laborer recently arrived from England, went to Concord with Lincoln's men-in-arms, but he got cold feet and left before the fighting occurred. Subsequently he served at Bunker Hill, and during the British evacuation of Boston. He served at Dorchester and in the Continental Army, evidently changing his residence between stints from Lincoln to Weston to Acton. After eight months in the Continental Army, he deserted, but he appears to have returned to service a short time later with a unit guarding Burgoyne's troops, who were being held as prisoners-of-war at Cambridge. He appears to have continued his itinerant ways, as he left no further trail in any of the nearby towns.

Tilly Mead answered the April 19th Alarm with a Watertown company, then stayed on and served at Cambridge. He survived the Battle of Bunker Hill, only to chop up his knee with an axe a month later. The wound must have been significant, as there is a record of liquor being requisitioned from the Commissary for him because of it. But it does not appear to have inhibited his continuing service. He remained in service for another 18 months, reenlisting twice, and serving on the relief expedition to Canada, at Ticonderoga, in New Jersey, and in the Battle of Rhode Island. Nevertheless, after the war, as a cabinetmaker living in Barre, he declared himself "wholly unable to labor on account of [the] wound rec'd in the war of the Revolution," and he was awarded an invalid pension.

Jeduthan Bemis claimed to have killed a Regular Soldier on April 19th; then he remained in service at Cambridge and participated in the Battle of Bunker Hill. The next year he went to Canada in the relief expedition, where he was evidently captured in a battle at The Cedars (near Montreal), then released in a prisoner exchange. He returned to service at New York, where he may have been wounded at the Battle of White Plains. Subsequently, he served at Saratoga and at Fishkill. After the war, he ended up in Connecticut, where he struggled as a farmer, becoming in his words, a "town pauper."

Three Lincoln men served as Life Guards for Generals Washington and Lee. *Jesse Smith* was drafted into Gen. George Washington's Life Guard, and served for several years, through several incarnations of the Commander-in-Chief's Guard. In this capacity, he appears to have participated in many of the important operations of the war, including the Battles of Long Island, White Plains, Trenton, Princeton, Brandywine, and Monmouth, as well as the winter encampment at Valley Forge. In one incarnation of the Guard, he served in the Virginia Line, as a dragoon.[1] *Aaron Parks* served as a Life Guard for Gen. Charles Lee briefly in 1776, in Boston and New York, whereupon he left General Lee's Guard and went to Canada with his regiment. At about the same time, *Samuel Hastings, Jr.,* was appointed to General Lee's Guard, serving in this capacity through the New York campaign. As the recalcitrant General Lee was dragging his feet through New Jersey on his

---

1 A cavalryman.

way to join Washington (who was regrouping on the opposite side of the Delaware River), Lee was surprised and captured by a British patrol at Basking Ridge on December 13, 1776. *Samuel Hastings, Jr.*, was also taken prisoner in the raid, and he was held until his release on parole sometime later. After his release, *Hastings* married a Lincoln girl and settled in Lincoln; *Smith* moved to Salem and became a mariner following his service; *Parks* settled in Charlestown, New Hampshire after the war.

And so the stories go on—stories as individual as the individuals who served. Lincoln's Revolutionary soldiers defy cardboard stereotypes. They were real people; their reasons for serving and their stories reflect the varied patterns of real life in a rural, eighteenth-century New England village. For some, the war had a profound impact on their lives; for others, it was largely incidental. In each case, the war and the individual stories of war became part of the tapestry of Lincoln tradition, woven into the rich history of this proud community.

Chapter 2

Incentives and Enlistment

Notwithstanding the Lincoln community's conviction in the importance of their charter rights and privileges, individual decisions to enlist in a war effort necessarily reflect a variety of other factors. It may be one thing to declare—as Lincoln had in December 1773—a collective readiness to *"encounter all the horrors of war"* and to *"join with our brethren to face the formidable forces"* long before it became clear that such steps would actually become necessary. It is quite another thing to make a personal choice to do so. Nevertheless, the Lincoln men were as good as their collective declaration; a very substantial percentage of Lincoln's male population of service age enlisted—at least briefly—in the war effort. For some, this was undoubtedly driven by conviction; for others, additional influences must certainly have been part of the equation.

Extended Kinships

Colonial Lincoln, like most eighteenth-century New England towns, was a closely knit community of extended family relationships and interconnections. Evidence of this is found in the large numbers of individuals with common surnames. Individuals with the same surname were often related to each other within two or three generations. And rare was the family, new to Lincoln, that had not intermarried with one or more of the other Lincoln families by the next generation.

A map of 1775 Lincoln, drawn from an extensive study of land records, shows six houses with members of the Brooks family, ten of the Parks, four of the Billings, three Farrars, four Adams, seven Browns, three Garfields, and so forth. There were more than twice as many dwelling units in town as there were surnames of families occupying them.[1] And consistent with the origin of the town itself, many of these families had cross-border connections as well, with family members, in-laws, and branches in Lincoln's neighboring parent towns of Concord, Lexington, and Weston.

In a small, rural community where just about everyone was knitted together by friendships, extended family ties, historically shared religious convictions, and/or intertwined economic interests, there were sure to be strong social pressures to serve the common cause. Their principled conviction in the justice of their cause was only a starting point; the shared community response and encouragement of friends and family would certainly have facilitated individual decisions to enlist for service either individually or in groups. There can be little doubt that the knitted social structure of the community was an important factor in explaining the high turnout for the war.[2]

---

1 Glass and Little Map of Lincoln.
2 Resch, *Suffering Soldiers* (p. 44), reports similar findings of "kin, peer, and community expectations to serve" in his study of Peterborough, New Hampshire, and concludes similarly that "fathers, sons, brothers, cousins, and in-laws" represented an important factor accounting for enlistments.

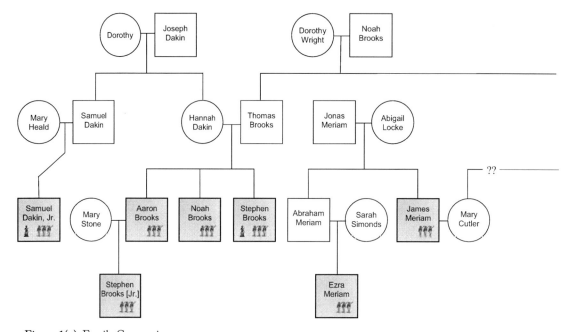

Figure 1(a). Family Connections.
An extended web of kinship connected more than 100 members of Lincoln's Army of the Revolution; each one was the father or son, brother or brother-in-law, nephew, uncle, or cousin of one or more others.

Not surprisingly, the family ties of the Lincoln individuals who served in the war appear to reflect those of the community. The links can be traced through a web of family connections involving more than a hundred members of Lincoln's Revolutionary army—every one a father/son, brother/brother-in-law, nephew/uncle, or cousin of one or more others (see Figure 1).[1]

Brothers *Nathan* and *Daniel Brown* were first cousins of *James Adams, Jr.*, and, through their sisters, were brothers-in-law of *Daniel Wesson* and *William Lawrence, Jr. William Lawrence, Jr.* was the first cousin of four *Adams* brothers *(Bulkley, Edward, Abel,* and *John)*. *Nathan Brown* was married to the sister of brothers *Solomon Garfield* and *Abraham Gearfield*, who in turn were nephews of *Elisha Gearfield* and brothers-in-law of *David Fisk*. Another sister of *Nathan* and *Daniel Brown* was married to *Phineas Allen's* brother.

Phineas Allen married *Jacob Foster's* sister. *Phineas Allen's* sisters married into the *Wesson, Tower, Billing, Wheeler,* and *Parks* families, which had other links between them, as well.

Edmond Wheeler married the sister of *Benjamin Munroe, Jr.*, and their daughter married *Leonard Hoar. Benjamin Munroe, Jr.'s* other sister was the mother of *Abner Mathis; Benjamin's* son, *Isaac Munroe*, married a *Hartwell*, while his daughter married *Edward Cabot*.

The *Flints* connect the *Hartwells* to the *Masons*, who connect back to the *Fosters* and *Allens*. The *Hartwell* brothers connect through *Moses Brown's* sisters to the *Farrars*, who in

---

[1] The limits of these family ties have not been fully probed; it is likely that the web extends even further than the diagram shows. Technically speaking, the *Cutler* brothers are a generation removed as cousins of the *Bond* brothers, but they are included in Figure 1 as another example of family bonds connecting even those with conflicting loyalties.

Chapter 2: Incentives and Enlistment

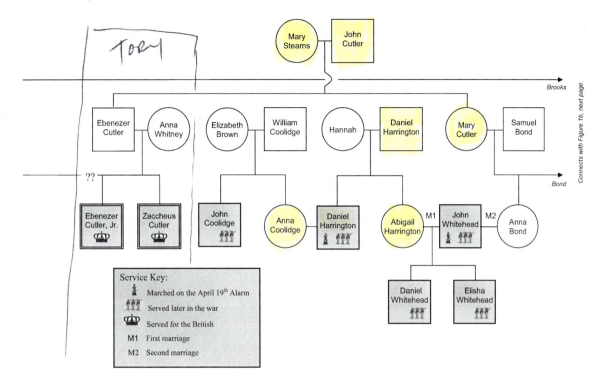

turn connect to the *Bonds* and *Hoars*. The *Hoars* connect to the *Abbots*, *Edmund Bowman*, and *Abijah Peirce*. The *Hartwell* brothers were also cousins of *Abner* and *Benjamin Brooks* and *Ephraim Brooks, Jr.*

And so on: the *Childs*; the *Meriams*; the *Meloneys*; the *Cutlers*; the *Whiteheads*. *John Coolidge, Daniel Harrington, Jonathan Smith*. This web is but one example of the intertwined family relationships. Similar webs draw in additional Lincoln men-in-arms. It is doubtful that there were many (if any at all) who were not connected in some way to at least one or more of these webs.

In fairness, it should be noted that not all of the inter-family marriages predate the war. And of course, family connections do not in and of themselves suggest unanimity of thought or action. Indeed, several individuals are found in the web who fought on the side of the Crown. But they do underscore the connectedness of the community, and they indicate intertwined interests likely to encourage common behavior when those interests are threatened.

So it was for many a Revolutionary soldier from Lincoln. He served for his family and community as well as for his country. And the soldier next to him in line might well have been a brother, a nephew, a cousin, or another relation.[1]

---

[1] See Appendix A, Units & Commanding Officers, to find cases of brothers, cousins, and even occasionally fathers and sons serving together in the same units during the same campaigns.

Part I: In Defense of Our Charter Rights and Privileges

Figure 1(b).

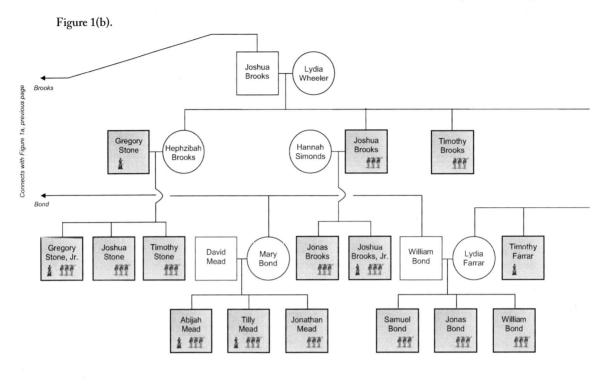

Figure 1(c).

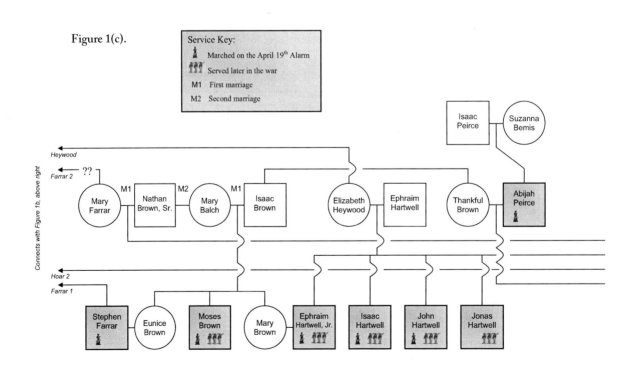

Chapter 2: Incentives and Enlistment

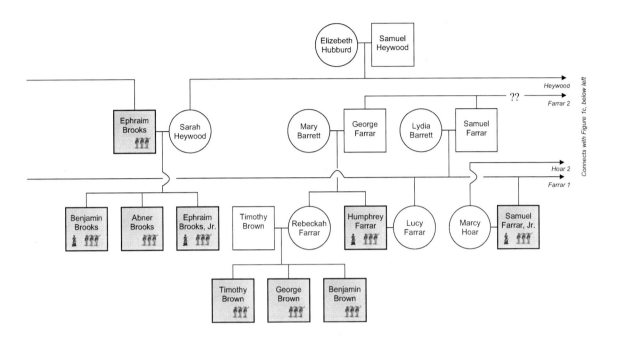

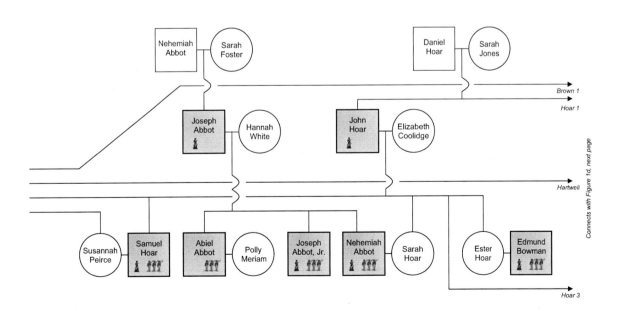

Part I: In Defense of Our Charter Rights and Privileges

Figure 1(d).

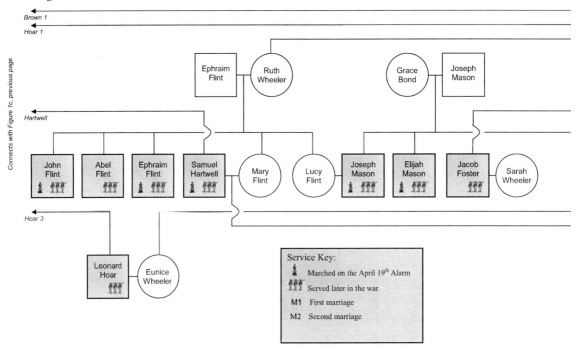

Figure 1(e).

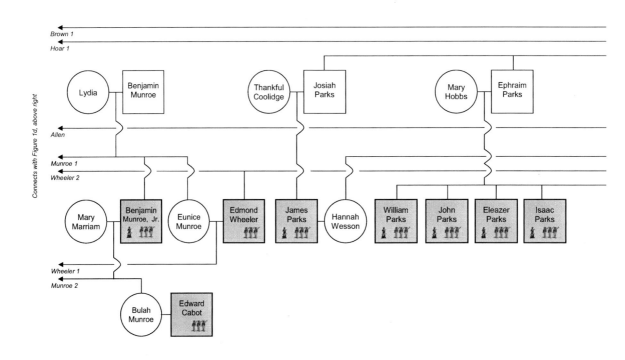

Chapter 2: Incentives and Enlistment

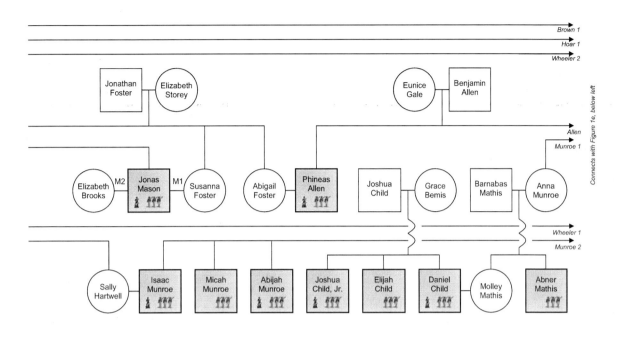

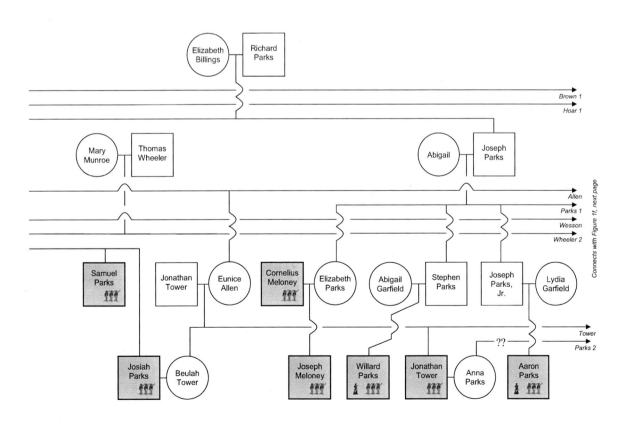

Part I: In Defense of Our Charter Rights and Privileges

Figure 1(f).

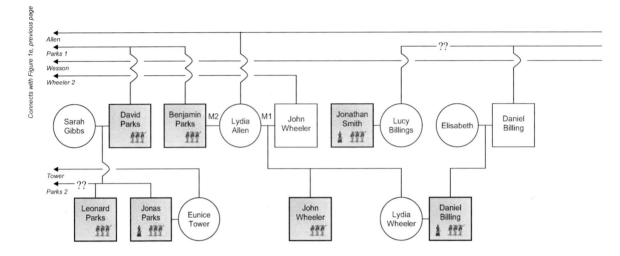

Figure 1(g).

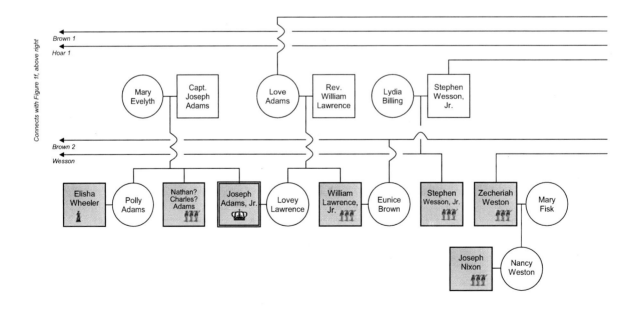

Chapter 2: Incentives and Enlistment

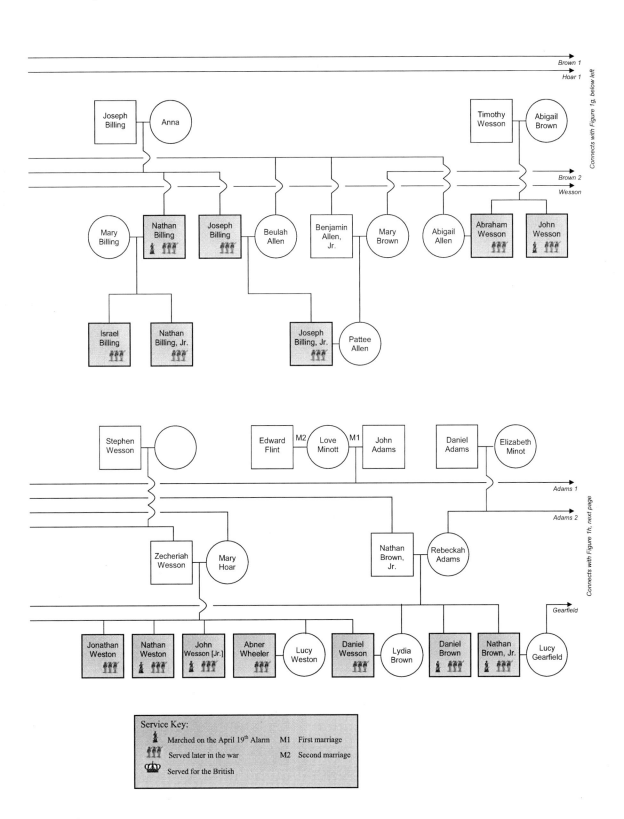

Figure 1(h).

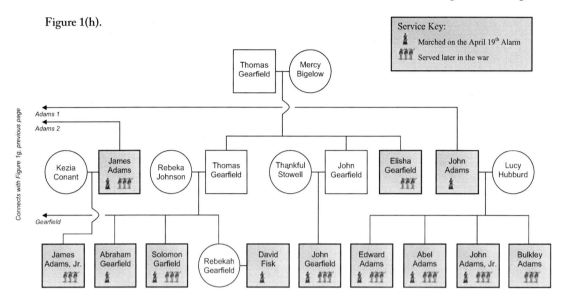

Economic Turbulence

The economic impact of the war is another factor which may to some extent have encouraged enlistment. Economic dislocation is inherent in any major war, and the American Revolution was certainly no exception. And as military recruiters have understood throughout history, the attractiveness of military service as an economic option is well correlated with economic difficulties.

The economic vicissitudes of the war were felt almost immediately in Massachusetts. The exodus of large numbers of refugees from Boston and Charlestown into the countryside, along with the sudden necessity of supplying the army in Cambridge, required immediate accommodation. The disruption of Atlantic trade routes by the Royal Navy and the loss of markets for American goods in England and elsewhere in the Empire, depressed the merchant economy of coastal New England. The American economy sank into recession, from which it would take 25 years to recover. Overall, average per capita incomes fell 20 percent from 1770 to 1780.[1]

Estimates of the amount of hard currency in America at the time vary widely. But it was certainly insufficient to pay for the cost of the war. Congress printed up $240 million in paper money from 1775 to 1779, and the states added another $200-plus million in paper currency.[2] The flood of paper fueled a crippling inflation, the magnitude of which is unimaginable by modern Americans. In the three years from January 1777 to January 1780, prices of basic supplies increased thirty to forty times their previous levels (see Table 1). Each year, paper currency lost one-half to two-thirds of its value, until by the end of 1780

---

1 Lindert and Williamson, "America's Revolution."
2 Baack, "The Economics of the American Revolutionary War." See also, Michener, "Money in the American Colonies."

Table 1. Prices of Basic Supplies

	Pre-1777	January 1778	*Inflation Rate*	January 1779	*Inflation Rate*	January 1780	*Inflation Rate*
Beef (1 pound)	3½ d	10½ d	*200%*	1/10d	*110%*	8/9d	*377%*
Indian corn (1 bushel)	4/-	18/-	*350%*	£2 12/-	*189%*	£8	*208%*
Wool (1 pound)	2/-	12/-	*500%*	15/-	*25%*	60/-	*300%*
Sole leather (1 pound)	3d	5/7½ d	*350%*	8/5½ d	*50%*	37/6d	*343%*

Source: Felt, *An Historical Account of Massachusetts Currency*, p. 186.
Note: 12 pence (symbol: d) equal one shilling (symbol: s or /); 20 shillings equal one pound (symbol: £). Fractions of a penny were fairly common.

Table 2. Depreciation of the Currency from 1777 through 1780
(The Value in Silver of £1 of paper currency)

	1777		1778		1779		1780	
	value	scale	value	scale	value	scale	value	scale
Jan	19/½d	914	6/1¼d	293	2/8¼d	129	8d	32
Feb	18/8¾d	899	5/8½d	274	2/3½d	110	7¼d	29
Mar	18/4d	880	5/4d	256	2/-	96	6¼d	25
Apr	17/10¼d	857	5/-	240	1/9¾d	87	6d	24
May	17/5¾d	839	5/-	240	1/7¾d	79	5¾d	23
Jun	16/8d	800	5/-	240	1/5¾d	71	5¾d	23
Jul	16/-	768	4/8¼d	225	1/4¾d	67	3¼d	13
Aug	13/4d	640	4/4¾d	211	1/2¾d	59	3¼d	13
Sep	11/5d	548	4/2½d	202	1/1¼d	53	3¼d	13
Oct	7/3d	348	4/-	192	11¾d	47	3¼d	13
Nov	6/8d	320	3/8d	176	10¾d	43	3¼d	13
Dec	6/5¼d	309	3/1¾d	151	9¼d	37	3¼d	13

Source: Daniels, *History of the Town of Oxford*, p. 765; Hudson, *History of the Town of Lexington*, p. 241.
Note: 12 pence (symbol: d) equal one shilling (symbol: s or /); 20 shillings equal one pound (symbol: £). Fractions of a penny were fairly common. Thus the designation 17/5¾d represents 17 shillings and 5¾ pence. Relative values are shown on the normalized decimal scale, with ¼d equal to 1 (£1 calculates to 960).

it was worth only 1.4 percent of its pre-1777 value (see Table 2). The Spanish dollar (one of the most common coins in eighteenth-century America, used here as an example of specie), would have circulated at close to par early in the war, but by 1781 it would not have traded for less than $75 in paper. The economic turbulence prompted regular and repeated conferences at the county, state, and regional levels in an effort to control prices and regulate the economy, but in the words of Concord historian Lemuel Shattuck, "Such a rapid depreciation introduced great embarrassment and distress into all commercial transactions, which no body of men could remove by resolutions, addresses, price-currents, or prosecutions."[1]

---

[1] Felt, *An Historical Account of Massachusetts Currency*, p. 169; Shattuck, *History of the Town of Concord*, p. 123.

The actual impact of the turbulent Revolutionary economy in Lincoln, however, is difficult to measure. Certainly (except for April 19, 1775) Lincoln was spared the direct impacts of warfare. It suffered almost none of the dislocations of civilian populations and the catastrophic property damage which invariably accompany battles, skirmishes, and campaigning armies. Lincoln farms were not subject to repeated invasion by foraging parties or theft by marauding soldiers.

On the other hand, Lincoln was certainly not spared the depredations of the wartime economy. Runaway prices were certainly no less rampant in Lincoln. Inflation, loss of purchasing power, economic uncertainty, and probably in many cases loss of income were as true in Lincoln as elsewhere.

It is reasonable to suppose, however, that as an agricultural community, Lincoln may have been less impacted by these factors than other, more commercially-centered towns. Trades and craft incomes may well have suffered the effects of the economic downturn. But regardless of what other ties they may have had with the commercial world, virtually everyone in Lincoln was also a farmer. The demand for local farm products did not go away; in addition, periodically during the war, Lincoln farms provided portions of the hay, beef, wood, and other supplies required to feed and provision the army.

Furthermore, many of the farms in Lincoln had been in family hands for at least a generation or two; it is probable that few were burdened with heavy debt. While it is true that after the war several Lincoln farms were lost to foreclosure, no record has been found of any such problem occurring during the war years.

Wage growth in Lincoln appears, at least anecdotally, to have kept pace with the spiraling inflation. This can be traced through the town's payments to its teachers. One example of teachers' pay in Lincoln shows that it increased by 75 times over the five years between the winters of 1775–76 and 1780–81. The town's expense for boarding the teacher increased between 65 and 70 times during the same period. A parallel example shows teachers' pay in Lincoln increasing more than 100 times between 1775 and 1780.[1]

Wages for farm labor are unknown, but there is evidence through service records of at least some movement of young people into (and out of) Lincoln, suggesting both the availability of jobs and the probability of a reasonably competitive pay scale. *Richard Winship* and *Jonathan Page* appear to have come to Lincoln as teenagers by 1779 or 1780, during the worst of the inflation. At least by 1781, *Ezra Meriam* and *Joseph Munroe* appear to have come from Lexington, and possibly *Jeduthan Bemis* from Weston. There is little reason to suspect that they joined the service for want of other opportunity.

Recruiting data tells a similar story. Lincoln reportedly recruited nine men from outside of town to meet its 1777 quota of enlistees for three years of service in the Continental Army, evidence that the economic turbulence of the times was not driving Lincoln men into service. Enlistment bounties, at least anecdotally, also appear to have kept reasonably apace with inflation, suggesting that even outside of Lincoln, large numbers of individuals were not enlisting in the service because of economic displacement. One should be cautious about reading too much into enlistment bounties because they were very specific to individual troop calls, but it does appear significant that in 1781, twelve Lincoln enlistees reportedly

---

1 MacLean, *A Rich Harvest*, p. 308; Wheeler, "Lincoln," in Hurd, Vol. 2, p. 620.

received their Continental Army bounties in "Hard money." Even inflated bounties seem to have lost much of their appeal if they were being paid in deflated paper currency.[1]

In the absence of aggregate data to suggest that enlistments were encouraged by the troubled economic times, it would do well to remember that aggregate data is a product of many different individual decisions, each representing a complex mix of circumstances and motivations. David Mead is one such example. He scratched out a living for his family as an innholder and farmer, never ranking very high on the economic ladder of Lincoln residents. He was heavily mortgaged before the war, and after the war ended he was jailed for his debts, then he lost his farm to foreclosure. Despite his economic struggles, he declined to enlist in military service, even paying a handsome fine in defiance of a draft order.[2]

James Miles also struggled economically. He, too, lost his farm after the war and was imprisoned as a debtor. He served for five days at Dorchester Heights, and for two months in 1777 at Rhode Island. Neither service was of sufficient duration to appear to have been motivated primarily by economic circumstances.[3]

For *Solomon Whitney*, on the other hand, military service may well have been an economic safety net. He appears to have been in such hard economic straits that he was receiving financial assistance from the town before the war broke out.[4] From April 19, 1775, through the end of the war, he served enlistment after enlistment: as a minute man and in the Siege of Boston in 1775–1776; in New York and New Jersey in 1776–1777; at Saratoga in 1777; in the Hudson Highlands in 1778; Rhode Island in 1779; and for three years in the Continental Army in 1780–1783. In all, he served nine separate enlistments; it is hard not to interpret an economic motivation to his repeated terms of service.

Other examples are ripe for individual interpretation. *John Hagar* seems to have been receiving economic support from the town prior to the outbreak of war, and he subsequently served 20 months in the Continental Army. *Artemas Reed* served continuously for nearly five years, from April 19, 1775, until December 31, 1779. The town provided wood, meat, meal (i.e., grain), and other provisions as assistance to his wife during this period. After a six-month break, he accumulated another two years of service. At age 40, *Samuel Avery* enlisted for a three-year term in the Continental Army in 1781. As a first tour of duty at that age, this represented, effectively, a career change. Seventeen-year-old *Peter Sharon*, believed to have been a former slave, enlisted for three-and-a-half years of service in the Continental Army, beginning in 1780.[5]

On a case by case basis, the reader may draw his or her own interpretation about financial need or an economic motivation for service. In some cases, it would be hard to deny economic motives. But beyond the time-honored notion that the attractiveness of military service is inversely correlated to economic prosperity, little evidence has been found to suggest that the depressed wartime economy in Massachusetts was much of a factor in encouraging Lincoln enlistments in the Army of the Revolution.

---

1 Wheeler, "Lincoln," in Hurd, Vol. 2, p. 620. See Table 3, Sampling of Bounties Offered for Enlistment, p. 34.
2 MacLean, *A Rich Harvest*, pp.309–310. See also sidebar, "The Price for Not Serving," p. 333.
3 MacLean, *A Rich Harvest*, pp.310–311.
4 "Treasurer's Accompts," December 7, 1775, and January 25, 1776.
5 For support of John Hagar, see "Treasurer's Accompts," February 21, 1775, December 7, 1775, January 25, 1776, and February 19, 1776. For the support of the wife of Artemas Reed, "Now in Continental Service," see "Treasurer's Accompts," July 15, 1778, and November 11, 1779.

Table 3. Sampling of Bounties Offered for Enlistment

Date	Service	Duration	Bounty offered
Resolve of May 4, 1775	in the Massachusetts Army	until December 31, 1775	20s advanced pay
Resolve of July 5, 1775	in the Massachusetts Army	until December 31, 1775	A "bounty coat"
Resolve of February 10, 1776	to reinforce the army in Canada	until January 1, 1777	40s in lieu of advanced pay
by December 1776	in the Continental Army	3 years	£20 bounty plus 20s per month, supplemental to Continental Army pay
Resolve of June 18, 1778	Detachment from the militia to serve as guards	until January 1, 1779	£5 per month, supplemental to Continental Army pay
Resolve of May 1, 1779	Enlistment in the Continental Army	3 years	$100 bounty in addition to the $200 Continental Army bounty, plus $200 after six months of service[a]

Source: Massachusetts Soldiers and Sailors, Vol. I, pp. xiii–xxxix.
a. A meaningful conversion between dollars and pounds has not been found.

Troop Calls

The demand for manpower to prosecute the war with Great Britain prompted regular and repeated troop calls (known as "resolves") from the Massachusetts General Court.[1] In the four years from January 1776 through December 1779, the General Court passed no fewer than 51 separate resolves calling for the enlisting or drafting of troops to serve in various campaigns, for terms ranging from two months to three years.[2]

Some of the resolves sought to raise new enlistments from the general population. Other resolves were to be fulfilled by recruiting or drafting individuals out of the militia units to be reassigned or organized into new militia units amalgamated and detached for specific assignments. In addition to the resolves, there were also occasional mobilizations of militia units as intact entities, in response to various urgent alarms.[3]

Some calls were for local service in defense of the coastal regions of Massachusetts and Rhode Island (through a cooperative agreement entered into by the New England states); other calls were for militia support for Continental Army campaigns; still other calls were to fulfill the enlistment quota (initially 15 battalions, later increased to 18 battalions) requested of Massachusetts by the Continental Congress for service in the Continental Army.

Such was the process by which many Lincoln men were attached and detached to and from a wide array of militia and Continental units throughout the war. Many of the units are identifiable (see Appendix A, "Units & Commanding Officers"). Unfortunately, in many other cases, the records of the different units and commands have not been found.

---

1 Initially, the resolves were passed by the Massachusetts Provincial Congress, which preceded the reestablishment of the Massachusetts General Court as the war progressed.

2 These resolves are itemized in *Massachusetts Soldiers and Sailors*, Vol. 1, pp. ix–xxxix.

3 For a detailed listing of the resolves, see *Massachusetts Soldiers and Sailors*, Vol. 1, pp. ix–xxxix. Eleazer Brooks Papers [Lincoln] contain several direct orders (not traceable to the resolves) received by *Col. Eleazer Brooks* for mobilizing his militia regiment.

Table 4. Sampling of Penalties for Avoiding Service

Date	Service	Penalty
Resolve of July 11, 1776	Draft (from the training bands and alarm lists)[a] of reinforcements for service in Canada until December 1, 1776	£10 fine for evading the draft, plus £3 additional fine if not paid within 24 hours
Resolve of Sept. 12, 1776	Draft from the militia for 2 months of service at New York	Fine as above, plus 2 months imprisonment for evading the draft
Resolve of August 15, 1777	Draft from the militia for 3 years of service to fill the state's delinquencies in the ranks of the Continental Army	Severe penalties levied against military officers, Selectmen, and others failing to enlist the required numbers
Resolve of April 20, 1778	Draft from the militia for 9 months of service from the time of arrival at Fishkill	Very severe penalties for evading the draft; also £100 per deficiency levied against the town
Resolve of June 5, 1780	Draft for 6 months of service from the time of arrival at the place of rendezvous	£150 fine for evading the draft; failure to pay the fine within 24 hours to be considered desertion

Source: Massachusetts Soldiers and Sailors, Vol. I, pp. xiii–xxxix.

a. Used together, the terms "alarm list" and "training band" certainly refer to all members of the militia, i.e., all males between the ages of 16 and 60. As discrete terms, their meanings seem to have been evolving during this period, the "alarm list" being typically older men (over age 50) who were no longer actively part of the "training band." See French, *The Day of Concord and Lexington*, pp. 22, 158; Fischer, *Paul Revere's Ride*, pp. 151-152.

Notwithstanding that Massachusetts contributed many more Revolutionary soldiers to the war effort than any other colony or state,[1] Massachusetts was perennially deficient (as were the other states) in enlisting enough troops to fill out the Massachusetts line of the Continental Army. With troop calls coming up short throughout the war, the General Court progressively raised the ante (which consisted of both carrot and stick) to attract recruits. The carrot consisted of a bounty which was paid to individuals just for signing up. The amount of the bounty was specific to each resolve, and the evidence shows progressive escalation over the course of the war (see Table 3). While some of the increase was undoubtedly a necessary response to the runaway wartime inflation, for the data points in which comparison can be made, the increase in the enlistment incentive appears to have exceeded the rate of inflation.

When voluntary enlistments failed to meet the demand, a draft for service was enacted, first appearing in the Resolve of July 11, 1776. As with enlistment bounties, the penalty for avoiding service when drafted thereafter escalated apace (see Table 4). In addition, within

---

1 In a report to Congress in 1790, Henry Knox, then Secretary of War, reported that Massachusetts provided 67,907 men for Continental service. By comparison, this is twice the number for Connecticut, the next most represented state, and more than all of the states south of the Mason/Dixon Line combined. According to these numbers, Massachusetts by itself made up nearly 30 percent of the Continental Army. The numbers change only slightly when militia estimates are added in. Combining the number of Continental troops and militia troops provided, Virginia takes over second place for total troops supplied, with 52,721. Massachusetts, with an estimated 24,655 militia, remains solidly in first place, with 92,562. These figures represent the number of enlistments, not discrete individuals, as many individuals enrolled for more than one enlistment.

Knox's figures have come under relentless attack from all sides, and many modern historians consider them grossly overstated. While the author acknowledges the limitations of Knox's figures, they remain the best contemporary estimates available with which to work. (See Knox, "Statement"; Lesser, *Sinews of Independence*, footnote 66 on page xxxiv. For further discussion, see Lesser, *Sinews of Independence*, pp. xxxiii–xxxv.)

Table 5. Response to Troop Calls by Lincoln Residents and Other Lincoln-Connected Individuals

Date of the call	quota	# who served	Service
Concord Alarm, April 18, 1775		129–143 (est.)	Service ranging from 2 to 26 days at Concord and Cambridge from April 19 on. 62 minute men in *Capt. William Smith*'s Company; at least 43–53 (est.) others (mostly militia) from Lincoln; 4 in Concord and Bedford companies; 2 in command structure. 18–22 others marched on the Alarm with other companies, but they were not at the North Bridge.[a]
Resolve of January 20, 1776	8	10–12	Service at Cambridge to reinforce the Continental Army during the Siege of Boston from February 4 to April 1, in Capt. Asahel Wheeler's Company, Col. John Robinson's Regiment (in service during the British evacuation of Boston).
March 1, 1776		64–65	59 men in *Capt. John Hartwell*'s Militia Company from Lincoln, at Dorchester Heights March 4–9 in anticipation of an assault on Boston; 5 in Concord, Weston, Lexington, Waltham companies; possibly 1 in a Bridgewater Company at Horse Neck.
May 7, 1776		5–6	August to December at Roxbury and Dorchester, in Capt. John Minot's Company, Colonel Dikes's Regiment.
Resolves of June 25 and July 11, 1776		10[b]	Service through December 1, 1776, to reinforce the Continental Army expedition to Canada.
		32–43	Militia service at Ticonderoga for 5 months from July until December 1; 18–21 in Colonel Reed's and Wheelock's Regiments; 14–22 in unknown units.
		4	Militia service at Ticonderoga for 4 months from August until December 1, in Colonel Brewer's Regiment.
Resolve of Sept 12, 1776		10–12[c]	2 months at North Castle and White Plains, NY, in *Col. Eleazer Brooks*'s Regiment (including *Brooks*).

thirteen months, penalties were imposed not only on those individuals who refused to serve, but also on the towns themselves and on the officials within the towns who were responsible for drafting troops. While certain specified exemptions existed, in general, one could escape the penalty for not serving only by finding another individual to serve as a "substitute" in one's place.[1]

Troop calls were typically apportioned among selected counties, with specific quotas required to be met by each town or militia unit through voluntary enlistments, or through a draft if necessary. Although Lincoln's specific quota is unknown in most cases, the number of Lincoln residents and recruits who responded to various troop calls frequently can be reconstructed (see Table 5). Many of these quotas were met through voluntary enlistments, others by a draft, and at least in the case of Continental service in 1777, by recruiting individuals from outside of Lincoln.

---

1 For one example, see service records for *Joshua Child, Jr.*, and for *Brister Hoar*. Another example is *David Mead*, father of *Abijah Mead, Jonathan Mead*, and *Tilly Mead*, who was fined £12 for declining to serve when called in response to a resolve. He paid the fine on January 4, 1777, to *Capt. Samuel Farrar*. Later, on February 10, 1777, the fine was reimbursed after he procured a man to serve in his place (see "Treasurer's Accompts," January 4, 1777, and February 10, 1777; see also sidebar, "The Price for Not Serving," p. 333).

Chapter 2: Incentives and Enlistment

Table 5 (continued)

Date of the call	quota	# who served	Service
Resolve of Nov. 14, 1776 (?)		4–11 [d]	3 months at New York and Woodbridge, NJ, in Capt. John Bridge's Company, Col. Samuel Thatcher's Regiment. Discharged probably late March 1777.
December 1, 1776		25–27	3 months at Dorchester; in Col. Nicholas Dike's Regiment, December to March, including 15 in *Capt. John Hartwell's* Company.
Resolves of January 26, 1777, April 30, 1777, and August 15, 1777	26	34–38 [e]	3 years of Continental service from February 28, 1777; Draft to fill quotas for Continental service from May 15; Penalties for unmet quotas for Continental service.
Resolve of April 12, 1777 (?)		6–8 [f]	2 months at Providence and Point Judith.
Resolve of August 9, 1777		16 [g]	August 16 to November 30 at Saratoga in Col. Samuel Bullard's Regiment, Capt. George Minot's Company (present at the surrender of Burgoyne).
September 22, 1777		15 [h]	September 29 to November 7 at Saratoga and Fort Edward, in Colonel Reed's Regiment; 14 in *Capt. Samuel Farrar's* Company, 1 in Capt. Asahel Wheeler's Company (present at the surrender of Burgoyne). Discharged at Cambridge after escorting Burgoyne's captured troops to Cambridge.
1777 (probably October)		8 [i]	Teams to Worthington, probably to supply Burgoyne's captured army and its American escort on the march from Saratoga to Cambridge.
November 28, 1777		16–19 [j]	5 months of guard duty at Cambridge, guarding Burgoyne's "Convention Army"; mostly in Capt. Simon Hunt's Company, *Col. Eleazer Brooks's* Regiment.
Resolve of April 20, 1778		10 [k]	Continental Army service first at Rhode Island, then Fishkill, NY. Served 9 months after arrival in Fishkill.
Resolve of April 27, 1779		5–6	2 months at Tiverton, Rhode Island in Lt. Col. Samuel Pierce's Regiment,[l] Capt. Lawson Buckminster's Company, May 17 to July 1.
September 1, 1779		7–9	2 months at Providence, Tiverton, and Newport, Rhode Island, from September 16 to November 16, in Col. John Jacobs's Light Infantry Regiment, Capt. Samuel Heald's Company.
Resolve of June 5, 1780		12 [m]	6 months of Continental service from the time of arrival at the place of rendezvous. Originally intended to march to Albany to quell Indian incursions, but diverted to Rhode Island. Capt. Abraham Andrews's Company, Col. Cyprian How's Regiment.
Resolve of December 2, 1780		14–17 [n]	3 years of service in the Continental Army.
Resolve of June 15, 1781		8 [o]	5 months of service at Rhode Island.

Sources: This table is compiled largely from Shattuck (pp. 124–125, 299–300, 352–359) and from MacLean, *A Rich Harvest* (p. 295), both of whom attribute their information to a May 8, 1778, report to Town Meeting.

Table 5 (continued)

Notes: The 1778 report to Town Meeting is a tally of bounties paid by the town, and thus it includes only those who were resident at the time of service or whose service was credited to Lincoln. Accordingly, the author has augmented the reported data as appropriate to reflect records of additional Lincoln service found in this work. Many other tours of duty were served by Lincoln men through individual initiatives.

a. See sidebar, "Accounting for Lincoln's Men-in-Arms on April 19th," p. 12.
b. The May 8, 1778, report to Town Meeting shows 7 bounties paid for service in Canada, indicative of 7 individuals having responded to the resolves. However, most of the 10 men recorded on the relief expedition to Canada appear already to have been serving in Continental units. It is not clear how many enlisted for Canada in response to the resolves.
c. The May 8, 1778, report to Town Meeting shows 12 bounties paid for service around New York. In addition to those in *Colonel Brooks*'s Regiment; there were 4–7 others in unidentified (probably militia) units; and 10–14 with the Continental Army.
d. The May 8, 1778, report to Town Meeting shows 8 bounties paid for this service; Shattuck credits Lincoln's participation at 13.
e. Because the town recruited 9 individuals from out of town to fill its quota, it is presumed that 9–14 of these individuals enlisted independently from the resolves. Some enlisted prior to the January 26 Resolve; others were already in Continental service and reenlisted upon the expiration of their terms.
f. The May 8, 1778, report to Town Meeting shows 4 bounties paid for two months at Providence.
g. The May 8, 1778, report to Town Meeting shows 10; a return dated Lincoln, August 14, 1777, from *Capt. Samuel Farrar, Jr.*, to *Col. Eleazer Brooks* lists 12 men in his Lincoln Militia Company who were "draughted and inlisted and agreeable to the order of the court." See sidebar, "Facing the Crisis", p. 99.
h. A return dated Lincoln, September 29, 1777, from *Capt. Samuel Farrar, Jr.*, to *Col. Eleazer Brooks* states that 14 men in his Lincoln Militia Company were in readiness for this service (see *Massachusetts Soldiers and Sailors*, Vol. V, p. 536). The May 8, 1778, report to Town Meeting shows 12.
i. The identity of the eighth teamster on this expedition (according to the May 8 report) is still undiscovered.
j. Eleazer Brooks Papers [Concord] shows eight. The May 8, 1778, report to Town Meeting shows nine. Both are understated. Shattuck dates this service to November 28, but they had to be in service at least by November 7. They were relieved by a subsequent April draft, which included 14–18 men from Lincoln.
k. Eleazer Brooks Papers [Concord] shows 5 for nine months of service (no date), 4 for the North River draft (March 1778), and 4 for Rhode Island service (June 1778). Other records identify at least 10 at Fishkill; but not all were in response to the April 20 Resolve. Brooks's North River and Rhode Island draftees are not identifiable from the records.
l. Shattuck, *History of the Town of Concord* (p. 357), incorrectly reports that this was in Colonel Jacobs's Regiment.
m. Shattuck, *History of the Town of Concord* (p. 359), credits Lincoln with 12; only 9 have been identified.
n. Shattuck, *History of the Town of Concord* (p. 359), credits Lincoln with 10; 14–17 are identifiable.
o. Shattuck, *History of the Town of Concord* (p. 359), credits Lincoln with this number; they have not been identified.

Against a Common Enemy

Service data shows that the men of Lincoln responded repeatedly, consistently, and in large numbers to the manpower needs of their war to secure their rights and liberties. There are 251 Lincoln individuals identified herein who answered the call for service during the Revolution. As well as can be determined from the record, approximately one half were in service on April 19, 1775. Most of these reenlisted for further service, in some cases serving virtually the entire war.

Of the other half, some joined the Massachusetts Provincial Army in Cambridge in the days immediately following the outbreak of war. Others, perhaps less eager to make a military commitment, enlisted in response to a later troop call for militia or Continental Army service. Some certainly waited to be drafted. Many were underage when the war

Table 6. Lincoln Demographics During the Revolution

	1776-1777		Comparison data			
			1765 census		1790 census	
	number	% of total	number	% of total	number	% of total
Total population	775		649		740	
Males over age 16	187	24.1%	145	22.3%	180	24.3%
Males under age 16	*(est.)* 183-193		153	23.6%	184	24.9%

Sources: Benton, *Early Census Making in Massachusetts*, pp. 80–81; 1790 Federal Census; *Vital Records of Lincoln*; "Several Drafts of Men since Nov 1777," found in Eleazer Brooks Papers [Concord].

broke out, enlisting as they aged onto the militia lists. A few jumped the gun and enlisted before they came of age.

Some members of Lincoln's Army of the Revolution served just once; most served multiple enlistments. In the aggregate, Lincoln soldiers enlisted for service an average of approximately three-and-a-quarter times.

By today's standards, the population of early America was comparatively young. Population data for Lincoln bears this out; it shows 775 residents in 1776, and 187 males over age 16 in 1777 (Table 6).[1] It can be reasonably estimated from other census data taken a decade before the war and a decade after the war that the under-age-16 population in Lincoln was roughly equivalent to the 16-and-over segment. Accordingly, we can estimate that in the six years of war following 1777, somewhere in the neighborhood of 66–72 Lincoln lads became age-eligible for military service; creating a total pool of service-eligible men of approximately 253–271.

The mobility of the young people in Lincoln and the surrounding towns, along with limitations in the historical record, makes it difficult in many cases to determine actual residency at the time of service, but the data suggests that approximately 200–210 of the Lincoln servicemen were resident in the town when they served; 15 others were sons of Lincoln who had left Lincoln before the war. The balance consisted of transients, non-residents recruited to fulfill Lincoln's quota, and people who were unconnected with Lincoln when they served, but who then came to Lincoln after the war.

The math is simple but somewhat startling. It indicates that upwards of 75–80 percent of Lincoln's service-eligible population actually served in the war. Reliable data with which to make meaningful comparisons with other areas is surprisingly sparse. In the immediate vicinity, Concord historian Lemuel Shattuck states simply that Concord's war service was "very great in proportion to her population, but how great cannot now be fully estimated."[2] A comparison of Lincoln and Concord enlistment numbers in various campaigns of the war reveals a wide variation, with no discernable pattern from campaign to campaign. In the

---

1 Population is from the 1776 Massachusetts census (see *Vital Records of Lincoln*). The figure for males age 16-and-over is found in *Col. Eleazer Brooks's* working notes, "Several Drafts of Men since Nov 1777," in Eleazer Brooks Papers [Concord]. It is given as 187 living in town, 2 living in Boston, and 10 Negroes, and it is most likely taken directly from the town's alarm list. Both figures are in line with census data from 1765 and 1790, and they reflect Shattuck's statement that the numbers "would not essentially vary" through a 50-year period. Shattuck, *History of the Town of Concord*, pp. 309–310.
2 Shattuck, *History of the Town of Concord*, p. 123.

aggregate, however, across multiple campaigns, the participation from each town appears roughly proportional to their respective populations.[1]

Elsewhere, information is equally anecdotal. Peterborough, New Hampshire, is purported to have participated at a rate of 64 percent. In Lancaster, it is reported proudly but unquantifiably that "almost every male citizen of military age must have served at some period of the war, either personally or by substitute."[2]

Aggregate service numbers for Massachusetts indicate that Massachusetts provided a disproportionate share of the total manpower to fight the war.[3] It would not be unreasonable to attribute this to prewar radicalization in Massachusetts, and to the fact that the war centered in Massachusetts during the first year. It would likewise not be unreasonable to suppose that the regions of the state most involved with the start and early progression of the war may have had a higher participation rate than other parts of the state. Thus one might postulate that Middlesex County residents may have participated in the war to a greater extent than residents of other counties, and that within Middlesex County, participation may have been higher in towns near the epicenter of the events of April 19th, perhaps peaking in Lincoln, Lexington, and Concord. Unfortunately, comparative data has not been found with which to test this hypothesis.

For many years, established wisdom has held that the American Revolution was supported by only about one-third of the American colonists, with one-third remaining loyal to the Crown and one-third staying neutral. Although the evidence for this is unclear, the premise has been widely disseminated by those wishing to make the point that the Revolution did not have the overwhelming support of the American people.[4] Despite some degree of variation around the one-third-each proportions, the underlying premise of proponents remains the same: that the Revolution was supported by only a minority of Americans.

It seems reasonable to believe that the percentage of individuals who served in the war must in some way have been roughly parallel to the amount of popular support for the war. Within this context, and to the extent there may be any validity to the "doctrine of minority support" elsewhere, Lincoln's participation rate of 75 to 80 percent stands in marked counterpoint!

A more populist view of the American Revolution is propounded by others. Writer/researcher Ray Raphael describes in great detail the almost instant transformation of the simmering conflict with the Crown, from a trade and tariff related dispute centered in the port towns into a (bloodless) populist uprising across all of Massachusetts during the summer and fall of 1774. Historian Robert Calhoon also details large mobs, typically numbering in

---

1 For examples of such campaigns, see Shattuck, *History of the Town of Concord*, pp. 124–25, 211, 299–300.

2 Peterborough statement is from Resch, *Suffering Soldiers*, pp. 19, 205–06. Precise details of Resch's methodology are not given, but it appears to be more or less similar to that used by the author. The Lancaster statement, from Nourse, *Military Annals of Lancaster* (p. 189), follows lists of individuals who served, but it is unsupported by any numeric analysis. Further, Nourse's words "by substitute" are a catch-all which includes individuals who *avoided* service by sending someone else to serve in their place. Thus the statement is essentially meaningless.

3 Knox, "Statement"; Heitman, *Historical Register of the Army*, pp. 280, 282. See also note 1 on p. 35.

4 This popular premise is purported to have its origins in the misreading of a January 1813 letter from John Adams to James Lloyd, in which he used it to describe American opinion of the French Revolution during the 1790s. Despite several historians having reported on the error, the theory has been strangely persistent (see Marina, "The Revolution as a People's War," who cites works by John R. Alden (1954), R. R. Palmer (1959), Herbert Aptheker (1960), and himself (1975) in exposing the error).

the thousands, that systematically forced the resignations all across the colony of officials appointed under the Coercive Acts. He comments that the Coercive Acts, "taken together, evoked a pattern of resistance that plunged the colony into revolution," and that the mobs "express[ed] the authentic sentiments of the entire community."[1] Lincoln's participation rate in the war certainly supports the more populist view of the American Revolution, at least as it pertains to the town of Lincoln.

In many ways, Lincoln was probably typical of small New England agricultural communities. Pragmatic and conservative in its approach to change, it was not in the forefront of the prewar rebellious movements. But when it became necessary to resort to arms to defend their liberties and to protect their families, the men of Lincoln responded with singular conviction and in vast numbers. In Lincoln, as elsewhere, this became a war "against a common enemy."[2]

Much has been made of the dedication and perseverance of the Americans in their long struggle to assert their Charter rights, and ultimately their independence from the British monarchy. Certainly, in this contest, there were few other advantages the Americans held. While acknowledging the invaluable assistance of the French, historians generally attribute the success of the American Revolution—against unbelievably long odds—to the resolute determination of a people who believed passionately in their cause and were determined to see it through. Aptly described by historian David Hackett Fischer, "Their greatest advantage was the moral strength of a just cause. They were fighting on their own ground, in defense of homes and families, for ideas of liberty and freedom.... The Americans were a deeply spiritual people, with an abiding faith that sustained them in adversity.... They had a different test of success. Their opponents had to conquer; the Americans needed only to survive."[3]

Fischer also explains that the men of Massachusetts "thought of fighting as a dirty business that had to be done from time to time if good men were to survive in a world of evil.... When they believed that their homes and their way of life were at stake, they fought with courage and resolve—not for the sake of fighting, but for the sake of winning."[4]

This commitment to principle, and the willingness to risk all, has become a material part of American mythology. And rightly so. Historical literature is replete with countless examples drawn from virtually every corner of what was then Colonial America.

So, too, Lincoln men served long and hard in the armed struggle to achieve victory. Two companies of Lincoln men were among the very first in the field at Concord in 1775; others were on Bunker Hill and Dorchester Heights. Many Lincoln men were in the field (now scattered among more than a dozen companies) at Saratoga in 1777. *George Brown, Asa Adams,* and *Jack Farrar* endured the hardships at Valley Forge during the winter of 1777–1778; *Silas Sharon, Nehemiah Abbot,* and *Isaac Bussell* fought the British to a standstill on the Monmouth battlefield the following spring. *Ezra Meriam, Joseph Munroe,* and

---

1 Marina, "The Revolution as a People's War"; Raphael, *The First American Revolution*, pp. 59–168; Calhoon, *Loyalists in Revolutionary America*, pp. 269, 279.
2 The author has found this phrase in the pension declarations of many of Lincoln's soldiers of the Revolution. These pension declarations were written many years later, but the phrase seems to capture their sense of communal solidarity and common cause during the Revolutionary War.
3 Fischer, *Washington's Crossing*, p. 368.
4 Fischer, *Paul Revere's Ride*, p. 155.

Lemuel Wheeler served multiple terms in the Hudson Valley; *Solomon Whitney, William Smith*, and *Edward Adams* served naval duty at sea. A few went south later in the war. *Isaac Bussell* and perhaps *Peter Sharon* helped defeat Lord Cornwallis at Yorktown in 1781. And when Washington finally dissolved the Army in 1783, *Levi Parker, Jonathan Tower, Joel Adams, William Orr,* and *Abner Richardson,* who were still in service, at last shouldered their backpacks and muskets and returned home.

Timothy Farrar, Nathaniel Baker, and *Edmund Bowman* served only a few days. *Peter Oliver, Benjamin Cleaveland, Elisha Willington,* and *Artemas Reed* spent more than five years in service. Overall, the town's soldiers appear to have suffered relatively few casualties, but perhaps nowhere did men of military age serve more consistently, more repeatedly, and in greater proportions than did the men from Lincoln.

"To them," wrote historian Howard W. Peckham as if speaking directly of the Lincoln soldiers, "independence and freedom had vivid and personal meaning for human life." Each one "was a citizen-soldier. He had volunteered because he had an idea of how his political life should be ordered. He introduced a new concept into war: patriotism. His loyalty was to his state or to the united states, in contrast to the Briton and German whose loyalty was to a ruler. [His] own honor was at stake. He was fighting to determine the destiny of his country and therefore of his children."[1]

As is always the case, each individual was different, and the individual stories played out differently. The story of Lincoln's Army of the Revolution is really a collection of some 250 different stories. They include desertions, capture by the enemy, prisoner exchanges, battle wounds, disease, and death. They include families torn apart by conflicting loyalties; others brought together by marriage and the birth of subsequent generations of Americans. Invariably, lives were forever altered. Farms were lost; fortunes were built. And when the war was over, a great wave of optimism for the economic and political future of the new republic swept many of them north and west to new opportunity in budding settlements on the edges of New England, New York, Pennsylvania, and Virginia. They and subsequently their descendants carried forth their faith in the ideals for which they had taken up arms, their individual stories eventually blending with others into American mythology.

Whether they volunteered or were drafted; whether their primary motivations for enlisting and serving were ideological or economic; whether driven by family and community relationships, or simply the individual's desire for youthful adventure, their stories continue to inspire generations of Americans possessed of a determination to preserve their cherished rights and liberties, and of a faith in their ability to make a difference in this world.

---

1 Peckham, *The War for Independence*, pp. 203–04.

Chapter 3

The War in Massachusetts Bay, 1775–1776

The Alarm on the morning of April 19, 1775, fanned out as ripples in a pond, the report that the Regulars were on the march spreading out in an ever increasing arc around Boston. Meeting House bells pealed the alarm. Musket fire relayed the urgency. Neighbors alerted neighbors. As in Lincoln, the response was similar in each town. Minute man and militia companies hurriedly mobilized, assembled, then marched to the defense of Concord. This much, at least, had been carefully scripted.

The previous September, the colonists had been caught flatfooted when General Gage had made a preemptive raid on the Powder House in Charlestown (now Somerville), carrying off 250 half-barrels of gunpowder that the provincials rightly or wrongly believed belonged to the province; the raid also secured two small cannons in Cambridge. Wild rumors alarmed the countryside, militia companies mobilized, and an angry mob of thousands of remonstrating citizens poured into Cambridge ready to do battle. But the powder was already gone.

It was a lesson learned. Determined not to be caught off guard again, provincial leaders put the fall and winter months to good use. Urged and directed by the Provincial Congress—newly formed in defiance of General Gage and meeting in Concord—the militia system was reorganized. Local towns began organizing, training, and equipping minute companies. The alarm system was revitalized, with an expanded network of alarm riders. In Boston, a clandestine network of volunteers organized eyes and ears to keep a close watch for clues of General Gage's next move. And large quantities of military supplies were procured and stockpiled in Worcester and Concord, in the growing expectation that they were likely to be needed.

The stockpiles were of considerable magnitude; weapons, equipment, and foodstuff sufficient to equip and sustain in the field a Provincial army of 15,000 men. For perspective, the entire British army in Boston at the time was about 4,500 men.[1] The supplies stockpiled at Concord alone included 60 barrels of beef, 318 barrels of flour, 47 hogsheads of salt, another 50 barrels of salt, 17,000 pounds of salt fish, 35,000 pounds of rice, 15 hogsheads of molasses, 18 casks of wine, 10 hogsheads of rum, plus innumerable quantities of tents, axes, iron spikes, billhooks, candles, and chests of medicine. In addition, there appear to have been a dozen pieces of artillery, 200 barrels of powder, another 14 hogsheads of powder, 20,000 pounds of musket balls and cartridges, along with an assortment of other ammunition.[2]

---

1 See Fischer, *Paul Revere's Ride*, p. 309.
2 Shattuck, *History of the Town of Concord*, pp. 94–99. Exact inventories of many items may never be known, but as large as these known quantities are, they appear to be a fraction of the procurements ordered by the Provincial Congress during the fall of 1774 and spring of 1775.

This, of course, was of no trivial concern to General Gage, who gathered intelligence during the winter and spring using both local informants and "spies" sent out from Boston. He sent other expeditions to secure powder in Portsmouth, New Hampshire, in December, and Salem in February; both came away empty-handed, thwarted by local action. By April, he concluded that another preemptive strike was necessary, this time to seize or destroy the supplies at Concord.

The eyes and ears in Boston picked up the preliminary preparations, and Paul Revere carried the warning out to Concord on April 8. The Provincials began removing supplies from

Many of the Provincial military supplies were stockpiled at Col. James Barrett's farm, before they were removed for safekeeping. Barrett was colonel of the regiment of local militia companies. (Sketch by E. C. Piexotto, *Scribner's Magazine*, January 1898)

Concord to dispersed locations in Acton, Groton, Sudbury, and other towns. Revere made a second preparatory ride to Concord a week later to report further military developments, check the readiness of the alarm system, and arrange some final details.

So it was that when the British expedition left Boston two nights later, the script played out almost flawlessly. Despite the British trap that snared Revere in Lincoln in the early hours of April 19th, the alarm continued to fan out across the countryside. In town after town, the mobilization of militia and minute companies manifested a collective determination to prevent the seizure of Provincial supplies, and to protect their Charter right of self-government. Except for the mobilization, however, there was no further script to follow, and little in the way of a coherent plan.

Concord

From the outflow of Flint's Pond by the home of *Samuel Dakin, Jr.*, where the minute men and militia companies from Lincoln met the *Baker* menfolk, the direct road to Concord skirted the swampy shoreline behind Great Ridge Hill, climbed away from the water, then turned northwesterly toward Concord. Minute man captain, *William Smith,* on horseback, probably rode with his men for awhile, before galloping ahead to confer with Concord's leadership.[1] As he was a relative newcomer to the town, it was unusual that his men should have elected him captain. But he was well connected. Before coming to Lincoln, he had been an active member of the Sons of Liberty in Boston; he was also the brother-in-law of the prominent patriot lawyer, John Adams.

---

1 Upon his arrival in Concord, Smith left his horse at Wright's Tavern, from where the British would later impress it into service for their return march to Boston.

Chapter 3: The War in Massachusetts Bay, 1775–1776

Lt. Samuel Farrar, Jr., and the other officers hurried the Lincoln men along through the moonlight. They covered the four miles to Concord quickly—the first men to arrive from another town. Within a couple of hours, they were busy assisting their next-town neighbors with last-minute preparations, removing and hiding the remaining provincial stores.

Morning dawned, as small groups from other towns dribbled into Concord. Concord's Reuben Brown, who had been detailed as a scout to the Lexington Green, galloped in with the report that he had seen the King's soldiers fire upon the Lexington militia. Anxiously, the men waited. The sun rose over Lincoln fields to the east. After a while, with still no sign of the Redcoats, a scouting party organized and marched off toward Lexington. They found their objective on the outskirts of town. Near the Concord/Lincoln boundary line, not far from the Brooks tannery, the vanguard of the column of Regulars appeared, cresting one of the undulations in the road. The locals paused momentarily, then wheeled about and marched back into Concord ahead of the Regulars, fifes and drums on both sides playing away, all making "grand musick."[1]

Despite the time to prepare, there was no plan or agreement in Concord about what to do when the Redcoats arrived. Cautiously, the Provincials withdrew, leaving the town to the custody of the unwanted visitors. Giving them wide berth, the locals crossed the North Bridge, regrouped briefly on the opposite side around Maj. John Buttrick's farm, then withdrew further north to Punkatasset Hill to watch and wait.

In command of the British forces, Lt. Col. Francis Smith went straight to work. He sent patrols to secure the two bridges that controlled access to the town from the southwest and north. Then he dispatched another four companies across the North Bridge to Col. James Barrett's farm about two miles beyond. Intelligence reports, gathered from loyal informants during the previous months, indicated that this was where they would find vast quantities of the military supplies stockpiled by the Massachusetts Provincials. His orders were to seize and destroy it. He put the rest of the troops to work searching suspect cellars, attics, and barns about the center of town. The searches were fruitful. A supply of musket balls and a large quantity of flour were dumped into the millpond. Gun carriages and other supplies were hauled onto the Town Common and set ablaze.[2]

On Punkatasset Hill, colonial numbers swelled with additional arrivals from surrounding towns. To better observe what was happening, they moved forward again, to Major Buttrick's place, and formed up in a field overlooking the river, a couple of hundred yards away. Three companies of Regulars patrolled the road below, which led from the bridge on the left,

---

1 The story is told by Amos Barrett of Concord; it can be found in Kehoe, *"We Were There!"* Part Six, p. 231. Undoubtedly, this patrol was comprised of both Concord and Lincoln men, but except for Barrett and Thaddeus Blood (who also wrote an account of the reconnaissance), no names have survived (see also Emerson, *Diaries and Letters*, p. 71).

2 The blaze on the Common quickly spread to the Courthouse and threatened other nearby buildings as well, but it was brought under control by the mutual efforts of Concord citizens and British Regulars. Concordians later retrieved most of the 500 pounds of musket balls from the millpond, and they saved about half of the 60 barrels of flour broken open (see Gross, *The Minutemen and Their World*, p. 123; Fischer, *Paul Revere's Ride*, p. 207; Shattuck, *History of the Town of Concord*, p. 107).

The expectations of the Redcoats dispatched to Colonel Barrett's farm were largely disappointed, as most of the supplies had been removed in recent days to towns further to the north and west. Of the supplies still remaining at Barrett's farm, most had been ingeniously hidden, including—according to tradition—cannons (or rows of muskets) that had been feverishly plowed into furrows in the fields just before the Redcoats arrived.

across a causeway through the marshy bottomland that extended toward Colonel Barrett's farm, some distance out of sight to the right. Across the river, the morning sun illuminated the fields and houses clustered about the town, about a mile away. *Capt. William Smith* volunteered the Lincoln men to dislodge the Redcoats from the bridge, but his bravado was rebuffed; indecision retaining the upper hand in this waiting game.

James Nichols, a "droll fellow and a fine singer" (and a fairly recent transplant from England to the colonies), was growing increasingly uneasy. At last, he asked one of his compatriots to hold his musket while he went down to talk with the Regular soldiers. At some length, he returned, retrieved his musket, and set off for home, becoming perhaps the first deserter of the American Revolution.[1]

Chimney smoke flitted and twirled above the scattered farmhouses. The spring morning was seasonably crisp. Above the village, smoke hovered. The small cloud was gaining strength, billowing as if fueled by something other than domestic hearths. All at once, an unthinkable realization rippled through the assembled militia. Watching in horrified disbelief, Concord's Joseph Hosmer finally turned to the officers, demanding, "Will you let them burn the town down?"[2]

Major Buttrick ordered his captains to mobilize their companies. With muskets loaded, but under strict orders not to fire unless first fired upon, the nearly 500 men marched double-file, down the hill.[3] The road descended to the right where, upon intersecting the river road, it switched back to the left toward the bridge.

Seeing the Colonials approach "in a very military manner," the three British companies (consisting of about 100 men altogether) consolidated, falling back toward the bridge.[4]

In the lead, the Acton company turned sharply left at the intersection and hurried forward, followed by the others in a continuous column.[5]

The Redcoats scrambled back across the bridge, pried up some of the planking, and quickly re-formed on the opposite side.

The Colonials were now nearly to the bridge. A warning shot rang out from the other side, then a scattering of two or three more, followed by a ragged volley. Several Colonials staggered and fell. Acton's Capt. Isaac Davis and Fifer Abner Hosmer were killed instantly.[6]

---

1 Baker Affidavit (1850).
2 Shattuck, *History of the Town of Concord*, p. 111.
3 Contemporary estimates of the colonial strength at the bridge vary from 300 to 500 (excepting some British accounts which place the number as high as 2,000). Fischer, *Paul Revere's Ride* (p. 209), places the number at about 500, comprised of companies from Lincoln, Concord, Bedford, and Acton, with portions of companies from Carlisle, Chelmsford, Groton, Littleton, Stow, and Westford. Surviving muster rolls of seven companies from Lincoln, Concord, Bedford, and Acton identify 288 individuals. Five other companies from these towns were also at the bridge, but no muster rolls survive. It is also unknown how many men were present in the partial companies from the other six towns, but modest assumptions would place the total number somewhere above 400, likely approaching or exceeding the 500 mark.
4 The quote is from a letter by Lt. William Southerland of the 38th Regiment, who was at the bridge, to Sir Henry Clinton, dated at Boston, April 26, 1775. He repeated the description in his report to General Gage the following day. The letters can be found in Kehoe, *"We Were There!"* Part Three; pp. 139–150.
5 Except for Acton being in the lead, the order of march to the bridge is for the most part unknown.
6 The only reported Lincoln casualty was *Joshua Brooks, Jr.,* who was grazed in the forehead. The wound appears to have been slight, but cut cleanly enough to cause the Lincoln men to joke that the Regulars must have been firing jackknives instead of ball (see Baker Affidavit (1850)).

With smoke rising from the center of Concord (right, above the horizon), the minute men return the fire of the Redcoats (far left) at the North Bridge. Acton Capt. Isaac Davis lies dead in the grass; Maj. John Buttrick (at right, sword raised) exhorts the locals to "Fire, fellow soldiers, for God's sake, fire." For several instants, musket fire poured back and forth across the river before the Redcoats were overwhelmed and retreated back to the center of town. The scene is depicted by Aiden Lassell Ripley. (Courtesy of Unum Group)

"Fire, fellow soldiers, for God's sake fire!" cried Major Buttrick. In an instant, the Colonial muskets roared back. For several additional instants, musket fire poured back and forth across the river. Then, as quickly as it began, the Redcoats gave way, turned, and fled back toward the town in equal parts haste and confusion—all but two Regulars, who lay unmoving on the moist ground.

The militia swarmed across the bridge but declined to give chase, their momentum blunted. Some turned back to assist wounded comrades. Others remained and took a defensive position behind a stone wall, on a nearby hill, expecting the British to regroup and return. They did not have long to wait.

Bayonets, Military Etiquette, and the Order of March to the Bridge

Except for Acton being in the lead, the order of march to the bridge remains unknown. At the time, it was evidently not thought important enough to record. By 1835, however, community pride had set elements in Concord and Acton to feuding over *why* Acton led instead of Concord.

Concord historian Lemuel Shattuck described the late arrival of the Acton Company, just as the march to the bridge was getting underway, implying (purportedly, at least) that Capt. Isaac Davis usurped the lead role by marching his troops to the front in ignorance of or in defiance of military etiquette—the honor of the lead position belonging by right to the men of Concord. Acton native Josiah Adams countered that Davis had moved his company to the front only after conferring with the other officers, and he charged that the Concord captains had declined (i.e., lacked the courage to take) the lead position. He excoriated Concord's lack of leadership, noting not only the indecisiveness before the march, but also that after Davis was killed at the bridge, command of the Provincial forces fell apart.

A popular theory among modern historians is that Acton was the only company equipped with bayonets. If this is true, then the logic certainly explains Acton's lead position. Support for this theory is offered by the fact that Isaac Davis was a gunsmith (who purportedly supplied his company with bayonets himself), and by Lincoln militiaman *Amos Baker,* who says in his 1850 affidavit that he "was the only man from Lincoln that had a bayonet."

Baker, however, appears to be mistaken. In March 1775, Lincoln Town Meeting voted funds to equip each minute man with "a bayonet belt Catrige Box Steal ramer gun stock and knapsack." Treasurer's Accounts show reimbursements by the town for 56 to 57 bayonets purchased by or for minute men. Consistent with *Baker's* statement, historians have typically concluded—because the reimbursements occurred after April 19, 1775—that the minute men acquired their accoutrements after the fact. The historical context suggests otherwise.

Cash was a tight commodity in Colonial New England. The economy ran on substantial amounts of debt, and slow payments were the rule, not the exception. Treasurer's accounts document payments typically running months and years—in some cases as many as four years—behind the actual rendering of the service or debt! It is simply not possible to apply a modern framework to associate the time of payment with the time of procurement. The fact that the reimbursements were paid the following February and later does not at all suggest that many or most of the accoutrements were procured after April 19th. More likely, it simply indicates when the reimbursement funds became available.

Against the backdrop of heightened tensions (including British forays into Charlestown, Portsmouth, and Salem, which had nearly sparked the outbreak of war before April 19th), the Lincoln minute men had been actively drilling twice a week for at least a month and a half (possibly as long as two and a half to three months) prior to the April 19th Alarm. The logic is compelling that most of them would have equipped themselves on a priority basis—before April 19th. Further, the minute men ▶

> dissolved very quickly after April 19th, replaced first by a Provincial Army, then in mid-summer by the Continental Army. It makes little sense to imagine that former minute men would have procured accoutrements after the fact. The reimbursements are explicit: "for a set of accoutrements as a minute man." There is no record of any such reimbursement by the town for militiamen or Continental Army enlistees.
>
> *Amos Baker* was not a minute man. Among his cohort of militiamen, he may have had the rare bayonet. And while many of his 75-year-old recollections in 1850 appear to be surprisingly good, he may also have been influenced by—perhaps even a partisan to—the Concord/Acton feud. Notwithstanding *Baker's* recollections, Acton appears not to have been the only company equipped with bayonets.
>
> Accordingly—and regardless of whatever else it may or may not say about Isaac Davis's motives or Concord's leadership—there must be some explanation other than bayonets for Acton's lead position in the march to the bridge.
>
> [See Adams, *Letter to Lemuel Shattuck*, pp. 7–13; Shattuck, *History of the Town of Concord*, p. 111; Baker, Affidavit (1850); Wiggin, 'Did the Lincoln Minute Men have Bayonets?".]

Colonel Smith soon appeared with a strong force of grenadiers to retake the bridge. He stopped out of musket range, studied the Colonials crouched behind the stone wall, and noted the others milling around across the river. After careful deliberation, he turned his men around and marched them back into town.

In due course, the Redcoats still at Colonel Barrett's farm finished their business and returned. They re-crossed the North Bridge unmolested, marching right past the Provincials crouched behind the stone wall on the hill. Muskets on both sides remained silent.

With his men now back from Barrett's farm, Colonel Smith's mission in Concord was complete. It was approaching midday. He was acutely aware of the increasing number of armed colonists continuing to gather from all directions. The reinforcements he had requested shortly after leaving Boston had not yet arrived. He confiscated carts and chaises for his wounded and pressed into service whatever extra horses he could find.[1] He reassembled his fatigued troops into a column for the long march back to Boston. Then he paused, waiting. The minutes ticked by, but still no reinforcements arrived. He moved a flanking company onto the ridge that paralleled the north side of the road to Lexington. At last, he called in the patrol holding the South Bridge and started moving the column back down the road leading from Concord, through Lincoln, toward Lexington and Boston.

The Bloody Angles

The column moved briskly, protected by the flankers on the ridge to its left. The Lincoln men, together with their counterparts from Concord, Acton, Bedford, and other towns—but more as a swarm than displaying any sort of organizational discipline—tracked the exodus as closely as they dared, just out of range of the flankers' muskets.

---

[1] Including the horse that Capt. William Smith left at Wright's Tavern.

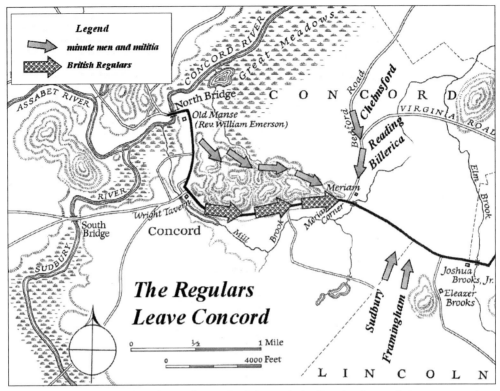

Protected by flankers on the ridge to the north of the road, the Regulars began their return march to Boston, while a swarm of minute men and militia from the North Bridge tracked their progress as closely as they dared—just out of musket range. (Base map, Brooks, *Trial by Fire*)

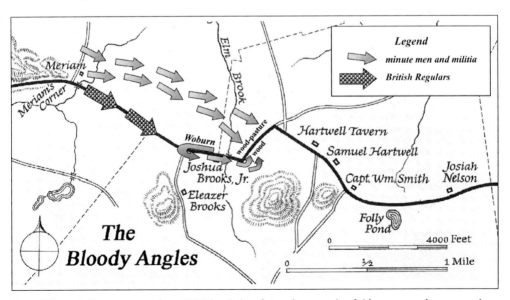

From Meriam's Corner, more than 1,000 locals leapfrogged across the fields to a wood-pasture where a bend in the road forms a dogleg. The Woburn militia, meanwhile, just arriving on the scene, abruptly turned around and took positions among the trees opposite, setting up a gauntlet through which the Regulars had to pass. (Base map, Brooks, *Trial by Fire*)

The Regulars reached Meriam's Corner, near the edge of Concord, without incident. As the main column maneuvered to cross the narrow bridge over Elm Brook,[1] the flankers descended the ridge. The swarm of minute men and militia pressed closely upon the jittery rear guard. Perhaps a little too closely. Newly arrived minute and militia companies from Chelmsford, Billerica, and Reading watched anxiously from positions along the road from Bedford.

Without warning, a spattering of uneasy musket fire fractured the tension.[2] It intensified as the Redcoats completed the bridge crossing and retreated down the Bay Road through the meadow and pastureland, toward the Lincoln hills. Other minute and militia companies from Framingham and Sudbury (including *Isaac Goodenow, Elisha Wheeler, Zebediah Farrar,* and *Timothy Sherman*), also newly arrived, had arrayed themselves along the south side of the road, and added accent to the echoing gunfire as the column of Regulars moved through. Their shots fell largely ineffectively, as Colonel Smith deployed his flankers to sweep the rebels back, away from his exposed troops in the road.

The swarming escort gave chase, its size growing with the newly arrived companies. Running ahead, the Provincials staked out locations from which to fire at the enemy. Disengaging as the flankers flushed them away, or as the column passed, they ran ahead again to stake out new spots to reengage.

Looking ahead into Lincoln, across the open fields on the north side of the road, the locals recognized a stand of trees on a small rise, some distance away. This marked a wood-pasture,[3] belonging to Thomas Brooks, where the road formed a dogleg, turning nearly perpendicular for about a hundred rods (550 yards) before resuming its easterly course. Many of them leapt a stone wall and made for the trees, realizing that by cutting across the fields and along a connecting lane, they could reach the wood-pasture ahead of the enemy, which was following the somewhat longer course of the road.

Meanwhile, from the east, three companies of Woburn militia still on their way to Concord were on a collision course with the enemy. Having come through the dogleg, they heard the rattle of musketry, and from a rise in the road near the Lincoln/Concord town boundary, they saw the Redcoats marching toward them. Quickly, they wheeled about, returned to the dogleg, and scattered among the trees in a young-growth maple wood opposite the wood-pasture.[4]

---

1 Also called Mill Brook. Another Elm Brook (also called Tanner's Brook) crosses the road about a mile further along, in Lincoln, just before the start of the dogleg that has become known today as the Bloody Angles.

2 Reports differ both as to who fired first, and as to the number of casualties. Amos Barrett later remembered, "a grait many Lay dead and the road was bloddy" (quoted in French, *The Day of Concord and Lexington,* pp. 218–219). Fischer, *Paul Revere's Ride,* (pp. 220–221), suggests as many as six Regulars may have been hit. Despite these indications to the contrary, other reports indicate that casualties at this point were light on both sides. Thaddeus Blood later recalled, "little injury was done on either side, at least I saw but one killed." Edmund Foster remembered that the British "faced about suddenly, and fired a volley of musketry upon us. They overshot; and no one, to my knowledge, was injured by the fire. The fire was immediately returned by the Americans, and two British soldiers fell dead at a little distance from each other, in the road near the brook" (quoted in Kehoe, *"We Were There!"* Part Six, pp. 205, 253).

3 A wood-pasture was a grazing area with scattered trees to provide an over-story of shade for the animals. Malcolm, *The Scene of Battle* (pp. 67–74), and Fischer, *Paul Revere's Ride* (pp. 223–225), give somewhat different terrain and land-use descriptions through this stretch of road. The author adheres to Fischer's description, which seems to be more consistent with firsthand accounts of the fight, and currently more accepted by historians at Minute Man National Historical Park.

4 Most accounts seem to imply that the Woburn men were just arriving on the scene at this point in time. Galvin, *The Minute Men* (pp. 172–173), goes to great length to describe that the Woburn men arrived at Concord just after the fight at the North Bridge and deliberately waited around on the outskirts of town

Harassed on their flank and rear, the Regulars pushed ahead. As the column turned into the dogleg, the flankers bogged down in the woods, and the column took unusually heavy fire on the right from the Woburn men pressing in at close range. The column staggered, but its momentum carried it forward. Moments later, an even heavier fire erupted on the left from the wood-pasture, now filled with 1,000 colonials, with others still arriving across the fields. The flankers on this side were driven in by the sheer intensity of the colonial fire. The column staggered again, briefly, but drove forward through the gauntlet, taking hits from both sides. Colonel Smith again "ordered out a flank guard on the left to dislodge the Americans from their posts behind large trees: but they only became a better mark to be shot at," recalled Edmund Foster of Reading. "A short but sharp contest ensued."[1] For ten to fifteen minutes the firefight raged, until the last of the Regulars cleared the woods and the dogleg.[2]

Free of the woods at last, the British flankers redeployed, moving quickly into the fields. Past the Mason house, the Hartwell Tavern, and the Smith farm, they traded musket fire with the growing army of Provincials. In the road, the instinct for self-preservation overcame growing fatigue, and the column picked up speed even as it began to lose order and discipline. Casualties continued to climb. Past the Foster farm and the Nelson farm, the battle raged, the Redcoats racing toward the safety of Boston. It was now simply a matter of survival.

Keeping pace with the enemy, *William Thorning* reportedly escaped flankers in his rear by dropping down into a shallow trench, then after they passed, he took a position behind a large boulder, resumed firing and killed two Redcoats. *Daniel Child* reportedly found himself caught between a flanking party and the main column of Regulars. They were near enough to each other that neither could fire at him without endangering the other. So the firing

---

to ambush the British on their return march. As a military historian, Galvin seems to relish discussing the strategic implications of his premise. However, the author has found no primary source to support an earlier arrival of the Woburn men. Whenever it was that they arrived, the Woburn men may have taken time in Lexington to assist their neighbors in the aftermath of the bloodshed on the Lexington Green; then they stopped near the meeting house in Lincoln for rest and refreshment before resuming their march toward Concord (Galvin, *The Minute Men*, p. 172; see also Loammi Baldwin's diary entry for April 19, 1775, in Hurd, *History of Middlesex County*, Vol. 1, p. 447).

1 Letter from Rev. Edmund Foster to Col. Daniel Shattuck, dated Littleton, March 10, 1825 (in Kehoe, *"We Were There!"* Part Six, p. 254). Edmund Foster had been in the wood-pasture as a participant in the fight. In 1783, he married Phebe Lawrence of Lincoln, daughter of Lincoln's Pastor, and sister of *William Lawrence, Jr.*

2 Galvin, *The Minute Men* (p. 176), estimates that it took the Regulars half an hour to fight their way through the Bloody Angles. While this underscores the intensity and severity of the fighting—by all accounts it was the most severe and deadly of any of the fighting along Battle Road, except perhaps portions of the bitter house-to-house combat in the village of Menotomy (now Arlington)—Galvin's estimate is overstated. The British column stretched about one-quarter of a mile in length. The dogleg (between the angles) is a quarter to a third of a mile in length. Under normal circumstances, and at a normal marching pace, it would have taken about 10 to 12 minutes from the time the first Redcoat entered the Bloody Angles until the last Redcoat exited the Bloody Angles. Doubtless, the forward progress of the British column slowed temporarily as it absorbed the shock and intensity of the Provincial fire. But by most accounts it exited the Bloody Angles at a trot—a perfectly normal reaction for troops trying to escape a gauntlet of deadly fire. The duration of the fight at the Bloody Angles was probably not too much different from the time it would have taken them to pass this part of the road without having been ambushed. Galvin's estimate would make sense if the roadway had actually been blocked, either by Provincial troops or by a physical barrier. Neither was the case, however.

The casualty count through the Bloody Angles is imprecise, both because of limited information, and because casualties in the Bloody Angles are often lumped with casualties that occurred further along the road at the Hartwell and Smith farms and beyond. Foster says eight Regulars were killed at the Bloody Angles, and typically three Provincials are said to have been killed there. See also Coburn, *The Battle of April 19, 1775*, p. 105. Fischer, *Paul Revere's Ride* (p. 226) estimates the number of British killed and wounded at 30.

Chapter 3: The War in Massachusetts Bay, 1775–1776   53

Unable to deploy their flankers effectively through the Bloody Angles, the British column suffered some of their worst casualties—an estimated thirty killed and wounded—along this brief stretch of road. Losing military discipline, they exited the gauntlet at a run. (Drawing by E. C. Peixotto, *Scribner's Magazine*, January 1898)

stopped, and he was able to run out from between them. Once he got out in the open, they commenced firing at him, but he successfully dodged the whizzing bullets and reached shelter behind a rock, as he said afterwards, "verily holding my breath in my hands." *Ephraim Flint* reportedly captured a Redcoat, then took him home and gave him work as a farmhand.[1]

---

[1] See Hersey, *Heroes*, pp. 27, 29; *An Account of the Celebration*, p. 174. Tales of individual exploits enrich the overall story, but they are impossible to verify. They are perpetuated through tradition and family lore, and to the extent that the stories may actually be true, they undoubtedly occurred at various locations along the road, not just in Lincoln, but also in Lexington, Menotomy, and Cambridge.

In disarray, the British column staggered out of Lincoln, leaving behind ten of their number killed or mortally wounded, to be buried in Lincoln soil.[1] The long-awaited British reinforcements finally brought them some relief in Lexington, but the long-simmering dispute between England and her American colonies had now boiled over. There could be no turning back. After a brief lull, the fight resumed and raged on through Menotomy and Cambridge—the Lincoln men among the now several thousand Provincials from more than two dozen towns giving chase. At last, as dusk approached, the weary Redcoats succeeded in crossing and securing Charlestown Neck, and the setting sun silenced the last of the muskets.

Chaos at Cambridge

Swept along by adrenalin and participating more as individuals than as members of functional units, most of Lincoln's men-in-arms at Concord pursued the retreating Redcoats back to Boston. Cambridge Common and the surrounding countryside teemed with confusion. The expectation of a counterattack by the Regulars kept most reasonably alert to what was happening around them.

Chaos continued the next morning, as members of the various minute and militia companies reconnected and regrouped. Many were now wet and chilled from the overnight rain. A steady stream of newcomers continued to pour into Cambridge from an ever expanding arc of towns.[2]

It is probable that some returned to Lincoln, to attend to hastily abandoned chores, to reassure anxious families, and to collect supplies needed to sustain themselves at Cambridge. Others may have wandered in search of information, or perhaps to forage for food or for whatever else they could find. We can assume that the sergeants attempted to reestablish some semblance of order, while *Col. Abijah Peirce*, *Capt. William Smith*, and *Lt. Samuel Farrar* undoubtedly conferred with higher command. The central question on everyone's mind was, "What happens next?"

The overnight sentinels at Charlestown Neck and Boston Neck remained at their posts, and patrols kept lookout for the expected counter attack. Units were sent to Roxbury and Dorchester and were deployed along the banks of the Charles. The counterattack never came. Instead, the British pulled out of Charlestown and beefed up their defenses in Boston.

The Committee of Safety called for thousands of additional volunteers, then turned to the tedious process of reorganizing largely autonomous units and un-enlisted volunteers into a new Provincial Army with a coherent, unified command structure.

---

1 Of the ten British soldiers reportedly buried in Lincoln, five rest in a common grave in the old Precinct Burial Ground; the other five are reportedly buried along the road near where they fell. See Hersey, pp. 16-17. The familiar story of Mary Hartwell accompanying her father-in-law transporting the five fallen soldiers in his oxcart to the cemetery the next morning—drawn by thoughts of the wives, sweethearts, and parents who would never again see their loved ones—is a local favorite. A similar story is told of Eunice Wheeler, daughter of *Edmond Wheeler*. While unverifiable, both are rooted in local family tradition. See *Edmond Wheeler* (q.v.), note 2, p. 431.

2 It is widely estimated that within a couple of days, as many as 20,000 men mobilized in response to the Alarm of April 19, 1775. They came from Connecticut, Rhode Island, and New Hampshire, as well as Massachusetts. The number is illusory, however. French, *The Siege of Boston* (p. 243), puts the proper perspective on this: "The very size of the army was uncertain. On paper there were more than twenty thousand men; as a matter of fact there can seldom have been more than four-fifths of that number." He cites more realistic numbers from Frothingham, *History of the Siege of Boston* (p. 101), as 11,500 from Massachusetts, 2,300 from Connecticut, 1,200 from New Hampshire, and 1,000 from Rhode Island. Even so, 16,000 men pouring into Cambridge (with a population of fewer than 1,600) is an extraordinary influx.

During the ensuing days and weeks, a dozen and a half new arrivals dribbled in from Lincoln. *Capt. William Smith* secured the command of a new company in Colonel Nixon's Regiment, which he set about populating with men from Lincoln and Acton. Other Lincoln men enlisted in Capt. Nathan Fuller's Company in Colonel Gardner's Regiment, and in a smattering of other units. *John Flint, Jeduthan Bemis,* and *John Viles* joined Capt. Abijah Child's Company in Colonel Brewer's Regiment, but two weeks later, they found the company reassigned to Colonel Gardner's Regiment. Bit by bit, nearly half of the Lincoln men who had answered the April 19th Alarm drifted back to Lincoln, recalled by domestic responsibilities, farming or occupational obligations, or personal priorities that precluded their enlistment for extended service at that point in time. About 70 to 75 Lincoln men remained in arms at Cambridge.

The Propaganda Coup

Having returned to Lincoln in the days immediately following April 19th, *John Whitehead, Abraham Gearfield,* and *Isaac Parks* went to Lexington, with others, on April 23 to give legal depositions about the fight at the North Bridge. "Seeing several fires in the Town, [we] thought the houses in Concord were in danger, and marched toward the said bridge," they testified, "and when we had got near the bridge they [i.e., the Regular Troops] fired on our men, first three guns, (one after the other,) and then a considerable number more, and then, and not before, (having orders from our commanding officer not to fire till we were fired upon,) we fired upon the Regulars, and they retreated. On their retreat through the Town of Lexington to Charlestown, they ravaged and destroyed private property, and burnt three houses, one barn, and one shop."[1]

"Without saying any thing to us, they discharged a number of guns on us," added *James Adams* in his sworn statement, "which killed two men dead on the spot, and wounded several others, when we returned the fire on them, which killed two of them and wounded several."[2]

Two days later, *Joseph Abbot, Sr.,* testified that, "being on Lexington common, and mounted on horses, we saw a body of Regular Troops marching up to the Lexington Company which was then dispersing. Soon after the Regulars fired first a few guns, which we took to be pistols from some of the Regulars who were mounted on horses, and then the said Regulars fired a volley or two before any guns were fired by the Lexington Company. Our horses immediately started and we rode off."[3]

For three days, ninety-five participants and witnesses to the events at Lexington and Concord, including three captured soldiers of the King, gave legal testimony about how the bloodshed had occurred. Together, they executed a total of twenty depositions, sworn under oath, duly testified by Justices of the Peace, and certified by a Notary Public.[4] These established a body of evidence that at both locations, the King's soldiers had fired first, unprovoked, on the

---

1 Deposition of John Hoar, et al.
2 Deposition of James Adams.
3 Deposition of Joseph Abbot.
4 Ten of the signatories on three of the depositions were Lincoln participants in the April 19th events. In addition, the deposition of one of the captured soldiers of the King (John Bateman of the 52nd Regiment) was executed in Lincoln, suggesting the likelihood that he was being held in Lincoln. Could this be the soldier reportedly captured by *Ephraim Flint,* who worked *"peacefully"* on the Flint farm for some time? See "Ephraim Flint's Prisoner of War," p. 284. While some of the captives were later exchanged, no record has been found that Bateman ever returned to his regiment (see Kehoe, "The Provincial Depositions," p. 147).

innocent citizens of Massachusetts. Orchestrated by the Provincial Congress, and with a cover letter addressed "To the Inhabitants of Great Britain," the depositions were put on a speedy packet out of Salem, and they arrived in London eleven days before General Gage's official report. This was political propaganda at its best.

Thus, Londoners received their first reports of the, "Hostilities… commenced in this Colony by the Troops under command of General Gage" and of "the ravages of the Troops as they retreated from Concord to Charlestown, …women in childbed were driven by the soldiery naked into the streets; old men, peaceably in their houses, were shot dead; and such scenes exhibited as would disgrace the annals of the most uncivilized Nation." The news created quite a stir.[1]

> Lincoln, April 23, 1775.
> I John Bateman, belonging to the fifty second regiment, commanded by Colonel Jones, on Wednesday morning, on the nineteenth day of April, instant, was in the party marching to Concord, being at Lexington, in the county of Middlesex, being nigh the meeting house in said Lexington, there was a small party of men gathered together in that place, when our said troops marched by, and I testify and declare, that I heard the word of command given to the troops to fire, and some of said troops did fire, and I saw one of said small party lay dead on the ground nigh said meeting house; and I testify that I never heard any of the inhabitants so much as fire one gun on said troops.
> John Bateman.

British soldier John Bateman was captured on April 19th and deposed a few days later in Lincoln. He may have been captured by Ephraim Flint and been working peacefully on the Flint farm. The deposition was published a month later. (*The New England Chronicle or The Essex Gazette*, May 25–June 1, 1775)

Public sentiment peaked against the "ministerial vengeance" and the "persecution and tyranny" of the King's government, and in favor of the "justice" of the Colonial cause. The opposition Whig party had a field day in Parliament, attacking the policies of the government, "which, if successful, must end in the ruin and slavery of Britain, as well as the persecuted American Colonies."[2] Embarrassed, defensive, and without contravening evidence, the King's ministers squirmed answerless except to ask everyone to wait for the arrival of the official report.

By the time General Gage's official report finally arrived, however, the Provincial Congress's version of the events had become firmly implanted in the public mind. There was not enough substantively different in the official version to quell the uproar, or to silence the Whigs in Parliament.

Bunker Hill

Amidst the ongoing organizational confusion at Cambridge, essential military readiness was maintained. On May 11, 19-year-old *Abraham Peirce* drew duty on picket guard close to enemy lines; *John Adams, Jr.*, may have served with a detachment on main guard on May 15; a week later, *Abel Adams* and *William Thorning* took their turns on picket guard.

Capt. William Smith's Company, containing approximately 23 Lincoln men, participated in a raid on Hog and Noddle's Islands on May 27. During a sharp skirmish with a contingent of Royal marines, the colonials seized, stripped, and burned a schooner that had run aground, drove off several-hundred head of livestock, and burned hay to deprive

---

1 Force, *American Archives*, p. 487.
2 The quotations are contained within the covering letter dated Watertown, April 26, 1775, and signed by "Jos. Warren, President pro tem.," as it appears in Force, *American Archives* (p. 487).

Chapter 3: The War in Massachusetts Bay, 1775–1776 57

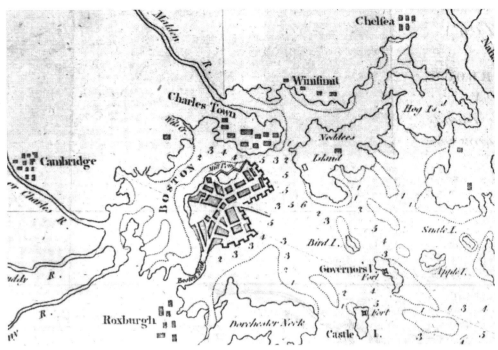

This 1775 chart of Boston Harbor identifies the location of Noddles and Hog islands (now part of East Boston), where on May 27, 1775, Lincoln men in Capt. William Smith's Company participated in a raid (known as the Battle of Chelsea Creek) to deprive the British garrison of supplies of hay and livestock. (Library of Congress)

the Regulars from using it for supply. The success of the raid elicited general acclaim in the Colonial camp.[1]

On June 14, *James Nichols* and *Jonas Parks* were sent to the armorer to get their muskets fitted for service. Early on the evening of June 16, *Peter Oliver* paraded on Cambridge Common as a member of Col. William Prescott's Regiment. Powder was distributed. Rumors began to circulate, but reliable information was nowhere to be found. About nine o'clock, as quietly as possible, Colonel Prescott's Regiment moved out. Under strict orders of silence, they marched to Charlestown Neck, crossed it, then marched up the back side of Bunker Hill. They dug themselves in on a forward knob, known as Breed's Hill, overlooking Boston.

Daybreak brought a swift response from the British. All morning long, British guns in the harbor pounded the hill, while Prescott's men worked resolutely to improve their defenses.

In Cambridge, Colonel Gardner's Regiment, with about a dozen and a half Lincoln men in three companies, moved up to the road to Lechmere's Point and stopped. The British guns, continuing to pound the hill, paid them no attention. Colonel Nixon's Regiment, with about two dozen Lincoln men in four companies, began to mobilize.

By early afternoon, British landing operations had ferried thousands of troops with light artillery to the base of the hill. Colonel Nixon's Regiment moved across Charlestown Neck and onto the heights. It is probable that they split themselves up, most filling in gaps along the rail fence to the left, others reinforcing Prescott's men in the redoubt.

---

1 French, *The Siege of Boston*, pp. 248–249; Frothingham, *History of the Siege of Boston*, pp. 109–110.

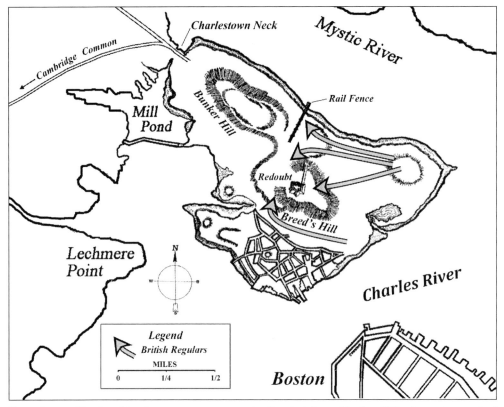

Forty-five to fifty-five Lincoln men were among the Provincials on Bunker Hill who twice repulsed British assaults, inflicting heavy losses. Their ammunition ran out during the third British assault, and they were forced to abandon the hill. British Gen. Henry Clinton reportedly said of the costly British victory, "another such would have ruined us." (Base map, National Park Service)

About mid-afternoon, the British burned the town of Charlestown and ceased cannonading the hill. In open order, a long wave of Redcoats advanced on colonial positions. In the redoubt, *Daniel Farrar* and *Lemuel Wheeler* waited, under strict orders to hold their fire. Along the fence, *Daniel Hosmer*, *Artemas Reed*, *Ensign John Hartwell*, and *Cato Smith*, under similar orders, choked down their anxieties about the meager protection offered by the freshly-cut hay that had been hastily raked in against the rails.[1]

The British Light Infantry advanced steadily and unmolested. Toward the left side of the rail fence, near the shoreline, and up the hill toward the redoubt they came. At close range, a sudden, withering volley fire from behind the hay and the breastworks repulsed the attack.

---

[1] The placement of these individuals in the redoubt or along the fence is strictly conjectural. Records and contemporary accounts are insufficiently detailed to know precisely how they were deployed. It is known only that these individuals were members of Colonel Nixon's Regiment, and there is evidence to suggest that elements of Colonel Nixon's Regiment were in both locations. But beyond that, French, *The Siege of Boston* (p. 264), aptly notes that it is "difficult to disentangle…who was on the field and who was not," much less to determine their exact locations. *Daniel Farrar* and *Lemuel Wheeler* were members of Capt. Joseph Butler's Company and Capt. Abishai Brown's Company, respectively; *Daniel Hosmer, Artemas Reed, John Hartwell,* and *Cato Smith* were members of *Capt. William Smith's* Company.

Chapter 3: The War in Massachusetts Bay, 1775–1776

British soldiers step over the fallen bodies of their compatriots in successive waves of their assault on Bunker Hill. (Painting by Howard Pyle, *Scribner's Magazine*, February 1898)

The Redcoats regrouped and advanced again. This time, the grenadiers advanced toward the middle of the rail fence; the focus of the attack shifting uphill toward the redoubt. Again, an explosion of Provincial volley fire at close range staggered their advance, forcing them to retreat.

As British forces regrouped once more, Colonel Gardner's Regiment now moved across the Neck and onto Bunker Hill, with 14-year-old *Leonard Parks* providing fife accompaniment. They assisted others already there in throwing up additional defenses. One company went forward to reinforce the men at the rail fence.

The long wave of Redcoats approached a third time, now advancing all along the Provincial line, marching uphill; steadily closer. The Provincials held their fire. Closer… Closer…. Suddenly erupting, a volley fire tore through the British ranks. But the intensity of the fire could not be sustained. Slowly it diminished as colonial munitions ran out; the Redcoats broke through the flanks and overwhelmed the redoubt. As the Provincials fell back, Colonel Gardner's Regiment moved up and covered their retreat, pouring a well-directed fire into the enemy between Breed's Hill and Bunker Hill. But the Provincials were now beaten. As they retreated back across Charlestown Neck, they left the battered but victorious British forces once again in full possession of the Charlestown peninsula.

Benjamin Cleaveland was hospitalized with a head wound and a broken leg. There are no other records of casualties among Lincoln men in the field that day. Loyalist *Dr. Charles Russell*, no longer Lincoln's most prominent citizen, went to work tending to the fallen soldiers of the King.

The Siege of Boston, and Dorchester Heights

Slowly the Provincials came to understand the defeat for its real significance: that undermanned, disorganized, and outgunned, they had held off everything that the King's army could throw at them until their ammunition had run out. The casualty count confirmed the moral victory. The roughly 2,000 home-grown citizen-soldiers had suffered approximately 400 casualties—most of those occurring in the final assault, as their ammunition gave out and the Redcoats swarmed the redoubt. In return, they had inflicted 1,100 casualties against a force of 2,500 professionally-trained British Regulars.[1] "A dear bought victory," noted British Gen. Sir Henry Clinton ruefully, "another such would have ruined us." Gen. Nathanael Greene of Rhode Island wrote, "I wish we could sell them another hill at the same price."[2]

Despite the confidence boost, however, the Provincials were unprepared for another engagement with the enemy. The continuing shortage of men, basic provisions, and military supplies remained a problem. And even after the Continental Congress adopted the New Englanders as the core of the new Continental Army, and General Washington arrived to take command, the uniquely "Yankee" notion of discipline—and a similar sense of individualism in the command structure—frustrated attempts to mold an effective army.

The routine of camp duty returned. Guard duty, fatigue duty, boredom—these were the constants. The men labored at strengthening defenses. On July 3, *Nathan Tidd, William Thorning, Daniel Child*, and probably *Jack Farrar* served duty on main guard with Col. Loammi Baldwin. Recruits arrived; others departed. In August, *Tilly Mead* chopped open his right knee, evidently while serving on wood detail. In September, *Daniel Hosmer* and *Abijah Munroe* became sick and left camp. *Capt. William Smith* and *Solomon Whitney* departed on furlough. *Edward Adams* arrived as a substitute first for *Joseph Peirce*, then for *Sgt. Elijah Willington*.

Despite a general order to punish any soldier who injured property, the town of Cambridge suffered the depredations of a large army suddenly encamped in its midst. Fields, gardens, and orchards were trampled, laid bare, and cut up into forts and entrenchments. Horses and cattle devoured whole fields of crops; demand for firewood destroyed countless wood lots and stands of trees. The camps were as varied "in their form as the Owners are in their Dress, and every tent is a Portraiture of ye Temper and Taste of ye Person that incamps in it," reported Rev. William Emerson of Concord, who expressed a sense of melancholy at the devastation to the town but found a strange, diverting beauty in the variety of temporary shelters. "Some are made of Boards, some of Sailcloth, and some partly of one and partly of the other. Others are made of Stone and Turf, and others again of Brick and others Brush. Some are thrown up in a hurry & look as if they could not help it—meer necessity—others are curiously wrought

---

1 No reliable count of numbers engaged or of the number of casualties has ever been agreed upon. Estimates of British troops engaged generally range from 2,200 to 3,000, and their casualties are typically estimated at between 1,050 and 1,150. On the colonial side, estimates of the number engaged typically fall between 1,500 and 2,400. Colonial casualty estimates range as low as 341 to as high as 451.

2 Both quotations are widely reported, but the author has been unable to find a primary source for Clinton's statement (see Morison, *Oxford History*, p. 217, as a secondary source for Clinton's statement. Greene's statement appears in a letter to his brother Jacob, found in Richard K. Showman, *The Papers of Nathanael Greene,* published for the Rhode Island Historical Society, Vol. 1 (Chapel Hill: University of North Carolina Press, 1976), p. 92 [as cited in Bobrick, *Angel in the Whirlwind*, p. 143]).

Chapter 3: The War in Massachusetts Bay, 1775–1776

The town of Cambridge suffered the depredations of a large army suddenly camped within its midst. The varied forms of shelter are shown in this drawing by B. West Clinedinst of General Washington escorting Benjamin Franklin and other members of a congressional committee on a tour of the camp. (*Scribner's Magazine*, March 1898)

with doors & windows, done with Wreaths and Withes, in manner of a Basket. Some are ye proper Tents and Markees that look as ye regular Camp of ye Enemy."[1]

Washington schemed and worked to put his army into a condition to strike at the British. Behind their fortifications, the Provincials had shown they could make a good account of themselves, but they were not sufficiently trained for an open engagement with the enemy, nor strong enough for a direct assault on British defenses. The lessons learned from Bunker Hill were many, but the game remained unchanged. Washington would have to find a way to provoke the Redcoats into leaving the protection of Boston to assault the Continental fortifications. Slowly, the elements of a bold plan began to take shape in his mind.

In January, Col. Henry Knox and his men arrived with 50-odd pieces of artillery from Fort Ticonderoga.[2] Soon thereafter, ten regiments detached from the militia reported to camp to reinforce the Continental Army. *Ephraim Hartwell, Jr.,* marched in as a quartermaster in Col. Josiah Whitney's Regiment. A few days later, *Daniel Child* may have come with Col. Simeon Cary's Regiment. On February 4, ten to twelve other members of the Lincoln militia arrived with Capt. Asahel Wheeler's Company, Col. John Robinson's Regiment. The 7,000 reinforcements raised troop strength to crucial levels. Throughout the Continental

---

1 Rev. William Emerson letter to Phebe Emerson (July 7, 1775), quoted in Emerson, *Diaries and Letters*, pp. 79–80.
2 Lincoln's *Solomon Whitney* may have participated in this expedition, but this is uncertain. He was wounded in western Massachusetts at about this time, requiring care in Stockbridge. Whether or not he was part of Knox's expedition, he probably did not return with Knox's men. He was back by February 4, however, when he went to Roxbury with Capt. Asahel Wheeler's Company, Col. John Robinson's Militia Regiment.

After Bunker Hill, the Regulars remained within their fortifications in Boston and Charlestown, while the Provincials erected a ring of fortifications around the two peninsulas. In order to provoke the Regulars into leaving the protection of Boston to assault Provincial earthworks, General Washington hatched a bold plan to fortify Dorchester Heights in March 1776. (Lossing, *Pictorial Field Book*)

camps, preparations swung into high gear. It was time to make a move before the British garrison could be reinforced.

Some of the Lincoln men doubtless worked with their fellow soldiers making *fascines*, bundles of branches used in making earthworks, and *chandeliers*, the frames to hold the fascines in place.[1] Thousands of pieces were needed. Perhaps other Lincoln men served with

---

[1] See sidebar, "Digging in at Dorchester Heights."

"Digging in" at Dorchester Heights

The ability of earthworks to withstand artillery fire in the eighteenth century often came from a wooden skeleton consisting of bundled branches called "fascines," held in place within wooden uprights known as "chandeliers," with the dirt piled against them. Without such an internal skeletal structure, dirt piled up into defensive earthworks has little inherent strength. For extended works, the number of fascines required could be considerable.

As a basic building block of military construction during campaigns afield, fascines were simple structures. They had a variety of other uses in addition to supporting earthworks, and they varied in size according to their use. An 1810 military manual explains that fascines "that are for making epaulements [i.e., breastworks] or chandeliers, or to raise works, or fill up ditches, are 10 feet long, and 1 or 1½ feet in diameter. They are made as follows: six small pickets are stuck into the ground, 2 and 2, forming little crosses, well fastened in the middle with willow bindings. On these tres[t]les the branches are laid, and are bound round with withes at the distance of every 2 feet. Six men are employed in making a fascine; 2 cut the boughs, 2 gather them, and the remaining 2 bind them. These six men can make 20 fascines every hour. Each fascine requires 5 pickets to fasten it."

The chandeliers designed for Dorchester Heights were described by Lt. Col. Rufus Putnam as each "constructed of one Sill, 10 feet long & 6 inch Square with two posts 5 feet long of the same size framed into the Sill 5 feet apart, each supported by a Brace on the out Side—they are placed on the ground at a proper distance from each other the open space between the post are then filled with bundels of Fasciens strongly picketed together."

Typically, the framework would be covered with dirt, but at Dorchester Heights, construction of the works was complicated by the frozen ground. Washington wrote that as the ground was "froze upwards of two feet deep, and as impenetrable as a Rock, nothing could be attempted with Earth; we were obligd, therefore to provide an amazing quantity of chandeliers and Fascines for the Work." ▶

Vast quantities of fascines and chandeliers were needed to erect the fortifications on the frozen ground of Dorchester Heights. (Courtesy of Sylva Native Nursery and Seed Co; Deidier, *Le Parfait Ingenieur Français*)

> Thus the Dorchester Heights fortifications were largely erected rather than dug. They were, said Colonel Putnam, "a Lodgment made of Chandeliers Fasciens &c." They were prefabricated and carted into place. By dawn, wrote Lt. Isaac Bangs, "our Forts were...then little besides Fashiens about 6 Feet thick."
>
> Notwithstanding the frozen ground, other contemporary reports indicate that entrenching was accomplished, and it is likely that at least some of the dirt was spread over the fascines, chandeliers, and hay. In addition, General Heath noted that, "Rows of barrels, filled with earth, were placed round the works." He explains their purpose: "They presented only the appearance of strengthening the works, but the real design was, in case the enemy made an attack, to have rolled them down the hill. They would have descended with such increasing velocity, as must have thrown the assailants into the utmost confusion, and have killed and wounded great numbers."
>
> [See Duane, *A Military Dictionary*, p. 153; Buell, *Memoirs of Rufus Putnam*, p. 58; George Washington letter to John A. Washington [March 31, 1776], in Washington *Papers*; Bangs, *Journal*, p. 11; Heath, *Memoirs*, pp. 32–33, quoted in Scheer and Rankin, *Rebels & Redcoats*, p. 106.]

details that collected and stockpiled hundreds of wagons and carts, barrels, teams of oxen, and tons of hay. Out of sight in the Charles River, other soldiers constructed two floating batteries and collected boats to ferry thousands of soldiers across the Back Bay. These would be used to counterattack undermanned British fortifications after the Redcoats were redeployed for the British assault. Artillerymen mounted some of the Fort Ticonderoga guns in the Cambridge and Roxbury batteries, and they readied the remainder for rapid deployment onto Dorchester's Heights. Bandages and medical supplies were secured, and nurses mobilized to treat the wounded.

On the night of March 2, Continental batteries in Cambridge opened fire on the British fortifications in Boston. The British answered with emphasis. The bombardment resumed the following night with greater intensity. The next day, March 4, the balance of Lincoln's militia company marched to Dorchester, 59 men under the command of *Capt. John Hartwell* in *Col. Eleazer Brooks's* 3rd Middlesex Regiment. Lincoln's *Zechariah Weston, John Coolidge, Abel Flint, Lemuel Wheeler,* and *Joseph Munroe* marched in with companies from Waltham, Concord, and Lexington.

The road approaching Dorchester was jammed with soldiers and militia. Teams of oxen yoked to wagons and carts—piled high with hay bales, fascines, chandeliers, and entrenching tools—waited in line, more than half a mile in length, and wedged together so tightly that the Lincoln men had to leave the road to make forward progress.

At nightfall, a heavy bombardment commenced again, this time from Roxbury as well as Cambridge. Again, the British guns responded threefold. The terrible roar shook houses and rattled windows as far away as Braintree, and the distant thunder may well have carried west into Lincoln. Anxious families in Lincoln slept fitfully, if at all.

Covered by the artillery barrage, 300 carts and 2,400 men—possibly including *Noah Bacon, Salem Middlesex,* and *John Lander*—moved across Dorchester Neck and onto the Heights. Hay silenced the wheels. Bales stacked as blinds and smoke from the Roxbury

Chapter 3: The War in Massachusetts Bay, 1775–1776

Dorchester Heights overlooked the shipping lanes into and out of Boston. By fortifying the heights in March 1776, the Provincials threatened to cut off vital British supply lines, forcing General Howe to evacuate Boston. In this 1774 view of Boston from Dorchester Heights, the main part of town is visible on the right, Beacon Hill is identifiable by its summit pole, and Boston Neck runs off to the left. (Lossing, *Pictorial Field Book*)

guns screened them from British view. Hour by hour, the fortifications took shape in the moonlight, the carts shuttling back and forth with more building supplies. Before daybreak, two strong Continental redoubts and four smaller works, with at least 20 pieces of artillery, overlooked Boston's wharfs from the hills and the lower slopes of Dorchester. American guns now commanded the entrance and exit to Boston Harbor. The fatiguers had retired to the rear, and a large force of fresh, well-armed men stared over the ramparts. "A very Great work for one Night," recorded Col. Jeduthan Baldwin with considerable satisfaction.[1]

By morning light, the British stared in disbelief, their surprise total. They turned their artillery on the new Continental fortifications, to little effect.

During the day, the Provincials continued to strengthen their positions. From the hill, with the Boston waterfront laid out before them, *Jacob Foster, Jube Savage,* and *Edmund Bowman* may have watched with others as the British prepared their assault.[2] They may

---

1 The quote is reported in French, *The Siege of Boston*, footnote on p. 304.
2 Unfortunately, it is not known for sure where and how the Lincoln men were deployed at Dorchester Heights, including whether they erected the fortifications or manned them after they were built. Brown, *Beneath Old Roof Trees* (p. 233) suggests that they were deployed as laborers in constructing the fortifications: "The Lincoln soldiers, like many others, took their ox-teams with them to aid in the work. 'When in service on the hills,' said Mr. [Samuel] Farrar, [Jr.], 'we were obliged to manage our oxen in silence, depending upon the prick of our bayonets to urge them along rather than our ordinary means of forcing them.'" His account is not referenced and impossible to authenticate. The other possibility exists that they may have served in neither capacity, deployed instead in some other supporting role. One of the other companies in *Colonel Brooks's* Regiment is recorded as having served at Roxbury, not Dorchester, but as Roxbury was only a mile from Dorchester (only slightly further from Dorchester Heights), this would not have precluded service on Dorchester Heights. The

> Extract of a letter from the camp at Cambridge, dated March 9, 1776.
> "We are just now on the eve of the long wished for hour. The enemy are embarking as fast as possible. All their heavy artillery are embarked with their ordnance stores. God knows where they intend to lodge next. The Selectmen of Boston have sent out, by permission of General Robinson, to acquaint us that if we will permit the Regulars to embark unmolested, they will leave the town standing, but as it was not authorized by General Howe, nor addressed by the Selectmen, his Excellency General Washington rejected it. We now intend, I believe, to pursue our intentions without remitting in the least. We shall occupy another post this night, and perhaps shall beat them off in greater haste than they imagine. On Thursday next, they say, the town shall be vacated, I rejoice with all my soul at the prospect of entering Boston. They give out they design for Halifax, but we understand them for Virginia."

Following the fortification of Dorchester Heights, it became clear by March 9, 1776, that the British army was preparing to vacate Boston. The threat of a British assault on the new fortifications having passed, the Lincoln Militia Company was discharged to return home. (*The Pennsylvania Evening Post*, March 16, 1776)

have watched the troops embark on the ships, and the ships in turn haul off and anchor in a line before them. As dusk approached, the British prepared to land their troops for a nighttime assault. It was March 5, the anniversary of the Boston Massacre. Impatiently and in high spirits, the Provincials waited, eager to eclipse the glories and reverse the outcome of Bunker Hill.[1]

A light rain began to fall. Without much warning, the breeze intensified into a heavy gale. Rain and howling winds roiled the sea and drove the boats from their anchors. The landing became impossible as the storm lashed the boats out of control and drove some of them aground on the shoals.

During the night and all the next day, the raging storm thwarted a British landing. As he watched the Provincials continue to strengthen their works, General Howe increasingly recognized the futility of his situation. By the end of the day, as the storm abated, he knew that even his professionally trained British troops would no longer be able to carry the hill. He understood that his only remaining option was to evacuate his troops and abandon Boston altogether.

By March 7, it became clear to the watching Continentals that the British army had begun packing. On March 9, the imminent threat of attack having subsided, the Lincoln company marched home. On March 17, 1776, the last of the British transports rode the tide out of Boston harbor and set sail for Halifax. The war in Massachusetts was now essentially over.

---

author believes it likely that some Lincoln men were actually in arms on the hill at least at some point during their deployment at Dorchester Heights. Nevertheless, the suggestion that these men were on the hill that day, watching the British prepare for their assault, is entirely speculative.

1   For the wonderful firsthand account of Maj. John Trumbull, see Scheer and Rankin, *Rebels & Redcoats*, pp. 106–107.

Chapter 4

Service to the Northward and Southward, 1775–1776

The war in Massachusetts may have been over, but elsewhere it had scarcely begun. Washington was convinced that the British would head southward and land troops in New York. He had already dispatched Gen. Charles Lee with a contingent of Continentals to guard that city. And northward, the campaign in Canada launched during the previous fall of 1775, was not going well.

Canada

The object of the dual-pronged expedition to Canada had been to capture Montreal and Quebec, thereby protecting the northern borders of New England and New York by denying British access to the Champlain Valley and the resources of the interior St. Lawrence region. In addition, although Canada had so far shown little active support for the 13 rebellious colonies to the south, the Continental Congress hoped that—freed from British military control—the former French colony would join the continental confederacy as the fourteenth "United Colony."

General Montgomery's troops embark from Crown Point, along the shore of Lake Champlain, on their invasion of Canada in August 1775. (Illustration by Sydney Adamson, engraved by J. W. Evans, *The Century Illustrated Monthly Magazine*, November 1902)

In August 1775, General Richard Montgomery had taken 1,200 men up the Champlain Valley from Fort Ticonderoga. With the help of another 1,000 men in two Canadian-raised militia regiments, he captured a string of British outposts, and by mid-November he occupied Montreal.

Benedict Arnold led the second prong of the campaign, taking 1,100 men, mostly New Englanders, straight up the Kennebec Valley through the heart of the Maine wilderness. It was an audacious undertaking, based as much on Arnold's arrogant confidence and dynamic leadership as it was on any realistic prospect of success. It had started to unravel almost immediately.

Arnold's men—slowed by the rigors of traversing the untamed Maine woods and out of reach of their sources of supply—were beset by foul weather, leaky boats, frequent portages, and spoiled rations. The route turned out to be twice as long as the survey reports indicated; the march became as much a survival journey as a military expedition. Lincoln's *Ephraim Brooks, Jr.*, must certainly have wondered what had possessed him to enlist. Three-hundred men turned back; others died of disease or exhaustion. Some drowned when boats overturned in the rapids. Still others, sickened by rancid

Characteristically bold and daring, Benedict Arnold is regarded by many historians as one of America's most brilliant military leaders before he defected to the enemy in 1780. This much-copied portrait, drawn from life by Swiss artist Pierre-Eugene du Simitiere in 1779, when Arnold was military governor of Philadelphia, is considered by many scholars to be the most faithful likeness of him. (see Darley, "Benedict Arnold's Portraits." Library of Congress portrait)

food and starving, subsisted on boiled leather and green bark. Only 600 soldiers finally straggled out of the snowy wilderness onto the banks of the St. Lawrence River, opposite Quebec City. Few were fit for service.

Montgomery arrived from Montreal with 500 troops. On December 31, 1775, in a howling snowstorm the day before the New England enlistments were to expire, Arnold's and Montgomery's combined forces attempted to storm Quebec. It ended in disaster. Montgomery was killed, Arnold wounded, and 400 were taken captive.

Arnold deployed his remaining troops for a siege of the city. But lacking sufficient manpower; the siege proved to be porous and largely ineffective. With the spring thaw approaching, there was little hope that he could prevent British ships from bringing relief.

With the British evacuation of Boston, Washington could now afford to send supporting troops to buttress the siege.

In April 1776, at least nine Lincoln men were among the four regiments of reinforcements who marched up the Champlain Valley from Fort Ticonderoga. *Daniel Child* and *Elisha Willington* served in Capt. Abijah Child's Company, *Aaron Parks* in Capt. Nathan

Chapter 4: Service to the Northward and Southward, 1775–1776

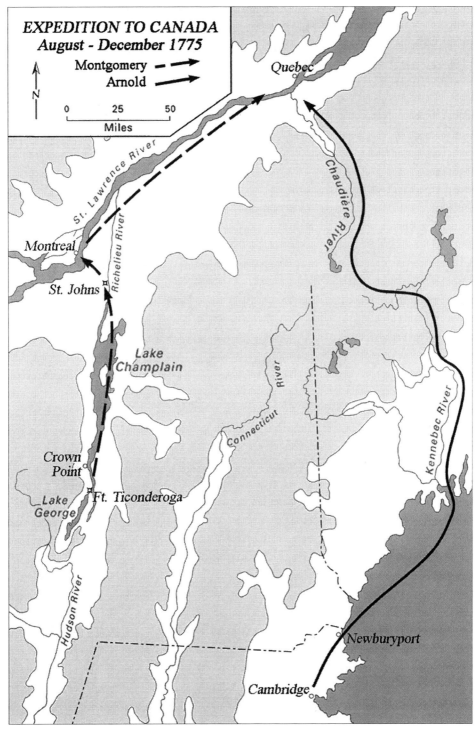

General Montgomery went north to Canada through the Champlain Valley, capturing Montreal in November 1775, while Arnold led his forces through the heart of the Maine wilderness. The Canadian expedition stalled, however, when Montgomery's and Arnold's combined forces failed to capture Quebec in December. (Base map, Stewart, ed., *American Military History*)

On the day their enlistments were to expire, Americans led by Benedict Arnold storm the city walls of Quebec in a howling snowstorm. The attack failed, General Montgomery was killed, and Arnold was seriously wounded. (Drawing by F. C. Yohn, *Scribner's Magazine,* February 1898)

Fuller's Company, and *Jeduthan Bemis* with Capt. Nailer Hatch—all three companies were part of Col. William Bond's Regiment. *George Brown*, along with brothers *Jonas* and *Leonard Parks*, marched in Col. John Paterson's Regiment.[1] The Continental forces headed north in high spirits, brimming with confidence. Together with the troops already in Canada, they expected little trouble overwhelming the meager British garrison guarding Quebec, bringing the Northern campaign to a successful close.

Gen. John Thomas went on ahead to assess the situation around Quebec City. As the senior Continental officer in Canada, he now had overall command. Colonel Bond's Regiment reached Canada in early May; they pushed on past Fort St. John and Chambly to Sorel on the banks of the St. Lawrence. Traveling downstream, they were now within a couple of days of reaching Quebec.

Suddenly, the picture changed. The first wave of retreating Continental soldiers straggled into Sorel. From them, the Lincoln men learned that General Thomas, having decided to abandon the ineffective siege, had ordered a general withdrawal. While this was underway, three British ships sailed into view with fresh supplies and fresh troops. Sir Guy Carleton, with 900 hastily disembarked and assembled troops, gave chase and panicked the retiring Continentals.

Worse was the news of smallpox in the American camp. For more than two months, its tentative appearance had been more or less checked—as much as smallpox could be held in check—by a combination of quarantine and inoculation, but neither approach was very effective. It had progressively weakened the American camp, and now it threatened the well-being of the entire Northern Army.[2]

---

1 The records of service in Canada are somewhat confused, and the number of Lincoln men involved is not entirely clear. "Treasurer's Accompts" identify eight individuals who were paid for service in Canada in 1776. Other records identify three additional individuals (including *Ephraim Brooks, Jr.*, who went north with Arnold).

MacLean, *A Rich Harvest* (p. 295), cites a May 8, 1778, town report indicating that the town paid bounties to seven men (unnamed) for 12 months of service in "Canady" in 1776. This is a curious record, as the author has found no record for service in Canada that lasted more than eight months. And the apparent discrepancy between seven bounties and eight payments for service is unexplained.

For *Daniel Child* and *Aaron Parks*, who were already in Continental service, it seems unlikely that they would have been paid a bounty for going to Canada. In any case, evidence exists of as many as ten Lincoln men serving in Canada in 1776 (*Ephraim Brooks, Jr.*, having probably returned to Massachusetts upon the expiration of his enlistment the day after the disastrous attack on Quebec City).

Confusing the issue further is the fact that General Sullivan took a fourth wave of soldiers north with him in late May. At least one Lincoln man, *Tilly Mead*, appears to have gone north at this time.

Still further confusion lies in the fact that the resolve of June 25, 1776, called for 3,000 men from the militia to reinforce the army in Canada. Ten days later, Lincoln Town Meeting voted to grant £6:6:8, "in addition to what the general Court has given as a bounty," as an "incouragement …to those non Commision officers and Solgers that shall inlist them selves into the present Expedition to Canaday." ["Lincoln First Book of Records," July 5, 1776.] Another resolve of July 11, 1776, called for two regiments (1,500 men) to reinforce the troops destined for Canada (evidently referring to the resolve of June 25). In both cases, these resolves occurred after the Northern Army had begun pulling out of Canada. By July 11, the Northern Army had returned to Fort Ticonderoga, and the new recruits appear to have been deployed to Ticonderoga, instead. Therefore, these resolves provide no meaningful clue about Canadian service by Lincoln men.

2 Krueger, "Troop Life at Champlain Valley Forts" (pp. 238-241) contains an interesting discussion of the competing views in the American camp on how best to deal with the smallpox. According to Krueger, smallpox had already reached epidemic proportions in the American camp by the end of February. If this is true, one would expect that this news would have been known further south, but within the scope of this work, the author has found no evidence that the reinforcements knew of or were prepared for encountering smallpox.

Typically, and for obvious reasons, eighteenth-century armies avoided exposing their troops to smallpox wherever possible. At Boston, for example, with reports of smallpox in the town, Washington segregated his

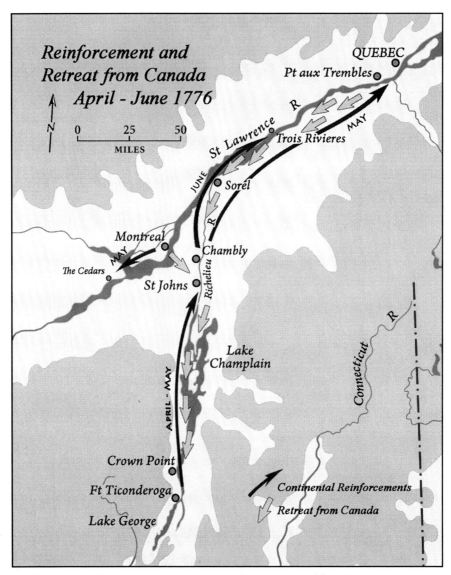

Waves of Provincial reinforcements streamed north to Quebec, then to Trois Rivieres, but they could not overcome smallpox and Crown reinforcements, which brought the Canadian campaign to a halt. By the end of June 1776, Americans had fallen back in disarray to Ticonderoga. (Base map, United States Army Center of Military History)

Harassed by Carleton and unable to stop the spread of smallpox, Thomas struggled to protect his weakened army and to prevent a complete collapse of the Canadian campaign. He pulled back to Trois Rivieres, then Sorel. But it was a losing battle. Carleton continued

---

troops, allowing only those who had already been exposed to the dread disease to reoccupy the town until after it had been determined that there was no threat to the rest of his troops. Inoculation was still largely experimental at this time, but within a year or two the Continental Army would begin routine programs to inoculate its troops in advance of any threatened exposure.

to pursue the Continentals with increasing numerical advantage. By May 19, nearly one in five of Thomas's Continental troops were reported sick, with some of his regiments reporting sick rates as high as 45 percent and 60 percent. A few days later, the smallpox hit him, too. He died on June 2, 1776.

Meanwhile, *Jeduthan Bemis* had been detached to The Cedars, a small outpost 30 miles west of Montreal, to counter increasing British and Iroquois activity in the area. In a series of skirmishes on May 19 and 20, both the garrison and a relief column surrendered to the enemy. *Bemis* was held for ten days before being released in a prisoner exchange.

Tilly Mead is assumed to have participated in another attempt by General Sullivan to push north. When this failed at Trois Rivieres on June 8, the Canadian campaign sputtered out. The Northern Army evacuated Montreal and retreated south from the St. Lawrence region. By June 13, nearly one-half of the retreating army was reporting sick and unfit.[1] Smallpox was claiming 10 to 15 lives each day. *John Flint, James Adams, Leonard Parks,* and other survivors limped south along the shores of Lake Champlain, arriving at Crown Point and Ticonderoga through early and mid-July, "emaciated and entirely broken down in strength, spirits and discipline." One of the officers described them as "not an army but a mob...ruined by sickness, fatigue, and desertion, and void of every idea of discipline or subordination." John Adams reported that, "Our Army at Crown Point is an object of wretchedness enough to fill a humane mind with horror; disgraced, defeated, discontented, dispirited, diseased, naked, undisciplined, eaten up with vermin; no clothes, beds, blankets, no medicines; no victuals, but salt pork and flour." Fifty-four percent of the returnees required hospitalization.[2]

It is not known how many of the Lincoln men suffered from the smallpox, dysentery, or the other camp diseases, but all seem to have survived. *Jonas Parks* suffered serious vision loss as a complication of his smallpox inoculation. *Ephraim Brooks, Jr.,* who had gone north in Arnold's leg of the expedition, returned home either from the travail of the Maine woods or in January 1776, when his enlistment ran out. He served alongside his father in the Lincoln Militia Company at Dorchester Heights in March. *Jeduthan Bemis* returned home after the prisoner exchange in May, then he went to New York in September with *Col. Eleazer Brooks's* Regiment. Others, who went north in April's aborted relief effort, served out the terms of their enlistments at Fort Ticonderoga before returning home in November 1776—all except *George Brown, Jonas Parks,* and *Leonard Parks,* who marched south with Colonel Paterson to join General Washington at the Battle of Trenton on the morning after Christmas.

Ticonderoga

Even as the campaign in the St. Lawrence Valley was becoming a lost cause, the Continental Congress was calling for more troops to reinforce the Northern Army in Canada. Massachusetts responded with resolves calling for six regiments (4,500 men) to be raised from the militia. The town of Lincoln sweetened the pot by voting an extra bounty for

---

1 Krueger, "Troop Life at Champlain Valley Forts," pp. 241–242.
2 Ketchum, *Saratoga*, p. 36. He attributes the initial quotations to British Lt. William Digby [Digby, *Journal 1776–1777* (Albany: Joel Munsell's Sons, 1887)] and Continental Lt. Col. John Trumbull [Trumbull, *Autobiography of John Trumbull, Patriot-Artist* (New Haven: Yale, 1953)]. John Adams letter from Philadelphia to Abigail Adams (July 7, 1776) in Adams, *Letters*, p. 130.

"those non Commision officers and Solgers that shall inlist them selves into the present Expedition to Canaday."[1] By the time these regiments were raised, there were no longer any Continental troops in Canada to reinforce. Instead, the regiments were deployed to Ticonderoga. Nineteen men from Lincoln made the march. *Thomas Blodget, Gregory Stone, Jr., Lemuel Wheeler,* and possibly *Josiah Nelson* served in Capt. Charles Miles's Company. *Lt. Samuel Hoar, Cpl. Joseph Abbot, Jr.,* and *Daniel Hosmer* marched with Capt. Asahel Wheeler. Both companies were part of Col. Jonathan Reed's Regiment.[2]

The collapse of the Canadian campaign exposed the "United Colonies" to the serious threat of an invasion from the north by the now heavily reinforced Crown forces in Canada. On the heels of the retreating Continentals, Carleton was poised with nearly 8,000 troops at Fort St. John, on the northern end of Lake Champlain, busily assembling a fleet of ships to transport his army south.

In disarray, the Northern Army was in no condition to resist. The Massachusetts reinforcements helped prop up the shattered and demoralized army. But despite its reputation as the "Gibraltar of the North," Fort Ticonderoga was of and by itself virtually indefensible. The decade and a half of maintenance neglect since the French and Indian War would have been problem enough, but advances in the destructive firepower of modern artillery had made its walls obsolete, defenseless even if they had been kept in good repair.

There was another factor, however, that trumped both of these issues. The fort had originally been built by the French to protect French Canada from the English colonies to the south. It was perfectly sited to withstand an invasion from the south. But now the French were gone, and the British were in the north. To defend against an invasion from the north, Fort Ticonderoga was in entirely the wrong location!

To correct the site problem, construction was begun at a new location on Rattlesnake Hill, directly across a narrows in the lake from the original fort. The new site had good sight lines down the lake to the north, and it would communicate with the original fort by means of a floating bridge. Whether or not this would have been the option of choice had they been starting from scratch is moot. Under the circumstances, it was a very satisfactory solution, except that construction had just begun. It would be some time before it would progress sufficiently to offer any defensive improvement.

In mid-July, news arrived from Philadelphia that the thirteen "United Colonies" had declared themselves the thirteen "United States." The assembled army listened as the Declaration of Independence was read, then cheered the thirteen-gun salute that followed. It was a time for celebration. Rattlesnake Hill became "Mount Independence," and the new site was christened Fort Independence. For many of those who had limped back from the debacle in Canada, however, knowing that 8,000 fresh, well supplied British troops were preparing to move south to destroy the remnants of the Northern Army, this must have

---

1 See note 1 on p. 71. The extra bounty, voted by Lincoln Town Meeting on July 5, 1776, underscores the urgency that must have been felt as news of the collapse of the Canadian Campaign filtered back to Massachusetts.

2 Shattuck, *History of the Town of Concord* (pp. 124, 354), gives the dates of service of Captain Miles's Company as June 25, 1776, for six months. This appears to be incorrect. June 25 was the date of the resolve, and it would typically have taken at least several days to carry it out. Further, the resolve specified that the term of service would be until December 1, 1776. From other records of service, Captain Miles's Company appears to have been in service from July 12 through November 30, 1776 (see *Massachusetts Soldiers and Sailors*, Vol. X, p. 732, and Vol. XI, p. 209).

Chapter 4: Service to the Northward and Southward, 1775–1776

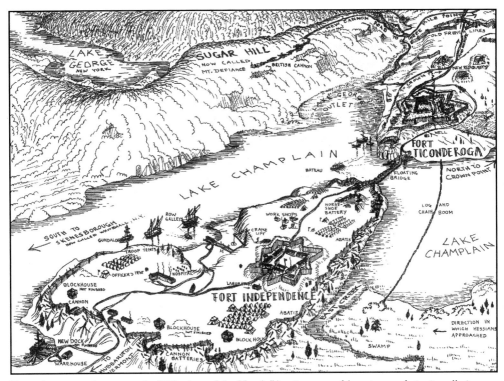

Ticonderoga was known as the "Gibraltar of the North," but its age and location made it virtually impossible to defend against an attack from the north. On the heels of the failed Canadian campaign, with the threat of a British attack hanging in the air, the "United Colonies" built Fort Independence as a new, supporting fortress across the lake. (Drawing by Ellen Viereck)

seemed like a desperate—and hollow—act of bravado. As if to underscore this point, Sugar Loaf Hill, just to the southwest of the original fort, was renamed "Mount Defiance."

Another 7 to 18 men from Lincoln appear to have marched to Ticonderoga during July and August. The Lincoln contingent at Ticonderoga now numbered at least 36, and perhaps as many as 47, including *Col. Eleazer Brooks,* who also appears to have gone to Ticonderoga at this time.[1]

Many Lincoln men undoubtedly served guard duty. Perhaps others went on scouting details to keep an eye on the British forces along the lake. Almost certainly, *Elisha Gearfield, Isaac Hartwell, Ezra Richardson,* and most of the others labored, muscles sore,

---

1 These numbers are difficult to reconstruct, as very few records have survived. The author has identified at least 32 and possibly as many as 43 individuals who served at Ticonderoga during this period (in addition to the 10 who retreated south from Canada). A May 8, 1778, committee report to Town Meeting indicates that the town paid bounties to 19 men sent to Ticonderoga in July, and four or five more in August, but this appears to understate the extent of service by Lincoln men. [See MacLean, *A Rich Harvest,* p. 295 and Shattuck, *History of the Town of Concord,* p. 299.] Unfortunately, only seven or eight individuals are identifiable as among the 19 bounties in July, and four individuals as among the four or five August bounties. No record has been found of *Colonel Brooks* being in command of any troops at Ticonderoga; it is probable that he was dispatched there on some other official business.

on construction details at Fort Independence. And possibly some of the Lincoln contingent volunteered for boatbuilding crews a few miles south at Skenesborough.

With little chance of defending Ticonderoga against Carleton's invasion army, the Continentals had settled on a plan to sail up the lake to stop the invaders on the open water. It was a crazy, desperate idea—the brainchild of Benedict Arnold—noteworthy primarily for its arrogant audacity. Never mind that the Continentals were an army of landlubbers, with scarcely a Jack Tar among them. Never mind that they had only a few lightly armed schooners with which to stop the British juggernaut; they would build a fleet of gunboats.

And so they set to work. As Fort Independence slowly began to take shape on the eastern shore of Lake Champlain, Benedict Arnold supervised the construction of a fledgling American Navy a short distance away.

New York

Meanwhile, convinced that following the evacuation of Boston, the British would next strike at New York, Washington had marched the bulk of his Continental forces southward. Accompanying them were Lincoln's fifer *Elijah Mason, Jack Farrar, Ezra Meriam,* and *Cato Smith,* along with 12-year-old fifer *Joseph Nixon,* each serving a one-year Continental enlistment in Col. John Nixon's Regiment. During May and June, they prepared for the defense of the city. And waited....

The Lincoln men were deployed building defensive works on Governor's Island. Other Continental soldiers built fortifications at Paulus Hook (now Jersey City) and Red Hook (on Long Island), in Brooklyn, and along the Manhattan shoreline. At the tip of Manhattan, they chopped up the New York streets into a maze of trenches and barricades and redoubts. They erected Fort Washington and Fort Lee on the heights overlooking the Hudson River, along with a *chevaux-de-frise* of boulders, floated in wooden cribs strung across the river to prevent enemy ships from sailing upstream and outflanking the American positions.[1]

Finally, in early July, as the sick and discouraged Northern Army was still straggling back to Ticonderoga, British sails appeared off of Sandy Hook, at the entrance to New York Harbor. Wave after wave of British transports arrived, anchored, and unloaded their troops on Staten Island. Soon 30,000 British troops were poised to invade New York. Some 150 British ships stood by, ready to land them anywhere along the long Manhattan shoreline. The Crown was taking no chances; this was the largest expeditionary force that Great Britain had ever assembled.[2] British General Howe took his time, planning carefully, not disclosing his next move.

Washington was kept guessing, unable to anticipate where and when Howe's attack would come, unsure how best to deploy his forces to resist the British landing. The Lincoln

---

1 See Scheer and Rankin, *Rebels & Redcoats,* pp. 143–46; Bobrick, *Angel in the Whirlwind,* pp. 209, 219. *Chevaux-de-frise* are defensive structures of various forms, typically multi-pronged and/or submerged. Many variations existed. In this case, the *Chevaux-de-frise* appear to have been more of a simple barrier than a device to tear apart ships' hulls. For the latter type, see note 1 on p. 101.
2 Bobrick, *Angel in the Whirlwind* (p. 206), puts the size of the force at 32,000 men, 170 transports, and 30 ships of war, which he says swelled to 35,000 men, 427 transports, and 52 ships of war when Clinton arrived from his unsuccessful expedition in South Carolina. Morison, *Oxford History* (p. 239), by contrast, estimates the British force at only 25,000 men.

Chapter 4: Service to the Northward and Southward, 1775–1776

Outflanked and routed by the British, Washington secretly evacuated his army from Long Island during the night of August 29–30. Masked first by rain then by dense fog at daybreak, the evacuation went off smoothly, saving the army from being surrounded and almost certainly forced to surrender. (Drawing by H.W. Ditzler, *Scribner's Magazine,* April 1898)

men, under Colonel Nixon, kept close watch on British ships from their advanced position on Governor's Island; the island batteries firing on any of His Majesty's ships attempting to sail up the Hudson.[1]

On August 22, Howe ferried his troops to Long Island. Washington moved his army across the East River to meet them. But the juggernaut was unstoppable. Slowly, systematically, professionally, Howe's Redcoats outflanked the Continentals, forcing them to evacuate Brooklyn on August 30, and then the British leapfrogged up the Manhattan coast, forcing the Continentals to abandon New York on September 15. The Continentals (including at least six or seven Lincoln men in Colonel Nixon's Regiment)[2] rallied and checked the British advance at Harlem Heights the following day, but the situation had become untenable. Outnumbered, outgunned, and outmaneuvered, Washington prepared to vacate the rest of Manhattan.

As the situation around New York worsened, *Col. Eleazer Brooks* was ordered south to the New York area on September 27 with a militia regiment of Middlesex County men to reinforce the beleaguered Continentals.[3] As many as 17 men from Lincoln may have accompanied him. *Edward Cabot, Abner Mathis, Michael Teny, Sgt. Jeremiah Knowlton,* and

---

1 Smith, *Governor's Island,* pp. 40, 41, 47.

2 Fischer, *Washington's Crossing,* p. 105.

3 This regiment was not a standing militia unit. It was created for this campaign by detaching men from their "home" militia companies and amalgamating them into a single, county-wide regiment. The officers were

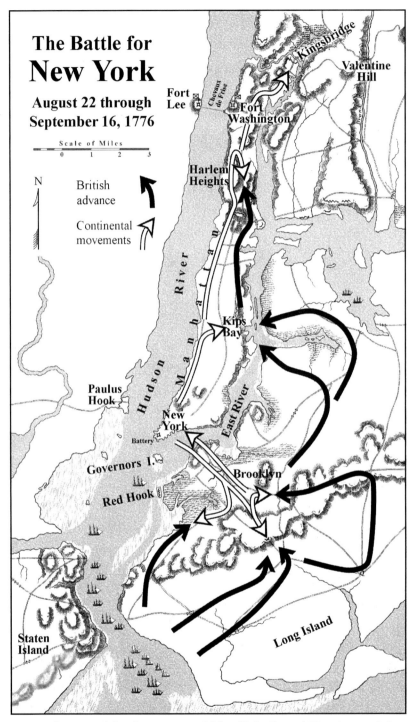

Despite extensive Continental fortifications around New York, General Howe's overwhelming British expeditionary force slowly and methodically outmaneuvered the Continentals, forcing General Washington to evacuate Brooklyn, and then to abandon New York City. After engaging the enemy at Harlem Heights, Washington pulled his men north, out of Manhattan. (Base map adapted from period maps at Brooklyn Historical Society and Library of Congress)

Chapter 4: Service to the Northward and Southward, 1775–1776

Lincoln men were among the Americans who counterattacked the advancing British at Harlem Heights, luring the British van into an area of low ground, then circling the flank and nearly surrounding them. The British escaped and regrouped, but they were forced to retreat further under American pressure. In addition to briefly checking the British advance, the victory served to boost American confidence after the dismal defeat on Long Island. (Engraving by A. R. Waud, *Harper's Weekly*, September 30, 1876)

Jeduthan Bemis marched in Capt. Simon Hunt's Company; *Keen Robinson* in Capt. John Walton's Company; and *Samuel Hartwell* as the regimental quartermaster. The detachment marched to Horse Neck, where they may have been employed temporarily as part of the supply line for Washington's Continental forces.[1]

Valcour Island

Up north, on the shores of Lake Champlain, during July and August, Arnold's mosquito fleet arose from the New York forest and took shape at the southernmost tongue of the lake. It was hardly impressive, except for the speed with which it was built. Perhaps *Abner Wheeler, Timothy Billing, Abel Child,* or *Moses Underwood* may have served on shipbuilding duty; the records do not tell us. By the end of August, Arnold's navy consisted of 16 small ships of assorted shapes and configurations, armed with an array of light-weight

---

similarly detached from the seven standing Middlesex County regiments. This became the model for calling Massachusetts militiamen into service during most of the rest of the war.

1 Horse Neck is located in the modern town of Greenwich, Connecticut, six miles up the coast from Rye, and six miles from Stamford. It appears to have been a staging area for New England militia units on their way to reinforce the Continental Army around New York. The employment is conjectural, although Bobrick, *Angel in the Whirlwind* (p. 220), reports that Washington's supply line was based in Connecticut.

Launched in August 1776, the gunboat *Philadelphia* was part of Benedict Arnold's mosquito fleet. Fifty-three-feet long and flat-bottomed, she carried three 12-pound guns and two 9-pound guns with a crew of 45 men. The *Philadelphia* was sunk in Valcour Bay during the first day of battle, and thus did not take part in the daring nighttime escape. Raised in 1935, she is now on display at the Smithsonian Institution in Washington, D.C. (Armed Forces History, Smithsonian Institution)

and medium-weight guns. "A very formidable fleet," Arnold had called it, leading General Gates to predict, "I am convinced he will add to that brilliant reputation he has so deservedly acquired."[1]

By contrast, British General Carleton had arrived at St. Johns well prepared. Using sleds, his army hauled scores of small transports around the rapids at Chambly and up the river to the lake. His larger ships had been specially constructed to be disassembled, carried around the rapids, and reassembled. At St. Johns, he put teams of engineers and carpenters to work building as many as 20 gunboats. Methodically, he prepared his fleet. By September, he had 30 heavily armed ships to protect the hundreds of bateaux he would use to transport his troops up the lake. They packed twice the firepower of the American cockleshell fleet, and they were manned with experienced crews from the Royal Navy.

---

1 The quotes are from Hubbard, "Battle at Valcour Island," who goes into wonderful detail about the preparation of both fleets, the lead up to the battle, and the battle itself. (For details about each of the ships, see Millard, "Orders Of Battle.")

Chapter 4: Service to the Northward and Southward, 1775–1776

After their desperate and brilliant nighttime escape from Valcour Bay, American gunboats and galleys retreat before the pursuing British fleet. Few returned safely, as most were destroyed or abandoned during the three-day chase. (Drawing by Carlton T. Chapman, *Scribner's Magazine,* February 1898)

Arnold sailed confidently north with his fleet. It is not known how many, if any, Lincoln men were among the landlubber crew.[1] Showing characteristic guile, he insolently demonstrated the strength of his fleet to the British near St. Johns. Then he withdrew and anchored off Valcour Island, where he believed he could neutralize British superiority in seamanship and firepower.

On October 11, he surprised the British fleet sailing south, and lured them into a pitched battle. With a wind and maneuvering advantage, he was able to string out the British ships somewhat, and to concentrate his fire on one at a time. It was not enough. Despite a brilliant nighttime escape, the American fleet was chased down and soundly beaten over the next three days, most of its ships abandoned as smoldering hulks along the lakeshore. The men who were not killed or captured limped back through the woods to Crown Point and Ticonderoga. The British fleet resumed its inexorable journey southward.

White Plains

From his Manhattan base, General Howe leapfrogged again on October 12, landing troops at Throgs Neck, and a few days later at Pell's Point, forcing Washington to pull his forces north once again to avoid being surrounded. Washington dug his army into a series of broken hills behind White Plains, and he ordered the New England militia units at Horse

---

1 At least some elements of Col. Jonathan Reed's Regiment were detached for service on the gunboats (see Lacroix, "Westford and the Battle of Valcour Island"). As there were a number of men from Lincoln serving with Colonel Reed, this at least establishes the possibility that one or more may have been detached for fleet duty. It is likely that men were similarly detached from other regiments in which Lincoln men were serving.

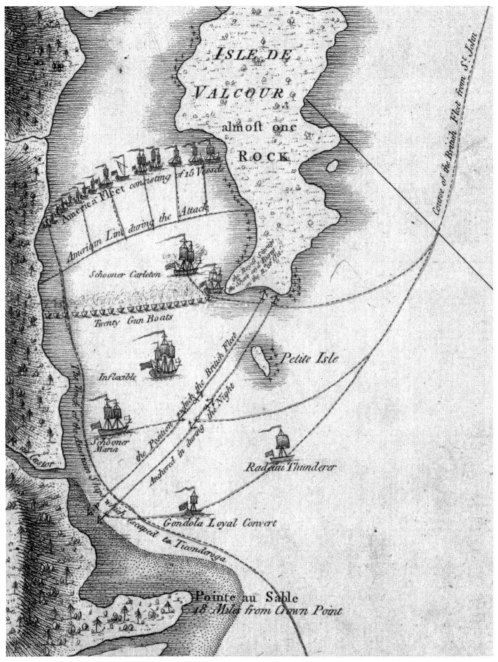

Benedict Arnold's "mosquito fleet" was soundly beaten by a more powerful British fleet at Valcour Island. This map, drawn by a British officer who was present, details the positions of the fleets and the course of the battle. (Map reproduction courtesy of the Richard H. Brown Revolutionary War Map Collection)

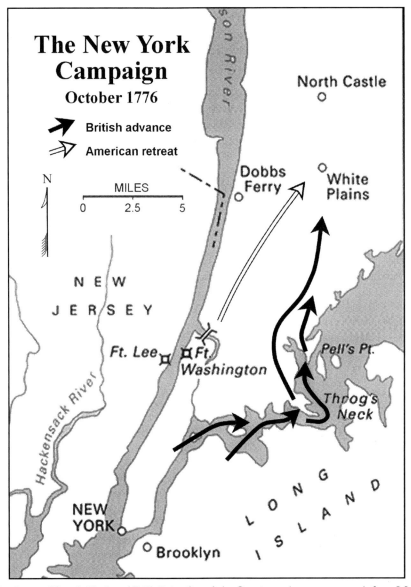

British landings at Throg's Neck and Pell's Point forced the Continentals to retreat north from Manhattan, setting the stage for the Battle of White Plains. (Base map, Stewart, ed., *American Military History*)

Neck to join him. He camped *Colonel Brooks* and his regiment with another militia regiment from New York on Chatterton's Hill, an otherwise unguarded hill on the extreme right of the American line.

From behind the stone fence beside their camp, on October 27 the Lincoln men looked east and southeast across the Bronx River to the broad, open terrain that gave the White Plains area its name. They could hear the distant crackle of musket fire and see a growing haze of smoke, as the British advance guard converged on and drove in their American counterpart. In short order, the whole camp was on full alert. They watched for the appearance of additional British units, but none came. Soon the firing petered out. Still, they knew this was just the start. Down the road, not very far, were as many as 25,000 British troops and their German mercenaries.

After a fitful night, the two militia units were joined at daybreak by additional troops from Delaware. As the bright sun rose higher in the sky, they watched, on the plain below, General Spencer's troops return from their morning foray, aimed at delaying the enemy and gathering intelligence. It was not long afterwards that two columns of neatly uniformed professional soldiers marched into view. Thousands of colorful uniforms—it was an impressive sight. As they watched, the enemy halted a short distance before the American center, then the British forces spread left and right into their line of battle. It was a brilliant but formidable scene. Wrote Massachusetts General Heath, "Their arms glistened; and perhaps troops never were shown to more advantage."[1]

Within minutes, the pageant turned suddenly and terrifyingly real, as the Royal Artillery roared its opening salvos. The crash of shells and grapeshot tore into the American lines. Only a few of the men in *Colonel Brooks's* Regiment had ever been this close to battle, and perhaps none had ever been targets of the gruesome destruction of an artillery barrage. Upon taking casualties, panic quickly spread through the ranks. Some scattered and fled; others were rallied only with the utmost difficulty.

Soon, additional troops from Maryland, New York, and Connecticut, under the command of Gen. Alexander McDougall, took up positions on their left and front.

Amid the chaos, the barrage concentrated on their position. Still jittery, crouching behind their stone fence, *James Adams, Jr.*, or *Michael Teny*, or perhaps *Sgt. Jeremiah Knowlton* may have watched some of the enemy units turn left and approach the base of their hill, pause briefly to bridge the river, cross, then reform. The cannonade stopped, and the enemy units marched toward them, bayonets fixed. On their left, a deafening clap of thunder from Continental guns slowed the enemy advance. The crisp, repeated blasts of musket volleys from the Maryland regiment punctuated additional thunder claps. The British and German troops fell back, reformed, then ascended again.

Around to their right, another unit of Germans appeared, battling their way toward the crest of the hill. The rattle of musketry was everywhere, and the smoke obscured their view. The German advance faltered, then resumed. The confusion was overwhelming. *Abner Mathis, Jeduthan Bemis,* and *Nathan Billing* probably struggled to make out the enemy to discharge their muskets to good effect. Suddenly, terrifyingly, the dragoons galloped upon them, sabers flying. Self-preservation welled to the fore; many reportedly broke and ran.[2] Overall, the Americans fought bravely, inflicting as many casualties as they were taking; but overwhelmed by numbers, slowly, the American line gave way. The enemy, content with taking the hill, declined to pursue. As the Americans retreated northward, off the hill, the battle subsided.

The actual conduct of the Lincoln men in *Colonel Brooks's* Regiment during this battle is in question. *Brooks* and his regiment reportedly distinguished themselves for bravery at White Plains, and they may have "received especial commendation from General Washington."

---

1 Heath, *Memoirs*, p. 70.

2 This was the first cavalry charge in American history. It was executed with devastating effect by the 17th Light Dragoons, commanded by Lt. Col. Samuel Birch. Within days after the battle, Washington began to incorporate light horse troops (cavalry units) into the Continental Army (see Moran, "Birth of the American Cavalry").

Chapter 4: Service to the Northward and Southward, 1775–1776

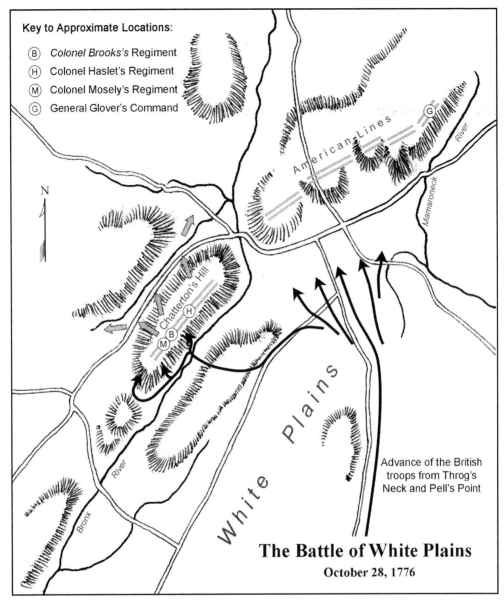

The Battle of White Plains
October 28, 1776

The British concentrated their attack on the American positions on Chatterton's Hill. The initial assaults were repelled, before the Americans were overwhelmed, scattering north and west. After taking the hill, however, the British failed to follow up. Washington repositioned his troops, then a few days later he withdrew to North Castle. (Map drawn by the author)

Accounts of the battle, on the other hand, typically heap blame on the militia for taking flight, and praise the Delaware and Maryland troops for their valiant defense of the hill. Although there were many militia units at White Plains, it is clear from the details of the battle that the condemnation is directed specifically at *Col. Eleazer Brooks's* Regiment.[1]

---

[1] The quote is from Wheeler, "Lincoln" in Drake, p. 42. See also Shattuck, *History of the Town of Concord*, pp. 319, 354. Neither identifies the source of this information. For blame, see Freeman, *George Washington*, pp. 229–231.

Commendation or Cowardice?

Lincoln historian William F. Wheeler credits *Col. Eleazer Brooks's* Regiment with a special commendation by General Washington for bravery at White Plains. Most historians' accounts of the battle, however, indicate that *Brooks's* militia broke and ran at the first sign of enemy fire. The truth may lie somewhere in between.

The source of the condemnation of *Brooks's* Regiment is identified as Col. John Haslet, who commanded a Continental regiment from Delaware, and who occupied a position on the hill near *Brooks's* Militia Regiment. It was not uncommon for militia units to be disparaged by the Continentals. And judging by the Lincoln men, at least, *Brooks's* Regiment had very little battle experience, so they were an obvious scapegoat.

Haslet seems to have been particularly adept at drawing attention to his own laudatory exploits while casting aspersions on the conduct of others. Historian David Hackett Fischer describes him as "bellicose." George Washington biographer, Douglas Freeman, notes that "Haslet's account [of the battle] is the only first-hand American narrative *and it most certainly does not depreciate its author or the troops he commanded*" [italics added].

Despite widespread acceptance of Haslet's account of the battle, other first-hand accounts do exist, and they paint a somewhat different picture. Gen. John Glover of Marblehead, in a letter written two weeks after the battle, reports that four regiments of militia (consisting of 1,000 men) ran away "upon the approach of the British cavalry." He appears to have accepted Haslet's scapegoating, but significantly, the cavalry charge occurred after the Americans had already withstood a couple of waves of enemy infantry. It should also be noted that Glover was positioned at the extreme opposite end of the American line, and he could have known this information only second or third hand (perhaps directly from Haslet, or from Haslet's correspondents).

Thomas Craige, a member of Colonel Mosely's Regiment (which was in the same brigade as *Brooks's*), suggests in his pension declaration that Brooks's Regiment may have put up credible resistance before they were overwhelmed: "Whether the men that dug that entrenchment were of Brook's Regiment—of McDugal's—or some other corps, the declarant is not certain; but it was soon done, and then Brook's Regiment, with some other troops, went into it—Brook's Reg^t was next to us. Then the British sent infantry forward, down into the ravine, or hollow way, who then turned to their left and came up to storm the entrenchment last mentioned. *The Americans twice repulsed the enemy's infantry back into the hollow* [italics added]. While they were rallying, the Highlanders came down—stacked their arms—drew their broadswords—and formed in rear of the infantry—then they all came up—our men opened their fire as before, and soon the enemy's infantry opened and the Highlanders marched into our entrenchments and the Americans retreated down the hill westwardly."

Regimental returns after the battle show that *Brooks's* Regiment suffered 6 killed, 10 missing, and 33 wounded (plus two who were "sent with the wounded"). Among ▶

those who lost items in the battle were *Edward Cabot, Michael Teny,* and David Fisk (it is uncertain if this is *David Fisk* from Lincoln). Archivist John Hannigan at the Massachusetts Archives calls the number of items reported missing in battle "unusually high" and consistent with a panicked departure from the scene of battle. The casualty count, however, seems to suggest that the panicked departure may have occurred *after* some pretty intense fighting. Strength reports compiled by historian Charles Lesser reinforce this idea: *Brooks's* regimental return after the battle shows more than twice as many "sick" (defined loosely as unfit, this includes the wounded) as any other regiment in his brigade. Among the other brigades on Chatterton's Hill, only Smallwood's, Haslet's, Wheedon's, and Read's regiments reported more.

> *Extract of a Letter from Camp White-Plains, October 29.*
>
> "This being a very Mountainous Country, and more extensive than the Number of Proprietors, it was Yesterday determined in Council, to dispose of Part of it at the dearest Rate; accordingly the Auction Room was opened at 9 o'Clock A. M. and a certain Eminence near to, and North West of the White-Plains, to us of inconsiderable Worth, was set up, and immediately loud and I believe generous Offers were made, which much increased till 3 o'Clock P. M. when a Part of our Right Wing struck it off o the whole Force of the Enemy's Left. This, Sir, I think, being myself a near Spectator, was sold at a Bunker-Hill Price. Our wounded were about 35 or 40, some killed, uncertain the Number. The Attack was expected at our Center and Left Wing, where was the Chief of our Force; but they discovering some loose dirt thrown up, wheeled off to the Left Wing, where the Ground was not broke. Colonel Book's Regiment of Militia, which assisted in disputing the Price, behaved with Courage. We took one Light House with his mounting, doubt not he will be of Service to his Excellency, who is ever upon the ride, and must be greatly Fatigued. ————

Penned the day after the Battle of White Plains, this colorful report credits Col. Eleazer Brooks's Militia Regiment with courageous behavior, giving no hint of the cowardice that many historians would later attribute to them, courtesy of a self-serving account by the bellicose, Col. John Haslet from Delaware. (*The Independent Chronicle and the Universal Advertiser*, November 14, 1776)

Contemporary newspaper accounts support this interpretation. A Pennsylvania newspaper reported from the battlefield, "… the part of our army which was engaged today was a brigade commanded by Genl McDougal, composed of Webb's, Ritzma's, Smallwood's, Haslet's, and Brooks's regiments—Ritzma's and Smallwood's suffered most, on this occasion, sustaining with great patience and coolness, a long and heavy fire—and finally retreated, with great sullenness, being obliged to give way to a superior force."

Three days later, a letter to the *Connecticut Journal* affirms that, "…Col. Brooks's, Smallwood's, and Ruzman's regiments who were drawn up on the hill near the [lines?] suffered considerably; our loss in the whole may be 70 or 80 killed and wounded.… Our sick and wounded are sent out 8 or 10 miles. Our men are in good spirits, and with much patience endure great hardships and fatigue."

The correspondent to a Boston paper filed his report the day after the battle: "…a certain Eminence near to, and North West of the White-Plains, to us of inconsiderable Worth was set up, and…was sold at a Bunker-Hill Price.…Colonel Brook's Regiment of Militia, which assisted in disputing the Price, behaved with Courage.…" ▶

> As for the commendation by Washington, no evidence of this has been found. Concord historian Lemuel Shattuck says that *Brooks* "distinguished himself for his cool and determined bravery," but offers no further elucidation.
>
> [See Fischer, *Washington's Crossing*, p. 255; Freeman, *George Washington*, p. 231, footnote; Upham, *John Glover*, p. 19; Thomas Craige's Pension Record # S12628; Muster Rolls of the Revolutionary War, Vol. 55, File L, p. 24; Lesser, *Sinews*, pp. 36–37; Wheeler, "Lincoln" in Drake, Vol. 2, p. 42; Shattuck, *History of the Town of Concord*, p. 319. Newspaper accounts are from the *Pennsylvania Evening Post* [Philadelphia], Vol. II, Issue 278 (October 31, 1776), p. 548; *Connecticut Journal* [New Haven], Issue 473 (November 6, 1776), p. 2; and *The Independent Chronicle and the Universal Advertiser* [Boston], Vol. IX, Issue 430 (November 14, 1776), p. 3. For other descriptions of the battle, see Freeman, *George Washington*, pp. 229–31; Irving, *Life of George Washington*, pp. 367–71; Ward, *The War of the Revolution*, pp. 261–66; Heath, *Memoirs*, pp. 69–70; Schecter, *The Battle for New York*, pp. 237–40; or Hickman, "American Revolution: Battle of White Plains."]

In any case, with his flank turned, Washington readjusted his right wing, then a few days later he withdrew once more, this time to stronger ground at North Castle, a few miles farther north. Still unsure of Howe's next move, but with multiple contingencies to prepare for, he divided up his army. As the British turned back and prepared to assault Fort Washington, the last remaining American outpost on the northern tip of Manhattan, the American Commander-in-Chief ferried a portion of his troops across the Hudson into New Jersey.[1] He sent 3,000 men north to guard the Hudson Highlands, leaving 7,000 troops under Gen. Lee to deter the British from invading New England. The disastrous New York campaign was drawing to a close.

Except for *Jesse Smith*, who crossed the Hudson into New Jersey with the Commander-in-Chief, most of the Lincoln men remained at North Castle with General Lee—*Samuel Hastings, Jr.*, as part of General Lee's Life Guard; and *Artemas Reed, Capt. Moses Brown*, drummer *Isaac Goodenow*, and probably *William Orr*, in Colonel Nixon's and Colonel Glover's regiments.

Their two-month enlistments expiring, *Colonel Brooks* and his regiment were discharged from North Castle to return home on November 16, the very day that Fort Washington fell to the British with a loss of 2,800 men taken prisoner. The Lincoln militiamen were credited with another 11 days of service to cover their travel time back home.

The records are sketchy, but at least 30 men from Lincoln appear to have participated in the New York campaign in at least three different regiments. With the possible exception of *Jeduthan Bemis*, who was "sent with the wounded" after the Battle of White Plains, no Lincoln casualties were reported.[2]

---

1 Estimates of the number of troops he took to New Jersey vary from 2,000 (Scheer and Rankin, *Rebels & Redcoats*, p. 196) to 5,000 (Bobrick, *Angel in the Whirlwind*, p. 221).

2 Muster Rolls of the Revolutionary War, Vol. 55, File L, p. 24. See sidebar, "Commendation or Cowardice?" (p. 86), for the casualty count. The author assumes that "sent with the wounded" means accompanied and assisted the wounded, rather than having some form of battle incapacity requiring care or observation, but this is not entirely certain.

Following the action at Valcour Island, British ships pursued the fleeing American fleet, destroying most of the remaining gunboats on their way to attack the American fortifications at Ticonderoga. General Carleton called off the attack, however, concluding that he was unprepared to maintain a garrison there during the approaching winter season. This painting by an unknown artist, circa 1925, shows the British ships destroying American gunboats off of Crown Point. (Library and Archives Canada, Acc. No. 1970-188-498 Coverdale Collection of Canadiana)

Reprieve for Ticonderoga

Meanwhile, having dispersed and destroyed most of Arnold's mosquito fleet, British General Carleton pursued the tattered remnants of the American navy up the lake. For the forty-plus Lincoln men and for the entire garrison at Ticonderoga, the crisis for which they had spent months preparing was now upon them. Clutching their muskets, they peered down the lake from behind the still unfinished fortifications, holding their breath.

Upon reaching Ticonderoga, Carleton surveyed the American fortifications and planned his next move. The Americans were better prepared than he had expected. At length, he concluded that the two forts could be taken only with a substantial loss of men. More than his battle plan, however, a bigger issue concerned him. His post-battle options were severely limited. It was already late October. The season was well advanced, and his supply lines were extended. He was not prepared to supply and sustain a garrison at Ticonderoga during the harsh northern-winter months. Upon capturing the forts, his only option would be to level and destroy them before returning to Canada. As there was little doubt that the Americans would regroup and return, they would likely have the fortifications substantially rebuilt by spring. What was to be gained from the loss of a large number of men?

Reluctantly, Carleton called off his invasion and withdrew his army north into winter quarters. But he had already formulated plans to return in the spring with an even stronger invasion force. As he pulled his forces north, he left behind a crew of artificers at St. Johns to build additional ships, gun boats, and floating batteries. In the spring, with an earlier start, nothing would be left to chance.[1]

As the Americans slowly exhaled, all understood that the reprieve was only temporary. Work resumed on the fortifications. For most of the Lincoln men, however, enlistments were expiring. A spring invasion would be the concern of other soldiers. They packed up and walked home to Lincoln in November.

---

1 Ketchum, *Saratoga*, p. 42.

Chapter 5

Fighting for Survival, 1776–1777

While Ticonderoga breathed a sigh of relief, the plight of Washington's army around New York continued to deteriorate after the surrender of Fort Washington. On top of the losses of the failed New York campaign (the loss of Fort Washington itself had cost nearly 3,000 men), expiring militia enlistments siphoned off much critically needed manpower. Of the nearly 22,000 Continentals stationed in and around New York in mid-August, there were now scarcely 10,000 men, scattered across a wide arc some distance north and west of the city, with no hope of regaining any lost ground.

In New Jersey, the Hudson River and the sheer cliffs of the Palisades proved to be little protection for Washington's small force of Continentals. Four days after capturing Fort Washington, taking advantage of intelligence gained from a local informant, Lord Cornwallis led 4,000 Regulars up a defile in the cliff to surprise the American garrison at Fort Lee. The garrison escaped in the nick of time, but they had to abandon much-needed supplies.

Day by day, the British expanded their foothold in New Jersey. Day by day, Washington's dwindling army lost ground to superior British strength. Washington ordered General Lee to join him from North Castle, north of White Plains. But with Cornwallis on his heels, the American Commander-in-Chief retreated south across New Jersey. It was a precipitous retreat in an increasingly desperate situation. The very survival of Washington's army was at risk, and with it the survival of the American nation.

Trenton and the "Petite Guerre"

In early December 1776, Washington crossed the Delaware into Pennsylvania, abandoning most of New Jersey to the British. To make matters worse, a large British and Hessian force sailed into Narragansett Bay and landed at Newport, Rhode Island, without opposition. For all appearances, the American Revolution was sputtering out.

For his part, Lee was in no hurry to join Washington. As sluggishly as he could justify, the borderline-insubordinate Lee worked his way south with his 3,000 men, including *fifer Elijah Mason, Ezra Meriam, Cato Smith, Artemas Reed,* and the other Lincoln men under Colonel Nixon and Colonel Glover. By December 13, he had gotten only as far as Basking Ridge when, under peculiar circumstances, a surprise British raid caught him (still in his bedclothes), and took him prisoner. *Samuel Hastings, Jr.,* was wounded in the struggle and also taken captive.

On December 16, *Joshua Stone, Joseph Bacon, Ebenezer Torrey,* and *James Meriam* may have been among as many as eleven Lincoln men detached to a new Massachusetts militia

Day by day, Washington's dwindling army retreated across the Jerseys. It was an increasingly desperate situation; the very survival of Washington's army was at risk, and with it the survival of the American nation. (Drawing by Howard Pyle, *Scribner's Magazine*, April 1898)

regiment, and ordered to Fairfield, Connecticut, under the command of Col. Samuel Thatcher. Marching through Providence, Danbury, and Tarrytown, their route meandered south to a point near Kingsbridge in the Bronx. There they peered out from their entrenchments, keeping an eye on the 2,000 Redcoats and Loyalists guarding the main access road onto Manhattan.[1]

Desperate for some reversal of fortune to revive the flickering flame of revolution, Washington hatched a bold plan to ferry his remaining army back across the Delaware River on Christmas night to attack the Hessian garrison holding Trenton. It was an all or nothing roll of the dice. A howling winter storm dampened the already slim chance of success. At Bristol, a few miles downriver from Trenton, *fifer Elijah Mason, Ezra Meriam,* and *Cato Smith* in Colonel Nixon's Regiment, struggled to break through the thick ice that packed dense and hard against the opposite shore. Shivering to the core, and unable to secure a landing, their unit was forced to turn back. Upriver at McConkey's Ferry, *Leonard Parks* and *George Brown,* in Colonel Paterson's Regiment, had more success getting through the ice pack, but they landed sleet-soaked and hours late. Two of Washington's three divisions failed to make it across the ice-choked river. The third was hopelessly behind schedule. But despite

---

1 Shattuck, *History of the Town of Concord* (pp. 354–355) says that the regiment commanded by Colonel Thatcher served from November 21, and "marched to New-York and New-Jersey before they returned, and were stationed at Woodbridge." (See also, *Massachusetts Soldiers and Sailors*, Vol. XV, p. 511. For stops at Providence, Danbury, Tarrytown, and Kingsbridge, see *Job Brooks's* pension record # S15345. The British strength at Kingsbridge is given in Fischer, *Washington's Crossing*, p. 383.)

Chapter 5: Fighting for Survival, 1776–1777

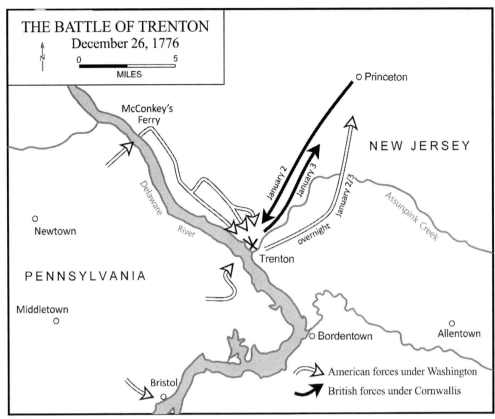

Washington's plan for his surprise attack on Trenton entailed river crossings at three points: at McConkey's Ferry, about ten miles upstream from Trenton; at Trenton Ferry, opposite Trenton; and at Bristol, about twelve miles downstream. Only the McConkey's Ferry crossing succeeded. The dense ice jam of drift ice—packed tightly by the interplay of the wind, current, and tide—foiled the Trenton Ferry and Bristol crossings. Nevertheless, Washington's attack routed the Hessian garrison defending Trenton. After surviving a strong British counterattack on January 2, Washington marched his army overnight to Princeton and secured another victory on January 3. (Base map by Ted Wiggin)

losing their cover of darkness, their movements went undiscovered. The surprise was complete. The Americans quickly rolled up the enemy guard posts, and swept through Trenton, inflicting heavy casualties and capturing most of the 1,500 Hessians holding the town.

Their enlistments expiring, some of the Lincoln men, including *Capt. Moses Brown* and *Leonard Parks,* started for home a few days later despite Washington's personal appeal. "Your country is at stake, your wives, your houses, and all that you hold dear," he had exhorted, pleading for them to remain and to "render that service to the cause of liberty and to your country, which you probably can never do under any other circumstances." Other Lincoln soldiers responded and reenlisted, including *Artemas Reed, Cato Smith,* and *George Brown.* Ironically and poignantly, *Cato Smith* was probably still a slave when he died in service a few weeks later, on January 23, 1777; it is not known whether from battle wounds or disease.[1]

---

1 Washington's appeal was recorded by a Sergeant R—, who was serving in a New England regiment. It was first reported in "The Battle of Princeton," Wellsborough, PA, *Phenix* (March 24, 1832) reprinted in *Pennsylvania*

The victory and the reenlistments brought renewed confidence. The Continentals successfully defended against a powerful British counterattack on Trenton on January 2, 1777, then they slipped away that night and audaciously marched to Princeton. At daybreak the next morning, they defeated the British garrison at Princeton.

Colonel Thatcher's Regiment at Kingsbridge was called to the Jerseys, where they took up a position at Woodbridge. During the following months, a series of pitched battles and skirmishes marked a *petite guerre* which kept the British on edge, allowing the Americans to recapture much of the New Jersey countryside they had lost the previous fall. The British concentrated defensively at Brunswick. In the lower line at Woodbridge in March, on the day the Lincoln terms of service were up, Continental troops under General Maxwell were filling in behind the Lincoln militiamen. The Lincoln men had packed to start for home, when the enemy attacked. *Job Brooks* supposed that the enemy knew they were disbanding. Eight of Colonel Thatcher's men were taken prisoner as they retreated. But as the drum beat for action, the men rallied, and soon they drove the enemy back. Afterwards, the Lincoln men were dismissed, and they set out for home. It was nearing the end of March 1777. With an 11 to 12 day journey, they might still make it back to Lincoln in time for spring planting.[1]

Coastal Defense and Continental Service

Despite the focus of activity in the Champlain Valley and around New York and New Jersey during the second half of 1776, the continued defense of Boston remained a critical Massachusetts priority. Even before Massachusetts started sending additional men to Canada, Ticonderoga, and New York, resolves during April and May 1776 had called for 1,500 militia men for coastal defense. Lincoln men turned out in force. The town paid at least twenty individuals for service in and around Boston during 1776. *Phineas Allen* and *Joseph Brown* served in Boston, as did *Joseph Peirce, Abijah Munroe,* and *Richard Wesson* on artillery duty; *Aaron Brooks* and *Samuel Farrar, Jr.,* served at Cambridge along with at least four other individuals who subsequently went to Ticonderoga with their units. *John Barrett* went to Hull; *John Gearfield, Samuel Dakin, Jr., Joseph Munroe,* and *Nathan Brown, Jr.,* served at Roxbury. *Lt. John Hartwell, Isaac Munroe, Isaac Peirce,* and *Jube Savage* were back in service at Dorchester in August with Capt. John Minot's Company.

In December 1776, the Lincoln contingent at Dorchester expanded to a couple of dozen when one-quarter of all eligible Massachusetts men not already in service were drafted for three months of service guarding the coast. *John Hartwell* became captain of a militia company that included *Bulkley Adams, Peter Brooks, Solomon Whitney, Brister Hoar,* and *Leonard Hoar*. Others, including *Sgt. Amos Baker, Abner Mathis, James Nichols,* and *William*

Magazine of History and Biography, 20 (1896), pp. 515–519, and cited in Fischer, *Washington's Crossing*, pp. 272–273.

1 Washington reached Morristown, New Jersey, where he set up his headquarters on January 6, 1777. The skirmishes were encouraged but not orchestrated by Washington. They were usually the work of independent Continental regiments (such as General Maxwell's) or of militia units. The term *petite guerre* is Fischer's term. The incident is reported in *Job Brooks's* pension record (# S15345). Shattuck, *History of the Town of Concord,* says Thatcher's Regiment served until March 6, 1777, but the evidence indicates that it served until the end of the month. Fischer, *Washington's Crossing* (p. 418) identifies skirmishes at Woodbridge on March 22 and March 28.

Hosmer, Jr., served in Capt. Moses Harrington's Militia Company. The term of service was until the first of March, but *James Nichols* departed in January and *Isaac Munroe* left in February to begin three-year enlistments in the Continental Army. Similarly, *Cpl. Joseph Peirce, Abraham Peirce,* and *Richard Wesson* were recruited out of Capt. Marett's Artillery Company for Continental service during the early months of 1777.

War stories fresh on the lips of returnees from Ticonderoga and the New York campaign may have prompted *Benjamin Cleaveland, Lt. John Whitehead,* and *Lt. Isaac Gage* to enlist for Continental Army service on January 1, 1777. Or perhaps they were simply responding to their country's urgent call for help. They were the first of more than 30 Lincoln men to report for Continental duty that year, most of whom marched off before the spring planting had even begun. Some were returning to service. For others, this was a first enlistment. *Jack Farrar* and *Peter Bowes,* probably still slaves, carried with them promises and expectations of earning their freedom through their war service. *Zodith Henderson, John Lander,* and *Adonijah Rice* were recruits from other towns, recruited to fulfill Lincoln's disproportionately high quota.[1] As the enlistees marched into service, weary soldiers from Trenton and Dorchester and Kingsbridge returned to Lincoln through the spring of 1777. Muskets in hand, Lincoln men crisscrossed the landscape, heading to and coming back from deployments near and far. Throughout 1776 and into 1777, Lincoln's army of the Revolution remained in motion, at once responding to the country's urgent calls for duty and service, and returning home to warm hearths and perhaps to unplowed fields.

Crisis in the North

In April 1777, the war dragged into its third inconclusive year. Despite having been soundly thrashed the previous fall, chased out of New Jersey, and nearly destroyed altogether, Washington's army had miraculously survived. Having been rejuvenated by victories at Trenton and Princeton, the Americans had retaken much of southern and western New Jersey, but closer to New York the British still maintained 14,000 troops on New Jersey soil.[2]

In Canada, General Carleton prepared to re-launch his invasion of the Champlain Valley. He had taken advantage of the winter months to move tons of provisions, ammunition, and needed supplies up the St. Lawrence and Richelieu rivers to staging areas at Sorel, St. John, and Île aux Noix. Teams of men were pressed into service, repairing facilities and defenses

---

1 Shattuck, *History of the Town of Concord*, p. 300. Recruiting soldiers from other towns appears not to have been an uncommon practice. Whether or not Lincoln's quota was in fact disproportionately high is beyond the scope of this work. Clearly the town believed it to be the case, however. In 1778, the town petitioned the Council for relief, explaining that, "The large farm of Dr. Charles Russell, now in the hands of the public, greatly augments the tax on the town, and consequently the number of men required." The Russell farm had been confiscated after *Dr. Russell,* a Tory, fled to the protection of the British Garrison in Boston at the start of the war. It is known today as the Codman House.

The town's petition suggests that the quota allocations may have been based on property tax rolls. However, the author has not discovered any other evidence to suggest that quotas were based on anything other than proportional allocations of the militia (including alarm list and training band) companies, or of the number of male inhabitants of the towns (typically with appropriate age and "able-bodied" qualifiers).

2 Ketchum, *Saratoga*, p. 51.

Burgoyne's invasion from Canada reached and captured Fort Ticonderoga in early July. From Ticonderoga, Burgoyne made his way south, capturing Fort Ann, Fort George, and Fort Edward, while militia units from around New England and New York urgently marched north to reinforce General Gates, who was concentrating his forces around Albany. Despite being checked at Bennington and at Fort Stanwix in the Mohawk Valley, Burgoyne's continuing advance and planned link-up with British forces coming north from New York City threatened to isolate New England from the other states and, in so doing, to cripple the American rebellion. (Base map, Stewart, ed., *American Military History*)

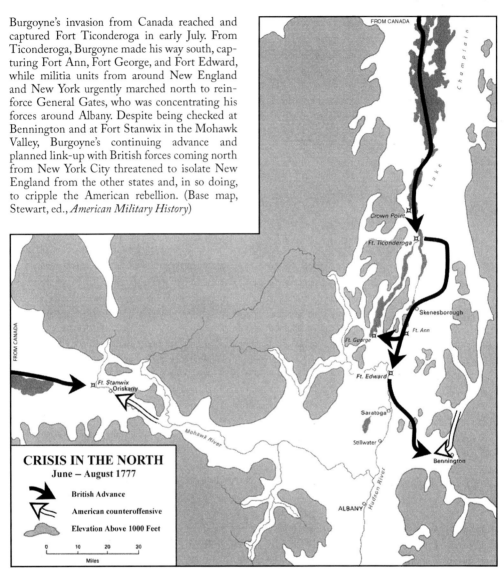

at these locations. This time, he would be ahead of the season, equipped to capture—and hold—Ticonderoga.

Early in May, as the river ice receded, British General John Burgoyne arrived back in Quebec. He had served under Carleton the previous year, and over the winter he had returned to England to attend to personal affairs. He had also used the opportunity for political advantage, playing his hand masterfully. Burgoyne had won approval for a plan to extend the campaign south from Ticonderoga into the Hudson Valley, linking up with British forces coming north from New York. This was a bold plan that would effectively cripple the American rebellion. But more important in his eyes, he also carried with him orders that placed *him* in command of the campaign, instead of Carleton.

By mid-June 1777, Burgoyne's carefully planned invasion of the Champlain and Hudson valleys from Canada was in full mobilization. Meeting with light resistance, his nearly

8,000 troops quickly penetrated deep into New York.[1] Fort Ticonderoga, the "Gibralter of the North," fell on July 6 without a fight, and seizing control of the surrounding territory, Burgoyne quickly dispersed the rebels' Northern Army. Now, little stood between him and Albany, except for a few remaining run-down frontier outposts, which he could quickly overrun.

After bringing up his baggage and supplies, Burgoyne slowly and methodically resumed his march southward. With the British also firmly in control of New York City, the Continental war effort faced an imminent danger. If Burgoyne gained control of the Hudson Valley, he would effectively split off and isolate New England from the rest of the American states. Massachusetts responded to the urgent call for reinforcements.

On August 14, *Capt. Samuel Farrar, Jr.*, mustered Lincoln's militia company on the Town Common. In the shadow of the Meeting House, he doubtlessly reminded his fellow townsmen of the proud response of the Lincoln companies to the April 19th Alarm, and of their patriotic service at Dorchester Heights. Few, if any, were not already aware of the urgency of the situation, but the 40-year-old captain must certainly have reiterated the dire consequences if Burgoyne succeeded in capturing Albany and linking up in the Hudson with Crown forces from New York City. Under orders to provide one-sixth of his men for 3½ months of service to reinforce the Northern Army, *Captain Farrar* called for volunteers. Amid foot shuffling and furtive glances, 19-year-old *Josiah Parks,* recently returned from a two-month stint in Rhode Island, slowly stepped forward, possibly accompanied by a few others. *Captain Farrar* paused, looking over his company. He waited.... Clearly, he would have to resort to a draft in order to fill his quota. One by one, he went down his list, selecting *Nehemiah Abbot, Abel Adams, Samuel Baker, Abner Brooks, Daniel Brown*. By the time he reached *Joshua Child, Jr.,* and *Nathaniel Colburn,* he was up to the requisite 12 names.[2] He ordered his volunteers and draftees to be ready to march in two days.

Joshua Child, Jr. did not have far to return home; he lived just up the hill, almost next door to the Meeting House. But second thoughts must quickly have begun to assert themselves. For reasons we can only guess, by the next day he had decided not to march north into service.[3] Having committed himself, however, his alternatives were few. He headed up the road and paid a visit to *John Hoar*. The financial arrangements have disappeared in the mists of history, but on August 16, 1777, *John Hoar's* Negro servant *Brister* marched into service in the place of *Joshua Child, Jr.*

---

1 Winsor, *Narrative and Critical History* (p. 294) places Burgoyne's strength at 4,135 British, 3,116 Germans, 148 Canadian militia, and 503 Indians, for a total of 7,902. Ketchum, *Saratoga* (p. 137) puts it closer to 7,000.

2 The twelve Lincoln men were reported as "draughted" for this service. The fact that (except for *Josiah Parks*) all of the names come at the beginning of the alphabet is a strong indication that the selection process was not random. The draft process evidently had an alphabetical component or bias, and *Parks* appears to have been a volunteer. See sidebar, "Facing the Crisis," p. 99.

3 The same day that *Joshua Child, Jr.,* was drafted for duty in the north, the *Massachusetts Spy* reported the sensational story of the lurid murder and horrific scalping of Jane McRae, an attractive young woman with long, red hair, by a band of Ottawa Indians employed by Burgoyne. Within a wave of almost daily butchery of northern settlers and soldiers by Burgoyne's Indians, this incident "fired the imagination of a thoroughly alarmed public." While some contemporary reports indicate that the McRea murder may have caused a surge of volunteer enlistments from residents of the area, it also added another dimension to the dangers inherent in service with the Northern Army. Quite possibly, *Joshua Child, Jr.,* may have been willing to face the risks of doing battle with the enemy he knew, but not the risk of inhuman mutilation by an Indian war party [see Ketchum, *Saratoga*, pp. 274–278, 505–506].

As the Lincoln men marched north, other New England militiamen under Gen. John Stark overwhelmed the redoubts of the combined British and German detachment at Bennington, sent there by Burgoyne to secure his flank and gather livestock and other needed supplies. The American victory was a major setback for Burgoyne, who otherwise continued to advance as the retreating rebels fell back toward Albany. (Drawing by F. C. Yohn, *Scribner's Magazine,* May 1898)

Brister Hoar and 15 other Lincoln men (without *Joshua Child, Jr.*) were detached to Capt. George Minot's Company, Col. Samuel Bullard's Middlesex County Regiment of Massachusetts Militia. Together, they headed north in unusually hot and rainy weather. Other militia units were on the move as well—from Massachusetts, Connecticut, New Hampshire, and New York—all headed to the Upper Hudson Valley, where it merges with the Mohawk Valley, above Albany.

As the militia reinforcements marched north, they were buoyed by news of a patriot victory at Bennington. A few days later, they learned that Benedict Arnold and a small force of Americans had broken the British siege of Fort Stanwix, and that the British had pulled north out of central New York.

Despite these checks to the British advance, however, the Northern Army continued to retreat south in the face of Burgoyne's superior force. Having already pulled out of Fort Ann, Fort George, and Fort Edward, the Americans consolidated whatever remaining strength they could muster around Albany.

Defense of Philadelphia

In New Jersey, Washington kept a worried eye on Burgoyne's progress, but his primary concern was second guessing Gen. William Howe, who commanded the much larger British force in New York City. Howe tried to lure the American commander out of the Jersey hills and into a decisive battle, but Washington was not taking the bait. Having recaptured much

Facing the Crisis

Prompted by the critical situation of the American forces after the capture of Ticonderoga by Burgoyne, the Resolve of August 9, 1777, called for one-sixth of the training band and alarm lists not already in service to be drafted without delay. *Capt. Samuel Farrar, Jr.'s* report to *Colonel Brooks*, dated August 14, identifies 12 Lincoln individuals "draughted, inlisted and agreeable to the order of court."

The record is clear enough, but it does not, by itself capture the fluidity or the urgency of the situation. Between the date of the report and the time the men marched north two days later on August 16, the picture changed.

Beneath the list of names is the notation, added later in a different hand, that "Brister Hoar appears in the room of Joshua Child, Junr," evidence of a change of heart by Child, and of the accepted practice of fulfilling a military obligation through substitution. The fact that Brister Hoar was a slave adds a whole additional dimension to the story.

Other evidence of substitution also exists. Draftee *Nathaniel Colburn* appears not to have served, but service by his younger brother *Joseph* is well documented. The presumption is that *Nathaniel* prevailed on his younger brother to substitute for him.

Similarly, no record of service has been found for draftees *Timothy Brown* and *Daniel Brown*; probably, they too found substitutes.

Nehemiah Abbot's name appears on the list. But he, too, appears to have had a change of heart. Instead, he enlisted for a three-year term in the Continental Army, perhaps deciding that if he was going to face the enemy for three months, he might as well make a serious commitment. It is not known who was subsequently drafted to fill his slot. ▶

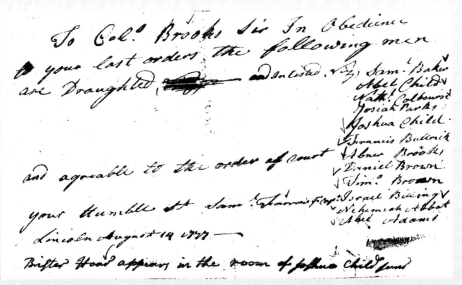

This report shows twelve militiamen from Lincoln drafted for the campaign to support the Northern Army around Saratoga. However, it was a different twelve men who appear to have reported for service. Joshua Child, Jr., having served two previous stints, arranged for Brister Hoar, a slave belonging to John Hoar, to substitute for him. Four others appear to have found substitutes, as well, but they were not identified on the list. (Massachusetts Archives)

> While it is not possible to trace the connections from person to person, the open slots were likely filled by *Amos Baker, Isaac Peirce*, perhaps *Daniel Farrar*, and/or *Amos Hosmer*, who appear to have marched north to Saratoga—one drafted as a replacement for *Nehemiah Abbot*, and probably two as substitutes.
>
> Of the 12 Lincoln individuals on the list, only seven marched north with Colonel Bullard's Regiment on August 16. They were accompanied by five substitutes (including *Abbot's* replacement) and by another four or five Lincoln individuals who are not on the list, but who were detached for this service from militia companies in other towns, where they were probably living or working at the time: *Jeduthan Bemis, Eleazer Parks,* and *Daniel Wesson* from Weston; and *Joseph Munroe* from Lexington.
>
> They were not the only Lincoln men to go north. They simply joined the approximately 16 Lincoln men already in service in the Northern Division of the Continental Army, in regiments commanded by Colonel Nixon, Colonel Greaton, and Colonel Vose. As General Gates prepared to march his forces toward an inevitable clash with Burgoyne, however, *James Nichols* and *Adonijah Rice* were discovered missing and reported deserted.
>
> As the situation became more critical, a second wave of Lincoln reinforcements was sent north in September; 14 more soldiers were detached to a company commanded by *Capt. Samuel Farrar, Jr.,* in Col. Jonathan Reed's regiment. They would not arrive until the fighting was over, but they had the honor of escorting the 6,000 British and German prisoners into detention at Cambridge.
>
> Along with other Lincoln individuals in other militia units and in Continental units, Lincoln's representation at Saratoga approximated 55 to 60 men-in-arms.

of New Jersey during the spring, the American general could afford to bide his time, scouting for intelligence, watching for clues, waiting for Howe to commit his next move.

Howe's skill as a tactician had been demonstrated by his brilliant flanking maneuvers the previous year that had forced Washington to abandon Long Island, then Manhattan, then most of New Jersey. He was systematic, careful, and deliberate. He knew that in order to win back the rebel colonies, he had to remain on the offensive. But he would not be rushed; he would act when ready.

During the winter and spring, he had considered multiple options for bringing the war to a successful close. First was the plan to secure the Hudson Valley north to Albany, and connect with Burgoyne, advancing south from Canada. With New England cut off, Royal troops could then march and retake Boston from their base in Rhode Island or from Ticonderoga. Alternatively he could move against Philadelphia, and squelch the Rebel government. This, he figured, would reenergize the large loyalist populace in the middle colonies, and cut Washington off from the southern colonies. Deprived of support, the Rebel army would fizzle away.[1]

---

1 Howe's various options and plans are laid out in correspondence between Howe and Lord George Germain, the American Secretary, during the winter of 1776–1777. Howe's ambitious first plan, advanced November 30, 1776, focused on the Hudson and New England. A second plan, focusing on Philadelphia, was advanced on December 20, and modified on April 2. Meanwhile, Germain had approved the second plan on March 3, 1777,

Washington was kept guessing. When British ships finally set sail from New York Harbor on July 23, 1777, Washington still had little idea where they were headed.

The ships turned south and entered the mouth of the Delaware River a week later; Washington ordered his army south to Philadelphia. Choosing not to challenge the *chevaux-de-frise*[1] in the river and the Rebel forts on either side, however, the fleet turned around and headed back out to sea. Rounding the capes, they sailed into Chesapeake Bay instead, where 15,000 British troops disembarked at Head of Elk, Maryland, on August 25.[2] In heavy rains over muddy, washed-out roads, Howe marched his troops northeast, toward the Rebel capital.

Washington's army, including *Isaac Munroe*, moved west to intercept them. Attempting to keep his army between Howe's flanking maneuvers and Philadelphia, Washington fell back to high ground behind Chadd's Ford, across the Brandywine Creek. Here *Nathan Tidd*, and perhaps *Benjamin Cleaveland* and *Asa Adams,* in Col. John Crane's Artillery Regiment, unlimbered the cannons and prepared to meet the advancing British column head on.[3]

Jesse Smith, with his mounted mates in the Virginia Light Dragoons that served as Washington's Guard, probably kept watch on the approaching enemy, and scouted the fords for miles on either side of Chadd's Ford. It is likely that they assisted the Commander-in-Chief in posting battalions at each of eight passable fords to guard against another possible British flanking move.[4]

---

shortly after he had approved Burgoyne's plan for a joint expedition to link up in the Hudson Valley. Howe's plan, however, contained only a token provision for supporting Burgoyne's Champlain/Hudson Valley campaign (which he further weakened in the April modification). Germain failed both to instruct Howe to march north to meet Burgoyne, and to provide the necessary troops with which to do so. (For a good summary of this planning process, see the National Park Service's white paper, "The British Campaign for Philadelphia.")

1 See note 1 on p. 76. In this case, the *Chevaux-de-frise* were heavy timbers, submerged and held in place by large cribs on the river bottom. Their iron-tipped points, facing downstream, were intended to tear apart the hulls of ships attempting to sail upriver.

2 At the mouth of the Elk River, near Elkton, Maryland. That Howe chose to move against Philadelphia instead of supporting Burgoyne is the subject of much historical curiosity. It appears self-evident that the British would have gained considerably more by closing off the Hudson to the Rebels than they actually did by occupying Philadelphia. On the other hand, many historians have noted that it was Burgoyne, not Howe, who would likely have gotten credit for success in the Hudson. Howe's troop strength was insufficient to provide meaningful support for Burgoyne and at the same time to undertake his own initiative. He perhaps never considered that he would later be blamed for Burgoyne's failure. The egos, rivalries, and resulting politics among the British command constitute an interesting story of hierarchical class privilege, insecurity, ambition, and style.

3 Brandywine Creek is also known as Brandywine River; it is a considerably larger stream than the term "creek" typically suggests.
   Col. John Crane's Artillery Regiment appears to have been split between the Northern Army at Saratoga and Washington's direct command. *Nathan Tidd* and *Benjamin Cleaveland* can be traced to Brandywine through their companies. *Tidd* was in Capt. David Briant's Company; Briant was killed at Brandywine. *Cleaveland* belonged to Capt. John Lillie's Company. (See Pension Declaration # W22807 for David Briant (also spelled Bryant); Pension Declaration # W10480 for Henry Burbeck [Briant's successor as captain]; and Pension Declaration # R6345 for John Lillie.) However, notwithstanding that Captain Lillie's Company was at Brandywine, *Cleaveland's* widow (in her Pension Declaration # W16908) places her husband at Saratoga. It is not likely that he could have been in both places. It has not been determined whether *Asa Adams*, in Capt. Benjamin Frothingham's Company, was at Brandywine or elsewhere. Placing them at the defense of Chadd's Ford is suppositional. Washington appears to have located most of his artillery there, but the actual location of Crane's artillery is unknown.

4 *Jesse Smith* may have been the only non-Virginian in Colonel Baylor's 3rd Continental Regiment of Light Dragoons. Washington had reconstituted his Guard in 1777 to be only Virginians (later, he changed it again to be representative of all the states). What ruse *Smith* used to remain part of the Guard is unknown. The indicated duty is suppositional, but it is consistent with the duties that the Guard performed.

Despite guarding the fords of the Brandywine Creek for miles on either side of Chadd's Ford, Washington's army was outflanked once again by General Howe's main force. Washington was forced to reposition his troops, thus weakening the American defense of Chadd's Ford and allowing the British to push their way across the creek at that point. The Americans put up stiff resistance, but by nightfall they were in full retreat. (Drawing by F. C. Yohn, *Scribner's Magazine*, June 1898)

The next morning, September 11, Howe marched a division of 7,000 troops forward to engage the Continentals at Chadd's Ford. They "fell in very early with large Bodies of the Enemy," recorded one of the British soldiers, "who form'd upon ev'ry advantageous Post & behind Fences fired on the Troops as they advanc'd—This galling fire was sustain'd the whole way."[1] The contest was sharp and bloody. Amid the smoke and confusion, *Tidd* and possibly *Adams* and *Cleaveland*, worked the guns. *Tidd's* commanding officer went down, fatally wounded. The American line held.

Despite the best efforts of the British officers to make their force appear larger than it was, Washington knew that he was facing only a portion of Howe's army. But conflicting reports of British troops heading north kept him guessing about Howe's real game plan. By the time Washington was able to confirm that the northern movement was real and not just a feint, he had already been outflanked.

With superior intelligence, Howe's larger division crossed the Brandywine at an unguarded ford two miles to the north of the northernmost Continental outpost. Washington readjusted his troops, who gave the enemy fierce resistance. Through the afternoon, the fight raged. "'Twas not like those at Covent Garden or Drury Lane," reported a British

---

1 The quote is from the diary entry of one of the British soldiers, but its source is not identified. (It is reported in "The Philadelphia Campaign 1777—Part 3." The site is well researched and detailed, but it lacks references.)

Chapter 5: Fighting for Survival, 1776–1777

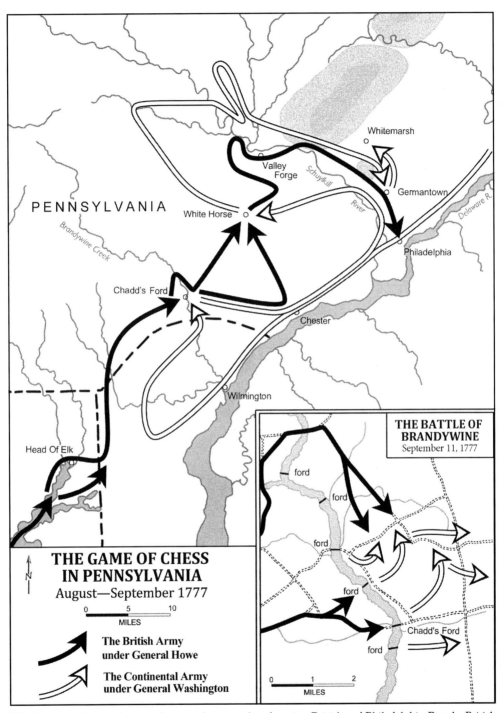

Washington endeavored to keep his army between the advancing British and Philadelphia. But the British victory at Brandywine, and their subsequent maneuvering, forced Washington to choose between defending Philadelphia and protecting his supply bases in the Pennsylvania interior. He chose the latter. On September 26, 1777, British General Howe marched his army into Philadelphia to the cheers of Tory sympathizers. (Base map courtesy of the Department of History, United States Military Academy; Stewart, ed., *American Military History*)

captain, "There was the most infernal Fire of cannon and musquetry. Most incessant shouting, 'Incline to the right! Incline to the left! Halt! Charge!' etc. The balls ploughing up the ground. The trees cracking over one's head. The branches riven by the artillery. The leaves falling as in autumn by the grapeshot...." Despite their fatiguing 17-mile end run, the British slowly began to roll up the right side of the American line.[1]

Washington shifted more troops north, perhaps including *Isaac Munroe*, to shore up his right. A soldier from New Jersey later recalled, "We broke and Rallied and Rallied & broke from height to height till we fell [back] on our main Army who reinforced us & about sunset we made a stand."[2] Washington's troop adjustments had weakened the Continental position at Chadd's Ford, however, and the British there began to push their way across the creek. Now caught between enemy divisions, slowly the Lincoln men and their compatriots yielded, and retreated into the darkening evening. They regrouped a few miles to the rear at Chester, the victorious British too fatigued to pursue.

For two weeks, the American and British armies continued to jockey for position on the southeastern Pennsylvania chessboard. Congress packed up and fled to safety at Lancaster, then York. Eventually, unable to protect both Philadelphia and his important supply base at Reading, Washington conceded the capital city to the British. On September 26, 1777, amid great pomp and procession, the British marched victoriously down Second Street, to the cheers of thousands of Tory sympathizers.

Washington was not through yet, however. Eight days later, on October 4, he launched a surprise, four-pronged, dawn attack on the British camp at Germantown, just outside of Philadelphia. The Americans penetrated the British perimeter and drove the Regulars back. *Nathan Tidd*, and perhaps *Benjamin Cleaveland*, again manned the guns and bombarded the enemy; *Jesse Smith* again provided guard service and other appropriate duties for the Commander in Chief. But in the heavy morning fog initial American success was met by stiffening enemy resistance, and poor coordination between the different American divisions doomed the effort. The British counterattacked. The Americans withdrew to Whitemarsh, about eight miles north. There, Washington rested his troops, addressed the scarcity of provisions, and planned his next move.

Saratoga

As the Massachusetts men approached the Upper Hudson Valley, it is likely that their optimism rose both with the number of reinforcements making their way north, and with the news that Gen. Horatio Gates had replaced Gen. Philip Schuyler in command of the Northern Army. General Gates was popular among New Englanders. He had served under Washington during the siege of Boston, and he had gained a reputation both as an organizer and as a leader with concern for the welfare of his men. He camped with his men,

---

1 The unsourced quote is reported in "The Philadelphia Campaign 1777—Part 7." Several cannons were lost during this phase of the battle. Quite possibly, the Lincoln artillerymen may have been engaged, and Captain Briant may have fallen at this time.

2 The unsourced quote is reported in "The Philadelphia Campaign 1777—Part 8." *Isaac Munroe's* deployment during the battle is unknown.

made sure they were fed and sheltered, and he was "always present with them in Fatigue and Danger."[1]

The 16 Lincoln men in Colonel Bullard's Regiment arrived near Albany probably around the end of August. By the end of the first week in September, General Gates's Northern Army had swelled to over 10,000 men. Most of the arriving troops probably went into camp on Van Schaicks Island, where the Mohawk and Hudson rivers converge. But there was little time to settle in. On September 7, Gates marched them north to Stillwater, then several miles further to Bemis Heights, where they were now within perhaps 20 miles of Burgoyne's slowly advancing troops. Here they dug themselves in and waited.

Bemis Heights was a superb defensive choice, a wooded plateau that came to within a few hundred feet of the Hudson River. The only road to Albany would take Burgoyne's army through the narrow pass along the river at the foot of the heights. Gates deployed his artillery so it could maul the enemy, should they attempt to force their way through. Burgoyne's only alternative would be to turn away from the river and attempt to get around the left wing of the entrenched Continentals. That would mean difficult going in unfamiliar, ravine-cut, wooded hillsides—just the type of terrain that would be likely to neutralize the disciplined effectiveness of European field maneuvers, and favor the less-disciplined American style of warfare.

On the morning of September 19, as a thick fog blanketed the valley, Burgoyne made his move. He turned his army right, away from the river, entered the wooded hills, and tried to flank the Continentals. In command of the Continental left wing, Benedict Arnold led his men out to meet them. The armies converged in a pasture on Freeman's farm. The fight raged all afternoon, seesawing back and forth across the field. The American army held. By dusk, they had blunted the British advance.

For the Americans, however, the situation remained precarious. Burgoyne would almost certainly try again. Amidst continuing calls for reinforcements, *Capt. Samuel Farrar, Jr.*, rallied another 14 Lincoln men. *Daniel Billing, Samuel Dakin, Jr., William Thorning*, and *Joseph Mason, Jr.*, had served previously both as minute men and subsequently during the fortification of Dorchester Heights. For *Peter Nelson*, a 14-year-old slave, this was probably a first enlistment. The Lincoln captain was chosen to command the company, and on September 29, they left Lincoln and marched north in Colonel Reed's Regiment. They were undoubtedly cheered by news of the Bemis Heights battle, which arrived probably just before they left, and they may anxiously have quickened their pace as a result. There was growing optimism that Burgoyne might be stopped, and this was reinforced by further news of a successful raid on the British garrison holding Fort Ticonderoga in Burgoyne's rear. That raid had captured 274 British prisoners and released 118 Americans.

As the men from Lincoln marched toward Bemis Heights, Burgoyne paused, waiting for the arrival of the troops from New York City. He had long since outdistanced his supply chain from Canada, and his supplies were now running dangerously low. Still, there was no sign of the British reinforcement from the south. The Lincoln men were still a day or two short of Bemis Heights on October 7, when Burgoyne, now desperate, once more

---

[1] The quote is attributed to Samuel Adams by Semkiw, "Return of the Revolutionaries." The author has been unable to locate the source of the quote but uses it here because it does seem to capture the essence of his reputation.

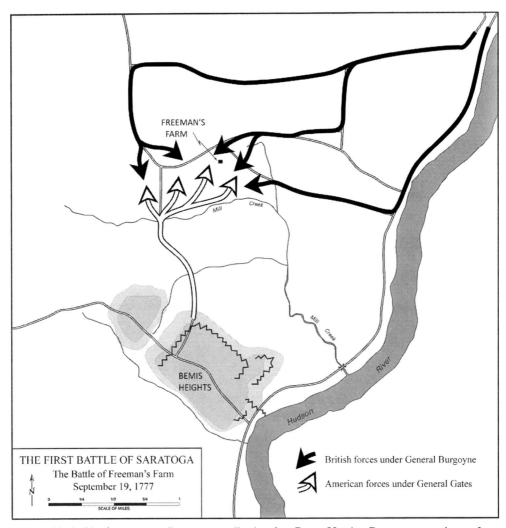

His way blocked by American artillery strategically placed on Bemis Heights, Burgoyne turned away from the river and tried to flank the American line, but he was stopped at Freeman's Farm on September 19 *(above)*. A second attempt *(right)* failed on October 7, when Benedict Arnold—disobeying orders from General Gates—took the field and rallied the American troops. Burgoyne then began a slow withdrawal north. By October 17, his luck had run out. Completely surrounded, out of supplies, and with no prospect of relief, he surrendered. (Base map courtesy of the Department of History, United States Military Academy)

moved to flank the American left. Once more, Benedict Arnold rallied the American left and stopped the determined British advance, inflicting heavy losses.[1]

---

1 Shattuck, *History of the Town of Concord* (p. 356) reports that a company commanded by Col. John Buttrick (in Colonel Reed's Regiment) left Concord on October 4 and arrived in Saratoga on October 10, by way of Rutland and Northampton. After a couple of days at Saratoga, they were sent to Ft. Edward, where they went on a scouting mission and "brought in 53 Indians, several Tories, and some women." They returned to Saratoga on the 17th to witness the surrender ceremony, and subsequently they were part of the escort for Burgoyne's troops to Cambridge. Although there is no certainty that *Capt. Samuel Farrar's* Company served similar duty, the author believes it likely that since they were in the same regiment, the experience of the Lincoln men was

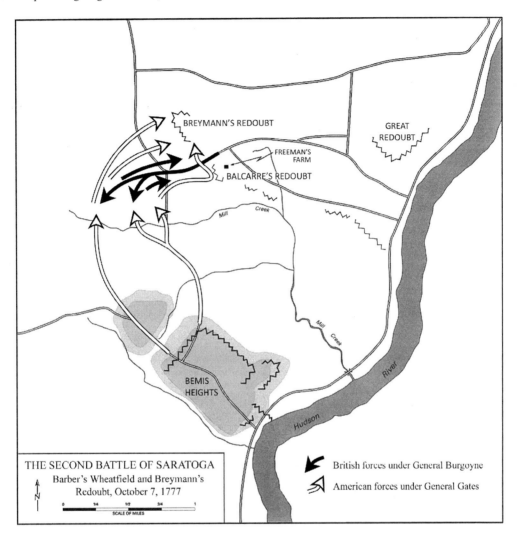

Out of options, Burgoyne began to withdraw his army northward the next night. Executed with reluctance and confusion, the retreat managed to log only a few miles each day, and by October 13 they found themselves completely surrounded by the Americans, whose numbers continued to swell with new militia arrivals. Burgoyne had played out his hand. On October 16, after negotiating unusually favorable terms and dragging his feet in the vain hope that relief might still arrive from the south, Burgoyne signed the surrender document. Stripped of any reference to capitulation or surrender, and instead called the

---

reasonably parallel. In his pension declaration (Pension Record # S29229), *Leonard Hoar* confirms that they arrived after the October 7 fighting occurred.

Arnold's heroic, maniacal leadership was a decisive element in the victory, notwithstanding that Gates had relieved him of his command before the battle, and that his actions were in direct violation of Gates's orders. The feud between these two individuals constitutes an interesting story of conflicting egos, insecurities, ambitions and style.

Saratoga "Convention," the result was nevertheless unmistakable. The next morning, with approximately 55 Lincoln soldiers of the Revolution present, the 5,900 surviving British and German troops under Burgoyne's command at Saratoga formally laid down their arms.

Despite the sanitized language of the document, the news of Burgoyne's surrender radiated from Saratoga with relief and renewed optimism. Within days, troops along the New England coastline discharged their cannons in celebration. The news was greeted with jubilation as it traveled south through the other states. Over in London, the King reportedly "fell into agonies," and at the French court at Versailles, it "occasioned as much general joy … as if it had been a Victory of their own troops over their own Enemies."[1]

Except for palpable excitement, however, there was little time for the troops at Saratoga to celebrate. Much of the Northern Army marched south the next day to reinforce Washington in New Jersey. The 16 Lincoln men in Colonel Bullard's Regiment served in New Jersey until their November 30 discharge. They arrived back home approximately ten days later.[2] *George Brown, Peter Oliver,* and the other Lincoln men serving in many of the Continental regiments, subsequently went into winter quarters with Washington's army at Valley Forge.

While most of their compatriots marched south, the 14 Lincoln men in *Capt. Samuel Farrar, Jr.'s* company prepared to escort Burgoyne's "Convention Army" to Boston to await repatriation across the Atlantic. By October 22, they were underway: 4,640 prisoners, nine companies of guards, wagon drivers, and bat-horsemen;[3] there were over 6,000 people in total, divided into two divisions, following slightly different routes. In marked contrast to the difficulty of provisioning the expedition–and the early snow that greeted it as it crossed the Berkshires–enthusiastic residents lined the roads and hillsides all along the route to gawk at the prisoners and cheer encouragement for the valiant American heroes.[4]

The Lincoln men escorted the British wing of the Convention, which marched by way of Williamstown and Northampton. As they descended the foothills of the Berkshires into Worthington, they likely rendezvoused with a group of Lincoln teamsters. Former minute men *John Parks* and *Elijah Willington,* in company with former slave *Cuff Hoar* and five other Lincoln men, arrived with teams of oxen carrying supplies for the weary prisoners and guards.[5]

---

1 Ketchum, *Saratoga,* pp. 436–439, 442, 225.
2 Ketchum, *Saratoga,* pp. 437, 440; Shattuck, *History of the Town of Concord,* p. 356. *Amos Baker* had been discharged September 30; *Nathan Brown* was discharged October 21, probably while they were en route to New Jersey. The reasons for the early discharges are unknown.
3 Bat-horsemen, or batmen, were those who attended the pack horses.
4 Upham, *A Memoir of General John Glover,* pp. 31–32; Shattuck, *History of the Town of Concord,* p. 356; Roads, *The History of Marblehead,* p. 162. This estimate of the number of prisoners and the size of the overall expedition is from a letter by Gen. John Glover, dated October 22, 1777, requesting provisioning assistance (as reported in Upham). General Glover was in charge of the escort operation. Most estimates of the number of prisoners are closer to the 5,900 figure given by Ketchum and used previously in this work. Shattuck says that nine companies provided the escort, five marching in front and four in back. As he makes no reference to the different divisions, it is unclear if this is nine companies per division or nine companies total.
5 Evidence that *Captain Farrar's* Company was assigned to guard the British division of the "Convention Army" is found in *Joseph Mason's* Pension Record (# S13820), which states that they guarded the prisoners to Prospect Hill, which is where the British prisoners were housed. The German soldiers were sent by a more southerly

Chapter 5: Fighting for Survival, 1776–1777

Disarmed British soldiers passed between the American lines, which extended for nearly a mile, as General Burgoyne silently handed his sword to General Gates in a ceremony of surrender attended by approximately 55 soldiers from Lincoln. (Drawing by F. C. Yohn, *Scribner's Magazine*, May 1898)

When the entourage arrived in Cambridge on November 6, the Americans delivered their prisoners to the dilapidated huts on Prospect Hill and Winter Hill that had been constructed two years before, in 1775, as barracks for the fledgling Continental Army. The Lincoln men were discharged the next day.[1]

Undoubtedly, some militia units remained in the Upper Hudson Valley to keep an eye on the remaining pockets of enemy troops at Lake George and Fort Ticonderoga. One by one over the next weeks, the enemy garrisons packed up and returned to Canada.

As the "Convention Army" neared Cambridge, *Col. Eleazer Brooks* was selected to command a regiment of militia to serve as camp guards. Half a dozen Lincoln men enlisted for this service in Capt. Simon Hunt's Company. *Noah Parkhurst, William Parks, James Adams, Jr.,* and *Amos Baker* had previously faced the British together at the North Bridge. *Leonard Hoar,* freshly discharged from having escorted the Convention from

---

route through Kinderhook, Great Barrington, and Springfield, and were housed at Winter Hill (see Upham, *A Memoir of General John Glover*, p. 31; Fleming, "Gentleman Johnny's Wandering Army").

The rendezvous of the Worthington teams with *Captain Farrar's* Company is speculative, as the specific dates and purpose of the Worthington supply expedition have not been identified. Worthington is, however, located approximately on the route of travel between Williamstown and Northampton. The speculation is based on the absence of any other apparent reason for carting supplies to Worthington, and it is given credence by Glover's letter (see note 4, p. 108) requesting that provisions be sent to meet them at Worcester. It also supposes that the supplies carried by the Lincoln teamsters were destined for the troops escorted by the Lincoln men.

1 *Daniel Billing* appears to have been discharged on October 24, probably en route. He must have returned to Lincoln independently of the escort.

Saratoga, probably had not even returned home. For 39-year-old *Abraham Wesson*, this was a first enlistment.[1] This was expected to be short duty, only as long as it took to repatriate the enemy soldiers.

---

1 *Samuel Hartwell* was the regimental quartermaster, as is made clear from various accounts for goods and services found in Eleazer Brooks Papers [Concord]. Another half-dozen Lincoln men appear to have served at this time, as well, in several different companies. Among them, *Enos Wheeler, Jonathan Smith*, and *Samuel Bacon* are recorded as having served guard duty in 1777 and 1778, but the specific dates and units are not given.

Chapter 6

A Renewed Spirit and Renewed Dangers, 1777–1780

The defeat of Burgoyne's army ended the immediate threat of New England being isolated from the rest of the rebellious colonies, and it changed the complexion of the war in the north. It also encouraged optimism about the eventuality of a successful outcome to the struggle. But few harbored any illusions. British troops were still firmly entrenched in New York and Philadelphia and Newport, and British ships could easily transport the troops to other locations along the coast. The war was far from over.

In southeastern Pennsylvania, Washington welcomed the Continental regiments marching in from Saratoga, among them Lincoln soldiers *George Brown* and *Peter Oliver*, and he prepared to move his troops into winter quarters on high ground along the west bank of the Schuylkill River. On an open hillside near an iron forge on Valley Creek, about 15 miles west of their Whitemarsh camp, the Continentals found defensive ground safe from a surprise British attack, where they could also prevent British foraging parties from raiding the interior of Pennsylvania.

Valley Forge

With the rest of Washington's army, *Zodith Henderson, Nehemiah Abbot,* and *Jack Farrar* marched into Valley Forge on December 19, 1777. They had no reason to expect conditions or the availability of provisions or supplies to get any better than they had been all year. Provisioning had always been barely adequate, meager, subsistence level—and three and a half months of campaigning across the cornucopia of southeast Pennsylvania had stripped the normally plentiful region of much of its bounty. Even foraging had become minimally productive. Beef was a rare treat, and the soldiers often had to subsist on Johnny cakes and watered-down gruel for days at a time.

Like many of the others, the Lincoln men were still wearing the same clothes they had brought with them into the army nearly a year before. What was left of them, at least. Patched or unpatched, torn or worn thin in spots—there had not been much chance to replace them. Shoes were the same way: holes worn in the soles, heels lost, seams separated, the stitching long gone. Most soldiers still had blankets, which provided some warmth, even if they were a little threadbare.

They were not exactly sure why they stayed. Except that they had agreed to this when they enlisted, and their enlistments still had two years to run. Probably most had not even seriously considered leaving. Sure, others had left, disappeared—deserted—but that stood for failure and dishonor. That was the easy way out, not the honorable thing to do.

"Dispersion was not thought of," wrote one Connecticut soldier, "at least I did not think of it. We had engaged in the defense of our injured country and were willing, nay, we were determined to persevere as long as such hardships were not altogether intolerable."[1]

Winter had already set in. They were now racing against the calendar to construct huts against the snow and wind. Equally important were the camp perimeters; redoubts to build and trenches to dig. General Howe had already tried to come after them in their last camp; he would be likely to do so again. Chop…Thud…Clank…construction echoed through the crisp air. Axes and saws felled trees, shaped the logs for huts, sharpened them for abatis.[2] Picks and shovels cut the frozen crust for entrenchments and piled the sod and dirt for redoubts. The whole army was at work. Day by day, as the skies flurried and temperatures fell with the season, the camp took shape: miles of trenches, five redoubts, and perhaps 2,000 huts laid out in parallel lines.

Only the sick were idle. Between turns with an axe or shovel or hammer, *Silas Sharon* and *Eden London* served guard duty; *Jesse Smith* and other dragoons left camp for advanced positions from which to scout the enemy; *Peter Oliver* and *Luke Fletcher* may have been detailed to foraging parties. *Nehemiah Abbot* was quarantined with his regiment at Lancaster for smallpox inoculation.

One visitor reported in *The New Jersey Gazette*, "I found them employed in building little huts for their winter quarters. It was natural to expect that they wished for more comfortable accommodations, after the hardships of a most severe campaign; but I could discover nothing like a sigh of discontent at their situation.… On the contrary, my ears were agreeably struck every evening, in riding through the camp, with a variety of military and patriotic songs and every countenance I saw, wore the appearance of cheerfulness or satisfaction."[3]

Working hard to maintain camp discipline, and to improve the flow of supplies, Washington lamented "the present dreadful situation of the army for want of provisions, and the miserable prospects before us." But he marveled at the endurance of his men, observing that "we cannot enough admire the incomparable patience and fidelity of the soldiery that they have not been ere this excited by their sufferings to a general mutiny and dispersion."[4]

Despite a unified command under General Washington, the Continental Army was less a national army than it was a collection of individual state regiments, each one recruited

---

[1] Martin, *Private Yankee Doodle*, p. 102.

[2] An important part of eighteenth-century fortifications, abatis are stakes or poles planted close together in rows, typically at the foot of earthworks, with pointed ends out, usually at an angle facing the enemy.

[3] Valley Forge National Park, Visitor brochure, GPO: 2010–357-940/80428. No formal citation for the quote is given, but it is attributed to an anonymous observer in *The New Jersey Gazette* on December 25, 1777. Consistent with recent scholarship, which shows that the Valley Forge winter of 1777–1778 was an average winter (i.e., not the brutally severe cold and extreme conditions traditionally associated with Valley Forge), the National Park Service has shifted its interpretive focus on Valley Forge away from the "myth" of an excessively harsh winter and the extreme suffering of the men, toward the emergence (from a collection of diverse state regiments) of a coherent national army, with a unified drill and renewed confidence. While the author concurs with the new interpretive focus, he notes that the observations of the anonymous visitor are rather more upbeat than most contemporary reports, which blame the want of adequate provisions and clothing for much suffering, sickness, and death.

[4] Washington letter to Governor George Clinton of New York (February 16, 1778), quoted in Scheer and Rankin, *Rebels & Redcoats*, p. 304.

Chapter 6: A Renewed Spirit and Renewed Dangers, 1777–1780

from, organized in, and accountable to its state of origin. There was little uniformity from one unit to another. Even within a unit, more often than not, little attention had been given to training individual soldiers on how to work together for maximum effectiveness in the art of warfare. Courage, spirit, and common purpose had served the army well, but in terms of military skill, the Continental Army was still no match for its professionally trained enemy.

In late February, a former Prussian staff officer presented his credentials at the camp, as a volunteer for the American cause. Although he could not speak a word of English, Baron von Steuben made an immediate impression. Resplendent in his uniform, astride his steed, the stout, balding Prussian officer reminded one soldier "of the ancient fabled God of War…he seemed to me a perfect personification of Mars. The trappings of his horse, the enormous holsters of his pistols, his large size, and his strikingly martial aspect, all seemed to favor

Baron Von Steuben—a stout, balding, former Prussian staff officer—arrived in camp in late February 1778. Astride his steed, resplendent in his uniform, he made an immediate impression on one soldier as the personification of "the ancient fabled God of War." (1780 painting by Charles Willson Peale, Pennsylvania Academy of Fine Arts)

the idea."[1] Unlike those of many of his European counterparts seeking fame and fortune in the American war, von Steuben's military credentials were solid. He was steeped in the military arts, and he understood their importance.

Von Steuben drafted a simplified set of drill instructions, which were translated, copied, and disseminated to the individual units. From the Commander-in-Chief's Guard, possibly including *Jesse Smith*, and from other companies representing each state, he selected 100 men to form a "model company." He drilled the model company in person, often coloring the air with strings of German and French expletives. When this failed to elicit the desired response from the amused Americans, he would turn to his aide to curse for him in English.

Day by day, he expanded the drill, drilled his model company, and then dispersed his trainees to the individual units as trainers. Day by day, as the Prussian volunteer drilled his charges, the model company disseminated the drill through the ranks.

As he worked, he discovered that this army was different from the European armies of his experience. Not only did he find it necessary to simplify the European drill standards, but also, as he wrote to a former colleague, "The genius of this nation is not in the least to be compared with that of the Prussians, Austrians, or French. You say to your soldier, 'Do

---

[1] Sheer & Rankin, pp. 305–306. The source of the quote is unidentified. It appears in the National Park Service's online article, "General von Steuben."

Speaking no English, General Von Steuben drilled his model company in German and French, filling the air with expletives, before turning to his aide to translate. Day by day, the model company learned the drill, and then dispersed to train the various regiments. (Painting by Edwin Austin Abbey, Pennsylvania State Capital Building)

this,' and he doeth it, but I am obliged to say, 'This is the reason why you ought to do that,' and then he does it."[1]

Day by day, a new, unified American army began to take shape. The soldiers learned effective use of the bayonet, and to load and fire their muskets rapidly and in unison. Individual units learned to maneuver together, to coordinate their movements. As their skills increased, their confidence rose.

Coincidentally, Gen. Nathanael Greene was appointed to oversee the procurement process, and the supply problems began to ease somewhat. It was still "life in the army," but the hardships became more bearable. For most, that is. *George Brown* was reported deserted on June 1.

As the leaf buds swelled and opened, and as the aroma of spring settled into Valley Forge, so too, a new spirit of hope and readiness permeated the air. May brought news of the new French alliance. Cannons roared their approval across the rolling terrain. On the Grand Parade in the center of the camp, the troops assembled and demonstrated their new skills with a *feu de joie*.[2] From their advanced positions, the scouts brought in reports of unusual activity in the British camp. Soon, their new-found training and confidence would be put to the test.

Guarding the Convention

In the Cambridge camps, Burgoyne's "Convention Army" bided its time awaiting repatriation. Days and weeks ticked by for the prisoners and for *Noah Parkhurst* and *Abraham Wesson*, serving guard duty.

---

1 Baron von Steuben letter to Baron von Gaudy (n.d.), quoted in Scheer and Rankin, *Rebels & Redcoats*, p. 307.

2 A *feu de joie* is a celebratory rolling musket fire which starts at one end of the line and works its way down the line to the other end.

By December, the politics of camp command began to wear on *Colonel Brooks*. As one of the ranking militia officers of the guard, he rankled at the "degrading" of militia officers by Continental counterparts. In a letter to General Heath, he observed that only militia officers were called upon to serve duty as Officers of the Day. He noted his understanding that Continental officers needed to be in direct command of troops in order for Continental command to supercede militia command. As the Continental officers were not serving duty as Officers of the Day, this indicated that they were not in direct field command. If this was so, he questioned, then why did the Continental command supercede militia command?[1]

With the British occupying Philadelphia, and Congress sitting in exile at York, Pennsylvania, pragmatic concerns had overcome the euphoria generated by the defeat of Burgoyne. The "Saratoga Convention" stipulated that the repatriated British soldiers could not return to fight in the American war. But there was no provision in the Convention to prevent them from being assigned duties that would free up other British troops to be sent to America. Congress balked; repatriation stalled. Winter dragged into spring.

At the beginning of April 1778, their five-month enlistments having expired, the Lincoln men (including *Colonel Brooks*) returned home. A second wave of guards served three months. Sixteen-year-old first-timers, *Nehemiah Farrar* and *Jonathan Page*, were among thirteen Lincoln men in Capt. Daniel Harrington's Company, Col. Jonathan Reed's Regiment of Guards. In turn, they were relieved in July by a third wave of guards, including first-timer *Joseph Billing, Jr.*, his cousin *Israel Billing*, who had marched the prisoners from Saratoga eight months before, and *Nehemiah Farrar*, who instead of going home, had reenlisted for another term.

By now, repatriation had become derailed. Increasing fear of a British raid on Boston to rescue the prisoners prompted consideration of relocating them to inland quarters. After some deliberation, finally, on November 7—exactly one year after arriving in Cambridge—the "Convention Army" was marched south to Charlottesville, Virginia.[2] The Lincoln guards returned home from Cambridge on December 15, 1778.

Monmouth

With the French entry into the war on the side of the Americans, the British vacated Philadelphia on June 18, 1778, in order to concentrate their forces in New York. Ten thousand soldiers, one thousand Loyalists, and a baggage train stretched as much as 12 miles across the New Jersey countryside. Moving slowly, the long procession presented a

---

1 Eleazer Brooks Papers [Lincoln], p. 19. Heath was the ranking Massachusetts general, who also held a Continental commission, and was in overall command of the forces guarding Burgoyne's "Convention Army." *Brooks's* letter actually asks if there were any Continental officers in command of their own units, but he must certainly have known the answer. The question appears to be a rhetorical ploy by which to register his unhappiness with the situation.

2 The snag in the repatriation provision of the Convention was never resolved, and the "Convention Army" remained prisoners of war until the end of the war in 1783. After Charlottesville, they were subsequently moved to Fredrick, Maryland, and to York, Pennsylvania, ahead of various perceived threats to their security from British campaigns during the war. During their captivity, many (particularly the Germans) were recruited for service in the Continental Army or allowed to assimilate into the local population. Others escaped or perished. By the end of the war, only 1,500 of the original 5,000 to 6,000 prisoners were still being held.

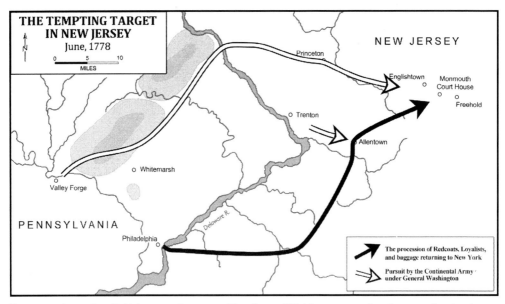

Pursuing a long, slow British procession across New Jersey, Washington sent detachments ahead to harass the British rear at Allentown and elsewhere before catching up with the main British force at Monmouth Court House. (Base map courtesy of the Department of History, United States Military Academy)

tempting target for General Washington. General Lafayette concurred that it "would be disgraceful and humiliating to allow the enemy to cross the Jerseys in tranquility."[1]

Leaving Valley Forge, the American army moved in pursuit. On June 24, *Stephen Lufkin* and *Zodith Henderson* went ahead with Colonel Cilley's Regiment to annoy the British left and rear at Allentown. Colonel Jackson's Regiment, perhaps with *Cpl. Ephraim Brooks, Jr.,* and *William Orr,* participated in capturing British "stragglers and marauders." A contingent of the Commander-in-Chief Guards, likely including *Jesse Smith,* was sent forward in support of Col. Daniel Morgan, attempting to gain the right flank of the British column. Near Squaw Creek, they encountered a unit of British Grenadiers and took 39 prisoners, in the process of which, reported one of Morgan's men, "the elegant Life Guards had been splattered with mud as they dashed through the swamps and then Morgan indulged himself in a stentorian laugh that made the woodlands ring."[2]

A few days later, on June 28, from their camp in Englishtown, Col. Henry Jackson's Regiment, possibly including *Cpl. Ephraim Brooks, Jr., Cpl. Nehemiah Abbot,* and *William Orr,* was sent ahead under General Lee[3] to engage the British left flank and rear near Monmouth Court House, several miles distant. In sweltering heat, they pushed hard—some thought too

---

1 Stryker, *The Battle of Monmouth*, p. 77.
2 Stryker, *The Battle of Monmouth*, pp. 78, 91. Moran, *C-in-C Guards*.
3 Gen. Charles Lee, who had been held by the British since his bizarre capture at Basking Ridge on December 13, 1776, was released on parole on April 5, 1778, then declared exchanged for British Gen. Richard Prescott on April 21. Despite Lee's previous arrogant rivalry (at times bordering on insubordination) with the Commander in Chief, Washington considered him an indispensable officer, and he gave him a lavish Hero's welcome upon his return to Valley Forge on April 23 (see Stryker, *The Battle of Monmouth*, p. 43, footnote). Lee was originally opposed to engaging the British at this time, and he petulantly declined Washington's offer of this command. After Washington gave the command to Lafayette, Lee reconsidered.

Chapter 6: A Renewed Spirit and Renewed Dangers, 1777–1780

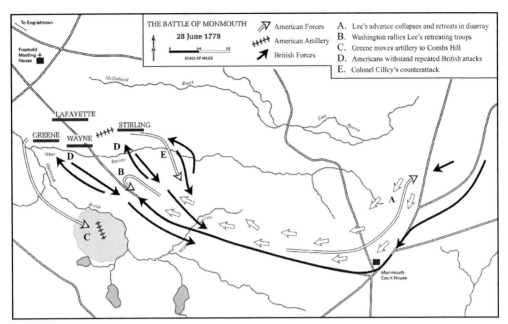

At Monmouth, Lincoln men participated in General Lee's botched engagement with the British rear guard, which was inadequately planned and executed in confusion. In disarray, the American advance fell back, pursued by the British. Washington rallied the retreating men and held off the enemy until additional units were brought up. After successive British attacks failed and before darkness ended the battle, other Lincoln men took part in a brief counterattack led by Colonel Cilley. (Base map courtesy of the Department of History, United States Military Academy)

hard—stopping only to distribute cartridges and load their muskets. Quickstepping the final mile, they moved right, through a small orchard to an open plain, and began to form a battle line. A cloud of dust galloped by on the right. "Form, for God sake! Form! The enemy is upon us!" shouted someone from the retiring party of American cavalrymen.

"Wheel to the right!" came the order, instantly. In perfect order, by platoons, they wheeled into line to cover the cavalry retreat.

"Recover!" Their muskets snapped vertically to their left temples, awaiting the follow-on commands to "Make Ready!" "Present!" then "Fire!"

"Hold fire!" "Don't fire until orders are given," echoed down the line, the officers pausing, waiting, and insistent that no musket be fired until the right moment. On the heels of the American Horse came the British Light Horse through the dust, nearly upon them. A fierce musket volley roared from Colonel Butler's Regiment on their left; the Light Horse turned and retreated.[1]

After a brief pause, muskets returned to "Shoulder!" on command. Wheeling left, they marched forward 100 yards and stopped. Shortly, they started taking casualties from enemy

---

[1] The fact of having held their fire was as important a deterrent to the oncoming Light Horse as the volley from Colonel Butler's forces. After a musket is fired, it takes 20 seconds or so to reload, and reloading soldiers are essentially defenseless. For a cavalry unit galloping upon an enemy, those 20 seconds are more than enough time to reach the enemy line and cut up its ranks. Having suffered the damage of one volley firing, and knowing what was in store for them at even closer range if they continued on, the British Light Horse opted to turn around, instead.

The artillery on the Monmouth battlefield roared fiercely for most of the afternoon, making the blisteringly-hot day even hotter. From advantageous positions on the ridge behind West Ravine and on Combs Hill, the American guns helped repel repeated enemy assaults. (Drawing by H. W. Ditzler, *Scribner's Magazine*, June 1898)

artillery fire, and with a vastly superior enemy force coming into view, they obliqued left to the cover of a wooded hollow. Again they halted, awaiting further orders. Confusion reigned. A number of men fainted from the oppressive heat and fatigue. Soon they were moving again, toward a hill on their left rear. An order arrived from General Lee to retreat. They turned, and in good order—minus further depletions from exhaustion and heatstroke—marched back to camp at Englishtown.[1]

As General Lee's other units retreated—in some disorder—Washington was bringing up his main force. Incredulous at finding Lee's advanced forces in retreat, the Commander in Chief spurred his horse forward. By the sheer weight of his presence, he rallied the retreating men, getting them to reform and make a stand. Lafayette marveled, as General Washington rode "all along the lines amid the shouts of the soldiers, cheering them by his voice and example and restoring to our standard the fortunes of the fight. I thought… that never had I beheld so superb a man."[2] Amidst increasing enemy fire, *Jesse Smith* and his fellow Guardsmen tried to protect the General. The Guard took losses; the General remained untouched.

---

1 "Col. Jackson's Court of Enquiry," pp. 209, 213–227. This sequence, including most of the dialog, is distilled from the proceedings of a Court of Enquiry into Colonel Jackson's conduct during the battle. The Court found that considering "the Confusion of the advanced Corps of Genl. Lee's Division on that Day," there appeared nothing "against Col°. Jackson sufficiently reprehensible to call him before a Court Martial."

2 Quoted in Scheer and Rankin, *Rebels & Redcoats*, p. 331.

Chapter 6: A Renewed Spirit and Renewed Dangers, 1777–1780

General Stirling brought other men from Lincoln up on the left wing, formed on the hill, and withstood repeated British assaults.[1] In Col. Thomas Marshall's 10th Massachusetts Regiment, *Silas Sharon* and *Eden London* wheeled, formed battle lines, loaded and volleyed on command. *Peter Oliver, Luke Fletcher,* and *Peter Bowes* did the same in Col. Timothy Bigelow's 15th Massachusetts Regiment. *Jack Farrar* stood his ground with Colonel Vose's 1st Massachusetts Regiment. Their lines held. *Nathan Tidd* and perhaps *Benjamin Cleaveland* manned their overheated guns, probably behind the west ravine or perhaps on Combs Hill,[2] sending shot and ball repeatedly into British lines in a fierce artillery battle, perhaps the hottest and fiercest yet seen on American soil.

In mid-afternoon, an enemy force drove against Stirling's left flank. *Stephen Lufkin, Zodith Henderson,* and perhaps *John Barter,* advanced with Colonel Cilley to counterattack. One member of their detachment reported:

> We instantly marched toward the enemy's right wing, which was in the orchard, and kept concealed from them as long as possible by keeping behind the bushes. When we could no longer keep ourselves concealed, we marched into the open fields and formed our line. The British immediately formed and began to retreat to the main body of their army. Colonel Cilly, finding that we were not likely to overtake the enemy before they reached the main body of the army…ordered three or four platoons from the right of our corps to pursue and attack them, and thus keep them in play till the rest of the detachment could come up.… I was in this party; we pursued without order.… We overtook the enemy just as they were entering upon the meadow, which was rather bushy.… They were retreating in line, though in some disorder. I singled out a man and took my aim directly between his shoulders.…
>
> By this time our whole party had arrived and the British had obtained a position that suited them, as I suppose, for they returned our fire in good earnest, and we played the second part of the same tune.… We gave it to poor Sawney (for they were Scotch troops) so hot that he was forced to fall back and leave the ground they occupied. When our commander saw them retreating and nearly joined with their main body, he shouted, "Come, my boys, reload your pieces and we will give them a set-off." We did so, and gave them the parting salute, and the firing on both sides ceased. We then laid ourselves down under the fences and bushes to take breath, for we had need of it.[3]

Darkness finally silenced the guns. The American army still held the field. All in all, the freshly trained American troops had passed the test. "Although the victory was not so *extensive* as we could wish," wrote Washington's secretary, "yet it has every substantial and unequivocal proof of its being one. We gained the field of battle before evening."[4]

---

1 Stirling's name was actually William Alexander, and he may more properly be referred to as General Alexander. He was a competent American officer who had claimed the title of Earl of Stirling, a Scottish peerage, which would have entitled him to a vast land grant in New England and Canada. Notwithstanding that his disputed title was not recognized by the British House of Lords, he continued to style himself Lord Stirling. Historians continue to refer to him by both names.

2 The location of their units has not been determined with certainty. If they were with General Stirling behind the west ravine, then they were battery-mates with the legendary Molly Pitcher, and they may have been recipients of the refreshing water she carried onto the battlefield.

3 Martin, *Private Yankee Doodle*, pp. 129–131.

4 James McHenry letter to John Cox (July 1, 1778), quoted in Scheer and Rankin, *Rebels & Redcoats*, p. 333.

The British withdrew during the night and sped toward Sandy Hook, where they were ferried to New York. Washington chose not to pursue them. Two days later, after a curious exchange of correspondence, the Commander-in-Chief arrested General Lee and ordered a Court Martial for disobedience, unnecessary and shameful retreat, and disrespect of the Commander-in-Chief.[1]

The exhausted army rested in the continuing heat wave. The young Republic, preparing to celebrate its second anniversary, greeted news of the "victory" at Monmouth with enthusiasm. On July 14, *Silas Sharon* died; it is not known whether or not his death was battle-related.

The Battle of Rhode Island

For a year and a half, since occupying Newport, Rhode Island, in December 1776 with 6,000 troops and a supporting fleet, the British had been interrupting shipping in Narragansett Bay and posing a constant threat of attack around southern New England. Against sparsely organized opposition, marauding British patrols had plundered the surrounding countryside. Multiple alarms had sent militia units marching to Rhode Island to counter perceived threats, and as many as fifteen Lincoln men may have been in Rhode Island at various times during 1777. As in New York, however, the enemy was too solidly entrenched to be expelled by land-based troops without naval support.

The arrival of the French fleet in American waters in July 1778 offered the realistic prospect for a successful joint American/French land and sea attack to recapture one of the British bases, either at New York or at Newport. It was generally believed—on the heels of Burgoyne's surrender at Saratoga—that another significant British defeat and surrender would destroy British resolve to continue the war, resulting in a final American victory. Washington moved his main army to White Plains, where it was positioned to march to either New York or Newport.

Notwithstanding French enthusiasm for an attack on the main British base in New York, harbor pilots determined that it was impossible to get their heavy, deep-draft ships across the bar into New York harbor. Rhode Island became the target.

Washington sent several regiments of Continental troops to join General Sullivan's command in Providence. Lincoln's *Peter Oliver, Peter Bowes,* and *Luke Fletcher* marched with Colonel Bigelow; *Jack Farrar* and *Isaac Bussell* with Colonel Vose; possibly *Cpl. Ephraim Brooks, Jr., Cpl. Nehemiah Abbot,* and *William Orr* with Colonel Jackson. From around New England, militia detachments marched toward Rhode Island. From Lincoln, 12 to 16 militia men marched south, including *Thomas Smith, Jonathan Abel,* and *James Meriam.*

On July 29, 17 French ships under Comte d'Estaing arrived at the entrance of Narragansett Bay and positioned themselves to blockade the British fleet. To prevent capture, the British were forced to scuttle their fleet, grounding and burning four frigates and destroying most of their remaining ships, resulting in the loss of 212 guns.[2] British troops were recalled from

---

1 Lee was found guilty of all three counts and suspended from further command for the term of 12 months. He never served again, but he continued to defend himself in the press and in copious correspondence, arrogantly maintaining his innocence and condemning his detractors.

2 Murray, *Gen. John Sullivan*, p. 11; Lippitt, *The Battle of Rhode Island*, p. 3 (who values each gun at 600 livres); Stone, *Our French Allies*, p. 67 (who itemizes ten ships accounting for 218 guns).

Conanicut Island, opposite Newport, and from other outposts, in order to concentrate their defensive position in Newport.

From Tiverton on August 9, *Bulkley Adams, Jeremiah Knowlton,* and *Tilly Mead* crossed Howland's Ferry onto the north end of Rhode Island with 10,000 American troops.[1] They occupied the recently abandoned British redoubts on Butt's Hill. The coordinated French landing of 4,000 troops on Conanicut Island, however, was interrupted by 20 British sail appearing off Brenton's Point.[2] Hastily, the French admiral reloaded the troops and put out to sea on August 10 to engage the enemy fleet. The French ships chased the British fleet out of sight of land, each side maneuvering for the weather helm.

The next day, a nor'easterly gale intensified into a raging storm. For several days, rain and howling winds raked and battered the American camp, blowing down many of the tents. Violent seas thrashed and scattered the fleets and heavily damaged many of the ships. Two British ships were captured during a limited engagement before the rest limped back to New York.

As the storm abated and the French ships regrouped, *Salem Middlesex, Jonathan Abel, James Adams, Jr.,* with their fellow soldiers extended the American siege lines toward Newport, and by August 20, probably took turns with *Isaac Hartwell, Abner Mathis, Jube Savage,* and *Samuel Bond* peering into enemy lines from their earthworks atop Honeyman's Hill on the outskirts of Newport. *Asa Adams,* or *Nathan Tidd,* or *Benjamin Cleaveland,* may have manned the guns that poured heavy fire into the British lines.[3] Bit by bit, the Americans tightened their siege lines. The enemy retrenched, and the "fire from their outworks visibly grew weaker."[4] Victory awaited only the return of the French fleet to provide necessary cover for ferrying American troops to Brenton's Neck, in the rear of the enemy fortifications.

Dismasted and rudderless, the regrouped French ships returned to Rhode Island on August 21. D'Estaing informed his allies that his fleet was "so disastered they could by no means afford us any assistance, but were gone to Boston to refit." The American's "most sanguine hopes" for victory "were cropped in the bud."[5] Despite the best efforts of the American generals, the French admiral could not be dissuaded from the urgency of making the needed repairs, fearful that another juncture with the British fleet would prove the ruin of his own crippled fleet.

---

1 Now more commonly known as Aquidneck Island. The name Rhode Island originally applied both to the state and to the island on which Newport is located.

2 Rev. Manasseh Cutler diary, reported in Stone, *Our French Allies*, p. xv. Reverend Cutler was pastor of a church in Hamilton, Massachusetts, and a volunteer chaplain in General Titcomb's Brigade at this time. He records the arrival of 18 to 20 British ships. Scheer and Rankin, *Rebels & Redcoats* (p. 339) number the British fleet at 30 sail.

3 All three individuals were part of Col. John Crane's Artillery Regiment, portions of which appear to have been detached at multiple locations. Colonel Crane was present at Rhode Island at this time; the author has been unable to determine whether any of the companies to which the Lincoln men belonged were there with him or were deployed elsewhere.

4 Gen. John Sullivan letter from Tiverton to the President of the Continental Congress (August 31, 1778), quoted in Murray, *Gen. John Sullivan*, p. 13.

5 Rev. Manasseh Cutler diary, op. cit., pp. xv–xix. Reverend Cutler records that the Admiral's flagship, the "Languedoc," had been dismasted and was rudderless, but he gives no other specifics. He says simply that the French fleet was "greatly damaged by the storm."

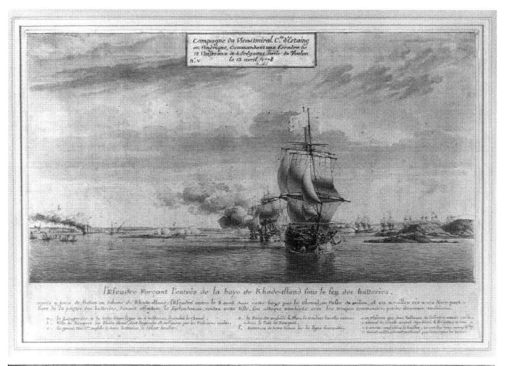

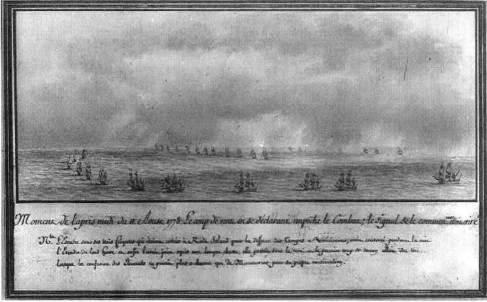

The tale of the French fleet (and with it the fate of the joint American/French operation to recapture Newport from the British) is recorded in a series of 1778 drawings made by Pierre Ozanne, a French artist who was with the fleet. *Top left,* the French fleet enters Newport Harbor on August 8 under fire from the British shore batteries; *bottom left,* the fleet later sets sail from Newport to engage the British fleet arriving from New York; *top right,* dismasted and rudderless from the storm, the flagship *Languedoc* battles the British ship *Renown* on August 14; and *bottom right,* after leaving Newport, the French fleet anchors at Boston to undergo repairs. (Library of Congress)

Chapter 6: A Renewed Spirit and Renewed Dangers, 1777–1780

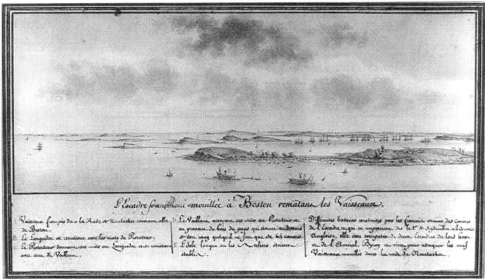

Disheartened, but in anticipation of the return of at least part of the fleet, General Sullivan kept the pressure on the British defenses. By August 27, he reported, the enemy "had removed their cannon from all the outworks except one."[1]

"This unexpected desertion of the fleet, which was the mainspring of the expedition, cast a universal gloom on the army, and threw us all into consternation," recorded Reverend Cutler in his diary.[2] "The [British] garrison would be all our own in a few days if the fleet

---
1 Gen. John Sullivan letter, op. cit., p. 14.
2 Rev. Manasseh Cutler diary, op. cit., pp. xv–xix.

would only cooperate with us; but alas, they will not," lamented General Greene to a friend. "I am afraid our expedition is now at an end."[1]

Discouraged by the departure of the French navy, and "upon a supposition that nothing could be done before the return of the French fleet," many volunteers departed for home.[2] General Greene wrote to General Washington that the departure of the ships "struck such a panic among the militia and volunteers that they began to desert in shoals. The fleet no sooner set sail than they began to be alarmed for their safety. This misfortune dampened the hopes of our army, and gave new spirits to that of the enemy."[3] General Sullivan reported losing 2,000 to 3,000 men in 24 hours, "and others still going off."[4]

Faced with the loss of troop strength, the Americans were obliged to pull back to await the French return. On the evening of August 28, the Lincoln men withdrew from the redoubts overlooking Newport and marched with their comrades-in-arms back to Butt's Hill.

Seizing the opportunity to break the siege and disrupt the American movement, British General Pigot gave chase. Marching north early the next morning, August 29, the British van was met by advance American units, including the Lincoln men under Colonel Jackson. *Cpl. Nehemiah Abbot* and *Cpl. Ephraim Brooks, Jr.*, may have been with Colonel Jackson at this time,[5] firing fearfully effective volleys into the ranks of the surprised Redcoats before slowly withdrawing. Against stiff American resistance, the British forces pushed forward.

Near Butt's Hill, *Luke Fletcher, Peter Oliver,* and *Peter Bowes* in General Glover's Brigade on the American left were waiting, watching the enemy approach. In a sharp fight, they withstood and repulsed the enemy attack. The enemy retired to Quaker Hill, opposite the American lines.

On the right, from Turkey Hill, and under covering fire from recently arrived British gunboats, Hessian troops attempted to turn the American right wing. They, too, were rebuffed, driven back with heavy losses, and in great confusion. They regrouped and tried again. Again, they were routed in fierce combat, the ground littered with bodies. The warm day and the heavy, still air compounded the heat and fatigue of battle. British reserves were brought forward; with increased resolve, the enemy formed for a third assault.

General Sullivan ordered two additional Continental regiments to support the exhausted right wing. Colonel Jackson, possibly with *Cpl. Nehemiah Abbot* and *William Orr*, was ordered around the back side of the hill to be in readiness for a counterattack. American batteries finally forced the gunboats to withdraw; the land-batteries on both sides continued to hammer away.

With renewed strength, the enemy drove against the American right a third time. With renewed fury, the contest raged bloody, and desperate. The outcome hung in the balance. Meanwhile, on the American left, General Lovell's Brigade—containing the Lincoln militia

---

[1] Gen. Nathanael Greene letter to Charles Pettit, quoted in Stone, *Our French Allies*, p. 77. Date and citation are not given.
[2] Gen. John Sullivan letter, op. cit., p. 14.
[3] Gen. Nathanael Greene letters to Gen. George Washington, quoted in Stone, *Our French Allies*, p. 77. Date and citation are not given.
[4] Gen. John Sullivan letter, op. cit., p. 14.
[5] Several months earlier, *Cpl. Nehemiah Abbot* and *Cpl. Ephraim Brooks, Jr.*, appear to have been detached to Col. David Henley's command. It is not known whether or not they had returned to Colonel Jackson's Regiment before the battle took place.

Chapter 6: A Renewed Spirit and Renewed Dangers, 1777–1780

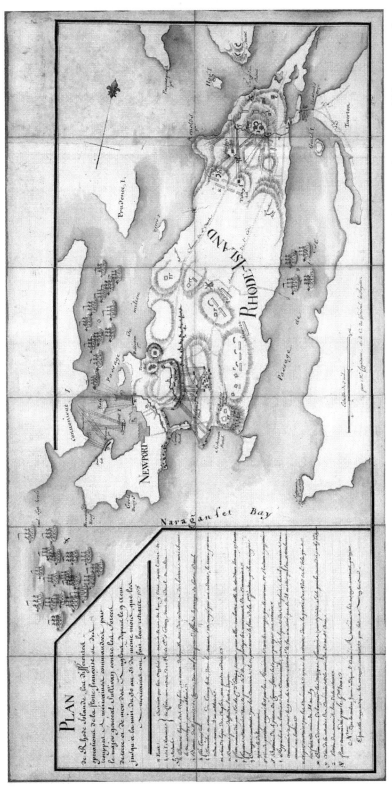

This map of the Battle of Rhode Island, drawn by an aide to General Lafayette, shows the advanced position of the American forces around Newport, standing ready to capture the city—as well as Butts Hill at the northern end of the island (*on the right*), where they put up a spirited and successful defense against a British counteroffensive. Despite the disheartening departure of the French fleet and the disappointing failure to re-capture Newport, Lafayette praised the effort as "the best fought action of the war." (Library of Congress)

men under Colonel McIntosh—engaged the other end of the British line; *Joshua Brooks, Jr., Jube Savage, Abner Mathis, Tilly Mead,* and *Salem Middlesex* gallantly pushed the attack on the British right and rear, successfully relieving some of the pressure of the British assault on the American right. At the critical moment, with fixed bayonets, *Cpl. Nehemiah Abbot* and *William Orr* may have been in company with their battalion-mates in Colonel Jackson's counterattack, when the battalion furiously charged and drove in the enemy flank. The tide shifted; the attack wavered; the enemy fell back in defeat.[1]

Fatigue dampened the American follow-up, and both armies lay on their arms that night, expecting to resume the fight with daybreak. Come morning, however, only the artillery reengaged, the guns on each side continuing to play on the other's lines during the day. With new intelligence that the British fleet was again approaching, and that the return of the French fleet could not be expected soon, General Sullivan evacuated his troops to the mainland that night.

With Colonel McIntosh's Regiment, *Joshua Brooks, Jr., Jeremiah Knowlton, Samuel Bond,* and *Bulkley Adams* were discharged to return home, followed several months later by *James Adams, Jr., Isaac Hartwell, Thomas Smith,* and *James Meriam.*

Disappointment and fault-finding persisted. Widespread criticism of the desertion of the French fleet by American officers and troops threatened to undo the new French alliance. Urging a "cultivation of harmony," Washington campaigned to patch the discord. Lafayette called it "the best fought action of the war," and Congress praised General Sullivan, all of the troops, and Comte d'Estaing. Only through patient diplomacy was the French admiral appeased, goodwill restored, and the alliance kept from unraveling.

Defense of the Hudson Highlands

If there was one constant during the war, it was the strategic imperative of maintaining control of the Hudson Valley. This was a vital link between New England and the rest of the states. From Massachusetts came most of the fighting men, while from Connecticut came a disproportionate quantity of foodstuff for the Continental Army. With the British army solidly ensconced in Manhattan and the Royal Navy controlling the seas, all communication, supplies, and manpower flowed across the Hudson at King's Ferry and points north, a region known as "the Highlands."

During the course of the war, the Americans had erected a series of forts along this stretch of the river. On either side of King's Ferry, Stony Point held a blockhouse with a 40-man garrison, and Verplanck's Point was home to Fort Lafayette with another 70 men. Further up the river were Fort Hill, Fort Independence, Fort Clinton, Fort Montgomery, Fort Constitution, and Fort Putnam.[2] American camps dotted the landscape at Peekskill, Robinson's Farm, Continental Village, Soldier's Fortune, Garrison, Cold Spring, and Fishkill. Anchoring the American position, about ten miles north of King's Ferry was a

---

1 The 1st Rhode Island Regiment, celebrated as the first all–African-American unit in American history, was one of the units on the American right in this contest. Recently recruited, this was their first time in combat. By all accounts they acquitted themselves bravely and honorably.

2 Forts Clinton, Montgomery, and Constitution, destroyed by the British in 1777, were now in ruins, but new fortifications had been constructed at the site of Fort Constitution, and Continental units camped in the vicinity of Forts Clinton and Montgomery.

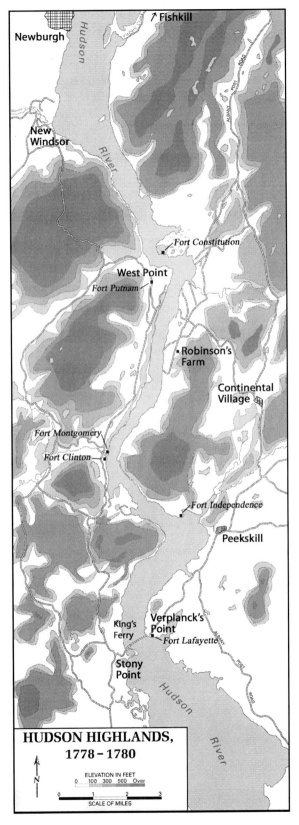

The highlands of the Hudson River were dotted with Continental camps and outposts, as control of the Hudson Valley was strategically critical to the fledgling nation. "There is nothing of greater importance," counseled General Von Steuben, than to prevent the enemy from "getting possession of [West] Point, and of the river as far as Albany...[upon which] depends—the fate of America." (Base map courtesy of the Department of History, United States Military Academy)

heavily fortified rocky head known as West Point, with a commanding view of the river for miles in both directions.

Even before Washington led his main army out of Valley Forge in the spring of 1778, the call had gone out in April for more troops to reinforce the army in the Hudson. In June and July—even as Lincoln men were involved in guarding the Convention and in the developing campaigns at Monmouth and Newport—13 to 15 more Lincoln men marched west to Fishkill for nine months of service.[1] For 18-year-old *Jonas Bond*, this was probably a first enlistment. Beside him marched *Abijah Munroe* and *William Thorning*, who, though just a couple of years older, had served repeated stints since marching to Concord three years before.

Fishkill was located on the east side of the Hudson, about ten miles north of West Point. It was the site of a large supply magazine. There can be little doubt that the Lincoln men there drilled as soldiers, learned the new von Steuben manual, and maintained a level of readiness to meet an enemy threat. But little was heard from the enemy. Instead, *Sgt. Joseph Mason* and his brother, *fifer Elijah Mason*, served duty as commissary guards, while *Jonas Bond* tended the commissary's beef cattle. Later, they were deployed in Connecticut in bridge building (probably across the Housatonic River), then in building huts at Soldier's Fortune (near West Point).

Other Lincoln men followed to other sites in the Highlands. *Peter Nelson*, a 15-year-old slave, was by now a seasoned veteran. He and 42-year old veteran *Solomon Whitney*, who had served together the previous fall at Saratoga, were deployed first at West Point and then at King's Ferry.

In the fall, Colonel Nixon's and Colonel Greaton's regiments meandered into the Highlands[2] with 15-year-old *Joseph Nixon*, 21-year-old *Lemuel Wheeler*, and 20-year-old *Sgt. Elisha Willington*, all with long records of service, and all in the middle of three-year Continental enlistments.[3] The region remained quiet, and the unusually mild winter passed without notable incident. The Fishkill terms expired in the early months of 1779, and the Lincoln nine-month men returned home in time for spring chores, having had no contact with the enemy.

After a desultory and largely reactive previous year, however, British General Clinton was now under increasing pressure to draw Washington's army into a general engagement. In May 1779, Clinton moved 6,000 men upriver to King's Ferry, and he quickly overran the American-held positions at Stony Point and Verplanck's Point on June 1. He was now within striking distance of West Point.

---

1 Even the geographically savvy reader may feel somewhat challenged by eighteenth-century designations. The Lower Hudson Valley (from Albany, south through the Hudson Highlands, to Westchester), which is, of course, largely west of Massachusetts, appears to have been known as the "southward" during 1778. Around New York City, in 1776, the Lincoln men had also served "at the southward." Defense of the Hudson River (also known as the North River) was largely the responsibility of the Northern Department. In 1776 and 1777, when the British were threatening from the north, and the Upper Hudson (north of Albany) and the Champlain Valley was the region of focus, the Lincoln men marched "north" to that area.

2 The record shows that these regiments were in Danbury, Connecticut in September; New Milford, Connecticut, in October; and in the Hudson Highlands in November. The bridge-building deployment of *Jonas Bond* and the *Mason* brothers appears to have been in the approximate vicinity of Danbury and New Milford in October. The bridge builders appear to have returned to the Hudson Highlands at approximately the same time as Nixon's and Greaton's regiments arrived. Colonel Nixon's Regiment wintered at Soldier's Fortune, perhaps in the very huts that the Lincoln nine-month men built.

3 Also, *Sgt. Joseph Peirce, Jonathan Gage, Artemas Reed*, and perhaps *John Gorden* and *John Lander*, all serving three-year terms in Colonel Greaton's Regiment.

Chapter 6: A Renewed Spirit and Renewed Dangers, 1777–1780

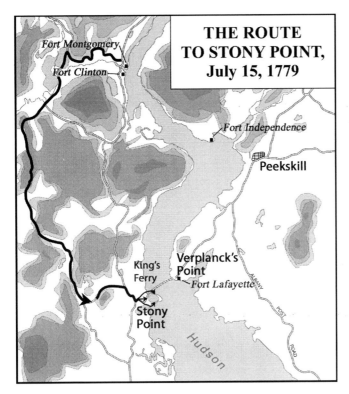

Under unusually strict orders for secrecy, Gen. Anthony Wayne marched his detachment of seasoned infantrymen west, away from the Hudson River, then south over and around the hills, along a rough track through the woods. Only near the end did he inform his men that their orders were to storm Stony Point by point of bayonet at midnight. (Base map courtesy of the Department of History, United States Military Academy)

Washington pulled his main army out of New Jersey, marched it north, and positioned it for the defense of West Point. The combined American armies awaited Clinton's next move. The tension and anticipation kept the Continentals on alert.

The British strengthened both forts. Instead of further advances against American positions, however, Clinton sent troops into Connecticut to impress cattle and to destroy ships and stores. For ten days, the raiders sacked New Haven, Fairfield, and Norwalk, burning hundreds of houses, seven churches, and countless barns, shops, and mills.[1]

Washington declined to be lured into Connecticut, but he reconnoitered closely the enemy posts at Fort Lafayette and Stony Point. Finding it "a very disagreeable aspect to remain in a state of inactivity," he formulated a bold plan.[2]

Benjamin Cleaveland was ordered to report for inspection "'fresh shaved and well powdered' and fully equipped and rationed," at General Wayne's Light Infantry camp near Fort Montgomery on July 15, 1779. He was probably puzzled. He was an artilleryman; the Lights were an elite corps of seasoned infantrymen. After inspection, about noon, he was marched west with

---

[1] Clinton's real aim, it turns out, was not to dislodge the Americans from the Hudson, but rather to draw Washington out of New Jersey, then to occupy the vacated American camp at Middlebrook and threaten the American supply depots at Easton, Pennsylvania, and Trenton. This was all calculated to draw Washington forward into an open engagement, or at least to create an opportunity to strike at him while his army was in motion. Because of the strategic importance of West Point, Washington responded to the first bait. But Clinton was unable to lure Washington far enough away (West Point was only about a two- or three-day forced march from Middlebrook) to execute the balance of his plan (see Johnston, *The Storming of Stony Point*, pp. 31, 43–44, 55–57, 142–43.

[2] Washington letter to General Wayne (July 9, [1779]), quoted in Dawson, *Assault on Stony Point*, p. 27.

the corps, under unusually strict orders. They marched away from the river, then along a rough track south, through the woods, over and around the hills, stopping at dusk after about thirteen miles.[1] Soon, they learned their mission: just a mile and a half away, but still out of sight, rising 150 feet above and almost surrounded by the river, the rocky prominence of Stony Point lay silhouetted in gray against the dark sky. At midnight, with unloaded muskets, they were to storm the heavily fortified British bastion by point of bayonet. The success of the mission depended upon complete surprise. Anyone who fired his musket, ordered General Wayne, would be instantly put to death. They fixed pieces of white paper to their hats, by which to identify friend from foe in the dark. At the appointed hour, they marched silently toward their target, shortly splitting into three columns.

Silently, invisibly, the first two columns approached opposite sides of the granite outcropping, while the smaller third division headed for the impregnable main gate to deliver a diversionary fire. On the right, an enemy picket discovered their movement and sounded the alarm. Musket fire erupted from the top of the rock, aimed down upon the silent attackers; it was answered quickly from the feint at the gate with a "perpetual and Gauling fire." The attackers "dashed forward, bayonet in hand, climbing up the rocks."[2] Scaling the precipices under heavy fire, they reached the top, scrambled into the works, and still without firing a shot, quickly subdued the defenders. Within minutes, the British captives were rounded up.[3] Then, the British guns were turned around, and *Benjamin Cleaveland* and his fellow artillerymen began hurling lead at the enemy garrison in Fort

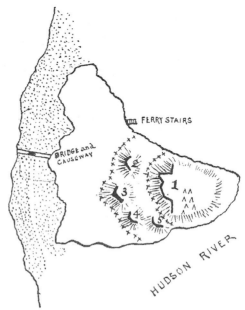

This pen-and-ink sketch of Stony Point is attributed to General Heath, July 3, 1779. It appears to have been prepared from reconnaissance information and used in planning the surprise assault on the British position. The features are identified as: "1, the capital work on the highest part of the point, commanding the out-flèches. Which is conformed to the broken eminence it is built on; 2,3,4,5, flèches built on so many little eminences, each with one embrasure; but in the principle work (1) the number of embrasures is uncertain, being covered by the works and the declivity of the hill. Two rows of abatis (xxx) cross the point from water to water." (Cornell University Library)

---

1 Despite the presence of 24 artillerymen, there is no evidence that they took any field pieces with them. Washington ordered up two guns, evidently as cover for having drafted the artillerymen, but these appear to have been deliberately left behind (see Dawson, *Assault on Stony Point*, p. 31; Johnston, *The Storming of Stony Point*, p. 72).

2 The first quote is from General Wayne's plan of battle, quoted in Dawson, *Assault on Stony Point*, p. 37. By all accounts, this is an accurate description of the fire they delivered. The second quote is of Dawson's description in Dawson, *Assault on Stony Point*, p. 51.

3 British Lieutenant Colonel Johnson claimed 472 were taken prisoner in his Report on July 24, 1779, as reported in Dawson, *Assault on Stony Point* (p. 55). The American tally was 575 prisoners, as reported in Johnston, *The Storming of Stony Point* (p. 212).

Chapter 6: A Renewed Spirit and Renewed Dangers, 1777–1780   131

"Mad Anthony" Wayne exhorts his troops onward in the midnight storming of Stony Point. As planned, the attackers "dashed forward, bayonet in hand, climbing up the rocks" under heavy fire, and quickly subdued the British defenders. The bold assault electrified American imaginations and reignited the flame of Independence in a war-weary nation. (1858 drawing by J. M. Nevin, engraved by J. Roberts, courtesy of Darlington Digital Library, University of Pittsburgh)

Lafayette, across the river, and at the enemy ship in the river below, forcing it to lift anchor and slip downriver, out of range.

As the shockwaves from the storming of Stony Point electrified American imaginations, *Jonathan Gage, Sgt. Joseph Peirce, Lemuel Wheeler, Artemas Reed, Sgt. Elisha Willington, Joseph Nixon,* and probably *John Lander* mobilized with their regiments to attack Fort Lafayette a day later, on July 17. It was an opportunity lost, however. They had scarcely begun bridging a creek on the approach to Fort Lafayette when the operation had to be aborted by the approach of an enemy relief column.[1]

---

1 The details of this piece of the Stony Point action are a bit sparse. Washington appears to have ordered Gen. John Nixon's Brigade, which contained both Col. Thomas Nixon's and Colonel Greaton's regiments, to Continental Village (apparently from Constitution Island opposite West Point) on the 14th. They were supposed to have been ready to attack Fort Lafayette on the 16th, pending the success of Wayne's assault on Stony Point. According to Colonel Putnam's account, however, they did not get underway until the 16th, and they arrived at Continental Village "without their field pieces, artillery men, or so much as an axe or spade, or any orders as to what they were to do." Putnam had done extensive reconnaissance on Fort Lafayette, and he knew that the artillery was necessary "on account of a block house which stood in the way of our approach to the main work on the point." The axes and entrenching tools were necessary not only for destroying and building fortifications, but also because "it was impossible to cross the creek without rebuilding the bridge, which had been destroyed." By the time they had scrounged together the needed equipment and begun operations against Fort Lafayette, late in the day on the 17th, Clinton's reinforcements were rapidly closing (see Johnston, *The Storming of Stony Point*, pp. 89, 220–25, who cites Colonel Putnam's MSS. Papers in possession of Marietta College, Marietta, Ohio).

There was little question about the Americans' ability to hold Stony Point. Washington ordered the fortifications destroyed, and abandoned the new prize to the British reinforcements on July 18. But he had made his point brilliantly. The moral victory counted for more than the ground itself. The bold, daring stroke of defiance energized the war-weary continent as proof of American resilience. Despite the deadening pace of the war, the flame of independence had not been extinguished.

The Continental forces concentrated around West Point, determined to hold the key to the Hudson Valley at all cost. General von Steuben summed up the imperative in a communiqué to the Commander-in-Chief:

> I am positive that their [i.e., British] operations are directed exclusively to getting possession of this post, and of the river as far as Albany.... On their success depends—the fate of America. The consequence is, therefore, that there is nothing of greater importance to us than to avert this blow. Let them burn whatever they have not burned already, and this campaign will add to their shame but not to their success. Were West Point strongly fortified, supplied with sufficient artillery, ammunition and provisions, and a garrison of two thousand men, we ought not to be induced to take our forces more than a day's march from it.... I go further and say, that our army should be destroyed or taken before we allow them to commence an attack on West Point.... Let us defend the North [i.e., Hudson] river and hold West Point, and the end of our campaign will be glorious.[1]

From Rhode Island, Colonel Bigelow's Regiment arrived with *Peter Bowes, Luke Fletcher,* and *Peter Oliver.* Colonel Vose's Regiment brought in *Isaac Bussell* and probably *Jack Farrar* (before he returned home, sick). During July and August, new levies arrived. *Ezra Meriam, Isaac Peirce, Joseph Meloney,* and *John Barrett* were assigned to Colonel Wesson's Regiment.

Notwithstanding British reoccupation and rebuilding of the bastion at Stony Point, the defeat deepened General Clinton's frustration, and it appears to have broken his spirit, at least temporarily. Convinced of his inability to bring the war to a satisfactory conclusion in the face of the persistent failing of the war ministry to provide adequate manpower, he submitted his resignation in August.[2] He abandoned his forward positions at King's Ferry in October 1779. A few days later, he withdrew his garrison from Newport, Rhode Island, as well, to concentrate his strength in New York City.

Another wave of militia support in October brought *Daniel Wesson, Stephen Brooks, Jr., Zebediah Farrar, Timothy Stone, Elijah Mason,* and probably *Sgt. Timothy Sherman.* With them came brothers *Abel* and *Solomon Billing,* whose brother *John* had been killed in the Penobscot debacle two months before.[3] They were posted to reinforce Continental troops at Claverack, well north of the Highlands on the Albany Post Road. Claverack was an

---

1 Dated at West Point, July 27, 1779, the document is reported in Kapp, *Life of Von Steuben*, pp. 232–35. Also quoted in Johnston, *The Storming of Stony Point*, pp. 59–60, 208–09.

2 General Clinton's letter of resignation, dated August 20, 1779, appears in Johnston, *The Storming of Stony Point*, pp. 138–40. His resignation request, however, was not accepted.

3 In July, a naval expedition out of Boston, supported by local militia, laid siege to a small, newly planted British garrison at the site of the modern town of Castine in Penobscot Bay. Despite many advantages, the American forces failed to take sufficient initiative to capture the garrison, then they panicked and fled upriver when British ships arrived in relief. The Americans lost all of their ships; survivors escaped overland through the Maine woods. The botched expedition itself was of relatively minor strategic significance, but it stands as America's worst naval defeat before Pearl Harbor. The debacle resulted in several courts martial,

important link in the Hudson River communication system, and an area with contentious partisan loyalties. Although the Massachusetts men had enlisted for a term of three months, they were discharged after six weeks, probably because, with both armies settling into wintry repose, they had become a superfluous drain on always scarce provisions.

The Blackest Dye

South of King's Ferry, between the Croton River and White Plains, there had developed a vast, lawless, no man's land between the British lines and the American lines. Raids, scouting parties, and troop movements on both sides destabilized the region, and gangs of partisan marauders roamed the countryside, preying opportunistically on unescorted strangers. In addition to professed partisan loyalties and objectives, for many gang members this was also a lucrative source of supplemental income.

Patrolling the northern expanse of this region, in the early part of 1780, was a detachment of 250 Massachusetts men.[1] Having stopped briefly in the town of Mt. Pleasant, northeast of Tarrytown, the patrol was posted in and about the home of Joseph Young on the morning of February 3, 1780. *Cpl. Jonathan Gage,* perhaps with other Lincoln men, was among them. Suddenly, they were alarmed by the approach through the snowpack of an enemy force of considerable strength on foot and on horseback. *Gage* and his company formed in front of the house; the other companies were called in from the flanks, and they formed on either side. The attack came head on. Resisting gallantly, the Americans met the enemy with a hot fire. In the melee, *Gage* received a major head wound from an enemy broadsword and several bayonet wounds to his body. After a stiff fight, the enemy overpowered the right flank and flooded into the orchard behind the house. Defeated, the Americans fled.[2] His escape cut off, *Gage* and 75 others were rounded up as prisoners. They were escorted to New York, where they were held for about ten months before being exchanged.

In the Highlands, *Jack Farrar* and *Peter Bowes* departed for home in February and March, no longer slaves, their three-year enlistments likely having earned them their freedom. *Luke Fletcher, Lemuel Wheeler,* and *Peter Oliver* also left for home upon the expiration of their enlistments in March.

By now, the war had turned south, and not much of significance was happening along the Hudson. The news elsewhere was mostly bleak. From New Jersey, word of a mutiny among Continental troops for want of provisions probably sparked a sympathetic reaction. From the south came news of a string of setbacks: the fall of Charleston to the British, along with the surrender of its 5,000-man Continental garrison in May; British Col. Banastre

---

including that of Col. Paul Revere, whose reputation was besmirched, even though he was eventually cleared of wrongdoing.

1 Dawson, *Battles of the United States*, p. 579. Ward, *The War of the Revolution* (p. 620) gives the figure as 450, which seems to be echoed in most other modern accounts of the affair. However, considering that the patrol consisted of five detached companies, 250 appears to be a more accurate estimate. In his pension declaration, *Jonathan Gage* later put the number at "about One hundred."

2 The enemy consisting of a mix of British, German, and Tory units, estimated strength of about 550 men. Citing a February 16, 1780, report in the *New Jersey Gazette*, Dawson, *Battles of the United States* (p. 581) comments, "The usual cruelties with which the Tories visited their countrymen were extended to the Americans in this case; and the bodies of the dead and the wounded bore evidence of their heartless barbarities." *Gage's* wounds attest to the ferocity of the fight.

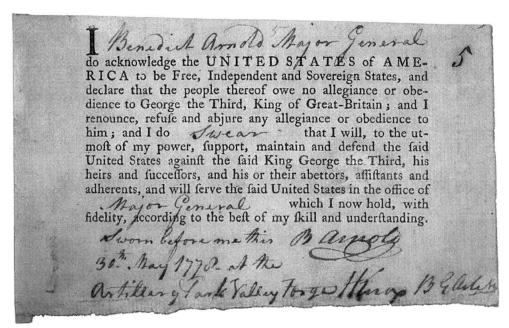

Scarcely two years after signing this Loyalty Oath at Valley Forge, Maj. Gen. Benedict Arnold, America's bold and brilliant military leader, became America's most infamous traitor. By the summer of 1780, he had wrangled an appointment as commander of West Point, and he was scheming to deliver it into the hands of the enemy. Had he succeeded, it would have severely crippled the American cause. (National Archives)

Tarleton's savage butchery of the Virginia militia as they were surrendering at Waxhaws, shortly afterward; General Gates's humiliating defeat at Camden. Except for some isolated pockets of local resistance, the American army in the south had been effectively routed.

Lemuel Wheeler, Peter Oliver, and *Ezra Meriam* returned to the Highlands in July 1780, with a new band of six-month enlistees, including *Artemas Reed, Richard Winship, John Meriam,* and *Solomon Whitney.* The Lincoln soldiers were detailed to normal camp routines, including guard duty, fatigue duty, and camp chores. When Gen. Benedict Arnold was appointed to command the Hudson Highlands, the fact seems to have passed with little notice.

With characteristic energy, Arnold studied the defenses and drew up detailed plans. He redeployed work parties, arranged and rearranged scattered detachments. *Richard Winship* remembered moving with his unit "to West Point, from thence across the North River to a place called Robinson's Farms; from thence to Peekskill, and crossed the river to Stoney Point; and from Stoney Point to Orangetown. The regiment moved to several other places, names not recollected, and returned to West Point."[1]

On September 23, near Tarrytown—in the middle of no man's land—three rogue freebooters accosted their mark; the lone traveler identified himself as John Anderson. When he claimed to have no money, the moonlighting militiamen searched him, and finding incriminating papers hidden in his boots, delivered him to American authorities.

---

1 Pension Record # S11786. Orangetown was also known as Tappan.

Chapter 6: A Renewed Spirit and Renewed Dangers, 1777–1780

On the evening of September 25, much of the army was suddenly in motion again, urgently being repositioned around West Point under fresh orders from General Washington. By the next morning, the American camp was abuzz with the news. *"Treason of the blackest dye was yesterday discovered!"* read the General Orders, continuing:

> *General Arnold who commanded at West Point, lost to every sentiment of honor, of public and private obligation, was about to deliver up that important Post into the hands of the enemy. Such an event must have given the American cause a deadly wound if not a fatal stab. Happily the treason has been timely discovered to prevent the fatal misfortune. The providential train of circumstances which led to it affords the most convincing proof that the Liberties of America are the object of divine Protection.*
>
> *At the same time that the Treason is to be regretted the General cannot help congratulating the Army on the happy discovery. Our Enemies despairing of carrying their point by force are practising every base art to effect by bribery and Corruption what they cannot accomplish in a manly way.*
>
> *Great honor is due to the American Army that this is the first instance of Treason of the kind where many were to be expected from the nature of the dispute, and nothing is so bright an ornament in the Character of the American soldiers as their having been proof against all the arts and seduction of an insidious enemy.*
>
> *Arnold has made his escape to the Enemy but Mr. André the Adjutant General to the British Army who came out as a spy to negotiate the Business is our Prisoner.*
>
> *His Excellency the Commander in Chief has arrived at West Point from Hartford and is no doubt taking the proper measures to unravel fully, so hellish a plot.*[1]

Washington continued to take steps to secure West Point against the prospect of an imminent attack. In addition, at the center of the West Point defenses, Fort Arnold was summarily renamed Fort Clinton.[2]

André was tried as a spy, convicted, and sentenced to hang. Curiously, with American rage riveted on Arnold's betrayal, André became a somewhat sympathetic figure. For many Continentals, the parallels with Nathan Hale—the American spy whose execution by the British in New York in 1776 had made him a symbol for America of selfless dignity and patriotism—were inescapable, and André was accorded the mantle of a noble victim. "I can

---

1 General Orders, September 26, 1780 (issued by General Greene from headquarters at Orangetown), in Washington, *Writings* [Fitzpatrick, ed.], XX, pp. 95–96. "John Anderson" revealed himself to be Maj. John André, Adjutant General to British General Clinton. He had just sealed the deal with Arnold, by which Arnold would continue to weaken West Point defenses and provide intelligence sufficient to ensure its fall to the enemy. Through an unplanned turn of events, André had been forced to return to the British lines overland rather than by boat. Arnold had provided him with a pass to get through the checkpoints, and as an added precaution he had issued an order directing that if a John Anderson were stopped, he was to be sent to Arnold. Upon Anderson's capture by the rogue militiamen, the officer in charge did in fact send him back to Arnold. In what Washington later called "an extraordinary concurrence of incidents," another officer intervened; André and his escort were recalled (Arnold was merely informed of the arrest), and the documents were sent to Washington. Arnold received notification of the arrest on the morning of September 25, and he quietly disappeared (escaping downriver) about an hour before Washington's arrival at Arnold's headquarters. Washington was still unaware of the treason. The plot remained undiscovered, even among Arnold's aides, until shortly thereafter the incriminating documents arrived for Washington's perusal.

2 This was a second Fort Clinton, not to be confused with the original Fort Clinton, which was several miles downriver near Fort Montgomery, and which had been destroyed by the British in October 1777, when they sailed upriver as far as Kingston. At that time, West Point had yet to be fortified.

remember no instance where my affections were so fully absorbed in any man," wrote an American officer.[1] For others, the parallels went too far. "He was but a man, and no better," wrote one Continental foot soldier, "nor had he better qualifications than the brave Captain Hale, whom the British commander caused to be executed as a spy…without the shadow of a trial, denying him the use of a bible or the assistance of a clergyman in his last moments, and destroying the letters he had written to his widowed mother and other relations. André had every indulgence allowed him that could be granted with propriety. See the contrast. Let all who pity André so much look at it and be silent."[2]

On the morning of October 2, *John Meriam*, probably with *Peter Oliver, Richard Winship, Artemas Reed, Ezra Meriam, Jonathan Mead, Joseph Nixon, Lemuel Wheeler*, and *Isaac Bussell*, each in his respective regiment, marched onto a lonely hilltop just west of the village of Tappan. Eighty files from each wing of the Army, and an immense throng of onlookers, stared silently at the tall gibbet and the composed British spy. At precisely noon, Major André was executed.

FISH-KILL, October 5.

We learn from Head-Quarters, that Major Andre, Adjutant-General of the British army, received the reward of his dear earned labours, the gallows, on last Monday. His unhappy fate was much regretted; tho' his life was justly forfeited by the law of nations. From his behaviour, it cannot be said, but that, if he did not die a good christian, he died like a brave soldier.—Thus died, in the bloom of life, Major Andre, the pride of the British army, the friend and confident of Sir Henry Clinton.

We farther learn, that the truly infamous Arnold, through whom this unfortunate gentleman lost his life, has lodged information against sundry persons in New-York, supposed friendly to our cause; in consequence of which, upwards of fifty of them were imprisoned.

Hanged as a spy, Major John André nevertheless became a somewhat sympathetic figure, seen by some as an honorable victim of Arnold's treachery. After escaping to the enemy and having lost all sentiment of honor, Arnold appears to have deepened his crime by exposing American informants who were behind enemy lines. (*The Connecticut Journal*, October 12, 1780)

---

1 Maj. Benjamin Tallmadge, quoted in Scheer and Rankin, *Rebels & Redcoats*, p. 385. Tallmadge was one of André's guards during his imprisonment.

2 Martin, *Private Yankee Doodle*, pp. 206–207.

Chapter 7

The War Turns South, 1780–1781

For two years after the Americans had successfully defended Charleston, South Carolina, against the British in 1776, both armies had abandoned the south to the festering anarchy of warring partisan bands, focusing instead on prosecuting the war in the northern provinces. By 1778, however, dissatisfied with the progress of the war in the north, British strategists again began to turn their hopes for ending the rebellion toward the south, where they still believed local sympathies favored the Crown. Under instructions from London, British General Clinton had sent troops into Georgia in late 1778, and they quickly captured Savannah then Augusta.

A year later, Clinton sailed south again with another 7,600 Regulars to Charleston, which capitulated in May 1780. He followed up quickly, dispatching troops into the South Carolina interior to crush remaining pockets of Rebel resistance and to reassert Royal authority. Within weeks, the British southern campaign had ruthlessly and indiscriminately slashed, hacked, and bludgeoned the population into a terrorized submission. Reporting "an end to all resistance in South Carolina," Lord Cornwallis, now in command of the British forces in the south, planned his next move: a march north into North Carolina, then Virginia.[1]

It was premature. By July and August, bands of patriot guerrillas had reformed and become active. Large parts of the state flared into rebellion, once again. Another Continental force, under Gen. Horatio Gates, made up largely of local militias, marched south to Camden on August 16, 1780, confident of a quick victory over its small British garrison. Instead, he found a heavily reinforced British garrison with Cornwallis in command. The militia units proved unreliable, and Gates's army was completely routed. Its remnants fled north in disarray.

Tango in the Carolinas

Small resurgent pockets of rebel militias continued to harass and frustrate Crown forces, but militarily, the American army in the south had been beaten.

Or so Cornwallis thought. He began to move his army north from South Carolina to reassert British authority in North Carolina and then Virginia, according to plan. On October 7, 1780, he was dealt a setback when patriot militias defeated the loyalist militia on his left wing at King's Mountain. He pulled back to Winnsboro, South Carolina, and regrouped.

From the beginning, the southern war had been fought largely as a civil war. Encouraged by Crown authorities, loyalist partisans, as loosely organized militias, had carried on a savage,

---

[1] Scheer and Rankin, *Rebels & Redcoats*, p. 403.

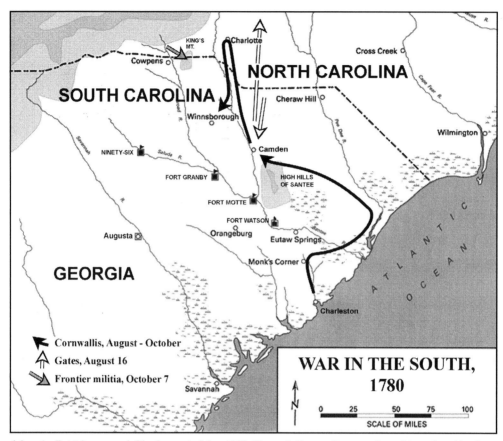

After the British captured Charleston in May 1780, General Cornwallis moved quickly and ruthlessly to wipe out pockets of resistance in the interior. Establishing a series of inland forts to consolidate his hold on Georgia and South Carolina, he then marched north to Camden, where he routed a combined Continental and militia force under Gen. Horatio Gates. But the victory of patriot militias at King's Mountain in October forced Cornwallis to pull back from his initial attempt to push into North Carolina. (Base map courtesy of the Department of History, United States Military Academy)

internecine campaign of bloodshed, pillaging, and devastation against anyone suspected of Rebel sympathies. Noted for the depths of its wretchedness, it was returned in kind by irregular patriot militias.[1]

For both armies, the fortunes of war in the Carolinas depended on their abilities to rally the support of local militias. But militia support proved a remarkably fickle and unreliable commodity. Militiamen appeared and disappeared at will, according to the risks, threats, and perceived prospects. As unreliable as they were, they represented both a disproportionate share of the American troop strength and an important supplement for the British regulars.

---

1 Bancroft, *History of the United States*, p. 300; Scheer and Rankin, *Rebels & Redcoats*, p. 390. See also Ward, *The War of the Revolution* (pp. 656–660) for the ethnic, religious, and geographic differences that served as the background for this conflict. "Nowhere else in the American colonies were the different opinions, so often, so continuously, and so ferociously expressed in action," he states.

Chapter 7: The War Turns South, 1780–1781

Through the woods, the patriot militias advanced upward on King's Mountain. Driven back by loyalist bayonets in one spot, the wave of backwoodsmen advanced higher in another, until they overran the enemy camp on top. This battle typified much of the war in the south, with friends, neighbors, and kinsmen often fighting on opposite sides. (Drawing by F. C. Yohn, *Scribner's Magazine,* August 1898)

General Greene arrived in Charlotte, North Carolina, in early December 1780 to rebuild the American southern army. He found more militiamen in the ranks than Continental soldiers. Of his total force of 2,300 men, he had fewer than 1,500 effectives, and only a third of his force was properly clothed and equipped. It was, in his words, "but the shadow of an army in the midst of distress."[1]

Cornwallis's force was larger, better trained, and better equipped. Most of his 4,000 men were professional soldiers; only 700 were Tory militiamen.

Around the first of the year 1781, both armies resumed their elaborate dance to check each other's progress: Cornwallis to consolidate British authority in South Carolina and to march north, asserting Royal hegemony; Greene to rally local support and to constrain the British army in the Carolinas. Into the spring, the dance dipped and pirouetted through the region to variations in relative troop strengths, determined by arrivals and departures of the fickle partisan militias.

As the armies stalked each other's movements, *Benjamin Cleaveland* reportedly was one of the Continentals in the detachment under Gen. Daniel Morgan on the morning of January 17, 1781, when British Colonel Tarleton caught up with them in a rolling pastureland in a

---

[1] Quotation is from Scheer and Rankin, *Rebels & Redcoats,* p. 425, without citation.

British Col. Banastre Tarleton clashes with Continental Light Dragoon Col. William Washington (cousin of General Washington) before making his escape at the battle of the Cowpens. Despite Tarleton's well-earned reputation for fierce bravery and efficient brutality, his dragoons were completely routed in this engagement, only a handful escaping death or capture. (Drawing by T. de Thulstrup, *Scribner's Magazine*, August 1898)

Chapter 7: The War Turns South, 1780–1781

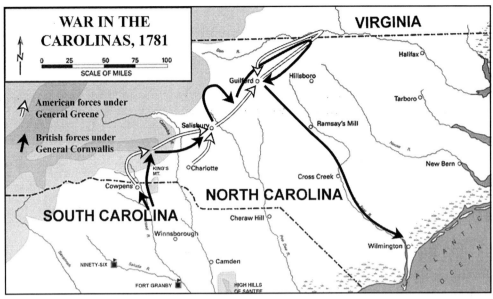

After pulling back the previous year, in 1781 Cornwallis again moved into North Carolina. To variations in relative troop strength determined by the fickleness of partisan militias, the American and British forces danced across the state from Cowpens to Guilford, each trying to gain a strategic advantage over the other. Despite Cornwallis's claim of victory at Guilford Court House, he had been effectively checked, and he was forced to retreat to the coast to rest and resupply. (Base map courtesy of the Department of History, United States Military Academy)

region known as the Cowpens.[1] Tarleton had developed a fearful reputation to match his aggressive style, and his dragoons galloped straight at the American lines. Morgan's battle plan was equal to the task, however, and the Americans withstood the successive waves that Tarleton threw forward. In an hour, the fighting was over; Tarleton had been completely routed. Nearly nine-tenths of Tarleton's force was killed or captured; only Tarleton himself, the baggage guard, and a handful of cavalry galloped off the field to safety.[2]

The dance of the armies carried them across North Carolina, where they met again at Guilford Court House in March. Logically, *Benjamin Cleaveland* was among the 1,600 Continentals under Greene's command, although no such claim has been found. They were supported by 2,600 militia, making this the largest American army thus far in the south. Morgan cautioned Greene about the large number of militia, "If they fight, you will beat Cornwallis, if not, he will beat you."[3] Some did fight, others fled. The fatigued American

---

[1] The report is found in his wife's pension declaration (Pension Record # W16908). As Benjamin Cleaveland was an artilleryman, and Morgan appears not to have had artillery with him, it is not clear why he would have been at Cowpens, unless he had joined the detachment in some other capacity.

[2] Ward, *The War of the Revolution* (pp. 755, 762) puts Tarleton's losses at 100 killed (including 39 officers) and 829 prisoners, out of a total force of 1,100. Without reconciling the math, Scheer and Rankin, *Rebels & Redcoats* (pp. 427, 432) put his losses at 110 killed (including 10 officers) and 702 prisoners out of a total force of 750. Bancroft, *History of the United States* (pp. 463, 465, 470) reports Tarleton's troop strength as 1,100, with losses numbering more than 110 (including 10 officers) killed; 200 wounded; and 29 officers, 500 privates, 70 Negroes, plus nearly 100 stragglers taken prisoner.

[3] Quoted in Ward, *The War of the Revolution*, p. 786.

commander yielded the field of battle, but not before his combined forces punished the British with disproportionately severe casualties.

Both sides claimed victory, but in truth, the British commander had been checked again. Faced with dwindling support from loyalist militias, his losses were paralyzing. Further, his dance with Greene had compelled him to shed his baggage, and it had lured him beyond his ability to supply his army. Desperate for provisions, he turned southeast and retreated toward more loyalist regions along the coast.

The Reemergence of Benedict Arnold

Meanwhile, at about the same time that Greene and Cornwallis began their Carolina tango, the British high command deployed its newly commissioned Brig. Gen. Benedict Arnold into Virginia. With Col. John Simcoe and 1,200 men, he sailed up the James River, virtually unopposed, and sacked Richmond on January 5, 1781. After destroying much public and private property, including a nearby foundry, gunpowder mill, and machine shops, he sailed back downriver and went into winter camp at Portsmouth.[1]

General von Steuben, with a token force of newly enlisted, untrained, Virginia Continentals hovered nearby, powerless as a counterforce, but keeping a trained eye on the enemy. Washington was no doubt still seething over Arnold's treachery at West Point, and he appears to have seen an opportunity to turn the table on the turncoat.[2]

Abel Billing had just returned to the Hudson Valley from detached duty at Ringwood, New Jersey, a few weeks before, when in mid-February he was detached again, and marched south with General Lafayette. He was accompanied by *Isaac Bussell*; the two Lincoln men were among 1,200 hand-picked New England and New Jersey troops, and marched under the immediate command of Colonel Vose.

Leaving the Highlands on February 19, the detachment marched through Morristown on the 24th, Somerset on the 26th, Princeton and Trenton on the 28th. Reaching Head of Elk, Maryland, on March 3, they had to wait for enough boats to transport them to Annapolis, evidently on March 8. The Lincoln men remained at Annapolis while Lafayette took a small escort to Yorktown and Williamsburg to confer with General von Steuben. During their conference, British General Phillips sailed into Portsmouth with 2,600 additional troops, raising British troop strength to uncontestable levels. In addition, a French naval squadron sent to support Lafayette had been turned back by British ships. His mission

---

1 See Dawson, *Battles of the United States*, Vol. 1, pp. 641–644.

2 Ward, *The War of the Revolution*, p. 870. "Lafayette's first objective was to capture the American traitor, Benedict Arnold....Washington [was] intent on bringing Arnold in," echoes the National Park Service, in "Lafayette and the Virginia Campaign 1781."

The notion that this was Washington's primary motive is compelling, although few historians seem to have picked up on this. The prevailing historical explanation for Lafayette's mission was to counter British presence in Virginia at the urgent request of Virginia Governor Thomas Jefferson. But Arnold seems to have gone into dormancy after his Richmond romp, and Lafayette's mission was launched before Arnold appears to have reawakened. Washington had a personal interest in Virginia, of course, and was undoubtedly sensitive to Jefferson's plea (notwithstanding Jefferson's apparent culpability for leaving his state completely unprepared). However, it seems unlikely that the small, inactive British force in Virginia would have caused the Commander-in-Chief major concern militarily or have warranted his draining critical manpower from the Hudson Valley had the enemy troops not been led by Arnold.

thus thwarted, Lafayette returned to Annapolis on April 3 and started north again with his detachment.[1]

Upon arriving at Head of Elk on April 8, the troops halted. A dispatch from Washington ordered Lafayette to take his detachment south to reinforce Greene in the Carolinas. A palpable groan passed through the New England ranks. Reportedly some deserted rather than return to the south, further from their homes. *Abel Billing's* enlistment had already expired. He opted to return to West Point, where he was discharged on April 18, 1781. *Isaac Bussell* had no such option; his enlistment ran for the duration of the war. He turned and marched south again with Lafayette and his men.

Converging in Virginia

By the time *Isaac Bussell* and his fellow soldiers marched through Baltimore, heading south with Lafayette on April 18 or 19, 1781, the British had initiated a campaign of raiding and destruction across the tidewater region of Virginia. They captured towns, burned warehouses and shipyards, and released slaves. Neither the militia nor the meager Continental force in the area had any chance of standing up to them.

New orders from Washington and Greene encouraged Lafayette to engage the British in Virginia, to keep them from heading south to support Cornwallis in the Carolinas. Lafayette force-marched his men south. He crossed the Potomac River into Virginia on April 21, intent on reaching Richmond as soon as possible.

Cornwallis, meanwhile, having retreated to coastal North Carolina, briefly rested and refitted his much reduced army. Then he crafted a justification for resuming his plan to march north into Virginia. Knowing that the move would not have the approval of General Clinton in New York, he took advantage of his opportunity: "It is very disagreeable to me to decide upon measures so very important and of such consequence to the general conduct of the war, without an opportunity of procuring your Excellency's directions or approbation," he wrote his superior officer, "but the delay and difficulty of conveying letters, and the impossibility of waiting for answers render it indispensably necessary."[2]

He reasoned that he had effectively restored legal government to much of South Carolina, having left British garrisons occupying outposts scattered across that colony. Notwithstanding that Greene was still afield, his mission had been accomplished. There was little justification for returning to South Carolina unless Greene threatened the outposts. On the other hand, if that were to happen, he discounted his ability to arrive in time or to provide much assistance. In order to consolidate British gains in the south, "a serious attempt upon Virginia would be the most solid plan, because successful operations might not only be attended with important consequences there, but would tend to the security of South Carolina and ultimately to the submission of North Carolina."[3] On April 25, 1781, he self-servingly pointed his army north toward Virginia.

---

1 For the route and dates of this journey, see Abel Billing's Pension Record (#W23614) and "Lafayette's Virginia Campaign (1781)."

2 Charles Cornwallis letter to Henry Clinton (April 23, 1781), quoted in Scheer and Rankin, *Rebels & Redcoats*, p. 468.

3 Charles Cornwallis (from Wilmington) letter to George Germain (April 18, 1781), quoted in Tarleton, *A History of the Campaigns*, p. 325; also in Ward, *The War of the Revolution*, p. 797. In addition to a strategic

Greene wasted no time in moving against the outposts. Even before Cornwallis started for Virginia, the first of the garrisons surrendered. By the time Cornwallis reached Petersburg, much of the British force in South Carolina was in retreat. By the end of June, South Carolina and Georgia, except for the coastal cities of Savannah and Charleston, and the British outpost at Ninety-Six in the interior, had been reconquered by patriot forces.

In Virginia, Generals Phillips and Arnold continued their campaign of destruction, ravaging the countryside. The militia and the meager force of Continentals under von Steuben attempted—with limited success—to move military stores out of the way of the marauding enemy.

With hard marches, *Isaac Bussell* with his fellow Continentals, marching with Lafayette, reached Richmond on April 29. Von Steuben joined the new arrivals, but even together, the combined American forces were not strong enough to risk an engagement. Instead, they could only shadow the British as an army of observation,

Cornwallis's army arrived near Richmond on May 20, followed by reinforcements from New York. British troop strength swelled to 7,000. Arnold was recalled to New York.

Lafayette could muster only a fraction of the enemy strength. He described his predicament to Washington, "Were I to fight a battle, I should be cut to pieces, the Militia dispersed, and the arms lost. Were I to decline fighting, the country would think itself given up. I am therefore determined to skirmish, but not to engage too far, and particularly to take care against their immense and excellent body of horse, whom the Militia fear as they would so many wild beasts....Were I anyways equal to the enemy, I should be extremely happy in my present command, but I am not strong enough even to get beaten."[1] He abandoned Richmond on May 28 and cautiously pulled north for safety, careful to keep a day's march between him and Cornwallis.

Cornwallis gave light pursuit, continuing to ravage the countryside. When he had chased the Continentals well north, he suddenly halted and sent Tarleton west to raid Monticello and Charlottesville. Completing his sweep of the interior, in mid-June he started back toward the coast.

In July, back at his base at Portsmouth, Cornwallis sifted through conflicting orders from General Clinton in New York. Clinton was feeling threatened by the prospect of a combined French and American operation against New York, and he vacillated about his best strategic option. He ordered Cornwallis to send 3,000 troops to New York, then to Philadelphia, then to New York again, before deciding that they should remain in Virginia. The only constant, besides the mutual jealousy and growing animosity between the two generals, was that Cornwallis was to establish and fortify a defensive post either at Old Point Comfort or at Yorktown. Cornwallis and his engineers surveyed both sites and decided that Yorktown was more defensible. There, during August 1781, he concentrated his forces and began to erect extensive earthworks.

---

objective of disrupting the flow of Rebel supplies into the Carolinas from Virginia, it is quite clear that Cornwallis simply wanted out of the Carolinas. Cornwallis's justification for moving north into Virginia is exposed for what it was—a decision in search of a rationale, lacking any real plan—in a letter to General Phillips dated April 10, 1781. He writes, "Now, my dear friend, what is our plan? Without one, we cannot succeed, and I assure you that I am quite tired of marching about the country in quest of adventures..." (quoted in Scheer and Rankin, *Rebels & Redcoats*, p. 469).

1 Lafayette letter to George Washington (May 24, 1781), quoted in Landers, *The Virginia Campaign*, p. 106.

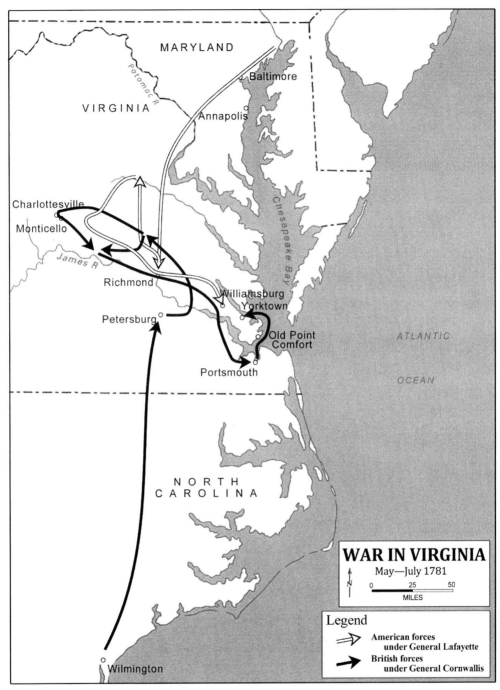

Marching south into Virginia, Lafayette reached Richmond on April 29, 1781, but he abandoned it a month later when Cornwallis, arriving from North Carolina, circled Richmond and threatened Lafayette's rear. Cornwallis chased the outnumbered Americans north. He then sent his campaign of destruction west to Charlottesville and Monticello before starting back toward the coast. Lafayette loosely followed, carefully keeping a wide margin between the two forces. (Base map, Stewart, ed., *American Military History*)

The Siege of Yorktown

The reinforcements poured in: French Admiral de Grasse landed 3,000 French troops on September 5; Admiral de Barras brought in 600 more four days later. Then, starting in mid-September, 2,000 Continentals under General Washington and another 4,800 French under General Rochambeau began to arrive at the end of their long, secretive march from the Hudson Highlands. The combined Allied force congregating in Virginia numbered over 16,000.[1]

After months of relative inactivity, the much enlarged army began to move again. It was a warm day. Optimism was high. *Isaac Bussell* and perhaps *Benjamin Cleaveland* were afoot with their units.[2] After an early start from Williamsburg and a rest en route, it was afternoon as they neared the extensive earthworks protecting the 7,600 British troops (plus about 2,000 Negro refugees used as laborers) encamped at Yorktown.[3]

The British fortifications had been slow to rise. Even after the unaccountable delays in developing the engineering plan, work had proceeded slowly in the summer heat. It had picked up hurriedly, however, at the end of August, when rumors began to circulate of the approaching French fleet. Now, on September 28, 1781, as the Allied army approached, the earthworks were still incomplete, but to many of the American troops, who had little previous experience with the science of military fortification or siege warfare, they looked impressive.[4]

The main line of defense consisted of a high parapet, palisaded in parts, rising eight to ten feet above the plateau on the landside of the town. The British had built eight redoubts and six batteries into the parapet; another three redoubts with a variety of redans were set at forward positions.[5]

---

1 French troops under de Grasse and de Barras are from Thompson, *Historic Preservation Study*, pp. 37, 40. Thompson (p. 37) gives Lafayette's strength as 1,500 Continentals, 400 recruits, and 2,000 ill-trained militia before the reinforcements began to arrive. Ward, *The War of the Revolution* (pp. 881, 883) says Washington marched in about 2,000 troops from the Hudson, and Rochambeau had 4,796. The numbers do not tally exactly, but Ward (pp. 886–87) totals the troop strength at 8,845 Americans and 7,800 French.

2 Benjamin Cleaveland's pension record (# W16908, filed by his wife) states that he was at the Battle of Cowpens on January 17, 1781. If this is accurate, then he may more probably have still been with Greene in South Carolina. On the other hand, Capt. John Lillie, in whose company he appears to have been serving, can be traced to Yorktown through his Pension Record (# R6345).

3 British troop count is from Thompson, *Historic Preservation Study*, pp. 25–26; it shows 5,600 present and fit for duty, 2,000 sick and wounded, and 1,500 absent or already POWs. Estimates of the number of African Americans range up to 3,000 (see Thompson, *Historic Preservation Study*, pp. 16–17).

4 Despite the outward appearance, the earthworks were comparatively weak. The earth out of which the parapets were formed was "sandy and gravelly," in the words of one British officer, "giving it an appearance of strength which it little merited." A Hessian officer characterized the works as "great heaps of sand." A French officer commented, "They are not solid; the parapets are not thick, and are made of sandy soil which obliges them to be propped up lest they fall down" (see Thompson, *Historic Preservation Study*, pp. 38–41, 67, 74–75; for the weakness of the construction; for the delays and pace of construction, see Thompson, *Historic Preservation Study*, pp. 15–19, 38).

5 The fortification wall is typically called a *rampart*, while a *parapet* refers to the narrower protective shield that surmounts the rampart, but at Yorktown the distinction seems to have been lost; the entire earthen wall being called the parapet. A *palisade* is a wooden wall, in this case often supported by a smaller parapet. A *redoubt* is a small earthen fort; a *battery* is a fortified artillery emplacement. A *redan* is a V-shaped earthen barrier, open in the back, for the protection of advanced troops and artillery.

The ditch from which came the dirt for the parapet ran along the front of the parapet. It was typically 8 feet deep, with a vertical palisade in its center. Thus, in making an assault on the parapet, an attacker would first have to enter the ditch and breach the palisade, then scale an effective height of 16 feet in order to reach the

Chapter 7: The War Turns South, 1780–1781   147

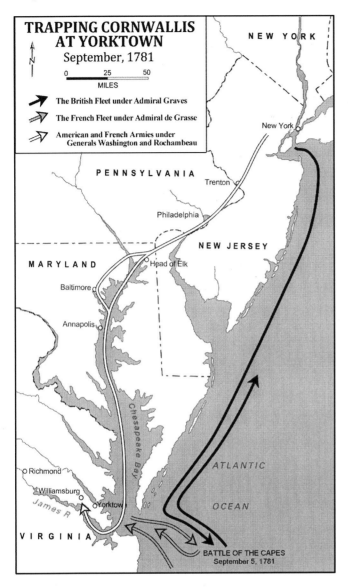

As Cornwallis was constructing his defensive earthworks around Yorktown, his supply line and escape route by sea were cut off by the victory of Admiral de Grasse's French fleet over the British in the Battle of the Capes, off the mouth of the Chesapeake Bay. General Washington with French General Rochambeau had already secretly begun marching their armies toward Virginia, with the hope of catching the elusive British general in a trap. (Base map courtesy of the Department of History, United States Military Academy)

    The French took up a position on the Allied left, where they could control access into and out of the town, as well as turn their cannon on some of the British ships in the river. The American position swung around to the right, connecting to the river east of the town. Together, with detachments on the opposite side of the river, they completely enveloped the enemy camp.

    While the officers began planning the siege, and the engineers surveyed the enemy fortifications, *Isaac Bussell,* as a Light Infantryman, probably alternated serving guard duty and constructing fascines, gabions, saucissons, and hurdles. A considerable inventory of

---

enemy (for a thorough study of the Yorktown defenses, see Thompson, *Historic Preservation Study*, pp. 56–64, 70–83, 85–87, 222–227).

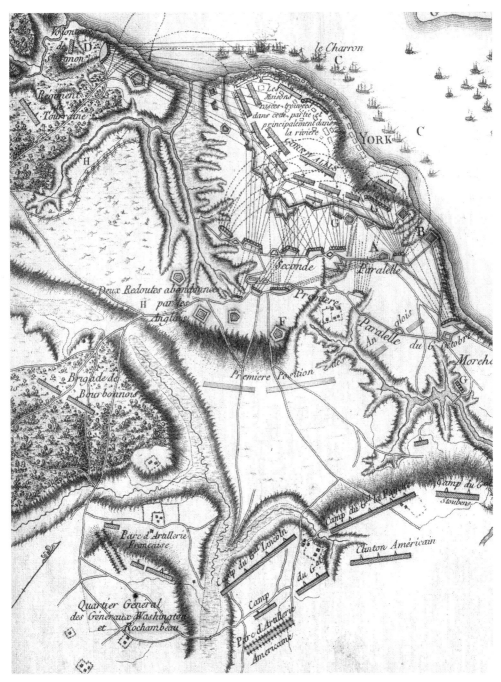

With the French fleet cutting off Cornwallis's escape route by sea, over 16,000 Continental and French troops circled Yorktown on the land side. This detail from a contemporary French map of the siege operations shows the British fortifications erected around the town (*top, center-right*), and the first ("premiere") and second parallels with which the Allies tightened their noose. Redoubts # 9 and # 10 (*indexed as* A *and* B) are visible on the right side of the second parallel. Outside of these parallels the landscape is dotted by outworks previously abandoned by the British. At the bottom right are the American camps, with the French camps in the woods to their left. (1781 map by George-Louis le Rouge; image from the author's collection)

these structural components would be needed before the active stage of the siege could get underway.[1]

Meanwhile, the French fleet had landed heavy siege-guns on the shore of the James River, about seven miles distant. The artillerymen, possibly including *Benjamin Cleaveland*, were detailed to haul the pieces into camp. With the scarcity of horses and oxen, this was backbreaking work. Others drew duty reworking some of the abandoned British outworks into American batteries.

Soon, all was in readiness. On the night of October 6, while enemy attention and fire was drawn to a decoy consisting of a battalion of soldiers on the move, silhouetted in a string of fires around on the left, the first parallel was laid out on the right, and the trenching begun.[2] Rotating between trenching, guarding the trenchers, and rest, *Isaac Bussell* and his messmates rotated shifts, night and day—digging and widening the trench, and strengthening the protective breastwork. The work progressed rapidly; within four days it extended 2,000 yards in length.

On the 9th, the American and French batteries commenced firing, and the shells tore into the enemy earthworks and the town. During the following week, gun crews watched their steady bombardment batter the sandy soil of the British parapets. The Allied guns did fearsome damage. One of the Hessian defenders noted in his diary:

> We could find no refuge in or out of the town. The people fled to the waterside and hid in hastily contrived shelters on the banks, but many of them were killed by bursting bombs. More than eighty were thus lost, besides many wounded, and their houses utterly destroyed. Our ships suffered, too, under the heavy fire, for the enemy fired in one day thirty-six hundred shot from their heavy guns and batteries. Soldiers and sailors deserted in great numbers. The Hessian Regiment von Bose lost heavily.... Our two regiments lost very heavily too. The Light Infantry posted at an angle had the worst position and the heaviest loss.[3]

On the night of the 11th, the second parallel was begun; by morning, it extended 750 yards to a depth of 3½ feet and a width of 7 feet. Allied soldiers were now within 300 yards of the enemy defenses.

---

1 *Gabions* were bottomless baskets of woven brush and twigs, three-feet high by about two-and-a-half feet in diameter. They were used for entrenching. Described one American soldier, "Three or more rows of them are sent [set?] down together (breaking joints), the trench is then dug behind and the dirt thrown into them, which, when full, together with the trench, forms a complete breastwork" (Martin, *Private Yankee Doodle*, p. 218).

Fascines and *saucissons* were bundles of branches, used for facing the interior walls of trenches and parapets, and also for the tops of powder magazines. Fascines (typically six-feet long by six inches in diameter at Yorktown) were smaller than saucissons (typically 15 to 16 feet long by 12 inches in diameter). Otherwise they were essentially identical.

Hurdles were woven mats, made essentially the same way, measuring six feet by three feet, and used similarly for facing the interior walls of earthworks (see Thompson, *Historic Preservation Study*, pp. 64–66).

2 *Parallels* were protective trenches dug by the besiegers successively closer to the fortifications, used to move men and firepower closer to the besieged works in order to weaken the defenses, tighten the siege, and ultimately launch an assault on the fortifications. Typically, three parallels were required to be in a position to assault the ramparts, but at Yorktown, the British surrendered shortly after completion of the second parallel (see Martin, *Private Yankee Doodle*, p. 232).

3 Stephan Popp, Journal, quoted in Scheer and Rankin, *Rebels & Redcoats*, p. 485.

Now the work stopped. On the right, inside a strong enemy redoubt, known as # 9, a garrison of 120 British and Hessian soldiers kept up a constant, pesky fire on the Allied work parties. Further to the right, beyond this redoubt, lay redoubt # 10, with another 70 British Regulars.

Washington and Rochambeau were working against a deadline. In eighteenth-century siege warfare, it was not uncommon for sieges to last for many months before they ended either successfully or by the arrival of a relief army. But time was running out for Admiral de Grasse, whose fleet maintained an airtight blockade at the mouth of the Chesapeake Bay that prevented British ships from coming to the relief of Cornwallis's army. Anxious to attend to other business in the Caribbean, he had informed the generals that he would depart by the end of the month. If Yorktown was still in enemy hands at that time, relief would be able to reach Cornwallis, and the entire effort would be lost.

As dusk faded to darkness on the evening of the 14th, *Isaac Bussell* waited silently at the edge of the American lines, his bayonet fixed on the end of his musket. Anxiously, he eyed redoubt # 10 silhouetted in the darkening twilight. The American batteries were silent. Jupiter and Venus shone brightly near the western horizon. With him were 400 New Englanders and New Yorkers under the command of Alexander Hamilton. A short distance away, another battalion of 400 French soldiers waited, studying what they could see of redoubt # 9. At last it was dark enough. Three shells arched into the sky, one after the other, and the men were off quickly, silently, right behind the sappers and miners, whose job it was to cut a passage through the thick abatis.

Across the field they ran, the ground pocked with large artillery-shell craters. As the sappers and miners reached the abatis, the enemy discovered their presence and opened a sharp fire. Soon, a passage was cleared through the abatis, and the infantry crowded through. Others forced a passage where the artillery shells had cut parts of it away. Across the trench they swarmed, enemy grenades raining from the parapet. "Rush on boys!" they cried, charging with bayonets, "The fort's our own." Scarcely breaking stride, they scrambled up the side and over the top, quickly overwhelming the garrison. In ten minutes, it was over.[1]

On the left, the action continued. Pouring a heavy fire on the French, the defenders charged. The French answered with a volley. *"Vive le Roi!"* they shouted and counter charged. They too soon overwhelmed the Hessian and British defenders and forced the redoubt. Within half an hour, the prisoners were being led away, and fatiguing parties arrived with trenching tools. By morning, the second parallel had been extended to include both redoubts.[2]

"My situation now becomes very critical," Cornwallis wrote to General Clinton. "We dare not show a gun to their old batteries, and I expect that their new ones will open tomorrow morning. Experience has shown that our fresh earthen works do not resist their powerful artillery, so that we shall soon be exposed to an assault in ruined works, in a bad position, and with weakened numbers."[3]

---

1 See Martin, *Private Yankee Doodle*, pp. 234–236.
2 Ward, *The War of the Revolution*, p. 892.
3 Charles Cornwallis letter to Henry Clinton (October 15, 1781), quoted in Scheer and Rankin, *Rebels & Redcoats*, p. 488.

Chapter 7: The War Turns South, 1780–1781

"Rush on, boys! The fort's our own!" the New Englanders and New Yorkers cried as they stormed Redoubt # 10, quickly overwhelming the British garrison after dark on October 14. With the simultaneous capture of Redoubt # 9 by the French, Yorktown was left virtually defenseless. It was the end of the line for Cornwallis, who requested surrender negotiations three days later. (Drawing by H. Charles McBarron, "Soldiers of the American Revolution")

There was little question that the game was almost up. But not quite. The British general, known as a hard campaigner, was not ready to give up if there was still a chance. That night, a party of Light Infantry and Guards sallied from the enemy earthworks and successfully spiked several American guns. The next night, Cornwallis began transporting troops across the river in a desperate attempt to save his army by escaping north through Gloucester. It was too little, too late. Whatever remote chance it had of success ended when a squall scuttled the operation.

As soon as the rain stopped, in the early morning of October 17, "the bombardment began again from the enemy side even more horribly than before," recorded a Hessian soldier. "Our detachment, which stood in the hornwork, could scarcely avoid the enemy's bombs, howitzer shot, and cannon balls any more. One saw nothing but bombs and balls raining on our whole line....

"Right after reveille, General Cornwallis came into the hornwork and observed the enemy and his works. As soon as he had gone back to his quarters, he immediately sent a flag of truce with a white standard over to the enemy."[1]

---

[1] Johann Conrad Döhla, *Tagebuch eines Bayreuther Soldaten* [Döhla's Journal], p. 148, quoted in Scheer and Rankin, *Rebels & Redcoats*, p. 490.

> Newport, October 25, 1781.
>
> YESTERDAY afternoon arrived in this Harbour Capt. Lovett, of the Schooner Adventure, from York-River, in Chesapeak-Bay (which he left the 20th Instant) and brought us the glorious News of the Surrender of Lord CORNWALLIS and his Army Prisoners of War to the allied Army, under the Command of our illustrious General, and the French Fleet, under the Command of his Excellency the Count de GRASSE.
>
> A Cessation of Arms took Place on Thursday the 18th Instant, in Consequence of Proposals from Lord Cornwallis for a Capitulation. His Lordship proposed a Cessation of Twenty-four Hours, but Two only were granted by His Excellency General WASHINGTON. The Articles were completed the same Day, and the next Day the allied Army took Possession of York-Town.
>
> By this glorious Conquest, NINE THOUSAND of the Enemy, including Seamen, fell into our Hands, with an immense Quantity of Warlike Stores, a forty Gun Ship, a Frigate, an armed Vessel, and about One Hundred Sail of Transports.

News of Cornwallis's surrender at Yorktown arrived in New England six days later. There, as elsewhere around the nation, the victory triggered widespread rejoicing and celebration. Despite a common belief that the victory signaled the end of the war, it would be two more years before peace was finally concluded. (*The Boston Evening-Post and the General Advertiser*, October 27, 1781)

On October 19, 1781, the surrender negotiations completed, two long files of Allied troops snaked about a mile and a half from the gates of the main parapet into a field in the center of the Allied camp. *Isaac Bussell* and his mates, possibly including *Benjamin Cleaveland,* stood their places in rank on the east side of the road, having cleaned and dressed themselves "in as good order as our circumstances would permit." Facing them on the west side of the road was a similar file of French troops in resplendent white uniforms. Between them, with solemn countenance, marched the files of defeated British and German regiments, their colors encased, "all armed, with bayonets fixed, drums beating, and faces lengthening....They marched to the place appointed and stacked their arms; they then returned to the town in the same manner they had marched out."[1]

---

1 Martin, *Private Yankee Doodle*, pp. 240–241.

Chapter 8
"To make a good peace..."
1781–1783

Rejoicing and celebration spread with the news, and with the widespread belief that the surrender of Cornwallis signaled the ending of the war. Cannons roared; French and American flags sprouted; bonfires lit up the sky; and all across the fledgling nation dinners, toasts, and other festivities celebrated the victory. Amidst the outpouring of joy and relief, *Isaac Bussell* marched with his detachment back to the Hudson Highlands.

The Lincoln men who had remained in the Hudson Highlands must certainly have participated with their fellow soldiers in extra rations of food and drink, the *feux-de-joies*, and in the burnings in effigy of Benedict Arnold. In one instance, the exuberance of the men led to a humorous incident: "The company collected had determined to burn General Arnold in effigy.... Just as they were going to commit the effigy to the flames, one of the company observed that one of Arnold's legs was wounded when he was fighting bravely for America, that this leg ought not to be burnt, but amputated; in which the whole company agreed, and this leg was taken off and safely laid by."[1]

General Washington was under no illusions about the end of the war. He was apprehensive that the victory at Yorktown, "instead of exciting our exertions, as it ought to do, should produce such a relaxation in the prosecution of the war, as will prolong the calamities of it;" he struggled to maintain army readiness.[2] He sent militia reinforcements to General Greene in the Carolinas, then he returned most of the Continental Army to the north. And he once again turned his attentions to the persistent problems of procuring needed supplies, maintaining discipline, and preparing for the next campaign.

At the end of November 1781, militia units that had been called into service in August to backfill for the French and Continental troops sent to Yorktown were discharged. *William Thorning, Sgt. Lemuel Wheeler,* and probably *Lt. Abel Adams* returned home from their deployments in Rhode Island.

In the Hudson Highlands, *Daniel Brooks* was discharged at the expiration of his enlistment on December 4. Reportedly, he walked home penniless, not having been paid. Without money for food, it was a difficult journey. Hungry and sick, he was taken in, fed, and nursed back to health by a kindly family en route.[3] *Peter Bowes* may have been discharged with him, but no such story of his journey home has survived.

Jonas Parks, probably in company with *Capt. Isaac Gage* and *Cpl. Jonathan Weston,* also finished his stint in the Highlands in early December; all three made their way back to

---

1 General William Heath, quoted in Scheer and Rankin, *Rebels & Redcoats*, p. 497. Arnold had been seriously wounded in the left leg at Saratoga.
2 Scheer and Rankin, *Rebels & Redcoats*, p. 497.
3 Brooks Family Notes.

Lincoln. *John Wood* and *Joseph Munroe* were discharged about this time as well. *Joseph Munroe* was too sick to return home, however, and remained in camp for another five or six weeks before he was well enough to travel.

Despite the intransigence of King George, who insisted that it would not make "the smallest alteration" in the principles and conduct of the war, the surrender by Cornwallis had deflated the initiative of the British field command, and British military campaigning ground to a virtual halt.[1] General Clinton was recalled to England in May 1782, by which time the winds of political change were sweeping London. His replacement, General Carleton—who had routed the Americans during the Canadian Campaign in 1776—now began to consolidate his southern forces. He withdrew his troops from Savannah in July.

The inactivity of the enemy seemed to confirm the persistent rumors of the end of the war, and it further compounded Washington's efforts to maintain a war footing. Peace talks commenced in Paris. In August, General Carleton wrote Washington to inform him that he had "suspended" all hostilities. Washington, however, was skeptical. "That the King will push the war as long as the nation will find men or money admits not of a doubt in my mind," he declared.[2] "To make a good peace," he insisted, "you ought to be well prepared to carry on the war."[3] In the Highlands, *Abner Richardson*, *Artemas Reed*, and probably *Peter Weston*, still serving their Continental enlistments, submitted to "soldier's rules and discipline, and soldier's fare."[4] Throughout the American camps, drill, guard duty, wood detail, and various other special assignments mixed invariably with boredom, camp fever, and all manner of soldierly entertainment, folly, and mischief.

Meanwhile, *Solomon Whitney*, now in Continental service as an artilleryman, was detached for marine duty, serving shipboard on Continental frigates for most of 1782.

In December 1782, British troops evacuated Charleston, leaving the south entirely in the hands of the Americans. *Benjamin Cleaveland* probably had the satisfaction of entering Charleston with General Greene, before his subsequent discharge in 1783.

The winter of 1782–1783 came early to the Hudson Highlands. "We passed this winter as contentedly as we could, under the hope that the war was nearly over, and that hope buoyed us up under many difficulties," wrote Connecticut soldier Joseph Plum Martin. "But we were afraid to be *too* sanguine, for fear of being disappointed." The men soldiered on, searching for clues as to the status of the war. "Simple stories would keep the men in agitation, often for days together…, when they would get some other piece of information …, which would entirely put the boot on the other leg."[5]

Artemas Reed, too, from his vantage point in the Hudson Highlands, pondered the status of the war, at least until his early discharge from Continental service at the end of December 1782. He returned home to his Littleton farm, having moved his family out of Lincoln by July 1780.

Abraham Wesson was furloughed in March 1783, then he decided not to return to service, perhaps because by this time rumors were confirmed that a conditional peace treaty had

---

1 Scheer and Rankin, *Rebels & Redcoats*, pp. 497–498.
2 Scheer and Rankin, *Rebels & Redcoats*, p. 499.
3 Washington letter to James McHenry (December 11, 1781), quoted in Washington, *Writings* [Ford, ed.], p. 418. Also in Scheer and Rankin, *Rebels & Redcoats*, p.498. Washington appears to have said this in many ways, as lots of variations of this statement appear in various historical accounts.
4 Martin, *Private Yankee Doodle*, p. 249.
5 Martin, *Private Yankee Doodle*, pp. 275, 278.

Massive transports evacuate the British troops from Charleston on December 14, 1782, as the winds of change in London prompted General Carleton to wind down the American war effort. Lincoln-connected *Benjamin Cleaveland* may have been among the American forces on hand to re-enter the city. (Drawing by Howard Pyle, *Scribner's Magazine*, September 1898)

been reached in Paris the previous November. Or possibly the 44-year-old carpenter chose not to return because he lost faith that he would ever be paid for his service. Nevertheless, his term remained unfilled, and he was formally listed as a deserter.

On April 19, 1783, one day after *Abraham Wesson* was formally listed as a deserter, and eight years to the day after war broke out in Lexington and Concord and Lincoln, the Continental Congress officially announced to the army the cessation of hostilities.

As the de facto peace descended on the war-weary nation, the soldiers awaited both their back pay and their discharges. Congress was noncompliant. Instead, in June, Washington granted furloughs to large parts of the Continental Army. In lieu of pay, furloughed soldiers were given certificates redeemable (so they were told, at least) for back pay. With mixed emotions, borne of their experiences together in the service of their country, many of the soldiers left camp. Some returned home; others, having come of age in the army, departed for new adventures in new locations. Many had to sell their back-pay certificates or their muskets to finance their journeys. "I received my discharge from Captain John Mills—," remembered *Isaac Bussell* later. "Three years pay was due me—I committed my note for clothing & it amounted to only thirty dollars & thirty three cents." *Lt. Elisha Willington*, and possibly *Aaron Parker* and *Peter Weston*, returned to Lincoln—with only furlough papers and at best an unfilled promise of being paid.[1]

---

1 Pension Record # S36948; see Martin, *Private Yankee Doodle*, pp. 279–282; Dann, *Revolution Remembered*, p. xvii. The furloughed soldiers were allowed to keep their muskets. It is unknown whether or not *Elisha*

Finally, on September 3, 1783, the formalities caught up with the realities. The Treaty of Paris was signed, bringing the war to an end. The independence of the American states from the British Crown was now fully established. No longer subjects of a Royal sovereign, the Lincoln men and their families were now citizens of a new Republic. In November, Washington officially dissolved the Continental Army, as the British vacated New York. *Jonathan Tower, Abner Richardson,* and perhaps *Ezra Meriam or Silas Whitney,* were still in service, and may have been among the last vestiges of the Continental Army that entered New York in late November, on the heels of the departing British troops. They were discharged in December 1783 or early 1784.[1] The war was over.

So marked the end of "one of the most unusual armies ever to win a war."[2] It was a home-grown army, consisting of a full range of "voluntary corps at the beginning of the conflict, Continental units, state lines fighting with the main army, state militia units usually organized on the county or town level, companies of Indian spies, and 'coast guards'…with men serving in the United States navy, state navies, and on privateers."[3] The Lincoln men were full participants in this conglomerate of a Revolutionary Army, and in the winning of American independence.

There was nothing particularly extraordinary about this group of people; they were everyday farmers, laborers, merchants, tradesmen, slaves, and former slaves, the cross-section of an eighteenth-century New England farming community. They answered multiple calls for service, and they demonstrated the tenacity, resilience, and faith in the rectitude of their cause to see it through. "No European army would suffer the tenth part of what the American troops suffer," wrote Lafayette in the midst of one crisis. "It takes *citizens* to support hunger, nakedness, toil, and the total want of pay, which constitute the condition of our soldiers, the hardiest and most patient that are to be found in the world."[4]

Willington, Aaron Parker, or *Peter Weston* arrived home with their muskets or their back-pay certificates.

1 Demobilization in full swing, Washington left the army and returned to Mt. Vernon with a series of emotional farewells in November 1783. The actual discharging of soldiers and decommissioning of units appears to have continued into December. *Abner Richardson* was discharged December 23, 1783; *Jonathan Tower* served through December 1783. It is unclear if either of them were part of the single consolidated Continental Regiment, commanded by Col. Henry Jackson, which remained in service until it was formally disbanded in June 1784. *Ezra Meriam* appears to have been part of this final regiment, but the date of his discharge is unknown. *Silas Whitney* claimed in his pension declaration to have been discharged in April 1784.

2 Dann, *Revolution Remembered,* p. xvi.

3 Ibid.

4 Lafayette letter to his wife, quoted in Bancroft, *History of the United States,* p. 417 [italics added]. The quote is widely reported, but the author has been unable to ascertain the date of the letter. It appears to have been written in conjunction with the mutiny of the Pennsylvania line in January 1781, for which one might have expected harsher condemnation. But the substance of the mutineers' complaints was well understood, and they remained loyal to the cause. As explained by Larned and Reiley, *History For Ready Reference* (Vol. V, p. 3276), "Whatever of discredit may attach to the revolt, it will never be unassociated with the fact that…it did not affect the fealty of the soldiers to the cause for which they took up arms." Indeed, the mutineers turned over to be hanged as spies two British agents, whom General Clinton had sent to persuade them to desert (see Avery, *History of the United States,* Vol. IV, p. 304).

Chapter 9

Honoring the Legacy

So the Revolutionary War passed into history—the events that swept across Lincoln soil on April 19, 1775, the protracted struggle that ensued, and the against-all-odds outcome which spawned the great American democratic experiment. With an abiding faith in the righteousness of their cause, ordinary citizens of Lincoln and elsewhere altered the course of history not only of their local communities and of their nation, but also of the entire world. These events and these ordinary citizens continue to define and inspire generations of Americans.

It took more than seven years for these ordinary citizens to secure American independence, and it has taken successive generations more years to affect subsequent improvements in the American democratic system. So too, recognition and homage to the historical legacy of these ordinary citizens has come about with time. The process is inherently an ongoing one. Influenced by initiative, culture, the times, and the pragmatic necessities of life; the process had a slow beginning.

The Unwelcomed Intrusion

There was little to celebrate in Lincoln, or elsewhere, in the immediate aftermath of the events of April 19, 1775. As *Noah Parkhurst* is reported to have said, "Now the war has begun, and no one knows when it will end." Despite the anticipation of the possibility of having to resort to arms in the defense of their charter rights and liberties, and the extensive preparations for the prospect of war, the war's outbreak was not a desired or welcome development.[1]

The hasty departure of large numbers of militia and minute men left fields unplanted, projects abandoned, and economic activity disrupted. Everywhere, routines of daily living were interrupted.

In Cambridge, the arrival of 4,000 uninvited, armed men with little discipline brought chaos to a previously peaceful, genteel community. Fields and gardens were trampled and laid bare. Privacies were invaded, and properties abused. And there would be no relief. Within months, the town was "covered over with American Camps, and cut up into Forts and Entrenchments, & all their Lands, Fields & Orchards laid common, ye Horses & other Cattle feeding in ye choicest mowing Land,—whole fields of corn eat down to the Ground. Large parks of well regulated Locusts cutt down for firewood & other public Uses."[2]

---

1 Quotation is in the Baker Affidavit (1850)
2 Rev. William Emerson letter to Phebe Emerson (July 7, 1775), quoted in Emerson, *Diaries and Letters*, p. 79. "This I must say looks a little melancholy," he understated.

Charlestown would suffer a similar fate from the British troops. That is, after the town was first destroyed, the houses and buildings intentionally burned to the ground during the Battle of Bunker Hill.

Lexington suffered eight of its citizens killed on the Green on the morning of April 19th, then that afternoon it suffered several more deaths. In addition, substantial losses occurred from looting, burning, and other destructions as the British relief column attempted to regain control of the increasingly desperate situation confronting the original expeditionary force.

In Lincoln, losses were minimal. But the outbreak of war was nevertheless accompanied by more disruption than celebration. For most, concern over the safety and well being of the husbands and sons who had marched to Concord and not yet returned (in many cases, for days and months) was paramount. On the opposite side of the issue, *Dr. Charles Russell*, no longer feeling safe in the rebellious countryside, packed a few belongings, and hastily departed with his family for Boston.

There was cleanup from the maelstrom that had swept along the Bay Road that afternoon, and the distasteful but essential job of burying the bodies left behind. *Ephraim Hartwell*, probably with the assistance of *Edmond Wheeler*, gathered up the bodies of five uniformed soldiers from the road and fields around his tavern and from the dogleg a quarter of a mile up the road, where the fighting had been so intense. Loading them into an oxcart, the men transported them to the Precinct Burying Ground and placed them in a common, unmarked grave. Up the Bay Road toward Lexington, members of the *Nelson family* similarly interred two more soldiers by the side of the road. Catherine Louisa Smith, wife of *Capt. William Smith*, did her best, unsuccessfully, to nurse a critically wounded Redcoat back to health. A few days later, he too was buried by the side of the road, near Folly Pond.

The sudden need to feed and equip an army of men in Cambridge, Charlestown, and Roxbury brought further disruption to prewar "normalcy." Care packages were no doubt prepared and delivered to Cambridge individually and collectively by family members and friends. Soon supply trains began moving food and munitions from storage points in Concord and beyond, down the Bay Road to distribution points around Cambridge. Community and Provincial budgets suddenly became burdened with the necessity of providing for the army in the field.

The routines of daily living would slowly reassert themselves. But the normalcy of peacetime activity would not return to Lincoln for more than eight years, during which conflicting loyalties split families apart, Lincoln men marched into service never to return, and families struggled to make ends meet in a wildly inflationary and radically changed economy. Even after peace finally returned to the land, the economic dislocation brought on by the war would cause Lincoln farms to be lost to foreclosure and Lincoln residents to serve time in debtor prison.

There is little room in such circumstances to entertain romantic notions of glory and honor. Through it all, there were mouths to feed; animals to tend; fields to plant; business matters to transact. Weddings to arrange; births to celebrate; and deaths of loved ones to mourn. Roads and buildings needed repair; schoolteacher appointments, the minister's salary, and other town issues needed resolution. Through it all, the events marking the start of the war—even as principled a war as this one—were not matters to be celebrated.

Indeed, without a passing glance backwards at the fateful events that occurred at Concord's North Bridge, the bridge was unceremoniously removed 18 years later, and a new one erected at a more convenient site downstream. It would be 24 years before the first memorials to the fallen heroes began to appear—when in 1799 Lexington erected a memorial obelisk to the men killed on the Lexington Green—and nearly 50 years before local commemorations began to attract widespread interest in celebrating the momentous events that had sparked America's war to secure its rights, privileges, and liberties.[1]

The Second Battle of Lexington and Concord

By the 1820s, the bold American experiment with self-government was secure enough, and the dislocation of the war a distant-enough memory, for Americans to begin to look back with increasing pride and "the haze of romance" at the momentous events that had brought about American independence.[2]

On the cusp of the 50th anniversary of the American Revolution, the Marquis de Lafayette returned to America in 1824 and began a triumphant Grand Tour. He was cheered and feted at every stop from one end of the country to the other. At Concord on September 2, 1824, the Revolutionary War hero was welcomed to the site of "the first forcible resistance" to the British army, in a speech by Concord's Hon. Samuel Hoar, a State Senator and son of Lincoln's *Samuel Hoar*.

The Lincoln native could scarcely have anticipated the bitter reaction his remarks would trigger in the town of Lexington. Lexingtonians saw the remarks as a calculated attempt "to give an erroneous impression to the world respecting *the place*, where the revolutionary war commenced," and "to deprive the town of Lexington of the honor of having raised the first standard of an armed opposition to the unjust and tyrannical measures of the mother country." They set out to prove, despite the lack of hard evidence, that the Lexington men had put up an armed resistance to the Regulars.[3]

Lexington Town Meeting appointed a committee to collect and publish a statement of facts "which may be calculated to place the transactions of that day [April 19, 1775] before the publick in their true light." New depositions were taken from ten of the aging individuals who had witnessed or been on the Lexington Green with Captain Parker's militia, nearly fifty years before. They were published in 1825, by Elias Phinney, as part of a 40-page brochure, which argued that at least eight named men (along with unnamed "others") in Lexington had returned the Regulars' fire. "History affords few examples," it trumpeted, "of men, called upon by their country to give such a sanguinary proof of unyielding courage and disinterested virtue. Yet these gallant men showed themselves equal to this great trial. Their purpose was accomplished. The mighty struggle was begun."[4]

---

1 See Purcell, *Sealed with Blood* (pp. 92–126) for a discussion of the growth and democratization of a national memory of the war during the decade of the 1790s. She focuses primarily on the arts and literature, but notes (p. 125) that Lexington was "yearly celebrat[ing] their own battle anniversary and the glory of the nation" before this time. These commemorations remained essentially local memorials for the fallen for many years.

2 The term "the haze of romance" is from Tourtellot, Introduction and Comments.

3 Quotation is in Phinney, *History of the Battle of Lexington*, p. 6.

4 Phinney, *History of the Battle of Lexington*, pp. 6, 20-22, 23.

Elias Phinney's 1825 tract purporting to prove that the Lexington men returned the fire of the British troops on the Green was a reflection of community pride more than verifiable historical evidence. It gained support, however, from an 1830 lithograph by John and William Pendleton, shown here as it was later reproduced in an 1875 reprint of Phinney's work, and described as "an old, well-authenticated picture." (Phinney, *History of the Battle of Lexington*)

Concord struck back. First in various articles in the *Yeoman's Gazette,* and then in an 1827 tract, *A History of the Fight at Concord, on the 19th of April, 1775,* Rev. Ezra Ripley rebutted Lexington's claims, and quoted additional accounts collected from aging participants. There was no return fire from the Lexington militia, Ripley concluded from a review of the evidence, expressing disbelief that anyone could seriously have thought otherwise. He credited the Lexington Company with being "prompt, patriotic, and courageous to admiration," but he scoffed at the word *battle* and painted the Lexington scene instead as a *horrid massacre.*[1]

Thus came about the Second Battle of Lexington and Concord.

From the beginning, this battle was more about community pride than about what actually happened on April 19, 1775. There was never any agreement about what was meant by the words "the first forcible resistance," nor was there ever any attempt to define the phrase in any sort of objective fashion. Instead, partisans on both sides defined and applied the terms and parameters to justify community self-interest, interpreting and reinterpreting the available evidence to bolster their partisan arguments. Invariably, historical objectivity was sacrificed to the geographical loyalties of the historian.

"Without any intentions of reviving the controversy," wrote Concord historian Lemuel Shattuck in 1835, "…or of casting a comparative shade over the honor acquired by the brave 'sons of liberty,' in either town for the part they acted…," he gives a detailed review of

---

[1] Ripley, *A History of the Fight at Concord,* pp. iv, 13, 37, 38, 48, 59.

Chapter 9: Honoring the Legacy

the historical evidence—from the perspective of a Concord historian. "Would two or three guns from behind the walls…on each one's own responsibility, after orders had been given by the commanding officers, 'to disperse and not to fire,' be considered…as returning the fire, and making a regular, forcible resistance?" he asks rhetorically, concluding predictably that, "As to resistance there [in Lexington], it is not contended by anyone that any was made or attempted, which could have impeded the progress of the troops. Mr. Clark speaks of the place, as 'the field, not of battle, but of murder and bloodshed.'"[1]

Showing no more objectivity than Shattuck, Lexington proponents clung to the opposite interpretation. They gained pictorial support from an 1830 lithograph by John and William Pendleton showing six Lexington men holding their ground and firing at the Redcoats, while two others were loading. Another drawing by Hammett Billings in 1855 showed a dozen Lexington men firing, loading, or preparing to fire. In 1868, Lexington historian, Charles Hudson reprinted the Billings drawing and echoed the Lexington line in his description of the the battle, "several of them [Lexington militiamen] immediately returned the fire of the British. Jonas Parker, John Munroe, and Ebenezer Munroe, Jr., and some others, fired before leaving the line … several of the Americans returned the fire after leaving the field.[2]

Phinney's brochure was reissued in 1875 with the addition of the Pendletons' lithograph, identified as "a cut of the battle, from an old, well-authenticated picture," to reassert "the facts in regard to the first resistance to British tyranny at Lexington."[3]

And so the rhetoric declaimed. In fact, the Second Battle of Lexington and Concord was never about historical objectivity or about where "the first forcible resistance" occurred. It was about establishing primacy. For each salvo fired, the conclusion was inescapable and emphatic: that the Revolutionary War had begun in Lexington, or in Concord, depending on which side it was that launched the salvo.

Amid the claims and counterclaims, it was not long before the town of Acton was drawn in, as well. This was over perceived slights by Concord to the honor of Capt. Isaac Davis and the Acton Company, which led the march to the North Bridge and suffered the brunt of the casualties in the brief fight. Shattuck had observed that the Acton Company had arrived on the scene late, just before the march got underway, implying that Capt. Isaac Davis had usurped the lead position—the honor of which rightly belonged to the men of Concord—by marching his troops to the front of the column in ignorance of, or in defiance of, military etiquette.[4]

Josiah Adams, arguing the case for Acton, countered that Captain Davis had moved his company to the front only after conferring with the other officers, and he charged that the Concord captains had declined (i.e., lacked the courage) to take the lead position. Adams excoriated Concord's lack of leadership, noting not only the indecisiveness before the march, but also that after Davis was killed at the bridge, the command of the Provincial forces fell apart.[5]

---

1 Shattuck, *History of the Town of Concord*, pp. 333, 340, 341. Mr. Clark refers to the Rev. Jonas Clark of Lexington, who made the statement in his Anniversary Sermon in 1776.
2 Hudson, *History of the Town of Lexington* (1868), Vol. I, p. 178, illus. opp. p. 183.
3 Phinney, *History of the Battle of Lexington*, p. 4.
4 Shattuck, *History of the Town of Concord*, p. 111.
5 Adams, *Letter to Lemuel Shattuck*, pp. 8–9, 11.

For nearly 200 years, with the honor of the towns at stake, Lexington and Concord have continued to bicker for primacy in the events of April 19, 1775, the intensity waxing and waning, at times seeming to rival the intensity of the original dispute between the colonies and the Crown. Commenting on this in 1916, historian Harold Murdoch lamented "the accumulation of a mass of questionable evidence, which in exaggerated forms has gradually become accepted as history," as well as "the time and ink that were wasted in the fruitless controversy, [and] the recriminations and bitterness of spirit…of neighboring towns."[1] Yet the battle continued.

Nearly 50 years later, historian Arthur Tourtellot commented, "The rivalry between Concord and Lexington for the glory of shedding the first British blood was carried to even greater extremes than Mr. Murdoch alleged. As the intertown feud went on, the heroics ascribed to the minutemen became so preposterous that if their bravery should not be questioned, their sanity could be doubted."[2] Even today, both Lexington and Concord still cling tenaciously to their separate claims of being the place where the American Revolution began.

Such is human nature that it matters. Cynics (or perhaps realists) may attribute the claims to commercial interests and tourist dollars. Possibly the tourists themselves invite the rivalry, often being less interested in historical nuance than in simplified answers and a story told in black and white.[3] Or perhaps it is a simple one-upmanship that marks the human spirit—an age-old quest for public recognition and the bragging rights that go with that. Glory and honor can be powerful drivers. But if it is not always clear exactly *why* it matters, the persistence of this question underscores the simple reality that to many people it *does* matter.

Adjudication of the claims of Lincoln's ancestral towns[4] is beyond the scope or the intention of this work. However, as the controversy has always had less to do with an objective analysis and interpretation of the historical record than with a human need to justify the claims made, a new perspective may be instructive.

This much is certain: that the simmering conflict between the colonists of Massachusetts Bay and the Crown turned ugly on the morning of April 19, 1775, in the nearby towns of Lexington and Concord. Eight Lexington residents lay dead or dying on the Green when the King's troops resumed their march to Concord. Two more, from Acton, fell at the North Bridge before the Provincials returned the fire, with similar deadly effect. Three Redcoats breathed their last.[5]

---

1 Murdoch, "Historic Doubts," pp. 361, 362.
2 Tourtellot, Introduction and Comments.
3 The author cites his own experience with tourists, both on the Lexington Green and at the North Bridge in Concord. One of the questions most frequently asked is, "Where did they fire 'the shot heard round the world?'" The question is almost never about the line from Emerson's famous poem, inscribed on the base of the Minute Man Statue at the Concord bridge. Nor is it about where the Colonial forces stood in relation to the Regulars. The question is not a nuanced one; nor, in most cases, is the inquirer looking for a nuanced answer. Invariably, the question translates as, "so where did the Revolution actually begin?" and the expected answer is a simple "Lexington" or "Concord."
4 The town of Lincoln was carved out of the towns of Lexington, Concord, and Weston when it was founded in 1754. As Weston is not on the route of the British march to and from Concord, it has not been a combatant in the Second Battle of Lexington and Concord.
5 Two Redcoats were killed outright, and are buried at the bridge; the third was mortally wounded, and lingered for a time before he died. He was later buried in the center of Concord.

Chapter 9: Honoring the Legacy 163

This heroic 1855 drawing by Hammatt Billings depicting the Lexington men actively engaged in battle with the British contributed to the growing revisionist myth in the nineteenth century that the Lexington men stood their ground and engaged in a pitched battle with the enemy. This is an example of what historian Harold Murdoch called "a mass of questionable evidence" which "has gradually become accepted as history." (Hudson, *History of the Town of Lexington* (1868))

Horrific as it was, the deadly massacre that took place on the Lexington Green was unplanned, unintended, and lacking in any strategic purpose (although after the fact, the propaganda value for the colonial cause was inestimable).[1] It was over as quickly as it began. Whether or not one accepts the revisionism of the nineteenth century, the musket fire on the Lexington Green ended quickly and without further ado.

The brief skirmish at the North Bridge in Concord was similarly tangential to the broader strategic objectives of either party. It, too, was over as quickly as it began, without the attainment of any recognized objective on either side.

Neither incident was worthy of being termed a "battle," in the usual sense of the word. The incidents were isolated and independent of each other, and in both cases the firing ended without further provocation or disturbance. Had no more shots been fired that day, the lid on the long simmering dispute between the Crown and the colonies would probably have

---

1 Finding it inexplicable from any logical or military perspective that the Lexington militia should have paraded on the Green that morning with the approach of an armed force ten times its size, Murdoch, "Historic Doubts" (pp. 373–374), posits the possibility that Captain Parker might have had orders to do so in order to provoke an incident. Tourtellot, Introduction and Comments, finds support for this notion among the papers of Rev. Jonas Clark, pastor of the Lexington church, and letters to General Gage from his mole, Dr. Benjamin Church, within the Provincial Congress. This theory, if it were to hold true, would certainly indicate strategic significance for the Colonial cause, but there was still nothing to be gained by the Regulars by firing on the Lexington men. Either way, for the Redcoats, this was an unintended event, without any strategic benefit.

remained in place. The lid would have rattled a bit as it let off another bolus of steam, but it is not likely to have been blown off completely. Despite the colonial military preparations and the escalation of tensions, war, per se, was not the objective.

Without a doubt, both incidents would have been played for all their worth in the propaganda war, which of course they were, in any case. Similar to the Boston Massacre and the Boston Tea Party, the incidents at Lexington and Concord would likely have played out politically, not militarily; steppingstones in American colonial history, but something short of the precipitators of an American Revolution. Similar British excursions to Charlestown, Portsmouth, and Salem in previous months for the purpose of disarming the colonists had significantly raised colonial anger and ire without sparking armed conflict.

But of course, more shots *were* fired. Layering anger erupted again a few hours later, near the border between Concord and Lincoln, and it escalated in Lincoln through the dogleg that became known as the "Bloody Angles." "Here," says Hudson, "may be said to have commenced the *battle* of the 19th of April. At Lexington Common and at Concord North Bridge but few guns had been fired by the Americans; … But now all restraint seems to have been removed." The battle raged along the Bay Road, which became known as the "Battle Road," reaching a ferocious intensity that nearly routed the British column. "In no part of the retreat were the British more sorely pressed than in passing through Lincoln. Their loss was severe.… The retreat here became a rout."[1]

Now the real battle had been joined, a full-scale battle from which there could be no turning back. By the time the British column exited Lincoln, the simmering dispute had boiled over, the lid blown completely off. No longer was the bloodshed unintended, episodic, or able to be patched over. Along the Battle Road in Lincoln, the casualty count surpassed the combined casualties at the Lexington Green and the North Bridge. The rapid escalation and intensity of the fighting eliminated any possibility of reconciliation. Here, both sides became mortal combatants, the point-of-no-return passing unnoticed in the hail of bullets, the clouds of swirling smoke, and the acrid stench of burning powder.

Wars begin when one side in a conflict pushes beyond a point acceptable to the opposing side; when civil or political discourse can no longer deal with the threat or crisis presented. By definition, this is the point-of-no-return. When you strip away community pride, entrenched interests, and doctrinaire passions, the historical record demonstrates that the lid blew off the pot neither on the Lexington Green, nor at the North Bridge, but during the British return march to Boston. On this basis, then, one could certainly make the case that the Revolutionary War actually began along Battle Road, between the outbreak of fighting at Meriam's Corner and the arrival of the British relief column at Munroe's Tavern.

Despite the clarity of the historical record, and broad consensus among historians on the significance of Battle Road, there is little chance that this interpretation of events will please Lexingtonians any more than the 1824 statement by Samuel Hoar. Or Concordians either, for that matter. The fact is that no convention exists for pinpointing the precise starting point of a war. Therefore, deciding that the American Revolution began on the Lexington Green, or at Concord's North Bridge, or along the Battle Road, remains largely dependant on individual definition, and this tends to be informed more by one's town of residence or affiliation than by the historical record.

---

1 Quotations are from Hudson, *History of the Town of Lexington* (1868), Vol. I, pp. 194, 195. Italics included.

Chapter 9: Honoring the Legacy

Despite the exclusive nature of the claims and counterclaims made by Lexington and Concord, the events of April 19, 1775, cannot be considered in isolation from one another. All occurred during, and as a consequence of, the British march to and from Concord. Together, the events formed a continuum, the significance of which exceeds the component parts. Each event was shaped by the events that preceded it, and in turn each event shaped the events that followed.

While the skirmish at the North Bridge was a separate incident from the massacre on the Lexington Green, the assembled companies in Concord knew that the Regulars had already fired on the Lexington men. Similarly, the outbreak of shooting along Battle Road was triggered separately from the previous events, but the acute jitteriness of the Regulars and the anger of the locals over the spilled blood certainly contributed to the rapid escalation of the fighting through Lincoln.

So another appropriate interpretation is that the Revolutionary War began *jointly* on the Lexington Green, *and* at the North Bridge, *and* along Battle Road. To single out Lexington or Concord to the exclusion of Lincoln or the other locations for the "honor" of being the place where the Revolution began is to demonstrate continuing partisan zealotry in the Second Battle of Lexington and Concord.

There is more than enough honor to go around. If one argues that "the first forcible resistance" to the Crown occurred in Concord, that does not detract from the honor of the Lexington martyrs, or the prudence of Captain Parker in dismissing his militia company in the face of an overwhelmingly superior force. If one argues that a few angry Lexingtonians fired back after their companions were massacred as they were dispersing from the Green, this does not undermine the significance of the skirmish at the North Bridge. Similarly, the fact that the Acton Company led the march to the bridge does nothing to denigrate the honor of Concord, or the collective resolve to march into town to prevent the Regulars from burning it down. Nor does the fact that the simmering conflict boiled over at the Bloody Angles diminish the significance of the bloodshed in Lexington and Concord.

Lincoln has largely steered clear of the Second Battle of Lexington and Concord. It has never sought primacy in the events of April 19, 1775, and has made few claims to the honor and glory thereof. Perhaps the sound and fury of its neighboring towns has diverted attention away from Lincoln's right to claim its own place of honor in the opening events of the war. Or perhaps individuals in Lincoln are simply content to take quiet, un-trumpeted pride in the town's role in the historic events of the day.

Rational perspectives notwithstanding, the competing claims of Lexington and Concord are not likely to go away. The fact is that to many people the precise black and white distinctions do matter, even more so as the haze of romance deepens, and local interests become more entrenched.

None of this denies Lexington and Concord the honor and glory associated with the opening events of the American Revolution. Rightfully, both towns deserve recognition for the events that took place within their borders on April 19th. But to be fair, similar recognition must be accorded Lincoln and Menotomy and Cambridge. And equal honor is due to the men of Acton and Bedford who stood shoulder to shoulder at the North Bridge with the men of Lincoln and Concord. Also to the other towns across the colony and throughout New England whose men, determined to defend their right of self-government, reached for their muskets upon receiving news of the Alarm of April 19th. The American

Revolution began in all of these towns together, spontaneously, collectively. All are equally deserving of such recognition. Whether or not any of their claims, however, will ever be heard above the din of the Second Battle of Lexington and Concord remains to be seen.

Recognition of a Proud Legacy

It would be more than 100 years after the bloody fight along Battle Road, before the town of Lincoln first commemorated anything to do with the Revolutionary War. Certainly, the town must have been well represented by individual citizens at the anniversary celebrations of April 19th in Concord and perhaps Lexington during the 1830s and 1840s. At Concord's 75th anniversary ceremonies in 1850, *Amos Baker* was fêted as the last living participant in the North Bridge fight.[1] But it would take the Centennial celebrations (held separately in Concord and Lexington) to inspire Lincoln's interest in undertaking commemorations of its own.

In 1884, the town erected a stone marker at the resting site of the five British soldiers in the old Precinct Burial Ground.

Eleven years later, Lincoln Town Meeting approved a proposal "to erect a monument… to designate the place where Paul Revere was captured." It created a committee and appropriated $100 to be put toward the project. In subsequent years, Town Meeting approved additional funding, as the proposal for a bronze tablet progressed. Finally, in 1899, the monument was erected at what was determined to be the exact location of Revere's arrest, as determined by "Rev. Edward G. Porter,[2] recognized as the highest authority" on the subject. The large bronze tablet attached to a slab of Quincy granite stood resolutely at that spot, near the edge of the Battle Road, for many years. By 1956, it had found a new location, set further back from the increasing traffic, and in 2000, the National Park Service relocated it for the convenience of visitors, incorporating it into an interpretive display still further back from the road.[3]

One hundred and nine years after the fact, Lincoln marked the spot where five British soldiers were buried in the old Precinct Burial Ground. Each April, the graves are decorated as part of the town's annual Patriots Day commemorations. (Photograph by Jack MacLean)

---

1 He executed his Affidavit a few days afterward, which was just in time, because he died about ten weeks later.
2 Of Lexington.
3 Wiggin, "Recognition of a Proud Legacy," p. 7. The original placement of the stone by Reverend Porter is known only by an old photograph that lacks identifiable landmarks. Subsequent locations are shown in Dietrich-Smith, *Cultural Landscape Report*, (pp. 65, 67, 68, 113, 156). The marker has been re-oriented and set

Chapter 9: Honoring the Legacy

Looking east along what is now Route 2A in Lincoln, this early-twentieth-century photograph shows the monument—embedded in a stone wall—marking the spot where Paul Revere was captured by a patrol of British officers. The monument has since been moved further back from the road, and it is now part of an interpretive display designed by the National Park Service. (*New England Magazine*, 1902)

Shortly after the end of World War II, the town began holding an annual ceremony to decorate the gravesites of Revolutionary War participants, including the British soldiers in the Precinct Burial Ground.

Then in 1966, by proclamation of the Selectmen, and in anticipation of the Bicentennial of the American Revolution, Lincoln reestablished its company of minute men, "to perpetuate the memory of the Minute Men of 1775, and their example of steady and solemn refusal to be subject to the whims and caprices of any man or body of men." For more than 45 years, the modern incarnation of the Lincoln Minute Men have kept this rich history alive, carrying it into Lincoln's schools, conducting the town's annual Patriots Day ceremonies, and representing Lincoln's proud Revolutionary history at appropriate events.

Every year, the Lincoln Minute Men decorate the graves of the Revolutionary War veterans buried in Lincoln, including the five British soldiers in the Precinct Burial Ground. Every year, they reenact the Alarm arriving by horseback from north Lincoln, and every year they march to Concord. They regularly march at Concord's Patriots Day celebration, and also at the Bunker Hill parade in honor of the 44 to 55 Lincoln men who served in that battle. The Lincoln Minute Men have served as Honor Guard for Queen Elizabeth's state visit to Boston, and as Honor Guard for returning Gulf War soldiers. In addition, they have appeared nationally, representing Lincoln and Massachusetts at the Inaugural Ceremonies of Presidents Bill Clinton and George W. Bush.

As the town's awareness and pride in its Revolutionary history grew, a plan was proposed and enthusiastically endorsed at a 1982 Town Meeting to place a historic marker on the field where the original minute men and militia companies mustered in the early morning hours of April 19, 1775, and began their march to Concord. It would take nearly 18 years to

---

further back from the road, but as nearly as can be determined, it remains in the same approximate location *along* the road as its original placement.

In time for the 225th anniversary of the April 19th Alarm, the modern company of Lincoln Minute Men erected historic markers on the Town Common (*top*), and at the intersection of Sandy Pond and Baker Bridge Roads (*bottom*) to commemorate the muster and march of the Lincoln men to Concord on that fateful morning. Shown here in 2004, the Lincoln Minute Men prepare to step off on their annual Patriots Day march to Concord. (Photographs by Jack MacLean)

resolve a plague of historic, political, and aesthetic roadblocks, but on April 19, 2000—the 225th anniversary of their historic march to Concord—the Lincoln Minute Men dedicated historic markers on the Town Common, where the minute men drilled and mustered, and in Dakin's Field (at the corner of Sandy Pond and Baker Bridge roads), where the *Baker* clan and perhaps the *Billings* joined the minute men en route to Concord.[1]

That the town of Lincoln and its people were richly woven into the tapestry of the American Revolutionary period is well understood. Consistent with the understated character of the town, it has never felt the need to compete with its neighbors for public recognition. In its own quiet way, it has recognized and honored the proud legacy of its forebears, the contributions they made, and the sacrifices they endured to secure their *Charter Rights and Privileges* for the benefit of future generations of Americans.

---

[1] See Wiggin, "Recognition of a Proud Legacy." See also the Lincoln Minute Men Collection in the Archives/Special Collections of the Lincoln Public Library.

PART II
Muster Rolls

During the climactic struggle against the army of British General Burgoyne at Saratoga, Col. Eleazer Brooks was ordered on September 24, 1777, to mobilize a second wave of men from his militia regiment to march northward in support of the Northern Department of the Continental Army under General Gates. Fourteen Lincoln men marched on this order, joining 16 or 17 Lincoln men who had marched north a month earlier, plus another 24 to 33 Lincoln men who were in the Northern Department with other militia companies and the Continental Army. (Courtesy of Lincoln Town Archives, Lincoln, MA)

Chapter 10

The Army of the Revolution

ABBOT, Abiel
[also ABBOTT, also Abial]

Abiel Abbot of Lincoln served at Dorchester as a private in Capt. John Hartwell's Company, Col. Nicholas Dike's Regiment, from December 14, 1776, to March 1, 1777.[1]

He may possibly be the Abiel Abbot who served as a private in Capt. John Bodwell's Company, Col. Jacob Gerrish's Regiment of Guards in Cambridge from April 2, 1778, to July 2, 1778 (credited with 2 months, 13 days of service). Attributing this service to Abiel Abbot of Lincoln, however, is uncertain, as there is a reasonable likelihood that it may have been provided by an Abiel Abbot from Essex County.[2]

He appears to have served on an alarm at Rhode Island, as a private in Capt. Samuel Heald's Company, Col. John Jacobs's Regiment of Light Infantry, from September 16, 1779, to November 16, 1779 (credited with 2 months, 4 days of service).[3]

Lincoln historian William Wheeler reports that he served at Rhode Island again in 1781, but this is unconfirmed.[4]

Abiel Abbot of Lincoln was age 15 when the war broke out; age 17 at the time of his initial service at Dorchester. He was the son of Joseph Abbot (Sr.) (q.v.) and Hannah (White)

---

[1] *Massachusetts Soldiers and Sailors*, Vol. I, pp. 5, 16. The town appears to have paid his father, Lt. Joseph Abbot, for this service (see "Treasurer's Accompts," June 10, 1779).

[2] *Massachusetts Soldiers and Sailors*, Vol. I, pp. 5, 16. Identical service by a Joseph Abbot (who on the face of it appears to be his brother) suggests the likelihood of this being Abiel Abbot of Lincoln (see *Massachusetts Soldiers and Sailors*, Vol. I, p. 11). However, this service is conspicuously absent from the pension record of his brother Joseph Abbot (Pension Record # W26972), and does not fit with his brother's marriage or previous ranks in service, casting reasonable doubt on the attribution of this service to Abiel Abbot of Lincoln. Further, the geography is not a good fit: Captain Bodwell was from Methuen and Colonel Gerrish was from Essex County. On the other hand, guard units do not appear to have been organized on strictly geographic lines. There were other Lincoln men serving with other companies under Colonel Gerrish at this time.

[3] *Massachusetts Soldiers and Sailors*, Vol. I, pp. 5, 16. While it is not absolutely certain that this is the same Abiel Abbot, this record is consistent with Wheeler, "Lincoln" (in Hurd, Vol. 2, p. 621), which asserts that he served at Rhode Island in 1779. Captain Heald was from Concord, and members of the company were from nearby towns, including Lincoln.

[4] Wheeler, "Lincoln," in Hurd, Vol. 2, p. 621. A confirming record of this service has not been found. In another more recent compilation of records, Miller, "Joseph Abbott" credits him with service at Saratoga in 1777, but this appears to be erroneous. There was an Abiel Abbot who marched to Saratoga with Capt. Enoch Shepard's Company, Col. John Moseley's Regiment, from September 21, 1777, to October 23, 1777 (credited with 1 month, 3 days of service) (see *Massachusetts Soldiers and Sailors*, Vol. I, pp. 4, 5, 16). Attributing this service to Abiel Abbot of Lincoln, however, is highly doubtful, as this was a Hampshire County regiment. Most Lincoln militiamen who went to Saratoga at this time served in Capt. Samuel Farrar, Jr.'s Company, Colonel Jonathan Reed's Regiment.

Abbot; brother of Joseph Abbot (q.v.) and Nehemiah Abbot (q.v.), both of whom were minute men. The family operated a grist mill in the northeastern part of town.

He married Polly Meriam in 1788 and died in 1817, apparently in Farmington, Maine.[1]

ABBOT, Joseph (Sr.)
[also ABBOTT, also Lt. Joseph]

Joseph Abbot was on horseback at the Lexington Green when the Regulars arrived and fired the first volley, then he rode off immediately without witnessing anything further. His purpose for being at the Lexington Green is unknown, and there is no record of his taking part in any further activity that day.[2]

Lt. Joseph Abbot was paid by the town for service at Cambridge in 1775, at Dorchester in 1776 and 1777, and in the Continental Army for three years.[3] This service, however, was actually provided by his sons: Abiel Abbot (q.v.) served at Dorchester from December 14, 1776, to March 1, 1777; and Nehemiah Abbot (q.v.) served at Cambridge from April 24, 1775, to at least September 30, 1775, and in the Continental Army from August 20, 1777, to August 19, 1780.

He was age 47 at the Lexington Green; the son of Nehemiah and Sarah (Foster) Abbot. He had been married to Hannah White since 1752; he was the father of Abiel Abbot (q.v.), Nehemiah Abbot (q.v.), and Joseph Abbot, Jr. (q.v.). He was a miller, operating a grist mill

---

1 *Vital Records of Lincoln*; *Lexington Births, Marriages and Deaths*; Abbot and Abbot, *Genealogical Register*, p. 154; Wheeler, "Lincoln," in Hurd, Vol. 2, p. 621; MacLean, *A Rich Harvest*, p. 175; Federal Census Records, 1810, 1820. Wheeler says he died in Lincoln, but his death is not recorded in *Vital Records of Lincoln*. Abbot and Abbot indicate that he died in Farmington, Maine. Census records confirm this. Miller, "Joseph Abbott," says he died in 1826 in Mason, New Hampshire. A number of Lincoln residents had indeed migrated to Mason after the war. However, Miller's information as to the date and location of his death appears to be incorrect.

Polly (also given as Mary) was from Lexington and was a second-cousin to Ezra Meriam (q.v.).

2 Deposition of Joseph Abbot. The deposition does not identify the deponent as Joseph Sr. or Joseph Jr. One theory holds that this was Joseph Jr., and that as a minute man, he may have been charged (probably by pre-arrangement) with scouting the road to the east before reporting his intelligence to Concord. However, Joseph Jr. is recorded as being in service at Cambridge when the deposition was taken at Lexington.

The author believes that in the chaos that was Cambridge in the aftermath of the events of April 19th, many individuals must have returned home for supplies or to attend to hastily interrupted matters. On the face of it, it seems quite plausible that Joseph Jr. could have been a deponent at Lexington, even while officially in service at Cambridge. However, among the 95 other deponents (including a few spectators and a couple of British soldiers), none of them is recorded as being in service on the date of his deposition. Even if Joseph Jr. had returned to Lincoln briefly, it would be inconsistent with this evidence to attribute the deposition to him. Therefore, the author concludes that the deponent in this case must have been Joseph Sr.

His co-deponent, Benjamin Tidd, was age 32 and (according to Coburn) a private in Capt. John Parker's Lexington Militia Company. Obviously, for whatever reason, he was not with his unit on the Green, nor is he recorded as serving in Cambridge until June 17–18.

3 "Treasurer's Accompts," June 10, 1779. The record shows consecutive payments, first to Lt. Joseph Abbot (for Cambridge in 1775, Dorchester in 1776–77, and three years in the Continental Army) and then to Joseph Abbot, Jr. (for Cambridge in 1776, and Ticonderoga in 1776).

It was not an unusual practice for the town to pay a father for his son's service.

There is no other record of either Abiel or Nehemiah being paid for these terms of service. The record also shows that Nehemiah was away when the transaction occurred, still serving his three-year term in the Continental Army. It is not clear why Abiel was not paid directly, but the logic is compelling that the payment that the town made to Lt. Joseph Abbot was for service by his sons. While it may be impossible to totally disqualify the elder Joseph Abbot from this service, neither can we infer service by the elder Joseph from the treasurer's accounts or from any other records found.

in the northeastern part of town, which eventually gave Mill Street its name. He died in Lincoln in 1794, shortly after turning age 67, and is buried in the Precinct Burial Ground on Lexington Road.[1]

ABBOT, Joseph, Jr.
[also ABBOTT]

Joseph Abbot, Jr., of Lincoln was a corporal in Capt. William Smith's Company of Minute Men from Lincoln, Col. Abijah Peirce's Regiment.[2] Following the engagement at Concord, he served for 25 days in Cambridge.[3] He was reimbursed by the town for a set of accoutrements as a minute man on February 29, 1776.[4]

Subsequently, he served as sergeant in Capt. John Hartwell's Company of Militia from Lincoln, Col. Eleazer Brooks's 3rd Middlesex County Regiment, which marched from Lincoln to fortify Dorchester Heights on March 4, 1776. The unit was discharged five days later, on March 9.[5]

Town records show that he was paid for service at Cambridge in 1776 and for service at Ticonderoga in 1776.[6] The details of the Cambridge service have not survived. At Ticonderoga, he served as an orderly corporal (doing duty as a sergeant) in Capt. Asahel Wheeler's Company, Col. Jonathan Reed's Regiment from June 1776 to December 1776. He was discharged at Albany at the end of his six-month term.[7]

Minute Man Cpl. Joseph Abbot, Jr., served on April 19th and at Ticonderoga the following year. After the war, he moved to Maine; he is buried in Livermore Falls. (Photograph by the author)

He was age 22 on April 19, 1775; the son of Joseph Abbot (Sr.) (q.v.) and Hannah (White) Abbot of Lincoln; brother of Nehemiah Abbot (q.v.), who was also a minute man, and Abiel Abbot (q.v.). The family operated a grist mill in the northeastern part of town.[8]

---

1 *Lexington Births, Marriages and Deaths*; *Vital Records of Lincoln*; MacLean, *A Rich Harvest*, p. 175; Biggs, "In Memorium," p. 189.
2 Coburn, *Muster Rolls*; Pension Record # W26972. In his pension declaration, he gives his rank as sergeant.
3 *Massachusetts Soldiers and Sailors*, Vol. I, p. 11.
4 "Treasurer's Accompts," February 26, 1776.
5 Hartwell, "A List of a Company of Militia." Also Pension Record # W26972. In his pension declaration, he said he served for one month, and he called himself an "orderly Sergeant."
6 "Treasurer's Accompts," June 10, 1779. Wheeler, "Lincoln," (in Hurd, Vol. 2, p. 621), credits him with service at Cambridge in 1775, but the record clearly says 1776.
7 Pension Record # W26972.
8 *Lexington Births, Marriages and Deaths*; MacLean, *A Rich Harvest*, p. 175. His birth was recorded in Lexington (four months after his parents were married), as Lincoln had not yet become a separate town.

He married Ruth Bucknam (also given as Buckingham) of Lexington on April 30, 1778. He left Lincoln for Sidney, Maine, and later moved to Livermore, Maine, in 1818. He died in 1832, age 80, in Livermore, Maine. He is buried in the Stricklands Ferry Cemetery in Livermore Falls.[1]

ABBOT, Nehemiah
[also ABBOTT]

Nehemiah Abbot was a private in Capt. William Smith's Company of Minute Men from Lincoln, Col. Abijah Peirce's Regiment.[2] He was reimbursed by the town for a part of a set of accoutrements as a minute man on February 29, 1776.[3]

Following the engagement at Concord, he served for five days in Cambridge before enlisting on April 24, 1775, for eight months of service in Capt. William Smith's Company, Col. John Nixon's 16th Massachusetts Regiment in the rapidly organizing Provincial Army of Massachusetts. He is presumed to have participated in the Battle of Bunker Hill with his unit on June 17, 1775.[4]

Subsequently, he served as corporal in Capt. John Hartwell's Company of Militia from Lincoln, Col. Eleazer Brooks's 3rd Middlesex County Regiment, which marched from Lincoln to fortify Dorchester Heights on March 4, 1776. The unit was discharged five days later, on March 9.[5]

On August 14, 1777, as members of the Lincoln Militia Company were being

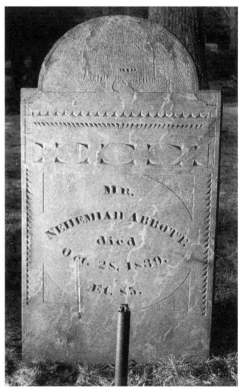

Buried in Lincoln's Precinct Burial Ground, Minute Man Nehemiah Abbot served repeatedly throughout much of the war. He was later described as "imperturbable." (Photograph by Fred Tingley)

---

1 *Lexington Births, Marriages and Deaths*; Wheeler, "Lincoln," in Hurd, Vol. 2, p. 621; Abbot and Abbot, *Genealogical Register*, p. 154; Pension Record # W26972; *SAR Revolutionary War Graves Register*. The move to Sidney is dated 1796 according to the pension record. Nevertheless, Joseph and Ruth appear to have remained in (or retained ties to) Lincoln at least through 1803, when the birth of their eleventh child is recorded in *Vital Records of Lincoln*. After Joseph died, Ruth moved back to Sidney. In her application for a widow's pension, she gives three different dates for her marriage to Joseph, suggesting that she may have been failing mentally.

2 Coburn, *Muster Rolls*.

3 "Treasurer's Accompts," February 26, 1776.

4 *Massachusetts Soldiers and Sailors*, Vol. I, pp. 13, 20, 25; "Treasurer's Accompts," June 10, 1779. The town paid Nehemiah Abbot's father, Lt. Joseph Abbot, for this service, as Nehemiah was away on Continental service at the time of the transaction. In August 1775, Colonel Nixon's 16th Massachusetts Regiment became known also as the 5th Continental Regiment under General Washington's command.

5 Hartwell, "A List of a Company of Militia."

called upon to reinforce the Northern Army under General Gates, he enlisted instead for a three-year term in the Continental Army. He served from August 20, 1777, to August 19, 1780, in Capt. Thomas Turner's 5th Company, Col. Henry Jackson's Regiment. Appointed a corporal, he probably arrived in southeastern Pennsylvania in time to participate in the concluding engagements of the unsuccessful American defense of Philadelphia. Presumably, he spent the winter of 1777 at Valley Forge. The following year Colonel Jackson's Regiment fought in the Battle of Monmouth on June 28, 1778, and the Battle of Rhode Island on August 29, 1778.

He appears to have taken on the duty of orderly sergeant and remained in Rhode Island through mid-1779. He shows up on muster rolls for April 1779, dated at Pawtuxet, and June 1779, dated at Camp at Providence. Jackson's Regiment returned to New Jersey and participated in the defense of Morristown during the summer of 1780. Nehemiah Abbot was discharged at the expiration of his term of service on August 19, 1780.[1]

He had the reputation of being a good soldier. Fifty years after his death, Lincoln historian William Wheeler notes, "Anyone who remembers the imperturbable old gentleman can readily believe that nothing less than an army with banners would terrify him."[2]

He was age 20 as a minute man; the son of Joseph Abbot (Sr.) (q.v.) and Hannah (White) Abbot of Lincoln; brother of Joseph Abbot (q.v.), who was also a minute man, and Abiel Abbot (q.v.).[3] The family operated a grist mill in the northeastern part of town.

He married Sarah Hoar in 1791. Sarah was the daughter of John Hoar (q.v.) and sister of Samuel Hoar (q.v.) and Leonard Hoar (q.v.). He died in Lincoln in 1839, age 85, and is buried in the old Precinct Burial Ground on Lexington Road.[4]

ABEL, Jonathan

Jonathan Abel appears on a list, dated July 28, 1778, of Lincoln men mustered into Rhode Island service, agreeable to a resolve of the General Court, to serve until the first day of January, 1779. The list was prepared by James Barrett, muster master for Middlesex County. The details of this service are unknown, but there is a reasonable likelihood that he participated in the Battle of Rhode Island on August 29, 1778.[5]

The identity of this individual has not been discovered.

---

1 *Massachusetts Soldiers and Sailors*, Vol. I, pp. 13, 20, 25; "Treasurer's Accompts," June 10, 1779; Pension Record # S5224. The town paid his father, Lt. Joseph Abbot, for this service.

Although Jackson's Regiment is credited with having fought at Monmouth, it is possible that Nehemiah Abbot may already have been sent to Rhode Island by the time of the battle. He appears on the April 1778 payroll dated at Providence, in Capt. Lemuel Trescott's Company, Col. David Henley's Regiment. While it is likely that the payroll was prepared sometime after April 1778, further study would be necessary to place Nehemiah Abbot on the field of battle at Monmouth with any degree of certainty.

2 Wheeler, "Lincoln," in Hurd, Vol. 2, p. 621.

3 *Vital Records of Lincoln*. Also *Lexington Births, Marriages and Deaths*.

4 *Vital Records of Lincoln*; Wheeler, "Lincoln," in Hurd, Vol. 2, p. 621; Biggs, "In Memorium," p. 189. Abbot and Abbot, *Genealogical Register* (p. 154), gives the date of his death as 1840.

5 Blake, "James Barrett's Returns of Men," p. 17. The resolve was dated June 12, 1778; the date of enlistment is unknown.

ADAMS, Abel

Abel Adams of Lincoln was a private in Capt. William Smith's Company of Minute Men from Lincoln, Col. Abijah Peirce's Regiment.[1] He was reimbursed by the town for his cartridge box as a minute man on April 1, 1776.[2]

Following the engagement at Concord, he appears to have served for five days in Cambridge, before enlisting on April 24, 1775, for service with Capt. William Smith's Company, Col. John Nixon's 16th Massachusetts Regiment in the rapidly organizing Provincial Army of Massachusetts. On May 23, 1775, he appears to have been with Capt. Reuben Dickenson's Company serving on picket guard under Maj. Loammi Baldwin. Presumably, this was temporary duty, and he was back serving with Captain Smith's Company during the Battle of Bunker Hill on June 17, 1775. He served again with Major Baldwin on July 16, 1775, on main guard. He served at Cambridge at least through September 30, 1775.[3]

Subsequently, he served as a private in Capt. John Hartwell's Company of Militia from Lincoln, Col. Eleazer Brooks's 3rd Middlesex County Regiment, which marched from Lincoln to fortify Dorchester Heights on March 4, 1776. The unit was discharged five days later, on March 9, after the threat of a British attack on the fortifications had subsided, and General Howe opted instead to evacuate Boston.[4]

He marched to Bennington, then to Ticonderoga on August 28, 1776, as a private in Capt. Zachariah Fitch's Company, Col. Samuel Brewer's Massachusetts Militia Regiment, which had been formed for the Ticonderoga service. He appears to have served into December 1776.[5]

He was recruited out of the Lincoln Militia Company on August 14, 1777, and was sent to reinforce the Northern Army under General Gates, in the face of continuing advances by Burgoyne. He served as a corporal in Capt. George Minot's Company, Col. Samuel Bullard's Middlesex County Regiment (Brig. Gen. Jonathan Warner's Brigade of Massachusetts Militia) from August 16, 1777, to November 30, 1777 (credited with 3 months 25 days of service), and he was present at the surrender of Burgoyne on October 17, 1777. He was paid by the town for this service.[6]

---

1 Coburn, *Muster Rolls*.
2 "Treasurer's Accompts," April 1, 1776; paid to his father, John Adams (q.v.).
3 *Massachusetts Soldiers and Sailors*, Vol. I, pp. 34, 84. In August, Colonel Nixon's 16th Massachusetts Regiment became known as the 5th Regiment under Washington's Continental command.
4 Hartwell, "A List of a Company of Militia"; *Massachusetts Soldiers and Sailors*, Vol. I, p. 34.
5 *Massachusetts Soldiers and Sailors*, Vol. I, pp. 34, 84; Green, *Groton During the Revolution*, pp. 52–65. An identical record in *Massachusetts Soldiers and Sailors* for Amos Addams suggests initially the likelihood of parallel service by Abel Adams and Amos Addams of Lincoln. However, the Amos Adams in the identical record is identifiable from pension records as from Pepperell, not Lincoln. The Abel Adams of this record, on the other hand, does appear to be from Lincoln, as his mileage reimbursement (Green, *Groton During the Revolution*, p. 53) was identical to that for Abijah Mead (q.v.), Zebediah Farrar (q.v.), and Daniel Billing (q.v.), and substantially different from that for Amos Adams of Pepperell. See Amos Adams (q.v.), note 3, p. 179.

Further, although *Massachusetts Soldiers and Sailors* documents service only until September 30, 1776, Green shows pay records into November and December. This conforms with resolves for Ticonderoga service running to December 31, 1776, and with the logic that Colonel Brewer's Regiment would not have been discharged prematurely in the face of the continuing threat of an attack on Ticonderoga by British General Carleton late into the fall of 1776.
6 "Treasurer's Accompts," Nov. 11, 1779; *Massachusetts Soldiers and Sailors*, Vol. I, p. 34.

He could be the Abel Adams who was commissioned on July 6, 1780, as a second lieutenant of the Massachusetts Militia, serving in Capt. Benjamin Fletcher's 1st Company, 7th Middlesex County Regiment, and who later appears as a lieutenant in Capt. Asa Drury's Company, Col. William Turner's Regiment from August 1, 1781, to December 1, 1781 (credited with 4 months, 4 days of service) on an alarm at Rhode Island. However, this is uncertain.[1]

He was age 18 on April 19, 1775; the son of John Adams (q.v.) and Lucy (Hubburd or Hubbart) Adams of Lincoln; brother of Edward Adams (q.v.), Bulkley Adams (q.v.), and John Adams, Jr. (q.v.). He married Rebecca Jones of Concord in 1786 and moved to Mason, New Hampshire. After she died, he married Mary Edwards of Sudbury in 1818 at Framingham. He died in 1826, either in Framingham or in Mason, New Hampshire.[2]

ADAMS, Amos

Amos Adams of Lincoln enlisted under a resolve of December 2, 1780, for three years of service in the Continental Army. He appears to have entered the service on February 15, 1781. He is described as age 30; five feet, six inches in height; dark complexion and dark eyes and hair. His occupation is listed as farmer.[3]

He was age 25 when the war broke out. He was the son of John Adams, Jr., and Elisabeth (Shaw) Adams; brother of Asa Adams (q.v.). He was also the brother-in-law of Nathaniel Gove (q.v.).[4]

ADAMS, Asa

Asa Adams of Lincoln (also of Concord) served as a fifer in Capt. Edmund Bemis's Company, Col. Asa Whitcomb's Regiment, probably around Cambridge during the Siege of Boston in 1775. He enlisted shortly after the war broke out, evidently on May 8, 1775, although he may have been in service as early as April 30. He may have participated in the Battle of Bunker Hill on June 17, 1775. He served at least until September 11, 1775, but he also appears on records dated October 4, 1775, and November 25, 1775, suggesting the likelihood that he served a full eight-month term.[5]

---

1 *Massachusetts Soldiers and Sailors*, Vol. I, pp. 34, 84.
2 *Vital Records of Lincoln*; *Concord, Massachusetts: Births, Marriages, and Deaths*; Baldwin, *Vital Records of Framingham*; Wheeler, "Lincoln," in Hurd, Vol. 2, p. 621; Farrar, comp., Excerpts from Adams, p. 4. Wheeler says he died in 1826 in Mason, but Farrar says that he settled in Mason, after which he moved to Framingham, where he died (no date indicated). His 1826 death record in Framingham gives no location, but identifies the source as the First Baptist Church, a strong suggestion that he was living in Framingham at the time.
3 *Massachusetts Soldiers and Sailors*, Vol. I, pp. 36, 84; "Treasurer's Accompts," February 1, 1782; Wheeler, "Lincoln," in Hurd, Vol. 2, p. 621. Actually, he was already 31 by February 1781 (see *Vital Records of Lincoln*). There is a record of an Amos Adams who served from August 23, 1776, to September 30, 1776 (1 month, 9 days of service), as a private in Capt. Zachariah Fitch's Company, Col. Samuel Brewer's Regiment at Ticonderoga. The record is intriguing because of an identical record for an Abel Adams. However, the Amos Adams of this record is identifiable from pension records as being from Pepperell, not Lincoln (see *Massachusetts Soldiers and Sailors*, Vol. I, pp. 36, 84; Pension Record # S18681). See also Abel Adams (q.v.), note 5, p. 178.
4 *Vital Records of Lincoln*; Bond, *Genealogies of the Families of Watertown*, p. 2. His father, John Adams, Jr., is not to be confused with the John Adams, Jr. (q.v.), who marched on the April 19th Alarm and served at the Battle of Bunker Hill.
5 *Massachusetts Soldiers and Sailors*, Vol. I, pp. 37–38. On June 15, 1779, the town paid a John Adams for service at Cambridge in 1775 and for a three-year campaign in the Continental Army. This fits the service record of Asa Adams (inst.) better than it fits the service records of John Adams (q.v.), or John Adams, Jr. (q.v.), or

In 1777, he was recruited into the Continental Army from Suffolk County. He is described as age 19; standing five-feet, six-inches tall; with brown complexion. His occupation is listed as "gentleman soldier." He enlisted on April 25, 1777, for the duration of the war.[1]

He served as a gunner in Capt. Benjamin Frothingham's Company, Col. John Crane's Artillery Regiment. This unit was deployed around Morristown, New Jersey, in 1777; fought at the Battle of Brandywine later that year; and spent the winter of 1777–78 at Valley Forge. In 1778, it may have been engaged at the Battle of Monmouth and perhaps at the Battle of Rhode Island. In January 1780, he appears to have been deployed near Morristown, New Jersey. He is reported to have deserted on May 25, 1780.[2]

He was age 15 when he entered service as a fifer. His age when he became a gunner appears to be overstated by two years. He was the son of John Adams, Jr., and Elisabeth (Shaw) Adams; brother of Amos Adams (q.v.). He was also the brother-in-law of Nathaniel Gove (q.v.).[3]

ADAMS, Bulkley
[also Bulckley]

Bulkley Adams of Weston (also of Lincoln) served as a private in Capt. John Hartwell's Company of Militia from Lincoln, Col. Eleazer Brooks's 3rd Middlesex County Regiment, which marched from Lincoln to fortify Dorchester Heights on March 4, 1776. The unit was discharged five days later, on March 9, after the threat of a British attack on the fortifications had subsided, and General Howe opted instead to evacuate Boston.

Subsequently, he served in Capt. John Hartwell's Company, Col. Nicholas Dike's Regiment for three months, from December 1, 1776, to March 1, 1777, reportedly making cartridges in Boston.

Three times, he responded to Rhode Island alarms. From May 10, 1777, to July 10, 1777, he served in Capt. Jesse Wyman's Company, Col. Josiah Whitney's Regiment at Point Judith (credited with 2 months, 9 days of service).

A year later, he went to Rhode Island in Capt. Francis Brown's Company, Col. William McIntosh's Regiment (Brig. Gen. Solomon Lovell's Brigade of Massachusetts Militia) from August 1, 1778, to Sept. 11, 1778 (credited with 1 month, 14 days of service), and he participated in the Battle of Rhode Island on August 29, 1778.

---

any of the sons of John Adams (q.v.). Therefore, the author concludes that the John Adams in this payment record was John Adams, Jr., the father of Asa Adams, who was away in his Continental service at the time of the transaction (see "Treasurer's Accompts," June 15, 1779). Asa's father, John Adams, Jr., is not to be confused with John Adams, Jr. (q.v.), or with John Adams (q.v.).

Quintal, *Patriots of Color* (p. 155), places Capt. James Burt's Company of Col. Asa Whitcomb's Regiment at the Battle of Bunker Hill. Accordingly, it is likely that Capt. Edmund Bemis's Company also participated in the battle, but the author has been unable to confirm this.

1 Ibid. Also Wheeler, "Lincoln," in Hurd, Vol. 2, p. 621. Actually, he was only age 17 in April 1777 (see *Vital Records of Lincoln*). The town appears to have paid his father, John Adams, Jr., for this Continental service as well as his Cambridge service (see "Treasurer's Accompts," June 15, 1779).

2 Ibid.

3 *Vital Records of Lincoln*; Bond, *Genealogies of the Families of Watertown*, p. 2. His father, John Adams, Jr., is not to be confused with the John Adams, Jr. (q.v.), who marched on the April 19th Alarm and served at the Battle of Bunker Hill.

He returned to Rhode Island a third time, from July 28, 1780, to August 7, 1780, in Capt. Lawson Buckminster's 2nd Company, Col. Abner Perry's Regiment (credited with 14 days of service).[1]

He was age 16 (a few days shy of turning 17) when he marched to Dorchester Heights. He was the son of John Adams (q.v.) and Lucy (Hubburd or Hubbart) Adams; brother of Edward Adams (q.v.), Abel Adams (q.v.), and John Adams, Jr. (q.v.). After the war, he served for a time as an innkeeper (c. 1784–1790), started a tannery (sometime after 1785), and later (c. 1793–1796) built Lincoln's first brick house (arguably the most fashionable house in Lincoln at the time). He married Persis Stone of Framingham in 1785, and after she died in 1797 he married Anna Harrington in 1798. He died in 1827 at age 68, and he is buried in Lincoln in the Meeting House Cemetery behind Bemis Hall.[2]

ADAMS, Edward

Edward Adams (originally of Lincoln) was living in Mason, New Hampshire, when he marched on the Alarm of April 19th. He served for one month at Cambridge as a private in Capt. Obadiah Parker's Company of Minute Men.

After his service at Cambridge, he returned to Lincoln. In September 1775, he enlisted as a private in Capt. William Smith's Company, Col. John Nixon's 5th Massachusetts Regiment, for one month as a substitute for Joseph Peirce (q.v.). Upon the completion of this service in October, he immediately reenlisted in the same unit and served as a sergeant for three months as a substitute for Sgt. Elijah Willington (q.v.); he then remained in service for another month as a sergeant in the same unit. Then, at the request of Colonel Nixon, he volunteered with twenty others for three-month's duty under Lieutenant Walker, chopping wood for the army at Wood End, near Woburn.[3]

He served as a private in Capt. John Hartwell's Company of Militia from Lincoln, Col. Eleazer Brooks's 3rd Middlesex County Regiment, which marched from Lincoln to fortify Dorchester Heights on March 4, 1776. The unit was discharged five days later, on March 9, after the threat of a British attack on the fortifications had subsided, and General Howe had chosen to evacuate Boston.[4]

---

1 *Massachusetts Soldiers and Sailors*, Vol. I, pp. 40, 84. Wheeler, "Lincoln" (in Hurd, Vol. 2, p. 621), indicates he was in Rhode Island in 1779, but this does not conform to the existing records of service.

2 *Vital Records of Lincoln*; *Concord, Massachusetts: Births, Marriages, and Deaths*; MacLean, *A Rich Harvest*, pp. 346, 350; Biggs, "In Memorium," p. 156. Anna's possible relationship to Daniel Harrington (q.v.) is undiscovered.

3 Pension Record # W20567. The timing of all this does not quite fit with his Dorchester Heights service. According to the pension testimony, he was in constant service from September 1775 through April 1776, without a break for Dorchester Heights (see note 4). By misstating the dates of his naval service (see note 1, p. 183), he strings together a narrative of continuous service from September 1775 through July 1776.

The author finds the detail in this sequence of service stints somewhat self-serving. The date of his pension application was 1833. Eligibility under the pension act of 1832 required six months of service, and pension benefits increased with the length of service (up to two years, which qualified for full pay). The imprecision of the service stints claimed in the pension declaration—and the mismatch between pension claims and the service records—suggests that the pension declaration may have been written with an eye toward maximizing pension benefits more than for a precise and accurate detailing of his war service.

4 Hartwell, "A List of a Company of Militia"; *Massachusetts Soldiers and Sailors*, Vol. I, pp. 43–44, 89. Curiously, he fails to mention this service in his pension declaration. The possibility that there might be a second Edward Adams does not seem to be borne out by the Vital Records of the nearby towns, so the author concludes that this must be the same individual. Quite possibly, Dorchester Heights represented an unnecessary or

Lincoln native Edward Adams was living in New Hampshire when the war began. In his pension declaration, he testifies to having served in 1775 as a substitute for Joseph Peirce of Lincoln, then as a substitute for Sgt. Elijah Willington of Lincoln. (National Archives)

Subsequently, he served as corporal in Capt. John Hartwell's Company, Col. Nicholas Dike's Regiment for 2½ months, from December 14, 1776, to March 1, 1777.[1]

---

troublesome complication in stringing together his narrative of continuous service from September 1775 through July 1776 (see note 3 on p. 181, and note 1 on p. 183). Or, giving him the benefit of the doubt, perhaps the omission is more properly explained as the flawed recollection of a 79-year-old in the last years of his life.

1 *Massachusetts Soldiers and Sailors*, Vol. I, pp. 43–44, 89; Pension Record # W20567.

Chapter 10: The Army of the Revolution

In June 1777, he went to sea as a privateer in the brigantine *Wilkes*, under the command of Capt. John Foster Williams and Lt. Samuel Laha. The *Wilkes* carried 14 guns. Edward Adams served as a bombardier. After about three months at sea, the *Wilkes* encountered three British frigates, one of whom, the *Milford* with 32 guns, gave chase. After a sixteen-hour chase into the evening hours, the *Wilkes* was badly beaten up and was run up onto the beach at Chatham. Several of the men were killed in the action, and others drowned. Those that escaped did so in barges and by swimming. The *Wilkes* was burned by the British before departing.[1]

Shortly after this, he was drafted out of the Lincoln Militia Company and urgently marched north on September 29, 1777, to reinforce the Northern Army under General Gates. He served 1 month, 10 days as a private in Capt. Samuel Farrar, Jr.'s Company, Col. Jonathan Reed's Middlesex County Regiment (Brig. Gen. James Bricket's Brigade of Massachusetts Militia). In his pension application, he says they marched to Bennington, Saratoga, and Stillwater and were present at the taking of Burgoyne. He was discharged on November 7, 1777, after escorting Burgoyne's captured troops to Cambridge.[2]

He was age 22 when he marched on the Alarm of April 19th. He was the son of John Adams (q.v.) and Lucy (Hubburd or Hubbart) Adams; brother of Abel Adams (q.v.), Bulkley Adams (q.v.), and John Adams, Jr. (q.v.).

After his war service, he moved back to Mason, New Hampshire. He married Patty Barret of Weston in 1779, and then moved to Templeton, Massachusetts. Subsequently, he moved to Alstead, New Hampshire, then to Concord, Vermont, where he lived for about 25 years, and where he died in 1834 at age 81.[3]

---

1 Pension Record # W20567. His pension declaration gives the dates of this service as running from May 1776 (at the conclusion of his wood-chopping detail) for three months, forming part of the continuous service discussed in note 3 on p. 181. In reality, the *Wilkes* was not commissioned until June 23, 1777 (see *Massachusetts Soldiers and Sailors*, Vol. XVII, p. 455, "Williams, John Foster").

   Officially, the *Milford* carried 28 guns, although various historical accounts run as high as 36 (see "Ships Built at Milford Shipyard").

2 *Massachusetts Soldiers and Sailors*, Vol. I, pp. 43–44, 89; Pension Record # W20567. The pension declaration mistakenly places Capt. Samuel Farrar, Jr.'s Company in Col. Francis Faulkner's Regiment. Faulkner at this time was lieutenant colonel of Col. Eleazer Brooks's 3rd Middlesex Militia Regiment, out of which Capt. Samuel Farrar, Jr.'s Company was formed for detached duty at Saratoga. Faulkner became colonel of the regiment upon Brooks's promotion to brigadier general in October 1778.

3 *Vital Records of Lincoln*; *Concord, Massachusetts: Births, Marriages, and Deaths*; *Town of Weston, Births, Deaths, & Marriages*; Pension Record # W20567. Farrar, "Adams Genealogy," p. 4, gives his wife's name as Martha Burrett, and it notes that five children of Edward and Martha are recorded in Lincoln, through 1788, then four more in Alstead. However, no such birth records are found in *Vital Records of Lincoln* (nor Weston, Templeton, or Mason Vital Records). Edward's age at the time of his death is given as 82 in Farrar, comp., *Excerpts from Adams* (p. 5), but this is inconsistent with his birth record. If his birth record and the date of his death given in Farrar, comp., *Excerpts from Adams* are both correct, he was age 81, which conforms to the information in his pension declaration (Pension Record # W20567).

ADAMS, James

James Adams of Lincoln was in arms at Concord on April 19, 1775, probably as a member of the militia company from Lincoln.[1]

He went to Dorchester Heights as a private in Capt. John Hartwell's Company of Militia from Lincoln, Col. Eleazer Brooks's 3rd Middlesex County Regiment, which marched from Lincoln on March 4, 1776. The unit was discharged five days later, on March 9, but he served only three days.[2] The fact that his wife was eight months pregnant at the time, and that she would have had her hands full with seven other children (ages 3 to 19, of whom five were under age 10), may possibly explain his abbreviated stay at Dorchester Heights.

Following the birth of his daughter a month later, he may possibly have served on the relief expedition to Canada. However, it is not clear whether it was he or his son, James Adams, Jr. (q.v.), who provided this service.[3]

---

1 Deposition of James Adams. A corrupted version of this deposition identifies James Adams as being from Lexington. This error appears to have originated in a June 1, 1775, printing of the depositions in the *New England Chronicle*, and it was repeated in Peter Force's *American Archives*. The deposition as originally published by Isaiah Thomas of Worcester, in May 1775, by order of the Provincial Congress (republished by the state in 1838 as part of the *Journals of Each Provincial Congress;* a copy of which is found in Sawtell, *The Nineteenth of April*), correctly identifies him as from Lincoln, as does Shattuck's copy of the depositions in an appendix to his *History of Concord* (1835). There does not appear to have been a James Adams from Lexington who could logically have been the deponent. [A remotely possible exception is an isolated reference found in *Lexington Births, Marriages and Deaths* to a James Adams, son of John and Ruth, who died August 24, 1776, but with no further information about his age or his parents' ages or identities; the author surmises that this is probably a minor child. No other evidence has been found of anyone from Lexington being in arms at Concord that morning.]

The record does not identify this individual as James Adams (inst.) or James Adams, Jr. (q.v.). At age 16, James Jr. was old enough to have been in arms at Concord. However, the likelihood that a 16-year-old could have been misidentified as "of lawful age" for the deposition is highly remote. Therefore, the conclusion is that the deponent must have been James Adams (inst.).

Co-deponent Bradbury Robinson was a Concord minute man (Capt. David Brown's Company), identified by Cutter, *Historic Homes of Middlesex County* (Vol. IV, p. 1536) as age 24 and the brother of Keen Robinson (q.v.). Co-deponent Thaddeus Bancroft was a Concord minute man (Capt. Charles Miles's Company), but he is otherwise unidentified. Co-deponent Samuel Spring is identified only for his August 22, 1779, marriage to a Lidia Roberson (possibly the sister of Bradbury Robinson?). [*Town of Weston, Births, Deaths, & Marriages* contains a Samuel Spring who was age 30 on April 19, 1775 (he married Ruth Mors in 1767, had a son born nine months later, who died at eleven months). This may be the same individual—Ruth may have died during the 1770s, allowing him to marry Lidia—but there is no particular evidence to support this.]

2 Hartwell, "A List of a Company of Militia." Again, the record does not indicate Jr. or Sr. Notwithstanding that Farrar, comp., Excerpts from Adams (p. 4) credits this service to James Jr., the fact that James Jr. makes no mention of this service in his pension declaration (Pension Record # S5231) is evidence that this was probably served by James Sr.

3 "Treasurer's Accompts," June 15, 1779. The town paid a James Adams for service in the campaign to Canada (no date given), New York in 1776, Cambridge in 1777 and 1778, and half of a three-year campaign in the Continental Army. The service at New York in 1776 and at Cambridge in 1777 and 1778 is traceable to James Jr. Whether or not the payment was made to James Jr. or James Sr., it was not uncommon for the town to pay a parent for war service by a son. Unfortunately, the records of Canadian service and Continental service are inconclusive.

It is not clear whether the Canada service might have been part of Col. Benedict Arnold's expedition from September 1775 through the winter and spring 1776, or part of Gen. John Thomas's forces in May 1776, or part of another wave in July 1776. Lincoln presence in Canada in both 1775 and 1776 is evidenced by Ephraim Brooks (q.v.) in 1775, and Daniel Child (q.v.) and Elisha Willington (q.v.) (among others) in 1776. On July 5, 1776, Lincoln's Town Meeting voted to grant £6:6:8, "in addition to what the general Court has given as a bounty," as an "incouragement … to those non Commision officers and Solgers that shall inlist them selves into the present Expedition to Canaday." A May 8, 1778, report to the town shows that seven men

Similarly, he may subsequently have served 18 months in the Continental Army. However, it is not clear whether the Continental service was provided by James Adams (inst.) or by his son, James Jr.[1]

He was age 43 when he went to Concord, the son of Daniel and Elizabeth (Minot) Adams; the uncle of Daniel Brown (q.v.) and Nathan Brown, Jr. (q.v.); and probably the cousin of John Adams (q.v.). He had married his first wife, Kezia Conant, in 1755. She had died ten years later at age 33, leaving him with three children. He had married his second wife, Deliverance Adams of Sudbury, in 1766. Of his fifteen children (from both wives), ten children survived into adulthood. He died in 1803 at age 71 and is buried in the Meeting House Cemetery behind Bemis Hall.[2]

ADAMS, James, Jr.

James Adams, Jr., served at New York for two months, from September 27, 1776, to November 16, 1776, as a private in Capt. Simon Hunt's Company, Col. Eleazer Brooks's Middlesex County Regiment of Massachusetts Militia. He marched with his regiment to Horse Neck, possibly to Kingsbridge and possibly to Valentine Hill. He participated in the Battle of White Plains on October 28, 1776, and was discharged at North Castle (credited with 2 months of service, including 11 days for travel home).[3]

---

from Lincoln received a bounty from the town to go to Canada in 1776 (see Shattuck, *History of the Town of Concord*, p. 299; MacLean, *A Rich Harvest*, p. 295).

The fact that James Jr. makes no mention of Canada in his pension declaration (Pension Record # S5231) indicates that this service was very likely provided by James Sr. (inst.). All of the various thrusts into Canada were brutal enough that it is hard to imagine that James Jr. would have failed to mention it had he served on one of them. Furthermore, the dates of the relief expeditions to Canada in 1776 overlap with the dates of James Jr.'s New York service in 1776. The only ways to reconcile the conflict of dates would be to place James Jr. on Arnold's 1775 expedition or to suggest that his service on one of the 1776 relief campaigns was truncated for some reason (see Jeduthan Bemis (q.v.)), but there is no evidence to indicate either of these.

James Sr. had no other sons of service age; nor is there any record of his owning any slaves. This supports the likelihood that it was James Sr. who served at Canada. On the other hand, the Canadian relief expedition was a brutal five-month campaign, and the possible explanation for James Sr.'s truncated service at Dorchester Heights may argue against the likelihood of his having gone to Canada shortly afterward.

1 "Treasurer's Accompts," June 15, 1779. Unfortunately, the record of who provided this service is inconclusive (see note 3, p. 184). James Adams (inst.) was age 44 and reasonably well established at this time, living with his second wife, Deliverance ("Delia") and eight children (including James Jr.), ages newborn to 19 years. Another child would be born during the time period in which this service would have occurred, and then another two would arrive before the end of the war. This would be sufficient logic to attribute this service to James Jr. rather than James Sr. However, there is a problem reconciling the probable dates of the Continental service with James Jr.'s service at New York, Cambridge, and Rhode Island. Notwithstanding James Sr.'s domestic circumstances, the author believes it likely that he may indeed have provided this service (see note 1, p. 187).

2 *Vital Records of Lincoln*; *Vital Records of Sudbury*; Farrar, "Adams Genealogy," p. 1; Biggs, "In Memorium," p. 154.

3 "Treasurer's Accompts," June 15, 1779; *Massachusetts Soldiers and Sailors*, Vol. I, pp. 49, 85, 89; Pension Record # S5231. Colonel Brooks's Regiment was made up of Middlesex County militiamen detached from their home units for this service. Horse Neck is in Greenwich, Connecticut; Kingsbridge is in the Bronx, near the northern tip of Manhattan; Valentine Hill is in Yonkers, New York. The locations of the regiment have been pieced together from anecdotal reports of different participants.

Notwithstanding the claim of three months of service in Adams's pension declaration, this unit was in service only two months. His pension declaration also says he was near Valentine Hill at the Battle of White Plains. If he was at Valentine Hill, this would have been several days before the battle. Colonel Brooks's Regiment was deployed on Chatterton's Hill during the Battle of White Plains.

Subsequently, he served at Cambridge from November 3, 1777, to April 3, 1778, as a private in Capt. Simon Hunt's Company, Col. Eleazer Brooks's Regiment of Guards, guarding the British and German troops that Burgoyne had surrendered at Saratoga. He may possibly have reenlisted and served additional time, but that is uncertain.[1]

On July 1, 1778, he enlisted and served at Rhode Island as a private in Capt. Joseph Griffith's Company, Col. John Jacobs's Regiment of Light Infantry through January 1, 1779. He says he was encamped about three miles from the north part of the Island when a violent storm blew down most of the tents and damaged both the British and French fleets. This was the beginning of the two week siege, which ended in the Battle of Rhode Island on August 29, 1778. He was evidently on temporary duty with Capt. Nathan Smith's Company in November 1778.[2]

Despite telling family members he would not sign up again, he served at Rhode Island a second time in 1779 as a private in Capt. Samuel Heald's Company, Col. John Jacobs's Regiment of Light Infantry, from September 15, 1779, to November 15, 1779 (credited with 2 months, 4 days of service). He says he marched to Providence, then to Tiverton. Then he crossed to the Island at Howland's Ferry, and "the next day took possession of Newport soon after the British had vacated it." He was discharged at Newport.[3]

James Adams, Jr., was probably age 17 at the time of his service at New York; probably age 19 and 20 when he served at Rhode Island. He was the son of James Adams (q.v.) and Kezia (Conant) Adams. He married Nancy Tarbell of Groton in 1796. After the war he moved to New Hampshire and later became a resident of Cambridge. By 1832, he was living in Boston. He reportedly died in 1842, age 82 or 83.[4]

[There is a slight possibility that he may have served additional stints at Dorchester Heights in 1776, on the campaign to Canada in 1775 or 1776, and in the Continental

---

1 Ibid. His pension declaration says he served nine months, until the prisoners were sent to Europe. This could not be accurate, however, as the prisoners were not sent to Europe after nine months. They were transferred to Virginia after twelve months. Furthermore, after the initial five-month term of service for the guards, the next term of service was three months (for a total of eight months), from the beginning of April through the beginning of July. Also, his pension record does not mention serving guard duty with Captain Hunt and Colonel Brooks, but it says he served in a company with Lieutenant Stearns of Waltham, in a regiment commanded by Colonel Wild of Scituate. The author has been unable to identify either of these individuals, but possibly he may have served under these officers if he reenlisted for a second stint after his five-month service in Captain Hunt's Company, Colonel Brooks's Regiment.

2 *Massachusetts Soldiers and Sailors*, Vol. I, pp. 49, 84, 85, 89; Pension Record # S5231. Also Blake, "James Barrett's Returns of Men," p. 17. Wheeler, "Lincoln" (in Hurd, Vol. 2, p. 621), says this service was for one year, beginning January 1, 1778, but this is inconsistent both with the record of his guard service and the record of his July enlistment. In his pension declaration, he says he served nine months in a regiment commanded by Col. Joseph Durfee of Freetown, and that Governor Hancock commanded the militia. He makes no mention of Capt. Joseph Griffith or Col. John Jacobs, but he does correctly identify Isaac Hartwell (q.v.) as a lieutenant in the company.

3 "Treasurer's Accompts," March 3, 1780. Also *Massachusetts Soldiers and Sailors*, Vol. I, pp. 49, 85, 89; Pension Record # S5231. His pension declaration says this service was for three months. Wheeler, "Lincoln" (in Hurd, Vol. 2, p. 621), says he was in Rhode Island in 1779 and 1780, but the records show this was 1778 and 1779.

4 *Vital Records of Lincoln*; Farrar, "Adams Genealogy," p. 3; Farrar, comp., Excerpts from Adams, p. 4; Pension Record # S5231. Also *Vital Records of Sudbury*. Kezia Conant was the first wife of the elder James Adams. James Jr.'s birth was recorded in Lincoln on January 14, 1759, but in his pension declaration, he gives 1760 as the year of his birth.

Army, but it is more probable that these stints were served by his father, James Adams (q.v.).][1]

ADAMS, Joel

Joel Adams of Lincoln was a private in Capt. William Smith's Company of Minute Men from Lincoln, Col. Abijah Peirce's Regiment.[2] He was reimbursed by the town for a part of a set of accoutrements as a minute man on June 18, 1776.[3]

Following the engagement at Concord, he served for eight days at Cambridge,[4] before enlisting for eight months of service in Capt. William Smith's Company, Col. John Nixon's 16th Massachusetts Regiment in the rapidly organizing Massachusetts Provincial Army. Presumably, he fought with his company at the Battle of Bunker Hill.[5]

Subsequently, he served for 1 month, 28 days as a private in Capt. Asahel Wheeler's Company, Col. John Robinson's Regiment, from February 4, 1776, through the departure of the British forces from Boston.[6]

Lincoln historian William Wheeler reports that he served in Rhode Island in 1779 and 1780, but this is unlikely.[7]

He enlisted again on March 6, 1781 (pursuant to a resolve of December 2, 1780) for a three-year service in the Continental Army. He is described as age 32; standing five-feet, eleven-inches tall; dark complexion, dark eyes, dark hair. His occupation is given as a farmer. He served as a private in Capt. Thomas Prichard's Company, Col. John Greaton's 3rd Massachusetts Regiment, and participated "in a battle near Kingsbridge NY at a place called Round Hill." He reports that he "was never paid for the last year [of service], 1783, as the paymaster went off with the money." He was discharged by General Knox on December 22, 1783, at West Point.[8]

---

1 "Treasurer's Accompts," June 15, 1779; Hartwell, "A List of a Company of Militia"; Pension Record # S5231. Farrar, comp., Excerpts from Adams (p. 4) credits the Dorchester Heights service to James Jr. However, James Jr.'s pension declaration makes no mention of service at Dorchester Heights or Canada, suggesting that it was James Sr. who served both of these stints. Although no dates for the Continental service survive, the payment date suggests that this service would likely have been completed before the end of 1778. There does not appear to be a sufficient window in which to fit the 18 months of Continental service in and around his other stints. (While it is quite possible that his service at New York and Rhode Island could have been considered Continental service, the record indicates that the payment for Continental service was separate and distinct from the payments for Cambridge, New York, and Canada.) This suggests that James Sr. must have provided the Continental service as well.
2 Coburn, *Muster Rolls*.
3 "Treasurer's Accompts," June 18, 1776.
4 *Massachusetts Soldiers and Sailors*, Vol. I, pp. 51, 85.
5 Pension Record # S45495. The pension file makes no mention of the Battle of Bunker Hill, but Capt. William Smith's Company did participate in the battle (without Captain Smith). With the absence of Smith and with the confusion of the day, it may be presumptive to place Smith's entire company on Bunker Hill (or Breed's Hill) during the battle, but there is no particular evidence to suggest otherwise. In August, Colonel Nixon's 16th Massachusetts Regiment became known also as the 5th Regiment under Washington's Continental command.
6 *Massachusetts Soldiers and Sailors*, Vol. I, pp. 51, 85.
7 Wheeler, "Lincoln," in Hurd, Vol. 2, p. 621. The fact that there is no mention of service at Rhode Island in his pension declaration casts doubt on Wheeler's assertion (see Pension Record # S45495); no other confirming record of such Rhode Island service has been found.
8 *Massachusetts Soldiers and Sailors*, Vol. I, pp. 51, 85; Pension Record # S45495. Kingsbridge is in the Bronx, just off the northern tip of Manhattan. The battle near Kingsbridge was a combined French/American operation

He was age 27 on April 19, 1775. He was originally from the town of Mendon, the son of Josiah and Grace (Hagar) Adams who moved from Mendon to Lincoln about 1754. He had married Lucy Whitney of Lincoln (sister of Solomon Whitney, q.v.) in 1772, and thus was the uncle of Leonard Whitney (q.v.) and Silas Whitney (q.v.).[1]

His wife Lucy died in 1777, and he married Rebecca Stratton of Watertown in 1778. Sometime after the war, he became a resident of Sharon, New Hampshire. In ill health and unable to work for a number of years, he sold his farm in 1823 to pay off his debts. He died at Sharon in 1828 at age 79.[2]

ADAMS, John

John Adams of Lincoln was in arms at Concord on April 19, 1775, probably as a member of the militia company from Lincoln.[3]

The identity of this individual is uncertain, but he is most probably the father of Abel Adams (q.v.), Bulkley Adams (q.v.), Edward Adams (q.v.), and John Adams, Jr. (q.v.); and probably the cousin of James Adams (q.v.). If so, he was the son of John and Love (Minott) Adams, age 51 and one of the leading political figures in Lincoln. He had married Lucy Hubburd (also Hubbart) in 1749. He died in 1809 at age 85, and he is buried in the Meeting House Cemetery behind Bemis Hall.[4]

[The town paid a John Adams for service at Cambridge in 1775 and for a three-year campaign in the Continental Army. However, this is probably a different John Adams,

---

on July 2, 1781, to probe the strength of the British fortifications around the outskirts of New York. They found the British defenses stronger than anticipated, and this contributed to Washington's decision to take his forces south, culminating in the victory at Yorktown in October 1781.

1 Wheeler, "Lincoln," in Hurd, Vol. 2, p. 621; *Vital Records of Lincoln*.
2 *Vital Records of Lincoln*; Pension Record # S45495; "Revolutionary Graves of New Hampshire", p. 1. In 1820, he reported living with a wife (unnamed) who was age 69 and "very infirm by reason of a Cancer in her leg," a daughter (unnamed, age 42), and a son (unnamed, age 27) who "has been sick for more than five years" (Pension Record # S45495).
3 Deposition of John Hoar, et al.
4 *Concord, Massachusetts: Births, Marriages, and Deaths*; *Vital Records of Lincoln*; Biggs, "In Memorium," p. 157. There were multiple individuals in Lincoln named John Adams. This putative John Adams had one son who was a minute man from Lincoln, and two sons who were minute men from New Hampshire. The putative identity is loosely supported by an analysis of the probable identities of his co-deponents on the April 23 deposition (Deposition of John Hoar, et al.):
   • Abraham Gearfield (q.v.) was age 27, and the brother-in-law of minute man David Fisk (q.v.).
   • Isaac Parks (q.v.) was age 32, and the brother of minute men Eleazer Parks (q.v.), John Parks (q.v.), and William Parks (q.v.).
   • William Hosmer (q.v.) was age 45, and the father of minute man William Hosmer, Jr. (q.v.).
   • Gregory Stone (q.v.) was age 46, and the father of minute man Gregory Stone, Jr. (q.v.).
   • John Hoar (q.v.) was age 68, and the father of minute man Samuel Hoar (q.v.).
   • Benjamin Munroe (q.v.) was probably age 52, and the father of minute man Abijah Munroe (q.v.).
   • John Whitehead (q.v.) was age (est.) 37, and the brother-in-law of minute man Daniel Harrington (q.v.).
The age range varies from 27 to 68, and all were closely related to minute men (four fathers, two brothers-in-law, and a brother). The putative John Adams fits within this profile.
   Another possible identity, perhaps only slightly less probable, could be the son of John Jr. and Elisabeth (Shaw) Adams, age 26 on April 19, 1775, and the brother of Amos Adams (q.v.) and Asa Adams (q.v.). Except for his being of a suitable age, however, there is no service record for him, and little in the service records of his brothers, to encourage this possible identity.

and the service for which he was paid was most probably provided by his son, Asa Adams (q.v.).]¹

ADAMS, John, Jr.

John Adams of Mason, New Hampshire, marched to Cambridge on the Alarm of April 19, 1775. Reportedly, "he was at meeting at New Ipswich…when the news came that the British were coming, and he went directly off." He served eight months in Capt. Josiah Crosby's Company, Col. James Reed's Regiment, at Winter Hill. He participated in the Battle of Bunker Hill on June 17, 1775. It is reported that "he fired till his gun was so hot he could not hold it, and that his ear lock was cut off by a bull[et]."²

He may possibly be the John Adams who served temporary duty on main guard at Cambridge under Major Baldwin on May 15, 1775, but this is uncertain.³

He may also be the John Adams who served at Ticonderoga during the summer and fall of 1776, in Capt. Asahel Wheeler's Company, Col. Jonathan Reed's Regiment, but this is uncertain.⁴

He was a Lincoln native son, the son of John Adams (q.v.) and Lucy (Hubburd or Hubbart) Adams, age 24 on April 19, 1775, and the brother of Abel Adams (q.v.) (a minute man), Bulkley Adams (q.v.), and Edward Adams (q.v.), all of whom served in the early part of the war. He married Mary (also Molly) Adams of New Ipswich, New Hampshire, in 1777. He died in 1807 in Mason, New Hampshire.⁵

ADAMS (?), [unidentified]

The town paid Capt. Joseph Adams for service at Ticonderoga in 1776, and for one half of a three-year campaign in the Continental Army.⁶

---

1 "Treasurer's Accompts," June 15, 1779. The John Adams of the payment record appears to be John Adams, Jr., father of Asa Adams (q.v.) and Amos Adams (q.v.). He is not to be confused either with the putative John Adams (who was in arms at Concord, but as a well-established town leader and father of four servicemen is not likely himself to have served three years in the Continental Army beginning at age 52 or 53) or with John Adams, Jr. (q.v.). The John Adams, Jr., of the payment record was of a similar age as the putative John Adams and was similarly unlikely to have served these stints. This payment record, however, does fit the service of his son, Asa Adams (q.v.), and does so better than it fits the service of any of the sons of the putative John Adams (none of whom is recorded as having provided three years of Continental service, nor could they have fit such service around their other service engagements). Further, Asa Adams was away in the service when the payment was made, which could explain why his father would have collected his pay.

2 Pension Record # W16093.

3 *Massachusetts Soldiers and Sailors*, Vol. I, p. 85. As this record does not identify his unit or residence, it is impossible to identify which of the several individuals in camp named John Adams served this duty. The fact that he was a New Hampshire soldier would have made no difference in his being assigned guard duty and other camp duties alongside the Massachusetts men; each of the units in camp contributed men for the various duty assignments necessary for operating and maintaining the camp.

4 Sudbury Miscellaneous Records, pay receipts dated September 30, 1776 (Doc. #109), and March 17, 1777 (Doc. # 2209).

5 Pension Record # W16093; *Vital Records of Lincoln*; Farrar, "Adams Genealogy," p. 4. The pension record makes no mention of Lincoln, but all of the pieces fit this identification, including a brother Jonas. Farrar, "Adams Genealogy" contains the notation, "S.A.R." next to his name. His brother, Edward Adams (q.v.), was also resident in Mason when the Alarm came.

6 "Treasurer's Accompts," June 15, 1779.

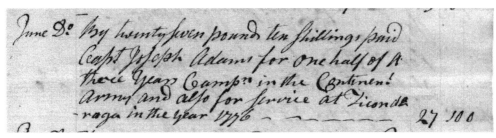

Capt. Joseph Adams was paid by the town of Lincoln for service at Ticonderoga and in the Continental Army, but he probably did not serve either enlistment himself. It is unclear who actually provided this service. (Courtesy of Lincoln Town Archives, Lincoln, MA)

He was one of the town fathers, having been involved in the earlier formation of the town, and having served as Selectman periodically in the early 1770s. He also had served in leadership positions in the Lincoln militia, appearing in town records as coronet in 1760 and as captain in 1766. Joseph Adams continued to be referred to by the honorific title of captain long after he relinquished command to younger individuals. He was age 52 at the time of Ticonderoga, probably 55 by the time he would have finished 1½ years of Continental Army service. Although it is theoretically possible that he could have provided the service for which he was paid, there is little logic in imagining him re-entering the military in his fifties, particularly in a non-leadership role.[1]

It is more likely that this service may have been provided either by his son Charles or by his son Nathan. Both possibilities are speculative, however, as no service record recognizable as belonging to either Charles or Nathan has yet been discovered.

Charles was a doctor, age 25 in 1776. He is often identified as a Tory, and he moved to Halifax after the war, in 1785. The author has found little to substantiate his Tory sentiments, however, and it is plausible to think that he may have gone to Halifax for reasons other than Tory sentiments, or perhaps that he may have served these stints prior to becoming a Tory.

Nathan was age 16 in 1776. Although little is known about his political sentiments, one can almost imagine him enlisting for Ticonderoga service and Continental service expressly to prove his loyalties in the face of his brothers' (real and perhaps perceived) disloyalties. Nathan subsequently married Hannah Soley McCarthy (or McCarty) of Billerica in 1796. He became a tanner, merchant, and auctioneer in Charlestown, where he died in 1830 at age 70.[2]

---

1 *Vital Records of Lincoln*; *Concord, Massachusetts: Births, Marriages, and Deaths*; MacLean, *A Rich Harvest*, p. 138; Farrar, comp., Excerpts from Adams, p. 2. The titles can be found in the birth records of his children, as well as in the treasurer's accounts. See Joseph Adams (q.v., Chapter 12).

2 *Vital Records of Lincoln*; Farrar, "Adams Genealogy," p. 2; Farrar, comp., Excerpts from Adams, p. 4. It was not unusual for the town to make a payment to a parent for service by a son, although in this instance, no corroborating record of service has been found for either son.

Another son, Joseph Jr., also a doctor and age 27 in 1776, can safely be ruled out as a possibility for having provided this service. Dr. Joseph had moved to Townsend several years before, was known to be an outspoken Tory, was arrested and fined at least twice for his loyalty to the Crown, escaped and served in the Royal Navy during the war, and moved to England permanently after the war (see MacLean, *A Rich Harvest*, pp. 204–205, 302–303). See also Joseph Adams, Jr. (q.v., Chapter 11).

Perhaps other possibilities, although probably less likely than Charles or Nathan, might be an unknown servant or slave of Captain Joseph, or Elisha Wheeler (q.v.), who had married Captain Joseph's daughter,

Through their sister Polly (also known as Mary), Charles and Nathan became brothers-in-law to Elisha Wheeler (q.v.) before the war was over.[1]

ALLEN, Phineas
[also ALIN, also Phinehas, Phinnehas]

Phineas Allen was most probably in arms at Concord as a private in Capt. David Brown's Company of Minute Men from Concord, Col. Abijah Peirce's Regiment, but it is not absolutely certain if the "Phineas Alin" appearing on the muster roll for Captain Brown's Company is the same individual as Phineas Allen of Lincoln.[2]

He was paid by the town for service in Boston in 1776, but no record survives of the precise dates of this service or the unit in which it was served.[3]

Subsequently, he served at Cambridge in 1778, detached from Capt. Samuel Farrar's Lincoln Militia Company, Col. Eleazer Brooks's 3rd Middlesex County Regiment to relieve the guards at Cambridge.[4] This duty was guarding the captured British and German soldiers surrendered by Burgoyne the previous fall at Saratoga.

He may possibly be the Phineas Allen appearing on a pay warrant as a private in Capt. John Robinson's Company (regiment not identified) on April 11, 1783, but there is no evidence that this individual is Phineas Allen of Lincoln.[5]

He was age 31 in 1776; the son of Benjamin and Eunice (Gale) Allen. His sister Beulah was married to Joseph Billing (q.v.) and was the mother of Joseph Billing, Jr. (q.v.); his sister Abigail was married to Abraham Wesson (q.v.); his sister Eunice was the mother of Jonathan Tower (q.v.); and his sister Lydia was the mother of John Wheeler (q.v.) and the wife of Benjamin Parks (q.v.). In addition, his brother, Benjamin Allen, Jr., was married to Mary Brown, sister of Nathan Brown, Jr. (q.v.), and Daniel Brown (q.v.).

He had married Abigail Foster in 1769; she had died 14 months later. In September 1775, he married Sarah Danforth. Reportedly three children were born in Lincoln. Sarah's death is not recorded, but he moved to Fitchburg about 1782, and in 1784 he married Dorothy Flagg of Leominster, with whom he had eight more children. He remained in

---

Mary, a few weeks before the payment. This possibility may require a somewhat greater leap of faith, but Joseph might well have been the appropriate surrogate, had Elisha perhaps provided this service and not been available on June 15, 1779, to receive the payment.

A search through Vital Records for surrounding towns to identify other possible interpretations of this record led only to further speculation about individuals who simply could not be contrived to fit the record any better than one of Captain Joseph's sons or his son-in-law. By virtue of their lineal kinship with Capt. Joseph Adams, Charles and Nathan (perhaps also Elisha Wheeler) remain logically the most likely identifiable individuals to have provided the indicated service.

1 *Vital Records of Sudbury; Vital Records of Lincoln.*
2 See Coburn, *Muster Rolls. Concord, Massachusetts: Births, Marriages, and Deaths* reveals no Phineas Alin nor any other individual who could fit this identity. Other individuals named Phineas Allen appear in *Massachusetts Soldiers and Sailors*, but none stand out as obvious candidates for Phineas Alin in Capt. David Brown's Company on April 19, 1775.
3 "Treasurer's Accompts," November 11, 1779.
4 "Treasurer's Accompts," November 11, 1779; *Massachusetts Soldiers and Sailors*, Vol. I, p. 183. The record identifies neither the unit to which he was assigned, nor the dates of service.
5 *Massachusetts Soldiers and Sailors*, Vol. I, p. 183.

Fitchburg until 1826, when he moved in with his son, Abijah, at Smyrna, New York, where he died in 1830.[1]

AVERY, Samuel

Samuel Avery of Lincoln enlisted in the Continental Army, March 10, 1781, for three years. He is described as age 40; standing five-feet, three-inches tall; blue eyes, dark hair, dark complexion. His occupation is given as farmer and housewright.[2]

He is otherwise unidentified.

BACON, Joseph

Joseph Bacon was paid by the town for service at New York in 1776 and 1777. He was probably assigned to Col. Samuel Thatcher's Regiment and marched south on December 16, 1776. This regiment served briefly around New York before being called to New Jersey in January 1777. They were stationed at Woodbridge and participated in the *petite guerre* in the Jerseys in the early months of 1777 before being dismissed to return home in March.[3]

He was the son of Capt. Samuel and Eunice (Bacon) Bacon of Bedford and Lincoln; brother of Noah Bacon (q.v.) and Samuel Bacon (q.v.). He was probably age 25 when he served at New York. He married Patty Rice of Sudbury on November 23, 1779.[4]

BACON, Noah

Noah Bacon served as a private in Capt. John Hartwell's Company of Militia from Lincoln, Col. Eleazer Brooks's 3rd Middlesex County Regiment, which marched from Lincoln to fortify Dorchester Heights on March 4, 1776. The unit was discharged five days later, on March 9, after the threat of a British assault on the fortifications had ended, General Howe having decided to evacuate his troops from Boston.[5]

In 1778, he was detached from Capt. Samuel Farrar's Lincoln Militia Company, Colonel Brooks's 3rd Middlesex County Regiment to relieve the guards at Cambridge,

---

1 *Vital Records of Lincoln*; *Proceedings of the Fitchburg Historical Society*, p. 219. See also MacLean, *A Rich Harvest*, p. 171, and *Town of Weston, Births, Deaths, & Marriages*. Malcolm, *The Scene of Battle* (pp. 50–51), describes him as a "landless farmer," a hired hand living along the Bay Road on the farm of either William Smith (q.v.) or Jacob Foster (q.v.). Abigail Foster was probably the sister of Jacob Foster (q.v.). Phineas was either living with or a neighbor of Jacob Foster, possibly a hired hand, as well as probably his brother-in-law.

Only two children are recorded in Lincoln: Benjamin, son of Phinehas and wife, bp. November 9, 1777; and Dolly, daughter of Phinehas and Abigail, bp. January 27, 1782. Presumably, Benjamin was Sarah's son, and Dolly was baptized as an 11-year-old.

2 *Massachusetts Soldiers and Sailors*, Vol. I, p. 369; "Treasurer's Accompts," October 15, 1781, February 8, 1783.

3 "Treasurer's Accompts," June 15, 1779. No actual record has been found of the unit in which he served. Attribution to Colonel Thatcher's Regiment is a supposition, consistent with records of service for other Lincoln men at this time. The *petite guerre* is David Hackett Fischer's term for the skirmishing that characterized the war in New Jersey following Washington's dramatic victories at Trenton and Princeton (see Fischer, *Washington's Crossing*, pp. 366–367).

4 Wheeler, "Lincoln," in Hurd, Vol. 2, pp. 621–622; *Vital Records of Bedford*; *Vital Records of Sudbury*; *Vital Records of Lincoln*. His parents, Samuel and Eunice, appear to have been living in Lincoln by 1774, when the baptisms of two daughters were recorded in Lincoln.

5 Hartwell, "A List of a Company of Militia"; *Massachusetts Soldiers and Sailors*, Vol. I, p. 421.

from April 2, 1778, to July 3, 1778. He served for 3 months, 2 days in Cambridge as a private in Capt. Daniel Harrington's Company, Col. Jonathan Reed's Regiment of Guards, guarding the British and German soldiers surrendered by Burgoyne at Saratoga the previous fall.[1]

He was the son of Capt. Samuel and Eunice (Bacon) Bacon of Bedford and Lincoln; brother of Joseph Bacon (q.v.) and Samuel Bacon (q.v.). He was age 20 when he marched to Dorchester Heights. He married Mary Brown, sister of Benjamin Brown (q.v.) and Timothy Brown (q.v.), in Weston in 1780 or 1781. By 1785, they were living in Bolton, where three children are recorded, and between 1791 and 1793 they moved to Princeton. After that their whereabouts is unknown.[2]

BACON, Samuel

Samuel Bacon was a private in Capt. John Moore's Bedford Militia Company, which responded to the Alarm of April 19, 1775, and marched to Concord. Following the engagement at Concord, he served for four days at Cambridge.[3]

He was paid by the town of Lincoln for service at New York. This was probably the New York campaign in 1776, and probably for service as a private with Col. Eleazer Brooks's Regiment of Massachusetts Militia, but no date or unit is specified.[4]

He was also paid by the town for service in a campaign at Providence. Again, the dates of service and the units in which he served have not survived.[5]

He was paid by the town for service at Cambridge in 1777 and 1778. Although the details of this service have not survived, this is presumed to be guard duty from November 1777 to April 1778, guarding the Convention Army surrendered by British General Burgoyne at Saratoga on October 17, 1777.[6]

He was the son of Capt. Samuel and Eunice (Bacon) Bacon of Bedford and Lincoln; brother of Joseph Bacon (q.v.) and Noah Bacon (q.v.). He was age 25 when he went to Concord on April 19, 1775. The record of his death has not been found, but he is reportedly buried in the First Church of Christ Congregational Cemetery in Bedford.[7]

---

1 *Massachusetts Soldiers and Sailors*, Vol. I, p. 421; "Treasurer's Accompts," June 15, 1779.
2 Wheeler, "Lincoln," in Hurd, Vol. 2, p. 622; *Vital Records of Bedford*; *Town of Weston, Births, Deaths, & Marriages*; *Vital Records of Lincoln*; *Vital Records of Bolton*; *Vital Records of Princeton*. His parents, Samuel and Eunice, appear to have been living in Lincoln by 1774, when the baptisms of two daughters were recorded in Lincoln. *Vital Records of Lincoln* lists Noah and Mary's marriage intention on January 25, 1781; *Town of Weston, Births, Deaths, & Marriages* lists their marriage on February 7, 1780. A fourth child is recorded in Princeton in 1793.
3 Coburn, *Muster Rolls*; *Massachusetts Soldiers and Sailors*, Vol. I, p. 422.
4 "Treasurer's Accompts," June 15, 1779. Wheeler, "Lincoln" (in Hurd, Vol. 2, p. 622), concurs that this was in 1776.
5 Ibid. Wheeler, "Lincoln" (in Hurd, Vol. 2, p. 622), places him at Rhode Island in 1777 and 1778.
6 "Treasurer's Accompts," June 15, 1779. The Convention Army refers to the British (and German) troops surrendered by Burgoyne at Saratoga who were being kept in Cambridge awaiting repatriation. The term "Convention" was a British euphemism to avoid the stigma of surrender, which Burgoyne cleverly negotiated along with very favorable terms into a Convention Agreement rather than a surrender agreement.
7 Wheeler, "Lincoln," in Hurd, Vol. 2, p. 622; *Vital Records of Bedford*; "Patriot Grave Search"; *SAR Revolutionary War Graves Register*. His parents, Samuel and Eunice, appear to have been living in Lincoln by 1774, when the baptisms of two daughters were recorded in Lincoln.

BAKER, Amos

Amos Baker went to Concord on April 19, 1775, probably as a member of the militia company from Lincoln. He crossed the bridge with the local forces and saw the dead bodies of the two British soldiers left behind. Then, in the confusion that followed in the wake of the fight, he headed back up the hill to Major Buttrick's house, where the bodies of the two Acton casualties had been carried.[1]

He was back in arms ten months later, as a private in Capt. John Hartwell's Militia Company from Lincoln, Col. Eleazer Brooks's 3rd Middlesex County Regiment, which marched from Lincoln to fortify Dorchester Heights on March 4, 1776. The unit was discharged five days later, on March 9, after the threat of a British assault on the fortifications had subsided, General Howe having instead decided to evacuate the British forces from Boston.[2]

Amos Baker was the last surviving participant of the fight at Concord. In his colorful affidavit, recorded just before he died in July 1850, he says, "I verily believe that I felt better that day, take it all the day through, than if I had staid at home." (Courtesy of Concord Free Public Library)

He returned to Dorchester on December 20, 1776, as a sergeant in Capt. Moses Harrington's Company, Col. Nicholas Dike's Regiment, in which unit he served until March 1, 1777. The town paid him for this service.[3]

He is probably the Amos Baker who served as a private in Capt. George Minot's Company, Col. Samuel Bullard's Massachusetts Militia Regiment for 1 month, 24 days, from August 16, 1777, to September 30, 1777, in the Northern Department (Saratoga), although it is not certain that this is the same individual. As he does not appear on the draft list for this service, he probably served as a substitute for one of the draftees.[4]

On November 3, 1777, he was drafted into Capt. Simon Hunt's Company, Col. Eleazer Brooks's Regiment of Guards for five months of service in Cambridge, guarding the British

---

1 Baker Affidavit (1850).

2 Hartwell, "A List of a Company of Militia." The duration of this service may have been too short to warrant a mention in his pension declaration.

3 *Massachusetts Soldiers and Sailors*, Vol. I, p. 468; "Treasurer's Accompts," November 11, 1779; Pension Record # S4922.

4 *Massachusetts Soldiers and Sailors*, Vol. I, p. 468. His failure to mention this service in his pension declaration may suggest that it was served by a different Amos Baker. On the other hand, the only other Amos Baker identified in the service records was from Wrentham, in Norfolk County, and thus outside of the geography and militia command structure (Middlesex County) from which Colonel Bullard's Regiment was drawn. Nor is any other Amos Baker identifiable living at this time in any of the towns in the Middlesex Third District, from which Capt. Minot's company was drawn (Lincoln, Lexington, Weston, Concord, and Acton). See also sidebar, "Facing the Crisis," p. 99.

and German troops surrendered by General Burgoyne at Saratoga. He was discharged on April 3, 1778.[1]

He was the son of Jacob and Grace (Billings) Baker and had just turned 19 on April 19, 1775. His father, Jacob Baker (q.v.); his brothers Jacob Baker, Jr. (q.v.), James Baker (q.v.), Nathaniel Baker (q.v.), and Samuel Baker (q.v.); and his brother-in-law Daniel Hosmer (q.v.), all went to Concord that morning. He was also the cousin of Silas Fay (q.v.).[2]

He married Ame Prescott (also given as Amy and Ama) of Concord in 1785.[3] He died in July 1850, at age 94, just a couple of months after being feted on the 75th Anniversary of the events of April 19, 1775, as the last surviving participant in the fight at Concord's North Bridge. He may be in the Baker tomb in the Meeting House Cemetery behind Bemis Hall.[4]

BAKER, Jacob
[also Jacob Sr.]

Jacob Baker went to Concord on April 19, 1775,[5] possibly as a member of the militia company from Lincoln, or possibly as a private citizen concerned about the well being of his five sons and son-in-law.

Born in Charlestown, he was age 52 on April 19, 1775. He had been married to Grace Billings (also Billing) since 1742, and he was on the muster roll of Lincoln's original militia company in 1757.[6] He was the father of Amos Baker (q.v.), Jacob Baker, Jr. (q.v.), James Baker (q.v.), Nathaniel Baker (q.v.), and Samuel Baker (q.v.), and the father-in-law of Daniel Hosmer (q.v.), all of whom went to Concord that morning. He was also the uncle of Silas Fay (q.v.).

Town records show a payment to Jacob Baker "toward procuring a man for three years service in the Continental Army."[7] There is no particular reason to conclude that he put in any additional service after April 19, 1775.

He is reported to have died in 1783, probably age 61.[8]

---

1 *Massachusetts Soldiers and Sailors*, Vol. I, p. 468. "Treasurer's Accompts," November 11, 1779.
2 Baker Affidavit (1850). See also *Vital Records of Lincoln*.
3 *Vital Records of Lincoln*. A November 1800 marriage between an Amos Baker and Eunice Dudley is found in *Concord, Massachusetts: Births, Marriages, and Deaths*. This appears to be a different Amos Baker, the existence of whom is confirmed in the 1800 Census Record (notwithstanding the Concord marriage record, the census finds him living in Lincoln). Census Records for 1800 and 1810 provide evidence that Ame was still living at this time.
4 *Soldiers and Sailors* [SAR], p. 30, lists him in an SAR marked grave in Lincoln, without identifying which cemetery. *SAR Revolutionary War Graves Register* lists his burial location simply as the Old Cemetery in Lincoln. The presumption of the Baker tomb is the author's, as no other record of him has been found in any of the Lincoln cemeteries.
5 Baker Affidavit (1850).
6 *Vital Records of Sudbury*; *Vital Records of Waltham*; Joslyn, *Vital Records of Charlestown*; Martin, "The Sons of Lincoln," p. 25.
7 "Treasurer's Accompts," June 15, 1779. Hiring another individual to serve in one's stead was a widespread practice, and this is not an unusual entry. Many individuals were paid for some service, and paid for procuring a man for other service. The point of mentioning his having procured a man for service is only to underscore that there appears to be no record of Jacob Sr. being paid for any service of his own.
8 Unpublished notes from Jack MacLean. The author has found no record of his death or burial. Despite the name Jacob Baker on the Baker vault in the Meeting House Cemetery, he is probably not buried there (see p.

Baker Farm (c. 1747–1749, shown here about 1880) was the home of Jacob Baker and his five sons and son-in-law, all of whom answered the Alarm on April 19, 1775. (Farrar, "Houses in Lincoln 100 Years Old")

BAKER, Jacob, Jr.

Jacob Baker, Jr., of Lincoln, was a private in Capt. William Smith's Company of Minute Men from Lincoln, Col. Abijah Peirce's Regiment.[1] Following the alarm of April 19, 1775, he served for four days.[2]

Subsequently, he was paid by the town for "a sixth part of a three years Camp^n in the Continental Army."[3]

He was age 31 on April 19, 1775, the son of Jacob and Grace (Billings) Baker.[4] His father, Jacob Baker, Sr. (q.v.); brothers Amos Baker (q.v.), James Baker (q.v.), Nathaniel Baker (q.v.), Samuel Baker (q.v.); and brother-in-law Daniel Hosmer (q.v.), all went to Concord that morning. He was also the cousin of Silas Fay (q.v.).

He had married Hannah Bell of Concord in 1770. He died in Lincoln in 1810, at age 65. He may be buried in the Baker tomb in the Meeting House Cemetery behind Bemis Hall, but this appears improbable.[5]

197, continuation of note 5 from below).

1 Coburn, *Muster Rolls*.

2 *Massachusetts Soldiers and Sailors*, Vol. I, p. 480.

3 "Treasurer's Accompts," March 3, 1780. There is a record of a Jacob Baker who served as a matross, in Captain Donnell's Company, Col. John Crane's Regiment, from May 9, 1778, through August 13, 1778, at which time he was reported deserted (see *Massachusetts Soldiers and Sailors*, Vol. I, p. 480). However, there is no evidence to indicate whether or not the Jacob Baker in this record is the same individual as Jacob Baker, Jr., of Lincoln (inst.).

4 *Concord, Massachusetts: Births, Marriages, and Deaths*. Lincoln had not yet become a town at the time of his birth.

5 *Vital Records of Lincoln* shows their intent to marry on April 7, 1770. *Concord, Massachusetts: Births, Marriages, and Deaths* shows their marriage on February 28, 1770. Obviously, both cannot be correct. *Vital Records of*

BAKER, James

James Baker of Lincoln was a private in Capt. William Smith's Company of Minute Men from Lincoln, Col. Abijah Peirce's Regiment.[1] He served for five days.[2]

He was age 25 on April 19, 1775, the son of Jacob and Grace (Billings) Baker.[3] His father, Jacob Baker, Sr. (q.v.); brothers Amos Baker (q.v.), Jacob Baker, Jr. (q.v.), Nathaniel Baker (q.v.), Samuel Baker (q.v.); and brother-in-law Daniel Hosmer (q.v.), all went to Concord that morning. He was also the cousin of Silas Fay (q.v.).

He was newly married (1774) to Hepzibah Taylor of Concord. He died in 1833 at age 84 in Concord, where he is buried in the Sleepy Hollow Cemetery.[4]

BAKER, Nathaniel

Nathaniel Baker was a private in Capt. William Smith's Company of Minute Men from Lincoln, Col. Abijah Peirce's Regiment.[5] He was reportedly visiting his girlfriend, Elizabeth Taylor of Concord, at a house she was staying at near the Lexington-Lincoln town line, when he received the alarm from Dr. Samuel Prescott in the early hours of April 19, 1775.[6] He marched to Concord on the alarm, and subsequently served for four days in Cambridge.[7]

He served as a private in Capt. John Hartwell's Company of Militia from Lincoln, Col. Eleazer Brooks's 3rd Middlesex County Regiment which marched from Lincoln to fortify Dorchester Heights on March 4, 1776. The unit was discharged five days later, on March 9, after the threat of a British assault on the fortifications had subsided in the wake of General Howe's decision to evacuate Boston.[8]

He was age 28 on April 19, 1775, the son of Jacob and Grace (Billings) Baker.[9] His father, Jacob Baker, Sr. (q.v.); brothers Amos Baker (q.v.), Jacob Baker, Jr. (q.v.), James Baker (q.v.), and Samuel Baker (q.v.); and brother-in-law Daniel Hosmer (q.v.), all went to Concord that morning. He was the cousin of Silas Fay (q.v.).

He married Elizabeth Taylor in February 1776. He died in Lincoln in 1838 at age 92.[10]

Lincoln lists his age at death as 66, but if his birth record and date of death are correct, he had not yet reached his 66th birthday.

The Baker tomb is identified as Jacob and James Baker, 1834. If either Jacob Jr. or Sr. is there, however, he would have to have been moved there, as both died many years before the tomb was built. Two other individuals named Jacob Baker may be more likely possibilities: Jacob Jr. (inst.) had a son Jacob, born in 1771; and a nephew Jacob, son of Nathaniel Baker (q.v.), born in 1784.

1 Coburn, *Muster Rolls*.
2 *Massachusetts Soldiers and Sailors*, Vol. I, p. 480.
3 *Vital Records of Lincoln*.
4 *Vital Records of Lincoln*; *Concord, Massachusetts: Births, Marriages, and Deaths*; "Find A Grave."
5 Coburn, *Muster Rolls*.
6 Baker Affidavit (1850).
7 *Massachusetts Soldiers and Sailors*, Vol. I, p. 492.
8 Hartwell, "A List of a Company of Militia."
9 *Concord, Massachusetts: Births, Marriages, and Deaths*. Lincoln had not yet become a town at the time of his birth.
10 *Vital Records of Lincoln. Concord, Massachusetts: Births, Marriages, and Deaths* indicates that Nathaniel Baker and Elizabeth Taylor were married in February 1775. The Lincoln record, containing both a (public) marriage intention and a (private) entry from the family Bible, is fundamentally more believable than the Concord

BAKER, Samuel

Samuel Baker of Lincoln went to Concord on April 19, 1775,[1] probably as a member of the militia company from Lincoln.

Subsequently, he served for 1 month, 28 days as a private in Capt. Asahel Wheeler's Company, Col. John Robinson's Regiment, in Roxbury, from February 4, 1776, through the departure of the British forces from Boston.

He was paid by the town of Lincoln for service at Cambridge in 1776.[2]

He appears to have served at Ticonderoga through November 1776, in Capt. Asahel Wheeler's Company, Col. Jonathan Reed's Regiment.[3]

He served as a corporal in Capt. Moses Harrington's Company, Col. Nicholas Dike's Regiment from December 20, 1776, to March 1, 1777, at Dorchester. He was paid by the town of Lincoln for this service.[4]

On August 14, 1777, he was detached from Capt. Samuel Farrar's Lincoln Militia Company, Col. Eleazer Brooks's 3rd Middlesex County Regiment, and sent to reinforce the Northern Department under General Gates. As a member of Capt. George Minot's Company, Col. Samuel Bullard's Regiment from August 16, 1777, to November 30, 1777, he served 3 months, 25 days in the Saratoga campaign, through the surrender of General Burgoyne. Town records confirm that he was paid for service at Saratoga in 1777.[5]

He was age 23 on April 19, 1775, the son of Jacob and Grace (Billings) Baker.[6] His father, Jacob Baker, Sr. (q.v.); brothers Amos Baker (q.v.), Jacob Baker, Jr. (q.v.), James Baker (q.v.), and Nathaniel Baker (q.v.); and brother-in-law Daniel Hosmer (q.v.), all went to Concord that morning. He was the cousin of Silas Fay (q.v.).

Little is known about his life after his war service. At some point in time, he went north. He also appears to have married a woman named Betsy. He died at Enosburg, Vermont, in 1828, age 75 or 76, and is buried in the Enosburg Center Congregational Cemetery.[7]

BALEY, Samuel
[also BAILEY]

Samuel Baley appears on a list of men enlisted into the Continental Army from Middlesex County (no year is indicated), and this enlistment was credited to the town of Lincoln.[8]

---

    record (which can be explained logically as a recording error). Another discrepancy exists in the recorded marriage date of Jacob Baker, Jr. (q.v.), and Hannah Bell (see note 5 on p. 196).

    It is presumed that he may have been buried in the Baker tomb in the Meeting House Cemetery behind Bemis Hall. However, no record of this has been found.

1 Baker Affidavit (1850).
2 "Treasurer's Accompts," November 11, 1779. It is not clear whether Cambridge refers unspecifically to his service around Boston (and thus would apply to his Roxbury service with Colonel Robinson), or specifically to Cambridge (in which case it must necessarily be for another service stint in Cambridge between April and December. Both interpretations can be inferred from the character of other payment records.
3 Pay receipt, December 16, 1776, Sudbury Miscellaneous Records, Doc. # 2204.
4 *Massachusetts Soldiers and Sailors*, Vol. I, p. 497; "Treasurer's Accompts," November 11, 1779.
5 Ibid.
6 *Vital Records of Lincoln*.
7 Wheeler, "Lincoln," in Hurd, Vol. 2, p. 622; *SAR Revolutionary War Graves Register*.
8 *Massachusetts Soldiers and Sailors*, Vol. I, p. 530.

Reportedly, he was not a Lincoln resident but was recruited from outside of town to fulfill the town's 1777 quota of 26 men to serve three-year terms in the Continental Army.[1]

He also appears on a list, dated June 23, 1778, of "nine months men" from "Westown," mustered presumably to support the Continental Army in the Hudson Highlands.[2]

Nothing more is known about him or his service.

BARRETT, John
[also BARRET, BARROT]

John Barrett marched on the Alarm of April 19th, probably as a private in Capt. Oliver Bates's Westford Militia Company, Col. James Prescott's Regiment. He pursued the British to Charlestown, serving for 12 days. Then he enlisted for eight months of service at Cambridge in the rapidly forming Massachusetts Provincial Army. After having served for one month, he recalled years later, "my mother being sick and my presence being necessary at home I found a substitute."[3]

Subsequently, he enlisted again and served at Hull for six months.[4]

He served for three months at New York with Capt. John Bridge's Company, Col. Samuel Thatcher's Regiment. They were ordered to march to Fairfield, Connecticut, on or before December 16, 1776, and served in the New York area. In January 1777, they were ordered to New Jersey and served at Woodbridge into March 1777.[5]

He served at Rhode Island, under Continental Gen. John Sullivan, as a corporal in Capt. Jesse Wyman's Company, Col. Josiah Whitney's Regiment, from his arrival on May 10, 1777, to July 10, 1777. He was discharged at Point Judith, credited with 2 months, 9 days of service (including travel to and from Rhode Island). The service record identifies him as a Lincoln person.[6]

Agreeable to the resolve of June 9, 1779, he enlisted on August 1, 1779, for nine months of service as a private in the Continental Army. He marched to Springfield, then to West Point, where he joined Captain Dix's Company, Colonel Wesson's 9th Regiment. He served for nine months and was discharged May 1, 1780. He is described as age 22 years; five feet, seven inches in stature; light complexion, and a resident of Lincoln. He may have served temporary duty at Claverack with Capt. Joseph Shed's Company, Col. Jacob Gerrish's 1st Regiment from October 18, 1779, to December 2, 1779 (1 month, 14 days), but this appears unlikely.[7]

---

1 Wheeler, "Lincoln," in Hurd, Vol. 2, p. 620.
2 Blake, "James Barrett's Returns of Men," p. 16. This record would appear to contradict Wheeler's crediting him with a three-year term beginning in 1777. There are a number of different individuals named Samuel Baley evident in *Massachusetts Soldiers and Sailors*; quite possibly Samuel Baley of "Westown" may be a different individual from Samuel Baley who served to the credit of Lincoln. Or possibly the records may reflect different enlistments for the same Samuel Baley.
3 Coburn, *Muster Rolls*, p. 37; *Massachusetts Soldiers and Sailors*, Vol. I, p. 693; quotation from Pension Record # R562.
4 Ibid.
5 Pension Record # R562. He recalls in the pension record that this was Colonel How's Regiment, but other records indicate that Cyprian How was lieutenant colonel of the regiment and not in command (see *Massachusetts Soldiers and Sailors*, Vol. II, p. 486, and Vol. VIII, p. 329).
6 *Massachusetts Soldiers and Sailors*, Vol. I, pp. 674, 675, 680; Pension Record # R562.
7 Ibid. As he was already in service in the Hudson Valley when Colonel Gerrish's regiment was raised (in Suffolk and Essex Counties, then discharged after short service), the Claverack duty may refer to a different John Barrett.

Town records show only that he was paid "for service done in the war."[1]

He was the son of Nathaniel and Martha Barret of Westford, age 18 at the time of the April 19th Alarm. He appears to have moved to Lincoln in 1776 or 1777. After his war service, he moved to Mason, New Hampshire (probably in 1781 or 1782), where he married Susanna Chambers in 1782. He was a cooper by trade. In 1818, he was a resident of Fairfield, Maine, in poor health, and unable to earn a living from his trade. He died in Dover, Maine, in 1837 at age 80.[2]

BARTER, John

John Barter served in Capt. Abijah Child's Company, Col. John Greaton's 2nd Regiment. He was mustered by Colonel Barrett, and his service was credited to the town of Lincoln. He was reportedly transferred by prior enlistment to Colonel Cilley's Regiment. The record shows that Capt. Abijah Child's Company, Col. John Greaton's 2nd Regiment was deployed at or around Albany in February 1778. It is not clear, however, whether John Barter's transfer to Colonel Cilley's Regiment occurred before or after the deployment of Captain Child's Company to Albany.[3]

His identity is undiscovered; it is possible that he is the same individual listed as John Porter (q.v.). It is likely that he may not have been a Lincoln resident, but that he may have been recruited from out of town as one of the 26 men the town was called upon to furnish in 1777 to serve for three years in the Continental Army.[4]

BEMIS, Jeduthan

Jeduthan Bemis of Weston (also given as Lincoln) marched on the alarm of April 19, 1775, as a private in Capt. Samuel Lamson's Militia Company from Weston. He reported later that he killed a British Regular during the ensuing battle.[5] He served for three days. Then on

---

1 "Treasurer's Accompts," February 8, 1781.

2 *Massachusetts Soldiers and Sailors*, Vol. I, pp. 674, 675, 680; Pension Record # R562; *Vital Records of Westford*. If the identification is correct, his father appears to have died in 1773. With five younger brothers and sisters, this may help to explain why his presence was necessary at home when his mother was sick.

   His age is understated by two years in his pension record. This appears to be a simple clerical error, reflecting an 1820 review of his 1818 application.

3 *Massachusetts Soldiers and Sailors*, Vol. I, p. 708, Vol. III, p. 410. He may be the John Bortor who was mustered into service in Capt. Abijah Child's Company, Col. John Greaton's Regiment, and paid a bounty, as reported by James Barrett, muster master for Middlesex County on February 26, 1777, but this is uncertain (see Blake, "James Barrett's Returns of Men," p. 469). See also John Porter (q.v.).

4 No record of him appears in the Vital Records of Lincoln or surrounding towns. For Lincoln's quota in 1777, see Wheeler, "Lincoln," in Hurd, Vol. 2, (p. 620) or Shattuck, *History of the Town of Concord* (p. 300).

   Wheeler does not list John Barter (inst.) among the men recruited from outside Lincoln (actually, Wheeler does not mention John Barter at all). Wheeler does, however, place John Porter (q.v.) among the men recruited from outside Lincoln, despite the fact that Porter's service record clearly shows a Lincoln residency. The author notes the phonetic similarity of Barter and Porter, and ponders the possibility that Wheeler may have mistaken John Porter for John Barter. Another possibility is that Barter may be a spelling corruption of Porter; that perhaps spelling irregularities may have created the appearance of different individuals when they may in fact have been the same individual. The possibility that John Barter and John Porter could be the same individual does not resolve the question of Lincoln residency, however. See John Porter (q.v.).

5 *Massachusetts Soldiers and Sailors*, Vol. I, pp. 926, 932; Pension Record # W17283. Samuel Lamson's Company does not appear in Coburn, *Muster Rolls*. Various accounts, however, indicate that Captain Lamson's Company started toward Concord but changed direction and entered the fight at Lincoln or Lexington (see Drake, *History of Middlesex County*, vol. 2, p. 497; Hurd, *History of Middlesex County*, vol. 1, p. 490; Lamson, *History of*

Chapter 10: The Army of the Revolution

April 27, 1775, he enlisted for eight months in the rapidly forming Massachusetts Provincial Army, serving in Capt. Abijah Child's Company, Col. Thomas Gardner's Regiment. He is described as five feet, seven inches in stature. He participated in the Battle of Bunker Hill on June 17, 1775. Colonel Gardner was mortally wounded in the battle, and Lt. Col. William Bond took over command of the regiment.[1]

In December 1775, near the expiration of his term, he reenlisted for a year in Capt. Nailer Hatch's Company, Colonel Bond's Regiment. In April 1776, Colonel Bond's Regiment was sent to reinforce the Northern Army in Canada. In Canada, he appears to have been captured by the British at The Cedars (30 miles upstream from Montreal), and he was released in a prisoner exchange on May 30.[2]

Subsequently, he went to New York as a private in Capt. Simon Hunt's Company, Col. Eleazer Brooks's Middlesex County Regiment of Massachusetts Militia. This unit was in service from September 27, 1776, when they marched to New York, through November 16, 1776, when they were discharged from North Castle, and credited with an additional 11 days of service to cover their march home. The regiment sustained heavy losses at the Battle of White Plains on October 28, and afterward he was reported away from camp, having been sent with the wounded.[3]

Apparently, he was drafted by Capt. Jonathan Fisk out of the Weston Militia Company in 1777, in response to the urgent call for men to support the Northern Army in the Upper Hudson Valley. He served as a private in Capt. George Minot's Company, Col. Samuel Bullard's Regiment from August 16, 1777, to November 30, 1777 (credited with 3 months, 14 days of service), under General Gates at Saratoga. On September 10, he was drafted into the artillery, and served as a matross in Lt. Ebenezer Mattoon's Company, Lt. James Furnivall's detachment until November 29. He fought in the Battle of Saratoga and was present at the surrender of Burgoyne.[4]

Later, agreeable to a resolve of April 20, 1778, he enlisted for Continental service for the term of nine months from the time of his arrival at Fishkill, on July 8, 1778, detached from Capt. Weston's Company, Colonel Brooks's 3rd Middlesex County Militia Regiment. He is described as age 24 years; five feet, seven inches in stature; and a resident of Weston.[5]

---

the town of Weston, pp. 78–79). Mike Ryan (private communication, 2008) says Captain Lamson's Company arrived at Lexington just before Lieutenant Colonel Smith's retreating British column reached the relative safety of Lord Percy's relief column.

1 *Massachusetts Soldiers and Sailors*, Vol. I, pp. 926, 932.
2 Pension Record # W17283. See sidebar, "Two Places at Once?" on p. 202. By mid-June, the Northern Army was pulling out of Canada, and Colonel Bond's Regiment served out its term at Ticonderoga. Colonel Bond died at Ticonderoga in August 1776. Jeduthan Bemis's claim of being discharged in Canada in December is undoubtedly the product of a faded memory.
3 *Massachusetts Soldiers and Sailors*, Vol. I, pp. 926, 932; *Muster Rolls of the Revolutionary War*, Vol. 55, file L, p. 24; Pension Record # W17283. Colonel Brooks's Regiment was made up of Middlesex County militiamen detached from their home units for this service. It is not clear whether his having been sent with the wounded after the Battle of White Plains indicates that he was wounded, or that he went along to assist those who had been wounded.
4 *Massachusetts Soldiers and Sailors*, Vol. I, pp. 926, 932–933; Pension Record # W17283. His pension record claims participation in "the action at Stilwater of the 19th September 1777" (i.e., the first battle at Saratoga), but does not mention the second, decisive battle which took place on October 7. He was undoubtedly on hand, but perhaps he did not participate in the actual fighting. Similarly, he undoubtedly witnessed the surrender ceremony.
5 *Massachusetts Soldiers and Sailors*, Vol. I, pp. 926, 932. Actually, he was age 25 by July 1778 (*Town of Weston, Births, Deaths, & Marriages*; see also Blake, "James Barrett's Returns of Men," p. 16). He makes no mention of this service in his pension declaration.

Two Places at Once?

How could Jeduthan Bemis have served at Canada through the fall of 1776 (discharged, he says, at "the Cedars of Canada" in December 1776), and also have participated in the Battle of White Plains in New York on October 28, 1776? His pension declaration is clear about having served at both places. Yet the incompatibility seems so obvious that one hundred fifty years later, in a 1929 summary of his service, the Acting Commissioner for the pension records dismissed his White Plains claim with the notation, "I did not say anything about the battle of White Plains as the time covered by that he was in the expe[dition] to Canada."

The record of his White Plains service, however, cannot be so easily dismissed. The facts of his service in the New York Campaign, of his being "sent with the wounded" after the battle of White Plains, and of his discharge at North Castle in mid-November, are all well documented.

There is another blatant problem with his pension claim: how is it possible that he could have remained in Canada until December, when the Northern Army was in full retreat by mid-June? The members of the disastrous Canadian expedition served out their terms (through November) at Ticonderoga. Bemis's claim of being discharged at "the Cedars of Canada" in December must undoubtedly be incorrect: he must have been discharged either at Ticonderoga in November or December, or at "the Cedars of Canada" before the collapse of the Canadian campaign. A Ticonderoga discharge would not resolve the conflict, but if the circumstances of an earlier discharge from Canada could be explained, then perhaps it might be possible to resolve the problem that eluded the Acting Commissioner of pension records.

The Cedars was a portage point around a section of rapids in the St. Lawrence River, about 30 miles west of Montreal. In the spring of 1776, as the Americans besieged Quebec, they also retained a tenuous hold on Montreal. In April, to forestall the threat of a combined British and Indian attack on Montreal, 400 Continental troops were sent to The Cedars to build and garrison a stockade fort. Under siege by an enemy force believed to be larger than it was in fact, both the garrison under the command of Maj. Isaac Butterfield and subsequently a 100-man relief force under Maj. Henry Sherborn surrendered on the 18th and 20th of May. A few days later, Benedict Arnold launched a counter-offensive, under the pressure of which a prisoner exchange was negotiated on May 30. By this time, the Canadian campaign was beginning to implode, and shortly afterward, a disorderly exodus from Canada was underway.

If, as Jeduthan Bemis states, he was discharged at "the Cedars of Canada," then this was undoubtedly on May 30, as a consequence of the prisoner exchange, not in December. The pension declaration makes no reference to having been captured, but there is little other rationale for his being discharged at The Cedars. It indicates that he had probably been detached either as part of the garrison at The Cedars, or to the relief force. The terms of the prisoner exchange undoubtedly required that the exchanged prisoners not return to the ranks. They would logically have been discharged to return home. ▶

> Thus, as the rest of the Northern Army staggered back to Ticonderoga, Jeduthan Bemis must have returned home in June, after which he was drafted in September for militia service in the New York campaign. In his pension declaration years later, he evidently remembered being in Canada and returning home in December 1776. Ignoring, overlooking, or forgetting the intervening details, both facts are consistent with his one-year enlistment in Colonel Bond's Regiment in December 1775. But he also remembered the Battle of White Plains. And while ordinarily he could not have been at both places, his misstatement contained the critical piece of information with which to thread together his story, and the particular circumstances of how, in fact, he did serve at both places—just not at the same time.
> [See *Massachusetts Soldiers and Sailors*, Vol. I, pp. 926, 932; *Muster Rolls of the Revolutionary War*, Vol. 55, file L, p. 24; Pension Record # W17283.]

He was back in the Hudson Valley in 1781, credited with 2 months, 22 days service in Capt. John Hayward's company, Colonel Webb's Regiment from September 22, through December 4.[1]

He was age 21 when he marched on the Alarm of April 19, 1775. He was the son of John and Hannah Bemis, born in Weston. He married Polley Stapels of Sudbury in 1780. There is no record in Weston, Lincoln, or Sudbury of any children, or of Polley's death. However, in 1787 he was living in Durham, Connecticut, when he married Statira Squires of Durham. For a while, he made his living as a farmer, but he described himself as a "town pauper" and unable to work when he was pensioned in 1819. He died in Durham in 1828, age 75.[2]

BILLING, Abel
[also BILLINGS]

Abel Billing was living in Sedgewick, Maine, in 1777, where he volunteered and served as a private in Capt. William Reed's Company for 1 month, 10 days from August 19, 1777, to September 28, 1777. He marched to Machias by order of Col. Jonathan Buck, to protect the town which had previously been taken and partly burned by the British.

He was a Lincoln native, and by 1779 he was back in Lincoln, where he enlisted for a three-month term, starting on October 23, 1779. Service records show that he served as a private in Capt. Joshua Walker's Company, Col. Samuel Denny's Regiment, detached to reinforce the Continental Army, and that he marched to Claverack, New York. His pension record, on the other hand, says that he served in Captain Butters's Company, Colonel Buttrick's Regiment, and marched from Concord to Albany, then to Schenectady, where they

---

1 *Massachusetts Soldiers and Sailors*, Vol. I, p. 933. He makes no mention of this service in his pension declaration.
2 *Town of Weston, Births, Deaths, & Marriages*; Pension Record # W17283. His connection with Lincoln is not well defined. His uncle, Abraham Bemis, appears to have been living in Lincoln with ten children, who were Jeduthan's cousins (see Farrar, Notes relating to Bemis Family, and Bond, *Genealogies of the Families of Watertown*, pp. 21, 23). He may also have worked transiently in Lincoln.

remained for four weeks. From Schenectady, they returned to Albany, where he was discharged in December, having served six weeks.[1]

Pursuant to a resolve of June 5, 1780, he enlisted for six months in the Continental Army. He is described as age 23; six feet, two inches in stature; and light complexion. He marched on October 7, 1780, arrived in Springfield on October 10, 1780, and then marched to Fishkill, Stony Point, and Camp Totoway (New Jersey) under the command of Lieutenant Cary on October 26, 1780. There he joined Capt. Adam Bailey's Company, Col. John Bailey's 2nd Massachusetts Regiment, and marched to West Point. In December, he was detached to Ringwood, New Jersey, until the end of January 1781. Back at West Point, he was again detached on February 19 with General Lafayette on a mission through Princeton, New Jersey, to Annapolis, Maryland. Upon his return to West Point, he was discharged on April 18, 1781, having served 6 months, 21 days.[2]

Born in Lincoln, Abel Billing was living in coastal Maine in 1777, when he enlisted in the war with his brother, Solomon. In 1781, he was detached with General Lafayette on a mission to capture Benedict Arnold in Virginia. He is buried in Sargentville, Maine. (Photograph by the author)

He was age 20 when he marched to Machias, the son of John and Hannah (Farrar) Billing of Lincoln, brother of John Billing (q.v.) and Solomon Billing (q.v.). In 1763, his parents had moved the family to Deer Isle, Maine. He married Elizabeth Farrar of Sudbury in May 1780. After his war service, he returned to Sedgewick, Maine, where he became a Deacon of the church and died in 1833, age 76. He is buried in the Settler's Rest Cemetery, Sargentville, Maine.[3]

---

1 *Massachusetts Soldiers and Sailors*, Vol. II, pp. 45, 46; Pension Record # W23614. The possibility that the Claverack service and the Schenectady service may have been provided by different individuals is rejected because of identical service records (at Machias and Claverack) by a Solomon Billings. The suggestion is compelling that the Abel Billings and Solomon Billings of these records must be kinsmen. As no other Abel Billing and Solomon Billing (with or without the s) combination has been found elsewhere, these must be the Lincoln brothers. See Solomon Billing (q.v.).

Reconciling the different units and locations is more problematic. In general, the detail provided in his pension declaration is sufficiently cogent and verifiable as to be credible. He says that the regiment was never all together except at Albany. This might explain different locations, but not the different units. Perhaps Colonel Denny's Regiment at Claverack was a temporary assignment on the way to Albany or Schenectady. Or perhaps Colonel Buttrick's Regiment delivered the enlistees to Colonel Denny's Regiment upon arrival at Albany.

2 *Massachusetts Soldiers and Sailors*, Vol. II, pp. 40, 45; Pension Record # W23614.

3 *Vital Records of Lincoln*; *Vital Records of Sudbury*; Wheeler, "Lincoln," in Hurd, Vol. 2, p. 622; Pension Record # W23614; Pierce, *Old Hancock County Families*, pp. 16–17; *SAR Revolutionary War Graves Register*. Neither

[Lincoln historian William Wheeler reports that he served at Rhode Island in 1780, but this appears doubtful.][1]

BILLING, Daniel
[also BILLINGS, also Daniel Jr.]

Daniel Billing was a private in Capt. William Smith's Company of Minute Men from Lincoln, Col. Abijah Peirce's Regiment.[2] Following the engagement at Concord, he served for 20 days in Cambridge.[3] He was reimbursed by the town for his bayonet and knapsack as a minute man on August 5, 1776.[4]

Subsequently, he served as a private in Capt. John Hartwell's Company of Militia from Lincoln, Col. Eleazer Brooks's 3rd Middlesex County Regiment, which marched from Lincoln to fortify Dorchester Heights on March 4, 1776. The unit was discharged five days later, on March 9, after the threat of a British assault on the fortifications ended in the wake of General Howe's decision to evacuate Boston.[5]

He was back in service for several months when he marched to Bennington, then to Ticonderoga on August 28, 1776, as a private in Capt. Zachariah Fitch's Company, Col. Samuel Brewer's Massachusetts Militia Regiment, which was formed for the Ticonderoga expedition. He appears to have served into December 1776 and was paid by the town for this service.[6]

In 1777, he served in Capt. Samuel Farrar, Jr.'s Company, Col. Jonathan Reed's Middlesex County Regiment (Brig. Gen. James Bricket's Brigade of Massachusetts Militia), which was drafted out of Colonel Brooks's Regiment and sent on September 29, 1777, to Saratoga to reinforce the Northern Army under General Gates. He served in the Northern Department for 26 days and was discharged on October 24, 1777, shortly after the surrender of General Burgoyne.[7]

He was paid by the town for a one-third part of a three-year man in the Continental Army.[8]

Hannah nor Elizabeth appears to be closely related to any of the Farrars in Lincoln. It is not known when Abel returned to Sedgewick, but no children are recorded in Lincoln or Sudbury.

1 Wheeler, "Lincoln," in Hurd, Vol. 2, p. 622. A confirming record of this service has not been found. As Billing fails to mention such service in his pension declaration, this service appears unlikely.
2 Coburn, *Muster Rolls*.
3 *Massachusetts Soldiers and Sailors*, Vol. II, pp. 41, 46.
4 "Treasurer's Accompts," August 5, 1776.
5 *Massachusetts Soldiers and Sailors*, Vol. II, pp. 41, 46.
6 Green, *Groton During the Revolution*, pp. 52–65; "Treasurer's Accompts," November 11, 1779. Service into December 1776 is derived from the similar service of Abijah Mead (q.v.), Abel Adams (q.v.), and Zebediah Farrar (q.v.), and it is consistent with pay receipts contained in Green. With British General Carleton threatening an attack on Ticonderoga, it is unlikely that they would have been discharged prematurely.
7 *Massachusetts Soldiers and Sailors*, Vol. II, pp. 41, 46. "Treasurer's Accompts," November 11, 1779, confirm his service at Saratoga.
8 Wheeler, "Lincoln" (in Hurd, Vol. 2, p. 622), interprets this as his having served a one-third part of a three-year campaign in the Continental Army. He is mistaken. The wording in the "Treasurer's Accompts" consistently distinguishes between service and providing a man for service. This very payment record specifically makes that distinction: "… for service at Ticonderoga in the year 1776 and for a third part of a three years man, and for service at Saratoga in the year 1777" ("Treasurer's Accompts," November 11, 1779).

He was age 21 on April 19, 1775; the son of Daniel and Elisabeth (Farrar) Billing of Lincoln. He was the nephew of Joseph Billing (q.v.), Nathan Billing (q.v.), and probably Jonathan Smith (q.v.); cousin of Joseph Billing, Jr. (q.v.), Nathan Billing, Jr. (q.v.), and Israel Billing (q.v.).[1]

He had married Anna Hunt of Concord on October 31, 1771, when he was age 17 and she was age 23 and about seven months pregnant. She died six years later, in 1777, and he married Lydia Wheeler on January 11, 1779; she was the sister of John Wheeler (q.v.). He reportedly left Lincoln around 1798 or 1799 for Livermore, Maine, and afterward for Bangor, Maine, where he died.[2]

BILLING, Israel
[also BILLINGS]

Israel Billing of Lincoln was drafted out of Capt. Samuel Farrar, Jr.'s Lincoln Militia Company, Col. Eleazer Brooks's 3rd Middlesex County Regiment on August 14, 1777, for service at Saratoga. He served as a private in Capt. George Minot's Company, Col. Samuel Bullard's Massachusetts Militia Regiment from August 16, 1777, to November 30, 1777 (credited with 3 months, 14 days of service), through the surrender of British General Burgoyne at Saratoga.

Subsequently, he served 4 months, 25 days at Winter Hill (now part of Somerville) as a private in Capt. Simon Hunt's Company, Col. Jacob Gerrish's Regiment of Guards from July 21, 1778, through December 15, 1778, guarding the German troops that Burgoyne surrendered at Saratoga.[3]

He enlisted again for a six-month term to reinforce the Continental Army, pursuant to a resolve of June 5, 1780. He is described as age 21; five feet, ten inches in stature; with a ruddy complexion. He marched to Springfield on July 11, 1780, and then marched to camp under the command of Capt. James Cooper on July 15, 1780. He seems to have passed muster at Camp Totoway, New Jersey, under Brigadier General Patterson, on October 25, 1780. He was discharged January 11, 1781, having served 6 months, 10 days.[4]

Lincoln historian William Wheeler reports that he served at Rhode Island in 1780, but this is unconfirmed.[5]

He was age 16 when the war broke out; age 18 in 1777 when he served at Saratoga. He was the son of Nathan Billing (q.v.) and Mary (Billing); the brother of Nathan Billing, Jr. (q.v.); nephew of Joseph Billing (q.v.) and probably Jonathan Smith (q.v.); cousin of Joseph Billing, Jr. (q.v.), and Daniel Billing (q.v.).[6]

---

1 *Concord, Massachusetts: Births, Marriages, and Deaths*; *Vital Records of Sudbury*; Billing Family Bible. Elizabeth does not appear to be closely related to any of the other Farrars in this book.
2 *Concord, Massachusetts: Births, Marriages, and Deaths*; *Vital Records of Lincoln*; Wheeler, "Lincoln," in Hurd, Vol. 2, p. 622. Ten children of Daniel and Lydia are recorded in Lincoln; the last in March 1799.
3 *Massachusetts Soldiers and Sailors*, Vol. II, pp. 42, 48. The German troops were housed at Winter Hill; the British troops were housed at Prospect Hill.
4 *Massachusetts Soldiers and Sailors*, Vol. II, pp. 42, 48.
5 Wheeler, "Lincoln," in Hurd, Vol. 2, p. 622. A confirming record of this service has not been found.
6 *Vital Records of Lincoln*; Billing Family Bible.

Chapter 10: The Army of the Revolution

The Penobscot Expedition ended in disaster with the arrival of British ships in Penobscot Bay. Lincoln-native John Billing was mortally wounded in the fiasco that followed, as the Americans fled up the Penobscot River. (Contemporary painting by Dominic Serres)

No record has been found of his ever having been married. He died in 1828 in Lincoln at age 69. His burial location is undetermined.[1]

BILLING, John
[also BILLINGS]

John Billing was killed in an engagement with British troops at Castine, Maine, on August 29, 1779.[2] This appears to have occurred in conjunction with the failed Penobscot Expedition, July 25, 1779, to August 13, 1779, but the details of this specific engagement have not been found. He was probably a militiaman recruited locally for this campaign.

The defeated American forces attempted to escape up the Penobscot River. "In the utter confusion that followed," reports one modern account, "coordinating an effective stand grew increasingly difficult over the ensuing days, as crews burned their vessels and took to the woods. A handful of vain attempts were made to gather troops and make a stand, but eventually, as Colonel Jonathan Mitchell of Maine revealed, all the participants made off for

---

1 Wheeler, "Lincoln," in Hurd, Vol. 2, p. 622; *Vital Records of Lincoln*.
2 Pierce, *Old Hancock County Families*, p. 16.

home '…without any leave from a superior officer.' Ultimately, all American armed ships and transports, save for at least one captured by the British, were destroyed along various portions of the river and upper bay."[1]

The fighting appears to have been over by August 13, and within a day or two all the troops seem to have departed for home. Colonel Mitchell, finding himself without troops to command, left for his home in North Yarmouth on the sixteenth, arriving home four days later. Accordingly, if the date of the death of John Billing is correct, it is likely that he was mortally wounded during the engagement, returned home, and lingered for a couple of weeks before he died.

He was age 20 when the war broke out, age 24 when he was killed. He was born in Lincoln, the son of John and Hannah (Farrar) Billing of Lincoln, brother of Abel Billing (q.v.) and Solomon Billing (q.v.). In 1763, his parents had moved the family to Deer Isle, Maine, where he was raised, and where he had married Mary Closson of Deer Isle. He is reported buried in an area cemetery in Sargentville, Maine.[2]

BILLING, Joseph
[also BILLINGS]

Joseph Billing served as a private in Capt. John Hartwell's Company of Militia from Lincoln, Col. Eleazer Brooks's 3rd Middlesex County Regiment, which marched from Lincoln to fortify Dorchester Heights on March 4, 1776. The unit was discharged five days later, on March 9, after the threat of a British assault on the fortifications ended in the wake of General Howe's decision to evacuate Boston.[3]

He was paid by the town for service at New York in 1776 and 1777. Logically, this was probably in Capt. John Bridge's Company, Col. Samuel Thatcher's Regiment, from November 21, 1776, to March 6, 1777, serving at Fairfield, Connecticut, and Woodbridge, New Jersey, but no confirming record has been found.[4]

Although he was age 43 at the time of the Dorchester Heights service, this is believed to be the son of Joseph and Anna Billing; brother of Nathan Billing (q.v.); father of Joseph Billing, Jr. (q.v.); uncle of Israel Billing (q.v.), Nathan Billing, Jr. (q.v.), and Daniel Billing (q.v.); probably the brother-in-law of Jonathan Smith (q.v.).[5]

He had been a member of Lincoln's original militia company in 1757, and he had been part of an expedition to Canada during the French and Indian War.[6]

---

1 "A Short History of the Penobscot Expedition." See also Goold, "Colonel Mitchell's Regiment."
2 *Vital Records of Lincoln*; Pierce, *Old Hancock County Families*, p. 16. His burial location is per *SAR Revolutionary War Graves Register*. The author has been unable to identify the specific location.
3 *Massachusetts Soldiers and Sailors*, Vol. II, pp. 43, 50.
4 "Treasurer's Accompts," June 15, 1779.
5 *Concord, Massachusetts: Births, Marriages, and Deaths*; Billing Family Bible. See also *Vital Records of Lincoln*. It is remotely possible that this service could have been provided by Joseph Billing, Jr. (q.v.), who was age 14 at the time of Dorchester Heights and may have turned age 15 before the end of the New York campaign. Other examples of underage service make it impossible to rule this out. However, underage service was the exception, not the norm. Unless there is evidence or a compelling reason (which there does not appear to be) to conclude that the elder Joseph could not have provided this service, or that Joseph Jr. actually did provide this service, the logic of age-appropriate service outweighs the exception of underage service.
6 Martin, "The Sons of Lincoln," pp. 20, 25.

Chapter 10: The Army of the Revolution

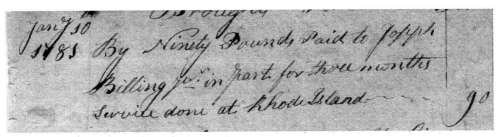

Joseph Billing, Jr., was age 13 when the war began, but later he served guard duty in Cambridge in 1778, and two campaigns in Rhode Island in 1779 and 1780. The "Treasurer's Accompts" of the town record the second of two payments made to him for his 1780 service. (Courtesy of Lincoln Town Archives, Lincoln, MA)

A cooper by trade, he had been married to Beulah (Allen), sister of Phineas Allen (q.v.), since 1761. Thus, he was also brother-in-law of Phineas Allen (q.v.); uncle of Jonathan Tower (q.v.) and John Wheeler (q.v.). He died in Lincoln in 1810 at age 77. His burial location is unknown.[1]

BILLING, Joseph, Jr.
[also BILLINGS]

Joseph Billing, Jr., volunteered or was drafted out of the Lincoln Militia Company to relieve the guards at Cambridge. He served as a private in Capt. Simon Hunt's Company, Col. Jacob Gerrish's Regiment of Guards from July 12, 1778, through December 15, 1778 (credited with 5 months, 4 days of service at Winter Hill), guarding the German troops surrendered by Burgoyne at Saratoga. Town records confirm his service at Cambridge as a guard to the Convention.[2]

The town paid him for service at Rhode Island, probably as a private in Capt. Samuel Heald's Company, Col. John Jacobs's Regiment of Light Infantry from September 15, 1779, to November 15, 1779 (credited with 2 months, 4 days of service).[3]

He returned to Rhode Island for a second campaign, evidently as a private in Capt. Abraham Andrews's Company, Col. Cyprian How's Middlesex County Regiment, which was detached to reinforce the Continental Army in Rhode Island. He served from July 27, 1780, to October 30, 1780 (credited with 3 months, 7 days of service).[4]

---

1 MacLean, *A Rich Harvest*, p. 179; *Vital Records of Lincoln*; Wheeler, "Lincoln," in Hurd, Vol. 2, p. 622.
2 *Massachusetts Soldiers and Sailors*, Vol. II, pp. 43, 50; "Treasurer's Accompts," June 15, 1779. The Convention refers to the British (and German) troops surrendered by Burgoyne at Saratoga, who were being kept in Cambridge awaiting repatriation. The term "Convention" was a British euphemism to avoid the stigma of surrender, which Burgoyne cleverly negotiated along with very favorable terms into a Convention Agreement rather than a surrender agreement. Burgoyne's troops were marched to Cambridge in expectation of a rapid repatriation. But compliance with the agreement broke down on both sides, and after a year, the troops were removed from Cambridge and marched to points south. While they were being held in Cambridge, the British troops were housed on Prospect Hill, while the Germans were housed on Winter Hill.
3 *Massachusetts Soldiers and Sailors*, Vol. II, p. 43; "Treasurer's Accompts," February 3, 1780. The pay record reads "for service in a late campaign at Rhode Island."
4 *Massachusetts Soldiers and Sailors*, Vol. II, p. 50; "Treasurer's Accompts," January 5, 1781, and January 10, 1781.

He was age 13 when the war began, age 16 when he served in Cambridge in 1778; the son of Joseph (q.v.) and Beulah (Allen) Billing; nephew of Phineas Allen (q.v.), Nathan Billing (q.v.), and probably Jonathan Smith (q.v.); cousin of Nathan Billing, Jr. (q.v.), Israel Billing (q.v.), Daniel Billing (q.v.), Jonathan Tower (q.v.), and John Wheeler (q.v.).[1]

He married his first cousin, Pattee Allen, who was also the niece of Phineas Allen (q.v.), in 1784. He died in 1825 at age 62, and he is buried in the Meeting House Cemetery behind Bemis Hall.[2]

BILLING, Nathan
[also BILLINGS]

Nathan Billing of Lincoln was a private in Capt. William Smith's Company of Minute Men from Lincoln, Col. Abijah Peirce's Regiment.[3] Including the engagement at Concord, he served for two days.[4] He was reimbursed for his accoutrements as a minute man on February 29, 1776.[5]

In 1776, he went to New York as a private in Capt. Simon Hunt's Company, Col. Eleazer Brooks's Middlesex County Regiment of Massachusetts Militia. He served for two months, from September 27, 1776, to November 16, 1776 (plus credit for 11 days of travel home). The regiment suffered heavy losses at the Battle of White Plains on October 28, but he was reported in camp and fit for service after the battle.[6]

He was also paid by the town for taking a team with supplies to Worthington in 1777. The purpose and details of this expedition are uncertain, but it may possibly have been to supply the Convention Army and its escort.[7]

There is a possibility that he may have served in Rhode Island during 1779, but this service is more logically attributed to his son, Nathan Billing, Jr. (q.v.).[8]

---

1 *Vital Records of Lincoln*; Billing Family Bible.
2 Ibid. Also, Wheeler, "Lincoln," in Hurd, Vol. 2, p. 622; Biggs, "In Memorium," p. 158. *Vital Records of Lincoln* lists his age at the time of death as 63. If the dates recorded for his birth and death are correct, he appears not yet to have reached his 63rd birthday. His headstone, which was erected ten years after he died, echoes the age given in the Vital Records.
3 Coburn, *Muster Rolls*.
4 *Massachusetts Soldiers and Sailors*, Vol. II, pp. 43, 50.
5 "Treasurer's Accompts," February 29, 1776.
6 "Treasurer's Accompts," June 15, 1779; *Massachusetts Soldiers and Sailors*, Vol. II, pp. 43, 50; *Muster Rolls of the Revolutionary War*, Vol. 55, file L, p. 24. Colonel Brooks's Regiment was raised out of the seven standing Middlesex County militia regiments and sent to New York to support the Continental Army.
7 "Treasurer's Accompts," June 15, 1779. The author's speculation that this was a supply mission for the march of the Convention Army being escorted to Boston is based on: (a) Worthington's location in west-central Massachusetts, approximately on the route by which the British arm of the Convention Army was escorted to Boston; (b) the difficulty experienced by General Glover in securing supplies in New York for this march; and (c) the absence of any other apparent reason for carting supplies to Worthington. However, the author has not found confirming evidence.
8 *Massachusetts Soldiers and Sailors*, Vol. II, pp. 43, 50. Wheeler, "Lincoln" (in Hurd, Vol. 2, p. 622), places Nathan Billings at Rhode Island in 1779, but he does not distinguish between Nathan Sr. and Nathan Jr. Nathan Billing, Jr. (q.v.), was age 16 at the time and could have served both of the Rhode Island stints (May 17 to July 1, 1779, and September 15 to November 17, 1779). The elder Nathan Billing (inst.) was evidently in Lincoln on June 15, collecting his pay for earlier service, so it is likely that Nathan Jr. provided the first Rhode Island service, and by extension probably also the service in the fall.

He was age 39 when he went to Concord on April 19, 1775. He was the son of Joseph and Anna Billing; father of Israel Billing (q.v.) and Nathan Billing, Jr. (q.v.); brother of Joseph Billing (q.v.); uncle of Joseph Billing, Jr. (q.v.) and Daniel Billing (q.v.); probably brother-in-law of Jonathan Smith (q.v.).[1]

He had been a member of Lincoln's original militia company in 1757, and he had been married to Mary (Billing) since 1759. He died in Lincoln in 1809, age 74.[2]

BILLING, Nathan, Jr.
[also BILLINGS]

Nathan Billing, Jr., probably served in Rhode Island twice during 1779.

He is probably the Nathan Billings who served as a private in Capt. Lawson Buckminster's Company, Lt. Col. Samuel Pierce's Regiment from May 17 to July 1, 1779 (credited with 1 month, 18 days service at Tiverton), but this remains uncertain.[3]

While likewise not certain, he is probably also the Nathan Billing who served as a private in Capt. Samuel Heald's Company, Col. John Jacobs's Regiment of Light Infantry from September 15 to November 15, 1779 (credited with 2 months, 4 days of service).[4]

Agreeable to a resolve of June 5, 1780, he enlisted for the term of six months to reinforce the Continental Army. He is described as age 17; five feet, eight inches in stature; with a light complexion. He marched to Springfield on July 11, 1780. Upon arriving in Springfield, he was marched to camp under the command of Capt. James Cooper on July 15, 1780. His unit and duty are unknown, but he was at Camp Totoway, New Jersey, in the fall, when he is recorded as having passed muster under Brigadier General Patterson, on October 25, 1780. He was discharged January 11, 1781, having served 6 months, 10 days.[5]

He was age 12 when the war started, age 16 for most of the likely Rhode Island service; the son of Nathan Billing (q.v.) and Mary Billing; brother of Israel Billing (q.v.); nephew of Joseph Billing (q.v.) and probably Jonathan Smith (q.v.); cousin of Joseph Billing, Jr. (q.v.), and Daniel Billing (q.v.).

He married Elizabeth Handcock on October 14, 1791. One son is recorded in Lincoln, in 1794, after which he and Elizabeth disappear from the local record.[6]

---

1 MacLean, *A Rich Harvest*, p. 256; *Vital Records of Lincoln*; Billing Family Bible.

2 Martin, "The Sons of Lincoln," p. 25; *Vital Records of Lincoln*; Wheeler, "Lincoln," in Hurd, Vol. 2, p. 622. Mary Billing appears to be the sister of Timothy Billing (q.v.), and thus she may have been Nathan's cousin, but this needs to be investigated further.

3 *Massachusetts Soldiers and Sailors*, Vol. II, p. 50.

4 *Massachusetts Soldiers and Sailors*, Vol. II, p. 43. Wheeler, "Lincoln" (in Hurd, Vol. 2, p. 622), places Nathan Billings at Rhode Island in 1779, but he does not distinguish between Nathan Sr. and Nathan Jr. The elder Nathan Billing (q.v.) can reasonably be ruled out for the first stint under Captain Buckminster. By extension, the second stint was probably served by Nathan Jr. as well. An identical service record in Colonel Jacobs's Regiment for Joseph Billing, Jr. (q.v.), a cousin of Nathan Billing, Jr. (inst.), is further evidence that the latter probably provided this service.

5 *Massachusetts Soldiers and Sailors*, Vol. II, pp. 43, 50.

6 *Vital Records of Lincoln*; Billing Family Bible.

BILLING, Solomon
[also BILLINGS]

Solomon Billing was in Sedgewick, Maine, in 1777, where he volunteered for service on August 19, 1777, as a private in Captain William Reed's Company. He marched to Machias by order of Col. Jonathan Buck to protect the town, which had previously been taken and partly burned by the British. He served for 1 month, 10 days, until September 28, 1777.

He was a Lincoln native, and was back in Lincoln in 1779, where he enlisted for a three-month term, starting on October 23, 1779. Service records show that he served as a private in Capt. Joshua Walker's Company, Col. Samuel Denny's Regiment, detached to reinforce the Continental Army, and that he marched to Claverack, New York. His brother's pension record, however, suggests that he may have served in Captain Butters's Company, Colonel Buttrick's Regiment, and marched from Concord to Albany, then to Schenectady where they remained for four weeks. From Schenectady, they returned to Albany, where he was discharged in December, having served six weeks.[1]

Lincoln-born Solomon Billing marched north with his brother, Abel, to defend Machias, Maine, in 1777; later he served with Abel in the Hudson Valley. (Photograph by the author)

He was age 16 when the war broke out, age 18 when he marched to Machias. He was the son of John and Hannah Billing of Lincoln, brother of Abel Billing (q.v.) and John Billing (q.v.). In 1763, when he was still very young, his parents had moved the family to Deer Isle, Maine. After his war service, he went back to Maine. He married Abigail Eaton of Deer Isle and settled in Brooksville, where he became a Deacon of the church. He died at Brooksville in 1821, at age 61, and is buried in the Lake Side Cemetery.[2]

---

1 *Massachusetts Soldiers and Sailors*, Vol. II, p. 52; Pension Record for Abel Billing, # W23614. Note the identical service records at Machias and Claverack for his brother, Abel Billings (q.v.) (see *Massachusetts Soldiers and Sailors*, Vol. II, pp. 45-46). The juxtaposition, and the fact that no other Abel Billing and Solomon Billing (with or without the s) combination has been found elsewhere, confirms the identity of the Solomon Billings in these records as Solomon Billing (inst.).

The author assumes that Abel's pension information regarding these two stints applies equally to Solomon's service. Reconciling the differences between the pension record and the service record, however, is a bit problematic. In general, the detail provided in Abel's pension record is sufficiently cogent and verifiable as to be credible. Perhaps Colonel Denny's Regiment at Claverack was a temporary assignment on the way to Albany or Schenectady. Or perhaps Colonel Buttrick's Regiment delivered the enlistees to Colonel Denny's Regiment upon arrival at Albany.

2 *Vital Records of Lincoln*; Pierce, *Old Hancock County Families*, p. 17; *SAR Revolutionary War Graves Register*. See also Dana, "John Billings of Deer Isle." His gravestone lists his age as 62, but he appears to have died three weeks shy of his 62nd birthday. The burial site is more commonly referred to as the Roberts Cemetery

BILLING, Timothy
[also BILLINGS, Timothy Jr.]

Timothy Billing was a private in Capt. William Smith's Company of Minute Men from Lincoln, Col. Abijah Peirce's Regiment.[1] Following the engagement at Concord, he served for nine days in Cambridge.[2]

Subsequently, he served as a private in Capt. John Hartwell's Company of Militia from Lincoln, Col. Eleazer Brooks's 3rd Middlesex County Regiment, which marched from Lincoln to fortify Dorchester Heights on March 4, 1776. The unit was discharged five days later, on March 9, after the threat of a British assault on the fortifications ended with General Howe's decision to evacuate Boston.[3]

Town records indicate that he was paid "for service at Ticonderoga in the year 1776 and at Saratoga [in 1777] and for a three-years campaign in the Continental Army." No details of this service have been found.[4]

He was age 26 when he went to Concord on April 19, 1775. He was the son of Timothy and Mary (Moor) Billing.[5]

He was a ropemaker, and his family was the largest producer of flax and hemp in the area. He had married Anna Gearfield of Weston in 1771. He died in Lincoln in 1812 at age 64 and is buried in the Meeting House Cemetery behind Bemis Hall.[6]

BLODGET, Thomas
[also BLODGETT]

Thomas Blodget was a private in Capt. William Smith's Company of Minute Men from Lincoln, Col. Abijah Peirce's Regiment.[7] Following the engagement at Concord, he served for 26 days in Cambridge.[8]

Subsequently, he enlisted as a private in Capt. Asahel Wheeler's Company, Col. John Robinson's Regiment, and served from February 4, 1776, to the beginning of April as reinforcement for Washington's army during the preparation and fortification of Dorchester

---

and the Herrick Road Cemetery, but the engraved boulder on site identifies it unmistakably as "Lake Side Cemetery."

1 Coburn, *Muster Rolls*.
2 *Massachusetts Soldiers and Sailors*, Vol. II, pp. 45, 52.
3 Ibid. Also, Hartwell, "A List of a Company of Militia"; which makes it clear that there was only one individual named Timothy Billing at Dorchester Heights, despite separate records in *Massachusetts Soldiers and Sailors* for Timothy Billings and Timothy Billing, Jr. Therefore, entries for Timothy Billing and Timothy Billing, Jr., are for the same individual.
4 "Treasurer's Accompts," June 15, 1779. See also Wheeler, "Lincoln" (in Hurd, Vol. 2, p. 622), who credits him with Continental service but provides no details.
5 *Concord, Massachusetts: Births, Marriages, and Deaths*; Billing Family Bible. Lincoln had not yet become a town at the time of his birth. His sister, Mary, was likely the wife of Nathan Billing (q.v.).
6 MacLean, *A Rich Harvest*, p. 170; *Town of Weston, Births, Deaths, & Marriages*; *Vital Records of Lincoln*; Wheeler, "Lincoln," in Hurd, Vol. 2, p. 622; Biggs, "In Memorium," p. 159. Anna's possible kinship with Abraham Gearfield (q.v.), Elisha Gearfield (q.v.), John Gearfield (q.v.), or Solomon Garfield (q.v.) has not been determined.
7 Coburn, *Muster Rolls*.
8 *Massachusetts Soldiers and Sailors*, Vol. II, pp. 198, 199.

Heights. He served for 1 month, 28 days, through the departure of the British forces from Boston.¹

He served at Ticonderoga, probably from July 1776 through November 1776, with Capt. Charles Miles's Company, Col. Jonathan Reed's Regiment, as he is reported discharged on the reverse side of a company roll dated Concord, December 20, 1776. A receipt for mileage home from Ticonderoga, dated Lexington, February 18, 1777, for members of Captain Miles's Company was signed on behalf of Thomas Blodget by Josiah Nelson (q.v.).²

Not much is known about him, as there are few qualifying Thomas Blodgets in state or local records.³

---

1 Ibid.

2 Ibid. The dates of service indicated are for the company; in the absence of other information, it is presumed that he served the full period. The fact that the receipt was signed by Josiah Nelson triggers speculation that Blodget may have served this stint as a substitute for Josiah Nelson (see "Are All Records Created Equal?" on p. 351).

3 The closest fit among recorded birth and baptism records may be a Thomas Blogget from Westford, son of "wid. Sarah," baptized in 1759. Widow Sarah may be the Sarah Spencer of Groton whose intention to wed Samuel Blodget was recorded in Westford in 1744, but this identification has not been verified. This was likely not an infant baptism (two of his siblings were baptized at the same time, and another less than a year later), so his possible service age is indeterminate—but this all remains speculative as there is no evidence to connect this individual with the Thomas Blodget (inst.) who served for Lincoln (*Vital Records of Westford*).

There are few other records of qualifying individuals. Lexington and Woburn were home to a large number of Blodgets, but none of those recorded fit this service record. Similar is the case for the towns of Brimfield and Monson.

Despite the paucity of records for qualifying Thomas Blodgets, other records of service by Thomas Blodget are probably different individuals. The Thomas Blodget who served at Ticonderoga in Capt. Reuben Munn's Company, Col. David Leonard's Regiment from March 1, 1777, to April 11, 1777, was almost certainly a resident of Brimfield or Monson, as this was a Brimfield/Monson company in a Hampshire County regiment. The Thomas Blodgett who served at Saratoga in Capt. Fortunatus Eager's Company, Col. Ephraim Sawyer's Regiment from October 2, 1777, through October 18, 1777, was logically a Lancaster-area resident, as both officers were Lancastrians. And the Thomas Blodget who served at Rhode Island as a private in Capt. David Moore's Company, Lt. Col. Enoch Hallet's Regiment from August 1, 1780, to October 31, 1780, was logically a Barnstable County resident, as that is where the regiment was raised (see *Massachusetts Soldiers and Sailors*, Vol. II, pp. 198, 199; Vol. V, p. 136; Vol. VII, p. 123; Vol. X, p. 917; Vol. XI, p. 206).

Another interesting reference to a Thomas Blodget is found in a Land Grant application in the Federal pension records. This is a claim that Thomas Blodget enlisted for the duration of the war in the 2nd New Hampshire Regiment, commanded by Colonel Reed, and that "he was slain by the enemy" in the fall of 1777. The possibility of this being the same individual as Thomas Blodget (inst.) is no less speculative, but if a connection were to be found, it would place Thomas Blodget (inst.) at Saratoga, and explain why as little is known about him after the war as there is about him before he marched to Concord. Pension Record # BLWT 2340-100. To the extent that the claim may be considered credible, Thomas Blodget must have enlisted in 1777, as Continental enlistments before 1777 were for one year at a time.

The reference to Colonel Reed is not well defined. The 2nd New Hampshire Regiment was commanded by Col. Nathan Hale (different from the legendary Nathan Hale who was hanged by the British) until he was captured at Hubbardstown in July 1777. Possibly the claimants refer to George Reid, who was appointed lieutenant colonel of the 2nd New Hampshire Regiment in 1777. Lieutenant Colonel Reid eventually succeeded to the command of the 2nd New Hampshire Regiment, but some sources suggest that this may not have occurred until much later in the war.

The 3rd New Hampshire Regiment (also known as the 2nd Continental Regiment), on the other hand, was commanded by a Col. James Reed during 1775 and 1776. He contracted smallpox on his way to Canada in 1776 and was effectively disabled. He was never in command of this regiment or another regiment after that. Both regiments were at Saratoga in 1777, but it is not clear that either was at that time commanded by a Colonel Reed (or Reid).

The application was made in 1844 by a Henry Blodgett of Lemington, Vermont, and a Howard Blodget of Stewartstown, New Hampshire, "heirs in law" of said Thomas Blodget. No genealogical information is

Town records show a "Thos Bladged" who came to Lincoln from Lexington in 1760 and was warned out in 1761. It is reasonable to presume that this may be the same individual as Thomas Blodget (inst.), but the evidence is circumstantial, at best. As there is no reference to any family members with him when he came to Lincoln, he presumably was old enough to have been on his own, suggesting (if he was the same individual) that he was probably in his mid-thirties when he answered the April 19th Alarm.[1]

BOND, Jonas

Jonas Bond of Lincoln appears to have served at Ticonderoga in 1776, in Capt. Asahel Wheeler's Company, Col. Jonathan Reed's Regiment.[2]

Jonas Bond did enlist in the Continental Army, pursuant to a resolve of April 20, 1778, for the term of nine months from his arrival in Fishkill. He was probably drafted, recruited, or chosen by lot for this service out of Captain Samuel Farrar, Jr.'s Lincoln Militia Company, Col. Eleazer Brooks's 3rd Middlesex County Regiment. He was described as age 18 and five feet, eight inches in stature. Upon his arrival in Fishkill on June 17, 1778, he was assigned to take care of the beef cattle for the provisioning commissary, in which capacity he served until October. Then he was ordered to Connecticut to build a bridge for Colonel Carleton across the Newtown River (probably the Housatonic River at Newtown), after which he joined Captain Dix's Company, Colonel Weston's Regiment at West Hartford. By Christmas, he was back in the Hudson Valley, near West Point, building huts at Soldiers Fortune. Subsequently, he joined Colonel Nixon's 4th Continental Regiment, and he was discharged in March 1779.[3]

"Some time after," he reported, "feeling my Duty towards my Country [I] returned to its Assistance & in some trying Conflicts lost my Discharge that I took at west point."[4]

He was age 15 at the outbreak of the war, age 16 at Ticonderoga, age 18 at Fishkill; the son of William and Lydia (Farrar) Bond; brother of Samuel Bond (q.v.), William Bond (q.v.), and perhaps Thomas Bond (q.v.); nephew of Samuel Farrar, Jr. (q.v.), Timothy Farrar

---

provided, and the proffered details are sparse at best. The sense of opportunism one gets from this document is enhanced by observing that the attestation was provided by a "Beach Blodgett, Justice of the Peace." Nevertheless, it does raise the interesting possibility that after returning from Ticonderoga, Thomas Blodget (inst.) may have enlisted in the Continental Army, in the 2nd (or 3rd) New Hampshire Regiment and been killed at Saratoga. Of course, without connective tissue, this remains entirely speculative.

1 Jack MacLean, private communication with the author.
2 "Treasurer's Accompts," June 15, 1779. The town paid Deacon Samuel Farrar for service at Ticonderoga in 1776 and for 18-months service in the Continental Army. The record does not identify who provided this service, but by a process of elimination, Jonas Bond appears to be a likely candidate. See the discussion under Samuel Farrar (q.v., Chapter 12).

Further, he signed a receipt dated March 17, 1777, for "all oure wagers and Rations & arrears Due to ous While we ware under him [Capt. Asahel Wheeler]." Sudbury Miscellaneous Records, Doc. # 2209.

His pension declaration contains no mention of service at Ticonderoga, as the Pension Act of 1818, under which it was submitted, covered Continental service, but did not include militia service.
3 *Massachusetts Soldiers and Sailors*, Vol. II, p. 258; Pension Record # W1132. See also Blake, "James Barrett's Returns of Men," p. 15. Colonel Nixon's 4th Continental Regiment was also known as the 6th Massachusetts Regiment.
4 Pension Record # W1132. Except for this statement in his pension declaration, no record of his return to service has been found.

(q.v.), Stephen Farrar (q.v.), and Humphrey Farrar (q.v.). His mother had died in 1774, two months after his 14th birthday, and his father, too, died a year later.[1]

He married Lydia Hapgood of Petersham on February 8, 1789, and began a journey northward. He was living in Guilford, Vermont, by 1791; Winslow, Maine, by 1798; St. Stephen, New Brunswick, by 1801; Calais, Maine by 1805; and subsequently Robbinston, Maine. He was a farmer, but by 1820 he was unable to work by reason of "Rheumatic complaints" in his back and hip. Lydia was then described as being "in feeble health." After she died, he married Eunice Eaton in 1834, in Calais. He reportedly died at St. Stephen, New Brunswick, in 1840 or 1841, at about age 81. He is buried at Brewer Cemetery in Robbinston, Maine.[2]

BOND, Samuel

Samuel Bond of Lincoln served as a private in Capt. John Hartwell's Company of Militia from Lincoln, Col. Eleazer Brooks's 3rd Middlesex County Regiment, which marched from Lincoln to fortify Dorchester Heights on March 4, 1776. The unit was discharged five days later, on March 9, after the threat of a British assault on the fortifications had subsided with General Howe's decision to evacuate Boston.[3]

He is reported by Lincoln historian William Wheeler to have served prior to this at Cambridge in 1775 and subsequently at New York in 1776. However, no confirming record of this service has been found.[4]

He is recorded as serving at Ticonderoga from September through November 1776, in Capt. Asahel Wheeler's Company, Col. Jonathan Reed's Regiment. Presumably, he had been at Ticonderoga since June or July, serving for four or five months.[5]

He had no sooner returned from Ticonderoga, when he was back in Dorchester as a corporal in Capt. John Hartwell's Company, Col. Nicholas Dike's Regiment from December 14, 1776 to March 1, 1777.[6]

Later in 1777, he was urgently drafted out of Capt. Samuel Farrar, Jr.'s Company, Col. Eleazer Brooks's 3rd Middlesex County Regiment, assigned to a new company commanded by Captain Farrar, in Col. Jonathan Reed's Middlesex Regiment (Brig. Gen. James Bricket's Brigade of Massachusetts Militia), and sent to Saratoga to reinforce General Gates on September 27, 1777. Following British General Burgoyne's surrender on October 17, he

---

1 *Vital Records of Lincoln*.
2 Bond, *Genealogies of the Families of Watertown*, p. 53; Wheeler, "Lincoln," in Hurd, Vol. 2, p. 622; Pension Record # W1132; *SAR Revolutionary War Graves Register*. His death in St. Stephen in 1840 or 1841 is reported in the pension record by a close friend of Eunice. Wheeler says he died in Robbinston, Maine, in 1843. *SAR Revolutionary War Graves Register* also lists his death as 1843. The author has not visited his headstone, but suspects this may be the source of the 1843 date. His journey north is traceable in the birth locations of his nine children, as reported in Bond, *Genealogies of the Families of Watertown* (p. 53).
3 *Massachusetts Soldiers and Sailors*, Vol. II, p. 261.
4 Wheeler, "Lincoln," in Hurd, Vol. 2, p. 622. By service at New York, Wheeler refers to service in the 1776 Campaign around New York City, which he clearly distinguishes from service at Ticonderoga in 1776. New York service would be in direct conflict with the record of his Ticonderoga service.
5 Sudbury Miscellaneous Records, Pay receipts, September 30, 1776 (Doc. # 109), December 16, 1776 (Doc. # 2204), December 26, 1776 (Doc. # 2208), March 17, 1777 (Doc. # 2209).
6 *Massachusetts Soldiers and Sailors*, Vol. II, p. 261; "Treasurer's Accompts," June 15, 1779.

served with his unit as part of the escort for marching Burgoyne's troops to Cambridge, where he was discharged on November 7, 1777 (credited with 1 month, 10 days of service).[1]

In addition, the town paid him for one-half of a three-year campaign in the Continental Army. The details of this service are unknown.[2]

He may possibly be the Samuel Bond who served at Rhode Island in 1778 as a private in Capt. Francis Brown's Company, Colonel McIntosh's Regiment (Brig. Gen. Solomon Lovell's Brigade of Massachusetts Militia) from August 1, 1778, to September 11, 1778 (credited with 1 month, 14 days of service). If so, he was present during the Battle of Rhode Island on August 29, 1778. However, it is uncertain if this is the same individual as Samuel Bond of Lincoln.[3]

He was age 18 at Dorchester Heights; the son of William and Lydia (Farrar) Bond; brother of Jonas Bond (q.v.), William Bond (q.v.), and perhaps Thomas Bond (q.v.); nephew of Samuel Farrar, Jr. (q.v.), Timothy Farrar (q.v.), Stephen Farrar (q.v.), and Humphrey Farrar (q.v.). His mother had died in 1774, and his father, too, had passed away about six months before his Dorchester Heights service.[4]

In 1779, he is reported to have sailed for France in a letter-of-marque ship, which was captured by the British and taken to St. Lucia. He died at St. Lucia of fever.[5]

BOND, Thomas

Thomas Bond of Lincoln enlisted in the Continental Army pursuant to a resolve dated April 20, 1778. His term of service was nine months from the time of his arrival in Fishkill. The dates and details of this service are unknown.[6]

Despite the logic for assuming kinship with Jonas Bond (q.v.), Samuel Bond (q.v.), and William Bond (q.v.), no clear record of his identity has been found.[7]

---

1 Ibid. Colonel Reed's Regiment was formed of men detached from all seven of the Middlesex County militia regiments.
2 "Treasurer's Accompts," June 15, 1779.
3 *Massachusetts Soldiers and Sailors*, Vol. II, p. 261. This service is attributed to a Samuel Bond, probably of Weston. *Town of Weston, Births, Deaths, & Marriages*, however, contains no Samuel Bond. There are two Samuel Bonds, identified in Bond, *Genealogies of the Families of Watertown* (pp. 60, 67), who may have provided this service instead of Samuel Bond (inst.). The first is the son of Col. William and Lucy (Brown) Bond of Watertown. Bond, *Genealogies of the Families of Watertown* attributes him with marine service during the Revolution, but no record of this can be found in *Massachusetts Soldiers and Sailors*. [Col. William Bond commanded several Lincoln men in the relief expedition to Canada, before he died at Ticonderoga in 1776.] The other possibility is the son of Henry and Mary (Cutting) Bond of Watertown, who would have been age 30 when and if he provided this service. Both individuals were distant cousins of Samuel (inst.). Neither has been identified with a connection to Weston or Lincoln.
4 *Vital Records of Lincoln*.
5 Wheeler, "Lincoln," in Hurd, Vol. 2, p. 622. Bond, *Genealogies of the Families of Watertown* (p. 53) incorrectly gives 1777 as the year in which he set sail for France, which would have precluded his possible 1778 service at Rhode Island, and more importantly is incompatible with the record of the town's having paid him for his war service in 1779.
6 *Massachusetts Soldiers and Sailors*, Vol. II, p. 263. Note the record of similar service by Jonas Bond (q.v.).
7 There was a Thomas Bond born in Waltham in 1739, son of Jonathan and Mary Bond. He had grown up in Mendon and Westborough, and at age 18 had been a soldier in the French and Indian War. He married Lydia Newton in 1765, lived in Westborough for a time, and then moved to North Brookfield before the start of the Revolutionary War. He would have been age 39 when and if he served at Fishkill.

BOND, William

William Bond of Lincoln served at Rhode Island, probably as a private in Capt. Samuel Heald's Company, Col. John Jacobs's Regiment of Light Infantry, for 2 months, 4 days, from September 15, 1779, to November 15, 1779.[1]

He was age 13 when the war started; age 18 when he served in Rhode Island. He was the son of William and Lydia (Farrar) Bond; brother of Jonas Bond (q.v.), Samuel Bond (q.v.), and perhaps Thomas Bond (q.v.); nephew of Samuel Farrar, Jr. (q.v.), Timothy Farrar (q.v.), Stephen Farrar (q.v.), and Humphrey Farrar (q.v.). He was age 12 when his mother died in 1774; age 14 when his father died in 1775.[2]

He married Rosanna Negus, probably in 1792 or 1793, and went to live in Whittingham, Vermont. He died in 1837 in Whittingham at age 76.[3]

BOWES, Peter

Peter Bowes of Lincoln served for three years as a private in the Continental Army from March 20, 1777, to March 20, 1780. He served at Saratoga as a member of Capt. Edmund Munroe's Company, Col. Timothy Bigelow's 15th Massachusetts Regiment, then marched

---

    Another Thomas Bond was born in Watertown in 1751, and after his father died, his mother married Timothy Wheeler of Concord in 1765. Thomas moved to Groton in 1773, married Esther Merriam of Concord in 1777, and settled in Groton. He would have been age 26 when and if he began his service at Fishkill.

    Both individuals appear to be distant cousins of Jonas, Samuel, and William. Unfortunately, no evidence has been found to equate either of these individuals with Thomas Bond (inst.) of Lincoln, and neither has an identifiable Lincoln connection (Bond, *Genealogies of the Families of Watertown*, pp. 56, 62, 688).

1 "Treasurer's Accompts," March 4, 1780; *Massachusetts Soldiers and Sailors*, Vol. II, p. 263. The Treasurer's Account transaction does not identify the year or dates of service. The record of service at Rhode Island in 1779 in Captain Heald's Company, Colonel Jacobs's Regiment does not identify William Bond as being from Lincoln, but this service is consistent with service records of other Lincoln men. Wheeler, "Lincoln" (in Hurd, Vol. 2, p. 622), says the Rhode Island service was in 1780, but apparently he has confused the date of service with the date of payment.

    Another William Bond who served at Rhode Island from July 31, 1778, to September 14, 1778 (during the period of the Battle of Rhode Island, August 29, 1778), in Capt. Joshua Whitney's Company, Col. Josiah Whitney's Regiment, is identifiable from his pension record as William Bond of Weston, born in 1758 (his pension declaration says 1760), the son of Benjamin and Abigail. According to his pension record, he had previously served in 1776 with Colonel Bond in Canada, and earlier in 1778 as a guard in Boston. He was a distant cousin of William Bond (inst.). He married Sarah Parks of Lincoln in 1783. Sarah may have been the sister of Jonas Parks (q.v.) or Willard Parks (q.v.) (see *Town of Weston, Births, Deaths, & Marriages* and Pension Record # S14976).

    Massachusetts Soldiers and Sailors (Vol. II, p. 263) also contains records for a William Bond of Weston, and a William Bond, Jr., of Weston, who marched on the Alarm of April 19th with Capt. Samuel Lamson's Company, serving one day and three days respectively. Neither record of service is consistent with the pension declaration of the foregoing William, indicating that there must have been three different William Bonds from Weston (in addition to William Bond (inst.) of Lincoln) who provided service during the war. Positive identification of the two William Bonds who marched on the April 19th Alarm is not possible from *Town of Weston, Births, Deaths, & Marriages*, and the absence of other identifiable candidates suggests the intriguing possibility that one of them might have been the father of William (inst.) and his brothers Jonas (q.v.) and Samuel (q.v.), before he died in August 1775. This possibility is considered remote, however, as in order to make this case, it would be necessary to explain away either the designation "Jr." in one record, or the additional service at Cambridge, Dorchester Heights, and Saratoga attributed to him in the other record.

2 *Vital Records of Lincoln*. Lydia was the sister of Samuel Farrar, Jr. (q.v.).

3 Ibid.; *Town of Weston, Births, Deaths, & Marriages*; Bond, *Genealogies of the Families of Watertown*, p. 53; Wheeler, "Lincoln," in Hurd, Vol. 2, p. 622.

> **What's in a (New England Slave) Name?**
>
> Few New England slaves had last names of their own. In most cases, they were known by the last names of their owners: "The Smith's boy, Cato," for example, or more simply "Cato Smith," was usually sufficient to identify a slave named Cato who was owned by the Smiths (see Cato Smith (q.v.)). Among Lincoln-related slaves in the 1770s, Salem Middlesex (q.v.) is the only one known to have had a last name apparently unrelated to his owner; he was owned by Braddyll Smith of Weston.
>
> Upon gaining freedom, it was often a different story. Almost as a rite of manumission, it was a widespread practice for former slaves to shed their owners' names and to adopt last names or family names of their own.
>
> Generally, a new name adopted by a former slave would reflect some familial link to an important family member or ancestor, or honor someone else meaningful to ▶

south with this unit to join Washington's forces at Valley Forge. His name appears on a muster return dated Valley Forge, February 1778. During 1778, he served at the Battle of Monmouth and the Battle of Rhode Island. The following year, from February 1779 through April 1779, he appears to have been deployed in Providence with the same unit. From January 1, 1780, until his discharge on March 20, 1780, he served in Captain Bowman's Company, Col. Timothy Bigelow's Regiment.[1]

He was back in service a year later, and served in Capt. John Hayward's Company, Colonel Webb's Regiment from September 1, 1781, through December 4, 1781 (credited with 3 months, 13 days of service). He was paid by the town of Lincoln for this service.[2]

He was African-American; a cordwainer (i.e., shoemaker) by trade. He paid a poll tax in 1780, indicating that he was by then a free man. He is identifiable almost certainly as the former slave of either Amos Brooks or Timothy Brooks, and he may have obtained his freedom through this three-year Continental service. He remained in Lincoln until about 1785, when he moved to Boston. No further information is known about his family, his service age, his life in Boston, or his death.[3]

There is substantial evidence to indicate that Peter Bowes (inst.) and Peter Brooks (q.v.) are in fact the same individual. If so, then as Peter Brooks, he had served previously at Cambridge in 1775 and at Dorchester in 1776–77.[4]

---

1 *Massachusetts Soldiers and Sailors*, Vol. II, p. 339. See also Blake, "James Barrett's Returns of Men" (p. 473) for a record of his being mustered and paid a bounty for this service, as reported by James Barrett, muster master, on April 25, 1777.

2 *Massachusetts Soldiers and Sailors*, Vol. II, p. 354. "Treasurer's Accompts," March 8, 1782. This service appears to have been in the Hudson Valley.

3 MacLean, *A Rich Harvest*, p. 306; Brooks deed to Bowes (1783); Bowes deed to Brooks (1785). See also sidebar, "What's in a (New England Slave) Name?" Former slaveholders in colonial New England were ethically and legally responsible to provide for the economic well-being of their former slaves. As evidence of that responsibility, the transfer of land from Amos Brooks to Bowes, and from Bowes back to Timothy Brooks is evidence of a former slave, former slaveholder relationship. The author's premise is that Peter Bowes is a former slave of Amos Brooks. Jack MacLean (private communication, 2009) hypothesizes that Peter may have been the former slave of Timothy Brooks, and that there may have been some sort of agreement between the families of the two Brooks cousins.

4 See Wiggin, "A Tale of Two or Three Peters."

A pair of land transactions fits the pattern of former slaveowners providing for their former slaves, showing evidence that Peter Bowes was the former slave of either Amos Brooks or Timothy Brooks. He served in the war first under the name Peter Brooks, then later under the name Peter Bowes. In 1783 *(above)*, the heirs of Amos Brooks sold to "Peter Bowes, a free Negro man of Lincoln aforesaid Cordwainer" an acre of land bordering Flint's Pond and land belonging to Timothy Brooks. Two years later *(right)*, Peter Bowes, "late of Lincoln now resident in Boston," sold the parcel to Timothy Brooks along with "a certain Dwelling house … standing on land of the said Timothy Brooks"— land that previously may have belonged to Amos Brooks's heirs. (*above*, courtesy of Lincoln Town Archives, Lincoln, MA; *right*, Middlesex County Registry of Deeds)

his or her life, or symbolize something—anything—of particular significance to the former slave. In some cases, the significance of the new name is obvious, as for example, "Freeman." In other cases, and without much thought to the difficulties they were creating for future historians, the link is more obscure. In Lincoln, Brister Hoar became Sippio Brister, Cuff Hoar became Cuff Kneeland, Peter Brooks became Peter Bowes, and Jack Farrar became Jack Freeman and Jack Hatch. The significance, in each case, of the adopted names Sippio, Kneeland, Bowes, and Hatch remains unknown.

The resulting difficulties in tracking slaves and former slaves are obvious. In rare cases, documents have survived which irrefutably link different names to the same individual. A single probate document, for example, provides incontrovertible evidence that the names Jack Farrar (q.v.), Jack Hatch, and Jack Freeman all referred to the same individual (see p. 273).

More often, it takes a bit of historical detective work to fit the pieces together. Consider the example of Peter Brooks (q.v.) and Peter Bowes (q.v.). Peter Brooks disappears from the historical record after his March 1, 1777, discharge from service at Dorchester. On March 20, 1777, a hitherto unknown individual named Peter Bowes enlisted for Continental service. The enlistment is reported by James Barrett, muster master, on April 25, 1777.

In colonial New England, deep Puritanical roots underpinned slaveholders' ethical and legal responsibility to provide for their former slaves and to prevent them from becoming economic wards of the town. This manifested itself in many forms, including the posting of a bond upon manumitting a slave, or providing the ▸

former slave with land, or with a house, or with employment, or with a bequest. Numerous examples exist in local records: Susanna Barron of Concord sold "four acres of plow land" in 1761 for £16 to John Jack, a former slave who had belonged to her deceased father, Benjamin Barron; Duncan Ingraham of Concord reportedly built a house for his former slave, Cato; Squire Cuming of Concord willed his former slave, Brister Freeman, £35 in 1788; John Headley of Lincoln, in his will, freed his slaves Prince and Rose upon his death (in 1779) but specifically provided for their continued support from his estate.

In 1783, the heirs of Amos Brooks sold one acre of land in Lincoln to Peter Bowes for £3:6. Two years later, Peter Bowes, now living in Boston, sold this land to Timothy Brooks (q.v.) along with his rights to "a certain Dwelling house in said Lincoln standing on land of said Timothy Brooks" for £12. Timothy Brooks and Amos Brooks were cousins, and they owned adjacent property. These were not arms-length transactions; they have all of the appropriate earmarks of former slaveholding family/former slave transactions. The fact that Amos Brooks and Peter Bowes were both cordwainers (shoemakers) is further evidence of a relationship, as it fits the typical pattern of slaves being trained in the trade or occupation of their owners. Timothy Brooks is also known to have been a slaveholder. There is little doubt that Peter Bowes is the former slave of either Amos Brooks or Timothy Brooks. Either way, as a slave, Peter Bowes probably had no surname of his own prior to manumission, and most likely he was known simply as the Brooks's boy, Peter, or as Peter Brooks for short.

Thus, while no single document has been found that explicitly identifies Peter Brooks and Peter Bowes as the same individual, the historical context provides reasonable certainty that this was the case.

The origin and significance of the name Bowes, however, is less clear. One possibility is a Rev. Nicholas Bowes, who was Pastor of the Bedford Church, just a few miles down the road. Reverend Bowes had eight children, born between 1734 and 1755, some of whom may have been approximately Peter's age. Possibly, the Reverend Bowes or his family may have been an important source of friendship, spiritual guidance, or support for Peter at some critical juncture during his life. Or perhaps Peter had a connection to the Bowes family even before he was with the Brooks family. Whatever reason Peter had for choosing the name Bowes, it was finally a name of his own.

[See MacLean, *A Rich Harvest,* pp. 220, 306; March 12, 1788, administrative paper for Jack Hatch, Middlesex County Probate; Brooks deed to Bowes (1783); Bowes deed to Brooks (1785); Wiggin, "A Tale of Two or Three Peters"; Blake, "James Barrett's Returns of Men," p. 473. See also Tolman, *John Jack and Daniel Bliss,* p. 17; and Elliott and Jones, *Concord: Its Black History,* pp. 31, 42.]

BOWMAN, Edmund
[also Edmond]

Edmund Bowman may have been in arms at Concord on April 19, 1775, probably as a member of the militia company from Lincoln.[1]

He served as a private in Capt. John Hartwell's Company of Militia from Lincoln, Col. Eleazer Brooks's 3rd Middlesex County Regiment, which marched from Lincoln to fortify Dorchester Heights on March 4, 1776. The unit was discharged five days later, on March 9, after the threat of a British assault on the fortifications had eased with General Howe's decision to evacuate Boston. A pay receipt dated Lincoln, September 21, 1776, relates to this service at Dorchester Heights.[2]

He was age 36 at Dorchester Heights; the son of Thaddeus and Sarah (Loring) Bowman of Lexington. He had been married to Ester (also Esther) Hoar since 1760. They were evidently living in Lincoln by 1766. Ester was the daughter of John Hoar (q.v.) and sister of Samuel Hoar (q.v.) and Leonard Hoar (q.v.). He was also the brother-in-law of Samuel Farrar, Jr. (q.v.), and Nehemiah Abbot (q.v.). After Ester died in 1780, he married Eunice Mead of Stow in October 1782. He died in Concord in 1805 at age 66; he may possibly be buried in Lincoln.[3]

---

1 Without giving names, Hoar, *Autobiography* (p. 20) states: "My grandfather, two great-grandfathers, and three of my father's uncles were at Concord Bridge in the Lincoln Company...on the 19th of April, 1775." Clearly identifiable are his grandfather, Samuel Hoar (q.v.), great-grandfathers John Hoar (q.v.) and Abijah Peirce (q.v.), and two of his father's uncles, Nehemiah Abbot (q.v.) and Samuel Farrar, Jr. (q.v.). Although some conjecture accompanies the identity of the third uncle, Edmund Bowman appears to be the best fit. Joseph Cutler of Lexington; Moses Stone, Jr., of Watertown; Joseph White of Lancaster; Nathaniel Peirce of Lincoln; and Thomas Wheeler of Lincoln are all qualifying uncles, but none can be placed at Concord. Cutler, Stone, and White simply cannot be connected with Lincoln or with any other town that had men at Concord (although it appears that White and Stone may have marched on the April 19th Alarm). Thomas Wheeler and Nathaniel Peirce are simply unsupportable; they lack both any direct evidence to suggest a presence at Concord, and also any record of war service at all to hint at the possibility of an initial, unrecorded presence at Concord. John Hoar, brother of Samuel Hoar and Leonard Hoar (q.v.), appears to have died some years before 1775. The only other possibility for the third uncle could be Leonard Hoar, but at age 16, he would have been younger than any of the other Lincoln men known to have been at Concord. In addition, there is a strong Hoar family tradition that places him firmly at the Hoar family homestead, with Brister Hoar (q.v.), keeping lookout for an assemblage of women and children. It is doubtful that family tradition would have placed him at both locations (i.e., also at the Bridge). Accordingly, if only by a process of elimination, Edmund Bowman was probably the third uncle at Concord.

2 Hartwell, "A List of a Company of Militia"; *Massachusetts Soldiers and Sailors*, Vol. II, p. 351.

3 *Lexington Births, Marriages and Deaths*; *Vital Records of Lincoln*; Bond, *Genealogies of the Families of Watertown*, p. 89; *Vital Records of Stow*; *Concord, Massachusetts: Births, Marriages, and Deaths*. The births of Edmund and Ester's first three children are recorded in Lexington. The baptisms of two of them are recorded in Lincoln. The death of one of them is recorded in Lexington (a second child must also have died, apparently unrecorded, because another child born in 1766 was given the same name). Thereafter, starting in 1766, six births are recorded in Lincoln but not Lexington. This suggests family ties in both towns, but residency in Lexington until they moved to Lincoln before 1766. Bond apparently agrees. Bowman's marriage to Eunice is recorded in Stow (Eunice's name is listed as Meeds) and Weston, and it clearly indicates that he was living in Weston at the time. However, the only record of children by Edmund and Eunice is in Lincoln, starting in 1783, so they must have been back in Lincoln by that time. Both *Vital Records of Lincoln* and *Concord, Massachusetts: Births, Marriages, and Deaths* (which understates his age by a year) show the death of Edmund, Eunice, and a daughter in the space of 15 months in Concord, strong evidence that the family was living in Concord by 1805. His burial in Lincoln is per Bond, *Genealogies of the Families of Watertown*; this may be because his wife, Esther (Hoar) Bowman, is buried in the Meeting House Cemetery behind Bemis Hall or also because

The home of Aaron Brooks and his son, Stephen [Jr.], was located just south of Battle Road. Aaron was age 49 and a former Selectman when he served at Cambridge and at Ticonderoga in 1776; Stephen served at Dorchester Heights in 1776, then in the Hudson Valley in 1779. (Farrar, "Houses in Lincoln 100 Years Old")

BROOKS, Aaron

Aaron Brooks was paid by the town for service in Cambridge in 1776 and for service at Ticonderoga in 1776.[1]

He is reported by Lincoln historian William Wheeler to have served at Saratoga in 1777, but no primary source has been identified.[2]

There was an Aaron Brookes who served for 21 days at Rhode Island in June 1778, as a private in Capt. John Putnam's Company, Col. John Holman's Regiment, but it is not at all certain that this is the same Aaron Brooks.[3]

He turned age 49 in 1776, probably during his Ticonderoga service; the son of Thomas Brooks (q.v., Chapter 12) and Hannah (Dakin) Brooks; brother of Noah Brooks (q.v.) and Stephen Brooks (q.v.); cousin of Samuel Dakin, Jr. (q.v.), Timothy Brooks (q.v.), Ephraim Brooks (q.v.), and Deacon Joshua Brooks (q.v.).[4]

He had been married to Mary (Stone) from Concord since 1755 and was the father of Stephen Brooks [Jr.] (q.v.). He had been a member of Lincoln's original militia company in 1757. He had also served as a Selectman immediately before the war broke out. He died in 1811 at age 84 and is buried in the Meeting House Cemetery behind Bemis Hall.[5]

Edmund Bowman's death in Concord was also recorded in Lincoln records, but no burial record for Edmund Bowman has been found either in the Meeting House Cemetery or in the old Precinct Burial Ground.

1 "Treasurer's Accompts," June 9, 1779, and June 10, 1779.
2 Wheeler, "Lincoln," in Hurd, Vol. 2, p. 622.
3 *Massachusetts Soldiers and Sailors*, Vol. II, p. 565.
4 *Concord, Massachusetts: Births, Marriages, and Deaths*; *Vital Records of Lincoln*.
5 Ibid. Also MacLean, *A Rich Harvest*, p. 240; Martin, "The Sons of Lincoln," p. 25; Wheeler, "Lincoln," in Hurd, Vol. 2, p. 622; Biggs, "In Memorium," p. 165.

BROOKS, Abner

Abner Brooks of Lincoln served as a private in Capt. John Hartwell's Company, Col. Nicholas Dike's Regiment at Dorchester from December 14, 1776 to March 1, 1777.

A few months later, on August 14, 1777, he was drafted out of Capt. Samuel Farrar, Jr.'s Lincoln Militia Company, Col. Eleazer Brooks's 3rd Middlesex County Regiment for service in the Northern Department. He went to Saratoga as a private in Capt. George Minot's Company, Col. Samuel Bullard's Massachusetts Militia Regiment, for 3 months, 25 days from August 16, 1777, to November 30, 1777, and was present at the surrender of Burgoyne.[1]

Quite possibly, he may also have served previously, as a 16-year-old at Ticonderoga, in 1776, although no confirming record has been found.[2]

He was the son of Ephraim Brooks (q.v.) and Sarah (Heywood) Brooks, brother of Benjamin Brooks (q.v.), Levi Brooks (q.v., Chapter 12), and Ephraim Brooks, Jr. (q.v.). He was also the nephew of Deacon Joshua Brooks (q.v.), Timothy Brooks (q.v.), and Gregory Stone (q.v.); cousin of Joshua Brooks, Jr. (q.v.), Jonas Brooks (q.v.), Ephraim Hartwell, Jr. (q.v.), Isaac Hartwell (q.v.), John Hartwell (q.v.), Jonas Hartwell (q.v.), Samuel Hartwell (q.v.), Gregory Stone, Jr. (q.v.), Joshua Stone (q.v.), and Timothy Stone (q.v.). He turned 17 during his service with Captain Hartwell, and died on December 4, 1777, four days after being discharged from his service at Saratoga, and about three months shy of his 18th birthday.[3] Except that it occurred so quickly on the heels of his discharge, no indication has been found to suggest that his death may or may not have been related to his service.

BROOKS, Benjamin

Benjamin Brooks was a private in Capt. William Smith's Company of Minute Men from Lincoln, Col. Abijah Peirce's Regiment.[4] Following the engagement at Concord, he served for 1 month, 4 days in Cambridge.[5]

---

1 *Massachusetts Soldiers and Sailors*, Vol. II, p. 568; "Treasurer's Accompts," February 18, 1780. The town appears to have paid his father, posthumously, for this service. On February 18, 1780, the town paid Ephraim Brooks (q.v.) for service at Ticonderoga in 1776, Dorchester in 1777, and Saratoga in 1777. As a man of 50-plus years, it is not likely that Ephraim provided this service. As Abner Brooks (inst.) served at Dorchester in 1777 and at Saratoga in 1777, it is probable that the payment was for his service.

Wheeler, "Lincoln" (in Hurd, Vol. 2, p. 622), says he served at Rhode Island in 1777 and was discharged November 30, 1777. No corroborating record of service at Rhode Island has been identified, and the discharge date Wheeler gives corresponds to Abner Brooks's discharge date from service at Saratoga. Perhaps Wheeler intended to credit him with service at Saratoga, not Rhode Island.

2 See note 1. The town's payment to Ephraim for Ticonderoga service is unmatched with a corresponding record of service. Of Ephraim's sons, Benjamin (q.v.) died before he could have served at Ticonderoga, and no record of any service by Levi (q.v., Chapter 12) has been found. Ephraim Jr. (q.v.) could have served at Ticonderoga. But as the Dorchester and Saratoga payments match service by Abner, there is some logic to suggest that Abner may have provided the Ticonderoga service as well.

3 *Vital Records of Lincoln*.

4 Coburn, *Muster Rolls*.

5 *Massachusetts Soldiers and Sailors*, Vol. II, p. 569; "Treasurer's Accompts," February 19, 1776. The town paid his father, Ephraim Brooks (q.v.), for his accoutrements as a minute man. As Ephraim was not a minute man, this payment was probably a posthumous reimbursement for Benjamin's accoutrements.

He was age 18 on April 19, 1775; the son of Ephraim Brooks (q.v.) and Sarah (Heywood) Brooks of Lincoln; brother of Ephraim Brooks, Jr. (q.v.), Levi Brooks (q.v., Chapter 12), and Abner Brooks (q.v.). He was also the nephew of Deacon Joshua Brooks (q.v.), Timothy Brooks (q.v.), and Gregory Stone (q.v.); cousin of Joshua Brooks, Jr. (q.v.), Jonas Brooks (q.v.), Ephraim Hartwell, Jr. (q.v.), Isaac Hartwell (q.v.), John Hartwell (q.v.), Jonas Hartwell (q.v.), Samuel Hartwell (q.v.), Gregory Stone, Jr. (q.v.), Joshua Stone (q.v.), and Timothy Stone (q.v.). He died three months after returning home, on August 29, 1775, age 19, evidently in Lincoln. Despite speculation that he may have caught Camp Fever at Cambridge, no indication has been found to suggest that his death may or may not have been related to his service.[1]

BROOKS, Daniel

Daniel Brooks served 3 months, 14 days as a private in Capt. John Hayward's Company, Colonel Webb's Regiment of the Continental Army, evidently in the Hudson River Valley. He enlisted September 1, 1781, for three months and was discharged December 4, 1781. He was paid by the town for three months of service.[2]

He was age 10 when the war broke out. He entered the service a few days prior to turning 17. He was the son of John and Lucy (Hoar) Brooks; brother of Job Brooks (q.v.); nephew of Eleazer Brooks (q.v.).[3]

He reportedly claimed to have been a witness to the events on April 19, 1775.[4]

After the war, he married Bathsheba Dakin, daughter of Samuel Dakin (q.v.) and Elizabeth Dakin, on December 20, 1786. By 1789, he was serving as a Deacon in the Lincoln Church, and by 1802, he was captain of the Lincoln Militia Company. Later, he appears to have become a colonel of the Middlesex County Militia. He opened his home

---

[1] *Vital Records of Lincoln*.

[2] *Massachusetts Soldiers and Sailors*, Vol. II, p. 570. "Treasurer's Accompts," March 12, 1782, and March 25, 1784; Brooks Family Notes. The service record in *Massachusetts Soldiers and Sailors* does not indicate where he was deployed, but according to family tradition (see Brooks Family Notes), he told his son that he served in New York, was discharged at Saratoga without having been paid, and walked home penniless. As he had no money for food, his journey was difficult. Hungry and sick, he apparently was taken in, fed, and nursed back to health by a kindly family en route. To the extent that the tradition may be factually based, he was more likely discharged around West Point, rather than at Saratoga.

In *An Account of the Celebration* (p. 197) his grandson, Lewis E. Smith, writes, "at the age of sixteen, he enlisted in the Continental Army and served a long term."

[3] *Vital Records of Lincoln*; Brooks Family Notes.

[4] *An Account of the Celebration*, p. 197; Brooks Family Notes. One story places him at Concord. It is told by Lewis E. Smith, Brooks's grandson, who recalled (in *An Account of the Celebration*, p. 197) his grandfather's tales of seeing "the British soldiers cut down the flagstaff of the Provincials [actually, it was the liberty pole, not the flagstaff, that the British soldiers cut down], watch[ing] the progress of the events, and [seeing] the beginning of the hasty retreat." Smith says his grandfather was age 14 at the time, but this is incorrect. Whether or not a 10-year-old would have wandered a couple of miles down the road on his own, and witnessed the action at Concord may be open to question. Another, perhaps more credible Brooks family tradition has the 10-year-old unable to resist the excitement of the events unfolding in and around Brooks Village (so called, the cluster of Brooks-family properties near the Lincoln/Concord town line) that morning. As the escalating fight swept through Brooks Village—and in direct defiance of his mother's demands to stay away—he crept close enough to become a spectator of the fight (Brooks Family Notes).

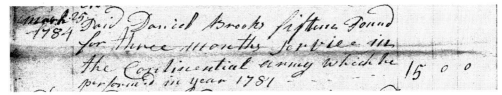

As a curious 10-year-old, Daniel Brooks is said to have witnessed the swirl of events in Concord and Lincoln at the start of the Revolutionary War. Six-and-a-half years later, he was in the army when the war climaxed—serving as backfill in the Hudson Valley for the troops that General Washington marched south to capture Lord Cornwallis at Yorktown. (Courtesy of the Lincoln Town Archives, Lincoln, MA)

as a tavern for a few years, after the turn of the century. He died in Lincoln in 1839, a few days after turning age 75, and he is reportedly buried in the Meeting House Cemetery behind Bemis Hall.[1]

BROOKS, Eleazer

Major Eleazer Brooks went to Concord on April 19, 1775, although it is unknown whether or not he held an official leadership position. Historian Lemuel Shattuck credits him with having cooled the ardor of Rev. William Emerson and others who wanted to engage the Regulars as soon as they arrived in Concord, with the caution, "No, it will not do for *us* to begin the war."[2]

Subsequently, he was commissioned as first major in Col. James Barrett's 3rd Middlesex County Regiment of the Massachusetts Militia on February 7, 1776, and the following day he was elected colonel to succeed Barrett in command of the regiment. His commission was dated February 14, 1776.[3]

Only a couple of weeks later, Colonel Brooks's 3rd Middlesex County Regiment was called into service, and he marched his troops from Lincoln to fortify Dorchester Heights on March 4, 1776. They were part of General Washington's grand surprise to the British the next morning. They served for five days, returning to Lincoln on March 9, after the threat of a British assault on Dorchester Heights had passed, and British General Howe had made the decision instead to evacuate Boston.[4]

---

1 Ibid. MacLean, *A Rich Harvest*, p. 332. His burial location is currently unmarked. Brooks Family Notes and *Soldiers and Sailors* [SAR] both indicate that his grave is marked by an SAR marker. Brooks Family Notes even identifies the location as plot # 2007, near Aaron Brooks # 2006, Levi Brooks # 2008, Noah Brooks # 2009, and Timothy Brooks # 2010. Biggs, however, gives mention to the others, but not to Daniel (Biggs, "In Memorium," pp. 163, 165, 166). Whatever stone may once have marked the spot must have disappeared by the time of Biggs's study.

2 See Shattuck, *History of the Town of Concord*, p. 106. MacLean, *A Rich Harvest* (pp. 269, 607), identifies Brooks as a major of the militia companies, but his name is strangely missing from listings of the officers of the Provincial forces at the bridge (see Shattuck, *History of the Town of Concord*, p. 110; Ripley, *A History of the Fight at Concord*, pp. 14–15). Whatever his official role (if any) may have been at Concord, his credentials as a leader were well understood. Within ten months, he would be named colonel of the militia regiment made up of the same companies that were at the bridge. The quote attributed to him may or may not be apocryphal, but it certainly reflects his standing among the Provincial military and community leaders.

3 *Massachusetts Soldiers and Sailors*, Vol. II, pp. 562, 564, 572. Also Eleazer Brooks Papers [Lincoln], p. 1.

4 Shattuck, *History of the Town of Concord* (p. 300), places Brooks at Dorchester Heights in 1777, but he probably meant 1776. No confirming record of service at Dorchester Heights in 1777 has been found.

His regiment was mobilized again on July 21, 1776, "to defend the lines of Fortifications near and about the Town of Boston," until December 1, 1776, as replacements for Continental regiments being sent to Ticonderoga and New York. He appears to have gone to Ticonderoga at this time on some official business, but there is no record of his being in command of any troops at Ticonderoga.[1]

On September 27, 1776, he marched a detached militia regiment to the New York area to support General Washington in the increasingly bleak New York campaign.[2] During 62 days of service through November 16, 1776, his regiment is reported to have served at Horse Neck (Greenwich), Kingsbridge (Bronx), Valentine Hill (Yonkers), White Plains, and North Castle. During the battle at White Plains (October 28, 1776), his position was the object of the first cavalry charge in American history; a devastatingly effective maneuver executed by a unit of British Light Dragoons. His regiment suffered heavy losses, and broke. Shattuck says "Col. Brooks distinguished himself for his cool and determined bravery." His 1806 obituary similarly credits that at White Plains "he exhibited a specimen of undaunted bravery." Lincoln historian William Wheeler credits him with receiving a commendation from General Washington. But most others have heaped blame on Colonel Brooks's Militia Regiment for breaking and running at the first exposure to enemy fire.[3]

Col. Eleazer Brooks (*above*) was commander of the 3rd Middlesex County Militia Regiment, and he led a regiment of Massachusetts Militia at the Battle of White Plains in 1776. He was promoted to Brigadier General in 1778 (*right*). Brooks was highly regarded as a brave officer, a distinguished leader, and an influential statesman during the Revolutionary period. Carved into his gravestone are the lines, "He was intrusted with many important offices, both military and political. In the defence of the rights of his Country he distinguished himself in Council and in the Field. As a statesman and Politician, he excelled." (Portrait courtesy of the Concord Museum, Concord, MA, www.concordmuseum.org; Commission courtesy of Lincoln Town Archives, Lincoln, MA)

---

1 Eleazer Brooks Papers [Lincoln], pp. 3–4; Brooks, *Trial by Fire*, pp. 47–48; "Treasurer's Accompts," June 10, 1779. The "Treasurer's Accompts" give no dates for his Ticonderoga service, but the troop calls suggest that it would have been at this time. There is no record that his regiment was actually called into service. More likely, it served as a source of manpower from which individuals were detached for service.

Another record attributed to him indicates he held the rank of major in the Continental Army in Colonel Webb's Regiment, Major General Sullivan's Division in 1776, but this is probably an error. This record appears more likely to apply to Maj. John Brooks of Reading than to Col. Eleazer Brooks, but the precise details warrant further investigation (*Massachusetts Soldiers and Sailors*, Vol. II, pp. 564, 576).

2 A record in *Massachusetts Soldiers and Sailors* (Vol. II, p. 572) seems to suggest that Colonel Brooks's Regiment marched to New York on November 28, 1776, but the Regiment had already returned from the New York service twelve days before. There is no evidence of a second march to New York. The November 28th date appears instead to be an administrative date, unrelated to the actual dates of service.

3 *Massachusetts Soldiers and Sailors*, Vol. II, pp. 562, 572; Shattuck, *History of the Town of Concord*, p. 319; *Newburyport Herald* (November 25, 1806), p. 3; Wheeler, "Lincoln," in Drake, Vol. 2, p. 42. The absence of

Chapter 10: The Army of the Revolution

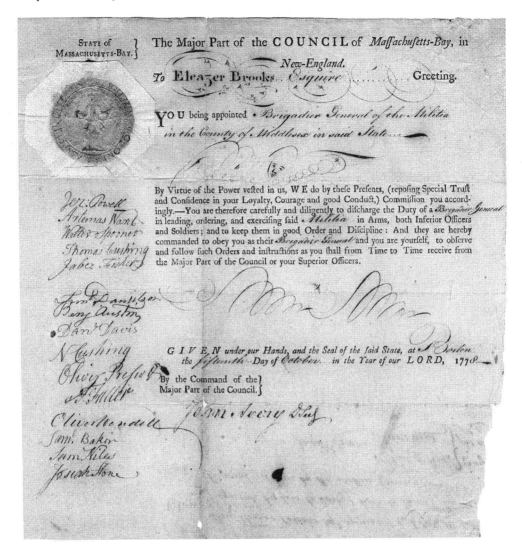

any evidence or reference in the Eleazer Brooks Papers [Lincoln] to distinguished service or a commendation from General Washington is interesting, and maybe telling. On the other hand, MacLean notes (private communication) that Wheeler may have had access to Brooks's papers, which had been passed down through his cousin, Horatio Wheeler (who was a grandson of Eleazer Brooks). "One could well imagine," writes MacLean, "a commendation from Washington being the one item Horatio might choose to retain, so I'm not sure it is necessarily telling that such a document is not in the collection." Wheeler's family connections provide a rationale for him to have known of such a commendation, if it existed. This warrants further investigation. The source of condemnation for the behavior of Brooks's Regiment is Colonel Haslet, who commanded a Delaware regiment in the Continental Line. Haslet's account of the battle is characteristically self-serving, and Colonel Brooks's Regiment is a convenient scapegoat. Nevertheless, historians have echoed Haslet's condemnation in most subsequent accounts of the battle. John Hannigan at the Massachusetts Archives believes that the "unusually high" number of items missing in battle is consistent with a panicked departure from the scene of battle. The author suggests, however, that the high casualty count (6 killed, 10 missing, 33 wounded) is inconsistent with running away at the first sign of battle. Brooks's Regiment may have made a panicked departure, but they must have stood their ground for awhile, until they were overwhelmed by the enemy. (See sidebar, "Commendation or Cowardice?", p. 86, for a further discussion of this issue. For Haslet's blame, see

On July 16, 1777, his regiment was mobilized again, bound for Rhode Island, but the order was cancelled seven days later, apparently before they got underway. During August and September, consistent with the Resolve of August 9, 1777, and with the increasing urgency of checking Burgoyne's advance toward Albany, significant numbers of men were detached (drafted or recruited) from his regiment, and sent north to support General Gates. Despite Shattuck's assertion, there is little evidence that Colonel Brooks himself was at Saratoga when Burgoyne surrendered, or that he was deployed in escorting Burgoyne's surrendered troops to Cambridge. Instead, he was called into active service on November 3 for five months, as the ranking militia officer in charge of guarding Burgoyne's Convention Army at Cambridge from the time of their arrival on November 7, 1777, until April 3, 1778. During this service, Colonel Brooks's correspondence suggests some friction with his Continental Army counterparts.[1]

Following the resolve of April 20, 1778, many individuals from his regiment were deployed for nine months at Fishkill. As the purpose of the resolve was to raise 2000 men to fill up the quota of the 15 battalions in the Continental Army for which Massachusetts was responsible, it is more probable that Brooks's Regiment served as a feeder for these men, rather than that it was actually called into service at Fishkill.[2]

He was commissioned brigadier general of the Middlesex County Militia on October 15, 1778.[3]

Eleazer Brooks was age 47 when the war broke out, the son of Job and Elizabeth Brooks. He was the uncle of Job Brooks (q.v.) and Daniel Brooks (q.v.).[4]

He had previously been captain of Lincoln's militia company in 1773. He was one of the town's most influential leaders in the period leading up to the outbreak of war, as well as during and after the Revolution. In addition to a succession of town offices, he served on Lincoln's Committee of Correspondence in 1773 and represented the town in the Provincial Congress in 1774. He became a delegate to the Massachusetts Constitutional Convention in

---

Freeman, *George Washington*, p. 231, footnote. Also Commager and Morris, *The Spirit of Seventy-Six*, p. 489. For battle returns, see *Muster Rolls of the Revolutionary War*, Vol. 55, File L, p. 24.)

1 Eleazer Brooks Papers [Lincoln], pp. 13, 19; Shattuck, *History of the Town of Concord*, pp. 300, 356; Wheeler, "Lincoln," in Hurd, Vol. 2, p. 620. Shattuck's placement of Eleazer Brooks at Saratoga, echoed by Wheeler, "Lincoln" (in Drake, Vol. 2, p. 42), and Brooks, *Trial by Fire* (p. 50), is confused and misleading. The August 14th drafting of troops from Brooks's Regiment for service at Saratoga under Col. Samuel Bullard and the September 27th detachment of more troops from Brooks's Regiment for service at Saratoga under Capt. Samuel Farrar, Jr., and Col. Jonathan Reed, does not indicate Brooks's presence at Saratoga. Regarding the escort of the captives to Cambridge, Shattuck's statement (p. 356) that "Nine companies guarded Burgoyne's troops down, five marching before and four behind," implies through its juxtaposition that the escort included Capt. Simon Hunt's Company "under Col. Eleazer Brooks and Gen. Heath." In fact, the escort included Capt. Samuel Farrar, Jr.'s Company under Col. Jonathan Reed and General Glover. Capt. Simon Hunt's Company was part of a new regiment under Colonel Brooks and General Heath, detached in early November to guard the captives after they arrived in Cambridge.

2 The resolve of April 20, 1778, provided for the militia companies to be assembled and the required number of men to be raised by draft, lot, or voluntary enlistment. This had become a pretty standard practice for raising men to fill out the ranks of the Continental forces.

3 *Massachusetts Soldiers and Sailors*, Vol. II, pp. 562, 564, 572. Surprisingly little information has survived about his military service after his promotion to brigadier general. He seems to have turned his attention increasingly to matters of civil governance and to the military cabinet.

4 *Concord, Massachusetts: Births, Marriages, and Deaths*. See also *Vital Records of Lincoln*.

1779, and he represented Lincoln during the postwar period in the Massachusetts General Court. He became a Deacon of the Lincoln Church in 1794.[1]

He had married Mary Taylor of Concord in 1763; she had died in 1769, apparently childless. In 1777 (probably June), he married Elizabeth Greenough of Boston, who was approximately 20 years his junior. They had one son, Eleazer, born the following year, and a daughter Elizabeth, born two years after that. The elder Eleazer Brooks died in 1806, at age 79, and is buried in the Meeting House Cemetery behind Bemis Hall.[2]

BROOKS, Eleazer, Jr.

The town paid Eleazer Brooks, Jr., for three months of service in Rhode Island. No details or dates are given, but this service was possibly in 1779 or 1780.[3]

The identity of Eleazer Brooks, Jr., is unknown. He appears on the town's 1780 north Assessors' list, assessed for one poll. Despite the similarity of names, there is no apparent relationship, linear or otherwise, to Eleazer Brooks (q.v.).[4]

BROOKS, Ephraim

Ephraim Brooks served alongside his son, Ephraim Jr., as a private in Capt. John Hartwell's Company of Militia from Lincoln, Col. Eleazer Brooks's 3rd Middlesex County Regiment, which marched from Lincoln to fortify Dorchester Heights on March 4, 1776. The unit was discharged five days later, on March 9, after the threat of a British assault on the fortifications had eased with General Howe's decision to evacuate his troops from Boston.[5]

He was age 50 when he served with his son at Dorchester Heights. He was a veteran of the French and Indian War, having been wounded on the Crown Point expedition. He was the son of Joshua and Lydia Brooks and had been married to Sarah Heywood since 1752.[6] He was the father of Ephraim Brooks, Jr. (q.v.), who served with him at Dorchester Heights, Benjamin Brooks (q.v.), who had died the previous August after service as a minute man, Levi Brooks (q.v., Chapter 12) and Abner Brooks (q.v.). He was also the brother of Deacon Joshua Brooks (q.v.) and Timothy Brooks (q.v.); brother-in-law of Gregory Stone (q.v.); nephew of Thomas Brooks (q.v., Chapter 12); cousin of Aaron Brooks (q.v.), Noah

---

1 MacLean, *A Rich Harvest*, pp. 297–300. Brooks, *Trial by Fire* (pp. 39–55) provides a nicely written, sympathetic biography of Eleazer Brooks, as a man and as a public servant. What little he says of Brooks's wartime service, however, is somewhat misleading, ignoring Brooks's participation in the New York campaign, and incorrectly presuming Brooks's participation at Saratoga (p. 50). In a portrayal of homespun humility, he asserts that Brooks "served as a private with the rebel forces" at the Concord Bridge (p. 47). Notwithstanding uncertainty about Brooks's official role at Concord, this is unsubstantiated and belies Brooks's strong influence.

2 His intention to marry Elizabeth Greenough is recorded as May 26, 1777 (*Concord, Massachusetts: Births, Marriages, and Deaths*; *Vital Records of Lincoln*; Biggs, "In Memorium," p. 161).

3 "Treasurer's Accompts," February 16, 1781. The timeframe for the service is suggested by similar payments to Joseph Billing, Jr. (q.v.), Elijah Child, (q.v.), and others.

4 Lincoln 1780 north Assessors' list. Eleazer Brooks's (q.v.) son, Eleazer Jr., was only two years old in 1780, so he could not be the Eleazer Brooks, Jr., of this record. No other individual named Eleazer Brooks or Eleazer Brooks, Jr., has been found. A separate entry on the Assessors' list for Eleazer Brooks with assessed real estate precludes any possibility that the Eleazer Brooks, Jr., listing could actually refer to Eleazer Brooks (q.v.).

5 *Massachusetts Soldiers and Sailors*, Vol. II, p. 572.

6 *Concord, Massachusetts: Births, Marriages, and Deaths*; Shattuck, *History of the Town of Concord*, p. 73.

Brooks (q.v.), and Stephen Brooks (q.v.); uncle of Joshua Brooks, Jr. (q.v.), Jonas Brooks (q.v.), Gregory Stone, Jr. (q.v.), Joshua Stone (q.v.), and Timothy Stone (q.v.).

He died in Lincoln in 1792 at age 66 and is buried in the Meeting House Cemetery behind Bemis Hall.[1]

The town paid Ephraim Brooks for service at Ticonderoga in 1776, Dorchester in 1777, and Saratoga in 1777. Most likely, these payments were for the service of his son, Abner, who died in 1777. Another possibility is that his son Ephraim Jr. might have provided the Ticonderoga service. In addition, the town reimbursed Ephraim (inst.) for accoutrements "as a minute man" on behalf of his son Benjamin who had died a few months after serving as a minute man.[2]

BROOKS, Ephraim, Jr.

Ephraim Brooks, Jr. served as a minute man on the Alarm of April 19th, in Capt. Charles Miles's Minute Company from Concord, Col. Abijah Peirce's Regiment.[3]

Subsequently, on May 30, 1775, he enlisted and served at Cambridge as a private in Capt. Joseph Butler's Company, Col. John Nixon's 16th Massachusetts Regiment, during which he is presumed to have participated with his regiment in the Battle of Bunker Hill.[4]

In September 1775, while serving at Cambridge, he enlisted in the campaign to Quebec, evidently under Col. Benedict Arnold. It is unknown whether he was part of Col. Roger Enos's Division, which turned back during the arduous trek through the Maine wilderness in late October, or whether he continued on, participated in the Battle of Quebec on December 31, 1775, and returned home upon the expiration of his enlistment on January 1, 1776.

In either case, he was back in Lincoln by March 1776, when he served alongside his father, as a private in Capt. John Hartwell's Company of Militia from Lincoln, Col. Eleazer Brooks's 3rd Middlesex County Regiment at Dorchester Heights. The company marched from Lincoln to fortify Dorchester Heights on March 4, 1776, and was discharged five days later, on March 9, after the threat of a British assault on the fortifications had eased with General Howe's decision to evacuate his troops from Boston.[5]

It is possible that he may have served at Ticonderoga in 1776, although this service may just as logically have been served by his brother, Abner.[6]

---

1 *Vital Records of Lincoln*; Biggs, "In Memorium," p. 163.

2 "Treasurer's Accompts," February 18, 1780, February 19, 1776. Ephraim Jr. was away in the Continental service at the time of the 1780 transaction, so that would explain the payment to Ephraim Sr. if indeed it was Ephraim Jr. who had provided the Ticonderoga service.

3 Coburn, *Muster Rolls*.

4 In August, Colonel Nixon's 16th Massachusetts Regiment became known also as the 5th Regiment under Washington's Continental command.

5 *Massachusetts Soldiers and Sailors*, Vol. II, p. 572; Hartwell, "A List of a Company of Militia." *Massachusetts Soldiers and Sailors* credits all of this service to an Ephraim Brooks of Concord. There is, however, no record of another Ephraim Brooks who could have provided this service. The likelihood is that he may have been living and working in Concord in 1775 when the war broke out, then returned from Canada to his family's home in Lincoln.

6 "Treasurer's Accompts," February 18, 1780. The town paid his father, Ephraim Brooks (q.v.), for service at Ticonderoga in 1776, Dorchester in 1777, and Saratoga in 1777. It is more likely that this payment was for the service of one or more of his sons than it is that Ephraim provided this service himself. The Dorchester and Saratoga payments match the service record of his son, Abner (q.v.). Abner may also have provided the

From June 26, 1777, to June 26, 1780, he was back in service for three years in the Continental Army. His enlistment was credited to the town of Marlborough. He served as a corporal in Capt. Joseph Fox's Company, Col. Henry Jackson's Regiment. Colonel Jackson's Regiment participated in the Battle of Brandywine on September 11, 1777, wintered over at Valley Forge, and engaged the enemy at Monmouth on June 28, 1778. Thereafter, they were deployed to Rhode Island, where they participated in the Battle of Rhode Island on August 29, 1778, and remained for much of 1779. Whether or not Brooks was at Monmouth is uncertain, as he seems to have served for a time with Capt. Lemuel Trescott in Col. David Henley's Regiment in Providence in April 1778. He was back with Captain Fox in Colonel Henley's Regiment in the fall of 1778, and by April 1779, he had moved with Captain Fox's Company back to Colonel Jackson's Regiment at Pawtuxet. By July 1779 they were back in Providence. He also appears to have been in Warwick.[1]

Ephraim Brooks, Jr., was age 21 on April 19, 1775; age 22 at Bunker Hill, Canada, and Dorchester Heights.[2] He was the son of Ephraim Brooks (q.v.) and Sarah (Heywood) Brooks; brother of Benjamin Brooks (q.v.), Levi Brooks (q.v., Chapter 12), and Abner Brooks (q.v.) He was also the nephew of Deacon Joshua Brooks (q.v.), Timothy Brooks (q.v.), and Gregory Stone (q.v.); cousin of Joshua Brooks, Jr. (q.v.), Jonas Brooks (q.v.), Gregory Stone, Jr. (q.v.), Joshua Stone (q.v.), Timothy Stone (q.v.), Ephraim Hartwell, Jr. (q.v.), Isaac Hartwell (q.v.), John Hartwell (q.v.), Jonas Hartwell (q.v.), and Samuel Hartwell (q.v.).

He married Susanna Estabrook of Concord in 1784 and settled in Concord. He appears to have died in Concord at age 45 in 1799.[3]

BROOKS, Job

Job Brooks of Lincoln served in Cambridge as a private in Capt. Asahel Wheeler's Company, Colonel Robinson's Regiment from February 4, 1776, through the departure of the British forces from Boston. He enlisted under the Resolve of January 20, 1776, and served for 1 month, 28 days, stationed first at "the old College" (Harvard), then at "the Barracks on a small rise west of the college." Once, while on guard at Lechmere Point, he saw General Washington. General Putnam was there also, but he says he "did not know him."[4]

Ticonderoga service, but that is uncertain. Another possibility is that Ephraim Jr. (inst.) may have provided the Ticonderoga service. Ephraim Jr. was away in the Continental service at the time the payment was made.

1 *Massachusetts Soldiers and Sailors*, Vol. II, p. 572. This service is credited to Ephraim Brooks of Concord (see note 5, p. 232).

2 *Vital Records of Lincoln*. See also *Concord, Massachusetts: Births, Marriages, and Deaths*.

3 *Concord, Massachusetts: Births, Marriages, and Deaths*. The first of eight children recorded in Concord was born 4½ months after their marriage. The death record lists his age as 42. Although Ephraim Brooks, Jr., would have been age 45, there do not appear to be other qualifying individuals named Ephraim Brooks in the Concord or Lincoln records. Jack MacLean points out (private communication with the author) that in the 1790 and 1800 census entries, there is no Ephraim Brooks as head of household in either Lincoln or Concord; that the 1798 Federal Direct Tax shows an Ephraim Brooks assessed for a house (no barn) and land in Concord (no entry under name Susanna Brooks); and that Concord has a Susanna Brooks as a head of household in 1800—all of which tends to support the notion that the death record is Ephraim Brooks, Jr. (inst.) despite the age issue.

4 *Massachusetts Soldiers and Sailors*, Vol. II, p. 574; Pension Record # S15345. He mistakenly recalls in his pension declaration that this was Colonel Barrett's Regiment. Colonel Barrett commanded the 3rd Middlesex Militia Regiment until he was succeeded on February 8, 1776, by Col. Eleazer Brooks. It is probable that Job

His name also appears on a list of men in service at Ticonderoga in 1776.[1]

He enlisted again in December 1776 for four-months service to help meet the quota of men from Concord. He says he joined Captain Bridge's Company, Col. Samuel Thatcher's Regiment at Watertown; marched to Providence, stayed there a few days; then went to Danbury, Connecticut. From there, he went to Tarrytown, then to a spot near Kingsbridge (in the Bronx), and then to the Jerseys. In New Jersey, he was stationed at Woodbridge. The British were at Brunswick. The Continental troops under General Maxwell lay behind his regiment in the lower line.

On the day his term of service expired, he had fixed his pack to start for home, when the enemy attacked. He supposed that the enemy knew that they were disbanding. Eight men were taken prisoner as they retreated. "The Adjutant beat up For volunteers to drive the enemy back," he recalled. The men rallied, and "they retired as we advanced upon them, there was some Firing, nothing important." This was the second skirmish in which he had been involved. He says he was dismissed at Woodbridge about the first of April or the first of May.[2]

He was the son of John and Lucy (Hoar) Brooks; brother of Daniel Brooks (q.v.); nephew of Eleazer Brooks (q.v.). He turned 19 a few days into his service with Captain Wheeler's Company. After his war service, he left Lincoln and married Sarah Hildreth of Townsend in 1779. He may have lived briefly in New Ipswich and Hancock, New Hampshire, before settling in Stoddard, New Hampshire, by about 1790. About 1830, he moved to Walpole, New Hampshire, where he died in 1832 at age 75. He is buried in the North Cemetery, Westmoreland, New Hampshire.[3]

BROOKS, Jonas

Jonas Brooks served at Rhode Island from July 27, 1780, to October 30, 1780 (credited with 3 months, 7 days of service), as a private in Capt. Abraham Andrews's Company, Col. Cyprian How's Middlesex County Regiment. The company was detached to reinforce the Continental Army.[4]

He was age 13 at the start of the war; he turned 19 years of age during his service at Rhode Island.[5] He was the son of Deacon Joshua Brooks (q.v.) and Hannah (Simonds) Brooks; brother of Joshua Brooks, Jr. (q.v.). He was also the nephew of Ephraim Brooks (q.v.), Timothy Brooks (q.v.), and Gregory Stone (q.v.); cousin of Ephraim Brooks, Jr. (q.v.),

---

Brooks (inst.) was detached from Colonel Barrett's Regiment (of which Lincoln's militia company was part) for service with Colonel Robinson's Regiment.

1 *Massachusetts Soldiers and Sailors*, Vol. II, p. 574. As no details of this service have survived, and as he makes no mention of Ticonderoga service in his pension declaration, it is possible that he appears on the list but did not actually go into service at Ticonderoga.
2 Pension Record # S15345. Shattuck, *History of the Town of Concord* (p. 355), gives their discharge date as March 6. Other records suggest it was about the first of April.
3 *Vital Records of Lincoln*; Hallowell, *Vital Records of Townsend*; Brooks Family Notes; Pension Record # S15345; *SAR Revolutionary War Graves Register*. His marriage record in *Vital Records of Townsend* identifies him as being from Temple, which is unclear, but it probably means Temple, New Hampshire.
4 "Treasurer's Accompts," February 6, 1781; *Massachusetts Soldiers and Sailors*, Vol. II, p. 272.
5 *Vital Records of Lincoln*.

Benjamin Brooks (q.v.), Levi Brooks (q.v., Chapter 12), Abner Brooks (q.v.), Gregory Stone, Jr. (q.v.), Joshua Stone (q.v.), and Timothy Stone (q.v.).

After the war, he settled in Pepperell and married Rachel Greenough of Boston in 1785. Nine children are recorded in Pepperell through 1802. Sometime thereafter they appear to have moved out of Pepperell. By 1820, they were living in Wiscasset, Maine, where he died in 1850 at age 88. He is buried in Evergreen Cemetery in Wiscasset.[1]

BROOKS, Joshua[2]

[also Deacon Joshua, Joshua Jr.]

Deacon Joshua Brooks was paid by the town for service at Cambridge in 1775, at Ticonderoga in 1776, and for one-quarter of a three-year campaign in the Continental Army.[3]

No details of this service have been found. Because Deacon Joshua Brooks was age 54 in 1775, and a town father with a substantial tanning business to run, he seems an unlikely candidate to have served these stints, amounting to an estimated 17 to 22 months of service during a period of approximately 30 to 40 months. On the other hand, the possibility that he may actually have provided at least some of this service cannot be ignored. The payment transaction says explicitly that Deacon Joshua Brooks was paid "for His service at Cambridge," but it is less explicit about the Ticonderoga and the Continental service.[4]

Perhaps a more likely candidate for some of this service would be his son, William Brooks, who was age 18 at the time of the Cambridge service in 1775. Another, only slightly less likely possibility would be his son, Abel Brooks, who was age 16 at that time, and later married Betsey Brooks in 1788. Neither son, however, left any identifiable record of service in the American Revolution.[5]

---

1 *Vital Records of Lincoln*; *Vital Records of Pepperell*; 1820 Federal Census, Wiscasset, Lincoln County, Maine; 1850 Federal Census, Wiscasset, Lincoln County, Maine; Maine Deaths and Burials, 1841–1910; "Find A Grave." Jonas seems to disappear from *Vital Records of Lincoln* after his birth in October 1761. But there is a death record that reads, "Brooks, Jonas Greenough, s. Jonas & Rachel of Pepperrell, Sept. 14, 1788, a. 4 m." *Vital Records of Pepperell* contains a similar record: "Brooks, _____, s. Jonas & Rachel, at Lincoln, Sept. 19, 1788, a. almost a year." There is nothing else in *Vital Records of Pepperell* that hints at a Lincoln connection, but the author speculates that the father of this child is Jonas Brooks (inst.). No birth record for this child exists in either town, but the marriage intention for Jonas and Rachel is recorded in Pepperell, along with the births of eight subsequent children (Rachel's name is also given as Nancy). No other deaths are recorded.

2 There were four consecutive generations of individuals named Joshua Brooks. This individual is the second generation, properly known as Joshua Jr. from 1720 to 1768, when Joshua Sr. died. Both he and his father were tanners, town fathers, selectmen, and deacons, which can make the historical record difficult to follow. For our purposes, consistent with the period of time we are primarily concerned with (1775–1783), we will refer to this individual simply as Joshua Brooks (the designation Jr. having been passed to his son) or as Deacon Joshua Brooks.

3 "Treasurer's Accompts," June 10, 1779.

4 The estimate for the duration of these stints is derived from Shattuck, *History of the Town of Concord* (p. 299). The significance to be placed on the word "His" for the Cambridge service, or the omission of it for the Ticonderoga service and the Continental service, is not at all clear.

5 *Vital Records of Lincoln*. No other information about William or Abel has been uncovered. Two other sons did leave service records, but they are logically less likely candidates for having provided this service. Joshua Brooks, Jr. (q.v.) served at Cambridge in 1775, and there is no record of his having been paid for this service. However, the "Treasurer's Accompts" contain a separate transaction on the same day (the transactions are sequential) for other service by Joshua Brooks, Jr. The author has found no logic with which to explain the possibility that the town might have paid Deacon Joshua for service by Joshua Jr., when at the same time it paid Joshua Jr. directly for other service. Jonas Brooks (q.v.) was not yet of service age for Cambridge in 1775

The home of Deacon Joshua Brooks and his sons, Joshua Jr. and Jonas, bore witness to the fight along Battle Road. As a minute man, Joshua Jr. was slightly wounded at the North Bridge; later he was at Dorchester Heights, Saratoga, and the Battle of Rhode Island. Deacon Joshua may have served at Cambridge in 1775, while Jonas served at Rhode Island in 1780. (Farrar, "Houses in Lincoln 100 Years Old")

Another reasonable possibility for this service could be a slave named Jupiter. Not much is known about Jupiter, except that he was owned by Joshua Brooks, Sr., before Joshua Sr. died in 1768. Jupiter married Peg (a Negro servant of William Reed of Lexington) in 1756, and he is presumed to be the father of Peter Nelson (q.v.).[1]

Unfortunately, all of these possibilities are entirely speculative.

Joshua Brooks was the son of Joshua and Lydia (Wheeler) Brooks. He had been married to Hannah Simonds of Lexington since at least 1746 and was the father of Joshua Jr. (q.v.) and Jonas Brooks (q.v.). He was also the brother of Ephraim Brooks (q.v.) and Timothy Brooks (q.v.); brother-in-law of Gregory Stone (q.v.); nephew of Thomas Brooks (q.v., Chapter 12); cousin of Aaron Brooks (q.v.), Noah Brooks (q.v.), and Stephen Brooks (q.v.);

---

or Ticonderoga in 1776. This does not rule out the possibility of his having provided the Continental service, but there appears to be little logic to support the possibility.

1 *Lexington Births, Marriages and Deaths*; Brooks bill of sale to Nelson (1765). Malcolm, *Peter's War* connects this Jupiter with a record of a Jupiter Free (q.v., Chapter 12) of Lexington who served in Capt. Edmund Munroe's Company (also in Captain Bowman's Company), Col. Timothy Bigelow's Regiment from March 10, 1777, to March 10, 1780 (see *Massachusetts Soldiers and Sailors*, Vol. XVI, p. 40, which corrupts his last name to "Tree"). Malcolm provides no evidence for making the connection, and her work lacks source citations. The author finds this possible connection intriguing, but lacking in sufficient basis to be considered anything other than highly speculative.

Chapter 10: The Army of the Revolution

Deacon Joshua Brooks was paid by the town for his son, Joshua Jr.'s accoutrements as a minute man. The elder Joshua may have served at Cambridge, Ticonderoga, and/or in the Continental Army. (Courtesy of Lincoln Town Archives, Lincoln, MA)

uncle to Ephraim Brooks, Jr. (q.v.), Benjamin Brooks (q.v.), Levi Brooks (q.v., Chapter 12), Abner Brooks (q.v.), Gregory Stone, Jr. (q.v.), Joshua Stone (q.v.), and Timothy Stone (q.v.).[1]

He had previously been part of the town's militia company, having served for a time as its quartermaster. He had been a Deacon of the Lincoln Church since 1763, a Selectman for several terms, and a member of the Committee of Correspondence. Like his father and grandfather, he was a tanner by trade, and he in turn ran the substantial family tanning and currier business on the Bay Road until he died in 1790 at age 69. He is buried in the Meeting House Cemetery behind Bemis Hall.[2]

BROOKS, Joshua, Jr.[3]
[also Joshua III]

Joshua Brooks, Jr., was a private in Capt. William Smith's Company of Minute Men from Lincoln, Col. Abijah Peirce's Regiment.[4] At the North Bridge, he was "struck with a ball that cut through his hat, and drew blood on his forehead, and it looked as if it was cut with a knife."[5] Following the engagement at Concord, he served for five days in Cambridge.[6]

He apparently served at Cambridge during 1775, but the record of this service has not been found.[7]

---

1 *Concord, Massachusetts: Births, Marriages, and Deaths;* Hudson, *History of the Town of Lexington (revised),* Vol. 2, p. 620. See also *Vital Records of Lincoln.*

2 MacLean, *A Rich Harvest,* pp, 148, 165, 230, 237; Shattuck, *History of the Town of Concord,* p. 308; Biggs, "In Memorium," p. 162.

3 There were four consecutive generations of individuals named Joshua Brooks, which can make the historical record difficult to follow. This individual is the third generation, properly known as Joshua III until 1768, when his grandfather died, then Joshua Jr. from 1768 until 1790, when his father died. To avoid generational confusion, historians sometimes refer to him as Joshua III even after he became Joshua Jr. For our purposes, however, consistent with the practice during the period of time we are primarily concerned with (1775–1783), we will refer to this individual as Joshua Brooks, Jr. His son was born as Joshua III in 1780.

4 Coburn, *Muster Rolls.* The town paid his father, Deacon Joshua Brooks, for his accoutrements as a minute man (see "Treasurer's Accompts," February 19, 1776).

5 Baker Affidavit (1850).

6 *Massachusetts Soldiers and Sailors,* Vol. II, p. 579.

7 Pension Record # R22013, # BLWT 16269-160-55. His widow reports that he used to speak of his service at Cambridge, but she provided no details. The pension application was filed in 1855 by widow Sarah, and was rejected for insufficient proof of service. There is no evidence that Joshua Brooks, Jr., himself, ever applied for a pension.

He served as a corporal in Capt. John Hartwell's Company of Militia from Lincoln, Col. Eleazer Brooks's 3rd Middlesex County Regiment, which marched from Lincoln to fortify Dorchester Heights on March 4, 1776. The unit was discharged five days later, on March 9, after the threat of a British assault on the fortifications eased following General Howe's decision to evacuate Boston.[1]

Subsequently, he served as a sergeant in Capt. Samuel Farrar, Jr.'s Company, which was made up of men drafted out of Col. Eleazer Brooks's 3rd Middlesex County Regiment, assigned to Col. Jonathan Reed's Middlesex County Regiment (Brig. Gen. James Bricket's Brigade of Massachusetts Militia), and sent to reinforce the Northern Division under General Gates at Saratoga. He served at or near Saratoga for 1 month, 10 days, from September 29, 1777, to November 7, 1777. The unit was sent to Fort Edward, was back in Saratoga for Burgoyne's surrender on October 17, 1777, then it escorted Burgoyne's Convention Army to Cambridge.[2]

The following year, he went to Rhode Island from August 1, 1778, to September 11, 1778 (credited with 1 month, 14 days of service), in Capt. Francis Brown's Company, Col. William McIntosh's Regiment (Brig. Gen. Solomon Lovell's Brigade of Massachusetts Militia) and participated in the Battle of Rhode Island on August 29, 1778. This may have been part of his three-years' service in the Continental Army, for which he was paid by the town.[3]

He was age 20 on April 19, 1775; the son of Deacon Joshua Brooks (q.v.) and Hannah (Simonds) Brooks; brother of Jonas Brooks (q.v.). He was the nephew of Ephraim Brooks (q.v.), Timothy Brooks (q.v.), and Gregory Stone (q.v.); cousin of Ephraim Brooks, Jr. (q.v.), Benjamin Brooks (q.v.), Levi Brooks (q.v., Chapter 12), Abner Brooks (q.v.), Gregory Stone, Jr. (q.v.), Joshua Stone (q.v.), and Timothy Stone (q.v.).

He was a tanner by trade, and after the war he carried on the family tannery business. He married Martha Barrett of Concord in 1780. She died of smallpox in 1792, and the following year he married Sarah (also Sally) Davis. He represented Lincoln in the Great and General Court from 1809 to 1811. He died in 1825 at age 70 and is buried in the Meeting House Cemetery behind Bemis Hall.[4]

BROOKS, Noah

Noah Brooks served as a private in Capt. John Hartwell's Company of Militia from Lincoln, Col. Eleazer Brooks's 3rd Middlesex County Regiment, which marched from Lincoln to fortify Dorchester Heights on March 4, 1776. The unit was discharged five days

---

1 Hartwell, "A List of a Company of Militia."

2 *Massachusetts Soldiers and Sailors*, Vol. II, p. 579; "Treasurer's Accompts," June 10, 1779; Pension Record # R22013, # BLWT 16269-160-55. For Fort Edward, see Shattuck, *History of the Town of Concord*, p. 356.
  Wheeler, "Lincoln" (in Hurd, Vol. 2, p. 622), reports that he "was in Capt. Farrar's Company before New York in 1777." This is obviously incorrect, unless it may be interpreted as an awkward introduction to Joshua Jr.'s service in Captain Farrar's Company at Saratoga. No record has been found of Capt. Samuel Farrar, Jr., commanding a company before New York City in 1777, or in any other year.

3 Ibid. *Massachusetts Soldiers and Sailors* indicates that he served as a private at Rhode Island; Wheeler, "Lincoln," in Hurd, Vol. 2, (p. 622) credits him with being a sergeant. Having already served at the rank of sergeant, the later seems likely.

4 *Concord, Massachusetts: Births, Marriages, and Deaths*; *Vital Records of Lincoln*; Shattuck, *History of the Town of Concord*, p. 312; Biggs, "In Memorium," p. 163.

later, on March 9, after the threat of a British assault on the fortifications had subsided with General Howe's decision to evacuate Boston. He was paid for this service the following September.[1]

He was paid by the town for service at Ticonderoga in 1776.[2]

He was age 42 when he served at Dorchester Heights. He was the son of Thomas Brooks (q.v., Chapter 12) and Hannah (Dakin) Brooks; brother of Aaron Brooks (q.v.) and Stephen Brooks (q.v.); cousin of Samuel Dakin, Jr. (q.v.), Timothy Brooks (q.v.), Ephraim Brooks (q.v.), and Deacon Joshua Brooks (q.v.); uncle of Stephen Brooks [Jr.] (q.v.). In 1757, he had been a member of the town's original militia company.

He had married Elizabeth Potter of Concord in January 1760. He died in Lincoln in 1790 in his 57th year, and he is buried in the Meeting House Cemetery behind Bemis Hall.[3]

BROOKS, Peter

Peter Brooks of Lincoln enlisted as a private in Capt. William Smith's Company, Col. John Nixon's 16th Massachusetts Regiment on April 24, 1775, five days after the war began. Presumably, he participated with his unit in the Battle of Bunker Hill. A muster roll dated August 1, 1775, credits him with 3 months, 15 days of service, but it is likely that he served out a typical eight-month term.[4]

It is possible that he may be the Peter Brooks who served in the New York campaign as a private in Capt. Simon Hunt's Company, Col. Eleazer Brooks's Middlesex County Regiment of Massachusetts Militia, from September 27, 1776, to November 16, 1776, and who was reported fit and in camp at North Castle after the Battle of White Plains.[5]

Subsequently, he served at Dorchester, in Capt. John Hartwell's Company, Col. Nicholas Dike's Regiment from December 14, 1776, to March 1, 1777. He was paid for his gun and blanket under a resolve of November 27, 1776.[6]

A Peter Brooks from Acton is credited with enlisting in the Continental Army (year not given), but this appears to be a different Peter Brooks.[7]

---

1 *Massachusetts Soldiers and Sailors*, Vol. II, p. 582.
2 "Treasurer's Accompts," June 10, 1779.
3 *Concord, Massachusetts: Births, Marriages, and Deaths*; *Vital Records of Lincoln*; Biggs, "In Memorium," p. 165; Martin, "The Sons of Lincoln," p. 25.
4 *Massachusetts Soldiers and Sailors*, Vol. II, p. 582. In August, Colonel Nixon's 16th Massachusetts Regiment became known also as the 5th Regiment under Washington's Continental command.
5 Ibid. Also *Muster Rolls of the Revolutionary War*, Vol. 55, file L, p. 24. Colonel Brooks's Regiment was raised in Middlesex County for the New York campaign, and consisted of men detached from their home militia units. *Massachusetts Soldiers and Sailors* indicates that this Peter Brooks was from Lexington, but *Lexington Births, Marriages and Deaths* contains no record of a Peter Brooks. If this is the same individual as Peter Brooks (inst.), it is not clear why he is listed as being from Lexington. On the other hand, it is not clear who Peter Brooks from Lexington could be if not Peter Brooks (inst.).
6 *Massachusetts Soldiers and Sailors*, Vol. II, p. 582.
7 Ibid. Peter Brooks (inst.) probably did serve in the Continental Army, but he appears to have done so under the name Peter Bowes (q.v.), enlisting just days after returning from his Dorchester service in Colonel Dike's Regiment in 1777. See note 1, p. 240; see also sidebar "What's in a (New England Slave) Name?", p. 219

Vital Records of Acton reveals a Peter Brooks, son of John and Lydia Brooks, born in 1745. Jack MacLean (private communication with the author) reports that this Peter Brooks moved to Ashburnham and married Judith Foster on March 29, 1769, at Ashburnham, that they had children born at Ashburnham between 1770

He has been identified as a slave, of either Amos Brooks or Timothy Brooks (q.v.), who changed his name to Peter Bowes (q.v.) upon enlisting for a three-year term in the Continental Army in 1777 (his name change is most likely associated with his manumission). His age and origin, however, are unknown.[1]

BROOKS, Stephen

Stephen Brooks was a minute man in Capt. Charles Miles's Company from Concord, Col. Abijah Peirce's Regiment, on April 19, 1775.[2]

---

and 1784, and that he was reportedly a doctor. Accordingly, it seems unlikely that this individual is the Peter Brooks from Acton who enlisted for Continental service.

Regardless of the identity of Peter Brooks from Acton, however, the record of his Continental service appears not to apply to Peter Brooks (inst.), who had become Peter Bowes (q.v.) of Lincoln, and who appears to have been serving a separate 3-year Continental Army enlistment by the time this service is likely to have taken place (see *Massachusetts Soldiers and Sailors*, Vol. II, p. 339, "Peter Bowes").

1 Brooks deed to Bowes (1783); Bowes deed to Brooks (1785); Wiggin, "A Tale of Two or Three Peters." Slaveholders in colonial New England had an ethical and legal responsibility to prevent former slaves from becoming economic wards of the town. Some of the many forms this took included providing the former slave with land, or with a house, or with employment, or with a bequest. Numerous examples exist in local records.

The 1783 sale of one acre of land by the heirs of Amos Brooks to Peter Bowes for £3:6 has all of the appropriate earmarks of such a former slave/former slaveholder transaction (Brooks deed to Bowes (1783)). Two years later, Peter Bowes, now living in Boston, sold his land to Timothy Brooks (q.v.) along with his rights to "a certain Dwelling house in said Lincoln standing on land of said Timothy Brooks" (Bowes deed to Brooks (1785)) Timothy Brooks and Amos Brooks were cousins; both owned adjacent property. The author's premise is that Peter Bowes is a former slave of Amos Brooks. Jack MacLean (private communication) hypothesizes that Peter may have been the former slave of Timothy Brooks, and that there may have been some sort of agreement between the families of the two Brooks cousins. Either way, as a slave, Peter Bowes would probably have had no surname of his own prior to manumission, and would probably have been known simply as the Brooks's boy, Peter, or as Peter Brooks for short.

Malcolm, *Peter's War*, lays out an alternative premise. Malcolm identifies Peter Brooks as the subject of a 1765 Bill of Sale of a 19-month-old Negro servant boy named Peter from Joshua Brooks to Josiah Nelson (q.v.), with the statement that it was customary for a slave to take as his last name "that of his original owners." If her premise is correct, then Peter Brooks (inst.) must be the same individual as Peter Nelson (q.v.), not the same individual as Peter Bowes (q.v.). It would mean that he was not yet 12 years old when he enlisted at Cambridge. As compelling a story line as this may be, the evidence to support it is simply not credible.

Malcolm is correct that New England slaves rarely had surnames of their own prior to manumission. A Brooks slave would have been known simply as Brooks's boy, or in this case as Peter Brooks. Similarly, a Nelson slave would have been known as Nelson's boy, or in this case as Peter Nelson. However, the author has found no examples in eighteenth-century New England of a slave retaining the name of an original owner. Further, none of the scholarship on the subject of slavery in colonial New England (see Greene, *The Negro in Colonial New England*; Piersen, *Black Yankees*; McManus, *Black Bondage*; Karttunen, *The Other Islanders*; Lemire, *Black Walden*) has identified such a practice.

[A few examples have indeed been identified in the antebellum south (see Gutman, *The Black Family in Slavery & Freedom*, pp. 230–251). These were exceptions to the rule, however, not indicative of a common or "customary" practice. More to the point, in each case studied, the slave had an established identity that transcended the change of ownership. In no case was the slave still a young boy when the change of ownership occurred.]

Malcolm's work contains no source citations. In a private communication with the author, she asserts that her "original owner" statement is based on her own research, but she has provided no details and the author has been unable to find any corroborating evidence or examples. Accordingly, the author finds the evidence that Peter Brooks became Peter Bowes to be much more compelling than the unsupported premise that Josiah Nelson's Peter retained the name Brooks after being sold out of the Brooks family at 19 months of age, and that he was in service at Cambridge before his 12th birthday (see Wiggin, "A Tale of Two or Three Peters" for a more thorough discussion of this issue and of the identities of Peter Brooks, Peter Bowes, and Peter Nelson).

2 Coburn, *Muster Rolls*.

He appears to have enlisted in the Continental Army on January 1, 1776, and served for one year as a private in Capt. Jonathan Minott's Company, Col. Loammi Baldwin's Regiment. The unit served throughout the New York campaign, and then, under the command of Gen. Charles Lee, headed south to join Washington in Pennsylvania. It crossed the Hudson River at Peekskill on December 2, 1776, and reached Morristown by December 10. After General Lee was captured in a surprise British raid on December 13, the regiment joined Washington's forces just in time to participate in the Battle of Trenton.

He appears, also, to be the Stephen Brooks who served at Rhode Island in 1777, as a private in Capt. Peter Penniman's Company, Col. Ezra Wood's Regiment for 21 days from April 18, 1777, to May 7, 1777.[1]

He was the son of Thomas Brooks (q.v., Chapter 12) and Hannah (Dakin) Brooks; the brother of Aaron Brooks (q.v.) and Noah Brooks (q.v.); cousin of Samuel Dakin, Jr. (q.v.), Timothy Brooks (q.v.), Deacon Joshua Brooks (q.v.), and Ephraim Brooks (q.v.); and the uncle of Stephen Brooks [Jr.] (q.v.). He was age 33 as a minute man. No record of any marriage and no record of his death have been found.[2]

BROOKS, Stephen [Jr.][3]

Stephen Brooks [Jr.] of Lincoln served as a private in Capt. John Hartwell's Militia Company from Lincoln, Col. Eleazer Brooks's 3rd Middlesex County Regiment, which marched from Lincoln to fortify Dorchester Heights on March 4, 1776. The unit was discharged five days later, on March 9, after the threat of a British assault on the fortifications had subsided, and General Howe had decided instead to evacuate Boston.

Subsequently, he served in Capt. John Hartwell's Company, Col. Nicholas Dike's Regiment at Dorchester from December 14, 1776, to March 1, 1777. He appears to have been paid for his gun and blanket under a resolve of November 27, 1776.[4]

---

1 *Massachusetts Soldiers and Sailors*, Vol. II, pp. 585–586; "Treasurer's Accompts," June 10, 1779. Neither of these service records identifies Stephen Brooks as being from Lincoln. Tentative identification is made on the basis of their being consistent with the town's payment to his father, Thomas Brooks (q.v., Chapter 12), for one year of service in the Continental Army, and for service at Providence in 1777. Thomas could not have served the stints, as he was age 74-plus. But the payment record matches these service records attributed to Stephen Brooks. Furthermore, his other sons, Noah Brooks (q.v.) and Aaron Brooks (q.v.), were each paid for service on the same day. If one of them had provided the service, then it is reasonable to presume that the town would have paid him directly rather than paying his father. No record has been found to indicate that Stephen was in service on June 10, 1779, nor has any other reason been discovered to explain why Stephen was unavailable to be paid directly for this service on that day.

2 *Concord, Massachusetts: Births, Marriages, and Deaths*; *Vital Records of Lincoln*.

3 There is no lineal relationship between Stephen Brooks and Stephen Brooks [Jr.]. The author's use of the designation "Jr.," in this case, is merely a convenience. It reflects the eighteenth-century practice of using Jr. to distinguish between two unrelated individuals with the same name. The author has set it off in brackets, however, because strictly speaking, its use in this case is incorrect. The two individuals were not in service together, as were John Wesson (q.v.) and John Wesson [Jr.] (q.v.), and the designation "Jr." is nowhere applied to Stephen Brooks in the historical record. The author trusts the reader will agree that this convenience is appropriate in the spirit of the period, if not in the precise practice of the times.

4 Hartwell, "A List of a Company of Militia"; *Massachusetts Soldiers and Sailors*, Vol. II, p. 586. Wheeler, "Lincoln" (in Hurd, Vol. 2, p. 622), credits this service to Stephen Brooks [Jr.] (inst.), and the author finds no reason to take issue. The other Stephen Brooks (q.v.) appears to have been serving in the Continental Army during both of these stints.

He appears to be the Stephen Brooks who enlisted for three months in Capt. Joshua Walker's Company, Col. Samuel Denny's Regiment on October 23, 1779. The company was detached to join the Continental Army and marched to Claverack on the Hudson. He was discharged November 23, 1779, after 1 month 11 days of service.[1]

He was the son of Aaron Brooks (q.v.) and Mary (Stone) Brooks; nephew of Noah Brooks (q.v.) and Stephen Brooks (q.v.); age 16 (a few days shy of turning 17) at the time of his service at Dorchester Heights. He married Rachel Taylor of Groton and moved to New Ipswich then to Rindge, New Hampshire, sometime after the war, where he reportedly died in 1848 at age 88. He is buried in Smithville Cemetery in New Ipswich, New Hampshire.[2]

BROOKS, Timothy

Timothy Brooks served as a private in Capt. John Hartwell's Militia Company from Lincoln, Col. Eleazer Brooks's 3rd Middlesex County Regiment, which marched from Lincoln to fortify Dorchester Heights on March 4, 1776. The unit was discharged five days later, on March 9, after the threat of a British assault on the fortifications had subsided, and General Howe had decided to evacuate Boston. He was paid for this service the following September.[3]

He was paid by the town for service in Cambridge in 1775, York in 1777, and for three-years' service in the Continental Army. The details of this service have not survived.[4]

He was the son of Joshua and Lydia Brooks; brother of Deacon Joshua Brooks (q.v.) and Ephraim Brooks (q.v.); probably age 41 at the start of his Cambridge service; age 42 when he marched to Dorchester Heights.[5] He was the nephew of Thomas Brooks (q.v., Chapter 12); brother-in-law of Gregory Stone; cousin of Aaron Brooks (q.v.), Noah Brooks (q.v.), and Stephen Brooks (q.v.); uncle of Joshua Brooks, Jr. (q.v.), Jonas Brooks (q.v.), Ephraim Brooks, Jr. (q.v.), Benjamin Brooks (q.v.), Levi Brooks (q.v., Chapter 12), Abner Brooks (q.v.), Gregory Stone, Jr. (q.v.), Joshua Stone (q.v.), and Timothy Stone (q.v.).

He had been a member of Lincoln's original militia company in 1757, and he had married Elizabeth Jones of Concord in 1762. He died in Lincoln in 1803 at age 70 and is buried in the Meeting House Cemetery behind Bemis Hall.[6]

---

1 *Massachusetts Soldiers and Sailors*, Vol. II, p. 586. No town is given for Stephen Brooks in the Claverack records. Wheeler, "Lincoln" (in Hurd, Vol. 2, p. 622), accepts the Claverack service as Stephen Brooks [Jr.] (inst.) of Lincoln. Brooks Family Notes also gives him credit for service at "Klaverick," but says this was in 1780. Although neither gives a source, the author finds no particular reason to dispute the attribution of this service to Stephen Brooks [Jr.] of Lincoln. The company appears to have been raised in Middlesex County.

2 Wheeler, "Lincoln," in Hurd, Vol. 2, p. 622; *Concord, Massachusetts: Births, Marriages, and Deaths*; *Vital Records of Lincoln*; Brooks Family Notes; "Find A Grave." The marriage is per Brooks Family Notes; no marriage record is found in either *Vital Records of Lincoln* or *Vital Records of Groton*, nor is Rachel Taylor's birth record found in *Vital Records of Groton*.

3 *Massachusetts Soldiers and Sailors*, Vol. II, p. 587.

4 "Treasurer's Accompts," June 9, 1779.

5 *Concord, Massachusetts: Births, Marriages, and Deaths*. Lincoln had not yet become a town at the time of his birth. The SAR marker at his gravesite reinforces this identity (see Biggs, "In Memorium," p. 166, and *Soldiers and Sailors* [SAR], p. 30).

6 *Vital Records of Lincoln*; Martin, "The Sons of Lincoln," p. 25; Biggs, "In Memorium," p. 166.

Chapter 10: The Army of the Revolution

Built by their grandfather in 1703, and still standing on Conant Road, the Benjamin Brown homestead was the home of brothers Benjamin, George, and Timothy Brown. George and perhaps Benjamin fought at the Battle of Bunker Hill, and both brothers later served in the Continental Army. Timothy served with militia units raised to reinforce the Continental Army, first around New York and New Jersey in 1776–1777, then at Saratoga in the fall of 1777. (Courtesy of Lincoln Town Archives, Lincoln, MA)

BROWN, Benjamin

Benjamin Brown was paid by the town for service at Cambridge in 1775, perhaps in Capt. Nathan Fuller's Company, Col. Thomas Gardner's Regiment. He may have been a participant in the Battle of Bunker Hill. He may have been detailed to serve on main guard at Prospect Hill under Lt. Col. Loammi Baldwin on July 16, 1775, although it is not certain if the Benjamin Brown of this record is the same individual.[1]

The town also paid him for one-half of a three-year service in the Continental Army. In the absence of any further information, it is speculative whether or not he might be the Benjamin Brown who enlisted in January 1776, and served in the Garrison at Fort George in Capt. Jeremiah Hill's Company, Col. Edmund Phinney's Regiment according to a roll dated December 8, 1776; or whether or not he might be the Benjamin Brown who was in

---

1 "Treasurer's Accompts," June 15, 1779. No record has been found to identify his unit. Possible service in Capt. Nathan Fuller's Company, Thomas Gardner's Regiment (and any presumption of participation with this unit in the Battle of Bunker Hill) is entirely speculative, suggested by the service of his brother, George Brown (q.v.).
  The record of Benjamin Brown who served on main guard at Prospect Hill under Lt. Col. Loammi Baldwin on July 16, 1775, is insufficiently detailed to identify him as Benjamin Brown of Lincoln. On one hand, he would not have been the only Lincoln man on this detail, as Abel Adams (q.v.) appears also to have served. On the other hand, he may be Benjamin Brown of Ipswich, who served at Cambridge in Capt. Benjamin Kimball's Company, Col. John Mansfield's Regiment, a possibility suggested by Captain Kimball's service on this detail, as well (*Massachusetts Soldiers and Sailors*, Vol. II, pp. 601, 603; Vol. IX, p. 205).

service at North Kingston, Rhode Island under Capt. Samuel Thomas on January 6, 1777; or whether or not he might be the Benjamin Brown who was detached from Capt. Thomas Bumstead's Company in Boston to serve for five weeks under Major General Heath, agreeable to an order dated May 7, 1777.[1]

He was age 22 during his service at Cambridge; the son of Timothy and Rebeckah (Farrar) Brown; brother of George Brown (q.v.) and Timothy Brown (q.v.); and nephew of Humphrey Farrar (q.v.).[2]

BROWN, Daniel

Daniel Brown of Lincoln was a drummer in Capt. William Smith's Company of Minute Men from Lincoln, Col. Abijah Peirce's Regiment.[3] Following the engagement at Concord, he served for eight days in Cambridge.[4] He was reimbursed for his accoutrements as a minute man on November 11, 1779.[5]

Subsequently, he served as a private in Capt. John Hartwell's Militia Company from Lincoln, Col. Eleazer Brooks's 3rd Middlesex County Regiment, which marched from Lincoln to fortify Dorchester Heights on March 4, 1776. The unit was discharged five days later on March 9. He was paid for this service the following September.[6]

He served in Capt. Caleb Brooks's Company, Col. Nicholas Dike's Regiment from December 18, 1776, to March 1, 1777, guarding stores at Boston.

His name appears on a list dated Lincoln, August 14, 1777, of men drafted out of Capt. Samuel Farrar, Jr.'s Company, Col. Eleazer Brooks's Regiment, for service at Saratoga. No evidence has been found that he actually served, however, and it is presumed that he sent a substitute, instead.[7]

He was age 17 on April 19, 1775, the son of Nathan Brown, Jr., and Rebeckah (Adams) Brown; brother of Nathan Brown, Jr.[8] (q.v.); brother-in-law of William Lawrence, Jr. (q.v.) and Daniel Wesson (q.v.); and nephew of James Adams (q.v.). There is an intriguing suggestion by the late stages of the war that he may have switched his loyalties from the patriot cause to the British cause, or perhaps that he may have been held as a prisoner of

---

1 "Treasurer's Accompts," June 15, 1779. *Massachusetts Soldiers and Sailors*, Vol. II, pp. 601–602.
2 *Vital Records of Lincoln*; Bond, *Genealogies of the Families of Watertown*, p. 121.
3 Coburn, *Muster Rolls*. Ironically, there was another Daniel Brown who was a drummer in Capt. Charles Miles's Company of Minute Men from Concord. How closely they may have been related has not been determined.
4 *Massachusetts Soldiers and Sailors*, Vol. II, p. 607. In addition to Lincoln, this record lists him as also being from Stow, but this appears to be a result of confusion with another Daniel Brown from Stow (see note 1, p. 245).
5 "Treasurer's Accompts," November 11, 1779.
6 *Massachusetts Soldiers and Sailors*, Vol. II, p. 607. Also Hartwell, "A List of a Company of Militia."
7 *Massachusetts Soldiers and Sailors*, Vol. II, p. 607. There is a record in *Massachusetts Soldiers and Sailors* (Vol. II, p. 703) of a Daniel Browne at Saratoga in Capt. Jonathan Rice's Company, Col. Samuel Bullard's Massachusetts Militia Regiment from August 17, 1777, to November 29, 1777 (credited with 3 months 13 days of service in the Northern Department). However, this individual is identifiable from his pension declaration (Pension Record # S34078) as Daniel Brown of Stow. Several cases of substitution have been identified for individuals on this draft list, and in addition, Saratoga service records exist for several other individuals who are not on this list. The absence of any evidence of Saratoga service by Daniel Brown (inst.) suggests that one of these others may have substituted for him (see sidebar, "Facing the Crisis," p. 99).
8 Often known to modern historians as Nathan Brown III. He became Nathan Brown, Jr., upon the death of his father in 1764.

war somewhere outside of the country. His grandfather, Nathan Brown, Sr., notes of him in 1781, "…now absent, uncertain whether he be alive and not permitted to return to his native country." He is reported to have died in the West Indies.[1]

BROWN, Ebenezer

Ebenezer Brown of Lincoln was a corporal in Capt. William Smith's Company of Minute Men from Lincoln, Col. Abijah Peirce's Regiment.[2] Following the engagement at Concord, he served for 15 days in Cambridge.[3] He was reimbursed by the town for his accoutrements as a minute man on March 25, 1776.[4]

He was age 23 on April 19, 1775; the son of Benjamin and Sarah (Dakin) Brown. He died in Lincoln on December 5, 1776, age 25.[5]

BROWN, Ephraim

Ephraim Brown served as a private in Capt. John Hartwell's Militia Company from Lincoln, Col. Eleazer Brooks's 3rd Middlesex County Regiment, which marched from Lincoln to fortify Dorchester Heights on March 4, 1776. The unit was discharged five days later, on March 9, after the threat of a British assault on the fortifications had subsided following

---

1 *Vital Records of Lincoln*; quotation in MacLean, *A Rich Harvest*, p. 303; Shattuck, "The Minot Family," p. 206. MacLean implies some uncertainty about this identity, but no other identity appears probable. As for his not being "permitted to return to his native country," MacLean suggests changed loyalty rather than the possibility of his being a prisoner of war (MacLean, *A Rich Harvest*, p. 303).

As the Treasurer's Accounts show that he was in Lincoln on November 11, 1779, the possibility of his being held as a prisoner of war would necessarily require that he was in service after that date. There is, in fact, no particular evidence of any service after Boston in 1777.

There is an intriguing record of a Daniel Brown of Stow (*Massachusetts Soldiers and Sailors*, Vol. II, p. 609) with a long record of service (none of which appears to conflict directly with known service by Daniel Brown (inst.) of Lincoln, who enlisted in the Continental Army for nine months agreeable to a resolve of June 9, 1779 (actual enlistment date is not recorded), and who is described as age 21, five-feet, six-inches in height (described a year earlier as five-feet, four-inches), light complexion, and living in Stow. *Daniel Brown (inst.) of Lincoln was age 21 at that time, also*. However, Daniel Brown of Stow is identifiable (from *Vital Records of Stow* and from Pension Record # S34078) as a different individual. He was the son of Jonas and Mary, who turned 21 in March 1779 (almost exactly six months younger than Daniel Brown (inst.)). The author judges that the suggested link between Daniel Brown of Lincoln and Daniel Brown of Stow is a case of confusion on the part of the compilers of the records in *Massachusetts Soldiers and Sailors*, between different individuals with the same name and of the same age.

There is another intriguing record of a Daniel Brown (the location of this individual's home or residence is not identified) who enlisted in Capt. Timothy Remick's Company, Col. Joseph Vose's Regiment on June 20, 1780, who was reported as having deserted on January 1, 1781, while serving at West Point. If this record could be connected with Daniel Brown (inst.) of Lincoln, this would probably suggest disillusionment and possibly changed loyalties, more than his having been captured as a prisoner (*Massachusetts Soldiers and Sailors*, Vol. II, p. 611).

Shattuck, "The Minot Family" (p. 260), reports that he died in the West Indies, but he offers no further information. This would make an interesting subject for further investigation.

2 Coburn, *Muster Rolls*
3 *Massachusetts Soldiers and Sailors*, Vol. II, p. 614.
4 "Treasurer's Accompts," March 25, 1776.
5 *Vital Records of Lincoln*; *Town of Weston, Births, Deaths, & Marriages*; Bond, *Genealogies of the Families of Watertown*, p. 125. Sarah Dakin's possible relationship to Samuel Dakin (q.v.) has not been determined, except that they were evidently not siblings.

General Howe's decision to evacuate Boston. He was paid for this service the following September.[1]

He was age 19 at Dorchester Heights; the son of Joseph and Abigail Brown.

He married Betsey Wyman of Weston in December 1779. After the war, he became fairly active in local affairs and town government. He died in Lincoln in 1813 in his 57th year and is buried in the old Precinct Burial Ground on Lexington Road.[2]

BROWN, George

George Brown served at Cambridge in 1775 as a private in Capt. Nathan Fuller's Company, Col. Thomas Gardner's Regiment. He was in service at least by June 14, 1775, when he received a certificate of service. Presumably, he served with his unit in the Battle of Bunker Hill, on June 17, 1775. After July, Colonel Gardner's Regiment was deployed at Prospect Hill, where he was still in service on October 6, 1775, in Captain Fuller's Company, now in Lt. Col. William Bond's (late Colonel Gardner's) Regiment.[3]

He reenlisted for service in Capt. Moses Ashley's Company, Col. John Paterson's 15th Continental Regiment on January 1, 1776. After the departure of the British from Boston, he went to New York City, then participated in the relief expedition to Canada. In November 1776, the regiment was sent south from Ticonderoga to join the main section of the Continental Army under General Washington. On Christmas night, he crossed the Delaware with Washington's troops, and participated in the Battle of Trenton on December 26, 1776. He was discharged at Trenton at year's end.[4]

He immediately reenlisted for another three years in the Continental Army on January 1, 1777, and served as a private in Capt. Moses Ashley's Company, Col. Joseph Vose's Regiment. He served in the Hudson Valley, and at Saratoga during the taking of Burgoyne, then he spent the legendary winter of 1777–1778 at Valley Forge. On June 1, 1778, he is reported as having deserted. Subsequently, he must have returned to service or enlisted again, because he appears again on a list of deserters in Colonel Vose's Regiment, dated

---

1 *Massachusetts Soldiers and Sailors*, Vol. II, p. 620.
   Another record in *Massachusetts Soldiers and Sailors* shows an Ephraim Brown serving at Ticonderoga in Capt. Zachariah Fitch's Company, Col. Samuel Brewer's Regiment from August 23 through September 30, 1776. Notwithstanding that Abijah Mead (q.v.), Zebediah Farrar (q.v.), Abel Adams (q.v.), and Daniel Billing (q.v.), all of Lincoln, served at Ticonderoga in the same unit at the same time, the Ephraim Brown of this record is identified by Green, *Groton During the Revolution* (pp. 13, 53–54), as Ephraim Brown of Townsend. Green shows that he was paid for 132 miles travel; the Lincoln men were paid for 151 miles (see also Hallowell, *Vital Records of Townsend*).
2 *Vital Records of Lincoln*; *Town of Weston, Births, Deaths, & Marriages*; MacLean, *A Rich Harvest*, p. 374; Biggs, "In Memorium," p. 190
3 *Massachusetts Soldiers and Sailors*, Vol. II, p. 623.
4 Pension Record # W18659; "Treasurer's Accompts," June 15, 1779. This service is not recorded in *Massachusetts Soldiers and Sailors*, but is reconstructed from the pension record and the "Treasurer's Accompts." His pension declaration curiously omits much of his Continental service, mentioning only his service in 1776 in Colonel Paterson's Regiment. Curiously, also, the pension record mentions Trenton, but not Canada. Perhaps this may reflect a lack of participation in an identifiable battle, per se, in Canada (despite the hardships of the campaign). The evidence of his service at Canada, however, is inescapable, as Colonel Paterson's Regiment is recorded as serving at both locations (the only unit to have done so).

Camp Highlands, New York, July 13, 1780. He is described as age 22; five feet, seven inches in height; light complexion, light hair.[1]

He was the son of Timothy and Rebeckah (Farrar) Brown; brother of Benjamin Brown (q.v.) and Timothy Brown (q.v.). He turned age 17 approximately at the time of his enlistment at Cambridge. After the war, he went west and settled as a farmer in Sheshequin, Pennsylvania, around 1790. He married Sally Brown in 1792. Sometime before 1829, he took up residence in Southport, New York, where he died in 1833 at age 75. He is buried in Roushy Cemetery in Ashland Township, New York.[2]

BROWN, Joseph

Joseph Brown was paid by the town for service at Boston in 1776, for service at New York in 1776, and for one-half of a three-year campaign in the Continental Army.[3]

He was probably age 20 when he began his service; probably the son of Joseph Jr. and Desire Brown.[4]

BROWN, Moses

Moses Brown marched on the Alarm of April 19, 1775, as a sergeant in Capt. Larkin Thorndike's 1st Beverly Company. They reached Arlington in time to participate in the fight along the Battle Road. He served for 2½ days.

---

1 *Massachusetts Soldiers and Sailors*, Vol. II, p. 623. See also Blake, "James Barrett's Returns of Men" (p. 471), for a record of his being mustered and paid a bounty for this service, which lists him in "Col Pattison Battal[ion] Capt Ashby Comp[any]" as reported by James Barrett, muster master, on March 24, 1777. The report was a few months out-of-date: Colonel Paterson's Regiment was consolidated with elements of the 6th and 18th Continental Regiments to form Colonel Vose's Regiment on January 1, 1777, when Paterson was promoted to brigadier general.

Actually, he turned age 23, two months before he was reported as having deserted in 1780. Curiously, he fails to mention this service (from 1777 to his 1780 desertion) in his pension declaration, perhaps out of a fear that his desertion(s) would disqualify the application.

It is tempting to think that his 1778 desertion ended his service, and that his appearance on the 1780 list refers to his 1778 desertion. His term of service would have been up on January 1, 1780 (unless it was extended by his desertion or another enlistment). However, the fact that the age given for him is approximately correct for 1780 (rather than 1778), suggests that this is a second desertion.

In an 1891 biographical note, probably supplied by his granddaughter, Bradsby, *History of Bradford County* (biographical sketch for Charles C. Thompson, #1225), credits George Brown (inst.) with "four years and eight months in the war, and [he] was taken a prisoner once." This is an accurate statement of his terms of enlistment, at least through January 1, 1780. One wonders what effect the desertions may have had on his actual time served. No other record has been found of his having been taken prisoner; one wonders if this could have been how he accounted for his absences in the stories he later told his family.

2 *Vital Records of Lincoln*; Bond, *Genealogies of the Families of Watertown*, p. 121; Pension Record # W18659; *SAR Revolutionary War Graves Register*. The pension record shows his birth date as a year earlier than appears in *Vital Records of Lincoln*. There is little likelihood that *Vital Records of Lincoln* is in error, however, as it clearly shows that he was born in 1758, fourteen months after the infant deaths of twin brothers George and Elijah, and thirteen months before the birth of another brother Elijah. Sally was about 16 years his junior. She was the daughter of Obadiah Brown of Sheshequin Township. Around the 1828 to 1831 timeframe, their home was destroyed by fire. It is unknown whether their move to Southport was related to the fire or whether they had moved to Southport before the fire.

3 "Treasurer's Accompts," June 15, 1779.

4 *Vital Records of Lincoln*.

Moses Brown served on the Concord Alarm, in the New York campaign, and at the Battle of Trenton. He was age 68 and had become a socially prominent Beverly merchant when he sat for this portrait by Gilbert Stuart in 1816. The original is at the Beverly Historical Society. (Engraving by H. W. Smith)

Subsequently, he obtained a commission to raise a company in Beverly to guard the seacoast, and he reentered the service as captain of this company, in Col. John Glover's Regiment, on July 11, 1775. He served for 6 months, 6 days at Beverly.

On January 1, 1776, he joined the Continental Army as captain of the 7th Company, Col. John Glover's 14th Regiment. After seacoast duty in the early months of 1776, the regiment was sent south and actively participated in the New York campaign on Long Island, in Brooklyn, in Manhattan, and at White Plains. He participated in the Battle of Trenton, on December 26, 1776, before which he reportedly addressed his men, "my friends in a few minutes we shall be in the presence of the enemy, and I hope you will behave like the men I take you to be." Upon the expiration of his enlistment on January 1, 1777, he left the service.[1]

He had been raised in Waltham and Lincoln, and was age 27 during the April 19th Alarm. He was the son of Isaac and Mary (Balch) Brown, and became the step-uncle of Nathan Brown, Jr. (q.v.) and Daniel Brown (q.v.) when his widowed mother married Nathan Brown, Sr., in 1760. He was the nephew of Abijah Peirce (q.v.); brother-in-law of Ephraim Hartwell, Jr. (q.v.) and Stephen Farrar (q.v.). He had graduated from Harvard College in 1768 and taught school in Framingham, Lexington, and Lincoln before settling in Beverly in 1772 and becoming a merchant. Subsequently, in 1774, he married Elizabeth Trask, who died in 1788. A year later, he married Mary Bridge. In 1779, he financed the privateer *Defence*, and by the 1780s he was investing in ships, shipbuilding, trade, and manufacturing. He achieved considerable prominence as a merchant, and he appears to have courted an accompanying social and political network. He died in Beverly in 1820 at age 72.[2]

---

1 Bond, *Genealogies of the Families of Watertown*, p. 126; *Massachusetts Soldiers and Sailors*, Vol. II, p. 664; Coburn, *Muster Rolls*, p. 68; Pension Record # W14400. As a member of Glover's Regiment, it is probable that he was involved in ferrying Washington's army across the ice-clogged Delaware River on Christmas night 1776, before the battle the next morning. The date on which he left the service in 1777 is not given, but as there is no indication that he participated in the Battle of Princeton, or in any subsequent action, and as it is likely that his enlistment was for one year, he probably departed on January 1, 1777.

2 MacLean, *A Rich Harvest*, pp. 206–208; Bond, *Genealogies of the Families of Watertown*, pp. 126–127; Mike Ryan, unpublished notes (information about his financing and investment activity). Isaac and Mary had set-

BROWN, Nathan, Jr.
[also Nathan, Nathan III, Capt. Nathan][1]

Nathan Brown, Jr. was a private in Capt. William Smith's Company of Minute Men from Lincoln, Col. Abijah Peirce's Regiment.[2] Following the engagement at Concord, he served for three days in Cambridge. He was reimbursed for his accoutrements as a minute man on June 18, 1776.[3]

Subsequently, he served as a corporal in Capt. John Hartwell's Militia Company from Lincoln, Col. Eleazer Brooks's 3rd Middlesex County Regiment, which marched from Lincoln to fortify Dorchester Heights on March 4, 1776. The unit was discharged five days later, on March 9, after the threat of a British assault on the fortifications had subsided following General Howe's decision to evacuate Boston. He was paid for this service the following September.[4]

The evidence suggests that he served at New York in 1776, but no details of this service have been found.[5]

He was paid by the town for service at Roxbury in 1776 and at Saratoga in 1777. Whether or not he actually served at Roxbury or at Saratoga is doubtful.[6]

---

tled on the Waltham Plain after they were married. In 1760, however, when Moses was age 12, his widowed mother married Nathan Brown, Sr., later moving her family to Lincoln.

Isaac's sister, Thankful, was the wife of Abijah Peirce (q.v.). Moses' sister, Mary, was the wife of Ephraim Hartwell, Jr. (q.v.). Moses' sister, Eunice, was the wife of Stephen Farrar (q.v.), who was a brother of Samuel Farrar, Jr. (q.v.) and Timothy Farrar (q.v.).

1 The *War Memorial Book* and *An Account of the Celebration* credit both Nathan Brown and Nathan Brown, Jr., with service. While there were three generations of Nathan Browns, the service records all belong, in fact, to the same individual: the third generation Nathan Brown. The first Nathan Brown was age 71 in 1775, obviously too old for service. The second Nathan Brown (frequently appearing as Nathan Brown, Jr.) died in 1764 at age 40. The third Nathan Brown became known as Nathan Brown, Jr., upon the death of his father. Modern historians variously refer to him as Nathan Brown III or Capt. Nathan Brown (he apparently became captain sometime after 1786) to distinguish Nathan Jr. (the father) from Nathan Jr. (the son) (see also Glass, *The Nathan Brown Farm*). At the risk of causing further confusion between the different Nathans, the author has chosen to refer to Nathan III as Nathan Brown, Jr., consistent with the way he was known in 1775.

2 Coburn, *Muster Rolls*.

3 *Massachusetts Soldiers and Sailors*, Vol. II, p. 667; "Treasurer's Accompts," June 18, 1776.

4 *Massachusetts Soldiers and Sailors*, Vol. II, p. 667.

5 "Treasurer's Accompts," November 11, 1779. This record reads, "paid Mr. Nathan Brown for *his* service at New York in 1776 and for service at Saratoga in 1777" [italics added]. The significance of the word "his" in the Treasurer's accounts is often difficult to determine, but in this case, it suggests both that the recipient of the payment was Nathan Brown, Jr. (inst.), not his grandfather Nathan Brown, Sr., and that he actually provided the service. By contrast, the word "his" is missing from the Saratoga reference. "His" is also missing from Roxbury and Saratoga service referenced in the town's July 15, 1779 payment (see note 6).

6 "Treasurer's Accompts," June 15, 1779. No service record for either location has been found. Nor does his name appear on the Saratoga draft list. Nor is either service referred to as "his" in the payment record (as is the New York service in the November 11, 1779, payment record; see note 5).

The fact that the June 15, 1779, payment was made to "Nathan Brown, Jr." and the November 11, 1779, payment was made to "Nathan Brown" appears to be the source of the *War Memorial Book* and *An Account of the Celebration* crediting both Nathan Brown and Nathan Brown, Jr. with service. However, as explained in notes 1 and 5, above, the elder Nathan Brown could not have served any of these stints, and is probably not the recipient of the November payment.

Massachusetts Soldiers and Sailors (Vol. II, p. 668) lists service by a Nathaniel Brown in Capt. Jonathan Rice's Company, Col. Samuel Bullard's Regiment from August 17, 1777, to October 21, 1777 (credited with 2 months, 14 days of service in the Northern Department), but this individual is identifiable from other records as Nathaniel Brown of Sudbury, not Nathan Brown, Jr. (inst.), of Lincoln. [See *Massachusetts Soldiers and*

Brothers Daniel Brown and Nathan Brown, Jr., answered the Alarm of April 19, 1775, from this house, still standing at the corner of Peirce Hill Road and Tower Road (shown here in 1960). The brothers served repeatedly during the war, before Daniel may have defected to the enemy. (Historic American Buildings Survey)

Who was the Widow Rebeckah Brown?

On June 15, 1779, the town paid the Widow Rebeckah Brown for service at Cambridge in 1775 and Canada in 1776. The record does not tell us who actually provided this service, nor does it identify the Widow Rebeckah Brown. At the time, there were in fact two widows named Rebeckah Brown:

a) Rebeckah (Adams) Brown, widow of Nathan Brown (Jr., who died in 1764), mother of Daniel Brown (q.v.) and Nathan Brown, Jr. (q.v.) [often known to modern historians as Nathan Brown III; he became Nathan Brown, Jr., upon the death of his father (see p. 249, note 1)], and

b) Rebeckah (Farrar) Brown, widow of Timothy Brown (who died in 1768), mother of Benjamin Brown (q.v.), George Brown (q.v.), Timothy Brown (q.v.), and Elijah Brown.

Historian Lemuel Shattuck (1835) reports that Rebecca Brown, widow of Nathan Brown, married Solomon Foster in 1790. *Vital Records of Lincoln* provides corroborating evidence of such a marriage, but it corrects the marriage date to 1770 (1790 is the year of Solomon's death). If the marriage attribution is accurate, then it would preclude her from being the Widow Rebeckah Brown who was paid for service, as she would have become Rebecca Foster (instead of the Widow Rebeckah Brown) upon her marriage to Solomon.

Considerable confusion attends the multiple generations of Nathan Brown and multiple individuals named Rebecca Brown, and a careful examination of the *Vital Records of Lincoln* reveals a quite different truth than reported by Shattuck. The death ▶

Chapter 10: The Army of the Revolution

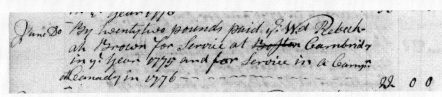

(Courtesy of Lincoln Town Archives, Lincoln, MA)

of Rebeccah Foster (widow of Solomon) is recorded in 1815, at age 64. This conforms to the 1751 baptism record of Rebecca Brown (daughter of Nathan Jr. and Rebeccah). The death of Rebecca Brown (widow of Nathan Jr.) is recorded in 1811, at age 84. We can reasonably conclude from these records that the Rebecca Brown who married Solomon Foster was the daughter, not the widow, of Nathan Brown, Jr. The marriage record in the *Vital Records of Lincoln* is missing the words "daughter of" in front of the identifying words, "[Rebeccah, [wid.] Nathan, C.R.I.]." Shattuck compounds his error by asserting that daughter Rebecca never married, which of course cannot be true.

Thus, the payment record for service at Cambridge (1775) and Canada (1776) could apply to either widow Rebecca Brown, for service by any of their sons.

For the identity of the son who provided the service, we can logically eliminate Benjamin, Nathan Jr., and Timothy, as they were paid directly for service on the same day that the town paid the Widow Rebeckah Brown (Benjamin for his Cambridge service; Nathan Jr. and Timothy for other service). There was obviously no need to pay the Widow Rebeckah if the service for which she was paid was provided by any of them.

Daniel is recorded as having served at New York in 1776, which overlapped with the Canadian service, so it is unlikely that he could have provided the service for which the Widow Rebeckah was paid.

Elijah turned age 16 in June 1775, so he could have served at Cambridge and Canada. But attributing the service to him would be entirely speculative, as we have no record of any service at all by Elijah.

George, on the other hand, is recorded as having served at Cambridge in 1775 (for which there is no other record of his being paid). Could he also have served in Canada? His pension declaration tells of service in 1776 in Colonel Paterson's Regiment in the Battle of Trenton, but there is no mention or record of service in Canada, which in any case would seem to conflict with service at Trenton. Colonel Paterson's Regiment, however, did go to Canada in 1776, and it was the only unit in Canada that also served at Trenton. So the records tie together. Further, another record tells us that he was in service and away from Lincoln on June 15, 1779, providing the logical justification for the town having paid his mother instead of paying him directly. Thus, it can be confidently concluded that the Widow Rebeckah Brown who was paid by the town was the widow of Timothy Brown, and that the service for which she was paid was provided by her son, George Brown.

[See "Treasurer's Accompts," June 15, 1779; Shattuck, "The Minot Family," p. 260; *Vital Records of Lincoln*; Pierce, *Foster Genealogy*, p. 196.]

He turned age 20 just three days before the events of April 19, 1775. He was the son of Nathan Jr.[1] and Rebeckah (Adams) Brown; brother of Daniel Brown (q.v.); brother-in-law of William Lawrence, Jr. (q.v.) and Daniel Wesson (q.v.); and nephew of James Adams (q.v.).[2]

Just a week before the events of April 19, 1775, he married Lucy Gearfield of Weston, sister of Abraham Gearfield (q.v.) and Solomon Garfield (q.v.). After the war, he became a lieutenant in the militia company and later a captain. In the turbulent postwar economy, he seems to have been in perpetual financial trouble, and by 1787 he had lost his title to the family farm and sawmill. About the same time, he also secured a court judgment against David Mead (q.v.) for a £43 debt. In 1814, at age 60, he was killed when he was run over in Concord by a wagon loaded with wood. He is buried in the Meeting House Cemetery behind Bemis Hall.[3]

BROWN, Timothy
[also Timothy Jr.]

Timothy Brown was drafted out of Lincoln's Militia Company on December 3, 1776, by Lt. James Parks to reinforce the Continental Army outside of New York. The draft call was probably for Col. Samuel Thatcher's Regiment, which marched south on December 16, 1776. This regiment served briefly around New York before being called to New Jersey in January 1777. They were stationed at Woodbridge and participated in the *petite guerre* in the Jerseys in the early months of 1777 before being dismissed to return home in March. As no matching service record has been found, however, it is uncertain whether he actually went into service or sent a substitute.[4]

His name also appears on a list dated Lincoln, August 14, 1777, of men drafted or recruited out of Capt. Samuel Farrar, Jr.'s Company, Col. Eleazer Brooks's Regiment, for

---

Sailors, Vol. II, pp. 667, 668; parallel records for Ebenezer Burbank, *Massachusetts Soldiers and Sailors,* Vol. II, p. 812; and Sudbury Town Meeting records which mention Nathaniel Brown on February 23, 1776, November 1776, March 1777, and October 26, 1778. The author thanks Jack MacLean for this identity.]

It is curious that the town seems to have paid Nathan Jr. twice for Saratoga service. Possibly the Saratoga payments were partial payments, but partial payments were usually indicated as such in the transaction records. The fact that Nathan's brother Daniel Brown (q.v.) was drafted for Saratoga service suggests some sort of connection, but none has been found. The possibility that Nathan might have served as a substitute for Daniel seems to belie the lack of any evidence to that effect.

Another possibility is that the service could possibly have been provided by slaves or indentured servants. Identified candidates might include Nero (slave of Nathan Jr.) and Salem Middlesex (probably no longer a slave, but the husband of a slave of Nathan Sr.). Other, unidentified, possibilities probably also exist. *Massachusetts Soldiers and Sailors* contains records of a number of individuals who could possibly qualify as the hypothetical slave, but none of the records are detailed enough to do any more than fuel speculation. Unfortunately, the identity of the individuals who provided the service at Roxbury and the two stints at Saratoga, and how their Saratoga service relates to the Saratoga draft list remains a mystery.

1 See note 1 on p. 249.
2 *Vital Records of Lincoln.*
3 MacLean, *A Rich Harvest,* p. 310; Glass, *The Nathan Brown Farm,* p. 33; Biggs, "In Memorium," p. 167; Shattuck, "The Minot Family," p. 260.
4 Eleazer Brooks Papers [Lincoln], p. 157. "Treasurer's Accompts," June 15, 1779. No actual record of his unit has been found. Assignment to Colonel Thatcher's Regiment is a supposition, consistent with the service of other Lincoln men at this time. The *petite guerre* is David Hackett Fischer's term for the skirmishing that characterized the war in New Jersey following Washington's dramatic victories at Trenton and Princeton. See Fischer, *Washington's Crossing,* pp. 366–367.

> To mr. Tim.º Brown S.r these are to inform you that agreable to a late act of the great and general court you are draughted as one to reinforce the Continental army
> Lincoln Dec.m 13.º 1776
> James Parks [foint?]

This draft notice ordered 25-year-old Timothy Brown into service for the first time. It gave him about two weeks' notice before he marched south for deployments around New York and New Jersey during the winter of 1776–1777. (Courtesy of Lincoln Town Archives, Lincoln, MA)

service at Saratoga. No evidence has been found that he actually served, however, and it is presumed that he sent a substitute, instead.[1]

He was age 25 at the time of his initial draft call for service around New York and New Jersey. He was the son of Timothy and Rebeckah (Farrar) Brown; brother of Benjamin Brown (q.v.) and George Brown (q.v.). He had married Hannah Lee of Concord in 1772. He died in Lincoln in 1796 at age 45 and is currently buried in the Arbor Vitae Cemetery.[2]

BUSSELL, Isaac
[also BUSEL, BUSELL, BUSSEL, BUZELL, BUZZEL, also Isaac Jr.]

Isaac Bussell enlisted as a drummer or a private in Capt. Noah Moulton Littlefield's Company on July 10, 1775, and served for six months, six days, at Wells and Arundel, guarding the Maine seacoast.[3]

From October 12. 1776, to July 28, 1777 (9 months, 16 days of service), he served as a private in Lt. Andrew Gilman's Company, stationed at Penobscot River. While in this service, he was recruited out of Capt. Joseph Keith's Company, Colonel Mitchell's Plymouth County Militia Regiment on July 16, 1777, for a three-year term in the Continental Army as a private in Capt. Abraham Hunt's Company, Col. Joseph Vose's Regiment. He listed his residence as Penobscot. His enlistment was credited to the town of Bridgewater.[4]

---

1 "Treasurer's Accompts," June 15, 1779. *Massachusetts Soldiers and Sailors*, Vol. II, p. 696. Several cases of substitution have been identified for individuals on this draft list, and in addition, Saratoga service records exist for several other individuals who are not on this list. The absence of any evidence of Saratoga service by Timothy Brown (inst.) suggests that one of these others may have substituted for him (see sidebar, "Facing the Crisis," p. 99).

2 *Vital Records of Lincoln*; Bond, *Genealogies of the Families of Watertown*. p. 121. The Arbor Vitae Cemetery was established more than thirty years after his death, so his remains must have been moved there at a later date.

3 *Massachusetts Soldiers and Sailors*, Vol. II, pp. 926, 936. Identical records exist for Isaac Bussell, who enlisted as a drummer, and an Isaac Busell, Jr., who is listed as a private. It is not clear if these records refer to the same or different individuals. Captain Littlefield's Company appears to have had roots in the Wells area.

4 *Massachusetts Soldiers and Sailors*, Vol. II, p. 936; Pension Record # S36948. Ignoring his militia service, he says in his pension declaration that he enlisted in the American Army in August at Kenduskeag, near Bangor. Bangor is on the Penobscot River; Kenduskeag is recognizable as a village about ten miles northwest of Bangor.

On July 28, 1777, he was detached north as part of an expedition against St. John, Nova Scotia, in Capt. Nicholas Crosby's Company, Col. Samuel McCobb's Regiment, but the expedition met with little success and they returned by September 4, 1777.[1]

He marched to Boston, where he served temporary duty in Captain Allen's Company, in the 7th Regiment, and was reported sick. In February 1778, he says he marched to Albany where he was "innoculated for the small pox," then in April he marched to Valley Forge, where he rejoined Colonel Vose's Regiment. Vose's Regiment participated in the Battle of Monmouth on June 28, 1778. Then, in July, the regiment was deployed at Providence, Rhode Island, and participated in the Battle of Rhode Island on August 29. He served in Rhode Island through the spring of 1779.[2]

He evidently spent the next year and a half in the Hudson Valley, including two months aboard an open boat on the river. In December 1779, at Peekskill, he appears to have extended his enlistment for the duration of the war. He is described as age 24; five feet, eight inches in height. This time, he listed his residence as Lincoln (also Penobscot). His enlistment was again credited to the town of Bridgewater. He served nine months as a corporal in 1780 before becoming a private again. Then, in the spring of 1781, he was drafted into Capt. Nathaniel Cushing's Company of Light Infantry, placed under the command of General Lafayette, and marched to Richmond, Virginia. He was at Yorktown for the surrender of Cornwallis, where he participated in the storming of redoubt 10 on the right of the line, "and carried it, at the point of the bayonet."[3]

He was discharged on June 8, 1783, at Snakehill, New York. He says he sold his three-years-back-pay certificate for clothing, and it netted him only "thirty dollars & thirty-three cents."[4]

He was born in Dover, New Hampshire, and was age 19 when he first served along the Maine coast. He returned to Maine after the war, residing successively at Robbinston, Plantation No. 23, and Columbia, where he received a land grant of 200 acres for his service during the war. His pension declaration makes reference to sons and daughters, but little information is given about his family. His wife's name appears to have been Prudence, and

---

1 *Massachusetts Soldiers and Sailors*, Vol. II, pp. 936, 978; Pension Record # S36948. This expedition appears to be part of a protracted border war involving northern Maine and the part of Nova Scotia which is now New Brunswick. Col. John Allen had led a small band comprised largely of local militia to St. John in June 1777, and they briefly held the town before being forced into retreat upon the arrival of British ships. This expedition may have been launched to reinforce Allen, but by the time it got off in late July, Allen's men had straggled back to Machias. In mid-August, British ships attacked Machias, and there appear to have been no further American incursions into Nova Scotia. The author's supposition is that Bussell and his fellow soldiers were probably deployed to bolster Machias's defenses (see Abel Billing (q.v.) and Solomon Billing (q.v.)).
2 *Massachusetts Soldiers and Sailors*, Vol. II, pp. 936, 978; Pension Record # S36948. This itinerary largely follows his pension declaration, although there is some uncertainty over the precise details. His name appears, for example, on a muster roll for December 1777, dated Camp near Valley Forge, suggesting that he may have spent the winter of 1777–78 at Valley Forge rather than at Boston and Albany.
3 *Massachusetts Soldiers and Sailors*, Vol. II, pp. 936, 979; Pension Record # S36948. His name appears on a muster roll for February through November 1781, dated Huts near West Point, but for much of this time, according to his pension declaration, he was actually in Virginia.
4 Pension Record # S36948. Although the precise location has not been determined, Snakehill is presumed to be in the Hudson Highlands.

he is reported to have died in 1844, at age 88, probably at Columbia. He is buried in the Mill River Cemetery in Harrington, Maine.[1]

BUTTRICK, Francis

Francis Buttrick was paid by the town for service at the Southward in 1776 and at Saratoga in 1777. His name appears on a list dated Lincoln, August 14, 1777, of men drafted or recruited out of Capt. Samuel Farrar, Jr.'s Lincoln Militia Company, Col. Eleazer Brooks's Regiment, for service in the Northern Department (i.e., Saratoga). He served as a corporal in Capt. George Minot's Company, Col. Samuel Bullard's Massachusetts Militia Regiment from August 16, 1777, to November 30, 1777 (credited with 3 months, 25 days of service in the Northern Department), and he was present at Burgoyne's surrender at Saratoga on October 17, 1777.[2]

His identity has not been determined, but he appears on Lincoln's tax roles as early as 1769. While no record of his connection with Lincoln has been found, a probable candidate is the son of Francis and Hannah (Gilson) Buttrick of Lunenburg; age 28 when he would

---

[1] Pension Record # S36948; *SAR Revolutionary War Graves Register*. At the time of his 1779 reenlistment, he listed his residence as Lincoln, but his connection to the town of Lincoln is not at all clear. It is possible that his Lincoln residency may refer to Lincoln County (Maine), not the town of Lincoln, but among the records found in *Massachusetts Soldiers and Sailors*, this appears to be a very unusual way for residency to have been stated. Although today there does exist a Lincoln, Maine, there appears not to have been such a place before the town of Mattanawcook changed its name to Lincoln in 1829. Accordingly, he appears to have had or imagined at least some fleeting connection to or residency within the town of Lincoln (in Middlesex County). This is all the more curious because he had been in the service continuously for more than three years, and he had previously listed his residence as Penobscot.

Possibly, he had lived and worked in Lincoln briefly before going to war. Perhaps he had lived in Lincoln briefly in his youth, perhaps with itinerant or peripatetic parents who had stopped for a time in the town.

A cursory scan of *Massachusetts Soldiers and Sailors* shows other Bussells from Penobscot, and it suggests other possible family connections along the Maine coast. In the 1770s, there was no specific location called Penobscot. The town of Penobscot was organized in 1787; Penobscot County was formed in 1816. In 1774, three homesteaders (one of whom was a Stephen Bussell) began carving a settlement out of the wilderness along the east bank of the Penobscot River, above the falls. A reasonable presumption is that Isaac and the other Bussell soldiers from Penobscot were sons of Stephen, and that they were referencing this settlement along the Penobscot River. By 1777, it seems that problems with the Penobscot Tribe forced the abandonment of the settlement (Force, *American Archives*, Vol. 2, pp. 729–730). Could Isaac's reference to Lincoln be simply an awkward reference to an uncertain location in Lincoln County, where his family had resettled?

Or could his parents have come to Lincoln after he entered the service, perhaps after leaving the Penobscot settlement? Perhaps he had never actually lived in Lincoln, but after several years in the service and with no other identifiable residence, his parents' new residence was the logical reference point. Lots of scenarios can be conjured up, all entirely speculative.

Massachusetts Soldiers and Sailors (Vol. II, p. 936) lists a Stephen Bussell who served with Isaac in Lieutenant Gilman's Company on the Penobscot. He appears to be the same individual as the Stephen Bussell who enlisted from Marlborough, Massachusetts, in December 1777, but who deserted later in the war. Could this service relate to a brother or, perhaps less likely, to his father? Without further investigation beyond the scope of this work, the best we can do is to speculate.

In the absence of such an investigation, the evidence of his Lincoln connection is regrettably thin. Equally so, his connection to Bridgewater, and to Plymouth County. Whatever truth lies behind it, the record indicates an apparent Lincoln residence in 1779, and accordingly, he finds a place in this compilation.

In a private communication with the author, Jack MacLean made the observation that in addition to Isaac Bussell, the records of John Conant (q.v.) and Benjamin Cleaveland (q.v.) also contain links to the town of Bridgewater. Whether or not this is a clue to understanding more about these individuals or about links between the towns is another subject for further investigation.

[2] "Treasurer's Accompts," February 18, 1780. *Massachusetts Soldiers and Sailors*, Vol. I, p. 555, Vol. II, p. 972.

have served at the Southward in 1776. This Francis Buttrick settled in Pepperell after the war (quite possibly, he may have been raised in Pepperell) and married Lydia Howe of Sterling in 1785. He died at Pepperell, "supposed in a fit," in 1829 at age 81.[1]

The Daughters of the American Revolution (DAR) credit this Francis Buttrick of Pepperell with having "served a short enlistment in the Middlesex county, Massachusetts militia, 1777," which is consistent with the service records for Francis Buttrick (inst.). If this identity is correct, then he may have been living and working on a Lincoln farm during the early years of the war. As no positive connection with Lincoln has been found, however, this putative identity remains speculative.[2]

CABOT, Edward

Edward Cabot was paid by the town for eight months of service at Cambridge in 1775.[3] He enlisted on May 19, 1775, as a private in Capt. William Smith's Company, Col. John Nixon's 16th Massachusetts Regiment, and served at least through September 30, 1775. He probably participated with his unit at the Battle of Bunker Hill on June 17, 1775.[4]

He served in the New York campaign in 1776, as a private in Capt. Simon Hunt's Company, Col. Eleazer Brooks's Middlesex County Regiment of Massachusetts Militia, marching to Horse Neck on September 27, 1776, and participating in the Battle of White Plains on October 28, 1776, during which he lost his knapsack, blanket, shoes, socks, and shirt. The unit was discharged on November 16, 1776, credited with 2 months of service, including 11 days of travel allowance to return home.[5]

He was in service at Cambridge again in 1778, this time for three months, from April 2, 1778, to July 3, 1778, in Capt. Daniel Harrington's Company, Col. Jonathan Reed's Regiment of Guards, guarding the "Convention Army" surrendered the previous October by General Burgoyne at Saratoga. He appears to have remained in service for a second term of guard duty in a company commanded by Maj. Samuel Lamson of Weston, probably until November or December 1778.[6]

He was originally from Boston but he had come to Lincoln and married Bulah Munroe in 1772. Bulah was the daughter of Benjamin Munroe (q.v.), and the sister of Micah Munroe (q.v.), Abijah Munroe (q.v.), and Isaac Munroe (q.v.). Edward Cabot is reported to have lived in Lincoln for about eight years.[7]

---

1 Lincoln Assessors Records, North Book, 1769; *Vital Records of Pepperell*; Davis, *Early Records of Lunenburg*, pp. 245, 274.

2 *Lineage Book of the DAR*, p. 116. The *SAR Patriot Index* also credits this Francis Buttrick with service but provides few other details that would link him with the service records of Lincoln's Francis Buttrick (inst.).

3 "Treasurer's Accompts," May 12, 1781

4 *Massachusetts Soldiers and Sailors*, Vol. III, p. 2. In August, Colonel Nixon's 16th Massachusetts Regiment became known also as the 5th Regiment under Washington's Continental command.

5 *Massachusetts Soldiers and Sailors*, Vol. III, p. 685; *Muster Rolls of the Revolutionary War*, Vol. 55, file L, p. 24. The regiment consisted of Middlesex County militiamen detached from their home units for this campaign.

6 *Massachusetts Soldiers and Sailors*, Vol. III, pp. 2, 685; Wheeler, "Lincoln," in Hurd, Vol. 2, p. 622. The dates of service in Major Lamson's Company are not given, but Major Lamson appears to have been engaged to serve guard duty from July through December 1778 (see *Massachusetts Soldiers and Sailors*, Vol. IX, p. 458). The Convention Army had been completely removed from Cambridge by early November 1778; it is unclear how much longer the guards served after that.

7 *Vital Records of Lincoln*; Wheeler, "Lincoln," in Hurd, Vol. 2, p. 622.

CHILD, Abel

[also CHILDS]

Abel Child served as a private in Capt. John Hartwell's Militia Company from Lincoln, Col. Eleazer Brooks's 3rd Middlesex County Regiment, which marched from Lincoln to fortify Dorchester Heights on March 4, 1776. The unit was discharged five days later, on March 9, after the threat of a British assault on the fortifications had subsided following General Howe's decision to evacuate Boston.[1]

He appears to have marched to Ticonderoga, and served during the summer and fall of 1776 in Capt. Asahel Wheeler's Company, Col. Jonathan Reed's Regiment. He was paid by the town for this service.[2]

His name appears on a list dated Lincoln, August 14, 1777, of men volunteered or drafted out of Capt. Samuel Farrar, Jr.'s Company, Col. Eleazer Brooks's Regiment to reinforce the Continental Army, and he served at Saratoga as a private in Capt. George Minot's Company, Col. Samuel Bullard's Massachusetts Militia Regiment, from August 16, 1777 to November 30, 1777 (credited with 3 months, 25 days of service in the Northern Department). He was present at the taking of Burgoyne.[3]

He later served as a private in Capt. Edward Richardson's Company, Col. Thomas Poor's Regiment, enlisting on June 25, 1778, and serving for 7 months, 11 days at North River, New York. Various muster roll and payroll records suggest that during this time he saw much of upstate New York, with deployments to Watertown, to West Point (in September), and to Kings Ferry (in November). He was discharged from this service on January 25, 1779.[4]

He was age 18 when he served at Dorchester Heights; the son of Isaac and Hannah Child; brother of Amos Child (q.v.). He married Polly Lewis on February 10, 1780. After the war, he made his living as a woodworker. He appears to have struggled financially, and even served time in a Cambridge prison for unpaid debts. He went north sometime after 1786, probably in search of new opportunity. He died at Stockbridge, Vermont, in 1831 at age 74.[5]

---

1 Hartwell, "A List of a Company of Militia"; *Massachusetts Soldiers and Sailors*, Vol. III, p. 410.

2 "Treasurer's Accompts," June 15, 1779. Neither his pension record (# R1921), nor *Massachusetts Soldiers and Sailors* contain any record of Ticonderoga service by Abel Child (inst.). However, a pay receipt at Ticonderoga in September, and another after he returned, place him in Captain Wheeler's Company (Sudbury Miscellaneous Records, September 30, 1776 (Doc. # 109), March 17, 1777 (Doc. 2209)).

Coincidentally, there was an Abel Childs of Framingham who served at Ticonderoga in Capt. Silas Gates's Company, Col. Reed's Regiment, from July to December 1776, as evidenced by Pension Record # W14459.

3 *Massachusetts Soldiers and Sailors*, Vol. III, pp. 401–402; Pension Record # R1921.

4 *Massachusetts Soldiers and Sailors*, Vol. III, p. 410; "Treasurer's Accompts," June 15, 1779; Pension Record # R1921. The town paid him for eight months of service "in the [illegible] Department" in 1778. Without being able to read the name of the Department, the author presumes that the payment record fits with his service record in Captain Richardson's Company in upstate New York. Wheeler, "Lincoln" (in Hurd, Vol. 2, p. 622), says he served eight months in Cambridge in 1778, but this appears to be inconsistent with the record.

Abel Childs is also recorded as serving at Rhode Island, as a private in Capt. Lawson Buckminster's 2nd Company, Col. Abner Perry's Regiment, from July 28, 1780, to August 7, 1780 (*Massachusetts Soldiers and Sailors*, Vol. III, p. 410). This service is missing from the pension record of Abel Child (inst.). It was more likely served by Abel Childs of Framingham. (See Pension Records # R1921 and # W14459.)

5 *Vital Records of Lincoln*; MacLean, *A Rich Harvest*, pp. 311, 353; Pension Record # R1921. One child is recorded in Lincoln in 1786.

CHILD, Amos
[also CHILDS]

Amos Child served as a private in Capt. John Hartwell's Militia Company from Lincoln, Col. Eleazer Brooks's 3rd Middlesex County Regiment, which marched from Lincoln to fortify Dorchester Heights on March 4, 1776. The unit was discharged five days later, on March 9, after the threat of a British assault on the fortifications had subsided following General Howe's decision to evacuate Boston.[1]

He was age 26 during this service; the son of Isaac and Hannah Child; brother of Abel Child (q.v.). No further record of him has been found.[2]

CHILD, Daniel

Daniel Child was a private in Capt. William Smith's Company of Minute Men from Lincoln, Col. Abijah Peirce's Regiment. Following the engagement at Concord, he followed the running fight all the way to Cambridge. It is reported that he knew Lord Percy by sight, and that he had an opportunity to take aim at him with his musket. Before he could pull the trigger, he realized he was caught between a flanking party and the main column of Regulars. However, they were so near each other that neither the column nor the flankers could fire without wounding the other. So the firing stopped, and he was able to run out from between them. Once he got out in the open, of course, they commenced firing at him. He continued to run for cover, successfully dodging the bullets whizzing about him, and eventually he found shelter behind a rock, "verily holding [his] breath in [his] hands."[3] He was reimbursed by the town on February 23, 1776, for his accoutrements as a minute man.[4]

He served for five days in Cambridge before signing up (on April 24, 1775) for service with Capt. William Smith's Company, Col. John Nixon's 16th Massachusetts Regiment, in the rapidly organizing Massachusetts Provincial Army. With his unit, he probably fought at the Battle of Bunker Hill on June 17, 1775. On July 3, 1775, he was probably deployed on main guard with Lt. Col. Loammi Baldwin, but it is not certain that this is the same Daniel Child. He served at Cambridge at least through September 30, 1775, when he was reported "on command with masons." He was paid by the town for his services at Cambridge in 1775.[5]

He was paid by the town for service at Canada in 1776. He served as a sergeant in Capt. Abijah Child's Company, Colonel Bond's Regiment, and was discharged from Ticonderoga on November 9, 1776.[6]

---

1 Hartwell, "A List of a Company of Militia"; *Massachusetts Soldiers and Sailors*, Vol. III, p. 410.
2 *Concord, Massachusetts: Births, Marriages, and Deaths*.
3 Coburn, *Muster Rolls*. The story is related in Hersey, *Heroes*, p. 29, but its source has not been found.
4 "Treasurer's Accompts," February 23, 1776.
5 *Massachusetts Soldiers and Sailors*, Vol. III, p. 403; "Treasurer's Accompts," June 10, 1779. "On command with masons" indicates that he was evidently deployed as a mason on a construction crew, probably working on fortifications, and probably deployed alongside Artemas Reed (q.v.). In August, Colonel Nixon's 16th Massachusetts Regiment became known also as the 5th Regiment under Washington's Continental command.
6 "Treasurer's Accompts," June 10, 1779; *Massachusetts Soldiers and Sailors*, Vol. III, p. 404.

He was paid by the town for three months of service in Rhode Island, probably in 1779.[1]

It is probable that he returned to Rhode Island on July 27, 1780, as a sergeant in Capt. Abraham Andrews's Company, Col. Cyprian How's Middlesex County Regiment, which was called in to reinforce the Continental Army. He served 3 months, 7 days until October 30, 1780.[2]

He was age 22 on April 19, 1775; the son of Joshua Child (q.v., Chapter 12) and Grace (Bemis) Child; brother of Joshua Child, Jr. (q.v.), who was also a minute man, and Elijah Child (q.v.). He married Molley Mathis, the sister of Abner Mathis (q.v.), on July 28, 1778.[3]

[He may also have served as a private in Capt. Micah Hamlin's Company, Col. Simeon Cary's Regiment, enlisting on February 2, 1776, and marching to strengthen the siege of Boston on February 8, 1776. This company appears to have been recruited under a resolve of January 20, 1776, and served until April 1, 1776. However, as the company was raised from Plymouth and Bristol Counties, it is likely that this may be a different Daniel Child.][4]

CHILD, Elijah
[also CHILDS]

Elijah Child was paid by the town for three months of service in Rhode Island, as a private in Capt. Abraham Andrews's Company, Col. Cyprian How's Middlesex County Regiment. The regiment was engaged to reinforce the Continental Army for three months. He enlisted on July 27, 1780, and served for 3 months, 10 days, until October 30, 1780.[5]

He was age 14 when the war broke out; age 19 at the time of his service in Rhode Island. He was the son of Joshua Child (q.v., Chapter 12) and Grace (Bemis) Child; brother of Daniel Child (q.v.) and Joshua Child, Jr. (q.v.). He appears to have married Mary Knight in 1807. Their child died shortly after birth in 1808, and Mary died the following March 1809. In November 1810, he married Anna Hosmer. No further record of him has been found.[6]

---

1 "Treasurer's Accompts," October 28, 1780. Wheeler, "Lincoln" (in Hurd, Vol. 2, p. 622), credits him with serving at Rhode Island in 1779. Given the date of his pay, it is unlikely that this service occurred after 1779.
2 *Massachusetts Soldiers and Sailors*, Vol. III, pp. 403–404, 411. The parallel with similar service by his brother, Elijah Child (q.v.), is strongly suggestive that this record does indeed apply to Daniel Child (inst.). As this could not be the service for which he was paid on October 28, 1780, this must have been a second term of service in Rhode Island.
3 *Vital Records of Lincoln*; MacLean, *A Rich Harvest*, pp. 152, 347.
4 *Massachusetts Soldiers and Sailors*, Vol. III, pp. 178, 411. It is also not clear how the dates of this possible service square with his February 23, 1776, reimbursement by the Town Treasurer. Because Col. Simeon Cary was from Bridgewater, it is tempting to view this as another possible link between Lincoln and Bridgewater. However, as Pembroke is in Plymouth County, it is perhaps more likely that this record applies to a Daniel Child of Pembroke. For other Bridgewater links (real and suggested), see Isaac Bussell (q.v.), John Conant (q.v.), and Benjamin Cleaveland (q.v.).
5 "Treasurer's Accompts," February 8, 1781; *Massachusetts Soldiers and Sailors*, Vol. III, p. 411.
6 *Vital Records of Lincoln*; Bond, *Genealogies of the Families of Watertown*, p. 154. If the marriage records are accurate and apply to him, he was age 47 when he married Mary and age 50 when he married Anna. The identities of Mary Knight and Anna Hosmer have not been determined with certainty. Mary may have been the daughter of Samuel and Ann Knight of Sudbury, who would have been age 40 when they were married; Anna may have been the daughter of William Hosmer (q.v.); brother of William Hosmer, Jr. (q.v.), twelve years junior to Elijah.

[Elijah Child may also have served at Governor's Island (in Boston Harbor) as a private in Capt. James Morton's Company, Colonel Pierce's Regiment for 36 days from March 3, 1778, to April 8, 1778, but it is unclear if the Elijah Childs in this record is the same individual as Elijah Child of Lincoln. He would have been age 17.][1]

CHILD, Elisha
[also CHILDS]

Elisha Child served as a private in Capt. John Hartwell's Militia Company from Lincoln, Col. Eleazer Brooks's 3rd Middlesex County Regiment, which marched from Lincoln to fortify Dorchester Heights on March 4, 1776. The unit was discharged five days later, on March 9, after the threat of a British assault on the American positions had subsided following British General Howe's decision to evacuate Boston.[2]

He appears to be the son of Elisha and Mary (Wheeler) Child; probably about 26 years old at Dorchester Heights. He married Abigail Winch of Concord on November 25, 1790, and made his living as a farmer, cordwainer, and general handyman. He died in Lincoln in 1823, probably at about 73 years of age.[3]

CHILD, Joshua, Jr.[4]
[also CHILDS, also Joshua]

Joshua Child, Jr., was a private in Capt. William Smith's Company of Minute Men from Lincoln, Col. Abijah Peirce's Regiment. Following the engagement at Concord, he served for ten days in Cambridge. He was reimbursed by the town on February 19, 1776, for a set of accoutrements as a minute man.[5]

Subsequently, he served as a private in Capt. John Hartwell's Militia Company from Lincoln, Col. Eleazer Brooks's 3rd Middlesex County Regiment, which marched from

---

1 *Massachusetts Soldiers and Sailors*, Vol. III, p. 411. The dates of this service abut the dates of another term of Cambridge service guarding the Convention Army by an Elijah Childs of Barnstable, suggesting some likelihood that this service may have been by said Elijah Childs of Barnstable.

2 Hartwell, "A List of a Company of Militia." Also *Massachusetts Soldiers and Sailors*, Vol. III, pp. 411.

3 *Vital Records of Lincoln*; *Concord, Massachusetts: Births, Marriages, and Deaths*; MacLean, *A Rich Harvest*, p. 347. Vital Records for Elisha Child are sparse. No birth record has been found, and the identity of his parents is at best an educated guess. His age is estimated by the 1748 marriage date of his purported parents and by the age of his wife. Abigail (also listed as Nabby) was born in 1754; she was age 21 at the time of Dorchester Heights, age 36 when they were married. Her birth record has not been found; her ages are calculated from her death record in Lincoln.

Bond, *Genealogies of the Families of Watertown* (p. 155), says he was the son of Elisha and (second wife) Mehitabel Garfield, born in 1770, but this would be inconsistent both with Abigail's age and with the record of his service at Dorchester Heights. One might rationalize placing the elder Elisha at Dorchester Heights (at age 55), but it is a little more difficult to imagine a 20-year-old Elisha marrying a 36-year-old Abigail.

4 Because the Muster Roll for April 19th lists Joshua Child, Jr., while Hartwell, "A List of a Company of Militia," lists Joshua Child (without the designation "Jr."), the *War Memorial Book* and *An Account of the Celebration* mistakenly list service by Joshua Child and Joshua Child, Jr., as different individuals. While it may be theoretically possible that Joshua Child, Sr., could have served at Dorchester, there is no rationale for thinking that this service was provided by anyone other than Joshua Jr. No record has been found of any service by a Joshua Child that does not fit Joshua Child, Jr. As far as war service goes, the logical conclusion is that entries for Joshua Child and for Joshua Child, Jr., are for the same individual.

5 Coburn, *Muster Rolls*; *Massachusetts Soldiers and Sailors*, Vol. III, pp. 407; "Treasurer's Accompts," February 19, 1776.

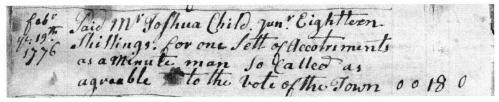

Joshua Child, Jr., was paid the following February by the town for his accoutrements as a minute man on April 19th. A set of accoutrements consisted of "a bayonet belt Catridge Box Steal ramer gun stock and knap sack." (Courtesy of Lincoln Town Archives, Lincoln, MA)

Lincoln to fortify Dorchester Heights on March 4, 1776. The unit was discharged five days later, on March 9, after the threat of a British assault on the fortifications had subsided following British General Howe's decision instead to evacuate Boston.[1]

He appears on a list dated Lincoln, August 14, 1777, of men who were drafted out of Capt. Samuel Farrar, Jr.'s Company, Col. Eleazer Brooks's Regiment, for service at Saratoga, and the town paid him for this service. However, this time he chose not to serve, and instead arranged for Brister Hoar (q.v.), a slave of John Hoar, to serve in his place.[2]

He was age 26 on April 19, 1775; the son of Joshua Child (q.v., Chapter 12) and Grace (Bemis) Child; brother of Daniel Child (q.v.), who was also a minute man, and Elijah Child (q.v.).

He married Elizabeth Hammond of Waltham (who was about 8½ years his junior) in 1781. He died in 1822 at age 73 and is buried in the Meeting House Cemetery behind Bemis Hall.[3]

CLEAVELAND, Benjamin
[also CLEVELAND]

Benjamin Cleaveland reportedly enlisted for a year in the service of the Massachusetts troops in the spring of 1775, and "was in the battle of Bunker Hill – was there wounded in the head and had a leg broken – and was afterwards confined in the Hospital."[4]

He enlisted in the Continental Army on January 1, 1777, for the duration of the war, in Col. John Crane's Artillery Regiment. He identified himself as a Boston resident, and his enlistment was credited to the town of Bridgewater. Eight days later, he enlisted again, on January 8, 1777, in Capt. Abijah Child's Company, Col. John Greaton's 2nd Regiment. This time his enlistment was credited to the town of Lincoln. His prior enlistment was discovered, and he was transferred back to Colonel Crane's Artillery Regiment.[5]

---

1 *Massachusetts Soldiers and Sailors*, Vol. III, pp. 407.
2 *Massachusetts Soldiers and Sailors*, Vol. III, pp. 407, Vol. VIII, p. 2. "Treasurer's Accompts," June 10, 1779. This was an accepted method of avoiding service. See "Facing the Crisis," p. 99.
3 *Vital Records of Lincoln*; *Vital Records of Waltham*; MacLean, *A Rich Harvest*, p. 152; Biggs, "In Memorium," p. 167. Intention to marry is recorded in Lincoln as December 18, 1780.
4 Pension Record # W16908. This enlistment was more probably a nominal eight-month enlistment (i.e., until December 31, 1775). His unit is not identified.
5 *Massachusetts Soldiers and Sailors*, Vol. III, pp. 609, 632. Multiple enlistments were not unusual as many "enterprising" young men tried to game the system and collect multiple bounties. He appears to have been a bit of a rogue at this time, as he was also soon to father a child out of wedlock (see note 4, p. 262). Col. Greaton's Regiment is listed as the 2nd Regiment in the *Massachusetts Soldiers and Sailors* record (Vol. III, p. 632), but

He served for two years as a matross in Colonel Crane's Regiment, then was promoted to bombardier. He appears to have served first in Captain Buckland's Company, then in Capt. John Lillie's Company. He is described as age 28; five feet, seven inches in height; and of dark complexion.[1]

He is reported to have served at Ticonderoga (probably before July 5–6, 1777, when it was hastily abandoned to Burgoyne's army), and "in the battle at the taking of Gen. Burgoyne" (Saratoga, September–October 1777). Instead, however, he may have been with his regiment at Morristown in early 1777, then at Brandywine in September 1777, and at Valley Forge during the winter of 1777–78.[2]

He is also reported to have been at the storming of Stony Point (July 16, 1779), and "in the battles of the Cowpens" (January 17, 1781). If he was in fact at Cowpens, then he may have remained under General Greene's command in the Carolinas, and re-entered Charleston upon the British departure in December 1782, or he may have participated in the siege of Yorktown in September and October 1781. He was discharged in 1783.[3]

He was born in Freetown, Massachusetts, the son of Benjamin and Jerusha (Round) Cleaveland; age 20 and living with his father in Tiverton, Rhode Island when the war broke out. In October or November 1777, Sarah Stratton of Weston bore him a son out of wedlock. He and Sarah were subsequently married on April 13, 1778, while he was on furlough, and the son was baptized 13 days later. They lived in Weston for about four years after the war, and then they moved to Claremont, New Hampshire. By 1795, they had settled in German, New York. He died of yellow fever in 1803 near Coeyman's Landing (present-day Ravena, New York), while traveling home from conducting business in Rhode Island. He was age 48.[4]

---

after January 1, 1777, it is usually given as the 3rd Massachusetts (also 24th Continental). See Heitman, *Historical Register of Officers* (pp. 37, 259).

1 Ibid. His term of enlistment seems not to have been understood, at least by his wife. She relates (Pension Record # W16908) paying Captain Lilley a visit when he returned north after three years to inquire about the discharge of her husband, apparently only then learning that he was in for the duration. He was age 21 when he enlisted in the Continental service; probably age 28 when he was discharged. The sequence of companies in which he served is not wholly clear. Captains Buckland and Lillie are mentioned in *Massachusetts Soldiers and Sailors*. The pension declaration by his widow suggests that he served under Captain Lilley for three years, then under Captain Winslow. However, Capt. John Winslow is recorded as having resigned from the service in November 1778 (see *Massachusetts Soldiers and Sailors*, Vol. XVII, pp. 635).

2 Pension Record # W16908. His widow remembered receiving letters from him while he was at Ticonderoga. On the other hand, Crane's Regiment is recorded stationed at Morristown in early 1777, then at Brandywine in September 1777, and Valley Forge during the winter of 1777–78. This discrepancy is not easily reconciled.

3 Pension Record # W16908. Gen. Daniel Morgan appears not to have had artillery with him at Cowpens. Therefore, unless he had joined the detachment in some other capacity, it is not entirely clear why, as an artillerist, he would have been at Cowpens at all. However, if we assume his widow's pension declaration to be correct and that he was indeed at Cowpens, then it is reasonable to presume that he remained in the Carolinas as there appears to be little evidence of Greene sending troops north during this campaign, even at the time of Yorktown.

On the other hand, the possibility that he may have served at Yorktown derives from the indication that he was serving in Capt. John Lillie's Company. Captain Lillie states that he was at Yorktown in his pension record (# R6345).

4 Pension Record # W16908; *Town of Weston, Births, Deaths, & Marriages*. The author is indebted to Jack MacLean for locating his baptism record among the New England Historic Genealogical Society's genealogical entries. The baptism record for Benjamin and Sarah's son reads, "b. last Oct^r." A birth record (probably recorded after they were married) reads, "Novr 6th 1777." In her pension declaration, Sarah lists his birth date as November 6, 1779, perhaps a family fiction originally invented to hide the stain of illegitimacy, but which had by then taken on the aura of fact.

Chapter 10: The Army of the Revolution

COCKRAN, Bacchus

Bacchus Cockran was paid a bounty by the town of Lincoln on September 10, 1781, for enlisting in the Continental Army for three years of service, agreeable to a resolve of December 2, 1780.[1]

His identity has not been determined. The name Bacchus suggests that he may have been a free African-American, but this is speculative. He may have been recruited from out of town for this service, but this is also uncertain.[2]

COLBURN, Joseph
[also COLBORN]

Joseph Colburn of Lincoln served in the 1st Company of Col. Thomas Craft's Artillery Regiment for one year, from early May 1776 to May 8, 1777, first under Capt. James Swan, then under Capt. Philip Marett. At first he served as a matross, then he became a gunner on February 1, 1777. This unit was part of the Massachusetts Militia, and most or all of this service was at Boston.[3]

There is a record of a Joseph Coburn who was drafted on May 12, 1777, to serve in a detachment commanded by Maj. Andrew Symmes for five weeks of service guarding stores in and about Boston under Major General Heath, but it is unclear whether this record applies to Joseph Colborn of Lincoln or to a different individual.[4]

He served at Saratoga as a private in Capt. George Minot's Company, Col. Samuel Bullard's Massachusetts Militia Regiment. He marched north with his company on August 16, 1777, via Hadley

Buried in Arbor Vitae Cemetery, Joseph Colburn served in the artillery guarding Boston Harbor for a year, following the departure of the British. Then in 1777, he substituted for his brother, Nathaniel, and marched north with the first wave of Lincoln militiamen to arrest British General Burgoyne's progress in the Champlain and Hudson valleys. (Photograph by the author)

---

1 *Massachusetts Soldiers and Sailors*, Vol. III, p. 700.

2 If he was African-American, the presumption of his being a former slave (or perhaps born free) rather than being a slave is that the bounty was paid to him rather than to an owner.

3 *Massachusetts Soldiers and Sailors*, Vol. III, p. 741; Pension Record # S18772. Captain Swan was promoted to major in November 1776. Marett, who became captain about this time, appears to have been Swan's replacement. The lieutenant colonel of this regiment was Paul Revere.

4 *Massachusetts Soldiers and Sailors*, Vol. III, p. 691. There is no mention of this service in his pension declaration. The individual in this record was drafted out of Lt. Col. Jabez Hatch's Regiment from Boston. No evidence has been found to suggest that Joseph Colburn (inst.) enlisted in this regiment upon the expiration of his artillery service.

and Northampton, Massachusetts, and Bennington, Vermont. There he saw some of the hundreds of "prisoners taken by General Stark" at the decisive Battle of Bennington the day they had begun their march. From Bennington, they marched to Stillwater, where he participated in the Battle of Saratoga and was present at the surrender of Burgoyne on October 17, 1777. He served until November 30, 1777, credited with 3 months, 24 days of service (including travel).[1]

He was back in service in 1778, guarding the British or German soldiers surrendered by Burgoyne at Saratoga. He appears on a list of men under Maj. Samuel Lamson of Weston returned to Lt. Col. Francis Faulkner as having been detached from Col. Eleazer Brooks's 3rd Middlesex County Regiment to relieve the guards at Cambridge. In this duty, he served as a private in Capt. Daniel Harrington's Company, Col. Jonathan Reed's Regiment of Guards from April 2, 1778, to July 3, 1778 (credited with 3 months, 2 days of service). He appears to have been on furlough on May 9.[2]

He was age 18 when he enlisted in the service in 1776; the son of Nathaniel Jr. and Tabitha (Headley) Colburn of Leominster; brother of Nathaniel Colburn (q.v.). Tabitha was a Lincoln native, and the family appears to have resettled in Lincoln on family property before the start of the war. After Joseph's service, he returned to settle in Lincoln. He married Elizabeth (Gleason) Wyman of Woburn (who was about four years older than he) in 1780. He died in Lincoln in 1841 at age 83 and is buried in the Arbor Vitae Cemetery.[3]

---

1 *Massachusetts Soldiers and Sailors*, Vol. III, p. 742; Pension Record # S18772. His name is not on the Saratoga draft list, but he appears to have served as a substitute for his brother Nathaniel Colburn (q.v.), whose name appears on the draft list but who evidently did not serve.

2 *Massachusetts Soldiers and Sailors*, Vol. III, pp. 735, 742; Wheeler, "Lincoln," in Hurd, Vol. 2, p. 622. There is no mention of this service in his pension declaration. Major Lamson and Lieutenant Colonel Faulkner were officers in Colonel Brooks's Militia Regiment. There is evidence that Major Lamson may have commanded a company of guards from July through December 1778 (see *Massachusetts Soldiers and Sailors*, Vol. IX, p. 458). If one interprets the list to be of those serving in Major Lamson's Company, then Joseph Colburn (inst.) probably served a second term of guard duty upon his discharge from Captain Harrington's Company. For a similar record, see Edward Cabot (q.v.).

3 Pension Record # S18772; *Vital Records of Leominster*; *Vital Records of Lincoln*; Johnson, *Woburn Records of Births, Deaths, and Marriages*; Wheeler, "Lincoln," in Hurd, Vol. 2, p. 622. *Vital Records of Leominster* indicates that Tabitha Headley was from Woburn, but this is in error, and Johnson, *Woburn Records of Births, Deaths, and Marriages*, contains no record of her. Her roots were in Weston's North Parish, the part of Weston which became part of Lincoln in 1754 (see *Historical Manual of the Lincoln Church*, p. 88; Bond, *Genealogies of the Families of Watertown*, p. 296; and *Town of Weston, Births, Deaths, & Marriages*).

Historical Manual of the Lincoln Church says the family moved to Lincoln in 1779. Jack MacLean, on the other hand (in private notes shared with the author), places their reestablishing connections to Lincoln in 1771, citing a 1771 deed transferring property from John Headley to Nathaniel and Tabitha. Whether Lincoln residency occurred in 1771 or sometime after, it is clear that the parents of Nathaniel Colburn (q.v.) and Joseph Colburn (inst.) were expanding their involvement in Lincoln during this period, probably to help manage the holdings and affairs of Tabitha's father (John Headley, who died in January 1779), and/or simply to reunite three generations of Tabitha's family. By 1776, in any case, Joseph Colburn (inst.) seems to have been calling Lincoln "home."

Elizabeth was the widow of Jonas Wyman of Woburn, who had taken sick during the New York campaign and died in service in October 1776.

COLBURN, Nathaniel
[also COLBOURN, COLBORN]

Nathaniel Colburn served at Boston in 1776 and 1777, for which he was paid by the town. Quite possibly this could have been as a private in Capt. Ebenezer Battle's Company, Col. William McIntosh's Regiment, including 19 days (December 11–30, 1776) under Lieutenant Colonel Weld at Castle Island, although this service was recorded as Nathan Colburn, not Nathaniel Colburn.[1]

His name appears on a list dated Lincoln, August 14, 1777, of men drafted out of Capt. Samuel Farrar, Jr.'s Company, Col. Eleazer Brooks's 3rd Middlesex County Regiment, for service at Saratoga. Town records show that he was paid for this service, but no evidence has been found that he actually served. It is supposed that he arranged for his brother Joseph to substitute for him.[2]

He was age 24 during his Boston service in 1776 and 1777. He was the son of Nathaniel Jr. and Tabitha (Headley) Colburn of Leominster; brother of Joseph Colburn (q.v.). Tabitha was a Lincoln native, and the family appears to have resettled in Lincoln on family property before the start of the war. Nathaniel's marriage to Jane Stratton of Concord is recorded in Lincoln shortly before his war service in 1776.[3]

Census records show that he had living in his household one of the six black residents of the town in 1790. Sometime later they evidently moved back to Leominster, where his death is recorded in 1840 at age 90 (actually he was age 88).[4]

---

1 "Treasurer's Accompts," June 10, 1779; *Massachusetts Soldiers and Sailors*, Vol. III, pp. 736, 742.
2 Ibid. See also Joseph Colburn (q.v.); "Facing the Crisis," p. 99.
3 *Vital Records of Leominster*; *Vital Records of Lincoln*. *Vital Records of Leominster* indicates that Tabitha Headley was from Woburn, but this in error, and Johnson, *Woburn Records of Births, Deaths, and Marriages* contain no record of her. Her roots were in Weston's North Parish, which became part of Lincoln in 1754 (See *Historical Manual of the Lincoln Church*, p. 88, Bond, *Genealogies of the Families of Watertown*, p. 296, and *Town of Weston, Births, Deaths, & Marriages*).

Historical Manual of the Lincoln Church says the family moved to Lincoln in 1779. Jack MacLean, on the other hand (in private notes shared with the author), places their reestablishing connections to Lincoln in 1771, citing a 1771 deed transferring property from John Headley to Nathaniel and Tabitha. Whether Lincoln residency occurred in 1771 or sometime after, it is clear that the parents of Nathaniel Colburn (inst.) and Joseph Colburn (q.v.) were becoming increasingly involved in Lincoln during this period, probably helping to manage the holdings and affairs of Tabitha's father (John Headley, d. January 1779), and/or simply reuniting three generations of Tabitha's family. By 1776, in any case, at least Nathaniel Colburn (inst.) seems to have been calling Lincoln "home."

Vital Records of Lincoln lists two children born to Nathaniel "Colbrun," Jr., and his wife Jane (Nathaniel in 1777 and William in 1779). The first matches a baptism record in Leominster, and four successive Leominster baptisms appear to be his children (although no mother's name is given, and there is no baptism record for William). No other birth records are found in either town. The evidence indicates that he remained resident in Lincoln; the baptisms were probably done in Leominster to celebrate with Colburn family members living in Leominster.

4 MacLean, *A Rich Harvest*, p. 307; *Vital Records of Leominster*. The black resident is unidentified but would logically have been one of the former slaves of John Headley, who had made provision for them to remain and to be cared for in his estate. Notwithstanding the age reported in his death record, his birth record indicates he was age 88 when he died. Jane appears to have died ten years earlier; she is nameless in her death record, identified only as "w. Nathaniel Sr."

CONANT, John

John Conant was paid by the town for service at Rhode Island. No dates or details are given, and he has not been positively identified.[1]

This record fits with the record of a John Conant from Bridgewater, who served at Rhode Island as a private in Capt. Francis Brown's Company, Colonel McIntosh's Massachusetts Militia Regiment (Brig. Gen. Solomon Lovell's Brigade) from August 1, 1778, to September 11, 1778 (credited with 1 month, 14 days of service). It is uncertain, however, if these are the same or different individuals.

John Conant of Bridgewater had previously marched to Horse Neck in Braintree (now Houghs Neck in Quincy) on March 4, 1776, for six days (probably as part of the broad militia mobilization at the time of the fortification of Dorchester Heights), in Capt. Abram Washburn's Company, Col. Edward Mitchell's Regiment.

He is reported also as being in service at Cambridge in January 1776, as a private in Capt. Jonathan Minott's Company, Col. Loammi Baldwin's Regiment.[2]

He is subsequently reported to have served as a corporal in Lt. William Dunbar's Company, Maj. Eliphalet Cary's Regiment for 11 days at Tiverton, Rhode Island, from July 30, 1780, to August 9, 1780, and as a private in Capt. Daniel Bowker's Company, Colonel Webb's Regiment in support of the Continental Army from August 20, 1781, through December 2, 1781 (credited with 3 months, 22 days of service).[3]

John Conant of Bridgewater was the son of John and Abigail Conant; age 26 when the war broke out. He was age 29 during his Rhode Island service in 1778. His wife's name was Deborah, although no marriage record has been found. He died in Bridgewater in 1845, reportedly age 95, and is buried in the Conant Street Cemetery.[4]

Whether or not he is the John Conant who was paid by the town for service at Rhode Island remains speculative, as there is little concrete evidence to connect him with Lincoln. Capt. Francis Brown was from Lexington, and his company contained many individuals from Lincoln and the surrounding towns, as well as John Conant of Bridgewater. It may be possible to impute a Lincoln connection from this, but the precise nature of such a connection is not at all clear.[5]

---

1 "Treasurer's Accompts," May 3, 1779. *Massachusetts Soldiers and Sailors*, Vol. III, p. 876.

2 Pension Record # S29728; *Massachusetts Soldiers and Sailors*, Vol. III, p. 876. If he was serving at Cambridge in January, he would have to have been discharged in order to have marched to Horse Neck in Colonel Mitchell's Regiment. It seems unlikely that he would have been discharged, as militia units were being called in and preparations were accelerating for the major battle expected to be provoked by the fortification of Dorchester Heights. It is reasonable to presume, therefore, either that the pay abstract which is the basis of this record applies to prior service in 1775, or that (the pension declaration by his son notwithstanding) this record applies to a different John Conant.

3 Ibid.

4 Pension Record # S29728. Also, Bridgewater Vital Records and the records of the Conant Street Cemetery in Bridgewater, for which information the author thanks Jack MacLean. If the dates are accurate, he would have been age 96 at the time of his death.

5 The author thanks Jack MacLean for his investigation into the geographic makeup of Capt. Francis Brown's Company.
  Another, even more speculative, possibility could be John Conant from Townsend, age 34 at the start of the war, one of several generations of John Conants from that town. His father, John Conant, had married Sarah

COOLIDGE, John
[also COLEDG, COOLIGE]

John Coolidge marched on the Alarm of April 19, 1775, as a private in Capt. Abraham Peirce's Militia Company from Waltham, Col. Thomas Gardner's Regiment. The company is reported to have served as guards until Saturday, the fourth day after the Concord fight. He served for three days.[1]

Subsequently, he served as a private in Capt. Abraham Peirce's Company, Col. Samuel Thatcher's Regiment, from March 4, 1776, to March 8, 1776. The unit was called out by order of General Washington to reinforce the Continental Army during the fortification of Dorchester Heights. He served five days, until the threat of a British assault on the fortifications had subsided.[2]

He may have served guard duty at Roxbury, from April 1 to July 2, 1778, as a private in Capt. Seth Newton's Company, Col. Abijah Stearns's Regiment, but it is uncertain if this is the same John Coolidge.

He may have served to reinforce the Continental Army in Rhode Island, from August 14 to October 29, 1780 (credited with 2 months, 20 days of service, including travel), as a private in Capt. David Moore's Company, Col. Enoch Hallet's Regiment, but it is uncertain if this is the same John Coolidge.[3]

He was from Waltham; age 17 when he marched on the Alarm of April 19, 1775; the son of William and Elizabeth (Brown) Coolidge; brother-in-law of Daniel Harrington (q.v.). In 1777 or 1778, he came to Lincoln, perhaps to work in Harrington's sawmill, but he appears to have left after a brief period. He died in Waltham in 1781 at age 23.[4]

Farrar of Concord in 1735. In 1771, he had also married a Sarah Farrar whose parents (Isaac Farrar and Sarah Brooks) were both from Concord. Both the Farrar and Brooks families, of course, had ample Lincoln connections, so it is entirely plausible that John could have served from Lincoln. However, no record has been found of Rhode Island service by this John Conant, so such a possibility is entirely speculative.

The difficulty with such a possibility is that this John Conant remained a resident and substantial landholder in Townsend, and he had apparently already served at least once from Townsend. On April 19, 1775, he had marched as a sergeant in Capt. James Hosley's Company of Minute Men, Col. William Prescott's Regiment, and served 21 days at Cambridge. There seems to be little reason to imagine him having been paid by the town of Lincoln to serve at Rhode Island. (Hallowell, *Vital Records of Townsend*; *Concord, Massachusetts: Births, Marriages, and Deaths*; *Massachusetts Soldiers and Sailors*, Vol. III, p. 876.)

1 *Massachusetts Soldiers and Sailors*, Vol. III, p. 792. The record seems to suggest that the company marched on April 20, the *day after* the Alarm and the opening battle of the war. This is consistent with the premise of most historians that the Alarm never quite reached Waltham, despite it being an adjacent town to Lexington and Lincoln. Fischer (p. 146) indicates that the Alarm did not even reach Waltham until well after the first casualties had been inflicted on the Lexington Green.
2 *Massachusetts Soldiers and Sailors*, Vol. III, p. 968.
3 *Massachusetts Soldiers and Sailors*, Vol. III, pp. 956, 966.
4 *Vital Records of Waltham*. His Lincoln residency is recorded in the 1778 North Assessment, which contains a £1 poll tax assessment for "Capt. William Coolidge for his son John." It is unclear why this assessment was charged to his father instead of to John directly. It is also unclear how long he remained in town. On June 9, 1779, the "Treasurer's Accompts" show, "One Pound paid Capt. John Hartwell for abatement of Capt. Coolidge's rates for his son John in the year 1778." (The author thanks Jack MacLean and Peg Martin for pointing out these records.)

DAKIN, Samuel, Jr.[1]
[also DAKEN]

Samuel Dakin, Jr., served as a private in Capt. William Smith's Company of Minute Men from Lincoln, Col. Abijah Peirce's Regiment. He served for four days. He was reimbursed by the town on June 18, 1776, for a set of accoutrements as a minute man.[2]

He served as a private in Capt. John Hartwell's Militia Company from Lincoln, Col. Eleazer Brooks's 3rd Middlesex County Regiment, which marched from Lincoln to fortify Dorchester Heights on March 4, 1776. The unit was discharged five days later, on March 9, after the threat of a British assault on the American positions had subsided with British General Howe's decision to evacuate Boston.[3]

Later in 1776, he served at Roxbury, for which he was paid by the town.[4]

In 1777, he was urgently detached from Col. Eleazer Brooks's 3rd Middlesex County Regiment, and sent to reinforce General Gates at Saratoga. He served as a sergeant in Capt. Samuel Farrar, Jr.'s Company, Col. Jonathan Reed's Middlesex County Regiment of Massachusetts Militia (Brig. Gen. James Bricket's Brigade), and marched to Saratoga on September 27, 1777. From various accounts, the unit was sent to Fort Edward, then recalled to Saratoga, arriving at camp "just after the firing ceased." They witnessed British General Burgoyne's surrender on October 17, and they served as part of the escort which marched Burgoyne's troops to Prospect Hill in Cambridge. He was discharged "after all things were settled at the hill" on November 7, 1777 (credited with 1 month, 10 days of service).[5]

He was paid by the town for a one-sixth part of a three-year service in the Continental Army. The record does not indicate where and when this was served, but he appears to have achieved the rank of lieutenant (probably in the militia company) by the time of the payment.[6]

---

1 Because he appears on the Muster Roll as Samuel Dakin, Jr., and on Hartwell, "A List of a Company of Militia," as Samuel Dakin (without the "Jr."), the *War Memorial Book* and *An Account of the Celebration* mistakenly list service by Samuel Dakin and Samuel Dakin, Jr., as different individuals. As Samuel Dakin, Sr., was age 75 (see *Concord, Massachusetts: Births, Marriages, and Deaths* and MacLean, *A Rich Harvest*, p. 181) at the time of Dorchester Heights, it defies logic to think that this service was not provided by Samuel Jr. All the records which have been found for service by a Samuel Dakin fit for Samuel Dakin, Jr. As far as war service goes, the conclusion is inescapable that entries for Samuel Dakin and Samuel Dakin, Jr., are the same individual. As if to concur, *Massachusetts Soldiers and Sailors* (Vol. IV, p. 364) makes no attempt to separate the records of Samuel Dakin from those of Samuel Dakin, Jr.

2 Coburn, *Muster Rolls*; *Massachusetts Soldiers and Sailors*, Vol. IV, p. 364; "Treasurer's Accompts," June 18, 1776.

3 Hartwell, "A List of a Company of Militia"; *Massachusetts Soldiers and Sailors*, Vol. IV, p. 364.

4 "Treasurer's Accompts," June 15, 1779.

5 *Massachusetts Soldiers and Sailors*, Vol. IV, p. 364; Goodway, *American Participants at the Battles of Saratoga*. For accounts of their deployment to Saratoga, see Shattuck, *History of the Town of Concord*, p. 356; Pension Record # S29229 for Leonard Hoar (q.v.).

6 "Treasurer's Accompts," June 15, 1779. Curiously, the town paid "Mr. Samuel Dakin Jr. for service at Roxbury in the year 1776 and for service at Saratoga in 1777," on the same day it paid "Lt. Samuel Dakin for one sixth part of a three years Campaign in the Continental Army." It is not immediately apparent why these should not have been handled as separate transactions, unless the payments were made from different accounts. Nor is it apparent why his name appears differently, unless Lt. Samuel and Samuel Jr. are in fact different individuals. Samuel Dakin, Sr. had been a lieutenant in the militia company many years before (MacLean, *A Rich Harvest*, p. 230). But birth records of Samuel Jr.'s children show that Samuel Jr. also appears to have achieved the rank

He was the son of Samuel Dakin (q.v., Chapter 12) and Mary or Mercy (Heald) Dakin; age 30 in 1775, when he responded to the April 19th Alarm. He had married Elizabeth Billing in 1765. He was a cooper by trade, and he also operated a limekiln, utilizing the limestone deposits on his farm at the corner of what we now call Sandy Pond Road and Baker Bridge Road. After the war, his daughter, Bathsheba, married Daniel Brooks (q.v.). By 1788, Samuel Dakin, Jr., had sold his farm and moved to Concord. He died in 1811 at age 67 in Concord.[1]

FARRAR, Daniel

Daniel Farrar may have been at Concord on April 19, 1775, either as a minute man in Capt. Charles Miles's Concord Company or as a member of the Lincoln Militia Company.[2]

He appears to have served at Cambridge thereafter, enlisting for eight months on April 26, 1775, as a private in Capt. Joseph Butler's 1st Company, Col. John Nixon's 16th Massachusetts Regiment. He was given advance pay on June 10, 1775, and was still in camp at Winter Hill on September 30, 1775. He appears to have participated with his regiment in the Battle of Bunker Hill on June 17, 1775, "where a musket ball clipped a lock of his whiskers."[3]

---

of lieutenant between May 3, 1779, and June 15, 1779. The author accepts that Samuel Jr. was the individual involved in both transactions, and that the elder Samuel does not figure into this.

The two separate transactions, while unusual, may likely be circumstantial rather than material. This is easier logic than to force the conclusion that the separate transactions necessarily evince different individuals, i.e., that the elder Samuel was paid for Continental service. In the latter case, the Continental service would have to have been provided either by his son, Amos (who was age 43 at the outbreak of the war, had been married to Thankful Sarah Minot of Concord since 1755, and had seven children recorded in Lincoln), or Timothy (who was age 37 at the outbreak of the war, but otherwise seems to have left little record). MacLean mentions another son, Nathan, but he appears to have died in infancy. Neither Amos nor Timothy left any other record of service during the war. Accordingly, there is little logic in attributing this service to one of them, rather than to Samuel Jr. (inst.) (see *Concord, Massachusetts: Births, Marriages, and Deaths* and *Vital Records of Lincoln*).

1 *Vital Records of Lincoln*; *Concord, Massachusetts: Births, Marriages, and Deaths*; MacLean, *A Rich Harvest*, pp. 179, 184. His house stood opposite from where the historical marker now sits; the limestone deposits and kiln were further to the southwest.

The Dakin family had long Concord roots, but his father Samuel and his mother Mary Heald both are reported to have been born in Newington, South Carolina (see McGhie, "Descendants of Thomas Dakin"). This source has not been substantiated, but it appears detailed, thorough, and well annotated.

Elizabeth Billing was not a sister to any of the Billings who served in the Revolution from Lincoln. Beyond that, the relationships between Elizabeth Billing and the Billings who served has not been determined. Both Samuel's and Elizabeth's deaths (14 years apart) are recorded in *Concord, Massachusetts: Births, Marriages, and Deaths*.

Elizabeth is buried in the South Burying Ground in Concord, but no record of Samuel's gravesite has been found.

2 Coburn, *Muster Rolls*, p. 10. Caverly, *Historical Sketch of Troy* (p. 54), states that Daniel (inst.) was "one of the minute men at Concord." If Caverly is right, then he must be the Daniel Farrar in Captain Miles's Company, which would also be consistent with subsequent identifications of Daniel Farror, Jr., of Concord (see note 3). Another possibility for the Daniel Farrar in Captain Miles's Company could be the son of Jacob and Mary, born in Concord May 20, 1756 (see *Concord, Massachusetts: Births, Marriages, and Deaths*). In that case, Daniel (inst.) may have been in the Lincoln Militia Company at Concord, misidentified by Caverly as a minute man rather than a militia man.

3 Wheeler, "Lincoln," in Hurd, Vol. 2, p. 622; *Massachusetts Soldiers and Sailors*, Vol. V, pp. 532, 533, 552. The quote is from Caverly, *Historical Sketch of Troy* (p. 54), who also says of him that he "took an active part in the various operations of the army in the vicinity of Boston." Two of the various records of this service in *Massachusetts Soldiers and Sailors* attribute it to a Daniel Farror (also Farrow), Jr., of Concord. *Concord, Massachusetts: Births, Marriages, and Deaths* does list a Daniel Farrar from Concord (b. May 20, 1756; son of Jacob and Mary). However, Jack MacLean's analysis of Butler's Company (communicated privately) suggests

He may be the Daniel Farrar who served as a private in Capt. Caleb Brooks's Company, Col. Nicholas Dike's Regiment during the fall of 1776, probably around Roxbury and Dorchester.[1]

He may have enlisted (probably as a substitute) on August 16, 1777, into Capt. George Minot's Company, Col. Samuel Bullard's Middlesex County Regiment of Massachusetts Militia, and marched to the Northern Department to reinforce General Gates at Saratoga. However, it is not certain if this record refers to Daniel Farrar of Lincoln. The Daniel Farrar in this record was present at the surrender of Burgoyne's army on October 17, 1777, then marched south to reinforce General Washington in New Jersey, serving 3 months, 25 days (including travel) until discharged on November 30, 1777.[2]

He likely served at Cambridge again in 1778, having been detached from Capt. Samuel Farrar, Jr.'s Militia Company from Lincoln, Col. Eleazer Brooks's 3rd Middlesex Regiment. He was sent to relieve the guards who were guarding the British and German soldiers surrendered by Burgoyne at Saratoga. He was paid by the town for this service.[3]

He was age 20 in 1775; the son of Daniel and Mary (Allen) Farrar; brother of George Farrar (q.v.), Nehemiah Farrar (q.v.), and Zebediah Farrar (q.v.). He married Lucy Bruce of Sudbury in August 1775, evidently while on furlough; she bore him a child five months later. At some point following his war service, he moved his family to New Hampshire. He died at Troy, New Hampshire, in 1825 or 1827 at age 70 or 72, and is buried in the old Village Cemetery in Troy.[4]

---

that "Concord" may have been applied loosely to individuals from a broader area than just the town itself. As there is no apparent reason for Daniel of Concord to have been designated as "Jr," the designation "Jr.," along with attribution by Wheeler and Caverly, suggests that this service probably belongs to Daniel Farrar of Lincoln.

In August, Colonel Nixon's 16th Massachusetts Regiment became known also as the 5th Regiment under Washington's Continental command.

1 *Massachusetts Soldiers and Sailors*, Vol. V, p. 533. This service was credited to the town of Sudbury. Daniel (inst.) had a cousin Daniel Farrar of Sudbury (son of Josiah and Hannah), who is reported to have died at age 16 (*Vital Records of Sudbury*; Farrar, *Memoir of the Farrar Family*, p. 11). The timing is tight, but not disqualifying; Daniel of Sudbury could have served this stint before he died. The author believes it equally likely to have been served by Daniel (inst.), who also had family connections in Sudbury; having married a Sudbury girl the previous year, he may possibly have been temporarily living in Sudbury at the time.

2 *Massachusetts Soldiers and Sailors*, Vol. V, p. 538. Either Daniel Farrar of Lincoln (age 22), or Daniel Farrar of Concord (age 21) could have provided this service. Whichever Daniel Farrar this is, he does not appear on the draft list of either town; therefore the presumption is that he served as a substitute for one of the draftees.

3 "Treasurer's Accompts," June 15, 1779; *Massachusetts Soldiers and Sailors*, Vol. V, p. 532.

4 *Vital Records of Lincoln*; Briggs, "Genealogical Chart of Farrar family"; *SAR Revolutionary War Graves Register*. *SAR Revolutionary War Graves Register* identifies the burial location as the Old Cemetery. Wheeler, "Lincoln" (in Hurd, Vol. 2, p. 622), says he died in Lincoln in 1810; this appears on its face to run counter to the evidence. Most sources report his death as 1837, but this is incorrect. His gravestone is indistinct, but appears to read either 1825 or 1827, at age 71. 1825 would be consistent with his being in his 71st year.

Lucy appears to be the sister of Bethiah Bruce, who married Daniel's brother, George Farrar (q.v.).

There are January 1776 and March 1778 birth records in Fitzwilliam, New Hampshire, which list Daniel and Lucy Farrar as parents. It is not quite clear how to reconcile these records with the records of Daniel's service from Lincoln and Sudbury. Norton and Whittemore, *History of Fitzwilliam* (pp. 143, 498, 552), indicate that Lucy's family moved to Fitzwilliam around 1775, and conclude from the birth records that Daniel and Lucy arrived about the same time. If this is so, then possibly, the service records could be applied to his father, Daniel Sr., who would have been age 53 in 1778. More likely, the birth records may have been added after Daniel and Lucy later moved to New Hampshire (perhaps recorded in 1781 when the second child died). This would be consistent with Caverly's narrative (*Historical Sketch of Troy*, pp. 54–55) attributing to him "an active part in the various operations of the army in the vicinity of Boston," and saying that after his marriage, he "settled in Lincoln, where he resided until 1779." It is also likely that Daniel and Lucy may have gone back

FARRAR, George

George Farrar of Weston served as a private at Ticonderoga in 1776, in Capt. Charles Miles's Company, Col. Jonathan Reed's Regiment.[1]

He responded to the Rhode Island Alarm in 1777, arriving at his rendezvous point on May 10, 1777, and serving as a private in Capt. Jesse Wyman's Company, Col. Josiah Whitney's Regiment. He was discharged at Point Judith on July 10, 1777 (credited with 2 months, 9 days of service, including 9 days of travel).[2]

After the surrender of Burgoyne's army at Saratoga, he returned to service on November 5, 1777, to guard the prisoners at Cambridge. He served for 4 months, 28 days, in Capt. Simon Hunt's Company, Col. Eleazer Brooks's Regiment, until his discharge on April 2, 1778.[3]

He enlisted in Capt. Daniel Bowker's Company, Col. Webb's Regiment on August 18, 1781, to reinforce the Continental Army in the Hudson Valley while General Washington marched much of the army south to Yorktown. He was discharged on November 30, 1781 (credited with 3 months, 22 days of service, including 10 days for travel home).[4]

He was a Lincoln native; age 16 at Ticonderoga; the son of Daniel and Mary (Allen) Farrar. He was the brother of Daniel Farrar (q.v.), Nehemiah Farrar (q.v.), and Zebediah Farrar (q.v.). He married Bethiah Bruce from Sudbury, and followed his brother Daniel to Marlborough, New Hampshire, about 1783. He appears to have died in 1824, three months shy of turning age 65. He is buried in the Village Cemetery in Troy, New Hampshire[5]

FARRAR, Humphrey

Humphrey Farrar was a private in Capt. William Smith's Company of Minute Men from Lincoln, Col. Abijah Peirce's Regiment.[6] Following the engagement at Concord, he served for 21 days in Cambridge.[7] He was reimbursed by the town on May 7, 1776, for a set of accoutrements as a minute man.[8]

He appears to have stayed or returned to Cambridge and served probably through the summer and fall of 1775 during the Siege of Boston, although the record of the dates and unit has not been found.[9]

---

and forth between Lincoln and Fitzwilliam for a period of time before they were ready to pull up stakes from Lincoln. See also "New Hampshire, Births and Christenings, 1714-1904."

1 *Massachusetts Soldiers and Sailors*, Vol. V, p. 533.
2 *Massachusetts Soldiers and Sailors*, Vol. V, p. 538.
3 Ibid.
4 Ibid.
5 *Vital Records of Lincoln*; Caverly, *Historical Sketch of Troy*, pp. 54–55; Bemis, *History of Marlborough*, pp. 63, 67; Farrar, *Memoir of the Farrar Family*, pp. 36–37; "Find A Grave." No marriage record has been found. His wife's given name appears in the 1784 birth record for their son, George Farrar, Jr. (see "New Hampshire, Birth Records, Early to 1900"); she appears to be the sister of Lucy Bruce, his brother Daniel's wife. Caverly says he lived with his brother Daniel for a year in Marlborough, then he purchased Daniel's farm in 1784, after Daniel moved into the farm of his deceased father-in-law. Bemis says he served for five or six years in the Continental Army, but this is clearly incorrect. Farrar gives his death as 1820, but his gravestone indicates it was in 1824.
6 Coburn, *Muster Rolls*.
7 *Massachusetts Soldiers and Sailors*, Vol. V, p. 539.
8 "Treasurer's Accompts," May 7, 1776.
9 "Treasurer's Accompts," June 15, 1779; Wheeler, "Lincoln," in Hurd, Vol. 2, p. 622.

Subsequently, he served as a private in Capt. John Hartwell's Militia Company from Lincoln, Col. Eleazer Brooks's 3rd Middlesex County Regiment, which marched from Lincoln to fortify Dorchester Heights on March 4, 1776. The unit was discharged five days later, on March 9, after the threat of a British assault on the fortifications had subsided, General Howe having instead begun preparations to evacuate Boston. He was paid for this service the following September.[1]

He was paid by the town for service at the Southward in 1776, following the British evacuation of Boston. The details of this service are not known, but it is likely to have been served by his slave, Jack Farrar (q.v.).[2]

He was age 35 when he went to Concord; son of George and Mary (Barrett) Farrar. He had been married to his first cousin, Lucy (Farrar), since 1770, making him the brother-in-law as well as cousin of Samuel Farrar, Jr. (q.v.), Stephen Farrar (q.v.), and Timothy Farrar (q.v.); uncle to William Bond (q.v.), Jonas Bond (q.v.), and Samuel Bond (q.v.). He is reported to have died at Colebrook, New Hampshire, in 1816, probably at age 76, and to be buried in the Colebrook Village Cemetery.[3]

FARRAR, Jack
[also John FARRAR, Jack FREEMAN, Jack HATCH]

Jack Farrar may have been in arms at Cambridge by July 3, 1775, serving temporary duty as a private on main guard under Lt. Col. Loammi Baldwin, but it is uncertain if the record of this John Farrar refers to Jack Farrar from Lincoln.[4]

He must have been in service before the end of 1775, in Capt. Adam Wheeler's 2nd Company, Col. John Nixon's 5th Continental Regiment, as he appears to have been paid "for wages due prior to January 1, 1776."[5]

He remained in service with Captain Wheeler's Company through 1776 and January 1777. We can follow his trail during the New York campaign: to Camp Mt. Washington on September 30, 1776; probably at the Battle of White Plains on October 28, 1776; at North Castle on November 9, 1776; and at the Battle of Trenton on December 26, 1776, where his unit failed to make it across the ice-choked river. He was in the Battle of Princeton on January 3, 1777, and at Springfield on January 25, 1777. He appears on

---

1 *Massachusetts Soldiers and Sailors*, Vol. V, p. 533. The pay receipt is signed by his wife Lucy.
2 "Treasurer's Accompts," June 15, 1779. MacLean, *A Rich Harvest* (p. 293), defines "Southward" as beyond New York. This is consistent with my observation of the Treasurer's accounts, which frequently mention New York, but scarcely if ever name anything further afield. As there is no record of any such service by Humphrey Farrar, and as his father George died of smallpox in 1777, this payment logically fits the 1776–1777 New York-New Jersey service of his father's slave (now his slave), Jack Farrar (q.v.).
3 *Vital Records of Lincoln*; *Concord, Massachusetts: Births, Marriages, and Deaths*; Briggs, "Genealogical Chart of Farrar family"; *SAR Revolutionary War Graves Register*. Lucy was the sister of Samuel Farrar, Jr. (q.v.), Stephen Farrar (q.v.), and Timothy Farrar (q.v.). Assuming *Concord, Massachusetts: Births, Marriages, and Deaths* to be correct, Briggs, "Genealogical Chart of Farrar family," and *SAR Revolutionary War Graves Register* both misstate his birth date by a year.
4 *Massachusetts Soldiers and Sailors*, Vol. V, p. 535. There appear to have been several John Farrars in service at Cambridge in 1775, but this record parallels similar records of main guard service by other Lincoln men.
5 *Massachusetts Soldiers and Sailors*, Vol. V, p. 539. This regiment was also known as the 16th Massachusetts. In 1776, it became the 4th Continental Regiment. From August 1776, it was commanded by Lt. Col. Thomas Nixon.

Chapter 10: The Army of the Revolution

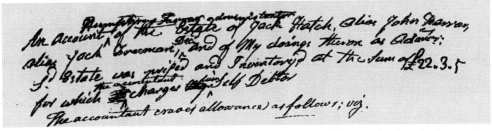

As shown in this probate document, slave Jack Farrar adopted the name Freeman, then Hatch after securing his freedom through his nearly five years of war service. He served at Dorchester Heights; in the New York campaign; at the battles of White Plains, Trenton, Princeton, Saratoga, Monmouth, and Rhode Island; and spent the winter of 1777–1778 at Valley Forge. (Middlesex County Probate Records)

a list dated Chatham, February 1, 1777, of men who returned the equipment used in the campaign of 1776.[1]

He reenlisted immediately for three years in the Continental service, serving from February 1, 1777, until February 1, 1780. His reenlistment was credited to the town of Lincoln. He served as a private in Capt. Moses Ashley's Company, Col. Joseph Vose's 15th Continental Regiment.[2] Again, we can follow segments of his trail: he marched to Peekskill, and arrived in camp by August 16, 1777; Colonel Vose's Regiment marched north to Albany, then to Bemis Heights; they participated in the defeat of General Burgoyne at Saratoga on October 17, 1777, then marched south to rejoin Washington's command outside of Philadelphia. The men endured the legendary winter of 1777–78 at Valley Forge; then participated in the Battle of Monmouth on June 28, 1778. The regiment was deployed to Rhode Island in July, and it may have participated in the Battle of Rhode Island on August 29, 1778. He served at Providence from January through April 1779, and he was reported sick and absent during July and August 1779. From January 1, 1780, until his apparent discharge on February 1, 1780, he served in Captain Hancock's Company, Colonel Vose's Regiment.[3]

He may have enlisted again for Continental service, as Jack Freeman, on August 29, 1781 (agreeable to a resolve of December 2, 1780, and credited to the town of Boston), possibly in Col. John Ashley's Berkshire County Regiment.[4]

---

1 *Massachusetts Soldiers and Sailors*, Vol. V, pp. 539, 869. Springfield and Chatham are in New Jersey. Chatham is about six miles southeast of Morristown, where Washington had established his headquarters on January 6, 1777, and about midway between Springfield and Morristown.

2 *Massachusetts Soldiers and Sailors*, Vol. V, p. 534. See also Blake, "James Barrett's Returns of Men," p. 471 for a record of his being mustered and paid a bounty for this service, which lists him as "Jack Farret" in Captain Ashby's Company, Colonel Pattison's Battalion, as reported by James Barrett, muster master, on March 24, 1777.

3 *Massachusetts Soldiers and Sailors*, Vol. V, p. 534. While the record of his service shows that he was at Providence during the early months of 1779, it is likely that he was at Providence as early as July 1778, when Colonel Vose's Regiment was deployed there prior to the Battle of Rhode Island, August 29, 1778. His 1779 sickness is from pay accounts found by Jack MacLean in the National Archives. Jack MacLean also found probate records (see note 1, p. 274) indicating that he appears to have returned to Lincoln during his 1779 illness, and probably during a 1778 illness, as his estate was assessed for board and care by Humphrey Farrar (q.v.), the Widow Rebecca Brown, and Stephen Hosmer.

4 *Massachusetts Soldiers and Sailors*, Vol. VI, p. 41. This record does not identify his unit. The author is indebted to Jack MacLean for information concerning his probate record (see note 1, p. 274), which indicates that his estate

Known in the records mostly as Jack Farrar, he was African-American; a slave of George Farrar and Humphrey Farrar (q.v.). He had been baptized into Lincoln's First Parish in 1772. By 1778, he appears to have become a free man, and subsequently he adopted the names Freeman and Hatch. After the war, he probably worked as a laborer. In October 1781, he boarded for a month with Jube Savage (q.v.). He died in 1784, evidently in Lincoln.[1]

FARRAR, Nehemiah

At age 16, Nehemiah Farrar went to Cambridge on April 2, 1778, as a private in Capt. Daniel Harrington's Company, Col. Jonathan Reed's Regiment of Guards. He served 3 months, 2 days, through July 3, 1778, guarding the "Convention Army" that Burgoyne had surrendered at Saratoga the previous October.

Within a few days of his discharge, he was back in service on July 12, 1778, in Capt. Simon Hunt's Company, Col. Jacob Gerrish's Regiment of Guards at Winter Hill, guarding Burgoyne's German troops. He served 5 months, 4 days, until December 15, 1778, about five weeks after the last of Burgoyne's troops had been marched out of Cambridge en route to a more secure holding area near Charlottesville, Virginia.[2]

He served again the next spring, at Tiverton, Rhode Island, from May 17, 1779, to July 1, 1779 (credited with 1 month, 18 days of service, including travel) in Capt. Lawson Buckminster's Company, Lt. Col. Samuel Pierce's Regiment.[3]

He was the son of Daniel and Mary (Allen) Farrar; age 13 when the war broke out. He was the brother of Daniel Farrar (q.v.), George Farrar (q.v.), and Zebediah Farrar (q.v.). He married Ruth Simonds of Boston in 1788. He died in Lincoln in 1808, age 46.[4]

---

was still owed pay for his "last Service in the Continental Army." In 1785, Humphrey Farrar (q.v.), administrator, wrote "to Esq. Walker of Leonix to draw a final settlement." Jack MacLean surmises that this was William Walker, who appears to have been an adjutant in the early years of the war. In a search of *Massachusetts Soldiers and Sailors*, he found 192 entries on a "descriptive list dated Lenox, August 20, 1781, of men raised in Berkshire Co. agreeable to a resolve of Dec. 2, 1780, and delivered to William Walker, Superintendent of said county; [in various companies] Col. Ashley's regt." Jack Farrar, in any of his known names, does not appear on this list, which predates his apparent Continental enlistment by nine days. Nevertheless, the probate reference to Esq. Walker of Lenox is intriguing. Whatever connection he may have had with Berkshire County is unclear.

1 MacLean, *A Rich Harvest*, p. 219, 306; MacLean, "Resources." MacLean says he died in 1787, but this date refers to probate records; MacLean, "Resources," makes it clear that he died in 1784. The fact that his estate was assessed £12 for nursing and board by Humphrey Farrar in 1778 indicates that he was by then a free man. (The probate records cited in MacLean, *A Rich Harvest*, and MacLean, "Resources," are Inventory of Jack Hatch, September 1, 1787, Middlesex Probate, General Records 70:204 (see also 71:347); Jack Hatch, March 11, 1784, administrative paper, Middlesex Probate, first series, #10,743; and Jack Hatch, March 12, 1788, administrative paper, Middlesex Probate, first series, #10,743.)

2 *Massachusetts Soldiers and Sailors*, Vol. V, pp. 535, 539. The town paid his father for his Cambridge service (see "Treasurer's Accompts," June 30, 1779).

3 Ibid. Wheeler, "Lincoln" (in Hurd, Vol. 2, p. 622), places him in Rhode Island in 1778, but this appears to be in error.

4 *Vital Records of Lincoln*; Wheeler, "Lincoln," in Hurd, Vol. 2, p. 622; Briggs, "Genealogical Chart of Farrar family"; Shattuck, Draft; *Essex Register*, (October 19, 1808), p. 3. Assuming *Vital Records of Lincoln* to be correct, Briggs misstates his birth date by nearly 2 years. His death is not recorded in *Vital Records of Lincoln*. Wheeler lists his death incorrectly as a year earlier. After his death, Ruth appears to have remarried in 1811, to Jonas Sherman.

FARRAR, Samuel, Jr.

Samuel Farrar, Jr., was a lieutenant in Capt. William Smith's Company of Minute Men from Lincoln, Col. Abijah Peirce's Regiment, and marched to Concord on April 19, 1775. It is probable that he may also have been in acting command of the militia company from Lincoln that morning.[1] He is reported to have received the alarm while he was "on his way to the mill," whereupon he immediately "threw the bars over the wall and hastened to call his men." Following the engagement at Concord, he served for 24 days in Cambridge.[2] He was reimbursed by the town for his accoutrements as a minute man, and reimbursed by the state for losses he sustained at the battles of Lexington and Bunker Hill.[3]

Subsequently, he served as a lieutenant in Capt. John Hartwell's Militia Company from Lincoln, Col. Eleazer Brooks's 3rd Middlesex County Regiment, which marched from Lincoln to fortify Dorchester Heights on March 4, 1776. "When in service on the hills," he was later quoted as saying, "we were obliged to manage our oxen in silence, depending on the prick of our bayonets to urge them along rather than our ordinary means of forcing them." The unit was discharged five days later, on March 9, after the threat of a British assault on the fortifications had subsided, General Howe having instead begun preparations to evacuate Boston.[4]

He was commissioned captain of the 6th Company from Lincoln, Col. Eleazer Brooks's 3rd Middlesex County Regiment of Militia, replacing John Hartwell on March 27, 1776.

He was paid by the town for service at Cambridge in 1776, for service at Ticonderoga in 1776, for 1½ years of service in the Continental Army, and for an additional three months of service in the Continental Army.[5]

On September 29, 1777, amidst rising anxiety about Burgoyne's unchecked penetration into the Hudson Valley, he was detached from Colonel Brooks's 3rd Middlesex County Regiment with 13 other men from his Lincoln company and put in command of a company made up of men from Lincoln and Lexington. Attached to Col. Jonathan Reed's Middlesex County Regiment (Brig. Gen. James Bricket's Brigade of Massachusetts Militia), he marched north via Rutland and Northampton to Saratoga. Arriving a day or

---

1 Coburn, *Muster Rolls*. In 1827, Ripley, *A History of the Fight at Concord* (p. 14) asserts that he was captain in command of the militia company from Lincoln. Since a muster roll for the militia company has never been found, the question of who commanded it will likely remain a subject of speculation. MacLean, *A Rich Harvest* (p. 607) applies some clear logic to this debate. Bearing in mind that minute companies were formed out of the militia units, the author concurs with MacLean's reasoning: Abijah Peirce (q.v.) was probably still the captain of the militia company, but was also colonel of the regiment of minute men. Samuel Farrar, Jr., was probably a lieutenant in both the militia and minute companies. With Peirce assuming regimental responsibilities on April 19, and with the militia ranks depleted somewhat by the detachment of the minute company, Farrar may well have served in the role of acting captain of the militia company, as well as or in lieu of his responsibilities as lieutenant of the minute company. This might also explain Shattuck's listing him (*History of the Town of Concord*, p. 110) as captain of the militia company.
2 *Massachusetts Soldiers and Sailors*, Vol. V, p. 536. MacLean, *A Rich Harvest* (p. 268), attributes the quote to Mary B. Farrar.
3 "Treasurer's Accompts," February 29, 1776; *Massachusetts Soldiers and Sailors*, Vol. V, p. 536. Administratively, claims stemming from both battles were handled at the same time and together. The juxtaposition of the two battles is not to suggest that he participated in or had losses associated with Bunker Hill. Neither is it clear what equipment losses he suffered on April 19, 1775.
4 *Massachusetts Soldiers and Sailors*, Vol. V, p. 536. The quote is in Brown, *Beneath Old Roof Trees*, p. 233.
5 Shattuck, *History of the Town of Concord*, p. 358; "Treasurer's Accompts," June 15, 1779.

The Farrar Homestead served as the home of Deacon Samuel Farrar; his sons Samuel Jr., Stephen, and Timothy; and possibly grandsons Jonas, Samuel, and William Bond, all of whom (excepting Deacon Samuel) served at various times during the war. (*An Account of the Celebration*)

two after the British were repulsed at Bemis Heights on October 7, his men appear to have been deployed to Fort Edward, where they engaged in scouting operations and rounded up Indians and Tories in Burgoyne's rear. On October 17, they were recalled to Saratoga, where they were present at the surrender of Burgoyne's army. Following the surrender, his company was deployed under General Glover in escorting Burgoyne's troops to Cambridge, and the unit was discharged upon arrival at Cambridge on November 7, 1777. He was paid for this service by the town.[1]

He was still serving as captain of Lincoln's 6th Company, 3rd Middlesex County Regiment of Militia as late as March 7, 1780.[2]

He was age 38 when he answered the April 19th Alarm; the son of Samuel Farrar (q.v., Chapter 12) and Lydia (Barrett) Farrar; brother of Stephen Farrar (q.v.) and Timothy Farrar (q.v.); first cousin and brother-in-law of Humphrey Farrar (q.v.); and uncle of William Bond (q.v.), Samuel Bond (q.v.), and Jonas Bond (q.v.). He had been a member of the militia company from Lincoln since its origin in 1757. In 1772, he had married Mercy (or Marcy) Hoar, sister of Samuel Hoar (q.v.) and Leonard Hoar (q.v.). He died in Lincoln in

---

1 *Massachusetts Soldiers and Sailors*, Vol. V, p. 536; "Treasurer's Accompts," June 15, 1779. Shattuck, *History of the Town of Concord*, p. 356. MacLean, *A Rich Harvest* (p. 294), numbers the contingent from Lincoln as Samuel Farrar plus 11 others. The Saratoga itinerary is that followed by Maj. John Buttrick's Company, Colonel Reed's Regiment; the assumption is that, as part of the same regiment, Capt. Samuel Farrar, Jr.'s Company was deployed in similar or parallel duty.

As for escorting Burgoyne's troops, Shattuck reports, "They guarded the prisoners to Cambridge...Capt. Simon Hunt, of Acton, commanded the company to which most of the Concord men were attached....Nine companies guarded Burgoyne's troops down, five marching before and four behind." Shattuck's narrative is unclear and a bit confused. Major Buttrick's Company and Captain Farrar's Company were deployed as escort guards en route to Cambridge. Captain Hunt was almost certainly not at Saratoga, but his company was engaged, as part of Col. Eleazer Brooks's Regiment, to guard the prisoners upon their arrival at Cambridge.

2 Shattuck, *History of the Town of Concord*, p. 358.

1829 at age 92 years, 7 months. He appears to be buried in the Farrar tomb in the Meeting House Cemetery behind Bemis Hall.[1]

On July 14, 1779, he and Abijah Peirce (q.v.) served as Lincoln's delegates to a state convention organized to try to bring some sanity to the economic chaos brought by the war, through the implementation of price controls or through some other means. Seven years later, with the economy still roiling from the impact of the war, he and Samuel Hoar (q.v.) represented Lincoln in a conference on August 23, 1786, to deal with the growing credit and foreclosure problem which sparked Shays' Rebellion in the central and western counties of Massachusetts.[2]

Following in his father's footsteps, he was elected Selectman in 1780 and chosen a Deacon of the church in Lincoln in 1784.[3]

FARRAR, Stephen

Stephen Farrar of New Ipswich, New Hampshire, marched to Cambridge on the Alarm of April 19, 1775, as a private in Capt. Thomas Heald's Company from New Ipswich. He served for 30 days.

He was born and raised in the section of Concord that in 1754 became Lincoln; the son of Samuel Farrar (q.v., Chapter 12) and Lydia (Barrett) Farrar; brother of Samuel Farrar, Jr. (q.v.), and Timothy Farrar (q.v.); brother-in-law of Moses Brown (q.v.); first cousin and brother-in-law of Humphrey Farrar (q.v.); and uncle of William Bond (q.v.), Jonas Bond (q.v.), and Samuel Bond (q.v.).

He was age 36 during his 30-days service at Cambridge. He had been a classmate of John Adams (the future president) at Harvard College, having graduated in 1755. He is reported to have been a soldier in the French and Indian War.

He appears to have settled in New Ipswich after the French and Indian War, probably on property belonging to his father. By 1760, he had organized the New Ipswich church and begun a long career as its first pastor. He had married Eunice Brown, sister of Moses Brown

---

1 *Vital Records of Lincoln*; *Concord, Massachusetts: Births, Marriages, and Deaths*; MacLean, *A Rich Harvest*, p. 255; Briggs, "Genealogical Chart of Farrar family." See Martin, "The Sons of Lincoln" for the muster roll of the original militia company. His final resting place has not been determined with certainty. *SAR Revolutionary War Graves Register* lists his burial place as "Old Cemetery" and "Old Three Cornered Cemetery." However, the Farrar–Munroe tomb in the Meeting House Cemetery has an SAR marker next to it with Samuel Farrar, Jr.'s name on it. It is presumed that he is probably entombed there, but no other evidence of him has been found in any of the town's burial grounds.

There is a curious record of a Samuel Farrar being recruited into the Continental Army for a three-year term (engaged for the town of Concord), subsequent to January 1, 1781. This Samuel Farrar was assigned to the 9th Massachusetts Regiment, but he was reported as unfit for duty. He is described as age 44 (also age 43); five feet, four inches. (also five feet, five inches) in height; light complexion, dark hair, and dark eyes. His occupation is listed as a laborer and also as a farmer (*Massachusetts Soldiers and Sailors*, Vol. V, pp. 536, 540). While the age matches Samuel Farrar, Jr., exactly, it is difficult to imagine that this record could be him. Shattuck, *History of the Town of Concord* (p. 359) also treats this individual as if he were a Concordian. What is baffling is that Vital Records do not reveal another Samuel Farrar in Concord or in any of the surrounding towns of the same or similar age, thereby preventing us from making a suitable alternative identification. For what it's worth, Farrar, "Record from Memoirs" (p. 4) appears to accept this service as Samuel Farrar (inst.), but this appears to be less an authoritative source than an uncritical collection of memoirs. This individual will remain a mystery.

2 Shattuck, *History of the Town of Concord*, pp. 122, 130.

3 MacLean, *A Rich Harvest*, p. 301; Shattuck, *History of the Town of Concord*, p. 308.

(q.v.), in 1764. After his brief Revolutionary War service, he returned to New Ipswich, where it is said he "held as strong an influence over his parishioners as that wielded by any prelate in the pomp of ecclesiastic authority and office," until he died in 1809 at age 70. He is reportedly buried in the Old Village Yard at New Ipswich.[1]

FARRAR, Timothy

Timothy Farrar of New Ipswich, New Hampshire, marched to Cambridge on the Alarm of April 19, 1775, as a private in Capt. Thomas Heald's Company from New Ipswich. He served for five days.[2]

He was born and raised in Lincoln; the son of Samuel Farrar (q.v., Chapter 12) and Lydia (Barrett) Farrar; brother of Samuel Farrar, Jr. (q.v.), and Stephen Farrar (q.v.); brother-in-law of Moses Brown (q.v.); first cousin and brother-in-law of Humphrey Farrar (q.v.); and uncle of William Bond (q.v.), Jonas Bond (q.v.), and Samuel Bond (q.v.).

He was age 27 when he responded to the Alarm and marched to Cambridge. He had graduated from Harvard in 1767, and he had been a teacher in or near Concord before moving to New Ipswich to teach in 1770. By the time the war broke out, he was an attorney and had become active in public affairs.

After his brief service on the Alarm of April 19, 1775, he returned to New Ipswich and was appointed a Judge of the Court of Common Pleas. Thus began a long

Lincoln native Timothy Farrar marched on the Alarm of April 19th with men from New Ipswich, New Hampshire. Afterward, he opted for civil service, becoming a highly respected judge, a Justice in the New Hampshire Superior Court, and a senior law partner to Daniel Webster. This portrait, by J. G. Cole (engraved by H. W. Smith), shows him at age 85. (Courtesy of the New York Public Library. www.nypl.org.)

---

1 *Register of Members* [SAR], p. 130; *Concord, Massachusetts: Births, Marriages, and Deaths*, Shattuck, *History of the Town of Concord*, p. 314; Bouvé, "Town History of New Ipswich"; Chandler, *History of New Ipswich*, pp. 74–76, 123–124, 395–396; Bond, *Genealogies of the Families of Watertown*, p. 728; *SAR Revolutionary War Graves Register*. His 30-day service is curious, as the longest service recorded for anyone else in the company was 13 days. Perhaps there was a shortage of chaplains in the army (such as it was) at the time, and he may have felt the need to stay and minister to others beyond his own company.

The quotation is from Bouvé; Chandler contains a more thorough account of his ministry. He appears to have been about age 16 when he graduated from Harvard; about age 22 when he assumed his pastoral duties at New Ipswich. Chandler mistakenly identifies Eunice as the *daughter* of Moses Brown (q.v.) of Beverly.

2 Chandler, *History of New Ipswich*, pp. 75, 397. Another report, published on the occasion of his 100th birthday (*Boston Evening Transcript*, August 31, 1847), says "on the report which went by express, that the British were coming out of Boston to Concord, he collected a small company and hurried to the expected scene of conflict, but at Peperell or Groton they were met by the news that the invaders had retreated to Boston, and they returned."

and respected judicial career, which included a brief tenure as Chief Justice of the New Hampshire Superior Court.

He married Anna Bancroft of Pepperell in 1779. In his final years he went to live with his daughter in Hollis, New Hampshire, where died in 1849, four months shy of his 102nd birthday.[1]

FARRAR, Zebediah

Zebediah Farrar served as a private in Capt. Nathaniel Cudworth's Company of Minute Men from Sudbury, Col. Abijah Peirce's Regiment, and marched on the Alarm of April 19th. He served for 1 month, 11 days in Cambridge.[2]

Subsequently, he served as a corporal in Capt. Asahel Wheeler's Company, Col. John Robinson's Regiment, during the Siege of Boston from February 4, 1776, through April 1, 1776. This service lasted 1 month, 28 days, through the fortification of Dorchester Heights and the British evacuation of Boston.[3]

He was back in service on August 23, 1776, as a corporal in Capt. Zachariah Fitch's Company, Col. Samuel Brewer's Massachusetts Militia Regiment, which marched to Bennington, then Ticonderoga on August 28. He served into December 1776.[4]

He appears to have made his first of several appearances in Rhode Island in 1777, where he was recorded as serving in Capt. John Gleason's Company, Col. Josiah Whitney's Regiment in North Kingston, on June 26, 1777. His length of service was not recorded.

He was back in North Kingston for a three-month term starting January 2, 1778, as a sergeant in Capt. Benjamin Monroe's Company.

No sooner had he completed that service, when he was enticed by an individual named Trobridge Taylor to serve for him in Captain Home's Company, Col. Jonathan Reed's Regiment, from April 20, 1778, to July 2, 1778, evidently guarding the "Convention Army" that Burgoyne had surrendered at Saratoga the previous October.

On July 2, 1778, he went to Fort No. 2 in Cambridge for seven days, until July 8, 1778, as a corporal in Lt. John Dix's Company, Col. Jacob Gerrish's Regiment of Guards.

He was back in Rhode Island the following May, as a sergeant in Capt. Lawson Buckminster's Company, Lt. Col. Samuel Pierce's Regiment at Tiverton, from May 17, 1779, to July 1, 1779 (credited with 1 month, 18 days of service).

---

1 Chandler, *History of New Ipswich*, pp. 75, 397–99; *Concord, Massachusetts: Births, Marriages, and Deaths*; MacLean, *A Rich Harvest*, p. 203; Shattuck, *History of the Town of Concord*, p. 314; Briggs, "Five hundred years of Farrar family." According to Chandler, Timothy eventually became senior law partner to a young Daniel Webster, who said he "never knew a judge more calm, dispassionate, impartial, and attentive, or more anxious to discover truth and to do justice" (Chandler, *History of New Ipswich*, p. 398).

2 *Massachusetts Soldiers and Sailors*, Vol. V, p. 537.

3 *Massachusetts Soldiers and Sailors*, Vol. V, p. 540. See also pay receipt dated April 17, 1777, Sudbury Miscellaneous Records, Doc. # 2217.

4 Ibid; Green, *Groton During the Revolution*, pp. 52–53. *Massachusetts Soldiers and Sailors* records 1 month, 9 days of service through September 30, 1776, but this does not necessarily indicate the expiration of the service. Pay records in Green, *Groton During the Revolution* (pp. 53–65), indicate service into December 1776. This accords with the author's premise that it is unlikely the regiment would have been discharged until near the expiration of its term (apparently, the end of December), particularly as Ticonderoga was under a serious threat of attack by British General Carleton late into the fall of 1776. Before Carleton called off his invasion, every available soldier was needed to help in the defense of Ticonderoga.

He served with Capt. Joshua Walker's Company, Col. Samuel Denny's Regiment from October 23, 1779, to November 23, 1779. The company was detached to march to Claverack (in the Hudson Valley) for three months with the Continental Army, but he served only 1 month, 11 days (including travel).[1]

He was the son of Daniel and Mary (Allen) Farrar of Lincoln; age 23 when he marched on the Alarm of April 19th. He was the brother of Daniel Farrar (q.v.), George Farrar (q.v.), and Nehemiah Farrar (q.v.). He had married Catherine Moor of Sudbury on July 11, 1771, and was evidently living in Sudbury throughout the war. Catherine must have died during the war years, because he married Eunice Sherman of East Sudbury (Wayland) in 1780. Eunice also died, and in 1785 he married Eunice's sister-in-law, the widow Abigail (Worcester) Sherman. He was living in Lincoln at least by 1790, where he died in 1825, age 74.[2]

FAY, Silas

Silas Fay marched on the alarm of April 19, 1775, from Princeton to Cambridge as a private in Capt. Joseph Sargent's Company, Colonel Sparhawk's Regiment. He served for six days before enlisting in the hastily forming Massachusetts Provincial Army.[3]

On April 26, he enlisted as a corporal in Capt. Samuel Wood's Company, Col. Jonathan Ward's Regiment at Cambridge. He may have participated in the Battle of Bunker Hill, but this is uncertain. On the day of the battle, his regiment reportedly had been retained at Cambridge to guard the American center. Then, shortly after noon, it was moved to Lechmere's Point to meet any attempt of the British to attack the center by way of Willis Creek. Later, when British movements rendered such an attack improbable, the regiment was ordered to advance to the Charlestown Peninsula to reinforce the troops on Bunker Hill. Part of the regiment may have gotten across Charlestown Neck, and in time to help cover the Provincial retreat.[4]

---

1 *Massachusetts Soldiers and Sailors*, Vol. V, pp. 531, 537, 540.

2 *Vital Records of Lincoln*; *Vital Records of Wayland*; Wheeler, "Lincoln," in Hurd, Vol. 2, p. 622; Briggs, "Genealogical Chart of Farrar family"; Pension Record # W14711 for Samuel Sherman; 1790 census records. Neither Catherine's nor Eunice's death is recorded. Eunice also appears as Unice; she and Timothy Sherman (q.v.) were first cousins. Abigail's maiden name also appears as Worster. She was originally from Littleton and had married Samuel Sherman (Eunice's brother) in 1772. Samuel Sherman had served on the April 19th Alarm as a private in Capt. Joseph Smith's Militia Company from Sudbury, then he enlisted for eight months at Cambridge in Capt. Thaddeus Russell's Company, Col. Jonathan Brewer's Regiment. Subsequently, he had enlisted for three years in the Continental Army, marched to Fishkill, and there reportedly died of a fever.

Zebediah Farrar's death is per Wheeler, "Lincoln" (in Hurd, Vol. 2, p. 622), and Abigail's pension declaration; it does not appear in the *Vital Records* of Lincoln or surrounding towns. Abigail was still living in Lincoln in 1837, age 93, when she made her pension application in the name of her first husband. She declared that Zebediah had also served for three years, but she provided no details.

3 *Massachusetts Soldiers and Sailors*, Vol. V, p. 580.

4 *Massachusetts Soldiers and Sailors*, Vol. V, p. 580; Martyn, *William Ward Genealogy*, p. 151. Martyn relates local tradition, which says that Colonel Ward's Regiment was halted on the mainland side of Charlestown Neck with orders that no more troops should go into action, and that in defiance of the order, part of the regiment (including Colonel Ward) nevertheless marched across the Neck toward the battlefield in time to help cover the retreat from the redoubt. Captain Wood is reported to have been wounded slightly in the battle, suggesting the probability that Fay may have been one of those who participated in the battle by helping to cover the retreat (see Allen, *Topographical Sketches of Northborough*, p. 42).

After the Battle of Bunker Hill, he was repositioned in July to Dorchester, and at the end of his enlistment on December 31, 1775, he served for another month at the request of Colonel Ward.[1]

On September 8, 1777, in response to the threat from Burgoyne's army in the Hudson River–Lake Champlain corridor, he marched north as a private in Lt. Amos Fairbanks's Company, Col. Job Cushing's Regiment. After the surrender of Burgoyne, his unit was marched south to Tarrytown, where he was discharged on November 29, 1777, credited with 3 months, 5 days of service, including travel.[2]

He was the son of Silas and Hannah (Billing) Fay; probably age 25 or 27 on the April 19th alarm. He appears to have been born in Westborough, but he grew up in Lincoln. He was living in Worcester County when the war broke out, and after his initial service at Cambridge, he married Anna Gleason of Princeton in 1776. He was the brother-in-law of Solomon Whitney (q.v.); uncle of Leonard Whitney (q.v.) and Silas Whitney (q.v.); nephew of Jacob Baker (q.v.); and cousin of Amos Baker (q.v.), Jacob Baker, Jr. (q.v.), James Baker (q.v.), Nathaniel Baker (q.v.), and Samuel Baker (q.v.). He settled in Princeton, where he lived until moving to Camden, Maine, in 1816. He died in Camden in 1838, at age between 88 and 91, and he is buried in Mountain View Cemetery.[3]

FIELD, Nathan

Nathan Field of Lincoln served in the Continental Army (dates not given). He is listed as a resident of Lincoln, and his service was credited to the town.[4]

His identity is unknown, as he does not appear in any of the Vital Records of Lincoln or the surrounding towns.[5]

FISK, David

[also FISKE]

David Fisk was a sergeant in Capt. William Smith's Company of Minute Men from Lincoln, Col. Abijah Peirce's Regiment.[6] Following the engagement at Concord, he served for six days in Cambridge.[7] He was reimbursed by the town for his accoutrements as a minute man.[8]

---

1 Pension Record # S31017.
2 *Massachusetts Soldiers and Sailors*, Vol. V, p. 581; Pension Record # S31017.
3 *Vital Records of Lincoln*; *Vital Records of Westborough*; *Vital Records of Princeton*; Pension Record # S31017; "Patriot Grave Search." His birth is recorded in Lincoln and not in Westborough, but the Lincoln record appears to have been recorded at a later date. In his pension declaration, he says he was born in Westborough, giving his date of birth as exactly two years later than the Lincoln record. His residence in 1775 is listed variously in his pension record as Princeton and Northborough.
4 *Massachusetts Soldiers and Sailors*, Vol. V, p. 652.
5 The only viable record of a Nathan Field found in Vital Records in Massachusetts, is a marriage intention of Nathan and Abigel Bullard, on Dec. 7, 1780, in *Vital Records of Oakham*. There is nothing in the record to indicate whether or not this individual could be Nathan Field (inst.).
6 Coburn, *Muster Rolls*.
7 *Massachusetts Soldiers and Sailors*, Vol. V, p. 719.
8 "Treasurer's Accompts," March 15, 1776.

He may be the David Fisk who served in the New York campaign in 1776, as a private in Capt. Simon Hunt's Company, Col. Eleazer Brooks's Middlesex County Regiment of Massachusetts Militia, from September 27, 1776, through November 16, 1776 (plus 11 days for travel home). After the Battle of White Plains on October 28, 1776, he is reported "in camp and fit for duty," having lost his knapsack, blanket, coat, stockings, and shirt in the battle. However, it is not certain if this is David Fisk (inst.).[1]

He seems not to have served again, as he was subsequently paid by the town for providing "a three years man in the Continental Army."[2]

He was originally from Woburn. In 1765, he had married Rebekah Gearfield of Lincoln, sister of Abraham Gearfield (q.v.) and Solomon Garfield (q.v.). She was 13 years his junior. He was age 43 when he marched on the Concord alarm. Later, in 1780, he was elected Selectman.

He died in 1800 at age 68. He is buried in the Meeting House Cemetery behind Bemis Hall.[3]

FLETCHER, Luke

Luke Fletcher of Lincoln served a three-year term in the Continental Army from March 20, 1777, to March 20, 1780. He served as a private in Capt. Edmund Munro's Company, Col. Timothy Bigelow's Regiment from March 20, 1777, to December 31, 1779. Colonel Bigelow's Regiment spent the winter of 1777–78 at Valley Forge, and participated in the Battle of Monmouth on June 28, 1778, and in the Battle of Rhode Island on August 29, 1778. He seems to have been at Providence during the months of February through April 1779, detailed for duty with the surgeon during March and April 1779. From January 1, 1780, to his discharge on March 20, 1780, he served in Captain Bowman's Company, Colonel Bigelow's Regiment.[4]

---

1 *Muster Rolls of the Revolutionary War*, Vol. 55, file L, p. 24. *Massachusetts Soldiers and Sailors* (Vol. V, p. 677) places a David Fish from Acton in this unit at White Plains, and also attributes Continental service to him, which matches another record for a David Fisk of Lexington (*Massachusetts Soldiers and Sailors*, Vol. V, p. 718). The trail is not clear. *Lexington Births, Marriages and Deaths* identifies a David Fiske who would have been age 39 at White Plains, and a David Fiske who would have been age 15. Neither has an identified Acton connection. Acton Vital Records contains only a David Fish from Westford, age unknown, who married Sarah Barns of Acton in 1767. These records raise the element of uncertainty about whether or not David Fisk (inst.) is the David Fisk who served at White Plains, but it is not apparent to the author that there is sufficient evidence to rule it out. The regiment was made up of Middlesex County militiamen detached from their home units for this campaign.

2 "Treasurer's Accompts," November 11, 1779. There is a record of a David Fisk (or Fish) who served at Providence for two months in 1779, as a private in Capt. Samuel Heald's Company, Col. John Jacobs's Regiment of Light Infantry from September 22, 1779, to November 22, 1779 (2 months, 7 days, including travel). This service, however, appears to conflict with his being in Lincoln to receive the November 11, 1779, payment. Accordingly, it does not appear that this could be David Fisk from Lincoln (see *Massachusetts Soldiers and Sailors*, Vol. V, pp. 678, 719).

There also is a record of a David Fisk being mustered into service into Captain Munroe's Company, Colonel Bigelow's Battalion (and paid a bounty), as reported by James Barrett, muster master, on June 23, 1777 (see Blake, "James Barrett's Returns of Men," p. 476). In view of Lincoln having paid him for providing a man for service, it would appear that this record must be a different David Fisk.

3 MacLean, *A Rich Harvest*, pp. 256, 301; *Vital Records of Lincoln*; Biggs, "In Memorium," p. 171.

4 *Massachusetts Soldiers and Sailors*, Vol. V, p. 780. See also Blake, "James Barrett's Returns of Men" (p. 473) for a record of his being mustered and paid a bounty for this service, as reported by James Barrett, muster master, on April 25, 1777.

FLINT, Abel

Abel Flint served as a private in Capt. Jonathan Fisk's Militia Company from Weston, Col. Eleazer Brooks's 3rd Middlesex County Regiment, which marched from Weston to fortify Dorchester Heights on March 4, 1776. The unit was discharged five days later, on March 9, after the threat of a British assault on the fortifications had subsided, General Howe having begun preparations to evacuate Boston.[1]

He was age 17 at Dorchester Heights. He was the son of Ephraim and Ruth (Wheeler) Flint; his father had died in Lincoln in 1762, and in 1766 his mother married Capt. Braddyll (or Bradyll) Smith of Weston, in whose Weston household Abel Flint was likely living at the outbreak of the war. He was the brother of Ephraim Flint (q.v.) and John Flint (q.v.); brother-in-law of Samuel Hartwell (q.v.) and Joseph Mason (q.v.); nephew of Edmond Wheeler (q.v.); and cousin of John Wheeler (q.v.). He graduated from Harvard College in 1780, and then taught school for several years at Haverhill and elsewhere. No record of any marriage has been found. In 1789, he died in Lincoln of consumption at age 30, and he is buried in the old Precinct Burial Ground.[2]

FLINT, Ephraim

According to Flint family lore, Ephraim Flint "shouldered his musket" on April 19, 1775, "and as one of the results, captured a British Soldier at Lexington, and took him home with him, where he worked some time on the farm of his captor *peacefully*."[3]

He is also reported to have participated in the Battle of Bunker Hill, in Col. John Nixon's 16th Massachusetts Regiment.[4]

He served as a private in Capt. John Hartwell's Militia Company from Lincoln, Col. Eleazer Brooks's 3rd Middlesex County Regiment, which marched from Lincoln to fortify Dorchester Heights on March 4, 1776. The unit was discharged five days later, on March 9, after the threat of a British assault on the fortifications had subsided as General Howe

---

He is reported to be a resident of Lincoln, and his enlistment was credited to the town of Lincoln. His identity is uncertain, as he is missing from the Vital Records of Lincoln and the surrounding towns.

---

1 *Massachusetts Soldiers and Sailors*, Vol. V, p. 790.
2 *Vital Records of Lincoln*; *Town of Weston, Births, Deaths, & Marriages*; Shattuck, *History of the Town of Concord*, p. 315; Biggs, "In Memorium," p. 192. Shattuck misstates his age at the time of his death by two years. Braddyll Smith served as lieutenant colonel of the 3rd Middlesex County Militia Regiment under Col. James Barrett, stepping down in favor of new leadership on February 7, 1776.
3 *An Account of the Celebration*, p. 174. It might logically be assumed that this may have been as a member of Lincoln's militia company. Unfortunately, no muster roll for the militia company has ever been found, nor has the author found other evidence to confirm this service. On the other hand, the fact that the British prisoner, John Bateman of the King's 52nd Regiment, was deposed in Lincoln and apparently never returned to his regiment (see sidebar, "Ephraim Flint's Prisoner of War," p. 284), offers wonderful opportunities for pondering just what the real story might be.
4 *Register of Members* [SAR], p. 131. The author has found no confirming evidence of this service. In August, Colonel Nixon's 16th Massachusetts Regiment became known also as the 5th Regiment under Washington's Continental command.

Ephraim Flint's Prisoner of War

Ephraim Flint "shouldered his musket" on April 19, 1775, "and as one of the results, captured a British Soldier at Lexington, and took him home with him, where he worked some time on the farm of his captor *peacefully."* So we are told, at least, by Flint family lore. The origin of the lore is somewhat obscure, and whatever details might once have filled out the story have long since been lost. The story survives as a one-sentence teaser, repeated by a descendant in the 1904 printed record of the 150th Anniversary Celebration of the incorporation of the town. Is it possible that there could be some truth to this story? And if so, where would one look to find corroborating evidence?

There is a record of a British soldier in Lincoln four days later, on April 23, 1775. John Bateman, of the 52nd Regiment, was deposed in Lincoln as part of the Provincial campaign to document that the British Regulars fired unprovoked upon the locals. His is the only deposition (of twenty taken over three days) that was executed in Lincoln. In it, he gives no hint as to how or why he happened to be in Lincoln, but he is presumed to be either a prisoner or a deserter. Concord's Rev. Ezra Ripley suggests that there may have been a fine line between the two. "Willing captives," he called them in 1827. "They designedly separated themselves from their companions, in order to be taken…prefer[ing] this method to desertion, which would be attended with danger." Nor is it clear from his deposition at what point he fell into the hands of the Provincials, or whether he may have been wounded. The content of the deposition ends with the firing on the Lexington Green, suggesting that he could have separated from the column before it reached Concord, or at least that he was probably not part of the patrol at the North Bridge. But this is speculative. All we know is that he was in Lincoln four days later.

Can anything be deduced from the fact that he was deposed in Lincoln? Nine Lincoln men had traveled to Lexington to be deposed on the same day; another was deposed in Lexington two days later. Is there a reason he could not have gone (or been taken) to Lexington, as well? Why was it necessary for the deposers to travel to Lincoln? Could John Bateman be Ephraim Flint's prisoner of war?

The reader may feel free to speculate. Individual tales often spark the imagination and provide wonderful color for the overall story, but too often they are impossible to verify. In this particular case, the story of Ephraim Flint's prisoner of war gains an element of credence by the evidence of John Bateman being in Lincoln. But it remains a mystery. John Bateman may not have remained in Lincoln for very long. No record of him can be found in Lincoln tax records, militia records, or census records. Historian Vincent J-R Kehoe also reports that while some of the captives were later exchanged, no record has been found that Bateman ever returned to his regiment. Until more evidence is found to elucidate this matter, this story offers a wonderful opportunity to ponder just what the real facts might be.

[See Francis Flint, "Remarks," in *An Account of the Celebration*, p. 174; Deposition of John Bateman; Ripley, *A History of the Fight at Concord*, p. 55; Kehoe, "The Provincial Depositions," p. 147.]

Chapter 10: The Army of the Revolution

The Flint homestead (c. 1709), home of Ephraim Flint, may have been temporarily home to a British prisoner of war after April 19, 1775. Shown here with nineteenth-century alterations and an 1870 barn, it has remained in the Flint family for eight generations. (*An Account of the Celebration*)

had begun preparations to evacuate Boston. He was paid for this service the following September.[1]

He was paid by the town for service in New York during 1776 and 1777. He was probably assigned to Col. Samuel Thatcher's Regiment and marched south on December 16, 1776. This regiment served briefly around New York before being called to New Jersey in January 1777. They were stationed at Woodbridge and participated in the *petite guerre* in the Jerseys in the early months of 1777 before being dismissed to return home in March.[2]

He was the son of Ephraim and Ruth (Wheeler) Flint, age 30 at Dorchester Heights; brother of Abel Flint (q.v.) and John Flint (q.v.); brother-in-law of Samuel Hartwell (q.v.) and Joseph Mason (q.v.); nephew of Edmond Wheeler (q.v.); and cousin of John Wheeler (q.v.). He had married Catherine Fox in 1772. She died in 1785 at age 33, and subsequently

---

1 Hartwell, "A List of a Company of Militia"; *Massachusetts Soldiers and Sailors*, Vol. V, p. 794.

2 "Treasurer's Accompts," November 11, 1779. No actual record has been found of the unit in which he served. Attribution to Colonel Thatcher's Regiment is a supposition, consistent with records of service for other Lincoln men at this time. The *petite guerre* is David Hackett Fischer's term for the skirmishing that characterized the war in New Jersey following Washington's dramatic victories at Trenton and Princeton.

Another possibility is that this may have been a payment for the service of his brother, John Flint (q.v.), for whom there is a record of service that appears to be a reasonable match (and no other record of payment). John appears to have gone to New Hampshire, probably by the time this payment was made, which could explain why it might have been made to Ephraim, instead. [Ordinarily, such a payment to a surrogate would have been made to the individual's father, but Ephraim Sr. died in 1762. The individual's mother would be next in line to be trusted with such a payment, but she had remarried and moved to Weston. Quite possibly, Ephraim (inst.) may have been the trusted surrogate of choice.] As this possibility hinges on a number of suppositions, it must remain speculative.

he married Rebecca Wright of Concord in 1798. He died in 1824 at age 79 and is buried in the old Precinct Burial Ground on Lexington Road.[1]

FLINT, John

John Flint marched on the Alarm of April 19, 1775, in Capt. Samuel Lamson's Company from Weston, served for three days at Cambridge, and subsequently (date unknown) enlisted in the Massachusetts Provincial Army.[2]

He was paid by the town of Lincoln for service at Cambridge in 1775 and at Canada in 1776. The details of these terms of service are not indicated. He may have served in Col. Thomas Gardner's Regiment and participated in the Battle of Bunker Hill on June 17, 1775, although it is not clear whether or not he was back in service at that time. From August through December 1775, he is recorded as having served as a corporal in Capt. Abijah Child's Company, Lt. Col. William Bond's 37th Continental Regiment. He was reimbursed by the state for losses incurred at the battles of Lexington and Bunker Hill. He is described as five feet, seven inches in height.[3]

He probably remained in Lieutenant Colonel Bond's Regiment for his service in Canada. After the collapse of the Canadian campaign, he served out his enlistment at Ticonderoga through the fall of 1776.[4]

He may be the John Flint who was detached to serve with Colonel Thatcher. No date is given in the record, but this probably refers to Col. Samuel Thatcher's Regiment, which marched southward on December 16, 1776. This regiment served briefly around New York before being called to New Jersey in January 1777. They were stationed at Woodbridge and participated in the *petite guerre* in the Jerseys in the early months of 1777, before being dismissed to return home in March.[5]

He was age 20 on April 19, 1775. He was the son of Ephraim and Ruth (Wheeler) Flint; his father had died in 1762 in Lincoln, and in 1766 his mother married Capt. Braddyll (or Bradyll) Smith of Weston. He was the brother of Abel Flint (q.v.) and Ephraim Flint (q.v.); brother-in-law of Samuel Hartwell (q.v.) and Joseph Mason (q.v.); nephew of Edmond Wheeler (q.v.); and cousin of John Wheeler (q.v.). He reportedly moved to Walpole, New Hampshire, in 1779, by which time he may have been known as "Capt." John Flint. He married Esther Fuller in Walpole in 1795, and he died in Walpole, New Hampshire, in 1810 at age 56.[6]

---

1 *Vital Records of Lincoln*; *Concord, Massachusetts: Births, Marriages, and Deaths*; Biggs, "In Memorium," p. 193.

2 *Massachusetts Soldiers and Sailors*, Vol. V, p. 796.

3 "Treasurer's Accompts," May 18, 1779; *Massachusetts Soldiers and Sailors*, Vol. V, p. 796. The record indicates that he was then from Weston, probably living in the Weston household of his stepfather, Braddyll Smith.
   Colonel Gardner was mortally wounded at Bunker Hill, and afterward the command of his regiment fell to Lt. Col. William Bond. Claims for losses at Lexington and Bunker Hill were adjudicated together; it is not clear whether his loss claim was for Lexington or Bunker Hill, or whether he was, in fact, the John Flint who incurred the loss.

4 Ibid. Service in Lieutenant Colonel Bond's Regiment in Canada is a supposition, based on his previous service in this regiment and on the logic of Lieutenant Colonel Bond's Regiment being a common link between his Cambridge service and his Canadian service.

5 *Massachusetts Soldiers and Sailors*, Vol. V, p. 796. It is not certain if this record applies to John Flint (inst.).

6 *Vital Records of Lincoln*; Flint and Flint, *Flint Family History*, Vol. I, pp. 74, 326; Wheeler, "Lincoln," in Hurd, Vol. 2, p. 622; New Hampshire Marriages, 1720–1920. Esther was nearly 14 years his junior. His marriage

FOSTER, Jacob

Jacob Foster was a private in Capt. William Smith's Company of Minute Men from Lincoln, Col. Abijah Peirce's Regiment. During the running fight along Battle Road, his hat was reportedly pierced by a British musket ball.[1] He served for eight days in Cambridge. He was reimbursed by the town for a part of a set of accoutrements as a minute man.[2]

Subsequently, he served as a private in Capt. John Hartwell's Militia Company from Lincoln, Col. Eleazer Brooks's 3rd Middlesex County Regiment, which marched from Lincoln to fortify Dorchester Heights on March 4, 1776. The unit was discharged five days later, on March 9, after the threat of a British assault on the fortifications had subsided, General Howe having begun preparations to evacuate Boston. He was paid for this service the following September.[3]

He served again in 1777 or 1778, when he was detached from Capt. Samuel Farrar, Jr.'s Militia Company from Lincoln to relieve the guards at Cambridge. This duty was the guarding of Burgoyne's "Convention Army," held in Cambridge from November 1777 to November 1778, but the precise details of his service are unknown.[4]

Town records indicate only that he was paid "for his service in the present war," without further detail.[5]

He was the son of Jonathan and Elizabeth (Storey) Foster, originally from Ipswich. The family was resident in Lincoln at least by 1764, when Jonathan and subsequently Jacob became tenant farmers on a farm belonging to the Dodge family, located along the Bay Road roughly proximal to the Paul Revere capture site. He was age 28 as a minute man, probably the brother-in-law of Phineas Allen (q.v.). He married Sarah Wheeler in Lincoln in 1780, and subsequently moved to Hanover, New Hampshire, where he may have died as early as 1788 at age 41 or 42. He is reportedly buried in the Dartmouth College Cemetery.[6]

---

to Esther, Esther's 1768 birth record, and the births of eight children between 1796 and 1810 are recorded in *Vital Records of Lincoln*. This, however, does not signify that Esther was a Lincoln person or that the births took place in Lincoln; as the listings come from a Family Bible record and not from Lincoln's town or church records. The basis for his being called captain in Flint and Flint is unexplained. Wheeler lists his birth date incorrectly.

1 Coburn, *Muster Rolls*; Peirce, *Foster Genealogy*, p. 173. The source of the hat piercing story is unidentified, but apparently he escaped injury.
2 *Massachusetts Soldiers and Sailors*, Vol. V, p. 905; "Treasurer's Accompts," February 29, 1776.
3 *Massachusetts Soldiers and Sailors*, Vol. V, p. 905.
4 Ibid. The record does not indicate his service dates. Enlistment periods were November 1777 to April 1778 (5 months), April to July 1778 (3 months), and July to December 1778 (5 months).
5 "Treasurer's Accompts," May 12, 1781.
6 Malcolm, *The Scene of Battle*, pp. 50–53; *Vital Records of Lincoln*; *Vital Records of Ipswich*. For the identity of Jacob Foster, along with his move to and death in Hanover, the author is indebted to Mike Ryan, who cites (in a communication with the author) the Mormon Genealogical Archives in Salt Lake City, Utah, cross referenced with "Descendants of Reginald Foster" in the New England Historic Genealogical Society Register. 1764 residency in Lincoln is determined by papers, *signed in Lincoln*, by which Jonathan sold land in Ipswich (see also Peirce, *Foster Genealogy*, pp. 146, 173).

The Mormon Genealogical Archives (accessed online as FamilySearch) indicate that he died in 1791 at age 45, and that Sarah died in 1799. Neither date is confirmed. "Find A Grave," which reports their burial location as Dartmouth College Cemetery, lists both Jacob's and Sarah's deaths in 1788 at age 40 (actually, he would

FOSTER, John[1]

John Foster served as a private in Capt. John Hartwell's Militia Company from Lincoln, Col. Eleazer Brooks's 3rd Middlesex County Regiment, which marched from Lincoln to fortify Dorchester Heights on March 4, 1776. The unit was discharged five days later, on March 9, after the threat of a British assault on the fortifications had subsided, and General Howe had begun preparations to evacuate Boston. He was paid for this service the following September.[2]

Probable kinship with Jacob Foster (q.v.) is logically assumed, but his identity is undiscovered.[3]

---

have been age 41 or 42; she appears to have been eight years younger). No record of either Jacob or Sarah is identifiable in the 1790 Census.

The Foster farm in Lincoln was essentially contiguous with the Smith farm, and on first glance, Malcolm appears to suggest that Foster became a tenant of William Smith (q.v.) after Smith's marriage to Catherine Louisa Salmon, step-daughter of William Dodge and daughter of Elizabeth Dodge. Closer examination of Malcolm suggests that the Foster farm may have remained a Dodge property when the Dodges gave a portion of their holdings (which became known as the Smith farm) to Catherine Louisa two months before she married William Smith. Thus it is unclear whether Jacob Foster remained a tenant farmer of the Dodges or became a tenant of William Smith (q.v.). It is also unclear whether Phineas Allen (q.v.) was Foster's or Smith's hired hand.

Jacob Foster had a sister, Abigail, who is logically the Abigail Foster who married Phineas Allen (q.v.). She was five years older than Phineas.

1 He is listed as "Jonathan" in the *An Account of the Celebration* and *War Memorial Book*, but the source of this apparent error is unidentified. Both Hartwell, "A List of a Company of Militia," and *Massachusetts Soldiers and Sailors* show him unmistakably as John. Presumably Hartwell, "A List of a Company of Militia," is the source of the listing in *Massachusetts Soldiers and Sailors*. However, if John Hartwell, who made out the Dorchester Heights muster roll, may possibly have confusedly written John instead of Jonathan (there are three Johns and no Jonathans on the muster roll), then perhaps John Foster (inst.) could reasonably be identified as Jonathan Foster, the brother of Jacob Foster (q.v.).

2 Hartwell, "A List of a Company of Militia"; *Massachusetts Soldiers and Sailors*, Vol. V, p. 911.

3 Several possible identities are hypothesized:
- If his name was incorrectly recorded on the muster roll as John instead of Jonathan, then this could possibly be Jonathan Foster, brother of Jacob Foster (q.v.), who would have been age 42 at Dorchester Heights, and who might have been resident on the farm in Lincoln during the spring of 1776 (see note 1). (Jonathan is not found in *Vital Records of Ipswich*. He is identified in Mike Ryan's communication with the author [see Jacob Foster (q.v.), note 6 on p. 287] and in Pierce, *Foster Genealogy*, p. 146). Jacob's father Jonathan would have been age 70, too old to have been at Dorchester Heights.
- A Solomon Foster from Andover who came to Lincoln for a while and married Rebecca Brown in 1770, had a brother, John, who would have been age 43 at Dorchester Heights, and who might possibly have been temporarily resident in Lincoln during the spring of 1776. Except for speculation associated with Solomon, however, nothing has been found to connect this John Foster to Lincoln. (MacLean, *A Rich Harvest*, p. 189; *Vital Records of Lincoln*; *Vital Records of Andover*. See also "Who was the Widow Rebeckah Brown?", p. 250.) MacLean points out (private communication with the author) that Solomon left Lincoln when he bought a farm in Littleton in 1770, and that there is no evidence of a return to Lincoln until 1784, when he bought land in Lincoln. This possible identity appears unlikely.
- A John Foster of Littleton (identifiable by an 1832 death record) would have been age 32 at Dorchester Heights. A birth record of a son born in April 1776 identifies a John Foster of Littleton (and his wife Ruth), perhaps the same individual, who would probably also have been of service age for Dorchester Heights. (*Records of Littleton*.) The Littleton connection is suggested by Solomon and Rebecca, who moved to Littleton in 1770 and in the 1780s moved back again to Lincoln. However, except for speculation associated with Solomon and Rebecca, nothing has been found to connect this (or these) John Foster(s) to Lincoln.
- A John Foster marched on the Alarm of April 19, 1775, in Capt. Jonathan Stickney's Company from Billerica. Other John Fosters marched on the Alarm of April 19, 1775, from Andover, Ashby, Attleborough,

GAGE, Isaac

Isaac Gage was a private in Capt. William Smith's Company of Minute Men from Lincoln, Col. Abijah Peirce's Regiment.[1] Following the engagement at Concord, he served for ten days in Cambridge.[2] He was reimbursed by the town for his accoutrements as a minute man.[3]

He appears to have remained in Cambridge, where he enlisted in the rapidly forming Massachusetts Provincial Army for eight months of service. He served as a sergeant in Capt. Nathan Fuller's Company, Colonel Gardner's 37th Regiment, at the Battle of Bunker Hill. The record picks him up again in the fall of 1775, after Colonel Gardner had died (of wounds received at Bunker Hill) and regimental command had devolved on Lt. Col. William Bond.[4]

He served as a lieutenant in Capt. Job Sumner's Company, Col. John Greaton's 2nd Regiment, in the Continental Army from January 1, 1777, to September 16, 1778, when he was discharged as a supernumerary officer.[5]

In 1781, he may have served as captain of a company detached from Colonel Dana's Regiment, placed under the command of Lt. Col. Joseph Webb, and sent to support the Continental Army at West Point for three months. This Isaac Gage marched on August 20, 1781, served for 3 months, 25 days (including travel), and was discharged on December 3, 1781. However, it is uncertain whether or not this is the same Isaac Gage.[6]

He was the son of Robert and Susannah (Smith) Gage; age 21 when he responded to the April 19th Alarm. He married Mary Allen of Weston on November 23, 1775, and she bore him a daughter four months later. After the war, he abandoned his wife and daughter, and "went off to parts unknown." It is supposed that he died in the early 1800s.[7]

Barnstable, Dorchester, Plymouth, and Roxbury. *Massachusetts Soldiers and Sailors*, Vol. V, pp. 907–912. Nothing has been found in these records to connect any of them to Lincoln or to Lincoln's militia company ten months after the Alarm of April 19, 1775; nor has anything been found to preclude any of them from having a Lincoln connection or from being the same individual as John Foster (inst.).

1 Coburn, *Muster Rolls*.
2 *Massachusetts Soldiers and Sailors*, Vol. VI, p. 215.
3 "Treasurer's Accompts," June 18, 1776. This was paid to Lt. James Parks.
4 *Massachusetts Soldiers and Sailors*, Vol. VI, p. 215; Wheeler, "Lincoln," in Hurd, Vol. 2, p. 622.
5 Wheeler, "Lincoln," in Hurd, Vol. 2, p. 622; *Massachusetts Soldiers and Sailors*, Vol. VI, p. 215; Pension Record # BLWT2237-200. A supernumerary officer was one considered expendable by reason of being overstaffed.
6 Wheeler, "Lincoln," in Hurd, Vol. 2, p. 622; *Massachusetts Soldiers and Sailors*, Vol. VI, p. 216. Wheeler asserts that this is Isaac Gage (inst.), although there is little about this record to provide corroboration for Wheeler's assertion.
7 *Vital Records of Lincoln*; *Town of Weston, Births, Deaths, & Marriages*; Pension Record # BLWT2237-200. Wheeler, "Lincoln" (in Hurd, Vol. 2, p. 622), gives his mother's name as Mary, evidently confusing her with his wife. Kinship with Jonathan Gage (q.v.) has not been determined, although they do not appear to have been closely related. Nevertheless, the parallels in their service records do suggest some level of kinship.

His pension record (actually a Land Grant application filed by his daughter Mary) contains a supporting statement from a Weston neighbor, dated June 23, 1838, which says, "Soon after the war [he] left his wife & child & went off to parts unknown & has not been heard of for more than twenty years; & it was reported & generally believed that he died as long ago as that."

GAGE, Jonathan

Jonathan Gage was a private in Capt. William Smith's Company of Minute Men from Lincoln, Col. Abijah Peirce's Regiment.[1] Following the engagement at Concord, he served for ten days in Cambridge.[2] He does not seem to have been reimbursed by the town for his accoutrements as a minute man.

He appears to have remained in Cambridge, where he enlisted in the rapidly forming Massachusetts Provincial Army for eight months of service as a corporal in Capt. Nathan Fuller's Company, Colonel Gardner's 37th Regiment. He presumably participated with his regiment in the Battle of Bunker Hill on June 17, 1775. Soon after, Colonel Gardner died of wounds received at Bunker Hill and regimental command devolved on Lt. Col. William Bond.[3]

He enlisted for three years in the Continental Army, starting March 1, 1777, and served in Capt. Abijah Child's Company, Col. John Greaton's 2nd Regiment, through December 31, 1779.[4] His residence is listed as Lincoln, and Lincoln was credited for his service. On January 1, 1780, he appears as a corporal, probably in Major Thompson's Company.[5]

He was surprised by the enemy a month later, while on patrol in advance of the American lines near New York. His pension declaration states, "On the 3^d of February 1780, I was in a party of about One hundred Commanded by Maj^r Thompson, we were taken prisoners & carried to New York, where I remained ten months & nine days, in the encounter I received a wound from a Broad sword on my head & several thrusts from a bayonet in my body, the effects from the wound on my head were very serious & still felt; when I was exchanged I returned to my regiment then stationed at West Point in order to receive my wages." Alas, the coffers were empty, and he was sent home with "a due bill from the paymaster to be taken up in Boston." He appears to have been credited with service through December 31, 1780, but he says, "The Field officers were then all at home on furlough so that I did not then, nor have I since ever received a formal discharge." For this period of service, his residence was listed as Weston.[6]

He was the son of Jonathan and Ruth (Underwood) Gage; age 19 when he responded to the April 19th Alarm. After the war, he was likely living in Northborough when he married Mary Brigham of Northborough in 1784; she was five years older than him. By 1818, he was living in Erving's Grant (now the town of Erving). He reportedly died in 1828.[7]

---

1 Coburn, *Muster Rolls*.
2 *Massachusetts Soldiers and Sailors*, Vol. VI, pp. 218.
3 Ibid.
4 Capt. Abijah Child resigned his commission in the spring of 1778 (*Massachusetts Soldiers and Sailors*, Vol. III, pp. 410). Jonathan Gage presumably continued to serve in the same company, now under the command of Capt. Thomas Prichard (see Pension Record # S32713).
5 *Massachusetts Soldiers and Sailors*, Vol. VI, pp. 218. In the record, the company is identified as "Major's Company." *Massachusetts Soldiers and Sailors* contains no record of an officer named Major in Colonel Greaton's Regiment. The presumption from his pension record is that this must have been Major Thompson's Company.
6 Pension Record # S32713; *Massachusetts Soldiers and Sailors*, Vol. VI, pp. 218. Also Wheeler, "Lincoln," in Hurd, Vol. 2, p. 622.
7 *Vital Records of Lincoln*; *Town of Weston, Births, Deaths, & Marriages*; Wheeler, "Lincoln," in Hurd, Vol. 2, p. 622; Pension Record # S32713; *Vital Records of Northborough*; Kinship with Isaac Gage (q.v.) has not been determined, but they do not appear to have been closely related. The parallels in their service records do, however, suggest some level of kinship. His death is per unpublished notes (without citation) from Mike Ryan.

GEARFIELD, Abraham
[also GARFIELD]

Abraham Gearfield was in arms at Concord on the morning of April 19, 1775, probably as a member of Lincoln's militia company.[1]

He was the son of Thomas and Rebeka (Johnson) Gearfield; age 27 when he responded to the April 19th Alarm. He was also the brother of Solomon Garfield (q.v.); brother-in-law of David Fisk (q.v.) and Nathan Brown, Jr. (q.v.); nephew of Elisha Gearfield (q.v.); and cousin of John Gearfield (q.v.). He died less than four months after his Concord service, on August 15, 1775, age 27, and is buried in the Meeting House Cemetery behind Bemis Hall.[2]

As an interesting postscript, he was the great-great-uncle of James A. Garfield, the twentieth President of the United States. The President's middle name Abram reportedly had been passed through the family in Abraham's memory.[3]

GEARFIELD, Elisha
[also GARFIELD]

Elisha Gearfield was paid by the town for one-half of a campaign at Ticonderoga in 1776.[4]

He was the son of Thomas and Mercy (Bigelow) Gearfield; age 48 at Ticonderoga; uncle of Abraham Gearfield (q.v.), Solomon Garfield (q.v.), and John Gearfield (q.v.). He had been married to Susanna Bemis since 1753, and he appears on the muster roll of Lincoln's original militia company in 1757. He appears to have been in the lumber business, owned a saw mill near the Weston town line, and served the town as Surveyor of Lumber. He died in September 1809, at age 80.[5]

As an interesting postscript, he was the great-great-great-uncle of James A. Garfield, the twentieth President of the United States.[6]

---

1 Deposition of John Hoar, et al. Wheeler, "Lincoln" (in Hurd, Vol. 2, p. 622), credits him with being a minute man, even though he doesn't appear on the Muster Roll. According to Wheeler, his name was left off the Muster Roll because he died before the Muster Roll was made up. Wheeler's premise seems to be that as the Muster Roll was used for pay purposes, and because he was now dead, there was no reason to have included him. Intriguing as it is to imagine the discovery of a previously undocumented minute man, Wheeler overlooks the fact that the pay obligation would not have been erased by his death. It would have passed to the next of kin. As Abraham doesn't appear to have been married, and his parents appear already to have passed away (see Bond, *Genealogies of the Families of Watertown*, p. 233), I presume that means his pay would have gone to his siblings, or somewhere else according to the way his estate was handled. Without further evidence, therefore, the author finds Wheeler's claim hard to accept.

2 *Vital Records of Lincoln; Town of Weston, Births, Deaths, & Marriages;* Wheeler, "Lincoln," in Hurd, Vol. 2, p. 622.

3 Ryan, "Presidential Relations," explains that Abraham's brother Solomon Garfield (q.v.) moved to New York, and had a grandson who was named Abram in memory of Abraham (inst.). Abram Garfield moved to Ohio, and named his son James Abram Garfield.

4 "Treasurer's Accompts," June 15, 1779.

5 *Vital Records of Lincoln; Town of Weston, Births, Deaths, & Marriages;* MacLean, *A Rich Harvest*, pp. 130, 177; Bond, *Genealogies of the Families of Watertown*, p. 234; Martin, "The Sons of Lincoln," p. 25. Notwithstanding his age, there is little doubt that he provided this service. Elisha and Susanna had two sons named Elisha, but neither of them could have provided this service. The first died shortly before his first birthday, in 1756; the second was age ten in 1776. He had three other sons, all younger.

6 See Ryan, "Presidential Relations"; Conwell, *Life of James A. Garfield*, p. 33.

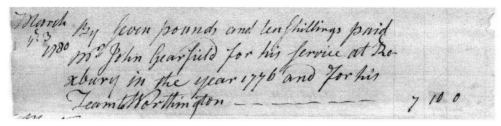

Lincoln's "Treasurer's Accompts" show that John Gearfield waited nearly four years to be paid for his 1776 service at Roxbury and two-and-a-half years to be paid for his 1777 service going to Worthington, Massachusetts. The Worthington mission was to supply the troops—including a dozen men from Lincoln—who were escorting Burgoyne's captured army from Saratoga to Cambridge. (Courtesy of Lincoln Town Archives, Lincoln, MA)

GEARFIELD, John
[also GARFIELD]

John Gearfield was a private in Capt. William Smith's Company of Minute Men from Lincoln, Col. Abijah Peirce's Regiment.[1] Following the engagement at Concord, he served for ten days in Cambridge.[2] He was reimbursed by the town for his accoutrements as a minute man.[3]

He was paid by the town for service at Roxbury in 1776 and for taking a team with provisions to Worthington.[4]

He was the son of John and Thankful (Stowell) Gearfield; age 23 at Concord; cousin of Abraham Gearfield (q.v.) and Solomon Garfield (q.v.); nephew of Elisha Gearfield (q.v.). He married Lucy Smith on July 6, 1775. After the war, he remained in Lincoln for approximately 10 to 15 years, but by 1796 he had taken up residence in Marlborough, New Hampshire.[5]

GARFIELD, Solomon
[also GEARFIELD]

Solomon Garfield was living in Westminster when he marched on the Alarm of April 19, 1775, as a private in Capt. Noah Miles's Company. The company joined Col. John Whitcom's Regiment at Cambridge, and he served for 11½ days.

---

1 Coburn, *Muster Rolls*.
2 *Massachusetts Soldiers and Sailors*, Vol. VI, p. 286.
3 "Treasurer's Accompts," July 10, 1777.
4 "Treasurer's Accompts," March 3, 1780. The following day he was paid for clothing for the army. Shattuck, *History of the Town of Concord* (p. 300) says the Worthington expedition occurred in 1777, but the precise dates and purpose remain unidentified. The author's hypothesis is that it was undertaken in October to supply the troops escorting Burgoyne's captured army from Saratoga to Cambridge. The escort included a contingent of Lincoln men in a company commanded by Lincoln's Capt. Samuel Farrar, Jr. (q.v.).
5 *Vital Records of Lincoln*; *Town of Weston, Births, Deaths, & Marriages*; Bond, *Genealogies of the Families of Watertown*, p. 233–234. See also Caverly, *Historical Sketch of Troy*, p. 90. Through April 1792, John and Lucy had ten children recorded in Lincoln. An eleventh child, baptized in February 1796, is also recorded in Lincoln, but that record clearly indicates that John and his wife were by that time living in Marlborough. Eckhardt, "John Garfield," notes that he sold his farm in 1792, but whether he left for Marlborough at that time or closer to 1796 remains a question.
  Interestingly, the record shows that he first sold the farm in 1788, but the sale did not go through. This was in the wake of the serious economic dislocation brought on by the war, and the credit and foreclosure problem that reached a peak in 1787 with Shays' Rebellion. Four years later, he may have gotten considerably greater value than he would have had the sale gone through in 1788.

Chapter 10: The Army of the Revolution

On April 19, 1775, Abraham Gearfield left his home (shown here c. 1900) and marched to Concord with Lincoln's militia company. His brother, Solomon Garfield, also grew up in this house; Solomon marched on the alarm of April 19th with a company from Westminster, where he was living at the time. (*An Account of the Celebration*)

In late September 1777, he was in service again as a corporal in Capt. Elisha Jackson's Company, which marched from Westminster under the command of Major Bridge to reinforce the Northern army under General Gates. He served for 27 days and was probably present at the surrender of General Burgoyne at Saratoga on October 17, 1777.[1]

He was the son of Thomas and Rebeka (Johnson) Gearfield; age 31 when he responded to the April 19th Alarm. He was the brother of Abraham Gearfield (q.v.). He was also the brother-in-law of David Fisk (q.v.) and Nathan Brown, Jr. (q.v.); nephew of Elisha Gearfield (q.v.); and cousin of John Gearfield (q.v.). He had married Sarah Stimpson of Sudbury in 1769 and settled in Westminster. He reportedly fared poorly in the economic turbulence caused by the war and lost his farm. Sometime after 1785, he moved his family to Worcester, New York, where he purchased another farm, and where he reportedly died in 1806, by accidentally falling from a beam in his barn.[2]

As an interesting postscript, he was the great-grandfather of James A. Garfield, the twentieth President of the United States.[3]

GILBERT, William

William Gilbert served in the Continental Army for three years in Captain Berton's Company, Colonel Sherbourn's Regiment. He appears on a list of men raised to serve in the

---

1 *Massachusetts Soldiers and Sailors*, Vol. VI, p. 287.
2 *Vital Records of Lincoln*; *Town of Weston, Births, Deaths, & Marriages*; *Vital Records of Sudbury*; *Vital Records of Westminster*; Brown, *Beneath Old Roof Trees*, p. 230. Also Conwell, *Life of James A. Garfield*, p. 31. Conwell misstates the date of his marriage, which is recorded in Sudbury. Five children are recorded in Westminster between 1770 and 1785.
3 Ryan, "Presidential Relations"; Conwell, *Life of James A. Garfield*, p. 33.

Continental Army, returned from Capt. Samuel Farrar, Jr., to Col. Eleazer Brooks, dated September 8, 1777. His service was credited to the town of Lincoln. He appears to have been recruited from outside of Lincoln to fulfill Lincoln's quota.[1]

He is otherwise unidentified, and no other Lincoln connection has been determined.

GOODENOW, Isaac
[also GOODENOUGH, also Isaac Jr.]

Isaac Goodenow of Framingham marched on the Alarm of April 19, 1775, as a private in Capt. Simon Edgel's Company, Col. Abijah Peirce's Regiment of Minute Men. He served for two days at Concord and Cambridge. It is unknown if this is Isaac Goodenow, Jr., or Isaac Goodenow, Sr.[2]

Within days or weeks, "some time in the month of April or May 1775," Isaac Goodenow, Jr., enlisted for eight months in Capt. David Moore's Company, Col. John Nixon's 16th Massachusetts Regiment. He is presumed to have served with his regiment at the Battle of Bunker Hill. He received advance pay on June 10, and appears to have served duty on main guard at Prospect Hill, under Col. Loammi Baldwin, on July 16, 1775.[3]

In 1776, he was back in service. He appears to have enlisted for a year in the Continental Army, "at the Expiration of [his] Eight months" service, and to have served in Capt. Adam Wheeler's Company, Col. John Nixon's 4th Continental Regiment. He was dispatched to Charlestown, New Hampshire, in June, under an agreement to serve until December 1, 1776. The perceived threat in the upper Connecticut Valley must have diminished, as he appears to have been serving as a drummer in Capt. Adam Wheeler's Company at the Battle of White Plains on October 28, 1776. His drum was destroyed by cannon shot, and he was ordered reimbursed for his loss.[4]

---

1 *Massachusetts Soldiers and Sailors*, Vol. VI, p. 422; *Muster Rolls of the Revolutionary War*, Vol. 53, p. 191a; Wheeler, "Lincoln," in Hurd, Vol. 2, p. 620. He appears on the September 8 list as belonging to "no town" before he engaged for this service. The fact that the list was returned from Capt. Samuel Farrar, Jr. (q.v.), to Col. Eleazer Brooks (q.v.) suggests the possibility that he may have been recruited from within the Lincoln Militia Company. If so, this would be an indication that he may have been at least temporarily living and working in Lincoln.

2 *Massachusetts Soldiers and Sailors*, Vol. VI, p. 569; Coburn, *Muster Rolls*. Coburn transcribes his name in *Muster Rolls* as "Isaace Goodman." Readers may argue whether or not this was Isaac Jr., age 17, or Isaac Sr. age 40. Isaac Jr.'s failure to mention this service in his Pension Declaration is most likely explained by the limitations of the 1818 Pension Act, which covered only Continental Service. For the same reason, he also fails to mention service at Rhode Island in 1777, and at Saratoga in 1777, which the evidence suggests was his.

The author acknowledges the possibility that this service may well have been by Isaac Sr. However, as no particular evidence has been found to support the argument in favor of the elder Isaac, and as no evidence of other service by Isaac Sr. seems to exist, the default position is to treat this service as if it were provided by Isaac Jr.

3 Pension Record # S32752; *Massachusetts Soldiers and Sailors*, Vol. VI, pp. 566, 570. The quotation is from his pension declaration, which gives substance to his claim of eight months of service. *Massachusetts Soldiers and Sailors*, on the other hand, indicates a June 7, 1775, enlistment date. Most enlistments at this time expired at the end of December. His pension declaration, which contains few details, does not mention Bunker Hill. Colonel Nixon's 16th Massachusetts Regiment became known as the 5th Continental Regiment in August 1775, under Washington's new command structure.

4 *Massachusetts Soldiers and Sailors*, Vol. VI, p. 570; Pension Record # S32752. The quotation is from his pension declaration, which otherwise contains few details. Colonel Nixon's 5th Continental Regiment was reconstituted as the 4th Continental Regiment on January 1, 1776. In August 1776, Lt. Col. Thomas Nixon succeeded his brother as commanding officer. The details (including the story of the drum) are found in *Massachusetts Soldiers and Sailors*. The *Massachusetts Soldiers and Sailors* record suggests the possibility that he may have

He appears to have served again in 1777 at North Kingston, Rhode Island, in Capt. John Gleason's Company, Col. Josiah Whitney's Regiment, for 2 months, 8 days during May and June, reportedly as a waiter.[1]

He went north to Saratoga on September 28, 1777, as a private in Capt. Asahel Wheeler's Company, Col. Jonathan Reed's Regiment. He served for 41 days, through the surrender of Burgoyne.[2]

Isaac Jr., was born in Framingham; the son of Isaac and Martha (Hunt) Goodenow; age 17 when he served at Cambridge. After the war, he moved to Lincoln sometime before 1800 and worked as a farmer on the Codman estate. He married Lydia Carrol of Sutton in 1800. He died in Lincoln in 1836 at age 78 and is buried in the Precinct Burial Ground.[3]

GORDEN, John
[also GORDON]

John Gorden appears on a list of men raised in Middlesex County for service in the Continental Army, probably in 1777. He was engaged for the town of Lincoln. His residence is listed as Lincoln. Lincoln historian William Wheeler indicates, however, that he was not a resident of the town, but was recruited from outside of town to fulfill the town's quota.[4]

He is probably the "John Grodin" who enlisted for the town of Lincoln, who served in Capt. Abijah Child's Company, Col. John Greaton's 2nd Regiment, and who was reported deserted (no dates given).[5]

No further information about his identity or Lincoln connection has been found.[6]

---

enlisted in June 1776 rather than in January 1776. The author, however, interprets the "enlistment agreement" so referenced as applying to the special duty, rather than to his Continental service.

1 *Massachusetts Soldiers and Sailors*, Vol. VI, p. 570. This service is not mentioned in his pension declaration, as militia service was not included in the 1818 Pension Act.

2 *Massachusetts Soldiers and Sailors*, Vol. VI, p. 565; Hudson, *History of Sudbury*, p. 398. This service is not mentioned in his pension declaration, as militia service was not included in the 1818 Pension Act.

3 *Vital Records of Lincoln*; Baldwin, *Vital Records of Framingham*; *Vital Records of Sudbury*; Pension Record # S32752; Biggs, "In Memorium," p. 195; Martin, *The Chambers–Russell–Codman House*, pp. 134, 142; Chapin, "Early History of the Codman House." Both his death record and his headstone give his age as 77, but this is inconsistent with his birth record.

Isaac Sr. was the son of Ebenezer and Elizabeth Goodnew of Sudbury; age 40 when (if) he responded to the Alarm on April 19, 1775. He had married Martha Hunt in Sudbury in 1757 and settled in Framingham. He reportedly became a farmer for the Russell estate (later the Codman estate) after the war. Suffering the infirmity and dependency of age, he had taken up residency with his son Isaac Jr. in Lincoln sometime before 1820. He died in 1821, at age 86, two days after his daughter-in-law (Lydia, wife of Isaac Jr.), and is buried with her in the Precinct Burying Ground. His headstone and his death record give his age as 87 and 88, but this is inconsistent with his birth record.

4 *Massachusetts Soldiers and Sailors*, Vol. VI, p. 633; Wheeler, "Lincoln," in Hurd, Vol. 2, p. 620. No dates are given in the record; 1777 is the author's supposition, consistent with Wheeler's indication that he was recruited to fulfill the town's 1777 quota. The question of Lincoln residency remains unresolved.

5 *Massachusetts Soldiers and Sailors*, Vol. VI, p. 904.

6 *Vital Records of Stow* contains a John Gordan who married Susanna Whitman in 1785. He has been suggested as a possible identity. However, Pension Record # W19515 for John Gordon (identifiable as said John Gordan of Stow) contains no information to encourage this suggested identity.

GOVE (?), [unidentified]

Deacon John Gove was paid by the town for service in the campaign to New York in 1776.[1] However, as he was age 69 at the time of the New York campaign, the likelihood that he participated in this campaign appears to be very remote.[2]

This campaign may have been served by one of his slaves. Tombo was about age 55 at the time, not out of the realm of possibilities. It is also possible that Deacon John Gove may also have had other slaves of a more appropriate age to have served.[3]

Equally probable is that this campaign may have been served by one of his sons, John, Jonathan, or Nathaniel. Little is known about son John, except that he would have been age 32 or 33 during the New York campaign.[4] Jonathan was age 30, had a medical degree from Harvard, and had settled in Groton six to eight years previously. He seems an unlikely possibility. Nathaniel (q.v.), age 27, had served as a Minute Man 18 months before during the Concord Alarm. He could certainly have served again in the New York campaign. If so, or if this service was provided by one of Deacon John's other sons, then the payment to Deacon John would indicate that the appropriate son was unavailable on that date to receive the payment directly.[5]

---

1 Wheeler, "Lincoln," in Hurd, Vol. 2, p. 622; "Treasurer's Accompts," November 11, 1779.

2 *Vital Records of Lincoln*; Bond, *Genealogies of the Families of Watertown*, p. 258. Bond even suggests that he may already have died by this time, as he lists John's wife Tabitha as a widow when she died in 1769. *Vital Records of Lincoln*, however, lists Tabitha when she died as wife of Deacon John. This, along with the record of his having been paid by the town ten years later, is good enough for the author to conclude that he was still very much alive in 1776. However, it does not establish that he actually served. See the listing for John Gove (q.v.) in Chapter 12.

Rawson, "The Gove Family," reports on deeds dated 1780 and 1787 from John Gove to Nathaniel Gove, each conveying one-half of his farm to Nathaniel, further proof if needed that John was still alive.

It should be further noted that Deacon John Gove is generally considered among some modern historians to have been "one of His Majesty's friends." This apparently stems from his supposed role in helping the spy John Howe escape from Concord. However, the John Howe saga first appeared in 1827, remains unsubstantiated, and has in its own right been discredited by most modern historians (see MacLean, *A Rich Harvest*, p. 303; Ryan, *Concord and the Dawn of Revolution*, pp. 52–54). The author has found no hard evidence to identify Deacon John Gove as a Tory.

3 See MacLean, *A Rich Harvest*, pp 217–218. *Vital Records of Lincoln* reports the baptism of Lot, a "negro Child belonging to Dea^n Gave" on July 12, 1767. While Lot's parents are not identified, this is a clear indication that Deacon John probably had more than one slave. Possibly, someone other than Tombo might have been Lot's father, and could have provided this service. Another possibility is that Lot's baptism may not have been an infant baptism, in which case Lot himself may have been old enough to have provided this service. So far, no service record has been found for either Tombo or Lot.

4 *Town of Weston, Births, Deaths, & Marriages* lists his birth date as January 16, 1744; Bond, *Genealogies of the Families of Watertown* (p. 258) lists his birth date as January 15, 1743. There is nothing to indicate whether or not he was still living in 1776.

5 For information about Jonathan, see Bond, *Genealogies of the Families of Watertown*, pp. 258–259. Also MacLean, *A Rich Harvest*, p. 205.

Substitution is another possibility to consider. However, because Deacon John was well past service age, a substitute would have been serving for someone other than Deacon John. We would still have to view Deacon John as merely a surrogate (i.e., payee) for the service obligation of probably a son or slave.

Typically the individual with the service obligation was the individual who was paid. When a surrogate was paid for service, it was because the individual providing the service (or substitute) was either: (a) a slave of the surrogate; or (b) a son of the surrogate, away from Lincoln (frequently serving another stint) on the date the payment was made. Individual circumstances undoubtedly account for other cases in which surrogates were paid for service, but these are much harder to tease out of the historical record. Invariably,

GOVE, Nathaniel

Nathaniel Gove was a private in Capt. William Smith's Company of Minute Men from Lincoln, Col. Abijah Peirce's Regiment.[1] Following the engagement at Concord, he served for five days in Cambridge.[2] He does not seem to have been reimbursed by the town for his accoutrements as a minute man.

There is a pay record to his father that suggests the possibility that he may have served at New York in 1776, but this is entirely speculative.[3]

He was the son of Deacon John Gove (q.v.) and Tabitha (Livermore) Gove; age 25 at the time of the Concord Alarm. He had married Elizabeth Adams in 1772, sister of Amos Adams (q.v.) and Asa Adams (q.v.). He died in Lincoln in 1811.[4]

HAGAR, John
[also HAGER]

John Hagar was paid by the town for part of a three-year campaign in the Continental Army.[5]

This individual has not been positively identified. He is presumably the John Hagar who owned a house along Weston Road near the town line.[6]

---

the surrogate occupied a fiduciary role vis-à-vis the service provider: slave owner, parent, or occasionally a senior officer.

Because (except in the case of slaves) payments to surrogates were clearly the exception, the assumption is that in each case a justifying circumstance must have existed. Accordingly, without evidence that Nathaniel or one of Deacon John's other sons provided the service or sent a substitute, and without evidence that he was unavailable to be paid directly, the identity of who might have provided this service remains speculative.

1 Coburn, *Muster Rolls*.
2 *Massachusetts Soldiers and Sailors*, Vol. VI, p. 692.
3 "Treasurer's Accompts," November 11, 1779. The payment was made to Deacon John Gove (q.v.). While this service could also have been served by Deacon John's other sons, John or Jonathan, neither of them left any other identifiable record of service. Further, Jonathan had left Lincoln some years before and settled into a medical practice at Groton. However, without evidence that Nathaniel provided this service, or without a discernible explanation for why he was unavailable to be paid directly, a presumption that he was the one who provided this service could be sustained only as speculation. See the listings for Gove (?), [unidentified] (q.v.), as well as John Gove (q.v., Chapter 12).
4 *Vital Records of Lincoln*. The birth of their first child is recorded in *Vital Records of Lincoln* just one month after Nathaniel and Elizabeth were married. Bond, *Genealogies of the Families of Watertown* (p. 258) lists his death 1½ months earlier than *Vital Records of Lincoln*, but both agree on the year 1811.
5 "Treasurer's Accompts," June 15, 1779. Wheeler, "Lincoln" (in Hurd, Vol. 2, p. 622), indicates that John Hager served the first 20 months of this campaign, and John More (q.v.) served the final 16 months. The author has found no primary source to corroborate Wheeler's assertion. It appears to be based on the juxtaposition of the pay records, and on pay amounts that could be interpreted as prorated portions of a three-year campaign. A three-year campaign appears to have paid £30; Hager was paid £17:7 for his part; More was paid £12:13 for his part. The math works, but whether or not Wheeler's interpretation of the data is correct is unconfirmed. *Massachusetts Soldiers and Sailors* has multiple listings for service by individuals named John Hager (or John Hagar) and John More (or John Moore), but the author has found no meaningful relationship between any of the listings which would support Wheeler's assertion, nor has he been able to identify the Continental service for which this John Hagar was paid. (See *Massachusetts Soldiers and Sailors*, Vol. VII, pp. 23, 24, 27; Vol. X, pp. 923–925; Vol. XI, pp. 5–6.)
6 Glass and Little, Map of Lincoln. *Vital Records of Lincoln* reveals no John Hagar. "Treasurer's Accompts" show that a John Hager was paid or supported by the town through payments to Edmond Wheeler in 1774 and to Samuel Farrar, Jr., in 1775. Despite a degree of similarity between these entries and other entries for individuals identified as school teachers, he appears to have been supported as one of the town's poor. MacLean

HARRINGTON, Daniel

Daniel Harrington was a private in Capt. William Smith's Company of Minute Men from Lincoln, Col. Abijah Peirce's Regiment.[1] Following the engagement at Concord, he served for six days in Cambridge.[2] He was reimbursed by the town for his accoutrements as a minute man.[3]

There is no record of further military service during the Siege of Boston, but he was paid by the town for "carting three Tons of hay to Cambridge for the Army."[4]

He served at Ticonderoga in 1776, and he took a team with supplies to Worthington in 1777; for both of these, he was paid by the town.[5]

Having been detached from Col. Eleazer Brooks's 3rd Middlesex County Militia Regiment to relieve the guards at Cambridge, he joined Capt. Daniel Harrington's Company, Col. Jonathan Reed's Regiment of Guards, as a sergeant, on April 2, 1778. He served until July 3, 1778, guarding the "Convention Army" surrendered the previous October by General Burgoyne at Saratoga.[6]

(private communication with the author) reports that just before the war, the Town Meeting directed the Selectmen to act as they felt proper about providing financial assistance for John Hagar and wife. These records imply residency in Lincoln, and logically are assumed to refer to John Hagar (inst.).

Pension Record # S29857 provides details about a John Hagar of Weston who was the son of John and Sarah (Child) Hagar, age 17 at the start of the war. He enlisted in the relief expedition to Canada in 1776, for guard duty for the Convention Army in 1777–1778, and for service at West Point in 1778. In 1780, he married Eunice Whitehead, daughter of John Whitehead (q.v.), sister of Daniel Whitehead (q.v.) and Elisha Whitehead (q.v.), settling in Phillipston about 1782 or 1783. Despite initial appearances as a likely candidate for John Hagar (inst.), he was paid for all of this service by the town of Weston, so it is unlikely that he could, in fact, be John Hagar (inst.). As for his being a town-supported pauper, had he come to Lincoln without a means of support, it is likely that he would have been warned out instead, remaining the responsibility of Weston.

Other possible identities include: (i) the son of Isaac and Prudence (Allen) Hagar of Weston, age 48 on April 19, 1775; (ii) the son of John and Hannah (Stearns) Hagar of Weston, age 20 on April 19, 1775; (iii) the father of the John Hagar in Pension Record # S29857, who married Sarah Child in January 1757 and was probably around age 40 at the time of this service; (iv) a John Hagar who married Martha Parkhurst in October 1770; (v) son of Samuel and Mary (Fiske) Hagar of Waltham; age 29 on April 19, 1775; (vi) the son of Jonas and Hannah (Ellis) Hagar of Weston; age 22 at the outbreak of fighting on April 19, 1775. (See *Town of Weston, Births, Deaths, & Marriages*; Bond, *Genealogies of the Families of Watertown*, pp. 265–266.)

The author makes no pretense of keeping the various John Hagars straight. Bond, *Genealogies of the Families of Watertown* and *Town of Weston, Births, Deaths, & Marriages* are not entirely consistent with each other. The husband of Hannah (Stearns) and the husband of Sarah (Child) may be the same individual. Bond says he settled in Groton with Hannah in 1755 and remained in Groton with Sarah. But *Town of Weston, Births, Deaths, & Marriages* lists five children of John Jr. and Hannah, followed by three children of John Jr. and Sarah. And there is nary a Hagar appearing in any vital record of any sort in Groton.

MacLean, *A Rich Harvest* (p. 180), identifies an Isaac Hagar as a ward of the town (after having been a carpenter). He gives no dates, but John (inst.) had both a father Isaac and a brother Isaac. The reader is free to speculate. Could there be any implied connection between John Hagar, whom the town supported, and Isaac Hagar, who was a ward of the town? And if so, what might that tell us about the identity of John Hagar (inst.)?

1 Coburn, *Muster Rolls*.
2 *Massachusetts Soldiers and Sailors*, Vol. VII, p. 775.
3 "Treasurer's Accompts," February 23, 1776.
4 Ibid.
5 "Treasurer's Accompts," June 10, 1779.
6 Ibid. Also, *Massachusetts Soldiers and Sailors*, Vol. VII, pp. 321, 775, in which record he is reported to have been detached from Major Lamson's Militia Company from Weston. This appears unlikely, however, as he was

He was age 24 as a minute man; age 27 on guard duty. He was the son of Daniel and Hannah Harrington of Waltham; brother-in-law of John Whitehead (q.v.) and John Coolidge (q.v.). He had married Anna Coolidge in 1772, four months before she bore him a daughter. He was apparently living in Lincoln at the Lexington and Waltham town lines, where he operated a saw mill, but apparently he did not switch his church affiliation to Lincoln until 1780.[1]

After the war, he became captain of the Lincoln Militia Company, and he was called out with 16 of his men to help put down Shays' Rebellion in 1787. He subsequently also served the town as a Selectman.[2]

He died in 1818 at age 68, and he is buried in the Meeting House Cemetery behind Bemis Hall.[3]

HARTWELL, Ephraim, Jr.

Ephraim Hartwell, Jr., was a private in Capt. Boaz Moore's Company of Minute Men from Princeton, Col. Ephraim Doolittle's Regiment. He marched on the April 19th Alarm, and served for nine days in Cambridge.

He served as quartermaster (commissioned February 14, 1776) in Col. Josiah Whitney's Worcester County Regiment, raised to reinforce the Continental Army before Boston (in preparation for fortifying Dorchester Heights), from January 23, 1776, to April 1, 1776.

Subsequently, he served as adjutant in Col. Josiah Whitney's Regiment and marched to the Northward, agreeable to an order of the General Court dated September 22, 1777, for 25 days of service in support of General Gates at Saratoga. He was present at the surrender of Burgoyne.

On June 17, 1779, he was commissioned captain of the 12th Company, Colonel Whitney's 2nd Worcester County Regiment of Massachusetts Militia, and served from October 14, 1779, to April 20, 1780 (6 months, 6 days) as captain of a company of guards at Rutland, Massachusetts.[4]

He grew up in Lincoln, the son of Ephraim Hartwell (q.v., Chapter 12) and Elizabeth (Heywood) Hartwell; brother of Samuel Hartwell (q.v.), John Hartwell (q.v.), Isaac Hartwell (q.v.), and Jonas Hartwell (q.v.); cousin of Abner Brooks (q.v.), Benjamin Brooks (q.v.), and

---

paid for this service by the town of Lincoln. Furthermore, his previous and subsequent service from Lincoln strongly suggests that he was a sergeant in Capt. Samuel Farrar, Jr.'s Militia Company at the time.

Who could resist being intrigued by Sgt. Daniel Harrington serving in Capt. Daniel Harrington's Company? Notwithstanding the obvious expectation, no relationship has been identified. Sergeant Daniel does not appear to have had any close relatives named Daniel (except his father, who had died some years before). Captain Daniel's identity is uncertain, but he could possibly be the son of Robert and Abigail Harrington of Lexington, age 39, probably distantly related at best (see Bond, *Genealogies of the Families of Watertown*, p. 274).

1 Bond, *Genealogies of the Families of Watertown*, p. 281; *Vital Records of Lincoln*; Glass and Little, Map of Lincoln; Wheeler, "Lincoln," in Hurd, Vol. 2, p. 622.
2 MacLean, *A Rich Harvest*, pp. 301, 312. Wheeler, "Lincoln" (in Hurd, Vol. 2, p. 623), says "Captain Daniel Harrington with his company started from Lincoln January 2, 1787, for Northampton, to aid in the suppression of Shays' Rebellion. When the company reached Marlborough they received intelligence that the insurgents had dispersed, and they returned home."
3 *Vital Records of Lincoln*; Biggs, "In Memorium," p. 173.
4 *Massachusetts Soldiers and Sailors*, Vol. VII, pp. 392.

Ephraim Brooks, Jr. (q.v.). He had married Mary Brown, the sister of Moses Brown (q.v.), in 1769, and he had settled in Princeton by 1770. He was age 30 as a minute man.[1]

After the war, he moved to New Ipswich, New Hampshire, where he reportedly died in 1815 at age 70. He appears to be buried in Central Cemetery.[2]

HARTWELL, Isaac

Isaac Hartwell was a private in Capt. William Smith's Company of Minute Men from Lincoln, Col. Abijah Peirce's Regiment. Following the engagement at Concord, he served for four days in Cambridge. He was reimbursed by the town for his accoutrements as a minute man.[3]

Subsequently, he served as a sergeant in Capt. John Hartwell's Militia Company from Lincoln, Col. Eleazer Brooks's 3rd Middlesex County Regiment, which marched from Lincoln to fortify Dorchester Heights on March 4, 1776. The unit was discharged five days later, on March 9, after the threat of a British assault on the fortifications had subsided, General Howe having instead begun preparations to evacuate Boston. He was paid for this service the following September.[4]

He was paid by the town for service at Ticonderoga in 1776 and for taking a team with provisions to Worthington.[5]

He enlisted on January 1, 1778, in Col. John Jacobs's Regiment, raised for the defense of the New England states, serving for one year as a lieutenant in Capt. Nathan Smith's Company and in Capt. Joseph Griffith's Company. It appears that this service was mostly in Rhode Island, and he likely participated in the Battle of Rhode Island on August 29, 1778.[6]

He was age 22 on the April 19th Alarm; son of Ephraim Hartwell (q.v., Chapter 12) and Elizabeth (Heywood) Hartwell; brother of Ephraim Hartwell, Jr. (q.v.), Samuel

---

1 Hicks, "The Hartwell Family"; *Vital Records of Lincoln*; Bond, *Genealogies of the Families of Watertown*, p. 127. Hicks says that Ephraim Sr. owned land in Princeton, and she advances the premise that Ephraim Jr. was living in Princeton, farming this land in 1775. His brother, Isaac, was also in Princeton before the war, as evidenced by a record of Ephraim Sr. having received an abatement from the town of Lincoln because Isaac Hartwell (q.v.) was subject to a poll tax in Princeton in 1773 ("Treasurer's Accompts," January 25, 1776). Isaac was back in Lincoln at least by the spring 1775, but Ephraim Jr. remained in Princeton throughout the war. Isaac appears to have been unmarried during this time; Ephraim Jr. was married with a daughter recorded in *Vital Records of Princeton* but not in *Vital Records of Lincoln*.

2 Hicks, "The Hartwell Family"; *Vital Records of Lincoln*; Bond, *Genealogies of the Families of Watertown*, p. 127. Bond skips over their years in Princeton, but tells us simply that Ephraim Jr. and Mary settled in New Ipswich, New Hampshire. His burial in Central Cemetery is per "Find A Grave," which reports his death in 1816.

There is a remote possibility that he may also have served nine months in the Continental Army, for which his father was paid by the town. "Treasurer's Accompts," June 10, 1779. There seems to be little logic to any idea that it may have been Ephraim Jr. who rendered this service, except that his being in Princeton in 1779 might explain why the town paid his father for the service. On the other hand, the likelihood of his enlisting in the Continental Army to the credit of Lincoln appears wholly inconsistent with his consistent and regular service in Colonel Whitney's Regiment. This service was more probably provided by Jonas Hartwell (q.v.).

3 Coburn, *Muster Rolls*; *Massachusetts Soldiers and Sailors*, Vol. VII, pp. 393; "Treasurer's Accompts," February 19, 1776.

4 *Massachusetts Soldiers and Sailors*, Vol. VII, p. 393.

5 "Treasurer's Accompts," June 10, 1779. The purpose and dates of the Worthington trek are not identified, but Shattuck, *History of the Town of Concord*, p. 300, says it occurred in 1777, leading to speculation that it might have been undertaken to supply the troops (including a contingent from Lincoln under the command of Lincoln's Capt. Samuel Farrar, Jr.) escorting Burgoyne's army to Cambridge.

6 *Massachusetts Soldiers and Sailors*, Vol. VII, pp. 393, 676. See also *Massachusetts Soldiers and Sailors*, Vol. VI, p. 888; Vol. VIII, p. 699; Vol. XIV, p. 505.

Hartwell (q.v.), John Hartwell (q.v.), and Jonas Hartwell (q.v.); cousin of Abner Brooks (q.v.), Benjamin Brooks (q.v.), and Ephraim Brooks, Jr. (q.v.). He appears to have settled in Princeton after the war, and married Eunice Myrick in 1786. He died in Princeton in 1831 at age 79, and he is buried in the Meeting House Cemetery in Princeton.[1]

[There is a remote possibility that he may have served nine months in the Continental Army, for which his father was paid by the town.][2]

HARTWELL, John

John Hartwell was a sergeant in Capt. William Smith's Company of Minute Men from Lincoln, Col. Abijah Peirce's Regiment.[3] Following the engagement at Concord, he served for five days in Cambridge.[4] He was reimbursed by the town for his accoutrements as a minute man.[5]

On April 24, he enlisted in Capt. William Smith's Company, Col. John Nixon's 16th Massachusetts Regiment. He was commissioned ensign on June 5, 1775, and participated with his unit in the Battle of Bunker Hill on June 17, 1775. Subsequently he became a second lieutenant, probably by August 1, 1775. He was still in service on September 30, 1775, and probably served out an eight-month term. He was paid for this service by the town.[6]

By March 1776, he had become captain of the Lincoln Militia Company, Col. Eleazer Brooks's 3rd Middlesex County Regiment, which was called out on March 4, 1776, and marched from Lincoln to fortify Dorchester Heights. The unit was discharged five days later, on March 9, after the threat of a British assault on the fortifications had subsided, General Howe having begun preparations to evacuate Boston instead.[7]

He was paid by the town for service at Ticonderoga in 1776. The details of this service are unknown, except that it must have been between March and mid-August.[8]

On August 21, 1776, he was back in service in Dorchester as a lieutenant in Capt. John Minot's Company, Col. Nicholas Dike's 2nd Massachusetts Regiment, which was raised for the defense of Boston. By December 1, 1776, he was serving as captain, either of the same company or of another company in the same regiment. His commission was finally issued in

---

1 *Concord, Massachusetts: Births, Marriages, and Deaths*; *Vital Records of Princeton*; "Treasurer's Accompts," January 25, 1776; *SAR Revolutionary War Graves Register*. He must have been in Princeton in 1773, as he was subject to a poll tax there in 1773, with his father receiving an abatement for his Poll Tax in Lincoln from the town of Lincoln. Obviously, he had returned to Lincoln by 1775. Hicks, "The Hartwell Family," miscalculated his age on the April 19th Alarm. Wheeler, "Lincoln" (in Hurd, Vol. 2, p. 623), incorrectly gives his death as 1822.
2 "Treasurer's Accompts," June 10, 1779. As there does not appear to be a town record of his being paid for his service in Colonel Jacob's Regiment, this could be the Continental service for which his father was paid, except that the town paid him for other service on the same day. The service itself appears to work as well or better than trying to fit his brothers with this service, but why would the town have paid his father for this service on the same day it paid him for other service? This seems unlikely. This service may more probably have been provided by Jonas Hartwell (q.v.).
3 Coburn, *Muster Rolls*
4 *Massachusetts Soldiers and Sailors*, Vol. VII, pp. 393–394.
5 "Treasurer's Accompts," February 29, 1776.
6 Ibid. Also "Treasurer's Accompts," June 10, 1779. Colonel Nixon's Regiment became known also as the 5th Regiment in August 1775, under Washington's Continental command structure.
7 *Massachusetts Soldiers and Sailors*, Vol. VII, pp. 393–94.
8 "Treasurer's Accompts," June 10, 1779

February 1777, retroactive to December 1. He had engaged to serve until March 1, 1777, but he may not have served out his duty. He was reported sick and absent in February, probably returning to Lincoln at least for a time. He was paid by the town for this service.[1]

He was age 27 at the time of the April 19th Alarm; son of Ephraim Hartwell (q.v., Chapter 12) and Elizabeth (Heywood) Hartwell; brother of Ephraim Hartwell, Jr. (q.v.), Samuel Hartwell (q.v.), Isaac Hartwell (q.v.), and Jonas Hartwell (q.v.); cousin of Abner Brooks (q.v.), Benjamin Brooks (q.v.), and Ephraim Brooks, Jr. (q.v.). In 1777, he took over running the tavern from his father, and in 1780 he was elected Selectman. He married Hebzibah Brooks in 1783, and that same year his aging parents moved into an addition built onto the tavern. In 1787, he closed the tavern but continued to live there with his family until he died in 1820 at age 73. He was chosen Deacon of the Lincoln church in 1804, and is buried in the Meeting House Cemetery behind Bemis Hall.[2]

HARTWELL, Jonas

Jonas Hartwell may possibly have marched to Concord on April 19, 1775, as part of the militia company from Lincoln.[3]

He served as a sergeant in Capt. John Hartwell's Company, Col. Nicholas Dike's 2nd Regiment, in Dorchester, from December 14, 1776, through the end of February 1777. This regiment had been raised for the defense of Boston, to serve until March 1, 1777. This service was credited to the town of Lincoln.[4]

There is a possibility that he may have served nine months in the Continental Army, for which his father was paid by the town.[5]

---

1 Ibid. Also Shattuck, *History of the Town of Concord*, p. 354.

2 *Concord, Massachusetts: Births, Marriages, and Deaths; Vital Records of Lincoln*; Hicks, "The Hartwell Family"; MacLean, *A Rich Harvest*, pp. 195, 301; Shattuck, *History of the Town of Concord*, p. 308; Biggs, "In Memorium," p. 174. Hebzibah was most likely the sister of Joshua Brooks, Jr. (q.v.) and Jonas Brooks (q.v.). There is an intriguing record in *Concord, Massachusetts: Births, Marriages, and Deaths* of a son John born to a John and Susannah Hartwell in 1774 and a son Willard born to John and Susannah Hartwell in July 1776. These individuals have not been identified, but there is nothing in the Concord record to support (or refute) any speculative notion that this might be John Hartwell (inst.), or that Hebzibah may have been his second wife; other records clearly show that John Hartwell (inst.) was a resident of Lincoln rather than Concord in 1775 and 1776, spending much of that period in military service.

There is a remote possibility that he may have served nine months in the Continental Army, for which his father was paid by the town. "Treasurer's Accompts," June 10, 1779. Actually, there is little to suggest that this was John (versus his brothers), particularly as the town paid him for other service on the same day it paid his father for this service. This payment was more probably for service by Jonas Hartwell (q.v.).

3 Ryan, *Concord and the Dawn of Revolution*, p. 23, suggests this possibility. This is entirely speculative, as no militia record has been found. Ryan notes that all four of his brothers were in service on April 19 as minute men.

4 *Massachusetts Soldiers and Sailors*, Vol. VII, p. 394. Jonas reportedly entered Harvard in the fall of 1776. Ryan, *Concord and the Dawn of Revolution* (p. 26) says that almost immediately, in November 1776, he took a leave of absence for "nervous disorders," the first of "an unusual number…throughout his student days." He cites evidence to support the possibility that these leaves may actually have been a cover for military service. Whether or not this developed into a pattern, the juxtaposition of the November 1776 leave of absence with this service from December 1776 through February 1777 certainly appears consistent with Ryan's theory. Ryan explains further (in notes to the author) that Gen. William Prescott signed a letter in June 1779 (apparently to Harvard officials) explaining Jonas's previous medical/mental episodes.

5 "Treasurer's Accompts," June 10, 1779. Actually, there is nothing in the record to suggest that this was Jonas (versus other possible candidates), so this is speculative. Whether Jonas might have accumulated nine months of service during his multiple leaves of absence, or how he might have missed nine months of study without

Chapter 10: The Army of the Revolution

Hartwell Tavern bore witness to the fight along Battle Road. It was the boyhood home of five Hartwell brothers who served as soldiers in the Revolution, three of whom (John, Isaac, and Jonas) were still living here when they served. John, Isaac, Samuel, and Ephraim Jr. were all minute men on April 19th. John Hartwell closed the tavern in 1787, but he continued to live here with his family until he died in 1820. The tavern, in disrepair in this photo (c. 1900), has been carefully restored by Minute Man National Historical Park. (*An Account of the Celebration*)

He was age 22 at the time of his service in Dorchester; son of Ephraim Hartwell (q.v., Chapter 12) and Elizabeth (Heywood) Hartwell; brother of Ephraim Hartwell, Jr. (q.v.), Samuel Hartwell (q.v.), Isaac Hartwell (q.v.), and John Hartwell (q.v.); cousin of Abner Brooks (q.v.), Benjamin Brooks (q.v.), and Ephraim Brooks, Jr. (q.v.). He shared his war service with studies at Harvard College, graduating in 1779 and receiving a Masters degree there in 1782. He had a short but evidently successful career as a ship owner and merchant, working with Moses Brown (q.v.) in the Spanish trade. While at Bilbao, Spain, with a cargo of tobacco, he was arrested in 1784 and imprisoned by order of the Spanish Inquisition. His crime apparently was expressing some contempt for the Catholic religion. As the United States government applied diplomatic pressure on Spanish officials for his release, he was being poisoned by his captors. He died in Spain in 1785 at age 30.[1]

---

delaying his graduation, or whether he might have served this time before entering Harvard, are all questions to ponder. Notwithstanding the speculative nature of attributing this service to Jonas, however, this record fits Jonas as well or better than any of his brothers. Jonas graduated from Harvard just about the same time the town paid for this service, so that might have been a reason for the town to have paid Ephraim Sr. instead of Jonas (assuming that Jonas was the individual who actually provided the service). See the listing for Ephraim Hartwell (q.v., Chapter 12).

1 Hicks, "The Hartwell Family"; Ryan, *Concord and the Dawn of Revolution*, p. 27; *Vital Records of Lincoln*. Hicks puts his death in 1784, a few weeks after his release from prison. Ryan, citing diplomatic and family sources, says he died in prison in March 1785, weeks before "he would certainly have had his liberty."

HARTWELL, Jonathan

Jonathan Hartwell served as a corporal in Capt. John Hartwell's Company, Col. Nicholas Dike's 2nd Regiment, in Dorchester, from December 14, 1776, through February 1777. This regiment had been raised for the defense of Boston, to serve until March 1, 1777. His service was credited to the town of Lincoln.[1]

There is a possibility that he may have served previously as a private in Capt. Job Shattuck's Company, Col. John Robinson's Regiment, for eight days in Cambridge, in March 1776, around the time of the British evacuation of Boston. However, it is uncertain if this is the same Jonathan Hartwell.[2]

His identity is uncertain. The service parallels with John Hartwell (q.v.) and Jonas Hartwell (q.v.) are strong evidence of a family relationship between this individual and the other Hartwells. A likely possibility is that he may have been the son of Jonathan and Sarah (Wheeler) Hartwell, who would have been age 35 at Dorchester. If so, then he was a second cousin of Samuel Hartwell (q.v.), John Hartwell (q.v.), Isaac Hartwell (q.v.), Ephraim Hartwell, Jr. (q.v.), and Jonas Hartwell (q.v.). His parents had Concord roots, but he was born in Westford and had married Elizabeth Tarbell of Concord in 1762 at Littleton.[3]

HARTWELL, Samuel

Samuel Hartwell was a sergeant in Capt. William Smith's Company of Minute Men from Lincoln, Col. Abijah Peirce's Regiment.[4] Following the engagement at Concord, he served for 1 month, 4 days in Cambridge.[5] He was reimbursed by the town for his accoutrements as a minute man.[6]

Subsequently, he served as a private in Capt. John Hartwell's Company of Militia from Lincoln, Col. Eleazer Brooks's 3rd Middlesex County Regiment, which marched from Lincoln to fortify Dorchester Heights on March 4, 1776. The unit was discharged five days later, on March 9, after the threat of a British assault on the fortifications had subsided, General Howe having begun preparations to evacuate Boston. He was paid for this service the following September.[7]

He served as quartermaster in Col. Eleazer Brooks's Middlesex County Regiment of Massachusetts Militia detached for the New York campaign from September 27, 1776, to November 16, 1776 (credited with 62 days of service, including 11 days for 212 miles of travel home). The regiment marched to Fairfield, Horse Neck, and Valentine Hill, before participating in the Battle of White Plains on October 28, 1776. After the battle, they were

---

1 *Massachusetts Soldiers and Sailors*, Vol. VII, p. 394. See identical service by Jonas Hartwell (q.v.).

2 Ibid.

3 *Vital Records of Westford, Concord, Massachusetts: Births, Marriages, and Deaths*. The author is indebted to Mike Ryan for this putative identity and associated genealogical data. Jonathan and Sarah had a previous son named Jonathan, who was born in Concord in 1721 and died in Westford in 1738. The putative Jonathan was born in 1741, the last child of Jonathan and Sarah. Sarah had died while he was still young; father Jonathan died in Littleton in 1778.

4 Coburn, *Muster Rolls*.

5 *Massachusetts Soldiers and Sailors*, Vol. VII, pp. 395, 396.

6 "Treasurer's Accompts," February 19, 1776.

7 *Massachusetts Soldiers and Sailors*, Vol. VII, pp. 395, 396.

The home of Samuel and Mary Hartwell is believed to have been built around 1690. After Samuel marched to Concord on April 19th as a sergeant in the minute company, Mary watched the column of Redcoats march by her front door. "If it hadn't been for the purpose they came for," she reportedly later told her grandchildren, "I should say it was the handsomest sight I ever saw in my life!" The house was destroyed by fire in 1968, but the building's site is preserved at Minute Man National Historical Park. (*An Account of the Celebration*)

deployed at North Castle, where they were discharged. He reportedly stayed behind to collect arrears of rations due the regiment.[1]

The following year, he served again as quartermaster in Colonel Brooks's Militia Regiment, called into service in early November to guard Burgoyne's "Convention Army" upon its arrival at Cambridge, about November 7. He served until about April 24, 1778, and was paid by the town for this service.[2]

---

1 Ibid.; "Treasurer's Accompts," November 11, 1779; Wheeler, "Lincoln," in Drake, Vol. 2, p. 42; Pension Record # W14841. Shattuck, *History of the Town of Concord* (pp. 124, 354) says he served for three months, starting September 12, 1776. However, September 12, 1776, is the date of the resolve, which called for two months of service. The dates of service appear to be as above. The pension declaration by his widow, Mary Hartwell, also says he served for three months, but this was executed in 1838, three years after Shattuck was published, so her recollection may have been influenced by Shattuck's assertion.

2 *Massachusetts Soldiers and Sailors*, Vol. VII, pp. 395, 396; "Treasurer's Accompts," November 11, 1779; Pension Record # W14841. Eleazer Brooks Papers [Concord] provide ample evidence to support the logic that this service was in Colonel Brooks's Regiment. The *Massachusetts Soldiers and Sailors* record, however, says he served with the Suffolk County Militia, that he was commissioned on September 27, 1777, and that he served at or near Charlestown. It is easy to link these records, as "at or near Charlestown" and Cambridge could certainly refer to the same place. Guard duty is quite typically given as at Cambridge. But it is not known why this guard duty would have been recorded as having been with the Suffolk County Militia. It is also not clear why he would have been commissioned for this duty in September 1777. Commissions invariably followed, not preceded, the assumption of or appointment to rank and duty. Quite possibly, these records may refer to separate stints, and he may have served with the Suffolk County Militia at or near Charlestown prior to his guard service with Colonel Brooks's Regiment. It seems more likely, however, that the *Massachusetts Soldiers*

In her 1838 pension application, after Congress voted to extend pension benefits to widows of soldiers, Mary Hartwell identified the locations where her husband, Samuel, had served as regimental quartermaster, first during the New York campaign and later guarding Burgoyne's "Convention Army" captured at Saratoga. (National Archives)

He was age 32 on April 19, 1775; the son of Ephraim Hartwell (q.v., Chapter 12) and Elizabeth (Heywood) Hartwell; brother of Ephraim Hartwell, Jr. (q.v.), Jonas Hartwell (q.v.), Isaac Hartwell (q.v.), and John Hartwell (q.v.); cousin of Abner Brooks (q.v.), Benjamin Brooks (q.v.), and Ephraim Brooks, Jr. (q.v.). He had married Mary Flint in 1769. Thus, he was the brother-in-law of John Flint (q.v.), Ephraim Flint (q.v.), Abel Flint (q.v.), and Joseph Mason (q.v.). Samuel and Mary lived next door to his parents, Ephraim and Elizabeth, in the house built by his grandfather, Samuel. He appears to have been a detail metalworker by trade, and made clocks, locks, and guns in his shop. He died in 1829 at age 87; he is buried in the old Precinct Burial Ground on Lexington Road.[1]

---

and Sailors information may have been recorded carelessly—that the Commission date may actually have been September 27, 1776, when he marched with Colonel Brooks on the New York campaign, and that his guard duty with Colonel Brooks's Regiment (which probably included militia detachments from several counties) may have been recorded incorrectly as Suffolk County.

1 *Vital Records of Lincoln*; *Concord, Massachusetts: Births, Marriages, and Deaths*; Hicks, "The Hartwell Family"; MacLean, *A Rich Harvest*, p. 189; Biggs, "In Memorium," p. 195.

There is a slight possibility that he may also have served nine months in the Continental Army, for which the town paid his father. "Treasurer's Accompts," June 10, 1779. Actually, there is nothing in the record to indicate when and where this service might have been served, or to suggest that it was served by Samuel, so this is entirely speculative. As Samuel was married and had a family of his own, he is probably a less likely candidate than his brother, Jonas Hartwell (q.v.). See Ephraim Hartwell (q.v., Chapter 12).

He also may have served at Rhode Island as a private in Capt. Samuel Heald's Company, Col. John Jacobs's Light Infantry Regiment, from September 15, 1779, to November 15, 1779 (2 months, 4 days including 80 miles of travel), but it is not clear if this is the same Samuel Hartwell (*Massachusetts Soldiers and Sailors*, Vol. VII, pp. 395, 396). Mary Hartwell makes no mention of this service in her pension declaration. In fact, Mary says specifically that "his last service was at Cambridge or [in] that vicinity." If this is accurate, then this would preclude the provider of this service from being the same Samuel Hartwell. On the other hand, Mary's pension declaration also understates the length of his service as a minute man, and it omits completely his service at Dorchester Heights. And, as Captain Heald was from Concord, it is likely that the Samuel Hartwell who provided this service was a local man.

It was not typical for individuals to step back in rank from one enlistment to another, particularly dropping from a commissioned rank to a non-commissioned rank. In this case, however, Samuel Hartwell had already stepped back from a sergeant at the start of the war, to a private at Dorchester Heights. Although he was then commissioned as a quartermaster, this did not have line-of-command responsibility, and it may be therefore less problematic to place him in service again as a private than if he had previously served as a lieutenant or captain.

Wheeler, "Lincoln" (in Hurd, Vol. 2, p. 623), goes a step further and says that Samuel (inst.) served at Rhode Island not only in 1779, but also in 1780. If so, then the 1780 service was as a corporal in Capt. John Ames's

HASTINGS, Samuel, Jr.

Samuel Hastings, Jr., mobilized with the Lexington militia mid-morning on April 19, 1775, when Capt. John Parker marched them to the edge of town to extract their revenge on the Redcoats returning from Concord.[1]

He enlisted on December 2, 1775, as a private in Capt. Nathaniel Wade's Company, Col. Moses Little's 12th Continental Regiment.[2] He was detached soon after, to serve as a bodyguard for Gen. Charles Lee. He went with General Lee to New York; then Philadelphia; then York, Pennsylvania, where he contracted smallpox. Upon his recovery, he returned to New York and rejoined Colonel Little's Regiment. He rejoined General Lee's bodyguard when Lee returned to New York.[3]

He was taken prisoner in the British raid that captured General Lee at Basking Ridge, New Jersey, on December 13, 1776. He appears to have been slashed in the head or neck during the scuffle, and reportedly he credited his queue with saving his life.[4] As a prisoner, he was taken to Trenton, then to New York, where he was held with the men who were captured at Fort Washington. The details and date of his release from captivity are unclear, but he says he was never exchanged. He says he "continued a prisoner in the actual custody of the British and on parole during the war, and never had a right to enlist again during the war."[5]

He sat out the balance of the war.[6]

He was age 17 on April 19, 1775; age 18 when he was captured by the British. He was the son of Samuel Hastings, Sr.[7] and Lydia (Tidd) Hastings of Lexington. He married

---

Company, Maj. Eliphalet Cary's Regiment for 11 days on an alarm from July 30 to August 9, 1780. However, Cary's was a Plymouth County regiment, so the likelihood that this could be Samuel Hartwell (inst.) of Lincoln is uncertain.

1 By some accounts (see Malcolm, *Peter's War*, p. 172), he mustered on the Green that morning, but Cain, "Samuel Hastings Jr.," is explicit in declaring that he was not on the Green, but was at "Parker's Revenge." This is evidently consistent with Hastings-family tradition. One of the Provincial depositions taken in the aftermath of the events of April 19th was by a Samuel Hastings, and it establishes that he was on the Green, but this is believed to have been executed by his father, Samuel Sr., in as much as Samuel Jr. would probably have been considered under the legal age for being deposed. There is no evidence to place Samuel Jr. on the Green.
2 *Massachusetts Soldiers and Sailors*, Vol. VII, p. 475.
3 Pension Record # S30460. In January 1775, General Lee left Boston for New York, where in March he was placed in command of the Southern Department. He shadowed the British fleet to Charleston, South Carolina, where he thwarted the British attempt to capture the city in June. He returned to New York in October, shortly before the Battle of White Plains.
4 Cain, "Samuel Hastings Jr."; Malcolm, *Peter's War*, p. 172. Malcolm inexplicably says they were captured at Long Island. This is clearly incorrect.
5 Pension Record # S30460.
6 Malcolm, *Peter's War* (pp. 172, 192), credits him with further service at Ticonderoga in May 1777, and then again in New York in November 1779, but this is obviously inconsistent with his own pension declaration. *Massachusetts Soldiers and Sailors*, Vol. VII, p. 475, does indeed record service by a Samuel Hastings as a corporal in Capt. Eli Parker's Company, Colonel Leonard's Regiment at Ticonderoga in May 1777, and also service by a Samuel Hastings as a private in Capt. Thomas Cowdin's Company, Col. Samuel Denny's Regiment at Claverack (New York) in November 1779. Neither record identifies the subject individual, and there are four other Samuel Hastings (from Amherst, Princeton, Lunenburg, and Greenfield) in the records who could equally qualify for this service. In neither record of service is there any evidence to attribute the service to Samuel Hastings (inst.). His pension declaration makes it quite clear that, as Cain, "Samuel Hastings Jr.," says, "Samuel sat out the remainder of the war."
7 Actually, father Samuel appears in *Lexington Births, Marriages and Deaths* mostly as Samuel Hastings, Jr. The author refers to him here as Sr. only to avoid confusion with son Samuel, who also appears in the records as Samuel

In November 1776, Samuel Hastings, Jr., was serving as a bodyguard to General Charles Lee when they were surprised by a British raiding party and captured in Basking Ridge, New Jersey. He details the story in his pension application in 1832. (National Archives)

Lydia Nelson of Lincoln in 1778 and moved into Lincoln, onto the property of Lydia's parents.[1] Although he lived in Lincoln and inherited the property from his father-in-law, he seems to have functioned primarily as part of the Lexington community. He continued to attend the Lexington church; he co-founded the Lexington Artillery Company (and served as its major); and reportedly he served as a Lexington Selectman. He died in Lincoln in 1834 at age 76. He is buried in the Old Burial Ground in Lexington.[2]

Hastings, Jr. It was common practice during this period to apply Sr. and Jr. to living generations, and to slide the terms down the ladder (as appropriate) with the passing of each generation. Thus, a Jr. would become Sr. upon the death of Sr., resulting (as in this case) in father and son both showing up in the record, sequentially, as Jr.

1 Lydia was the niece of Josiah Nelson (q.v.). The Nelson property straddled the Lincoln/Lexington town line, but the house occupied by Samuel and Lydia was located in Lincoln. See Malcolm, *The Scene of Battle* (pp. 3, 25–30) for an explanation of the Nelson-Hastings house and of the property of Lydia's parents.

2 *Vital Records of Lincoln; Lexington Births, Marriages and Deaths;* Cain, "Samuel Hastings Jr." See also Malcolm, *Peter's War*, p. 172. Cain reports that Samuel Hastings was born in Lincoln and raised in a house on the Lincoln/Lexington town line in what is now Minute Man National Historical Park. Clearly he has confused properties and generations. Samuel's birth is recorded in Lexington, not Lincoln, and there is no indication in either Malcolm or the Glass and Little Map of Lincoln of any Hastings property along the town line until he married Lydia and moved onto the farm of her parents.

His reported service as a Lexington Selectman is curious. While presumably he remained a property owner in Lexington, he appears to have remained a resident of Lincoln. The births of eight of Samuel (inst.) and Lydia's children were recorded in Lincoln (from 1780 to 1793), while their baptisms (also the baptism of a ninth child) were recorded in Lexington. Marriage records for the children are found in both towns: six of them (from 1807 to 1821) clearly state or imply a Lincoln residency; two of them (from 1819 and 1824) indicate a Lexington residency. Thus it is pretty clear that the family remained in Lincoln at least through this period.

Chapter 10: The Army of the Revolution

HENDERSON, Zodith
[also "Zoth," Zoath]

"Zoth" Henderson from Lincoln served in Capt. Abijah Child's Company, Col. John Greaton's 2nd Regiment, in 1777. His residence is listed as Lincoln, and his enlistment was credited for the town of Lincoln. He was reported transferred by prior enlistment to Colonel Cilley's Regiment.[1]

This individual is unidentified from the vital records of Lincoln and surrounding towns. Notwithstanding his residence being listed as Lincoln, Lincoln historian William Wheeler identifies him as an individual who was not from Lincoln, but was recruited to fulfill Lincoln's quota of 26 men for Continental service in 1777.[2]

HOAR, Brister[3]
[also Sippio BRISTER; Sipeo BRISTER; Bristol HOARE]

Brister Hoar served at Ticonderoga in 1776, in Capt. Asahel Wheeler's Company, Col. Jonathan Reed's Regiment.[4]

Brister Hoar was a slave belonging to John Hoar during his war service at Dorchester and Saratoga. After he became free, he changed his name to Sippio Brister. His gravestone in the old Precinct Burial Ground marks the only identified grave in Lincoln for a slave or former slave. (Photograph by Jack MacLean)

---

1 *Massachusetts Soldiers and Sailors*, Vol. VII, p. 721; Blake, "James Barrett's Returns of Men," p. 469. Note similarities in the enlistment records for Stephen Lufkin (q.v.) and John Barter (q.v.).
   Multiple enlistments in different units by a single individual, for purposes of collecting multiple enlistment bounties, was a fairly common scam. The record indicates that he was paid a bounty when he was mustered into Captain Child's Company, suggesting that he may have gotten away with it, at least initially.

2 Wheeler, "Lincoln," in Hurd, Vol. 2, p. 620. There is a Zoath Henderson in the Revolutionary War Land Grant Records (Pension Record # BLWT 2301-100), who was from Dover, New Hampshire, and who served in the Continental Army under Col. Enoch Poor and Col. George Reed. He died in 1790. There is, however, nothing in the pension declaration (made by his "lawful heir") to indicate any connection with or residence in the town of Lincoln. Accordingly, it is uncertain whether or not said Zoath Henderson is the same individual as "Zoth" Henderson (inst.).

3 Not to be confused with Brister Freeman of Concord, who was originally known as Brister Cuming, a slave of John Cuming of Concord, and is the individual after whom Brister Hill Road (off of Route 126, north of Route 2 in Concord) was named. He is said to have taken up residency near there after he received his freedom. Many chroniclers (including Henry David Thoreau) have made the error of confusing these two individuals, and the reader is alerted to be appropriately cautious concerning material relating to either of them.
   Brister Cuming served at Saratoga in Col. John Buttrick's Company of volunteers in 1777, then in 1779 he enlisted as Brister Freeman for nine months in the Continental Army.

4 "Treasurer's Accompts," June 10, 1779; Sudbury Miscellanous Records, pay receipts September 30, 1776 (Doc. # 109), December 16, 1776 (Doc. # 2204), December 26, 1776 (Doc. # 2208). The town paid John Hoar (q.v.) for this service, along with service at Dorchester in 1776, Saratoga in 1777, and Cambridge in 1778. However, this service cannot logically be attributed to John Hoar, who was age 69 at the time of the Ticonderoga service. The major portion of the payment seems to fit most closely with the service record of

He served at Dorchester during the winter of 1776–77, as a private in Capt. John Hartwell's Company, Col. Nicholas Dike's Regiment. He began his service on December 14, 1776, and served until March 1, 1777. This service was credited to the town of Lincoln.

Subsequently, he appears on the list, dated Lincoln, August 14, 1777, submitted by Capt. Samuel Farrar, Jr., to Col. Eleazer Brooks, of men raised to serve in the Continental Army; he is reported as serving in place of Joshua Child, Jr. (q.v.). He marched to the Northern Department, as a private in Capt. George Minot's Company, Col. Samuel Bullard's Regiment, to reinforce the army under General Gates. He served from August 16, 1777, through November 30, 1777 (credited with 3 months, 25 days of service, including 11 days for 220 miles of travel home), and he was present at the surrender of Burgoyne at Saratoga.[1]

In 1778, there is a possibility that he may have been back in service, at Cambridge, but this is speculative.[2]

Brister was a slave, belonging to John Hoar (q.v.). He was most likely in his early to mid-20s during his service at Saratoga. He subsequently received his freedom, and by 1791 he had changed his name to Sippio Brister. He remained in Lincoln until his death in 1820. He is buried in the old Precinct Burial Ground on Lexington Road.[3]

Leonard Hoar (q.v.). However, Ticonderoga service is missing from Leonard's pension declaration, suggesting that the Ticonderoga portion of this payment was for this service by Brister Hoar (inst.).

1 *Massachusetts Soldiers and Sailors,* Vol. VIII, pp. 2, 9; "Treasurer's Accompts," June 10, 1779. The town's payment to John Hoar (q.v.) for service at Dorchester and at Saratoga appear at first glance to apply to this service by Brister. However, the town's payment on the same day to Joshua Child, Jr. (q.v.), appears to cover Brister's Saratoga service. Leonard Hoar (q.v.) also served at both locations, and he appears to be the better fit for having provided the service for which John Hoar was paid (see note 4, p. 309). Accordingly, no payment record for Brister's Dorchester service has been found (or identified).

2 See note 4, p. 309. Leonard Hoar (q.v.) is recorded as having served at Cambridge in 1778, and he is the other likely candidate for the service covered by the Cambridge portion of the payment to John Hoar (q.v.).

3 MacLean, *A Rich Harvest,* pp. 294, 306; *Vital Records of Lincoln*; Biggs, "In Memorium," p. 190. Wheeler, "Lincoln" (in Hurd, Vol. 2, p. 623), says he was a slave until 1780. *Vital Records of Lincoln* indicates that he was age 64 when he died. This appears to be the source of MacLean's listing his age as 21 at Saratoga, and his having been born in 1756. Wheeler also says he was born in Boston in 1756. His headstone is the town's only marker for one of its former slaves.

Vital Records of Lincoln contains an entry for the January 14, 1753, baptism of "Brister, Negro boy of Mr. Timothy Wesson." If the reader may be tempted to speculate about connecting this record with Brister Hoar (inst.), then he or she is warned that this is the same trap that ensnared Thoreau and many others (see note 3, p. 309). Timothy Wesson's Brister appears logically to be the same individual as Brister Freeman. The connection is straightforward and direct: Timothy Wesson's daughter Abigail married Dr. John Cuming later that same year. It was Dr. John Cuming's slave, known as Brister Cuming, who became Brister Freeman upon manumission. Meredith, "People of Concord," pp. 105, 141, speculates that the child Brister may have been a wedding present to the wedded couple from the bride's father.

Wheeler's assertion that he was born in Boston is consistent with a story passed down through Hoar family lore about how Brister came to belong to the Hoar family. The story is attributed to Leonard Hoar, Jr., son of Leonard Hoar (q.v.): "It was the custom of farmer's wives to ride on horseback to Boston to do the marketing. Suspended across the back of the horse were two panniers or baskets for carrying market produce. One day, my grandmother [Elizabeth Hoar, wife of John Hoar (q.v.)] on her way to Boston was passing through Cambridge. A colored woman came out and begged her to take her baby, as she feared that if he remained with her, he would be sold as a slave. My grandmother could not decide so important a question on the spur of the moment, and promised to give an answer on her return. On her return, she found the colored woman waiting. She had in her arms a little black baby, with a bundle of his clothes. The baby and clothes were put in the saddle bags, and my grandmother proceeded home to Lincoln. Here, Scipio, the baby spent the rest of his life. In his boyhood he was the playmate of the Hoar children" ("Notes on the Hoar family"; "Family

Chapter 10: The Army of the Revolution

> Know all men by these presents that I John Hoar of Lincoln in the county of Midd.x in the colony of Massachusetts Bay in New England Gentleman — in consideration that my Negro man servant named Cuff hath been a good and faithfull servant unto me — and he now desiring to be made free: I do therefore by these presents for my self fully and absolutely free ~~him~~ and Discharge him the sd Cuff to act for himself so long as he behaves and conducts himself regularly and well — without the denial or contradiction of me his sd master
>
> Witness my hand
>
> Lincoln may 28th 1776
>
> Benjamin Danforth   John Hoar
> Abijah Pierce

"In consideration [of his] good and faithful" service, Cuff Hoar was freed by his master, John Hoar, in 1776. A year later, Cuff served with seven other Lincoln men on a mission to Worthington to supply the expedition escorting Burgoyne's captured army from Saratoga to Cambridge. (Courtesy of the New England Historic Genealogical Society, www.AmericanAncestors.org)

HOAR, Cuff
[also Cuff KNEELAND]

Cuff Hoar was paid by the town for taking a team with supplies to Worthington (in west-central Massachusetts) in 1777.[1]

There is a remote possibility that he may also have served at Ticonderoga in 1776, and/or at Dorchester in 1776.[2]

He had been a slave belonging to John Hoar, but he had been freed on May 28, 1776, and he was a free man when he went to Worthington. In 1778, he paid a poll tax and owned some personal property. In 1780, he changed his name to Cuff Kneeland. In 1781, he married Dinah Young of Sudbury. He died just a month later.[3]

HOAR, John

John Hoar from Lincoln went to Concord on the morning of April 19, 1775. He appears from his deposition to have been in arms, possibly as an un-enlisted volunteer, or possibly as a member of Lincoln's militia company.[4]

---

history on the Hoar family"). It is interesting that the story seems to imply that Brister was not a slave. And as fascinating as the story is to contemplate, it is of course unverifiable. (For a slightly different version of this story—whether ultimately from the same source or a different source is uncertain—see Hafner, "Sippio Brister"). Hafner concludes that given the plight of many urban slave women, giving away a child was often preferable and more hopeful than most other courses of action.

1 "Treasurer's Accompts," November 11, 1779. Shattuck, *History of the Town of Concord*, p. 300, says the Worthington expedition occurred in 1777, but the precise dates and purpose remain unidentified. The author speculates that it might have been undertaken in October to supply the troops escorting Burgoyne's captured army from Saratoga to Cambridge. The escort included a contingent of Lincoln men in a company commanded by Lincoln's Capt. Samuel Farrar, Jr. (q.v.). While the Worthington expedition appears not to have been military service in a formal sense, i.e., as part of a formally constituted military unit, per se, this was clearly considered by the town at the time to be a material part of its war effort, and it was unmistakably included in the town's accounting of expenses incurred in the war. Shattuck and MacLean, *A Rich Harvest* (p. 295), have also treated it accordingly. Notwithstanding the uncertainty of its precise dates and purpose, as a measure of its importance, by contrast, the carting of supplies into Cambridge for the Army was not included in the town's war accounting.

2 "Treasurer's Accompts," June 10, 1779. The town paid John Hoar (q.v.) for service at Ticonderoga in 1776, at Dorchester in 1776, at Saratoga in 1777, and at Cambridge in 1778. However, at age 69, John Hoar assuredly did not provide this service; Leonard Hoar (q.v.) and Brister Hoar (q.v.) are the most likely candidates for this service, but the possibility that Cuff might have provided service at Ticonderoga or Dorchester cannot be ruled out entirely.

3 MacLean, *A Rich Harvest*, p. 306; *Vital Records of Lincoln*; *Vital Records of Sudbury*. His manumission document, dated Lincoln, May 28, 1776, is found in the Library of the New England Historic Genealogical Society (document # Mss A 6628). The fact that the town paid him (rather than John Hoar) for the Worthington expedition is consistent with his being a free man by this time. Service at Saratoga in 1777 and at Cambridge in 1778, for which the town paid John Hoar (q.v.), was therefore probably not provided by Cuff, who would likely have been paid directly for such service (see note 2).

His marriage intention is recorded in Lincoln, January 3, 1781; the marriage itself is recorded in Sudbury (as "Cuff Reland") as having occurred in Wayland (then still known as East Sudbury), February 8, 1781; his death is recorded in Lincoln, March 11, 1781.

4 Deposition of John Hoar, et al.; Bond, *Genealogies of the Families of Watertown*, p. 298; Hoar, *Autobiography*, p. 20. A general premise seems to exist among many modern chroniclers that individuals who went to Concord on April 19th, who were not members of the Minute Company, must have been members of the militia company. There is an easy logic to this, but there are a couple of individuals for whom a personal logic might be more appropriate. Because John Hoar was age 68, it is not likely that he was considered any longer of service

Chapter 10: The Army of the Revolution

The home of John Hoar was built in about 1712. John was sixty-nine years old when he went to Concord on April 19, 1775, with his son, Samuel, who was a lieutenant in the minute company. His other son, Leonard, and slaves Cuff and Brister also served subsequently in the war. (Courtesy of Lincoln Town Archives, Lincoln, MA)

Subsequently, he was paid by the town for service at Ticonderoga in 1776, at Dorchester in 1776, at Saratoga in 1777, and at Cambridge in 1778.[1] He was also reimbursed for clothing for the army. However, as he was age 69 at the time of the Ticonderoga campaign, there is no logic to believing that he actually provided this service.

This service may have been served by his son, Leonard Hoar (q.v.), but it is likely that at least a piece of it may have been served by his slave, Brister Hoar (q.v.). The additional possibility that his son, Samuel Hoar (q.v.), or another of his slaves, Cuff Hoar (q.v.), might have provided pieces of this service cannot be ruled out.[2]

---

age for the militia. He probably went to Concord for personal reasons (perhaps to accompany his son, Samuel (q.v.), with the idea of helping if needed, or perhaps as an act of personal defiance to the British incursion).

Notwithstanding his age at the time, there is no doubt that this is the John Hoar who went to Concord. He had two sons named John; the first had died young, the second was born in 1768. Therefore, we cannot attribute this Concord service to a John Jr.

Hoar family tradition says that while John Hoar and his son Samuel were in arms at Concord, the house served as a gathering spot for women and children in the neighborhood, where they hid in the woods, with John's 15-year-old [actually, he was age 16 at the time] son, Leonard Hoar (q.v.), and slave Brister Hoar (q.v.) keeping lookout (see MacLean, *A Rich Harvest*, pp. 276–77). A wonderful account of this story, including their feeding of a militia company that had been marching all night, can be found in "Notes on the Hoar family" and "Family history on the Hoar family": They "passed from the front door to back, filling their pockets, without stopping to eat, went over the brook, and proceeded on their way to Concord." The story may be apocryphal (see note 1, p. 316).

1 "Treasurer's Accompts," June 10, 1779.
2 The initial presumption is that the four stints covered by the transaction were all served by the same individual, which makes Leonard the compelling choice. Not only is he recorded as being at Dorchester in 1776, at Saratoga in 1777, and at Cambridge in 1778, but also he appears not to have been otherwise paid for that service. In addition, he was in service at Rhode Island at the time of the transaction, which explains why the

John Hoar was the son of Lt. Daniel Hoar and Sarah (Jones) Hoar; born in 1707. He had married Esther Peirce in 1734, then Elizabeth Coolidge in 1740. He was the father of Leonard Hoar (q.v.) and Samuel Hoar (q.v.); father-in-law of Edmund Bowman (q.v.), Nehemiah Abbot (q.v.), and Samuel Farrar, Jr. (q.v.).

He had previously served in King George's War (1744–1748). He had been taken captive from Fort Drummer (now Brattleboro, Vermont) in 1748 and held prisoner by the Indians for three months. He died in 1786 at age 79 and is buried in the Meeting House Cemetery behind Bemis Hall.[1]

HOAR, Leonard

Leonard Hoar may have served at Ticonderoga in 1776, but this is uncertain.[2]

He did serve as a private in Capt. John Hartwell's Company, Col. Nicholas Dike's Regiment, guarding the coastline at Dorchester Heights from December 14, 1776, to March 1, 1777. He served as a waiter to Captain Hartwell, and his service was credited to the town of Lincoln.

Later in 1777, he volunteered to go to Saratoga with Capt. Samuel Farrar, Jr.'s Company, which was urgently drafted out of Col. Eleazer Brooks's Regiment, assigned to Col. Jonathan Reed's Middlesex County Regiment (Brig. Gen. James Bricket's Brigade of Massachusetts Militia), and sent to reinforce General Gates on September 29, 1777. He arrived at camp "just after the firing ceased" but witnessed British General Burgoyne's surrender on October 17. He served with his unit as part of the escort which marched Burgoyne's troops to Prospect Hill in Cambridge. There he was discharged "after all things were settled at the hill" on November 7, 1777 (credited with 1 month, 10 days of service).

Instead of returning to Lincoln, however, he appears to have transferred into Capt. Simon Hunt's Company, Col. Eleazer Brooks's Regiment, which had been activated on November 3, 1777, for five months of guard duty over Burgoyne's troops, from their November 7, 1777, arrival at Cambridge through April 3, 1778.

He appears to have reenlisted for a second stint of guard duty on April 1, 1788, serving as a private in Capt. Daniel Harrington's Company, Col. Jonathan Reed's Regiment of

---

payment would have been made to John. However, the fact that Leonard's pension declaration makes no mention of Ticonderoga service casts doubt on the initial presumption.

While it is not a given that the four stints were necessarily all served by the same individual, there is little in the records of Samuel Hoar (q.v.) or Cuff Hoar (q.v.) to encourage attributing the stints to them. Samuel Hoar was at Ticonderoga and was paid by the town directly for his service. Cuff Hoar left no record of formal military service, at all. But while there is little to encourage this, there also is little to preclude it.

Brister Hoar (q.v.), on the other hand, is recorded as having been at Saratoga (for which the town paid Joshua Child Jr. (q.v.) on June 10, 1779), and at Dorchester (for which no payment record has been found). He appears to be the logical candidate for the Ticonderoga service covered by this payment.

1 *Concord, Massachusetts: Births, Marriages, and Deaths*; *Vital Records of Lincoln*; *Lexington Births, Marriages and Deaths*; Hoar, *Autobiography*, p. 20; Biggs, "In Memorium," pp. 175, 176. See also Nourse, *The Hoar Family*. His age at the time of his death is given on his headstone as 80. This appears to be incorrect, as he seems to have died before reaching his 80th birthday. He died before the marriage of his daughter Sarah to Nehemiah Abbot (q.v.).

2 "Treasurer's Accompts," June 10, 1779. The town paid John Hoar (q.v.) for this service, but at age 69, he was too old to have provided this service. Cuff Hoar (q.v.) and Brister Hoar (q.v.) are possible candidates to have done so, but overall the transaction seems to be a better fit for service by Leonard. On the other hand, the omission of Ticonderoga service from Leonard's pension declaration suggests that this service may not have been provided by him (see note 1, p. 315).

Guards, from April 2, 1778, to July 3, 1778 (credited with 3 months, 2 days of service) at Cambridge.[1]

On May 18, 1779, he was back in service in Capt. Lawson Buckminster's Company, Lt. Col. Samuel Pierce's Regiment, at Rhode Island. He served at Providence, Taunton, Howland's Ferry, and Tiverton, until July 1, 1779 (credited with 1 month, 17 days of service, including 72 miles of travel home).

He returned to Rhode Island with Capt. Samuel Heald's Light Infantry Company, Col. John Jacobs's Regiment, from September 16, 1779, to November 16, 1779 (credited with 2 months, 4 days of service, including 72 miles of travel home).[2]

From July 27, 1780, to October 30, 1780, he served with Capt. Abraham Andrews's Company, Col. Cyprian How's Regiment, detached for three months from the Middlesex County Militia to reinforce the Continental Army at Rhode Island. He marched to Newport and served for 3 months, 7 days.[3]

He was age 18 during his initial service, possibly at Ticonderoga, or later at Dorchester; son of John Hoar (q.v.) and Elizabeth (Coolidge) Hoar; brother of Samuel Hoar (q.v.); brother-in-law of Edmund Bowman (q.v.) and Samuel Farrar, Jr. (q.v.); later brother-in-law of Nehemiah Abbot (q.v.). He married Eunice Wheeler, daughter of Edmond Wheeler (q.v.), in 1785. Later, he became active in town affairs and served as toll keeper on the Cambridge Turnpike, where he also operated the family farm as an inn. Eunice died in 1820 at age 56, and in 1822 he married Pamela Hodgman of Stoddard, New Hampshire,

---

1 *Massachusetts Soldiers and Sailors*, Vol. VIII, pp. 6, 10; "Treasurer's Accompts," June 10, 1779; Pension Record # S29229. The town paid John Hoar (q.v.) for service at Ticonderoga in 1776, at Dorchester in 1776, at Saratoga in 1777, and at Cambridge in 1778 (See "Treasurer's Accompts," June 10, 1779). At age 69, it is apparent that John Hoar did not provide this service. As Leonard is recorded as serving at Dorchester in 1776, at Saratoga in 1777, and at Cambridge in 1778, this payment (except for the Ticonderoga portion) appears to be a better fit for known service by Leonard than by Samuel Hoar (q.v.), Brister Hoar (q.v.), or Cuff Hoar (q.v.). Furthermore, Leonard does not appear to have been otherwise paid for this service, and as he was serving at Rhode Island at the time of the town's payment, a logical explanation exists for the payment having been made to John rather than to Leonard directly.

Leonard's five months of service in Simon Hunt's Company is from his pension declaration, but it does not appear in *Massachusetts Soldiers and Sailors*. Inversely, his three-months of service in Capt. Daniel Harrington's Company is from *Massachusetts Soldiers and Sailors*, but it does not appear in his pension declaration. It would be easy to conclude from this confusion that there was probably only one stint of guard duty at Cambridge, but both records contain sufficient detail to be credible. As unusual as it may have been to have served three consecutive terms of guard duty (including the escort of the prisoners to Cambridge), the author cannot impeach any of the three records.

2 *Massachusetts Soldiers and Sailors*, Vol. VIII, pp. 6, 10; Pension Record # S29229. In his pension declaration, he rounds his terms of service up to two months with Colonel Pierce, and three months with Colonel Jacobs.

3 Ibid. Also "Treasurer's Accompts," July 10, 1782, and March 25, 1784. Both "Treasurer's Accompts" records were for three months of service at Rhode Island in 1780. While it appears that he may have been paid twice for this service, several more benign explanations may exist. Most probably, since no other record exists of his having been paid for either of the 1779 stints, possibly the 1782 payment may have mistakenly recorded 1780, but may actually have been for one or both of the 1779 Rhode Island services. Alternatively, the payments may have been partial payments (although they are not recorded as such). It is remotely possible that he may have served two stints in Rhode Island in 1780.

There is even the possibility that he may have served again at Rhode Island in 1781, and that the 1784 payment was for service in 1781. The legibility of the handwriting in this record leaves this possibility open (without having to attribute a mistake in the record). However, as there is no evidence (or any such claim in his pension record) to corroborate the speculation of further service at Rhode Island after service with Colonel How, the author considers such possibilities unlikely.

who died seven years later at age 52. He died in 1842 at age 84 and is buried in the Meeting House Cemetery behind Bemis Hall.[1]

HOAR, Samuel

Samuel Hoar was a second lieutenant in Capt. William Smith's Company of Minute Men from Lincoln, Col. Abijah Peirce's Regiment.[2] Following the engagement at Concord, he served for 26 days in Cambridge.[3] He was reimbursed by the town for his accoutrements as a minute man.[4]

He served as a second lieutenant in Capt. John Hartwell's Militia Company from Lincoln, Col. Eleazer Brooks's 3rd Middlesex County Regiment, which marched from Lincoln to fortify Dorchester Heights on March 4, 1776. The unit was discharged five days later, on March 9, after the threat of a British assault on the fortifications had subsided, General Howe having begun preparations to evacuate Boston.

On March 27, 1776, he was commissioned first lieutenant in Capt. Samuel Farrar, Jr.'s 6th Company, Col. Eleazer Brooks's 3rd Middlesex County Regiment of Militia.[5]

Subsequently, he served at Ticonderoga as a second lieutenant in Capt. Asahel Wheeler's Company, Col. Jonathan Reed's Regiment, probably from July through November 1776. He was paid by the town for this service.[6]

---

1 *Vital Records of Lincoln*; MacLean, *A Rich Harvest*, pp. 331, 374; Bond, *Genealogies of the Families of Watertown*, p. 298; Biggs, "In Memorium," p. 175.

Hoar family lore says that while John Hoar (q.v.) and Samuel Hoar (q.v.) were in arms at Concord, the family home became the gathering spot for women and children in the neighborhood, with sixteen-year-old Leonard, and Brister Hoar (q.v.), keeping lookout. There appears to have been a lookout spot hidden in the woods, but in one particular version of the story, Leonard and Brister were hiding in the cellar, when they saw troops approaching. At first they thought the troops to be British Regulars, but they soon realized that they were a militia unit. The men had been "traveling all night" and were hungry. Whereupon, they brought up cider from the cellar, laid out a whole cheese and seven loaves of freshly baked bread on the bar, and opened the front and back doors. The troops then "passed from the front door to back, filling their pockets, without stopping to eat, went over the brook, and proceeded on their way to Concord." (This account, evidently as recorded by Senator George Frisbie Hoar, is found in "Notes on the Hoar family" and "Family history on the Hoar family"; see also MacLean, *A Rich Harvest*, pp. 276–277.) The prodigious quantity of food and cider along with the reference to the bar appear to be anachronistic to the story, as the home was not opened as a tavern until many years later.

2 Coburn, *Muster Rolls*.

3 *Massachusetts Soldiers and Sailors*, Vol. VIII, pp. 7–8.

4 "Treasurer's Accompts," February 19, 1776.

5 *Massachusetts Soldiers and Sailors*, Vol. VIII, pp. 7–8.

6 *Massachusetts Soldiers and Sailors*, Vol. VIII, pp. 7–8; "Treasurer's Accompts," June 15, 1779; Shattuck, *History of the Town of Concord*, pp. 124, 299, 354. *Massachusetts Soldiers and Sailors* gives September 30, 1776, to November 1, 1776, as the dates for this service, but this record is a payroll receipt for a specific pay period, and therefore it does not necessarily indicate the starting and ending times of this service. Shattuck's date of June 25, 1776, appears to be the date of the resolve rather than the commencement of service. Shattuck gives the length of service variably as four, five, and six months, but the resolve specifies until December 1, 1776, unless sooner discharged. Colonel Reed was allowed rations from June 26 through Nov. 30; Captain Wheeler was allowed rations from July 25 through Nov. 30 (see *Massachusetts Soldiers and Sailors*, Vol. XIII, p. 77; Vol. XVI, p. 962). Accordingly, it appears likely that Samuel Hoar served from approximately July 25, 1776, through November 30, 1776. The author has made no attempt to reconcile the existence of the payroll receipt (recorded in *Massachusetts Soldiers and Sailors*) with the town's payment (recorded in the "Treasurer's Accompts"). See also Sudbury Miscellaneous Records, pay receipts December 16, 1776 (Doc. # 2204).

He was age 31 when he answered the Alarm on April 19, 1775; son of John Hoar (q.v.) and Elizabeth (Coolidge) Hoar; brother of Leonard Hoar (q.v.) and brother-in-law of Edmund Bowman (q.v.) and Samuel Farrar, Jr. (q.v.). He had married Susanna Peirce, daughter of Abijah Peirce (q.v.), in 1773. Later, he became the brother-in-law of Nehemiah Abbot (q.v.).

After the war, he served as a captain of the Lincoln Militia Company, and he became one of Lincoln's leading political figures, an influential judge, and one of the region's most respected patriarchs. In 1786, with the economy still roiling from the impact of the war, he and Samuel Farrar, Jr. (q.v.) represented Lincoln in a conference to deal with the growing credit and foreclosure problem which sparked Shays' Rebellion in the central and western counties of Massachusetts (and which affected a number of families in Lincoln, as well). He died in 1832 at age 88, and he is buried in the Meeting House Cemetery behind Bemis Hall.[1]

HOSMER, Amos

Amos Hosmer may have marched to Dorchester Heights as a 16-year old private, in Capt. Joseph Hosmer's Militia Company from Concord, Col. Eleazer Brooks's Regiment on March 4, 1776. The unit participated in the fortification of Dorchester Heights, and served for five days until it became clear that British General Howe had called off his plan to attack the fortifications, and that he was instead preparing to evacuate his troops from Boston. It is uncertain whether this record applies to Amos Hosmer of Lincoln, or to another Amos Hosmer of Concord.[2]

A year later, he appears to have served at Rhode Island, in Capt. Jesse Wyman's Company, Col. Josiah Whitney's Regiment, from May 10, 1777, to July 10, 1777, credited with 2 months, 9 days of service (including 8 days of travel to and from).[3]

He served in the Saratoga Campaign, marching northward on August 16, 1777, in Capt. George Minot's Company, Col. Samuel Bullard's Regiment. Following the surrender of British General Burgoyne, Col. Bullard's Regiment marched south and served through the end of November, but for some reason, Amos Hosmer was discharged on October 17, 1777, having served 2 months, 11 days (including 9 days travel home).[4]

He served again from September 22, 1778, through December 31, 1778, in Capt. David Goodwin's Company, Col. Cogswell's Regiment, to reinforce elements of the Continental Army on coastal defense in and around Boston.[5]

He was the son of William Hosmer, Sr. (q.v.) and Anna (Heald) Hosmer; brother of William Hosmer, Jr. (q.v.); age 15 when the war broke out on April 19, 1775.[6] Between stints, he went to Chester, Vermont with his brother William, where he appears on a list of

---

1 *Vital Records of Lincoln*; MacLean, *A Rich Harvest*, pp. 271, 301, 311; Biggs, "In Memorium," p. 176.
2 *Massachusetts Soldiers and Sailors*, Vol. VIII, p. 287. Amos (inst.) had an uncle Amos Hosmer in Concord, who was age 41 at the time of Dorchester Heights. This service record could belong to Uncle Amos or to an unidentified Amos Hosmer.
3 *Massachusetts Soldiers and Sailors*, Vol. VIII, p. 261. This record is credited to an Amos Hosmer of Weston. No Amos Hosmer is identifiable in Weston, but Amos's (inst.) family lived next to the Lincoln–Weston boundary.
4 *Massachusetts Soldiers and Sailors*, Vol. VIII, p. 287.
5 *Massachusetts Soldiers and Sailors*, Vol. VIII, p. 291.
6 *Vital Records of Lincoln*. His mother's name also appears as Ann.

Freemen dated September 7, 1778.[1] He married Sibbil Parker of Chester in 1784. He died in Chester in 1831, at age 71, and is buried in Brookside Cemetery.[2]

HOSMER, Daniel

Daniel Hosmer was a private in Capt. William Smith's Company of Minute Men from Lincoln, Col. Abijah Peirce's Regiment.[3] Following the engagement at Concord, he served for five days in Cambridge.[4]

On May 8, 1775, he enlisted for eight months as a private in Capt. William Smith's Company, Col. John Nixon's 16th Massachusetts Regiment in the rapidly organizing Massachusetts Provincial Army. Presumably, he participated with his unit at the Battle of Bunker Hill, on June 17. A company return, dated September 30, 1775, lists him as sick and absent, but he appears to have served out his term and been discharged on January 1, 1776.[5]

He enlisted again, and served as a private in Capt. Asahel Wheeler's Company, Col. John Robinson's Regiment, from February 4, 1776, through the departure of the British forces from Boston, until April 1776 (credited with 1 month, 28 days of service).[6]

He served at Ticonderoga as an ensign in Capt. Asahel Wheeler's Company, Col. Jonathan Reed's Regiment, probably from around July 25, 1776, through the end of November 1776.[7]

He appears to have served at Saratoga during the climactic battle in October 1777, but this is uncertain. The unit with which he may have served, and the dates of service, are unknown, but his name appears on a list of "men who went at the time of taking Burgoyne."[8]

He was age 29 when he responded to the Alarm of April 19, 1775; the son of Daniel and Bethia Hosmer of Concord. He had been married to Hannah Baker of Lincoln since 1768. Hannah was the sister of Amos Baker (q.v.), Jacob Baker, Jr. (q.v.), James Baker (q.v.), Nathaniel Baker (q.v.), and Samuel Baker (q.v.), and the daughter of Jacob Baker, Sr. (q.v.).

---

1 Aldrich and Holmes, *History of Windsor County*, pp. 670–671. Evidently, he had already begun to put down roots in Chester, despite his subsequent departure for further service.
2 Aldrich and Holmes, *History of Windsor County*, p. 821; "Find A Grave"; Heald, "Heald Family of Concord"; "Vermont Vital Records." Sibbil appears to be the sister of Hannah, who married his brother William.
3 Coburn, *Muster Rolls*.
4 *Massachusetts Soldiers and Sailors*, Vol. VIII, pp. 261, 286, 287.
5 *Massachusetts Soldiers and Sailors*, Vol. VIII, pp. 261, 286, 287; Pension Record # S29244. A record in *Massachusetts Soldiers and Sailors* indicates that he appears on a list of eight-month men, without dates or particulars. This record logically applies to his eight-month service at Cambridge in 1775. In August 1775, Colonel Nixon's Regiment became known as the 5th Regiment under Washington's Continental command.
6 Ibid. A receipt for wages, rations, etc. dated Sudbury, April 10, 1778, appears to apply to this service in 1776, rather than to separate service in 1778.
7 Shattuck, *History of the Town of Concord*, p. 354. For an explanation of the indicated dates, see note 6, p. 316.
8 *Massachusetts Soldiers and Sailors*, Vol. VIII, pp. 261, 286, 287; Pension Record # S29244. The precise meaning of "men who went at the time of taking Burgoyne" is not clear, but the supposition that the men on this list served at Saratoga seems reasonable. On the other hand, the absence of any mention in his pension declaration of service at Saratoga is curious, suggesting a different interpretation. The author is at a loss to identify any such different interpretation, so the reader is left to speculate not only about the details of this service, but also about whether or not any such different interpretation of the list may be appropriate.

In 1819, Hosmer moved to Temple, Maine, and then in 1830, he moved to Farmington, Maine.[1]

HOSMER, William, Jr.[2]

William Hosmer was a private in Capt. William Smith's Company of Minute Men from Lincoln, Col. Abijah Peirce's Regiment. This was probably William Hosmer, Jr.[3] Following the engagement at Concord, he served for nine days in Cambridge.[4] He was reimbursed by the town for part of a set of accoutrements as a minute man.[5]

The following summer, in June or July 1776, he marched to Ticonderoga in Capt. Asahel Wheeler's Company, Col. Jonathan Reed's Regiment, and served for four or five months, through November 1776.[6]

Upon his return from Ticonderoga, he enlisted on December 20, 1776, to serve on coastal defense around Dorchester. He served in Capt. Moses Harrington's Company, Colonel Dike's Regiment, and his service was credited to the town of Lincoln. This regiment was raised to serve until March 1, 1777, but Hosmer is reported to have been discharged on February 22, 1777.[7]

He was the son of William Hosmer, Sr. (q.v.) and Anna (Heald) Hosmer; brother of Amos Hosmer (q.v.); age 17 when he answered the Alarm on April 19, 1775.[8] After his service, he went with his brother Amos to Chester, Vermont, where he appears on a list of Freemen dated September 7, 1778.[9] He married Hannah Parker of Chester in 1781. He served as a Selectman and State Representative, and died in Chester in 1813, at age 55. He is buried in Brookside Cemetery.[10]

---

1 *Concord, Massachusetts: Births, Marriages, and Deaths*; *Vital Records of Lincoln*; Pension Record # S29244. Interestingly, *Vital Records of Lincoln* lists their intent to marry 17 days after *Concord, Massachusetts: Births, Marriages, and Deaths* indicate that they were married.

2 The designations "Jr." and "Sr." have been added for clarity. The historical record contains no such designations.

3 Coburn, *Muster Rolls*. The historical records do not indicate whether this was William Hosmer, Jr., or William Hosmer, Sr. (q.v.). MacLean, *A Rich Harvest* (p. 257) concludes that this is William Jr., presumably because he fits the age profile of the Minute Company better than does William Sr. [According to MacLean, there were four Minute Men who were age 17 (including Hosmer), three who were age 18, and six who were age 19. At the other end of the scale, there were four at age 35/36, three at age 39, one at age 40, and one at age 43. William Hosmer, Sr. was age 45.] While no hard evidence one way or the other seems to exist, MacLean's interpretation appears reasonable.

  Supporting logic is the evidence that William Sr. was at Lexington on April 23 executing a deposition. Therefore, the individual who remained in service at Cambridge until April 28 must have been William Jr.

4 *Massachusetts Soldiers and Sailors*, Vol. VIII, pp. 257, 291.

5 "Treasurer's Accompts," July 10, 1777.

6 Sudbury Miscellaneous Records, pay receipts dated September 30, 1776 (Doc. # 109), December 16, 1776 (Doc. # 2204), and March 17, 1777 (Doc. # 2209).

7 *Massachusetts Soldiers and Sailors*, Vol. VIII, pp. 257, 291. Attributing this service to William Hosmer, Jr., follows logically from his being identified as the William Hosmer who was a minute man. However, there is no hard evidence to rule out the possibility that this service may have been provided by William Hosmer, Sr.

8 *Vital Records of Lincoln*. His mother's name also appears as Ann.

9 Aldrich and Holmes, *History of Windsor County*, pp. 670-671.

10 Aldrich and Holmes, *History of Windsor County*, pp. 672-673; "Find A Grave"; Heald, "Heald Family of Concord"; "Vermont Vital Records." Hannah appears to be the sister of Sibbil, who married his brother Amos.

HOSMER, William, Sr.[1]

William Hosmer, Sr., was in arms at Concord on the morning of April 19, 1775, probably as a member of Lincoln's militia company.[2]

It is possible that he may subsequently have served at Dorchester as a private in Capt. Moses Harrington's Company, Colonel Dike's Regiment, from December 20, 1776, to February 22, 1777, but this service is more logically attributable to William Hosmer, Jr. (q.v.).[3]

He was the son of Nathaniel and Elizabeth Hosmer of Concord; a housewright and joiner; age 45 when he took up arms on April 19, 1775. He had been married to Ann Heald since 1753, and had been a member of Lincoln's original militia company in 1757. He was the father of William Hosmer, Jr. (q.v.) and Amos Hosmer (q.v.). He died in Mason, New Hampshire, in 1802 at age 72, and he is buried in Pleasant View Cemetery in Mason.[4]

JONES, Amos

Amos Jones of Weston marched on the Alarm of April 19, 1775, as a private in Capt. Samuel Lamson's Company. He served for three days.[5]

Subsequently, on April 29, 1775, he enlisted as a private in Capt. Abijah Child's Company, Colonel Gardner's Regiment, and served in the Battle of Bunker Hill. He reported that he was on Charlestown Neck during the battle and saw Colonel Gardner "after he received his mortal wound." After Colonel Gardner's death, the regiment was commanded by Lt. Col. William Bond.[6]

His stature is given as five feet, five inches. Despite the claim in his pension record that he served for 8 months, 15 days, he appears to have served for only about four months. A company return dated October 6, 1775, reports that he was discharged on October 1, 1775, and that his place was taken by Solomon Jones.[7]

---

1 The historical record contains no such "Jr." or "Sr." designation for William Hosmer. These have been added for clarity.

2 Deposition of John Hoar, et al. The deposition states that the deponents were of lawful age, which the prevailing wisdom suggests was age 18 or 21 in colonial Massachusetts. William Hosmer, Jr., at age 17, would have been considered under the legal age for the deposition. In addition, William Jr. was in service at Cambridge on April 23, when the depositions were taken at Lexington. Therefore, the deposition is believed to have been executed by William Hosmer, Sr.

3 *Massachusetts Soldiers and Sailors*, Vol. VIII, pp. 257, 291. Attributing this service to William Hosmer, Jr. (q.v.), follows logically from his being identified as the William Hosmer who was a minute man. However, there is no hard evidence to rule out the possibility that this service may have been provided by William Hosmer, Sr.

4 *Concord, Massachusetts: Births, Marriages, and Deaths; Vital Records of Lincoln;* MacLean, *A Rich Harvest*, p. 179; Martin, "The Sons of Lincoln," p. 25; *SAR Revolutionary War Graves Register*. Ann also appears in the record as Anna.

5 *Massachusetts Soldiers and Sailors*, Vol. VIII, p. 898.

6 Pension Record # S13560; *Massachusetts Soldiers and Sailors*, Vol. VIII, p. 898.

7 Ibid. See also *Massachusetts Soldiers and Sailors*, Vol. VIII, p. 959. Despite the similarity of names, Solomon Jones was probably not closely related. He is most likely the son of Moses and Hannah, age 33, who is listed in *Town of Weston, Births, Deaths, & Marriages* as a Revolutionary soldier. *Town of Weston, Births, Deaths, & Marriages* lists another Solomon, who is another possibility. He appears to be Amos's uncle (son of James and Abigail), also age 33. Uncle Solomon, however, was a blacksmith by trade, unmarried, and had left Weston for Barre in 1768 or 1769. Because these two Solomons were of the same age, considerable confusion accompanies

He was age 20 during his service at Cambridge; the son of Lemuel and Anna (Stimson) Jones of Weston. He married Azubah Russell of Weston in 1779. They moved to Lincoln in the 1800s, where he died in 1836 at age 81.[1]

KNOWLTON, Jeremiah

Jeremiah Knowlton served in the campaign at New York from September 27, 1776, for two months as a sergeant in Capt. Simon Hunt's Company, Col. Eleazer Brooks's Massachusetts Militia Regiment from Middlesex County. Following the Battle of White Plains on October 28, he was reported sick and in camp. He was discharged from North Castle on November 16, 1776, with an 11-day travel allowance home.[2]

A year later he served in the campaign to reinforce General Gates at Saratoga, although the details of this service are not known.[3]

On August 1, 1778, he enlisted as a private in Capt. Francis Brown's Company, Colonel McIntosh's Massachusetts Militia Regiment (Brig. Gen. Solomon Lovell's Brigade) in Rhode Island. He served 1 month, 14 days, until September 11, 1778, during which he participated in the Battle of Rhode Island on August 29, 1778.[4]

He was the son of Jeremiah and Sarah (Allen) Knowlton of Sudbury; age 31 during his 1776 service. Originally from Concord, he is identified as a resident of Lexington when he married Abigail Pierce of Waltham in 1771.[5] Abigail died in February 1776, and he married Hannah Goffe about seven months later (just 18 days before marching on the New York campaign). He remained in Lincoln at least through 1780, but he appears to have been living in Weston when he died in 1785 at age 40.[6]

---

their identities. *Town of Weston, Births, Deaths, & Marriages* (p. 571) attempts to straighten out the facts, declaring Bond, *Genealogies of the Families of Watertown* to be wrong.

1 *Town of Weston, Births, Deaths, & Marriages*; *Vital Records of Lincoln*; Pension Record # S13560. It was most likely after 1802 and before 1832 when Amos and Azubah moved to Lincoln. They had nine children recorded in Weston through 1802; none are recorded in Lincoln. Three sons and two daughters appear to have been living in Weston when they were married (1806, 1810, 1813, 1819, and 1823). On the other hand, daughters Betsey and Elmira were listed as "of Lincoln" in their marriage records (1807, 1827). Their ties to Weston evidently remained strong, even when they resided in Lincoln; both character witnesses (including a minister) in Amos's pension application were from Weston. *Vital Records of Lincoln* lists his age at death as 79, but if his birth record in *Town of Weston, Births, Deaths, & Marriages* is correct, he was actually two years older than that.

2 *Massachusetts Soldiers and Sailors*, Vol. XI, p. 503. He was paid by the town for this service. (See "Treasurer's Accompts," June 15, 1779. See also Wheeler, "Lincoln," in Hurd, Vol. 2, p. 623; *Muster Rolls of the Revolutionary War*, Vol. 55, file L, p. 24.)

3 "Treasurer's Accompts," June 15, 1779; Wheeler, "Lincoln," in Hurd, Vol. 2, p. 623. Wheeler's source is unidentified, but it is probable that it may be the "Treasurer's Accompts".

4 *Massachusetts Soldiers and Sailors*, Vol. IX, p. 383. Also Wheeler, "Lincoln," in Hurd, Vol. 2, p. 623.

5 *Concord, Massachusetts: Births, Marriages, and Deaths*; *Lexington Births, Marriages and Deaths*; *Vital Records of Sudbury*. Notwithstanding their apparent Lexington/Waltham residencies, the birth of their first child six weeks before they were married was recorded in *Vital Records of Lincoln*, not in Lexington or Waltham. If both dates are correct, then it would appear that they settled in Lincoln after getting married, and that they simply waited to record the birth of their child until after they had taken up residence.

6 *Vital Records of Lincoln*; *Town of Weston, Births, Deaths, & Marriages*. His third child with Hannah (Abigail previously bore him two) is recorded in Lincoln in 1780. His death is recorded in Weston, with the notation that Hannah and the family moved to Concord thereafter. However, *Concord, Massachusetts: Births, Marriages, and Deaths* contains no further information, suggesting that she may have moved from Concord before she died.

LANDER, John

[also LANDA, LANDEA, LANDY, LANCTAY, LANGTRY[1]]

John Lander served as a private in Capt. John Hartwell's Lincoln Militia Company, Col. Eleazer Brooks's 3rd Middlesex County Regiment, which marched from Lincoln to fortify Dorchester Heights on March 4, 1776. The unit was discharged five days later, on March 9, after the threat of a British assault on the fortifications had subsided, and General Howe had begun preparations to evacuate Boston. He was paid for this service the following September.[2]

He appears to have gone to Ticonderoga during the summer of 1776, serving through November 1776 in Capt. Asahel Wheeler's Company, Col. Jonathan Reed's Regiment. The service record has not been found, but his name appears on a receipt dated Sudbury, March 17, 1777, declaring "Received of Capt. Asahel Wheeler two pound in full of all our wagers and Rations & arrears Due to ous While we ware under him."[3]

Subsequently, he served in the Continental Army, in Capt. Abijah Child's Company, Col. John Greaton's 2nd Regiment. He was mustered into Captain Child's Company and paid a bounty by February 3, 1777, according to a report filed by James Barrett, muster master of Middlesex County. The service record identifies him as being a resident of Lincoln, and his service was credited to the town of Lincoln, but Lincoln historian William Wheeler says that he was recruited from outside of Lincoln to fulfill the town's 1777 quota of 26 men to serve three years in the Continental Army. He appears to have died in service, but no details are provided.[4]

His identity is unknown. There is a possibility that he may have served previously at Cambridge in 1775, although it is not clear if either the John Landey in Captain Curtis's Company, Colonel Glover's Regiment, or the John Landy of Marblehead in Capt. John Glover, Jr.'s Company, Col. John Glover's Regiment is the same individual as John Lander (inst.) of Lincoln.[5]

---

1 Wheeler, "Lincoln" (in Hurd, Vol. 2, pp. 620, 621), treats John Lander and John Langtry as separate individuals. Although the possibility exists that he is correct in doing so, the author believes that the various records all apply to a single individual.

    Massachusetts Soldiers and Sailors lists no one under the name Lander. However, on the handwritten Dorchester Heights muster roll (Hartwell, "A List of a Company of Militia"), the name Lander is easily mistaken as "Landa," which is how *Massachusetts Soldiers and Sailors* lists his Dorchester Heights service (along with a similar listing under "Landea." Another listing under "Landy" is unmistakably the same individual.

    Wheeler lists John Langtry as a non-Lincoln resident recruited to fill the town's 1777 quota. Except for Wheeler's assertion of non-residency, *Massachusetts Soldiers and Sailors'* listing for John Lanctay of Lincoln is a compelling match. But *Massachusetts Soldiers and Sailors* also lists "Lanctay," "Landa," and "Landea" as variants of "Landy." Indeed, all the records seem to fit, as well. Accordingly, the author concludes that this is all one individual (perhaps a transient Lincoln resident), which he lists under the name Lander (according to his best reading of the spelling on Hartwell, "A List of a Company of Militia") (see *Massachusetts Soldiers and Sailors*, Vol. IX, pp 463, 468).

2 *Massachusetts Soldiers and Sailors*, Vol. IX, p. 463.

3 Sudbury Miscellaneous Records, pay receipt, March 17, 1777 (Doc. # 2209).

4 *Massachusetts Soldiers and Sailors*, Vol. IX, pp. 463, 468; Blake, "James Barrett's Returns of Men," pp. 468, 469. Wheeler, "Lincoln" (in Hurd, Vol. 2, p. 620), says specifically that he was not a citizen or resident of the town. Note the parallels in the records of Continental service with Benjamin Cleaveland (q.v.), John Gorden (q.v.), and Zodith Henderson (q.v.), all of whom Wheeler says were recruited to fill the town's 1777 quota.

5 *Massachusetts Soldiers and Sailors*, Vol. IX, pp. 466, 468.

LAWRENCE, William, Jr.

William Lawrence, Jr., served for three years in the Continental Army. He was paid by the town for this service.[1] The precise details of this service are unknown.

He was the son of Rev. William Lawrence, Minister of the Gospel in Lincoln, and Love (Adams) Lawrence; age 23 when the war broke out; probably age 24 or 25 when he joined the Continental service. The sympathies of his family had more than once been called into question. His father had been temporarily barred from preaching in 1774 because of suspect loyalties, and his sister, Lovie, had married a known Loyalist in November 1774. William Jr. operated a retail establishment with a liquor license in the center of town from 1772 to 1776. In 1780, he married Eunice Brown, sister of Nathan Brown, Jr. (q.v.), and Daniel Brown (q.v.). He died in Lincoln in 1804 at age 52.[2]

LONDON, Eden
[also Edom]

Eden London served at Cambridge, in Capt. James Burt's Company, Col. Asa Whitcomb's Regiment, enlisting for eight months of service on May 10, 1775. His name appears on an order for advance pay dated June 3, 1775, and he is believed to have fought at Bunker Hill. He was in service at least into October.

He enlisted on December 7, 1776, for three years of service in the Continental Army, serving in Capt. William Warner's Company, Col. Thomas Marshall's 10th Massachusetts Regiment. This unit fought at both battles of Saratoga, forcing Burgoyne to surrender on October 17, 1777. They then marched south and spent the legendary winter of 1777–1778 at Valley Forge. They fought in the stifling heat at Monmouth on June 28, 1778. From January to April 1779 he served at West Point. He was discharged on December 7, 1779.[3]

He was an African-American slave, probably born in Fitchburg, age 31 during his Cambridge service. He had had a succession of owners before briefly becoming the property of William Bond of Lincoln (probably approximately 1772–1773).[4] Several years before the war broke out, he was back in Fitchburg with still another owner. During the course

---
1 "Treasurer's Accompts," June 10, 1779.
2 *Vital Records of Lincoln*; MacLean, *A Rich Harvest*, pp. 99, 120, 198, 243–244; *Historical Manual of the Lincoln Church*, p. 57. From the record of his death, he achieved the rank of lieutenant (probably in the Lincoln Militia Company after the war). See also MacLean, *A Rich Harvest* (pp. 303–305) for more on the divided loyalties of Rev. William Lawrence's family and the resulting difficulties. *Historical Manual of the Lincoln Church* says Eunice was the daughter of Capt. Nathan Brown. Clearly she was the daughter of Nathan Brown (second generation), while "Capt. Nathan Brown" usually refers to her brother, also referred to as Nathan Brown III or Nathan Brown, Jr. (q.v.). For an explanation of the three generations of Nathan Browns, see Nathan Brown, Jr. (q.v.).

He apparently had a reputation for drinking too much. After his marriage to Eunice Brown, he acquired and moved into the old Nathan Brown house on Pierce Hill in 1792. Despite an assertion (in Family record of William Lawrence) that he drank so much that he lost the place, William still owned the property when he died. Bond, *Genealogies of the Families of Watertown* (p. 835), reports that he died insolvent.
3 Quintal, *Patriots of Color*, pp. 155–158.
4 Ibid. Previously (in 1757), he had been owned briefly before the war by a Samuel Bond, possibly of Weston, and possibly the father of the said William Bond of Lincoln. William Bond of Lincoln appears to be the father of Jonas Bond (q.v.), Samuel Bond (q.v.), William Bond (q.v.), and possibly Thomas Bond (q.v.); brother-in-law of Samuel Farrar, Jr. (q.v.), Stephen Farrar (q.v.), and Timothy Farrar (q.v.).

of 19 years, he had no less than 11 different owners. He reportedly received his freedom in return for taking his master's place in the three-year Continental service.[1]

In 1806, as "a poor negro man," he became the subject of a lawsuit by the town of Winchendon against the town of Hatfield over which town was responsible for supporting him. He died in Winchendon in 1810, probably age 65, and is buried in the Old Centre Cemetery.[2]

LOVELL, Nathaniel
[also LOVEL, Nathan]

Nathaniel Lovell was paid a bounty by Gen. Eleazer Brooks (as chairman of Class #2 for the town of Lincoln) on March 29, 1782, for three years of service in the Continental Army. He was engaged for the town of Lincoln. He also appears on a list of recruits who were sent by Massachusetts as a portion of its quota of men for the Continental Army subsequent to January 1, 1781, and who were reported unfit for duty.[3]

His identity is unknown.

Notwithstanding his lack of fitness for duty in 1782, he may possibly have served previously at Cambridge (possibly Bunker Hill) in 1775, and at Rhode Island, but this is speculative.[4]

---

1 Quintal, *Patriots of Color*, pp. 155–158.
2 Ibid.
3 *Massachusetts Soldiers and Sailors*, Vol. IX, pp. 1000, 1009. Class #2 was one of the economic classes set up in 1781 to maintain economic fairness in enlisting recruits. For a brief overview of the system of economic classes, see MacLean, *A Rich Harvest*, p. 296.
4 There are multiple records of a Nathaniel Lovell (also Lovel) from the Medway/Medfield area, who:
   a) marched on the Alarm of April 19, 1775, and served nine days as a private in Capt. Ephraim Chenery's Medfield Company, Col. John Smith's Regiment.
   b) marched from Medway to Rhode Island on the Alarm of December 8, 1776, as a private in Capt. Joseph Lovell's Company, 4th Suffolk County Regiment of Massachusetts Militia. He is credited with three days of service, although Captain Lovell's Company served 21 days, and Captain Lovell "tarried at Providence" another 22 days in command of an independent company drafted out of the 4th Regiment.
   c) was drafted out of Capt. Sabin Mann's Company of Medfield Militia in accordance with a warrant from Col. Benjamin Hawes, dated September 25, 1777, and marched on a secret mission to Rhode Island on the last day of September, for 30 days of service starting October 1, 1777. Assigned to Capt. Ezekiel Plimpton's Company, Colonel Hawes's 4th Suffolk County Regiment, he was discharged October 28, 1777, and was credited with 1 month, 7 days of service (including 3 days for 60 miles of travel home).
   d) appears on a list of men reported by a committee of the town of Medway, dated April 13, 1778, as having rendered service at various times subsequent to April 19, 1775.
   e) was back in Rhode Island on the Alarm of July 29, 1780, as a private in Capt. John Ellis's Company, 4th Suffolk County Regiment (Maj. Seth Bullard commanding) at Tiverton. He was discharged August 7, 1780, with 12 days of service.
   (See *Massachusetts Soldiers and Sailors*, Vol. IX, pp. 1001, 1007–09.) The possibility exists that these records could apply to more than one individual. However, the common thread of the 4th Suffolk County Regiment, and the proximity of Medway and Medfield, strongly suggests the same person. *Vital Records of Medfield* reveals a Nathan Lovill, age 33 at the time of the April 19th Alarm, son of David and Hannah Lovill, who could possibly fit this profile. His connection to Lincoln, if any, is unclear.
   There is also a record of a Nathan Lovell (also Lovel) from Holden, who
   a) reportedly served at Bunker Hill.
   b) served as a private in Captain Belknap's Company, Colonel Wade's Regiment at Rhode Island (North Kingston and East Greenwich) from May 1, 1778, through January 1, 1779.
   c) "was in the war a considerable part of the time previous to [his] marriage" in 1781.
   (See Pension Record # W26151; *Massachusetts Soldiers and Sailors*, Vol. IX, p. 1000.) The pension record contains very few details about his service. It was executed in 1848 by his 90-year-old widow, 36 years after his

LUFKIN, Stephen
[also LOUCKIN]

Stephen Lufkin appears on a list of men raised to serve in the Continental Army, dated February 26, 1777. He was engaged for the town of Lincoln. He was enlisted into Capt. Abijah Child's Company, Col. John Greaton's 2nd Regiment, but was reported transferred by prior enlistment to Colonel Cilley's Regiment.[1]

His identity has not been determined.[2]

LUNT, John

John Lunt appears on a list of men raised to serve in the Continental Army. He was engaged for the town of Lincoln.[3] Lincoln historian William Wheeler says that he was neither a citizen nor a resident of Lincoln, but that he was recruited from outside of town to fulfill the town's quota of 26 men to serve three years in the Continental Army.[4]

His identity has not been determined.[5]

MANN, Christopher

Christopher Mann of Lexington went to Rhode Island in 1779 as a private in Capt. Thomas Hovey's Company, Col. Nathan Tyler's Regiment. He served from August 13, 1779, through December 25, 1779 (credited with 4 months, 17 days of service, including 4 days for 80 miles travel home).[6]

Subsequently, he was paid by the town of Lincoln for three months of service in the Continental Army. He enlisted on August 26, 1781, and served in the Hudson Highlands as a private in Capt. John Hayward's Company, Colonel Webb's Regiment. The regiment was raised to reinforce the Continental Army. He was discharged on November 11, 1781, having served 3 months, 14 days, including 10 days for 200 miles travel home.[7]

His identity is unknown.[8]

---

death. *Vital Records of Holden* identifies this individual as the son of Jonathan and Rachel Lovell. He was age 14 at the time of the Battle of Bunker Hill (casting an element of doubt on the report of his participation); just age 17 when he went to Rhode Island in Captain Belknap's Company. In 1781, he married Anna Inglesbee of Shrewsbury, and he died in Sodus, New York, in 1812. His connection to Lincoln, if any, is unclear.

1 *Massachusetts Soldiers and Sailors*, Vol. IX, p. 983, Vol X, p. 29; Blake, "James Barrett's Returns of Men," p. 469. The service records of John Barter (q.v.), Benjamin Cleaveland (q.v.), John Gorden (q.v.), Zodith Henderson (q.v.), and John Lander (q.v.) offer some interesting and possibly intertwined parallels.

   Multiple enlistments in different units by a single individual, for purposes of collecting multiple enlistment bounties, was a fairly common scam. The record indicates that he was paid a bounty when he was mustered into Captain Child's Company, suggesting that he may have gotten away with it, at least initially.

2 *Vital Records of Gloucester* reveals a Stephen Lufken, son of Stephen (mother's name not given); age 18 in 1777. Except for the matching name, however, the author has found no evidence to connect him with the Stephen Lufkin who served for Lincoln.

3 *Massachusetts Soldiers and Sailors*, Vol X, p. 49.

4 Wheeler, "Lincoln," in Hurd, Vol. 2, p. 620.

5 A John Lunt appears in *Vital Records of Newbury*, son of Elkanah and Elisabeth Lunt; age 17 in 1777. Except for the matching name, however, the author has found no evidence to connect him with the John Lunt who served for Lincoln.

6 *Massachusetts Soldiers and Sailors*, Vol. X, p. 180.

7 "Treasurer's Accompts," March 8, 1782; *Massachusetts Soldiers and Sailors*, Vol. X, p. 162.

8 The logical supposition that he may be the son of Oliver and Lucy Mann of Lincoln gets little encouragement from *Vital Records of Lincoln*, which contains no record at all of a Christopher Mann and lists only two

MASON, Elijah

Elijah Mason was a fifer in Capt. William Smith's Company of Minute Men from Lincoln, Col. Abijah Peirce's Regiment.[1] Following the engagement at Concord, he served for five days in Cambridge.[2] He was reimbursed by the town for his accoutrements as a minute man.[3]

On April 24, 1775, he enlisted as a fifer in Capt. William Smith's Company, Col. John Nixon's 16th Massachusetts Regiment in the rapidly organizing Massachusetts Provincial Army. He was "stationed at the college." He participated in the Battle of Bunker Hill on June 17, 1775, after which he moved to the barracks on Winter Hill. He served eight months, until the end of 1775.[4]

On January 1, 1776, he enlisted in the Continental Army for one year as a fifer in Capt. Adam Wheeler's 2nd Company, Col. John Nixon's 4th Regiment. He was detached to the party which entered Boston with General Washington, following the British evacuation of the city on March 17, 1776. Soon after, back in Captain Wheeler's Company, he marched south to New York, via Providence and New London. In New York, he was deployed on Governor's Island, where he remained until the British took Long Island on August 27, 1776. He retreated with Washington out of New York, participated in the Battle of White Plains on October 28, 1776, and was at North Castle on November 9, 1776. Subsequently he went to New Jersey with a division under General Lee to reinforce Washington's army. After General Lee was taken prisoner, he continued marching south, crossing the Delaware River to join Washington's army in Pennsylvania. He attempted to re-cross the Delaware with Washington's army to attack Trenton on December 25, 1776, but was turned back by the snow and ice. Afterward, he may have participated in retaking southern New Jersey, driving the British back to New Brunswick.[5]

In June 1778, he again enlisted for Continental service as a fifer, agreeable to a resolve of April 20, 1778, for a period of nine months from the time of their arrival at Fishkill. He is described as age 18; five feet, eight inches in height, and a resident of Lincoln. He was engaged for the town of Lincoln, detached from Capt. Samuel Farrar, Jr.'s Company,

---

children of Oliver and Lucy (both daughters born in 1780 and 1781). Nor has any record of a Christopher Mann been found in the *Vital Records* of any of the nearby towns.

1 Coburn, *Muster Rolls*.
2 *Massachusetts Soldiers and Sailors*, Vol. X, p. 320.
3 "Treasurer's Accompts," February 19, 1776. This was paid to his father, Joseph.
4 *Massachusetts Soldiers and Sailors*, Vol. X, p. 320; Pension Record # S17559; Wheeler, "Lincoln," in Hurd, Vol. 2, p. 623. The college means Harvard. Colonel Nixon's Regiment became known as the 5th Regiment in August 1775, under the Continental numbering system. The town appears to have paid Elijah's father for this Cambridge service (see Joseph Mason (Sr.) (q.v., Chapter 12); "Treasurer's Accompts," June 10, 1779).
5 *Massachusetts Soldiers and Sailors*, Vol. X, p. 320; Pension Record # S17559. This appears to be the "service at the Southward in the year 1776" for which the town paid his father ("Treasurer's Accompts," June 10, 1779). In his pension declaration, he says, "After the battle at Trenton, we crossed the River and drove the British into New Brunswick—soon after this my time expired and I returned home." However, the timing is difficult to reconcile. Driving the British back to New Brunswick occurred after his enlistment would have been up on January 1, 1777. Possibly he may have extended his enlistment briefly (there is no mention of so doing), or perhaps his one-year enlistment began sometime after January 1, 1776, or perhaps he did not actually participate in the events which followed on pretty quickly after his discharge. On January 1, 1776, Col. John Nixon's 5th Regiment was reconstituted as the 4th Regiment; Lt. Col. Thomas Nixon succeeded his brother in command, in August 1776.

Col. Eleazer Brooks's 3rd Middlesex Militia Regiment for this service. He arrived in Fishkill on June 17, 1778, and served in Capt. John Santford's Company, Colonel Malcom's Regiment. He served three or four months as a commissary guard, assigned to guard the stores on the road. Then he was ordered to help build a bridge, probably over the Housatonic River. After that, he went to Peekskill as a member of Col. Rufus Putnam's Regiment. He was discharged from Peekskill in 1779.[1]

He may have been back in New York's Hudson Valley as a private in Capt. Thomas Cowdin's Company, Col. Samuel Denny's Regiment, raised to reinforce the Continental Army in New York for three months, but it is not clear if this is the same Elijah Mason. This individual enlisted November 1, 1779, and was discharged November 23, 1779, credited with 1 month, 2 days of service at Claverack (including 9 days, 180 miles of travel back home).[2]

He was the son of Joseph and Grace (Bond) Mason; brother of Jonas Mason (q.v.) and Joseph Mason (q.v.); age 17 at the time of the Concord Alarm. He never married. At some point in time before 1832, he moved to Woodstock, Connecticut. He died in 1849 at age 91 in West Woodstock, and he is buried in the Woodstock Hill Cemetery.[3]

MASON, Jonas

Jonas Mason was a sergeant in Capt. William Smith's Company of Minute Men from Lincoln, Col. Abijah Peirce's Regiment.[4] This was the first minute company to arrive in Concord in response to the Alarm of April 19, 1775, and they followed the action into Cambridge. He served for five days.[5] He was reimbursed by the town for his accoutrements as a minute man.[6]

On April 24, 1775, he enlisted as a sergeant in Capt. William Smith's Company, Col. John Nixon's 16th Massachusetts Regiment in the rapidly organizing Massachusetts Provincial Army. He is presumed to have participated with his unit at the Battle of Bunker Hill on

---

1 *Massachusetts Soldiers and Sailors*, Vol. X, p. 320; Pension Record # S17559. See also, Blake, "James Barrett's Returns of Men," p. 15. Actually, he was age 20 when he went to Fishkill. In his pension declaration, he says of the bridge, "over the Housatonik or some other river."

  The town evidently paid him for this service on June 10, 1779. Why the town paid his father for his service at Cambridge in 1775 and "at the Southward" in 1776 on the same day it paid him directly for his service in the Continental Army in 1778 is not entirely clear. However, as neither of his brothers served at the Southward in 1776, the £20 payment to his father must be for Elijah's service (see notes 4 and 5 on p. 326). The £69/2/3 payment to Elijah for "service in the Continental Army at the Southward" reflects considerable inflation, strong evidence that this payment was not for his 1776 Continental service, but for his 1778 Continental service.

2 *Massachusetts Soldiers and Sailors*, Vol. X, p. 320. This service is not mentioned in his pension record, indicating the likelihood that it may have been served by a different Elijah Mason.

3 *Vital Records of Lincoln*; Wheeler, "Lincoln," in Hurd, Vol. 2, p. 623. Wheeler incorrectly identifies his father as Jonas. Grace does not appear to have been closely related to Jonas Bond (q.v.), Samuel Bond (q.v.) and William Bond (q.v.) (see Bond, *Genealogies of the Families of Watertown*, pp. 52, 358, 362). He was living in Woodstock when he filed his pension application in 1832.

4 Coburn, *Muster Rolls*

5 *Massachusetts Soldiers and Sailors*, Vol. X, p. 324.

6 "Treasurer's Accompts," February 19, 1776.

June 17, 1775. He received advance pay on July 7 and was still in service on September 30, 1775, but reportedly he became sick and had to leave the service shortly afterward.[1]

Subsequently, he served as a sergeant in Capt. John Hartwell's Company of Militia from Lincoln, Col. Eleazer Brooks's 3rd Middlesex County Regiment, which marched from Lincoln to fortify Dorchester Heights on March 4, 1776. The unit was discharged five days later, on March 9, after the threat of a British assault on the American positions had subsided, and British General Howe had begun preparations to evacuate Boston, instead. He was paid for this service the following September.[2]

He was the son of Joseph and Grace (Bond) Mason; brother of Joseph Mason (q.v.), and Elijah Mason (q.v.); age 26 at the time of the Concord Alarm. He married Susanna Foster in 1778, making him the brother-in-law of Phineas Allen (q.v.) and Jacob Foster (q.v.). He moved to Sidney, Maine about 1804. Susanna died in Sidney in 1811. In 1814, he married Elizabeth Brooks. He died in 1827 in Sidney, Maine, age 78, and is buried in the Longley Yard Cemetery.[3]

Minute man Sgt. Jonas Mason went to Concord with the Lincoln company. Subsequently he served at the Battle of Bunker Hill and in the fortification of Dorchester Heights. After the war, he moved his family to Sidney, Maine, where he died in 1827. (Photograph by the author)

---

1 *Massachusetts Soldiers and Sailors*, Vol. X, p. 324. Abijah Mead (q.v.) claims he took his place, reportedly about October 1, 1775, and completed the last two months of his eight-month term of service. The dates and times are not wholly consistent, suggesting that it may have been later in October that Jonas Mason took sick and left the service (see Pension Record # S18507 for Abijah Mead). Colonel Nixon's Regiment is often referred to as the 5th Regiment, which it became in August 1775, under the Continental numbering system.

2 Hartwell, "A List of a Company of Militia"; *Massachusetts Soldiers and Sailors*, Vol. X, p. 324.

3 *Vital Records of Lincoln*; Bond, *Genealogies of the Families of Watertown*, p. 359; Mason, *Descendants of Capt. Hugh Mason*; *SAR Revolutionary War Graves Register*. His gravestone lists his age as 79, but if Bond is correct, then he was still 4½ months short of turning age 79. Wheeler, "Lincoln" (in Hurd, Vol. 2, p. 623), incorrectly identifies his father as Jonas. Grace does not appear to have been closely related to Jonas Bond (q.v.), Samuel Bond (q.v.) and William Bond (q.v.). See Bond, *Genealogies of the Families of Watertown*, pp. 52, 358. Susanna Foster was probably the sister of Jacob Foster (q.v.). It is not known if Elizabeth Brooks was from Sidney, or if she may have been from Lincoln, possibly the sister of Abner Brooks (q.v.), Benjamin Brooks (q.v.), Ephraim Brooks, Jr. (q.v.), and Levi Brooks (q.v., Chapter 12), or possibly the daughter of Timothy Brooks (q.v.).

MASON, Joseph
[also Joseph, Jr.][1]

Joseph Mason was a fifer in Capt. William Smith's Company of Minute Men from Lincoln, Col. Abijah Peirce's Regiment.[2] This was the first minute company to arrive in Concord in response to the April 19, 1775, Alarm, and they followed the action into Cambridge. He served for five days.[3] He was reimbursed by the town for his accoutrements as a minute man.[4]

On April 24, 1775, he enlisted for eight months as a fifer in Capt. William Smith's Company, Col. John Nixon's 16th Massachusetts Regiment in the rapidly organizing Massachusetts Provincial Army. He also appears on the roll as a private, and was stationed at the "Old College" as part of Gen. John Sullivan's Brigade. He participated in the Battle of Bunker Hill on June 17, 1775, received advance pay on July 7, and was promoted to corporal on July 18, 1775. He served out his eight-month term through the end of December at Winter Hill.[5]

He served as a fifer in Capt. Asahel Wheeler's Company, Col. John Robinson's Regiment from February 4, 1776, for 1 month, 28 days through the departure of the British forces from Boston.[6]

Subsequently, on September 29, 1777, he was detached from Col. Eleazer Brooks's Militia Regiment, having volunteered to serve in Capt. Samuel Farrar, Jr.'s Company, Col. Jonathan Reed's Middlesex County Regiment (Brig. Gen. James Bricket's Brigade of Massachusetts Militia), which was sent to reinforce the Northern army under General Gates. From various accounts, the unit marched to Saratoga and Stillwater by way of Bennington, arriving at camp

---

1 Because most of the service records do not distinguish between Joseph Mason and Joseph Mason, Jr., the *War Memorial Book*, *An Account of the Celebration*, and Wheeler, "Lincoln" (in Hurd, Vol. 2, p. 623), mistakenly credit both Joseph Mason and Joseph Mason, Jr., with service. Wheeler inexplicably credits both of them with nearly identical service records (Cambridge, 1775; New York, 1776; Rhode Island, 1778/9; Continental Army), despite the absence of evidence of two Joseph Masons at any of the locations. *An Account of the Celebration* compounds the error, inexplicably crediting Joseph Mason for service as a minute man, and Joseph Mason, Jr., with the other service. Pension Record # S13820 confirms the identity of the minute man as Joseph Mason, Jr., and similarly confirms that the other records refer to Joseph Mason, Jr., as well. While it may be theoretically possible for the elder Joseph Mason (age unknown) to have served during the war, no record has been found of any service by a Joseph Mason that does not fit Joseph Mason, Jr. The only evidence suggesting any possibility of different individuals is a June 10, 1779, payment by the town to Joseph Mason for service at Cambridge in 1775 and at the Southward in 1776, followed by a November 11, 1779, payment to Joseph Mason, Jr., for service at Cambridge in 1775 and at Saratoga in 1777. The June payment to the elder Joseph Mason, however, conforms to service provided by Elijah Mason (q.v.), for which Elijah does not appear to have been otherwise paid by the town. This appears to be a more logical explanation for the payment than crediting the elder Joseph Mason with otherwise uncorroborated service. See the listing for Joseph Mason (Sr.) (q.v., Chapter 12).

2 Coburn, *Muster Rolls*.

3 *Massachusetts Soldiers and Sailors*, Vol. X, p. 325.

4 "Treasurer's Accompts," February 19, 1776.

5 *Massachusetts Soldiers and Sailors*, Vol. X, p. 325; Pension Record # S13820; "Treasurer's Accompts," November 11, 1779. Colonel Nixon's Regiment is often referred to as the 5th Regiment, which it became in August 1775, under the Continental numbering system. The "Old College" refers to Harvard. In his pension application, he claims to have stayed an extra month at the expiration of his eight-month enlistment. As he makes no mention of his service in Capt. Asahel Wheeler's Company, per se, the author assumes that the extra month refers to this service (actually nearly two months) in February and March 1776, although this would have been discontiguous with his December 31, 1775, discharge.

6 *Massachusetts Soldiers and Sailors*, Vol. X, p. 338; Sudbury Miscellaneous Records, pay receipt, April 17, 1777 (Doc. # 2217).

"just after the firing ceased." They were sent to Fort Edward, and then recalled to Saratoga, where they witnessed British General Burgoyne's surrender on October 17. Subsequently, they were part of the escort which guarded Burgoyne's troops to Cambridge. He served through November 7, 1777 (credited with 1 month, 10 days of service), but stayed on as a guard at Prospect Hill for an extra month, serving in place of Josiah Reed of Lexington.[1]

Agreeable to a resolve of April 20, 1778, he enlisted in the Continental Army for the period of nine months from the time of their arrival at Fishkill. He is described as age 24; five feet, three inches in height, and a resident of Lincoln. Engaged for the town of Lincoln, he was recruited out of Capt. Samuel Farrar, Jr.'s Militia Company, Col. Eleazer Brooks's Regiment. He arrived in Fishkill on June 17, 1778, and served in Capt. John Santford's Company, Colonel Malcom's Regiment. He served as sergeant of a commissary guard until the fall, when he joined Col. Rufus Putnam's Regiment and built huts at Soldiers Fortune (a few miles upstream of Peekskill). He was discharged at Peekskill at the expiration of his term.[2]

On July 14, 1779, he entered service again as a sergeant in Capt. Thomas Hovey's Company, Col. Nathan Tyler's Regiment in Rhode Island. He served at Providence until the British evacuated Newport on October 25, 1779, then marched to Newport. He was discharged at Newport on December 22, 1779, having served 5 months, 13 days at Rhode Island (including 80 miles of travel home).[3]

---

1 *Massachusetts Soldiers and Sailors*, Vol. X, p. 325; Pension Record # S13820; "Treasurer's Accompts," November 11, 1779. See also Joseph Mason's affidavit in John Wheeler's (q.v.) Pension Record # W27876. For accounts of their deployment around Saratoga, see Shattuck, *History of the Town of Concord*, p. 356; Pension Record # S29229 for Leonard Hoar (q.v.); Pension Record # W20567 for Edward Adams. The quotation belongs to Leonard Hoar.

Josiah Reed's identity is uncertain. His first name was inserted into Joseph Mason's pension declaration after the fact, and somewhat illegibly. It could possibly be read as Joseph or Isaiah, but neither of these offers much clarity. In Mason's affidavit in John Wheeler's pension file, his first name is not given, but he is identified as being from Lexington.

There is a Josiah Reed of Lexington, who was serving at Rhode Island during this time, through approximately the end of December 1777. It is not clear, however, how he might have been selected for guard duty which began nearly two months before the expiration of the term he was already serving. Further, no record of his guard service has been found (even in his own Pension Record # S30671). The author speculates that perhaps it might have been served entirely by substitutes.

There is also a Joseph Reed who served with Mason at Cambridge in 1775, and who later appears to have served with Mason at Fishkill in 1778. This individual appears to have begun serving guard duty on January 12, 1778, reasonably consistent with Mason's having substituted for a month. However, this Joseph Reed was from Acton, not Lexington, raising a question about this possible identity, as well (see *Massachusetts Soldiers and Sailors*, Vol. XIII, pp. 21, 78, 82).

2 *Massachusetts Soldiers and Sailors*, Vol. X, p. 325; Pension Record # S13820; Blake, "James Barrett's Returns of Men," p. 15. Also "Treasurer's Accompts," September 28, 1779. He was actually age 27 when he went to Fishkill. The *Massachusetts Soldiers and Sailors* record seems to imply that he went to Fishkill under the command of Capt. Samuel Farrar, Jr. and Col. Eleazer Brooks. However, neither Farrar nor Brooks were at Fishkill; the standing militia units such as theirs were used as sources of men raised for service at Fishkill and elsewhere. Wheeler, "Lincoln" (in Hurd, Vol. 2, p. 623), incorrectly credits the Fishkill service to the elder Joseph Mason and mistakenly places Joseph Mason, Jr.'s Rhode Island service in 1778.

3 *Massachusetts Soldiers and Sailors*, Vol. X, p. 325; Pension Record # S13820. Also "Treasurer's Accompts," February 19, 1780. In his pension declaration, he claims nine months of service in this stint. Note that Joseph Mason, Jr., was serving in Rhode Island on September 28 and November 11, 1779, when the "Treasurer's Accompts" records payments to him for service at Cambridge, Saratoga, and Fishkill. The author is unsure how to account for this discrepancy. The record of his service appears unimpeachable.

Wheeler, "Lincoln" (in Hurd, Vol. 2, p. 623), credits him additionally with three years of service in the Continental Army, but this appears improbable. In addition to not being able to find any corroborating

He was the son of Joseph and Grace (Bond) Mason; brother of Jonas Mason (q.v.), and Elijah Mason (q.v.); age 24 at the time of the Concord Alarm. After the war, he resided in Carlisle briefly. In 1786, he married Lucy Flint, sister of Ephraim Flint (q.v.), Abel Flint (q.v.), and John Flint (q.v.), and by 1787 or 1788 he moved to Walpole, New Hampshire, where he died in 1834 at age 82. He is buried in the Carpenter Hill Cemetery.[1]

MATHIS, Abner
[also MATHAIS, MATHIES, MATTHIS, MATTHES, MATHER, MATHEWS, MATTHEWS, METHES][2]

Abner Mathis was drafted to serve in the campaign at New York in 1776. On September 27, 1776, he marched to "Hells Gate or Kingsbridge, in New York, thence to White Plains." He served as a private in Capt. Simon Hunt's Company, Col. Eleazer Brooks's Middlesex County Regiment of Massachusetts Militia. After the Battle of White Plains on October 28, 1776, he is reported in camp at White Plains. He was discharged at North Castle on November 16, 1776 (credited with 2 months service, including 11 days for travel home).[3]

In December 1776, he volunteered for three months of service at Dorchester Heights, as a private in Capt. Moses Harrington's Company, Colonel Dike's Regiment. He served through the end of February 1777, and his service was credited to the town of Lincoln.[4]

On September 29, 1777, he marched to reinforce the Northern Army under General Gates, as a volunteer in Samuel Farrar, Jr.'s Company, Col. Jonathan Reed's Middlesex County Regiment (Brig. Gen. James Bricket's Brigade of Massachusetts Militia), which was detached from Col. Eleazer Brooks's Regiment. They marched to Saratoga by way of Bennington. Arriving a day or two after the Battle of Bemis Heights on October 7, 1777, they were sent to Fort Edward. On October 17, they were recalled to Saratoga, where they were present at General Burgoyne's surrender. With his unit, he was part of the guard that escorted the British prisoners to Cambridge, and was discharged at Cambridge on November 7, 1777 (having served 1 month, 10 days).[5]

He served 1 month, 14 days on an expedition to Rhode Island from August 1, 1778, to September 11, 1778, as a private in Capt. Francis Brown's Company, Colonel McIntosh's Regiment (Brig. Gen. Solomon Lovell's Brigade of Massachusetts Militia). He participated

---

evidence of this service, there does not appear to be much room in the record of his other service to fit three years of Continental service except possibly starting sometime in 1780. Joseph Mason, Jr., himself, gives no hint of such service in his pension application.

1 *Vital Records of Lincoln*; Bond, *Genealogies of the Families of Watertown*, p. 359; Wheeler, "Lincoln," in Hurd, Vol. 2, p. 623. Wheeler compounds his errors by incorrectly identifying his father as Jonas. Grace does not appear to have been closely related to Samuel Bond (q.v.) and William Bond (q.v.) (see Bond, *Genealogies of the Families of Watertown*, pp. 52, 358).

2 The author has found no consistency in the spelling of his name, and enough variation to make one question what his name actually was. He has chosen to use Mathis, following MacLean's lead, and one of three different spellings found in *Vital Records of Lincoln*. After the war, Mathews seems to have become the preferred form.

3 *Massachusetts Soldiers and Sailors*, Vol. X, p. 355; Pension Record # W15066.

4 *Massachusetts Soldiers and Sailors*, Vol. X, p. 356; Pension Record # W15066.

5 *Massachusetts Soldiers and Sailors*, Vol. X, p. 715. For accounts of their deployment around Saratoga, see Shattuck, *History of the Town of Concord*, p. 356; Pension Record # S29229 for Leonard Hoar (q.v.); Pension Record # W20567 for Edward Adams.

in the Battle of Rhode Island on August 29, 1778, as one of the picket guards, and retreated, firing for four or five miles before crossing over Howland's Ferry to Tiverton.[1]

He was age 16 during the New York campaign; the son of Barnabas and Anna (Munroe) Mathis; nephew of Benjamin Munroe (q.v.); cousin of Abijah Munroe (q.v.), Isaac Munroe (q.v.), and Micah Munroe (q.v.). He was born in Marlborough. When Barnabas died, Anna moved back to Lincoln with her two children in 1762 to live in her parents' home. They were promptly warned out of town. They stayed, and later Abner became an active member of the community, a cordwainer by trade, and the brother-in-law of Daniel Child (q.v.). He married Lydia Smith of Lexington in 1789. He appears to have served as captain of the Lincoln Militia Company (after 1790 and before 1794). He moved to Billerica about 1805 or 1807. He died in Billerica in 1837, age 77.[2]

MEAD, Abijah

Abijah Mead was a corporal in Capt. William Smith's Company of Minute Men from Lincoln, Col. Abijah Peirce's Regiment.[3] Theirs was the first minute company to arrive in Concord in response to the April 19, 1775, Alarm, and they followed the action into Cambridge. He served for seven days.[4] He was reimbursed by the town for his accoutrements as a minute man.[5]

In the fall of 1775, he enlisted in Capt. William Smith's Company, Col. John Nixon's 5th Regiment, in place of Sgt. Jonas Mason (q.v.), who was sick and unable to complete his eight-month term. He served about two months, until the end of December 1775.[6]

He served as a sergeant in Capt. Asahel Wheeler's Company, Col. John Robinson's Regiment from February 4, 1776, for 1 month, 28 days through the departure of the British forces from Boston.

Subsequently, he enlisted about August 23, 1776, as a sergeant in Capt. Zachariah Fitch's Company, Col. Samuel Brewer's Massachusetts Militia Regiment and marched through Northampton and Bennington to Skenesborough (now Whitehall, New York), where he was transported by boat to Ticonderoga. He served for about three months and was discharged at Ticonderoga.[7]

---

1 *Massachusetts Soldiers and Sailors*, Vol. X, p. 346; Pension Record # W15066; Wheeler, "Lincoln," in Hurd, Vol. 2, p 623. He was temporarily a Weston resident at the time of this service. His pension declaration appears to string two days of action into one. The four- or five-mile retreat as a picket guard was logically during the initial American withdrawal from the outskirts of Newport to Butt's Hill. It was two nights later, after the battle was over, that the Americans crossed Howland's Ferry onto the mainland, without opposition.

2 Wheeler, "Lincoln," in Hurd, Col. 2, p. 623; MacLean, *A Rich Harvest*, pp. 212, 347; *Vital Records of Lincoln*; *Lexington Births, Marriages and Deaths;* Pension Record # W15066. *Vital Records of Lincoln* lists their marriage intention in November 1788.

3 Coburn, *Muster Rolls*.

4 *Massachusetts Soldiers and Sailors*, Vol. X, p. 578.

5 "Treasurer's Accompts," July 10, 1777.

6 Pension Record # S18507. Colonel Nixon's 5th Continental Regiment was also known as the 16th Massachusetts Regiment. He entered this service, reportedly, about October 1, 1775. However, this date is not consistent with having completed the last two months of Jonas Mason's eight-month term of service. It is probable that it may have been later in October that he replaced Jonas Mason in the service.

7 *Massachusetts Soldiers and Sailors*, Vol. X, p. 578; Pension Record # S18507. On April 17, 1777, he signed a receipt along with Zebediah Farrar (q.v.) and Joseph Mason, Jr. (q.v.) for payment from Capt. Asahel Wheeler of "all oure wagers and arrears of all kinds." This appears to apply to his February and March service at Roxbury rather than to his Ticonderoga service (see Sudbury Miscellaneous Records, Doc. 2217, April 17,

Chapter 10: The Army of the Revolution

The Price for Not Serving

David Mead's two sons, Abijah Mead (q.v.) and Tilly Mead (q.v.), were both in service on April 19, 1775, and in Cambridge during the Siege of Boston. They were in arms during the fortification of Dorchester Heights the following spring, before going north—Tilly to Canada and Abijah to Ticonderoga. Another son was still underage, but there was probably little doubt that he, too, would serve if the war persisted.

As 1776 wound down, Tilly was still suffering from a serious injury incurred during his Cambridge service the year before. Abijah may have just returned from Ticonderoga, but Tilly—despite his wound—was still in service, now at Morristown (New Jersey). At age 53, David may have thought that his family was making a sufficient contribution to the war effort. When the draft notice for Continental service arrived, he declined to report for service.

On January 4, 1777, David Mead was fined £12 by Capt. Samuel Farrar, Jr., "for not Marching when ordered according to an Act of the Court."

During the previous year, Massachusetts authorities had found it increasingly difficult to fill the ranks of the army. Enlistment bounties were no longer sufficient by themselves to attract prospective soldiers. As early as July, a draft had been instituted. ▶

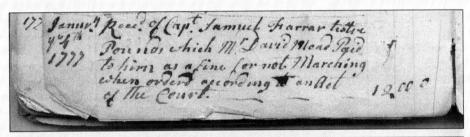

After first fining David Mead for not serving, the town refunded the fine when he found a substitute. Upon the completion of the substitute's three-year term of service, the town also paid Mead for the substitute's service. (Courtesy of Lincoln Town Archives, Lincoln, MA)

> Still, Massachusetts, like most states, remained delinquent in fulfilling its quota, so the penalties for ignoring the draft had begun to escalate.
>
> What's interesting about this record, is not that David Mead failed to report for service, but that he was actually fined. It was accepted practice for anyone wishing to avoid service to simply find a substitute to serve for him. Perhaps Mead had difficulty finding a substitute; Lincoln historian William Wheeler indicates that fully one-third of Lincoln's 1777 quota of 26 men for three years of Continental service was recruited from out of town.
>
> He appears to have persisted, however, because on February 10, 1777, the town refunded Mead's £12 fine "on account of his having Procured a man to inlist into ye Continental army." Three years later, on March 3, 1780, he was paid £30 for "one three years Continental Man." This was the going rate for Continental service, and it appears to have been paid more or less upon the completion of service by his substitute. No record has been found to indicate any service by David Mead himself, or to identify who it was that served his draft call. But taken together, the records that do survive highlight the increasingly complex system by which Massachusetts authorities attempted to fulfill the manpower needs of a protracted war effort.
>
> For his part, David Mead seems not to have prospered economically during or after the war. In 1787, he was ordered to be jailed for his debts, before he lost his heavily-mortgaged farm altogether. His wife Mary (Bond) Mead had died in 1780, at age 52, and is buried in the Meeting House Cemetery behind Bemis Hall. He appears to have moved to central Massachusetts to live with one of his sons.
>
> ["Treasurer's Accompts," January 4, 1777, February 10, 1777, March 3, 1780; MacLean, *A Rich Harvest*, p. 295; Biggs, "In Memorium," p. 178; MacLean, *A Rich Harvest*, p. 309–310; Wheeler, "Lincoln," in Hurd, Vol. 2, p. 620.]

He was the son of David and Mary (Bond) Mead; brother of Jonathan Mead (q.v.) and Tilly Mead (q.v.); age 26 at the time of the Concord Alarm. He ran an inn and tavern with his father until 1782. In 1787, he moved to Fitchburg, and a year later married Hepsibah Graves of Wayland. He left Fitchburg in 1799, possibly for Barre, where he was living at the time of his pension application in 1832. He died in Lincoln in 1837, age 88, identified as "a Revolutionary Pentioner an[d] town Pauper."[1]

1777). *Massachusetts Soldiers and Sailors* records 1 month, 9 days of service at Ticonderoga through September 30, 1776, but this does not necessarily indicate the expiration of the service. His pension application says he served 3 months. This accords with the author's belief that it is unlikely that Colonel Brewer's Regiment was discharged until near the expiration of their term (which was probably in December), as Ticonderoga was under a very serious threat of attack by British General Carleton until late into the fall of 1776, when he called off his invasion, and every available soldier was needed to help in its defense. Records in Green, *Groton During the Revolution* (pp. 53–65), appear to corroborate service into December 1776.

Wheeler, "Lincoln" (in Hurd, Vol. 2, p. 623), credits him additionally with a three-year enlistment in the Continental Army in 1777, but this appears unlikely. No confirming record has been found, and there is no mention of this service in his pension declaration.

[1] *Vital Records of Lincoln*; Wheeler, "Lincoln," in Hurd, Vol. 2, p. 623; MacLean, *A Rich Harvest*, p. 195; Bond, *Genealogies of the Families of Watertown*, p. 365; *Proceedings of the Fitchburg Historical Society*, p. 226. Bond

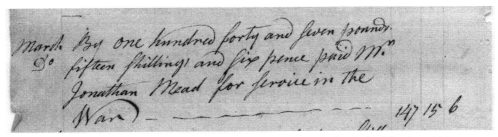

While Lincoln's "Treasurer's Accompts" usually provide more specific detail, this March 3, 1780, payment to Jonathan Mead was recorded only as "for service in the war." He may have served a stint in Rhode Island in 1778, before he enlisted into the Continental Army in November 1779 for the duration of the war. (Courtesy of Lincoln Town Archives, Lincoln, MA)

MEAD, Jonathan

Jonathan Mead may possibly have served in Rhode Island in 1778, but this is uncertain.[1]

Agreeable to a resolve of June 9, 1779, he was recruited in late November for service in the Continental Army. He appears on a list dated November 24, 1779, of men raised from Middlesex County, described as age 18, light complexion, five-feet, nine-inches tall. Evidently, his service began at Fishkill on December 12, 1779, as a private in Capt. John Williams's Company, Col. Joseph Vose's 1st Massachusetts Regiment. His enlistment was credited to the town of Lincoln, and his enlistment term was for the duration of the war. He appears again on a list dated February 3, 1781, on which he is described as age 27, light complexion, light hair; five feet, ten inches in height. His occupation is given as blacksmith, his birthplace and residence are given as Lincoln. He was reported as deserted on January 1, 1781, but he appears on the muster roll for January 1781, dated West Point, and on subsequent muster rolls through April 1781. He was reported sick in the general hospital during February and March, 1781.[2]

He was paid by the town for "service in the war."[3]

He was the son of David and Mary (Bond) Mead; brother of Abijah Mead (q.v.) and Tilly Mead (q.v.); age 18 at the time of his 1779 enlistment. After the war, he lived in Petersham before he settled in Hardwick. He appears to have been married twice; the second time to Lydia Hutchinson in 1800 in Petersham. Bond reports that he had two sons and four daughters. He died at Hardwick in 1814, age 53.[4]

---

makes him out to be four years younger, and *Vital Records of Lincoln* lists his age at the time of his death as 87. Both appear to be incorrect. His brother Tilly Mead (q.v.) was living in Barre by 1795, and beginning in 1822, an Abijah Mead, Jr., appears in *Vital Records of Barre* for marriage and children. Census records suggest the likelihood that Abijah Mead (inst.) may have been living in Barre with his brother, Tilly Mead (q.v.), in 1820, but Tilly makes no mention of him as a member of his household in his 1823 pension declaration. Perhaps by 1823, he may have taken up residence with Abijah Jr.'s family.

1 Wheeler, "Lincoln," in Hurd, Vol. 2, p. 623. No corroborating record of this service has been found.
2 *Massachusetts Soldiers and Sailors*, Vol. X, pp. 581, 599. Wheeler, "Lincoln" (in Hurd, Vol. 2, p. 623), says his enlistment was for three years. Notwithstanding the rigors of war, it is unlikely that he gained nine years of age in just over two calendar years; he was just about one month shy of turning 21 on February 3, 1781.
3 "Treasurer's Accompts," March 3, 1780.
4 *Vital Records of Lincoln*; Wheeler, "Lincoln," in Hurd, Vol. 2, p. 623; Bond, *Genealogies of the Families of Watertown*, p. 365; Baldwin, *Vital Records of Hardwick*, p. 310. *Vital Records of Hardwick* incorrectly lists his age as 50 when he died. No definitive record of a first marriage has been found, although it appears from the

MEAD, Tilly

Tilly Mead served as a private in Capt. Samuel Barnard's Militia Company from Watertown, Col. Thomas Gardner's Regiment, which marched on the Alarm of April 19, 1775. He served six days.[1]

In May, he enlisted for eight months in Capt. Abner Craft's Company, Col. Thomas Gardner's Regiment at Cambridge. He participated with his regiment in the Battle of Bunker Hill on June 17, 1775. On August 2, 1775, Abraham Watson, surgeon, requisitioned liquor from the Commissary of Stores at Watertown for use by Mead, who was wounded. He had chopped up his right knee "by the stroke of an axe." Despite his wound, he appears to have served out his term.[2]

On January 1, 1776, he reenlisted for one year of Continental service in Capt. Abner Craft's Company, now assigned to Col. John Greaton's Regiment. Following the Siege of Boston, he went to New York at the end of March, then went north in relief of the Canadian expedition. They reached Canada by the end of May, but by mid-June they were in full retreat. He served at Ticonderoga until November, when he was sent south to Morristown, New Jersey. He was discharged at Morristown in January 1777.

He was back in service in 1778, as a private in Capt. Francis Brown's Company, Colonel McIntosh's Regiment (Brig. Gen. Solomon Lovell's Brigade of Massachusetts Militia) for 1 month, 14 days (including 3 days, 60 miles of travel home), on an expedition to Rhode Island from August 1, 1778, to September 11, 1778. He participated in the Battle of Rhode Island on August 29, 1778.[3]

He was the son of David and Mary (Bond) Mead; brother of Abijah Mead (q.v.), and Jonathan Mead (q.v.); age 17 at the time he marched on the Alarm of April 19, 1775. He reportedly never married. He had become a Barre resident by 1790. In 1823, his 30-year-old niece Lucinda Mead was living with him, possibly as a caregiver. He died in Barre in 1848 at age 90.[4]

1849 death record of son Tilly Mead, age 54 years, 9 months, in Hardwick that his wife's name was Lydia, and that Tilly was reportedly born in Petersham. *Vital Records of Petersham* contains a marriage record of Jonathan Mead and Lydia Hutchinson in 1800. This is seven years after Tilly was reportedly born, suggesting that Jonathan may have been married previously. The Lydia in Tilly's death record must therefore be either a first wife of Jonathan, also named Lydia, or Tilly's stepmother, Lydia (Hutchinson) Mead, who raised him.

1 *Massachusetts Soldiers and Sailors*, Vol. X, pp. 582–84. He was evidently living in Watertown when the war broke out, but it is not known precisely why. It is easy to presume that he may have been working in Watertown as a laborer, perhaps on a farm. He was age 17 and had been raised in Lincoln. His pension application makes no mention of service on April 19, 1775.

2 *Massachusetts Soldiers and Sailors*, Vol. X, pp. 582–84; Pension Record # S33400; *Memorial of the American Patriots*, p. 9. Curiously, this wound does not appear to have inhibited his continuing service in the war, or his occupation (at least initially) as a cabinetmaker, but in 1794, he successfully applied for an invalid pension on the basis of this wound, and in 1823 he declared himself "wholly unable to labor on account of a wound rec'd in the war of the Revolution."

3 *Massachusetts Soldiers and Sailors*, Vol. X, pp. 582–84.
   Wheeler, "Lincoln" (in Hurd, Vol. 2, p. 623), credits him additionally with a three-year enlistment in the Continental Army, but this appears unlikely. No corroborating record of such service has been found, nor is it mentioned in his pension declaration.

4 *Vital Records of Lincoln*; Wheeler, "Lincoln," in Hurd, Vol. 2, p. 623; Bond, *Genealogies of the Families of Watertown*, p. 365; *Vital Records of Barre*; Pension Record # S33400. *Vital Records of Barre* incorrectly gives his age as 91 when he died. In his pension application he describes Lucinda as "a weakly & infirm person," raising some doubt about her possible role as a caregiver. She must have been the daughter of either Abijah Mead

MELONEY, Cornelius
[also MALONE, MELONY, MELONIA]

Cornelius Meloney enlisted for a six-month term to reinforce the Continental Army, agreeable to a resolve of June 5, 1780, and his enlistment was credited to the town of Lincoln. He is described as age 47 years; five feet, nine inches in stature; and light complexion. He marched to camp at Springfield on October 24, 1780, under the command of Captain Parker. Where and how he was deployed is not recorded, but he was discharged on December 2, 1780, probably from somewhere around New York or along the Hudson Valley, having served 1 month. 18 days (including 200 miles of travel home).[1]

He appears not to have been a Lincoln native, but appears to have been resident in Lincoln when he married Elizabeth Parks in 1756. He served in the French and Indian War on an expedition in 1756 and was a member of the original militia company from Lincoln the following year. He was the father of Joseph Meloney (q.v.); brother-in-law of Benjamin Parks (q.v.) and David Parks (q.v.); uncle of Aaron Parks (q.v.), Willard Parks (q.v.), Leonard Parks (q.v.), and Jonas Parks (q.v.). He may have left Lincoln shortly after the war. No record of his death has been found.[2]

There was a Cornelius Meloney who is said to have married Love Farrar, the sister of Daniel Farrar (q.v.), Nehemiah Farrar (q.v.), and Zebediah Farrar (q.v.). Love was about the same age as Cornelius's (inst.) sons. However, no marriage date is given, and no record has been found of Elizabeth's death. It is uncertain if this is the same Cornelius Meloney.[3]

MELONEY, Joseph
[also MALONE, MELONY]

Joseph Meloney enlisted for a nine-month term to reinforce the Continental Army, agreeable to a resolve of June 9, 1779. He entered the service on August 1, 1779, as a member of Captain Dix's Company, Colonel Wesson's 9th Regiment. He was engaged for the town of Lincoln. He is described as age 21; five feet, seven inches in stature, and light complexion. At the conclusion of his term, he is reported to have reenlisted.[4]

He was the son of Cornelius Meloney (q.v.) and Elizabeth (Parks) Meloney; nephew of Benjamin Parks (q.v.) and David Parks (q.v.); first cousin of Aaron Parks (q.v.), Jonas Parks (q.v.), Leonard Parks (q.v.), and Willard Parks (q.v.); age 21 on the date of the resolve, but

---

(q.v.) or Jonathan Mead (q.v.), as he seems to have had no other brothers. Wheeler says he was unmarried, but Census records for 1790, 1800, and 1810 show individuals living in his household consistent with his having a wife and children. His pension record indicates that by 1823, his household consisted of just him and Lucinda.

1 *Massachusetts Soldiers and Sailors*, Vol. X, pp. 618, 619.
2 *Vital Records of Lincoln*; Martin, "The Sons of Lincoln," pp. 21, 25. His leaving Lincoln is entirely speculative, but after the 1764 baptism of three surviving children, he and his family all disappear from the *Vital Records of Lincoln*. Census records reveal a Corns Melony in Boston in 1790, but the presence of three males under the age of 16 suggests the likelihood that this is probably a different individual, possibly a son of Cornelius Meloney (inst.).
3 Farrar, *Memoir of the Farrar Family*, p. 11. No further information is revealed, except that, "Love died in 1806, leaving eight children, one of whom, Cornelius, took the name of Daniel Farrar, and went to New Orleans."
4 *Massachusetts Soldiers and Sailors*, Vol. X, pp. 619, 620.

age 22 by the time he entered the service. He was born in Lincoln, but no further information has been found.[1]

MERIAM, Ezra

Ezra Meriam of Lexington enlisted in January 1776 for one year in the Continental Army, as a private in Capt. Joseph Butler's 8th Company, Col. John Nixon's 4th Regiment, which became Col. Thomas Nixon's Regiment in August 1776. Following the Siege of Boston, he was sent to New York, where he was at Camp Mt. Washington on September 30, 1776, and at North Castle on November 9, 1776. Doubtless, he was a participant in the Battle of White Plains, October 28, 1776, after which he went south with Washington's army. He attempted to cross the Delaware River on December 25 for the attack on Trenton the next morning, but he was turned back by the snow and ice. He extended his service through January 1777 and probably participated in driving the British back to New Brunswick.[2]

Agreeable to a resolve of April 20, 1778, he was back in service, recruited from Captain Brown's Company, Colonel Brooks's 3rd Middlesex County Militia Regiment, for nine months from the time of their arrival at Fishkill on June 21, 1778. He served as a private in Capt. Thomas Barns's Company, Col. Thomas Nixon's Regiment. He is described as age 18; five feet, seven inches in stature, and a resident of Lexington.[3]

The following year, agreeable to a resolve of June 9, 1779, he did another nine-month stint in the Continental Army, this time serving with his brothers Abraham and Silas, in Capt. Nathan Dix's Company, Col. James Wesson's 9th Regiment in the Hudson Highlands from July 18, 1779, to April 1, 1780.[4]

He enlisted for a six-month term in the Continental Army for the town of Lexington, under a resolve of June 5, 1780. Apparently, he set out on July 5 and arrived in Springfield on July 9, 1780. He is described as age 20; five feet, seven inches in stature, with a ruddy complexion. He was marched to camp under the command of Ensign Bancroft on July 11, 1780. He appears to have served in Capt. Othniel Taylor's Company, Col. Thomas Marshall's Regiment. He passed muster at Camp Totoway on October 25, 1780, and was discharged December 20, 1780, having served 5 months 26 days (including 200 miles of travel home).[5]

He was paid by the town of Lincoln for three months of service in the Continental Army in 1781, to reinforce American strength in the Hudson Valley when Washington marched much of the army south to Yorktown. He appears to have served as a private in Capt. John Hayward's Company, Colonel Webb's Regiment from August 26, 1781, to

---

1 *Vital Records of Lincoln.*
2 *Massachusetts Soldiers and Sailors,* Vol. X, p. 638; Pension Record # W16044.
3 Ibid. See also Blake, "James Barrett's Returns of Men," p. 17. His pension declaration misidentifies his officers as Capt. Oliver Barns and Col. John Nixon. The record indicates that the unit was commanded by Capt. Thomas Barns and Col. Thomas Nixon.
4 *Massachusetts Soldiers and Sailors,* Vol. X, pp. 638–639, 689. The resolve of June 9, 1779, called for 2000 troops for Continental Service, to be filled from the ranks of the militia. He appears to have been received at Springfield on July 19, 1779, detached from Captain Bridge's Company, now Colonel Faulkner's 3rd Middlesex County Militia Regiment. No Lincoln connection has been found for Abraham and Silas.
5 *Massachusetts Soldiers and Sailors,* Vol. X, pp. 638–639, 648, 656, 823; Pension Record # W16044.

November 30, 1781. He served for 3 months, 14 days (including 10 days for 200 miles of travel home).[1]

He enlisted again in June 1782 for a term of three years in the Continental Army and served until the end of the war. As the Continental Army demobilized and consolidated during 1783, he appears to have served in multiple companies, first in Col. Henry Dearborn's 1st New Hampshire Regiment, then in Colonel Reed's 2nd New Hampshire Regiment, finally in Capt. Isaac Frye's Company, Col. Henry Jackson's last remaining, consolidated, Continental Regiment. He was discharged probably in 1784.[2]

He was the son of Abraham and Sarah (Simonds) Meriam of Lexington; nephew of James Meriam (q.v.); age 16 during the campaign at New York, and age 21 when he served to the credit of Lincoln. After the war, he settled in Mason, New Hampshire, as a farmer, where he married Susannah Elliot in 1785. He died in Mason in 1827, age 67.[3]

MERIAM, James

James Meriam was paid by the town for service at New York in 1776 and 1777, and for service at Rhode Island in 1778. No record of the actual service has been found.[4]

The New York service is consistent with service by other Lincoln soldiers in Col. Samuel Thatcher's Regiment, which marched southward on December 16, 1776. This regiment served briefly around New York before being called to New Jersey in January 1777. They were stationed at Woodbridge, and participated in the *petite guerre* in the Jerseys in the early months of 1777, before being dismissed to return home in March.[5]

Consistent with service by other Lincoln men, his Rhode Island service is likely to have been in August and September 1778, and he may have participated in the Battle of Rhode Island on August 29, 1778.[6]

---

1 "Treasurer's Accompts," April 23, 1782; *Massachusetts Soldiers and Sailors*, Vol. X, p. 639. It is not immediately clear why Lincoln (and not Lexington) should have paid for this service. See parallel service by Joseph Munroe (q.v.), i.e., Lexington boys with previous service from Lexington (including similar stints at Fishkill), now serving identical stints for Lincoln. This service is not identifiable among his various claims of service in his pension declaration. The author speculates that he may have been working in Lincoln (perhaps on his uncle's farm) when he enlisted, and that the Lincoln connection may have influenced a subsequent decision to go to Mason, New Hampshire, after his discharge.

2 Pension Record # W16044. He appears to have gone to Mason, New Hampshire, after his November 1781 discharge, because this stint was clearly served in the New Hampshire line.

  His discharge date from this stint has not survived, but Colonel Jackson's consolidated Continental regiment remained in service until it was formally disbanded in June 1784.

3 *Lexington Births, Marriages and Deaths;* Pension Record # W16044.

4 "Treasurer's Accompts," November 11, 1779.

5 Placing him in Colonel Thatcher's Regiment is a supposition, based on the service of other Lincoln men at this time and on the description, "service at New York in the years 1776 and 1777." The *petite guerre* is David Hackett Fischer's term for the skirmishing that characterized the war in New Jersey following Washington's dramatic victories at Trenton and Princeton.

  According to Wheeler, "Lincoln" (in Hurd, Vol. 2, p. 623), the 1777 service was at Saratoga, but this is unlikely. Typically, the "Treasurer's Accompts" identify service at Saratoga as "Saratoga" or "Northward," not as New York. "New York in the years 1776 and 1777" usually refers to service with Colonel Thatcher's Regiment from December 1776 to March 1777.

6 Once again, this is suppositional, as no record of the actual service has been found.

He was originally from Lexington, the son of Jonas and Abigail (Locke) Meriam; uncle of Ezra Meriam (q.v.); age 37 during the 1776 campaign at New York. He had been married to Mary Cutler of Lincoln since 1764. He was a farmer and shoemaker by occupation. He died in Lincoln in 1816 at age 77.[1]

MERIAM, John
[also MERRIAM]

John Meriam enlisted for six months of service to reinforce the Continental Army in July 1780, and served from August 8, 1780, to February 8, 1781. He marched from Concord to Springfield, then to Pope Pond, New Jersey, where he joined Captain Williams's Company, Colonel Sprout's 5th Massachusetts Regiment. After the treason of Benedict Arnold on September 24, 1780, he "witnessed the execution of [Maj. John] Andre" at Tappan, New York, on October 2, 1780. He is reported to have passed muster at Camp Totoway on October 25, 1780, and "after marching in different parts of the country, went to West Point in December to Winter Quarters." He reports that at the expiration of his term on February 8, 1781, he "applied to General Putnam for a discharge, who put him off for a few days saying that he must wait for he [Putnam] wants a chance to have a brush with the enemy." A few days later, he received his discharge.[2]

He was from East Sudbury (present-day Wayland); the son of John and Mary (Bancroft) Meriam; age 13 when the war broke out, age 18 when he entered the Continental Service.[3]

---

1 Wheeler, "Lincoln," in Hurd, Vol. 2, p. 623; *Vital Records of Lincoln*; *Lexington Births, Marriages and Deaths*; Merriam Ancestry. Mary may have been the sister of Ebenezer Cutler (q.v., Chapter 11) and Zaccheus Cutler (q.v., Chapter 11), but this is speculative. James and Mary were married two months before the birth of their first child.

The story is told in Merriam Ancestry, that shortly after their marriage, Mr. Merriam (evidently James, inst.) went to Mason, New Hampshire, and bought one of the best farms in the town. His wife, however, was unwilling to move there, so he sold the farm, taking as payment Continental money, which he believed to be sound, but which "sank in value so much as to discourage his spirit of enterprise." If the story is accurate, it appears that the money in question was not the Continental Currency issued by the Continental Congress to pay for the war, but rather Colonial paper, issued by many of the colonies during most of the 1700s. Issued in various denominations, they must have been subject to some value fluctuation, in any case. However, in 1764, the British declared Colonial currency illegal. This must have seriously undercut its value, and the timing seems about right for this possibly to have been the triggering event that discouraged James Meriam's spirit of enterprise. For Colonial currency being declared illegal in 1764, see the American Currency Exhibit.

2 Pension Record # S30584; *Massachusetts Soldiers and Sailors*, Vol. X, pp. 639–640. The handwriting is unclear; Pope Pond may also be read as Pops Pond. Its location has not been identified. Camp Totoway was located in the present town of Totowa, New Jersey. He says he joined the service to meet the enlistment quota of the town of East Sudbury. Considerable confusion exists in the numbering of regiments; Col. Ebenezer Sprout is also credited with commanding the 12th Massachusetts Regiment in 1780 (see *Massachusetts Soldiers and Sailors*, Vol. X, p. 777).

3 *Vital Records of Sudbury*. *Proceedings of the Fitchburg Historical Society*, pp. 226–227, evidently confusing him with his father, appears to credit him with service as a corporal in Capt. Joseph Smith's Militia Company from Sudbury, Col. James Barrett's Regiment, on the Alarm of April 19th, and as a private in Capt. Asahel Wheeler's company, Col. John Robinson's Regiment at the time of Dorchester Heights. See also Coburn, *Muster Rolls*; *Massachusetts Soldiers and Sailors*, Vol. X, p. 640. At age 13, John Meriam (inst.) could not possibly have served as a corporal on April 19, 1775. Nor is he likely to have been at Dorchester Heights

After his war service, he married Dinah Hudson of Sudbury. By occupation a carpenter and builder, he moved from East Sudbury to Lincoln about 20 years after his return from the war. Subsequently, he moved to Concord, to Dedham, to Mendon, and by about 1818 to Uxbridge. Sometime after 1833, he moved to Fitchburg, where he died in 1843 at age 81. He is buried in the Laurel Hill Cemetery.[1]

MIDDLESEX, Salem[2]

Salem Middlesex served as a private in Capt. John Hartwell's Militia Company from Lincoln, Col. Eleazer Brooks's 3rd Middlesex County Regiment, which marched from Lincoln to fortify Dorchester Heights on March 4, 1776. The unit was discharged five days later, on March 9, after the threat of a British assault on the fortifications had subsided, and General Howe had begun preparations to evacuate Boston. He was paid for this service the following September.

Subsequently, he served as a private in Captain Brown's Company, Colonel McIntosh's Massachusetts Militia Regiment (Brig. Gen. Solomon Lovell's Brigade) at Rhode Island during July, August, and September 1778, and participated in the Battle of Rhode Island on August 29, 1778.[3]

He enlisted for Rhode Island service again, on July 27, 1780, in Capt. Abraham Andrews's Company, Col. Cyprian How's Regiment, detached from the Middlesex County Militia to reinforce the Continental Army for three months. He was discharged on October 30, 1780, having served for 3 months, 7 days.[4]

He was a slave of Col. Braddyll Smith of Weston, at least through 1774 when he married Vilot, a slave of Nathan Brown of Lincoln. He had become a free man probably by 1776, but at least by 1777, when he and Vilot joined the covenant of the Lincoln church. Vilot

---

at age 14. Both stints were almost certainly served by the elder John Meriam, who appears to have died in East Sudbury in 1798. See *Vital Records of Wayland*.

Other records in *Massachusetts Soldiers and Sailors* (Vol. X, pp. 639, 640) for service by a John Meriam at Ticonderoga and on guard duty at Cambridge belong logically either to the elder John Meriam, or to other John Meriams from Barre, Bedford, or Walpole. John Meriam (inst.) was age 16 by the time of the guard service, but his failure to mention it in his pension declaration reinforces the notion that it was likely served by a different John Meriam.

1 *Proceedings of the Fitchburg Historical Society*, p. 227; Pension Record # S30584. His marriage record does not appear in either *Vital Records of Sudbury* or *Vital Records of Wayland*.

2 The name Salem Middlesex is also associated with Peter Salem of Framingham (see Temple, *History of Framingham*, p. 324; Barry, *History of Framingham*, p. 64; Baldwin, *Vital Records of Framingham*, p. 337). Much has been written about Peter Salem, who is reputed to have fired the shot that killed British Maj. John Pitcairn at Bunker Hill. However, nothing has been found in the record of either Peter Salem of Framingham or Salem Middlesex of Lincoln/Weston to suggest the possibility that they could be the same individual or that there might be a link between them. It is not difficult to imagine an African-American man named Salem, from Middlesex County, being referred to as "Salem [from] Middlesex." My thanks to George Quintal for help sorting out this confusion. (For more information about Peter Salem, see Quintal, *Patriots of Color*, pp. 190–193.)

3 *Massachusetts Soldiers and Sailors*, Vol. X, pp. 720, 723.

4 Ibid. Also *Town of Weston, Births, Deaths, & Marriages*. He was paid by the town of Weston for this service, but he appears still to have been living in Lincoln at the time.

died in 1781, after which he moved back to Weston and married Catharine of Weston, who bore him two daughters. He died in 1799 in Weston.[1]

MILES, James

James Miles served as a private in Capt. John Hartwell's Company of Militia from Lincoln, Col. Eleazer Brooks's 3rd Middlesex County Regiment, which marched from Lincoln to fortify Dorchester Heights on March 4, 1776. The unit was discharged five days later, on March 9, after the threat of a British assault on the fortifications had subsided, and General Howe instead had begun preparations to evacuate Boston. He was paid for this service the following September.

On May 10, 1777, he arrived at his destination point (which is not identified) to join Capt. Jesse Wyman's Company, Col. Josiah Whitney's Regiment, which was raised for two months of service at Rhode Island. He was discharged at Point Judith on July 10, 1777. Including 3 days (60 miles) of travel allowed to join his company, and 5 days for travel home, he was credited with 2 months, 9 days of service, for which he was paid by the town.[2]

He appears to be the son of John and Elizabeth Miles; age 35 when he served at Dorchester Heights.[3]

After the war, he seems to have suffered from financial problems. In 1785, he lost title to his house and 30 acres after they were attached for non-payment of his debts. In addition, he was jailed for a time for his debts.[4]

---

1 *Vital Records of Lincoln*; *Town of Weston, Births, Deaths, & Marriages*; MacLean, *A Rich Harvest*, p. 306. Col. Braddyll Smith is also listed as Capt. Braddwell Smith; since 1766, he had been married to Ruth Flint, mother of Abel Flint (q.v.), Ephraim Flint (q.v.), and John Flint (q.v.). The fact that Salem Middlesex was paid directly for his service at Dorchester Heights in 1776 is a strong indication that he was a free man by that time. It is particularly interesting to note that the word "slave" was not typically used in recording the Vital Records of the towns. Instead, consistent with the practice of the time, the wedding records for Salem & Vilot refer to them as "Negro servant" and "Negro maid servant," or more simply as "servant."

The Archives at the Lincoln Public Library contains a Bill of Manumission for a Negro slave girl named Vilot, dated Sept. 17, 1774, filed in a section identified with Vilot Middlesex [document # 2003.063.15.1, located in box 1, folder 17]. The implication that this document refers to Vilot Middlesex, however, is misleading. The marriage record for Vilot and Salem Middlesex is dated December 22, 1774, and specifically identifies her as "Negro maid Servant of Mr Nathan Brown." In addition to predating the marriage record, the Bill of Manumission is signed by a John Russell of Dartmouth (whatever connection there may be to Lincoln is unclear), and it specifically states that Vilot will remain with him as an apprentice until her 18th birthday (the date of which is not given). The two Vilots are clearly different individuals.

2 *Massachusetts Soldiers and Sailors*, Vol. X, p. 733. "Treasurer's Accompts," June 15, 1779. The town's payment record identifies the service as Providence in the year 1777. He may possibly have served at other times during the war, as (allowing for wide variations in the spelling of Miles) there seem to be a number of other records in *Massachusetts Soldiers and Sailors* that possibly could be him. However, none of these other records contain an identifiable hint by which to connect the record to this individual.

3 *Concord, Massachusetts: Births, Marriages, and Deaths*. There are no other qualifying individuals named James Miles in the *Vital Records of Lincoln* or the surrounding towns. Two others named James Miles appear in *Concord, Massachusetts: Births, Marriages, and Deaths*, both sons of James and Hannah Miles. The first, born in 1753, died just before his 6th birthday; the second, born in 1761, would have been underage to have marched to Dorchester Heights.

4 MacLean, *A Rich Harvest*, p. 310.

Chapter 10: The Army of the Revolution 343

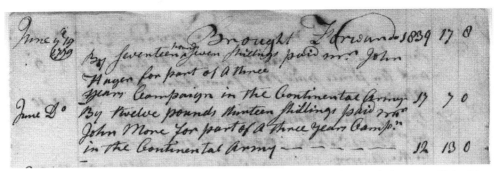

From the amounts and juxtaposition of these payment records in the "Treasurer's Accompts," John More and John Hagar appear to have shared a three-year term in the Continental Army, John Hagar serving the first 20 months and John More the final 16 months. No other records have been found to confirm this, and the details of such an arrangement are unidentified. Substitution was an accepted practice, however, for fulfilling service obligations, and that may have occurred here. (Courtesy of Lincoln Town Archives, Lincoln, MA)

MORE, John

John More was paid by the town for part of a three-year campaign in the Continental Army.[1]

His identity is uncertain, but there is a John Moore who shows up on the tax rolls of the town in 1779.[2]

---

1 "Treasurer's Accompts," June 15, 1779. Wheeler, "Lincoln" (in Hurd, Vol. 2, p. 622), indicates that John Hager (q.v.) served the first 20 months of this campaign, and John More served the final 16 months. The author has found no primary source to corroborate Wheeler's assertion. It appears to be based on the juxtaposition of the pay records, and on pay amounts that could be interpreted as prorated portions of a three-year campaign. A three-year campaign appears to have paid £30; Hager was paid £17:7 for his part; More was paid £12:13 for his part. The math works, but whether or not Wheeler's interpretation of the data is correct is unconfirmed. *Massachusetts Soldiers and Sailors* has multiple listings for service by individuals named John Hager (or John Hagar) and John More (or John Moore), but the author has found no meaningful relationship between any of the listings which would support Wheeler's assertion. The author has also been unable to identify the Continental service for which this John More was paid (see *Massachusetts Soldiers and Sailors*, Vol. VII, pp. 23, 24, 27, Vol. X, pp. 923–25, Vol. XI, pp. 5–6).

Blake, "James Barrett's Returns of Men" (p. 476), lists a John Moors, mustered (and paid a bounty) into Captain Smith's Company, Colonel Bigelow's Regiment, as reported by James Barrett, muster master, on June 6, 1777. However, this individual is identifiable as from Shirley, and his service was credited to Shirley. Accordingly, this record does not apply to John More (inst.) (see *Massachusetts Soldiers and Sailors*, Vol. X, pp. 941, 945).

2 There is no John More or John Moore identified in *Vital Records of Lincoln* or the Vital Records of most of the surrounding towns. *Vital Records of Sudbury* lists several possible candidates named John Moore:
- son of Edward and Kezia, age 36 at the start of the war
- son of Nathan and Agnice, age 29 at the start of the war
- son of Daniel and Elizabeth, age 21 at the start of the war

In addition, *Vital Records of Sudbury* lists the marriage of John Moore (possibly the son of Daniel and Elizabeth, but this is not identified) to Mary Bruce in 1775.

Coburn, *Muster Rolls*, reveals a John Moore, who was captain of a militia company from Bedford, and a John Moor, who was a minute man in Capt. John Nixon's Company from Sudbury, both of whom served on the Alarm of April 19, 1775.

Concord, Massachusetts: Births, Marriages, and Deaths lists the death of an Abel Moore, son of John and Anne, who must have been born about 1789. This suggests that John might have been of service age in the late 1770s, but there is little to suggest a Concord connection (much less, Lincoln) for John or any of his family before Abel's death in 1848.

There is simply insufficient information to connect any of these possible candidates with the Continental Army service of John More (inst.).

MUNROE, Abijah
[also MONROE, MUNRO]

Abijah Munroe was a private in Capt. William Smith's Company of Minute Men from Lincoln, Col. Abijah Peirce's Regiment.[1] This was the first minute company to arrive in Concord in response to the April 19, 1775, Alarm, and they followed the action into Cambridge. He served for five days.[2] He was reimbursed by the town for his accoutrements as a minute man.[3]

On April 24, 1775, he enlisted as a private in Capt. William Smith's Company, Col. John Nixon's 16th Massachusetts Regiment in the rapidly organizing Massachusetts Army. Presumably, he participated with his unit in the Battle of Bunker Hill on June 17, 1775. He was still on the rolls on September 30, 1775, when he was reported sick and absent. He was paid by the town for this service.[4]

He served as a corporal in Capt. John Hartwell's Lincoln Militia Company, Col. Eleazer Brooks's 3rd Middlesex County Regiment, which marched from Lincoln to fortify Dorchester Heights on March 4, 1776. The unit was discharged five days later, on March 9, after the threat of a British assault on the fortifications had subsided, and General Howe had begun preparations to evacuate Boston. He was paid for this service the following September.[5]

Next, he enlisted in Col. Thomas Craft's Artillery Regiment as a corporal in Capt. James Swan's 1st Company in Boston. It is likely that he was in service as early as June 8, 1776, when he received advance pay, but he is recorded as having served from August 1, 1776. On December 1, 1776, Capt. Philip Marett took over command of the company, and on February 1, 1777, he was promoted to sergeant. He served through May 8, 1777. He was paid by the town for this service.[6]

Agreeable to a resolve of April 20, 1778, he enlisted on June 4, 1778, to reinforce the Continental Army for a period of nine months from his arrival at Fishkill on June 17, 1778. He was detached from Capt. Samuel Farrar, Jr.'s Company, Colonel Brooks's Militia Regiment, and he appears to have served as a private in Capt. John Santford's Company, Colonel Malcom's Regiment, and also in Captain Jabez Lane's Company, Colonel Nixon's Regiment. He is described as age 22; five feet, nine inches in stature, and a resident of Lincoln. He was engaged for the town of Lincoln. He was stationed at Fishkill and at Innman's Ferry (near Woodbury, Connecticut), and he was discharged on March 17, 1779, from Verplanck's Point (near Peekskill). He was paid by the town for this service.[7]

---

1 Coburn, *Muster Rolls*.
2 *Massachusetts Soldiers and Sailors*, Vol. XI, p. 215.
3 "Treasurer's Accompts," March 15, 1776. This was paid to his father, Benjamin.
4 *Massachusetts Soldiers and Sailors*, Vol. XI, p. 215; "Treasurer's Accompts," June 10, 1779. Colonel Nixon's 16th Massachusetts Regiment became known as the 5th Regiment under the Continental numbering system adopted in August 1775.
5 *Massachusetts Soldiers and Sailors*, Vol. X, p. 882, Vol. XI, p. 215.
6 *Massachusetts Soldiers and Sailors*, Vol. XI, p. 215; "Treasurer's Accompts," June 10, 1779.
7 *Massachusetts Soldiers and Sailors*, Vol. XI, pp. 207, 215; "Treasurer's Accompts," June 10, 1779; Pension Record # S37264. See also Blake, "James Barrett's Returns of Men," p. 15. He had turned 23 by the time he reached Fishkill. His pension declaration makes no mention of any of his service at Concord, Cambridge, Dorchester Heights, or Boston, presumably because that service was militia or state service rather than Continental service, and thus was not qualifying service as defined under the Pension Act of 1818.

He was the son of Benjamin Munroe, Jr. (q.v.), and Mary (Merriam) Munroe; brother of Isaac Munroe (q.v.) and Micah Munroe (q.v.); brother-in-law of Edward Cabot (q.v.); nephew of Edmond Wheeler (q.v.); and cousin of Abner Mathis (q.v.). He was age 19 when he responded to the Concord Alarm. He married Salley Wheeler of Temple, New Hampshire, in 1786, and settled in Livermore, Maine, in 1795. He served as a Selectman of Livermore from 1798 to 1800, and he was granted a liquor retailing license in 1823. He reportedly died in Livermore, Maine, age and date unknown.[1]

MUNROE, Benjamin
[also MUNRO, also Benjamin, Jr.]

Benjamin Munroe was in arms at Concord on April 19, 1775, probably as a member of the militia company from Lincoln, or possibly as an un-enlisted volunteer.[2]

Subsequently, the town paid Lt. Benjamin Munroe for service at Dorchester in 1776 and 1777, and for nine months (one-quarter of a three-year service) in the Continental Army. No details of either of these terms of service are provided, but it is unlikely that he provided this service. More probably, the town's payment to Lt. Benjamin Munroe was for the service of his son, Isaac Munroe (q.v.), who was still serving in the Continental Army when the payment was made.[3]

The identity of the Benjamin Munroe who was in arms at Concord is most likely Lt. Benjamin Munroe, Jr.; he had been a lieutenant in the Lincoln militia prior to 1774. He was the son of Benjamin and Lydia Munroe; father of Abijah Munroe (q.v.), Isaac Munroe (q.v.), and Micah Munroe (q.v.); age 52 at Concord. He had been married since 1745 to Mary Merriam (also given as Marriam) from Lexington. He was also the brother-in-law

---

1 *Vital Records of Lincoln*; Bond, *Genealogies of the Families of Watertown*, p. 371; Wheeler, "Lincoln," in Hurd, Vol. 2, p. 623. Their marriage intention was recorded in Lincoln on October 2, 1785. Wheeler and "New Hampshire Marriage Records, 1637-1947" give January 9, 1786, as the date of their marriage. His death in Livermore is per Wheeler. Other Livermore information is from Michell and Daggett, *East Livermore and Livermore Register* (pp. 75, 104).

2 Deposition of John Hoar, et.al. No record survives of the members of the militia company. All of the Lincoln men we can place at the bridge who were over age 50 had sons who were minute men, suggesting a possible paternal reason for their presence, even if they had not been members of the militia company.

3 "Treasurer's Accompts," June 10, 1779. *Massachusetts Soldiers and Sailors* (Vol. XI, p. 208) offers little encouragement to suggest this payment was for service provided by Benjamin Munroe (inst.), either at Dorchester or in the Continental Army: There is a Benjamin Munro who served as a private in Lt. John Dryer's Company, Col. Thomas Carpenter's Regiment, which marched from Rehoboth to Bristol, Rhode Island, and served for 16 days on an Alarm of December 8, 1776. There is also a Benjamin Munro who was a corporal in John Boynton's Company, Col. Nathan Sparhawk's Regiment, and served for 34 days (including 6 days, 113 miles travel home), under Col. Job Cushing on the expedition to Bennington from July 27, 1777, to August 23, 1777. And there is a Benjamin Munro who served for 1 month, 6 days in Nathaniel Goodwin's Company, Col. Theophilus Cotton's Regiment, detached September 25, 1777, on a secret expedition to Newport, Rhode Island, and discharged October 31, 1777. It is possible that one of these records may be Benjamin Munroe (inst.) of Lincoln, but the author has found nothing in these records to encourage connecting Benjamin Munroe of Lincoln with Rehoboth, the Bennington Alarm, or a secret mission to Newport, much less Dorchester.

He would have turned age 54 at Dorchester, probably somewhat older during any Continental service. While this is not beyond the realm of possibilities, it does suggest the likelihood that the service for which he was paid may have been provided by someone else. Indeed, we find records of such service by his son, Isaac, no record of Isaac having been paid for that service, and evidence that Isaac was away from Lincoln, in service, when the payment was made.

of Edmond Wheeler (q.v.); father-in-law of Edward Cabot (q.v.); uncle of Abner Mathis (q.v.). He died in Lincoln in 1804 at age 81.[1]

MUNROE, Isaac
[also MONRO, MONROE, MONROW]

Isaac Munroe claimed that he was in arms at Concord on April 19, 1775, serving as a volunteer for one week, and that subsequently he volunteered for another week of service in June 1775, participating in the Battle of Bunker Hill. He also stated that he served six weeks at Winter Hill in the winter of 1775–1776 in Capt. Adam Wheeler's Company, Col. John Nixon's Regiment. If his claim of service is correct, his recollection of the details appears somewhat flawed.[2]

He served as a private in Capt. John Hartwell's Lincoln Militia Company, Col. Eleazer Brooks's 3rd Middlesex County Regiment, which marched from Lincoln to fortify Dorchester Heights on March 4, 1776. The unit was discharged five days later, on March 9, after the threat of a British assault on the fortifications had subsided, and General Howe had instead begun preparations to evacuate Boston. He was paid for this service the following September.[3]

He was back in service at Roxbury and Dorchester Heights later that year, first in Capt. John Minot's Company, Colonel Dike's Regiment, for three months from September through November 30, 1776, and then as a private in Capt. Moses Harrington's Company, Colonel Dike's Regiment for the months of December 1776 through February 1777. The regiment was raised to serve through March 1, 1777, but he was reported discharged on February 22, 1777, evidently in consequence of having enlisted for a three-year term of service in the Continental Army. He served from February 21, 1777, through December

---

1 Several other possibilities exist, but each requires a significant leap of faith: 1) Benjamin Jr. and Mary had a son Benjamin who was baptized in January 1767. If he was baptized as an infant (there is no pattern to suggest otherwise), then he would certainly have been too young to have been at Concord. Bond, *Genealogies of the Families of Watertown*, however, hints that Benjamin may have been a first child, which would have made him approximately age 29 at the time of Concord. The author has found nothing to corroborate this, and the regular birth (and baptism) pattern of their 11 children suggests that Benjamin was most likely born in the winter of 1766–1767; 2) There was recorded a 1748 marriage intention between a Benjamin Munroe of Weston and a Prudence Esterbrook of Lexington. No further information has been found about this Benjamin Munroe, nor anything to connect him to Lincoln, but his age can be loosely estimated as about 49 at the time of the Concord Alarm; 3) David Munroe of Lexington had a son, Benjamin, who was baptized in 1736, which would make him about age 38 at the time of the Concord Alarm. Benjamin's mother is not identified, but David had married Abigail in 1735. They had a second son, Abraham, born two years later. This is intriguing, because MacLean reports that David Munroe, wife Abigail, and son Abraham, from Lexington, came to live in Lincoln (then still part of Concord) in 1751. They were in "Low Circumstances," and were warned out of town. There is no mention of Benjamin, but at age 15 or 16, he may have been elsewhere, earning his keep. It may nevertheless be possible to connect the dots and place him in arms at Concord, with other Lincoln folk, in 1775 (see *Vital Records of Lincoln*; *Lexington Births, Marriages and Deaths; Town of Weston, Births, Deaths, & Marriages*; Bond, *Genealogies of the Families of Watertown*; MacLean, *A Rich Harvest*, pp. 210–11, 230).

2 Pension record # S13999. His pension declaration appears confused in comparison with the historical record. His claim of service on April 19th and at Bunker Hill is uncorroborated, yet he makes no claim for service at Dorchester Heights in March 1776, which is clearly documented. Further, he states that he enlisted in January 1776 in Capt. Adam Wheeler's Company, Colonel Nixon's Regiment and served for six weeks at Winter Hill. However, Capt. Adam Wheeler's Company is recorded as being at Winter Hill in the fall of 1775, in Colonel Doolittle's Regiment. Subsequently, Captain Wheeler was part of Colonel Nixon's Regiment around New York in the fall of 1776 (see *Massachusetts Soldiers and Sailors*, Vol. XVI, p. 959).

3 Hartwell, "A List of a Company of Militia"; *Massachusetts Soldiers and Sailors*, Vol. X, p. 882, Vol. XI, p. 216.

31, 1779, in Captain Pollard's (also Captain Parker's) Company, Col. Jeduthan Baldwin's Regiment of Artificers. He marched through Hartford to New York, then to Raritan, New Jersey, until the end of the 1776–1777 winter season. He then marched through Pennsylvania into Maryland, being present at the Battle of Brandywine in September 1777. He wintered along the Schuylkill (probably at or near Valley Forge) and was present at the Battle of Monmouth in June 1778. Subsequently, he wintered at Morristown. In addition to duty as an artificer, he also served as a substitute quartermaster and as a waiter to Captain Pollard. He was discharged in March 1780.[1]

Somewhere along the line, he seems to have put in three months at Rhode Island, as the town paid him for this service. However, no details of this service have been found.[2]

On July 27, 1780, he enlisted in Col. Cyprian How's Regiment, which was detached from the Middlesex County Militia to reinforce the Continental Army for three months. He marched through Weston, Natick, and Tiverton, to Butts Hill at Rhode Island. He was discharged on October 30, 1780, having served 3 months, 7 days in Rhode Island with Capt. Abraham Andrews's Company. He was paid for this service by the town.[3]

He was the son of Benjamin Munroe (q.v.) and Mary (Merriam) Munroe; brother of Abijah Munroe (q.v.) and Micah Munroe (q.v.); brother-in-law of Edward Cabot (q.v.); nephew of Edmond Wheeler (q.v.); cousin of Abner Mathis (q.v.). He was a few days short of his eighteenth birthday when he first served at Dorchester Heights. He married Grace Bigelow of Weston in 1798. When Grace died in 1812, he married Sally Hartwell, daughter of Samuel Hartwell (q.v.), the following January. Both women were about 15 years his junior. He died in Lincoln in 1840 at age 82.[4]

MUNROE, Joseph
[also MONROE, MUNRO]

Joseph Munroe was paid by the town for three months of service in the Continental Army. This appears to have been served as a private in Capt. John Hayward's Company, Colonel Webb's Regiment, from August 26, 1781, to November 30, 1781. The regiment was raised, in accordance with a resolve of June 30, 1781, to reinforce the Continental Army for three months at West Point or elsewhere. He served near West Point and at Continental Village. He was discharged on December 1, 1781, but was very sick and had to remain five or six

---

1 *Massachusetts Soldiers and Sailors*, Vol XI, pp. 216–17; "Treasurer's Accompts," June 10, 1779; Pension Record # S13999. It appears that the town paid his father for the Dorchester Heights service and part of the Continental Army service; see Benjamin Munroe (q.v.). Capt. Benjamin Pollard commanded the company of artificers in Colonel Baldwin's Regiment until his resignation in August 1778. Capt. Phineas Parker succeeded Captain Pollard (see *Massachusetts Soldiers and Sailors*, Vol. XII, p. 500).
2 "Treasurer's Accompts," October 28, 1780. Interestingly, the date of this payment appears to conflict with the dates of his subsequent Rhode Island service in Colonel How's Regiment from July 27 to October 30, 1780. Accordingly, either he must have arrived home early, or the payment date must have been recorded incorrectly. In any case, he was paid for his 1780 service at Rhode Island in Colonel How's Regiment on October 21, 1782, so this payment must have been for a previous tour of duty.
3 *Massachusetts Soldiers and Sailors*, Vol. X, p. 882; "Treasurer's Accompts," October 21, 1782; Pension record # S13999. With multiple records in *Massachusetts Soldiers and Sailors* of an Isaac Munroe who served as a fifer variously during 1775, 1776, 1778, 1779, and 1781, it was tempting to try to connect this individual with Isaac Munroe of Lincoln. The effort was unconvincing, both for the absence of connective tissue, and for conflicts in the service records. Isaac Munroe the fifer is a different individual from Isaac Munroe of Lincoln.
4 *Vital Records of Lincoln*. His death record lists his age as 85, but this is inconsistent with his birth record.

weeks before he was well enough to return home. He was credited with 3 months, 14 days of service including 10 days for 200 miles of travel home.[1]

He was the son of Jedediah Munroe and Abigail (Loring) Munroe of Lexington, about age 23 at West Point. His father was wounded on the Lexington Green the morning of April 19, 1775, then killed during the fighting that afternoon.[2]

He had served several previous tours of duty. His first service was as a member of Capt. John Bridge's Company, Col. Eleazer Brooks's 3rd Middlesex County Regiment of Militia, which marched to Roxbury and served from March 4, 1776, to March 8, 1776, during the fortification of Dorchester Heights.[3]

In October 1776, he served a week on guard duty in Roxbury, followed by another term of two weeks.[4]

He served at Saratoga, in Capt. George Minot's Company, Col. Samuel Bullard's Regiment (drafted from Capt. Francis Brown's Lexington Company, Col. Eleazer Brooks's Militia Regiment, as one of every sixth man from the training band and alarm lists) from August 16, 1777, to November 30, 1777. He served short-term duty in various locations around Saratoga and was present at the surrender of General Burgoyne, but he did not participate in either of the climactic battles at Saratoga. Following Burgoyne's surrender, he marched south with his regiment, and was discharged near New York City, having served for 3 months, 14 days.[5]

He returned to Roxbury for 14 days as a private in Capt. Lemuel May's Company, Colonel McIntosh's Regiment, from March 23, 1778, to April 5, 1778.[6]

Then, agreeable to a resolve of April 20, 1778, he enlisted for nine months of service (from the time of his arrival at Fishkill) to reinforce the Continental Army. Once again, he was recruited out of Captain Brown's Militia Company, Colonel Brooks's Regiment, and is described as age 18; standing five feet, seven inches high, and a Lexington resident.[7]

Following his war service, he married Rhoda Leathe of Woburn in 1783. Except for a couple of years when he lived in Woburn, he remained a lifelong Lexington resident. He died in 1832, just weeks after filing his pension claim. He was age 74.[8]

---

1 "Treasurer's Accompts," May 2, 1782; *Massachusetts Soldiers and Sailors,* Vol XI, p. 218; Pension Record # W18542. It is not immediately clear why Lincoln (and not Lexington) should have paid for this service. See parallel service by Ezra Meriam (q.v.), i.e., both Lexington boys with previous service from Lexington, now serving identical stints for Lincoln. Both served similar stints previously at Fishkill.

2 *Lexington Births, Marriages and Deaths.* His date of birth is not given; his age is estimated based upon the baptismal record. Jedediah's fate on April 19, 1775, is recorded in Hudson, *History of the Town of Lexington* (revised, Vol. I, p. 185).

3 *Massachusetts Soldiers and Sailors,* Vol XI, pp. 211.

4 Pension Record # W18542. Details of this service are not disclosed, but the short stints suggest that this may have been as a temporary substitute for another or other individuals (see also note 6).

5 *Massachusetts Soldiers and Sailors,* Vol XI, pp. 211, 218; Pension Record # W18542. Selection was consistent with the resolve of August 9, 1777, which directed that one-sixth part of the able bodied men of the training band and alarm lists, not already in service, be drafted at once to reinforce the northern army.

6 Quite possibly, this could be the second (two-week) Roxbury stint he mentions in his pension declaration. If so, his juxtaposition is confused and misleading (see note 4).

7 *Massachusetts Soldiers and Sailors,* Vol XI, pp. 211, 218. It is possible that there is more than one Joseph Munroe responsible for these terms of service, but they seem to fit the profile of a single individual just as well. There appears to be no particular reason to think this is more than one individual. If the identification is correct, and the Vital Record is accurate, then he would have been at least age 20 at Fishkill. He would have been age 18 during his initial service at Dorchester Heights in 1776.

8 Pension Record # W18542.

MUNROE, Micah
[also MONROW]

Micah Munroe enlisted on July 27, 1780, in Col. Cyprian How's Regiment, which was detached from the Middlesex County Militia to reinforce the Continental Army for three months. He was discharged on October 30, 1780, having served 3 months, 7 days in Rhode Island as a private in Capt. Abraham Andrews's Company. He was paid for this service by the town.[1]

He was the son of Benjamin Munroe (q.v.) and Mary (Merriam) Munroe; brother of Abijah Munroe (q.v.) and Isaac Munroe (q.v.); brother-in-law of Edward Cabot (q.v.); nephew of Edmond Wheeler (q.v.); cousin of Abner Mathis (q.v.); age 18 at the time of his service. He never married. He reportedly died in Livermore, Maine, date unknown.[2]

NELSON, Josiah

Josiah Nelson was paid by the town of Lincoln for service at Cambridge in 1776, and subsequently at Ticonderoga in 1776. The details of neither term of service are known, and the possibility exists that he may not have actually served either term.[3]

He was also paid for service at Saratoga in 1777, but the record shows that he did not provide that service. The Saratoga service was provided by his slave, Peter Nelson (q.v.).[4]

Josiah Nelson was the son of Thomas and Tabitha (Hobbs) Nelson; age 48 at the time of the Concord Alarm. He had been married to Elizabeth Flagg since 1750 and was living on the North Road near the Lexington town line (now called Nelson Road, as part of the Minute Man National Historical Park). He appears to have been assigned to carry the Alarm (if and when it should come) into the southern part of Bedford, and he is generally credited with having done so. Elizabeth died, childless, in 1776, and he married Mellacent Bond of Lexington, 20 years his junior, in 1777. Mellacent bore him seven children, starting

---

1 *Massachusetts Soldiers and Sailors*, Vol. X, p. 883; "Treasurer's Accompts," February 16, 1781.

2 *Vital Records of Lincoln*; Wheeler, "Lincoln," in Hurd, Vol. 2, p. 623.

3 "Treasurer's Accompts," June 10, 1779. Wheeler, "Lincoln" (in Hurd, Vol. 2, p. 623; also repeated in Hersey, *Heroes*, p. 20, and Malcolm, *The Scene of Battle*, p. 33), lists his Cambridge service as 1775, which the author takes to be an editing error.

  The absence of concrete evidence that he actually provided this service has fueled some debate about whether the actual service was by him or by someone else. Hafner, "The First Blood" (p. 13), takes the position that in the absence of a service record for him in *Massachusetts Soldiers and Sailors* and among Lincoln's militia records, the logic of his personal circumstances (age 48-plus, large farm, pregnant wife) makes it "rather certain he was never…a soldier in arms during the Revolution." The author respectfully disagrees. Neither Lincoln's militia records nor *Massachusetts Soldiers and Sailors* are sufficiently comprehensive to equate omission with lack of service. As good a compiled source as *Massachusetts Soldiers and Sailors* is, there are a number of Lincoln individuals who do not appear in *Massachusetts Soldiers and Sailors*, but whose service has been documented from other sources. The "Treasurer's Accompts" constitute prima facie evidence of his service. To reach a contrary conclusion would require some sort of disqualifier, evidence of an alternative explanation, or compelling logic to the contrary.

  Service in Capt. Charles Miles's Company, Col. Jonathan Reed's Regiment at Ticonderoga is suggested by a mileage receipt he signed for Thomas Blodget (q.v.). However, as Josiah does not appear on any of the returns from that company, it appears equally likely that Blodget may have been serving as Josiah's substitute (see sidebar, "Are All Records Created Equal?", p. 351).

4 "Treasurer's Accompts," June 10, 1779. Although Peter was still only age 14 at the time, the record of his service at Saratoga, as recorded in *Massachusetts Soldiers and Sailors* (Vol. XI, p. 321), is unmistakable.

According to tradition, the first blood drawn in the Revolutionary War was at the Josiah Nelson farm (seen as it looked c. 1900). Possibly bleeding from a forehead gash inflicted by the sword of a British officer, Josiah is generally credited with galloping the alarm into Bedford in the early hours of April 19th. Later, in 1776, he may have served at Cambridge and at Ticonderoga. (*An Account of the Celebration*)

with Josiah Jr., in January 1778. The elder Josiah (inst.) died in Lincoln in 1810, at the age of 83. He is buried in the Old Burial Ground in Lexington.[1]

Tradition has it that in the early hours of April 19th, he was awakened by the British patrol escorting Paul Revere back to Lexington as a captive. Thinking that the sounds were from a local farmer taking his goods to market, he rushed outside to inquire if there was any news about the Regulars being about. Before he realized his mistake, one of the officers is said to have raised his sword and struck him in the head, drawing blood and declaring, "We

---

1 Hafner, "The First Blood," pp. 7–8; *Lexington Births, Marriages and Deaths; Vital Records of Grafton*. Hafner lists his age at the time of his death as 84; actually he appears to have died 6½ months prior to his 84th birthday (see also Malcolm, *The Scene of Battle*, pp. 32–35).

Josiah's first wife's name is often given as Elizabeth Abrams, but this appears to be in error. Elizabeth Flagg was born in Concord, but she had been living in Grafton with her mother (her father had died when she was about age 16), where the marriage intention was recorded. Hafner details an ingenious bit of genealogical sleuthing by Justine Gengras to get this record straight.

Malcolm, *The Scene of Battle* (p. 35) erroneously states that he deteriorated substantially in his later years, was declared insane, and placed under the guardianship of his family. A careful reading of the Nelson Family Papers makes it clear that this record applies to his son, Josiah Nelson, Jr., not to Josiah Nelson (inst.) (see Hafner, "The First Blood," pp. 9–10, footnote; Patch Deed to Nelson (1827)).

His Lexington burial is per Malcolm, *Peter's War*, p. 233; *SAR Revolutionary War Graves Register*.

Are All Records Created Equal?
Drawing Cautious Interpretations from Limited Evidence

Connected to the "midnight ride" of Paul Revere, Josiah Nelson's story on April 19th is a fascinating part of America's legendary history. First recorded in 1890, Nelson-family tradition tells us that Josiah Nelson helped to spread the Alarm that the Regulars were coming, and that in the early hours of that fateful day, *his* was the first blood to be shed in the Revolutionary War.

Lacking period records to verify the tradition, it may always remain a legend. So, too, sparse records on his possible later military service prompt questions about whether or not he subsequently served in the war.

No records of service by Josiah Nelson are listed in *Massachusetts Soldiers and Sailors*, but as good a compiled source as that is, it is not definitive. There are a number of Lincoln individuals who do not appear in *Massachusetts Soldiers and Sailors* whose service has been documented from other sources. Indeed, Lincoln's "Treasurer's Accompts" record town payments to Josiah Nelson for services rendered at Cambridge, Ticonderoga, and Saratoga. His signing a receipt for mileage home from Ticonderoga may further the case. But there are differing views on how to interpret these records. Did he serve himself, or was he being paid for the services of others?

It was an accepted practice for an individual to avoid a military obligation by providing a substitute to serve in his place. The "Treasurer's Accompts" distinguish many of these instances of "providing a man for service." Other instances of substitution are not so noted. Nor, typically, are individuals who were paid for the service provided by a son or a slave. These cases can be difficult to ferret out, and to identify who actually provided the service indicated.

Josiah Nelson had no sons who could have provided any of this service, but he did own a slave. He is known to have acquired a "Negro Servant boy named Peter," age about 19 months, in January 1765. The town's payment to Josiah Nelson for Saratoga service matches a service record for a Peter Nelson (q.v.), at Saratoga. This fits the pattern of slave owners being paid for the service provided by their slaves, and it is likely that the Saratoga payment to Josiah was in fact for the service provided by his slave Peter.

No such service record has been identified to explain the payment to Josiah Nelson for Cambridge or Ticonderoga. His slave Peter was age 12—turning 13 about June 1776—probably too young to have provided this service (although it should be noted that Peter was age 14 when he served at Saratoga the following year, and that service by a 13-year-old, while exceptionally rare, was not unknown; see Joseph Parker (q.v.)). While it is possible that Josiah also could have had an older slave who served, this would be entirely speculative.

The town's payment record specifically states "for His service at Cambridge in the year 1776." The word "His" is presumably significant; it is notably missing from the reference to Ticonderoga and Saratoga service, and that certainly makes it difficult ▶

to attribute "His service at Cambridge" speculatively to another individual. This fact, and the absence of other identified or logical candidates in the first place, forces us to conclude that the Cambridge service was most likely provided by Josiah himself.

Josiah Nelson would have been age 48 or 49 at Cambridge, a bit older than the norm, but not all that rare. Other individuals of a similar age or older who served in various campaigns are Aaron Brooks (q.v.), Ephraim Brooks (q.v.), Joshua Brooks (q.v.), Elisha Gearfield (q.v.), and Cornelius Meloney (q.v.).

The death of Josiah's wife Elizabeth in March 1776 argues both for and against his Cambridge service. On one hand, he could certainly have been too overwhelmed with grief, personal obligations, and/or farm chores to have enlisted for service. On the other hand, he may have been in need of getting away from it all for a period of time, and service at Cambridge may have provided a means of escape. In either case, he had a brother and a sister living next door, and at least one young slave who might have been able to help run the farm while he was away.

Similar arguments would apply to the question of whether he served at Ticonderoga a few months later, or sent a substitute instead. In this case, however, the payment record does not specifically state "His" service. *Massachusetts Soldiers and Sailors* (Vol. II, p. 198) contains a record of Josiah Nelson signing a receipt for mileage home from Ticonderoga on behalf of Thomas Blodget (q.v.), who served in Captain Miles's Company. Juxtaposed with the town's payment for service at Ticonderoga, one interpretation of this record suggests that Nelson served in Captain Miles's Company. On the other hand, the receipt proves only that Nelson was on location in Lexington on February 18, 1777, to collect Blodget's travel allowance and sign the receipt. An equally valid interpretation is that Blodget may have been Nelson's substitute.

In the absence of any other evidence, the author is left to presume that it was Josiah Nelson who served at Cambridge, that he likely was paid for Blodget's service at Ticonderoga, and that the payment for Saratoga was for his slave Peter's service. Indeed, not all records are equal, and further records may either suggest contrary conclusions or confirm these cautious interpretations.

[See "Treasurer's Accompts," June 10, 1779; Hafner, "The First Blood"; *Massachusetts Soldiers and Sailors*; MacLean, *Rich Harvest*.]

will let you know when they are coming!" Although the legend is unverifiable, this episode is regarded by some as "the first blood shed in the American Revolution."[1]

---

1 There are several versions of this story, all somewhat similar but with variations in the detail. This one is from Hersey, *Heroes* (pp. 18–20). Wheeler, "Lincoln" (in Hurd, Vol. 2, p. 619), published the earliest known version in 1890. Josiah's grandson, George Nelson, appears to be directly linked as the source of several of the published accounts. Because none of Josiah's children were born until 1778, and George was born 12 years after Josiah's death, the story (if one assumes there to be at least some basis in fact) was at least third-hand by the time it appeared in print. Hafner, "The First Blood," has done a superb job of deconstructing the legend and trying to reconcile the different versions with the historical record. A detail of Josiah's supposed lameness first appears in 1904, in the version of the story that is related in *An Account of the Celebration*. Even if lameness could be verified, Hafner (p. 11) appropriately notes that we do not know if it might have been permanent or temporary.

NELSON, Peter

Peter Nelson served as a private in Capt. Samuel Farrar, Jr.'s Company, Col. Jonathan Reed's Middlesex County Regiment (Brig. Gen. James Bricket's Brigade of Massachusetts Militia) at Saratoga. This company was urgently detached from Col. Eleazer Brooks's 3rd Middlesex County Regiment of Militia on September 29, 1777, and sent northward to reinforce the Northern Army under General Gates. They marched to Saratoga by way of Bennington, arriving a day or two after the Battle of Bemis Heights on October 7, 1777. They were deployed to Fort Edward, and on October 17, they were recalled to Saratoga, where they were present at General Burgoyne's surrender. With his unit, he was part of the guard that escorted the British prisoners to Cambridge. He was discharged at Cambridge on November 7, 1777, credited with having served 1 month, 10 days.[1]

He enlisted again on June 14, 1778, and three days later marched back to the Hudson Valley (this time a little further south) with Capt. Edward Richardson's Company, Col. Thomas Poor's Regiment. Through muster roll and payroll records, we can trace him to West Point (September 1778), and King's Ferry (November 1778). He was discharged from the Hudson Valley on February 24, 1779, having served 8 months, 21 days, including an allowance of 11 days for 220 miles of travel home.[2]

He was a slave belonging to Josiah Nelson (q.v.); age 14 when he served at Saratoga; not yet age 16 when he completed his service in the Hudson Valley in 1779. He may have been the son of Jupiter (a slave belonging to Joshua Brooks of Lincoln) and Peg (a slave belonging to William Reed of Lexington).[3]

---

1 *Massachusetts Soldiers and Sailors*, Vol. XI, p. 321. For accounts of their deployment around Saratoga, see Shattuck, *History of the Town of Concord*, p. 356; Pension Record # S29229 for Leonard Hoar (q.v.); Pension Record # W20567 for Edward Adams.

2 *Massachusetts Soldiers and Sailors*, Vol. XI, p. 321. Malcolm, *Peter's War* (p. 173), says he was discharged in 1779 at Watertown, but clearly "Watertown" represents the roll's administrative processing. The record specifically indicates his discharge at North River, New York (i.e., the Hudson Valley). This is consistent with the more typical practice for soldiers to be discharged from the field rather than to be marched home before their discharge. Note that his discharge date is 11 days short of his credited service time (reflecting the 20 miles per day allowance for the time it would take him to travel home).

3 MacLean, *A Rich Harvest*, p. 217. See also Brooks bill of sale to Nelson (1765). In January 1765, Josiah Nelson paid £4 to Joshua Brooks for a "neagro servant boy named peter about one year and seven months old." Parentage is a reasonable supposition. Jupiter and Peg had been married with the consent of their owners in 1756 (see also *Vital Records of Lincoln*). The Joshua Brooks who sold Peter is the father of Joshua Brooks (q.v.); grandfather of Joshua Brooks, Jr. (q.v.). His wife Mary, who is mentioned in the bill of sale, is his second wife (born Mary Munroe, widow of Thomas Wheeler), whom he married in 1751 (see also *Concord, Massachusetts: Births, Marriages, and Deaths*).

Malcolm, *Peter's War* (pp. 5–6), reports Peter's baptism on October 2, 1763, and credits him with a twin sister, baptized a month later. The record in question, found in *Lexington Births, Marriages and Deaths*, reads "Peter, s. of Robbin & Peggy, bp. Oct. 2, 1763." The companion record reads "Peggy, d. of Robbin & Peggy, bp. Nov. 6, 1763." Robbin and Peggy are identifiable from other Vital Records as Robbin (also given as Robin, Robing) and Peggy (also given as Margaret) Tulop (also given as Tulip), who were the parents of four other children between 1735 and 1759. Robbin was the slave of John Bridge, and he died in 1784. Peggy died in 1794. This baptism record cannot belong to Peter Nelson (inst.).

> Know all men by these presence that of Joshua Broocks of lincoln in the County of middelsir and prouence of the maschusits bay in newingland gentelman for and in consideration of the sum of four pounds to me in hand before the in sealing hear of paid by Josiah nellson of lincoln yeaman in full satisfaction do hear by sell con uay and deliuer to him the sd Josiah nellson his eirs and asines for euer a sartain neagro seruant boy named peter a bout one year and seuen months old and of the said Joshu broocks for my selfe and for my eirs exetors and administrators do couenant and ingage to and with him the said josiah nellson that before the in sealing hear of I am the true and proper owner of the aforesaid peter and I do warant to secure and defend him the said Josiah nellson and his eirs against the lawfull claims or demands of any parson or parsons what soeuer in witness whear of I the said Joshu Broocks with mary my wife haue hear unto set our hands and seals this twenty ninth day of Janwary anodomony 1765
> in presence of us
> Jhn Brooks
> Lucy Brooks
>
> Joshua Brooks
> her
> Mary X Brooks
> Mark

This bill of sale for "a sertain neagro servant boy named peter a bout one year and seven months old" establishes the identity of Peter Nelson, who was a fourteen-year-old slave of Josiah Nelson when he served at Saratoga. A year later he served in the Hudson Valley as a fifteen-year-old. After that, his trail becomes indistinct; he may have changed his name after gaining his freedom. (Courtesy of Lincoln Town Archives, Lincoln, MA)

No further information has been found about Peter Nelson. It has been suggested that he may have changed his name in 1779 or 1780, and reenlisted for additional service as Peter Sharon (q.v.), but this is entirely speculative.[1]

---

1 Malcolm, *Peter's War*, p. 193. See also Wiggin, "A Tale of Two or Three Peters." Malcolm lays out the premise that Peter Nelson enlisted for further service in 1780 as Peter Sharon (q.v.) on the promise of manumission

NICHOLS, James
[also NICHOLLS, NICKELS, NICKOLLS]

James Nichols of Lincoln went to Concord on the morning of April 19th, either as a member of the militia company or as a private citizen. He is described as "an Englishman, and a droll fellow, and a fine singer." Before the fight at the bridge, he is reported to have conversed for a time with the Regulars, then picked up his musket and gone home.[1]

He served at Bunker Hill, as evidenced by a communication, dated June 14, 1775 (three days before the battle), by Capt. Nathan Fuller to the armorer requesting him to receive the guns belonging to Nichols and other members of his company, and fit them for service. Fuller's company was part of Colonel Gardner's 37th Regiment; Gardner was mortally wounded in the battle. Nichols was reported still serving as a private in Captain Fuller's Company, now Lt. Col. William Bond's Regiment, in a return dated Prospect Hill, October 6, 1775.[2]

He is reported to have served at Dorchester Heights, from where he deserted to the British lines. This reported desertion appears to be incorrect.[3]

---

following the completion of his term of service. Name changes were a widespread practice among slaves upon manumission, and the records establish that Peter Nelson and Peter Sharon were approximately the same age (within a year's difference). The possibility that Peter Nelson and Peter Sharon could be the same individual cannot be denied. However, beyond the similarities in age, the author has found no evidence with which to connect them, or connections that might explain Peter Nelson's adopting the name Sharon, which elsewhere appears to have been adopted by former Lincoln slaves associated with the Headley family. Drawing a link between Peter Nelson and Peter Sharon is speculative, representing a leap of faith that the author finds intriguing but unconvincing on the available evidence.

Malcolm, *Peter's War* (p. 76), further asserts that Peter Nelson had served earlier in the war, at Cambridge in 1775, at age not yet 12, under the name of Peter Brooks (q.v.). She explains that it was customary for a slave to take as his last name "that of his original owners." As compelling a story line as this makes, the author finds this assertion unsustainable both logically and by reason of contrary evidence.

The author has been unable to validate Malcolm's premise of such a customary practice, or to find any examples in eighteenth-century New England of a slave taking the name of an original owner after being sold to another owner. Nor has he found any scholarship on the subject of slavery in colonial New England that has identified or hinted at such a practice (see, for example, Greene, *The Negro in Colonial New England*; Piersen, *Black Yankees*; McManus, *Black Bondage*; Karttunen, *The Other Islanders*; Lemire, *Black Walden*). [The author was able to find a few examples of this in scholarship associated with the antebellum south (see Gutman, *The Black Family in Slavery & Freedom*, pp. 230–251). Whether or not examples from the antebellum south are applicable to colonial New England is questionable. But in either case, these examples were exceptions to the rule, and were not indicative of a common or "customary" practice. In each case, the slave had an established identity that transcended the change of ownership. In no case was the slave still a young boy when the change of ownership occurred.]

Malcolm's work contains no source citations. In correspondence with the author, Malcolm attributed the finding of such a customary practice to her "own research," but failed to provide particulars. Further, if her premise were correct, it is logically unclear why such a customary practice would not still have applied two years later when (according to Malcolm) Peter abandoned the name Brooks and enlisted as Peter Nelson.

Beyond the above questions, the evidence itself counters the hypothesis that Peter Brooks and Peter Nelson were the same individual. A pair of land transactions in 1783 and 1785 provides strong evidence that Peter Brooks became known as Peter Bowes upon manumission. This evidence would preclude Peter Brooks from being the same individual as Peter Nelson. See sidebar, "What's in a (New England Slave) Name?", pp. 219-222, including illustrations, pp. 220-221; see also note 1, p. 240.

See also Wiggin, "A Tale of Two or Three Peters," for a more thorough discussion of this issue and of the identities of Peter Brooks, Peter Bowes, and Peter Nelson.

1 Baker Affidavit (1850). See sidebar, "A 75-Year-Old Recollection," p. 356.
2 *Massachusetts Soldiers and Sailors*, Vol. XI, p. 414.
3 Baker Affidavit (1850). Not surprisingly, given his age (94) and the 75 years that had passed since the events, Baker appears to have confused some of his facts. Nichols does not appear in Hartwell, "A List of a Company

A 75-Year-Old Recollection: Teasing out the Rest of the Story

In 1850, 75 years after the battle at Concord's North Bridge, Lincoln's Amos Baker (q.v.) recalled an interesting anecdote about one of the men present. "Before the fighting begun, when we were on the hill," Baker remembered, "James Nichols, of Lincoln, who was an Englishman, and a droll fellow, and a fine singer, said, 'If any of you will hold my gun, I will go down and talk to them.' Some of them held his gun, and he went down alone to the British soldiers at the bridge and talked to them some time. Then he came back and took his gun and said he was going home, and went off before the fighting. Afterwards he enlisted to go to Dorchester and there deserted to the British, and I never heard of him again."

The story has fascinated generations of history buffs. Amos Baker may never have "heard of him again," but James Nichols did leave a small trail in the historical records through which we can piece together the rest of the story…and test the mental acuity of the 94-year-old Baker.

The record tells us that shortly after leaving Concord, Nichols enlisted in the Provincial Army besieging Boston, and he participated in the Battle of Bunker Hill. He served through that summer and fall, and into the following spring. He appears to have served through the fortification of Dorchester Heights—but without deserting to the British. Baker, too, served at Dorchester Heights, albeit in a different unit.

That summer (1776), Nichols appears to have left Lincoln, gone to Weston, then taken up residence in Acton, perhaps an itinerant worker moving from job to job. By wintertime, he was back in militia service at Dorchester—this time in the same unit as Baker, and they evidently renewed their friendship. During their three-month stint, Nichols was recruited into the Continental Army, and one January day Baker discovered his friend gone.

The Continental unit Nichols joined had a handful of other Lincoln men in it. They were marched northward in chase of the British army of General Burgoyne, who was threatening to split the country along the Hudson River/Lake Champlain corridor. In September 1777, after eight months of Continental service, Nichols was reported as having deserted. He may have become disillusioned at the not-so-rosy life of a Continental soldier. Or gotten cold feet with the approach of what was certain to be a climactic battle. Or perhaps he simply succumbed to itinerant tendencies. The historical record does not reveal what was going on in his head. Two months later, he appears to have returned to militia service in Cambridge, guarding the British and German troops surrendered by General Burgoyne following the climactic battles at Saratoga.

Somewhere along the line, Amos Baker learned of the reported desertion by Nichols, probably from one of the Lincoln men serving in the same unit. Perhaps in the years that followed, he occasionally thought about the good times they had together—the singing, the humor, the storytelling. He recalled the incident at the bridge. He remembered last seeing his friend at Dorchester.… ▶

> Seventy-plus years later, Baker was feted as the last known surviving participant of the fight at the Concord bridge. Old memories returned, a little worn with age. He was coaxed to write them down for posterity. And he left us with a wonderful snippet of the human side of the developing conflict. He got it almost right; he passes the acuity test. But even he did not know the rest of the story.
>
> [See Baker Affidavit (1850); *Massachusetts Soldiers and Sailors*, Vol. XI, pp. 414, 421, 422, 440, 441, 452.]

More probably, he seems to have served through the time of Dorchester Heights, as a private in Capt. James Perry's Company, 16th Regiment, from January 1, 1776, to April 6, 1776 (during which he was hospitalized for a time). While not certain, this appears to be the same James Nichols.[1]

He was back in service from December 20, 1776, to January 13, 1777, as a private in Capt. Moses Harrington's Company, Colonel Dike's Regiment. The regiment was raised to serve to March 1, 1777. This service was credited to the town of Weston, and it appears to overlap his subsequent service in the Continental Army.[2]

He served in the Continental Army as a private in Capt. Abijah Child's Company, Col. John Greaton's 2nd Regiment, from January 1, 1777, to September 5, 1777, at which time he is reported as having deserted. He appears to have left Lincoln by this time, as he is described as a resident of Acton, and this service was credited to Acton.[3]

Notwithstanding his reported desertion, he seems to have been back in service two months later, in Capt. Miles Greenwood's Company, Col. Jacob Gerrish's Regiment of Guards, from November 11, 1777, to April 3, 1778 (4 months, 23 days), at Winter Hill, guarding General Burgoyne's Convention Army, although once again, it is not certain if this is the same James Nichols.[4]

Nichols appears not to have left much of a trail in the Vital Records. As he was later described as an Englishman, he was presumably a fairly recent arrival in America, and evi-

---

of Militia," which omission would make sense if he had deserted to British lines, but it would not make sense if he had not deserted. However, Nichols's desertion to the British lines at Dorchester Heights would be inconsistent with subsequent service for which documentation has been found (see sidebar "A 75-Year-Old Recollection").

1 *Massachusetts Soldiers and Sailors*, Vol. XI, p. 440.
2 *Massachusetts Soldiers and Sailors*, Vol. XI, p. 452. This service matches service by Amos Baker (q.v.) and appears to have been the Dorchester service that Baker connected years later with Nichols's desertion. Baker served through March 1, 1777, but after January 13 he must have realized that Nichols was no longer there. He may not have known, or may subsequently have forgotten, where Nichols went. The overlapping service credit was probably a Continental enlistment bonus.
3 *Massachusetts Soldiers and Sailors*, Vol. XI, pp. 421, 441. This listing also reports an undated return crediting his enlistment to Lincoln. It is not clear if the Lincoln and Acton credits pertain to the same service (which would appear to be an unlikely circumstance) or to different service (the dates of which are not reported) in the same unit.
4 *Massachusetts Soldiers and Sailors*, Vol. XI, p. 422. Colonel Gerrish and Captain Greenwood were both residents of Essex County, suggesting that this unit may have been made up mostly of Essex County residents. While this might ordinarily discourage the identity of this James Nichols as the same individual, James Nichols (inst.) appears to have been sufficiently peripatetic for this to have been plausible.

dently moved about somewhat (from Lincoln, possibly to Weston, then to Acton). He may have worked as a farmhand or laborer, moving about from job to job, but this, of course, is all speculative, as no further information has been found.

NIXON, Joseph
[also NIXEN]

Joseph Nixon enlisted in the rapidly forming Massachusetts Provincial Army on April 24, 1775, and served at Cambridge as a fifer in the regiment commanded by his father, Col. John Nixon. He participated in the Battle of Bunker Hill on June 17, 1775, probably in Captain Moore's Company. In August, he is recorded as serving in Capt. Jeremiah Gilman's Company, and on September 30, he is recorded in Capt. Joseph Butler's Company. He served through the end of December.[1]

Enlisting in the Continental Army, he appears to have remained in service in his father's regiment through August 12, 1776, "at which time," according to his pension declaration, "I was honorably and regularly discharged from said service by His Excellency George Washington, Commander in Chief."[2]

He was back in Continental service, as a fifer and private, possibly as early as May 1, 1777. He enlisted for three years in Capt. Abel Holden's Company, Col. Thomas Nixon's 6th Massachusetts Regiment. He participated in the Saratoga campaign in the fall of 1777 and was deployed in the Hudson Valley during most of 1779. On January 1, 1780, he became a member of Capt. Matthew Chambers's Company, and on January 1, 1781, Colonel Nixon was succeeded by Col. Calvin Smith. He was discharged on May 1, 1781.[3]

He was from Sudbury, the son of Col. John and Thankful (Berry) Nixon; age 11 when he fifed at Bunker Hill. In 1780, he listed his residence as Framingham, and after his war service he lived in Waltham, where he married Nancy Weston, daughter of Zechariah Weston (q.v.), in 1791. She was age 14; he was age 28. He was by occupation a housewright. He remained in Waltham at least through 1810. He appears to have moved to Lincoln by

---

1 *Massachusetts Soldiers and Sailors,* Vol. XI, p. 481.

2 Pension Record # W20277 / BLWT19812-160-55. Many of the Massachusetts regiments, including Col. John Nixon's Regiment, were absorbed into the Continental Army by the end of 1775. With his original term expiring on December 31, 1775, Joseph Nixon's reenlistment would normally have been for the calendar year, 1776. His discharge by Gen. George Washington in August, before the commencement of serious fighting around New York, suggests a bit of deference accorded Colonel Nixon regarding the continued service of his 13-year-old son. It was about mid-August that Col. John Nixon appears to have been given additional responsibility and was succeeded in regimental command by his brother, Col. Thomas Nixon. The author surmises that Colonel Nixon arranged the discharge because he was no longer able to exercise personal involvement in his son's safety. Col. John Nixon was later named brigadier general (see *Massachusetts Soldiers and Sailors,* Vol. XI, p. 480).

3 *Massachusetts Soldiers and Sailors,* Vol. XI, p. 481; Pension Record # W20277 / BLWT19812-160-55. His pension declaration says he enlisted in May 1778 for three years, which is consistent with his discharge, but the service record clearly shows that he enlisted for three years on or before August 15, 1777. The author surmises that his three-year enlistment began on May 1, 1777, and that subsequently he extended it for a year. Col. Thomas Nixon was reported deranged (i.e., removed from office as a consequence of the reorganization and reform of the army by an act of Congress), and left the service on December 31, 1780 (see *Massachusetts Soldiers and Sailors,* Vol. XI, p. 482; *Massachusetts Soldiers and Sailors,* Vol. XIV, p. 358; for the obsolete meaning of the word "deranged," see the *Oxford English Dictionary*.)

1813, and to have remained in Lincoln through 1817. By the spring of 1818, he was living in Cambridge, and in 1820 we find him in Brookline. He died in 1832 at age 68.[1]

He is reportedly buried in a Lincoln cemetery, but this is uncertain.[2]

OLIVER, Peter

Peter Oliver of Lincoln served at Cambridge as a private in Capt. Abijah Wyman's Company, Col. William Prescott's Regiment from May 30, 1775, at least through August 1, 1775 (2 months, 3 days of service), and presumably through October 3, 1775, when he shows up again on a company return in Cambridge. He most likely participated in the Battle of Bunker Hill. An order for a bounty coat or its equivalent in money was issued on November 11, 1775.[3]

During 1776, he served at Ticonderoga, as a private in Capt. Timothy Stow's Company, Col. Ephraim Wheelock's Regiment.[4]

On March 20, 1777, now residing in Littleton, he enlisted in the Continental Army for three years, serving as a private in Capt. Edmund Munroe's Company, Col. Timothy Bigelow's 15th Massachusetts Regiment. This regiment served at Saratoga in October 1777, and spent the legendary winter of 1777–1778 at Valley Forge. It also served in the Battle of Monmouth in June 1778 and in the Battle of Rhode Island in August 1778. He appears to have been serving in Providence in February 1779, but he was reportedly on furlough in March and April 1779. After Captain Munroe's death at Monmouth, he continued to serve in this company, now led by Captain Bowman, until his discharge on March 20, 1780. This service was credited to the town of Littleton.[5]

Four months later, he was back in Continental service for six months, agreeable to a resolve of June 5, 1780. He marched on July 15, 1780, arriving in Springfield on July 19, 1780. He is described as a Negro, age 23, five feet, nine inches in stature. He was at Camp

---

1 *Vital Records of Sudbury; Massachusetts Soldiers and Sailors*, Vol. XI, p. 481; Bond, *Genealogies of the Families of Watertown*, p. 376; *Vital Records of Waltham*; *Vital Records of Lincoln*; Pension Record # W20277 / BLWT19812-160-55. Nancy's birth is recorded in Waltham. Waltham Vital Records also lists the birth of six children between 1792 (five months after their marriage; Nancy was still age 14) and 1804. Census records confirm his Waltham residency through 1810. *Vital Records of Lincoln* lists the 1813 baptism of three children not recorded elsewhere. These were probably added many years later, along with a birth record for Nancy (as Nancy Nixon, not Nancy Weston), as they are identified as children of "Nancy, wid." *Vital Records of Lincoln* also contains the 1817 death of Joseph Nixen, Jr., identified as "s. Capt. Joseph and Nancy, a. 23." The honorific "Captain" is probably from postwar service in the Waltham militia.

His Lincoln residency is an educated guess, based upon the author's reading of *Vital Records of Lincoln*, and may have been related to Nancy's parents, who were clearly living in Lincoln by this time.

2 *Soldiers and Sailors* [SAR], p. 30. Biggs, "In Memorium" (p. 179) shows a "Mr. Joseph Nixon, Jr. son of Cap. Joseph and Mrs. Nancy Nixon, who died Oct. 12, 1817, Æ t. 23," and a "Mrs. Nancy W. Nixon, Born Oct. 28, 1777. Died Dec. 18, 1869. Aged 92," both in the Meeting House Cemetery. These stones are next to Nancy's parents, Zechariah Weston (q.v.) and Mary Weston. Joseph Nixon (inst.) does not appear to be with them, although there is a possibility that he could be in unmarked space beside Joseph Jr. The location of Joseph Sr.'s death and burial remain unknown. According to the pension record (# W20277), Nancy lived in Boston for thirty years after Joseph's death. Notwithstanding her Lincoln burial, her death is not recorded in Lincoln.

3 *Massachusetts Soldiers and Sailors*, Vol. XI, p. 642; Quintal, *Patriots of Color*, pp. 40, 166.

4 *Massachusetts Soldiers and Sailors*, Vol. XI, p. 643.

5 *Massachusetts Soldiers and Sailors*, Vol. XI, p. 642; Quintal, *Patriots of Color*, pp. 42–43, 166; Blake, "James Barrett's Returns of Men," p. 471. He appears to have had family connections in Littleton, which may explain his enlisting for the credit of Littleton (see note 2, p. 360).

Totaway in New Jersey on October 25, 1780, and was discharged on December 6, 1780, having served 5 months, 2 days (including 220 miles of travel home). This service was credited to Littleton.

Agreeable to a resolve of December 2, 1780, he reenlisted in the Continental Army for another three-year term on July 4, 1781. He is described as age 24; five feet, eight inches in stature; black complexion, black eyes, and black hair. His occupation is listed as farmer, but it is also given as laborer. This service was credited to the town of Carlisle.[1]

He was African American, possibly of mixed race; the son of Margaret Oliver; born in Lincoln, age 19 during his service at Bunker Hill.[2]

ORR, William

William Orr enlisted for a three-year tour of duty in the Continental Army, agreeable to a resolve of December 2, 1780. He is described as age 24; five feet, nine-and-a-half inches in stature; light complexion, brown hair, gray eyes. His occupation is listed as farmer (also laborer). He appears to have begun his service on February 12, 1782. This service was credited to the town of Lincoln. The town appears to have reimbursed at least eleven individuals for moneys paid to Orr for this service, presumably in conjunction with the system of economic classification adopted in February 1781.[3]

Because the war was beginning to wind down in the aftermath of General Cornwallis's surrender at Yorktown in October 1781, and the Continental Army was completely disbanded by June 1784, he certainly did not serve his full term. However, no date has been found for his discharge.[4]

---

1 *Massachusetts Soldiers and Sailors*, Vol. XI, p. 642. His three-year enlistment in 1781 is almost an exact match with the enlistment of a Philip Boston of Carlisle, who appears to be his nephew (see *Massachusetts Soldiers and Sailors*, Vol. II, p. 295; see also note 2).

2 *Vital Records of Lincoln*; Quintal, *Patriots of Color*, p. 166. Quintal (p. 40) incorrectly lists his age at Bunker Hill as 18. The fact that his baptism record indicates a last name and conspicuously omits any information about being a "Negro servant belonging to..." suggests the likelihood that he was free born rather than as a slave. Further, *Concord, Massachusetts: Births, Marriages, and Deaths* shows four children born to Margaret and Peter Oliver between 1742 and 1749 (7–14 years before Peter's baptism). Mary, the oldest of these, is identified as "a free molatto woman" in the record of her 1761 marriage to Jack (identified as a Negro Servant of a Stoneham man). The logic is compelling that Peter must have been the brother or half brother of Mary, almost certainly born free.

There is an intriguing record of a Lucy Oliver who was taken in by Jube Savage (q.v.) for a month, probably during 1780 (for which he was paid by the town; see "Treasurer's Accompts," January 22, 1781). Could she have been the sister of Peter Oliver, or perhaps a wife in need of community support while Peter was off in service?

Records of Littleton (p. 224) lists the marriage of Elisabeth Oliver and Phillip Boston in 1762. Elisabeth appears to be Peter's sister (see *Concord, Massachusetts: Births, Marriages, and Deaths*). Jack MacLean (private notes) indicates that they had a son, Phillip, who is almost certainly the Philip Boston from Carlisle who enlisted with Peter for three years in 1781 (see note 1).

3 *Massachusetts Soldiers and Sailors*, Vol. XI, p. 681; "Treasurer's Accompts," March 25, 1782, September 14, 1782, October 31, 1782. The details of this service are unknown. The individuals paid by the town include Lt. James Parks, Benjamin Parks, Samuel Bacon, John Whitney, Nathan Brown, Daniel Parks, Leonard Parks, Eleazer Parks, Moses Underwood, John Parks, and Isaac Parks. For a brief overview of the system of economic classes, see MacLean, *A Rich Harvest* (p. 296).

4 If, as Robertson and McDonald, "Brief Profile of the Continental Army" (on the page titled "The Armies of 1783 and 1784") indicate with some logic, the men furloughed in June 1783 were largely those who had enlisted for the duration of the war, and that those remaining in service after June 1783 were those with unex-

Chapter 10: The Army of the Revolution

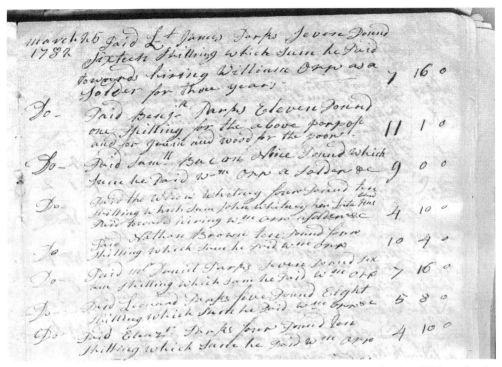

On March 25, 1782, the town reimbursed eight individuals for money they paid to hire William Orr for Continental Army service. This reflects the town's new system (adopted the previous year) for fulfilling its quota of men for service; intended to achieve a more equitable burden across the economic strata of the community, the town grouped residents into economic classes of equal aggregate wealth, with each class then required to hire a man. (Courtesy of Lincoln Town Archives, Lincoln, MA)

William Orr's identity has not been determined.

There is a record of a William Orr who served in the New York campaign in the fall of 1776, as a private in Captain Butler's Company, Col. Thomas Nixon's 4th Regiment, but it is uncertain if this is the same William Orr.[1]

There is also a record of a William Orr who served a three-year term in the Continental Army from May 12, 1777, through May 12, 1780, as a private in the colonel's company, Colonel Jackson's Regiment. Colonel Jackson's Regiment was at Valley Forge during the winter of 1777–78, at the Battle of Monmouth in June 1778, and at the Battle of Rhode Island in August 1778. This individual appears to have served most of his term at Rhode Island, but he may have spent the bitterly cold winter of 1779–80 at Morristown. His residence is listed variously as Merrimac, Walpole, and Boston, and the service was credited to the town of Walpole. It is uncertain if this could be the same William Orr (inst.) who later served to the credit of Lincoln.[2]

---

pired fixed terms, then it is likely that he served into the fall of 1783 and possibly until the final remnants were discharged in June 1784.

1 *Massachusetts Soldiers and Sailors*, Vol. XI, p. 681.
2 *Massachusetts Soldiers and Sailors*, Vol. XI, pp. 680–81.

PAGE, Jonathan

Jonathan Page enlisted on April 1, 1778, for three months of guard duty in Cambridge, as a private in Capt. Daniel Harrington's Company, Col. Jonathan Reed's Regiment. He reported for duty the following day and served 3 months, 2 days, until July 3, 1778, guarding the "Convention Army" surrendered the previous October by General Burgoyne at Saratoga. If this is Jonathan Page of Lincoln, he was age 16.[1]

He was paid by the town for "a late campaign" to Rhode Island, but it appears that he may have served twice, in fairly rapid succession. He is probably the Jonathan Page who served at Tiverton from May 18, 1779, to July 1, 1779 (credited with 1 month, 17 days of service), in Capt. Lawson Buckminster's Company, Lt. Col. Samuel Pierce's Regiment. He appears to have returned to Rhode Island as a private in Capt. Samuel Heald's Company, Col. John Jacobs's Light Infantry Regiment, from September 16, 1779, to November 16, 1779 (credited with 2 months, 4 days of service, including 72 miles of travel home).[2]

Agreeable to a resolve of June 5, 1780, he enlisted on July 11, 1780, to reinforce the Continental Army for six months. He arrived in Springfield on July 15, 1780, and was marched to camp under the command of Capt. James Cooper. He is described as age 18; five feet, eight inches in height, with a ruddy complexion. The record places him at Camp Totoway (present-day Totowa, New Jersey) on October 25, 1780, under the command of Brig. Gen. John Paterson in the 3rd Massachusetts Brigade. He was discharged December 16, 1780, having served 5 months, 15 days, including 200 miles of travel home. This service was credited to the town of Lincoln.[3]

Agreeable to a resolve of December 2, 1780, he enlisted in the Continental service again on May 19, 1781, this time for a three-year tour of duty. He was paid a bounty by a class of the town of Lincoln on June 1, 1781, and the town appears to have reimbursed a number of individuals for moneys paid to Page for this service, presumably in conjunction with the system of economic classification adopted in February 1781. He is described as age 19; five feet, six inches in height; with a light complexion, light hair, gray eyes. He listed his occupation as a farmer (also a laborer).

He served as a non-commissioned officer in Capt. Haffield White's Company, Col. Rufus Putnam's 5th Massachusetts Regiment, around West Point. With the war winding down in the aftermath of General Cornwallis's surrender at Yorktown in October 1781, he served only 2 years, 2 months. He was discharged in July 1783 at New Windsor, New York.[4]

---

1 *Massachusetts Soldiers and Sailors*, Vol. XI, p. 762; Pension Record # S34462. The service record does not identify him as being from Lincoln, and his pension declaration does not mention this service specifically. This appears to be part of the 15 months he says he served in various enlistments (without providing details) prior to his 2 years, 2 months of Continental service from May 1781 to July 1783. If his statement is accurate, there remain a couple of months of service unaccounted for.

2 "Treasurer's Accompts," December 17, 1779; *Massachusetts Soldiers and Sailors*, Vol. XI, p. 762. It is unclear for which campaign (or perhaps both) the town's payment was made. In either case, it is remarkably fast compared with other payments for service found in the Treasurer's accounts, which perhaps explains the notation "a late campaign." Neither record of service identifies Jonathan Page as being from Lincoln, but the travel allowance in both cases is very consistent with a Lincoln residency. In addition, both terms of service fit within the 15 months of service prior to May 1781, which he claims in his pension declaration (see note 1).

3 *Massachusetts Soldiers and Sailors*, Vol. XI, p. 761.

4 *Massachusetts Soldiers and Sailors*, Vol. XI, p. 761; "Treasurer's Accompts," September 30, 1781, October 29 and 31, 1782, January 27, 1783, August 4, 1783; Pension Record # S34462. Among the individuals paid by

He must have been on furlough in January 1783, as he married Lydia Munroe of Lexington at that time. Some years later, he became a colonel of the militia, and during the War of 1812, he superintended some of the fortifications in Boston Harbor. By 1820, he was destitute and living in Cambridge. "I have children," he states in his pension declaration, "but none of them are in a position to be with me or to contribute to my support. My family…was broken up many years since." There is no mention of his wife.[1]

PARKER, Aaron

Aaron Parker enlisted in the Continental Army on March 28, 1781, for the duration of the war. His enlistment was credited to the town of Lincoln, and he was paid a bounty on April 28, 1781. He served as a private in Capt. Elnathan Haskell's Company, Col. William Shepard's 4th Regiment. He appears to have been stationed at York Hutts from October 1781 through February 1782, and to have been assigned to commissary guard during October and November. The regiment was disbanded at West Point on November 3, 1783. The town appears to have reimbursed a number of individuals for moneys paid to him for this service, presumably in conjunction with the system of economic classification adopted in February 1781.[2]

He was the son of Joseph and Eunice (Hobbs) Parker, who lived at the intersection of present-day Sandy Pond and Baker Bridge Roads; brother of Joseph Parker (q.v.) and Levi Parker (q.v.); age 15 at the time of his enlistment. After the war, in 1791, he and his brother, Jonathan, joined Gen. Arthur St. Clair's campaign against the Miami tribes in the Northwest Territories. They were both killed in Ohio on November 4, 1791, at the Battle of the Wabash. He was a month shy of his 26th birthday.[3]

---

 the town are: Lt. Daniel Harrington, widow Abigail Fox, Gregory Stone, Joseph Abbot, John Fox, William Thorning, Lt. John Hoar, Leonard Hoar. For a brief overview of the system of economic classes, see MacLean, *A Rich Harvest* (p. 296).

 His claim to being a non-commissioned officer is unsubstantiated. His pension was granted on the basis of three years of service as a private soldier.

1 Wheeler, "Lincoln," in Hurd, Vol. 2, p. 623; *Vital Records of Lincoln*; *Lexington Births, Marriages and Deaths*; Pension Record # S34462; Hudson, *History of the Town of Lexington (revised)*, Vol. II, pp. 457, 459. The marriage record identifies him as a resident of Lincoln, with marriage intentions recorded in *Vital Records of Lincoln*. His identity has otherwise not been determined.

 Lydia was the daughter of John and Anna (Kendall) Munroe. Her father served at Lexington and Bunker Hill in 1775, and in New Jersey in 1776. Inexplicably, Hudson lists her parents also as John and Lydia (Bemis) Munroe.

 Hudson credits Jonathan and Lydia with four children, but no records have been found. It is unknown what became of his family, or when and where he died.

2 *Massachusetts Soldiers and Sailors*, Vol. XI, p. 832; "Treasurer's Accompts," April 23, 1782, October 31, 1782, January 27, 1783, August 4, 1783. Among the individuals paid by the town are Jonas Peirce (q.v., Chapter 12), Nathaniel Colburn, Abijah Munroe, and Lt. Benjamin Munroe. For a brief overview of the system of economic classes, see MacLean, *A Rich Harvest* (p. 296).

 Wheeler, "Lincoln" (in Hurd, Vol. 2, p. 623), mistakenly attributes this service to Aaron Parks (q.v.).

 If, as Robertson and McDonald, "Brief Profile of the Continental Army" (on the page titled "The Armies of 1783 and 1784"), indicate with some logic, the men furloughed in June 1783 were largely those who had enlisted for the duration of the war, and that those remaining in service after June 1783 were those with unexpired fixed terms, then it is likely that he left the Hudson Highlands and returned home in June 1783.

3 *Vital Records of Lincoln*; Hudson, *History of the Town of Lexington (revised)*, Vol. II, p. 514; Glass and Little, Map of Lincoln. If the Vital Records are correct, he was actually eight months shy of his 16th birthday when he enlisted in 1781. Jonathan was age 22 when they died in 1791. His father Joseph was a cooper by trade, with

PARKER, Joseph

Joseph Parker lied about his age to join the Continental Army, evidently at age 13. Agreeable to a resolve of December 2, 1780, he entered the service on July 4, 1781, for a three-year term. He is described as age 16; four feet, ten inches in height; light complexion, light hair, and light eyes. His occupation is given as farmer. The town of Lincoln was credited for this service.[1]

Because the war was beginning to wind down in the aftermath of General Cornwallis's surrender at Yorktown in October 1781, it is probably unlikely that he served his full term, but this is speculative, as no date has been found for his discharge.

He was the son of Joseph and Eunice (Hobbs) Parker, who lived at the intersection of present-day Sandy Pond and Baker Bridge Roads. He was the brother of Aaron Parker (q.v.) and Levi Parker (q.v.). He appears to have been age 13, still three months shy of his 14th birthday, when he entered the service. After the war, he appears to have moved to Weston. He married Polly Fisk of Weston in 1791. They returned to Lincoln for a few years (probably 1793 to 1795), but they moved back to Weston, where they settled on a small farm and reportedly spent the remainder of their lives. He was a blacksmith and a farmer. A record of his death has not been found.[2]

PARKER, Levi

Levi Parker served in Captain Stearns's Company, at North Castle, New York during the summer of 1780. He appears to have gambled or bartered away his service pay to Sgt. John Bingham.[3]

Agreeable to a resolve of December 2, 1780, he enlisted again on March 16, 1781, for a three-year term in the Continental Army, for which he was paid a bounty on May 21, 1781. He served in Captain Hastings's Company, Colonel Whitney's Regiment. He is described as age 18; five feet, six inches in height, with a light complexion; and he listed his occupation as a farmer. His service was credited to the town of Princeton. He was discharged on December 31, 1783, by Gen. Henry Knox.[4]

Lexington roots, the brother of Capt. John Parker of the Lexington Militia Company. Joseph moved from Lexington and settled his family in Lincoln in 1768 (see MacLean, *A Rich Harvest*, pp. 179, 182).

1 *Massachusetts Soldiers and Sailors*, Vol. XI, pp. 880–81.
2 *Vital Records of Lincoln*; *Town of Weston, Births, Deaths, & Marriages*; Wheeler, "Lincoln," in Hurd, Vol. 2, p. 623; Hudson, *History of the Town of Lexington (revised)*, Vol. II, p. 514; Parker, *Genealogy of John Parker*, p. 161; Glass and Little, Map of Lincoln. Wheeler lists his birthday as December 5, 1765, but this is evidently incorrect, as *Vital Records of Lincoln* shows this as the birth date of his brother, Aaron. *Vital Records of Lincoln* gives Joseph's birth date as October 4, 1767.

Two of their nine children were born in Lincoln; four are recorded in Weston; the rest appear to have been born in Weston, but they are not found in *Town of Weston, Births, Deaths, & Marriages*.

The elder Joseph was a cooper by trade, with Lexington roots, the brother of Capt. John Parker of the Lexington Militia Company. Joseph moved from Lexington and settled his family in Lincoln in 1768 (see MacLean, *A Rich Harvest*, pp. 179, 182).

3 *Massachusetts Soldiers and Sailors*, Vol. XI, p. 887. An April 30, 1781, order, signed by him, directs that his wages were payable to Sergeant Bingham.
4 *Massachusetts Soldiers and Sailors*, Vol. XI, pp. 887–88; Pension Record # W21914. The pension office reported in a 1937 letter that he served in the 4th Massachusetts Regiment. This regiment was commanded by Col. William Shepard, not Colonel Whitney. The author has not identified Colonel Whitney's Regiment in the Continental service during 1781–1783, but supposes that if he served into late 1783 (as also the Pension

He was the son of Joseph and Eunice (Hobbs) Parker, who lived at the intersection of modern-day Sandy Pond and Baker Bridge roads; the brother of Aaron Parker (q.v.) and Joseph Parker (q.v.). He was reportedly living in Roxbury by age 13, perhaps as an apprentice, where by family tradition he witnessed the Battle of Bunker Hill.[1]

By 1779, he was living in Princeton, where at age 17 he enlisted in the service with Captain Stearns. After the war, he bought a farm in Hubbardston, and in 1786 he married Mary Lyon of that town. He is said to have been a mason by trade. In 1798 or 1799, he moved his growing family to Royalton, Vermont, where he cleared the woods for a 100-acre farm. He died in Royalton in 1813, age 50.[2]

PARKHURST, Noah
[also PARKES]

Noah Parkhurst went to Concord on April 19, 1775, probably as a member of the militia company from Lincoln. After the skirmish at the North Bridge, he is reported to have said, "Now the war has begun, and no one knows when it will end."[3]

Soon, he was in service at Cambridge, as a private in Capt. Nathan Fuller's Company, Lt. Col. William Bond's Regiment (late Col. Thomas Gardner's 37th Regiment). The dates of this service have not survived, but he shows up on a return dated Prospect Hill, October 6, 1775. Colonel Gardner's Regiment fought at Bunker Hill on June 17, 1775, so if he was in service as early as May or June, he was undoubtedly in that battle.

He was back in Cambridge as a private in Capt. Simon Hunt's Company, Col. Eleazer Brooks's Regiment for five months, from November 3, 1777, to April 3, 1778. This unit was detached from the militia to guard the "Convention Army" surrendered by General Burgoyne at Saratoga a few weeks before, on October 17.[4]

He appears to have served for 13 days at Rutland Barracks, as a private in Capt. Josiah Wilder's Company, Col. Nathan Sparhawk's Regiment, commanded by Maj. Daniel Clap, from July 4, 1778, to July 15, 1778. The company was raised for 20 days of service. However, it is uncertain if this is the same individual as Noah Parkhurst (inst.).[5]

Office letter indicates), he must have been re-assigned to one of the ten Massachusetts regiments that were not demobilizing until that time. The 4th Massachusetts was disbanded at West Point in November 1783.

1 Parker, *Genealogy of John Parker*, p. 158; *Vital Records of Lincoln*.
2 Parker, *Genealogy of John Parker*, p. 158; Pension Record # W21914; Glass and Little, Map of Lincoln; *Vital Records of Lincoln*; *Hubbardston Vital Records*. His father Joseph was a cooper by trade, with Lexington roots, the brother of Capt. John Parker of the Lexington Militia Company. Joseph moved his family from Lexington and settled in Lincoln in 1768 (see MacLean, *A Rich Harvest*, pp. 179, 182). Mary was also known as Polly. After Levi died, she remained in Royalton until 1837, when she moved to Potsdam, New York, to live with her son, Samuel.
3 Baker Affidavit (1850).
4 *Massachusetts Soldiers and Sailors*, Vol. XI, p. 916.
5 *Massachusetts Soldiers and Sailors*, Vol. XI, p. 911. Rutland Barracks were in Rutland, Massachusetts. The fact that the roll is dated Templeton suggests that this may be a different individual, but if so, he seems to be the only other Noah Parkhurst (or Parkes) in the historical record for Massachusetts service. A matching record for a Jonathan Parkes, who appears to be his brother (see Bond, *Genealogies of the Families of Watertown*, p. 390), reinforces the notion that this record belongs to Noah Parkhurst (inst.). The short duration of service suggests a specialized call-up, fulfilled by individuals from a somewhat wider geography than might otherwise be the case. Templeton is an administrative notation; the home of Captain Wilder. The author speculates that

He may have served again for six months in 1780, as a private in Capt. Ephraim Stone's Company, in the New Hampshire line at Coos, but it is uncertain if this is the same Noah Parkhurst.[1]

He enlisted in the Continental Army for a three-year term in November 1781, credited to the town of Weston. He served in Capt. Zebulon King's Company, Lt. Col. John Brooks's Regiment, evidently into 1783. He is described as age 24 (upon enlistment); having a light complexion, light brown hair, and blue eyes; five feet, five-and-a-half inches (also five feet, four inches) in height; and a farmer or laborer by occupation. He gives his residence both as Weston and as Kittery.[2]

He was from Waltham and then Weston, the son of Nathaniel and Eunice (Harrington) Parkhurst. He came to Lincoln in 1773, at age 16, and was warned out in 1774. He was age 18 at Concord and Bunker Hill, age 20 when he joined Captain Hunt's Company in Cambridge.[3]

PARKS, Aaron

Aaron Parks served as a private in Capt. William Smith's Company of Minute Men from Lincoln, Col. Abijah Peirce's Regiment.[4] Following the engagement at Concord, he served for ten days in Cambridge.[5] He was reimbursed by the town for part of a set of accoutrements as a minute man.[6]

He appears to have remained in service in Cambridge, enlisting in the rapidly forming Massachusetts Provincial Army for eight months. He served in Capt. Nathan Fuller's Company, Col. Thomas Gardner's 37th Regiment, and participated in the Battle of Bunker Hill. Command of the 37th Regiment passed to Lt. Col. William Bond following the death of Colonel Gardner from wounds received at Bunker Hill. On October 6, he was reported in camp at Prospect Hill, and he served out his eight-month term in December 1775.[7]

---

this service may have been related to a plan to move some of Burgoyne's army from Cambridge to Rutland, where they would be safer from a possible British rescue attempt.

1 Hammond, *Town Papers*, pp. 524, 525. A pay authorization and pay order connect this individual and service with the town of Swanzey, New Hampshire.

2 *Massachusetts Soldiers and Sailors*, Vol. XI, p. 911.

3 Bond, *Genealogies of the Families of Watertown*, p. 390; MacLean, *A Rich Harvest*, p. 212. His birth is recorded in *Vital Records of Waltham*, along with twelve brothers and sisters. His record of Continental service, however, lists his birthplace as Kittery.

His death in 1783 at Concord, age 26, is reported in the genealogical databases of the Church of Jesus Christ of Latter Day Saints. However, the author has been unable to find corroborating evidence of this. Alternatively, the 1790 and 1800 censuses show a Noah Parkhurst, who appears to be age-appropriate for Noah Parkhurst (inst.), living in Sharon, Vermont, with what appears to be a wife, two daughters, and (by 1800) six sons. The author has found no more evidence to connect the Sharon, Vermont, resident with Noah Parkhurst (inst.), than he has in corroborating a 1783 death of Noah Parkhurst (inst.) at Concord.

4 Coburn, *Muster Rolls*.

5 *Massachusetts Soldiers and Sailors*, Vol. XI, pp. 923.

6 "Treasurer's Accompts," March 15, 1776. This was paid to his father, Joseph Parks, Jr.

7 Pension Record # W9590; *Massachusetts Soldiers and Sailors*, Vol. XI, pp. 923. Parks, *Genealogy of the Parke Family* (p. 66), seems to follow Wheeler, "Lincoln" (in Hurd, Vol. 2, p. 623), who says he served at Winter Hill, which record the author has not found, but for practical purposes represents the same service (i.e., Cambridge) as Prospect Hill. He appears to have been paid by the town for this service ("Treasurer's Accompts," November 11, 1779).

Thereupon, he reenlisted for another year in the same company and regiment. For a time he served duty in Gen. Charles Lee's Life Guard. When General Lee left for New York in January 1776, he returned to his unit and served through the fortification of Dorchester Heights. Subsequently, he served on the relief expedition to Canada (for which he was paid by the town), completing his term of enlistment at Ticonderoga in December.[1]

He was the son of Joseph Jr. and Lydia (Garfield) Parks; age 17 on April 19, 1775. He was the nephew of Benjamin Parks (q.v.) and David Parks (q.v.), and first cousin to Jonas Parks (q.v.), Leonard Parks (q.v.) and Willard Parks (q.v.). He married Anna Jennison of East Sudbury (now Wayland) in 1783, and settled in Charlestown, New Hampshire, by 1792. Anna died in 1825, and he married Lucinda Nesmith of Charlestown in 1826. He died in 1832, age 74, at Charlestown, New Hampshire, and is buried in the Forest Hill Cemetery.[2]

PARKS, Benjamin

Benjamin Parks may have served at Cambridge for eight months in 1775, following the outbreak of fighting on April 19, 1775, but this is somewhat doubtful.[3]

He served as a private in Capt. John Hartwell's Company of Militia from Lincoln, Col. Eleazer Brooks's 3rd Middlesex County Regiment, which marched from Lincoln to fortify Dorchester Heights on March 4, 1776. Although the unit was discharged five days later, on March 9 (after the threat of a British assault on the fortifications had subsided, and General Howe had begun preparations to evacuate Boston), the record shows that he served only two days.[4]

---

1 Pension Record # W9590; "Treasurer's Accompts," November 11, 1779. In his pension declaration, he says that his pay for this service was in arrears, and that in an attempt to collect it, he gave his discharge to an individual who never returned it. Perhaps he was a victim of a scam, or at least of hollow promises.

Wheeler, "Lincoln" (in Hurd, Vol. 2, p. 623), incorrectly credits him with further service in 1781, saying that he enlisted in the Continental Army on March 28, 1781, for the duration of the war. Parks, *Genealogy of the Parke Family* (p. 66), seems to follow Wheeler into this error. Wheeler has confused Aaron Parks for Aaron Parker (q.v.). This service is correctly attributable to Aaron Parker (q.v.). (See *Massachusetts Soldiers and Sailors*, Vol. XI, p. 832, and "Treasurer's Accompts," April 23, 1782, October 31, 1782, January 27, 1783, August 4, 1783.)

2 *Vital Records of Lincoln*; *Concord, Massachusetts: Births, Marriages, and Deaths*; *Vital Records of Wayland*; Bond, *Genealogies of the Families of Watertown*, p. 388; Parks, *Genealogy of the Parke Family*, pp. 50, 66; Pension Record # W9590; *SAR Revolutionary War Graves Register*. No birth record has been found. His parentage is from Wheeler, "Lincoln" (in Hurd, Vol. 2, p. 623), and appears to be generally accepted. His age is from his pension record and from Parks, *Genealogy of the Parke Family*. MacLean, *A Rich Harvest* (p. 257) lists his age as 27 on April 19, 1775, probably a typographical error.

Saunderson, *History of Charlestown, New Hampshire* (p. 711), lists him as a taxpayer in Charlestown in 1792.

He had 12 children with Anna, and two more with Lucinda.

Lucinda was either 14 or 33 years younger than Aaron (she gives conflicting ages in her pension declaration). In 1832 (approximately six to eight months after Aaron's death), she married Robert Kennedy and lived in Lebanon, New Hampshire. In 1860, she divorced him and resumed using the name Parks. She was living at Galena, Ohio, at the time.

3 Wheeler, "Lincoln" (in Hurd, Vol. 2, p. 623), credits him with this service, but the author has found no record to corroborate this (see also note 1, p. 368). Parks, *Genealogy of the Parke Family* (p. 51), also credits him with this service, but it appears that Wheeler is his source.

4 Hartwell, "A List of a Company of Militia"; *Massachusetts Soldiers and Sailors*, Vol. XI, p. 924.

Subsequently, he served two terms in the Continental Army, although the details of this service have not been found. He was paid by the town for one-quarter of a three-year campaign, probably in 1777, and then for eight months of service in the Continental Army, probably in 1778.[1]

He was the son of Joseph and Abigail Parks; age 42 at Dorchester Heights. He had been a member of Lincoln's original militia company in 1757. He had married Lois Gibbs of Sudbury in 1754; she had borne him two children before she died in 1758. He had subsequently married Sarah (family name unknown), probably in 1760 or 1761; she had borne him five more children before she died in 1771. The following year (1772), he had married Lydia Wheeler (sister of Phineas Allen (q.v.); widow of John Wheeler; mother of John Wheeler (q.v.) and five other children). Together, they had two more children, making 15 (including the six step-children) in all.[2]

He was the brother of David Parks (q.v.); uncle of Aaron Parks (q.v.), Willard Parks (q.v.), Jonas Parks (q.v.), Leonard Parks (q.v.), Jonathan Tower (q.v.), Joseph Billing, Jr. (q.v.), and Joseph Meloney (q.v.); stepfather of John Wheeler (q.v.); brother-in-law of Phineas Allen (q.v.), Joseph Billing (q.v.), Abraham Wesson (q.v.) and Cornelius Meloney (q.v.); cousin of James Parks (q.v.), William Parks (q.v.), Samuel Parks (q.v.), John Parks (q.v.), Isaac Parks (q.v.), Eleazer Parks (q.v.), and Josiah Parks (q.v.).

He moved to Livermore, Maine, about the year 1800, where he died in 1825 at age 92.[3]

PARKS, David

David Parks served at Cambridge in 1775, at Canada in 1776, and at Cambridge again in 1778, for which he was paid by the town.[4] In a separate transaction, he was paid by the town for service at Ticonderoga in 1776, and for one-quarter of a three-year campaign in the Continental Army. No details for any of this service have been found.[5]

---

1 "Treasurer's Accompts," June 8, 1779, and June 15, 1779. Although the juxtaposition of the pay records might cause one to question whether or not these payments could have been for the same term of service, it is apparent that they were for different stints. He was paid £7 10s for his first nine months, evidently early in the war (1777 or before, when £30 was the going rate for three years of service). He was paid £53 12s for his eight months of service, obviously somewhat later. The amount he was paid for his first service is more or less in line with the £8 that Willard Parks (q.v.) and Eleazer Parks (q.v.) were each paid for their Cambridge service, so it is possible that this could be the Cambridge service with which Wheeler, "Lincoln" (in Hurd, Vol. 2, p. 623), credits him in 1775 (see note 3, p. 367). However, this service is listed as "one fourth part of a three years campn," instead of "service at Cambridge" which is the way Cambridge service appears in most other "Treasurer's Accompts" records. Accordingly, the author judges the Cambridge service to be Wheeler's error, and the actual service to be Continental service as stated in the record.

2 *Vital Records of Lincoln*; *Concord, Massachusetts: Births, Marriages, and Deaths*; *Vital Records of Sudbury*; Bond, *Genealogies of the Families of Watertown*, p. 386; Martin, "The Sons of Lincoln," p. 25. Lois does not appear to be closely related to Sarah Gibbs, the wife of his brother, David Parks (q.v.).

3 Wheeler, "Lincoln," in Hurd, Vol. 2, p. 623.

4 "Treasurer's Accompts," June 15, 1779.

5 Ibid. It is not clear why two separate payments were made on the same day, unless perhaps this may have had something to do with accounting for possibly different sources of funds. The second transaction could possibly be read as "Daniel Parks," but this does not help much in identifying the individual who provided the service. There appears to be only one Daniel Parks who could have provided this service. He was the uncle of David Parks (inst.), age at least 51 at Ticonderoga (determined by the death of his father in 1725). He was the son of Richard and Elizabeth (Billing) Parks. He married first Elizabeth (who died sometime after 1757), then Lydia Priest in 1763. He appears, at least on the basis of age, to be no more likely than David to have served

Chapter 10: The Army of the Revolution

David Parks lived in this house in the southern part of town with his sons, Jonas and Leonard. Jonas went to Concord as a minute man on April 19th. He and Leonard served together at the Battle of Bunker Hill, at Canada, and at the Battle of Trenton. David may have served at Ticonderoga at age 51. (Photograph by Jack MacLean)

It is not clear how much, if any, of this service he actually served.[1]

He was the son of Joseph and Abigail Parks; age 50 during his first tour of duty at Cambridge. He had been married to Sarah Gibbs of Sudbury since 1755. He probably moved to Springfield, Vermont, before 1790.[2]

---

at Ticonderoga and in the Continental Army. Nor did he have any living sons of service age to whom one could attribute this service. Finally, no service records have been found by which to connect any of this service to Daniel. While it remains possible that Daniel could have served these tours of duty, the author has found nothing to encourage this possibility, and concludes that the second transaction must also read David.

1 Cambridge in 1775 and 1778, Canada in 1776, and nine months Continental service match the service provided by his son, Leonard Parks (q.v.), for which no payment record has been found. It is quite possible that this payment to David is for moneys due Leonard for this service. The payment for service at Ticonderoga in 1776 is not as easily explained. The author has found no other record or individual to connect to the Ticonderoga payment. Nor does there appear to be any evidence that David owned any slaves who might have served at Ticonderoga. Therefore, and with little else to go on, one has to presume that David Parks (inst.) likely served at least at Ticonderoga.

2 *Concord, Massachusetts: Births, Marriages, and Deaths*; *Vital Records of Sudbury*; Bond, *Genealogies of the Families of Watertown*, p. 386; Parks, *Genealogy of the Parke Family*, p. 50. Bond incorrectly gives his wife's name as Mary. Sarah does not appear to be closely related to Lois Gibbs, the first wife of his brother, Benjamin Parks (q.v.).

He was the brother of Benjamin Parks (q.v.); father of Jonas Parks (q.v.) and Leonard Parks (q.v.); uncle of Aaron Parks (q.v.), Willard Parks (q.v.), and Joseph Meloney (q.v.); brother-in-law of Cornelius Meloney (q.v.); cousin of James Parks (q.v.), William Parks (q.v.), Samuel Parks (q.v.), John Parks (q.v.), Isaac Parks (q.v.), Eleazer Parks (q.v.), and Josiah Parks (q.v.); and probably father-in-law of Jonathan Tower (q.v.).

PARKS, Eleazer
[also Ebenezer]

Eleazer Parks was a private in Capt. William Smith's Company of Minute Men from Lincoln, Col. Abijah Peirce's Regiment. Following the Concord alarm, he served for ten days in Cambridge.[1] He was reimbursed by the town for his accoutrements as a minute man.[2]

He appears to have remained in service in Cambridge, enlisting in the rapidly forming Massachusetts Provincial Army. He participated in the Battle of Bunker Hill, in Capt. Nathan Fuller's Company, Colonel Gardner's 37th Regiment, and appears on the roll of Capt. Nathan Fuller's Company, now Lt. Col. William Bond's 37th Regiment, dated at Prospect Hill, on October 6, 1775. He served for eight months, and was paid for this service by the town.[3]

There is an October 20, 1775, order for a bounty coat for an Eleazer Parkes, in Capt. Asa Lawrence's Company, Col. William Prescott's Regiment. Possibly, he changed units, or more likely this may refer to a different individual.[4]

Subsequently, he served as a private in Capt. John Hartwell's Militia Company from Lincoln, Col. Eleazer Brooks's 3rd Middlesex County Regiment, which marched from Lincoln to fortify Dorchester Heights on March 4, 1776. The unit was discharged five days later, on March 9, after the threat of a British assault on the fortifications had subsided, and General Howe had begun preparations to evacuate Boston, instead.

That summer, in June or July 1776, he marched to Ticonderoga in Capt. Asahel Wheeler's Company, Col. Jonathan Reed's Regiment, and served for 4 or 5 months, through November 1776.[5]

He appears to have served at Rhode Island as a private in Capt. Jesse Wyman's Company, Col. Josiah Whitney's Regiment, from May 10, 1777, to July 10. 1777 (credited with 2

---

1 Coburn, *Muster Rolls*; *Massachusetts Soldiers and Sailors*, Vol. XI, p. 924. He appears as Ebenezer Parks on the Muster Roll, but the records make it clear that this is the same individual. The *War Memorial Book* and *An Account of the Celebration* give Ebenezer Parks and Eleazer Parks separate listings, perpetuating the error that they were different individuals.

2 "Treasurer's Accompts," July 24, 1776. The record indicates he was paid for a bayonet, ramrod, and knapsack.

3 "Treasurer's Accompts," June 15, 1779; *Massachusetts Soldiers and Sailors*, Vol. XI, pp. 924–25; Pension Record # W15162; Wheeler, "Lincoln," in Hurd, Vol. 2, p. 623. His wife's pension declaration says he served in Capt. William Smith's Company, Colonel Nixon's Regiment. [The source of her confusion about Eleazer's unit is unclear.] Both regiments were engaged at Bunker Hill. Note the parallels between Eleazer's service records and those for Aaron Parks (q.v.), John Parks (q.v.), Jonas Parks (q.v.), Leonard Parks (q.v.), and Willard Parks (q.v.).

4 *Massachusetts Soldiers and Sailors*, Vol. XI, p. 911.

5 Sudbury Miscellaneous Records, pay receipts dated September 30, 1776 (Doc. # 109), December 16, 1776 (Doc. # 2204), and March 17, 1777 (Doc. # 2209).

months, 9 days of service, including 3 days for travel to the rendezvous point and 5 days for travel home from Point Judith), but it is not certain if this is the same Eleazer Parks.

He served at Saratoga, in Capt. George Minot's Company, Col. Samuel Bullard's Regiment from August 16, 1777, to November 30, 1777 (credited with 3 months, 25 days of service, including 11 days for 220 miles of travel home), and he was present at the surrender of General Burgoyne.[1]

He was the son of Ephraim and Mary (Hobbs) Parks; age 20 on April 19, 1775. He married Elizabeth Whitney of Stow in 1782 and remained resident in Lincoln for a couple of years after that. About 1784, they moved to Winchendon, where he died in 1817 at age 62. He rests in the Old Centre Burial Ground.[2]

He was the brother of Isaac Parks (q.v.), John Parks (q.v.), Josiah Parks (q.v.), Samuel Parks (q.v.), and William Parks (q.v.); cousin of David Parks (q.v.), Benjamin Parks (q.v.), and James Parks (q.v.).

PARKS, Isaac

Isaac Parks was in arms at Concord on April 19, 1775, probably as a member of the militia company from Lincoln.[3]

Subsequently, he served as a private in Capt. John Hartwell's Militia Company from Lincoln, Col. Eleazer Brooks's 3rd Middlesex County Regiment, which marched from Lincoln to fortify Dorchester Heights on March 4, 1776. The unit was discharged five days later, on March 9, after the threat of a British assault on the fortifications had subsided, and General Howe instead had begun preparations to evacuate Boston. He was paid for this service the following September.[4]

Later in 1776, he served in New York, but the details of this service have not been found.[5]

---

1 Hartwell, "A List of a Company of Militia"; *Massachusetts Soldiers and Sailors*, Vol. XI, p. 925. The Rhode Island service is attributed to Eleazer Parks of Weston. Wheeler, "Lincoln" (in Hurd, Vol. 2, p. 623), credits Eleazer Parks (inst.) with the Rhode Island service. This is consistent with his wife's estimate of time served in 1777. Although his wife makes no mention of Rhode Island service, per se, she says in the pension declaration that he served "three or five months in the year 1777, marched to Ticonderoga and other places, and was present when Burgoyne surrendered." "Other places" could be interpreted to include his two months' service in Rhode Island, or the various locations between Saratoga and Ticonderoga at which Colonel Bullard's Regiment was deployed (Ticonderoga remained in enemy hands until after Burgoyne's surrender, so he may well have been near Ticonderoga, but almost certainly not at Ticonderoga), or New Jersey, where the regiment served briefly after Burgoyne's surrender. He does not appear on the Saratoga draft list from Lincoln, suggesting either that he went as a substitute for one of the draftees, or more likely that he enlisted from the Weston militia company (which would also be consistent with the record of his Rhode Island service).

2 MacLean, *A Rich Harvest*, p. 257; Wheeler, "Lincoln," in Hurd, Vol. 2, p. 623; *Vital Records of Lincoln*; *Vital Records of Stow*; *Vital Records of Winchendon*; Pension Record # W15162; Bond, *Genealogies of the Families of Watertown*, p. 386, Parks, *Genealogy of the Parke Family*, p. 43; "Find A Grave." In her pension declaration, Elizabeth gives their marriage date incorrectly, as April 10, 1781; the Stow Town Clerk testified to a date of April 10, 1782. *Vital Records of Stow* backs him up, and *Vital Records of Lincoln* confirms this with a record of their marriage intention on December 3, 1781.

3 Deposition of John Hoar, et al.

4 *Massachusetts Soldiers and Sailors*, Vol. XI, p. 925.

5 "Treasurer's Accompts," June 15, 1779. There is an intriguing record in Muster Rolls of the Revolutionary War (Vol. 19, p. 112) of an Isaac Parkis of Waltham, who was a fifer at New York in Capt. Edward Fuller's Company, Col. Eleazer Brooks's Regiment, and who was reported as sick after the Battle of White Plains. The

He was a twin son of Ephraim and Mary (Hobbs) Parks; age 32 on April 19, 1775. He had married Rhoda Faugason of Weston in 1768. After the war, he moved to Thompson, Connecticut, by 1790. He reportedly died in 1823, at age 80 or 81, and is buried in the Aspinwall Cemetery in Putnam, Connecticut.[1]

He was the brother of Eleazer Parks (q.v.), John Parks (q.v.), Josiah Parks (q.v.), Samuel Parks (q.v.), and William Parks (q.v.); cousin of David Parks (q.v.), Benjamin Parks (q.v.), and James Parks (q.v.).

PARKS, James

James Parks was a private in Capt. William Smith's Company of Minute Men from Lincoln, Col. Abijah Peirce's Regiment.[2] Following the Concord Alarm, he served for 14 days in Cambridge.[3] He was reimbursed by the town for his accoutrements as a minute man.[4]

On March 27, 1776, he was commissioned a second lieutenant in Capt. Samuel Farrar, Jr.'s 6th Company, Col. Eleazer Brooks's 3rd Middlesex County Regiment of Militia.[5]

He served at Ticonderoga in 1776, at Cambridge in 1777 and 1778, for which he was paid by the town. The details of this service have not been found, but the resolves calling for troops for Ticonderoga were passed on June 25 and July 11, 1776, and specified service until December 1, 1776. His Cambridge service was guarding the "Convention Army" surrendered by General Burgoyne at Saratoga in October 1777, and appears to have been served probably from November 7, 1777, through April 2, 1778, as the Ensign in Capt. Simon Hunt's Company, Colonel Brooks's Regiment.[6]

There is a record of a James Park who served on an alarm at Rhode Island, as a corporal in Capt. Thomas Mellen's Company, Col. Abner Perry's Regiment for 14 days from July 28, 1780, to August 10, 1780, but the record lacks sufficient evidence to connect this service with James Parks of Lincoln.[7]

He was the son of Josiah and Thankful (Coolidge) Parks; age 34 on April 19, 1775. He had married Hannah Wesson in 1771. She died in 1778, at age 26, and is buried in the

---

record also notes that he lost items in the battle. This individual is not Isaac Parks (inst.), however, as he is identifiable in *Vital Records of Waltham* as Isaac Parkhurst, son of Isaac and Sarah, age 20 during the New York campaign (see also *Massachusetts Soldiers and Sailors*, Vol. XI, p. 920).

1 *Concord, Massachusetts: Births, Marriages, and Deaths*; *Vital Records of Lincoln*; Bond, *Genealogies of the Families of Watertown*, p. 387; Parks, *Genealogy of the Parke Family*, p. 43; *SAR Revolutionary War Graves Register*. Bond gives Rhoda's name as Fergerson. She appears to be the sister of Anna Faugason, who had married Isaac's brother John Parks (q.v.) seven years before.

2 Coburn, *Muster Rolls*.

3 *Massachusetts Soldiers and Sailors*, Vol. XI, p. 925.

4 "Treasurer's Accompts," April 1, 1776.

5 *Massachusetts Soldiers and Sailors*, Vol. XI, p. 925. As early as June 1775, he is listed as Lt. James Parks in the birth record of his son Josiah. *Vital Records of Lincoln*.

6 "Treasurer's Accompts," June 15, 1779; *Massachusetts Soldiers and Sailors*, Vol. I, pp. xxi–xxii. See also John Wheeler (q.v.)'s Pension Record # W27876, in which he identifies James Parks as Ensign of Capt. Simon Hunt's Company, with whom he (Wheeler) served at Cambridge from December 1777 through April 2, 1778.

7 *Massachusetts Soldiers and Sailors*, Vol. XI, p. 824.

Meeting House Cemetery behind Bemis Hall. He is reported to have died in Lincoln, about 1790.[1]

James Parks was the cousin of David Parks (q.v.), Benjamin Parks (q.v.), William Parks (q.v.), Samuel Parks (q.v.), John Parks (q.v.), Isaac Parks (q.v.), Eleazer Parks (q.v.), and Josiah Parks (q.v.); brother-in-law of Stephen Wesson, Jr. (q.v.).

PARKS, John

John Parks was a private in Capt. William Smith's Company of Minute Men from Lincoln, Col. Abijah Peirce's Regiment.[2] Following the engagement at Concord, he served for ten days in Cambridge.[3]

Following his service as a minute man, he appears to have remained in service in Cambridge, enlisting in the rapidly forming Massachusetts Provincial Army. He served for eight months, and participated in the Battle of Bunker Hill in Capt. Nathan Fuller's Company, Colonel Gardner's Regiment. He appears again on the roll of this unit (in Lt. Col. William Bond's 37th Regiment following the death of Colonel Gardner after Bunker Hill), dated Prospect Hill, October 6, 1775. He was paid for this service by the town.[4]

The following summer, in June or July 1776, he marched to Ticonderoga in Capt. Asahel Wheeler's Company, Col. Jonathan Reed's Regiment, and served for 4 or 5 months, through November 1776.[5]

In 1777, he took a team with supplies to Worthington, for which he was paid by the town. This may have been to supply the expedition (including Lincoln men under Capt. Samuel Farrar, Jr.) escorting Burgoyne's "Convention Army" to Cambridge.[6]

There is a record of a John Park who served 2 months, 22 days at Cambridge, guarding General Burgoyne's "Convention Army" from January 12, 1778, to April 3, 1778, as a private in Capt. Abraham Peirce's Company, Col. Eleazer Brooks's Regiment of Guards, but it is not certain if this is the same individual.[7]

---

1 *Vital Records of Lincoln*; Bond, *Genealogies of the Families of Watertown*, p. 386; Wheeler, "Lincoln," in Hurd, p. 623; Biggs, "In Memorium," p. 180; Parks, *Genealogy of the Parke Family*, p. 52. MacLean, *A Rich Harvest* (p. 257) lists his age as 20 at Concord, Wheeler says age 35, but both appear to be incorrect, based on the information given in Bond and Parks. His death is reported in Parks; the 1817 death record in *Vital Records of Lincoln* apparently belongs to his son James. During private discussions, George Quintal expressed the opinion that James Parks died in Lincoln, and is buried next to his wife, but no confirming evidence of this has been found. Hannah appears to be the sister of Stephen Wesson Jr. (q.v.).

2 Coburn, *Muster Rolls*.

3 *Massachusetts Soldiers and Sailors*, Vol. XI, p. 925.

4 "Treasurer's Accompts," June 15, 1779; *Massachusetts Soldiers and Sailors*, Vol. XI, p. 925; Wheeler, "Lincoln," in Hurd, Vol. 2, p. 623. The "Treasurer's Accompts" record does not itemize the £9 10s he was paid for service at Cambridge and for going to Worthington. The going rate for eight months of service at Cambridge was £8, and Cuff Hoar (q.v.) was paid £1 10s for Worthington, so the math works. The parallels between his service records and those for Aaron Parks (q.v.), Eleazer Parks (q.v.), Jonas Parks (q.v.), Leonard Parks (q.v.), and Willard Parks (q.v.) further supports the case for his participation at Bunker Hill.

5 Sudbury Miscellaneous Records, pay receipts dated September 30, 1776 (Doc. # 109), December 16, 1776 (Doc. # 2204), and March 17, 1777 (Doc. # 2209).

6 "Treasurer's Accompts," June 15, 1779. The suggested purpose of this expedition is the author's hypothesis; the actual purpose is undiscovered.

7 *Massachusetts Soldiers and Sailors*, Vol. XI, p. 825.

There is another record of a John Parks who served 3 months, 4 days at Cambridge, guarding General Burgoyne's "Convention Army" starting April 1, 1778, as a private in Capt. Isaac Wood's Company, Col. Jonathan Reed's Regiment of Guards, but it is not certain if this is the same individual.[1]

Possibly, he may have served at Rhode Island, as reinforcement to the Continental Army from July 24, 1780, to October 30, 1780 (credited with 3 months, 10 days of service; including 3 days for 60 miles of travel home). This service was as a corporal in Capt. Walter McFarland's Company, Col. Cyprian How's Regiment, but it is not certain if this is the same individual.[2]

He was the son of Ephraim and Mary (Hobbs) Parks; age 35 on April 19, 1775. He had been married to Anna Faugason of Weston since 1761. He was the brother of Isaac Parks (q.v.), Eleazer Parks (q.v.), Josiah Parks (q.v.), Samuel Parks (q.v.), and William Parks (q.v.); cousin of David Parks (q.v.), Benjamin Parks (q.v.), and James Parks (q.v.).[3]

PARKS, Jonas

Jonas Parks was a private in Capt. William Smith's Company of Minute Men from Lincoln, Col. Abijah Peirce's Regiment.[4] Following the engagement at Concord, he served for ten days in Cambridge.[5] He was paid by the town for his accoutrements as a minute man.[6]

Following his service as a minute man, he appears to have remained in Cambridge, where he enlisted for eight months of service in the rapidly forming Massachusetts Provincial Army. He served at Bunker Hill, as evidenced by a communication, dated June 14, 1775 (three days before the battle), by Capt. Nathan Fuller to the armorer, requesting him to receive the guns belonging to Parks and other members of his company, and fit them for service. Fuller's company was part of Colonel Gardner's 37th Regiment; Gardner was mortally wounded in the battle. Parks was reported still serving in Captain Fuller's Company, now Lt. Col. William Bond's Regiment, in a return dated at Prospect Hill, October 6, 1775, but now he is listed as a fifer. He remained in service until the end of December 1775, and was paid for this service by the town.[7]

Whereupon, he enlisted for another year of service, now in Col. John Paterson's Regiment. He served on the relief expedition to Canada. There, he developed complications from his

---

1 *Massachusetts Soldiers and Sailors*, Vol. XI, p. 926.
2 *Massachusetts Soldiers and Sailors*, Vol. XI, p. 825.
3 *Vital Records of Lincoln*; *Concord, Massachusetts: Births, Marriages, and Deaths*; MacLean, *A Rich Harvest*, p. 257; Bond, *Genealogies of the Families of Watertown*, pp. 386–87. Bond gives him a slightly different birth date than *Concord, Massachusetts: Births, Marriages, and Deaths*. Anna appears to be the sister of Rhoda Faugason, who married John's brother, Isaac Parks (q.v.). Bond gives Anna's name as Ann Fergerson.
4 Coburn, *Muster Rolls*.
5 *Massachusetts Soldiers and Sailors*, Vol. XI, p. 927.
6 "Treasurer's Accompts," July 10, 1777. The record does not mention Jonas at all. This payment was made to David Parks, who was not a minute man but was Jonas's father.
7 "Treasurer's Accompts," June 15, 1779; *Massachusetts Soldiers and Sailors*, Vol. XI, p. 927. MacLean, *A Rich Harvest* (p. 294), says he was a fifer at Bunker Hill, and his Pension Record (# W15154) provides loose support. But the service record suggests that he may well have been carrying a weapon in the battle. Whether he may have traded his fife for a weapon on the day of the battle, or perhaps traded his weapon for a fife sometime after the battle is not clear from the record.

smallpox inoculation, which cost him his sight in one eye and impaired his vision in the other.[1]

Following the retreat from Canada, he assisted in the defense of Ticonderoga. In November 1776, after British General Carlton pulled back his troops and returned north, he marched south with his regiment to join General Washington in New Jersey (Washington had retreated into Pennsylvania by the time they arrived). He participated at the Battle of Trenton on December 26, 1776, having crossed the ice-choked Delaware with Washington's forces the night before.[2]

In 1777, he enlisted for another tour of duty in the Continental Army, probably in Capt. Job Sumner's Company, Lt. Col. John Greaton's Regiment, and was present at the taking of Burgoyne on October 17, 1777.[3]

He appears to have served again in 1781, in Capt. Isaac Gage's Company, Col. Joseph Webb's Regiment from August to December 3, 1781, in the highlands of the Hudson Valley (near West Point and Peekskill).[4] This was as part of a large militia call-up to reinforce the Continental Army in the Hudson while Washington marched a sizeable portion of the army south to Yorktown.

He was the son of David Parks (q.v.) and Sarah (Gibbs) Parks; age 19 on April 19, 1775. He was the brother of Leonard Parks (q.v.); cousin of Aaron Parks (q.v.) and Willard Parks (q.v.); nephew of Benjamin Parks (q.v.); after the war, brother-in-law of Jonathan Tower (q.v.).

He married Eunice Tower, sister of Jonathan Tower (q.v.) in 1783 and moved to Charlestown, New Hampshire, probably shortly thereafter. He reportedly died about 1802 by drowning in the Connecticut River. He would have been about age 46. Eunice returned to Lincoln.[5]

---

1 "Treasurer's Accompts," June 15, 1779; Pension Record # W15154. While his unit is not identified in either record, Colonel Paterson's Regiment is the only Massachusetts regiment that served both in Canada and at Trenton. It is also consistent with the service of his brother, Leonard. Curiously, his loss of vision does not appear to have impaired his continuing service throughout most of the rest of the war. Later, in 1795, he applied for an invalid pension because of the loss of his sight, but his application appears to have been rejected because that condition was not covered under the invalid pension law.

2 Pension Record # W15154. His widow's declaration states he was "at the taking of the Hessians at Trenton." Patterson's Regiment was part of Gen. John Sullivan's Division.

3 Ibid. The pension declaration (filed 62 years later by his widow) mentions Lt. Isaac Gage (q.v.) with some degree of uncertainty. Lieutenant Gage appears to have been serving in Capt. Job Sumner's Company, Colonel Greaton's Regiment at Saratoga (see *Massachusetts Soldiers and Sailors*, Vol. VI, p. 215). The specific dates of this service are unknown, but, consistent with 1777 enlistments, it was probably a three-year term, lasting until the end of December 1779.

4 Pension Record # W15154; Parks, *Genealogy of the Parke Family*, p. 67. Parks (p. 67) says Jonas was paid for three months of Continental service in 1781, but neither the payment record nor the actual service record has been found. The pension declaration claims three or four months service at New York with Captain Gage's Company, Colonel Webb's Militia Regiment, but it gives no dates for the service, and juxtaposes the claim with the taking of Burgoyne in 1777. Isaac Gage is recorded as a lieutenant serving in Col. John Greaton's Regiment in 1777, however, and as a captain in Lt. Col. Joseph Webb's Militia Regiment near West Point (militia serving with the Continental Army would have been considered in Continental service) from August 20, 1781, to December 3, 1781. This appears to corroborate Parks's statement (see *Massachusetts Soldiers and Sailors*, Vol. VI, pp. 215, 216, and Vol. XVI, pp. 748–49).

5 Wheeler, "Lincoln," in Hurd, Vol. 2, p. 623; *Vital Records of Lincoln*; Parks, *Genealogy of the Parke Family*, p. 67; Saunderson, *History of Charlestown, New Hampshire*, p. 711. MacLean, *A Rich Harvest*, p. 257, incorrectly gives his age at Concord as 35. Bond, *Genealogies of the Families of Watertown* (p. 387), gives Sarah's name as

PARKS, Josiah

Josiah Parks served as a private in Capt. John Hartwell's Militia Company from Lincoln, Col. Eleazer Brooks's 3rd Middlesex County Regiment, which marched from Lincoln to fortify Dorchester Heights on March 4, 1776. The unit was discharged five days later, on March 9, after the threat of a British assault on the fortifications had subsided, and General Howe had begun preparations to evacuate Boston.[1]

He was back in service from December 20, 1776, to March 1, 1777, in Capt. Moses Harrington's Company, Colonel Dike's Regiment, at Dorchester. This service was credited to the town of Lincoln.[2]

He served at Rhode Island from May 10, 1777, to July 10, 1777, as a private in Capt. Jesse Wyman's Company, Col. Josiah Whitney's Regiment. He marched to Providence, then to Point Judith. The duration of this service was 2 months, 9 days, including 3 days for 50 miles of travel to the place of destination and 5 days for travel from Point Judith home. He is listed as being from Weston.[3]

A more modern stone has replaced the original marker at the grave of Josiah Parks in the Arbor Vitae Cemetery. He served at Dorchester Heights, Rhode Island, and Saratoga. (Photograph by the author)

Mary. Eunice was the sister of Bulah, who married Josiah Parks (q.v.) in 1780. Jonas and Eunice's marriage occurred less than a month before the birth of their first child, Jonas, who is recorded in Lincoln. Parks says that after Eunice died, he married Elizabeth Rollins. This is clearly incorrect, as Eunice was still alive in 1839 (long after Jonas's death), when she filed a pension application. Elizabeth Rollins is unidentified.

His move to Charlestown probably occurred in the mid-1780s, between the birth of their first child (1783) and the birth of their second child (Parks reports this as 1786). Parks credits Jonas and Eunice with nine children born between 1786 and 1800, none of whom were recorded in Lincoln. In any case, Jonas is listed as a taxpayer in Charlestown in 1792.

There may be a story around his drowning death (reported in Parks), but the author has not discovered it. It appears that Eunice must have been pregnant at the time, and that following his death, she returned to Lincoln fairly quickly, as their youngest child, Jonas, is recorded in Lincoln in 1803. The record lists Eunice as the mother, but it makes no mention of Jonas.

Unable to recall the date of Jonas's death in her pension declaration in 1839, Eunice dismisses it as "over 30 years since." The pension office recorded this as "about 1808."

1 *Massachusetts Soldiers and Sailors,* Vol. XI, p. 927; "Treasurer's Accompts," June 15, 1779.
2 *Massachusetts Soldiers and Sailors,* Vol. XI, p. 927; "Treasurer's Accompts," June 15, 1779; Pension Record # W18715. His pension declaration says that this service was for three months from November 1776, and that upon the expiration of the three months, he immediately reenlisted in the same unit for "one month longer."
3 The precise meaning of "place of destination" is unclear, but presumably this means either their initial march to Providence, or his travel to an initial rendezvous point. His pension record claims three months at Point Judith.

On August 14, 1777, he was detached from Capt. Samuel Farrar, Jr.'s Company of Militia from Lincoln, Colonel Eleazer Brooks's 3rd Middlesex County Regiment to reinforce the Northern Army. He was sent northward as a private in Capt. George Minot's Company, Col. Samuel Bullard's Regiment, from August 16, 1777, through November 30, 1777 (credited with 3 months, 25 days of service; including 11 days for 220 miles, of travel home). He marched "from Concord to Northampton, then to Bennington & then to a place called Pollet [Pawlet, Vermont]," where he joined a growing American force that was harassing Burgoyne's rear. Then he marched to Stillwater, participated in the Battle of Bemis Heights, and was present when British General Burgoyne surrendered at Saratoga.[1]

He was the son of Ephraim and Mary (Hobbs) Parks; age 18 when he marched to Dorchester Heights. He married Beulah Tower, sister of Jonathan Tower (q.v.), in 1780. He was the brother of Isaac Parks (q.v.), Eleazer Parks (q.v.), John Parks (q.v.), Samuel Parks (q.v.), and William Parks (q.v.); brother-in-law of Jonathan Tower (q.v.); cousin of David Parks (q.v.), Benjamin Parks (q.v.), and James Parks (q.v.). He died in Lincoln in 1841 at age 83, and he is buried in the Arbor Vitae Cemetery. After his death, Beulah moved to Waltham.[2]

PARKS, Leonard

Leonard Parks may have been a fifer at Concord on April 19, 1775, but this seems unlikely.[3]

Following the outbreak of fighting, he went to Cambridge to join his brother, Jonas (q.v.), in Capt. Nathan Fuller's Company, Col. Thomas Gardner's 37th Regiment. He served for eight months as a fifer, and participated in the Battle of Bunker Hill. He appears on a roll of Captain Fuller's Company (now Lt. Col. William Bond's Regiment), dated at Prospect Hill, October 6, 1775.[4]

Immediately upon the expiration of the foregoing term, he and his brother enlisted in 1776 in Captain Ashley's Company, Col. John Paterson's Regiment. He marched from Boston to New London and went thence to New York by water. Ordered to Canada, the regiment marched to Albany, then through Ticonderoga to Montreal, where the army was

---

1 *Massachusetts Soldiers and Sailors*, Vol. XI, p. 927; Pension Record # W18715.
2 *Vital Records of Lincoln*; Bond, *Genealogies of the Families of Watertown*, p. 387; Parks, *Genealogy of the Parke Family*, p. 55; Pension Record # W18715. His birth was recorded in Lincoln as August 9, 1757, but in his pension declaration he gives his date of birth as August 18, 1756. Wheeler, "Lincoln" (in Hurd, Vol. 2, p. 623), misstates his birth year as 1747. *Vital Records of Lincoln* lists his age at the time of death as 86, but he appears to have been only 83 based upon his birth record. The record of his death describes him as a "stone layer," presumably his trade or occupation. Bulah (Tower) was the sister of Eunice, who married Jonas Parks (q.v.) in 1783.
3 Parks family tradition, as reported in MacLean, *A Rich Harvest*, p. 294. Parks, *Genealogy of the Parke Family* (p. 68), quotes an 1838 newspaper article (evidently an obituary) which places him in the "Battle of Lexington." No evidence of this service has been found, and he makes no mention of it in his pension declaration. In the absence of any corroborating evidence, or compelling logic this is at best unsubstantiated, and more likely an unnecessary later embellishment to his otherwise suitably impressive Revolutionary War resume (see note 2, p. 378).
4 *Massachusetts Soldiers and Sailors*, Vol. XI, p. 927; Pension Record # S5144; MacLean, *A Rich Harvest*, p. 294; Wheeler, "Lincoln," in Hurd, Vol. 2, p. 623. Fifty years later, he identified himself as "Fife Master" in Colonel Gardner's Regiment when he attended the laying of the cornerstone for the Bunker Hill Monument in 1825 (see *Proceedings of the Bunker Hill Monument Association* (1895), p. 47). This appears to be a little bit of self-aggrandizement; he was only age 14 during the battle.

exposed to smallpox. After their retreat from Canada, and their defense of Ticonderoga against the British incursion, they went to Albany where in November they were ordered to join General Washington in New Jersey. Marching south, they arrived in time to re-cross the Delaware on Christmas night and participate in the Battle of Trenton on December 26, 1776. He was discharged in Trenton after the battle and returned home.[1]

He is reported to have served at the Battle of Brandywine on September 11, 1777, but this is highly improbable.[2]

He served at Saratoga as a fifer in Capt. Samuel Farrar, Jr.'s Company, Col. Jonathan Reed's Middlesex County Regiment (Brig. Gen. James Bricket's Brigade of Massachusetts Militia), urgently sent north on September 29, 1777, in a second wave of troops detached from Col. Eleazer Brooks's Militia Regiment to reinforce the Northern Army under General Gates. He marched via Northampton to Stillwater, was present at the surrender of Burgoyne, and was part of the escort which marched the prisoners to Cambridge. He served 1 month, 10 days, and was discharged upon delivering the prisoners to Prospect Hill on November 7, 1777.[3]

He served for three months guarding General Burgoyne's troops in Cambridge, as a private in Capt. Daniel Harrington's Company, Col. Jonathan Reed's Regiment of Guards, from April 1st or 2nd, 1778, through July 3, 1778. He may possibly have served a second three-month term on the heels of the first, but this is not probable.[4]

---

1 Pension Record # S5144. Washington's Army had retreated into Pennsylvania by the time they arrived. The 1838 newspaper account in Parks, *Genealogy of the Parke Family* (p. 68), credits him with having been at the Battle of Princeton on January 3, 1777, but this appears to be incorrect. He makes no claim to having been at Princeton, nor is there any record of his having been there. His enlistment would have been up December 31, 1776, and he says he was discharged and returned home.

2 The 1838 newspaper account in Parks, *Genealogy of the Parke Family* (p. 68), reads, "He enlisted in the northern army, and was at the taking of Burgoyne, and being transferred to the main army, he was also at the battles of Trenton, Princeton, and Brandywine." The sequence is obviously out of order, and the account offers little assistance in distinguishing fact from folklore. No corroborating record of service at Brandywine (or of any 1777 service at all prior to his service at Saratoga) has been found, nor does his pension declaration make any such claim. Furthermore, the pragmatic details make it nearly impossible for him to have been at both Brandywine and Saratoga. In the aftermath of the American defeat at Brandywine, it would have taken at least several days for Leonard Parks to be discharged and processed out. Travel itself, back to Lincoln, would have taken upwards of 17 days (at the standard allowance of 20 miles/day). Perhaps, if he had pushed hard, he might have made it in less time. Even so, his having been prepared to march northward on September 29 is highly improbable. The record of his being drafted for Saratoga service on August 14, 1777 (see note 3), casts further doubt on his presence at Brandywine.

Leonard Parks himself was undoubtedly the source (perhaps via second- and third-hand re-tellers) of much of the information in the newspaper account about the battles in which he served. The article tells us that, "From that time [i.e., of his war service], until his age prevented, he was an eminent fifer in this neighborhood." He was evidently a popular figure who enjoyed entertaining his Cambridge neighbors. The author speculates that perhaps he may have enjoyed entertaining his neighbors with tales of his exploits in the war (real and embellished), as much as he evidently did with his fifing. To the extent that he may have been so inclined, he certainly had a much freer hand to tell stories among friends and family than he did within the legal context and sworn testimony of his pension declaration, which makes no mention of Brandywine.

3 *Massachusetts Soldiers and Sailors*, Vol. XI, pp. 927–28; Pension Record # S5144. The *Massachusetts Soldiers and Sailors* record indicates that he was drafted in Acton, on August 14, 1777, for the first wave of reinforcements for the Northern Army. This is presumed to be Leonard Parks (inst.), as no Leonard Parks of Acton is identifiable. It is not clear why he did not go north at that time, rather than five weeks later in the second wave.

4 *Massachusetts Soldiers and Sailors*, Vol. XI, pp. 826, 928. He shows up on a "list dated July 1, 1778, of men detached from Capt. Samuel Farrar's co. to march to relieve men "now" serving as guards over troops of convention [i.e., Burgoyne's army] at or near Cambridge, as returned by said Capt. Farrar to Col. Eleazer Brooks";

He was paid by the town for service at Boston in 1778, as a private in Capt. David Goodwin's Company, Colonel Cogswell's Regiment from September 22, 1778, to December 31, 1778, (3 months, 11 days). This company was detached to guard and fortify posts in and around Boston.[1]

He was the son of David Parks (q.v.) and Sarah (Gibbs) Parks; age 14 at Bunker Hill. He was the brother of Jonas Parks (q.v.); cousin of Aaron Parks (q.v.) and Willard Parks (q.v.); nephew of Benjamin Parks (q.v.). He married Betsey Bucknam (or Buckman) of Malden in 1785. During the 1790s, he moved to Cambridgeport, where he died in 1838 at age 77. He is reported to have remained an "eminent fifer" all his life.[2]

PARKS, Samuel

Samuel Parks of Lincoln had settled in Stoddard, New Hampshire, by the time the Revolutionary War broke out, and he was a member of Stoddard's Committee of Correspondence and Safety. He served as an ensign in Capt. Silas Wright's Company of Militia during the Royalton Alarm in 1780. Duration of service: one month.

He was age 25 when the war broke out, age 30 during the Royalton Alarm. He was the son of Ephraim and Mary (Hobbs) Parks; born in Lincoln; the brother of Isaac Parks (q.v.), Eleazer Parks (q.v.), John Parks (q.v.), Josiah Parks (q.v.), and William Parks (q.v.); cousin of David Parks (q.v.), Benjamin Parks (q.v.), and James Parks (q.v.). He married Hannah Richardson possibly in Townsend. Subsequently, he moved to Winchendon, but eventually returned to Lincoln, where he died in 1832 at age 83.[3]

PARKS, Willard

Willard Parks was a private in Capt. William Smith's Company of Minute Men from Lincoln, Col. Abijah Peirce's Regiment.[4] Following the engagement at Concord, he served

---

also, on a similar "list of men detached from [Captain Farrar's Company] Col. Brooks's regt. to relieve guards at Cambridge, as returned to Lieut. Col. Francis Faulkner [undated]." Faulkner was on Colonel Brooks's staff. The date of the first list suggests a second term of guard duty, or it may more probably have been a lag in recordkeeping for a term of duty that was about to end. His pension declaration makes no mention of a second three-month tour of guard duty, and is sufficiently detailed for the omission to be material.

Typically, the terms of service for guarding the Convention ran from November 1777 through the beginning of April 1778 (five months), April 1778 through the beginning of July (three months), and July 1778 through November (five months).

1 "Treasurer's Accompts," May 5, 1779; *Massachusetts Soldiers and Sailors,* Vol. XI, p. 928; Pension Record # S5144. In his pension declaration, he claimed to be fife major. Whether or not this is valid (he turned just age 19 during this service), it reflects his self-image as a skilled fifer, and his claim of being "Fife Master" (perhaps an errant transcription of "fife major") at the Bunker Hill ceremony in 1825 (see note 4, p. 377).

2 Wheeler, "Lincoln," in Hurd, Vol. 2, p. 623; *Vital Records of Lincoln*; Bond, *Genealogies of the Families of Watertown,* p. 386; Parks, *Genealogy of the Parke Family,* p. 68. His marriage intention was recorded in Lincoln in December 1784; the marriage record is found in Corey, *Births Marriages and Deaths in Malden.*

3 Parks, *Genealogy of the Parke Family,* p. 54; *Vital Records of Lincoln*; Marvin, *History of the Town of Winchendon,* p. 464. His marriage date is estimated as about 1783 in the genealogical databases of the Church of Jesus Christ of Latter Day Saints. However, the author has been unable to find corroborating evidence. Marvin indicates he was living in Winchendon before his brother, William (i.e., before 1790). He references three children by name, but he gives no ages or dates. Their birth records do not appear in *Vital Records of Winchendon.* Census records show a Samuel Parks in Sutton in 1790, but not in Winchendon or in Townsend. The 1800 census shows him back in Lincoln.

4 Coburn, *Muster Rolls.*

for nine days in Cambridge.¹ He was reimbursed by the town for his accoutrements as a minute man.²

He was paid by the town for service at Cambridge in 1775, but the details of this service have not been found.³

Subsequently, he served as a private in Capt. John Hartwell's Militia Company from Lincoln, Col. Eleazer Brooks's 3rd Middlesex County Regiment, which marched from Lincoln to fortify Dorchester Heights on March 4, 1776. The unit was discharged five days later, on March 9, after the threat of a British assault on the fortifications had subsided, and General Howe had begun preparations to evacuate Boston.⁴

He was age 22 at Concord; the son of Stephen and Abigail (Garfield) Parks; nephew of Benjamin Parks (q.v.) and David Parks (q.v.), and first cousin to Aaron Parks (q.v.), Jonas Parks (q.v.) and Leonard Parks (q.v.). He married Lucy Parks (possibly a distant cousin, but her identity has not been discovered), probably in 1776. His death is recorded in Lincoln in 1816. He was age 63.⁵

PARKS, William

William Parks was a private in Capt. William Smith's Company of Minute Men from Lincoln, Col. Abijah Peirce's Regiment.⁶ Following the engagement at Concord, he served for nine days in Cambridge.⁷ He was reimbursed by the town for his accoutrements as a minute man.⁸

Having watched two drafts of men from Lincoln's militia company march north for service at Saratoga, his number came up on November 3, 1777. He was detached from the militia company, and served five months at Cambridge (through April 3, 1778) in Capt. Simon Hunt's Company, Col. Eleazer Brooks's Regiment, guarding the British and German soldiers surrendered by Burgoyne at Saratoga.⁹

He was the son of Ephraim and Mary (Hobbs) Parks, age 40 as a minute man. He was the brother of Isaac Parks (q.v.), Eleazer Parks (q.v.), John Parks (q.v.), Josiah Parks (q.v.), and Samuel Parks (q.v.); cousin of David Parks (q.v.), Benjamin Parks (q.v.), and James

---

1 *Massachusetts Soldiers and Sailors*, Vol. XI, p. 930.
2 "Treasurer's Accompts," February 19, 1776.
3 "Treasurer's Accompts," June 15, 1779. Wheeler, "Lincoln" (in Hurd, Vol. 2, p. 623), credits him with eight months of service at Cambridge. Parks, *Genealogy of the Parke Family* (p. 66), agrees, but he appears to use Wheeler as his source. Nevertheless, this is likely. Eight months (until December 31, 1775) was the typical term of enlistment in the days immediately following the April 19th Alarm, and a reasonable assumption, unless the individual did not enlist right away, or perhaps failed to complete his term for some reason (e.g., illness).
4 *Massachusetts Soldiers and Sailors*, Vol. XI, p. 930.
5 Wheeler, "Lincoln," in Hurd, Vol. 2, p. 623; *Vital Records of Lincoln*; Bond, *Genealogies of the Families of Watertown*, p. 387; Parks, *Genealogy of the Parke Family*, p. 66. Their probable marriage date is imputed from the birth record of their son, Cady, in early 1777. Parks, *Genealogy of the Parke Family* (p. 66), gives their marriage date as January 11, 1777. While this is entirely possible, no corroboration has been found. It was less than one month before Cady was born.
6 Coburn, *Muster Rolls*.
7 *Massachusetts Soldiers and Sailors*, Vol. XI, p. 930.
8 "Treasurer's Accompts," July 10, 1777.
9 *Massachusetts Soldiers and Sailors*, Vol. XI, p. 930; "Treasurer's Accompts," November 11, 1779.

Chapter 10: The Army of the Revolution

The childhood home of six Parks brothers who served in the Revolutionary War stood near the corner of what is now Tower Road and Route 117. William, John, and Eleazer were minute men on April 19th, while Isaac also went to Concord as a militiaman. William, John, Eleazer, Isaac, and Josiah all subsequently served multiple enlistments from Lincoln; their brother Samuel was living in New Hampshire and served from there. (Courtesy of Lincoln Town Archives, Lincoln, MA)

Parks (q.v.). He married Lydia (surname unknown), probably before 1758. He moved to Winchendon sometime before 1790.[1]

[He may have served for two days on a Rhode Island Alarm on July 22, 1777, as a private in Capt. Hezekiah Whitney's Company, Col. Josiah Whitney's Regiment, but this seems unlikely. This record probably refers to a different William Parke.][2]

---

1 *Concord, Massachusetts: Births, Marriages, and Deaths*; *Vital Records of Lincoln*; Parks, *Genealogy of the Parke Family*, p. 53. No marriage record has been found. His wife's name is from Parks, but it is confirmed in the birth records of four of their children in *Vital Records of Lincoln*. Their marriage date is estimated from the birth of their first child, Elezibeth, in 1758. *Vital Records of Lincoln* contains baptism records of four more children, through 1777. It also contains marriage records of two of the children, as late as 1783. Marriage records for other children appear in Winchendon, starting in 1788, suggesting that he moved the family to Winchendon between 1783 and 1788. The 1790 census records him as living in Winchendon.

2 *Massachusetts Soldiers and Sailors*, Vol. XI, p. 828. It is most likely that the men who made up this unit were already in service when the alarm came in. Both Whitneys were from Harvard, and Col. Josiah Whitney seems to have been serving from a base near Hull in the fall 1776. He had supplied at least a company of men to General Washington in New Jersey from December 1776 through March 1777. In May and June 1777, he spent two months in Rhode Island with a regiment raised for that purpose from Worcester, Bristol, Middlesex, and Barnstable counties. In August, his regiment was ordered to Vermont on the Bennington Alarm. There seems to be little chance, if William Parks (inst.) had not already been in service (for which we have no record), that he could have been tapped and mobilized for the Rhode Island alarm.

PEIRCE, Abijah
[also PIERCE]

Abijah Peirce was colonel of a regiment of minute men which included Capt. William Smith's Company from Lincoln, Capt. David Brown's Company from Concord, Capt. Charles Miles's Company from Concord, Capt. Isaac Davis's Company from Acton, Capt. Jonathan Willson's Company from Bedford, Capt. Simon Edgel's Company from Framingham, and Capt. John Nixon's Company from Sudbury.[1] He appears to have been the captain of Lincoln's militia company from before August 1774, at least through March 1775, and probably still captain on April 19th. He appears to have been named colonel only the day before the April 19th Alarm.[2] He is widely reported to have gone to Concord armed only with a cane, and to have picked up the musket of one of the British soldiers killed in the action at the Bridge. This was reputed to be the first trophy taken in battle in the Revolutionary War.[3] He was reimbursed by the town for two sets of accoutrements as a minute man.[4]

Following the opening engagement of the war, he was paid by the town for two campaigns in Cambridge in 1775, and for a three-year campaign in the Continental Army. No details of this service have been found, and it is quite possible that he may not have provided this service.[5]

---

1 This list is from Coburn, *Muster Rolls*, p. 8. It agrees with Shattuck, *History of the Town of Concord*, p. 110.

2 See MacLean, *A Rich Harvest*, p. 607; Hoar, *Autobiography*, p. 20. There is considerable confusion and speculation about the precise command structure of Colonial forces on April 19, 1775. Ripley, *A History of the Fight at Concord* (p. 14), and Shattuck, *History of the Town of Concord* (p. 110), assert that Samuel Farrar, Jr. (q.v.), was captain of Lincoln's militia company, but the author accepts MacLean's logic that Peirce was still officially captain and that Farrar was in acting command.

Coburn, *Muster Rolls* (p. 7), and MacLean have provided some reasoned sense to the holes in the record. As captain of Lincoln's militia company, and a highly respected individual, Peirce would undoubtedly have had a hand in the formation of Lincoln's minute company, and he was probably influential in getting the various minute companies organized into a regiment during that spring. Ripley (p. 14) refers to him as a Major, but he may or may not have had a formal title before being named Colonel. Hoar indicates that on April 19th, he had not yet received his commission, his equipment, or taken his oath. It is probably not surprising that on the morning of April 19th, James Barrett, as the senior Colonel, took command of all the companies and effectively amalgamated them into a single regiment. Major Buttrick was ordered to lead the attack. However, Hoar's contention that Peirce served as a private soldier is ludicrous. He would have been given some deference befitting his rank (even without his new commission), and his actual role at Concord would likely have devolved to something on the order of an informal aide or staff officer rather than as part of the rank and file. Mike Ryan, in notes shared with the author, points out (citing the example of Warren at Breed's Hill) that without his official commission, Pierce may simply have deferred as a gentleman to those who held formal commissions.

3 Baker Affidavit (1850); Hoar, *Autobiography*, p. 20. The musket is in the collection of the Concord Museum. David Wood, Curator of the Concord Museum, however, informed the author that it is actually a trade fusil, more likely to have belonged to an American than to a British Regular.

4 "Treasurer's Accompts," February 28, 1776.

5 "Treasurer's Accompts," June 10, 1779. Wheeler, "Lincoln" (in Hurd, Vol. 2, p. 623), indicates that he served at Cambridge during the summer of 1775, and he does not mention Continental service at all (the entry is in quotation marks as if quoting another source, but the source is not identified). *Massachusetts Soldiers and Sailors* does not mention him at all. And it is hard to imagine him serving in a non-officer's role, or that as an officer there would not be a surviving service record. The Treasurer's account is also curious. The £40 he was paid appears to be scarcely more than the going rate for a foot soldier. [Three years of Continental service as a private seems to have paid £30. Cambridge service (8 months) as a private seems to have paid £8.] For him to have served two campaigns at Cambridge, they would have to have been partial campaigns. But unless only part of a three-year Continental service is included (which would normally be indicated, but in this case is not), it is hard to see where there is any room for an officer's pay scale. A more likely possibility is that this pay could have been for service by someone else (or perhaps two people, as suggested by two Cambridge cam-

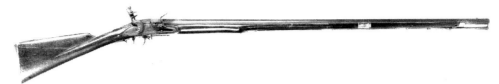

Minute man Col. Abijah Peirce went to Concord on April 19th armed only with a cane. After the fight at the North Bridge, he reportedly picked up this musket, purported to be a British musket—the first trophy taken in a Revolutionary War battle. It has been identified as a trade fusil, however, which is more likely to have been carried by a colonist than a British Regular. (Courtesy of the Concord Museum, Concord, MA, www.concordmuseum.org)

He was the son of Isaac and Susanna (Bemis) Peirce, born in Watertown (in the portion that became Waltham); age 47 during the Concord Alarm. He had been married to Thankful (Brown) since 1751. He was the father-in-law of Samuel Hoar (q.v.); uncle of Moses Brown (q.v.). He died in Lincoln in 1800 at age 73, from a fall from a high beam in his barn. He is buried in the Meeting House Cemetery behind Bemis Hall.[1]

He had been a leading citizen of the town since shortly after its founding, said to be "of commanding personal presence and strong individuality." Over the years, he had served Lincoln as Deer Reeve, Tythingman, Surveyor of Highways, Selectman, Treasurer, and Town Clerk. In 1773, he had been named to Lincoln's newly-formed Committee of Correspondence, along with Eleazer Brooks (q.v.) and Deacon Samuel Farrar (q.v., Chapter 12). The following year, in the wake of the Coercive Acts, he represented the town at a County Convention held in August at Concord, then at the Provincial Congress, which commenced meeting in Concord in October. As economic dislocation increased during the war, he was appointed a delegate to a state convention called at Concord in 1779, to establish a state-wide pricing schedule and adopt other measures to prevent monopoly, extortion, and unfair dealings.[2]

PEIRCE, Abraham
[also PIERCE]

Abraham Peirce was a private in Capt. William Smith's Company of Minute Men from Lincoln, Col. Abijah Peirce's Regiment.[3] Following the engagement at Concord, he served

---

paigns or two sets of accoutrements). Normally this would have meant a son or slave. The fact that MacLean, *A Rich Harvest*, does not include Abijah on his list of known slaveholders (p. 220) casts an element of doubt on the possibility of a slave. But Abijah did have a son, Nathaniel, age 20 and just graduated from Harvard, who could have served. Unfortunately, we can find no service record for Nathaniel to encourage the possibility that the service might have been his. As a colonel and respected individual, it is possible that Abijah may have been entrusted with pay for individuals other than sons or slaves. The logic of this (particularly in the absence of logical alternatives) is appealing. However, one supposes that, notwithstanding the respect accorded Abijah, there would still need to be some rationale for using him as the conduit. Without ready candidates for this service, and in the absence of such an explanation, the service for which this payment was made remains a mystery.

1 Biggs, "In Memorium," p. 176; *Vital Records of Lincoln*; Hoar, *Autobiography*, p. 21; Peirce, *Peirce Genealogy* pp. 44, 59; *Watertown Records, Second Book*, p. 84.
2 Peirce, *Peirce Genealogy*, p. 59; MacLean, *A Rich Harvest*, p. 138; Shattuck, *History of the Town of Concord*, pp. 82, 91, 122, 312. The descriptive quotation is from Shattuck. Others who represented Lincoln at these meetings were Samuel Farrar (q.v., Chapter 12), Samuel Farrar, Jr. (q.v.), and Eleazer Brooks (q.v.).
3 Coburn, *Muster Rolls*.

for five days in Cambridge.[1] He was reimbursed by the town for part of a set of accoutrements as a minute man.[2]

On April 24, 1775, he enrolled with his brother, Joseph Peirce (q.v.), in the hastily forming Massachusetts Provincial Army, as a private in Capt. William Smith's Company, Col. John Nixon's 16th Massachusetts Regiment, serving in Cambridge at least through September. On May 11, we find him on picket guard duty under Maj. Loammi Baldwin. He is presumed to have participated with his unit in the Battle of Bunker Hill on June 17, 1775.[3]

The following year, along with his brother, Joseph, he joined the artillery, appearing as a matross in Capt. James Swan's 1st Company, Col. Thomas Craft's Artillery Regiment by June 8, 1776. By August 1, 1776, he had become a gunner; he became a bombardier six months later, on February 1, 1777, perhaps replacing his brother, Joseph, who became a corporal. Meanwhile, Capt. Philip Marett had taken over command of the company from Captain Swan on December 1, 1776. Abraham Peirce continued to serve in this company until May 8, 1777, when he appears to have been recruited into the Continental Army.

He appears on a return dated May 20, 1777, as a private in Capt. Andrew Samson's Company, stationed at the fort at the Gurnet.[4]

He was the son of Jonas and Mary (Adams) Peirce; age 19 when he responded to the Concord Alarm. He was the brother of Isaac Peirce (q.v.), Jonas Peirce (q.v., Chapter 12), and Joseph Peirce (q.v.). After his war service, he went to Rindge, New Hampshire, where he married Phebe Towne, probably in 1779. He died at Rindge, in 1802, at age 47.[5]

PEIRCE, Isaac
[also PIERCE]

Isaac Peirce served as a private in Capt. John Hartwell's Company of Militia from Lincoln, Col. Eleazer Brooks's 3rd Middlesex County Regiment, which marched from Lincoln to fortify Dorchester Heights on March 4, 1776. The unit was discharged five days later, on March 9, after the threat of a British assault on the fortifications had subsided, and General Howe had begun preparations to evacuate Boston.[6] Most of the company was paid in September, but there is a record allowed in Council of a pay abstract for mileage to and from Dorchester Heights, on which he appears in Capt. John Minot's Company, Colonel

---

1 *Massachusetts Soldiers and Sailors*, Vol. XII, p. 363.
2 "Treasurer's Accompts," March 15, 1776. This was paid to his father, Jonas.
3 *Massachusetts Soldiers and Sailors*, Vol. XII, pp. 72, 363. Smith's company was involved in the Battle of Bunker Hill, although William Smith (q.v.) himself appears to have been sick and "confined to his chamber." Colonel Nixon's Regiment was also known as the 5th Regiment under the Continental numbering system adopted after Washington took command of the Provincial forces.
4 Ibid. The Gurnet is the hill that sits at the end of a long sand spit at the entrance to Plymouth Harbor. The towns of Plymouth, Kingston, and Duxbury erected Fort Andrew there, in 1776. The fort mounted three twelve-pounders, two nine-pounders, and one six-pounder. It held a garrison of about sixty men (see Morris, "The Gurnet.")
5 Peirce, *Peirce Genealogy*, pp. 48, 68; *Vital Records of Lincoln*. The date of his marriage is not given, but Peirce notes that he had a son, Elipha, born in June 1780. Phebe had just turned age 17 when she gave birth to Elipha. Following Abraham's death, she married Lt. Nathaniel Thomas, who reportedly had served in a Lexington company during the Revolutionary War (although Peirce gives his birth date as August 4, 1787).
6 *Massachusetts Soldiers and Sailors*, Vol. XII, p. 81.

Dike's Regiment. This indicates that he was probably back in Dorchester Heights from August 1776 until November 1776.[1]

He followed his brothers, Abraham Peirce (q.v.) and Joseph Peirce (q.v.), into the artillery service, showing up by November 1, 1776 as a matross in Capt. James Swan's 1st Company, Col. Thomas Craft's Artillery Regiment. A month later, the company command devolved to Capt. Philip Marett. Isaac Peirce served until May 8, 1777.[2]

On August 16, 1777, he enlisted (evidently as a substitute) for service in the Northern Department. He served for 3 months, 14 days, until November 30, 1777, as a private in Capt. George Minot's Company, Col. Samuel Bullard's Regiment, serving through the surrender of General Burgoyne at Saratoga.[3]

He may have served on guard duty for General Burgoyne's troops in Cambridge, possibly as early as January 12, 1778, through April 3, 1778 (2 months, 22 days), as a private in Capt. Abraham Peirce's Company, Col. Eleazer Brooks's Regiment, but clearly from April 2, 1778, through July 3, 1778 (3 months, 2 days), as a private in Capt. Daniel Harrington's Company, Col. Jonathan Reed's Regiment of Guards.[4]

He probably served on an expedition to Rhode Island, from August 1, 1778, through September 11, 1778 (credited with 1 month, 14 days of service, including 3 days for 60 miles of travel home), as a private in Capt. Francis Brown's Company, Col. William McIntosh's Regiment (Brig. Gen. Solomon Lovell's Brigade of Massachusetts Militia). This individual participated in the Battle of Rhode Island on August 29, 1778. However, it is not certain if this is the same Isaac Peirce.[5]

Subsequently, he enlisted for nine months in the Continental Army, pursuant to a resolve of June 9, 1779. He is described as age 21; six feet in stature, light complexioned. His enlistment was credited to Lincoln. Details of his unit and deployment have not survived, but it is likely that he was in service by August 1, 1779, when an Isaac Pearce is recorded in Captain Dix's Company, Colonel Wesson's 9th Regiment. If this is he, he appears to have reenlisted, and his trail seems to have taken him to Rhode Island several times under different commands during the next 15 months.[6]

---

1 *Massachusetts Soldiers and Sailors*, Vol. XII, p. 370.

2 *Massachusetts Soldiers and Sailors*, Vol. XII, p. 81.

3 Ibid. He does not appear on the draft list for Saratoga, suggesting that this service was as a substitute, probably for either Timothy Brown (q.v.), Nehemiah Abbot (q.v.), or Daniel Brown (q.v.), who do appear on the draft list, but who evidently did not go north on this campaign.

4 *Massachusetts Soldiers and Sailors*, Vol. XII, pp. 81, 370–71. Capt. Abraham Peirce was a distant (third or fourth) cousin from Waltham, probably not a close enough relationship to be relevant to identifying this record with certainty as being Isaac Peirce (inst.). It is just as likely that it may have been another Isaac Peirce who provided this service. Likely alternative candidates may be the brother of the captain, age 46, also of Waltham; his son (nephew of the captain), age 20; and the brother of Col. Abijah Peirce (q.v., distant cousin of the captain), age 39–40, who lived in Waltham and later became a Waltham Selectman. The latter's marriage to Hannah Mason of Watertown in 1764 is recorded in *Vital Records of Lincoln*, but they probably had left Lincoln before the outbreak of the war.

5 *Massachusetts Soldiers and Sailors*, Vol. XII, p. 370. The mileage allowance is consistent with what other Lincoln men on this service were allowed, suggesting the likelihood that this record applies to Isaac Peirce (inst.). In an apparent confusion of his Saratoga service with this Rhode Island service, Wheeler, "Lincoln" (in Hurd, Vol. 2, p. 624), places him "in Captain John Minot's company in the expedition to Rhode Island in 1778," which record does not appear in *Massachusetts Soldiers and Sailors*.

6 *Massachusetts Soldiers and Sailors*, Vol. XII, pp. 17, 81–82, 370–71. Except for the certainty of his having enlisted in the Continental Army, it is by no means certain that these stints in Rhode Island were served by

He was the son of Jonas and Mary (Adams) Peirce; age 18 at Dorchester Heights. He was the brother of Abraham Peirce (q.v.), Jonas Peirce (q.v., Chapter 12), and Joseph Peirce (q.v.). He married Anna Sanderson in Waltham in 1786. No record of his death has been found.[1]

PEIRCE, Joseph
[also PIERCE]

Joseph Peirce served on April 19, 1775, as a private in Capt. William Smith's Company of Minute Men from Lincoln, Col. Abijah Peirce's Regiment.[2] As a minute man, he served for five days in Cambridge, whereupon he enlisted in Capt. William Smith's Company, Col. John Nixon's 16th Massachusetts Regiment, in the rapidly forming Massachusetts army. He is presumed to have participated with his unit in the Battle of Bunker Hill on June 17, and he remained in service at Cambridge into the fall of 1775.[3]

Subsequently, he served as a private in Capt. John Hartwell's Militia Company from Lincoln, Col. Eleazer Brooks's 3rd Middlesex County Regiment, which marched from Lincoln to fortify Dorchester Heights on March 4, 1776. The unit was discharged five days later, on March 9, after the threat of a British assault on the fortifications had subsided, and General Howe had begun preparations to evacuate Boston.

Later that year, along with his brother, Abraham Peirce (q.v.), he joined the artillery, appearing by June 8, 1776, as a bombardier in Capt. James Swan's 1st Company, Col. Thomas Craft's Artillery Regiment in Boston. He seems to have served in that capacity until February 1, 1777, when he became a corporal. Meanwhile, Capt. Philip Marett had taken over command of the company from Captain Swan on December 1, 1776. Joseph Peirce served as a corporal in this company until May 8, 1777.

In January 1777, he was recruited out of the artillery regiment to serve in the Continental Army, which service began officially on May 1, 1777. He served for three years in Capt. Abijah Child's Company, Col. John Greaton's 2nd Regiment, during which he was promoted to sergeant, and served at Saratoga. He also served in Capt. Thomas Prichard's Company before being discharged on May 1, 1780. This service was credited to Lincoln.[4]

He was the son of Jonas and Mary (Adams) Peirce; age 22 on the Alarm of April 19th. He was the brother of Abraham Peirce (q.v.), Isaac Peirce (q.v.), and Jonas Peirce (q.v., Chapter 12). He married Mehitable Peirce on March 17, 1778, who died soon after, and Mary Headley (who also appears in the record as "Polley") in 1780, with whom two children are recorded in Lincoln. By 1818, he was living in Sterling. He married Lucy Parks

---

him. In fact, in a couple of cases, the record indicates that the unit was detached from the militia, suggesting that this was not the service of a Continental soldier.

1 Peirce, *Peirce Genealogy*, p. 48; *Vital Records of Lincoln*; Wheeler, "Lincoln," in Hurd, Vol. 2, p. 624.
2 Coburn, *Muster Rolls*.
3 *Massachusetts Soldiers and Sailors*, Vol. XII, pp. 89, 377. Capt. William Smith's Company is recorded as having been engaged at Bunker Hill. Colonel Nixon's 16th Massachusetts Regiment was also known as the 5th Regiment under the Continental numbering system adopted after General Washington assumed command of the Provincial forces.

Edward Adams (q.v.) served as a substitute for Joseph Peirce (inst.) for a month during September and possibly into October 1775. The circumstances of the substitution, and whether or not he returned to finish his term of service, are unknown (see Edward Adams's Pension Record # W20567).
4 *Massachusetts Soldiers and Sailors*, Vol. XII, pp. 89–90, 377; Pension Record # S34475.

of Lincoln in 1820, and appears to have returned to Lincoln, where he died in 1825 at age 72.[1]

PORTER, John
[also POTTER]

John Porter of Lincoln enlisted May 10, 1775, as a private in Capt. William Smith's Company, Col. John Nixon's 16th Massachusetts Regiment, in the rapidly forming Massachusetts Provincial Army, on May 10, 1775. He is presumed to have participated with his unit in the Battle of Bunker Hill on June 17, 1775. He remained in service at least through September 1775, when he appears on a company return, and probably through the end of December, when a typical eight-month enlistment would have expired.[2]

He appears to have served subsequently in the Continental Army, as his name appears on a list of men raised for that purpose, engaged for the town of Lincoln. No dates or information about this service are given in the record, but it is likely that this may have been in 1777, when the town had a quota of 26 men to furnish for three-year terms in the Continental Army.[3]

He may be the John Bortor who was mustered into service in Capt. Abijah Child's Company, Col. John Greaton's Regiment, and paid a bounty, as reported by James Barrett, muster master for Middlesex County on February 26, 1777, but this is uncertain.[4]

His identity is undiscovered; it is likely that he is the same individual listed as John Barter (q.v.).

---

1 MacLean, *A Rich Harvest*, p. 257; *Vital Records of Lincoln*; Wheeler, "Lincoln," in Hurd, Vol. 2, p. 624; Peirce, *Peirce Genealogy*, p. 48; Bond, *Genealogies of the Families of Watertown*, pp. 296, 397; Pension Record # S34475. Some confusion seems to exist about his marriages.

   Vital Records of Lincoln shows a marriage intention for Joseph Peirce and "Polley" Headley on July 24, 1780, but subsequently lists "Mary" as the mother of his children, Joseph (b. February 24, 1781) and Mary (b. February 3, 1782). Bond lists the marriage of Joseph Peirce to Polly Hadley on July 25, 1780, and the marriage of Mary Headly to Joseph Peirce in 1780, confirming that Mary and Polley are the same individual. She was a cousin of Nathaniel Colburn (q.v.) and Joseph Colburn (q.v.).

   Peirce incorrectly identifies Lucy Parks of Lincoln as wife number two (after Mehitable), and the mother of the children (Joseph and Mary). *Vital Records of Lincoln* correctly shows Lucy Parks marrying Joseph Peirce of Sterling on May 27, 1820.

   Neither Mehitable nor Lucy appear to be closely related to any of the Peirces or Parkses referenced herein.

   Wheeler gives his date of birth incorrectly by three years.

2 *Massachusetts Soldiers and Sailors*, Vol. XII, p. 629. Colonel Nixon's Regiment was also known as the 5th Regiment under the Continental numbering system adopted after Washington assumed command of the Provincial Army.

3 *Massachusetts Soldiers and Sailors*, Vol. XII, p. 593. For Lincoln's quota in 1777, see Wheeler, "Lincoln" (in Hurd, Vol. 2, p. 620), or Shattuck, *History of the Town of Concord* (p. 300). Wheeler lists John Porter as one of the men recruited in 1777 from outside of Lincoln to fulfill the quota, but the *Massachusetts Soldiers and Sailors* record clearly indicates a Lincoln residency. It is likely that he may have been a transient, as no record of him appears in the *Vital Records of Lincoln* or surrounding towns.

4 Blake, "James Barrett's Returns of Men," p. 469. See also John Barter (q.v.). The phonetic similarity between John Porter, John Bortor, and John Barter (q.v.), coupled with the records connecting both John Bortor and John Barter with Capt. Abijah Child's Company, Col. John Greaton's Regiment, suggest a strong likelihood that John Porter (inst.) may be the same individual as John Barter (q.v.).

REED, Artemas
[also READ]

Artemas Reed was a private in Capt. William Smith's Company of Minute Men from Lincoln, Col. Abijah Peirce's Regiment.[1] Following the engagement at Concord, he served for five days in Cambridge, before enlisting for eight months in Capt. William Smith's Company, Col. John Nixon's 16th Regiment in the rapidly forming Massachusetts Army. Presumably, he participated with his unit in the Battle of Bunker Hill on June 17. On September 30, he was reported "on Command in the mason business."[2]

He remained in service, enlisting at the beginning of 1776, for a year in Capt. Jeremiah Gilman's 6th Company, Col. John Nixon's 4th Regiment. After the British evacuated Boston, he went Southward and participated in operations around New York.[3] After the Battle of White Plains, he is reported at North Castle on November 9, 1776. The regiment marched south in December to join Washington's forces, which had retreated across the Delaware River. At the Battle of Trenton, on Christmas night, his unit was unsuccessful in its attempt to re-cross the ice-choked Delaware River, and thus it failed to engage with the enemy. He was paid by the town for this term of service.[4]

Perhaps inspired by Washington's personal appeal, or simply because he enjoyed the life of a soldier, he immediately reenlisted for three years, and presumably participated in the Battle of Princeton. He joined Capt. Abijah Child's Company, Col. John Greaton's 2nd Regiment as a private, and he was at the taking of Burgoyne at Saratoga. After Captain Childs resigned in the spring of 1778, he served under the command of Lt. Thomas Prichard until his discharge on December 31, 1779. This service was credited to Lincoln. His residence is listed as Lincoln.[5]

He returned to Lincoln just long enough to move to Littleton, where on July 15, 1780 (agreeable to a resolve of June 5, 1780), he enlisted for another six months, this time to the credit of Littleton. He is described as age 34; five feet, five inches in height, with a ruddy complexion. He served as a private in Capt. James Tisdale's Company, Col. John Greaton's 3rd Regiment. He is recorded as having: marched to Springfield on July 15, 1780, served at Camp Orangetown during August and September, and been stationed at Camp Totoway,

---

1 Coburn, *Muster Rolls*.
2 *Massachusetts Soldiers and Sailors*, Vol. XIII, pp. 6, 53. Colonel Nixon's Regiment was also known as the 5th Regiment under the Continental numbering system adopted after General Washington assumed command of the Provincial forces. "The mason business" evidently indicates he was deployed with construction crews, probably working on fortifications. He was a bricklayer by trade.
3 Col. John Nixon's 5th Regiment was re-designated the 4th Regiment on January 1, 1776. In mid-August, Col. John Nixon was promoted, and regimental command passed to his brother, Lt. Col. Thomas Nixon.
4 *Massachusetts Soldiers and Sailors*, Vol. XIII, pp. 6, 53; Pension Record # S38326; "Treasurer's Accompts," July 20, 1779. The town's payment was "paid [to] Lt. Benjamin Munroe per order of Artemas Read for [said] Read's service in a campaign at the Southward in the year 1776." This transaction occurred during Reed's three years of service in the Continental Army.
5 *Massachusetts Soldiers and Sailors*, Vol. XIII, pp. 6, 53; Pension Record # S38326. Colonel Greaton's Regiment was at Morristown at the time of his reenlistment at Trenton. Accordingly, he must have joined Greaton's Regiment after operations around Trenton and Princeton. The record is imprecise. Participation in the battle at Princeton is conjecture, based on the presumption that he must have been moving north with Washington's army in early January 1777. It is unclear in whose command he served during this interim period.

New Jersey, in October. He was discharged December 6, 1780, having served 5 months, 2 days, including 220 miles of travel home.[1]

Once again, he apparently was unable to resist the allure or pay of army life, because he was back in service again by March 20, 1781, serving 21 months, 12 days (of a three-year enlistment) through December 31, 1782, as a private in Capt. Ebenezer Smith's Company, Lt. Col. Calvin Smith's 6th Regiment. He is described as age 35; five-feet, five-inches in height; light complexion, brown hair, blue eyes, and a farmer by occupation. The record indicates that he was on furlough in March 1782, that he deserted on May 19, 1782, that he returned on May 29, 1782, and that he was absent (probably on temporary assignment) during August and September 1782. He was discharged at West Point on January 2, 1784. This service was credited to Littleton.[2]

He was about age 28 during the April 19th Alarm, probably born in Lexington. He reportedly married Anna Johnson of Greenwich in 1768. He is recorded as living in Lincoln at least by 1773, when the baptism of two daughters (probably twins) was recorded. He resided in Littleton at least through the 1786 birth of another child. He reportedly also lived in Vermont. By 1818, however, he was living in Brooke County, Virginia (now West Virginia), where he died in 1826, age about 79. He is buried next to Anna in Wellsburg, West Virginia.[3]

RICE, Adonijah

Adonijah Rice appears to have been recruited from outside Lincoln to serve in the Continental Army to fulfill the 26 man quota for the town of Lincoln in 1777. He enlisted for a three-year term, and served in Capt. Abijah Childs's Company, Col. John Greaton's 2nd Regiment. He is reported as having deserted.[4]

---

1 *Massachusetts Soldiers and Sailors*, Vol. XIII, pp. 6, 53–54; Pension Record # S38326. His 1818 pension declaration says he served eight months in Capt. Nay Smith's Company, but the service records indicate a faulty recollection on this point. In addition to July 15, 1780, the service records also give an enlistment date of July 23, 1780, but this does not square with the 5 months, 2 days of service for which he was credited. July 23, 1780, appears to be the date he was processed out of Springfield and marched to his assigned unit.

Col. John Greaton's Regiment is variously referred to as the 2nd and the 3rd. Presumably, these were sequential designations, but the author has not found an authoritative source or a recognizable pattern to indicate when the designation changed.

2 *Massachusetts Soldiers and Sailors*, Vol. XIII, pp. 6, 53–54; Pension Record # S38326. He had a child born approximately February 1783, indicating that he probably returned home to Littleton during his desertion in May 1782 (see *Records of Littleton*; see also note 3).

3 MacLean, *A Rich Harvest*, p. 257; *Lexington Births, Marriages and Deaths*; Pension Record # S38326. Unfortunately, much of this information is pieced together from unsubstantiated sources. *Lexington Births, Marriages and Deaths* contains a baptism record dated March 1, 1747, with no information about his parents. His marriage date and his wife's identity is also unconfirmed, but it may possibly be found in Greenwich Vital Records (Greenwich, in Hampshire County, disappeared as a town when the Quabbin Reservoir was created). Four children are recorded in Lincoln, through 1777. A child is recorded in *Records of Littleton* in January 1781; another appears to have died in March 1783 at about six weeks of age, evidence that he must have made it back to Littleton during his desertion. No information is given about the mother of either Littleton child, but Anna is identified as the mother in one of the Lincoln birth records. Burial in Wellsburg is according to George Quintal (in discussion with the author).

4 Wheeler, "Lincoln," in Hurd, Vol. 2, p. 620; *Massachusetts Soldiers and Sailors*, Vol. XIII, pp. 142, 190. One of these *Massachusetts Soldiers and Sailors* records lists him as, "Adon— Rich," but the record is unmistakably Adonijah Rice (inst.). No dates are given for his service.

Another record similarly shows that he served in Captain Childs's Company, Colonel Greaton's Regiment from January 1, 1777, through September 5, 1777, when he is reported as having deserted. In this record, he was recruited in Suffolk County, out of the 1st Medway Company, Col. Benjamin Hawes's 4th Suffolk County Militia Regiment, and his service was credited to the town of Medway.[1]

There is another record of an Adonijah Rice who was serving in the Continental Army as a private in Capt. William Hawes's Company of Harness-makers in the Artillery Artificers at Springfield, commanded by David Mason, lieutenant colonel of artillery and director of ordinance, between August 11, 1779, and December 31, 1779, but it is uncertain if this is the same individual.[2]

The identity of this individual has not been determined.[3]

RICHARDSON, Abner

Abner Richardson enlisted as a Continental soldier for a term of three years. Agreeable to a resolve of December 2, 1780, he enlisted and served from February 20, 1781. He is described as age 16; five feet, six inches in stature; light complexion, dark hair, dark eyes, and a farmer by occupation.[4]

After enlisting in Lincoln, he joined the Army at West Point and served in Capt. Thomas Turner's Company, Col. Henry Jackson's 9th Massachusetts Regiment. He remained at West Point "during most of the first year," then was deployed "at Nelson's Point, at Newburgh, and at Verplanck's Point on the Hudson until the restoration of Peace." Then he was transferred

---

1 *Massachusetts Soldiers and Sailors*, Vol. XIII, p. 142. This is a curious record, and it may be that it confuses two different individuals named Adonijah Rice. This record clearly links to the service from Lincoln, but it is not exactly clear how the service could have been credited to both towns. Nor does it appear likely that we could be looking at different tours of duty for the same individual, as both are given as three-year terms, and the time period for both appears to be the years 1777 through 1779. Improbable as it may seem, it is certainly possible that there might have been two different individuals named Adonijah Rice in the same unit at the same time.

Another possibility is that he may have enlisted twice (i.e., in both towns at the same time). This was a fairly common scam, whereby the enlistee would try to claim enlistment bounties from both towns, while actually engaging in a single term of service. In such cases, one record will usually note a prior enlistment. No such notation exists on either record.

2 Wheeler, "Lincoln," in Hurd, Vol. 2, p. 620; *Massachusetts Soldiers and Sailors*, Vol. XIII, p. 142. This record fits within the enlistment period of his Continental service, but there is little else to connect it to Adonijah Rice (inst.). It also occurs during his reported desertion, which suggests: 1) a different individual; 2) a separate enlistment by him (and bounty claim) during his desertion; or, 3) that someone failed to record his (temporary?) reassignment to the harness-makers, causing him to be listed mistakenly as a deserter.

As unusual as this name appears to be, there are actually several other service records pertaining to several (apparently) different individuals named Adonijah Rice. However, except for the possibilities suggested herein, it would be difficult to connect any of the records with the service credited to Lincoln. It may be possible, with further research, to connect one or more of these records to different terms of service by Adonijah Rice (inst.), but the author has found insufficient evidence to do so here.

3 There is no Adonijah Rice found in the Vital Records of the towns bordering Lincoln. Other possibilities may be (a) the son of Charles and Rachael (Wheeler) Rice of Marlborough or Westborough; age 50 when he would have entered the service for Lincoln; married to Hannah Crosby since 1751, or (b) his son Adonijah, born in 1761, who would have thus entered the service a few months before his 16th birthday, or (c) the son of Adonijah and Persis (Gates) Rice of Worcester; probably age 34 when he would have entered the service for Lincoln. By age and geography, however, the later appears more likely to fit the service record of a different Adonijah Rice (see *Vital Records of Westborough*; *Worcester Births, Marriages and Deaths*). Further investigation is needed.

4 *Massachusetts Soldiers and Sailors*, Vol. XIII, p. 224.

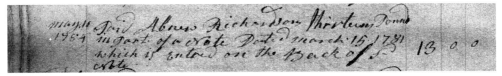

After Abner Richardson's father died in 1772, his family probably struggled financially, likely motivating Abner's enlistment into the Continental Army on February 20, 1781, at age 16. Following his three years of service, he received a payment from the town on a note dating from his period of enlistment. The note was likely part of the financial arrangement Abner's guardian had made with the town in connection with his service. (Courtesy of Lincoln Town Archives, Lincoln, MA)

to Capt. Adam Bailey's Company, Colonel Sprout's 2nd Massachusetts Regiment, and he was ordered to Philadelphia to quell some disturbances. He was discharged from West Point on December 23, 1783, having served 2 years, 10 months.[1]

His service was credited to the town of Lincoln. He was engaged by a class of the town that included Deacon Joshua Brooks, John Brooks, Joseph Mason, and others.[2]

He was the son of Abijah and Sarah (Stewart) Richardson; age 16 when he entered the service. He married Anna Moore in 1797 in Kingsbury, New York, with whom he had 11 children. He died at age 90 in Lake Luzerne (Warren County), New York, in 1855, and is buried in Luzerne Cemetery. He is believed to be Lincoln's last surviving veteran of the Revolutionary War.[3]

RICHARDSON, Barnabas

Barnabas Richardson of Lincoln served as a private in Capt. Jesse Wyman's Company, Col. Josiah Whitney's Regiment in 1777. This company was raised for two months of service at Rhode Island. On May 10, 1777, he arrived at his place of rendezvous, and he was discharged from Point Judith on July 10, 1777. His length of service was 2 months, 9 days (including 3 days of travel, 60 miles, to the rendezvous point; and 5 days of travel home).[4]

---

1 Pension Record # W5710 (also # BLWT18218-60-55). His pension declaration claims 2 years, 11 months of service.

2 *Massachusetts Soldiers and Sailors*, Vol. XIII, p. 224; "Treasurer's Accompts," September 30, 1781, April 23, 1782, January 27, 1783, February 8, 1783. Deacon Joshua Brooks appears as "Dr. Joshus Brooks." The author has made no particular effort to follow the money, but the town evidently reimbursed the members of a class for the moneys they paid to the individual who served. For a brief overview of the system of economic classes, see MacLean, *A Rich Harvest* (p. 296). See also "Treasurer's Accompts," May 10, 1784, for a partial payment from the town of a note dated March 15, 1781. The record does not explain the nature of the note, but the dates suggest that it may have been a form of payment for his service.

3 *Town of Weston, Births, Deaths, & Marriages*; Wheeler, "Lincoln," in Hurd, Vol. 2, p. 624; Pension Record # W5710 (also # BLWT18218-60-55); "Find A Grave." Wheeler incorrectly says he was age 94 when he died, as does his headstone. The pension record lists his birth date as November 19 (but the year is illegible); however, he was baptized in Weston on December 23, 1764, when he was listed as being "a week old" (*Town of Weston, Births, Deaths, & Marriages*, p. 481). His mother died when he was about 15 months old; his father remarried four months later. The family had evidently moved to Lincoln by 1769, as *Vital Records of Lincoln* list a sister baptized in Lincoln that year. His father died in 1772, before Abner's 8th birthday.

He was living at Argyle, New York, when he filed a pension application on April 8, 1818, reportedly in his 55th year (the math does not quite work out), and at Saratoga, New York, on June 25, 1822, at age 59 (math still faulty), when the pension was reviewed.

4 *Massachusetts Soldiers and Sailors*, Vol. XIII, p. 294.

The identity of this individual has not been determined, but it appears likely that he was from Woburn and had only a temporary connection with Lincoln.[1]

RICHARDSON, Ezra

Ezra Richardson was paid by the town for service at Ticonderoga in 1776 and for service in the Continental Army. No details of this service have been found.[2]

The identity of this individual is tentative. The obvious candidate is Ezra Richardson of Lincoln, who was a cordwainer, age 55 when he would have served at Ticonderoga. He was the son of John and Abigail (Swan) Richardson of Woburn, who had come to Lincoln and married Love Parks in 1749. He had been a member of Lincoln's original militia company in 1757. After making his home on the Bay Road for a while, by the time of the Revolution he was living on today's Tower Road. He died in Lincoln in 1787 at age 65.[3]

However, at age 55-plus, his serving two campaigns in the army would be unusual. No record of any sons has been found, nor is there any suggestion of his having had any slaves. So, his age notwithstanding, it is not clear who, other than him, would have provided the service for which he was paid.

ROBINSON, Keen
[also ROBENSON, also Cain, Cane, Kane]

Keen Robinson served as a private in Capt. John Walton's Company, Col. Eleazer Brooks's Middlesex County Regiment of Massachusetts Militia from September 27, 1776, to November 16, 1776. He is presumed to have participated with his unit at the Battle of

---

1 The author has found only two individuals named Barnabas Richardson in Massachusetts at this time. Both were born, married, and died in Woburn:

The first is the son of Edward and Jerusha Richardson of Woburn, who would have been age 43 during this service. He had been married to Rebecca Tidd (also of Woburn) since 1758. He died in Woburn in 1816, at age 82. Chiles, "The Henry & Sarah Ballinger Chiles Family" reports that he served at Dorchester Heights in 1776 as a private in Caleb Brooks's Company, Col. Nicholas Dike's Regiment (which record is not found in *Massachusetts Soldiers and Sailors*). He may also be the Barny Richardson who marched on the Alarm of April 19th to Concord and Cambridge, in Capt. Jonathan Fox's Company from Woburn (Coburn, *Muster Rolls*, p. 32; also listed as Barnabas Richrdson in *Massachusetts Soldiers and Sailors*, Vol. XIII, p. 295).

Although highly speculative, it would be possible to conjure a connection to Lincoln through David Fisk (q.v.), who was about the same age, originally from Woburn, and had been in Lincoln since at least 1765. Perhaps through a friendship with Fisk, Barnabas Richardson had been lured to Lincoln for a period of time during the war.

Perhaps a more likely possibility is Barnabas and Rebecca's son, Barnabas Jr. He would have been age 18 during this service. He married Mary Richardson of Woburn in 1782 and died in Woburn in 1823 at age 64. Although equally speculative, it would be easy to imagine the younger Barnabas in Lincoln, perhaps employed by Fisk for a period of time, or perhaps employed elsewhere in town through the hypothetical friendship between Fisk and the elder Barnabas (see Johnson, *Woburn Records of Births, Deaths, and Marriages*).

2 "Treasurer's Accompts," June 15, 1779.

3 Johnson, *Woburn Records of Births, Deaths, and Marriages*; *Vital Records of Lincoln*; *Concord, Massachusetts: Births, Marriages, and Deaths*; Glass and Little Map of Lincoln; MacLean, *A Rich Harvest*, p. 168; Martin, "The Sons of Lincoln," p. 25. His death in 1787 is established by the Richardson, Ezra, Estate Inventory.

Vital Records of Lincoln contains the 1755 baptism record for his daughter Abigail, but no birth or baptism records for any other children. Unsubstantiated online genealogical postings credit him with another daughter named Love, born variously in 1752 or in 1755. There is no hint of any sons.

White Plains on October 28, 1776. After the battle, he is recorded on a roll taken at North Castle. He served 2 months, 1 day, including 11 days for 223 miles of travel home.[1]

On April 1, 1778, he enlisted for three months as a private in Capt. Daniel Harrington's Company, Col. Jonathan Reed's Regiment of Guards in Cambridge. He served for 3 months, 2 days, from April 2, 1778, to July 3, 1778, guarding the "Convention Army" surrendered by General Burgoyne at Saratoga.[2]

Agreeable to a resolve of April 20, 1778, he was drafted from Captain Weston's Company, Col. Eleazer Brooks's Regiment, to support the Continental Army for the term of nine months from his arrival at Fishkill. He is described as age 23; five feet, four inches in stature, and a resident of Weston. This service was credited to the town of Weston. He arrived in Springfield on June 11, 1778, and in Fishkill on June 21, 1778. He served in Capt. Thomas Barns's Company, Col. Thomas Nixon's Regiment. He is recorded on July 20, 1778, as being transferred from the command of Jonathan Warner, commissioner, to the command of Col. R. Putnam; this was probably a logistical matter. He was discharged at Fishkill in March 1779.[3]

He was the son of Dr. Jeremiah and Eunice (Amsden) Robinson of Marlborough, age 22 at White Plains and North Castle. He was a cordwainer by trade, having been indentured to his half-brother for training as such some years before. He settled in Lincoln, and in 1780 or 1781 he married Achsah (also listed as Acsah, or Atchsah) Leathe of Watertown. Sometime after 1804 he appears to have left Lincoln, and eventually he moved his family to Lisle, New York, where he died in 1843 at age 89.[4]

SAVAGE, Jube

Jube Savage served as a private in Capt. John Hartwell's Company of Militia, Col. Eleazer Brooks's 3rd Middlesex County Regiment, which marched from Lincoln to fortify Dorchester Heights on March 4, 1776. The unit was discharged five days later, on March 9, after the threat of a British assault on the fortifications had subsided, and General Howe had begun preparations to evacuate Boston.

---

1 Wheeler, "Lincoln," in Hurd, Vol. 2, p. 624; *Massachusetts Soldiers and Sailors*, Vol. XIII, p. 435. He does not mention this service in his pension declaration. Wheeler gives the company commander's name as Capt. John Watson.

2 *Massachusetts Soldiers and Sailors*, Vol. XIII, p. 435. He does not mention this service in his pension declaration.

3 *Massachusetts Soldiers and Sailors*, Vol. XIII, p. 458; Pension Record # W22119. See also Blake, "James Barrett's Returns of Men," p. 16. Notwithstanding that he is recorded as being detached from the militia company, it appears that he was recruited for service at Fishkill while he was on guard duty in Cambridge. The overlapping dates are curious, but it is probable that they were ignored, and credited to him as an enlistment bonus.

4 *Vital Records of Marlborough*; *Concord, Massachusetts: Births, Marriages, and Deaths*; *Vital Records of Lincoln*; Pension Record # W22119; Cutter, *Historic Homes of Middlesex County*, Vol. IV, p. 1536; *Robinsons and Their Kin Folk*, p. 117. He was the brother of Bradbury Robinson, who was a Concord minute man and co-deponent of James Adams (q.v.). In her pension declaration in 1844, Achsah (age 80) is less than precise about their marriage date, giving it as "April 1780 or 1781." The marriage record has not been found. Achsah's maiden name and origin are unconfirmed but are as reported in "Gunn Family Tree." Interestingly, seven surviving children are recorded in *Concord, Massachusetts: Births, Marriages, and Deaths* between 1783 and 1804, while two others who died in infancy in 1795 and 1797 appear in *Vital Records of Lincoln*. Cutter says that he settled near the boundary line between Weston and Concord; of course, the line no longer existed after 1754. The location is not identified on the Glass and Little Map of Lincoln.

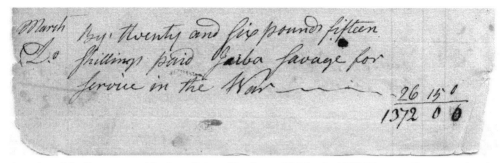

As a slave, Jube Savage served in the militia at Dorchester Heights in 1776. He was a free man when he served again at Dorchester in 1776–1777, and in the Battle of Rhode Island in 1778. The service covered by this March 3, 1780, payment from the town of Lincoln is not identified. (Courtesy of Lincoln Town Archives, Lincoln, MA)

He was in service again at Roxbury and Dorchester, in Capt. John Minot's Company, Colonel Dike's Regiment, possibly in November 1776 or earlier. He appears on a December 21, 1776, muster roll of Captain Minot's Company, listed as being age 40 and from Lincoln. On December 23, 1776, he evidently reenlisted in the same unit, and he served through March 1, 1777.[1]

He served on an expedition to Rhode Island from July through September 1778, as part of Capt. Francis Brown's Company, Col. William McIntosh's Regiment (Brig. Gen. Solomon Lovell's Brigade of Massachusetts Militia) and participated in the Battle of Rhode Island, on August 29, 1778.[2]

He was paid by the town "for service in the war," without further details.[3]

He was the "Negro servant of Mr. Saml Ph[illips] Savage of Weston" when he married Judith, the "Negro servant of Capt. Daniel Adams" of Lincoln in 1771. He became a free man on April 27, 1776, when Samuel Phillips Savage records in his diary, "Jubee by my consent, left me." As a free man, Jube acquired some land and owned a home in Lincoln. He boarded Jack Farrar (q.v.) in 1781 for four weeks. Sometime later, he left Lincoln and went to Temple, New Hampshire, where the 1790 census records him living with two other individuals in his household. What became of him after that is unknown.[4]

---

1 Waters, *History of Chelmsford*, pp. 266, 268; *Massachusetts Soldiers and Sailors*, Vol. XIII, p. 840. A pay abstract for travel to and from Dorchester Heights, which was allowed in Council on November 30, 1776, identifies him as in Capt. John Minot's Company, Colonel Dike's Regiment. This suggests that he must have been in service with this unit at least by November 30, 1776, and perhaps as early as August 21, 1776, when Captain Minot's Company was engaged.

The travel allowance could not have been for his March Dorchester Heights service, as he was credited with 36 miles at that time (see Hartwell, "A List of a Company of Militia"). The standard allowance for travel time was figured as 20 miles per day, which makes this pay abstract (for 40 miles travel and one day travel time) appear somewhat unusual. However, at the same time, Captain Minot was awarded 62 miles (from Chelmsford) and two days of travel time, suggesting that there must have been a different set of rules in place for this deployment.

2 Ibid.

3 "Treasurer's Accompts," March 3, 1780.

4 *Vital Records of Lincoln*; 1790 Census; Dickson and Lucas. *One Town*, p. 31; notes communicated privately by Jack MacLean, which notes reference Jack Hatch administrative papers, March 11, 1784, and March 12, 1788, in Middlesex Probate records, first series, 10,743. Little is known about Jube's origin. Fitts, *Inventing New England's Slave Paradise* (p. 176) and Kolchin, *American Slavery* (p. 45) identify the name "Juba" as a Gold

SHARON, Peter

Peter Sharon is reported to have served at Rhode Island in 1780.[1]

He is also reported to have enlisted December 31, 1779, in the Continental Army for six months of service in the 13th Massachusetts Regiment at West Point.[2]

He did enlist in the Continental Army for six months, agreeable to a resolve of June 5, 1780. He marched to camp on July 11, 1780, under the command of Capt. James Cooper (arriving at Springfield on July 15), and later passed muster at Camp Totoway, New Jersey, on October 25, 1780, by Brigadier General Paterson. He was described as age 17; five feet, nine inches in stature, and a Negro. He was discharged January 15, 1781, credited with 6 months, 14 days of service, including 200 miles travel home. This service was credited to Lincoln's quota for supplying soldiers for the war.[3]

He enlisted again on June 27, 1781, for three years in the Continental Army (agreeable to a resolve of December 2, 1780). Again, this service was credited to the town of Lincoln. He is described as age 18; stature five feet, nine inches; complexion black, hair black, eyes black; occupation farmer (also laborer). Reportedly, he went south with Washington's army in September 1781 and participated in the Siege of Yorktown, but this is uncertain.[4]

The identity of Peter Sharon is unknown. He may possibly have been the son of Prince and Rose, Negro servants of John Headley, and if so, he may possibly have been the brother of Silas Sharon (q.v.). The evidence for this is circumstantial.[5]

Coast day name for Monday. If Piersen's theory is correct (see Piersen, *Black Yankees*, pp. 7, 129) that the use of African names in northern slave populations was inversely related to their lengths of time in America and to their acculturation as African-Americans (rather than as transplanted Africans), then we may suppose that Jube or his parents may have been born in Africa. Dickson and Lucas suggest that Samuel Phillips Savage probably brought Jube with him when he moved from Boston to Weston in 1765.

1 Wheeler, "Lincoln," in Hurd, Vol. 2, p. 624. No corroborating evidence of this service has been found.

2 Malcolm, *Peter's War*, p. 193. No corroborating evidence of this service has been found (see note 3).

3 *Massachusetts Soldiers and Sailors*, Vol. XIV pp. 17, 150. This was certainly not the Rhode Island service with which Wheeler credits him. Camp Totoway was located in the present town of Totowa, New Jersey, and the mileage home suggests that he was discharged from somewhere in New Jersey or New York.

Malcolm, *Peter's War* (p. 205) says he had already been at West Point for six months (see note 2), and says further that he reenlisted in the 13th Massachusetts on July 15, 1780, at West Point. This is inconsistent with the records in *Massachusetts Soldiers and Sailors*, which show him passing through Springfield at this time, being processed into the service, and thus casts doubt on her claim to his first six months at West Point (i.e., from December 31, 1779 to July 15, 1780). *Massachusetts Soldiers and Sailors* also makes no mention of West Point or of the 13th Massachusetts in the July 1780 to January 1781 service, but it does place him at Camp Totoway, which Malcolm does not reflect. The source of Malcolm's information is not clear, as her work contains no citations.

4 *Massachusetts Soldiers and Sailors*, Vol. XIV pp. 17, 150; "Treasurer's Accompts," September 30, 1781, February 1, 1782, May 29, 1782, October 31, 1782, February 8, 1783. His going south to Yorktown is per Malcolm, *Peter's War* (pp. 217–221) but corroborating evidence of this has not been found.

Under the system of economic classification used for hiring men for service during the later years of the war, the practice seems to have been for the members of the class to pay the soldier directly, then seek reimbursement from the town. The "Treasurer's Accompts" show payments made to various individuals, evidently members of the class which sponsored his service. The author has made no effort to follow the money. For a brief overview of the system of economic classes, see MacLean, *A Rich Harvest* (p. 296). In addition to the transaction dates above, Sharon was paid a bounty for this service on June 25, 1781, by John Adams (q.v.) and other members of a class of the town of Lincoln. (See also *Massachusetts Soldiers and Sailors*, Vol. XIV p. 20.)

5 The case for this is as follows: Four sons of Prince and Rose are recorded in Lincoln: Silas, (bp. 1752), Prince (bp. 1755), Festus (bp. 1758, probably died), and Festus (bp. 1760). In his will, dated 1773, John Headley provided for the freedom of Prince and Rose upon his death. He also provided for their continued support

Another hypothesis that has been advanced is that he may be the same individual as Peter Nelson (q.v.), who had served previously at Saratoga in 1777 and in the highlands of the Hudson Valley in 1778 and 1779. This is entirely speculative.[1]

He is reported to have died in Lincoln in the winter of 1792–1793.[2]

SHARON, Silas

Silas Sharon of Leominster enlisted in the Continental Army for a three-year term of service beginning April 1, 1777. He served as a private in Capt. William Warner's 6th Company, Col. Thomas Marshall's 10th Regiment, and participated in the Saratoga campaign. He is also listed as a servant.

---

from his estate. He died in January 1779, and that same year, a Prince Sharon appeared on the poll list of the town (see MacLean, *A Rich Harvest*, pp. 219, 306; Malcolm, *Peter's War*, p. 194). Circumstantially, Prince Sharon appears to be the recently freed slave of John Headley. At approximately this time, three other individuals named Sharon appeared in the records, as well. All have at least a circumstantial connection with Lincoln: Silas Sharon (q.v.) from Leominster enlisted in the Continental service in 1777; Peter Sharon (inst.) from Lincoln enlisted in the Continental service in 1780; and Dinah Sharron from Lincoln married a man from Concord in 1781 (see *Vital Records of Lincoln*). From his service records, we can reasonably estimate Peter's birth year as 1762 or 1763. Although it is much harder to estimate age from a marriage record, Dinah's birth year may reasonably be "guess-timated" between 1761 and 1764. While neither birth nor baptism records exist to provide evidence of the link, a reasonable hypothesis is that both Peter and Dinah were children of Prince and Rose, all taking Sharon as the family name at about this time. This would be consistent with existing scholarship about slave families and naming practices (scholarship on the subject is sparse, but the reader is directed to: Greene, *The Negro in Colonial New England*, pp. 201, 280; Piersen, *Black Yankees*, pp. 7, 35, 92, 129; Kolchin, *American Slavery*, pp. 45–46, 57, 119–120; and Gutman, *The Black Family in Slavery & Freedom*, pp. 194, 230–237, 245, 250–251). Malcolm, *Peter's War* (p. 194) speculates on a possible source of the name Sharon, but the actual source (assuming the hypothesis to be true) is unknown.

The hypothesis is bolstered by a supposition that Silas Sharon of Leominster may also be the son of Prince and Rose. John Headley's daughter, Tabitha, had married Nathaniel Colburn, Jr., of Leominster, and they had settled there. It is logically supposed that John Headley may have given Silas to his daughter's family, and that Silas may have been the slave or former slave of Nathaniel and Tabitha Colburn at the time of his 1777 enlistment. Tabitha's sons, Nathaniel (q.v.) and Joseph (q.v.) returned from Leominster and took up residence in Lincoln before their war service, evidently followed by Tabitha and her husband in 1779 (see *Historical Manual of the Lincoln Church*, p. 88). [Jack MacLean (in private notes shared with the author) cites a 1771 deed transferring property from John Headley to Nathaniel and Tabitha as the time of their return to Lincoln, but the author sees no reason to match the date of their return with the property transfer. If the property transfer is interpreted as part of John Headley's estate planning, then it does not conflict with the evidence of their 1779 return to Lincoln.] See Nathaniel Colburn (q.v.), note 3, p. 265. The pieces fit together to build a plausible hypothesis. The evidence, however, remains circumstantial.

1 Malcolm, *Peter's War*, p. 193. See also Wiggin, "A Tale of Two or Three Peters." Without citing sources or evidence, Malcolm lays out the premise that Peter Nelson (q.v.) enlisted for further service in 1780 as Peter Sharon on the promise of manumission following the completion of his term of service. Name changes were a widespread practice among slaves upon manumission, and the records establish that Peter Nelson and Peter Sharon were approximately the same age (within a year's difference). The possibility that Peter Nelson and Peter Sharon could be the same individual cannot be denied. However, the author has found no evidence with which to connect them. The records of these two individuals are separate, discrete, and unconnected (except for a common first name and an approximate age). Drawing a link between these two individuals is entirely speculative; a leap of faith that the author finds intriguing but unconvincing.

See also Wiggin, "A Tale of Two or Three Peters" for a further discussion of this issue and of the identities of Peter Brooks (q.v.), Peter Bowes (q.v.), and Peter Nelson (q.v.).

2 Wheeler, "Lincoln," in Hurd, Vol. 2, p. 624. Malcolm, *Peter's War* (p. 234) reports this as the winter of 1791–1792.

He spent the winter of 1777–1778 at Valley Forge, and he was present at the Battle of Monmouth on June 28, 1778. He died in service on July 14, 1778.[1]

His identity and his connection with Lincoln are tentative. It is supposed that he was the son of John Headley's slaves, Prince and Rose, baptized in Lincoln, possibly the brother of Peter Sharon (q.v.), and probably age 24 when he entered the Continental service (age 25 when he died). The evidence for this, however, is circumstantial.[2]

SHERMAN, Timothy
[also SHARMAN, SHARMON, SHEARMAN]

Timothy Sherman was at Concord on April 19, 1775, either as a private in Capt. Nathaniel Cudworth's Company of Minute Men from Sudbury, Col. Abijah Peirce's Regiment, or as a member of Capt. Isaac Locker's Sudbury Militia Company, Col. James Barrett's Regiment. He served 3 days.[3]

---

1 *Massachusetts Soldiers and Sailors*, Vol. XIV p. 17; Nourse, *Military Annals of Lancaster*, p. 193; Blake, "James Barrett's Returns of Men," p. 473. It is unknown whether his death was from wounds suffered at Monmouth, or from some other cause.

2 *Vital Records of Lincoln* identifies a Silas, s. Prince, "Negro," bp. Dec. 3, 1752. His mother, Rose, is identified in similar baptism records for his siblings, and together, Prince and Rose are identified as "Negro Servants of M[r] John Headley." The tentative connection between this Silas and Silas Sharon from Leominster (inst.) is as follows:

In his will, in 1773, John Headley provided for the freedom of Prince and Rose upon his death. His will also provided for their continued support from his estate. He died in January 1779, and that same year a Prince Sharon appeared on the poll list of the town (see MacLean, *A Rich Harvest*, pp. 219, 306; Malcolm, *Peter's War*, p. 194). Circumstantially, Prince Sharon appears to be the recently freed slave of John Headley.

At approximately this time, three other individuals named Sharon also appeared in the records. Silas Sharon (inst.) from Leominster enlisted in the Continental service in 1777; Peter Sharon (q.v.) from Lincoln enlisted in the Continental service in 1780; and Dinah Sharron from Lincoln married a man from Concord in 1781. Except for Dinah's marriage, which appears in *Vital Records of Lincoln*, there are no Sharons to be found in the Vital Records of Lincoln, Leominster, or any of the towns around Lincoln. That these Sharons all appear at approximately the same time suggests a possibility that they may all somehow be related.

In addition to the name, a logical connection between Silas, son of Prince and Rose, and Silas Sharon of Leominster can be drawn through the Headley family. John Headley's daughter, Tabitha, married Nathaniel Colburn, Jr., of Leominster, and settled in Leominster. Their sons, Nathaniel (q.v.) and Joseph (q.v.) returned from Leominster and took up residence in Lincoln before their war service. Tabitha and her husband appear to have remained in Leominster until 1779, when they moved to Lincoln, following John Headley's death. See Nathaniel Colburn (q.v.), note 3, p. 265. It is supposed that Silas Sharon of Leominster may be the son of Prince and Rose; that John Headley had passed him on to his daughter's family, and that he was the slave or former slave of Nathaniel and Tabitha Colburn at the time of his 1777 enlistment.

From his service records, we can reasonably estimate Peter's birth year as 1762 or 1763. Although it is much harder to estimate age from a marriage record, Dinah's birth year may reasonably be "guess-timated" between 1761 and 1764. While neither birth nor baptism records exist to provide evidence of the link, a reasonable hypothesis is that both Peter and Dinah may also be children of Prince and Rose, and that they all took Sharon as the family name at about this time (1777–1779). Scholarship on the subject of slave families and naming practices is sparse, but this would be consistent with the scholarship that does exist. (The reader is directed to: Greene, *The Negro in Colonial New England*, pp. 201, 280; Piersen, *Black Yankees*, pp. 7, 35, 92, 129; Kolchin, *American Slavery*, pp. 45–46, 57, 119–120; and Gutman, *The Black Family in Slavery & Freedom*, pp. 194, 230–237, 245, 250–251.) Malcolm, *Peter's War* (p. 194) speculates on a possible source of the name Sharon, but the actual source is unknown.

The pieces fit together to build a plausible hypothesis, notwithstanding the circumstantial nature of the evidence.

3 *Massachusetts Soldiers and Sailors*, Vol. XIV, pp. 16, 146. Coburn, *Muster Rolls*, shows a Timothy Sherman in Captain Cudworth's Company *and* a Timothy Sharmon in Captain Locker's Company. It is not clear whether these are two different individuals, or the same individual listed twice. Neither *Vital Records of Sudbury* nor those of surrounding towns give any hint of a second Timothy Sherman (or Sharmon), suggesting that these

Subsequently, he appears to have served again, as evidenced by a 1777 payment by the town of Sudbury. The record does not specify the service, but it may likely have been six months at Castle William in Boston Harbor, probably beginning in April 1776. No such service record has been found, so he may have hired a substitute instead of actually serving himself.[1]

He was born in Lincoln; son of Jonathan and Elizabeth (Bruce) Sherman; age 26 when he marched to Concord. He had married Mary Maynard in Sudbury in 1771. He died in 1819 in Wayland (then East Sudbury) at age 71, and is buried in Wayland's North Cemetery.[2]

SMITH, Cato

Cato Smith from Lincoln served as a private in Capt. William Smith's Company, Col. John Nixon's 16th Massachusetts Regiment in Cambridge from April 24, 1775, through at least September 30, 1775. It is probable that he was involved in the Battle of Bunker Hill. He signed a receipt for advance pay on June 26, 1775. It is likely that he served until the end of December 1775.

He reenlisted in Colonel Nixon's 4th Regiment sometime during 1776. In April 1776, following the British evacuation of Boston, the regiment marched south to New York. In August, Col. John Nixon became brigadier general, and Lt. Col. Thomas Nixon became commander of the regiment. It is not clear when Cato Smith reenlisted, but pay receipts establish that he served in Capt. Joseph Butler's Company, Lt. Col. Thomas Nixon's Regiment during the New York campaign, from September through November 1776. It is probable that he saw action in the battles at Long Island, Turtle Bay, Harlem Heights, and White Plains. A regimental return places him at North Castle, New York, on November 9, 1776.

---

listings refer to the same individual. As the Muster Rolls were usually made up months later (sometimes many months) from memory, and as minute companies were drawn from the ranks of militia companies, it is quite probable that Sherman may have been a member of both companies; that he marched on the Alarm of April 19th as a member of Cudworth's Minute Company, and that later Locker mistakenly included him as one of the men under his command.

1 Hudson, *History of Sudbury*, pp.402-403, 406. The payment of £12 was approved by Sudbury Town Meeting on October 26, 1778, along with other amounts reflecting service by the other members of the town's four militia companies. The composition of the £12 allocated for Timothy Sherman is not itemized, but from the amounts in the approved schedule it can be surmised that he was paid either as a minute man (£3) and one of the "Six month men to the Castle" (£9) or as one of the "Two months men to Providence" (£12). The Castle appears to be Castle William. Service at Providence could fit a record of a Timothy Sharmon who served as a corporal in Capt. Joseph Sibley's Company, Col. Danforth Keyes's Regiment from August 12, 1777, through December 31, 1777, during which he was stationed at North Kingston on December 8, 1777 (see *Massachusetts Soldiers and Sailors*, Vol. XIV, pp. 16, 146). However, this unit appears to have been raised in Worcester County, and it served for 4½ months. As two other Timothy Shermans are identifiable in that area (Worcester and Hamden Counties), this service (along with Continental service in 1779 in the Hudson Highlands by the same individual) is probably a different Timothy Sherman. See *Vital Records of Sturbridge*; *Vital Records of Brimfield*; Census Records for 1790.

2 *Vital Records of Lincoln*; *Vital Records of Sudbury*; *Vital Records of Wayland*. Also, private communication from Jack MacLean, September 13, 2007. MacLean notes that he was born in the 2nd Precinct of Concord (i.e., Lincoln), at or near the current 62 Oxbow Road, on the Lincoln/Wayland town line. The current house on the site (reportedly built after his birth) actually straddles the Lincoln/Wayland town line. He later settled on what is now Sherman's Bridge Road in Wayland.

Thereafter, the regiment went south following Washington's main army, and participated in the Delaware River crossing on Christmas night, before the Battle of Trenton. It was unsuccessful at making it across the ice-choked river and had to turn back. As most Continental enlistments expired December 31, 1776, it is presumed Cato must have reenlisted, and that he probably participated in the Battle of Princeton on January 3, 1777, in Colonel Nixon's Regiment. He reportedly died in service on January 23, 1777.[1]

His identity is unknown. He is reported to be an African-American, probably a slave.[2]

SMITH, Jesse

Jesse Smith served as a private in Capt. William Smith's Company of Minute Men from Lincoln, Col. Abijah Peirce's Regiment. Including the engagement at Concord and along the Battle Road, he served for five days at Cambridge before enlisting, on April 24, 1775, in the rapidly forming Massachusetts Provincial Army in Cambridge. He was reimbursed by the town for his knapsack as a minute man.[3]

In Cambridge, he served in Capt. William Smith's Company, Col. John Nixon's 16th Regiment, and he was a participant in the Battle of Bunker Hill on June 17, 1775. He remained in service through the expiration of his eight-month term at the end of December 1775.[4]

---

1 *Massachusetts Soldiers and Sailors*, Vol. XIV, p. 358; Quintal, *Patriots of Color*, pp. 41, 202. Colonel Nixon's 16th Massachusetts Regiment became known as the 5th Regiment in August 1775, under Washington's Continental command structure. On January 1, 1776, Colonel Nixon's 5th Regiment was reconstituted as the 4th Continental Regiment.

2 Quintal, *Patriots of Color*, p. 202. The author hypothesizes that he may have been a slave belonging to William Smith (q.v.). No hard evidence has been found to confirm that Cato was a slave, but the preponderance of African Americans in Lincoln at the time appear to have been slaves. And if he were, then his last name certainly suggests ownership by an individual named Smith. According to Ryan, "The Incomplete Life" (p. 2), William Smith's father, the Rev. William Smith of Weymouth, purchased a Negro boy named Cato in 1761 for £200. Malcolm, *The Scene of Battle* (p. 55), states that Lincoln tax records for 1774 and 1777 show William Smith to be a slave owner in Lincoln. While the author has found no evidence that Cato was passed through the family and came to Lincoln with William Jr., this would certainly be a logical possibility. What makes this possibility particularly intriguing is that William Smith (q.v.) was paid for service at the southward, which service he apparently did not serve himself. If this possible identity is accurate, then Cato's New York service would explain the town's payment to William. Unfortunately, this theory does not explain the pay receipts for September, October, and November that Cato signed (evidently while he was in New York). It is also unclear whether William Smith was paid for a second (i.e., Cato's) Cambridge service. The record shows £28 paid to "Capt. William Smith for his service at Cambridge in the year 1775 and for service at the southward in the year 1776" (see "Treasurer's Accompts," November 11, 1779). Pay for New York service in 1776 seems to have varied from £6 to £12, probably depending on the duration. Cambridge service in 1775 paid £8 for an enlisted man (captain's pay is unknown). Without more details, this must remain an intriguing theory.

Another possibility is that he may be "Cate," listed in *Vital Records of Lincoln* as one of two "Negro Servant Children of Mr. Ephraim Flint," baptized on June 22, 1755. We do not know if "Cate" was male or female. If male, it is conceivable that "Cate" may have become Cato Smith (inst.) when Ephraim Flint's widow married Braddyll Smith of Weston in 1766. While this would explain "Cate" or Cato's acquiring the Smith name, the problem with this theory is that no slaves were enumerated in the 1765 probate inventory of Ephraim Flint's estate (Middlesex Probate, First Series, #7990).

3 Coburn, *Muster Rolls*; *Massachusetts Soldiers and Sailors*, Vol. XIV, pp. 435–437; "Treasurer's Accompts," November 21, 1776. This was paid to Joseph Wheat (q.v.).

4 *Massachusetts Soldiers and Sailors*, Vol. XIV, pp. 436–437; Pension Record # S19469. See also Frothingham, *History of the Siege of Boston*, footnote, p. 132. Colonel Nixon's 16th Massachusetts Regiment became known as the 5th Regiment in August 1775, under Washington's Continental command structure.

He reenlisted for the calendar year 1776, serving first in Capt. Adam Wheeler's 2nd Company, Col. John Nixon's 4th Regiment. In the spring, he was drafted into Capt. Caleb Gibbs's Company of Guards to serve in the Commander-in-Chief's Guard.[1]

He enlisted again in the Continental Army for three years, starting January 1, 1777, and continued his service in General Washington's Life Guards. He served as a private in Capt. George Lewis's Company of Horse, Colonel Baylor's 3rd Regiment of Light Dragoons. After Colonel Baylor was captured in a surprise British raid at Tappan, New York, in September 1778, regimental command devolved to Lt. Col. William Washington. The record lists Jesse Smith's residence as Lincoln (also Newburyport). He was paid by the town of Lincoln for this service, which was credited to the town of Lincoln. He served through December 13, 1779.[2]

Possibly, he may have been back in service on July 23, 1780, in Capt. Samuel Holden's Company, Col. Ebenezer Thayer's Regiment, for 3 months, 10 days, until October 30, 1780. This regiment was raised in Suffolk County to reinforce the Continental Army for three months. However, it is uncertain if this is the same Jesse Smith.[3]

He was a few days past his 19th birthday when he answered the alarm as a minute man on April 19, 1775. He was the son of Ephraim and Abigail (Munroe) Smith of Concord. While his father's death is not recorded, his mother appears to have married widower John Wheat of Lincoln in 1764. John Wheat was the father of Joseph Wheat (q.v.). Jesse Smith's sister, Mary, may subsequently have married Joseph Wheat, which would make Jesse Smith both a step-brother and a brother-in-law of Joseph Wheat.[4]

---

1 Pension Record # S19469. On January 1, 1776, Colonel Nixon's 5th Regiment was reconstituted as the 4th Continental Regiment. Washington created his Guard Company on March 11, 1776, by ordering the selection of four men from each Continental regiment present at the Siege of Boston. His order called "for good Men, such as they can recommend for their sobriety, honesty, and good behaviour… from five feet, eight Inches high, to five feet, ten Inches; handsomely and well made… neat, and spruce… They should be drill'd men" (General Orders [March 11, 1776], in Washington, *Writings* [Fitzpatrick, ed.], IV, pp. 387–388). Initially the Guard consisted of 50 men.

2 Wheeler, "Lincoln," in Hurd, Vol. 2, p. 624; *Massachusetts Soldiers and Sailors*, Vol. XIV, pp. 436–437; "Treasurer's Accompts," February 12, 1780; Pension Record # S19469. The reported residency at Newburyport remains unexplained.

  Washington reorganized the Commander-in-Chief's Guard (popularly called his Excellency's "Life Guard") in the spring of 1777, selecting only Virginia men, and adding a troop of cavalry. Caleb Gibbs remained Captain Commandant of the Life Guard, but the precise organizational details are difficult to follow. Lt. George Lewis (who had been second-in-command and was a nephew of General Washington) appears to have been detached at the end of 1776 for the purpose of raising a troop of cavalry. Jesse Smith (inst.) appears to be one of 20 in the Life Guard with expiring terms of service, who enlisted in Lewis's cavalry troop. The troop was formally assigned to Colonel Baylor's 3rd Regiment of Dragoons (part of the Virginia Line), but it was detached and serving in conjunction with the Life Guard from May 1, 1777, through September 1778. Col. William Washington, who took over command of Baylor's Regiment of Dragoons following the brutal loss at Tappan, was a cousin of the commander-in-chief. During Jesse Smith's service with the Life Guard, they are said to have participated in the Battles of White Plains, Trenton, Princeton, Brandywine, and Monmouth. They also spent the winter of 1777–1778 at Valley Forge (see Ward, *George Washington's Enforcers*, pp. 59–63; Moran, "History of the Commander-in-Chief Guards").

3 *Massachusetts Soldiers and Sailors*, Vol. XIV, pp. 436–437. No mention of this service appears in his pension declaration. An unconfirmed biographical sketch in "Find A Grave" says that after he left the army, he served on a privateer out of Salem, was captured, and spent the rest of the war at Mill Prison in Plymouth, England. However, there is no mention of this service in his pension record, either.

4 *Concord, Massachusetts: Births, Marriages, and Deaths*; *Vital Records of Lincoln*; Quintal, Unpublished research. It is not absolutely certain that Mary Smith (the sister of Jesse) and Mary Smith (the wife of Joseph Wheat)

After the war, he settled in Salem and became a mariner. He married Sarah Grant (also known as Sallie) of Salem in 1785. As a mariner, he was the master of several ships, including the brigantine *Fanny* in 1798, and the schooner *Hero* in 1805–1806 (of which he was also co-owner). By 1820, having been too old and infirm to go to sea "for several years," he was working periodically as a tax collector for the town. Failing eyesight left him nearly blind before he died in Salem of a fever in 1844 at age 88. He is buried in Harmony Grove Cemetery. He was incorrectly believed to be the last surviving member of Washington's Life Guards.[1]

SMITH, Jonathan

Jonathan Smith of Lincoln served as a private in Capt. William Smith's Company of Minute Men from Lincoln, Col. Abijah Peirce's Regiment.[2] Following the engagement at Concord, he served for 12 days at Cambridge.[3] He was reimbursed by the town for part of a set of accoutrements as a minute man.[4]

He was paid by the town for service at Cambridge in 1775, at New York in 1776, and at Cambridge in 1777 and 1778. The details of this service have not been found; he may possibly have hired a substitute for one or more of these stints. It is likely that the service at Cambridge in 1777 and 1778 was guarding the British and German troops captured at Saratoga.[5]

His identity is uncertain. He appears to have been age 27 during the April 19th Alarm. He had come to Lincoln by 1771, and he married Lucy Billings in 1772. Lucy was probably the sister of Joseph Billing (q.v.) and Nathan Billing (q.v.). Accordingly, he appears also to have been the uncle of Israel Billing (q.v.), Joseph Billing, Jr. (q.v.), Daniel Billing (q.v.), and Nathan Billing, Jr. (q.v.).

He died in Lincoln in 1832, at age 84 or 85, and is buried in the Meeting House Cemetery behind Bemis Hall.[6]

[There is a record of a Jonathan Smith who served at the northward (at Stillwater, near Saratoga) with Capt. Joseph Fuller's Company, Col. Samuel Bullard's Regiment, from August 20, 1777, through the surrender of Burgoyne. The regiment then marched south,

---

are the same individual, but this seems quite probable. MacLean, *A Rich Harvest* (p. 257), speculates that Jesse Smith may have been apprenticed to a Wheat, but with the realization that John Wheat was the step-father of Jesse Smith, he concurs that such an apprenticeship arrangement appears less likely (Jack MacLean, private communication with author).

1 *Vital Records of Salem*; Quintal, Unpublished research; Pension Record # S19469; Hitchings and Phillips, *Ship Registers*, pp. 59, 85; "Find A Grave"; Whipple, "History of the Salem Light Infantry," p. 201. Calling him "the last of Washington's Life Guard," the Salem Light Infantry Company turned out in uniform to attend his funeral on June 7, 1844. Actually, there were apparently several who out-survived him, the prize going to Uzal Knapp of New Windsor, New York, who survived to 1856, at age 96 (see Custis, et al., *Recollections and Private Memoirs of Washington,* p. 263).

2 Coburn, *Muster Rolls*.

3 *Massachusetts Soldiers and Sailors*, Vol. XIV, p. 468.

4 "Treasurer's Accompts," March 25, 1776.

5 "Treasurer's Accompts," June 15, 1779. The nature of the Cambridge service in 1777 and 1778 is suppositional, but it is based on similar service by other Lincoln individuals, and on the principal military activity in Cambridge at the time.

6 *Vital Records of Lincoln*; MacLean, *A Rich Harvest*, p. 257; Wheeler, "Lincoln," in Hurd, Vol. 2, p. 624; Biggs, "In Memorium," p. 182. MacLean gives his age as 27 at Concord, which is consistent with his death record,

and served briefly in New Jersey. He was discharged on November 29, 1777 (credited with 3 months, 22 days, including 12 days for 240 miles of travel home). However, it is uncertain whether or not this is the same Jonathan Smith.]¹

SMITH, Thomas

Thomas Smith appears on a list, dated July 28, 1778, of Lincoln men mustered into Rhode Island service, agreeable to a resolve of the General Court, to serve until the first day of January, 1779. The list was prepared by James Barrett, muster master for Middlesex County.²

The details of this service are unknown, but there is a reasonable likelihood that he participated in the Battle of Rhode Island on August 29, 1778.

The identity of this individual is uncertain. He may possibly have been the son of Benjamin Jr. and Anna (Parker) Smith from Lexington, age 18 at the time of this service. If so, he had served previously at Roxbury and Dorchester in the fall and winter of 1776–1777 (at age 16) in Capt. John Minot's Company, Colonel Dike's Regiment, then at Rhode Island from May 10, 1777, to July 10, 1777 (plus eight days credited for travel to and from). He was discharged at Point Judith. After his war service, this Thomas Smith returned to Lexington and settled there, married Sarah Taylor of Charlestown in 1782, and died in Lexington in 1809 at age 49. However, no evidence has been found to connect him to Lincoln.³

---

which lists his age as both 84 and 85. No Lincoln birth record has been found, and only three Jonathan Smiths close to the right age are identifiable in vital records of the surrounding towns:
- Jonathan Smith of Lexington, son of Jonathan and Abigail (Stratton) Smith, would have been age 26 as a minute man, and age 83 had he died in 1832. This is tantalizingly close. However, his death is recorded in Lexington in 1819, at age 71, as are his three marriages in 1771, 1788, and 1795 (none of them to Lucy Billings). This individual cannot be Jonathan Smith of Lincoln.
- A Jonathan Smith of Reading, son of Jonathan and Martha Smith, would have been age 29 as a minute man, and age 86 when he died if he became Jonathan Smith of Lincoln.
- Another Jonathan Smith, son of Amos and Susanna Smith (recorded in Sudbury) would have been age 30 as a minute man. However (notwithstanding the "Jr." designation), this individual appears to be the Jonathan Smith, Jr. who married Ann Willis in 1766, recorded nine children in Sudbury, and is buried next to Ann in Sudbury's Old Revolutionary Cemetery. Thus, he could not be Jonathan Smith of Lincoln.

1 *Massachusetts Soldiers and Sailors*, Vol. XIV, p. 471. This record is noteworthy primarily because at least 16 Lincoln men went north with Colonel Bullard's Regiment. There is little other reason for supposing that this record applies to Jonathan Smith (inst.) of Lincoln. Capt. Joseph Fuller was from Newton; his company was made up of men from a different Middlesex district.

2 Blake, "James Barrett's Returns of Men," p. 17. The resolve was dated June 12, 1778; the date of enlistment is unknown.

3 *Lexington Births, Marriages and Deaths*; Parker, *Genealogy of John Parker*, p. 72; *Massachusetts Soldiers and Sailors*, Vol. XIV, pp. 558, 561. No particular reason has been found to connect this individual with Lincoln, except for the proximity of the towns, and except for the fact that no other likely candidates have been identified.

There was a Thomas Smith of Sudbury, age 22 at the time of this service, who had served previously at Roxbury from December 1, 1775 through February 1, 1776, in Capt. Asahel Wheeler's Company, Col. Joseph Reed's Regiment; also in the New York campaign (including the Battle of White Plains) in Capt. Amasa Cranston's Company, Col. Eleazer Brooks's Regiment, for two months, September to November 1776; also at Saratoga in Capt. Asahel Wheeler's Company, Col. Joseph Reed's Regiment, from September 28, 1777, to his return 41 days later escorting Burgoyne's captured army; also for one month in the fall of 1779, in the Hudson Valley, in Capt. Amasa Cranston's Company, Col. Samuel Denny's Regiment at Claverack (credited with 1 month, 10 days of service, including travel). He married Polly Haynes of Sudbury in 1788, and remained in Sudbury until his later years. He died in Harvard in 1837. Because his service records and his pension declaration give a fairly detailed and consistent account of his war service, but neither gives any hint of Rhode Island service in 1778, or of a Lincoln connection, this Thomas Smith of Sudbury is probably not Thomas

SMITH, William

As captain, and on horseback, William Smith led Lincoln's Company of Minute Men, Col. Abijah Peirce's Regiment, to Concord on April 19, 1775, leaving his horse in town at the tavern when the Provincial forces pulled back across the river. Before the fight occurred, he volunteered the services of the Lincoln Company to endeavor to dislodge the Regulars from possession of the North Bridge, but Maj. John Buttrick wisely chose to use the combined force of the assembled companies. Later, upon leaving Concord, the British troops absconded with Smith's horse and pressed it into service to carry off the wounded.[1] He was subsequently reimbursed by the town for his accoutrements as a Minute Man.[2]

Including the engagement at Concord, Smith served for five days at Cambridge, before, on April 24, 1775, in the rapidly forming Massachusetts Provincial Army in Cambridge, he was appointed captain of a company in Col. John Nixon's 16th Regiment. He was commissioned on June 5, 1775, and later, on September 30, 1775, he was reported on furlough.[3]

On May 26 and 27, 1775, he probably participated in raids on Hog Island and Noddle's Island to drive away livestock and destroy the hay. On June 17, 1775, his company participated in the Battle on Bunker Hill, but he was evidently unwell at the time, and confined to his bed. Instead, his company was led by Lt. John Heald and Ensign John Hartwell (q.v.).[4]

Subsequently, the town paid him for service at the southward, i.e., the New York campaign, in 1776, but he probably did not actually serve in this campaign. There is an intriguing possibility that this service may have been provided by Cato Smith (q.v.).[5]

Smith (inst.) (see *Vital Records of Sudbury*; *Massachusetts Soldiers and Sailors*, Vol. XIV, pp. 560, 561; Pension Record # W15359).

1 Coburn, *Muster Rolls*; Deposition of John Buttrick, November 1776, in support of Smith's claim for loss for reimbursement to the Provincial Congress (as quoted in Ryan, "The Incomplete Life," p. 1). The horse was never recovered, but the claim appears to have been allowed (see also Ryan, "The Incomplete Life," pp. 14, 15).

   The position of the Lincoln Company in the line of march to the bridge has been debated actively through the years. It is beyond the scope of this work to unravel the various claims and explanations, except to note that Smith's offer was declined and the job was prudently assigned to the entire body of assembled troops. Ryan places the Lincoln Company fourth in the line of march (presumably behind Acton and two Concord companies). French, *The Siege of Boston* (p. 190), suggests that Lincoln was fifth or sixth.

2 "Treasurer's Accompts," February 19, 1776.

3 *Massachusetts Soldiers and Sailors*, Vol. XIV, p. 572. Colonel Nixon's 16th Massachusetts Regiment became known as the 5th Regiment in August 1775, under Washington's Continental command structure.

4 Ryan, "The Incomplete Life," pp. 17, 18. Ryan cites a June 25, 1775, letter from Smith's uncle, Isaac Smith, to John Adams (Smith's brother-in-law) as confirming evidence that Smith was not on the battlefield. Capt. William Smith is, however, one of 14 officers who signed a petition dated December 5, 1775, commending "under our own observation" Salem Poor for meritorious conduct during the battle (see also Quintal, *Patriots of Color*, pp. 175–180, 232). While this would seem to contradict Uncle Isaac, the author concurs with Ryan's interpretation that Captain Smith likely signed the petition upon the good authority of others whom he trusted, and that in the face of the contrary evidence, this does not necessarily place him in the midst of the battle. Ryan also cites Frothingham, *History of the Siege of Boston* in noting that the muster roll for Smith's Company on the day of the battle lists no captain.

5 "Treasurer's Accompts," November 11, 1779, show £28 paid to "Capt. William Smith for his service at Cambridge in the year 1775 and for service at the southward in the year 1776." Wheeler, "Lincoln" (in Hurd, Vol. 2, p. 624), indicates that the New York service was in Col. Eleazer Brooks's Regiment, but this is unverified. From a review of Adams family letters, however, Ryan, "The Incomplete Life" (p. 21) concludes that Smith was not in service at this time, and that he was "spending much time away from home and family as he continued his search for a means of support and a purposeful life." Smith had applied for a commission, which had not

Built about 1693, the home of minute man Capt. William Smith is probably the oldest surviving house in Lincoln. Its distinctive chimney design and under-the-eaves plaster cove are visible in this late-nineteenth-century photograph. On April 19, 1775, the bloody battle raged through this property. Smith's family subsequently nursed a wounded Redcoat for several days before he died. (Farrar, "Houses in Lincoln 100 Years Old")

Frustrated in obtaining a Continental Army commission, on May 22, 1777, he set sail from Salem, as captain of marines, with a contingent of 30 to 35 provincial marines aboard *American Tartar* (24 guns, 350 tons, crew of 150 men), commissioned as a privateer and under the command of Capt. John Grimes. Initially, they were part of a fleet of 11 vessels hired by the province to capture the H.M.S. *Milford*, a British ship that was wreaking havoc on American shipping along the New England coast, but by July 12, *American Tartar* was cruising off the coast of Scotland. After getting beaten up by the British ship *Pole*, they achieved notorious success by capturing seven British ships during the next several weeks. In early August, Smith was assigned to head the prize crew aboard the captured *Royal Bounty*, and sail it back to Salem. Their luck had run out. On August 28, *American Tartar* was captured, and on September 17, *Royal Bounty* was overtaken and captured off Cape Cod by H.M.S. *Diamond*. A month later, Smith and his prize crew were put ashore and

---

come through, and in September 1776, Abigail Adams noted that her brother had not been seen or heard from since the application. It may or may not be significant, but notice also that the payment record omits the word "his" from "service at the southward." The case for Cato Smith (q.v.) having provided the New York service is based entirely upon the theory that Cato may have been a slave belonging to William Smith. Tax records for 1774 and 1777 show that William Smith owned a slave (see Malcolm, *The Scene of Battle*, p. 55). Ryan, "The Incomplete Life" (p. 2) says that Smith's father, Rev. William Smith, Sr., purchased a Negro boy named Cato for £200 in 1761. The pieces appear to fit fairly well, but unfortunately they are insufficient to be considered conclusive. See also Cato Smith (q.v.).

Chapter 10: The Army of the Revolution

jailed in Halifax. The timing was fortuitous, however, as a prisoner exchange was already being negotiated. On November 9, 1777, he was returned to Boston.[1]

He was age 28 at the outbreak of the war on April 19, 1775; the son of Rev. William and Elizabeth (Quincy) Smith of Weymouth; brother of Abigail Adams. In the midst of a struggling career as a maritime merchant in Boston, persistent debts, and growing connections within Boston's radical politic scene, he had married Catherine Salmon (of Medford, but with Harvard and Lunenburg roots) in 1771. Through her family, Catherine had become the absentee owner of one of the largest farms in Lincoln. In 1773 or 1774, William gave up his maritime ambitions, moved his family onto the Lincoln farm, and became a lieutenant in the Lincoln Militia Company. He taught school briefly in Lincoln in 1773.

His debts, which were evidently exacerbated by gambling and excessive drinking, continued to plague him during and after the war, and he was prone to disappear from his family for increasingly long periods of time. By 1783, he abandoned his family altogether, and shadowy reports from New York or Philadelphia tell of a tragic life caught in the downward spiral of alcohol, gambling, women, more alcohol, further business failure, and involvement in a counterfeiting scheme (for which he was acquitted in a jury trial in 1785). It is believed that he died somewhere around Philadelphia or New York in 1787, at age 40, of "the black jaundice."[2]

[There are a couple of records of war service by a William Smith later in the war, which may possibly be this William Smith (inst). Agreeable to a resolve of June 5, 1780, a William Smith from Lincoln enlisted for six months in the Continental Army. He was engaged for the town of Lincoln, and was in service as early as July 22, 1780, when he marched to camp. The record picks him up in Springfield on August 26, 1780, and again on September 7, 1780. He passed muster by Brigadier General Paterson (according to a return dated at Camp Totoway, October 25, 1780) before being discharged on October 15, 1780, having served for 3 months, 3 days, including 200 miles of travel home. He is described as age 29; five feet, seven inches in stature, with a fresh complexion. This is an intriguing record with few other candidates who could qualify, but it is not certain if this is indeed the same William Smith.][3]

---

1 Ryan, "The Incomplete Life," pp. 22–26; *Massachusetts Soldiers and Sailors*, Vol. XIV, p. 579. Ryan's account of Smith's venture as a privateer is wonderfully researched and detailed, and is explained within the context of his commercial maritime failures, his inability to secure a commission in the army, and his desire to redeem himself in the eyes of his family.

2 Ryan, "The Incomplete Life," pp. 1–8, 27–34. Also Wheeler, "Lincoln," in Hurd, Vol. 2, p. 624; MacLean, *A Rich Harvest*, pp. 206, 256. Ryan and MacLean miscalculate his age on April 19, 1775. He appears to have been age 28, not 29. Catherine's mother had remarried after her father died, and Smith's in-laws were named Dodge.

3 *Massachusetts Soldiers and Sailors*, Vol. XIV, pp. 572, 582. Although William Smith (inst.) was age 33 at this time, Vital Records of Lincoln and surrounding towns reveal no other individuals who could fit this record. In addition to age, however, there are two other problems with concluding that this is the same individual: 1) Ryan, "The Incomplete Life" (p. 3) pegs William's height at six feet, two inches at age 15. Eighteen years later, could he have been measured (or eyeballed) at seven inches shorter? 2) It requires a leap of faith to think that an individual from a proud family of standing, who had aspirations and had already served as captain, would have entered the service as a foot soldier, even in the face of recurring failures, disappointments, and financial troubles. It cannot be ruled out, but it is by no means certain.

On the other hand, if this record is not William Smith (inst.), then who could it be? There is no shortage of other William Smiths floating around, but the difficulty is connecting them with Lincoln. Braddyll Smith of Weston had a brother, William, who (with his wife Hannah (Fiske) Smith) had a son William, who was age 31 at this time. Braddyll Smith shows up periodically in Lincoln records, but there seems to be little else

[Agreeable to a resolve of December 2, 1780, a William Smith, described as age 35, enlisted for a three-year term in the Continental Army. He entered the service on April 23, 1781, engaged for the town of Cambridge. He is further described as five feet, six inches in height; light hair and complexion, blue eyes, and a laborer (also farmer) by occupation. Although the bounty paid on July 6, 1781, may well have helped with his debts, there is little beyond the age to connect this record with William Smith (inst.) of Lincoln.][1]

STONE, Gregory, Jr.

Gregory Stone, Jr., of Lincoln served as a private in Capt. William Smith's Company of Minute Men from Lincoln, Col. Abijah Peirce's Regiment. Including the engagement at Concord, he served for 1 month, 2 days at Cambridge.[2] He was reimbursed by the town for his accoutrements as a minute man.[3]

He was paid by the town for service at Cambridge in 1776. This is reported to be in Capt. Asahel Wheeler's Company for two months during January and February 1776, but this appears unlikely.[4]

He served as a private in Capt. John Hartwell's Militia Company from Lincoln, Col. Eleazer Brooks's 3rd Middlesex County Regiment, which marched from Lincoln to fortify Dorchester Heights on March 4, 1776. The unit was discharged five days later, on March 9, after the threat of a British assault on the fortifications had subsided, and General Howe instead had begun preparations to evacuate Boston. He was paid for this service the following September.[5]

---

to connect his nephew with Lincoln or with this record (see Bond, *Genealogies of the Families of Watertown*, p. 440). William Smith (inst.) had a cousin William (son of Uncle Isaac), who appears to have been about nine years younger. Here again, it is not easy to conjure up a Lincoln connection, particularly in the face of William's (inst.) increasing estrangement from the family.

The identity of the William Smith of this record remains a mystery.

1 *Massachusetts Soldiers and Sailors*, Vol. XIV, p. 582. William Smith (inst.) was age 34 at this time.
2 Coburn, *Muster Rolls*; *Massachusetts Soldiers and Sailors*, Vol. XV, p. 95.
3 "Treasurer's Accompts," February 19, 1776. This may have been paid to his father, as Gregory Jr. is reported to have been in service at this time.
4 "Treasurer's Accompts," November 11, 1779; Pension Record # W25087. The details of this service are found in his widow's pension declaration, but they are uncertain. Capt. Asahel Wheeler reportedly served in the Siege of Boston from February 4, 1776, to April 1, 1776, in Col. John Robinson's Regiment. There is no record of Wheeler being in Cambridge in January. Similarly, if Stone had served with Captain Wheeler in February, it is doubtful that he would have been discharged to march with Captain Hartwell's Company to Dorchester Heights on March 4. A two-month term of service in January and February dovetails nicely with the record of his Dorchester Heights service, but the circumstances and the unit associated with such a service at that time are not at all clear. This service may more plausibly have been served, if at all, after his Dorchester Heights service.
5 *Massachusetts Soldiers and Sailors*, Vol. XV, p. 95; Pension Record # W25087; Hartwell, "A List of a Company of Militia." Presumably because of the absence of the "Jr." designation in this record, *An Account of the Celebration* (p. 238) incorrectly indicates that this is a different individual from Gregory Stone, Jr. The pension declaration is evidence that this was, in fact, served by Gregory Stone, Jr. The fact that he was at Ticonderoga in September 1776, when he was supposedly paid for this service, is a potential complication. However, since the evidence of payment in this case is a receipt signed by multiple Lincoln men in a Lincoln Company (whose captain was also back in service at this time), there is little question that the date is an administrative date and that these payments were made and signed for over some period of time.

In July 1776, he went to Ticonderoga, possibly in Capt. Charles Miles's Company, or more probably in Capt. Asahel Wheeler's Company, Col. Jonathan Reed's Regiment. He served for five months.[1]

On September 17, 1777, he marched with Capt. Charles Miles's Company to convey stores from Concord to Boston, traveling 21 miles to Roxbury on an alarm, and returned with empty teams, as certified by Ephraim Wood, Concord Town Clerk.[2]

He was the son of Gregory Stone (q.v.) and Hephzibah (Brooks) Stone; age 21 as a minute man. He was the brother of Joshua Stone (q.v.) and Timothy Stone (q.v.); nephew of Deacon Joshua Brooks (q.v.), Timothy Brooks (q.v.), and Ephraim Brooks (q.v.), cousin of Joshua Brooks, Jr. (q.v.), Jonas Brooks (q.v.), Ephraim Brooks, Jr. (q.v.), Benjamin Brooks (q.v.), Levi Brooks (q.v., Chapter 12), and Abner Brooks (q.v.). After the war, he married Lucy Jones in 1788. He died in Lincoln in 1807, at age 53, and is buried in the old Precinct Burial Ground on Lexington Road.[3]

STONE, Gregory (Sr.)[4]

Gregory Stone, Sr., went to Concord on the morning of April 19, 1775. He appears from his deposition to have been in arms, probably as a member of the militia company from Lincoln.[5]

He was age 46; a native of Lexington. He had been married to Hephzibah Brooks, sister of Deacon Joshua Brooks (q.v.), Timothy Brooks (q.v.), and Ephraim Brooks (q.v.), since 1750. He was the father of Gregory Stone, Jr. (q.v.), Joshua Stone (q.v.), and Timothy

---

1 Lawrence, "Gregory Stone," p. 1; Pension Record # W25087; Sudbury Miscellaneous Records, pay receipts dated September 30, 1776 (Doc. # 109), December 26, 1776 (Doc. # 2208). His widow's pension declaration says he served in Captain Miles's Company, but the pay receipts provide evidence that he served in Captain Wheeler's company. His widow seems to have correctly identified his captains, but incorrectly matched them with the campaigns.

2 *Massachusetts Soldiers and Sailors*, Vol. XV, p. 95; Lawrence, "Gregory Stone," p. 2.

3 *Vital Records of Lincoln*; Wheeler, "Lincoln," in Hurd, Vol. 2, p. 624; Biggs, "In Memorium," p. 197.

4 The designation "Sr." is not found anywhere in the records. It is used here only for convenience. Because records for Gregory Stone, Jr., appear variously with and without the designation "Jr.," some service by Gregory Jr. has erroneously been attributed to Gregory Sr. Except for Concord, however, the author has found no evidence to suggest that any of the service records apply to the elder Gregory Stone; all of the service is clearly attributable to Gregory Stone, Jr.

5 Deposition of John Hoar, et al. The deposition does not identify the deponent as Gregory Sr. or Gregory Jr. The Muster Roll provides clear evidence that Gregory Stone, Jr., was at Concord, and thus it would be logical to assume that it was he who provided the deposition. However, the record shows that Gregory Jr. was in service at Cambridge on April 23, when the deposition was taken in Lexington.

The author believes that in the chaos that was Cambridge in the aftermath of the events of April 19th, many individuals must have returned home for supplies or to attend to hastily interrupted matters. On the face of it, it seems quite plausible that Gregory Jr. could have been a deponent at Lexington, even while officially in service at Cambridge. However, among the 95 other deponents (including a few spectators and a couple of British soldiers), none of them is recorded as being in service on the date of his deposition. Even if Gregory Jr. had returned from Cambridge briefly, it would be inconsistent with this evidence to attribute the deposition to him. Therefore, the author concludes that the deponent in this case must have been Gregory Sr.

Gregory Sr. was still within the age of militia service. On the other hand, the presence of others who were not members of militia and minute companies has been documented, as well. So possibly he could have been an un-enlisted volunteer. It seems plausible to this author, in view of his not having served again, that he may have had personal reasons for being at Concord, as well as (or in place of) a militia obligation. He would certainly have had a paternal interest in the welfare of his son, Gregory Jr., who was a minute man, or he may have gone to Concord in a support role or as an act of personal defiance against the Crown authority (see also John Hoar (q.v.)).

Stone (q.v.); uncle of Joshua Brooks, Jr. (q.v.), Jonas Brooks (q.v.), Ephraim Brooks, Jr. (q.v.), Benjamin Brooks (q.v.), Levi Brooks (q.v., Chapter 12), and Abner Brooks (q.v.). He died in Lincoln in 1782 at age 53, and he is buried in the old Precinct Burying Ground.[1]

STONE, Joshua

Joshua Stone served as a private in Capt. John Hartwell's Militia Company from Lincoln, Col. Eleazer Brooks's 3rd Middlesex County Regiment, which marched from Lincoln to fortify Dorchester Heights on March 4, 1776. The unit was discharged five days later, on March 9, after the threat of a British assault on the fortifications had subsided, and General Howe had begun preparations to evacuate Boston, instead. He was paid for this service the following September.[2]

He was paid by the town for service at New York in 1776 and 1777. He served in Capt. John Bridge's Company, Col. Samuel Thatcher's Regiment, from November 21, 1776, into March 1777, in Fairfield, Connecticut, and Woodbridge, New Jersey.[3]

On September 29, 1777, he was again detached from Colonel Brooks's 3rd Middlesex County Militia Regiment, and sent northward to reinforce the Northern Army under General Gates at Saratoga, as a member of Capt. Samuel Farrar, Jr.'s Company, Col. Jonathan Reed's Middlesex County Regiment (Brig. Gen. James Bricket's Brigade of Massachusetts Militia). He served for 1 month, 10 days, through the surrender of General Burgoyne, and escorted the British captives to Cambridge, where he was discharged on November 7, 1777.[4]

He was age 24 at Dorchester Heights; the son of Gregory Stone (q.v.) and Hephzibah (Brooks) Stone; the brother of Gregory Stone, Jr. (q.v.), and Timothy Stone (q.v.); nephew of Deacon Joshua Brooks (q.v.), Timothy Brooks (q.v.), and Ephraim Brooks (q.v.); cousin of Joshua Brooks, Jr. (q.v.), Jonas Brooks (q.v.), Ephraim Brooks, Jr. (q.v.), Benjamin Brooks (q.v.), Levi Brooks (q.v., Chapter 12), and Abner Brooks (q.v.). After the war, he married Sarah Avery of Chelmsford in 1789 and settled in Concord. He died in Concord in 1822 at age 71, and he is buried in the Hill Burial Ground in Concord.[5]

STONE, Timothy

Timothy Stone served as a private in Capt. John Hartwell's Militia Company from Lincoln, Col. Eleazer Brooks's 3rd Middlesex County Regiment, which marched from Lincoln to fortify

---

1 *Vital Records of Lincoln*; *Lexington Births, Marriages and Deaths*; Biggs, "In Memorium," p. 196. His Lexington birth record does not identify his parents, but similarities with other records suggest the possibility that his father was also Gregory Stone.
2 *Massachusetts Soldiers and Sailors*, Vol. XV, p. 110.
3 "Treasurer's Accompts," June 10, 1779; Wheeler, "Lincoln," in Hurd, Vol. 2, p. 624. Wheeler says that this was in Capt. Samuel Farrar's Company, Colonel Brooks's Regiment, but he is confused. Stone was detached from Capt. Farrar's company to serve in Colonel Thatcher's Regiment (see Shattuck, *History of the Town of Concord*, pp. 354–355). For a fuller description of this service, see Job Brooks (q.v.)
4 *Massachusetts Soldiers and Sailors*, Vol. XV, p. 110.
5 *Lexington Births, Marriages and Deaths*; *Concord, Massachusetts: Births, Marriages, and Deaths*; *Vital Records of Chelmsford*; Wheeler, "Lincoln," in Hurd, Vol. 2, p. 624; Lawrence, "Gregory Stone," p. 2; *SAR Revolutionary War Graves Register*. The baptismal record in Lexington does not identify his parents, but it conforms to the age given in his death record in Concord. His parents are identified by his father Gregory's will, dated April 4, 1782, which mentions Joshua as one of his sons. The marriage record is found in *Vital Records of Chelmsford*.
    Wheeler says he was baptized in the precinct in 1752. Although he seems to be off by a year, the Stone family resided in that part of Lexington which became part of Lincoln in 1754.

Dorchester Heights on March 4, 1776. The unit was discharged five days later, on March 9, after the threat of a British assault on the fortifications had subsided, and General Howe had begun preparations to evacuate Boston. He was paid for this service the following September.[1]

He is probably the Timothy Stone who enlisted on October 23, 1779, as a private in Capt. Joshua Walker's Company, Colonel Denny's Regiment. This regiment was recruited from the militia, detached to join the Continental Army, and ordered to march to Claverack for three months. He was discharged on November 23, 1779, credited with serving just 1 month, 11 days (including 10 days for 200 miles of travel home).[2]

He was age 17 at Dorchester Heights; son of Gregory Stone (q.v.) and Hephzibah (Brooks) Stone; brother of Gregory Stone, Jr. (q.v.) and Joshua Stone (q.v.); nephew of Deacon Joshua Brooks (q.v.), Timothy Brooks (q.v.), and Ephraim Brooks (q.v.); cousin of Joshua Brooks, Jr. (q.v.), Jonas Brooks (q.v.), Ephraim Brooks, Jr. (q.v.), Benjamin Brooks (q.v.), Levi Brooks (q.v., Chapter 12), and Abner Brooks (q.v.). He died in Lincoln in 1780 at age 22.[3]

TENY, Michael
[also TENNEY, also Micah]

Michael Teny of Lincoln served as a private in Capt. Simon Hunt's Company, Col. Eleazer Brooks's Middlesex County Regiment of Massachusetts Militia in the New York campaign in 1776. After the Battle of White Plains on October 28, 1776, he is reported on a company return as being in camp and fit for duty at White Plains, having lost his knapsack, blanket, coat, stockings, and shirt in the battle.[4]

Subsequently, he served as a private in Capt. Oliver Titcomb's Company, Col. Jacob Gerrish's Regiment of Guards, guarding General Burgoyne's troops at Charlestown and Winter Hill, from November 11, 1777, to February 2, 1778 (credited with 81 days of service).[5]

He is reported to be the son of Thomas and Hannah (Boynton) Tenney of Rowley; age 30 during the New York campaign. He never married. Sometime after his war service, he returned to Rowley, where he died in 1815 at age 68, identified as a "pauper."[6]

---

1 *Massachusetts Soldiers and Sailors*, Vol. XV, p. 123.
2 *Massachusetts Soldiers and Sailors*, Vol. XV, p. 124. While the identity of this individual as Timothy Stone (inst.) is not absolutely certain, it appears likely. The roll is dated Woburn, which was the residence location of Captain Walker. Colonel Denny was from Leicester. Because the troop call was small (only 2,000 men), the regiment appears to have been made up of men from a wider geographic area than was typically the case with larger mobilizations. See the similar record of service by Daniel Wesson (q.v.).
3 *Vital Records of Lincoln*. The cause of death is unspecified, but as it came ten months after his return from the service, there appears little reason to suspect it was service related.
4 *Massachusetts Soldiers and Sailors*, Vol. XV, p. 490; *Muster Rolls of the Revolutionary War*, Vol. 55, file L, p. 24.
5 *Massachusetts Soldiers and Sailors*, Vol. XV, p. 486. This record is associated with a William Tenney, evidently of Rowley, who served in the same unit from the next day, February 3, to April 2, 1777. The connection between the records is not explained, but it appears that William Tenney, who evidently must have been a kinsman, substituted for him for the remainder of his service (see *Massachusetts Soldiers and Sailors*, Vol. XV, p. 487). Neither *Vital Records of Rowley*, nor *Vital Records of Newbury* offers an apparent identity for William Tenney.
6 Tenney, *The Tenney Family*, pp. 44, 79; *Vital Records of Rowley*. His birth was also recorded in Newbury, from where his mother came. In both records, his given name is recorded as Micah. His death record overstates his age by a year.

THORNING, John

John Thorning of Lincoln served as a private in Capt. William Smith's Company of Minute Men from Lincoln, Col. Abijah Peirce's Regiment. Including the engagement at Concord, he served for 20 days at Cambridge.[1] He was reimbursed by the town for his accoutrements as a Minute Man.[2]

The following summer, in June or July 1776, he marched to Ticonderoga in Capt. Asahel Wheeler's Company, Col. Jonathan Reed's Regiment, and served for 4 or 5 months, through November 1776.[3]

He was no sooner back from Ticonderoga, when he enlisted on December 14, 1776, and served through February 1777 at Dorchester, in Capt. John Hartwell's Company, Col. Nicholas Dike's Regiment. This regiment was raised to serve until March 1, 1777.[4]

In 1780, he enlisted again, this time for six months in the Continental Army. Although the enlistment was to the credit of Lincoln, he apparently never actually served, on account of sickness.[5]

He was age 18 as a minute man; son of John and Sarah (Clarke) Thorning; brother of William Thorning (q.v.). He moved to Lexington in 1781, where he boarded with and worked as a husbandman for Thomas Cutler. He married Betsy Russell of Concord in 1789 and settled in Concord, where he died in 1802 at age 45.[6]

[The town paid John Thorning for service at Cambridge in 1775, but this appears to be a payment made to his father John Thorning for service by his brother, William Thorning (q.v.).][7]

[The town paid John Thorning for service at Saratoga in 1777, but once again this appears to be a payment made to his father John Thorning for service by his brother, William Thorning (q.v.).][8]

THORNING, William

William Thorning of Lincoln served as a private in Capt. William Smith's Company of Minute Men from Lincoln, Col. Abijah Peirce's Regiment. According to family tradition,

---

1 *Massachusetts Soldiers and Sailors*, Vol. XV, p. 692.
2 "Treasurer's Accompts," July 22, 1776
3 Sudbury Miscellaneous Records, pay receipts dated September 30, 1776 (Doc. # 109) and December 26, 1776 (Doc. # 2208).
4 *Massachusetts Soldiers and Sailors*, Vol. XV, p. 692; "Treasurer's Accompts," November 11, 1779.
5 *Massachusetts Soldiers and Sailors*, Vol. XV, p. 692.
6 *Vital Records of Lincoln*; *Lexington Births, Marriages and Deaths*; *Concord, Massachusetts: Births, Marriages, and Deaths*; Wheeler, "Lincoln," in Hurd, Vol. 2, p. 624; Cutter, *Historic Homes of Middlesex County*, pp. 1988–1989. Their children are recorded in Concord. Betsy may also have been known as Betty, as she is often listed as Betty in *Concord, Massachusetts: Births, Marriages, and Deaths*.
7 "Treasurer's Accompts," November 11, 1779. Wheeler, "Lincoln" (in Hurd, Vol. 2, p. 624), gives John credit for this service, probably on the strength of this record, but this appears to be only a partial reading of the record. The absence of any details of Cambridge service by John, coupled with the town's apparent failure to pay William for amply-documented Cambridge service, suggests the probability of this payment being for William's service. The fact that William was serving in Rhode Island at the time the payment was made provides the explanation for why this payment was made to John, who would almost certainly have been William's father John, and not his brother, John Thorning (inst.).
8 "Treasurer's Accompts," November 11, 1779. See note 7. No record exists of Saratoga service by John. Nor was William otherwise paid for his Saratoga service.

Chapter 10: The Army of the Revolution

From behind this boulder, seventeen-year-old minute man, William Thorning, is said to have shot and killed two Regular soldiers on April 19, 1775. He served nine separate enlistments during the war, participating in the Battle of Bunker Hill, the fortification of Dorchester Heights, and Burgoyne's surrender at Saratoga, as well as serving other stints in the Hudson Valley and Rhode Island. (Hersey, *Heroes*)

he carried his invalid sister in his arms to a hut in the woods for safety. Tradition also says that later in the day, during the fight along Battle Road, he got caught in a cross-fire between Regulars in the road and a flanking party. He escaped by dropping down into a shallow trench, then quickly he took a position behind a large boulder, from where he shot and killed two Regulars. Including the engagement at Concord and along the Battle Road, he served for five days at Cambridge before enlisting on April 24, 1775, in the rapidly forming Massachusetts Provincial Army.[1]

He served in Capt. William Smith's Company, Col. John Nixon's 16th Regiment, and on May 23, 1775, he was detailed as a picket guard under Capt. Reuben Dickenson and Maj. Loammi Baldwin. He was a participant in the Battle of Bunker Hill, on June 17, 1775, and a couple of weeks later, on July 3, 1775, he is recorded as serving on the main

---

1 *Massachusetts Soldiers and Sailors*, Vol. XV, p. 692; Hersey, *Heroes*, pp. 27–29; Cutter, *Historic Homes of Middlesex County*, Vol. 4, p. 1989. Carrying his sister to safety conjures up wonderful heroic images, but it seems unlikely that he would have done that in the cold, early morning hours before marching off to Concord, and it is unclear when else he would have had the opportunity to do so. The Battle Road story is told by both Cutter and Hersey. Earlier accounts may exist, but the author has made no attempt to trace its origin, deconstruct it, or pass judgment on its veracity. Whether or not they were killed by Thorning, two Regulars are believed to be buried along that stretch of Battle Road, now called Nelson Road in Minute Man National Historical Park.

guard at Prospect Hill under now Lieutenant Colonel Baldwin. He served at least through September 30, 1775, and probably through the end of December 1775 (typically, the expiration date of enlistments during 1775).[1]

On February 4, 1776, he marched back into service for 1 month, 28 days in Capt. Asahel Wheeler's Company, Col. John Robinson's Regiment, serving through the evacuation of the British forces from Boston.[2]

That summer, in June or July 1776, he marched to Ticonderoga in Capt. Asahel Wheeler's Company, Col. Jonathan Reed's Regiment, and served for 4 or 5 months, through November 1776.[3]

It appears that he may have decided to try his hand at artillery, probably serving as a matross in Capt. Daniel Lathrop's Company, Colonel Craft's Artillery Regiment for 5 months, 10 days, from November 26, 1776, to May 7, 1777.[4]

On September 29, 1777, amidst a growing sense of urgency about Burgoyne's penetration into the Hudson Valley, he was detached from Colonel Brooks's 3rd Middlesex County Militia Regiment, and was sent northward to reinforce the Northern Army under General Gates at Saratoga, as a member of Capt. Samuel Farrar, Jr.'s Company, Col. Jonathan Reed's Middlesex County Regiment (Brig. Gen. James Bricket's Brigade of Massachusetts Militia). He served for 1 month, 10 days, through the surrender of General Burgoyne, and was discharged November 7, 1777, after escorting the prisoners of war to Cambridge.[5]

Agreeable to a resolve of April 20, 1778, he was again detached from Capt. Samuel Farrar, Jr.'s Company, Colonel Brooks's Militia Regiment, and sent to reinforce the Continental Army for nine months from his arrival at Fishkill on June 17, 1778. He appears to have served under Capt. John Santford, Colonel Malcolm's Regiment, and in Captain Jabez Lane's Company, Colonel Nixon's Regiment. He is described as age 23; five feet, ten inches in stature, and a resident of Lincoln. His service was credited to Lincoln. He was discharged with Abijah Munroe (q.v.) at Verplanck's Point on March 17, 1779.[6]

On July 14, 1779, he was back in service as a private in Capt. Thomas Hovey's Company, Col. Nathan Tyler's Regiment at Rhode Island. He was discharged December 25, 1779,

---

1 *Massachusetts Soldiers and Sailors*, Vol. XV, p. 692–693. Colonel Nixon's 16th Massachusetts Regiment became known also as the 5th Regiment in August 1775, under Washington's Continental command structure. The town appears to have paid his father, John Thorning, for this Cambridge service (see "Treasurer's Accompts," November 11, 1779). William was in service at Rhode Island when the payment was made. See also John Thorning (q.v.), note 7, p. 410.

2 *Massachusetts Soldiers and Sailors*, Vol. XV, p. 693.

3 Sudbury Miscellaneous Records, pay receipts dated September 30, 1776 (Doc. # 109), December 16, 1777 (Doc. # 2204), and December 26, 1776 (Doc. # 2208).

4 *Massachusetts Soldiers and Sailors*, Vol. XV, pp. 693, 854.

5 *Massachusetts Soldiers and Sailors*, Vol. XV, p. 693. The town seems to have paid his father John for this service. See "Treasurer's Accompts," November 11, 1779. See also John Thorning (q.v.), notes 7 and 8, p. 410.

6 *Massachusetts Soldiers and Sailors*, Vol. XV, p. 693, 854; Pension Record # W20090; Blake, "James Barrett's Returns of Men," p. 15. See also Pension Record # S37264 for Abijah Munroe (q.v.). Actually, he was only age 20 when he went to Fishkill. Wheeler, "Lincoln" (in Hurd, Vol. 2, p. 624), says he was "drafted" for this service, but this is unconfirmed. Notwithstanding the tortured geography (Fishkill is more west of Lincoln than south), this may be the service "at the southward" for which the town paid him on May 27, 1779 (see "Treasurer's Accompts," May 27, 1779).

having served for 5 months, 16 days (including 4 days for 80 miles of travel home). He was paid by the town for this service.[1]

He reenlisted for six months service in the Continental Army, agreeable to a Resolve of June 5, 1780. He marched to camp on July 11, 1780, under the command of Capt. James Cooper, and arrived in Springfield on July 15, 1780. He is described as age 22; five feet, eleven inches in height, with a ruddy complexion. He passed muster by Brigadier General Paterson, according to a return dated at Camp Totoway, October 25, 1780. He was discharged on December 5, 1780, with 5 months, 4 days of service (including 10 days for 200 miles of travel home).

He was back in Rhode Island for five months of service as a sergeant in Capt. Asa Drury's Company, Col. William Turner's Regiment on August 13, 1781. He served only 3 months, 22 days (including 4 days for 80 miles of travel home), having been discharged on November 30, 1781.[2]

He was age 17 as a minute man; son of John and Sarah (Clarke) Thorning; brother of John Thorning (q.v.). He went to Lexington with his brother John, in 1781 (probably before his final stint in the service), to board with and work as a husbandman for Thomas Cutler. He married Eunice Phillips of Lexington in 1782. He continued to reside in Lexington, where he prospered as a farmer and a shoemaker. He is said to have had a jovial disposition, and he loved to sing and play the violin. His death is recorded in Lexington in 1829 at age 71; he is buried in the Old Burying Ground.[3]

TIDD, Nathan

Nathan Tidd of Lincoln served as a private in Capt. William Smith's Company of Minute Men from Lincoln, Col. Abijah Peirce's Regiment. Including the engagement at Concord and along the Battle Road, he served for five days at Cambridge, before enlisting on April 24, 1775, in the rapidly forming Massachusetts Provincial Army in Cambridge.[4]

He served as a private in Capt. William Smith's Company, Col. John Nixon's 16th Regiment. He is presumed to have participated with his unit in the Battle of Bunker Hill on June 17, 1775, and a couple of weeks later is recorded serving on the main guard at Prospect Hill under Lt. Col. Loammi Baldwin on July 3, 1775. He served at least through September 30, 1775, and probably until the end of his eight-month term on December 31, 1775.[5]

He served as a private in Capt. John Hartwell's Company of Militia from Lincoln, Col. Eleazer Brooks's 3rd Middlesex County Regiment, which marched from Lincoln to fortify Dorchester Heights on March 4, 1776. The unit was discharged five days later, on March 9,

---

1 *Massachusetts Soldiers and Sailors*, Vol. XV, p. 693; "Treasurer's Accompts," February 21, 1780. This payment was unusually prompt compared with most of the other service pay transactions.
2 *Massachusetts Soldiers and Sailors*, Vol. XV, p. 693.
3 *Vital Records of Lincoln*; *Lexington Births, Marriages and Deaths*; *Records of Littleton*; Wheeler, "Lincoln," in Hurd, Vol. 2, p. 624; "Find A Grave"; Cutter, *Historic Homes of Middlesex County*, p. 1989. He appears to have eloped with Eunice, as the marriage ceremony was performed by a Justice of the Peace in Littleton.
4 Coburn, *Muster Rolls*; *Massachusetts Soldiers and Sailors*, Vol. XV, p. 732.
5 *Massachusetts Soldiers and Sailors*, Vol. XV, p. 732. Colonel Nixon's 16th Massachusetts Regiment became known as the 5th Regiment in August 1775, under Washington's Continental command structure.

after the threat of a British assault on the fortifications had subsided, and General Howe had begun preparations to evacuate Boston.

He joined Col. Thomas Craft's Artillery Regiment on June 8, 1776, and served in Boston as a gunner in Capt. James Swan's 1st Company until August 1, 1776, when he became a bombardier. On December 1, 1776, Capt. Philip Marett took over command of the company from Captain Swan. Nathan Tidd served another 5 months, 7 days in this company, until May 8, 1777.

Upon his discharge from Colonel Craft's Regiment, he enlisted in the Continental Army, in Col. John Crane's Artillery Regiment, for the duration of the war, perhaps enticed by the state bounty. He appears to have served in Capt. David Briant's Company, from May 21, 1777, through the Battle of Brandywine in September 1777, then as a corporal in Capt. Henry Burbeck's Company from October 1777. He spent the legendary winter of 1777–1778 at Valley Forge, and probably participated in the Battle of Monmouth the following June. He may also have participated in the Battle of Rhode Island before he died on October 28, 1778. This service was credited to the town of Lincoln.[1]

He was age 19 when he served as a minute man on April 19, 1775; the son of Amos and Elizabeth (Smith) Tidd of Lexington. He was age 23 when he died in service.[2]

TORREY, Ebenezer

Ebenezer Torrey was paid by the town for his service at New York in the years 1776 and 1777. No details of this service have been found, but it is probable that he served at Fairfield, Connecticut and Woodbridge, New Jersey, in Capt. John Bridge's Company, Col. Samuel Thatcher's Regiment, from November 21, 1776, to March 6, 1777.[3]

His identity has not been determined, but he appears to have remained in Lincoln at least through 1779.[4]

[Possibly, he may be the same individual who served as a private in Capt. Thomas Bumstead's Company, which was drafted out of Col. Jabez Hatch's Boston Regiment, agreeable to an Order of Council dated May 7, 1777, to guard the stores for five weeks at and around Boston under Major General Heath. Subsequently, this individual served again

---

1 *Massachusetts Soldiers and Sailors*, Vol. XV, pp. 732–733. The record also indicates a Holliston connection, and a tie to Oliver Tidd from Holliston (also Hopkinton), who served concurrently in Colonel Crane's Artillery Regiment. Oliver Tidd is identifiable as his brother (see *Lexington Births, Marriages and Deaths*).

2 *Lexington Births, Marriages and Deaths*. Despite being away from Lincoln in the service for most of the time since he was age 19, he appears to have been assessed a poll tax in Lincoln, as the "Treasurer's Accompts" contain a record of a March 1779 tax abatement for being in the "Continental Service." Note that this is a few months after his death; perhaps the news of his death had not yet reached the town.

It is reported, without substantiation, in the genealogical databases of the Church of Jesus Christ of Latter Day Saints that his death was from sunstroke. The author has been unable to find any sort of corroboration for this. On the face of it, sunstroke would seem to be a rather unlikely cause of death for that time of year.

3 "Treasurer's Accompts," June 15, 1779. *Massachusetts Soldiers and Sailors* (Vol. XV, pp. 853, 877) contains records of two individuals with this surname serving in New York in late 1776, but neither of these records appear to be connected to Ebenezer Torrey of Lincoln. The probable service indicated is consistent with the service at this time by several others from Lincoln.

4 He appears on the tax rolls of the town in 1779. Notes conveyed to the author by Mike Ryan suggest an Ebenezer Torrey of Boston; son of Samuel Jr. and Silence Torrey. He would have been age 39 during the New York service. He had married Suzannah Torrey of Mendon (possibly a cousin) in 1759, and then Sarah Barron in 1765. He died in Boston in 1790, age 52. It is unclear what, if any, connection he may have had with Lincoln.

under General Heath, in Capt. John Hinkley's Company, Lieutenant Colonel Symmes's detachment of guards at Boston for three months, from February 13, 1778, to May 13, 1778. However, it is uncertain if this is the same Ebenezer Torrey.]¹

TOWER, Jonathan
[also Jonathan Jr., John]

Jonathan Tower enlisted in the Continental Army on February 19, 1781, for three years, agreeable to a resolve of Dec. 2, 1780. He is described as age 16; stature five feet, four inches; dark complexion, dark hair, dark eyes; and a farmer by occupation. He was engaged for the town of Lincoln by a class of the town that included Ephraim Hartwell, Noah Brooks, and Josiah Nelson, among others.²

He served as a private in Capt. Jonathan Maynard's 6th Company, Lt. Col. John Brooks's 7th Massachusetts Regiment. Muster rolls trace some of his service locations: May 1781 at West Point; August 1781 at Peekskill; and September 1781 on command with Colonel Swift. On Feb. 20, 1782, after a year of service, he is described as age 16; stature five feet, four inches (also five feet, four and a half inches); dark complexion, dark hair; occupation laborer; birthplace Lincoln, residence Lincoln. He served in this unit through November 1782.

At the end of November 1782, he joined Capt. Nathaniel C. Allen's 8th Company, in the same regiment. After his second year of service he is described as age 18; stature five feet, five inches; dark complexion, dark hair; occupation farmer; residence Lincoln.

In May 1783, without changing companies, he became part of the 4th Massachusetts Regiment. He was reported sick at the huts at New Windsor during May and June 1783. He served through December 1783, when he was discharged.³

He was age 16 when he enlisted; son of Jonathan and Eunice (Allen) Tower; nephew of Phineas Allen (q.v.), Benjamin Parks (q.v.), Joseph Billing (q.v.), and Abraham Wesson (q.v.); cousin of John Wheeler (q.v.), and Joseph Billing, Jr. (q.v.); brother-in-law of Josiah Parks (q.v.) and Jonas Parks (q.v.). After the war, he married Anna Parks in 1789, and thus he became the brother-in-law of Leonard Parks (q.v.). There is no record of any children, or of Anna's death. However, in 1802 he married Abigail Dudley, and by 1818 he had two minor children. After Abigail died in 1820, he apparently lived out his years meagerly. He

---

1 *Massachusetts Soldiers and Sailors*, Vol. XV, p. 857. Another record exists of an Ebenezer Torrey who was commissioned a captain on June 7, 1780, in the Boston Regiment of the Massachusetts Militia. This individual was the son of William and Bethia (Bass) Torrey of Boston and was a baker, with a shop (in 1769) on Water Street, near Oliver's Dock, "at the sign of the Wheat Sheaff" in Boston. He was a member of the Ancient and Honorable Artillery Company. He moved to Lancaster during the Siege of Boston, where he reportedly resided until his death in 1818, at age 77. He reportedly became quite prosperous, may also have kept a residence in Boston, and was buried in Boston's Granary Burial Ground (see also Roberts, *History of the Military Company of the Massachusetts*, pp. 135–136, 403; Grivetti and Shapiro, *Chocolate*, p. 828). If the 1776–1777 New York service can be attributed to him, he would have been age 37 during that service, but it is not clear if this is the same Ebenezer Torrey or what, if any, connection he may have had with Lincoln.

2 *Massachusetts Soldiers and Sailors*, Vol. XV, pp. 893–894. Also "Treasurer's Accompts," September 12, 1781. The author has made no particular effort to follow the money, but the town evidently reimbursed the members of a class for the moneys they paid to the individual who served. Evidently, Ephraim Hartwell, et al., paid him a bounty on April 2, 1781; the September 12 reimbursement by the town was paid to Noah Brooks and Josiah Nelson. For a brief overview of the system of economic classes, see MacLean, *A Rich Harvest* (p. 296).

3 *Massachusetts Soldiers and Sailors*, Vol. XV, pp. 893–894, 901; Pension Record # S33808.

died in Lincoln in 1835 at age 70, described as a "revolutionary pensioner" and as a "town pauper."[1]

UNDERWOOD, Moses

Moses Underwood was paid by the town for service at Ticonderoga in 1776. No details of this service have been found.[2]

He probably turned age 41 during this service. He was the son of Joseph and Ruth Underwood, initially of Lexington and then of Concord and Lincoln. He had been living in Lincoln since before the French and Indian War, in which he had served in Captain Cutler's Company in 1757. He also appears on the 1757 muster roll of Lincoln's original militia company. He was by occupation a carpenter and yeoman. He had married Mary Peirce in 1771, and he died in Lincoln in 1806 at age 70.[3]

VILES, John
[also VILA, VILEY, VILS]

John Viles marched on the Alarm of April 19, 1775, as a private in Capt. Abraham Peirce's Waltham Company of Militia, Col. Thomas Gardner's Regiment. He served for two days.[4]

After a few days to consider the matter, or perhaps to settle some personal affairs, he returned to Cambridge and joined Capt. Abijah Child's Company, Col. Thomas Gardner's 37th Regiment on May 2, 1775, as a private. He is presumed to have participated with his regiment in the Battle of Bunker Hill on June 17, 1775. He served into the fall, appearing on a company return dated Prospect Hill, October 6, 1775, and he may have been in service as late as December 25, 1775. He is described as five feet, ten inches in stature. He was paid by the town of Lincoln for this service.[5]

---

1 *Vital Records of Lincoln*. The death record lists his age both as 75 and as 73. Neither appears to be correct.
   In his 1818 pension declaration, he said he had a wife and two minor children, with no means of providing for them. He had been dangerously sick the previous spring, and been left with a broken constitution. In 1820, after Abigail died, he had no family, and he had been assigned a guardian.

2 "Treasurer's Accompts," June 15, 1779. Typically, Ticonderoga service in 1776 was for four or five months, from July or August through November or December.

3 *Lexington Births, Marriages and Deaths*; *Vital Records of Lincoln*; MacLean, *A Rich Harvest*, p. 180; Underwood, *The Underwood Families*, pp. 321–322, 362; Martin, "The Sons of Lincoln," p. 25. His baptism was recorded in Lexington. MacLean indicates that he grew up in the southeast portion of Lincoln. This is not the part of Lincoln that was originally part of Lexington. The Glass and Little Map of Lincoln shows Moses Underwood's house in 1775 as being on today's Tower Road, near Rte. 117. His death record identifies him simply as "Mr. Moses," containing no age or information. Mary, who was about ten years his junior, is listed as a widow when she died in 1832 at age 86 or 87. Her identity is uncertain, but she does not appear to be closely related to any of the Peirces listed herein.

4 *Massachusetts Soldiers and Sailors*, Vol. XVI, pp. 329, 330. Evidently, Captain Peirce's Company was not in motion on April 19th, but was called out four days later. Two older brothers (Nathan, age 35; and Jonas, age 28) also marched on the Alarm with Captain Peirce's Militia Company, and served for three days (see also Bond, *Genealogies of the Families of Watertown*, p. 616).

5 *Massachusetts Soldiers and Sailors*, Vol. XVI, pp. 329; "Treasurer's Accompts," June 15, 1779. Lt. Col. William Bond took over command of the regiment after Colonel Gardner was mortally wounded at Bunker Hill. The December 25, 1775 record is a pay receipt for money in lieu of a bounty coat, so it does not necessarily mean he was still in service. On the other hand, the terms of service generally ran until December 31, 1775.

In December 1776, he was back in service briefly, detached for four days of service on Noddle's Island in Capt. John Walton's Company from December 9–12, 1776.[1]

In the aftermath of Burgoyne's surrender at Saratoga, he served with Col. Eleazer Brooks's Regiment of Guards, guarding the troops of the convention (i.e., Burgoyne's troops) at Cambridge. He is recorded as having served for 2 months, 22 days, from January 12, 1778, to April 3, 1778, in Capt. John Walton's Company, and also in Capt. Abraham Peirce's Company. He was paid by the town of Lincoln for this service.[2]

He was age 24 when he marched on the April 19th Alarm; the son of John and Suzanna (Bemis) Viles of Waltham. He married Hannah Warren in November 1775, probably on leave from his service at Cambridge. Hannah died in 1784 at age 30, and 4½ months later he married Hannah's older sister, Mary Warren. He appears to have settled in Weston, where he died in 1820 at age 70. He is buried in Weston's Central Cemetery.[3]

His connection with Lincoln has not been determined. He appears to have lived in Waltham throughout the war. Why the town of Lincoln paid him for service at Cambridge in 1775 and at Cambridge in 1778 is not at all clear.[4]

WESSON, Abraham
[also WESTON, also Abram]

Abraham Wesson was detached from the Lincoln Militia Company in November 1777 for duty at Cambridge, guarding the British and German troops surrendered by Burgoyne at Saratoga. He served from November 6, 1777, to April 2, 1778, as a private in Capt. Simon Hunt's Company, Col. Eleazer Brooks's Regiment. He was credited with only 4 months, 16

---

1 *Massachusetts Soldiers and Sailors*, Vol. XVI, pp. 328. This record appears in the name of John Vila. It is not clear if he was already in service at this time or if he was called up and detached from the militia company. He was paid for the Noddle's Island service on May 9, 1777.

2 *Massachusetts Soldiers and Sailors*, Vol. XVI, pp. 328, 329; "Treasurer's Accompts," June 15, 1779. The normal term of service for this guard shift ran from November 7, 1777, to April 3, 1778. Otherwise identical records (not counting spelling differences of the name) exist which place him in Capt. John Walton's Company and in Capt. Abraham Peirce's Company at the same time. Further investigation is needed to explain this apparent conflict.

3 Bond, *Genealogies of the Families of Watertown*, p. 616; *Vital Records of Waltham*; *Town of Weston, Births, Deaths, & Marriages*; "Find A Grave." Interestingly, his brother Jonas also married two sisters: first, Suzanna Hastings in 1782, who died in 1784; then Suzanna's younger sister, Irene Hastings, in 1787.

4 Notwithstanding the near perfect match between the service for which the town paid John Viles, and the service record of John Viles of Waltham, it may be possible that the putative identification of John Viles may be incorrect. The different pieces of this record fit together so well that it is impossible not to have confidence in making this identification. Nevertheless, it is not clear what connection John Viles of Waltham may have had with Lincoln.

Notwithstanding the multiple spellings of his name, there is no question that the fragmented pieces of this service record all belong to the same individual. Nor has the author found any other individual in the service records or the Vital Records who could qualify as the individual who was paid by the town.

The only other possible candidate is a John Villa who marched on the Alarm of April 19, 1775, as a private in Capt. Samuel Barnard's Watertown Company of Militia, Col. Thomas Gardner's Regiment, and served for six days (see *Massachusetts Soldiers and Sailors*, Vol. XVI, pp. 329). This individual, however, has no other record of service, so he can hardly be matched with the payment for Cambridge service in 1775 and 1778.

Town lines, of course, rarely serve as demarcations of economic interests, employment opportunities, familial relationships, or friendships. That cross-fertilization between Lincoln and surrounding towns was common in the 1700s should be apparent from the many stories in this volume. Further investigation may identify a tangible link between John Viles and Lincoln.

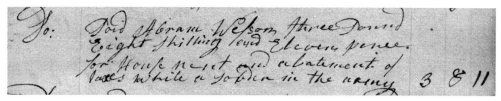

In this June 2, 1784, transaction, the town abated Abram Wesson's taxes during his 1782 Continental Army service. The house rent is unexplained and probably unrelated. When the 44-year-old soldier failed to return to service following a 1783 furlough, he was listed as a deserter. (Courtesy of Lincoln Town Archives, Lincoln, MA)

days of service, however, as he was reported absent for 11 days prior to February 3, 1778. He was paid by the town of Lincoln for this service.[1]

In the spring of 1782, he was recruited and paid a bounty to serve a three-year term in the Continental Army. He enlisted in April 1782 and served in Capt. William Mills's Company, Lt. Col. John Brooks's 7th Regiment. He is described as age 43; five feet, five inches in stature; light complexion, light hair, and a carpenter by occupation. His birthplace and residence are given as Lincoln, and Lincoln was credited for his service. On March 6, 1783, he was given a furlough for 40 days to return to Lincoln from New Windsor, New York. Apparently, he never returned to the army. The record of his service concludes with a notation next to his name on a list of deserters: "deserted April 18, 1783, from furlough." Notwithstanding his having deserted with two-thirds of his term unserved, the town subsequently granted him on June 2, 1784, an "abatement of taxes while a soldier in the army."[2]

He was age 39 when he served at Cambridge; the son of Timothy and Abigail (Brown) Wesson; brother of John Wesson (q.v.). He had been a member of Lincoln's original militia company in 1757. He had been married to Abigail Allen, the sister of Phineas Allen (q.v.), since 1764. Thus, he was the brother-in-law of Phineas Allen, Joseph Billing (q.v.), and Benjamin Parks (q.v.); uncle of Joseph Billing, Jr. (q.v.), Jonathan Tower (q.v.), and John Wheeler (q.v.). He was a carpenter by trade. By 1790, he was living near Livermore Falls, Maine, where he died in 1801 at age 62.[3]

---

1 *Massachusetts Soldiers and Sailors*, Vol. XVI, p. 881; "Treasurer's Accompts," February 18, 1780.

2 *Massachusetts Soldiers and Sailors*, Vol. XVI, p. 881; "Treasurer's Accompts," June 2, 1784. His age is also listed as 45 (although 43 appears to be correct), and his stature is also given as five feet, five inches and a half His enlistment was probably on April 4, 1782, when the bounty was paid in Boston by David Fisk (q.v.), chairman of Class 4 for the town of Lincoln. For a brief overview of the system of economic classes, see MacLean, *A Rich Harvest* (p. 296).

Listed as "Windsor" in the record, New Windsor is north of West Point, the site of the 1782–1783 winter encampment of a large portion of the Continental Army, and the location from which Washington mustered out most of the Continental Army in 1783. MacLean, *A Rich Harvest* (p. 287), attributes his desertion to his not being paid. Whether or not this is accurate, many soldiers were in fact not getting paid. Clearly the war effort was winding down during this period. The entire 7th Regiment was furloughed on June 12, 1783, and never recalled to service. It was formally dissolved on November 15, 1783.

3 *Concord, Massachusetts: Births, Marriages, and Deaths*; *Vital Records of Lincoln*; Wheeler, "Lincoln," in Hurd, Vol. 2, p. 624; Bond, *Genealogies of the Families of Watertown*, p. 7; MacLean, *A Rich Harvest*, p. 180; Martin, "The Sons of Lincoln," p. 25. Census records show him to be living in Jay, Maine (just upriver from Livermore Falls) in 1800.

WESSON, Daniel
[also WESTON]

Daniel Wesson appears to have served in Capt. John Minot's Company, Colonel Dike's Regiment at Dorchester Heights, evidently during the fall of 1776. While the dates or details of this service have not survived, he was credited with 40-miles travel allowance to and from Dorchester Heights, along with pay for a day of travel, which was allowed in Council on November 30, 1776.[1]

He appears to have enlisted again on December 1, 1776, as a private in Capt. John Hartwell's Company, Col. Nicholas Dike's Regiment. This regiment was raised to serve until March 1, 1777. During January and February, he appears to have been detailed making cartridges at Boston. The service was credited to the town of Lincoln.[2]

He appears to have gone to Weston (possibly for seasonal employment) upon the conclusion of his service in Captain Hartwell's Company, as he was drafted out of the Weston Militia Company, for the urgent support of General Gates in the Northern Department. He served as a private in Capt. George Minot's Company, Col. Samuel Bullard's Regiment, from August 16, 1777, through the surrender of Burgoyne at Saratoga, to November 30, 1777. He was credited with 3 months, 25 days of service, including 11 days for 220 miles of travel home.[3]

On April 1, 1778, he was detached from Captain Farrar's Company, Colonel Brooks's Regiment, to relieve the guards at Cambridge. He served until July 3, 1778 (credited with 3 months, 2 days of service) as a private in Capt. Daniel Harrington's Company, Col. Jonathan Reed's Regiment of Guards.[4]

He served at Tiverton, Rhode Island, from May 18, 1779, to July 1, 1779 (1 month, 17 days), as private in Capt. Lawson Buckminster's Company, Lt. Col. Samuel Pierce's Regiment.[5]

He appears to have served as a private in Joshua Walker's Company, Col. Samuel Denny's Regiment, in October and November 1779. This regiment was detached to serve in the Continental Army for three months at Claverack, but he served only 1 month, 11 days (including 200 miles of travel home), from October 23, 1779, to November 23, 1779.[6]

---

1 *Massachusetts Soldiers and Sailors*, Vol. XVI, p. 882. His widow's pension application in 1839 (Pension Record # W20123) makes no mention of this service.

2 *Massachusetts Soldiers and Sailors*, Vol. XVI, p. 882, Vol. XVII, p. 560. His widow's pension application in 1839 (Pension Record # W20123) makes no mention of this service.

3 *Massachusetts Soldiers and Sailors*, Vol. XVI, pp. 882, 909. Pension Record # W20123 confirms that this is indeed Daniel Wesson (inst.), despite the initial appearance of being a different Daniel Wesson.

   That he shows up as a member of the militia company in Weston is less surprising if one looks at the pattern of service by his brothers. Two brothers responded to the Alarm of April 19th, one in Lincoln's minute company, the other in an artillery company from Weston. At Dorchester Heights in March 1776, one brother was in Lincoln's militia company, another in a Waltham company, and possibly a third brother was in a third company (made up of individuals from a mix of towns). See John Wesson [Jr.] (q.v.), Nathan Weston (q.v.), and Zechariah Weston (q.v.).

4 Ibid. The record suggests that he was probably back in Lincoln at this time, or at least now a member of the militia company in Lincoln rather than in Weston.

5 *Massachusetts Soldiers and Sailors*, Vol. XVI, p. 909; Wheeler, "Lincoln," in Hurd, Vol. 2, p. 624; Pension Record # W20123. The pension declaration claims three months of service at this time.

6 Ibid. Despite the fact that this record is dated at Woburn, and thus appears initially to be a different Daniel Wesson, the author has been unable to find a record of another Daniel Wesson in Woburn or another town. Nor is another Daniel Wesson necessary to account for the various service records for Daniel Wesson that are

He was age 18 when he first served in 1776; the son of Zechariah and Mary (Hoar) Wesson; brother of John Wesson [Jr.] (q.v.), Jonathan Weston (q.v.), Nathan Weston (q.v.), and Zechariah Weston (q.v.); probably nephew of John Hoar (q.v.); cousin of Stephen Wesson, Jr. (q.v.), and probably of Samuel Hoar (q.v.) and Leonard Hoar (q.v.). In 1793, he married Lydia Brown, sister of Daniel Brown (q.v.) and Nathan Brown, Jr. (q.v.), and began operating an inn the same year. He closed the inn the next year. Years later, he became the brother-in-law of Abner Wheeler (q.v.). He died in Lincoln in 1822 at age 64. His burial spot is unknown.[1]

WESSON, John
[also WESTON]

John Wesson of Lincoln was a private in Capt. William Smith's Company of Minute Men from Lincoln, Col. Abijah Peirce's Regiment.[2] Following the engagement at Concord, he served for five days in Cambridge.[3]

On February 4, 1776, he may have been back in service for 1 month, 28 days in Capt. Asahel Wheeler's Company, Col. John Robinson's Regiment, from February 4, 1776, through the departure of the British forces from Boston. It is not certain, however, if this is the same John Wesson.[4]

He was age 24 at the time of the April 19th Alarm; the son of Timothy Wesson and Abigail (Brown) Wesson; brother of Abraham Wesson (q.v.). He died in 1777 at age 27 and is buried in the Meeting House Cemetery behind Bemis Hall.[5]

---

found in *Massachusetts Soldiers and Sailors*. Wheeler, "Lincoln" (in Hurd, Vol. 2, p. 624), credits him with service at "Klaverick on the Hudson" in 1780, which convinces the author that this record probably does indeed apply to Daniel Wesson (inst.), despite the mismatching years, and Wheeler's failure to identify the source record.

Further investigation suggests that the Woburn date is probably less indicative of the geographic region of the soldiers making up the unit than of the residence of Captain Walker. Colonel Denny was from Leicester. Because the troop call was small (only 2,000 men), the regiment appears to have been made up of men from a wider geographic area than was typically the case with larger mobilizations. See the similar record of service by Timothy Stone (q.v.).

Pension Record # W20123 makes no mention of this service. As the pension declaration was filed by his wife, 17 years after his death, and also omits other service by him, the author places little importance on this omission.

1 Wheeler, "Lincoln," in Hurd, Vol. 2, p. 624, *Vital Records of Lincoln*; *Genealogy of the Family of Weston*; MacLean, *A Rich Harvest*, p. 346. Wheeler incorrectly gives the year of his death as 1823. Mary is probably the sister of John Hoar (q.v.). The rationale is as follows: Bond, *Genealogies of the Families of Watertown* (p. 298) and Nourse, *The Hoar Family* (p. 37) both show that John's sister Mary married Zachariah Whittemore, and Bond identifies the source of this information as Lemuel Shattuck. However, this appears to be in error, as no Zachariah Whittemore can be found either in area vital records or in Whittemore, *Genealogy of Several Branches*, nor can Mary Hoar be found in Whittemore. *Concord, Massachusetts: Births, Marriages, and Deaths* records the 1750 marriage of Mary Hoar to Zachariah Wesson, and the 1754 marriage of Elisabeth Hoar to Jacob Whittemore. Bond and Nourse concur with Whittemore (p. 32) in the marriage of John's sister Elizabeth to Jacob Whittemore, and the juxtaposition suggests that Shattuck mistakenly transcribed Zachariah Wesson as Zachariah Whittemore.
2 Coburn, *Muster Rolls*.
3 *Massachusetts Soldiers and Sailors*, Vol. XVI, p. 884.
4 Ibid. This service is attributed to a John Wesson of Concord. It is entirely feasible that John Wesson (inst.) of Lincoln, may have had a Concord connection. However, two other possibilities exist. *Concord, Massachusetts: Births, Marriages, and Deaths* tells us of a John Wesson, son of Joseph and Eunice Wesson, who was age 17 at this time. And the possibility cannot be ruled out that this record could apply to John Wesson [Jr.] (q.v.).
5 *Concord, Massachusetts: Births, Marriages, and Deaths*; *Vital Records of Lincoln*; MacLean, *A Rich Harvest*, p. 257; Biggs, "In Memorium," p. 184.

WESSON, John [Jr.][1]
[also WESTON]

John Wesson [Jr.] of Lincoln was a private in Capt. William Smith's Company of Minute Men from Lincoln, Col. Abijah Peirce's Regiment.[2] Following the engagement at Concord, he served for 20 days in Cambridge.[3]

He may have been back in service on February 4, 1776, for 1 month, 28 days, in Capt. Asahel Wheeler's company, Col. John Robinson's regiment, from February 4, 1776 through the departure of the British forces from Boston. It is uncertain, however, whether this record applies to John Wesson [Jr.] (inst) or to a different John Wesson.[4]

Lincoln historian William Wheeler credits him with service at Point Judith in 1777, and again at Rhode Island in 1779, but corroborating records have not been found.[5]

He was age 19 as a minute man; the son of Zechariah and Mary (Hoar) Wesson; brother of Daniel Wesson (q.v.), Jonathan Weston (q.v.), Nathan Weston (q.v.), and Zechariah Weston (q.v.); probably nephew of John Hoar (q.v.); cousin of Stephen Wesson, Jr. (q.v.), and probably of Samuel Hoar (q.v.) and Leonard Hoar (q.v.). He died in Lincoln in 1809 at age 54.[6]

[He may have served in Captain Smith's Company, Colonel Bigelow's Regiment in the Continental Army from June 1777 to January 10, 1778, but this appears more likely to be a different John Wesson.][7]

[There is a record of a John Wesson serving as a private in Capt. Joseph Winch's Company, Col. Samuel Bullard's Regiment, in the Northern Department, from Sept 15, 1777, to Nov 29, 1777 (credited with 2 months, 26 days of service, including 11 days for 220 miles of

---

1   There is no lineal relationship between John Wesson (q.v.) and John Wesson [Jr.] (inst.). The term Junior in the eighteenth century was sometimes used pragmatically, as today, to distinguish individuals with the same name, but different ages, without necessarily connoting kinship. Because both Johns were minute men, his name appears this way on the Muster Roll. However, as a rule, we should not expect to find this individual identified as Junior elsewhere.

2   Coburn, *Muster Rolls*.

3   *Massachusetts Soldiers and Sailors*, Vol. XVI, p. 884.

4   Ibid. This service is attributed to a John Wesson of Concord. John Wesson [Jr.] (inst.) may well have had a connection with Concord, but this has not been discovered. Other possible identities for this record are John Wesson (q.v.), and another John Wesson (son of Joseph and Eunice Wesson, age 17) of Concord (see *Concord, Massachusetts: Births, Marriages, and Deaths*).

5   Wheeler, "Lincoln," in Hurd, Vol. 2, p. 624. Unfortunately, Wheeler gives no source information.

   Wheeler also credits him with a year in the Continental Army, which appears to be incorrect. There is a record of the town paying John Wesson for "1/3 part of a three year man" in the Continental Army. We cannot say for certain if this was the same John Wesson, but the record clearly indicates that he provided a man for service rather than that he served the time himself. See "Treasurer's Accompts," November 11, 1779.

6   *Vital Records of Lincoln*; *Genealogy of the Family of Weston*; Wheeler, "Lincoln," in Hurd, p. 624; MacLean, *A Rich Harvest*, p. 257. Mary is probably the sister of John Hoar (q.v.) (see note 1, p. 420, for the rationale behind this premise). *Vital Records of Lincoln* contains a death record for a Mr. John Weston, who is otherwise unidentified. As there do not appear to be other likely candidates for this death record, this is deemed to be John Wesson [Jr.] (inst.).

7   Blake, "James Barrett's Returns of Men," p. 477. The John Wesson of this record is unidentified, but there is a parallel enlistment record by John Moors (Blake, "James Barrett's Returns of Men," p. 476) which matches a parallel service record for John Moors of Shirley (*Massachusetts Soldiers and Sailors*, Vol. X, p. 945), suggesting that this record more likely belongs to a John Wesson of Shirley, identified in *Massachusetts Soldiers and Sailors* (Vol. XVI, p. 884) as having enlisted in the Continental Army (date and unit not given). See John More (q.v.), note 1, p. 343.

travel home). The regiment was at or near Saratoga when Burgoyne surrendered, then it marched south, and served briefly in New Jersey before being discharged. This appears, however, also more likely to be a different John Wesson.][1]

[There is also a record of a John Wesson who served at Rhode Island in 1780, as a private in Capt. Walter McFarland's Company, Col. Cyprian How's Regiment, from July 24 to October 30 (credited with 3 months, 10 days of service), but this appears more likely to be a different John Wesson.][2]

WESTON, Jonathan
[also WESSON]

Jonathan Weston is reported to have served at Roxbury in 1778, as a private in Capt. Edward Fuller's Company, Col. William McIntosh's Regiment, for 29 days from March 19 to April 16, 1778, but it is uncertain if the Jonathan Weston of this record is the same individual as Jonathan Weston of Lincoln.[3]

He reportedly served near West Point in 1781. This service was as a corporal in Capt. Isaac Gage's Company, Lt. Col. Joseph Webb's Regiment from September 5, 1781, to December 3, 1781 (credited with 3 months, 10 days of service, including 11 days for 220 miles of travel from camp). The company was detached from Colonel Dana's Regiment. Again, it is uncertain if the Jonathan Weston of this record is the same individual as Jonathan Weston of Lincoln.[4]

He was age 17 when (if) he served at Roxbury; the son of Zechariah and Mary (Hoar) Wesson; brother of Daniel Wesson (q.v.), John Wesson [Jr.] (q.v.), Nathan Weston (q.v.), and Zechariah Weston (q.v.); probably nephew of John Hoar (q.v.); cousin of Stephen Wesson, Jr. (q.v.), and probably of Samuel Hoar (q.v.) and Leonard Hoar (q.v.). Years later, he became the brother-in-law of Abner Wheeler (q.v.). No further information about him has been found.[5]

---

1 *Massachusetts Soldiers and Sailors*, Vol. XVI, p. 884. The John Wesson of this record is unidentified, but Capt. Joseph Winch was from Framingham (part of the 5th Middlesex militia district that included Hopkinton) suggesting that this record more likely belongs to a John Wesson of Hopkinton (age 46 during this service). See *Massachusetts Soldiers and Sailors*, Vol. XVII, p. 590, *Vital Records of Hopkinton*.

2 *Massachusetts Soldiers and Sailors*, Vol. XVI, p. 884. Capt. Walter McFarland was from Hopkinton, suggesting that this record more likely belongs to a John Wesson of Hopkinton (age 49 during this service) than to John Wesson of Lincoln. See *Vital Records of Hopkinton*.

3 Wheeler, "Lincoln," in Hurd, Vol. 2, p. 624; *Massachusetts Soldiers and Sailors*, Vol. XVI, p. 922. Wheeler credits him with service at Roxbury in 1778. If Wheeler is correct, then this must be the unit and dates in which he served. Beyond Wheeler's assertion, however, there is little else to connect the "Jonathan Westson" in this record to Lincoln. This record is a roll dated Newton (i.e., Captain Fuller's residence, not necessarily the proximal area of the soldiers' residences). This is not inconsistent with the application of this record to Jonathan Wesson (inst.) of Lincoln. However, as Wheeler cites no sources, the author cannot confirm Wheeler's assertion.

4 Wheeler, "Lincoln," in Hurd, Vol. 2, p. 624; *Massachusetts Soldiers and Sailors*, Vol. XVI, p. 916. Wheeler credits him with service near West Point in 1781. Beyond Wheeler's assertion, however, there is little evidence to connect this service record to Jonathan Weston of Lincoln. As Wheeler cites no sources, the author cannot confirm Wheeler's assertion. Colonel Dana is unidentified, but he may be Col. Stephen Dana of Cambridge; Jonathan Weston may have been living and working outside of Lincoln at the time and a member of Colonel Dana's Militia Regiment.

5 *Vital Records of Lincoln*; Wheeler, "Lincoln," in Hurd, Vol. 2, p. 624. Mary is probably the sister of John Hoar (q.v.) (see note 1, p. 420, for the rationale behind this premise).

[He may have served for three days at Cambridge in expectation of a British landing of troops at Boston, from September 2, 1778, to September 6, 1778, in Capt. Abraham Peirce's Waltham Company, Col. Samuel Thatcher's Regiment.[1] Or, he may have served in the Hudson Valley, from August 1, 1778, to January 29, 1779, as a private in Capt. Caleb Moulton's Company (Lt. Eliphalet Hastings's Company after October 11, 1778), Col. Thomas Poor's Regiment (credited with 6 months, 9 days of service, including 11 days for 220 miles of travel home).[2] It is not clear if either of these records applies to Jonathan Weston of Lincoln.][3]

WESTON, Nathan
[also WESSON]

Nathan Weston served as a private in Capt. Israel Whitemore's Artillery Company in Weston, which marched on the Alarm of April 19th. He served for three days.[4]

Subsequently, he served as quartermaster sergeant in Capt. Nathan Fuller's Company in Cambridge. It is likely that he may have been a participant in the Battle of Bunker Hill, as Captain Fuller's Company was part of Col. Thomas Gardner's 37th Regiment, and it was involved in that fight. However, it is unknown if he was in service as early as mid-June, when the battle was fought. The record of this service is dated October 6, 1775, after command of the regiment had passed to Lt. Col. William Bond (following Colonel Gardner's death from wounds received in the battle). He was paid by the town of Lincoln for this service.[5]

He served as a sergeant in Capt. John Hartwell's Militia Company from Lincoln, Col. Eleazer Brooks's 3rd Middlesex County Regiment, which marched from Lincoln to fortify Dorchester Heights on March 4, 1776. The unit was discharged five days later, on March 9, after the threat of a British assault on the fortifications had subsided, and General Howe

---

1 *Massachusetts Soldiers and Sailors*, Vol. XVI, pp. 885, 914. He appears concurrently as a private on the roll of Capt. John Walton's Company, from September 4 to September 11, with the words "No Duty" next to his name. However, an amount due for four days of service is credited to him, and Captain Peirce is reported as receiving wages for him and three others.
2 *Massachusetts Soldiers and Sailors*, Vol. XVI, p. 885. The record finds him at Fort Clinton in September, King's Ferry in December, and North River (all in New York) from where he was discharged in January.
3 Insufficient information has been found to identify the individuals who provided these services.
   Other records found in *Massachusetts Soldiers and Sailors* (Vol. XVI, pp. 678, 884–885, 886, 916) for service by Jonathan Weston (i.e., April 19th, Cambridge 1775, White Plains 1776, Saratoga 1777, Continental Army 1777, Cambridge 1778, Rhode Island 1778) are identifiable as either Jonathan Wesson from Sudbury or Jonathan Weston of Reading (through his Pension Record # S29535 and/or identical service by his brother Nathaniel) and are clearly not for service by Jonathan Wesson (inst.).
4 *Massachusetts Soldiers and Sailors*, Vol. XVI, p. 918. This record lists him as Nathan Weston of Weston.
5 *Massachusetts Soldiers and Sailors*, Vol. XVI, p. 917; "Treasurer's Accompts," June 15, 1779. The *Massachusetts Soldiers and Sailors* record lists him as being from Lincoln, but notes that the record also indicates he was from Weston. Wheeler, "Lincoln" (in Hurd, Vol. 2, p. 624), says he was "quartermaster's sergeant in the regiment commanded by Col. Thomas Gardner, who was mortally wounded in the battle of Bunker Hill, and was quartermaster in the same regiment, afterwards known as Lieut.-Col. William Bond's regiment." His sources are unidentified, but the careful (and uncharacteristic) distinctions he makes may be revealing. If Nathan Weston served under Colonel Gardner (who succumbed to his wounds 16 days after the battle), then we can reasonably identify him as a participant in the battle.

had begun preparations to evacuate Boston. He was paid for this service the following September.[1]

He was age 21 at the time of the Alarm of April 19th; the son of Zechariah and Mary (Hoar) Wesson; brother of Daniel Wesson (q.v.), Jonathan Weston (q.v.), John Wesson [Jr.] (q.v.), and Zechariah Weston (q.v.); brother-in-law of Abner Wheeler (q.v.); probably nephew of John Hoar (q.v.); cousin of Stephen Wesson, Jr. (q.v.) and probably of Samuel Hoar (q.v.) and Leonard Hoar (q.v.). In 1783, he married Abigail Fox, who died four years later at age 31. The following year, in 1788, he married her sister, Nancy Fox (also known as Anna), who died in 1800 at age 36. Years later, he became the brother-in-law of Abner Wheeler (q.v.). Nathan Weston died in Lincoln in 1825 at age 72. He and Abigail and Anna are all buried in the Meeting House Cemetery behind Bemis Hall.[2]

WESTON, Peter

Peter Weston was recruited and paid a bounty in 1782 to serve a three-year term in the Continental Army. His service was credited to the town of Lincoln, but otherwise the details of this service are unknown.[3]

His identity has not been discovered.[4]

WESSON, Richard
[also WESTON]

Richard Wesson of Lincoln served as a matross in the 1st Company of Col. Thomas Craft's Artillery Regiment, from August 1, 1776, to May 8, 1777 (9 months, 7 days of service), in

---

1 *Massachusetts Soldiers and Sailors*, Vol. XVI, pp. 880, 886, 917.

  Wheeler, "Lincoln" (in Hurd, Vol. 2, p. 624), notes, also, that he was paid for one-third of a three-year campaign in the Continental Army, but the implication that he served in the Continental Army is incorrect. The record actually indicates otherwise. The town paid Nathan Wesson for providing a man for Continental service (see "Treasurer's Accompts," June 15, 1779), not for undertaking the Continental service himself. The "Treasurer's Accompts" make this distinction quite clearly. Whether the one-third part represents an installment, or the length of time the man served, or part of a consortium that provided the man, and who actually provided the service, are all undetermined.

  Other records found in *Massachusetts Soldiers and Sailors* (Vol. XVI, pp. 678, 886) for service by a Nathaniel Wesson in Capt. Abraham Foster's Company, Col. Samuel Bullard's Regiment at Saratoga in 1777, and in Capt. Nathaniel Cowdry's Company, Col. Jacob Gerrish's Regiment of Guards at Winter Hill in July 1778, are identifiable as the brother of Jonathan Wesson of Reading and are clearly not service by Nathan Weston (inst.) (see Jonathan Weston (q.v.); Baldwin, *Vital Records of Reading*).

2 Wheeler, "Lincoln," in Hurd, Vol. 2, p. 624; *Vital Records of Lincoln*; *Genealogy of the Family of Weston*; Biggs, "In Memorium," p. 185. *Vital Records of Lincoln* lists his mother's name as "Moly." She was probably the sister of John Hoar (q.v.) (see note 1, p. 420, for the derivation of this premise). *Vital Records of Lincoln* lists Nathan's age at the time of his death as 74, as does his headstone, but this does not conform with his birth date as recorded in *Vital Records of Lincoln*.

3 *Massachusetts Soldiers and Sailors*, Vol. XVI, p. 918. The bounty was paid in Lincoln by Col. Abijah Peirce (q.v.), chairman of Class 3 for the town of Lincoln. For a brief overview of the system of economic classes, see MacLean, *A Rich Harvest* (p. 296).

4 In the absence of any record of him in the Vital Records of Lincoln, Concord, Sudbury, Weston, or Lexington, it is not possible to determine whether or not he may have been in some way related to other members of the Wesson (or Weston) family who, at that time, resided in Lincoln and the surrounding area.

  A Peter Wesson appears in *Vital Records of Groton*, born in 1757, the son of Ephraim and Lydia Wesson. No further record of him has been found, so there is no evidence that would connect him with Lincoln. He would have turned age 25 in 1782.

Boston. This company was commanded by Capt. James Swan through November 1776, and thereafter by Capt. Philip Marett. However, an abstract for advanced pay, sworn to at Boston on October 22, 1776, lists him as being in Capt. Joseph Balch's Company.[1]

He appears to have been recruited out of the artillery company for service in the Continental Army. He enlisted for a three-year term and was credited with service from April 25, 1777, as a private in Capt. Edmund Munroe's Company, Col. Timothy Bigelow's 15th Regiment. He served until August 20, 1777, when he is reported as deceased.[2]

His identity is undetermined. He does not show up in the Vital Records of Lincoln or the surrounding towns.

WESSON, Stephen, Jr.
[also WESTON]

Stephen Wesson, Jr., was detached from Capt. Samuel Farrar, Jr.'s Lincoln Company of Militia, Colonel Brooks's Regiment, on April 1, 1778, to relieve the guards at Cambridge. He served as a private in Capt. Daniel Harrington's Company, Col. Jonathan Reed's Regiment of Guards at Cambridge from April 2, 1778, until July 3, 1778 (credited with 3 months, 2 days of service). This service was guarding the so called "Convention Army," the British and German troops surrendered by Burgoyne at Saratoga.[3]

He may have served previously at Boston in 1776 and 1777, but this is uncertain.[4]

He was age 17 on guard duty in 1778; son of Stephen Jr. and Lydia (Billing) Wesson; first cousin of Abel Billing (q.v.), and Solomon Billing (q.v.), Zechariah Weston (q.v.), Nathan Weston (q.v.), John Wesson [Jr.] (q.v.), Daniel Wesson (q.v.), and Jonathan Weston

---

1 *Massachusetts Soldiers and Sailors*, Vol. XVI, pp. 886, 918. Note that this service seems to match the town's payment to widow Lydia Wesson "for service at Boston in the years 1776 and 1777" ("Treasurer's Accompts," June 15, 1779). Although Richard's identity is unknown, perhaps he could be an unidentified slave of Stephen and Lydia Wesson (see Stephen Wesson, Jr. (q.v.), note 4, below).

2 *Massachusetts Soldiers and Sailors*, Vol. XVI, p. 886; Blake, "James Barrett's Returns of Men," p. 474. His name shows up again on a return dated February 2, 1778, but this appears to be administrative paperwork, rather than any indication that he survived beyond his reported death on August 20, 1777.

3 *Massachusetts Soldiers and Sailors*, Vol. XVI, pp. 887, 920; "Treasurer's Accompts," June 15, 1779. The town paid his mother, the widow Lydia Wesson, for this service.

4 "Treasurer's Accompts," June 15, 1779. The town paid his mother, the widow Lydia Wesson for this service, but he was underage in 1776. An equally likely possibility is that the Boston stint(s) may have been served by an unknown slave. Perhaps the payment was for the Boston service of Richard Wesson (q.v.), who remains unidentified, but could possibly have been such an unidentified slave.

There were at least four generations of Stephen Wessons. Within our frame of reference, this individual is number three. Grandfather Stephen (#1) lived into his 100th year, before dying in 1789. Father Stephen (#2, and husband of Lydia) was known as Stephen Jr. until his death in May 1776, in his 56th year. Stephen (inst.), #3, became Stephen Jr. upon the death of his father. He was age 15 at the time. He carried the designation "Jr." until Stephen #1 died 13 years later, and the designation passed to his son, Stephen #4 (born in 1786). Thus within a reasonably short period of time, three different individuals were known as Stephen Wesson, Jr. For clarity, they will be identified herein as Stephen #2, #3, and #4.

As to who served at Boston in 1776 and 1777, Stephen #2 could have served in 1776, if the service occurred before his death in May 1776, but at age 55, this is probably unlikely. Furthermore, the payment transaction suggests (consistent with similar notations) that this service probably occurred from December 1776 until March 1, 1777. Stephen #3 may have served such a stint, but as he was still underage until after March 1, 1777, we are obliged to look for alternatives before we can conclude in the affirmative. Stephen #3 did have six older siblings, but they were all sisters. His only surviving brother was little more than a toddler in 1776. Therefore, underage in 1776 or not, Stephen #3 is the only family member (other than possibly his father in a separate (q.v.). He married Susanna Whitney of Stow in 1784. He was a cordwainer by trade, which he plied from a small shop he erected on land belonging to Zechariah Weston (probably his uncle), until he sold the building to Daniel Wesson (q.v.) in 1792. He appears to have moved to Winchendon at about this point in time. His death is recorded in Winchendon in 1841, having just turned 80. He is buried in the Old Centre Burial Ground.[1]

WESTON, Zechariah
[also WESSON, also Zachariah]

Zechariah Weston served as a private in Capt. Abraham Peirce's Waltham Company, Col. Samuel Thatcher's Regiment, which marched on March 4, 1776, on orders from General Washington as part of the mobilization to fortify Dorchester Heights. The unit was discharged five days later, on March 8, after the threat of a British assault on Dorchester Heights had subsided, and General Howe had begun preparations to evacuate Boston.[2]

He was paid by the town of Lincoln for service at Dorchester again in 1777, and for service at Cambridge in 1778, and for a year of service in the Continental Army.[3]

He was paid by the town of Lincoln for service at Roxbury in 1779. This appears to have been as a private in Capt. Abner Crane's Company, from February 6 to May 4, 1779 (credited with 2 months, 28 days of service), apparently on guard duty at Boston.[4]

He may have been recruited for a Penobscot expedition in 1779. A Zachariah Weston appears in Capt. Alexander McLellan's Company, Col. Jonathan Mitchell's Regiment, from July 7 to September 25, 1779 (credited with 2 months, 18 days of service), but it is uncertain if this is the same individual.[5]

He was born in Lincoln; probably age 24 when he marched to Dorchester Heights; the son of Zechariah and Mary (Hoar) Wesson; brother of Daniel Wesson (q.v.), Jonathan Weston (q.v.), John Wesson [Jr.] (q.v.), and Nathan Weston (q.v.); probably nephew of John Hoar (q.v.); cousin of Stephen Wesson, Jr. (q.v.), and probably of Samuel Hoar (q.v.)

1776 stint) who could have served. See apparently similar service at Dorchester and Boston in 1776–1777 by his cousin, Daniel Wesson (q.v.).

MacLean, *A Rich Harvest* (p. 220) lists Stephen Jr. as a slaveholder. Presumably, he means Stephen #2. While we do not know if he had any male slaves of service age, this supports the possibility that his widow might have been paid for the service of such an unknown slave (perhaps Richard Wesson (q.v.)).

1 *Vital Records of Lincoln*; *Vital Records of Stow*; *Concord, Massachusetts: Births, Marriages, and Deaths*; *Vital Records of Winchendon*; MacLean, *A Rich Harvest*, p. 168; Crane, *Historic Homes of Worcester County*, Vol. II, p. 98; "Find A Grave." The baptisms of two children (1786 and 1790) are recorded in Lincoln. In the deed for the sale of his shop, dated March 31, 1792, he identifies its location as near his residence, evidence that he was still living in Lincoln (see Weston deed to Weston (1792)) Both he and Susanna appear as "Weston" in their death records (Susanna is listed as "Susan W.").

2 *Massachusetts Soldiers and Sailors*, Vol. XVI, p. 921.

3 "Treasurer's Accompts," June 15, 1779. The date of the Continental service is not recorded.

4 "Treasurer's Accompts," June 15, 1779; *Massachusetts Soldiers and Sailors*, Vol. XVI, p. 921.

5 *Massachusetts Soldiers and Sailors*, Vol. XVI, p. 921.
Wheeler, "Lincoln" (in Hurd, Vol. 2, p. 624), credits him with additional service at Rhode Island in 1780, but this appears to be doubtful. *Massachusetts Soldiers and Sailors* contains a record of a Zachariah Weston serving for nine days on a Rhode Island alarm, from August 1 through August 9, 1780, in Capt. Jonah Washburn's Company, Col. Ebenezer White's Regiment. However, the roll is dated at Middleborough, and the same individual had previously answered two different alarms at Dartmouth in May and September 1778 (also, evidently from Middleborough). As there does not appear to be any reason to connect Zechariah Weston (inst.) to Middleborough, this is likely a different Zachariah Weston.

and Leonard Hoar (q.v.). In 1777, he married Mary (also known as Polly) Fisk of Sudbury, five months before the birth of their first child. He was living in Waltham. He appears after the war to have attained the rank of captain, probably in Lincoln's or Waltham's militia company. In 1791, he became the father-in-law of Joseph Nixon (q.v.), and years later the brother-in-law of Abner Wheeler (q.v.). He died in Lincoln in 1833 at age 81. He is buried in the Meeting House Cemetery behind Bemis Hall.[1]

WHEAT, Benjamin

Benjamin Wheat enlisted in the Massachusetts Provincial Army at Cambridge on May 4, 1775, and served for eight months as a private in Capt. Seth Murray's Company, Col. Benjamin Ruggles Woodbridge's 25th Regiment. He is presumed to have participated with his regiment at the Battle of Bunker Hill on June 17. He received advance pay for his enlistment on June 22, and a bounty coat was ordered for him on October 25. His enlistment expired at the end of December 1775.[2]

Despite being left off of a roll of men fit to bear arms in 1777, he was drafted on September 23, 1777, during a second major mobilization of militia forces to reinforce the Northern Army in its pending showdown with British General Burgoyne's forces. He served for 23 days as a private in Capt. Thomas French's Company, Col. David Wells's Regiment, before his discharge on October 18, immediately following the surrender of General Burgoyne at Saratoga.[3]

By this time, it appears that his arms had become palsied, and he served no further military duty in the Revolutionary War.[4]

He was age 32 during his Cambridge service; the son of John and Grace (Brown) Wheat; brother of Joseph Wheat (q.v.). His mother had died when he was age 19, and a year and a half later, in 1764, his father married Abigail Smith, the mother of Jesse Smith (q.v.). He married Sarah Wright of Westford in 1766.[5]

That same year, he went to New Ipswich, New Hampshire, where he lived and worked as a housewright until 1771, when he and Sarah returned to Westford. In 1773, he moved onto a 65-acre parcel in Conway, purchased for him by his father, where he remained until 1795. Then he moved his family to Phelps, New York, where he died in 1817 at age 74. He is buried at Orleans, New York.[6]

---

1 Wheeler, "Lincoln," in Hurd, Vol. 2, p. 624; *Vital Records of Lincoln*; *Genealogy of the Family of Weston*; *Vital Records of Sudbury*; *Vital Records of Waltham*; Biggs, "In Memorium," p. 185. His death record and his headstone both indicate that he died at age 83. This appears to be inconsistent with the apparent date of his birth as found in *Vital Records of Lincoln* and the *Genealogy of the Family of Weston*. The record is actually a baptism record, but the inconsistency goes away only if one assumes that he was not baptized as an infant. As there is no evidence to support such an assumption from an examination of the birth and baptism records of his siblings, his baptism date is deemed to be a close approximation of his birth date, and therefore the record of his age at the time of his death appears to be overstated by two years. His mother was probably the sister of John Hoar (q.v.) (see note 1, p. 420, for the derivation of this premise).

He and Polly appear to have remained in Waltham at least through 1793, when the birth of their fifth child was recorded. No children are recorded in Lincoln.

2 *Massachusetts Soldiers and Sailors*, Vol. XVI, p. 950.
3 *Massachusetts Soldiers and Sailors*, Vol. XVI, p. 950; Wheat and Scranton, *Wheat Genealogy*, p. 56.
4 Ibid.
5 *Vital Records of Lincoln*; *Concord, Massachusetts: Births, Marriages, and Deaths*; Wheat and Scranton, *Wheat Genealogy*, p. 56.
6 Wheat and Scranton, *Wheat Genealogy*, pp. 15, 55–56.

Families Divided

To most modern Americans, it was the Civil War that split families apart. But for many Lincoln families, the Revolutionary War was equally destructive of family cohesiveness. The sons of Joseph Adams (q.v., Chapter 12) appear to have fought on both sides of the conflict. Brothers Ebenezer and Zaccheus Cutler (q.v., Chapter 11) took up arms for the Crown, while their father remained a patriotic citizen of the town. William Lawrence, Jr. (q.v.) served in the patriot army, while his sister awaited an opportunity to join her Loyalist husband in England, and their father—the town's pastor—faced outspoken criticism for his suspected Tory sympathies. Daniel and Nathan Brown (q.v.) served multiple stints in the service of their country before Daniel may have fled to the opposite side. But nowhere are family divisions more vividly documented than in the Wheat family.

John Wheat raised seven children (plus five step-children) on a large farm where the towns of Lincoln, Concord, and Bedford come together, portions of the farm having been inherited from earlier generations. His two sons, Benjamin and Joseph, and stepson Jesse Smith were all active in supporting the Provincial war effort. Joseph Wheat (q.v.) was a minute man at Concord. He and his brother, Benjamin (q.v.), both joined the Massachusetts Provincial Army at Cambridge, later serving both during the siege of Boston and in support of the Continental Army. Jesse Smith (q.v.) served for much of the war, and he became a member of General Washington's Life Guard.

For two of John Wheat's daughters, however, it was a different story. Sisters Betty and Mary Wheat had married brothers John and Robert Semple, Boston merchants who remained loyal to the Crown. In 1774, John Semple expressed support for Royal authority in a farewell letter to Governor Hutchinson. When the war broke out, he joined a Loyalist militia in Boston. John and Robert were both well-wishers to General Gage in October 1775, when he was recalled to England.

Betty's and Mary's sentiments naturally fell with their husbands. When the British evacuated Boston in 1776, Mary and Robert (evidently with a child), and John (presumably with Betty, but this detail has been lost) were among the refugees that left for Halifax with the troops. About four months later, en route from Halifax to New York aboard the ship *Peggy*, Mary and Robert and John were captured and taken to Marblehead, then imprisoned in Boston. Details of their release are unknown, but in 1778 John and Robert were officially proscribed and banished, as having "left this state…and joined the enemies thereof…manifesting an inimical disposition to the said states, and a design, to aid and abet the enemies thereof in their wicked purposes.…"

The following year, in 1779, John Wheat made out his will, amply providing for his sons and daughters. He made two notable exceptions. "To my daughter Betty Semple," he wrote, "only six shillings, because she has left this state and gone as a friend to the enemies of this continent, to be paid only on condition that she return a friend to America." And, "To my daughter Mary Semple six shillings for she has gone from this state an enemy to the country."

▶

> What became of Betty and Mary is unknown. Despite his 1778 banishment, John Semple is reported to have returned and died in Marlborough in 1793. Other than that, no record has been found to suggest any sort of reconciliation.
>
> The Wheats were only one of many families in and outside of Lincoln to be torn apart by divided loyalties during the Revolution. Many years later, the Civil War would divide families again, making an indelible imprint on the American consciousness. But by no means was the Civil War the first war in which American families had experienced such tribulations.
>
> [Wheat and Scranton, *Wheat Genealogy*, pp. 14–17; Sabine, *The American Loyalists*, Vol. 2, pp. 274, 451; Stark, *The Loyalists of Massachusetts*, pp. 125, 132, 135, 138; Siebert, "Loyalist Troops," p. 119; Muster Roll of the 5th Company of Associators (1775); *Massachusetts Soldiers and Sailors*, Vol. XVI, pp. 950–951.]

WHEAT, Joseph
[also WHEET]

Joseph Wheat was a private in Capt. William Smith's Company of Minute Men from Lincoln, Col. Abijah Peirce's Regiment.[1] Following the engagement at Concord, he served for 20 days in Cambridge.[2] He was reimbursed by the town for two knapsacks as a minute man.[3]

Following his service as a minute man, he enlisted in the rapidly organizing Massachusetts Provincial Army at Cambridge in 1775. The details of this service are unknown, but he was paid for this service by the town of Lincoln.[4]

Subsequently, he served as a private in Capt. John Hartwell's Militia Company from Lincoln, Col. Eleazer Brooks's 3rd Middlesex County Regiment, which marched from Lincoln to fortify Dorchester Heights on March 4, 1776. The unit was discharged five days later, on March 9, after the threat of a British assault on the fortifications had subsided, and General Howe had begun preparations to evacuate Boston.[5]

He served for nine months in the Continental Army, for which he was paid by the town of Lincoln. The dates and details of this service are unknown.[6]

He was age 29 as a minute man; the son of John and Grace (Brown) Wheat; brother of Benjamin Wheat (q.v.). His mother died when he was age 17, and a year and a half later, in 1764, his father married Abigail Smith, the mother of Jesse Smith (q.v.). In 1770, he married Mary Smith, probably a sister of Jesse Smith. Thus, he was both brother-in-law and step-brother of Jesse Smith. In 1786, he sold the farm to Abner Wheeler (q.v.) and settled

---

1 Coburn, *Muster Rolls*.
2 *Massachusetts Soldiers and Sailors*, Vol. XVI, p. 1017.
3 "Treasurer's Accompts," November 21, 1776.
4 "Treasurer's Accompts," June 10, 1779.
5 *Massachusetts Soldiers and Sailors*, Vol. XVI, p. 951.
6 "Treasurer's Accompts," June 10, 1779.

as a husbandman in Hollis, New Hampshire, for six years before moving on to an unknown location.[1]

WHEELER, Abner

Abner Wheeler enlisted for eight months of service, probably at Cambridge in 1775, but the details have not survived.

Subsequently, he served at Ticonderoga in 1776.[2]

He was age 29 during his probable service at Cambridge in 1775; probably age 30 at Ticonderoga. He was the son of Benjamin and Rebekah (Lee) Wheeler of Concord. He had been married to Elizabeth Hunt since 1769. Elizabeth died in March 1811, and before the year was out, he married Lucy Weston, 55-year-old spinster sister of Zechariah Weston (q.v.), Nathan Weston (q.v.), John Wesson [Jr.] (q.v.), Daniel Wesson (q.v.), and Jonathan Weston (q.v.). He died in Lincoln in 1820, at age 74, and is buried in the Meeting House cemetery behind Bemis Hall.

He appears to have grown up in Concord on a farm abutting Lincoln's north border, and through the years, he appears to have maintained connections in both towns. His marriage record in 1769 identifies both Elizabeth and him as residents of Lincoln, but this must have been a temporary situation. All of their children are recorded in Concord, not Lincoln, and there is nothing to suggest that his military service was credited to Lincoln. Lincoln historian Jack MacLean implies that he continued to live on the Concord side of the border until he bought the 70-acre Wheat farm (on Virginia Road, north of the Bay Road) in 1786. However, even the two children who were born after his purchase of the Wheat farm (and apparent move to Lincoln) are recorded only in Concord. He appears to have made a prosperous living as a housewright, a trade which undoubtedly he plied in both towns.[3]

---

1 *Vital Records of Lincoln*; *Concord, Massachusetts: Births, Marriages, and Deaths*; Wheat and Scranton, *Wheat Genealogy*, p. 57.

2 *Massachusetts Soldiers and Sailors*, Vol. XVI, p. 958. There is no record of his being in service on April 19th. Instead, an apocryphal old tale in the *Concord Freeman*, January 22, 1880, relates that prior to April 19, 1775, "Mr. Abner Wheeler used [to] often brag of what he would do if the British came, but the old colored woman [from a nearby house, while out spreading the word that night that the Regulars were coming,] on her way to give warning, found him hiding in the woods." Quoted in MacLean "Hot Topics."

3 *Concord, Massachusetts: Births, Marriages, and Deaths*; *Vital Records of Lincoln*; MacLean, *A Rich Harvest*, pp. 180, 353–357; Biggs, "In Memorium," p. 186; *Genealogy of the Family of Weston*. His marriage to Elizabeth is recorded in both Concord and Lincoln. *Vital Records of Lincoln* is silent about their residency, which generally would imply they were living in Lincoln. *Concord, Massachusetts: Births, Marriages, and Deaths* is more explicit, identifying them as "both of Lincoln."

The *Genealogy of the Family of Weston* contains a curious notation suggesting that Mary Weston may have been the first wife of Abner Wheeler. Not only has no record of this been found, but also the record of his marriage to Elizabeth would appear to preclude this. In addition, Mary Weston is identified in another document (see below) as a spinster in 1807.

Abner Wheeler (with Daniel Brooks) held a power of attorney for "Mary Weston and Lucy Weston, spinsters," executed in 1807 (see Weston Indenture and Power of Attorney). When Elizabeth died 4½ years later, he married Lucy.

His farm had grown to 130 acres, with a 14-room house, wood shed, two barns, a two-story joiner's shop, and other outbuildings by the time he died (see MacLean, "Hot Topics"). *Vital Records of Lincoln* misstates the year of his death as 1830, evidently a transcription error.

WHEELER, Edmond
[also Edmund]

Edmond Wheeler served at Cambridge in 1776, and at Ticonderoga in 1776, the details of which have not survived. He was paid by the town of Lincoln for this service.[1]

He was age 45 at Cambridge and Ticonderoga; the son of Thomas and Mary (Munroe) Wheeler. He had been married to Eunice Munroe since 1756. He was the uncle of John Wheeler (q.v.), Abel Flint (q.v.), Ephraim Flint (q.v.), and John Flint (q.v.); after the war he became the father-in-law of Leonard Hoar (q.v.). Previous to the war, he had served as ensign in the town's militia company. He was also active as a town leader, including multiple terms as Treasurer and Selectman before and after the war. He died in 1805 at age 74 and is buried in the old Precinct Burial Ground on Lexington Road.[2]

WHEELER, Elisha
[also WHELER, WHELOR]

Elisha Wheeler of Sudbury responded to the April 19th alarm, and marched to Concord as a private in Capt. John Nixon's Company of Minute Men, Col. Abijah Peirce's Regiment. He served for 24 days.[3]

---

1 "Treasurer's Accompts," November 11, 1779. Wheeler, "Lincoln" (in Hurd, Vol. 2, p. 624), reports that he served at Cambridge in 1775, but the transaction clearly reads 1776.

   Wheeler also credits him with one-third of a three-year campaign in the Continental Army, but the record actually indicates otherwise. The "Treasurer's Accompts" make a careful distinction between serving in the Continental Army, and finding a person to serve in one's stead. In both cases, the town paid, but the records clearly delineate which was the case. In this case, the town paid Ens. Edmond Wheeler for providing a man for Continental service, not for undertaking the Continental service himself. Crane, *Historic Homes of Worcester County* (Vol. IV, p. 401), echoes Wheeler's error.

2 *Vital Records of Lincoln*; *Concord, Massachusetts: Births, Marriages, and Deaths*; MacLean, *A Rich Harvest*, pp. 60, 134, 137, 230, 301; Biggs, "In Memorium," p. 198. Eunice Munroe was the sister of Lt. Benjamin Munroe, Jr. See Benjamin Munroe (q.v.). Eunice Wheeler, daughter of Edmond and Eunice, married Leonard Hoar (q.v.) in 1785 (see Wheeler, "The Wheelers in Heretic Court," p. 5).

   Wheeler, "The Wheelers in Heretic Court" (p. 3) relates the following story of Edmond Wheeler: that he was a Selectman, and therefore also effectively a member of the board of health, and that upon learning that five dead British soldiers were lying by the roadside on April 20, 1775, he went with his oxcart to the North Road, picked up the bodies, and buried them in the town cemetery. His daughter Eunice (age 11) thought that it was a disgrace for the bodies to be buried without anyone to mourn them, so she went with him, a total distance of about five miles.

   This is virtually identical to the widely circulated Mary Hartwell story. The fact that it appears to have originated well after the appearance of the Mary Hartwell story raises a question about its authenticity. On the other hand, Don Hafner points out in a private communication, that the Mary Hartwell story does mention unidentified others manning the cart (in addition to Ephraim Hartwell), and thus that the stories are not mutually incompatible. Mary Hartwell's account as later recorded made no mention of an 11-year-old compatriot.

   Edmond Wheeler appears to have served as Selectman in 1773 and 1774, but not 1775 (see MacLean, *A Rich Harvest*, p. 134).

3 *Massachusetts Soldiers and Sailors*, Vol. XVI, p. 966. In this record, his name appears as "Eleshai," obviously a corruption of Elisha. Interestingly, there is another record that shows Elisha Wheeler serving on the Alarm of April 19th, as a lieutenant in Capt. Moses Stone's Company of Sudbury Militia, Col. Ezekiel How's Regiment, which marched to "headquarters." In this record, he served two days and is reported as having left the company "without a proper dismission." This second record is logically his father, who was almost certainly on the high side of age 45 at the time. Wheeler, *Genealogical History of the Wheeler Family* (p. 356), reports that

He was age 25 at the time of the April 19th Alarm; the son of Elisha and Mary (Loring) Whelor of Sudbury. He had married Sarah Goodenow in 1773. Tragically, a few months after the death of their first son, Sarah died (evidently of complications following the birth of a second child) in 1775. Subsequently, he married Polly Adams (also known as Mary) of Lincoln in 1779. They appear to have lived in Sudbury at least through 1783, but at some point in time thereafter, they moved to Lincoln. Polly (Mary) died in childbirth in 1791, and he died in 1794 at age 43; both are buried in the Meeting House Cemetery behind Bemis Hall.[1]

[There may be a remote possibility that he may also have served at Ticonderoga in 1776 and for 18 months in the Continental Army.][2]

WHEELER, Enos

Enos Wheeler was a private in Capt. William Smith's Company of Minute Men from Lincoln, Col. Abijah Peirce's Regiment.[3] Following the engagement at Concord, he served for two days.[4]

Subsequently, he served as a private in Capt. John Hartwell's Company of Militia from Lincoln, Col. Eleazer Brooks's 3rd Middlesex County Regiment, which marched from Lincoln to fortify Dorchester Heights on March 4, 1776. The unit was discharged five days later, on March 9, after the threat of a British assault on the fortifications had subsided, and General Howe had begun preparations to evacuate Boston.[5]

He served at New York in 1776 and 1777, probably in Colonel Thatcher's Regiment at Woodbridge, and at Cambridge in 1777 and 1778. The Cambridge service was probably served guarding the British and/or German troops surrendered by Burgoyne at Saratoga. In both cases, he was paid by the town for his service.[6]

---

in addition to Elisha Wheeler (inst.), his father and five brothers turned out on the Alarm of April 19th, and that his father had his horse shot out from under him in the fight.

"Headquarters" is an unusual designation within the context of April 19th records. Certainly, they marched to Cambridge, where most of the April 19th respondents ended up, and which became the center of operations for the spontaneous, rapidly organizing Massachusetts Provincial Army.

1 *Vital Records of Sudbury*; *Vital Records of Lincoln*; Farrar, "Adams Genealogy," p. 2; Wheeler, *Genealogical History of the Wheeler Family*, p. 356; Biggs, "In Memorium," p. 185. Polly (Mary) was the daughter of Captain Joseph and Mary Adams. See Joseph Adams (q.v., Chapter 12). A typographical error in *Vital Records of Sudbury* erroneously postdates his second marriage by 20 years. His first three children with Polly (in 1780, 1781, and 1783) were recorded in Sudbury but not Lincoln. Two more (in 1786 and 1791), listed in Farrar, "Adams Genealogy," are recorded in neither Lincoln nor Sudbury. Elisha's and Mary's deaths are both recorded in Lincoln but not Sudbury.

2 "Treasurer's Accompts," June 15, 1779, records a payment to Capt. Joseph Adams for this service, which he is not likely to have served. See Joseph Adams (q.v., Chapter 12). Elisha Wheeler had just married Joseph Adams's daughter Mary a few weeks before. While a more probable case can be made for this service having been provided by Charles or Nathan Adams (see [unidentified] Adams (q.v.)), neither case is made with much confidence. If Elisha Wheeler came to Lincoln following the death of Sarah and his son, perhaps he might have provided this service, and if he had not been available to receive payment on June 15, 1779, perhaps the town might have paid Capt. Joseph Adams, a respected, upstanding citizen into whose family Wheeler was now married. This is speculative, at best.

3 Coburn, *Muster Rolls*.

4 *Massachusetts Soldiers and Sailors*, Vol. XVI, pp. 966–967.

5 Ibid.

6 "Treasurer's Accompts," June 15, 1779.

He was age 36 as a minute man; the son of Joseph and Ruth (Fox) Wheeler of Acton. He had come to Lincoln and married Mary Garfield in 1765. He reportedly moved to Weston in 1782.[1]

WHEELER, John

John Wheeler entered the service in December 1777, as a substitute for John Cole of Concord. He served in Cambridge through April 2, 1778, in Capt. Simon Hunt's Company, Col. Eleazer Brooks's Regiment, guarding the prisoners taken at Saratoga the previous October.[2]

He served a second term at Cambridge, guarding Burgoyne's "Convention Army" from April 2, 1778, through July 3, 1778, in Capt. Daniel Harrington's Company, Col. Jonathan Reed's Regiment of Guards.[3]

In 1780, he volunteered with nine others from Lincoln, to serve at Rhode Island in a company raised to reinforce the Continental Army for three months. He marched to Tiverton and arrived on July 29. He served in Capt. Abraham Andrews's Company, Col. Cyprian

---

1 *Vital Records of Lincoln*; *Vital Records of Acton*; Wheeler, "Lincoln," in Hurd, Vol. 2, p. 624; MacLean, *A Rich Harvest*, p. 257. Mary's possible kinship with Abraham Gearfield (q.v.), Elisha Gearfield (q.v.), or John Gearfield (q.v.), is undiscovered.

Vital Records of Lincoln lists the birth of six children from 1766 through 1779. *Town of Weston, Births, Deaths, & Marriages* contains no birth records for his children. His move to Weston is per Wheeler; corroboration is found in his appearance on the Weston tax rolls in 1782, and in a November 20, 1782, sale by "Enos Wheeler of Weston, laborer,…to his brother Joseph [of] all his right and title in the lands and buildings of their late father Joseph Wheeler of Acton, deceased" (see Tolman, *Wheeler Families*).

Several internet postings suggest that he may have died in the town of Canaan (Somerset County) Maine, in 1820, but no reliable source for this has been found. Census records record an Enos Wheeler in Somerset County in 1810 and 1820. Weston Town Records contain a curious entry: at the May 8, 1786, Town Meeting, a committee (of one) was appointed to enquire whether or not Mr. Enos Wheeler was an inhabitant of the town. The committee reported back before the meeting adjourned that it had made proper enquiry and could not find that he was an inhabitant of the town. This is believed to be related to the town's legal obligation to provide assistance for its poor residents.

2 Pension Record # W27876. *Massachusetts Soldiers and Sailors* (Vol. XVI, p. 976; echoed by Wheeler, "Lincoln," in Hurd, Vol. 2, p. 624) contains a John Wheeler who served at Saratoga in Capt. Samuel Farrar, Jr.'s Company, Col. Jonathan Reed's Middlesex County Regiment of Massachusetts Militia from September 29, 1777, through Burgoyne's surrender, and was discharged on November 7, 1777 after escorting the prisoners-of-war to Cambridge. However, despite the fact that this company was commanded by a Lincoln captain, and that it had many other Lincoln men in it as well, this individual was probably not John Wheeler of Lincoln. Saratoga service is missing from John Wheeler's (inst.) Pension Record (# W27876), which is otherwise detailed and complete enough for such an omission to be material. And at least six other John Wheelers, of an age appropriate for this service, have been identified in Middlesex County. Accordingly, the author concludes that this record probably belongs to another John Wheeler and not John Wheeler of Lincoln.

Further, John Wheeler (inst.) states in his pension declaration that he served with Joseph Mason (q.v.) "for a small part of the time," and the pension file contains a confirming affidavit from Joseph Mason identifying the common service as Mason's one month of substitute guard duty in Captain Hunt's Company, Colonel Brooks's Regiment (Mason says they quartered together). However, as Mason did serve with Captain Farrar and Colonel Reed at Saratoga, but omitted that service from his affidavit, one can reasonably assume that John Wheeler (inst.) was not also in the same service.

Curiously, the mutual claims are not wholly consonant. Mason's own pension declaration (# S13820) says he stayed on and served the extra month of substitute guard duty following his November 7, 1777, discharge from Saratoga service. Wheeler says his guard duty began in December 1777. It would appear either that Mason stayed longer than one month, or that Wheeler's service began before December.

3 *Massachusetts Soldiers and Sailors*, Vol. XVI, p. 977; Pension Record # W27876. The service record says he was drafted; his pension declaration says he volunteered for this service.

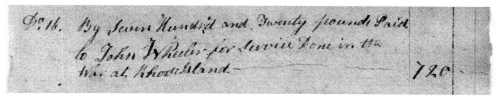

John Wheeler served for three months at Rhode Island in 1780, for which he was paid £720 on February 16, 1781. This is substantially inflated from the pay for similar Rhode Island service the prior year. (Courtesy of Lincoln Town Archives, Lincoln, MA)

How's Middlesex County Regiment, and was probably discharged on October 30, 1780, having served a full three months. He was paid by the town of Lincoln for this service.[1]

He was age 16 and living in Concord when he substituted for John Cole on guard duty at Cambridge. He was the son of John Wheeler and Lydia (Allen) Wheeler of Lincoln. He was nephew of Edmond Wheeler (q.v.), Phineas Allen (q.v.), Joseph Billing (q.v.), and Abraham Wesson (q.v.); cousin of Joseph Billing, Jr. (q.v.), Abel Flint (q.v.), Ephraim Flint (q.v.), John Flint (q.v.), and Jonathan Tower (q.v.). His father had died when he was age four, and seven years later his mother had married Benjamin Parks (q.v.) in 1772. Through his step-father, he was (step) nephew of David Parks (q.v.) and Cornelius Meloney (q.v.); (step) cousin of Aaron Parks (q.v.), Jonas Parks (q.v.), Leonard Parks (q.v.), Willard Parks (q.v.), and Joseph Meloney (q.v.). After his war service, he went to Walpole, New Hampshire, where a number of Lincoln people were settling. There he married Abigail Flint from Lincoln, in 1784. About 1799, he moved his family to Westmoreland, New Hampshire, where Abigail died in 1813. In 1816, he married Sally Read of Westmoreland. He died at Westmoreland in 1845, two months shy of turning age 84. He is buried in Westmoreland's North Cemetery.[2]

WHEELER, Lemuel

Lemuel Wheeler was in service at Cambridge in 1775, having enlisted in the rapidly forming Massachusetts Provincial Army within days of the outbreak of fighting. He served as a private in Capt. Abishai Brown's Company, Col. John Nixon's 5th Regiment from April 28, 1775, through the end of December 1775. He probably participated with his regiment in the Battle of Bunker Hill, on June 17.[3]

---

1 "Treasurer's Accompts," February 16, 1781; *Massachusetts Soldiers and Sailors*, Vol. XVI, pp. 957; Pension Record # W27876. The indicated service is per his pension declaration, and it is consistent with the service of others from Lincoln, including Jonas Brooks (q.v.), Joseph Billing, Jr. (q.v.), and Elijah Child (q.v.). The *Massachusetts Soldiers and Sailors* record shows that he served as a private in Capt. Thomas Brintnal's Company, Col. Cyprian How's Regiment, from August 11, 1780, to Oct. 10, 1780 (credited with 2 months, 3 days of service, including 3 days for 60 miles of travel home). The reference to Captain Brintnal is unclear, but it may have been a duty assignment. If so, this would likely also explain the abbreviated service dates.

2 *Vital Records of Lincoln*; Wheeler, "Lincoln," in Hurd, p. 624; Bond, *Genealogies of the Families of Watertown*, p. 7; Pension Record # W27876; *SAR Revolutionary War Graves Register*. The ages indicated here are based on his birth record. His pension declaration shows him to be a year older than his birth record. However, the birth record appears to be correct, on the basis of the spacing of his siblings' birth dates.

3 *Massachusetts Soldiers and Sailors*, Vol. XVI, p. 981. The record identifies him as being from Concord. Colonel Nixon's Regiment was known as the 16th Regiment before becoming the 5th Regiment under General Washington's command.

He marched to the defense of Dorchester Heights as a private in Capt. George Minot's Company, Col. Eleazer Brooks's 3rd Middlesex County Regiment on March 4, 1776. He was in service for five days, until the threat of a British assault on their positions subsided in the wake of the British decision to evacuate Boston.[1]

A few months later, probably around mid-summer 1776, he went to Ticonderoga for six months as a private in Capt. Charles Miles's Company, Col. Jonathan Reed's Regiment. He appears on a pay abstract dated February 16, 1777, evidently shortly before or after returning home. He was allowed 180 miles of travel home.[2]

He was back in service almost immediately, having enlisted for a three-year term in the Continental Army. He served in the Hudson River Valley, as a private in Col. Thomas Nixon's 6th Massachusetts Regiment, from March 3, 1777, through March 3, 1780. He was at Saratoga during the taking of Burgoyne (October 1777), and later served at Soldier's Fortune (February 1779), Camp near Peekskill, and Camp Highlands (May 1779). He served under Capt. Adam Wheeler (through October 15, 1778), Capt. Lt. Benjamin Haywood (June through September 1779), Capt. Lieut. Matthew Chambers (November and December 1779), and Capt. Lt. Peter Clayes (January through March 1780). He was discharged at Soldier's Fortune.[3]

In July 1780, after a few months off, and agreeable to a resolve of June 5, 1780, he was back in the Hudson Valley for a six-month stint in the Continental Army. He is described as age 23; six feet in stature, with a ruddy complexion. He appears to have begun his service on July 10, 1780, when he marched to camp at Springfield under the command of Capt. James Cooper, arriving on July 15. Subsequently, he marched to his post along the Hudson. He served in Col. Nixon's Regiment and spent at least part of the fall in New Jersey, having passed muster by Brigadier General Paterson, according to a return dated Camp Totoway (now Totowa, New Jersey), October 25, 1780. He was discharged on December 20, 1780, credited with 5 months, 20 days of service, including 10 days for 200 miles of travel home.[4]

On August 13, 1781, he enlisted for five months of service in Rhode Island, as a sergeant in Capt. Asa Drury's Company, Col. William Turner's Regiment. He served through November 28, 1781 (credited with 3 months, 20 days of service, including 80 miles of travel

---

1 *Massachusetts Soldiers and Sailors*, Vol. XVI, p. 981.

2 *Massachusetts Soldiers and Sailors*, Vol. XVI, p. 981; Pension Record # S44052. The record identifies him as being from Concord.

3 *Massachusetts Soldiers and Sailors*, Vol. XVI, p. 981; Pension Record # S44052. Colonel Nixon's 6th Massachusetts Regiment was also known as the 4th Continental Regiment. This service (1777–1780) was credited to the town of Concord. See also Blake, "James Barrett's Returns of Men" (p. 472) for James Barrett's April 9, 1777, report of mustering him into "Col Nixon batl Capt Wheeler" company.

Capt. Adam Wheeler was reported on October 15, 1778, to be a supernumerary officer (i.e., expendable by reason of being overstaffed) and "deranged" (i.e., removed from office as a consequence of the reorganization of the army by an act of Congress) (see *Massachusetts Soldiers and Sailors*, Vol. XVI, p. 959; for the obsolete meaning of the word "deranged," see the *Oxford English Dictionary*). Captain Lieutenants Haywood, Chambers, and Clayes were evidently successive commanders of the colonel's company.

Shattuck, *History of the Town of Concord* (p. 358) says he served at Rhode Island for two months in September 1779, but this clearly conflicts with the record of his Continental Service.

4 *Massachusetts Soldiers and Sailors*, Vol. XVI, p. 981; Pension Record # S44052. The records of this service identify him as being from Concord, and his service was credited to the town of Concord.

home). He appears to have been living in Lincoln by this time, and to have been paid for this service by the town of Lincoln.[1]

He was age 18 at Cambridge; the son of Timothy Wheeler, 3rd, and Sarah (Bond) Wheeler. He married Catherine Whitney of Stow in 1783. He appears to have left Massachusetts by 1790, and at some point in time after 1810, he moved his family to Lorraine (Jefferson County), New York, where he was living at least by 1818–1820. His pension record lists his occupation as farmer, but he evidently became crippled around 1797. The record of his death has not been found.[2]

WHITAKER, Jonas
[also WHITTAKER]

Jonas Whitaker of Lincoln served in Capt. Simon Hunt's Company, Col. Jacob Gerrish's Regiment of Guards, July 14, 1778, to September 14, 1778 (credited with 2 months, 2 days of service), at Cambridge, guarding the German prisoners surrendered by Burgoyne at Saratoga.[3]

He served again, briefly, in the Continental Army in 1780. He is described as age 53; five feet, six inches in stature, ruddy complexion. Agreeable to a resolve of June 5, 1780, he enlisted for a six-month term, and he appears to have arrived at Springfield on July 12, 1780. On July 19, 1780, under the command of Captain Clark, he was marched from Springfield to "camp," probably along the Hudson. Perhaps he failed to make the grade, or perhaps the march exposed a lack of fitness for service; whatever the reason, he was discharged on July 23, 1780, credited with having served 21 days, including 10 days for 200 miles of travel home.[4]

Lincoln historian William Wheeler credits him with being a veteran of the French and Indian War, first in Capt. Thomas Adams's Company in 1758, and then in Capt. William Barron's Company in 1762. Pinning down his identity is a bit problematical, however. There was a Jonas Whittaker, son of Nathaniel Whittaker (who had owned a large farm along the

---

1 *Massachusetts Soldiers and Sailors*, Vol. XVI, p. 981; "Treasurer's Accompts," May 29, 1782; Pension Record # S44052. This is the only one of the service records that identifies him as from Lincoln. Unfortunately, the purpose of the payment record is not entirely clear. It was a payment to Samuel Hartwell (q.v.) "for money paid Jonathan Tower and money paid Lemuel Wheeler," along with other sums due him by the town. It does not identify what the payment to either man was for, but Jonathan Tower (q.v.) was also in service later in the war, and the transaction has all the characteristics of similar reimbursements made to Tower and various other townspeople for moneys they paid to other Lincoln soldiers in Continental service. Accordingly, it appears to be a payment for service in the war, consistent with the system of economic classification adopted by the state toward the end of the war. As both of his Hudson Valley stints were served to the credit of Concord, the payment was obviously not for that service. Applying the payment to this Rhode Island service is a logical presumption. For a brief overview of the system of economic classification, see MacLean, *A Rich Harvest* (p. 296).

2 *Vital Records of Lincoln*; Pension Record # S44052. Two children of Lemuel and Catherine are recorded in Lincoln, the second baptized in 1786. Three other children (born approximately 1798 through 1804) are identified in his pension declaration. How many other children there were between 1786 and 1798 is unknown. It is supposed that he left Lincoln shortly after 1786. Census records suggest he left Massachusetts either for Dublin, New Hampshire, or for Litchfield, Connecticut, followed by Hardwick, Massachusetts, and that he remained in Dublin or Hardwick until at least 1810.

3 *Massachusetts Soldiers and Sailors*, Vol. XVII, p. 151.

4 *Massachusetts Soldiers and Sailors*, Vol. XVII, p. 22. Wheeler, "Lincoln" (in Hurd, Vol. 2, p. 624), says he served at Rhode Island in 1780. If so, it would appear to have been a different campaign (for which the author has found no record), as the travel distance home in this case is considerably further than it would have been from anywhere in Rhode Island.

Bedford border). If this is Jonas Whitaker (inst.), he would have been age 65 at Cambridge and age 67 along the banks of the Hudson. Ordinarily, this would seem very unlikely, but it might explain his apparent lack of fitness for service. Further, this Jonas may have become quite poor, which could explain his enlistment, lying about his age (in reverse!) in order to be accepted. No other Jonas Whitaker has been found in the records.[1]

WHITEHEAD, Daniel

Daniel Whitehead enlisted in the Continental Army on February 14, 1777, for the duration of the war. He served with his father and brother in Capt. Benjamin Pollard's Company of Artificers (later commanded by Phineas Parker), Col. Jeduthan Baldwin's Regiment of Artificers. He died in service on August 27, 1777.[2]

He was age 12 when he joined the service, age 13 when he died; the son of John Whitehead (q.v.) and Abigail (Harrington) Whitehead; brother of Elisha Whitehead (q.v.); nephew of Daniel Harrington (q.v.); step-cousin of Jonas Bond (q.v.), Samuel Bond (q.v.), and William Bond (q.v.). He was born in Waltham and raised in Lincoln. His mother had died shortly after his ninth birthday, and his father had married Anna Bond and moved the family to Weston.[3]

WHITEHEAD, Elisha

Elisha Whitehead of Weston served at Cambridge in 1775 as a private in Capt. Nathan Fuller's Company, Lt. Col. William Bond's Regiment. His enlistment date is not recorded, but he was in service on July 16, when he was recorded as on guard detail with Col. Loammi Baldwin at Prospect Hill. If he was in service as early as June 17, then it is probable that he participated with his unit in the Battle of Bunker Hill. The regiment was then commanded by Col. Thomas Gardner, who was mortally wounded in the battle. Elisha Whitehead appears to have remained in service at least through October 1775, and probably through December 31, 1775, when Cambridge terms of service typically expired.

He enlisted in the Continental Army for the duration of the war on March 27, 1777, and served with his father and brother in Capt. Benjamin Pollard's Company of Artificers (later commanded by Phineas Parker), Col. Jeduthan Baldwin's Regiment of Artificers. He died in service in July 1777 (credited with service through July 27).[4]

He was age 15 when he served at Cambridge; age 17 when he died; the son of John Whitehead (q.v.) and Abigail (Harrington) Whitehead; brother of Daniel Whitehead (q.v.);

---

1 Wheeler, "Lincoln," in Hurd, Vol. 2, p. 624; MacLean, *A Rich Harvest*, pp. 214–215; *Concord, Massachusetts: Births, Marriages, and Deaths*; *Lexington Births, Marriages and Deaths*. *Concord, Massachusetts: Births, Marriages, and Deaths* identifies the mother of the 65 and 67-year-old Jonas as Hanah.

2 *Massachusetts Soldiers and Sailors*, Vol. XVII, p. 148.

3 *Vital Records of Waltham*; *Vital Records of Lincoln*; *Town of Weston, Births, Deaths, & Marriages*. The fact that his father, John Whitehead (q.v.), was a lieutenant in the same unit was undoubtedly a primary factor in his underage enlistment. Jack MacLean reasoned in a private note to the author, "While Daniel was rather young, the special nature of the unit [i.e., artificers] and the fact that his father was serving would help to explain his involvement (the fact that Anna was a stepmother rather than mother could also come into play in family dynamics)." John Whitehead resigned his commission shortly after the death of his two sons. See also Elisha Whitehead (q.v.), John Whitehead (q.v.), and the sidebar "A Shattered Family," p. 439.

4 *Massachusetts Soldiers and Sailors*, Vol. XVII, pp. 148–149.

nephew of Daniel Harrington (q.v.); step-cousin of Jonas Bond (q.v.), Samuel Bond (q.v.), and William Bond (q.v.). He was born in Waltham and raised in Lincoln. His mother had died when he was 13; his father had married Anna Bond and moved the family to Weston.[1]

WHITEHEAD, John

John Whitehead of Lincoln was in arms at Concord on April 19, 1775, perhaps as a member of Lincoln's militia company, or perhaps more likely as an unenlisted volunteer.[2]

Notwithstanding his being at Concord on the morning of April 19th, he apparently served for four days on the Alarm of April 19th as a private in Capt. Israel Whitemore's Artillery Company from Weston.[3]

On January 1, 1777, he enlisted for a three-year stint in the Continental Army and served as a lieutenant in Capt. Benjamin Pollard's Company of Artificers (later commanded by Phineas Parker), Col. Jeduthan Baldwin's Regiment of Artificers. He reportedly resigned March 27, 1778.[4]

His origins are unknown. He is reported as having served as a soldier at Lake George in 1758. The following year (1759) in Waltham, he had married Abigail Harrington, sister of Daniel Harrington (q.v.), and they appear to have been living in Lincoln at least by 1765, when he was operating an inn on the main road (now Old Concord Road) between Concord and Sudbury's East Parish (later East Sudbury, now Wayland).

When Abigail died in 1773 at age 30, he moved to Weston. Seven months later, he married Anna Bond (also listed as Hannah) of Lincoln, aunt of Jonas Bond (q.v.), Samuel

---

1 *Vital Records of Waltham*; *Vital Records of Lincoln*; *Town of Weston, Births, Deaths, & Marriages*. The fact that his father, John Whitehead (q.v.), was a lieutenant in the same unit was undoubtedly a primary factor in his enlistment in 1777. Jack MacLean also surmises in a private note to the author, that the family dynamics of a step-mother may have contributed to his stints in the service. John Whitehead resigned his commission shortly after the death of his two sons. See also Daniel Whitehead (q.v.), John Whitehead (q.v.), and the sidebar, "A Shattered Family," p. 439.

2 Deposition of John Hoar, et al. His residence is stated as Lincoln. As it seems unlikely that he would have been a member of both units at the same time, he may very well have been at Concord unofficially.

3 *Massachusetts Soldiers and Sailors*, Vol. XVII, p. 149. In this record, his residence is listed as Weston. It would be easy to dismiss this record as a different person, but as there does not appear to be any evidence of the existence of another John Whitehead, this must be the same person. According to a private communication by Mike Ryan, Captain Whitemore's Company started to Concord on April 19th, but on learning that the British had already left Concord and were on their way back to Boston, they altered their route and marched to Lexington, instead, arriving in the afternoon about the same time as did the British troops. If this is accurate, Whitehead must have joined them at that point, or perhaps shortly after. After four days of service, his return from Cambridge on the 22nd (possibly the morning of the 23rd) would have been in time for his being deposed in Lexington on the 23rd. *Historical Memoranda* [SAR] (pp. 466–467), places Captain Whitemore's Company in the 8th Artillery Regiment.

4 Ibid. Also *Historical Memoranda* [SAR], pp. 466–467. His resignation in mid-term appears a bit irregular, but it is probably better understood within the context of the death of his two sons, Daniel Whitehead (q.v.) and Elisha Whitehead (q.v.), who were serving in the same unit. Both died within a month of each other, in July and August 1777. As lieutenant, it is a certainty that he had recruited them both to the unit. Jack MacLean reasoned in a private note to the author, "While Daniel was rather young, the special nature of the unit [i.e., artificers] and the fact that his father was serving would help to explain his involvement (the fact that Anna was a stepmother rather than mother could also come into play in family dynamics)." One can imagine that, following their deaths, he may have had difficulty maintaining an attitude conducive to carrying out his duties appropriately. He may possibly have been tendering his resignation since August, awaiting its eventual acceptance seven months later. MacLean also notes that Weston records list him as "Capt. John Whitehead" (probably a militia title) beginning in 1777.

Chapter 10: The Army of the Revolution

A Shattered Family

John Whitehead's (q.v.) wife of 14 years died in 1773, leaving him with seven young children from age thirteen to less than one year old. He sold the Lincoln inn and farm they had run together for at least eight years. He moved to Weston, remarried, and started fresh. In December of that year, he participated in the Boston Tea Party. He joined an artillery company, and he probably stayed abreast of the escalating tensions between the colony and her mother country. The morning of April 19, 1775, saw him in arms at the North Bridge with his old Lincoln neighbors, and with them he chased the Redcoats back to Lexington before his mates in the artillery company arrived to participate in the running fight. After four days in service at Cambridge, he stopped in Lexington to record—under oath—just how the fight had broken out in Concord.

Notwithstanding his apparent zeal for the Provincial cause, he appears not to have been in arms during the next year and a half, perhaps devoting himself to private or family matters rather than community interests or public affairs. But by the end of 1776, he was on his way back into service for a three-year term in the Continental Army. He secured a commission as a lieutenant and entered the service as an artificer on January 1, 1777. His precise reasons for joining are unknown—perhaps economic, perhaps a commitment to the cause of liberty, perhaps an unavoidable draft call. Whatever his primary motivation, the evidence suggests that family discord also may have been on the rise, and this may have been a contributing factor.

Scarcely a month after he entered the service, he arranged for his 12-year-old son Daniel (q.v.) to join him in the service. A month later, at the end of March, his now 17-year-old son Elisha (q.v.) also joined them. That something was terribly wrong at home is evidenced by a public notice that John placed in a Boston newspaper a few days later, informing readers not to trust his wife, Anna, and disavowing any debt that she might incur. No further details are known, but it seems reasonable to suppose that Daniel and Elisha had joined their Dad in the service to escape an untenable situation at home with their stepmother.

> I *John Whitehead,* of *Weston,* for several Reasons, forbid all Persons trusting ANNA, my Wife, any Thing whatsoever, on my Account; as I declare I will not pay any Debt she may contract after the Date hereof.
> Weston, April 5th, 1777.

John Whitehead disavowed his wife's debts in this public notice, which appeared in the Boston newspaper, *The Independent Chronicle and the Universal Advertiser*, on April 10, 1777 [IX:451, 3].

Unfortunately, the story turns tragic. Four months after entering the service, Elisha died on July 27, 1777. Daniel died in service shortly afterward, on August 27, 1777. It is hard to imagine John's devastation. It is likely that he attempted to resign his ▶

> commission immediately. But it would be seven months before his resignation was accepted. He left the service on March 27, 1778, apparently never to serve again.
>
> [*Massachusetts Soldiers and Sailors*, Vol. XVII, pp. 148–149; *Town of Weston, Births, Deaths, & Marriages*; *Vital Records of Lincoln*; *Vital Records of Waltham*; MacLean, *A Rich Harvest*, pp. 195, 198.]

Bond (q.v.), and William Bond (q.v.). Just a few days after marrying Anna, he reportedly participated in the Boston Tea Party. According to the deposition, he appears to have been back in Lincoln by 1775, or at least to have retained a strong Lincoln affiliation.

He is estimated to have been around age 37 at Concord. He was the father of Daniel Whitehead (q.v.) and Elisha Whitehead (q.v.). He died at Weston in 1783, perhaps around age 45. Probate records indicate that his widow Anna was again residing in Lincoln when she died in 1796. His daughter, Eunice, married John Hagar (q.v.) in 1780.[1]

WHITNEY, Leonard

Agreeable to a resolve of December 2, 1780, Leonard Whitney enlisted in the Continental Army for a three-year term on January 31, 1781. He served in Capt. Thomas Prichard's Company, Col. John Greaton's Regiment, and is described in the record as age 17; five feet, five inches in stature; dark complexion, dark hair, black eyes. His occupation is given as a laborer and farmer. The enlistment was credited to the town of Concord. After passing muster in Boston and "Gard[ing] some Deserters" for fourteen days, he marched to West Point where he remained through the summer. Then he went into winter quarters at New Boston.[2] He returned to West Point in the spring of 1782, where he served until the following year.

---

1 *Town of Weston, Births, Deaths, & Marriages*; *Vital Records of Lincoln*; *Vital Records of Waltham*; Bond, *Genealogies of the Families of Watertown*, pp. 50, 281, 642; MacLean, *A Rich Harvest*, pp. 195, 198. Tea Party participation is given in *Historical Memoranda* [SAR] (p. 466) for which the author is indebted to George Quintal. In the absence of a birth record, the estimates of his age are based on a guess that he may have been around 20 at Lake George. Abigail appears to have been age 16 when they were married in 1759. She is buried in the Meeting House Cemetery behind Bemis Hall (see Biggs, "In Memorium," p. 187).

Eunice's 1761 birth is recorded in Waltham, not Lincoln, indicating that he and Abigail were not yet living in Lincoln. Her 1780 marriage to John Hagar (q.v.) was recorded in Weston, listing them both as Weston residents.

It is unclear whether he moved back and forth between Lincoln and Weston, or whether he may have had sufficient interest in both towns to have considered himself and/or been listed circumstantially, according to convenience, as a resident of either one. His 1773 marriage record specifically lists him as from Weston, in contrast to Anna from Lincoln. Possibly, he may not have moved back to Lincoln, per se, but simply chose not to worry about that detail in the deposition.

2 *Massachusetts Soldiers and Sailors*, Vol. XVII, p. 237; Pension Record # S43300. New Boston was a Continental camp in the Hudson Highlands, a short distance from the Hudson River, but its precise location is unknown. Following the destruction of Fort Montgomery and Fort Clinton by the British in 1777, new camps had been laid out to defend the passes through the hills, but at the same time situated close enough to the river for the troops to rally to resist enemy ships sailing upstream. Massachusetts troops had built new huts at New Boston during the winter of 1780–1781, which afforded "a very convenient and comfortable accommodation." [Thatcher, *Military Journal*, p. 369; Calver, "Researches," pp. 152, 154.]

In July, 1783, he was sent to Philadelphia, "on account of the Pennsylvanians rising against Congress. When we got there the insurrection was over and the Pennsylvanians had withdrawn."[1]

He returned to West Point in September and was assigned to wood-cutting detail. After they had achieved their quota of wood, the whole wood-cutting detail was discharged at the end of October or early November, 1783.[2]

He was born in Lincoln, the son of Solomon Whitney (q.v.) and Mary (Fay) Whitney; age 17 at the time of his enlistment. He was the brother of Silas Whitney (q.v.); nephew of Joel Adams (q.v.) and Silas Fay (q.v.). After the war, he married Cate Wheeler of Concord during the winter of 1785–1786, and sometime thereafter moved to Canterbury, New Hampshire. He became lame when a tree fell on him and broke his thigh and shoulder, and injured his right arm. He died of dropsy in Canterbury in 1827, probably age 63 or 64.[3]

WHITNEY, Silas

Silas Whitney enlisted for a three-year term in the Continental Army in July 1782. Having just turned 16, he had hired into the family of Benjamin Williams in New Ipswich, New Hampshire, when he decided to enlist. He served in Capt. Isaac Frye's Company, Col. Henry Dearborn's 1st New Hampshire Regiment. He passed muster at Amherst (New Hampshire) before joining his regiment at Saratoga. In November, the unit moved downriver to winter quarters at New Windsor.[4]

Sometime the following year, the company deployed downriver further to Stony Point, and divided up; one half on one side of the river, the other half on the other side. Capt. Moody Dustin succeeded Captain Frye in command of the company.[5]

He relates in his pension declaration that the unit returned to West Point and spent the winter of 1783-1784 on Constitution Island. He recalled that he was discharged in April 1784, having served 21 months, and that his discharge paper was signed by General Washington.[6]

He was born in Lincoln, the son of Solomon Whitney (q.v.) and Mary (Fay) Whitney; age 16 at the time of his enlistment. He was the brother of Leonard Whitney (q.v.); nephew

---

1 Pension Record # S43300. The Philadelphia mutiny in June 1783 was one of a number of uprisings of Continental soldiers for non-payment of service wages. It involved as many as 400 soldiers, and it caused the Continental Congress to abandon Philadelphia temporarily and move to Princeton.

2 Ibid.

3 *Vital Records of Lincoln;* Pension Record # S43300; *New Hampshire Patriot & State Gazette,* March 19, 1827. His age at the time of his death is reported as 64, but this is uncertain, as no birth record has been found. His ages as indicated in his enlistment record, his pension declarations, and his death notice are not consistent with one another. His baptism record is reasonably consistent with his age given at enlistment, suggesting that he may have been slightly younger than the ages subsequently reported in his pension documents and at the time of his death.

4 Pension Record # W8311, BLWT38, 336-160-55.

5 Ibid.

6 Ibid. Other documents in his pension file suggest that he may have been discharged in July or December 1783, but his claim to having wintered on Constitution Island has enough specificity to be credible. If so, however, it is not likely that his discharge was signed by General Washington, as the Commander-in-Chief had resigned from the army and returned to Mt. Vernon by the end of 1783. Interestingly, the Pension Office calculated his pension on the basis of only fourteen months of service, determining that the war officially ended on September 3, 1783, with the signing of the Treaty of Paris.

of Joel Adams (q.v.) and Silas Fay (q.v.). When he returned to Lincoln from war service in the spring of 1784, his younger brother, Otis, later wrote, "I well recollect the return of my brother, Silas Whitney,…from the war of the Revolution to my parents, then living in said Lincoln—that my mother did not recognize him till after I said who it was…he had then been out in said war between one & a half & two years & had not been home during that time."[1]

After the war, he returned to New Hampshire to live, first at Concord, then from about 1792 at Thornton. He married Hopestill Sargent in 1798, then Sarah Lovejoy in 1815. He died at Thornton in 1850, at age 84, where he is buried in Pine Grove Cemetery.[2]

WHITNEY, Solomon

Solomon Whitney was a private in Capt. William Smith's Company of Minute Men from Lincoln, Col. Abijah Peirce's Regiment.[3] Following the engagement at Concord, he served for five days at Cambridge.[4]

On April 24, 1775, he enlisted in the rapidly forming Massachusetts Provincial Army, in Capt. William Smith's Company, Col. John Nixon's 5th Regiment. He received advance pay the day before going into battle at Bunker Hill. He was still in service in Cambridge September 30, when he was reported on furlough.[5]

Possibly, he may have been part of the Knox expedition to transport the cannons from Fort Ticonderoga to Boston during the winter of 1775–1776. He appears to have been in western Massachusetts at about this time in some sort of military role. Whether or not this was related to the Knox expedition is speculative. He was wounded, and for a time confined to the town of Stockbridge for care, before being well enough to journey home.[6]

By February 4, 1776, he had recovered from his wounds sufficiently to return to the Siege of Boston to reinforce the Continental Army, as a private in Capt. Asahel Wheeler's Company, Col. John Robinson's Regiment. He served for 1 month, 28 days, through the evacuation of the British forces from Boston.[7]

That summer, in June or July 1776, he marched to Ticonderoga in Capt. Asahel Wheeler's Company, Col. Jonathan Reed's Regiment, and served for 4 or 5 months, through November 1776.[8]

---

1 *Vital Records of Lincoln;* Pension Record # W8311, BLWT38, 336-160-55.
2 Pension Record # W8311, BLWT38, 336-160-55; "Family: Whitney, Silas"; "Find A Grave."
3 Coburn, *Muster Rolls*.
4 *Massachusetts Soldiers and Sailors*, Vol. XVII, pp. 249–250.
5 Ibid. Colonel Nixon's Regiment was originally designated the 16th Massachusetts Regiment. The 5th Regiment is a Continental designation.
6 "Treasurer's Accompts," May 7, 1776. This is a tantalizing record of the town reimbursing Col. Eleazer Brooks for what he "paid ye Selectmen of Stockbridge for taking care of Solomon Whitney when confined in that town by a wound." No confirming record has been found of his being on the Knox expedition; the speculation is based on the timing and location, and on the absence of other apparent interpretations of this record.
7 *Massachusetts Soldiers and Sailors*, Vol. XVII, p. 249. This record identifies him as being from Concord, but there can be no question that this is Solomon Whitney (inst.). This company was raised from the towns of Concord, Sudbury, Weston, Acton, and Lincoln.
8 Sudbury Miscellaneous Records, pay receipts dated September 30, 1776 (Doc. # 109) and March 17, 1777 (Doc. # 2209).

Chapter 10: The Army of the Revolution

This transaction provides evidence that Solomon Whitney was probably part of Henry Knox's Expedition to Ticonderoga during the fall and winter of 1775–1776 to transport cannons to Boston, and that he was wounded in the process. No other explanation has been found for Whitney being in western Massachusetts at this time on a matter of public expense. (Courtesy of Lincoln Town Archives, Lincoln, MA)

He served as a private in Capt. John Hartwell's Company, Col. Nicholas Dike's Regiment in Dorchester, from December 14, 1776, to March 1, 1777.[1]

He went north in the second wave of reinforcements for the Northern Army under General Gates. Detached from Col. Eleazer Brooks's Regiment of Militia, he served as a private in Capt. Samuel Farrar, Jr.'s Company, Col. Jonathan Reed's Middlesex County Regiment (Brig. Gen. James Bricket's Brigade of Massachusetts Militia), from September 29, 1777, to November 7, 1777 (credited with 1 month, 10 days of service), and was engaged in escorting Burgoyne's army to Cambridge.[2]

On June 14, 1778, he enlisted for service along the Hudson River as a private in Capt. Edward Richardson's Company, Col. Thomas Poor's Regiment. The record shows him at West Point in September and at King's Ferry in December. He was at North River when he was discharged on February 13, 1779 (credited with 8 months, 10 days of service, including 11 days for travel home).

He was at Rhode Island from September 15, 1779, until November 15, 1779 (credited with 2 months, 4 days of service including 80 miles of travel) as a private in Capt. Samuel Heald's Company, Col. John Jacobs's Light Infantry Regiment.

He reenlisted in the Continental Army for six months, agreeable to a resolve of June 5, 1780. He is described as age 45; five feet, eleven inches in stature, with a ruddy complexion. He was engaged for the town of Lincoln. There are conflicting records about how long he served. In one record, he entered the service on July 11, 1780, and was discharged almost immediately, on July 22, 1780 (credited with 21 days of service, including 200 miles of travel home). Another record indicates he enlisted on July 9, 1780, was garrisoned at West Point, and served in Capt. Joshua Benson's Light Infantry Company, Col. Rufus Putnam's 5th Regiment, until his discharge on January 15, 1781.[3]

He was back in Continental service on February 24, 1781 (agreeable to a resolve of December 2, 1780), for a three-year term. He is described as age 46; five feet, eleven inches

---

1 *Massachusetts Soldiers and Sailors*, Vol. XVII, p. 250.

2 Ibid.

3 *Massachusetts Soldiers and Sailors*, Vol. XVII, pp. 249–250, 255. The listing for his Rhode Island service appears under the headings, "Hartwell Brook the first Everidge" and "Resolve of Sept 1779."

in stature; with a dark complexion, dark hair, and dark eyes. His occupation is listed as a farmer. His service was credited to the town of Lincoln.

By July 1781, he appears to have been recruited from the infantry into the artillery, where he served as a private in Capt. Amos Lincoln's Company of Matrosses. On February 25, 1782, he appears to have been detached for duty as a Marine, aboard the Continental frigate *Deane* under the command of Capt. Samuel Nicholson. He served 3 months, 6 days on shipboard, until May 31, 1782, but reportedly reengaged. He subsequently served aboard the frigate *Hague*, commanded by Capt. John Manley. He was back on shore and back in Capt. Amos Lincoln's Company of Matrosses by November 1, 1782, where he was reported as among "rejected recruits detailed for garrison duty." He served out his term, as a matross in Captain Lincoln's Company in Boston (8 months, 18 days), until his discharge on July 18, 1783.[1]

He was born in the part of Weston that became Lincoln. He was age 39 at Concord; son of Solomon and Martha (Fletcher) Whitney. He had served several campaigns in the French and Indian War, when he had been in his early 20s, and he appears to have been sick or wounded on the Crown Point Expedition in 1756. He appears on the muster roll of Lincoln's original militia company in 1757. He had been married to Mary Fay since 1762, and was the father of Leonard Whitney (q.v.) and Silas Whitney (q.v.). He was also the brother-in-law of Joel Adams (q.v.) and Silas Fay (q.v.). He is reported to have moved to Canterbury, New Hampshire in 1794. The date and location of his death are unknown.[2]

---

1 *Massachusetts Soldiers and Sailors*, Vol. XVII, pp. 249–250; "Treasurer's Accompts," September 6, 1781, October 15, 1781, April 2, 1783. He was recruited and paid for this service through the system of economic classes mandated by the state. The "Treasurer's Accompts" show that the members of the class paid the soldier, and that the town reimbursed the members of the class. However, *Massachusetts Soldiers and Sailors* records an account dated September 10, 1781, rendered by the Selectmen of Lincoln of a bounty paid to Solomon Whitney, who "marched to join the army without a receipt having been obtained from him." For a brief overview of the system of economic classes, see MacLean, *A Rich Harvest* (p. 296). According to his birth record, he would have been age 45 when he began this service; Wheeler, "Lincoln" (in Hurd, Vol. 2, p. 624), evidently confusing his 1780 and 1781 enlistments, calls him age 47 when he enlisted in 1780 for three years in the Continental Army.

2 *Town of Weston, Births, Deaths, & Marriages*; *Concord, Massachusetts: Births, Marriages, and Deaths*; *Vital Records of Lincoln*; Wheeler, "Lincoln," in Hurd, p. 624; Bond, *Genealogies of the Families of Watertown*, p. 650; Shattuck, *History of the Town of Concord*, pp. 72–73; Martin, "The Sons of Lincoln," p. 25. MacLean, *A Rich Harvest* (p. 257) indicates that he was from Concord, or at least that his father was from Concord. *Town of Weston, Births, Deaths, & Marriages* contains his parents' marriage record, which clearly indicates that his father was from Weston and his mother was from Concord. The couple appears to have settled in Concord, but there can be little doubt that they affiliated with the Weston church. Solomon's birth record is found in *Concord, Massachusetts: Births, Marriages, and Deaths*, but his baptism is listed in *Town of Weston, Births, Deaths, & Marriages*. A similar pattern was followed for most of his siblings. It is apparent from multiple church records found in *Town of Weston, Births, Deaths, & Marriages*, that the family was part of the Weston Church until they were dismissed to the North Precinct in 1750. Bond says they "probably resided in that part of Weston which became a part of Lincoln," but from Concord tax records, Jack MacLean (private communication) has determined that at least between 1747 and 1750, the family was living in that part of Concord that became Lincoln. He has found no evidence that they owned real estate.

According to Mike Ryan (private communication, 2008), following his Crown Point service, he had served in Capt. Jonathan Brooks's Company to relieve Fort William Henry in 1757.

The "Treasurer's Accompts" document at least six transactions (from Jan. 23, 1775, through April 15, 1776) reimbursing various individuals for supporting Solomon Whitney and his family (two children were recorded, 1763 and 1766, in *Vital Records of Lincoln*) during April and May 1774 and at other (unspecified) times. If these suggest hard economic circumstances, this might possibly explain Solomon's regular stints in

WILLINGTON, Elijah
[also WELLINGTON]

Elijah Willington of Lincoln was a corporal in Capt. William Smith's Company of Minute Men from Lincoln, Col. Abijah Peirce's Regiment.[1] Following the engagement at Concord, he served for five days in Cambridge.[2] He was later reimbursed by the town for his accoutrements as a minute man.[3]

On April 24, 1775, he enlisted in the rapidly forming Massachusetts Provincial Army. He served as a sergeant in Capt. William Smith's Company, Col. John Nixon's 16th Regiment, probably participated with his unit in the Battle of Bunker Hill, and received advanced pay in Cambridge on July 7, 1775. He remained in service into the fall but was reported sick and absent on Sept. 30, 1775.[4]

A minute man on April 19th, Elijah Willington also participated in the Battle of Bunker Hill, and he later went on the supply mission to Worthington in 1777. After the war, he went north to Livermore, Maine, where he died in 1828. (Photograph by the author)

He may have been in service in 1776, but no record of this has been found.[5]

He took a team with provisions to Worthington in 1777, for which he was paid by the town.[6]

He was age 25 at Concord; the son of Jonathan Willington and Lydia (Gove) Willington; uncle of Elisha Willington (q.v.). He married Phoebe Brown in 1786, by which time he appears to have been a lieutenant in the militia company. He moved to Livermore,

---

the service. On the other hand, he appears to have owned a slave (Jenny, baptized in 1770), which is more suggestive of economic prosperity (or at least the pretensions of economic prosperity), than of being a ward of the town. Because the town's welfare predates the outbreak of the war, it does not seem likely that the support could be in any way related to his wound and incapacity at Stockbridge.

Whatever the economic implications, it is apparent from his multiple stints in both the French and Indian War and the Revolutionary War that he must have enjoyed the life of a soldier.

Wheeler erroneously lists the date of his marriage to Mary Fay as 1771; Bond lists it as 1761, which could be when the marriage intention may have been recorded.

1 Coburn, *Muster Rolls*. Wheeler, "Lincoln" (in Hurd, Vol. 2, p. 624), incorrectly lists him as a sergeant.
2 *Massachusetts Soldiers and Sailors*, Vol. XVII, p. 495.
3 "Treasurer's Accompts," February 19, 1776.
4 *Massachusetts Soldiers and Sailors*, Vol. XVI, p. 829, Vol. XVII, p. 495; Treasurer's Accompts," June 10, 1779. His illness appears to have prevented him from completing his term of service. Edward Adams (q.v.) substituted for him for the three months remaining until his term was up on December 31, 1775.
5 Wheeler, "Lincoln" (in Hurd, Vol. 2, p. 624), credits him with this service but offers no details.
6 "Treasurer's Accompts," June 10, 1779. The dates and purpose of the Worthington mission are not identified, but Shattuck, *History of the Town of Concord* (p. 300) says it occurred in 1777, leading to speculation that it might have been undertaken to supply the expedition returning from Saratoga, escorting Burgoyne's captured army to Cambridge.

Maine, reportedly about 1810, where he died in 1828. He is buried in Strickland's Ferry Cemetery, in Livermore Falls.[1]

WILLINGTON, Elisha
[also WELLINGTON]

Elisha Willington of Lincoln served as a private in Capt. John Hartwell's Company of Militia from Lincoln, Col. Eleazer Brooks's 3rd Middlesex County Regiment, which marched from Lincoln to fortify Dorchester Heights on March 4, 1776. The unit was discharged five days later, on March 9, after the threat of a British assault on the fortifications had subsided, and General Howe had begun preparations to evacuate Boston, instead. He was paid for this service the following September.[2]

He served on the relief expedition to Canada in 1776, as a member of Capt. Abijah Child's Company, Col. William Bond's 25th Continental Regiment. He appears to have been in service at least from July through November, when they returned from Fort Ticonderoga.[3]

On March 1, 1777, he was recruited (in Suffolk County) for a three-year term in the Continental Army. He served in Capt. Abijah Child's Company, Col. John Greaton's Regiment, as a corporal. He was promoted to sergeant on August 15, 1778, and to ensign on November 26, 1779.

---

1 *Vital Records of Lincoln*; Wheeler, "Lincoln," in Hurd, Vol. 2, p. 624; *SAR Revolutionary War Graves Register*. MacLean, *A Rich Harvest* (p. 257) lists his age as 28 at Concord; this appears to be a typographical error. No birth record has been found, but *Vital Records of Lincoln* contains his baptism record. Evidence from Jonathan's earlier children indicates close correlation between birth and baptism dates (see *Town of Weston, Births, Deaths, & Marriages*). On this basis he appears to have been age 25 at Concord. The baptism record does not identify Elijah's mother.

Wheeler identifies him as the son of Jonathan Jr. and Lydia (Fisk) Willington. MacLean echoes that, listing his father as Jonathan Jr. However, upon a closer reading of the record, this appears to be unlikely. *Town of Weston, Births, Deaths, & Marriages* contains a June 5, 1736, birth record for Jonathan Willington, the second recorded child of Jonathan and Lydia (both of Weston, whose marriage intention was recorded January 3, 1731). This Jonathan appears to be the Jonathan Jr. who married Lydia Fisk (intentions December 9, 1756) as recorded in *Vital Records of Lincoln*. See also Bond, *Genealogies of the Families of Watertown* (pp. 634, 637). Thus, when Elijah was born in 1750, Jonathan Jr. was only age 13, and still seven years away from marrying Lydia Fisk. *Town of Weston, Births, Deaths, & Marriages* contains three additional children of (the elder) Jonathan and Lydia through 1744, then a child of "Jonathan & ____, of this town," baptized April 10, 1748, in the North Precinct. Elijah is the first of three children of Jonathan recorded in a similar fashion in *Vital Records of Lincoln* (i.e., a baptism record with no mother's name) in 1750, 1762, and 1767. Taken together, these records demonstrate that Elijah's father was Jonathan Sr.

Elijah's move to Maine "about 1810" is according to Wheeler; his last child recorded in Lincoln was born in 1806.

2 *Massachusetts Soldiers and Sailors*, Vol. XVI, p. 829. Vol. XVII, p. 496.

3 Wheeler, "Lincoln," in Hurd, Vol. 2, p. 624; *Massachusetts Soldiers and Sailors*, Vol. XVI, p. 829; "Treasurer's Accompts," May 12, 1781. The town paid him "for service he performed at Cannady, this war." He must have been home on furlough from his Continental service in May 1781 to have received this payment.

Colonel Bond's Regiment reached Canada in early May, but it was back at Ticonderoga at least by early July and served at Ticonderoga into November, when it marched to Morristown, New Jersey, for the winter. The surviving record of Willington's service is a pay receipt for the period July through November 3, 1776. His enlistment and discharge dates are not known. He may have been with Colonel Bond's Regiment in April when it was ordered to Canada. Or perhaps he responded to the resolves of June 25, 1776, or July 11, 1776, calling for reinforcements for the Continental Army in Canada. In the later case it is unlikely that he ever made it into Canada, as colonial forces were pulling out of Canada by the end of June.

It is also unclear how to reconcile the pay receipt with the subsequent payment for this service by the town of Lincoln.

Captain Child resigned in April 1778, and Willington appears to have been serving in Capt. Abraham Watson's Company, when he reenlisted for another three-year term. The reenlistment was credited to the town of Lincoln. He transferred to the light infantry, in Capt. Joseph Williams's Company, on August 1, 1780.[1]

Subsequently, Colonel Greaton's Regiment appears to have been reorganized; sometime after January 19, 1781, he transferred to Lt. Col. John Brooks's 7th Regiment and was commissioned a lieutenant on July 26, 1782.[2]

He served as a lieutenant in Capt. John Maynard's 6th Company in November 1782, and in Capt. Nathaniel C. Allen's 8th Company from December 1782 through February 1783. He was reported on furlough from February 16 to March 15, 1783, in order to return to Massachusetts from New Windsor, New York. On April 1, 1783, he was transferred again, this time to the 3rd Company. He remained in service until June 13, 1783, when he was reported retired by General Washington while he was on furlough.[3]

He appears to have been a good soldier, as evidenced by his promotions and recommendations for promotion.

He was age 17 at Dorchester Heights; son of Jonathan Jr. and Lydia (Fiske) Willington; nephew of Elijah Willington (q.v.). After he returned from Continental service, he married Lucy Cutter in 1784. They settled in Concord, where their first child was born four months later. He died in Concord in 1799 at age 40.[4]

WINSHIP, Richard

Richard Winship of Lincoln enlisted in July 1780 to reinforce the Continental Army for a term of 6 months, agreeable to a resolve of June 5, 1780. He is described as age 17; five feet, seven inches in stature, with a ruddy complexion. He appears to have begun his service on July 10, 1780, when he marched to camp at Springfield under the command of Capt. James Cooper, arriving on July 15. He marched to West Point and served largely in the Hudson Valley, in Capt. Daniel Pilsbury's Company, Col. Timothy Bigelow's Regiment. From West Point, he was deployed across the river to Robinson's Farms, then to Peekskill, Stony Point, and Orangetown. He marched to New Jersey, where he passed muster by Brigadier General Paterson, according to a return dated Camp Totoway, October 25, 1780. He was discharged at West Point on March 1, 1781, credited with 8 months of service, including 10 days for 200 miles of travel home.[5]

---

1 *Massachusetts Soldiers and Sailors*, Vol. XVII, pp. 495–496.

2 Ibid. In another record, Lieutenant Colonel Brooks recommends him on October 28, 1782, for a promotion to lieutenant to fill a vacancy. He is listed as ensign. This date appears to be an administrative date, as he already held a commission as a lieutenant at that time.

3 Ibid. Listed as Windsor in the record, New Windsor is north of West Point, the site of the 1782–1783 winter encampment of a large portion of the Continental Army, and the location from which Washington mustered out most of the Continental Army in 1783.

4 *Vital Records of Lincoln*; *Concord, Massachusetts: Births, Marriages, and Deaths*; Wheeler, "Lincoln," in Hurd, Vol. 2, p. 624; Bond, *Genealogies of the Families of Watertown*, p. 634. *Concord, Massachusetts: Births, Marriages, and Deaths* lists his age as 41 when he died, but this does not conform to his birth record in *Vital Records of Lincoln*.

5 *Massachusetts Soldiers and Sailors*, Vol. XVII, p. 626; Pension Record # S11786. This service was credited to the town of Lexington, even though he is identified as being from Lincoln. According to his pension declaration, Colonel Bigelow's Regiment was commanded by Col. Kilby Smith, but the record indicates that this was

He was the son of Richard and Prudence Winship of Lexington. He married Salley Turrell of Bedford in 1788. He settled in Bedford for a few years, then subsequently moved to Milo (Yates County), New York, where he was living in 1832.[1]

WOOD, John

John Wood was paid by the town of Lincoln for three months of service in the Continental Army. He served probably as a private in Capt. John Hayward's Company, Colonel Webb's Regiment from August 26, 1781, through November 30, 1781. He was credited with 3 months, 10 days of service, including 10 days for 200 miles of travel home.[2]

His identity is uncertain.[3]

Lt. Col. Calvin Smith. Robinson's Farms was located across the river from West Point. Camp Totoway was located in what is now Totowa, New Jersey. His pension declaration states that Baron Von Steuben accompanied them during most of these travels.

1 *Lexington Births, Marriages and Deaths*; *Vital Records of Lincoln*; *Vital Records of Bedford*; Pension Record # S11786. His connection with Lincoln is unclear. The author supposes that at age 17, he may have been working and possibly living in Lincoln as a farm laborer. Notwithstanding the fact that he served for Lexington, he evidently returned to Lincoln, as his marriage intention is recorded in Lincoln (without indicating a non-Lincoln residence). There is no marriage record in Lexington. *Vital Records of Bedford* gives his bride's name as Sale Farrel. The birth of their first child is recorded in Bedford approximately 6½ months after their marriage. A third child is recorded in Bedford in 1792, indicating that they were probably still living in Bedford at least into 1792. The date and location of his death is unknown, but it is presumed that he died at or near Milo, New York.

2 "Treasurer's Accompts," April 23, 1782; *Massachusetts Soldiers and Sailors*, Vol. XVII, p. 749.

3 Three possible candidates include:
- John Wood of Concord, son of John and Elisabeth Wood, who was age 36 at the time of this service. This individual appears to be the same John Wood who was living in Leominster when he married Lidia Hosmer of Concord in 1770, and who died in Leominster in 1832 at age 87 or 88, but that is uncertain. His age is given as 87 and 88 in his death record in *Vital Records of Leominster*, but if this is the same individual, and if his birth record is correct, then he was age 86 when he died. No evidence has been found to connect this individual with Lincoln. Even if he may have been born in the section of Concord that became Lincoln, it is not clear why as a Leominster resident he would have been paid for this service by Lincoln instead of by Leominster (*Concord, Massachusetts: Births, Marriages, and Deaths*; *Vital Records of Leominster*).
- John Wood, who shows up in Lincoln records as the father of two children born in 1755 and 1758, and in Concord records as the father of an earlier child in 1751 (by which his age may reasonably be estimated to have been around 50 during this service). This is the only John Wood with an identifiable Lincoln connection (*Vital Records of Lincoln*; *Concord, Massachusetts: Births, Marriages, and Deaths*).
- John Wood or Woods from Cambridge, who married Dorcas Smith of Lexington in 1764 (which would probably make him around age 40 during this service). No evidence has been found to connect this individual with Lincoln (*Lexington Births, Marriages and Deaths*).

Chapter 11

The Army of the King

ADAMS, Joseph, Jr.

Joseph Adams, Jr., of Lincoln was a physician and an outspoken Tory who fled to New York in September 1777 and joined the Massachusetts Company of Volunteers, a loyalist militia unit commanded by Col. Abijah Willard.[1]

On May 18, 1778, he was appointed a surgeon to the store-ship *Greenwich*, where he served for 11 months. He was recommended for a promotion by the commander of the *Greenwich* on February 29, 1779.[2]

He appears subsequently to have been deployed away from the war in America, as in 1780 he saw action against the Spaniards off Cape Finisterre, aboard the *Pegasus*.[3]

By early in 1783, he was in England, serving as surgeon's mate aboard the hospital ship *Tyger*, located in Plymouth harbor. Once again, he was recommended for a promotion, this time to naval surgeon. He retired from service on April 12, 1783, and settled in Cornwall on a pension.[4]

He was born in Lincoln, the son of Capt. Joseph Adams (q.v., Chapter 12) and Mary (Evelyth) Adams; age 26 when the war broke out. He had become a doctor and settled in the town of Townsend before marrying Lovey Lawrence of Lincoln (daughter of Rev. William Lawrence; sister of William Lawrence, Jr. (q.v., Chapter 10)) in November 1774. Probably at about this time, he began communicating information to the Crown authorities in Boston about the storage of Provincial military supplies and about the proceedings of Town Meetings.[5]

Within days of the outbreak of fighting on April 19, 1775, he was placed under house arrest for six months. During the next couple of years, he paid several fines for refusing to serve

---

1 Jones, *The Loyalists of Massachusetts*, pp. 1–2.
2 Ibid. Coldham, *American Migrations* (p. 43), says "he was imprisoned in Philadelphia in July 1778 after being taken by a privateer," but this appears to conflict with the record of his service on the *Greenwich*.
3 Lawrence, *Historical Sketches*, p. 75.
4 Jones, *The Loyalists of Massachusetts*, pp. 1–2.
5 Farrar, comp., Excerpts from Adams, p. 2; *Vital Records of Lincoln*; MacLean, *A Rich Harvest*, pp. 204–205, 302–303; Jones, *The Loyalists of Massachusetts*, p. 1; Bradley and Porter, *Proceedings of The First Church in Lincoln*, p. 65; Lawrence, *Historical Sketches*, pp. 74–76, 140. *Vital Records of Lincoln* shows him already living in Townsend at the time of his marriage intention in September 1774. Jones erroneously gives his marriage as four years earlier, as does *Historical Manual of the Lincoln Church* (p. 57). Lovey's marriage to Joseph Adams (inst.) could not have helped her father's standing in town as a suspected loyalist. He was temporarily barred from preaching one Sabbath morning in the fall of 1774, had some of his letters opened by the Committee of Safety, and he was challenged again over his loyalties in 1779.

According to Coldham, *American Migrations* (p. 43), his career in naval medicine appears to have begun early. He seems to have been a surgeon's mate aboard the H.M.S. *Liberty* on July 19, 1769, when it was boarded, then burned by a colonial mob at Newport, Rhode Island.

against the British, and he was arrested again. He is credited with doing everything in his power to take care of the sick and wounded British prisoners of war in Massachusetts. One night in September 1777, he buried all his manuscripts and account books on his property in Townsend, and fled. "Leaving his wife and property to the mercy of the rebels," he spent 30 days traveling to New York "at the hazard of his life."[1]

A year later, he was specifically named (among others) in the Banishment Act, passed by Massachusetts in September 1778, as having left the state "and joined the enemies thereof, …manifesting an inimical disposition to the said states, and a design, to aid and abet the enemies thereof in their wicked purposes.…" The act provided for his imprisonment and deportation should he return, and for his execution upon returning a second time.[2]

In 1780, his property was seized, rented out, then forfeited, leaving Lovey "destitute of the necessities of life." In 1784, she sailed to join him in England. He died in 1803 in Liskeard, Cornwall, England, at age 54.[3]

Dr. Joseph Adams [Jr.] fled to New York in 1777, where he joined a loyalist militia. Subsequently, he served for five years as a surgeon and surgeon's mate in the Royal Navy before retiring on a pension in Cornwall. His wife was the daughter of Lincoln's pastor; she joined him in England after the war. (Lawrence, *Historical Sketches*)

CUTLER, Ebenezer
[also Ebenezer Jr.]

Ebenezer Cutler was arrested in Northborough on May 17, 1775, as "an avowed enemy of his Country" and was allowed to go to Boston "without his effects." At least by July 5, he

---

1 Jones, *The Loyalists of Massachusetts*, p. 1. One of the fines was for £14, paid to Lt. James Parks (q.v.) of Lincoln in March 1777. A subsequent arrest is indicated in notes communicated privately by Mike Ryan, which report that he was arrested July 1777 in Townsend as an "internal enemy." One of his letters of commendation to British authorities in England comments on his "unremitting attention to the relief and comfort of the British prisoners of war in Massachusetts," for which he suffered considerable abuse, and which apparently triggered his flight. It is not clear what this references, as he had fled Massachusetts before Burgoyne's army was defeated at Saratoga and marched to Cambridge in November 1777.

2 Stark, *The Loyalists of Massachusetts*, pp. 137–140.

3 Notwithstanding the quotation (from Jones, *The Loyalists of Massachusetts*, p. 1), Lovey had probably returned to live with her family in Lincoln. MacLean, *A Rich Harvest*, gives her departure for England both as 1783 (p. 305) and as June 1784 (p. 120). Martin, "The Sons of Lincoln" (p. 103), citing both Lawrence and Adams family sources, says she sailed aboard the *Active*, under Captain Lyde, in June 1784 (traveling coincidently with Abigail Adams, who was on her way to join John in London). Lovey took with her to England her youngest brother, Abel (age 12 at the time of sailing).

MacLean, *A Rich Harvest*, p. 204, and Lawrence, *Historical Sketches*, p. 76, both give Joseph Jr.'s death as 1803. Jones lists his death in 1807, evidently confusing the year with that of Capt. Joseph Adams, his father. 1803 appears to be correct, as that is the year that Lovey reportedly began receiving a pension (see Jones, *The Loyalists of Massachusetts*, p. 2).

was serving in Capt. Abijah Willard's 2nd Company of Associators, a loyalist militia unit, and is presumed to have served until the evacuation of the British army from Boston in March 1776. He is reported to have served with the British army until 1778, when he sailed for England.[1]

Subsequently, he reportedly returned to America, going to New York, where he joined another company of Loyalists.

He is also reported to have served military duty in South Carolina.[2]

In 1781, he appears to have accompanied a detachment of Dragoons to the eastern end of Long Island, New York, and there assisted them in the successful capture of a number of rebel officers.[3]

He was probably about age 34 when the war started; the son of Ebenezer and Anna (Whitney) Cutler; brother of Zaccheus Cutler (q.v.); born in the part of Weston that became Lincoln. He appears to have prospered as a trader, and perhaps as an importer of English goods. For a while, he was a business partner with his brother Jonas in Groton. By 1764, he was living in Oxford, where he married Miriam Eager of Westborough. He operated a store, licensed to sell tea, coffee, and chinaware. He was also a licensed innkeeper.[4]

---

1 Muster Roll of the 2nd Company of Associators (1775); Stark, *The Loyalists of Massachusetts*, p. 469; Jones, *The Loyalists of Massachusetts*, pp. 107–108. Martin, "The Sons of Lincoln" (p. 105), citing records in the Archives of Canada, says he arrived in Boston on June 19, 1775, and that "while in Boston he joined Colonel Willard on an expedition to procure stock for the garrison, and later became a clerk in the Quarter Master General's Department."

 The Associators were also known as the Loyal American Association, consisting of five companies (reduced to three in November, when Timothy Ruggles appears to have been promoted to command, at which time Captain Willard's 2nd Company became the 1st Company). They served less as soldiers, per se, than as a cross between a police force and a type of civil defense agency "to support order and good government" and to promote "the peace, order, and security of the town." They were not uniformed, but they were distinguished by a white scarf tied on their left arm (see Mollo and McGregor. *Uniforms*, p. 172; The On-Line Institute of Advanced Loyalist Studies; Siebert, "Loyalist Troops," p. 118).

 The Associators disbanded at the time the British army left Boston in March 1776. Ebenezer sailed with the British troops to Halifax (see Siebert, "Loyalist Troops," p. 134), then probably to New York. It is presumed that he was probably serving in the New York area before going to England.

2 Jones, *The Loyalists of Massachusetts*, pp. 107–108. The details of service are unknown. Coldham, *American Migrations* (p. 60) reports that after he fled to Boston, "he went first to Halifax and then to NJ, RI, PA, MD and Carolina with the Army," all before he went to England in 1778.

3 Ibid. He was reportedly operating a store on Long Island at this time, certainly under the protection of the British troops in New York. After this mission, the store failed as the locals refused to do business with him.

4 Jones, *The Loyalists of Massachusetts*, pp. 107–108; Daniels, *History of the Town of Oxford*, pp. 237, 456–457; *Town of Weston, Births, Deaths, & Marriages*; *Vital Records of Oxford*.

 Daniels, along with Stark, *The Loyalists of Massachusetts* (p. 468), Cutter, *Historic Homes of Middlesex County* (vol. III, p. 1347), and Cutler, *Cutler Memorial* (pp. 331, 559) all list him as the son of Ebenezer Cutler of Salem (b. 1695) who settled in Sutton and married Mary Stockwell in 1732. But Cutler cautiously tacks Ebenezer and Zaccheus at the end of the list of children, without detail (in distinct contrast to the other names), and hedges: "The compiler has been unable to find church or town records fully verifying the theory that Ebenezer and Zacheus were children of Ebenezer and Mary (Stockwell) Cutler." The records are found in Weston, not Sutton or Salem, and they clearly show the theory to be wrong: Ebenezer and Zaccheus were the sons of Ebenezer and Anna Cutler living in Weston. Neither birth is recorded, and their baptisms in Weston were clearly not infant baptisms. Ebenezer's age is estimated from Daniels, who gives his age at death as 90, and from Martin, "The Sons of Lincoln" (p. 25), who finds him on the muster roll of Lincoln's 1757 militia company, at which time he would have been at least age 16.

 Miriam was the sister of Hazadiah Eager, who later married his brother, Zaccheus Cutler (q.v.).

In June 1770, while on a supply run to Boston, he appears to have flaunted his disgust with the non-importation agreement, and purchased a large quantity of British goods, including tea, from another non-compliant merchant. Upon embarking on his return journey, he was overtaken and set upon by a mob, which made a spectacle of parading him through the streets of Boston before absconding with his merchandise. Subsequently, he sued the ringleaders for redress, but the court returned only a token judgment.[1]

He appears to have been living at Northborough when the war broke out. After taking him into custody, Northborough's Committee of Correspondence was unsure what to do with him, so they turned his case over to the Committee of Safety in Cambridge. The case was sent up to Congress for examination and trial. After reviewing the case, and concluding that all of Cutler's offending comments against the Continental and Provincial Congresses "were uttered some time ago," the Provincial Congress voted not to imprison him, but to allow him instead to go to Boston as he desired.[2]

He was specifically named (among others) in the Banishment Act, passed by Massachusetts in September 1778, as having left the state "and joined the enemies thereof,…manifesting an inimical disposition to the said states, and a design, to aid and abet the enemies thereof in their wicked purposes…." The act provided for his imprisonment and deportation should he return, and for his execution upon returning a second time.[3] His property was confiscated the next year.

After his war service, he received a 1442-acre land grant in Digby Township, Annapolis County, Nova Scotia, where he settled. He continued to make a living as a merchant, and he also became the chief clerk of the Court of Annapolis County. Miriam remained in Northborough, where she died in 1784. Subsequently, he married Mary Hicks, daughter of a British officer, in England. He died at Annapolis in 1831, reportedly age 90.[4]

CUTLER, Zaccheus

Zaccheus Cutler was living in Amherst, New Hampshire, when having "in a very daring manner proved himself inimical to his country," he fled "and joined our unnatural enemies

---

1 Martin, "The Sons of Lincoln" (pp. 42–45) contains a more detailed summary of the incident, taken from court documents. (She cites: The 1771 Book of the Superior Court of the Judicature, p. 140. Massachusetts Archives, Book 1772:124–125; Plea of Review, 15 September 1772; Books 90, 97; Reels 635, 152615.)
  Stark, *The Loyalists of Massachusetts* (p. 468) indicates that it was this incident that turned him into an avowed loyalist. This may or may not be true, but it would appear that he had little sympathy for the radical movement in the first place.

2 Stark, *The Loyalists of Massachusetts*, p. 469; Jones, *The Loyalists of Massachusetts*, pp. 107–108; Cutler, *Cutler Memorial*, p. 561; *Journals of Each Provincial Congress*, pp. 253, 552–553. See also Sabine, *The American Loyalists*, pp. 238–239. Notwithstanding the arrest and official ruling, there appears to be more to the story. Stark says of his arrest, he "had many enemies among the revolutionists, and a price was set on his capture. He had many narrow escapes before they got him. Once he was hidden in a farmhouse between the chimney and outer wall, most suffocated by smoke." Jones, drawing on documents archived in London, does not mention his arrest and passage to Boston, but says "he escaped to Portsmouth, New Hampshire, and thence to HMS Scarborough and to Boston."

3 Stark, *The Loyalists of Massachusetts*, pp. 137–140.

4 Daniels, *History of the Town of Oxford*, p. 457; Cutler, *Cutler Memorial*, p. 561; Cutler, *Invoice Book*. Stark, *The Loyalists of Massachusetts* (p. 469), says Miriam died at Worcester.

Chapter 11: The Army of the King

The home of Zaccheus Cutler in Amherst, New Hampshire (shown here in the early 1900s), was confiscated and sold after he joined "our unnatural enemies in Boston." The Lincoln native was reportedly lost at sea while on a British military mission in 1780. (Courtesy of the Historical Society of Amherst, NH)

in Boston." In Boston, he reportedly helped regain the allegiance of the soldiers who had deserted the town on March 10, 1775.[1]

In Boston, he appears on the July 5, 1775, muster roll of Capt. Abijah Willard's 2nd Company of Associators, a loyalist militia unit. He reportedly did garrison duty as a lieutenant before going to Halifax with the evacuating British army in March 1776, but this is uncertain.[2]

Subsequently, he appears to have gone to New York with the British army. The details of this service are not reported.[3]

He was the son of Ebenezer and Anna (Whitney) Cutler; born in the part of Weston that became Lincoln; brother of Ebenezer Cutler (q.v.). He may have been in his early 30s

---

1 Coldham, *American Migrations*, p. 122; Secomb, *History of the Town of Amherst*, pp. 381, 389. The quotes are from the May 30, 1776, Amherst Town Meeting action dealing with his abandoned property. His having helped to regain the allegiance of the deserted soldiers is a curious report about an incident that is unexplained. It is not known just *when* Zaccheus went to Boston, but as a prosperous merchant and prominent citizen, it is likely that he may have remained in New Hampshire at least until the fighting broke out on April 19, 1775—well *after* the apparent date of the desertion. Whether he went to Boston before or after the war started, if the soldiers had left the town of Boston, and he had arrived as a refugee, then it seems unlikely that he would have ventured out after them. This would be particularly so after April 19th. On the other hand (if this be the case), perhaps it is a measure of the respect he may still have commanded, for a time at least, that he could still mediate such an affair, even in the rebellious countryside. Another possibility is that the date may be misstated—that these may have been March 10, *1776*, desertions in the face of the British evacuation of Boston. Further identification and investigation of this incident would be interesting.

2 Muster Roll of the 2nd Company of Associators (1775); Coldham, *American Migrations*, p. 122. Jones, *The Loyalists of Massachusetts* (p. 108), says he did military service as a lieutenant in New Hampshire, but this is probably in error. No New Hampshire military record has been found; nor is it clear how such a record would accord with the records of his being a Loyalist. Jones may have meant to place this service in Boston, which would be consistent with Coldham. However, he is not listed as a lieutenant (or as an officer) on any of the surviving muster rolls of the Associators. (For more information about the Associators, see note 1, p. 449.)

3 Coldham, *American Migrations*, p. 122.

when the war broke out. He had married Hazadiah Eager (sister of Miriam Eager, wife of his brother, Ebenezer) of Northborough, Massachusetts, in 1771.[1]

He is reported to have settled in New Hampshire before 1768, where he appears to have prospered as a trader. He had been appointed Justice of the Peace, and also served as a Justice of the Court of General Sessions. In 1772, he bought additional property in Amherst.[2]

He was banished from the state in November 1778. The act provided for his imprisonment and deportation should he return, and for his execution upon returning a second time. His property was formally confiscated the same year.[3]

In 1780, he was lost at sea en route between London and South Carolina, evidently on some sort of military mission.[4] His age when he died may have been mid-thirties to late thirties.

RUSSELL, Charles

Charles Russell of Lincoln was a physician and a prominent Tory who fled Lincoln for the safety of the British garrison in Boston when war broke out in April 1775. Serving as a volunteer, he attended British casualties after the Battle of Bunker Hill.[5]

He had been one of Lincoln's leading citizens, having served multiple terms as the Town Moderator and a term as Selectman. He was the son of Judge James Russell and Katherine (Graves) Russell of Charlestown; age approximately 37 when he fled Lincoln. He had graduated from Harvard College in 1757, and earned his M.D. in Aberdeen, Scotland, in 1765, before having married Elizabeth Vassall of Cambridge in 1768. Elizabeth was the daughter of Col. Henry Vassall, who lived on the infamous Tory Row (i.e., Brattle Street, many of the residents of which were Tories). Economically and socially prominent, Russell had a considerable medical practice and owned a large estate in Lincoln. He held the official positions of Justice of the Peace, and Registrar of the Vice Admiralty Court.[6]

---

1 *Vital Records of Northborough; Town of Weston, Births, Deaths, & Marriages.* No birth record exists to determine his age. His age is at best a guess from a baptism record that is clearly not an infant baptism.

  Cutter, *Historic Homes of Middlesex County* (Vol. III, p. 1347) and Cutter, *Cutler Memorial* (pp. 331, 559), both list him as the son of Ebenezer Cutler of Salem (b. 1695) who settled in Sutton and married Mary Stockwell in 1732. But Cutter cautiously tacks Ebenezer and Zaccheus at the end of the list of children, without detail (in distinct contrast to the other names), and hedges: "The compiler has been unable to find church or town records fully verifying the theory that Ebenezer and Zacheus were children of Ebenezer and Mary (Stockwell) Cutler." The records are found in Weston, not Sutton or Salem, and they clearly show the theory to be wrong: Ebenezer and Zaccheus were the sons of Ebenezer and Anna Cutler living in Weston.

2 Cutler, *Cutler Memorial*, p. 559; Secomb, *History of the Town of Amherst*, p. 389; Hurd, *History of Hillsborough County*, p. 6. He appears to have lived in New Boston for a time before moving to Amherst.

3 Cutler, *Cutler Memorial*, p. 559; Secomb, *History of the Town of Amherst*, p. 389.

4 Jones, *The Loyalists of Massachusetts*, p. 108.

5 Jones, *The Loyalists of Massachusetts*, p. 253.

6 MacLean, *A Rich Harvest*, pp. 138, 140, 163, 242, 282, 302; Jones, *The Loyalists of Massachusetts*, p. 253. He inherited the estate, which is now known as the Codman House, from his uncle, Judge Chambers Russell, in 1766. MacLean says that after Charles Russell fled from Lincoln, his father occupied the estate until it was confiscated in May 1777. Jones indicates that his father was also a Tory, but MacLean disagrees. The author concurs with MacLean. Had the elder Russell been a Tory, logically, he would not have been allowed to occupy the estate, nor been elected Selectman and Moderator of the town as he was, in the early 1780s. Jones evidently confuses his father James with his Tory brother, James, who became a successful British privateer (see Martin, *The Chambers–Russell–Codman House*, pp. 110, 128, 141).

Chapter 11: The Army of the King

Dr. Charles Russell fled Lincoln when the war broke out. He tended British soldiers wounded at the Battle of Bunker Hill, then he left Boston for Antigua. This painting is a fragment of the original full-length portrait, cut out in 1819 by his daughter, Catherine, who was piqued because the portrait had been bequeathed to her sister, Penelope, instead. (Courtesy of the Massachusetts Historical Society)

In September 1774, someone shot at his carriage. His father-in-law, Henry Vassall, was riding in it at the time. Vassall was unhurt, but Russell understood that he, rather than his father-in-law, had probably been the intended target. The incident inflamed tensions between loyalist and patriot factions in Lincoln. When fighting broke out on April 19, 1775, Russell fled with his family to Boston.[1]

Shortly after the Battle of Bunker Hill, Russell left Boston and settled in Antigua, where he continued to practice medicine.

In September 1778, he was specifically named (among others) in the Banishment Act, passed by Massachusetts, as having left the state "and joined the enemies thereof,... manifesting an inimical disposition to the said states, and a design, to aid and abet the enemies thereof in their wicked purposes...." The act provided for his imprisonment and deportation should he return, and for his execution upon returning a second time.[2]

He died at Antigua in 1780 (at approximately age 42). Elizabeth and their four daughters returned to Lincoln for a while after the war.[3]

---

1 For more details of the shooting incident, see Martin, *The Chambers–Russell–Codman House* (pp. 107–108).
2 Stark, *The Loyalists of Massachusetts*, pp. 137–140.
3 MacLean, *A Rich Harvest*, pp. 138, 140, 163, 242, 282, 302; Jones, *The Loyalists of Massachusetts*, p. 253. *Historical Manual of the Lincoln Church* (p. 93), apparently erroneously, places his death at Martinique.

Chapter 12

The "Detachment" of Unsubstantiated Claimants

Author's note: The nature of historical information is that much misinformation circulates side-by-side with well-documented evidence. Historical integrity requires that occasionally the chaff be separated from the wheat, a process that has sometimes been missing from the assorted compilations and credits for Revolutionary War participation by Lincoln individuals. The individuals profiled in this chapter came to the attention of the author through the same records, secondary sources, lists, and other reports of service as those named in Chapters 10 and 11. However, in each case, the author's investigation has failed to find satisfactory evidence either of service for the individual or of a reliable Lincoln connection.

Inclusion in this chapter does not necessarily mean that the individual positively did not serve; it means simply that the author has not found reliable evidence that he did. Some of the names are clearly reporting errors that have accumulated through the years. Others may reflect differences of historical interpretation. For still others, reliable evidence of a Lincoln connection or of Revolutionary service may yet be discovered. Indeed, the missing muster roll for the militia company on April 19, 1775, highlights the caution required in interpreting a missing record as evidence of non-service. Each circumstance is different, and the possibility remains that for some members of this "detachment" a previously undiscovered primary source or compelling argument may warrant a future attribution of service which the author cannot now make.

ADAMS, Joseph
[also Captain Joseph]

The town paid Capt. Joseph Adams for service at Ticonderoga in 1776, for half of a three-year campaign in the Continental Army.[1]

He was age 52 at the time of Ticonderoga, probably 55 by the time he would have finished 1½ years of Continental Army service. He had served in leadership positions in the Lincoln militia, appearing in town records as coronet in 1760 and as captain in 1766. He continued to be referred to by the honorific "Captain" long after he relinquished command to younger individuals.

He had been married to Mary Evelyth of Stow since 1746. He was one of the town fathers, having been active in the formation and early history of the town, and having served as Selectman periodically in the early 1770s. He died in 1807 at age 83, and he is buried in the Meeting House Cemetery behind Bemis Hall.

---

1 "Treasurer's Accompts," June 15, 1779.

Although it is theoretically possible that he could have provided the service for which he was paid, in the absence of a service record, per se, there is little logic in imagining him re-entering the military in his 50s, particularly in a non-leadership role.[1]

It is likely that this service was provided either by his son, Charles (age 25 in 1776), or by his son, Nathan (age 16 in 1776), or perhaps by his son-in-law, Elisha Wheeler (q.v.). However, this is entirely speculative, as no service records for this service, recognizable as belonging to any of these three individuals, has yet been discovered. See also [unidentified] Adams (?) (q.v., Chapter 10).

BROOKS, John

John Brooks's headstone in the Meeting House Cemetery was marked, in the early twentieth century, with a Sons of the American Revolution marker.[2]

He was paid by the town for "the fourth part of a Man for three years and for part of a man at Ticonderoga in the year 1776." The transaction does not suggest that he actually put in any service, himself.[3]

Massachusetts Soldiers and Sailors contains a number of records for service by various individuals named John Brooks. However, there is nothing in any of the records to connect the John Brooks of the record with Lincoln.[4]

Interestingly, he does not show up on a 1901 SAR listing of marked gravesites. The origin or justification for the SAR marker is unclear.[5]

---

1 *Vital Records of Lincoln*; *Concord, Massachusetts: Births, Marriages, and Deaths*; MacLean, *A Rich Harvest*, p. 138; Farrar, comp., Excerpts from Adams, p. 2. The honorific can be found in the birth records of his children, as well as in the "Treasurer's Accompts." Notwithstanding that his grave was marked by the Sons of the American Revolution (see *Soldiers and Sailors* [SAR], p. 30), Biggs, "In Memorium" (p. 155), makes no mention of an SAR marker at his grave in the Meeting House Cemetery. It may or may not be significant that Farrar, "Adams Genealogy," which contains "SAR" notations beside several names, omits such a notation for Joseph Adams.

2 Biggs, "In Memorium," p. 160.

3 "Treasurer's Accompts," June 10, 1779. The practice of providing a surrogate for service was a standard and accepted method for avoiding military service oneself during the Revolutionary War. The "Treasurer's Accompts" clearly distinguish between service and providing a man for service. The town made a number of payments to individuals for providing a man for service. It is assumed that the payment was the same as if the individual had served himself, and that the individual made some sort of private deal with the person who actually served, but the author has not attempted to "follow the money." His purpose has been simply to determine whether or not an individual actually served. In this case, no reliable evidence has been found of any service by a John Brooks of Lincoln.

4 *Massachusetts Soldiers and Sailors*, Vol. II, pp. 574–577.

5 *Soldiers and Sailors* [SAR], p. 30. The headstone provides no information about him. *Vital Records of Lincoln* contains a John Brooks who died in 1812 at age 89. If this is the same John Brooks who is in the Meeting House Cemetery, he would have been age 52 or 53 when he hired a man for Ticonderoga. He appears to be the brother of Eleazer Brooks (q.v., Chapter 10); father of Daniel Brooks (q.v., Chapter 10) and Job Brooks (q.v., Chapter 10).

BROOKS, Levi

Levi Brooks is credited by Lincoln historian William Wheeler with service at Saratoga in Captain Minot's Company, from August 14, 1777, to November 30, 1777. No reliable record of this service has been found. Levi Brooks was only age 14 in August 1777.[1]

He was the son of Ephraim Brooks (q.v., Chapter 10) and Sarah Brooks; brother of Ephraim Brooks, Jr. (q.v., Chapter 10), Benjamin Brooks (q.v., Chapter 10), and Abner Brooks (q.v., Chapter 10); age 12 when the war broke out. He would have been old enough to have served by 1779, but in fact, no meaningful record of any service by Levi Brooks has been found. He married Lydia Stone, sister of Gregory Stone (q.v., Chapter 10) in 1794. He died in Lincoln in 1833 at age 70.[2]

He is buried in the Meeting House Cemetery behind Bemis Hall, with an SAR marker, the justification for which is unclear.[3]

BROOKS, Thomas

Thomas Brooks was paid by the town for one-third of a three-year campaign in the Continental Army. No dates of service are indicated. He was also paid for service at Providence in the year 1777.[4]

He certainly did not serve either of these stints, as he was age 73 when the war broke out. It is likely that this service was provided by his son, Stephen Brooks (q.v., Chapter 10).

Thomas was the son of Noah and Dorothy Brooks; father of Aaron Brooks (q.v., Chapter 10), Noah Brooks (q.v., Chapter 10), and Stephen Brooks (q.v., Chapter 10); uncle of Samuel Dakin, Jr. (q.v., Chapter 10). He had been married to Hannah Dakin since 1725. He owned the wood pasture at the Bloody Angles, where 1,000 Provincials ambushed the column of

---

1 Wheeler, "Lincoln," in Hurd, Vol. 2, p. 622; *Vital Records of Lincoln*. It is not inconceivable for a 14-year-old to have served at Saratoga. There is ample evidence of underage service during the war. Underage service was the exception, however, not the rule. Accordingly, there must be evidence which cannot be otherwise explained to conclude, case by case, that underage service occurred. Unfortunately, Wheeler is not necessarily a reliable source, and we have found no other evidence (either primary source or secondary source) to support Wheeler's assertion, or of any service at all by a Levi Brooks of Lincoln. Both *An Account of the Celebration* (p. 238) and the *War Memorial Book* in the Historical Room at the Lincoln Public Library do credit him with service. However, both of these lists appear to have been derived largely from Wheeler; and in the absence of any verifiable source information, neither list rises to the standard of a meaningful or reliable record

It is not clear what Wheeler had in mind, what his source information was, or how the error came about. *Massachusetts Soldiers and Sailors* (Vol. II, p. 580) does reveal a Levi Brooks from Westminster who was at Saratoga, but he was neither a Lincoln person nor a member of Captain Minot's Company. His Pension Record (# S19568) confirms that he is a different person from Levi Brooks (inst.).

Unfortunately, proving the negative is nearly impossible; without further information, one cannot even conclude with any confidence that Levi Brooks (inst.) positively *did not* serve. One cannot declare that Wheeler is necessarily wrong, in this case. It is not difficult to imagine Levi watching his father and brothers go off to war, and wishing he could join them. One can even imagine a 14-year-old furtively plotting to join his brother, Abner Brooks (q.v., Chapter 10), on the march northward to Saratoga. But the author has simply found no evidence that he did, or any evidence to support a conclusion that Levi Brooks provided any service during the Revolutionary War, at all.

2 *Vital Records of Lincoln*

3 Biggs, "In Memorium," p. 163; *Soldiers and Sailors* [SAR], p. 30. The SAR marker may possibly be the result of Wheeler's unsupported assertion.

4 "Treasurer's Accompts," June 10, 1779.

Regulars during their return march to Boston on April 19, 1775. He died in Lincoln in 1790, at age 89, and is buried in the Old Hill Burying Ground in Concord.[1]

BROWN, Nathan (Sr.)

There were three generations of Nathan Browns, and considerable confusion has ensued over which one was which. The *War Memorial Book* and *An Account of the Celebration* credit both Nathan Brown and Nathan Brown, Jr., with service.

The first Nathan Brown was age 71 in 1775, obviously too old for service. The second Nathan Brown (frequently appearing as Nathan Brown, Jr.) died in 1764 at age 39. Obviously, he could not have served, either.[2]

In fact, the service records all belong to the same individual: the third generation Nathan Brown. The third Nathan Brown became known as Nathan Brown, Jr., upon the death of his father. Modern historians variously refer to him as Nathan Brown III or Capt. Nathan Brown (he apparently became captain sometime after 1786) to distinguish Nathan Jr. (the father) from Nathan Jr. (the son). At the risk of causing further confusion between the different Nathans, the author has chosen to refer to Nathan III as Nathan Brown, Jr. (q.v., Chapter 10), consistent with the way he was known in 1775. No other Nathan Brown from Lincoln served in the Revolutionary War.

CHILD, Joshua (Sr.)

Because the muster roll for Capt. William Smith's Company of Minute Men lists Joshua Child, Jr., while the Dorchester Heights Muster Roll lists Joshua Child (without the designation Jr.), the *War Memorial Book* and *An Account of the Celebration* list service by Joshua Child and Joshua Child, Jr., as different individuals.[3]

The elder Joshua Child had just turned age 59 at the time of Dorchester Heights. He was the son of David and Beriah (Bemis) Child of Waltham, and he had been married to Grace Bemis since 1741.[4]

While it may be theoretically possible that the elder Joshua Child could have served at Dorchester, it defies logic to think that this service was not provided by Joshua Jr. No record has been found of any service by a Joshua Child that does not fit Joshua Child, Jr. (q.v., Chapter 10). As far as war service goes, the logical conclusion is that Joshua Child and Joshua Child, Jr., are the same individual. See Joshua Child, Jr. (q.v., Chapter 10).

DAKIN, Samuel (Sr.)

Because he appears on the muster roll for Capt. William Smith's Company of Minute Men as Samuel Dakin, Jr., and on the Dorchester Heights Muster Roll as Samuel Dakin

---

1 *Concord, Massachusetts: Births, Marriages, and Deaths*; *Vital Records of Lincoln*; Malcolm, *The Scene of Battle*, p. 72. See also Fischer, *Paul Revere's Ride*, p. 223; "Find a Grave."
2 *Concord, Massachusetts: Births, Marriages, and Deaths*; *Vital Records of Lincoln*.
3 See Coburn, *Muster Rolls*; Hartwell, "A List of a Company of Militia."
4 Bond, *Genealogies of the Families of Watertown*, p. 154.

(without the Jr.), the *War Memorial Book* and *An Account of the Celebration* mistakenly list service by Samuel Dakin and Samuel Dakin, Jr., as different individuals.[1]

As Samuel Dakin, Sr., was age 75 at the time of Dorchester Heights, it defies logic to think that this service was not provided by Samuel Jr.[2] All the records which have been found for service by a Samuel Dakin fit for Samuel Dakin, Jr. As far as war service goes, the conclusion is inescapable that Samuel Dakin and Samuel Dakin, Jr., are the same individual. This is entirely consistent with *Massachusetts Soldiers and Sailors*, which makes no attempt to separate the records of Samuel Dakin from those of Samuel Dakin, Jr.[3] See Samuel Dakin, Jr. (q.v., Chapter 10).

FARRAR, Samuel
[also Deacon Samuel]

Deacon Samuel Farrar was paid by the town for service at Ticonderoga in 1776 and for one-half of a three-year term of service in the Continental Army.[4] As he would have been age 67 at Ticonderoga, probably age 68 or 69 in the Continental service, there is virtually no possibility that he actually served this time.[5]

Deacon Samuel Farrar was one of the founding fathers of the town of Lincoln. He served as a Selectman for 21 years, as the Town Clerk, as the Town Moderator, and as the town's Representative to the Great and General Court. In the year and a half leading up to the war, he also served on the town's Committee of Correspondence.[6]

He was the son of George and Mary (Howe) Farrar, and he had married Lydia Barrett in 1732. He was also the father of Samuel Farrar, Jr. (q.v., Chapter 10), Stephen Farrar (q.v., Chapter 10), and Timothy Farrar (q.v., Chapter 10); the father-in-law (and uncle) of Humphrey Farrar (q.v., Chapter 10); the grandfather of William Bond (q.v., Chapter 10), Samuel Bond (q.v., Chapter 10), and Jonas Bond (q.v., Chapter 10). In 1756, he donated the land for the Meeting House Cemetery, where he was laid to rest in 1783 at the age of 75.[7]

If Deacon Samuel Farrar did not serve at Ticonderoga and in the Continental Army, then who did? As the town paid Samuel Jr. for identical service on the same day it paid Deacon Samuel, we can logically rule him out. Similarly, the Deacon's son-in-law, Humphrey, was

---

1 See Coburn, *Muster Rolls;* Hartwell, "A List of a Company of Militia."
2 *Concord, Massachusetts: Births, Marriages, and Deaths;* MacLean, *A Rich Harvest*, p. 181.
3 *Massachusetts Soldiers and Sailors*, Vol. IV, p. 364.
4 "Treasurer's Accompts," June 15, 1779
5 *Concord, Massachusetts: Births, Marriages, and Deaths.* Although few scholars of the events at Concord are guilty of confusing Deacon Samuel Farrar (inst.), who was not at Concord, with Samuel Farrar, Jr. (q.v.), who was lieutenant of the minute company (and probably also acting captain of the militia company), the Farrar family clung for many years to the myth of Deacon Samuel having served at Concord and beyond. See Briggs, "Five hundred years of Farrar family," and Farrar, "Record from Memoirs," p. 7. Notwithstanding such unexamined reporting of family lore, it is simply not credible that a 66-year-old would have led a company at Concord or served in subsequent campaigns.
6 MacLean, *A Rich Harvest*, p. 139.
7 *Concord, Massachusetts: Births, Marriages, and Deaths; Vital Records of Lincoln;* MacLean, *A Rich Harvest*, p. 402; Biggs, "In Memorium," p. 170. The SAR marker on his tombstone evidently came about because of the entry in the Treasurer's accounts, without anyone having investigated his age or critically evaluated the reasonableness of the conclusion.

paid for other service on the same day. There would seem little reason for the town not to have paid Humphrey directly if he had provided the service.

Deacon Samuel Farrar had three other sons, Stephen, James, and Timothy. Stephen attended Harvard, was ordained as a minister, and became Pastor of a church in New Ipswich, New Hampshire in 1760. He married Eunice Brown of Lincoln in 1764. James is reported to have died in New Ipswich in 1767. Timothy attended Harvard, also settled in New Ipswich, New Hampshire, and by 1775 had become a lawyer. Both Stephen and Timothy served on the April 19th Alarm, then returned to New Ipswich. Neither appears to have left any record of further service in the Revolutionary War[1] (see Stephen Farrar (q.v., Chapter 10) and Timothy Farrar (q.v., Chapter 10)).

Another possibility might be an unidentified slave or indentured servant of Deacon Samuel. MacLean does list Samuel Farrar as a slaveholder, and specifically references Kate, but provides no information about the possibility of a slave who might have served in the war. Similarly, we have yet to uncover any records of individuals who might have provided this service and on whom Samuel might have held an indenture.[2]

Another possibility appears to be his grandson, Jonas Bond (q.v., Chapter 10). Jonas was orphaned in 1775, at age 15, and Deacon Samuel was the closest surviving lineal relation. If the Bond family had not already been living in close proximity to the Farrars, the Farrars appear to have taken Jonas and his brothers under their wings following the death of their parents. Deacon Samuel would certainly have been the appropriate surrogate, if the town could not pay Jonas directly.

The town paid Jonas's brothers, Samuel Bond (q.v., Chapter 10) and William Bond (q.v., Chapter 10), directly for their service during the war. There is no record of the town paying Jonas for his Ticonderoga service, for his nine months of service in the Continental Army, or for further Continental service at West Point that Jonas mentions briefly and cryptically in his pension declaration. Accordingly, the author concludes that Jonas Bond was probably the provider of the service for which Deacon Samuel was paid.

FREE, Jupiter

Jupiter Free of Lexington enlisted in the Continental Army for three years on March 10, 1777. He served in Capt. Edmund Munroe's Company, Col. Timothy Bigelow's Regiment. After Captain Munroe was killed in June 1778, he served in Captain Bowman's Company until the expiration of his term on March 10, 1780. During the early months of 1779, they were stationed at Providence. He is listed as a resident of Lexington, and his service was credited to Lexington.[3]

---

1 MacLean, *A Rich Harvest*, pp. 202–203; Shattuck, *History of the Town of Concord*, p. 314; Briggs, "Five hundred years of Farrar family." There is a record of Ticonderoga and Continental service for a Timothy Farrar of Chelmsford (see *Massachusetts Soldiers and Sailors*, Vol. V, pp. 537, 540), but he appears to be unconnected to Lincoln or to Timothy Farrar (q.v., Chapter 10). Timothy (q.v., Chapter 10) eventually became a prominent New Hampshire attorney, a senior law partner to Daniel Webster, Justice of the New Hampshire Superior Court, and Chief Justice of the Circuit Court of Common Pleas. He lived into his 102nd year and died at Hollis, New Hampshire, in 1849.

2 MacLean, *A Rich Harvest*, pp. 219–220.

3 *Massachusetts Soldiers and Sailors*, Vol. XVI, p. 40. This record is recorded as Jupiter Tree, but this is believed to be in error. See also Blake, "James Barrett's Returns of Men" (p. 471), which confirms the enlistment (without indicating the term), and says he was paid a bounty.

He may be the Jupiter Free of Attleborough who served on an alarm at Tiverton in Capt. Samuel Robinson's Company, Col. Isaac Dean's Regiment, from August 5, 1780, through August 8, 1780 (credited with 3 days of service plus 2 days of travel home), but this is speculative.[1]

It is reasonable to presume that he was a slave or former slave who adopted the name Free either at the time of his manumission or at the time of his Continental enlistment, in anticipation of his manumission upon the completion of his three year term of Continental service.[2] However, the record provides no information as to his identity, and no information to connect him with Lincoln.

There is a record of a Lincoln slave named Jupiter, owned by Joshua Brooks in 1756. His marriage to Peg, a slave of William Reed of Lexington, was duly recorded in Lexington Vital Records. He is presumed to be the father of Peter Nelson (q.v., Chapter 10), the 19-month-old boy who was sold by Joshua Brooks to Josiah Nelson (q.v., Chapter 10) in 1765.[3]

In her narrative about a slave named Peter, Joyce Malcolm asserts this identity for Jupiter Free. Connecting the two Jupiters, however, is highly speculative. The author has found no evidence to support this supposition, and no record to connect Jupiter Free to Lincoln.[4]

GOVE, John
[also Deacon John]

Deacon John Gove was, according to Lincoln historian William Wheeler, a veteran of the French and Indian War, who returned to service in 1776 for the campaign to New York. Indeed, town records indicate that he was paid for this service by the town.[5]

However, he was age 69 during the New York campaign. The likelihood that he participated in this campaign seems very remote.[6]

More probable is that this campaign may have been served by one of his slaves, Tombo, Lot, or another (unidentified) slave, or by one of his sons, John, Jonathan, or Nathaniel. See [Unidentified] Gove (?) (q.v., Chapter 10).

---

1 *Massachusetts Soldiers and Sailors*, Vol. VI, p. 27. Outside of the name, there is little to connect this record with the Jupiter Tree who provided Continental service. For these records to be the same person, he would have had to leave Lexington and take up residence in Attleborough following his discharge from Continental service.

2 The fact that he was paid a bounty (see Blake, "James Barrett's Returns of Men," p. 471) suggests that he was probably already a free man at the time of his enlistment.

3 *Lexington Births, Marriages and Deaths*. See also Brooks bill of sale to Nelson (1765); Wiggin, "A Tale of Two or Three Peters"; Malcolm, *Peter's War*, pp. 3–7.

4 Malcolm, *Peter's War*; Wiggin, "A Tale of Two or Three Peters." Malcolm's assertion appears to be a leap of faith, as she offers no evidence to support her identification. Despite the lack of evidence, the possibility exists that her identification could be correct, but this is suppositional at best. With no source citations, little evidence, and a number of identified errors, the author finds little credence in the supposition advanced by Malcolm that Jupiter Free was a Lincoln person.

5 Wheeler, "Lincoln," in Hurd, Vol. 2, p. 622; "Treasurer's Accompts," November 11, 1779.

6 *Vital Records of Lincoln*; Bond, *Genealogies of the Families of Watertown*, p. 258. Bond even suggests that he may already have died by this time, as he lists John's wife Tabitha as a widow when she died in 1769. *Vital Records of Lincoln*, however, lists Tabitha when she died, as wife of Deacon John. This, along with the record of his having been paid by the town ten years later, is good enough for the author to conclude that he was still very much alive in 1776. However, it does not establish that he actually served.

Interestingly, there is a curious suggestion that Deacon John may have harbored loyalist sympathies. MacLean cites a fictional 1827 account of the events of 1775, in which the author seems to have portrayed his characters knowingly. Deacon John is characterized as "one of His Majesty's friends."[1]

He had married Tabitha Livermore in 1738; she had died in 1769. No record of when or where he died has been found, except that Concord historian Lemuel Shattuck says he served as a Deacon for "about 40 years" from 1749.[2]

HARTWELL, Daniel

Daniel Hartwell's name appears in the *War Memorial Book* as having served in the American Revolution. However, no record has been found of any service by a Daniel Hartwell who could possibly have been connected with Lincoln.[3]

HARTWELL, Ephraim

Coronet Ephraim Hartwell was paid by the town for nine months of service in the Continental Army.[4] There is no record of when and where that service was provided. However, as he was in the neighborhood of 70 years old at the time, we can be reasonably certain that this service was provided by someone other than Coronet Ephraim Hartwell.

Just who did provide this service remains a mystery. It could possibly have been any one of his sons, Samuel (q.v., Chapter 10), Ephraim Jr. (q.v., Chapter 10), John (q.v., Chapter 10), Isaac (q.v., Chapter 10), or Jonas (q.v., Chapter 10).[5] Another possibility is that it might

---

1 See MacLean, *A Rich Harvest*, p. 303. MacLean refers to the story of John Howe, a supposed British spy who traveled to Concord under the guise of a gunsmith, and succeeded in collecting vast amounts of intelligence for General Gage. The story is told in *The Journal Kept by John Howe While He was Employed as a British Spy*, published by Luther Roby in Concord, New Hampshire in 1827. While the story of John Howe has been discredited by historians as a hoax, MacLean suggests that the context and the supporting characters may be more true-to-life than the central character. Much of Howe's story appears to have been plagiarized from the accounts of Ensign de Berniere's real-life scouting expedition to Concord and Worcester in February 1775.

2 *Vital Records of Lincoln*; Bond, *Genealogies of the Families of Watertown*, p. 258; Shattuck, *History of the Town of Concord*, p. 308.

3 The source of this appears to be *Soldiers and Sailors* [SAR] (p. 30), which lists a "Daniel Hartwell (Captain)." This listing is obviously intended to be Captain Daniel Harrington, not Captain Daniel Hartwell, making this a perfect example of a careless error that gets perpetuated by a subsequent party. Biggs, "In Memorium" (p. 173), correctly connects the SAR marker with Daniel Harrington (q.v., Chapter 10), correctly showing no evidence of a Daniel Hartwell buried in Lincoln.

   Even if we could find a record of service for a Daniel Hartwell who could have been from Lincoln, there does not appear to have been a Daniel Hartwell from Lincoln who could have qualified. In *Concord, Massachusetts: Births, Marriages, and Deaths*, we find a Daniel Hartwell, son of William and Ruth Hartwell, born in 1709. He would have been age 66 when the war broke out. There is also a Daniel R. Hartwell of Weston, who recorded his intention to marry Sarah A. Britton of Watertown in 1749. Although it is impossible to ascertain his age from the record, he would almost certainly have been at least age 45 when the war broke out. *Vital Records of Bedford* reveal a Danel Hartwell, son of Danel and Sarah, born in 1735 (age 40 when the war broke out), and a Daniel Hartwell, son of Solomon and Abigail, born in 1762 (age 13 when the war broke out). None of these individuals has an identifiable connection with Lincoln (*Concord, Massachusetts: Births, Marriages, and Deaths*; *Town of Weston, Births, Deaths, & Marriages*; *Vital Records of Bedford*).

4 "Treasurer's Accompts," June 10, 1779.

5 For a discussion of each possibility, see each listing. Although any of them could have provided this service, a ready explanation as to why the town might have paid father rather than son for the service exists only for Jonas (who appears to have been finishing up his studies at Harvard at the time), and possibly for Ephraim

have been served by a slave; Ephraim is known to have been a slave owner. While there is no clear record that he owned a male slave who might have provided this service, there is at least one piece of family lore to suggest the existence of such an individual, named Crispus.[1]

Ephraim Hartwell was the son of Samuel and Abegail (Stearnes) Hartwell, born in 1707. He had been married to Elizabeth Heywood since 1732; their five children (ages six to less than a year) all died of throat distemper within 22 days in 1740; they started all over again and had nine additional children, all of whom survived to adulthood.

Making his living as a cordwainer, farmer, and innkeeper, he was one of the town's most prosperous residents. His farm was one of the largest in the town. Before the war, he served for many years as a Selectman. He died in 1793 in his 87th year, and he is buried in the Meeting House Cemetery behind Bemis Hall.[2]

MASON, Joseph (Sr.)

Because most of the service records do not distinguish between Joseph Mason and Joseph Mason, Jr., the *War Memorial Book*, *An Account of the Celebration*, and Lincoln historian William Wheeler all credit both Joseph Mason and Joseph Mason, Jr., with service.[3] Wheeler credits both of them with similar service records (Cambridge, 1775; New York, 1776; Rhode Island, 1778/1779). *An Account of the Celebration* compounds the issue, inexplicably crediting Joseph Mason for service as a Minute Man, and Joseph Mason, Jr., with the other service. Lincoln historian Jack MacLean logically identifies the Minute Man as Joseph Mason, Jr., which appears correct. It follows logically that the other records also refer to Joseph Mason, Jr., as well.[4]

While it may be theoretically possible for the elder Joseph Mason (age unknown; probably at least mid-40s) to have served during the war, no service record has been found for service by Joseph Mason that does not more logically fit for Joseph Mason, Jr. (q.v., Chapter 10).

On June 10, 1779, the town paid Joseph Mason for service at Cambridge in 1775 and at the southward in 1776. On November 11, 1779, the town paid Joseph Mason, Jr., for service at Cambridge in 1775 and at Saratoga in 1777.[5] The June payment was thus evidently made to Joseph Sr. However, it conforms to service provided by Elijah Mason (q.v., Chapter 10), for which Elijah does not appear otherwise to have been paid. The author finds more compelling logic in attributing the payment made to the elder Joseph Mason to service by his son, Elijah, than in supposing that Joseph Sr. provided this service himself.

Jr. (who is believed to have been a Princeton resident at the time). Ephraim Jr.'s continuing service in a Worcester County Regiment, however, makes him an unlikely choice.

1 See MacLean, *A Rich Harvest*, p. 266.
2 *Concord, Massachusetts: Births, Marriages, and Deaths*; *Vital Records of Lincoln*; MacLean, *A Rich Harvest*, pp. 133, 154, 197; Hicks, "The Hartwell Family"; Biggs, "In Memorium," p. 174.
3 *War Memorial Book*; *An Account of the Celebration*, pp. 237-238; Wheeler, "Lincoln," in Hurd, Vol. 2, p. 623.
4 MacLean, *A Rich Harvest*, p. 256.
5 "Treasurer's Accompts," June 10, 1779 and November 11, 1779.

Joseph Mason's house stood near the Bloody Angles, where it bore witness to the bloody fight on April 19th. His three sons (Joseph Jr., Elijah, and Jonas) were minute men, and thereafter they served multiple enlistments during the war. No evidence of any service has been found for the elder Joseph. (Photograph by the author)

MONROE, Josiah

Josiah Monroe is listed in *An Account of the Celebration* and in the *War Memorial Book* as having served in the Revolutionary War. However, no evidence of any kind has been found to support this listing.[1]

There is a record of a Josiah Munro who served as a private in Capt. Nathaniel Carpenter's Company, stationed at Brookline for six weeks, until he was dismissed on January 15, 1776.[2] There is no evidence or any particular reason to connect this individual to Lincoln.

The identity of this individual is equally tenuous. The best fit seems to be the son of Marrett and Deliverance Monroe of Lexington; age 30 during the six weeks prior to January 15, 1776. He appears to have been still living in Lexington at the time of his marriage to

---

1 This appears to be another example of an erroneous piece of information being passed from one listing to another without any attempt at verification. What is curious in this case is only that we have few clues as to how the original error came about.

2 *Massachusetts Soldiers and Sailors*, Vol XI, p. 211. There are also records for a Josiah Monro (or Monrow) of Peterborough, a Josiah Mero of Stoughton, and a Josiah Munroe (or Merow, Munrow, Murrow) of Dorchester, all of whom seem to have service records distinct from this Josiah Munro, with even less reason (because they are specifically identified as being from other localities) to connect them with Lincoln.

Susanna Fitch of Bedford in 1768.¹ It is not known what connection, if any, he might have had with Lincoln.

NELSON, Thomas

Thomas Nelson was paid by the town for clothing for the army. No record has been found of any military service by him.²

He was the son of Thomas and Tabitha (Hobbs) Nelson, age 53 at the time of the Concord Alarm. He was the brother of Josiah Nelson (q.v., Chapter 10). He had been married to his wife Lydia since the late 1750s, and he became the father-in-law of Samuel Hastings, Jr. (q.v., Chapter 10), in 1778. He died in Lincoln in 1802.³

PARKER, Isaac

Isaac Parker is listed by Lincoln author Frank Hersey as having been at Concord on the morning of April 19th. This appears to be in error. While the record shows five different individuals named Isaac Parker who marched on the April 19th Alarm, these individuals were from Chelmsford, Deerfield, Princeton, Reading, and Westford. Nothing has been found to connect any of these individuals with Lincoln.⁴

Furthermore, there is no Isaac Parker in *Vital Records of Lincoln* or any other town records found, who could have been at Concord on the morning of April 19th. It is apparent, not only that Isaac Parker of Lincoln did not serve at Concord, but that Isaac Parker of Lincoln does not even exist.

PARKS, Abraham

Abraham Parks is credited in the *War Memorial Book* and *An Account of the Celebration* with having served in the Revolutionary War, but it is apparent that this is in error.⁵

No record of any service by an Abraham Parks (from Lincoln or any surrounding town) has been found. In fact, no individual named Abraham Parks has been found even to have

---

1 *Lexington Births, Marriages and Deaths*. The author has not investigated Susanna's relationship to the Fitch family and tavern in Bedford. It is quite possible that it might reveal an extensive Revolutionary pedigree. It is, however, still not clear how it could be connected with Lincoln.
2 "Treasurer's Accompts," November 11, 1779. In many of these records, payments for clothing for the army parallel payments for service, suggesting that the town was reimbursing the soldiers for their clothing. This interpretation parallels the town's payments to individual minute men for their accoutrements. However, there are enough cases of payments for clothing for the army without parallel records of service to suggest an alternative explanation. The town may in some cases have been purchasing clothing from individual residents to fulfill its quota of supplies for the army in the field. The absence of any records of service for Thomas Nelson of Lincoln either in the "Treasurer's Accompts" or in *Massachusetts Soldiers and Sailors* suggests the latter explanation in this case. His age when the war started only reinforces this interpretation. There appears to be no reason to conclude that Thomas Nelson served during the war.
3 Hafner, "The First Blood," p. 4; Malcolm, *The Scene of Battle*, pp. 28, 30; *Vital Records of Lincoln*.
4 Hersey, *Heroes*, p. 32. It would be hard to imagine that Hersey could have intended to claim one of the other five Isaac Parkers as a Lincoln individual. Evidently, he meant Isaac Parks (q.v., Chapter 10), not Isaac Parker. Curiously, however, he also has Isaac Parks on the same list, suggesting a bit of editing confusion (see *Massachusetts Soldiers and Sailors*, Vol. XI, pp. 860–861).
5 *An Account of the Celebration* (p. 237) erroneously lists Abraham Parks as a minute man instead of Aaron Parks, and the *War Memorial Book* seems to have replicated the error.

existed from Lincoln or surrounding towns, who could have served during the Revolutionary War.

PARKS, Ebenezer

It is clear from service records that Ebenezer Parks and Eleazer Parks are the same individual.[1] Both the *War Memorial Book* and *An Account of the Celebration* give them separate listings, however, perpetuating the error that they were different individuals. The record is confusing. His name appears as Ebenezer Parks on the muster roll of minute men in 1775, but in subsequent service at Cambridge and Dorchester Heights his name appears both ways. By 1777, at Rhode Island and Saratoga, he seems to have dropped Ebenezer in favor of Eleazer. Vital Records and Pension records all list him as Eleazer, suggesting that Ebenezer may have been a nickname that he outgrew during his first year of service. See Eleazer Parks (q.v., Chapter 10).

PARKS, Joseph

Joseph Parks is credited by *An Account of the Celebration* and the *War Memorial Book* with having served in the Revolutionary War, but it is apparent that this is in error.[2]

No record has been found of any service by a Joseph Parks who could reasonably be connected with Lincoln. Nor has any individual named Joseph Parks been found from Lincoln who would have been of an appropriate age to have served during the Revolutionary War.

There is a record of a Joseph Parks (also listed as Joshua) who served in the northern campaign against General Burgoyne, from August 20, 1777, to November 29, 1777 (credited with 3 months, 22 days of service, including 12 days for 240 miles of travel home), first as a private in Capt. Joseph Fuller's Company, Col. Samuel Bullard's Regiment at Stillwater, then on September 10, 1777, drafted as a matross into an artillery detachment commanded by Capt. Lt. James Furnivall. However, there is nothing about this record to suggest a Lincoln connection.[3]

PEIRCE, Jonas
[also PIERCE]

Jonas Peirce was paid by the town of Lincoln "for service at Cambridge in 1775 and for service at Boston in 1776 and for service at Dorchester in 1776." There were two individuals

---

1 *Massachusetts Soldiers and Sailors*, Vol. XI, p. 924.

2 *An Account of the Celebration*, p. 239; *War Memorial Book. An Account of the Celebration* erroneously lists Joseph Parks as having served in the war at times other than on April 19th or at Dorchester Heights. Conspicuously missing from this list is Josiah Parks (q.v., Chapter 10) (although Josiah's service at Dorchester Heights is properly credited). It is apparent that this is an editing error; that Joseph Parks should read Josiah Parks, and that the *War Memorial Book* has simply replicated the error.

3 *Massachusetts Soldiers and Sailors*, Vol. XI, p. 927. With the possible exception of Jonathan Smith (q.v., Chapter 10), who may have served in Capt. Joseph Fuller's Company, individuals from Lincoln who served in Colonel Bullard's Regiment at Saratoga served in Capt. George Minot's Company.

named Jonas Peirce (father and son) with identifiable Lincoln connections. It is probable that neither of them provided this service.[1]

Matching service records for Jonas Peirce have not been found. The payment record does, however, match the service provided by Joseph Peirce (q.v., Chapter 10), son of Jonas Sr. (and brother of Jonas Jr.). Joseph served at all three locations, does not appear otherwise to have been paid for his service, and was away serving in the Continental Army at the time the payment was made. Pretty clearly, this payment was made to Jonas Sr., for service provided by Joseph.

The elder Jonas was the son of Joseph and Abigail Peirce; age 57 at the outbreak of the war. He had been married to Mary Adams since 1743. He appears to have been a lifelong resident of Lincoln who died in 1805 at age 87.

The younger Jonas was the son of the elder Jonas and Mary (Adams) Peirce; age 24 at the outbreak of the war. He was the brother of Abraham Peirce (q.v., Chapter 10), Isaac Peirce (q.v., Chapter 10), and Joseph Peirce (q.v., Chapter 10). Born in Lincoln, he was living in Weston by the early 1770s. After his marriage to Anna Gearfield of Lincoln in 1780, they settled in Lincoln. Sometime after 1794, they moved to Shrewsbury. Anna died in 1808, and he married Lavina Pool in 1811. At some point in time, he moved his family to Wardsboro, Vermont, where he died in 1840 at age 90.[2]

Lincoln historian William Wheeler credits the younger Jonas with service at Dorchester in 1776, Cambridge in 1778, and Rhode Island in 1779 and 1780. The service records for Cambridge in 1778 and Rhode Island in 1779, however, belong to a different Jonas Peirce. Service records for service by a Jonas Peirce at Dorchester in 1776 and Rhode Island in 1780 have not been found.[3]

---

1 "Treasurer's Accompts," June 19, 1779.

2 Wheeler, "Lincoln," in Hurd, Vol. 2, p. 624; *Vital Records of Lincoln*; *Town of Weston, Births, Deaths, & Marriages*; Peirce, *Peirce Genealogy*, pp. 48, 68. The elder Jonas is recorded as age 88 at the time of his death, but this is inconsistent with his birth record. Interestingly, Jonas (Jr.) and Anna's marriage intention was recorded in February 1778, but the marriage did not occur until April 1780. This is significantly longer than the typical pattern that emerges from the vital records of the period.

The date for his having moved to Shrewsbury is indicated by the fact that four of his first six children (as listed in Peirce, *Peirce Genealogy*) were recorded in *Vital Records of Lincoln*.

Anna Gearfields was the daughter of Elisha Gearfield (q.v., Chapter 10); cousin of Abraham Gearfield (q.v., Chapter 10), John Gearfield (q.v., Chapter 10), and Solomon Garfield (q.v., Chapter 10) (see Bond, *Genealogies of the Families of Watertown*, pp. 233–234, 397).

3 Wheeler, "Lincoln," in Hurd, Vol. 2, p. 624. The source of Wheeler's information is unclear. However, the records of service at Cambridge in 1778, and at Rhode Island in 1779 are identifiable as belonging to a Jonas Peirce of Weston, who does not appear to be Lincoln-connected (see Pension Record # W19990). He was the son of Jonas and Sarah (Bridge) Peirce of Weston; age 15 when he marched on the Alarm of April 19, 1775, as a private in Capt. Samuel Lamson's Militia Company from Weston. He served two days.

He enlisted for eight months of service at Cambridge during 1775 and participated at the Battle of Bunker Hill in Capt. Nathan Fuller's Company, Col. Thomas Gardner's Regiment (later, Lt. Col. William Bond's Regiment, after Colonel Gardner died of wounds received at Bunker Hill). He reenlisted in the same unit at the beginning of 1776, serving on the expedition to Canada, and returning by way of Ticonderoga. In September 1776, he took sick (apparently at Ticonderoga) and was sent to Albany. There he recuperated

PEIRCE, Joseph, Jr.

For some reason, *An Account of the Celebration* lists both a Joseph Pierce and a Joseph Pierce, Jr., as having served at Dorchester Heights in March 1776.[1] This mistake was parroted in the *War Memorial Book*. The author has found no other reference to a Joseph Peirce, Jr., nor any individual who could logically be identified as such. No such person appears to have existed.

PHILLIPS, Benjamin

Benjamin Phillips was an avowed Loyalist living in Boston during the war. He was an officer in the Ancient and Honorable Artillery Company, and appears not to have aroused any particular antipathy for his Loyalist views until he was drafted on December 18 or 19, 1776 to reinforce the Continental Army at or near New York. Possibly, he may have found a substitute, because there is no evidence that he served and he appears not to have been fined. However, the following May, 1777, he was identified as among Bostonians who "are suspected as being inimical to the States of America," and tried in a special court. The outcome of the trial is unknown. No evidence has been found of service with a Loyalist militia unit in Boston early in the war, or that he may have been exiled and served for the Crown after his trial.

After the war, he lived in Lincoln, possibly as early as 1786 or 1787, when his daughter Lucy was married in Lincoln. He reportedly died in Lincoln in 1792 at age 76.[2]

---

until late November, when he set out for home. Two weeks of travel got him only as far as Palmer, and he was subsequently returned to Weston with the aid of a horse and litter.

He served as a private in Capt. Daniel Harrington's Company, Col. Jonathan Reed's Regiment of Guards, from April 2 to July 3, 1778 (a total of 3 months, 2 days), guarding the British and German troops surrendered by Burgoyne at Saratoga the previous October.

He was again called into duty, this time to Rhode Island a year later. He served as a Sergeant in Capt. Samuel Heald's Company, Col. John Jacobs's Light Infantry Regiment from September 15, 1779, to November 15, 1779 (2 months, 4 days, including 80 miles of travel home).

He married Lois Clark in Sherborn in 1787, and Susanna Allen of East Sudbury (i.e., Wayland) probably in 1792. He appears to have remained a resident of Weston at least until the 1799 birth of their 5th child, after which at some point in time they moved to Milford, where he died in 1835 at age 75 (Pension Record # W19990; *Massachusetts Soldiers and Sailors*, Vol. XII, pp. 88, 375, and Vol. XI, p. 958; Petition for recovery of expenses, found in the Massachusetts Archives Collection, Vol. 183, #287 in the Massachusetts Archives; *Town of Weston, Births, Deaths, & Marriages*; Peirce, *Peirce Genealogy*, p. 106). *Town of Weston, Births, Deaths, & Marriages* lists his birth in 1760; Peirce inexplicably lists it on the same date in 1759. Curiously, *Town of Weston, Births, Deaths, & Marriages* gives his marriage to Susanna in 1792, but Susanna says 1793 in her pension declaration, which is confirmed by the attestation of the Weston Town Clerk. If Susanna and the Town Clerk are correct, this was a month after the birth of their first child.

In any case, despite some confusion with Jonas Peirce (the younger) of Lincoln (who also lived in Weston before and probably during the war years), this Jonas Peirce appears never to have lived in Lincoln or to have served for the credit of Lincoln.

1 Hartwell, "A List of a Company of Militia," shows only one Joseph Peirce, without a "Jr." designation.
2 Jones, *The Loyalists of Massachusetts*, p. 316; Roberts, *History of the Military Company of the Massachusetts*, pp. 75, 187-188; Bolton, *Marriage Notices*, p.69; *Vital Records of Lincoln*.

APPENDICES
Order of Battle

Although the Lincoln men and most others who responded to the April 19th Alarm did so as members of specific companies, organizational discipline gave way to individual initiative during the return march to Boston. Individuals crept as close as they dared to the Redcoats' column in the road or to flanking parties in the fields. "Now all restraint," says Lexington historian Charles Hudson, "seems to have been removed," as they staked out locations from which to fire at the enemy, then disengaged and ran ahead to find new spots to engage. For them, quite literally, this became a running battle. Here, artist Aiden Lassell Ripley catches the Regulars passing through the hills of Menotomy (Arlington), the Provincials keeping up a steady—if disorganized—fire, soon to be swept away by flankers approaching on the right. Across the road, other flankers are seen chasing away locals from around the house. "After the fight at the [Concord] bridge," Lincoln militiaman *Amos Baker* later remembered, "I saw nothing more of [my father, four brothers, and brother-in-law], and did not know whether they were alive or dead, until I found two of my brothers engaged in the pursuit near Lexington meeting-house. Nathaniel followed the enemy to Charlestown." *Baker* concludes with characteristic Yankee understatement, "I verily believe that I felt better that day, take it all the day through, than if I had staid at home." (Courtesy of Unum Group)

Appendix A
Units & Commanding Officers

Author's Note: A "(?)" denotes a degree of uncertainty as to the service, the identification of the individual, his connection to Lincoln, or the interpretation of the record(s), logic, or supposition by which the service is attributed. For more information in each case, please refer to the individual profiles in Chapter 10.

1775

1. The Alarm of April 19, 1775

Col. Abijah Peirce's Regiment, **Capt. William Smith**'s Company of Minute Men from Lincoln

Cpl. Joseph Abbot, Jr.	Sgt. David Fisk	John Parks
Nehemiah Abbot	Jacob Foster	Jonas Parks
Abel Adams	Isaac Gage	Willard Parks
Joel Adams	Jonathan Gage	William Parks
Jacob Baker, Jr.	John Gearfield	Abraham Peirce
James Baker	Nathaniel Gove	Joseph Peirce
Nathaniel Baker	Daniel Harrington	Artemas Reed
Daniel Billing	Isaac Hartwell	Jesse Smith
Nathan Billing	Sgt. John Hartwell	Jonathan Smith
Timothy Billing	Sgt. Samuel Hartwell	Capt. William Smith
Thomas Blodget	2nd Lt. Samuel Hoar	Gregory Stone, Jr.
Benjamin Brooks	Daniel Hosmer	John Thorning
Joshua Brooks, Jr.	William Hosmer, Jr.	William Thorning
Drummer Daniel Brown	Fifer Elijah Mason	Nathan Tidd
Cpl. Ebenezer Brown	Sgt. Jonas Mason	John Wesson
Nathan Brown, Jr.	Fifer Joseph Mason	John Wesson [Jr.]
Daniel Child	Cpl. Abijah Mead	Joseph Wheat
Joshua Child, Jr.	Abijah Munroe	Enos Wheeler
Samuel Dakin, Jr.	Aaron Parks	Solomon Whitney
Humphrey Farrar	Eleazer Parks	Cpl. Elijah Willington
Lt. Samuel Farrar, Jr.	James Parks	

Col. Abijah Peirce's Regiment, **Capt. David Brown**'s Company of Minute Men from Concord
  Phineas Allen

Col. Abijah Peirce's Regiment, **Capt. Nathaniel Cudworth**'s Company of Minute Men from Sudbury

Zebediah Farrar	Timothy Sherman (?)

Col. Abijah Peirce's Regiment, ***Capt. Simon Edgel's*** Company of Minute Men from Framingham
  Isaac Goodenow

Col. Abijah Peirce's Regiment, ***Capt. Charles Miles's*** Company of Minute Men from Concord
  Ephraim Brooks, Jr.   Stephen Brooks   Daniel Farrar (?)

Col. Abijah Peirce's Regiment, ***Capt. John Nixon's*** Company of Minute Men from Sudbury
  Elisha Wheeler

Col. James Barrett's Regiment, ***Capt. Abijah Peirce's*** (?) Militia Company from Lincoln (probably commanded by ***Lt. Samuel Farrar, Jr.***, and including others who were at Concord as unenlisted volunteers)[1]

  James Adams   Daniel Farrar (?)   James Nichols
  John Adams   Abraham Gearfield   Noah Parkhurst
  Amos Baker   Jonas Hartwell (?)   Isaac Parks
  Jacob Baker   John Hoar   Fifer Leonard Parks (?)
  Samuel Baker   William Hosmer, Sr.   Col. Abijah Peirce
  Edmund Bowman (?)   Benjamin Munroe   Gregory Stone
  Eleazer Brooks   Isaac Munroe (?)   John Whitehead[2]

Col. James Barrett's Regiment, ***Capt. Isaac Locker's*** Militia Company from Sudbury
  Timothy Sherman (?)

Col. Ephraim Doolittle's Regiment, ***Capt. Boaz Moore's*** Company of Minute Men from Princeton
  Ephraim Hartwell, Jr.

Col. Thomas Gardner's Regiment, ***Capt. Samuel Barnard's*** Militia Company from Watertown
  Tilly Mead

Col. Thomas Gardner's Regiment, ***Capt. Abraham Peirce's*** Militia Company from Waltham
  John Coolidge   John Viles

Col. James Prescott's Regiment, ***Capt. Oliver Bates's*** Militia Company from Westford
  John Barrett

Col. William Prescott's Regiment, ***Capt. James Hosley's*** Company of Minute Men from Townsend
  Sgt. John Conant (?)

Col. John Smith's Regiment, ***Capt. Ephraim Chenery's*** Company from Medfield
  Nathaniel Lovell (?)

Col. Nathan Sparhawk's Regiment, ***Capt. Joseph Sargent's*** Company from Princeton
  Silas Fay

---

1 No muster roll for the militia company has ever been found. The captain appears to have been *Abijah Peirce*, who went to Concord as the newly appointed colonel of the regiment of minute men; *Lt. Samuel Farrar, Jr.*, who was also a lieutenant of the minute company, was probably in command on April 19, but this is conjectural.

2 See also **Capt. Israel Whitemore's** Artillery Company from Weston, p. 475.

Appendix A: Units & Commanding Officers

***Col. John Whitcom's** Regiment (?),* **Capt. Noah Miles's** *Company from Westminster*
Solomon Garfield

***Capt. Thomas Heald's** Company from New Ipswich, New Hampshire*
Stephen Farrar Timothy Farrar

***Capt. Samuel Lamson's** Militia Company from Weston*
Jeduthan Bemis John Flint Amos Jones

***Capt. John Moore's** Militia Company from Bedford*
Samuel Bacon

***Capt. John Parker's** Militia Company from Lexington*
Samuel Hastings, Jr.

***Capt. Obadiah Parker's** Company from Mason, New Hampshire*
Edward Adams John Adams, Jr. (?)

***Capt. Larkin Thorndike's** Company from Beverly*
Sgt. Moses Brown

***Capt. Israel Whitemore's** Artillery Company from Weston*
Nathan Weston John Whitehead[1]

[at the Lexington Green]
Joseph Abbot, Sr.

[unit unknown]
Ephraim Flint (?)

2. Cambridge service, Siege of Boston (including the Battle of Bunker Hill, June 17, 1775)

***Col. John Nixon's** 16th Massachusetts Regiment,* **Capt. William Smith's** *Company*

Nehemiah Abbot
Abel Adams
Joel Adams
Peter Brooks
Edward Cabot
Daniel Child
Ens. John Hartwell
Daniel Hosmer
Fifer Elijah Mason
Sgt. Jonas Mason
Fifer Joseph Mason
Abijah Munroe
Abraham Peirce
Joseph Peirce
John Porter
Artemas Reed
Cato Smith
Jesse Smith
William Thorning
Nathan Tidd
Solomon Whitney
Sgt. Elijah Willington

***Col. John Nixon's** 16th Massachusetts Regiment,* **Capt. Abishai Brown's** *Company*
Lemuel Wheeler

---

1 See also **Col. James Barrett's** Regiment, **Capt. Abijah Peirce's** Militia Company from Lincoln, p. 474.

***Col. John Nixon's** 16th Massachusetts Regiment, **Capt. Joseph Butler's** Company*
   Ephraim Brooks, Jr.   Daniel Farrar (?)

***Col. John Nixon's** 16th Massachusetts Regiment, **Capt. David Moore's** Company*
   Isaac Goodenow   Fifer Joseph Nixon

***Col. John Nixon's** 16th Massachusetts Regiment, [company unknown]*
   Ephraim Flint (?)   Isaac Munroe (?)

***Col. Thomas Gardner's** 37th Regiment, **Capt. Nathan Fuller's** Company*

Benjamin Brown (?)	James Nichols	John Parks
George Brown	Noah Parkhurst (?)	Jonas Parks
Sgt. Isaac Gage (?)	Aaron Parks	Fifer Leonard Parks
Jonathan Gage	Eleazer Parks	Elisha Whitehead (?)

***Col. Thomas Gardner's** 37th Regiment, **Capt. Abijah Child's** Company*

Jeduthan Bemis	Amos Jones	John Viles
John Flint (?)		

***Col. Thomas Gardner's** 37th Regiment, **Capt. Abner Craft's** Company*
   Tilly Mead

***Col. Thomas Gardner's** 37th Regiment*
   QM Sgt. Nathan Weston (?)

***Col. William Prescott's** Regiment, **Capt. Abijah Wyman's** Company*
   Peter Oliver

***Col. James Reed's** Regiment, **Capt. Josiah Crosby's** Company*
   John Adams, Jr.

***Col. Jonathan Ward's** Regiment, **Capt. Samuel Wood's** Company (?)*
   Cpl. Silas Fay

***Col. Asa Whitcomb's** Regiment, **Capt. Edmund Bemis's** Company (?)*
   Fifer Asa Adams

***Col. Asa Whitcomb's** Regiment, **Capt. James Burt's** Company*
   Eden London

***Col. Benjamin Ruggles Woodbridge's** 25th Regiment, **Capt. Seth Murray's** Company*
   Benjamin Wheat

[units unknown]
   Benjamin Cleaveland   Nathaniel Lovell (?)

3. Cambridge service, Siege of Boston, other (cannot be placed at the Battle of Bunker Hill)

***Col. Loammi Baldwin's** Regiment, **Capt. Jonathan Minott's** Company*
  John Conant (?)

***Col. William Bond's** Regiment, **Capt. Nathan Fuller's** Company*
  Fifer Jonas Parks (after Bunker Hill).

***Col. John Nixon's** 5th Regiment, **Capt. Joseph Butler's** Company*
  Fifer Joseph Nixon (after Bunker Hill).

***Col. John Nixon's** 5th Regiment, **Capt. Jeremiah Gilman's** Company*
  Fifer Joseph Nixon (after Bunker Hill).

***Col. John Nixon's** 5th Regiment, **Capt. William Smith's** Company*
  Sgt. Edward Adams   Abijah Mead   Capt. William Smith

[units and dates of service unknown]
  John Barrett   Benjamin Brown   Col. Abijah Peirce (?)
  Samuel Bond (?)   Humphrey Farrar   Jonathan Smith
  Joshua Brooks (?)   John Farrar (?)   Joseph Wheat
  Joshua Brooks, Jr. (?) Benjamin Parks (?)   Abner Wheeler (?)
  Timothy Brooks   Willard Parks

4. Coastal service, 1775

***Col. John Glover's** Regiment, guarding the seacoast in Beverly*
  Capt. Moses Brown

***Capt. Noah Moulton Littlefield's** Company, guarding the Maine seacoast at Wells and Arundel*
  Isaac Bussell

[units and dates of service unknown] at Hull
  John Barrett (?)

5. Knox Expedition to Ticonderoga, Winter 1775–1776

***Col. Henry Knox's** detachment to transport artillery to Boston*
  Solomon Whitney (?)

6. The Campaign to Canada, 1775–1776

***Col. Benedict Arnold's** expedition to Quebec, September 1775*
  Ephraim Brooks, Jr.

1776

1. Dorchester Heights, March 4–9, 1776
(including the Siege of Boston, January and February, 1776)

Col. Eleazer Brooks's Regiment, at or near Dorchester Heights
Col. Eleazer Brooks

Col. Eleazer Brooks's Regiment, **Capt. John Hartwell's** Company, at or near Dorchester Heights

Sgt. Joseph Abbot, Jr.	Daniel Brown	James Miles
Cpl. Nehemiah Abbot	Ephraim Brown	Cpl. Abijah Monroe
Abel Adams	Cpl. Nathan Brown, Jr.	Isaac Munroe
Bulkley Adams	Abel Child	Benjamin Parks
Edward Adams	Amos Child	Eleazer Parks
James Adams	Elisha Child	Isaac Parks
Noah Bacon	Joshua Child, Jr.	Josiah Parks
Amos Baker	Samuel Dakin, Jr.	Willard Parks
Nathaniel Baker	Humphrey Farrar	Isaac Peirce
Daniel Billing	Lt. Samuel Farrar, Jr.	Joseph Peirce
Joseph Billing	Ephraim Flint	Jube Savage
Timothy Billing	Jacob Foster	Gregory Stone, Jr.
Samuel Bond	John Foster	Joshua Stone
Edmund Bowman	Sgt. Isaac Hartwell	Timothy Stone
Ephraim Brooks	Capt. John Hartwell	Nathan Tidd
Ephraim Brooks, Jr.	Samuel Hartwell	Sgt. Nathan Wesson
Cpl. Joshua Brooks, Jr.	Lt. Samuel Hoar	Joseph Wheat
Noah Brooks	John Lander	Enos Wheeler
Stephen Brooks [Jr.]	Sgt. Jonas Mason	Elisha Willington
Timothy Brooks	Salem Middlesex	

Col. Eleazer Brooks's Regiment, **Capt. John Bridge's** Company, at Roxbury
Joseph Munroe

Col. Eleazer Brooks's Regiment, **Capt. Jonathan Fisk's** Company, at or near Dorchester Heights
Abel Flint

Col. Eleazer Brooks's Regiment, **Capt. Joseph Hosmer's** Company, at or near Dorchester Heights
Amos Hosmer (?)

Col. Eleazer Brooks's Regiment, **Capt. George Minot's** Company, at or near Dorchester Heights
Lemuel Wheeler

Col. John Robinson's Regiment, **Capt. Asahel Wheeler's** Company, February 4 to April 1, 1776, at Roxbury

Joel Adams	Daniel Hosmer	John Wesson (?)
Samuel Baker	Fifer Joseph Mason	John Wesson [Jr.] (?)
Thomas Blodget	Sgt. Abijah Mead	Solomon Whitney
Job Brooks	Gregory Stone, Jr. (?)	
Cpl. Zebediah Farrar	William Thorning	

Appendix A: Units & Commanding Officers

***Col. John Robinson's** Regiment,* **Capt. Job Shattuck's** *Company, at Cambridge*
Jonathan Hartwell (?)

***Col. William Bond's** 25th Continental Regiment,* **Capt. Nathan Fuller's** *Company*
Aaron Parks

***Col. Simeon Cary's** Regiment,* **Capt. Micah Hamlin's** *Company, February 8 to April 1, 1776, at Roxbury*
Daniel Child (?)

*Gen. **Charles Lee's** Life Guard*[1]
Samuel Hastings, Jr.   Aaron Parks

***Col. Moses Little's** 12th Continental Regiment,* **Capt. Nathaniel Wade's** *Company*
Samuel Hastings, Jr.

***Col. Edward Mitchell's** Regiment,* **Capt. Abram Washburn's** *Company, at Horse Neck (Braintree)*
John Conant (?)

***Col. Samuel Thatcher's** Regiment,* **Capt. Abraham Peirce's** *Company, at or near Dorchester Heights*
John Coolidge   Zechariah Weston

***Col. Josiah Whitney's** Regiment, January 23 to April 1, 1776*
QM. Ephraim Hartwell, Jr.

16th Regiment, **Capt. James Perry's** *Company, January 1 to April 6, 1776*
James Nichols (?)

2. The Relief Expedition to Canada, 1776

***Col. William Bond's** 25th Continental Regiment,* **Capt. Abijah Child's** *Company, April to November 1776, Canada and Fort Ticonderoga*
Daniel Child   Cpl. John Flint (?)   Elisha Willington

***Col. William Bond's** 25th Continental Regiment,* **Capt. Nathan Fuller's** *Company, April to September 1776, Canada and Fort Ticonderoga*
Aaron Parks

***Col. William Bond's** 25th Continental Regiment,* **Capt. Nailer Hatch's** *Company, April 1776, to Canada*
Jeduthan Bemis

***Col. John Greaton's** 24th Continental Regiment,* **Capt. Abner Craft's** *Company, April 1776 to November 1776 at Canada and Ticonderoga, then Morristown in December 1776*
Tilly Mead

---

1 General Lee was reassigned to New York in January 1776, before the fortification of Dorchester Heights. Hastings went with him; Parks rejoined his old unit.

***Col. John Paterson**'s 15th Continental Regiment,* **Capt. Moses Ashley**'s *Company, April 1776 to November 1776 at Canada and Ticonderoga, then Trenton in December 1776*

   Leonard Parks   Jonas Parks (?)

***Col. John Paterson**'s 15th Continental Regiment, [company unknown], April 1776 to November 1776 at Canada and Ticonderoga, then Trenton in December 1776*

   George Brown   Jonas Parks

[units and dates of service unknown] 1775 or 1776

   James Adams (?)

3. Ticonderoga, 1776

***Col. Jonathan Reed**'s Militia Regiment,* **Capt. Asahel Wheeler**'s *Company, June or July 1776 to December 1776*

Cpl. Joseph Abbot, Jr.	Brister Hoar	John Parks
John Adams, Jr. (?)	Lt. Samuel Hoar	Gregory Stone, Jr.
Samuel Baker	Daniel Hosmer	John Thorning
Jonas Bond	William Hosmer, Jr.	William Thorning
Samuel Bond	John Lander (?)	Solomon Whitney
Abel Child	Eleazer Parks	

***Col. Jonathan Reed**'s Militia Regiment,* **Capt. Charles Miles**'s *Company, June or July 1776 to December 1776*

Thomas Blodget	Josiah Nelson (?)	Lemuel Wheeler
George Farrar		

***Col. Samuel Brewer**'s Militia Regiment,* **Capt. Zachariah Fitch**'s *Company, August 28, 1776, to December 1776*

Abel Adams	Cpl. Zebediah Farrar	Sgt. Abijah Mead
Daniel Billing		

***Col. Ephraim Wheelock**'s Militia Regiment,* **Capt. Timothy Stow**'s *Company, June or July 1776*

   Peter Oliver

[units and dates of service unknown]

[unidentified] Adams	Noah Brooks	James Parks
Timothy Billing	Samuel Farrar, Jr.	Ezra Richardson
Aaron Brooks	Elisha Gearfield	Moses Underwood
Abner Brooks (?)	Daniel Harrington	Abner Wheeler
Col. Eleazer Brooks (?)	Isaac Hartwell	Edmond Wheeler
Ephraim Brooks, Jr. (?)	John Hartwell	Elisha Wheeler (?)
Job Brooks (?)	Leonard Hoar (?)	
Joshua Brooks (?)	David Parks (?)	

Appendix A: Units & Commanding Officers

4. New York Campaign, 1776

Col. Eleazer Brooks's Regiment, September 27, 1776, to November 16, 1776, at Horse Neck, White Plains, and North Castle
- Col. Eleazer Brooks
- QM Samuel Hartwell

Col. Eleazer Brooks's Regiment, **Capt. Simon Hunt**'s Company, September 27, 1776, to November 16, 1776, at Horse Neck, White Plains, and North Castle
- James Adams, Jr.
- Jeduthan Bemis
- Nathan Billing
- Peter Brooks (?)
- Edward Cabot
- David Fisk (?)
- Sgt. Jeremiah Knowlton
- Abner Mathis
- Michael Teny

Col. Eleazer Brooks's Regiment, **Capt. John Walton**'s Company, September 27, 1776, to November 16, 1776, at Horse Neck, White Plains, and North Castle
- Keen Robinson

Col. Loammi Baldwin's 26th Regiment, **Capt. Jonathan Minott**'s Company
- Stephen Brooks

Col. John Glover's Regiment, **Capt. Moses Brown**'s Company, at Brooklyn, Manhattan, Fort Lee, White Plains, and North Castle
- Capt. Moses Brown

Gen. Charles Lee's Life Guard
- Samuel Hastings, Jr.

Col. Thomas Nixon's 4th Regiment, **Capt. Joseph Butler**'s 8th Company, at Governor's Island, Turtle Bay, Harlem Heights, White Plains, and North Castle
- Ezra Meriam
- William Orr (?)
- Cato Smith

Col. Thomas Nixon's 4th Regiment, **Capt. Jeremiah Gilman**'s 6th Company, at Governor's Island, Turtle Bay, Harlem Heights, White Plains, and North Castle
- Artemas Reed

Col. Thomas Nixon's 4th Regiment, **Capt. Adam Wheeler**'s 2nd Company, at Governor's Island, Turtle Bay, Harlem Heights, White Plains, and North Castle
- Jack Farrar
- Drummer Isaac Goodenow
- Fifer Elijah Mason

Col. John Nixon's 4th Regiment, at Governor's Island, through mid-August 1776
- Joseph Nixon

Col. Samuel Thatcher's Regiment, **Capt. John Bridge**'s Company, December 1776 to March 1777, at Fairfield, Connecticut; Kingsbridge, New York; and Woodbridge, New Jersey
- Joseph Bacon (?)
- John Barrett
- Joseph Billing
- Job Brooks
- Timothy Brown (?)
- Ephraim Flint (?)
- John Flint (?)
- James Meriam (?)
- Joshua Stone
- Ebenezer Torrey (?)
- Enos Wheeler (?)

Gen. George Washington's Life Guard, **Capt. Caleb Gibbs**'s Company
- Jesse Smith

[units and dates of service unknown], service "at the southward," 1776
  Francis Buttrick   Humphrey Farrar (?)

[units and dates of service unknown], service in the New York Campaign, 1776
  Samuel Bacon (?)   Nathan Brown, Jr. (?)   Isaac Parks
  Samuel Bond (?)   *[unidentified]* Gove   Jonathan Smith
  Joseph Brown

5. Trenton, 1776

*Col. Thomas Nixon's 4th Regiment, **Capt. Joseph Butler's** 8th Company*
  Ezra Meriam   William Orr (?)   Cato Smith

*Col. Thomas Nixon's 4th Regiment, **Capt. Adam Wheeler's** 2nd Company*
  Jack Farrar   Drummer Isaac Goodenow   Fifer Elijah Mason

*Col. Thomas Nixon's 4th Regiment, **Capt. Jeremiah Gilman's** 6th Company*
  Artemas Reed

*Col. Loammi Baldwin's 26th Regiment, **Capt. Jonathan Minott's** Company*
  Stephen Brooks

*Col. John Glover's Regiment, **Capt. Moses Brown's** Company*
  Capt. Moses Brown

*Col. John Paterson's 15th Continental Regiment, **Capt. Moses Ashley's** Company*
  Leonard Parks   Jonas Parks (?)

Col. John Paterson's 15th Continental Regiment, [company unknown]
  George Brown   Jonas Parks

*Gen. George Washington's Life Guard, **Capt. Caleb Gibbs's** Company*
  Jesse Smith

6. Continental Army, other (not included in The Relief Expedition to Canada, Ticonderoga, The New York Campaign, or Trenton), 1776

*Col. John Nixon's 4th Regiment, **Capt. Adam Wheeler's** 2nd Company, spring 1776 (before the New York Campaign)*
  Jesse Smith

[unit and dates of service unknown]
  Benjamin Parks (?)

7. Coastal Service, 1776–1777

*Col. Thomas Craft's Artillery Regiment, **Capt. Joseph Balch's** Company*
  Richard Wesson

Appendix A: Units & Commanding Officers

Col. Thomas Craft's Artillery Regiment, **Capt. Daniel Lathrop's** *Company*
William Thorning

Col. Thomas Craft's Artillery Regiment, **Capt. James Swan's** *(then* **Capt. Philip Marett's***) Company, May 1776 to May 1777, at Boston*

Joseph Colburn	Isaac Peirce	Nathan Tidd
Sgt. Abijah Munroe	Cpl. Joseph Peirce	Richard Wesson
Abraham Peirce		

Col. Nicholas Dike's 2nd Regiment, **Capt. John Minot's** *Company, August 1776 through November 1776, at Roxbury and Dorchester; then December 1776 to March 1, 1777, at Dorchester*

Lt. John Hartwell	Isaac Peirce	Thomas Smith (?)
Isaac Munroe	Jube Savage	Daniel Wesson

Col. Nicholas Dike's 2nd Regiment, **Capt. Caleb Brooks's** *Company, November 1776, around Roxbury and Dorchester*
Daniel Farrar (?)

Col. Nicholas Dike's 2nd Regiment, **Capt. John Hartwell's** *Company, December 1776 to March 1, 1777, at Dorchester*

Abiel Abbot	Peter Brooks	Brister Hoar
Bulkley Adams	Stephen Brooks [Jr.]	Leonard Hoar
Cpl. Edward Adams	Capt. John Hartwell	John Thorning
Samuel Bond	Sgt. Jonas Hartwell	Daniel Wesson
Abner Brooks	Cpl. Jonathan Hartwell	Solomon Whitney

Col. Nicholas Dike's 2nd Regiment, **Capt. Caleb Brooks's** *Company, December 1776 to March 1, 1777, guarding stores at Boston*
Daniel Brown

Col. Nicholas Dike's 2nd Regiment, **Capt. Moses Harrington's** *Company, December 1776 to March 1, 1777, at Dorchester*

Sgt. Amos Baker	Abner Mathis	James Nichols
Cpl. Samuel Baker	Isaac Munroe	Josiah Parks
William Hosmer, Jr.		

Col. Jabez Hatch's Regiment, **Capt. Thomas Bumstead's** *Company, guarding stores in Boston*
Ebenezer Torrey (?)

Col. William McIntosh's Militia Regiment, **Capt. Ebenezer Battle's** *Company, 1776 and 1777, at Boston*
Nathaniel Colburn (?)

4th Suffolk County Militia Regiment, **Capt. Joseph Lovell's** *Company, December 8, 1776, on Alarm at Rhode Island*
Nathaniel Lovell (?)

Lt. Andrew Gilman's *Company, October 1776 to July 1777, at the Penobscot River*
Isaac Bussell

Capt. John Walton's Company, December 9–12, 1776, at Noddle's Island
John Viles

[units and dates of service unknown], *1776, at Castle William*
Timothy Sherman (?)

[units and dates of service unknown], *1776, at Boston*
Phineas Allen   Joseph Brown

[units and dates of service unknown], *1776–1777, at Boston*
Nathaniel Colburn   Stephen Wesson, Jr. (?)

[units and dates of service unknown], *1776, at Cambridge*
Joseph Abbot, Jr.   Samuel Farrar, Jr.   Gregory Stone, Jr.
Aaron Brooks   Josiah Nelson   Edmond Wheeler

[unit and dates of service unknown], *1776–1777, at Dorchester*
Benjamin Munroe

[unit and dates of service unknown], *1776, at Hull*
John Barrett (?)

[units and dates of service unknown], *1776, at Roxbury*
Nathan Brown, Jr.   John Gearfield   Joseph Munroe
Samuel Dakin, Jr.

1777

1. Coastal Service, 1777

Col. Jonathan Buck's Regiment, Capt. William Reed's Company, *August to September 1777 at Machias*
Abel Billing   Solomon Billing

Capt. Charles Miles's Company, *September 17, 1777, conveying stores to Roxbury*
Gregory Stone, Jr.

Capt. Andrew Samson's Company, *1777, at the Gurnet in Plymouth Harbor*
Abraham Peirce

Maj. Andrew Symmes's detachment, *May 1777, guarding stores in Boston*
Joseph Colburn (?)

[unit and dates of service unknown], *1777, at Dorchester*
Zechariah Weston

[unit and dates of service unknown], *1777, at York*
Timothy Brooks

Appendix A: Units & Commanding Officers

2. Rhode Island Alarm, 1777

Colonel Hawes's 4th Suffolk County Militia Regiment, **Capt. Ezekiel Plimpton's** *Company, September 25, 1777, on a secret mission to Rhode Island*
  Nathaniel Lovell (?)

Col. Josiah Whitney's *Regiment,* **Capt. John Gleason's** *Company, service at North Kingston*
  Zebediah Farrar   Isaac Goodenow

Col. Josiah Whitney's *Regiment,* **Capt. Hezekiah Whitney's** *Company*
  William Parks (?)

Col. Josiah Whitney's *Regiment,* **Capt. Jesse Wyman's** *Company, service at Point Judith*
  Bulkley Adams   Amos Hosmer   Josiah Parks
  John Barrett   James Miles   Barnabas Richardson
  George Farrar   Eleazer Parks (?)   Thomas Smith (?)

Col. Ezra Wood's *Regiment,* **Capt. Peter Penniman's** *Company*
  Stephen Brooks (?)

[unit and dates of service unknown]
  John Wesson [Jr.] (?), at Point Judith

3. Saratoga Campaign, 1777

Col. Samuel Bullard's *Regiment,* **Capt. George Minot's** *Company*
  Cpl. Abel Adams   Cpl. Francis Buttrick   Joseph Munroe
  Amos Baker (?)   Abel Child   Eleazer Parks
  Samuel Baker   Joseph Colburn   Josiah Parks
  Jeduthan Bemis   Daniel Farrar (?)   Isaac Peirce
  Israel Billing   Brister Hoar   Daniel Wesson
  Abner Brooks   Amos Hosmer

Col. Samuel Bullard's *Regiment,* **Capt. Joseph Fuller's** *Company*
  Jonathan Smith (?)

Col. Jonathan Reed's *Regiment,* **Capt. Samuel Farrar, Jr.'s** *Company*
  Edward Adams   Capt. Samuel Farrar, Jr.   Fifer Leonard Parks
  Daniel Billing   Leonard Hoar   Joshua Stone
  Samuel Bond   Joseph Mason   William Thorning
  Sgt. Joshua Brooks, Jr. Abner Mathis   Solomon Whitney
  Sgt. Samuel Dakin, Jr. Peter Nelson

Col. Jonathan Reed's *Regiment,* **Capt. Asahel Wheeler's** *Company*
  Isaac Goodenow

Col. Timothy Bigelow's *15th Massachusetts Regiment,* **Capt. Edmund Munroe's** *Company*
  Peter Bowes   Luke Fletcher   Peter Oliver

***Col. Joseph Cilley's** Regiment*
John Barter (?)   Zodith Henderson (?)   Stephen Lufkin (?)

***Col. John Crane's** Artillery Regiment, **Captain Buckland's** or **Capt. John Lillie's** Company*
Benjamin Cleaveland (?)

***Col. Job Cushing's** Regiment, **Lt. Amos Fairbanks's** Company*
Silas Fay

***Col. John Greaton's** 2nd Regiment, **Capt. Abijah Child's** Company*

Jonathan Gage	James Nichols	Adonijah Rice
John Gorden (?)	Sgt. Joseph Peirce	Cpl. Elisha Willington
John Lander (?)	Artemas Reed	

***Col. John Greaton's** 2nd Regiment, **Capt. Job Sumner's** Company*
Lt. Isaac Gage   Jonas Parks (?)

***Col. Thomas Marshall's** 10th Massachusetts Regiment, **Capt. William Warner's** Company*
Eden London   Silas Sharon

***Col. Thomas Nixon's** Regiment, **Capt. Abel Holden's** Company*
Joseph Nixon

***Col. Thomas Nixon's** Regiment, **Capt. Adam Wheeler's** Company*
Lemuel Wheeler

***Col. Joseph Vose's** Regiment, **Capt. Moses Ashley's** Company*
George Brown   Jack Farrar

***Col. David Wells's** 15th Massachusetts Regiment, **Capt. Thomas French's** Company*
Benjamin Wheat

***Col. Josiah Whitney's** Regiment*
Adj. Ephraim Hartwell, Jr.

***Capt. Elisha Jackson's** Company*
Solomon Garfield

[units and dates of service unknown]

Timothy Billing	Nathan Brown, Jr. (?)	Jeremiah Knowlton
Aaron Brooks (?)	Daniel Hosmer	

4. Expedition to Worthington, 1777

Nathan Billing	Isaac Hartwell	John Parks
John Gearfield	Cuff Hoar	Elijah Willington
Daniel Harrington		

Appendix A: Units & Commanding Officers

5. Continental Army, other service, 1777

Col. Jeduthan Baldwin's *Regiment of Artificers,* ***Capt. Benjamin Pollard's*** *Company*
   Isaac Munroe   Elisha Whitehead   Lt. John Whitehead
   Daniel Whitehead

Colonel Baylor's *3rd Regiment of Light Dragoons,* ***Capt. George Lewis's*** *Company of Horse (detached as* ***Gen. George Washington's*** *Life Guard)*
   Jesse Smith

Col. Timothy Bigelow's *15th Massachusetts Regiment,* ***Capt. Edmund Munroe's*** *Company*
   Peter Bowes   Peter Oliver   Richard Wesson
   Luke Fletcher

Col. Joseph Cilley's *Regiment*
   John Barter (?)   Zodith Henderson (?)   Stephen Lufkin (?)

Col. John Crane's *Artillery Regiment,* ***Capt. Benjamin Frothingham's*** *Company, at Morristown and at the Battle of Brandywine*
   Asa Adams

Col. John Crane's *Artillery Regiment,* ***Capt. David Briant's*** *Company, at the Battle of Brandywine*
   Nathan Tidd

Col. John Crane's *Artillery Regiment,* ***Captain Buckland's*** *Company*
   Benjamin Cleaveland

Col. John Crane's *Artillery Regiment,* ***Capt. Henry Burbeck's*** *Company*
   Cpl. Nathan Tidd

Col. John Crane's *Artillery Regiment,* ***Capt. John Lillie's*** *Company*
   Benjamin Cleaveland

Col. John Greaton's *2nd Regiment,* ***Capt. Abijah Child's*** *Company*
   John Barter (?)   Zodith Henderson (?)   Sgt. Joseph Peirce
   Benjamin Cleaveland (?) John Lander   Artemas Reed
   Jonathan Gage   Stephen Lufkin (?)   Adonijah Rice
   John Gorden (?)   James Nichols   Cpl. Elisha Willington

Col. John Greaton's *2nd Regiment,* ***Capt. Job Sumner's*** *Company*
   Lt. Isaac Gage   Jonas Parks (?)

Col. Henry Jackson's *Regiment,* ***Capt. Thomas Turner's*** *5th Company, at the Battle of Brandywine*
   Cpl. Nehemiah Abbot

Col. Henry Jackson's *Regiment,* ***Capt. Joseph Fox's*** *Company, at the Battle of Brandywine*
   Cpl. Ephraim Brooks, Jr.

Col. Henry Jackson's Regiment, **Colonel's** Company, *at Morristown and at the Battle of Brandywine*
William Orr (?)

Col. Thomas Marshall's *10th Massachusetts Regiment,* **Capt. William Warner's** Company
Eden London   Silas Sharon

Col. Samuel McCobb's Regiment, **Capt. Nicholas Crosby's** Company, *expedition against St. John's, Nova Scotia, July to September 1777*
Isaac Bussell

Col. Thomas Nixon's Regiment, **Capt. Abel Holden's** Company
Joseph Nixon

Col. Thomas Nixon's Regiment, **Capt. Adam Wheeler's** Company
Lemuel Wheeler

Colonel Sherbourn's Regiment, **Captain Berton's** Company
William Gilbert

Col. Joseph Vose's Regiment, **Capt. Moses Ashley's** Company, *in the Hudson Valley*
George Brown   Jack Farrar

[units and dates of service unknown]
Samuel Baley   Benjamin Parks (?)

6. Naval, 1777

"Wilkes" commanded by **Capt. John Foster Williams**, *June 1777*
Edward Adams

"American Tartar" commanded by **Capt. John Grimes**, *May 22, 1777, to August 1777*
Capt. William Smith

"Royal Bounty" (prize crew), *August 1777 to September 17, 1777*
Capt. William Smith

7. Guarding the Convention Army, 1777–1778

Col. Eleazer Brooks's Regiment, *November 3, 1777, to April 3, 1778, at Cambridge*
Col. Eleazer Brooks   QM Samuel Hartwell

Col. Eleazer Brooks's Regiment, **Capt. Simon Hunt's** Company, *November 3, 1777, to April 3, 1778, at Cambridge*
James Adams, Jr.   Leonard Hoar   William Parks
Amos Baker   Noah Parkhurst   Abraham Wesson
George Farrar   Ens. James Parks   John Wheeler

Appendix A: Units & Commanding Officers

Col. Eleazer Brooks's Regiment, **Capt. Abraham Peirce**'s Company, November 1777 to April 3, 1778, at Cambridge

John Parks (?)   Isaac Peirce (?)   John Viles

Col. Eleazer Brooks's Regiment, **Capt. John Walton**'s Company, January 12, 1778, to April 3, 1778, at Cambridge

John Viles

Col. Jacob Gerrish's Regiment, **Capt. Miles Greenwood**'s Company, November 11, 1777, to April 3, 1778, at Cambridge (Winter Hill)

James Nichols (?)

Col. Jacob Gerrish's Regiment, **Capt. Oliver Titcomb**'s Company, November 11, 1777, to April 3, 1778, at Cambridge (Winter Hill)

Michael Teny

[units unknown] November 1777 to April 1778, at Cambridge

Samuel Bacon   Jonathan Smith   Enos Wheeler
Joseph Mason

Col. Jonathan Reed's Regiment, **Capt. Daniel Harrington**'s Company, April 2, 1778, to July 3, 1778, at Cambridge

Noah Bacon   Leonard Hoar   Keen Robinson
Edward Cabot   Jonathan Page (?)   Daniel Wesson
Joseph Colburn   Leonard Parks   Stephen Wesson, Jr.
Nehemiah Farrar   Isaac Peirce   John Wheeler
Daniel Harrington

Col. Jonathan Reed's Regiment, **Capt. John Homes**'s Company, April 1, 1778, to July 4, 1778, at Cambridge

Zebediah Farrar

Col. Jonathan Reed's Regiment, **Capt. Isaac Wood**'s Company, April 1, 1778, to July 4, 1778, at Cambridge

John Parks (?)

Col. Jacob Gerrish's Regiment of Guards, **Capt. John Bodwell**'s Company, April 2, 1778, to July 1778, at Cambridge

Abiel Abbot (?)

Col. Jacob Gerrish's Regiment of Guards, **Lt. John Dix**'s Company, July 2, 1778, to July 8, 1778, at Cambridge

Cpl. Zebediah Farrar

Col. Jacob Gerrish's Regiment of Guards, **Capt. Simon Hunt**'s Company, July 1778 to December 15, 1778, at Winter Hill

Israel Billing   Nehemiah Farrar   Jonas Whitaker
Joseph Billing, Jr.

Appendices: Order of Battle

Col. Jacob Gerrish's** Regiment of Guards,* ***Maj. Samuel Lamson's *Company, July 1778 to December 1778, at Cambridge*
  Edward Cabot (?)

Col. Nathan Sparhawk's** Regiment (commanded by **Maj. Daniel Clap**),* ***Capt. Josiah Wilder's *Company, July 4, 1778, to July 15, 1778, at Rutland Barracks*
  Noah Parkhurst (?)

[unit and dates of service unknown] 1777 or 1778
  Jacob Foster

[units and dates of service unknown] 1778

Phineas Allen	Daniel Farrar	Zechariah Weston

8. Valley Forge, 1777–1778

Colonel Baylor's** 3rd Regiment of Light Dragoons,* ***Capt. George Lewis's *Company of Horse (detached as **Gen. George Washington's** Life Guard)*
  Jesse Smith

Col. Timothy Bigelow's** 15th Massachusetts Regiment,* ***Capt. Edmund Munroe's *Company*

Peter Bowes	Luke Fletcher	Peter Oliver

***Col. Joseph Cilley's** Regiment, [company unknown]*

John Barter (?)	Zodith Henderson	Stephen Lufkin

Col. John Crane's** Artillery Regiment,* ***Captain Buckland's** or **Capt. John Lillie's *Company*
  Benjamin Cleaveland (?)

Col. John Crane's** Artillery Regiment,* ***Capt. Henry Burbeck's *Company*
  Cpl. Nathan Tidd

Col. John Crane's** Artillery Regiment,* ***Capt. Benjamin Frothingham's *Company*
  Asa Adams

Col. Henry Jackson's** Regiment,* ***Capt. Joseph Fox's *Company*
  Cpl. Ephraim Brooks, Jr.

Col. Henry Jackson's** Regiment,* ***Capt. Thomas Turner's *5th Company*
  Cpl. Nehemiah Abbot

Col. Henry Jackson's** Regiment,* ***Colonel's *Company*
  William Orr (?)

Col. Thomas Marshall's** 10th Massachusetts Regiment,* ***Capt. William Warner's *Company*

Eden London	Silas Sharon

Col. Joseph Vose's** Regiment,* ***Capt. Moses Ashley's *Company*

George Brown	Jack Farrar

Col. Joseph Vose's Regiment, Capt. Abraham Hunt's Company
Isaac Bussell

1778

1. Battle of Monmouth, June 28, 1778

Colonel Baylor's 3rd Regiment of Light Dragoons, **Capt. George Lewis's** *Company of Horse (detached as* **Gen. George Washington's** *Life Guard)*
Jesse Smith

Col. Timothy Bigelow's 15th Massachusetts Regiment, **Capt. Edmund Munroe's** *Company*
Peter Bowes   Luke Fletcher   Peter Oliver

Col. Joseph Cilley's Regiment, [company unknown]
John Barter (?)   Zodith Henderson   Stephen Lufkin

Col. John Crane's Artillery Regiment, **Captain Buckland's** *or* **Capt. John Lillie's** *Company*
Benjamin Cleaveland (?)

Col. John Crane's Artillery Regiment, **Capt. Henry Burbeck's** *Company*
Cpl. Nathan Tidd

Col. John Crane's Artillery Regiment, **Capt. Benjamin Frothingham's** *Company*
Asa Adams (?)

Col. Henry Jackson's Regiment, **Capt. Joseph Fox's** *Company*
Cpl. Ephraim Brooks, Jr. (?)

Col. Henry Jackson's Regiment, **Capt. Thomas Turner's** *5th Company*
Cpl. Nehemiah Abbot (?)

Col. Henry Jackson's Regiment, **Colonel's** *Company*
William Orr (?)

Col. Thomas Marshall's 10th Massachusetts Regiment, **Capt. William Warner's** *Company*
Eden London   Silas Sharon

Col. Joseph Vose's Regiment, **Capt. Moses Ashley's** *Company*
Jack Farrar

Col. Joseph Vose's Regiment, **Capt. Abraham Hunt's** *Company*
Isaac Bussell

2. Battle of Rhode Island, August 29, 1778

Col. William McIntosh's** Regiment,* ***Capt. Francis Brown's *Company*
Bulkley Adams	Jeremiah Knowlton	Salem Middlesex
Samuel Bond (?)	Abner Mathis	Isaac Peirce (?)
Joshua Brooks, Jr.	Tilly Mead	Jube Savage
John Conant (?)		

Col. Timothy Bigelow's** 15th Massachusetts Regiment,* ***Capt. Edmund Munroe's *Company*
Peter Bowes	Luke Fletcher	Peter Oliver

Col. John Crane's** Artillery Regiment,* ***Captain Buckland's *or* ***Capt. John Lillie's*** *Company*
Benjamin Cleaveland (?)

Col. John Crane's** Artillery Regiment,* ***Capt. Henry Burbeck's *Company*
Cpl. Nathan Tidd (?)

Col. John Crane's** Artillery Regiment,* ***Capt. Benjamin Frothingham's *Company*
Asa Adams (?)

Col. David Henley's** Regiment,* ***Capt. Lemuel Trescott's *Company*
Cpl. Nehemiah Abbot (?)	Cpl. Ephraim Brooks, Jr. (?)

Col. Henry Jackson's** Regiment,* ***Capt. Joseph Fox's *Company*
Cpl. Ephraim Brooks, Jr. (?)

Col. Henry Jackson's** Regiment,* ***Capt. Thomas Turner's *5th Company*
Cpl. Nehemiah Abbot (?)

Col. Henry Jackson's** Regiment,* ***Colonel's *Company*
William Orr (?)

Col. John Jacobs's** Regiment,* ***Capt. Joseph Griffith's *Company*
James Adams, Jr.	Lt. Isaac Hartwell

Col. Joseph Vose's** Regiment,* ***Capt. Moses Ashley's *Company*
Jack Farrar

Col. Joseph Vose's** Regiment,* ***Capt. Abraham Hunt's *Company*
Isaac Bussell

Col. Nathaniel Wade's** Regiment,* ***Capt. Ebenezer Belknap's *Company*
Nathaniel Lovell (?)

[units and dates of service unknown]
Jonathan Abel	James Meriam (?)	Thomas Smith

3. Rhode Island, 1778 (other than the Battle of Rhode Island)

Col. Timothy Bigelow's** 15th Massachusetts Regiment,* ***Capt. Edmund Munroe's *Company*
Peter Bowes	Luke Fletcher	Peter Oliver

Appendix A: Units & Commanding Officers

***Col. David Henley**'s Regiment*, ***Capt. Lemuel Trescott**'s Company*
Cpl. Nehemiah Abbot   Cpl. Ephraim Brooks, Jr.

***Col. John Holman**'s Regiment*, ***Capt. John Putnam**'s Company*
Aaron Brooks (?) [before the battle]

***Col. John Jacobs**'s Regiment*, ***Capt. Nathan Smith**'s Company*
James Adams, Jr.   Lt. Isaac Hartwell

***Col. Joseph Vose**'s Regiment*, ***Capt. Moses Ashley**'s Company*
Jack Farrar

***Col. Joseph Vose**'s Regiment*, ***Capt. Abraham Hunt**'s Company*
Isaac Bussell

***Col. Nathaniel Wade**'s Regiment*, ***Capt. Ebenezer Belknap**'s Company, at North Kingston and East Greenwich*
Nathaniel Lovell (?)

***Capt. Benjamin Monroe**'s Company. at North Kingston*
Sgt. Zebediah Farrar

[units and dates of service unknown]
Jonathan Mead (?)

4. Coastal Service, 1778

***Lieutenant Colonel Symmes**'s detachment, **Capt. John Hinkley**'s Company, February 13, 1778, to May 13, 1778, guarding stores in Boston*
Ebenezer Torrey (?)

***Col. William McIntosh**'s Regiment*, ***Capt. Edward Fuller**'s Company, March to April 1778, at Roxbury*
Jonathan Weston

***Col. William McIntosh**'s Regiment*, ***Capt. Lemuel May**'s Company, March to April 1778, at Roxbury*
Joseph Munroe

***Colonel Pierce**'s Regiment*, ***Capt. James Morton**'s Company, March to April 1778, at Governor's Island*
Elijah Child (?)

***Col. Abijah Stearns**' Regiment*, ***Capt. Seth Newton**'s Company, April 1 to July 2, 1778, at Roxbury*
John Coolidge (?)

***Col. Samuel Thatcher**'s Regiment*, ***Capt. Abraham Peirce**'s Company, September 2–6, 1778, in Boston*
Jonathan Weston (?)

Colonel Cogswell's *Regiment,* ***Capt. David Goodwin's*** *Company, September 22 to December 31, 1778, in and about Boston*
Amos Hosmer   Leonard Parks

5. Continental Army (including militia attachments), other service, 1778

Col. Jeduthan Baldwin's *Regiment of Artificers,* ***Capt. Benjamin Pollard's*** *(then* ***Capt. Phineas Parker's****) Company*
Isaac Munroe   Lt. John Whitehead

Col. Timothy Bigelow's *15th Massachusetts Regiment,* ***Capt. Edmund Munroe's*** *(then* ***Captain Bowman's****) Company*
Peter Bowes   Luke Fletcher   Peter Oliver

Col. Joseph Cilley's *Regiment, [company unknown]*
John Barter (?)   Zodith Henderson (?)   Stephen Lufkin (?)

Col. John Crane's *Artillery Regiment,* ***Capt. Benjamin Frothingham's*** *Company*
Asa Adams

Col. John Crane's *Artillery Regiment,* ***Captain Buckland's*** *or* ***Capt. John Lillie's*** *Company*
Benjamin Cleaveland

Col. John Crane's *Artillery Regiment,* ***Capt. Henry Burbeck's*** *Company*
Nathan Tidd

Col. John Greaton's *2nd Regiment,* ***Capt. Thomas Prichard's*** *Company*
Sgt. Joseph Peirce   Artemas Reed

Col. John Greaton's *2nd Regiment,* ***Major Thompson's*** *(?) Company*
Jonathan Gage

Col. John Greaton's *2nd Regiment,* ***Capt. Job Sumner's*** *Company*
Lt. Isaac Gage   Jonas Parks (?)

Col. John Greaton's *2nd Regiment,* ***Capt. Abraham Watson's*** *Company*
Sgt. Elisha Willington

Col. Henry Jackson's *Regiment,* ***Capt. Thomas Turner's*** *5th Company*
Cpl. Nehemiah Abbot

Col. Henry Jackson's *Regiment,* ***Capt. Joseph Fox's*** *Company*
Cpl. Ephraim Brooks, Jr.

Col. Henry Jackson's *Regiment,* ***Colonel's*** *Company*
William Orr (?)

Colonel Malcom's *Regiment,* ***Capt. John Santford's*** *Company, at Fishkill and elsewhere in the Hudson Valley*
Fifer Elijah Mason   Abijah Munroe   William Thorning
Sgt. Joseph Mason

Appendix A: Units & Commanding Officers

Col. Thomas Marshall's 10th Massachusetts Regiment, **Capt. William Warner's** *Company*
  Eden London

Col. Thomas Nixon's Regiment, **Capt. Thomas Barns's** *Company, at Fishkill and the Hudson Valley*
  Ezra Meriam   Keen Robinson

Col. Thomas Nixon's Regiment, **Capt. Jabez Lane's** *Company, in the Hudson Valley*
  Abijah Munroe   William Thorning

Col. Thomas Nixon's Regiment, **Capt. Abel Holden's** *Company, in the Hudson Valley*
  Joseph Nixon

Col. Thomas Nixon's Regiment, **Capt. Adam Wheeler's** *Company, in the Hudson Valley*
  Lemuel Wheeler

Col. Thomas Poor's Regiment, **Capt. Edward Richardson's** *Company, in the Hudson Valley*
  Abel Child   Peter Nelson   Solomon Whitney

Col. Thomas Poor's Regiment, **Capt. Caleb Moulton's** *(later* **Lt. Eliphalet Hastings's***) Company, in the Hudson Valley*
  Jonathan Weston (?)

Colonel Sherbourn's Regiment, **Captain Berton's** *Company*
  William Gilbert

Colonel Wesson's 9th Regiment, **Captain Dix's** *Company, June 1778, at Fishkill*
  Jonas Bond

[units and dates of service unknown]
  Samuel Baley   Jeduthan Bemis

(Fishkill, July 1778)
  Thomas Bond   Joseph Munroe   Benjamin Parks (?)

1779

1. Penobscot Expedition, July–August 1779

Col. Jonathan Mitchell's Regiment, **Capt. Alexander McLellan's** *Company*
  Zechariah Weston (?)

[unit and dates of service unknown]
  John Billing

2. Rhode Island, 1779

Col. Timothy Bigelow's 15th Massachusetts Regiment, **Capt. Edmund Munroe's** *Company*
  Peter Bowes   Luke Fletcher   Peter Oliver

***Col. Henry Jackson's** Regiment, **Capt. Joseph Fox's** Company*
Cpl. Ephraim Brooks, Jr.

***Col. Henry Jackson's** Regiment, **Capt. Thomas Turner's** Company*
Sgt. Nehemiah Abbot

***Col. Henry Jackson's** Regiment, **Colonel's** Company*
William Orr (?)

***Col. John Jacobs's** Light Infantry Regiment, **Capt. Samuel Heald's** Company, September 16, 1779, to November 16, 1779, at Providence, Tiverton, and Newport*

Abiel Abbot	Nathan Billing, Jr. (?)	Leonard Hoar
James Adams, Jr.	William Bond	Jonathan Page
Joseph Billing, Jr.	Samuel Hartwell (?)	Solomon Whitney

***Lt. Col. Samuel Pierce's** Regiment, **Capt. Lawson Buckminster's** Company, May 17, 1779, to July 1, 1779, at Tiverton*

Nathan Billing, Jr. (?)	Sgt. Zebediah Farrar	Jonathan Page
Nehemiah Farrar	Leonard Hoar	Daniel Wesson

***Col. Nathan Tyler's** Regiment, **Capt. Thomas Hovey's** Company*

Christopher Mann	Sgt. Joseph Mason	William Thorning

***Col. Joseph Vose's** Regiment, **Capt. Moses Ashley's** Company*
Jack Farrar

***Col. Joseph Vose's** Regiment, **Capt. Abraham Hunt's** Company*
Isaac Bussell

[units and dates of service unknown]

Eleazer Brooks, Jr. (?)	Daniel Child (?)	John Wesson [Jr.] (?)

3. Militia service, other, 1779

***Capt. Abner Crane's** Company, February to May 1779, guard duty at Roxbury*
Zechariah Weston

***Col. Josiah Whitney's** 2nd Worcester County Regiment, **Capt. Ephraim Hartwell's** 12th Company, guard duty at Rutland*
Capt. Ephraim Hartwell, Jr.

4. Continental Army, other, 1779

***Col. Jeduthan Baldwin's** Regiment of Artificers, **Capt. Phineas Parker's** Company*
Isaac Munroe

***Col. Timothy Bigelow's** 15th Massachusetts Regiment, **Captain Bowman's** Company*

Peter Bowes	Luke Fletcher	Peter Oliver

Appendix A: Units & Commanding Officers

***Colonel Buttrick's** Regiment,* ***Captain Butters's** Company, at Albany and Schenectady*
Abel Billing (?)

***Col. Joseph Cilley's** Regiment, [company unknown]*
John Barter (?)   Zodith Henderson (?)   Stephen Lufkin (?)

***Col. John Crane's** Artillery Regiment,* ***Captain Buckland's** or* ***Capt. John Lillie's** Company*
Benjamin Cleaveland

***Col. John Crane's** Artillery Regiment,* ***Capt. Benjamin Frothingham's** Company*
Asa Adams

***Col. Samuel Denny's** Regiment,* ***Capt. Thomas Cowdin's** Company, in the Hudson Valley*
Elijah Mason (?)

***Col. Samuel Denny's** Regiment,* ***Capt. Joshua Walker's** Company, at Claverack*
Abel Billing   Stephen Brooks [Jr.]   Timothy Stone
Solomon Billing   Zebediah Farrar   Daniel Wesson

***Col. Jacob Gerrish's** Regiment,* ***Capt. Joseph Shed's** Company, at Claverack*
John Barrett (?)

***Col. John Greaton's** 2nd Regiment,* ***Capt. Thomas Prichard's** Company*
Sgt. Joseph Peirce   Artemas Reed

***Col. John Greaton's** 2nd Regiment,* ***Capt. Job Sumner's** Company*
Jonas Parks (?)

***Col. John Greaton's** 2nd Regiment,* ***Major Thompson's** (?) Company*
Jonathan Gage

***Col. John Greaton's** Regiment,* ***Capt. Abraham Watson's** Company*
Ens. Elisha Willington

***Col. Thomas Marshall's** 10th Massachusetts Regiment,* ***Capt. William Warner's** Company, at West Point*
Eden London

***Lt. Col. David Mason's** Regiment of Artillery Articifers,* ***Capt. William Hawes's** Company of Harness Makers, at Springfield*
Adonijah Rice

***Col. Thomas Nixon's** Regiment,* ***Colonel's** Company (commanded by* ***Capt. Lieut. Benjamin Haywood**, then* ***Capt. Lieut. Matthew Chambers**), in the Hudson Valley*
Lemuel Wheeler

***Col. Thomas Nixon's** Regiment,* ***Capt. Abel Holden's** Company, in the Hudson Valley*
Joseph Nixon

***Colonel Sherbourn's** Regiment,* ***Captain Berton's** Company*
William Gilbert (?)

***Col. Joseph Vose's** Regiment,* **Capt. Moses Ashley's** *Company*
Jack Farrar

***Col. Joseph Vose's** Regiment,* **Capt. Abraham Hunt's** *Company, in the Hudson Valley*
Isaac Bussell

***Col. James Wesson's** 9th Regiment,* **Capt. Nathan Dix's** *Company, at West Point*
John Barrett Ezra Meriam Isaac Peirce (?)
Joseph Meloney

[unit and dates of service unknown]
Samuel Baley

1780

1. Rhode Island, 1780

***Maj. Seth Bullard's** 4th Suffolk County Militia Regiment,* **Capt. John Ellis's** *Company, July 29, 1780, at Tiverton*
Nathaniel Lovell (?)

***Maj. Eliphalet Cary's** Regiment,* **Lt. William Dunbar's** *Company*
Cpl. John Conant (?)

***Col. Enoch Hallet's** Regiment,* **Capt. David Moore's** *Company*
John Coolidge (?)

***Col. Cyprian How's** Regiment,* **Capt. Abraham Andrews's** *Company*
Joseph Billing, Jr. Elijah Child Isaac Munroe
Jonas Brooks Leonard Hoar Micah Munroe
Sgt. Daniel Child (?) Salem Middlesex John Wheeler

***Col. Cyprian How's** Regiment,* **Capt. Walter McFarland's** *Company*
Cpl. John Parks (?)

***Col. Abner Perry's** Regiment,* **Capt. Lawson Buckminster's** *2nd Company*
Bulkley Adams

***Col. Abner Perry's** Regiment,* **Capt. Thomas Mellen's** *Company*
Cpl. James Parks (?)

***Col. Ebenezer White's** Regiment,* **Capt. Jonah Washburn's** *Company*
Zechariah Weston (?)

[units and dates of service unknown]
Abel Billing (?) Eleazer Brooks, Jr. (?) Peter Sharon (?)
Israel Billing (?)

Appendix A: Units & Commanding Officers 499

2. *Continental Army, 1780*

***Col. John Bailey**'s 2nd Massachusetts Regiment, **Capt. Adam Bailey**'s Company*
Abel Billing

***Col. Timothy Bigelow**'s 15th Massachusetts Regiment, **Captain Bowman**'s Company*
Peter Bowes Luke Fletcher Peter Oliver

***Col. Timothy Bigelow**'s Regiment (commanded by **Lt. Col. Calvin Smith**), **Capt. Daniel Pilsbury**'s Company, in the Hudson Valley*
Richard Winship

***Col. Jeduthan Baldwin**'s Regiment of Artificers, **Capt. Phineas Parker**'s Company*
Isaac Munroe

***Col. John Crane**'s Artillery Regiment, **Capt. Benjamin Frothingham**'s Company*
Asa Adams

***Col. John Crane**'s Artillery Regiment, **Capt. John Lillie**'s Company*
Benjamin Cleaveland (?)

***Col. John Greaton**'s 2nd Regiment, **Capt. Thomas Prichard**'s Company*
Sgt. Joseph Peirce

***Col. John Greaton**'s Regiment, **Major Thompson**'s (?) Company*
Cpl. Jonathan Gage

***Col. John Greaton**'s Regiment, **Capt. James Tisdale**'s Company*
Artemas Reed

***Col. John Greaton**'s Regiment, **Capt. Abraham Watson**'s Company*
Sgt. Elisha Willington

***Col. John Greaton**'s Regiment, **Capt. Joseph Williams**'s Light Infantry Company*
Sgt. Elisha Willington

***Col. Henry Jackson**'s Regiment, **Capt. Joseph Fox**'s Company, at Morristown*
Cpl. Ephraim Brooks, Jr.

***Col. Henry Jackson**'s Regiment, **Capt. Thomas Turner**'s Company, at Morristown*
Sgt. Nehemiah Abbot

***Col. Henry Jackson**'s Regiment, **Colonel**'s Company, at Morristown*
William Orr (?)

***Col. Thomas Marshall**'s Regiment, **Capt. Othniel Taylor**'s Company*
Ezra Meriam

***Col. Thomas Nixon**'s Regiment, **Capt. Matthew Chambers**'s Company*
Joseph Nixon

***Col. Thomas Nixon's** Regiment,* **Colonel's** *Company, commanded by* **Capt. Lieut. Peter Clayes,** *in the Hudson Valley*
  Lemuel Wheeler

***Col. Rufus Putnam's** Regiment,* **Capt. Joshua Benson's Light Infantry Company**
  Solomon Whitney

***Colonel Sprout's** 5th Regiment,* **Capt. Abraham Williams's** *Company*
  John Meriam

***Col. Ebenezer Thayer's** Regiment,* **Capt. Samuel Holden's** *Company*
  Jesse Smith (?)

***Colonel Sherbourn's** Regiment,* **Captain Berton's** *Company*
  William Gilbert (?)

***Col. Joseph Vose's** Regiment,* **Capt. Belcher Hancock's** *Company*
  Jack Farrar

***Col. Joseph Vose's** Regiment,* **Capt. Abraham Hunt's** *Company, in the Hudson Valley*
  Cpl. Isaac Bussell

***Col. Joseph Vose's** Regiment,* **Capt. John Williams's** *Company*
  Jonathan Mead

***Col. Joseph Vose's** Regiment,* [Company unknown], at the Hudson Valley*
  George Brown (?)

***Col. James Wesson's** 9th Regiment,* **Capt. Nathan Dix's** *Company, at West Point*
  John Barrett   Ezra Meriam   Isaac Peirce (?)
  Joseph Meloney

***Captain Stearns's** Company, at North Castle*
  Levi Parker

[unit and dates of service unknown]
  Israel Billing   Peter Oliver   William Smith (?)
  Nathan Billing, Jr.   Jonathan Page   William Thorning
  Cornelius Meloney   Peter Sharon   Jonas Whitaker

3. Other (militia) service, 1780

7th Middlesex County Regiment, **Capt. Benjamin Fletcher's** *1st Company, August 1, 1781, to December 1, 1781*
  Lt. Abel Adams (?)

Capt. Ephraim Stone's *Company, New Hampshire line, at Coos*
  Noah Parkhurst (?)

Capt. Silas Wright's *Company, on the Royalton Alarm*
  Samuel Parks

1781

1. Rhode Island, 1781

Col. William Turner's Regiment, **Capt. Asa Drury's** Company, August 1, 1781, to December 1, 1781

    Lt. Abel Adams (?)   William Thorning   Sgt. Lemuel Wheeler

[unit and dates of service unknown]
    Abiel Abbot (?)

2. Hudson Valley, 1781

Lt. Col. John Brooks's 7th Massachusetts Regiment, **Capt. Zebulon King's** Company
    Noah Parkhurst

Lt. Col. John Brooks's 7th Massachusetts Regiment, **Capt. Jonathan Maynard's** 6th Company, at West Point and Peekskill
    Jonathan Tower   Elisha Willington (?)

Col. John Greaton's 3rd Massachusetts Regiment, **Capt. Thomas Prichard's** Company
    Joel Adams   Leonard Whitney

Col. Henry Jackson's Regiment, **Capt. Thomas Turner's** Company, at West Point
    Abner Richardson

Col. William Shepard's Regiment, **Capt. Elnathan Haskell's** Company
    Aaron Parker

Lt. Col. Calvin Smith's 6th Massachusetts Regiment, **Capt. Daniel Pilsbury's** Company
    Richard Winship

Col. Joseph Vose's Regiment, **Capt. John Williams's** Company, at West Point
    Jonathan Mead

Lt. Col. Joseph Webb's Regiment, **Capt. Daniel Bowker's** Company, August 20, 1781, to December 2, 1781
    John Conant (?)   George Farrar

Lt. Col. Joseph Webb's Regiment, **Capt. Isaac Gage's** Company, at West Point
    Capt. Isaac Gage (?)   Jonas Parks   Cpl. Jonathan Weston (?)

Lt. Col. Joseph Webb's Regiment, **Capt. John Hayward's** Company, in the Hudson Highlands
    Jeduthan Bemis   Christopher Mann   Joseph Munroe
    Peter Bowes   Ezra Meriam   John Wood
    Daniel Brooks

3. Continental Army, other, 1781

Col. John Ashley's *Berkshire County Regiment, [Company unknown]*
Jack Freeman (?)

Col. John Crane's *Artillery Regiment,* ***Capt. John Lillie's*** *Company.*
Benjamin Cleaveland (?)

Col. John Greaton's *3rd Massachusetts Regiment,* ***Capt. Thomas Prichard's*** *Company, service at Kingsbridge, July 2, 1781*
Joel Adams   Leonard Whitney

Col. Rufus Putnam's *Regiment,* ***Capt. Haffield White's*** *Company*
Jonathan Page

Col. Calvin Smith's *Regiment,* ***Capt. Matthew Chambers's*** *Company*
Joseph Nixon

Col. Calvin Smith's *Regiment,* ***Capt. Ebenezer Smith's*** *Company*
Artemas Reed

Colonel Sprout's *5th Regiment,* ***Capt. Abraham Williams's*** *Company*
John Meriam

Col. Joseph Vose's *Regiment,* ***Capt. Nathaniel Cushing's*** *Light Infantry Company, at Richmond and Yorktown, Virginia*
Isaac Bussell

Colonel Whitney's *Regiment,* ***Captain Hastings's*** *Company*
Levi Parker

9th Massachusetts Regiment, [Company unknown]
Samuel Farrar, Jr. (?)

Capt. Amos Lincoln's *Company of Matrosses*
Solomon Whitney

[units and dates of service unknown]
Amos Adams   Peter Oliver   Peter Sharon
Bacchus Cockran   Joseph Parker   William Smith (?)

1782

1. Continental Army, 1782

Lt. Col. John Brooks's *7th Massachusetts Regiment,* ***Capt. Nathaniel C. Allen's*** *8th Company*
Lt. Elisha Willington   Jonathan Tower

Appendix A: Units & Commanding Officers

***Lt. Col. John Brooks's** 7th Massachusetts Regiment,* **Capt. Zebulon King's** *Company*
Noah Parkhurst

***Lt. Col. John Brooks's** 7th Massachusetts Regiment,* **Capt. Jonathan Maynard's** *6th Company*
Jonathan Tower   Lt. Elisha Willington

***Lt. Col. John Brooks's** 7th Massachusetts Regiment,* **Capt. William Mills's** *Company*
Abraham Wesson

***Col. Henry Dearborn's** 1st New Hampshire Regiment,* **Capt. Isaac Frye's** *Company*
Silas Whitney

***Col. Henry Dearborn's** 1st New Hampshire Regiment, [Company unknown]*
Ezra Meriam

***Col. John Greaton's** 3rd Massachusetts Regiment,* **Capt. Thomas Prichard's** *Company, in the Hudson Highlands*
Joel Adams   Leonard Whitney

***Col. Henry Jackson's** Regiment,* **Capt. Isaac Frye's** *Company*
Ezra Meriam

***Col. Rufus Putnam's** Regiment,* **Capt. Haffield White's** *Company*
Jonathan Page

*Colonel **Reed's** 2nd New Hampshire Regiment, [Company unknown]*
Ezra Meriam

***Col. William Shepard's** Regiment,* **Capt. Elnathan Haskell's** *Company*
Aaron Parker

***Col. Calvin Smith's** Regiment,* **Capt. Ebenezer Smith's** *Company*
Artemas Reed

*Colonel **Sprout's** 2nd Massachusetts Regiment,* **Capt. Adam Bailey's** *Company*
Abner Richardson

***Col. Joseph Vose's** Regiment,* **Capt. Francis Green's** *(?) Company, in the Hudson Highlands*
Isaac Bussell

*Colonel **Whitney's** Regiment,* **Captain Hastings's** *Company*
Levi Parker

***Capt. Amos Lincoln's** Company of Matrosses*
Solomon Whitney

[units and dates of service unknown]
Amos Adams   William Orr   Peter Weston
Benjamin Cleaveland Joseph Parker

2. Naval, 1782

"Deane" commanded by **Capt. Samuel Nicholson**, *February 1782*
Solomon Whitney

"Hague" commanded by **Capt. John Manley**, *June (?) 1782*
Solomon Whitney

1783

1. Continental Army, 1783

Col. John Brooks's 7th Massachusetts Regiment, **Capt. Zebulon King's** *Company*
Noah Parkhurst

Col. John Brooks's 7th Massachusetts Regiment, **Capt. William Mills's** *Company*
Abraham Wesson

Col. John Brooks's 7th Massachusetts Regiment, 3rd Company
Lt. Elisha Willington

Col. Henry Dearborn's 1st New Hampshire Regiment, **Capt. Moody Dustin's** *Company*
Silas Whitney

Col. John Greaton's 3rd Massachusetts Regiment, **Capt. Thomas Prichard's** *Company, in the Hudson Highlands*
Joel Adams   Leonard Whitney

Col. Henry Jackson's Regiment, **Capt. Isaac Frye's** *Company*
Ezra Meriam

Col. Rufus Putnam's Regiment, **Capt. Haffield White's** *Company*
Jonathan Page

Col. William Shepard's Regiment, **Capt. Elnathan Haskell's** *Company*
Aaron Parker

Colonel Sprout's 2nd Massachusetts Regiment, **Capt. Adam Bailey's** *Company*
Abner Richardson

Col. Joseph Vose's Regiment, **Capt. Francis Green's** *(?) Company, in the Hudson Highlands*
Isaac Bussell

Colonel Whitney's Regiment, Captain Hastings's Company
Levi Parker

4th Massachusetts Regiment, **Capt. Jonathan Maynard's** *6th Company*
Jonathan Tower

Appendix A: Units & Commanding Officers

[units and dates of service unknown]
- Amos Adams
- Benjamin Cleaveland
- William Orr
- Joseph Parker
- Peter Weston

Year Not Indicated

1. Continental Army, year not indicated

[units and dates of service unknown]
- James Adams (?)
- *[unidentified]* Adams
- Samuel Avery
- Jacob Baker, Jr.
- Timothy Billing (?)
- Jonas Bond (?)
- Samuel Bond
- Joshua Brooks (?)
- Joshua Brooks, Jr.
- Timothy Brooks
- Benjamin Brown
- Joseph Brown
- Lt. Samuel Dakin, Jr.
- Samuel Farrar, Jr.
- Nathan Field
- John Hagar
- Jonas Hartwell (?)
- William Lawrence, Jr.
- Nathaniel Lovell
- John Lunt
- John More
- Abijah Peirce (?)
- John Porter
- Ezra Richardson
- Zechariah Weston
- Joseph Wheat
- Elisha Wheeler (?)

2. Rhode Island, year not indicated

[units and dates of service unknown]
- Samuel Bacon

Appendix B

Ages

Author's Note: A "(?)" denotes a degree of uncertainty in the record. For more information in each case, please refer to the individual profiles in Chapter 10.

1. Age at the outbreak of the war on April 19, 1775

Age 7
Joseph Parker

Age 8
Silas Whitney

Age 9
Aaron Parker

Age 10
Daniel Brooks
Jonathan Tower

Age 11
Peter Nelson
Joseph Nixon
Abner Richardson (?)
Daniel Whitehead
Leonard Whitney (?)

Age 12
Nathan Billing, Jr.
Micah Munroe
Peter Sharon (?)
Richard Winship

Age 13
Joseph Billing, Jr.
William Bond
Jonas Brooks
Nehemiah Farrar
John Meriam
Jonathan Page
Levi Parker

Age 14
Elijah Child
Jonathan Mead
Leonard Parks
Thomas Smith (?)
Jonathan Weston
Stephen Wesson, Jr.
John Wheeler

Age 15
Abiel Abbot
Asa Adams
Nathan Adams
Jonas Bond
Abner Brooks
George Farrar
Amos Hosmer
Abner Mathis
Ezra Meriam
Elisha Whitehead

Age 16
Bulkley Adams
James Adams, Jr.
Israel Billing
Solomon Billing
Stephen Brooks [Jr.]
George Brown
Abel Flint
Leonard Hoar
Joseph Munroe (?)
Barnabas Richardson (?)
Daniel Wesson
Elisha Willington

Age 17
Samuel Bond
Daniel Brown
Joseph Colburn
John Coolidge
Isaac Goodenow
Samuel Hastings, Jr.
William Hosmer, Jr.
Elijah Mason
Tilly Mead
Joseph Meloney
Isaac Munroe
Aaron Parks
Josiah Parks (?)
Isaac Peirce
William Thorning
Timothy Stone

Age 18
Abel Adams
John Barrett
Abel Billing
Benjamin Brooks
Job Brooks
Ephraim Brown
Abel Child
Brister Hoar (?)
Peter Oliver
Noah Parkhurst
Josiah Parks (?)
John Thorning
Lemuel Wheeler

Appendix B: Ages

Age 19
Noah Bacon
Amos Baker
Joseph Brown (?)
Isaac Bussell
Jonathan Gage
Abijah Munroe
Jonas Parks
Abraham Peirce
Jesse Smith
Nathan Tidd
John Wesson [Jr.]

Age 20
Nehemiah Abbot
John Billing
Joshua Brooks, Jr.
Nathan Brown, Jr.
Benjamin Cleaveland
Daniel Farrar
Jonas Hartwell
Amos Jones
Eleazer Parks

Age 21
Jeduthan Bemis
Daniel Billing
Ephraim Brooks, Jr.
John Flint
Isaac Gage
Gregory Stone, Jr.
Nathan Weston

Age 22
Joseph Abbot, Jr.
Edward Adams
Benjamin Brown
Daniel Child
Nathaniel Colburn
John Hagar (?)
Isaac Hartwell
Willard Parks
Joseph Peirce
Silas Sharon (?)

Age 23
Joseph Bacon
Samuel Baker
Ebenezer Brown
Timothy Brown (?)
Zebediah Farrar
John Gearfield
William Lawrence, Jr.
Joshua Stone
Zechariah Weston

Age 24
Charles Adams
John Adams, Jr.
Timothy Brown (?)
Daniel Harrington
Joseph Mason, Jr.
John Viles
John Wesson

Age 25
Amos Adams
Samuel Bacon
James Baker
Amos Child
Elisha Child (?)
Silas Fay (?)
Nathaniel Gove
Samuel Parks
Elisha Wheeler
Elijah Willington

Age 26
Timothy Billing
Joshua Child, Jr.
John Conant (?)
Jonas Mason
Abijah Mead
Timothy Sherman

Age 27
Joel Adams
Moses Brown
Francis Buttrick (?)
Timothy Farrar
Silas Fay (?)
Abraham Gearfield
John Hartwell
Jonathan Smith (?)

Age 28
Nathaniel Baker
Jacob Foster
Artemas Reed
William Smith
Michael Teny

Age 29
Ephraim Flint
Daniel Hosmer
Joseph Wheat
Abner Wheeler

Age 30
Phineas Allen
Samuel Dakin, Jr.
Ephraim Hartwell, Jr.
Jeremiah Knowlton
Eden London (?)

Age 31
Jacob Baker, Jr.
Solomon Garfield
Samuel Hoar

Age 32
Samuel Hartwell
Isaac Parks
Benjamin Wheat

Age 33
Stephen Brooks
Jonathan Hartwell (?)

Age 34
Samuel Avery (?)
John Conant (?)
James Miles
James Parks

Age 35
Edmund Bowman
Humphrey Farrar
John Parks

Age 36
Stephen Farrar
James Meriam
Abraham Wesson
Enos Wheeler

Age 37
John Whitehead (?)

Age 38
Samuel Farrar, Jr.

Age 39
Nathan Billing
Moses Underwood
Solomon Whitney

Age 40
William Parks

Age 41
Noah Brooks
Timothy Brooks
Benjamin Parks
Barnabas Richardson (?)

Age 42
Joseph Billing
Cornelius Meloney (?)

Age 43
James Adams
David Fisk

Age 44
Edmond Wheeler

Age 45
William Hosmer, Sr.

Age 46
Elisha Gearfield
Gregory Stone (Sr.)

Age 47
Joseph Abbot, Sr.
Eleazer Brooks
Abijah Peirce

Age 48
Aaron Brooks
Josiah Nelson

Age 49
Ephraim Brooks

Age 50
David Parks

Ages 51–53
John Adams
Jacob Baker
Benjamin Munroe
Ezra Richardson (?)

Ages 54–56
Joshua Brooks

Ages 57–59
—

Age over 60
John Hoar
Jonas Whitaker (?)

Ages unknown
Jonathan Abel
[unidentified] Adams
Samuel Baley
John Barter
Thomas Blodget
Thomas Bond
Peter Bowes
Peter Brooks
Edward Cabot
Bacchus Cockran
Jack Farrar
Nathan Field
Luke Fletcher
John Foster
William Gilbert
John Gorden
[unidentified] Gove
Zodith Henderson
Cuff Hoar
John Lander
Nathaniel Lovell
Stephen Lufkin
John Lunt
Christopher Mann
Salem Middlesex
John More
James Nichols
William Orr
John Porter
Adonijah Rice
Jube Savage
Cato Smith
Ebenezer Torrey
Richard Wesson
Peter Weston
John Wood

2. Age on the commencement of service

Age 11
Joseph Nixon

Age 12
Daniel Whitehead

Age 13
Joseph Parker

Age 14
Peter Nelson
Leonard Parks

Age 15
Asa Adams
Aaron Parker
Elisha Whitehead

Appendix B: Ages

Age 16
Bulkley Adams
Nathan Adams (?)
Joseph Billing, Jr.
Nathan Billing, Jr.
Jonas Bond (?)
Abner Brooks (?)
Daniel Brooks
Stephen Brooks [Jr.]
George Farrar
Nehemiah Farrar
Amos Hosmer
Abner Mathis
Ezra Meriam
Jonathan Page
Abner Richardson (?)
Jonathan Tower
John Wheeler
Silas Whitney

Age 17
Abiel Abbot
James Adams, Jr.
Abner Brooks (?)
Daniel Brown
George Brown
John Coolidge
Abel Flint
Isaac Goodenow
Samuel Hastings, Jr.
William Hosmer, Jr.
Elijah Mason
Jonathan Mead (?)
Tilly Mead
Isaac Munroe
Joseph Munroe (?)
Levi Parker
Aaron Parks
Peter Sharon (?)
Timothy Stone
William Thorning
Stephen Wesson, Jr.
Jonathan Weston (?)
Leonard Whitney
Elisha Willington
Richard Winship

Age 18
Abel Adams
John Barrett
Israel Billing
Solomon Billing
Jonas Bond (?)
Samuel Bond
William Bond
Benjamin Brooks
Job Brooks
Jonas Brooks
Abel Child
Joseph Colburn
Leonard Hoar
Jonathan Mead (?)
John Meriam
Micah Munroe
Noah Parkhurst
Josiah Parks (?)
Isaac Peirce
Barnabas Richardson (?)
Thomas Smith (?)
John Thorning
Daniel Wesson
Lemuel Wheeler

Age 19
Amos Baker
Ephraim Brown
Isaac Bussell
Elijah Child
Joseph Colburn
Jonathan Gage
Abijah Munroe
Peter Oliver
Jonas Parks
Josiah Parks (?)
Abraham Peirce
Jesse Smith
Nathan Tidd
John Wesson [Jr.]

Age 20
Nehemiah Abbot
Noah Bacon
Abel Billing
Joshua Brooks, Jr.
Joseph Brown (?)
Nathan Brown, Jr.
Daniel Farrar (?)
Brister Hoar (?)
Amos Jones
Eleazer Parks

Age 21
Jeduthan Bemis
Daniel Billing
Ephraim Brooks, Jr.
Benjamin Cleaveland
John Flint
Isaac Gage
Gregory Stone, Jr.
Nathan Weston

Age 22
Joseph Abbot, Jr.
Edward Adams
Benjamin Brown
Daniel Child
Isaac Hartwell
Jonas Hartwell
Joseph Meloney
Willard Parks
Joseph Peirce
Keen Robinson

Age 23
Samuel Baker
Ebenezer Brown
Zebediah Farrar
John Gearfield

Age 24
John Adams, Jr.
John Billing
Nathaniel Colburn (?)
John Hagar (?)
Daniel Harrington
Joseph Mason, Jr.
Silas Sharon (?)
Joshua Stone
John Viles
John Wesson
Zechariah Weston (?)

Age 25
Charles Adams (?)
Joseph Bacon
Samuel Bacon
James Baker
Timothy Brown
Silas Fay (?)
Nathaniel Gove
William Lawrence, Jr.
Elisha Wheeler
Elijah Willington

Age 26
Timothy Billing
Amos Child
Elisha Child (?)
Joshua Child, Jr.
John Conant (?)
Jonas Mason
Abijah Mead
Timothy Sherman

Age 27
Joel Adams
Moses Brown
Timothy Farrar
Silas Fay (?)
Abraham Gearfield
John Hartwell
Jonathan Smith (?)

Age 28
Nathaniel Baker
Francis Buttrick (?)
Jacob Foster
Artemas Reed
William Smith

Age 29
Daniel Hosmer
Joseph Wheat
Abner Wheeler

Age 30
Phineas Allen
Samuel Dakin, Jr.
Ephraim Flint
Ephraim Hartwell, Jr.
Eden London (?)
Samuel Parks
Michael Teny

Age 31
Amos Adams
Jacob Baker, Jr.
Solomon Garfield
Samuel Hoar
Jeremiah Knowlton

Age 32
Samuel Hartwell
Isaac Parks
Benjamin Wheat

Age 33
Stephen Brooks

Age 34
John Conant (?)
James Parks

Age 35
Humphrey Farrar
Jonathan Hartwell (?)
James Miles
John Parks

Age 36
Edmund Bowman
Stephen Farrar
Enos Wheeler

Age 37
James Meriam
John Whitehead (?)

Age 38
Samuel Farrar, Jr.

Age 39
Nathan Billing
Abraham Wesson
Solomon Whitney

Age 40
Samuel Avery
William Parks
Moses Underwood

Age 41
Benjamin Parks (?)

Age 42
Noah Brooks
Timothy Brooks
Benjamin Parks (?)

Age 43
James Adams
Joseph Billing
David Fisk
Barnabas Richardson (?)

Age 44
—

Age 45
William Hosmer, Sr.
Edmond Wheeler

Age 46
Gregory Stone (Sr.)

Age 47
Joseph Abbot, Sr.
Eleazer Brooks
Cornelius Meloney
Abijah Peirce

Appendix B: Ages

Age 48
Elisha Gearfield

Age 49
Aaron Brooks
Josiah Nelson

Age 50
Ephraim Brooks
David Parks (?)

Ages 51–53
John Adams
Jacob Baker
Benjamin Munroe

Ages 54–56
Joshua Brooks (?)
Ezra Richardson (?)

Ages 57–59
—

Age over 60
John Hoar
Jonas Whitaker (?)

Ages unknown
Jonathan Abel
[unidentified] Adams
Samuel Baley
John Barter
Thomas Blodget
Thomas Bond
Peter Bowes
Peter Brooks
Edward Cabot
Bacchus Cockran
Jack Farrar
Nathan Field
Luke Fletcher
John Foster
William Gilbert
John Gorden
[unidentified] Gove
Zodith Henderson
Cuff Hoar
John Lander
Nathaniel Lovell
Stephen Lufkin
John Lunt
Christopher Mann
Salem Middlesex
John More
James Nichols
William Orr
John Porter
Adonijah Rice
Jube Savage
Cato Smith
Ebenezer Torrey
Richard Wesson
Peter Weston
John Wood

Appendix C
Rank and Non-infantry Roles

Author's Note: A "(?)" denotes a degree of uncertainty in the record. For more information in each case, please refer to the individual profiles in Chapter 10.

1. Rank Achieved

Brigadier General
Eleazer Brooks

Colonel
Abijah Peirce

Adjutant
Ephraim Hartwell, Jr.

Quartermaster
Ephraim Hartwell, Jr.
Samuel Hartwell

Captain
Moses Brown
Samuel Farrar, Jr.
John Flint (?)
Isaac Gage (?)
Ephraim Hartwell, Jr.
John Hartwell
William Smith
Ebenezer Torrey (?)

Lieutenant
Abel Adams (?)
Samuel Dakin
Isaac Gage
Isaac Hartwell
Samuel Hoar
James Parks
John Whitehead
Elisha Willington

Ensign
Daniel Hosmer
James Parks
Samuel Parks

Sergeant
Joseph Abbot, Jr.
Nehemiah Abbot (?)
Edward Adams
Joshua Brooks, Jr.
Daniel Child
John Conant (?)
Zebediah Farrar
David Fisk
Daniel Harrington
Jonas Hartwell
Samuel Hartwell
Jeremiah Knowlton
Jonas Mason
Joseph Mason, Jr.
Abijah Mead
William Thorning
Lemuel Wheeler
Elijah Willington

Corporal
Nehemiah Abbot
Abel Adams
Samuel Baker
John Barrett
Samuel Bond
Ephraim Brooks, Jr.
Ebenezer Brown
Nathan Brown, Jr.
Isaac Bussell
Francis Buttrick
John Conant (?)
Silas Fay
Jonathan Gage
Solomon Garfield
Jonathan Hartwell
Abijah Munroe
Jonathan Page (?)
John Parks (?)
Joseph Peirce
Nathan Tidd
Jonathan Weston (?)

Appendix C: Rank and Non-infantry Roles

2. Non-infantry roles:

Dragoon
Jesse Smith

Artillery
Bombardier
Benjamin Cleaveland
Abraham Peirce
Joseph Peirce
Nathan Tidd
Gunner
Asa Adams
Joseph Colburn
Matross
Isaac Peirce
William Thorning
Richard Wesson
Solomon Whitney

Music
Drummer
Daniel Brown
Isaac Goodenow
Fifer
Asa Adams
Elijah Mason
Joseph Mason, Jr.
Joseph Nixon
Jonas Parks
Leonard Parks

Artificer
Isaac Munroe
Adonijah Rice
Daniel Whitehead
Elisha Whitehead
John Whitehead

Marine
Edward Adams
Jesse Smith (?)
Capt. William Smith
Solomon Whitney

Waiter
Isaac Goodenow
Leonard Hoar
Isaac Munroe

Appendix D
Length of Service

Author's Note: Categories are approximate, as in many cases, the records are imprecise as to length of service. A "(?)" denotes a particular degree of uncertainty in the service records. For more information in each case, please refer to the individual profiles in Chapter 10.

Up to 3 months of cumulative service

Joseph Abbot, Sr.
James Adams
John Adams
Phineas Allen
Noah Bacon
Jacob Baker
James Baker
Nathaniel Baker
John Billing (?)
Joseph Billing
Nathan Billing
Solomon Billing
William Bond
Edmund Bowman
Benjamin Brooks
Daniel Brooks
Ephraim Brooks
Jonas Brooks
Ebenezer Brown
Ephraim Brown
Timothy Brown

Amos Child
Elijah Child
Elisha Child
Joshua Child, Jr.
Nathaniel Colburn
John Conant (?)
John Coolidge
Stephen Farrar
Timothy Farrar
David Fisk
Abel Flint
Ephraim Flint
Jacob Foster (?)
John Foster (?)
Solomon Garfield
Abraham Gearfield
Elisha Gearfield
John Gearfield
Nathaniel Gove
Jonas Hartwell
Jonathan Hartwell

Cuff Hoar
John Hoar
William Hosmer, Sr.
Cornelius Meloney
James Miles
Benjamin Munroe
Micah Munroe
Isaac Parks
Samuel Parks
Abijah Peirce
Barnabas Richardson
Timothy Sherman (?)
Gregory Stone (Sr.)
Timothy Stone
Ebenezer Torrey
John Wesson
John Wesson [Jr.] (?)
Elisha Wheeler
Jonas Whitaker
John Wood

Appendix D: Length of Service

4 to 6 months of cumulative service

Abiel Abbot
Jonathan Abel
Joseph Bacon (?)
Jacob Baker, Jr.
Daniel Billing
Nathan Billing (?)
Nathan Billing, Jr.
Abner Brooks
Job Brooks
Noah Brooks
Stephen Brooks [Jr.]
Daniel Brown
Nathan Brown, Jr.
Francis Buttrick (?)
Elijah Child (?)
John Conant (?)
John Coolidge (?)
Jacob Foster (?)
[unidentified] Gove
Brister Hoar
Samuel Hoar
Amos Jones
Jeremiah Knowlton
Jonas Mason
James Meriam
John Meriam
Salem Middlesex
William Parks
Jube Savage (?)
Timothy Sherman (?)
Thomas Smith
Joshua Stone
Michael Teny
Ebenezer Torrey (?)
Moses Underwood (?)
Daniel Whitehead

7 to 9 months of cumulative service

Abiel Abbot (?)
Joseph Abbot, Jr.
Bulkley Adams
John Adams, Jr.
Samuel Bacon
Amos Baker
Abel Billing
Nathan Billing, Jr. (?)
Timothy Billing
Thomas Blodget
Jonas Bond
Thomas Bond
Aaron Brooks
Humphrey Farrar
Daniel Harrington
Ephraim Hartwell, Jr.
Amos Hosmer
William Hosmer, Jr. (?)
Christopher Mann
Abner Mathis
Abijah Mead
Josiah Nelson (?)
John Parks
Josiah Parks
Willard Parks
Adonijah Rice
Jube Savage (?)
Gregory Stone, Jr.
John Thorning
Benjamin Wheat
Stephen Wesson, Jr. (?)
Nathan Weston (?)
Edmond Wheeler (?)
Enos Wheeler
John Wheeler (?)
Elijah Willington (?)
Richard Winship

10 months up to 1 year of cumulative service

Edward Adams
Joseph Billing, Jr.
Abner Brooks (?)
Daniel Brown (?)
John Conant (?)
Samuel Dakin, Jr.
Daniel Farrar
Nehemiah Farrar
Jonas Hartwell (?)
Samuel Hartwell
Brister Hoar (?)
Peter Nelson
James Parks
John Viles
Jonathan Weston (?)
Elisha Whitehead (?)

1 year up to 1½ years of cumulative service

Abel Adams
James Adams, Jr.
Samuel Baker
Israel Billing
Eleazer Brooks (?)
Peter Brooks
Stephen Brooks
Moses Brown
Edward Cabot
Abel Child
Joseph Colburn
Daniel Farrar (?)
George Farrar
Zebediah Farrar
Silas Fay
John Flint
John Gorden (?)
John Hagar (?)
Isaac Hartwell
John Hartwell
Samuel Hastings, Jr. (?)
Daniel Hosmer
John Lander (?)
Nathaniel Lovell (?)
Jonathan Mead
Joseph Meloney (?)
John More (?)
Joseph Munroe
William Orr (?)
Noah Parkhurst (?)
Benjamin Parks (?)
Adonijah Rice (?)
Keen Robinson
Silas Sharon
Cato Smith
Jonathan Smith
William Smith
Abraham Wesson
Daniel Wesson
Richard Wesson
Peter Weston (?)
Joseph Wheat
Abner Wheeler (?)
John Whitehead

1½ years up to 2 years of cumulative service

Abel Adams (?)
James Adams (?)
[unidentified] Adams
John Barrett
Jonas Bond
Joseph Brown
Daniel Child
Bacchus Cockran (?)
Joseph Colburn (?)
John Flint (?)
Isaac Goodenow
Leonard Hoar
Tilly Mead
James Nichols
Aaron Parks
Eleazer Parks
John Parks (?)
Abraham Peirce
Cato Smith (?)
Jonathan Smith (?)
Zechariah Weston
Elisha Wheeler (?)
Silas Whitney

2 years up to 2½ years of cumulative service

Samuel Avery
Jeduthan Bemis
Benjamin Brown (?)
Bacchus Cockran (?)
Samuel Farrar, Jr. (?)
Elijah Mason
Joseph Mason, Jr.
Abijah Munroe
Joseph Parker (?)
Benjamin Parks (?)
Leonard Parks
Isaac Peirce
Peter Sharon

2½ years up to 3 years of cumulative service

Amos Adams
Samuel Baley
John Barter
Samuel Bond
Nathan Field (?)
Luke Fletcher
Isaac Gage
William Gilbert
Zodith Henderson (?)
William Lawrence, Jr.
Stephen Lufkin (?)
John Lunt (?)
Jonathan Page
Aaron Parker (?)
Levi Parker
Noah Parkhurst (?)
Jonas Parks
Isaac Peirce (?)
Abner Richardson
William Smith (?)
Jonathan Tower
Leonard Whitney

Appendix D: Length of Service

3 years up to 4 years of cumulative service

Nehemiah Abbot
Asa Adams
Joel Adams
Timothy Billing (?)
Peter Bowes
Ephraim Brooks, Jr.

Joshua Brooks, Jr.
Timothy Brooks
George Brown
Eden London
Jonathan Page (?)
Abijah Peirce (?)

John Porter
William Thorning
Nathan Tidd
Lemuel Wheeler

4 years up to 5 years of cumulative service

George Brown (?)
Jack Farrar
Samuel Farrar, Jr. (?)

Jonathan Gage
Ezra Meriam
Isaac Munroe

William Orr (?)
Joseph Peirce
Jesse Smith

More than 5 years of cumulative service

Isaac Bussell
Benjamin Cleaveland
Jack Farrar (?)

Joseph Nixon
Peter Oliver
Artemas Reed

Solomon Whitney
Elisha Willington

Appendix E

Lincoln Residency

Author's Note: In the eighteenth century, life was no less of a changing dynamic than it is today, and it has not always been possible to determine precise residence locations at particular points in time. This is particularly true among some of the young people who sometimes moved about somewhat before settling down. Even among established Lincoln individuals, cross-boundary interests occasionally confuse the residency picture. Further, it is beyond the scope of this work to pinpoint the precise birth locations of individuals born to longstanding Lincoln families whose births were recorded before 1754 in the parent towns of Lexington, Concord, and Weston. Accordingly, unless there is a birth record that clearly indicates otherwise, individuals born anywhere in Lexington, Concord, and Weston before 1754 to longstanding Lincoln families are considered "Born in Lincoln." A "(?)" denotes a more-than-usual degree of uncertainty in the record. For information in each case, please refer to the individual profiles in Chapter 10.

Born in Lincoln / Living in Lincoln during first service

Abiel Abbot
Joseph Abbot, Jr.
Joseph Abbot, Sr.
Nehemiah Abbot
Abel Adams
Amos Adams
Asa Adams
Bulkley Adams
James Adams
James Adams, Jr.
John Adams
[unidentified] Adams (?)
Phineas Allen
Amos Baker
Jacob Baker, Jr.
James Baker
Nathaniel Baker
Samuel Baker
Daniel Billing
Israel Billing
Joseph Billing
Joseph Billing, Jr.
Nathan Billing

Nathan Billing, Jr.
Timothy Billing
Jonas Bond
Samuel Bond
William Bond
Aaron Brooks
Abner Brooks
Benjamin Brooks
Daniel Brooks
Eleazer Brooks
Ephraim Brooks
Ephraim Brooks, Jr.
Job Brooks
Jonas Brooks
Joshua Brooks
Joshua Brooks, Jr.
Noah Brooks
Stephen Brooks
Stephen Brooks [Jr.]
Timothy Brooks
Benjamin Brown
Daniel Brown
Ebenezer Brown

Ephraim Brown
George Brown
Joseph Brown
Nathan Brown, Jr.
Timothy Brown
Abel Child
Amos Child
Daniel Child
Elijah Child
Elisha Child
Joshua Child, Jr.
Samuel Dakin, Jr.
Daniel Farrar
Humphrey Farrar
Nehemiah Farrar
Samuel Farrar, Jr.
Ephraim Flint
John Flint
Isaac Gage
Jonathan Gage
Abraham Gearfield
Elisha Gearfield
John Gearfield

Appendix E: Lincoln Residency

Nathaniel Gove
Isaac Hartwell
John Hartwell
Jonas Hartwell
Samuel Hartwell
John Hoar
Leonard Hoar
Samuel Hoar
Amos Hosmer (?)
Daniel Hosmer
William Hosmer, Jr.
William Hosmer, Sr.
William Lawrence, Jr.
Elijah Mason
Jonas Mason
Joseph Mason, Jr.
Abijah Mead
Jonathan Mead
Joseph Meloney
Abijah Munroe
Isaac Munroe
Micah Munroe
Peter Nelson (?)
Peter Oliver
Aaron Parks
Benjamin Parks
David Parks
Eleazer Parks
Isaac Parks
James Parks
John Parks
Jonas Parks
Josiah Parks
Leonard Parks
Willard Parks
William Parks
Abraham Peirce
Isaac Peirce
Joseph Peirce
Peter Sharon (?)
Jesse Smith
Gregory Stone, Jr.
Gregory Stone (Sr.)
Joshua Stone
Timothy Stone
John Thorning
William Thorning
Jonathan Tower
Abraham Wesson
Daniel Wesson
John Wesson
John Wesson [Jr.]
Stephen Wesson, Jr.
Jonathan Weston
Nathan Weston
Zechariah Weston
Joseph Wheat
Edmond Wheeler
John Wheeler
Leonard Whitney
Solomon Whitney
Elijah Willington
Elisha Willington

Born in Lincoln / Living outside of Lincoln during first service

Edward Adams
John Adams, Jr.
Joseph Adams*
Abel Billing
John Billing
Solomon Billing
Moses Brown
Ebenezer Cutler*
Zaccheus Cutler*
George Farrar (?)
Stephen Farrar
Timothy Farrar
Zebediah Farrar (?)
Abel Flint (?)
Solomon Garfield
Ephraim Hartwell, Jr.
Amos Hosmer (?)
Tilly Mead
Samuel Parks
Silas Sharon (?)
Timothy Sherman
Benjamin Wheat
Lemuel Wheeler (?)
Silas Whitney

*Served for the Crown

Non-native, but Lincoln connected prior to first service

Joel Adams
Joseph Bacon
Noah Bacon
Jacob Baker
Thomas Blodget
Edmund Bowman
Edward Cabot
Joseph Colburn
Nathaniel Colburn
Silas Fay
David Fisk
Jacob Foster
Daniel Harrington
Zodith Henderson (?)
Brister Hoar
Jeremiah Knowlton
John Lander
Abner Mathis
Cornelius Meloney
James Meriam
Salem Middlesex (?)
James Miles
Benjamin Munroe
Josiah Nelson
Jonathan Page (?)
Aaron Parker
Joseph Parker
Levi Parker
Noah Parkhurst
Abijah Peirce
Artemas Reed
Abner Richardson
Ezra Richardson
Keen Robinson (?)
Charles Russell*
Jube Savage

Cato Smith (?)
Jonathan Smith
Thomas Smith (?)
William Smith

Nathan Tidd
Moses Underwood
Abner Wheeler
Enos Wheeler

Daniel Whitehead
Elisha Whitehead
John Whitehead
Richard Winship (?)

*Served for the Crown

Moved into Lincoln during or between service stints

Samuel Bacon (?)   John Barrett   Elisha Wheeler

Enlisted to the credit of Lincoln (non-resident or residency unknown)

Samuel Baley
John Barter
Benjamin Cleaveland
William Gilbert

John Gorden
Nathaniel Lovell
Stephen Lufkin
John Lunt

Ezra Meriam
Joseph Munroe
John Porter
Adonijah Rice

Transient/Itinerant

Jeduthan Bemis (?)
John Coolidge

Eden London
James Nichols

Barnabas Richardson (?)
Michael Teny (?)

Moved into Lincoln after their service

Isaac Goodenow
Samuel Hastings, Jr.

Amos Jones
John Meriam

Joseph Nixon

Unknown

Jonathan Abel
Samuel Avery
Thomas Bond
Peter Bowes
Eleazer Brooks, Jr.
Peter Brooks
Isaac Bussell
Francis Buttrick
Bacchus Cockran

John Conant
Jack Farrar
Nathan Field
Luke Fletcher
John Foster
[unidentified] Gove
John Hagar
Jonathan Hartwell
Cuff Hoar

Christopher Mann
John More
William Orr
Ebenezer Torrey
John Viles
Richard Wesson
Peter Weston
Jonas Whitaker
John Wood

Appendix F
Identified Patriots of Color

Author's Note: Several cases are indicated in which substantial evidence links different names as belonging to the same individual. Possibly other pairings may also exist. A "(?)" denotes an uncertain identity, and therefore only a supposition that the individual may have been a Patriot of Color. For more information in each case, please refer to the individual profiles in Chapter 10.

Peter Bowes (*probably the individual previously known as* Peter Brooks)
Peter Brooks (*probably the individual later known as* Peter Bowes)
Jack Farrar (*a.k.a.* Jack Freeman, Jack Hatch)
Bacchus Cockran (?)
[unidentified] Gove (?)
Brister Hoar (*a.k.a.* Sippio Brister)
Cuff Hoar (*a.k.a.* Cuff Kneeland)
Eden London
Salem Middlesex
Peter Nelson
Peter Oliver
Jube Savage
Peter Sharon
Silas Sharon
Cato Smith

Appendix G

Deserted, Captured, Wounded, or Died in Service

Author's Note: A "(?)" denotes uncertainty in the record. For more information in each case, please refer to the individual profiles in Chapter 10.

1. Reported Deserted

Asa Adams	reported deserted on May 25, 1780
Jacob Baker, Jr. (?)	reported deserted on August 13, 1778
George Brown	reported deserted on June 1, 1778
George Brown	reported deserted on July 13, 1780
John Gorden (?)	(unknown)
Jonathan Mead	reported deserted on January 1, 1781
James Nichols	reported deserted on September 5, 1777
Artemas Reed	reported deserted on May 19, 1782 (returned May 29, 1782)
Adonijah Rice	reported deserted on September 5, 1777
Abraham Wesson	reported deserted on April 18, 1783, from furlough

2. Captured by the Enemy

Jeduthan Bemis	at the Cedars of Canada, May 19–20, 1776
Daniel Brown (?)	
George Brown (?)	
Jonathan Gage	at the Battle of Young's House, Mount Pleasant, New York, February 3, 1780
Samuel Hastings, Jr.	at Basking Ridge, New Jersey, December 13, 1776
Jesse Smith (?)	at sea, possibly 1780 or 1781 (?)
William Smith	off Cape Cod, by *HMS Diamond*, September 17, 1777

3. Reported Wounded in Battle

Jeduthan Bemis (?)	at White Plains, October 28, 1776
Joshua Brooks, Jr.	at Concord, April 19, 1775
Benjamin Cleaveland	at Bunker Hill, June 17, 1775
Jonathan Gage	at Young's House, February 3, 1780
Samuel Hastings, Jr.	at Basking Ridge, New Jersey, December 13, 1776

Appendix G: Deserted, Captured, Wounded, or Died in Service

4. Other Injuries Reported

Tilly Mead	axe wound in the knee, August 1775
Jonas Parks	loss of sight from complications of smallpox inoculation, Canada, 1776
Solomon Whitney	unidentified wound, Stockbridge, winter 1775–1776

5. Reported Died in Service

John Billing	killed in action, Penobscot Expedition, August 29, 1779
Thomas Blodget (?)	killed in action (?), Saratoga Campaign, fall of 1777
John Lander (?)	(unknown)
Silas Sharon	(unknown cause), July 14, 1778
Cato Smith	(unknown cause), January 23, 1777
Nathan Tidd	(unknown cause), October 28, 1778
Richard Wesson	(unknown cause), August 20, 1777
Daniel Whitehead	(unknown cause), August 27, 1777
Elisha Whitehead	(unknown cause), July 1777

6. Others who died shortly after discharge
(it is unknown whether or not their deaths were related to their service)

Abner Brooks	4 days after his November 30, 1777, discharge from the Saratoga Campaign
Benjamin Brooks	3 months after his May 23, 1775, discharge from service at Cambridge
Abraham Gearfield	4 months after his April 19, 1775, service

Appendix H

Pension Recipients

Author's Note: Tilly Mead was awarded a disability pension by the state of Massachusetts as early as 1794, but for most former Lincoln soldiers, pension benefits became available only much later. In 1818, Congress provided pensions for "needy" former Continental Army soldiers, but it failed to require financial disclosure until 1820. Consequently, many pensioners under the 1818 Act, including William Thorning, were stricken from the pension roles. In 1832, Congress began to broaden the eligibility requirements to include state and militia service, and increasingly over subsequent years to include widows. The following Lincoln individuals were awarded pensions under the various pension acts.

1. Lincoln Soldiers who were awarded pensions for their service

Joseph Abbot, Jr.	Isaac Goodenow	Jonathan Page
Nehemiah Abbot	Samuel Hastings, Jr.	Aaron Parks
Edward Adams	Leonard Hoar	Josiah Parks
James Adams, Jr.	Daniel Hosmer	Leonard Parks
Joel Adams	Amos Jones	Joseph Peirce
Amos Baker	Elijah Mason	Artemas Reed
John Barrett	Joseph Mason, Jr.	Abner Richardson
Jeduthan Bemis	Abner Mathis	Keen Robinson
Abel Billing	Abijah Mead	Jesse Smith
Jonas Bond	Tilly Mead	William Thorning
Job Brooks	Ezra Meriam	Jonathan Tower
George Brown	John Meriam	John Wheeler
Isaac Bussell	Abijah Munroe	Lemuel Wheeler
Joseph Colburn	Isaac Munroe	Leonard Whitney
Silas Fay	Joseph Munroe	Silas Whitney
Jonathan Gage	Joseph Nixon	Richard Winship

2. Widows of Former Soldiers who had been awarded pensions

Ruth Abbot, *widow of* Joseph Abbot, Jr.
Patty Adams, *widow of* Edward Adams
Statira Bemis, *widow of* Jeduthan Bemis
Elizabeth Billing, *widow of* Abel Billing
Eunice Bond, *widow of* Jonas Bond
Sally Brown, *widow of* George Brown
Lydia Mathews, *widow of* Abner Mathis
Susannah Meriam, *widow of* Ezra Meriam
Rhoda Munroe, *widow of* Joseph Munroe
Nancy Nixon, *widow of* Joseph Nixon
Bulah Parks, *widow of* Josiah Parks
Lucinda Parks, *widow of* Aaron Parks
Anna Richardson, *widow of* Abner Richardson
Achsah Robinson, *widow of* Keen Robinson
Eunice Thorning, *widow of* William Thorning
Sally Wheeler, *widow of* John Wheeler
Sally Whitney, *widow of* Silas Whitney

3. Widows who were later awarded pensions even though their husbands had not received pensions

Molly Adams, *widow of* John Adams, Jr.
Mary Brown, *widow of* Moses Brown
Sarah Cleaveland, *widow of* Benjamin Cleaveland
Mary Hartwell, *widow of* Samuel Hartwell
Mary Parker, *widow of* Levi Parker
Elizabeth Parks, *widow of* Eleazer Parks
Eunice Parks, *widow of* Jonas Parks
Lucy Stone, *widow of* Gregory Stone, Jr.
Lydia Weston, *widow of* Daniel Wesson

Appendix I
Burial Location

Author's Note: The names of burial grounds are as reported by credible sources, but they may not accord with local usage. Where a specific burial location is undetermined, the location given is typically either his residence at the time of death or the location where his death was recorded or reported. A "(?)" denotes uncertainty about the location attributed. For more information in each case, please refer to the individual profiles in Chapter 10.

1. Massachusetts

***Lincoln**—Precinct Burial Ground*
Joseph Abbot, Sr.
Nehemiah Abbot
Ephraim Brown
Abel Flint
Ephraim Flint
Isaac Goodenow
Samuel Hartwell
Brister Hoar (as Sippio Brister)
Gregory Stone, Jr.
Gregory Stone (Sr.)
Edmond Wheeler

***Lincoln**—Meeting House Cemetery*
Bulkley Adams
James Adams
John Adams
Amos Baker (?)
Jacob Baker, Jr. (?)
Nathaniel Baker (?)
Joseph Billing, Jr.
Timothy Billing
Aaron Brooks
Daniel Brooks (?)
Eleazer Brooks
Ephraim Brooks
Joshua Brooks
Joshua Brooks, Jr.
Noah Brooks
Timothy Brooks
Nathan Brown, Jr.

Joshua Child, Jr.
Samuel Farrar, Jr. (?)
David Fisk
Abraham Gearfield
Daniel Harrington
John Hartwell
John Hoar
Leonard Hoar
Samuel Hoar
Isaac Munroe (?)
Joseph Nixon (?)
Abijah Peirce
Jonathan Smith
John Wesson
Nathan Weston
Zechariah Weston
Abner Wheeler
Elisha Wheeler

***Lincoln**—Arbor Vitae Cemetery*
Timothy Brown
Joseph Colburn
Josiah Parks

***Lincoln**—undetermined location*
Jacob Baker
Israel Billing
Joseph Billing
Nathan Billing
Edmund Bowman (?)
Abner Brooks (?)
Benjamin Brooks

Appendix I: Burial Location

Ebenezer Brown
Elisha Child
Jack Farrar
Zebediah Farrar
Elisha Gearfield
Nathaniel Gove
Cuff Hoar
Amos Jones
William Lawrence, Jr.
Abijah Mead
James Meriam
Benjamin Munroe
James Parks (?)
Samuel Parks
Willard Parks
Joseph Peirce
Ezra Richardson
Peter Sharon
Timothy Stone
Jonathan Tower
Moses Underwood
Daniel Wesson
John Wesson [Jr.]

Barre—*undetermined location*
Tilly Mead

Bedford—*First Church of Christ Congregational Cemetery*
Samuel Bacon

Beverly—*undetermined location*
Moses Brown

Billerica—*undetermined location*
Abner Mathis

Bridgewater—*Conant Street Cemetery*
John Conant (?)

Cambridgeport—*undetermined location*
Leonard Parks

Concord—*Hill Burial Ground*
Joshua Stone

Concord—*Sleepy Hollow Cemetery*
James Baker

Concord—*undetermined location*
Edmund Bowman (?)
Ephraim Brooks, Jr.
Samuel Dakin, Jr.
Noah Parkhurst (?)
John Thorning
Elisha Willington

Erving—*undetermined location*
Jonathan Gage

Fitchburg—*Laurel Hill Cemetery*
John Meriam

Framingham—*undetermined location*
Abel Adams (?)

Hardwick—*undetermined location*
Jonathan Mead

Leominster—*undetermined location*
Nathaniel Colburn

Lexington—*Old Burying Ground*
Samuel Hastings, Jr.
Josiah Nelson
William Thorning

Lexington—*undetermined location*
Joseph Munroe
Thomas Smith (?)

Pepperell—*undetermined location*
Francis Buttrick (?)

Princeton—*Meeting House Cemetery*
Isaac Hartwell

Rowley—*undetermined location*
Michael Teny

Salem—*Harmony Grove Cemetery*
Jesse Smith

Townsend—*undetermined location*
John Conant (?)

Waltham—*undetermined location*
John Coolidge

Wayland—*North Cemetery*
Timothy Sherman

***Weston**—Central Cemetery*
John Viles

***Weston**—undetermined location*
Jeremiah Knowlton
Salem Middlesex
Joseph Parker
John Whitehead

***Winchendon**—Old Centre Burial Ground*
Eden London
Eleazer Parks
Stephen Wesson, Jr.

2. Maine

***Bangor**—undetermined location*
Daniel Billing

***Brooksville**—Lake Side Cemetery (a.k.a., Roberts Cemetery; Herrick Road Cemetery)*
Solomon Billing

***Camden**—Mountain View Cemetery*
Silas Fay

***Dover**—undetermined location*
John Barrett

***Farmington**—undetermined location*
Abiel Abbot
Daniel Hosmer

***Harrington**—Mill River Cemetery*
Isaac Bussell

***Livermore**—undetermined location*
Abijah Munroe
Micah Munroe
Benjamin Parks

***Livermore Falls**—Strickland's Ferry Cemetery*
Joseph Abbot, Jr.
Elijah Willington

***Livermore Falls**—undetermined location*
Abraham Wesson

***Robbinston**—Brewer Cemetery*
Jonas Bond (reportedly died at St. Stephen, New Brunswick)

***Sargentville**—Settler's Rest Cemetery*
Abel Billing (died in Sedgewick)

***Sargentville**—undetermined location*
John Billing (died in Castine)

***Sidney**—Longley Yard Cemetery*
Jonas Mason

***Wiscasset**—Evergreen Cemetery*
Jonas Brooks

3. New Hampshire

***Canterbury**—undetermined location*
Leonard Whitney

***Charlestown**—Forest Hill Cemetery*
Aaron Parks

***Charlestown**—undetermined location*
Jonas Parks

***Colebrook**—Colebrook Village Cemetery*
Humphrey Farrar

***Hanover**—Dartmouth College Cemetery*
Jacob Foster

***Marlborough**—undetermined location*
John Gearfield

***Mason**—Pleasant View Cemetery*
William Hosmer, Sr.

***Mason**—undetermined location*
Abel Adams (?)
John Adams, Jr.
Ezra Meriam

Appendix I: Burial Location

New Ipswich—*Central Cemetery*
 Ephraim Hartwell, Jr.

New Ipswich—*Old Village Yard*
 Stephen Farrar

New Ipswich—*Smithville Cemetery*
 Stephen Brooks [Jr.]

New Ipswich—*undetermined location*
 Timothy Farrar

Rindge—*undetermined location*
 Abraham Peirce

Sharon—*Jarmany Hill Cemetery*
 Joel Adams

Temple—*undetermined location*
 Jube Savage (?)

Thornton—*Pine Grove Cemetery*
 Silas Whitney

Troy—*Village Cemetery*
 Daniel Farrar
 George Farrar

Walpole—*Carpenter Hill Cemetery*
 John Flint
 Joseph Mason, Jr.

Westmoreland—*North Cemetery*
 Job Brooks
 John Wheeler

4. Vermont

Chester—*Riverside Cemetery*
 Amos Hosmer
 William Hosmer, Jr.

Concord—*undetermined location*
 Edward Adams

Enosburg—*Enosburg Center Congregational Cemetery*
 Samuel Baker

Royalton—*undetermined location*
 Levi Parker

Sharon—*undetermined location*
 Noah Parkhurst (?)

Springfield—*undetermined location*
 David Parks

Stockbridge—*undetermined location*
 Abel Child

Whittingham—*undetermined location*
 William Bond

5. Connecticut

Durham—*undetermined location*
 Jeduthan Bemis

Putnam—*Aspinwall Cemetery*
 Isaac Parks

Woodstock—*Woodstock Hill Cemetery*
 Elijah Mason

6. New York

Ashland Township—*Roushy Cemetery*
 George Brown

German—*undetermined location*
 Benjamin Cleaveland (?)

Lisle—*undetermined location*
 Keen Robinson

Lorraine—*undetermined location*
 Lemuel Wheeler

Lake Luzerne—*Luzerne Cemetery*
Abner Richardson

Milo—*undetermined location*
Richard Winship (?)

Orleans—*undetermined location*
Benjamin Wheat

Smyrna—*undetermined location*
Phineas Allen

Worcester—*undetermined location*
Solomon Garfield

7. Ohio

undetermined location
Aaron Parker (killed at the Battle of the Wabash)

8. West Virginia

Wellsburg—*undetermined location*
Artemas Reed

9. St. Lucia

undetermined location
Samuel Bond

10. West Indies

undetermined location
Daniel Brown (?)

11. Spain

Bilbao—*undetermined location*
Jonas Hartwell

12. Undetermined location

Jonathan Abel
Amos Adams
Asa Adams
James Adams, Jr.
[unidentified] Adams
Samuel Avery
Joseph Bacon
Noah Bacon
Samuel Baley
John Barter

Nathan Billing, Jr.
Thomas Blodget
Thomas Bond
Peter Bowes
Peter Brooks
Stephen Brooks
Benjamin Brown
Joseph Brown
Edward Cabot
Amos Child

Daniel Child
Elijah Child
Bacchus Cockran
Nehemiah Farrar
Nathan Field
Luke Fletcher
John Foster
Isaac Gage
William Gilbert
John Gorden

Appendix I: Burial Location

[unidentified] Gove
John Hagar
Jonathan Hartwell
Zodith Henderson
John Lander
Nathaniel Lovell
Stephen Lufkin
John Lunt
Christopher Mann
Cornelius Meloney
Joseph Meloney
James Miles
John More

Peter Nelson
James Nichols
Peter Oliver
William Orr
Jonathan Page
John Parks
William Parks
Isaac Peirce
John Porter
Adonijah Rice
Barnabas Richardson
Silas Sharon
Cato Smith

William Smith
Nathan Tidd
Ebenezer Torrey
Richard Wesson
Jonathan Weston
Peter Weston
Joseph Wheat
Enos Wheeler
Daniel Whitehead
Elisha Whitehead
Solomon Whitney
Jonas Whitaker
John Wood

Bibliography

1. Manuscripts and Special Collections

Billing Family Bible, photocopies of family records. In Archives/Special Collections of the Lincoln Public Library, Lincoln Founding Families Collection, Doc. # 2003.055.5.1.

Bowes, Peter, deed to Timothy Brooks, August 1785. Middlesex County Registry of Deeds, South District. Vol. 89, pp. 315–16.

Briggs, Peter Steele. "Five hundred years of the Farrar family, 1494–1994." 1997. In Archives/Special Collections of the Lincoln Public Library, Farrar Family Collection, Doc. # 2003.009.1.4.

———. "Genealogical Chart of the Farrar family through 14 generations." 1997. In Archives/Special Collections of the Lincoln Public Library, Farrar Family Collection, Doc. # 2003.009.1.5.

Brooks, Amos, heirs of, deed to Peter Bowes, 1783. In Archives/Special Collections of the Lincoln Public Library, Manuscript Records Collection, Doc. # 2003.050.1.2.

Brooks Family Notes, historical and genealogical notes on the Brooks family from ca. 1680s to ca. 1900, compiled at various dates. In Archives/Special Collections of the Lincoln Public Library, Lincoln Family Records Collection, Doc. # 2003.057.1.3.

Brooks, Joshua, bill of sale [for a 19-month-old Negro servant boy named Peter] to Josiah Nelson, January 29, 1765. In Archives/Special Collections of the Lincoln Public Library, Nelson Family Papers, Doc. # 2002.006.1.1.

Eckhardt, Mary. "John Garfield (Gearfield)." In Archives/Special Collections of the Lincoln Public Library, Lincoln Family Records Collection, Doc. # 2003.057.1.18.

Eleazer Brooks Papers, 1776–1793. In Special Collections of the Concord Free Public Library, Vault A45, Brooks, Unit 2.

Eleazer Brooks Papers, 1776–1825. Including a bound volume of photocopies of the collection. In Archives/Special Collections of the Lincoln Public Library, Eleazer Brooks Papers, Doc. # 2003.067.1.1. The individual documents in the collection were unbound shortly before this work went to press, but they had not yet been individually catalogued. Brooks's December 1777 letter to General Heath is page 19 in the bound photocopies; document number 12 in the uncatalogued collection.

"Family history and genealogical notes on the Hoar family." 1977. In Archives/Special Collections of the Lincoln Public Library, Lincoln Family Records Collection, Doc. # 2003.057.1.23.

Family record and genealogical notes relating to the family of William Lawrence. n.d. In Archives/Special Collections of the Lincoln Public Library, Lincoln Founding Families Collection, Doc. # 2003.055.23.1.

Farrar, Edith Biggs. "Adams Genealogy, ca.1650–1820." n.d. In Archives/Special Collections of the Lincoln Public Library, Lincoln Founding Families Collection, Doc. # 2003.055.1.7.

———. Notes relating to Bemis family from 1619 to 1924. n.d. In Archives/Special Collections of the Lincoln Public Library, Lincoln Founding Families Collection, Doc. # 2003.055.4.5.

———, comp. Excerpts from Andrew N. Adams, *A Genealogical History of Henry Adams of Braintree, Mass., 1632-1897* (1898). n.d. In Archives/Special Collections of the Lincoln Public Library, Lincoln Founding Families Collection, Doc. # 2003.055.1.4.

Farrar, Edward. "Record from Memoirs of the Farrar family, with extracts from Shattuck's History of Concord, Mass., by a member of the Historical Genealogical Society." 1930. In Archives/Special Collections of the Lincoln Public Library, Farrar Family Collection, Doc. # 2003.009.1.6.

Farrar, Edward R., and Samuel Farrar. "Houses in Lincoln 100 Years Old and Over With Some of Their Owners." 1935. In John C. MacLean Collection. Also available in Archives/Special Collections of the Lincoln Public Library, Farrar Historical Houses Manuscript, Doc. # 2004.002.1.1.

Farrar, Samuel, Jr., to Colonel Brooks. A list of men "draughted, inlisted and agreeable to the order of court," Lincoln, August 14, 1777. In the Massachusetts Archives, Muster Rolls of the Revolutionary War, Vol. 53, p. 191e.

Genealogy of the Family of Weston, Wesson and Wessen. 1837. Printed form in Archives/Special Collections of the Lincoln Public Library, Wesson & Smith Family Papers, Doc. # 2003.045.1.59.

Hafner, Donald L. "'The First Blood Shed in the Revolution' The Tale of Josiah Nelson on April 19, 1775." December 2007. Unpublished manuscript, expanded from a shorter version published in *The Lincoln Review* (July–August 2006). In Author's Collection.

Hartwell, John, to Eleazer Brooks, "A List of a Company of Militia men under the Command of Capt. John Hartwell in Col. Eleazer Brooks Regiment Called down on the Fortifying Dorchester Hills March fourth one thousand seven & seventy six," Middlesex, August 8, 1776. In the Massachusetts Archives, Muster Rolls of the Revolutionary War, Vol. 19, p. 193. A similar record is found in Vol. 54, File G, p. 1a.

Hatch, Jack, Middlesex County Probate, first series, 10,743.

Hicks, Margie. "The Hartwell Family." October 2002. Unpublished notes summarizing research as interpretive ranger at Minute Man National Historical Park. In Author's Collection.

Knox, H[enry]. "Statement of the number of non-Commissioned Officers and privates of the Regular Troops and Militia furnished by the several States taken from time to time, for the support of the late War." May 10, 1790. Report to the House of Representatives. In National Archives and Records Administration (NARA, 1st Congress, House, SecWarReports, RG233).

Lawrence, Priscilla. "Gregory Stone—Minute Man from Lincoln." n.d. In Archives/Special Collections of the Lincoln Public Library, Lincoln Family Records Collection, Doc. # 2003.057.1.31.

Lincoln Assessors Records. North Book, 1769. In Archives/Special Collections of the Lincoln Public Library, Doc. # 2003.021.1.2.

"Lincoln First Book of Records, 1754–1806." In Archives/Special Collections of the Lincoln Public Library, Administrative Records Collection, bound volume, Doc. # 2003.015.1.2.

Lincoln Minute Men Collection. In Archives/Special Collections of the Lincoln Public Library, Collection # 2005.03.

Martin, Margaret Mutchler. "The Sons of Lincoln in the American Revolution." n.d. Unpublished manuscript. In Author's Collection.

Massachusetts Archives Collection, a compilation of early records of Massachusetts. In Massachusetts Archives.

Merriam ancestry detailed in a letter, 1800. Transcription in Archives/Special Collections of the Lincoln Public Library, Lincoln Founding Families Collection, Doc. # 2003.055.24.2.

Miller, Paula R. "Joseph Abbott (Abbot)—A Chronology." n.d. In Archives/Special Collections of the Lincoln Public Library, Lincoln Founding Families Collection, Doc. # 2003.055.3.2.

Muster Rolls of the Revolutionary War, a compilation of Revolutionary War records and muster rolls. In Massachusetts Archives.

"Notes on the Hoar family from 1775 to 1820." n.d. In Archives/Special Collections of the Lincoln Public Library, Lincoln Family Records Collection, Doc. # 2003.057.1.24.

Patch, Stephen, Guardian, Administrator's Deed to John Nelson, March 31, 1827. In Archives/Special Collections of the Lincoln Public Library, Nelson Family Papers Collection, Doc. # 2002.006.1.54.

Quintal, George, Jr. Unpublished research into Revolutionary War Pension Records at the National Archives. Collection of George Quintal, Jr.

Rawson, Nancy. "The Gove Family." n.d. In Archives/Special Collections of the Lincoln Public Library, Lincoln Family Records Collection, Doc. # 2003.057.1.21.

Richardson, Ezra. Estate inventory, March 8, 1787. Middlesex County Probate. Copy in Archives/Special Collections of the Lincoln Public Library, Lincoln Family Records Collection, Doc. # 2003.057.2.1.

Ryan, Michael. "The Incomplete Life of Captain William Smith of Lincoln, MA." 2008. Draft manuscript, unpublished. In Author's Collection.

Shattuck, Lemuel. Draft portions of and notes compiled in preparing Lemuel Shattuck's 1835 printed *A History of the Town of Concord, Middlesex County, Massachusetts*, 1830–1835, In Special Collections of the Concord Free Public Library, Vault A45, Shattuck, U.1, F.3.

"Treasurers Accompts in Lincoln, 1755[–1788], The Book of the." In Archives/Special Collections of the Lincoln Public Library, Town of Lincoln, Treasurer's Records, Doc. # 2003.022.1.1.

War Memorial Book. 1960. Unpublished calligraphic record of Lincoln individuals who have served during America's wars. In Archives/Special Collections of the Lincoln Public Library. The *War Memorial Book* was being updated to reflect the results of the author's research, as reported herein, at the time of this book going to press.

Weston, Mary, and Lucy Weston, Indenture and Power of Attorney to Abner Wheeler and Daniel Brooks, March 6, 1807. In Archives/Special Collections of the Lincoln Public Library, Wesson & Smith Family Papers, Doc. # 2003.045.1.51.

Weston, Stephen, deed to Daniel Weston, March 31, 1792. In Archives/Special Collections of the Lincoln Public Library, Wesson & Smith Family Papers, Doc. #2003.045.1.74.

Wheeler, Mary L. "The Wheelers in Heretic Court." 1950. In Archives/Special Collections of the Lincoln Public Library, Miscellaneous Lincoln Family Papers, Doc. # 2003.063.16.1.

Wiggin, Richard C. "A Tale of Two or Three Peters." July 2009. Unpublished manuscript revised from Richard C. Wiggin, "A Tale of Two Peters," published in *The Lincoln Review*. Vol. 33, No. 3 (Jan./Feb. 2009), pp. 32–34. In Author's Collection; also in Lincoln Public Library.

2. Published Works

Abbot, Abiel, and Ephraim Abbot. *A Genealogical Register of the Descendents of George Abbot of Andover*. Boston: James Munroe & Co., 1847.

Account of the Celebration By The Town of Lincoln, Massachusetts April 23rd, 1904, of the 150th Anniversary of its Incorporation, 1754–1904, An. Lincoln, MA: Printed for the Town, 1905.

Adams, John. *Letters of John Adams, Addressed to his Wife*. Vol. 1. Edited by Charles Francis Adams. Boston: Charles C. Little and James Brown, 1841.

Adams, Josiah. *Letter to Lemuel Shattuck, Esq. of Boston, From Josiah Adams, Esq. of Framingham, in Vindication of the Claims of Capt. Isaac Davis, of Acton, to his Just Share in the Honors of the Concord Fight*. Boston: Damrell & Moore, 1850.

Aldrich, Lewis Cass, and Frank R. Holmes, eds. *History of Windsor County, Vermont, with Illustrations and Biographical Sketches of Some of its Prominent Men and Pioneers*. Syracuse, NY: D. Mason & Co., 1891.

Allen, Joseph. *Topographical and Historical Sketches of the Town of Northborough with the Early History of Marlborough in the Commonwealth of Massachusetts*. Worcester, MA: W. Lincoln & C. C. Baldwin, 1826.

Avery, Elroy McKendree. *History of the United States and its People, From Their Earliest Records to the Present Time*. Cleveland: The Burrows Brothers Co., 1909.

Baker, Amos. Affidavit of Amos Baker, April 22, 1850. In Robert Rantoul, Jr. *An Oration Delivered at Concord on the Celebration of the Seventy-Fifth Anniversary of the Events of April 19*,

1775. Boston: 1850, Appendix; also in Frank Hersey. *Heroes of the Battle Road* (1930). Reprint. Lincoln, MA: Lincoln Historical Society, 1983, Appendix, pp. 33–37.

Baldwin, Thomas W. *Vital Records of Framingham Massachusetts, to the Year 1850*. Boston: Wright & Potter Print Co., 1911.

———. *Vital Records of Hardwick Massachusetts, to the Year 1850*. Boston: Wright & Potter Print Co., 1917.

———. *Vital Records of Reading Massachusetts, to the Year 1850*. Boston: Wright & Potter Print Co., 1912.

Bancroft, George. *History of the United States, from the Discovery of the American Continent*. Vol. 10. Boston: Little, Brown, and Company, 1874.

Bangs, Edward, ed. *Journal of Lt. Isaac Bangs, April 1 to July 29, 1776*. Cambridge, MA: John Wilson and Son, 1890.

Barry, William. *A History of Framingham, Massachusetts, Including the Plantation, with an Appendix, Containing a Notice of Sudbury and its First Proprietors; also a Register of the Inhabitants of Framingham before 1800, with Genealogical Sketches*. Boston: James Munroe and Company, 1847.

Bemis, Charles A. *History of the Town of Marlborough, Cheshire County, New Hampshire*. Boston: Press of G.H. Ellis, 1881.

Benton, J. H., Jr. *Early Census Making in Massachusetts, 1643–1765; With a Reproduction of the Lost Census of 1765 (Recently Found) and Documents Relating Thereto*. Boston: Charles W. Goodspeed, 1905.

Biggs, Edith. "In Memorium: Inscriptions copied from the Tomb Stones in the Original Town Cemetery and the Second Town Cemetery made at the request of the Late Hon. Charles Francis Adams." In *Report of the Officers of the Town of Lincoln for the Year 1926* [1926 Annual Report], Boston: Town of Lincoln, pp. 151–199.

Blake, Francis E. "James Barrett's Returns of Men Mustered into Service, 1777–1778." *The New England Historical and Genealogical Register*. Vol. 50, no. 197 (January 1896), pp. 15–19, continued in Vol. 50, no. 200 (October 1896), pp. 468–482.

Bobrick, Benson. *Angel in the Whirlwind: The Triumph of the American Revolution*. New York: Simon & Schuster, 1997.

Bolton, Charles Knowles. *Marriage Notices 1785–1794 for the Whole United States, Copied from the Massachusetts Centinel and the Columbian Centinel*. Salem, MA: Eben Putnam, 1900.

Bond, Henry. *Genealogies of the Families and Descendants of the Early Settlers of Watertown, Massachusetts* (1860). Reprint. Boston: New England Historic Genealogical Society, 1978.

Boston Evening-Post and the General Advertiser, The. Vol. 1, Issue 2 (October 27, 1781).

Boston Evening Transcript, August 31, 1847.

Bradley, Edward Ernest, and Edward Griffin Porter. *Proceedings in Observation of the One Hundred and Fiftieth Anniversary of the Organization of The First Church in Lincoln Massachusetts, August 21 and September 4, 1898*. Cambridge, MA: University Press, 1899.

Brooks, Paul. *Trial by Fire: Lincoln Massachusetts and the War for Independence*. [Lincoln, MA]: Lincoln 1975 Bicentennial Commission, 1975.

Brown, Abram English. *Beneath Old Roof Trees*. Boston: Lee and Shepard, 1896.

Buell, Rowena W., comp. *The Memoirs of Rufus Putnam and Certain Official Papers and Correspondence*. Boston: Houghton Mifflin, 1903.

Calhoon, Robert M. *The Loyalists in Revolutionary America, 1760–1781*. New York: Harcourt Brace Jovanovich, 1965.

Calver, William L. "Researches into the American Army Button of the Revolutionary War." *The Journal of the American Military History Foundation*. Vol. 1, no. 4 (Winter 1937–1938), pp. 151–164.

Caverly, A. M. *An Historical Sketch of Troy, and her Inhabitants, from the First Settlement of the Town, in 1764, to 1855*. Keene, NH: N. H. Sentinel, 1859.

Century Illustrated Monthly Magazine, The. Vol. LXV, No. 1 (November 1902).

Chandler, Charles H. *The History of New Ipswich, New Hampshire, 1735–1914: With Genealogical Records of the Principal Families.* Fitchburg, MA: Sentinel Printing Company, 1914.

Chapin, R. Curtis. "The Early History and Federalization of the Codman House," *Old-Time New England.* 71 (1981), pp. 28–29, 34.

Clark, Murtie June. *The Pension Lists of 1792–1795 with Other Revolutionary War Pension Records.* Baltimore: Genealogical Publishing Co., 1991.

Clarke, George Kuhn. *History of Needham, Massachusetts, 1711–1911, Including West Needham Now the Town of Wellesley to its Separation from Needham in 1881, with Some References to its Affairs to 1911,* Cambridge: University Press, 1912.

Coburn, Frank Warren. *Muster Rolls of the Participating Companies of American Militia and Minute-Men in the Battle of April 10, 1775* (1912). Reprinted in Frank Warren Coburn. *The Battle of April 19, 1775.* Philadelphia: Eastern National Park & Monument Association, 1988.

———. *The Battle of April 19, 1775, in Lexington, .Concord, Lincoln, Arlington, Cambridge, Somerville and Charlestown, Massachusetts* (1912); Reprint. Philadelphia: Eastern National Park & Monument Association, 1988.

"Col. Jackson's Court of Enquiry," The Lee Papers, Vol. 3, 1778–1782, *Collections of the New-York Historical Society for the year 1873.* New York: New-York Historical Society, 1874, pp. 209–228.

Coldham, Peter Wilson. *American Migrations, 1765–1799.* Baltimore: Genealogical Publishing Co., 2000.

Commager, Henry Steele, and Richard B. Morris, eds. *The Spirit of Seventy-Six: The Story of the American Revolution as Told by Participants.* New York: Harper & Row, 1967.

Concord, Massachusetts: Births, Marriages, and Deaths, 1635–1850. Printed by the Town, 1891.

Connecticut Journal [New Haven]. Issue 473 (November 6, 1776).

Connecticut Journal [New Haven]. Issue 676 (October 12, 1780).

Conwell, Russell H. *The Life, Speeches, and Public Services of James A. Garfield, Twentieth President of the United States.* Boston: B. B. Russell, 1881.

Corey, Deloraine P., comp. *Births Marriages and Deaths in the Town of Malden Massachusetts 1649–1850.* Cambridge, MA: University Press for the City of Malden, 1903.

Crane, Ellery Bicknell, ed. *Historic Homes and Institutions and Genealogical and Personal Memoirs of Worcester County, Massachusetts.* Vols. 2, 4. New York: Lewis Publishing Co., 1907.

Custis, George Washington Parke, Mary Randolph Custis Lee, and Benson John Lossing. *Recollections and Private Memoirs of Washington.* Philadelphia: J. W. Bradley, 1861.

Cutler, Nahum S. *A Cutler Memorial and Genealogical History.* Greenfield, MA: E. A. Hall & Co., 1889.

Cutter, William Richard, ed. *Historic Homes and Places and Genealogical and Personal Memoirs Relating to the Families of Middlesex County, Massachusetts.* Vols. 3, 4. New York: Lewis Historical Publishing Co., 1908.

Dana, Harold Ward. "John Billings of Deer Isle, Maine." *New England Historical and Genealogical Register.* Vol. 97 (October 1943), pp. 347–353.

Daniels, George F. *History of the Town of Oxford, Massachusetts, With Genealogies and Notes on Persons and Estates.* Oxford, MA: The Author with the co-operation of the town, 1892.

Dann, John C., ed. *The Revolution Remembered: Eyewitness Accounts of the War for Independence.* Chicago: University of Chicago, 1980.

Davis, Walter A. *The Early Records of the Town of Lunenburg, Massachusetts, 1719–1764.* Fitchburg, MA: Sentinel Printing Company for Fitchburg City Council, 1896.

Dawson, Henry B. *Battles of the United States, by Sea and Land.* New York: Johnson, Fry & Co., 1858.

———. *The Assault on Stony Point, by General Anthony Wayne, July 16, 1779.* Prepared for the New York Historical Society and read at its regular monthly meeting, April 1, 1862. Morrisania, NY: 1863.

Deidier, Antoine. *Le Parfait Ingenieur Francais ou la Fortification Offensive et Defensive*. Amsterdam: la Compagnie des Libraires, 1734.

Deposition of Benjamin Tidd and Joseph Abbot, Lexington, April 25, 1775. In *A Narrative of the Excursion and Ravages of the King's Troops, Under the Command of General Gage, on the Nineteenth of April, 1775: Together with the Depositions Taken by Order of Congress to support the Truth of it*. Worcester, MA: Isaiah Thomas by order of the Provincial Congress, 1775. Reprinted in Clement C. Sawtell, *The Nineteenth of April, 1775: A Collection of First Hand Accounts*. Lincoln, MA: Sawtells of Somerset, 1968.

Deposition of Bradbury Robinson, Samuel Spring, Thaddeus Bancroft, and James Adams, Lexington, April 23, 1775. In *A Narrative of the Excursion and Ravages of the King's Troops, Under the Command of General Gage, on the Nineteenth of April, 1775: Together with the Depositions Taken by Order of Congress to support the Truth of it*. Worcester, MA: Isaiah Thomas by order of the Provincial Congress, 1775. Reprinted in Clement C. Sawtell. *The Nineteenth of April, 1775: A Collection of First Hand Accounts*. Lincoln, MA: Sawtells of Somerset, 1968.

Deposition of John Bateman, Lincoln, April 23, 1775. In *A Narrative of the Excursion and Ravages of the King's Troops, Under the Command of General Gage, on the Nineteenth of April, 1775: Together with the Depositions Taken by Order of Congress to support the Truth of it*. Worcester, MA: Isaiah Thomas by order of the Provincial Congress, 1775. Reprinted in Clement C. Sawtell, *The Nineteenth of April, 1775: A Collection of First Hand Accounts*. Lincoln, MA: Sawtells of Somerset, 1968.

Deposition of John Hoar, John Whitehead, Abraham Garfield, Benjamin Munroe, Isaac Parks, William Hosmer, John Adams, Gregory Stone, Lexington, April 23, 1775. In *A Narrative of the Excursion and Ravages of the King's Troops, Under the Command of General Gage, on the Nineteenth of April, 1775: Together with the Depositions Taken by Order of Congress to support the Truth of it*. Worcester, MA: Isaiah Thomas by order of the Provincial Congress, 1775. Reprinted in Clement C. Sawtell. *The Nineteenth of April, 1775: A Collection of First Hand Accounts*. Lincoln. MA: Sawtells of Somerset, 1968.

Dickson, Brenton H., and Homer C. Lucas. *One Town in the American Revolution – Weston Massachusetts*. Weston, MA: Weston Historical Society, 1976.

Dietrich-Smith, Deborah. *Cultural Landscape Report for Battle Road Unit, Minute Man National Historical Park*. Brookline, MA: National Park Service, Olmstead Center for Landscape Preservation, 2005.

Drake, Samuel Adams, ed. *History of Middlesex County, Massachusetts*. Vol. 2. Boston: Estes and Lauriat, 1880.

Duane, William. *A Military Dictionary*. Philadelphia: William Duane, 1810.

Eckenrode, H. J. *Virginia State Library List of the Revolutionary Soldiers of Virginia (Supplement), Special Report of the Department of Archives and History for 1912*. Richmond, VA: Davis Bottom, Superintendent of Public Printing, 1913.

Elliott, Barbara K., and Janet J. Jones. *Concord: Its Black History, 1636–1860*. Concord, MA: Concord Public Schools, 1976.

Emerson, William, *Diaries and Letters of William Emerson, 1743–1776, Minister of the Church in Concord, Chaplain in the Revolutionary Army*. Edited by Amelia Forbes Emerson. Boston: Thomas Todd, 1972.

Esposito, Vincent J., ed. *The West Point Atlas of American Wars*. Vol. 1, 1689–1900. Compiled by the Department of Military Art and Engineering, the United States Military Academy. New York: Frederick A. Praeger, 1959.

Essex Register [Salem, MA]. New Series, no. 130 (October 19, 1808).

Farrar, Timothy. *Memoir of the Farrar Family, by A Member of the N. E. Hist. Gen. Society*. Boston: Press of Thomas Prince, 1853.

Felt, Joseph B. "Statistics of Population in Massachusetts." In *American Statistical Association Collections*. Vol. 1. Boston: 1897, pp. 121–216. Reported in Evarts B. Greene and Virginia

D. Harrington. *American Population Before the Federal Census of 1790.* New York: Columbia University Press, 1932.

Felt, Joseph Barlow. *An Historical Account of Massachusetts Currency.* Boston: Perkins and Marvin, 1839.

Fischer, David Hackett. *Paul Revere's Ride.* New York: Oxford University Press, 1994.

———. *Washington's Crossing.* New York: Oxford University Press, 2004.

Fitts, Robert K. *Inventing New England's Slave Paradise: Master/Slave Relations in Eighteenth-Century Narragansett, Rhode Island.* New York: Routledge, 1998.

Flint, Edward E., and Gwendolyn S. Flint. *Flint Family History of the Adventurous Seven.* Vol. 1. Baltimore: Gateway Press, 1984.

Force, Peter. *American Archives: Consisting of a Collection of Authentick Records, State Papers, Debates, and Letters and Other Notices of Publick Affairs....* 4th Series, Vol. 2, Washington, D.C.: Published by M. St. Clair Clarke and Peter Force, 1837–1846.

Freeman, Douglas Southall. *George Washington: A Biography.* Vol. 4. New York: Scribner's, 1951.

French, Allen. *The Day of Concord and Lexington: The Nineteenth of April, 1775* (1925). Reprint. Eastern National Park & Monument Association, 1984.

———. *The Siege of Boston.* New York: MacMillan, 1911.

Frothingham, Richard, Jr. *History of the Siege of Boston and the Battles of Lexington, Concord, and Bunker Hill.* Boston: Charles C. Little & James Brown, 1851.

Galvin, John R. *The Minute Men: A Compact History of the Defenders of the Colonies, 1645–1775* (1967). Reprint. Washington, D.C.: Pergamon-Brassey's, 1989.

Glass, Kerry. *The Nathan Brown Farm.* Lincoln, MA: The Lincoln Historical Commission, 1977.

Glass, Kerry, and Elizabeth Little. [Map of] *LINCOLN, County of Middlesex in His Majesty's Province of the Massachusetts Bay in New England, 1775.* Sponsored by the Lincoln Historical Commission, 1975.

Goold, Nathan. "Colonel Jonathan Mitchell's Cumberland County Regiment, Bagaduce Expedition, 1779." Read before the Maine Historical Society (October 27, 1898). In *Collections and Proceedings of the Maine Historical Society.* Second Series, Vol. 10, Portland: Maine Historical Society, 1899, pp. 52–80, 143–174.

Green, Samuel Abbott. *Groton During the Revolution: With an Appendix.* Cambridge, MA: University Press, 1900.

Greene, Evarts B. and Virginia D. Harrington. *American Population Before the Federal Census of 1790.* New York: Columbia University Press, 1932.

Greene, Lorenzo Johnston. *The Negro in Colonial New England* (1942). Reprint. New York: Atheneum, 1974.

Grivetti, Louis Evan, and Howard-Yana Shapiro, eds. *Chocolate; History, Culture, and Heritage.* Hoboken: John Wiley & Son, 2009.

Gross, Robert A. *The Minutemen and Their World.* American Century Series. New York: Hill and Wang, 1976.

Gutman, Herbert G. *The Black Family in Slavery & Freedom, 1750–1925.* New York: Pantheon, 1976.

Hallowell, Henry C. ed. *Vital Records of Townsend, Massachusetts: Town Records to 1850, with Marriage Intentions to 1873 and Cemetery Inscriptions.* Boston, MA: New England Historic Genealogical Society, 1992.

Hammond, Isaac W. *Town Papers. Documents Relating to Towns in New Hampshire, New London to Wolfeborough, with an Appendix.* Vol. 13. Concord, NH: Parsons B. Cogswell, State Printer, 1884.

Harper's Weekly (September 30, 1876).

Haslet, John to Caesar Rodney. Letter dated Nov. 12, 1776. In Henry Steele Commager and Richard B. Morris, eds. *The Spirit of Seventy-Six: The Story of the American Revolution as Told by Participants.* New York: Harper & Row, 1967.

Heath, William. *Memoirs of Major-General William Heath* (1798). Reprint. New York: William Abbott, 1901. Reprint. New York Times and Arno Press, 1968.

Heitman, Francis Bernard. *Historical Register and Dictionary of the United States Army, From its Organization, September 29, 1789, to March 2, 1903.* Vol. 2. Washington, D.C.: U.S. Government Printing Office, 1903.

———. *Historical Register of Officers of the Continental Army During the War of the Revolution, April 1775 to December 1783.* Washington, D.C.: The Rare Book Shop Publishing Co., 1914.

Hersey, Frank. *Heroes of the Battle Road: A Narrative of Events in Lincoln on the 18th and 19th of April, 1775...* (1930). Reprint. Lincoln, MA: Lincoln Historical Society, 1983.

Historical Manual of the Church of Christ, Lincoln, Massachusetts. Boston: Tolman & White, 1872.

Historical Memoranda with Lists of Members and their Revolutionary Ancestors. Boston: Massachusetts Society of the Sons of the American Revolution, 1897.

Hitchings, A. Frank, and Stephen Willard Phillips. *Ship Registers of the District of Salem and Beverly, Massachusetts, 1789–1900.* Salem, MA: The Essex Institute, 1906.

Hoar, George F. *Autobiography of Seventy Years.* Vol. 1. New York: Charles Scribner's Sons, 1905.

Hudson, Alfred Sereno. *The History of Sudbury, Massachusetts, 1638–1889* (1889). Reprint. Sudbury, MA: The Sudbury Press, 1968.

Hudson, Charles. *History of the Town of Lexington, Middlesex County, Massachusetts, From its First Settlement to 1868.* 2 vols. Boston: Wiggin & Lunt, 1868.

———. *History of the Town of Lexington, Middlesex County, Massachusetts; Revised and Continued to 1912 by the Lexington Historical Society*, Bi-Centenary edition. 2 vols. Boston: Houghton Mifflin, 1913.

Hurd, D. Hamilton, ed. *History of Hillsborough County, New Hampshire.* Philadelphia: J. W. Lewis, 1885.

———, ed. *History of Middlesex County, Massachusetts.* Vol. I. Philadelphia: J. W. Lewis, 1890.

Independent Chronicle and the Universal Advertiser, The [Boston]. Vol. IX, Issue 430 (November 14, 1776).

Independent Chronicle and the Universal Advertiser, The [Boston]. Vol. IX, Issue 451 (April 10, 1777).

Irving, Washington. *Life of George Washington.* Vol. 2. New York: Putnam, 1860.

Johnson, Edward F., ed. *Woburn Records of Births, Deaths, and Marriages, from 1640 to 1873.* Woburn: Andrews, Cutler & Co., 1890.

Johnston, Henry P. *The Storming of Stony Point on the Hudson, Midnight, June 15, 1779, Its Importance in the Light of Unpublished Documents.* New York: James T. White & Co., 1900.

Jones, E. Alfred. *The Loyalists of Massachusetts: Their Memorials, Petitions and Claims.* Baltimore: Genealogical Publishing Company, 1969.

Joslyn, Roger D., ed. *Vital Records of Charlestown, Massachusetts, to the Year 1850.* Boston: New England Historic Genealogical Society, 1985.

Journals of Each Provincial Congress of Massachusetts in 1774 and 1775, and of the Committee of Safety. Boston: Dutton and Wentworth, 1838.

Kapp, Friedrich. *The Life of Frederick William Von Steuben, Major General in the Revolutionary Army.* New York: Mason Brothers, 1859.

Karttunen, Frances Ruley. *The Other Islanders.* New Bedford, MA: Spinner Publications, 2005.

Kehoe, Vincent J-R. "The Provincial Depositions taken on the 23rd and 25th of April, 1775." In *History of the 10th Regiment of Foot, 1767–1778.* Vol. 2. Ventura, CA: Vincent J-R Kehoe, 1995, Appendix A, pp. 135–148.

———. *"We Were There!" April 19, 1775.* Vol. 2. *The American Rebels.* Published by the author, 1974.

Ketchum, Richard M. *Saratoga: Turning Point of America's Revolutionary War.* New York: Henry Holt, 1997.

Kolchin, Peter. *American Slavery, 1619–1877.* New York: Hill and Wang, 1993.

Krueger, John W. "Troop Life at the Champlain Valley Forts During the American Revolution." In *Bulletin of the Fort Ticonderoga Museum.* Vol. XIV, no. 4 (Fall 1983), pp. 220–249.

Lamson, Daniel S. *History of the Town of Weston, Massachusetts, 1630–1890.* Boston: Geo. H. Ellis, 1913.

Landers, H. L. *The Virginia Campaign And The Blockade And Siege Of Yorktown, 1781, Including A Brief Narrative Of The French Participation In The Revolution Prior To The Southern Campaign.* Army War College. Historical Section. Washington, D.C.: United States Government Printing Office, 1931.

Larned, J. N., and Alan C. Reiley. *History For Ready Reference From the Best Historians, Biographers, and Specialists; Their Own Words in a Complete System of History.* Vol. V, Springfield, MA: C. A. Nichols, 1895.

Lawrence, Robert Means. *Historical Sketches of Some Members of the Lawrence Family.* Boston: Rand Avery, 1888.

Lemire, Elise V. *Black Walden: Slavery and its Aftermath in Concord.* Philadelphia: University of Pennsylvania Press, 2009.

Lesser, Charles H. *The Sinews of Independence: Monthly Strength Reports of the Continental Army.* Chicago: University of Chicago, 1976.

Lexington, Massachusetts, Record of Births, Marriages and Deaths to January 1, 1898. [Lexington Vital Records]. Boston: Wright & Potter, 1898.

Lineage Book, National Society of the Daughters of the American Revolution. Vol. 35, 1901. Washington, D.C.: Daughters of the American Revolution, 1912.

Lippitt, Charles Warren. *The Battle of Rhode Island.* Newport, RI: Mercury Publishing Company, 1915.

Lossing, Benson J. *Pictorial Field Book of the Revolution,* Vol. 1. New York: Harper Brothers, 1850.

MacLean, John C. *A Rich Harvest: The History, Buildings, and People of Lincoln, Massachusetts.* Lincoln, MA: Lincoln Historical Society, 1987.

Mahan, A. T. "The Naval Campaign of 1776 on Lake Champlain." *Scribner's Magazine,* Vol. 23, No. 2 (February 1898), pp. 147–160.

Malcolm, Joyce Lee. *Peter's War: A New England Slave Boy and the American Revolution.* New Haven: Yale University Press, 2009.

———. *The Scene of Battle, 1775: Historic Grounds Report, Minute Man National Park.* Boston: North Atlantic Regional Office, National Park Service, U.S. Department of the Interior, 1985.

Martin, Joseph Plum. *Private Yankee Doodle: Being a Narrative of Some of the Adventures, Dangers and Sufferings of a Revolutionary Soldier.* Edited by George F. Scheer. (1962). Reprint. Eastern Acorn Press, publishing arm of Eastern National Park & Monument Association, 1995.

Martin, Margaret Mutchler. *The Chambers—Russell—Codman House and Family in Lincoln, Massachusetts.* Lincoln, MA: Lincoln Historical Society, 1996.

Martyn, Charles. *The William Ward Genealogy : The History of the Descendants of William Ward of Sudbury, Mass., 1638–1925.* New York: A. Ward, 1925.

Marvin, Abijah Perkins. *History of the Town of Winchendon (Worcester County, Mass.) from the Grant of Ipswich Canada in 1735 to the Present Time.* Winchendon, MA: The Author, 1868.

Massachusetts Soldiers and Sailors of the Revolutionary War. 17 vols. Compiled under the Secretary of the Commonwealth. Boston: Wright & Potter Printing Co., 1896–1908.

McManus, Edgar J. *Black Bondage in the North.* Syracuse: Syracuse University Press, 1973.

Memorial of the American Patriots who fell at the Battle of Bunker Hill, June 17, 1775. With an account of the Dedication of the Memorial Tablets on Winthrop Square, Charlestown, June 17, 1889, A. Fourth Ed. Boston: by order of the City Council, 1896.

Mollo, John, and Malcolm McGregor. *Uniforms of the American Revolution.* New York: Macmillan, 1975.

Morison, Samuel Eliot. *The Oxford History of the American People.* New York: Oxford University Press, 1965.

Murdoch, Harold. "Historic Doubts on the Battle of Lexington," presented to the Massachusetts Historical Society in May 1916. In *Proceedings of the Massachusetts Historical Society.* Vol. 49, (October 1915–June 1916), pp. 361–386.

Murray, Thomas Hamilton. *Gen. John Sullivan and the Battle of Rhode Island: A Sketch of the Former and a Description of the Latter.* Providence: American-Irish Historical Society, 1902.

New England Chronicle: or, The Essex Gazette [Cambridge, MA]. Vol. VII, Issue 358 (June 1, 1775).

New England Magazine. An Illustrated Monthly. (April 1902).

New Hampshire Patriot & State Gazette [Concord, NH]. Vol. XIX, Issue 937 (March 19, 1827).

New-Hampshire Sentinel [Keene, NH]. Vol. XXVIII, Issue 52 (December 29, 1826).

Norton, John F. and Joel Whittemore. *The History of Fitzwilliam, NH, from 1752–1887 with a Genealogical Record of Many Fitzwilliam Families.* New York: Burr Printing House, 1888.

Nourse, Henry Stedman. *The Hoar Family in America and its English Ancestry.* Boston: David Clapp & Son, 1899.

———. *The Military Annals of Lancaster, Massachusetts, 1740–1865. Including Lists of Soldiers Serving in the Colonial and Revolutionary Wars for the Lancastrian Towns: Berlin, Bolton, Harvard, Leominster, and Sterling.* Lancaster, MA: W. J. Coulter, 1889.

Oxford English Dictionary. Compact Edition, New York: Oxford University Press, 1971.

Parker, Theodore. *Genealogy and Biographical Notes of John Parker of Lexington and his Descendants; Showing his Earlier Ancestry in America from Dea. Thomas Parker of Reading Mass. From 1635 to 1893.* Worcester, MA: Charles Hamilton, 1893.

Parks, Frank Sylvester, comp. *Genealogy of the Parke Family of Massachusetts; Including Richard Parke, of Cambridge, William Park, of Groton, and Others.* Washington, D.C.: Privately Printed, 1909.

Peckham, Howard H. *The War for Independence: A Military History.* The Chicago History of American Civilization, edited by Daniel J. Boorstin. Chicago: University of Chicago, 1958.

Peirce, Frederick Clifton. *Peirce Genealogy, Being the Record of the Posterity of John Pers, an Early Inhabitant of Watertown, in New England, who Came from Norwich, Norfolk County, England; with Notes on the History of other families of Peirce, Pierce, Pearce, etc.* Worcester, MA: Press of Chas. Hamilton, 1880.

Pennsylvania Evening Post [Philadelphia]. Vol. II, Issue 180 (March 16, 1776).

Pennsylvania Evening Post [Philadelphia]. Vol. II, Issue 278 (October 31, 1776).

Phinney, Elias. *History of the Battle of Lexington, on the Morning of the 19th April, 1775.* Boston: Phelps and Farnham, 1825. Also reprint. Boston: Rand, Avery & Co., 1875.

Pierce, Frederick Clifton. *Foster Genealogy, Being the Record of the Posterity of Reginald Foster, an Early Inhabitant of Ipswich in New England.* Chicago: W.B. Conkey Co., 1899.

Pierce, William Macbeth. *Old Hancock County Families.* Ellsworth, ME: Hancock County Publishing Co., 1933.

Piersen, William D. *Black Yankees: The Development of an Afro-American Subculture in Eighteenth Century New England.* Amherst, MA: University of Massachusetts Press, 1988.

Potter, J., "The Growth of Population in America, 1700–1860." In D. V. Glass and D. E. C. Eversley, eds. *Population in History, Essays in Historical Demography.* London: Edward Arnold, 1965.

Proceedings of the Bunker Hill Monument Association at the Annual Meeting, June 17, 1895. Boston: Bunker Hill Monument Association, 1895.

Proceedings of the Fitchburg Historical Society and Papers Relating to the History of the Town. Vol. 4. Fitchburg, MA: Fitchburg Historical Society, 1908.

Purcell, Sarah J. *Sealed with Blood: War, Sacrifice, and Memory in Revolutionary America.* Philadelphia: University of Pennsylvania Press, 2002.

Quimby, Ian M. G. "The Doolittle Engravings of the Battle of Lexington and Concord." *Winterthur Portfolio*. Vol. 4 (1968), pp. 83–108.

Quintal, George, Jr. *Patriots of Color, African Americans and Native Americans at Battle Road & Bunker Hill*. Boston National Historical Park and Minute Man National Historical Park, National Park Service, U.S. Department of the Interior, 2002.

Raphael, Ray. *A People's History of the American Revolution: How Common People Shaped the Fight for Independence*. New York: The New Press, 2001 (Perennial Edition, 2002).

———. *The First American Revolution, Before Lexington and Concord*. New York: The New Press, 2002.

Records of Littleton, Massachusetts; Births, Marriages, Deaths to 1850. Littleton, MA: Town of Littleton, 1900.

Register of Members, 1916. Boston: Massachusetts Society of the Sons of the American Revolution, 1916.

Resch, John Phillips. *Suffering Soldiers: Revolutionary War Veterans, Moral Sentiment, and Political Culture in the Early Republic*. Amherst, MA: University of Massachusetts Press, 1999.

Ripley, Ezra. *A History of the Fight at Concord, on the 19th of April, 1775....* Concord, MA: Allen & Atwill, 1827.

Roads, Samuel, Jr. *The History and Traditions of Marblehead*. Boston: Houghton, Osgood & Co., 1880.

Roberts, Oliver Ayer. *History of the Military Company of the Massachusetts, Now Called The Ancient and Honorable Artillery Company of Massachusetts, 1637–1888*. Vol. 2. Boston: Alfred Mudge, 1897.

Robinsons and Their Kin Folk, The. Third series, July 1906. New York: The Robinson Family Genealogical and Historical Association, 1906.

Ryan, D. Michael. *Concord and the Dawn of Revolution: The Hidden Truths*. Charleston, SC: The History Press, 2007.

Ryan, Michael, "Presidential Relations a Bridge to Revolution," *Concord Journal* [Concord, MA], (January 15, 2004).

Sabine, Lorenzo. *The American Loyalists, or Biographical Sketches of Adherents to the British Crown in the War of the Revolution*. Boston: Charles C. Little and James Brown, 1847.

SAR Patriot Index. Edition III, CD-ROM, compiled by the National Society of the Sons of the American Revolution. Wolfville, NS: Progeny Publishing, 2002.

SAR Revolutionary War Graves Register. 2000 edition, CD-ROM, compiled by the National Society of the Sons of the American Revolution. Wolfville, NS: Progeny Publishing, 2000.

Saunderson, Henry Hamilton. *History of Charlestown, New Hampshire: The Old No. 4, Embracing the Part Borne by Its Inhabitants in the Indian, French and Revolutionary Wars, and the Vermont Controversy. Also Genealogies and Sketches of Families, From Its Settlement to 1876*. Claremont, NH: The Claremont Manufacturing Company, 1876.

Sawtell, Clement C., ed. *The Nineteenth of April, 1775; A Collection of First Hand Accounts*. Lincoln, MA: Sawtells of Somerset, 1968.

Schecter, Barnet. *The Battle for New York*. New York: Walker & Co., 2002.

Scheer, George F., and Hugh F. Rankin. *Rebels & Redcoats: The American Revolution Through the Eyes of Those Who Fought and Lived It*. (1957). Reprint. Da Capo Press, n.d.

Scribner's Magazine. Vol. 23 (January—June 1898), pp. 17, 25, 130, 157, 208, 331, 389, 395, 565, 567, 711, 720.

Scribner's Magazine. Vol. 24 (July—December 1898), pp. 220, 234, 341.

Secomb, Daniel F. *History of the Town of Amherst, Hillsborough County, New Hampshire....* Concord, NH: Evans Sleeper & Woodbury, 1883.

Shattuck, Lemuel. *A History of the Town of Concord; Middlesex County, Massachusetts; From its Earliest Settlement to 1832; and of the Adjoining Towns of Bedford, Acton, Lincoln, and Carlisle....* Boston: Russell, Odiorne, & Company, 1835.

———. "The Minot Family." *New England Historical and Genealogical Register.* Vol. 1 (July 1847), p. 260.

Siebert, Wilbur H. "Loyalist Troops of New England." *New England Quarterly.* Vol. 4, no. 1 (January 1931), pp. 108–147.

Smith, Edmund Banks. *Governor's Island:* Its Military History under Three Flags, 1637–1913. New York: The Author, 1913.

Smith, Samuel Stelle. The Battle of Monmouth (1964). Revised ed.. Trenton, NJ: The New Jersey Historical Commission, 1975.

Soldiers and Sailors, Whose Graves Have Been Designated by the Marker of the Society. Boston: Massachusetts Society of the Sons of the American Revolution, 1901.

Stark, James Henry. *The Loyalists of Massachusetts and the Other Side of the American Revolution.* Boston: James H. Stark, 1910.

Stone, Edwin Martin. *Our French Allies: Rochambeau and his Army, Lafayette and his Devotion, D'Estaing, DeTernay, Barras, DeGrasse, and their Fleets, in the Great War of the American Revolution, From 1778 to 1782.* Providence, RI: Providence Press Company, 1884.

Stryker, William S. *The Battle of Monmouth.* Princeton, NJ: Princeton University Press, 1927.

Tarleton, Banastre. *A History of the Campaigns of 1780 and 1781, in the Southern Provinces of North America.* London: T. Cadell, 1787.

Temple, J. H. *History of Framingham, Massachusetts, Early Known as Danforth's Farms, 1640–1880; with a Genealogical Register.* Framingham, MA: The Town of Framingham, 1887.

Tenney, Jonathan. *The Tenney Family, or The Descendants of Thomas Tenney of Rowley, Massachusetts, 1638–1904.* Revised by M. J. Tenney. Concord, NH: The Rumford Press, 1904.

Thatcher, James. *A Military Journal During the American Revolutionary War, from 1775 to 1783.* Boston: Richardson and Lord, 1823.

Thompson, Erwin N. *Historic Preservation Study: The British Defenses of Yorktown, 1781, Colonial National Historical Park, Virginia.* Denver: Denver Service Center, Historic Preservation Division, National Park Service, U.S. Department of the Interior, 1976.

Tolman, George. *John Jack, the Slave, and Daniel Bliss, the Tory.* Concord, MA: Concord Antiquarian Society, 1902.

Town of Weston, Births, Deaths, & Marriages, 1707–1850. Boston: McIndoe Bros., 1901.

Underwood, Lucien Marcus. *The Underwood Families of America.* Lancaster, PA: New Era Printing, 1913.

Upham, William P. *A Memoir of General John Glover, of Marblehead.* Salem, MA: The Essex Institute, 1863.

Vital Records of Acton, Massachusetts, to the Year 1850. Boston: New England Historic Genealogical Society, 1923.

Vital Records of Andover, Massachusetts, to the End of the Year 1849. 2 vols. Topsfield, MA: Topsfield Historical Society, 1912.

Vital Records of Barre, Massachusetts, to the End of the Year 1849. Worcester, MA: Franklin P. Rice, 1903.

Vital Records of Bedford, Massachusetts, to the Year 1850. Boston: New England Historic Genealogical Society, 1903.

Vital Records of Bolton, Massachusetts, to the End of the Year 1849. Worcester, MA: Franklin P. Rice, 1910.

Vital Records of Brimfield, Massachusetts, to the Year 1850. Boston: New England Historic Genealogical Society, 1931.

Vital Records of Chelmsford, Massachusetts, to the End of the Year 1849. Salem, MA: Essex Institute, 1914.

Vital Records of Gloucester, Massachusetts, to the End of the Year 1849. 3 vols. Salem, MA: Essex Institute, 1923–1924.

Published Works

Vital Records of Grafton, Massachusetts, to the End of the Year 1849. Worcester, MA: Franklin P. Rice, 1906.

Vital Records of Groton, Massachusetts, to the End of the Year 1849. Salem, MA: Essex Institute, 1923.

Vital Records of Holden, Massachusetts, to the End of the Year 1849. Worcester, MA: Franklin P. Rice, 1904.

Vital Records of Hopkinton, Massachusetts, to the Year 1850. Boston: New England Historic Genealogical Society, 1911.

Vital Records of Ipswich, Massachusetts, to the End of the Year 1849. Salem, MA: Essex Institute, 1910.

Vital Records of Leominster, Massachusetts, to the End of the Year 1849. Worcester: Franklin P. Rice, 1911.

Vital Records of Lincoln, Massachusetts, to the Year 1850. Boston: New England Historic Genealogical Society, 1908.

Vital Records of Marlborough, Massachusetts, to the End of the Year 1849. Worcester, MA: Franklin P. Rice, 1908.

Vital Records of Medfield, Massachusetts, to the Year 1850, Boston: New-England Historic Genealogical Society, 1903.

Vital Records of Newbury, Massachusetts, to the End of the Year 1849. 2 vols. Salem, MA: Essex Institute, 1911.

Vital Records of Northborough, Massachusetts, to the End of the Year 1850. Worcester, MA: Franklin P. Rice, 1901.

Vital Records of Oakham, Massachusetts, to the End of the Year 1849. Worcester, MA: Franklin P. Rice, 1905.

Vital Records of Oxford, Massachusetts, to the End of the Year 1849. Worcester, MA: Franklin P. Rice, 1905.

Vital Records of Pepperell, Massachusetts, to the Year 1850. Compiled by George A. Rice. Boston: New England Historic Genealogical Society, 1985.

Vital Records of Petersham, Massachusetts, to the End of the Year 1849. Worcester, MA: Franklin P. Rice, 1904.

Vital Records of Princeton, Massachusetts, to the End of the Year 1849. Worcester, MA: Franklin P. Rice, 1902.

Vital Records of Rowley, Massachusetts, to the End of the Year 1849. Salem, MA: Essex Institute, 1928.

Vital Records of Salem, Massachusetts, to the End of the Year 1849. 6 vol. Salem, MA: Essex Institute, 1916–1925.

Vital Records of Stow, Massachusetts, to the Year 1850. Boston: New England Historic Genealogical Society, 1911.

Vital Records of Sturbridge, Massachusetts, to the Year 1850. Boston: New England Historic Genealogical Society, 1906.

Vital Records of Sudbury, Massachusetts, to the Year 1850. Boston: New-England Historic Genealogical Society, 1903.

Vital Records of Sutton, Massachusetts, to the End of the Year 1849. Worcester, MA: Franklin P. Rice, 1907.

Vital Records of Waltham, Massachusetts, to the Year 1850. Boston: New England Historic Genealogical Society, 1904.

Vital Records of Wayland, Massachusetts, to the Year 1850. Boston: New England Historic Genealogical Society, 1910.

Vital Records of Westborough, Massachusetts, to the end of the year 1849. Worcester, MA: Franklin P. Rice, 1903.

Vital Records of Westford, Massachusetts, to the End of the Year 1849. Salem, MA: Essex Institute, 1915.

Vital Records of Westminster, Massachusetts, to the end of the year 1849. Worcester, MA: Franklin P. Rice, 1908.

Vital Records of Winchendon, Massachusetts, to the end of the year 1849. Worcester, MA: Franklin P. Rice, 1909.

Ward, Christopher. *The War of the Revolution.* New York: MacMillan, 1952.

Ward, Harry M. *George Washington's Enforcers: Policing the Continental Army.* Carbondale, IL: Southern Illinois University Press, 2006.

Washington, George. *The Writings of George Washington.* Vol. 9, 1780–1782. Edited by Worthington Chauncey Ford. New York: G. P. Putnam's Sons, 1891.

———. *The Writings of George Washington from the Original Manuscript Sources, 1745–1799.* 39 vols. Edited by John Clement Fitzpatrick. Washington, D.C.: United States Government Printing Office, 1931–1944.

Waters, Wilson. *History of Chelmsford, Massachusetts.* Lowell, MA: Courier-Citizen Co., 1917.

Watertown Records, Comprising the Third Book of Town Proceedings and the Second Book of Births Marriages and Deaths to the End of Year 1737 also Plan and Register of Burials in Arlington Street Burying Ground. Watertown, MA: Fred G. Barker, 1900.

Wells, Robert V. *The Population of the British Colonies in America before 1776: A Survey of Census Data.* Princeton, NJ: Princeton University, 1975.

Wheat, Silas Carmi, and Helen Love Scranton. *Wheat Genealogy.* Guilford, CT: Shore Line Times Publishing Co., 1960.

Wheeler, Albert Gallatin, Jr. *The Genealogical and Encyclopedic History of the Wheeler Family in America.* Boston: American College of Genealogy, 1914.

Wheeler, William F. "Lincoln." In D. Hamilton Hurd. *History of Middlesex County, Massachusetts.* Vol. 2, Philadelphia: J. W. Lewis & Co., 1890, pp. 612–639.

———. "Lincoln." In Samuel Adams Drake. *History of Middlesex County, Massachusetts.* Vol. 2. Boston: Estes and Lauriat, 1880, pp. 34–43.

Whipple, George M. "History of the Salem Light Infantry." *Essex Institute Historical Collection.* Vol. 26. Salem: Essex Institute, 1889.

White, Virgil D. *Genealogical Abstracts of Revolutionary War Pension Files.* Waynesboro, TN: The National Historical Publishing Co., 1992.

———. *Index to Revolutionary War Service Records.* Waynesboro, TN: The National Historical Publishing Co., 1995.

Whittemore, B. B. *A Genealogy of Several Branches of the Whittemore Family.* Nashua, NH: Francis P. Whittemore, 1890.

Wiggin, Richard C. "Did the Lincoln Minute Men have Bayonets?" *The Lincoln Review,* Vol. 34, No. 5 (September–October 2010), pp. 33–37.

Wiggin, Rick. "Recognition of a Proud Legacy." *The Lincoln Review.* Vol. 24, No. 1 (January–February 2000), pp. 5–10.

Winsor, Justin, ed. *Narrative and Critical History of America.* Vol. 6, Part I. Boston: Houghton Mifflin, 1887.

———, ed. *The American Revolution: A Narrative, Critical and Bibliographical History.* Reprinted from Justin Winsor, ed. *Narrative and Critical History of America*, Vols. 6–8 (1887–89). Compiled by Jack Brussel. New York: Sons of Liberty Publications, 1972.

Worcester Births, Marriages and Deaths. Worcester, MA: Worcester Society of Antiquity, 1894.

Worthington, Erastus. *The History of Dedham, from the Beginning of its Settlement in September, 1625 to May, 1827.* Boston: Dutton and Wentworth, 1827.

3. Internet Sources

American Currency Exhibit, Era of Independence. n.d. Online, Federal Reserve Bank of San Francisco, http://www.frbsf.org/currency/independence/index.html (accessed July 2008).

Avalon Project, The. Online, Yale Law School, http://avalon.law.yale.edu/17th_century/mass07.asp (accessed May 2012).

Baack, Ben. "The Economics of the American Revolutionary War." Online, The Economic History Association (posted February 5, 2010), http://eh.net/encyclopedia/article/baack.war.revolutionary.us (accessed, February 2012).

Bouvé, Pauline Carrington. "Town History of New Ipswich," (including source material from *The New England Magazine,* New Series, Vol. 22, no. 1 [Mar 1900]). Online, Town of New Ipswich, http://www.townofnewipswich.org/ (accessed August 2009).

Bradford, Charles H. "Dorchester Heights: Prelude to Independence." n.d. Online, Dorchester Atheneum, http://www.dorchesteratheneum.org/pdf/Dorchester%20Heights.pdf (accessed March 2012).

Bradsby, H. C. *History of Bradford County, Pennsylvania with Biographical Sketches* (1891). Online, http://www.joycetice.com/bradsby/bio1225.htm (accessed July 2010).

British Library, The. Online, http://www.bl.uk/treasures/magnacarta/index.html (accessed May 2012).

Brooklyn Historical Society. Online, http://www.brooklynhistory.org/default/index.html.(accessed June 2012).

Cain, Alexander R. "Samuel Hastings Jr." Committee of Study, Character Biographies of Those Who Were Present at the Battle of Lexington, April 19, 1775. n.d. Online, Lexington Minute Men, http://lexingtonminutemen.com/images/samuelhastings.pdf (accessed December 2011).

Chiles, Henry. "The Henry & Sarah Ballinger Chiles Family." Online, http://www.henrychiles.com/i580.html (accessed November 2007).

Cutler, Ebenezer. "Invoice Book 1814–1830." Public Archives of Nova Scotia, item # PANS MG 3, Vol.2. Microfilm in The Loyalist Collection, Harriet Irving Library, University of New Brunswick, item # MIC-Loyalist FC LFR.C8E215. Finding aid online, at http://www.lib.unb.ca/collections/loyalist/seeOne.php?id=425&string, (accessed October 2011).

Darley, Stephen. "Benedict Arnold's Portraits." *The Early America Review, A Journal of People, Issues, and Events in 18th Century America,* Vol. 3, No. 3 (Winter/Spring 2001). Online, http://www.earlyamerica.com/review/2001_winter_spring/benedict_arnold.html (accessed June 2012)

Darlington Digital Library, University of Pittsburgh. Online, http://digital.library.pitt.edu/d/darlington/images.html (accessed August 2012).

FamilySearch. Online, https://familysearch.org (accessed May 2012).

"Family: Whitney, Silas (1766-1850)." Online, Whitney Research Group, http://wiki.whitneygen.org/wrg/index.php/Family:Whitney,_Silas_(1766-1850) (accessed February 2012).

Federal Census Records, United States, 1790–1850. Online, http://persi.heritagequestonline.com (accessed December 2011).

"Find A Grave." Online, http://www.findagrave.com/cgi-bin/fg.cgi (accessed May 2012).

Fleming, Thomas, "Gentleman Johnny's Wandering Army," *American Heritage Magazine.* Vol. 24, no. 1 (December 1972). Online, http://www.americanheritage.com/content/gentleman-johnny%E2%80%99s-wandering-army (accessed December 2010).

"General von Steuben." Online, Valley Forge National Park, National Park Service, http://www.nps.gov/vafo/historyculture/vonsteuben.htm (accessed January 2011).

Glasco, Jeff, comp. "Monmouth, New Jersey, June 28, 1778," Order of Battle, compiled July 7, 2004. Online (posted June 13, 2009), www.jdglasco.files.wordpress.com/2009/06/raw-monmouth-ob.doc (accessed February 2011).

Goodway, Frank. "American Participants at the Battles of Saratoga." 1997. Online, Heritage Hunters of Saratoga County in cooperation with Saratoga National Historical Park http://saratoganygenweb.com/sarapk.htm#Source (accessed December 2011).

"Gunn Family Tree." Online, http://gunn.familytreeguide.com/getperson.php?personID=I01477&tree=T1&PHPSESSID=fa48507b411cf29613f54c3287ddf4c2 (accessed March 2010).

Hafner, Donald L. "Sippio Brister: 'He is Styled ... 'A Man of Color.'" *The Lincoln Minute Men Dispatch* (June 2000). Online, The Lincoln Minute Men, http://www.lincolnminutemen.org/history/articles/hafner_sippio_brister.html (accessed June 2008).

Heald, Larry. "Heald Family of Concord Mass, Chester VT, and Canton, ILL." Online, http://wc.rootsweb.ancestry.com/cgi-bin/igm.cgi?op=REG&db=larrypdx&id=I362 (accessed May 2012).

Hickman, Kennedy. "American Revolution: Battle of White Plains." Online, www.militaryhistory.about.com/od/americanrevolution/p/whiteplains.htm (accessed March 2009).

Historic American Buildings Survey. Online, Library of Congress, http://www.loc.gov/pictures/collection/hh/ (accessed July 2012).

Hubbard, Timothy William. "Battle at Valcour Island: Benedict Arnold as Hero." American Heritage Magazine. Vol. 17, issue 6 (October 1966). Online, http://www.americanheritage.com/articles/magazine/ah/1966/6/1966_6_8.shtml (accessed December 2008).

Hubbardston, Massachusetts, Vital Records to 1850. Boston: New England Historic Genealgical Society, 1907. Transcribed for the web by Corolynn Brown. Online, http://www.rays-place.com/town/ma/hubbardston/ (accessed March 2010).

Lacroix, D.P. "Westford and the Battle of Valcour Island." 2004. Online, Westford Colonial Minutemen, http://lacroixfam.home.comcast.net/~lacroixfam/wmm/Valcour_Island_History.html (accessed December 2008).

"Lafayette and the Virginia Campaign 1781." Online, National Park Service, http://www.nps.gov/york/historyculture/lafayette-and-the-virginia-campaign-1781.htm (accessed March 2011).

"Lafayette's Virginia Campaign (1781)." Online, Xenophon Group Military History Database, http://xenophongroup.com/mcjoynt/laf_va.htm (accessed March 2011).

Library and Archives Canada, Coverdale Collection of Canadiana. Online, http://collectionscanada.gc.ca/pam_archives/index.php?fuseaction=genitem.displayItem&lang=eng&rec_nbr=2837814&rec_nbr_list=2837814 (accessed April 2012).

Library of Congress. Online, http://memory.loc.gov/ammem/gmdhtml/armhtml/armhome.html (accessed May 2012).

Lindert, Peter H., and Jeffrey G. Williamson. "America's Revolution: Economic disaster, development, and equality." Online (posted July 15, 2011), http://www.voxeu.org/index.php?q=node/6751 (accessed February 2012).

MacLean, John C. "Hot Topics: Farm for Sale: Finding Family History in Early Nineteenth-Century Newspapers." Online, New England Historic Genealogical Society, http://www.newenglandancestors.org/research/services/articles_farms_forsale.asp (accessed April 2010).

———. "Resources for Researching Massachusetts Slaves and Slaveholders." Online, New England Historic Genealogical Society, http://www.newenglandancestors.org/research/services/articles_resources_mass_slaves.asp (accessed February 2009).

"Maine Deaths and Burials, 1841–1910," Jonas Brooks (1850). Online, FamilySearch, https://familysearch.org/pal:/MM9.1.1/F48J-G48 (accessed December 2011).

Marina, William. "The Revolution as a People's War." July 1, 1976. Online, The Independent Institute, http://www.independent.org/newsroom/article.asp?id=1485 (accessed September 2008).

Mason, Edna Warren. *Descendants of Capt. Hugh Mason in America,* New Haven, CT: Tuttle, Morehouse & Taylor, 1937. Compiled and reported in Stephen M. Lawson. *Capt. Hugh Mason Genealogy.* Online, http://kinnexions.com/kinnexions/mason/rr01/rr01_065.htm (accessed December 2009).

McBarron, H. Charles. "Soldiers of the American Revolution." Print collection, U. S. Army Center of Military History, 1976. Online, http://www.history.army.mil/catalog/pubs/70/posters/70-5/70-5.html (accessed August 2012).

Internet Sources

McGhie, Myrna Doble. "Descendants of Thomas Dakin, 8th Great Grandfather." Online, http://familytreemaker.genealogy.com/users/m/c/g/Myrna-Lee-Mcghie/FILE/0030page.html (accessed October 2011).

Meredith, Austin, comp. "People of Concord During the 18th Century." 2007. Online, "Stack of the Artist of Kouroo" Project, http://www.kouroo.info/kouroo/places/towns/ConcordMA_18thCentury.pdf (accessed April 2010).

Michell, [H. E.], and [F. E.] Daggett. *The East Livermore and Livermore Register, 1903–4.* Kent's Hill, ME: H.E. Mitchell Publishing Company, 1903. Online, http://books.google.com/books?id=LbUTAAAAYAAJ&pg=PA104&dq=%22abijah+munroe%22&hl=en&sa=X&ei=p8nrTu2kHujz0gGL8fykCQ&ved=0CDQQ6AEwAA#v=onepage&q=%22abijah%20munroe%22&f=false (accessed December 2011).

Michener, Ron. "Money in the American Colonies." Online, The Economic History Association (posted February 1, 2010), http://eh.net/encyclopedia/article/michener.american.colonies.money (accessed, February 2012).

Millard, James P. "Orders Of Battle, Battle Of Lake Champlain At Valcour Island, American Revolution." Online, America's Historic Lakes (South Hero, VT), http://www.historiclakes.org/Valcour/valcour_chart.htm (accessed December 2008).

Moran, Donald N. "A Brief History of the Commander-in-Chief Guards with Roster." Online, Sons of Liberty Chapter, Sons of the American Revolution, http://www.revolutionarywararchives.org/cncguard.html (accessed March 2010).

———. "The Birth of the American Cavalry." *Liberty Tree Newsletter* (January 2008). Online, Sons of Liberty Chapter, Sons of the American Revolution, http://www.revolutionarywararchives.org/cavalry.html (accessed May 2009).

Morris, Charles W. E. "The Gurnet," *Pilgrim Society Note*, Series One, Number 30 (July 1982). Online, Pilgrim Hall Museum, http://www.pilgrimhall.org/PSNote30.htm (accessed November 2011).

Muster Roll of the 2nd Company of Associators, Loyal American Association. July 5, 1775. In Thomas Gage Papers, Vol. 131, William L. Clements Library, University of Michigan. Transcription online, The On-Line Institute of Advanced Loyalist Studies, http://www.royalprovincial.com/military/musters/loyamassoc/laasecondco.htm (accessed October 2011).

Muster Roll of the 5th Company of Associators, Loyal American Association. July 5, 1775. In Thomas Gage Papers, Vol. 131, William L. Clements Library, University of Michigan. Transcription online, The On-Line Institute of Advanced Loyalist Studies, http://www.royalprovincial.com/military/musters/loyamassoc/laafifthco.htm (accessed January 2012).

National Archives and Records Administration. Online, http://research.archives.gov/description/300357 (accessed August 2012). Also, Our Archives. Online, http://www.ourarchives.wikispaces.net/Archivist+of+the+United+States+David+Ferriero's+Favorite+Records (accessed August 2012), Benedict Arnold's Oath of Allegiance to the United States of America.

National Park Service. "The British Campaign for Philadelphia and the Occupation of Valley Forge in 1777." Online, http://www.nps.gov/vafo/historyculture/upload/Philadelphia%20Campaign.pdf (accessed November 2011).

"New Hampshire, Birth Records, Early to 1900," index and images. Online, FamilySearch, https://familysearch.org/pal:/MM9.1.1/FLLB-SJD (accessed December 2012), George Farrar, 08 Dec 1784.

"New Hampshire, Births and Christenings, 1714-1904," index. Online, FamilySearch, https://familysearch.org/pal:/MM9.1.1/FDX2-6JF (accessed April 2012), Daniel Farrar (1778).

"New Hampshire Marriage Records, 1637–1947," index. Online, FamilySearch, https://familysearch.org/pal:/MM9.1.1/FLFH-W84 (accessed December 2011), Abijah Munroe (1786).

On-Line Institute of Advanced Loyalist Studies, The. Online, http://www.royalprovincial.com/index.htm (accessed October 2011).

"Patriot Grave Search," Online, National Society of the Sons of the American Revolution, https://memberinfo.sar.org/patriotsearch/search.aspx (accessed March 2012).

"Philadelphia Campaign 1777, The." Online, Independence Hall Association (Philadelphia), http://www.ushistory.org/march/index.html, (accessed January 2011).

"Philadelphia Campaign 1777, The Battle of Brandywine:—Part 3, The." Online, Independence Hall Association (Philadelphia), http://www.ushistory.org/march/phila/brandywine_3.htm (accessed January 2011).

"Philadelphia Campaign 1777, The Battle of Brandywine:—Part 7, The." Online, Independence Hall Association (Philadelphia), http://www.ushistory.org/march/phila/brandywine_7.htm (accessed January 2011).

"Philadelphia Campaign 1777, The Battle of Brandywine:—Part 8, The." Online, Independence Hall Association (Philadelphia), http://www.ushistory.org/march/phila/brandywine_8.htm (accessed January 2011).

"Revolutionary Graves of New Hampshire." Online, The New Hampshire Society of the Sons of the American Revolution, http://www.nhssar.org/NH%20Revolutionary%20War%20Burials.pdf (accessed June 2010).

Richard H. Brown Revolutionary War Map Collection, The. Norman B. Leventhal Map Center at the Boston Public Library. Online, http://maps.bpl.org/id/rb15259 (accessed June 2012)

Robertson, John K., and Bob McDonald. "A Brief Profile of the Continental Army." Online, Orderly Books of the Continental Army, 1775–1784, http://www.revwar75.com/ob/profile.htm (accessed September 2011).

Semkiw, Walter. "Return of the Revolutionaries." Online, http://www.johnadams.net/cases/samples/Gore-Gates/index.html (accessed November 2011).

"Ships Built at Milford Shipyard and H.M. Dockyard, Pembroke." Online, The Great War Primary Document Archive, http://www.gwpda.org/naval/images/pembroke_app_a.pdf (accessed December 2011).

"Short History of the Penobscot Expedition, A." Online, http://penobscot1779.tripod.com/PE%20history.htm (accessed October 2011).

Stewart, Richard W., ed. *American Military History, Vol. 1, The United States Army and the Forging of a Nation, 1775-1917*. Washington, D.C.: Center of Military History, U.S. Army, 2004. Online, http://www.history.army.mil/books/AMH-V1/index.htm (accessed July 2012).

Sudbury Miscellaneous Records. Sudbury Town Clerk's Office, Bound Volume. Online, http://www.town.sudbury.ma.us/archives/ (accessed March 2012)

Tolman, George, comp. *The Wheeler Families of Old Concord, Massachusetts*. 1908 (revised by Joseph C. Wheeler, 2006). Online, Special Collections of the Concord Free Public Library, Concord, Massachusetts, http://www.concordlibrary.org/scollect/wheeler.htm (accessed April 2010)

Tourtellot, Arthur Bernon. Introduction and comments to "The Nineteenth of April 1775," republication of excerpts of Harold Murdoch's paper [see Murdoch], *American Heritage Magazine*. Vol. 10, issue 5 (August 1959). Online, http://www.americanheritage.com/content/harold-murdock%E2%80%99s-%E2%80%9C-nineteenth-april-1775%E2%80%9D (accessed October 2011).

United States Army Center of Military History. Online, http://www.history.army.mil/index.html (accessed July 2012).

"Vermont, Vital Records, 1760-1954," index and images. Online, FamilySearch, https://familysearch.org/pal:/MM9.1.1/XFVV-86J (accessed May 2012).

Washington, George. "The George Washington Papers." Online, Library of Congress, http://lcweb2.loc.gov/learn/features/timeline/amrev/north/johnwash.html (accessed November 2008).

Index

Names appearing CAPITALIZED are Lincoln individuals for whom records of Revolutionary service have been found, and who are therefore profiled in Chapters 10 and 11. Page numbers in **bold** represent the individual profiles in Chapters 10, 11, and 12. Page numbers in *italics* represent illustrations.

A

ABBOT, ABIEL, **173–174**, 506, 509, 515, 518, 528; family relationships of, *25*, 175,177; unit listings for, 483, 489, 496, 501

Abbot, Hannah (White), *25*, 173, 174, 175, 177

ABBOT, JOSEPH, JR. (Cpl.), *11*, 74, **175–176**, 363, 507, 509, 512, 515, 518, 524, 525, 528; family relationships of, *25*, 173, 174, 177; gravestone of, *175*; unit listings for, 473, 478, 480, 484

ABBOT, JOSEPH (SR.) (Lt.), 9, *11*, 13, **174–175**, 176, 508, 510, 514, 518, 526; deposition of, 9, 55, 174; family relationships of, *25*, 173, 175, 177; unit listing for, 475. *See also* Depositions of April 1775

ABBOT, NEHEMIAH, *11*, 41, 97, 99, 100, 111, 112, 116, 120, 124, 126, **176–177**, 385, 507, 509, 512, 517, 518, 524, 526; family relationships of, *25*, 174, 175, 223, 314, 315, 317; gravestone of, *176*; unit listings for, 473, 475, 478, 487, 490, 491, 492, 493, 494, 496, 499

Abbot, Nehemiah (father of JOSEPH (SR.)), *25*, 174

Abbot, Polly (Meriam), *25*, 174

Abbot, Ruth (Bucknam), 176, 525

Abbot, Sarah (Foster), *25*, 174

Abbot, Sarah (Hoar), *25*, 177, 314

Abbott. *See* Abbot

ABEL, JONATHAN, 120, 121, **177**, 508, 511, 515, 520, 530; unit listing for, 492

Aberdeen, Scotland, 454

Acton, MA, 44, 55, 194, 382, 442; feud with Concord, 48–49, 161; mentioned as residence location, 19, 239, 240, 276, 282, 330, 356, 357, 358, 378, 433; minute men and militia at Concord, 46–49, 47, 162, 165, 403; not the only company with bayonets, 48–49

ADAMS, [UNIDENTIFIED], **189**, 432, 458, 508, 511, 516, 518, 530; unit listings for, 480, 505

ADAMS, ABEL, *11*, 56, 97, 153, **178–179**, 205, 243, 246, 506, 509, 512, 516, 518, 527, 528; family relationships of, 22, *30*, 181, 183, 188, 189; unit listings for, 473, 475, 478, 480, 485, 500, 501

Adams, Abel (of Pepperell), 179

Adams, Abigail (Smith), 404, 405, 450

ADAMS, AMOS, 178, **179**, 507, 510, 516, 518,530; family relationships of,180,188, 189, 297; unit listings for, 502, 503, 505

Adams, Amos (of Pepperell). *See* Addams, Amos (of Pepperell)

Adams, Anna (Harrington), 181

ADAMS, ASA, 13, 41, 101, 121, **179–180**, 180, 506, 508, 513, 517, 518, 522, 530; family relationships of, 188, 189, 297; unit listings for, 476, 487, 490, 491, 492, 494, 497, 499

ADAMS, BULKLEY, 94, 121, 126, **180–181**, 506, 509, 515, 518, 526; family relationships of, 22, *30*, 179, 183, 188, 189; unit listings for, 478, 483, 485, 492, 498

Adams, Charles, 190, 432, 458, 507, 510; family relationships of, *28*, 458

Adams, Daniel (Capt.), *29*, 185, 394

Adams, Deliverance, 185

ADAMS, EDWARD, xv, xvi, 18, 42, 60, **181–183**, 386, 445, 507, 509, 512, 513, 515, 519, 524, 525, 529; family relationships of, 22, *30*, 179, 188, 189; pension declaration of, *182*; unit listings for, 475, 477, 478, 483, 485, 488

Adams, Elisabeth (Shaw), 179, 180, 188

Adams, Elizabeth. *See* Gove, Elizabeth (Adams)

Adams, Elizabeth (Minot), *29*, 185

Adams, Grace (Hagar), 188

Adams, Hannah Soley (McCarthy), 190

ADAMS, JAMES, 8, *10*, 73, **184–185**, 393, 508, 510, 514, 516, 518, 526; deposition of, 55, 184; family relationships of, *30*, 186, 188, 244, 252; unit listings for, 474, 478, 480, 505. *See also* Depositions of April 1775

ADAMS, JAMES, JR., 84, 109, 121, 126, 184, **185–187**, 506, 509, 516, 518, 524, 530; family relationships of, 22, *30*; unit listings for, 481, 488, 492, 493, 496

ADAMS, JOEL, 42, **187–188**, 507, 510, 517, 519, 524, 529; family relationships of, 441, 442, 444; unit listings for, 473, 475, 478, 501, 502, 503, 504

ADAMS, JOHN, *11*, 15, 178, **188–189**, 395, 508, 511, 514, 518, 526; deposition of, 188; family relationships of, 22, *30*, 179, 180, 181, 183, 185; unit listing for, 474. *See also* Depositions of April 1775

Adams, John (father of JOHN), *29*, 188

Adams, John (future president), 73, 277

ADAMS, JOHN, JR., 56, **189**, 507, 510, 515, 519, 525, 528; family relationships of, *30*, 179, 180, 181, 183, 188; unit listings for, 475, 476, 480

Adams, John, Jr. (father of AMOS; ASA), 179, 180

Adams, Joseph (Capt.), 12, 189, 190, 428, **457–458**, 519; family relationships of, *28*, 432, 449; payment for unidentified service to, *190*

ADAMS, JOSEPH, JR. (Dr.), 12, 15, 16,190, **449–450**; family relationships of, *28*, 190; portrait of, *450*

Adams, Josiah, 188

Adams, Kezia (Conant), *30*, 185, 186

Adams, Love. *See* Lawrence, Love (Adams)

Adams, Love (Minott), *29*, 188

Adams, Lovey (Lawrence), *12*, *28*, 323, 449

Adams, Lucy (Hubburd), *30*, 179, 181, 183, 188, 189

Adams, Lucy (Whitney), 188

Adams, Mary. *See* Peirce, Mary (Adams); Wheeler, Polly (Adams)

Adams, Mary (wife of JOHN, JR.), 189, 525

Adams, Mary (Edwards), 179

Adams, Mary (Evelyth), *28*, 432, 449, 457

Adams, Molly. *See* Adams, Mary (wife of JOHN, JR.)

Adams, Nancy (Tarbell), 186

Adams, Nathan, 16, 190, 432, 458, 506, 509; family relationships of, *28*, 458

Adams, Patty (Barret), 183, 525

Adams, Persis (Stone), 181

Adams, Polly. *See* Wheeler, Polly (Adams)

Adams, Rebecca (Jones), 179

Adams, Rebecca (Stratton), 188

Adams, Rebeckah. *See* Brown, Rebeckah (Adams)

Adams, Thomas (Capt.), 436

Addams, Amos (of Pepperell), 178

African-Americans, 15, 39, 97, 126, 141, 146, 219–222, 240, 351; individual soldiers identified as, 219, 236, 240, 263, 274, 310, 312, 323, 341, 353–355, 360,

394, 395, 396–397, 399, 521. *See also* Slaves and slavery
Alarm lists. *See* Militia system
Alarm of April 19, 1775. See April 19, 1775
Alarm riders. *See* April 19, 1775, alarm riders for
April 19, 1775, *vi,* vii–viii, *x,* 3, 4, 7–13, *8,* 14, 43–54, *47, 50 (maps), 53,* 97, *472;* alarm riders for, 7, *8,* 43, 349, 350, 351; commemoration of, 167, *168;* delay in alarm reaching Waltham, 267; preparations for 43–44, 49; residence locations of Lincoln men-in-arms on, *10–11;* supplies stored at Concord before, 43; unit listings of individual participants on, 473–475. *See also* Amos Baker, affidavit of; Depositions of April 1775; Lexington and Concord, Second Battle of; profiles of individual participants
Albany, NY, 37, 127, 128, 132; as a focal point of the Saratoga campaign, 96, 97, 98, 100, 105; mentioned as service location, 175, 200, 203, 204, 212, 230, 254, 273, 377, 378, 497
Alexander, William (Gen.), Lord Stirling. *See* Stirling (General)
ALIN, PHINEAS. *See* ALLEN, PHINEAS
Allen, Abigail. *See* Wesson, Abigail (Allen)
Allen, Abigail (Foster), *27,* 191, 192, 288
Allen, Benjamin, *27,* 191
Allen, Benjamin, Jr., *29,* 191
Allen, Beulah. *See* Billing, Beulah (Allen)
Allen, Dorothy (Flagg), 191
Allen, Eunice. *See* Tower, Eunice (Allen)
Allen, Eunice (Gale), *27,* 191
Allen, John (Col.), 254
Allen, Lydia. *See* Wheeler, Lydia (Allen)
Allen, Mary. *See* Farrar, Mary (Allen); Gage, Mary (Allen)
Allen, Mary (Brown), *29,* 191
Allen, Nathaniel C. (Capt.), 502; mentioned as unit commander, 415, 447
Allen, Pattee. *See* Billing, Pattee (Allen)
ALLEN, PHINEAS, xii, 12, 16, 94, **191–192**, 288, 507, 510, 514, 518, 530; family relationships of, 22, *27,* 209, 210, 287, 328, 368, 415, 418, 434; unit listings for, 473, 484, 490
Allen, Prudence. *See* Hagar, Prudence (Allen)
Allen, Sarah. *See* Knowlton, Sarah (Allen)
Allen, Sarah (Danforth), 191
Allen, Susanna. *See* Peirce, Susanna (Allen)
Allentown, NJ, 116
Alstead, NH, 183
American Tartar (privateer), 404, 488
Ames, John (Capt.), 306
Amherst, NH, 441, 452, 453, 454
Amsden, Eunice. *See* Robinson, Eunice (Amsden)
Ancient and Honorable Artillery Company, 415, 470
Anderson, John, 134, 135. *See also* André, John (Maj.)

Andover, MA, 288
André, John (Maj.), 135, 136, 340. *See also* Anderson, John
Andrews, Abraham (Capt.), 498; mentioned as unit commander, 37, 209, 234, 259, 315, 341, 347, 349, 433
Annapolis, MD, 142, 143, 204
Annapolis County, Nova Scotia. *See* Digby Township, Annapolis County, Nova Scotia
Antigua, 391, 455
Argyle, NY, 391
Arlington, MA. *See* Menotomy, MA
Arnold, Benedict (Col.; Brig. Gen.; Maj. Gen.); burned in effigy, 153; expedition to Canada, 68, *69 (map),* 70, 71, 73, 184–185, 202, 232, 477, gunboat fleet of, 76, 79–81, *80, 81, 82 (map),* 89; loyalty oath of, *134;* portrait of, *68;* reemergence as a British general, 142, 144, 204; in the Saratoga campaign, 98, 105, 106, 107, *106–107 (maps),* 153; treason of, 134–136, *136,* 340
Arundel, ME, 253, 477
Ashland Township, NY, 247, 529
Ashley, John (Col.), 502; mentioned as unit commander, 273
Ashley, Moses (Capt.), 480, 482, 486, 488, 490, 491, 492, 493, 496, 498; mentioned as unit commander, 246, 273, 377
Associators, 2nd Company of, 451, 453. *See also* Loyalist militias
Attleborough, MA, 288, 463
AVERY, SAMUEL, 33, **192**, 507, 510, 516, 520, 530; unit listing for, 505
Avery, Sarah. *See* Stone, Sarah (Avery)

B

Bacon, Eunice (Bacon), 192, 193
BACON, JOSEPH, 91, **192**, 507, 510, 515, 519, 530; family relationships of, 193; unit listing for, 481
Bacon, Mary (Brown), 193
BACON, NOAH, 64, **192–193**, 507, 509, 514, 519, 530; family relationships of, 192, 193; unit listings for, 478, 489
Bacon, Patty (Rice), 192
BACON, SAMUEL, 12, 110, **193**, 360, 507, 510, 515, 520, 527; family relationships of, 192; unit listings for, 475, 482, 489, 505
Bacon, Samuel (Capt.) (father of Samuel), 192, 193
Bailey, Adam (Capt.), 499, 503, 504; mentioned as unit commander, 204, 391
Bailey, John (Col.), 499; mentioned as unit commander, 204
BAILEY, SAMUEL. *See* BALEY, SAMUEL
Baker, Ame (Prescott), 195
BAKER, AMOS, *10,* 48–49, 94, 100, 108, 109, 166, **194–195**, *472,* 507, 509, 515, 518, 524, 526; 1850 affidavit of, 48–49 356–357; family relationships of, 195, 196, 197, 198, 281, 318; house of, *196;* portrait of, *194;* unit listings for, 474, 478, 483, 485, 488
Baker, Betsy, 198

Baker, Elizabeth (Taylor), 197
Baker, Eunice (Dudley), 195
Baker, Grace (Billings), 195, 196, 197, 198
Baker, Hannah. *See* Hosmer, Hannah (Baker)
Baker, Hannah (Bell), 196, 198
Baker, Hepzibah (Taylor), 197
BAKER, JACOB (Sr.), *10,* 16, **195**, 508, 511, 514, 519, 526; family relationships of, 196, 197, 198, 281, 318; house of, *196;* unit listing for, 474
BAKER, JACOB, JR., 3, *10,* **196**, 507, 510, 515, 518, 522, 526; family relationships of, 195, 197, 198, 281, 318; house of, *196;* unit listings for, 473, 505
BAKER, JAMES, 3, *10,* **197**, 507, 510, 514, 518, 527; family relationships of, 195, 196, 198, 281, 318; house of, *196;* unit listing for, 473
BAKER, NATHANIEL, 7, 9, *10,* 42, **197**, *472,* 507, 510, 514, 518, 526; family relationships of, 195, 196, 198, 281, 318; house of, *196;* unit listings for, 473, 478
BAKER, SAMUEL, *10,* 97, **198**, 507, 509, 512, 516, 518, 529; family relationships of, 195, 196, 197, 281, 318; house of, *196;* unit listings for, 474, 478, 480, 483, 485
Balch, Joseph (Capt.), 482; mentioned as unit commander, 425
Balch, Mary. *See* Brown, Mary (Balch)
Baldwin, Jeduthan (Col.), 65, 487, 494, 496, 499; mentioned as unit commander, 347, 437, 438
Baldwin, Loammi (Maj.; Lt. Col.; Col.), 60, 65, 477, 481, 482; mentioned as unit commander, 178, 189, 241, 243, 258, 266, 272, 294, 384, 411, 412, 413, 437
BALEY, SAMUEL, **198–199**, 508, 511, 516, 520, 530; unit listings for, 488, 495, 498
Baltimore, MD, 143
Bancroft, Anna. *See* Farrar, Anna (Bancroft)
Bancroft, Mary. *See* Meriam, Mary (Bancroft)
Bancroft, Thaddeus; deposition of, 184. *See also* Depositions of April 1775
Bangor, ME, 206, 253, 528
Banishment Act, 450, 452, 455
Barnard, Samuel (Capt.), 474; mentioned as unit commander, 336, 417
Barns, Oliver (Capt.). *See* Barns, Thomas (Capt.)
Barns, Thomas (Capt.), 495; mentioned as unit commander, 338, 393
Barnstable, MA, 260, 289
Barnstable County, MA, 214, 381
Barre, MA, 19, 320, 334, 335, 336, 341, 527
Barret, Martha, 200
Barret, Nathaniel, 200
Barret, Patty. *See* Adams, Patty (Barret)
Barrett, James (Col.), 45–46, 49, 382, 474; house of, *44;* mentioned as unit commander, 227, 283, 340, 397; as muster master, 177, 200, 221, 247, 273, 282, 322, 387, 402
BARRETT, JOHN, xvi, 94, 132, **199–200**, 506, 509, 512, 516, 520, 524, 528; unit

Index

listings for, 474, 477, 481, 484, 485, 497, 498, 500
Barrett, Lydia. *See* Farrar, Lydia (Barrett)
Barrett, Martha. *See* Brooks, Martha (Barrett)
Barrett, Mary. *See* Farrar, Mary (Barrett)
Barrett, Susanna (Chambers), 200
Barron, Benjamin, 222
Barron, Sarah. *See* Torrey, Sarah (Barron)
Barron, Susanna, 222
Barron, William (Capt.), 436
BARTER, JOHN, xvii, 119, 200, 309, 325, 387, 508, 511, 516, 520, 530; unit listings for, 486, 487, 490, 491, 494, 497
Basking Ridge, NJ, 20, 91, 116, 307, 308, 522
Bass, Bethia. *See* Torrey, Bethia (Bass)
Bateman, John, deposition of, 55, *56*, 283, 284. *See also* Depositions of April 1775
Bates, Oliver (Capt.), 474; mentioned as unit commander, 199
Battle, Ebenezer (Capt.), 483; mentioned as unit commander, 265
Battle Green. *See* Lexington, MA, bloodshed on the Lexington Green
Battle Road, vii, x, 13, *50 (map)*, 52, *53*, 164, 165, 166, 224, 236, 247, 287, 303, 399, 411, 413. *See also* Bay Road; Bloody Angles
Battles. *See* individual listings by name of battle
Baylor (Colonel), 400, 487, 490, 491
Bay Road, 7, 8, 9, 51, 158, 164, 192, 237, 287, 392, 430. *See also* Battle Road
Bedford, MA, 51, 192, 193, 222, 341, 428, 437, 448, 467, 527; alarm delivered to, 7, 349, 350; minute men and militia on April 19th, vii, 12, 13, 36, 46, 49, 165, 193, 343, 382, 475
Belknap, Ebenezer (Capt.), 492, 493; mentioned as unit commander, 324
Bell, Hannah. *See* Baker, Hannah (Bell)
Bemis, Beriah. *See* Child, Beriah (Bemis)
Bemis, Edmund (Capt.), 476; mentioned as unit commander, 179, 180
Bemis, Grace, 460. *See* Child, Grace (Bemis)
Bemis, Hannah, 203
BEMIS, JEDUTHAN, xvii, 32, 55, 71, 73, 79, 84, 88, 100, 185, **200-203**, 507, 509, 516, 520, 522, 524, 525, 529; at the Cedars of Canada, 202-203; unit listings for, 475, 476, 479, 481, 485, 495, 501
Bemis, John, 203
Bemis, Polley (Stapels), 203
Bemis, Statira (Squires), 203, 525
Bemis, Susanna. *See* Gearfield, Susanna (Bemis); Peirce, Susanna (Bemis); Viles, Suzanna (Bemis)
Bemis Heights, NY, Battle of, 105, *106-107 (maps)*, 273, 276, 331, 353, 377. *See also* Saratoga campaign
Bennington, VT, *96 (map)*, 178, 183, 205, 264, 279, 329, 331, 332, 345, 353, 377, 381; Alarm, 345, 381; Battle of, *98*, 264, 345
Benson, Joshua (Capt.), 500; mentioned as unit commander, 443

Berry, Thankful. *See* Nixon, Thankful (Berry)
Berton (Captain), 488, 495, 497, 500; mentioned as unit commander, 293
Beverly, MA, 15, 248, 477, 527; Captain Thorndike's company on April 19th, 13, 247, 475
Bigelow, Grace. *See* Munroe, Grace (Bigelow)
Bigelow, Mercy. *See* Gearfield, Mercy (Bigelow)
Bigelow, Timothy (Col.), 119, 120, 132, 485, 487, 490, 491, 492, 494, 495, 496, 499; mentioned as unit commander, 218, 219, 236, 282, 291, 343, 359, 421, 425, 447, 462
Bilbao, Spain, 18, 303, 530
Billerica, MA, 190, 332, 527; minute men and militia on April 19th, 51, 288
BILLING, ABEL, 132, 142, 143, **203-205**, 254, 506, 509, 515, 519, 524, 525, 528; family relationships of, 208, 212, 425; gravestone of, *204*; unit listings for, 484, 497, 498, 499
Billing, Abigail (Eaton), 212
Billing, Anna, *29*, 208, 211
Billing, Anna (Gearfield), 213
Billing, Anna (Hunt), 206
Billing, Beulah (Allen), *29*, 191, 209, 210
BILLING, DANIEL, *10*, 105, 109, 178, **205-206**, 246, 507, 509, 515, 518, 528; family relationships of, *28*, 208, 210, 211, 401; unit listings for, 473, 478, 480, 485
Billing, Daniel (father of DANIEL), *28*, 206
Billing, Elisabeth (Farrar) (mother of DANIEL), *28*, 206
Billing, Elizabeth. *See* Dakin, Elizabeth (Billing)
Billing, Elizabeth (Farrar) (wife of ABEL), 204, 525
Billing, Elizabeth (Handcock), 211
Billing, Hannah. *See* Fay, Hannah (Billing)
Billing, Hannah (Farrar), 204, 208, 212
BILLING, ISRAEL, 115, **206-207**, 506, 509, 516, 518, 526; family relationships of, *29*, 208, 210, 211, 401; unit listings for, 485, 489, 498, 500
BILLING, JOHN, 132, **207-208**, 507, 510, 514, 519, 523, 528; family relationships of, 204, 212; unit listing for, 495
Billing, John (father of ABEL; JOHN; SOLOMON), 204, 208, 212
Billing, Joseph (father of JOSEPH (Sr.); NATHAN), *29*, 208, 211
BILLING, JOSEPH (Sr.), **208-209**, 508, 510, 514, 518, 526; family relationships of, *29*, 191, 206, 210, 211, 368, 401, 415, 418, 434; unit listings for, 478, 481
BILLING, JOSEPH, JR., 115, **209-210**, 231, 506, 509, 515, 518, 526; family relationships of, *29*; 191, 206, 208, 211, 368, 401, 415, 418, 434; payment for service of, *209*; unit listings for, 489, 496, 498
Billing, Lydia. *See* Wesson, Lydia (Billing)
Billing, Lydia (Wheeler), *28*, 206, 368
Billing, Mary (Billing), *29*, 206, 211
Billing, Mary (Closson), 208

Billing, Mary (Moor), 213
BILLING, NATHAN, 84, **210-211**, 508, 510, 514, 515, 518, 526; family relationships of, *29*, 206, 208, 211, 213, 401; unit listings for, 473, 481, 486
BILLING, NATHAN, JR., **211**, 506, 509, 515, 518, 530; family relationships of, *29*, 206, 208, 210, 211, 401; unit listings for, 496, 500
Billing, Pattee (Allen), *29*, 210
BILLING, SOLOMON, 132, **212**, 254, 506, 509, 514, 519, 528; family relationships of, 204, 208, 425; gravestone of, *212*; unit listings for, 484, 497
BILLING, TIMOTHY, 79, 211, **213**, 507, 510, 515, 517, 518, 526; unit listings for, 473, 478, 480, 486, 505
Billing, Timothy (father of TIMOTHY), 213
Billings. *See also* Billing
Billings, Grace. *See* Baker, Grace (Billings)
Bladged, Thomas. *See* BLODGET, THOMAS
Blodget, Samuel, 214
Blodget, Sarah (Spencer), 214
BLODGET, THOMAS, 74, **213-215**, 349, 352, 508, 511, 515, 519, 523, 530; unit listings for, 473, 478, 480
Blogget, Thomas (of Westford), 214. *See also* BLODGET, THOMAS
Bloody Angles, vii, xvii, 49-52, *50 (map)*, *53*, 164, 165, 459, 466. *See also* Battle Road
Bodwell, John (Capt.), 489; mentioned as unit commander, 173
Bodyguards. *See* Lee, Charles (Gen.), Life Guard; Washington, George (Gen.), Life Guard
Bolton, MA, 193
Bond, Abigail, 218
Bond, Anna. *See* Whitehead, Anna (Bond)
Bond, Benjamin, 218
Bond, Esther (Merriam), 218
Bond, Eunice (Eaton), 216, 525
Bond, Grace. *See* Mason, Grace (Bond)
Bond, Hannah. *See* Whitehead, Anna (Bond)
BOND, JONAS, xv, 128, **215-216**, 506, 509, 515, 516, 518, 524, 525, 528; family relationships of, *24*, 217, 218, 272, 276, 277, 278, 323, 327, 328, 437, 438, 461, 462; house of, *276*; unit listings for, 480, 495, 505
Bond, Jonathan, 217
Bond, Lydia (Farrar), *24*, 215, 217, 218
Bond, Lydia (Hapgood), 216
Bond, Lydia (Newton), 217
Bond, Mary, 217
Bond, Mellacent. *See* Nelson, Mellacent (Bond)
Bond, Rosanna (Negus), 218
BOND, SAMUEL, 121, 126, **216-217**, 506, 509, 512, 516, 518, 530; family relationships of, *24*, 215, 217, 218, 272, 276, 277, 278, 323, 327, 328, 331, 437, 438, 461, 462; house of, *276*; unit listings for 477, 478, 480, 482, 483, 485, 492, 505
Bond, Sarah. *See* Wheeler, Sarah (Bond)
Bond, Sarah (Parks), 218

BOND, THOMAS, **217**, 508, 511, 515, 520, 530; family relationships of, 215, 218, 323; unit listing for, 495
Bond, Thomas (of Waltham), 217
Bond, Thomas (of Watertown), 218
BOND, WILLIAM, 71, 218, 506, 509, 514, 518, 529; family relationships of, *24*, 215, 217, 272, 276, 277, 278, 289, 320, 323, 327, 328, 331, 365, 373, 423, 437, 438, 440, 446, 461, 462; house of, *276*; unit listing for, 496
Bond, William (father of JONAS; SAMUEL; WILLIAM), *24*, 215, 217, 218
Bond, William (Lt. Col.; Col.), 17, 217, 446, 477, 479; mentioned as unit commander at Cambridge, 201, 246, 286, 289, 290, 320, 355, 365, 366, 370, 373, 374, 377, 416, 423, 437, 469; mentioned as unit commander in Canada, 201, 203, 218, 258, 286, 446, 469
Bond, William (of Weston), 218
Bond, William (of Weston, husband of Sarah Parks), 218
Bond, William, Jr. (of Weston), 218
Boston, Siege of, 36, 54–55, 56–66; mentioned as a participant in, 33, 104, 179, 259, 271, 279, 299, 333, 356, 406, 428, 442; unit listings of individual participants in, 475–477, 478–479. See also Bunker Hill, Battle of; Dorchester Heights, fortification of
Boston, MA; 30, 44, 273, 290, 363, 452; British evacuation of, 19, 66, 68, 71, 326; British garrison in, 6, 9, 43; British return march from Concord to, *x*, 44, 49–54, *50 (maps)*, *53*, 164, 438, *472*; French fleet refits at, 121, 122, *123*; mentioned as a resident of, 186, 219, 220, 222, 231, 235, 240, 256, 261, 274, 310, 359, 361, 395, 405, 414, 415, 428, 470; mentioned as serving at, 94, 180, 191, 198, 218, 244, 247, 254, 260, 263, 265, 269, 270, 301, 302, 304, 317, 344, 379, 386, 398, 407, 414, 419, 423, 425, 426, 440, 444, 468; patriot eyes and ears in, 17, 43, 44, 405; spies and Tories informants in, 12, 44, 449, 464; Tory safe haven in, 15, 95, 158, 428, 450, 451, 452, 453, 454. *See also* Boston, Siege of
Boston, Phillip, 360
Boston Massacre, 66, 164
Boston Tea Party, 2, 3, 6, 164, 439, 440
Bounties. *See* Enlistment bounties
Bowes, Nicholas (Rev.), 222
BOWES, PETER, xiv, 95, 119, 120, 124, 132, 133, 153, **218–222**, 239, 240, 355, 396, 508, 511, 517, 520, 521, 530; bills of sale for property of, *220–221*; unit listings for, 485, 487, 490, 491, 492, 494, 495, 496, 499, 501; *See also* BROOKS, PETER
Bowker, Daniel (Capt.), 501; mentioned as unit commander, 266, 271
Bowman (Captain), 494, 496, 499; mentioned as unit commander, 219, 282, 359
BOWMAN, EDMUND, 23, 42, 65, **223**, 224, 507, 510, 514, 519, 526, 527; family relationships of, *25*, 314, 315, 317; unit listings for, 474, 478
Bowman, Ester (Hoar), *25*, 223
Bowman, Eunice (Mead), 223
Bowman, Sarah (Loring), 223
Bowman, Thaddeus, 223
Boynton, Hannah. *See* Tenney, Hannah (Boynton)
Boynton, John (Capt.), 345
Brandywine, Battle of, 18, 19, 101–104, *102*, *103 (map)*, 487, 488; mentioned as a participant in, 180, 233, 262, 347, 378, 400, 414
Brandywine Creek. *See* Brandywine, Battle of
Breed's Hill. *See* Bunker Hill, Battle of
Brewer, Jonathan (Col.), 280
Brewer, Samuel (Col.), 480; mentioned as unit commander, 178, 179, 205, 246, 279, 332
Briant, David (Capt.), 101, 487; mentioned as unit commander, 414
Bricket, James (Brig. Gen.); mentioned as brigade commander, 183, 205, 216, 238, 268, 275, 314, 329, 331, 353, 378, 408, 412, 443
Bridge, John (Capt.), 37, 478, 481; mentioned as unit commander, 199, 208, 348, 408, 414
Bridge, Mary. *See* Brown, Mary (Bridge)
Bridge, Sarah. *See* Peirce, Sarah (Bridge)
Bridgewater, MA, 36, 253, 254, 255, 259, 261, 266, 527
Brigham, Mary. *See* Gage, Mary (Brigham)
Brintnal, Thomas (Capt.), 434
BRISTER, SIPPIO. *See* HOAR, BRISTER
Bristol, PA, 92, 93
Bristol, RI, 345
Bristol County, MA, 259, 381
Brooke County, VA, 389
Brooke County, WV. *See* Brooke County, VA
Brookline, MA, 359, 466
Brooklyn, NY, 76, 248, 481; evacuation of, 77, *78 (map)*. *See also* Long Island, Battle of
BROOKS, AARON, 15, 94, **224**, 227, 352, 508, 511, 515, 518, 526; family relationships of, *22*, 231, 236, 239, 241, 242, 459; house of, *224*; unit listings for, 480, 484, 486, 493
BROOKS, ABNER, 97, **225**, 232, 506, 509, 515, 518, 523, 526; family relationships of, 23, *25*, 226, 231, 233, 235, 237, 238, 242, 299, 301, 302, 303, 306, 328, 407, 408, 409, 459; unit listings for, 480, 483, 485
Brooks, Amos, 219, 222, 240; deed to PETER BOWES, *220*
Brooks, Bathsheba (Dakin), 226, 269
BROOKS, BENJAMIN, *11*, **225–226**, 232, 506, 509, 514, 518, 523, 526; family relationships of, 23, *25*, 231, 233, 235, 237, 238, 242, 299, 301, 302, 303, 306, 328, 407, 408, 409, 459; unit listings for, 473
Brooks, Caleb (Capt.), 483; mentioned as unit commander, 244, 270

BROOKS, DANIEL, 18, 153, **226–227**, 430, 506, 509, 514, 518, 526; family relationships of, 230, 234, 269, 458; payment record for, *227*; unit listing for, 501
Brooks, Dorothy, *22*, 459
BROOKS, ELEAZER (Col.; Gen.), *11*, 12, 64, 65, 75, **227–231**, *228*, 324, 442, 508, 510, 512, 516, 518, 526; civic activity of, 3, 4, 230–231, 383; commendation by Washington, 84, 86, 88, 228, 229; commission as general, *229*; disparaged for unit cowardice, xvi, 85, 86–88; family relationships of, 226, 231, 234, 458; guarding the Convention, 37, 109, 115; mentioned as home unit commander for detached militia, 183, 191, 192, 198, 201, 205, 206, 215, 216, 225, 233, 238, 244, 252, 255, 257, 261, 264, 265, 268, 270, 275, 294, 298, 310, 314, 329, 330, 331, 348, 353, 377, 378, 379, 393, 408, 412, 425, 443; mentioned as unit commander at Dorchester Heights, 175, 176, 178, 180, 181, 184, 192, 194, 197, 205, 208, 213, 216, 223, 231, 232, 238, 241, 242, 244, 245, 249, 257, 258, 260, 268, 272, 275, 283, 287, 288, 300, 301, 304, 316, 317, 322, 328, 341, 342, 344, 346, 348, 367, 370, 371, 376, 380, 384, 386, 393, 406, 408, 413, 423, 429, 432, 435, 446; mentioned as unit commander guarding the Convention, 186, 194, 271, 276, 305, 314, 365, 373, 380, 385, 417, 419, 433; mentioned as unit commander in New York campaign, 185, 193, 201, 210, 239, 256, 282, 304, 306, 321, 331, 371, 392, 402, 403, 409; draft of militia for Saratoga, 38, 99–100, *172*; on the New York campaign, 36, 38, 73, 77, 83–85, 88; officers in the home militia regiment of, 275, 316, 372; payment to the town of Stockbridge by, 442, *443*; portrait of, *228*; unit listings for, 474, 478, 480, 481, 488–489
BROOKS, ELEAZER, JR., **231**, 496, 498, 520
Brooks, Elizabeth. *See* Mason, Elizabeth (Brooks)
Brooks, Elizabeth (mother of ELEAZER), 230
Brooks, Elizabeth (Greenough), 231
Brooks, Elizabeth (Jones), 242
Brooks, Elizabeth (Potter), 239
BROOKS, EPHRAIM (Sr.), 12, 16, 184, **231–232**, 352, 508, 511, 514, 518, 526; family relationships of, *25*, 224, 225, 232, 233, 234, 236, 238, 239, 241, 242, 407, 408, 409, 459; unit listing for, 478
BROOKS, EPHRAIM, JR., 16, 68, 71, 73, 116, 120, 124, **232–233**, 507, 509, 512, 517, 518, 527; family relationships of, 23, *25*, 225, 231, 234, 237, 238, 242, 300, 301, 302, 303, 306, 328, 407, 408, 409, 459; unit listings for, 474, 476, 477, 478, 480, 487, 490, 491, 492, 493, 494, 496, 499
Brooks, Hannah (Dakin), *22*, 224, 239, 241, 459
Brooks, Hannah (Simonds), *24*, 234, 236, 238

Index

Brooks, Hebzibah. *See* Hartwell, Hebzibah (Brooks)
Brooks, Hephzibah. *See* Stone, Hephzibah (Brooks)
BROOKS, JOB, 92, 94, **233–234**, 408, 506, 509, 515, 518, 524, 529; family relationships of, 226, 230, 458; unit listings for, 478, 480, 481
Brooks, Job (father of ELEAZER), 230
Brooks, John, 391, **458**; family relationships of, 226, 234
Brooks, John (Maj.; Lt. Col.; Col.), 228, 501, 502, 503, 504; mentioned as unit commander, 366, 415, 418, 447
Brooks, John (of Acton), 239
BROOKS, JONAS, **234–235**, 302, 434, 506, 509, 514, 518, 528; family relationships of, *24*, 225, 226, 232, 233, 236, 238, 242, 407, 408, 409; house of, *236*; unit listing for, 498
Brooks, Jonathan (Capt.), 444
BROOKS, JOSHUA (Deacon), 15, **235–237**, 352, 391, 508, 511, 518, 526; family relationships of, *24*, 224, 225, 226, 231, 233, 234, 238, 239, 241, 242, 353, 407, 408, 409; house of, *236*; payment for accoutrements to, *237*; unit listings for, 477, 480, 505
Brooks, Joshua (father of JOSHUA (Deacon)), *24*, 231, 235, 236, 242; sale of a negro servant boy, 236, 240, 353, *354*, 463
BROOKS, JOSHUA, III. See BROOKS, JOSHUA, JR.
BROOKS, JOSHUA, JR., *11*, 126, 235, **237–238**, 507, 509, 512, 517, 518, 522, 526; family relationships of, *24*, 225, 226, 232, 233, 234, 235, 236, 242, 302, 353, 407, 408, 409; house of, 236; payment for accoutrements of, *237*; unit listings for, 473, 477, 478, 492, 505
Brooks, Judith (Foster), 239
Brooks, Levi, 227, **459**; family relationships of, 225, 226, 231, 233, 235, 237, 238, 242, 328, 407, 408, 409
Brooks, Lucy (Hoar), 226, 234
Brooks, Lydia (of Acton), 239
Brooks, Lydia (Stone), 459
Brooks, Lydia (Wheeler), *24*, 231, 236, 242
Brooks, Martha (Barrett), 238
Brooks, Mary (Munroe), 353, *354*. *See also* Wheeler, Mary (Munroe)
Brooks, Mary (Stone), *22*, 224, 242
Brooks, Mary (Taylor), 231
BROOKS, NOAH, 227, **238–239**, 415, 508, 510, 515, 518, 526; family relationships of, *22*, 224, 231, 236, 241, 242, 459; unit listings for, 478, 480
Brooks, Noah (father of Thomas), *22*, 459
BROOKS, PETER, xiv, 15, 94, 219, *220–221*, 222, **239–240**, 355, 396, 508, 511, 516, 520, 521, 530; unit listings for, 475, 481, 483. *See also* BOWES, PETER; NELSON, PETER
Brooks, Peter (of Acton), 239
Brooks, Rachel (Greenough), 235
Brooks, Rachel (Taylor), 242
Brooks, Sally (Davis). *See* Brooks, Sarah (Davis)

Brooks, Sarah (Davis), 238
Brooks, Sarah (Heywood), 225, 226, 231, 233, 459
Brooks, Sarah (Hildreth), 234
BROOKS, STEPHEN, 12, **240–241**, 507, 510, 516, 518, 530; family relationships of, *22*, 224, 232, 236, 239, 242, 459; unit listings for, 474, 481, 482, 485
BROOKS, STEPHEN [JR.], 132, **241–242**, 506, 509, 515, 518, 529; house of, *224*; family relationships of, *22*, 224, 239, 241; unit listings for, 478, 483, 497
Brooks, Susanna (Estabrook), 233
Brooks, Susanna (Foster), 328
Brooks, Thomas, 51, **459–460**; family relationships of, *22*, 224, 231, 236, 239, 241, 242, 459
BROOKS, TIMOTHY, 15, 219, 220, *221*, 222, **242**, 508, 510, 517, 518, 526; bill of sale or property to, *221*; family relationships of, *24*, 224, 225, 226, 227, 231, 233, 234, 236, 238, 239, 240, 241, 328, 407, 408, 409; unit listings for, 477, 478, 484, 505
Brooks Village (Lincoln, MA), 226
Brooksville, ME, 212, 528
Brown, Abigail. *See* Wesson, Abigail (Brown)
Brown, Abigail (mother of EPHRAIM), 246
Brown, Abishai (Capt.), 475; mentioned as unit commander, 58, 434
BROWN, BENJAMIN, **243–244**, 507, 509, 516, 518, 530; family relationships of, *25*, 193, 247, 250, 253; house of, *243*; unit listings for, 476, 477, 505
Brown, Benjamin (father of EBENEZER), 245
Brown, Betsey (Wyman), 246
BROWN, DANIEL, 8, *11*, 16, 97, 99, **244–245**, 385, 428, 506, 509, 513, 515, 518, 522, 530; family relationships of, *22*, *29*, 185, 191, 248, 250, 252, 323, 420; house of, *250*; unit listings for, 473, 478, 483
Brown, Daniel (of Stow), 244, 245
Brown, David (Capt.), 473; mentioned as unit commander, 12, 184, 191, 382
Brown, Desire, 247
BROWN, EBENEZER, *11*, **245**, 507, 509, 512, 514, 518, 527; unit listing for, 473
Brown, Elizabeth. *See* Coolidge, Elizabeth (Brown)
Brown, Elizabeth (Trask), 248
BROWN, EPHRAIM, **245–246**, 506, 509, 514, 518, 526; unit listing for, 478
Brown, Ephraim (of Townsend), 246
Brown, Eunice. *See* Farrar, Eunice (Brown); Lawrence, Eunice (Brown)
Brown, Francis (Capt.), 492; mentioned as unit commander, 180, 217, 238, 266, 321, 331, 336, 341, 348, 385, 394
BROWN, GEORGE, xv, 41, 71, 73, 92, 93, 108, 111, 114, 243, **246–247**, 250–251, 506, 509, 517, 518, 522, 524, 525, 529; family relationships of, *25*, 244, 250, 251, 253; house of, *243*; unit listings for, 476, 480, 482, 486, 488, 490, 500
Brown, Grace. *See* Wheat, Grace (Brown)
Brown, Hannah (Lee), 253

Brown, Isaac, *24*, 248
Brown, Jonas (of Stow), 245
BROWN, JOSEPH, 94, **247**, 507, 509, 516, 518, 530; unit listings for, 482, 484, 505
Brown, Joseph (father of EPHRAIM), 246
Brown, Joseph, Jr. (father of JOSEPH), 247
Brown, Lucy (Gearfield), *29*, 252
Brown, Lydia. *See* Wesson, Lydia (Brown)
Brown, Mary. *See* Allen, Mary (Brown); Bacon, Mary (Brown); Hartwell, Mary (Brown);
Brown, Mary (of Stow), 245
Brown, Mary (Balch), *24*, 248
Brown, Mary (Bridge), 248, 525
BROWN, MOSES (Capt.), 13, 15, 88, 93, **247–248**, 303, 507, 510, 512, 516, 519, 525, 527; family relationships of, *22*, *24*, 277, 278, 300, 383; portrait of, *248*; unit listings for, 475, 477, 481, 482
BROWN, NATHAN, JR., xiv, 8, *11*, 16, 94, 108, **249–252**, 428, 460, 507, 509, 512, 515, 518, 526; family relationships of, *22*, *29*, 185, 191, 244, 248, 291, 293, 323, 420; house of, *250*; unit listings for, 473, 478, 482, 484, 486
Brown, Nathan, Jr. (father of DANIEL; NATHAN, JR.), *29*, 244, 250
Brown, Nathan, Sr., xiv, 245, **460**; family relationships of, *24*, 245, 248, 249
Brown, Nathaniel (of Sudbury), 249
BROWN, NATHAN III. *See* BROWN, NATHAN, JR.
Brown, Phoebe. *See* Willington, Phoebe (Brown)
Brown, Rebecca. *See* Foster, Rebecca (Brown)
Brown, Rebeckah (Adams), *29*, 244, 250–251, 252
Brown, Rebeckah (Farrar), xv, *25*, 244, 247, 250–251, 253
Brown, Reuben (of Concord), 45
Brown, Sally (Brown), 247, 525
Brown, Sarah (Dakin), 245
Brown, Thankful. *See* Peirce, Thankful (Brown)
Brown, Timothy (father of BENJAMIN; GEORGE; TIMOTHY (Jr.)), *25*, 244, 247, 250
BROWN, TIMOTHY (Jr.), 99, 251, **252–253**, 385, 507, 510, 514, 518, 526; draft notice for, *253*; family relationships of, *25*, 193, 244, 247, 250; house of, *243*; unit listing for, 481
Bruce, Bethia. *See* Farrar, Bethia (Bruce)
Bruce, Elizabeth. *See* Sherman, Elizabeth (Bruce)
Bruce, Lucy. *See* Farrar, Lucy (Bruce)
Bruce, Mary. *See* More, Mary (Bruce)
Brunswick, NJ. *See* New Brunswick, NJ
Buck, Jonathan (Col.), 484; mentioned as unit commander, 203, 212
Buckland (Captain), 486, 487, 490, 491, 492, 494, 497; mentioned as unit commander, 262
Buckman, Betsey. *See* Parks, Betsey (Bucknam)

Buckminster, Lawson (Capt.), 37, 257, 496, 498; mentioned as unit commander, 181, 211, 274, 279, 315, 362, 419
Bucknam, Betsey. *See* Parks, Betsey (Bucknam)
Bucknam, Ruth. *See* Abbot, Ruth (Bucknam)
Bullard, Samuel (Col.), 37, 98, 100, 105, 108, 230, 485; mentioned as unit commander, 178, 194, 198, 201, 206, 225, 244, 249, 255, 257, 263, 270, 310, 317, 348, 371, 377, 385, 401, 419, 421, 424, 468
Bullard, Seth (Maj.), 498; mentioned as unit commander, 324
Bumstead, Thomas (Capt.), 483; mentioned as unit commander, 244, 414
Bunker Hill, Battle of, 56–59, *58 (map), 59*; personal accounts of, 189, 261, 269, 280, 320; underage fifers at, 13, 18; unit listings of individual participants in, 475-476
Burbeck, Henry (Capt.), 487, 490, 491, 492, 494; mentioned as unit commander, 414
Burgoyne, John (Gen.), invasion from Canada, 16, 96–98, *96 (map)*, 99–100, 101, 105–108, *106–107 (maps)*; surrender at Saratoga, 37, 107–108, *109*; 172, 468, 470; mentioned as being present at the surrender of, 178, 183, 201, 225, 238, 246, 255, 257, 262, 264, 268, 270, 276, 293, 299, 310, 314, 330, 331, 348, 353, 371, 375, 377, 378, 388, 435. *See also* Convention Army; Saratoga campaign; Saratoga Convention
Burt, James (Capt.), 180, 476; mentioned as unit commander, 323
BUSSELL, ISAAC, 41, 42, 120, 132, 136, 153, 155, **253–255**, 259, 507, 509, 512, 517, 520, 524, 528; in the Virginia campaign, 142, 143, 144, 146, 147, 149, 150, 152; unit listings for, 477, 483, 488, 491, 492, 493, 496, 498, 500, 502, 503, 504
Bussell, Prudence, 254
Bussell, Stephen, 255
Butler, Joseph (Capt.), 476, 477, 481, 482; mentioned as unit commander, 58, 232, 269, 338, 358, 398
Butler, Richard (Col.), 117
Butterfield, Isaac (Maj.), 202
Butters (Captain), 497; mentioned as unit commander, 203, 212
BUTTRICK, FRANCIS, **255–256**, 507, 510, 512, 515, 520, 527; unit listings for, 482, 485
Buttrick, Francis (father of FRANCIS), 255
Buttrick, Hannah (Gilson), 255
Buttrick, John (Maj.; Col.), 497; at Concord on April 19th, 45, 46, 47, 194, 382, 403; at Saratoga, 106, 276; mentioned as unit commander, 203, 204, 212, 309
Buttrick, Lydia (Howe), 256
Butts Hill, RI, 123, 124, 125, 332, 347. *See also* Rhode Island, Battle of

C

Cabot, Bulah (Munroe), *26*, 256
CABOT, EDWARD, 77, 87, **256**, 264, 508, 511, 516, 519, 530; family relationships of, 22, *26*, 345, 346, 347, 349; unit listings for, 475, 481, 489, 490
Calais, ME, 216
Cambridge, MA; Powder House Alarm at, 43; British retreat through, 53, 54; Provincial Army encamped at, 36, 38, 54–57, 60–61, 61, *62 (map)*, 64, 157–158; coastal defense at, 94; escort of the Convention Army to, 100, 106, 109; guarding the prisoners at, 19, 37, 114–115, 488–490; unit listings of individuals serving at, 475–477, 488–490. *See also* profiles of individuals serving at
Cambridgeport, MA, 18, 527
Camden, ME, 281, 528
Camden, SC, 134, 137, *138 (map)*
Camp Highlands (NY), 247, 435
Camp Mt. Washington, *272,* 338
Camp Orangetown (NY). *See* Orangetown
Camp Totoway (NJ), 204, 206, 211, 338, 340, 362, 388, 395, 405, 413, 435, 447, 448
Canaan, ME, 433
Canada, Campaign to, 19, 34, 35, 36, 38, 67–73; Arnold expedition to, 68, *69 (map)*, 232, 477; Battle of the Cedars, xvii, 19, 73, 201, 202; Battle of Quebec, 68, *70;* collapse of the Northern Army, 73–74; Lincoln's enlistment incentive for, 71, 184; Montgomery's expedition to Montreal, 67, 68, *69 (map)*; relief expeditions, 68, 71, *72 (map)*; unit listings of individuals serving in, 477, 479–480. *See also* profiles of individual participants
Canterbury, NH, 441, 444, 528
Cape Cod, 404, 522. *See also* Chatham, MA
Cape Finisterre, 449
Capes, Battle of the, *147 (map)*
Carleton, Guy (Gen.), 178, 205, 279, 334; command of the British army in Canada, 71, 72, 74, 76, 80, 89, 95, 96; winding down the war, 154, 155
Carlisle, MA, 331, 360; minute men and militia on April 19th, 46
Carpenter, Nathaniel (Capt.), 466
Carpenter, Thomas (Col.), 345
Carrol, Lydia. *See* Goodenow, Lydia (Carrol)
Cary, Eliphalet (Maj.), 498; mentioned as unit commander, 266, 307
Cary, Simeon (Col.), 61, 259
Castine, ME, 132, 207, 528
Castle William (Boston Harbor), 398, 484
Cato (slave of Duncan Ingraham), 222
Cavalry. *See* Dragoons
Cedars, Battle of the. *See* Canada, Campaign to
Chadd's Ford, PA, 101–104, *102, 103 (map)*
Chambers, Matthew (Capt. Lieut.; Capt.), 497, 499; mentioned as unit commander, 358, 435
Chambers, Susanna. *See* Barrett, Susanna (Chambers)
Champlain Valley, 128, 263, 281, 356. See also Canada, campaign to; Saratoga campaign
Charleston, SC, 133, 137, *138 (map)*, 144, 154, *155,* 262, 307
Charlestown, MA, 30, *62 (map)*, 158, 190, 195, 402, 409, 454; British retreat through, 54-56, 272; Powder House Alarm, 43, 48, 164. *See also* Bunker Hill, Battle of
Charlestown, NH, 20, 294, 367, 375
Charlotte, NC, 139
Charlottesville, VA, 115, 144, *145 (map)*, 274
Charter. *See* Massachusetts Charter of 1629; Massachusetts Charter of 1691
Charter Rights and Privileges, 3–7, *6,* 21, 169
Chatham, MA, 18, 183
Chatham, NJ, 273
Chatterton's Hill, 83, *85 (map)*, 87, 185
Chelmsford, MA, 394, 408, 462; minute men and militia on April 19th, 46, 51, 467
Chelsea Creek; Battle of, 56–57, *57 (map)*
Chenery, Ephraim (Capt.), 474; mentioned as unit commander, 324
Chesapeake Bay, 101, *147 (map)*, 150
Chester, PA, 104
Chester, VT, 317, 318, 319, 529
CHILD, ABEL, 79, **257**, 506, 509, 516, 518, 529; family relationships of, 258; unit listings for, 478, 480, 485, 495
Child, Abigail (Winch), 260
Child, Abijah (Capt.), 476, 479, 486, 487; mentioned as unit commander, 55, 68, 200, 201, 258, 261, 286, 290, 295, 309, 320, 322, 325, 357, 386, 387, 388, 416, 446
CHILD, AMOS, 258, 507, 510, 514, 518, 530; family relationships of, 257; unit listing for, 478
Child, Anna (Hosmer), 259
Child, Beriah (Bemis), 460
CHILD, DANIEL, 8, 11, 16, 52, 60, 61, 68, 71, 184, **258–259**, 507, 509, 512, 516, 518, 530; family relationships of, 27, 259, 261, 332; unit listings for, 473, 475, 479, 496, 498
Child, David, 460
CHILD, ELIJAH, 231, **259–260**, 434, 506, 509, 514, 515, 518, 530; family relationships of, 27, 261; unit listings for, 493, 498
CHILD, ELISHA, 260, 507, 510, 514, 518, 527; unit listing for, 478
Child, Elisha (father of ELISHA), 260
Child, Elizabeth (Hammond), 261
Child, Grace (Bemis), 27, 259, 261
Child, Hannah, 257, 258
Child, Isaac, 257, 258
Child, Joshua (Sr.), **460**; family relationships of, 27, 259, 261
CHILD, JOSHUA, JR., xv, 8, *11,* 15, 16, 36, 97, 98, 99, **260–261**, 310, 460, 507, 510, 514, 518, 526; family relationships of, 27, 259; payment for accoutrements of, *261;* unit listings for, 473, 478
Child, Mary (Knight), 259
Child, Mary (Wheeler), 260
Child, Molley (Mathis), 27, 259
Child, Polly (Lewis), 257

Child, Sarah. *See* Hagar, Sarah (Child)
Childs. *See* Child
Church, Benjamin (Dr.), 163
Cilley, Joseph (Col.), 116, 117, 119, 486, 487, 490, 491, 494, 497; mentioned as unit commander, 200, 309, 325
Clap, Daniel (Maj.), 490; mentioned as unit commander, 365
Claremont, NH, 262
Clark, Jonas (Rev.), 161, 163
Clark, Lois. *See* Peirce, Lois (Clark)
Clarke, Sarah. *See* Thorning, Sarah (Clarke)
Claverack, NY, 132, 199, 203, 204, 212, 242, 280, 307, 327, 402, 409, 419, 497
Clayes, Peter (Capt. Lieut.), 500; mentioned as unit commander, 435
CLEAVELAND, BENJAMIN, 15, 42, 59, 95, 101, 104, 119, 121, 129, 130, 139, 141, 146, 149, 152, 154, 155, 255, 259, **261–262**, 322, 325, 507, 509, 513, 517, 520, 522, 525, 529; unit listings for, 476, 486, 487, 490, 491, 492, 494, 497, 499, 502, 503, 505
Cleaveland, Benjamin (father of BENJAMIN), 262
Cleaveland, Jerusha (Round), 262
Cleaveland, Sarah (Stratton), 262, 525
Clinton, Henry (Gen.), 46, 58, 60, 76, 154, 156; initiatives in the Hudson Valley, 128, 129, 131, 132, 135; war in the south, 137, 143, 144, 150, 154
Closson, Mary. *See* Billing, Mary (Closson)
Coastal defense, 34, 94, 156; mentioned as type of service, 248, 253, 314, 317, 319; unit listings of individuals serving on, 477, 482–483, 484, 493–494
COCKRAN, BACCHUS, **263**, 508, 511, 516, 520, 521, 530; unit listing for, 502
Codman House, 12, 95, 295, 454
Coercive Acts, 6, 7, 41, 383
Cogswell (Colonel), 494; mentioned as unit commander, 317, 379
Colborn. *See* Colburn
Colbourn. *See* Colburn
Colburn, Elizabeth (Gleason), 264
Colburn, Jane (Stratton), 265
COLBURN, JOSEPH, 99, **263–264**, 506, 509, 513, 516, 519, 524, 526; family relationships of, 265, 387, 396, 397; gravestone of, *263*; unit listings for, 483, 484, 485, 489
COLBURN, NATHANIEL, 97, 99, **265**, 363, 507, 510, 514, 519, 527; family relationships of, 263, 264, 387, 396, 397; unit listings for, 483, 484
Colburn, Nathaniel, Jr., 264, 265, 396, 397
Colburn, Tabitha (Headley), 264, 265, 396, 397
Cole, John, 433, 434
Colebrook, NH, 272, 528
Columbia, ME, 254, 255
Commander-in-Chief's Guard. *See* Washington, George (Gen.), Life Guard of
Committee of Correspondence. *See* Lincoln, MA, Committee of Correspondence of; Northborough, MA, Committee of Correspondence of
Committee of Safety, 54, 449, 452
Conant, Abigail, 266
Conant, Deborah, 266
CONANT, JOHN, **266**, 507, 510, 512, 514, 515, 520, 527; unit listings for, 474, 477, 479, 492, 498, 501
Conant, John (of Townsend), 266
Conant, John (father of JOHN), 266
Conant, John (father of John Conant of Townsend), 266
Conant, Kezia. *See* Adams, Kezia (Conant)
Conant, Sarah (Farrar) (mother of John Conant of Townsend), 266
Conant, Sarah (Farrar) (wife of John Conant of Townsend), 267
Concord, MA; feud with Acton, 48, 161; feud with Lexington, 159, 160, 162; Meriam's Corner, *50 (map)*, 51, 164; minute men and militia at, vii–viii, 12–13, 36, 44–45, 46, *47*; North Bridge fight, *vi*, vii, xiii, 45–49, *47*, 55; North Bridge removed, 159; supplies stored at, 43–44; unit listings of participants at, 473–474. *See also* April 19, 1775; Lexington and Concord, Second Battle of; profiles of individual participants
Concord, NH, 464
Concord, VT, 183
Concord Alarm. *See* April 19, 1775
Connecticut River, 375
Connecticut Valley, 294
Constitutional Convention. *See* Massachusetts Constitutional Convention
Constitution Island (NY), 131, 441
Continental Army; unit listings of individual soldiers in, 479–482, 485–488, 490–505. *See also* profiles of individual soldiers; specific campaigns and battles
Continental currency. *See* Currency
Continental Village (NY), 126, 127 (map), 131, 347
Convention Army, 37; escort to Cambridge of, 108–109; guarding at Cambridge of, 109–110, 114–115; unit listings of individual guards of, 488–490. *See also* Burgoyne, John (Gen.); profiles of individual guards; Saratoga campaign
Conway, MA, 427
Coolidge, Anna. *See* Harrington, Anna (Coolidge)
Coolidge, Elizabeth. *See* Hoar, Elizabeth (Coolidge)
Coolidge, Elizabeth (Brown), *23*, 267
COOLIDGE, JOHN, 23, 64, **267**, 506, 509, 514, 515, 520, 527; family relationships of, *23*, 299; unit listing for, 474, 479, 493, 498
Coolidge, Thankful. *See* Parks, Thankful (Coolidge)
Coolidge, William (Capt.), *23*, 267
Cooper, James (Capt.); mentioned as detachment commander, 206, 211, 362, 395, 413, 435, 447
Coos, NH, 366, 500
Cornwall, England, 449, 450
Cornwallis, Charles (Gen.), 91; campaign in the Carolinas, 137–142, *138 (map)*, *141 (map)*; campaign in Virginia, 143–145, *145 (map)*; at Yorktown, 146–152; surrender of, 152, 153, 154, 227, 254
Cornwallis, Lord. *See* Cornwallis, Charles (Gen.)
Cotton, Theophilus (Col.), 345
Cowdin, Thomas (Capt.), 497; mentioned as unit commander, 307, 327
Cowdry, Nathaniel (Capt.), 424
Cowpens (SC), Battle of, 139–141, *140*, 146, 262
Craft, Abner (Capt.), 476, 479; mentioned as unit commander, 336
Craft, Thomas (Col.), 482, 483; mentioned as unit commander, 263, 344, 384, 385, 386, 414, 424
Crane, Abner (Capt.), 496; mentioned as unit commander, 426
Crane, John (Col.), 486, 487, 490, 491, 492, 494, 497, 499, 502; mentioned as unit commander, 101, 121, 180, 196, 261, 414
Cranston, Amasa (Capt.), 402
Crispus (slave of Ephraim Hartwell), 465
Crosby, Hannah. *See* Rice, Hannah (Crosby)
Crosby, Josiah (Capt.), 476; mentioned as unit commander, 189
Crosby, Nicholas (Capt.), 488; mentioned as unit commander, 254
Crown Point, NY, *67*, 73, 81, *89*
Crown Point expedition. *See* French & Indian War
Cudworth, Nathaniel (Capt.), 473; mentioned as unit commander, 279, 397
Cuming, Brister, xiv, 309, 310. *See also* Freeman, Brister
Cuming, John (Dr.), xiv, 222, 309, 310
Cuming, Squire. *See* Cuming, John (Dr.)
Currency; Colonial, 340; Continental, 340; hard, 30, 33; inflation of, 30, 32, 35, 327; paper money as, 30, 31, 33, 340; specie, 31
Curtis (Captain), 322
Cushing, Job (Col.), 486; mentioned as unit commander, 281, 345
Cushing, Nathaniel (Capt.), 502; mentioned as unit commander, 254
Cutler, Anna (Whitney), 23, 451, 453, 454
CUTLER, EBENEZER, 15, 428, **450–452**, 519; family relationships of, *23*, 340, 451, 453
Cutler, Ebenezer (father of EBENEZER; ZACCHEUS), *23*, 451, 453, 454
Cutler, Ebenezer (of Salem and Sutton), 451, 454
Cutler, Hazadiah (Eager), 451, 454
Cutler, Mary. *See* Meriam, Mary (Cutler)
Cutler, Mary (Hicks), 452
Cutler, Mary (Stockwell), 451, 454
Cutler, Miriam (Eager), 451, 454
Cutler, Thomas, 410, 413
CUTLER, ZACCHEUS, 15, 428, **452–454**, 519; house of, *453*; family relationships of, *23*, 340, 451

Cutter, Lucy. *See* Willington, Lucy (Cutter)

D

Dakin, Amos, 269
Dakin, Bathsheba. *See* Brooks, Bathsheba (Dakin)
Dakin, Elizabeth (Billing), 226, 269
Dakin, Hannah. *See* Brooks, Hannah (Dakin)
Dakin, Mary (Heald), *22*, 269
Dakin, Mercy (Heald). *See* Dakin, Mary (Heald)
Dakin, Samuel (Sr.), **460–461**; family relationships of, *22*, 268, 269
DAKIN, SAMUEL, JR., *10*, 44, 94, 105, **268–269**, 507, 510, 515, 512, 518, 527; family relationships of, *22*, 224, 226, 239, 241, 245, 459, 460–461; unit listings for, 473, 478, 484, 485, 505
Dakin, Sarah. *See* Brown, Sarah (Dakin)
Dakin, Thankful Sarah (Minot), 269
Dakin, Timothy, 269
Dana (Colonel), 289, 422
Danbury, CT, *92*, 128, 234
Danforth, Sarah. *See* Allen, Sarah (Danforth)
Danvers, MA; minute men and militia on April 19th, 13
Davis, Isaac (Capt.), 46, *47*, 48, 161, 382
Davis, Sally. *See* Brooks, Sarah (Davis)
Davis, Sarah. *See* Brooks, Sarah (Davis)
Dawes, William, 7
de Barras, Comte (Adm.), 146
de Berniere, Henry (Ens.), 464
de Grasse, Comte (Adm.), 146, *147 (map)*, 150
Dean, Isaac (Col.), 463
Deane (frigate, privateer), 444, 504
Dearborn, Henry (Col.), 503, 504; mentioned as unit commander, 339, 441
Declaration of Independence, 74
Dedham, MA, 341
Deerfield, MA, 467
Deer Isle, ME, 204, 208, 212
Defence (privateer), 248
Delaware River; Washington's crossing of, *92*, *93 (map)*, 248, 338, 388, 399. *See also* Trenton (NJ), Battle of
Denny, Samuel (Col.), 497; mentioned as unit commander, 203, 204, 212, 242, 280, 307, 327, 402, 409, 419
Depositions; of April 1775, 55–56, 174, 184, 188, 284, 319–320, 407, 440; of 1825, 159
Desertion, 19, 100, 111, 114, 143, 522; individual reports of, 180, 196, 245, 246, 247, 255, 295, 335, 355–357, 389–390, 418
d'Estaing, Comte (Adm.), 120, 121, 126
Diamond, H.M.S. (British frigate), 404
Dickenson, Reuben (Capt.), 178, 411
Digby Township, Annapolis County, Nova Scotia, 452
Dike, Nicholas (Col.), 37, 483; mentioned as unit commander, 173, 180, 182, 194, 198, 216, 225, 239, 241, 244, 270, 301, 302, 304, 310, 314, 319, 320, 331, 346, 357, 376, 384, 392, 394, 402, 410, 419, 443, 483

Dix, John (Lt.), 489; mentioned as unit commander, 279
Dix, Nathan (Capt.), 495, 498, 500; mentioned as unit commander, 199, 215, 337, 338, 385
Dodge, Elizabeth, 288
Dodge, William, 288
Doolittle, Amos, vi, x
Doolittle Engravings, vi, x
Doolittle, Ephraim (Col.), 474; mentioned as unit commander, 299,
Dorchester, MA, 18, 19, 36, 37, 54, *62*, 64, 65, 94; unit listings of individual soldiers at, 483–484. *See also* profiles of individual participants
Dorchester Heights, MA, fortification of, 12, 16, 33, 36, 41, 61–66, *62*, 73, 97, 105; unit listings of individual soldiers at, 478–479. *See also* profiles of individual participants
Dover, ME, 200, 528
Dover, NH, 254, 309
Draft, 35, 97, 99, 333; draft notice, *253*. *See also* Enlistment; Troop calls
Dragoons (cavalry), 19, 84, 86, 101, 112, 117, 140, 141, 228, 400
Drury, Asa (Capt.), 501; mentioned as unit commander, 179, 413, 435
Dryer, John (Lt.), 345
Dublin, NH, 436
Dudley, Abigail. *See* Tower, Abigail (Dudley)
Dudley, Eunice. *See* Baker, Eunice (Dudley)
Dunbar, William (Lt.), 498; mentioned as unit commander, 266,
Durfee, Joseph (Col.), 186
Durham, CT, 203, 529
Dustin, Moody (Capt.), 504; mentioned as unit commander, 441,

E

Eager, Fortunatus (Capt.), 214
Eager, Hazadiah. *See* Cutler, Hazadiah (Eager)
Eager, Miriam. *See* Cutler, Miriam (Eager)
East Greenwich, RI, 324, 493
East Sudbury, MA, 280, 312, 340, 341, 367, 398, 438, 470. *See also* Wayland, MA
Eaton, Abigail. *See* Billing, Abigail (Eaton)
Eaton, Eunice. *See* Bond, Eunice (Eaton)
Economic impact of the war, 30–33
Edgel, Simon (Capt.), 382, 474; mentioned as unit commander, 294
Edwards, Mary. *See* Adams, Mary (Edwards)
Eighteenth-century practices; of military, xiv–xvi; naming conventions in, xiii–xiv; record keeping in, xvi–xvii; spelling variations in, xiii
Elliot, Susannah. *See* Meriam, Susannah (Elliot)
Ellis, Hannah. *See* Hagar, Hannah (Ellis)
Ellis, John (Capt.), 498; mentioned as unit commander, 324
Emerson, William (Rev.), 60–61, 227
Englishtown, NJ, 116, 118

Enlistment; bounties, 32, 34, 35, 71, 75, 261, 309, 325, 390; economic incentive for, 32–33, 333; extra bounties for Canada, 71, 184; quotas, 32, 36, 95, 230; substitution, xv–xvi, 36, 97, 99–100, 333; under-age 13–14, 39, 364. *See also* Draft; Troop calls
Enos, Roger (Col.), 232
Enosburg, VT, 198, 529
Erving, MA, 290, 527
Essex County, MA, 173, 357
Estabrook, Susanna. *See* Brooks, Susanna (Estabrook)
Evelyth, Mary. *See* Adams, Mary (Evelyth)

F

Fairbanks, Amos (Lt.), 486; mentioned as unit commander, 281
Fairfield, CT, 92, 199, 208, 408, 414, 481
Fairfield, ME, 200
Families; extended relationships of, 21–30; split loyalties of, 16, 190, 323, 428–429
Farmington, ME, 174, 319, 528
Farrar, Abigail (Worcester), 280
Farrar, Anna (Bancroft), 279
Farrar, Bethiah (Bruce), 270, 271
Farrar, Catherine (Moor), 280
FARRAR, DANIEL, 58, 100, **269–270**, 337, 507, 509, 515, 516, 518, 529; family relationships of, 271, 274, 280; unit listings for, 474, 476, 483, 485, 490
Farrar, Daniel (father of DANIEL), 270, 271, 274, 280
Farrar, Daniel (of Concord), 270
Farrar, Daniel (of Sudbury), 270
Farrar, Elisabeth. *See* Billing, Elisabeth (Farrar)
Farrar, Elizabeth. *See* Billing, Elizabeth (Farrar)
Farrar, Eunice (Brown), *24*, 249, 277, 323, 462
Farrar, Eunice (Sherman), 280
FARRAR, GEORGE, **271**, 506, 509, 516; family relationships of, *25*, 270, 274, 280; unit listings for, 480, 485, 488, 501
Farrar, George (father of HUMPHREY), 272
Farrar, Hannah. *See* Billing, Hannah (Farrar)
Farrar, Hannah (mother of Daniel Farrar of Sudbury), 270
FARRAR, HUMPHREY, 8, *10*, **271–272**, 273, 274, 462, 507, 510, 515, 518, 528; family relationships of, *25*, 216, 217, 218, 244, 276, 277, 278, 461; unit listings for, 473, 477, 478, 482
FARRAR, JACK, 41, 60, 133, **272–274**, 394, 508, 511, 517, 520, 521, 527; Continental Army service of, 76, 95, 111, 119, 120, 132; name change upon manumission of, xiv, 221, *273*; probate record for, *273*; unit listings for, 477, 481, 482, 486, 488, 490, 491, 492, 493, 496, 498, 500. *See also* FREEMAN, JACK
Farrar, Jacob, 269
FARRAR, JOHN. *See* FARRAR, JACK
Farrar, Josiah, 270
Farrar, Love. *See* Meloney, Love (Farrar)

Farrar, Lucy (Bruce), 270, 271
Farrar, Lucy (Farrar), *25*, 272
Farrar, Lydia. *See* Bond, Lydia (Farrar)
Farrar, Lydia (Barrett), *25*, 276, 277, 278, 461
Farrar, Marcy (Hoar), *25*, 276
Farrar, Mary (mother of Daniel Farrar of Concord), 269
Farrar, Mary (Allen), 270, 271, 274, 280
Farrar, Mary (Barrett), *25*, 272
Farrar, Mary (Howe), 461

FARRAR, ZEBEDIAH, 51, 132, 178, 205, 246, **279–280**, 332, 507, 509, 512, 516, 519, 527; family relationships of, 270, 271, 274, 337; unit listings for, 473, 478, 480, 485, 489, 493, 496, 497
Faugason, Anna. *See* Parks, Anna (Faugason)
Faugason, Rhoda. *See* Parks, Rhoda (Faugason)
Faulkner, Francis (Lt. Col.; Col.), 183, 264, 338, 379
Fay, Anna (Gleason), 281
Fay, Hannah (Billing), 281
Fay, Mary. *See* Whitney, Mary (Fay)
FAY, SILAS, **280–281**, 507, 510, 512, 516, 519, 524, 528; family relationships of,

195, 196, 197, 198, 441, 442, 444; unit listings for, 474, 476, 486
Fay, Silas (father of SILAS), 281
FIELD, NATHAN, **281**, 505, 508, 511, 516, 520, 530
First blood shed in the Revolutionary War, 350, 352
Fishkill, NY, 19, 35, 37, 38, 126, 128, 204, 280, 335, 494, 495; mentioned as a nine-month man at, 201, 215, 217, 230, 326–327, 330, 338–339, 344, 348, , 412

See also Fiske
, DAVID, 8, *11*, 87, **281–282**, 392, , 508, 510, 512, 514, 519, 526; fam- relationships of, 22, *30*, 188, 291, ; unit listings for, 473, 481
Jonathan (Capt.), 478; mentioned nit commander, 201, 283
Lydia. *See* Willington, Lydia (Fisk)
Mary. *See* Weston, Mary (Fisk)
Polly. *See* Parker, Polly (Fisk); ston, Mary (Fisk)
Rebekah (Gearfield), *30*, 282
. *See also* Fisk
, Mary. *See* Hagar, Mary (Fiske)
, Susanna. *See* Monroe, Susanna tch)
, Zachariah (Capt.), 480; mentioned nit commander, 178, 179, 205, 246, , 332
burg, MA, 191, 192, 323, 334, 341, 527
William, NH, 270, 271
g, Dorothy. *See* Allen, Dorothy (Flagg)
g, Elizabeth. *See* Nelson, Elizabeth agg)
her, Benjamin (Capt.), 500; men- ned as unit commander, 179
TCHER, LUKE, 112, 119, 120, 124, 2, 133, **282–283**, 508, 511, 516, 520,); unit listings for, 485, 487, 490, 491, 2, 494, 495, 496, 499
cher, Martha. *See* Whitney, Martha etcher)
NT, ABEL, 64, **283**, 506, 509, 514, 519, 6; family relationships of, *26*, 285, 6, 306, 331, 342, 431, 434; unit list- ; for, 478
t, Abigail. *See* Wheeler, Abigail lint)
t, Catherine (Fox), 285
NT, EPHRAIM, 8, *11*, 53, 55, 56, **283–** 6, 399, 507, 510, 514, 518, 526; family relationships of, 283, 286, 306, 331, 342, 431, 434; house of, *285*; unit listings for, 475, 476, 478, 481
Flint, Ephraim (father of ABEL; EPHRAIM; JOHN), *26*, 283, 285, 286
Flint, Esther (Fuller), 286
FLINT, JOHN, 55, 73, **286**, 507, 509, 512, 516, 518, 529; family relationships of, *26*, 283, 285, 306, 331, 342, 431, 434; unit listings for, 475, 476, 479, 481
Flint, Lucy. *See* Mason, Lucy (Flint)
Flint, Mary. *See* Hartwell, Mary (Flint)
Flint, Rebecca (Wright), 286
Flint, Ruth (Wheeler), *26*, 283, 285, 286, 342
Folly Pond (Lincoln, MA), 158

Fort Clinton (NY), 126, *127 (map)*, 129 *(map)*, 135, 423, 440
Fort Constitution, 126
Fort Drummer. *See* King George's War
Fort Edward (NY), 37, 96, 98, 238, 268, 276, 330, 331, 353
Fort Independence (NY), 74, *75 (map)*, 76, 126
Fort Lafayette. *See* Verplanck's Point, NY
Fort Lee, NJ, 76, *83 (map)*, 91, 481
Fort No. 2 (Cambridge, MA), 279
Fort Stanwix (NY), *96 (map)*, 98
Fort Ticonderoga. *See* Ticonderoga, NY
Fort Washington (NY), 76, *83 (map)*, 91
Foster, Abigail. *See* Allen, Abigail (Foster)
Foster, Abraham (Capt.), 424
Foster, Elizabeth (Storey), *27*, 287
FOSTER, JACOB, *11*, 65, 192, **287**, 288, 507, 510, 514, 515, 519, 528; family relationships of, 22, *26*, 192, 288, 328; unit listings for, 473, 478, 490
FOSTER, JOHN, **288**, 289, 508, 511, 514, 520, 530; unit listing for, 478
Foster, Jonathan (brother of JACOB), *27*, 288
Foster, Jonathan (father of JACOB), 287
Foster, Judith. *See* Brooks, Judith (Foster)
Foster, Rebecca (Brown), 251, 288
Foster, Sarah. *See* Abbot, Sarah (Foster)
Foster, Sarah (Wheeler), *26*, 287
Foster, Solomon, 250, 251, 288
Foster, Susanna. *See* Mason, Susanna (Foster)
Fox, Abigail. *See* Weston, Abigail (Fox)
Fox, Anna. *See* Weston, Anna (Fox)
Fox, Catherine. *See* Flint, Catherine (Fox)
Fox, Jonathan (Capt.), 392
Fox, Joseph (Capt.), 487, 490, 491, 492, 494, 496, 499; mentioned as unit com- mander, 233
Fox, Nancy. *See* Weston, Anna (Fox)
Fox, Ruth. *See* Wheeler, Ruth (Fox)
Framingham, MA, 179, 181, 248, 257, 295, 341, 358, 422, 527; minute men and militia on April 19th, 13, 51, 294, 382, 474
France. *See* French alliance
Free, Jupiter, 236, **462–463**
Freeman, Brister, xiv, 222, 309, 310
FREEMAN, JACK, 502. *See also* FARRAR, JACK
Freeman's Farm, Battle of. *See* Saratoga campaign
Freetown, MA, 186, 262
French alliance, 41, 114, 115, 120, 144; French fleet at Rhode Island, 120–124, *122–123*, 126; French fleet in the Ches- apeake, 142, 146, *147 (map)*, 148, 149, 150; French assistance at Yorktown, 146–152, *147 (map)*, *148 (map)*
French and Indian War, 4, 9, 74; men- tioned as veteran of, 208, 217, 231, 277, 337, 416, 436, 444, 445, 463; served on the Crown Point Expedition, 231, 444
French, Thomas (Capt.), 486; mentioned as unit commander, 427
Frothingham, Benjamin (Capt.), 487, 490, 491, 492, 494, 497, 499; mentioned as unit commander, 180

Frye, Isaac (Capt.), 503, 504; mentioned as unit commander, 339, 441
Fuller, Edward (Capt.), 493; mentioned as unit commander, 371, 422
Fuller, Esther. *See* Flint, Esther (Fuller)
Fuller, Joseph (Capt.), 485; mentioned as unit commander, 401, 402, 468
Fuller, Nathan (Capt.), 476, 477, 479; mentioned as unit commander, 55, 68, 243, 246, 289, 290, 355, 365, 366, 370, 373, 374, 377, 423, 437, 469
Furnivall, James (Lt.; Capt. Lt.), 201, 468

G

Gage, Isaac (Capt.), 95, 153, **289**, 507, 509, 512, 516, 518, 530; family relationships of, 290; mentioned as unit commander, 375, 422; unit listings for, 473, 476, 486, 487, 494, 501
Gage, Jonathan, 128, 131, 133, **290**, 507, 509, 512, 517, 518, 522, 524, 527; family relationships of, 289; unit listings for, 473, 476, 486, 487, 494, 497, 499
Gage, Jonathan (father of Jonathan), 290
Gage, Mary (Allen), 289
Gage, Mary (Brigham), 290
Gage, Robert, 289
Gage, Ruth (Underwood), 290
Gage, Susannah (Smith), 289
Gage, Thomas (Gen.), 6, 9, 43, 44, 46, 56, 163, 428, 464
Gale, Eunice. *See* Allen, Eunice (Gale)
Gardner, Thomas (Col.), 474, 476; mentioned as unit commander, 201, 243, 246, 267, 286, 336, 365, 366, 377, 416, 417, 423, 437, 469
Garfield. *See also* Gearfield
Garfield, Abigail. *See* Parks, Abigail (Garfield)
Garfield, James A. (President), 291, 293
Garfield, Lydia. *See* Parks, Lydia (Garfield)
Garfield, Mary. *See* Wheeler, Mary (Garfield)
Garfield, Solomon, **292–293**, 507, 510, 512, 514, 519, 530; family relationships of, 22, *30*, 213, 252, 282, 291, 292, 469; house of, *293*; unit listings for, 475, 486
Gates, Horatio (Gen.), 80; at Camden, 137, *138 (map)*; mentioned as commanding the Northern Department, 177, 178, 183, 198, 201, 205, 216, 230, 238, 268, 270, 293, 299, 310, 314, 321, 329, 331, 353, 378, 408, 412, 419, 443; in the Saratoga campaign, *96 (map)*, 100, 104–107, *106–107 (map)*, *109*, 172
Gates, Persis. *See* Rice, Persis (Gates)
Gearfield. *See also* Garfield
Gearfield, Abraham, 8, *11*, **291**, 507, 510, 514, 518, 523, 526; deposition of, 55, 188, 291; family relationships of, 22, *30*, 213, 252, 282, 292, 293, 469; house of, *293*; unit listing for, 474. *See also* Depositions of April 1775
Gearfield, Anna. *See* Billing, Anna (Gearfield); Peirce, Anna (Gearfield)
Gearfield, Elisha, 75, **291**, 352, 508, 511, 514, 518, 527; family relationships of, 22, *30*, 213, 292, 293, 433, 469; farm of, *14*; unit listing for, 480
Gearfield, John, *11*, 94, **292**, 507, 509, 514, 518, 528; family relationships of, *30*, 213, 291, 293, 433, 469; payment for service of, *292*; unit listings for, 484, 486
Gearfield, John (father of John), *30*, 292
Gearfield, Lucy. *See* Brown, Lucy (Gearfield)
Gearfield, Lucy (Smith), 292
Gearfield, Mercy (Bigelow), *30*, 291
Gearfield, Rebeka (Johnson), *30*, 291, 293
Gearfield, Rebekah. *See* Fisk, Rebekah (Gearfield)
Gearfield, Sarah (Stimpson), 293
Gearfield, Susanna (Bemis), 291
Gearfield, Thankful (Stowell), *30*, 292
Gearfield, Thomas (father of Abraham; Solomon), *30*, 293
Gearfield, Thomas (father of Elisha), *30*, 291
General Court. *See* Massachusetts General Court
Germain, Lord George, 100, 143
German, NY, 262
German soldiers, 84, 97, 98, 100, 108, 115, 133, 152; mentioned as prisoners held in Cambridge, 186, 191, 193, 195, 206, 209, 264, 270, 274, 356, 380, 401, 417, 425, 432, 436, 470. *See also* Hessians
Germantown, PA; Battle of, 104
Gerrish, Jacob (Col.), 489, 490, 497; mentioned as unit commander, 173, 199, 206, 209, 274, 279, 357, 409, 424, 436
Gibbs, Caleb (Capt.), 481, 482; mentioned as unit commander, 400
Gibbs, Lois. *See* Parks, Lois (Gibbs)
Gibbs, Sarah. *See* Parks, Sarah (Gibbs)
Gilbert, William, **293–294**, 508, 511, 516, 520, 530; unit listings for, 488, 495, 497, 500
Gilman, Andrew (Lt.), 483; mentioned as unit commander, 253
Gilman, Jeremiah (Capt.), 477, 481, 482; mentioned as unit commander, 358, 388
Gilson, Hannah. *See* Buttrick, Hannah (Gilson)
Gleason, Anna. *See* Fay, Anna (Gleason)
Gleason, Elizabeth. *See* Colburn, Elizabeth (Gleason)
Gleason, John (Capt.), 485; mentioned as unit commander, 279, 295
Gloucester, VA. *See* Yorktown, VA
Glover, John (Col.; Gen.), 86, 88, 91, 124, 248, 477, 481, 482; escort of prisoners to Cambridge, 108, 109, 210, 230, 276; mentioned as unit commander, 248, 322
Glover, John, Jr. (Capt.), 322
Goffe, Hannah. *See* Knowlton, Hannah (Goffe)
Goodenough, Isaac. *See* Goodenow, Isaac
Goodenow, Isaac, 51, 88, **294–295**, 506, 509, 513, 516, 520, 524, 526; unit listings for, 474, 476, 481, 482, 485
Goodenow, Isaac (father of Isaac), 295
Goodenow, Lydia (Carrol), 295
Goodenow, Martha (Hunt), 295
Goodenow, Sarah. *See* Wheeler, Sarah (Goodenow)
Goodwin, David (Capt.), 494; mentioned as unit commander, 317, 379
Goodwin, Nathaniel (Capt.), 345
Gorden, John, 128, **295**, 322, 325, 508, 511, 516, 520, 522, 530; unit listings for, 486, 487
Gove, [unidentified], **296**, 508, 511, 515, 520, 521, 531; unit listing for, 482
Gove, Elizabeth (Adams), 297
Gove, John (Deacon), **463–464**; family relationships of, 296, 297
Gove, John (son of John (Deacon)), 296, 463
Gove, Jonathan, 296, 463
Gove, Lydia. *See* Willington, Lydia (Gove)
Gove, Nathaniel, 8, *11*, **297**, 507, 510, 514, 519, 527; family relationships of, 179, 180, 296, 463; unit listing for, 473
Gove, Tabitha (Livermore), 296, 297, 463, 464
Governor's Island, MA, 260, 493
Governor's Island, NY, 76, 77, 326, 481
Grafton, MA, 350
Grant, Sallie. *See* Smith, Sarah (Grant)
Grant, Sarah. *See* Smith, Sarah (Grant)
Graves, Hepsibah. *See* Mead, Hepsibah (Graves)
Graves, Katherine. *See* Russell, Katherine (Graves)
Graves, Thomas (Adm.), *147 (map)*
Greaton, John (Col.), 479, 486, 487, 494, 497, 499, 501, 502, 503, 504; mentioned as unit commander, xvii, 187, 200, 261, 289, 290, 295, 309, 322, 325, 336, 357, 375, 386, 387, 388, 389, 440, 446
Green, Francis (Capt.), 503, 504
Greene, Nathanael (Gen.), 60, 114, 124, 135, 139, *141 (map)*, 153, 154, 262
Greenough, Elizabeth. *See* Brooks, Elizabeth (Greenough)
Greenwich, CT, 79, 185
Greenwich, H.M.S. (British store-ship), 449
Greenwich, MA, 389
Greenwood, Miles (Capt.), 489; mentioned as unit commander, 357
Griffith, Joseph (Capt.) 492; mentioned as unit commander, 186, 300
Grimes, John (Capt.), 488; mentioned as unit commander, 404
Groton, MA, 44, 186, 214, 218, 242, 278, 296, 297, 298, 451; minute men and militia on April 19th, 46
Guard duty; as camp routine, 56, 60, 75, 134, 147, 154; mentioned as duty at the Siege of Boston, 178, 189, 243, 258, 272, 294, 384, 411, 413; mentioned as guarding the Convention Army, 186, 191, 193, 194, 206, 209, 230, 256, 260, 264, 270, 274, 279, 287, 298, 305, 306, 314, 315, 330, 362, 378, 385, 393, 425, 433. *See also* Convention Army
Guards. *See* Guard duty; Lee, Charles (Gen.), Life Guard of; Washington, George (Gen.), Life Guard of

Index

Guilford, Vermont, 216
Guilford Court House, NC; Battle of, 141, *141 (map)*
Gunboat *Philadelphia*. *See Philadelphia* (gunboat)
Gurnet, The. *See* Plymouth, MA

H

Hadley, MA, 263
Hagar, Eunice (Whitehead), 298, 440
Hagar, Grace. *See* Adams, Grace (Hagar)
Hagar, Hannah (Ellis), 298
Hagar, Hannah (Stearns), 298
Hagar, Isaac, 298
HAGAR, JOHN, 33, **297**, 343, 507, 510, 516, 520, 531; family relationship of, 440; payment for service of, *343*; unit listing for, 505
Hagar, John (father of John Hagar (of Weston)), 298
Hagar, John (of Waltham), 298
Hagar, John (of Weston), 298
Hagar, Jonas, 298
Hagar, Martha (Parkhurst), 298
Hagar, Mary (Fiske), 298
Hagar, Prudence (Allen), 298
Hagar, Samuel, 298
Hagar, Sarah (Child), 298
Hague (frigate, privateer), 444, 504
Hale, Nathan, 135, 214
Hale, Nathan (Col.), 214
Halifax, Nova Scotia, 18, 66, 190, 405, 428, 451, 453
Hallet, Enoch (Lt. Col; Col.), 214, 267
Hamilton, Alexander, 150
Hamlin, Micah (Capt.), 479; mentioned as unit commander, 259
Hammond, Elizabeth. *See* Child, Elizabeth (Hammond)
Hancock, Belcher (Capt.), 500; mentioned as unit commander, 273
Hancock, John (Gov.), 186
Hancock, NH, 234
Handcock, Elizabeth. *See* Billing, Elizabeth (Handcock)
Hanover, NH, 287, 528
Hapgood, Lydia. *See* Bond, Lydia (Hapgood)
Hardwick, MA, 335, 336, 436, 527
Harlem Heights, NY; Battle of, 77, *78 (map)*, 79
Harrington, Abigail. *See* Whitehead, Abigail (Harrington)
Harrington, Anna. *See* Adams, Anna (Harrington)
Harrington, Anna (Coolidge), *23*, 299
HARRINGTON, DANIEL, 8, *11*, 23, 115, **298–299**, 363, 464, 507, 510, 512, 515, 519, 526; family relationships of, *23*, 181, 188, 267, 437, 438; unit listings for, 473, 480, 486, 489
Harrington, Daniel (Capt.), 489; mentioned as unit commander, 115, 193, 256, 264, 274, 298, 299, 314, 315, 362, 378, 385, 393, 419, 425, 433, 464, 470
Harrington, Daniel (father of DANIEL), *23*, 299

Harrington, Eunice. *See* Parkhurst, Eunice (Harrington)
Harrington, Hannah, *23*, 299
Harrington, ME, 255
Harrington, Moses (Capt.), 95, 483; mentioned as unit commander, 194, 198, 319, 320, 331, 346, 357, 376
Hartford, CT, 135, 347
Hartwell, Abegail (Stearnes), 465
Hartwell, Abigail (mother of Daniel (of Bedford)), 464
"Hartwell Brook the first Everidge", 443
Hartwell, Danel, 464
Hartwell, Daniel, 464
Hartwell, Daniel (of Bedford), 464
Hartwell, Daniel (of Concord), 464
Hartwell, Daniel R. (of Weston), 464
Hartwell, Elizabeth (Heywood), *24*, 299, 300, 302, 303, 306, 465
Hartwell, Elizabeth (Tarbell), 304
Hartwell, Ephraim (Sr.), 158, 415, 431, **464–465**; family relationships of, 16, *24*, 299, 300, 302, 303, 306; house of, *303*
HARTWELL, EPHRAIM, JR. (Capt.), xii, **299–300**, 507, 510, 512, 515, 519, 529; family relationships of, 22, *24*, 61, 225, 226, 233, 248, 249, 300, 302, 303, 304, 306, 464; mentioned as unit commander, 496; unit listings for, 474, 479, 486, 496
Hartwell, Eunice (Myrick), 301
Hartwell, Hebzibah (Brooks), 302
HARTWELL, ISAAC, *11*, 75, 121, 126, 186, **300–301**, 507, 509, 512, 516, 519, 527; family relationships of, 22, *24*, 225, 226, 233, 299, 302, 303, 304, 306, 464; house of, *303*; unit listings for, 473, 478, 480, 486, 492, 493
HARTWELL, JOHN (Ens.; Lt.; Capt.), *11*, 36, 37, 64, 267, **301–302**, 403, 507, 510, 512, 516, 519, 526; family relationships of, 22, *24*, 225, 226, 233, 299, 301, 303, 304, 306, 464; house of, *303*; mentioned as unit commander in Dorchester, 173, 180, 182, 216, 225, 239, 241, 302, 304, 310, 314, 410, 419, 443; mentioned as unit commander at fortification of Dorchester Heights, 175, 176, 178, 180, 181, 184, 192, 194, 197, 205, 208, 213, 216, 223, 231, 232, 238, 241, 242, 244, 245, 249, 257, 258, 260, 268, 272, 275, 283, 287, 288, 300, 304, 316, 322, 328, 341, 342, 344, 346, 367, 370, 371, 376, 380, 384, 386, 393, 406, 408, 413, 423, 429, 432, 446; unit listings for, 473, 475, 478, 480, 483
HARTWELL, JONAS, 18, **302–303**, 507, 509, 512, 514, 515, 519, 530; family relationships of, 22, *24*, 225, 226, 233, 299, 300, 301, 302, 304, 306, 464; house of, *303*; unit listings for, 474, 483, 505
HARTWELL, JONATHAN, **304**, 507, 510, 512, 514, 520, 531; unit listings for, 479, 483
Hartwell, Jonathan (father of JONATHAN), 304
Hartwell, Mary (Brown), *24*, 249, 300
Hartwell, Mary (Flint), 7, 9, *26*, 54, 431; house of, *305*; pension of, 305, *306*, 525

Hartwell, Ruth, 464
Hartwell, Sally. *See* Munroe, Sally (Hartwell)
HARTWELL, SAMUEL, *11*, 79, 110, **304–306**, 307, 436, 507, 510, 512, 515, 519, 525, 526; family relationships of, 22, *26*, 225, 226, 233, 283, 285, 286, 299, 300, 302, 303, 304, 347, 464; house of, *305*; unit listings for, 473, 478, 481, 488, 496
Hartwell, Samuel (father of Ephraim), 465; house built by, *305*, 306
Hartwell, Sarah (Wheeler), 304
Hartwell, Solomon, 464
Hartwell Tavern, 52; as it appeared circa 1900, *303*
Hartwell, William, 464
Harvard College, 18, 233, 248, 277, 278, 283, 296, 302, 303, 326, 329, 383, 454, 462, 464
Harvard, MA, 381, 402, 405
Haskell, Elnathan (Capt.), 501, 503, 504; mentioned as unit commander, 363
Haslet, John (Col.), xvi, 86, 87, 229
Hastings (Captain), 502, 503, 504; mentioned as unit commander, 364
Hastings, Eliphalet (Lt.), 495; mentioned as unit commander, 423
Hastings, Lydia (Nelson), 308
Hastings, Lydia (Tidd), 307
HASTINGS, SAMUEL, JR., 13, 19, 20, 88, 91, 307, **307–308**, 506, 509, 516, 520, 522, 524, 527; family relationship of, 467; pension declaration of, *308*; unit listings for, 475, 479, 481
Hastings, Samuel, Sr., 307
Hatch, Jabez (Col.), 483; mentioned as unit commander, 263, 414
HATCH, JACK. *See* FARRAR, JACK
Hatch, Nailer (Capt.), 479; mentioned as unit commander, 71, 201
Hatfield, MA, 324
Haverhill, MA, 283
Hawes, Benjamin (Col.), 485; mentioned as unit commander, 390
Hawes, William (Capt.), 497; mentioned as unit commander, 390
Haynes, Polly. *See* Smith, Polly (Haynes)
Hayward, John (Capt.), 501; mentioned as unit commander, 203, 219, 226, 325, 338, 347, 448
Haywood, Benjamin (Capt. Lieut.), 497; mentioned as unit commander, 435
Head of Elk, MD, 101, 142, 143
Headley, John, 222, 264, 265, 395, 396, 397
Headley, Mary. *See* Peirce, Mary (Headley)
Headley, Polley. *See* Peirce, Mary (Headley)
Headley, Tabitha. *See* Colburn, Tabitha (Headley)
Heald, Ann. *See* Hosmer, Anna (Heald)
Heald, Anna. *See* Hosmer, Anna (Heald)
Heald, John (Lt.), 403
Heald, Mary. *See* Dakin, Mary (Heald)
Heald, Mercy. *See* Dakin, Mary (Heald)
Heald, Samuel (Capt.), 37, 496; mentioned as unit commander, 173, 186, 209, 211, 218, 282, 306, 315, 362, 443, 470

Heald, Thomas (Capt.), 475; mentioned as unit commander, 277, 278
Heath, William (Gen.), 64, 84, 130; mentioned on command in Boston, 244, 263, 414, 415; as senior officer guarding the Convention, 115, 230
Hells Gate (NY), 331
HENDERSON, ZODITH, 95, 111, 116, 119, **309**, 322, 325, 508, 511, 516, 519, 531; unit listings for, 486, 487, 490, 491, 494, 497
Henley, David (Col.), 492, 493; mentioned as unit commander, 177, 233
Hessians, 91, 92, 93, 124, 146, 149, 150, 151, 375. *See also* German soldiers
Heywood, Elizabeth. *See* Hartwell, Elizabeth (Heywood)
Heywood, Sarah. *See* Brooks, Sarah (Heywood)
Hicks, Mary. *See* Cutler, Mary (Hicks)
Hildreth, Sarah. *See* Brooks, Sarah (Hildreth)
Hill, Jeremiah (Capt.), 243
Hinkley, John (Capt.), 493; mentioned as unit commander, 415
Hoar family ancestry, 223
HOAR, BRISTER, xiv, xv, 15, 16, 18, 36, 94, 98, 99, 221, 223, 261, **309–310**, 312, 313, 314, 315, 316, 506, 509, 515, 519, 521, 526; gravestone of, *309*; home of, *313*; unit listings for, 480, 483, 485
HOAR, CUFF, 15, 108, 221, **312**, 313, 314, 315, 373, 508, 511, 514, 520, 521, 527; home of, *313*; manumission of, *311*; unit listing for, 486
Hoar, Daniel (Lt.), 25, 314
Hoar, Elizabeth (Coolidge), 25, 310, 314, 315, 317
Hoar, Ester. *See* Bowman, Ester (Hoar)
Hoar, Esther (Peirce), 314
Hoar, Eunice (Wheeler), 26, 54, 315, 431
HOAR, JOHN, xv, *11*, 12, 13, 15, 309, 311, **312–314**, 316, 363, 508, 511, 514, 519, 526; deposition of, 55, 188, 312; family relationships of, 25, 177, 188, 223, 315, 317, 420, 421, 422, 424, 426, 427; house of, *313*; mentioned as slave holder, xiv, 15, 16, 18, 97, 99, 261, 309, 310, 311, 312; unit listing for, 474. *See also* Depositions of April 1775
HOAR, LEONARD, xv, 94, 107, 109, 310, 312, 313, **314–316**, 363, 506, 509, 513, 516, 519, 524, 526; family relationships of, 22, 26, 177, 223, 276, 314, 317, 420, 421, 422, 424, 427, 431; home of, *313*; unit listings for, 480, 483, 485, 488, 489, 496, 498
Hoar, Lucy. *See* Brooks, Lucy (Hoar)
Hoar, Marcy. *See* Farrar, Marcy (Hoar)
Hoar, Mary. *See* Wesson, Mary (Hoar)
Hoar, Mercy. *See* Farrar, Marcy (Hoar)
Hoar, Pamela (Hodgman), 315
HOAR, SAMUEL, *11*, 16, 74, 159, 277, 313, **316–317**, 383, 507, 510, 512, 515, 519, 526; family relationships of, 25, 177, 188, 223, 276, 314, 315, 420, 421, 422, 424, 426; unit listings for, 473, 478, 480
Hoar, Samuel (Hon.) (son of SAMUEL), 159, 164

Hoar, Sarah. *See* Abbot, Sarah (Hoar)
Hoar, Sarah (Jones), 25, 314
Hoar, Susanna (Peirce), 317
Hobbs, Eunice. *See* Parker, Eunice (Hobbs)
Hobbs, Mary. *See* Parks, Mary (Hobbs)
Hobbs, Tabitha. *See* Nelson, Tabitha (Hobbs)
Hodgman, Pamela. *See* Hoar, Pamela (Hodgman)
Hog Island (Boston Harbor), 56, *57 (map)*, 403
Holden, Abel (Capt.), 486, 488, 495, 497; mentioned as unit commander, 358
Holden, MA, 324
Holden, Samuel (Capt.), 500; mentioned as unit commander, 400
Hollis, NH, 279, 430, 462
Holman, John (Col.), 493; mentioned as unit commander, 224
Homes, John (Capt.), 489; mentioned as unit commander, 279
Horse Neck (Braintree, MA), 36, 266, 479
Horse Neck (Greenwich, CT), 79, 185, 228, 256, 304, 481
Hosley, James (Capt.), 474; mentioned as unit commander, 267
HOSMER, AMOS, 100, **317–318**, 506, 509, 515, 519, 529; family relationships of, 319, 320; unit listings for, 478, 485, 494
Hosmer, Ann (Heald). *See* Hosmer, Anna (Heald)
Hosmer, Anna. *See* Child, Anna (Hosmer)
Hosmer, Anna (Heald), 317, 319, 320
Hosmer, Bethia, 318
HOSMER, DANIEL, 3, 58, 60, 74, **318–319**, 507, 510, 512, 516, 519, 524, 528; family relationships of, 195, 196, 197, 198; unit listings for, 473, 475, 478, 480, 486
Hosmer, Daniel (father of DANIEL), 318
Hosmer, Elizabeth, 320
Hosmer, Hannah (Baker), 318
Hosmer, Hannah (Parker), 318, 319
Hosmer, Joseph (Capt.), 478; mentioned as unit commander, 317
Hosmer, Joseph (of Concord), 46
Hosmer, Lidia. *See* Wood, Lidia (Hosmer)
Hosmer, Nathaniel, 320
Hosmer, Sibbil (Parker), 318, 319
HOSMER, WILLIAM, JR., 8, *11*, 16, 94, **319**, 506, 509, 515, 519, 529; family relationships of, 188, 259, 317, 318, 320; unit listings for, 473, 480, 483
HOSMER, WILLIAM, SR., 8, *11*, 16, **320**, 508, 510, 514, 519, 528; deposition of, 188, 320; family relationships of, 188, 259, 317, 319; unit listings for, 474, 480. *See also* Depositions of April 1775
Hough's Neck (Quincy, MA). *See* Horse Neck (Braintree, MA)
Housatonic River (CT), 128, 215, 327
Hovey, Thomas (Capt.), 496; mentioned as unit commander, 325, 330, 412
How, Cyprian (Col.), 37, 498; mentioned as unit commander, 209, 234, 259, 315, 341, 347, 349, 374, 422, 433–434
How, Ezekiel (Col.), 431
Howe, John, 296, 464

Howe, Lydia. *See* Buttrick, Lydia (Howe)
Howe, Mary. *See* Farrar, Mary (Howe)
Howe, William (Gen.), 65, 66, 112; on campaign around New York, 76, *78 (map)*, 81; on the campaign for Philadelphia, 98, 100–103, *102, 103 (map)*; mentioned in evacuation of Boston, 178, 180, 181, 192, 194, 197, 205, 208, 213, 216, 223, 227, 231, 232, 238, 239, 241, 242, 246, 249, 257, 258, 260, 261, 268, 272, 275, 283, 287, 288, 300, 301, 304, 316, 317, 322, 328, 341, 342, 344, 346, 367, 370, 371, 376, 380, 384, 386, 393, 406, 408, 409, 414, 423, 426, 429, 432, 446
Howland's Ferry (RI), 123, 186, 315, 332
Hubbardston, MA, 365
Hubbart, Lucy. *See* Adams, Lucy (Hubburd)
Hubburd, Lucy. *See* Adams, Lucy (Hubburd)
Hudson, Charles, 161, 164, 472
Hudson, Dinah. *See* Meriam, Dinah (Hudson)
Hudson Highlands, defense of, 88, 97, 126–136, *127 (map)*, *129 (map)*, *130 (map)*. *See also* Hudson River Valley; Saratoga campaign
Hudson River Valley; mentioned as serving in, 13, 16, 19, 33, 42; forts along, 76, 91, 126, *127 (map)*; British activity along, 77, 91; British plan to split the colonies along; 96–98, 100–101; deployments to and about, 37, 88, 98, 153–155; mentioned as serving in, 13, 16, 19, 33, 42, 142, 199, 201, 203, 212, 215, 219, 224, 226, 227, 241, 242, 246, 254, 263, 271, 275, 280, 281, 325, 327, 337, 338, 353, 354, 356, 358, 363, 375, 390, 396, 398, 402, 411, 412, 420, 423, 435, 436, 437, 440, 443, 447, unit listings of individuals deployed to, 488, 494–495, 497–498, 500, 501, 503, 504. *See also* Hudson Highlands, defense of; Saratoga campaign
Hull, MA, 94, 199, 381, 477, 484
Hunt, Abraham (Capt.), 491, 492, 493, 496, 498, 500; mentioned as unit commander, 253
Hunt, Anna. *See* Billing, Anna (Hunt)
Hunt, Elizabeth. *See* Wheeler, Elizabeth (Hunt)
Hunt, Martha. *See* Goodenow, Martha (Hunt)
Hunt, Simon (Capt.), 37, 79, 109, 481, 488, 489; mentioned as unit commander guarding the Convention, 186, 194, 206, 209, 230, 271, 274, 276, 314, 315, 365, 372, 380, 417, 433, 436; mentioned as unit commander in the New York campaign, 185, 201, 210, 239, 256, 282, 321, 331, 409
Hutchinson, Lydia. *See* Mead, Lydia (Hutchinson)

I

Inauguration, Presidential. *See* Presidential Inaugural Ceremonies
Inflation. *See* Currency, inflation of

Index

Inglesbee, Anna. *See* Lovell, Anna (Inglesbee)
Ingraham, Duncan, 222
Innman's Ferry (Woodbury, CT), 344
Inquisition, Spanish. *See* Spanish Inquisition
Intolerable Acts. *See* Coercive Acts
Ipswich, MA, 243, 287

J

Jack, John, 222
Jackson, Elisha (Capt.), 486; mentioned as unit commander, 293
Jackson, Henry (Col.); at the Battle of Monmouth, 116, 118; at the Battle of Rhode Island, 120, 124, 126; last remaining Continental unit, 156, 339; mentioned as unit commander, 177, 233, 339, 361, 390; unit listings for, 487, 488, 490, 491, 492, 494, 496, 499, 501, 503, 504
Jacobs, John (Col.), 37, 492, 493, 496; mentioned as unit commander, 173, 186, 209, 211, 218, 282, 300, 306, 315, 362, 443, 470,
Jay, ME, 418
Jefferson County, NY, 436
Jefferson, Thomas, 142
Jennison, Anna. *See* Parks, Anna (Jennison)
Johnson, Anna. *See* Reed, Anna (Johnson)
Johnson, Rebeka. *See* Gearfield, Rebeka (Johnson)
JONES, AMOS, xii, **320–321**, 507, 509, 515, 520, 524, 527; unit listings for, 475, 476
Jones, Anna (Stimson), 321
Jones, Azubah (Russell), 321
Jones, Elizabeth. *See* Brooks, Elizabeth (Jones)
Jones, Lemuel, 321
Jones, Lucy. *See* Stone, Lucy (Jones)
Jones, Rebecca. *See* Adams, Rebecca (Jones)
Jones, Sarah. *See* Hoar, Sarah (Jones)
Jones, Solomon, 320
Jupiter (slave of Joshua Brooks), 236, 353, 463

K

Keith, Joseph (Capt.), 253
Kenduskeag, ME, 253
Kennebec River (ME), 68, *69 (map)*
Keyes, Danforth (Col.), 398
Kimball, Benjamin (Capt.), 243
King's Ferry, NY, *127 (map)*, 126, 128, *129 (map)*, *130 (map)*, 132, 133; mentioned as service location, 353, 423, 443
King's Mountain, SC; Battle of, 137, *138 (map)*, 139
King, Zebulon (Capt.), 501, 503, 504; mentioned as unit commander, 366
King George's War, 314
Kingsbridge, NY, 92, 94, 95; mentioned as service location, 185, 187, 228, 234, 331, 481, 502
Kingsbury, NY, 391
Kip's Bay. *See* New York (City), New York campaign
Knapp, Uzal, 401

KNEELAND, CUFF. *SEE* HOAR, CUFF
Kneeland, Dinah (Young), 312
Knowlton, Abigail (Pierce), 321
Knowlton, Hannah (Goffe), 321
KNOWLTON, JEREMIAH, 77, 84, 121, 126, **321**, 507, 510, 512, 515, 519, 528; unit listings for, 481, 486, 492
Knowlton, Jeremiah (father of JEREMIAH), 321
Knowlton, Sarah (Allen), 321
Knox, Henry (Col.; Gen.), 35; Expedition to Ticonderoga, 61, 442, 443, 477; mentioned as discharged by, 187, 364
Knox Expedition to Ticonderoga. *See* Knox, Henry (Col.; Gen.), Expedition to Ticonderoga

L

Lafayette (General), 156; at the Battle of Monmouth, 116, 118; at the Battle of Rhode Island, 125, 126; Grand Tour in 1825, 159; in the Virginia campaign, 142–144, *145 (map)*; mentioned as unit commander, 204, 254
Lake Champlain. *See* Canada, campaign to; Ticonderoga; Valcour Island, Battle of
Lake George, 109, 438, 440
Lamson, Samuel (Capt.; Maj.), 475, 490; mentioned as unit commander, 200, 218, 256, 264, 286, 320, 469
Lancaster, MA, 40, 214, 223, 415
Lancaster, PA, 104, 112
LANCTAY, JOHN. *SEE* LANDER, JOHN
LANDA, JOHN. *SEE* LANDER, JOHN
LANDEA, JOHN. *SEE* LANDER, JOHN
LANDER, JOHN, 64, 95, 128, 131, **322**, 325, 508, 511, 516, 519, 523, 531; unit listings for, 478, 480, 486, 487
LANDY, JOHN. *SEE* LANDER, JOHN
Lane, Jabez (Capt.), 495; mentioned as unit commander, 344, 412
LANGTRY, JOHN. *SEE* LANDER, JOHN
Languedoc (French flagship), *123*
Lathrop, Daniel (Capt.), 483; mentioned as unit commander, 412
Lawrence, Asa (Capt.), 370
Lawrence, Eunice (Brown), *28*, 323
Lawrence, Love (Adams), *28*, 323
Lawrence, Lovey. *See* Adams, Lovey (Lawrence)
Lawrence, William (Rev.), 12, 16, *28*, 323, 428
LAWRENCE, WILLIAM, JR., 15, **323**, 428, 507, 510, 516, 519, 527; family relationships of, 22, *28*, 52, 244, 252, 449; unit listing for, 505
Leathe, Achsah. *See* Robinson, Achsah (Leathe)
Leathe, Rhoda. *See* Munroe, Rhoda (Leathe)
Lechmere Point (MA), 57, 233, 280
Lee, Charles (Gen.); arrest and court martial, 120; at the Battle of Monmouth, 116, *117 (map)*, 118; capture at Basking Ridge, 20, 91, 116, 307, 308; in the New York campaign, 67, 88, 307; Life Guard of, 19, 88, 307, 367, 479, 481; mentioned as unit commander, 241, 307, 326

Lee, Hannah. *See* Brown, Hannah (Lee)
Lee, Rebekah. *See* Wheeler, Rebekah (Lee)
Leominster, MA, 191, 264, 265, 396, 397, 448, 527
Leonard, David (Col.), 214
Lewis, George (Capt.), 487, 490, 491; mentioned as unit commander, 400
Lewis, Polly. *See* Child, Polly (Lewis)
Lexington, MA; militia company on April 19th, x, 13, 160, 163, 348, 475; bloodshed on the Lexington Green, vii, x, 4, 9, 45, 52, 158, *160*, *162*, 162–163; arrival of Percy's relief column, x, 54; depositions taken in, 55, 159, 174, 284; commemorative obelisk, 159; feud with Concord, 159, 161, 162; Lexington Artillery Company, 308. *See also* April 19, 1775; depositions of April 1775; depositions of 1825; Lexington and Concord, Second Battle of
Lexington Alarm. *See* April 19, 1775
Lexington and Concord, Second Battle of, 159–166. *See also* Concord, MA; Lexington, MA; Lincoln, MA
Liberty, H.M.S. (British revenue ship), 449
Life Guards; of General Lee. *See* Lee, Charles (Gen.), Life Guard of; of General Washington. *See* Washington, George (Gen.), Life Guard of
Lillie, John (Capt.), 486, 487, 490, 491, 492, 494, 497, 499, 502; mentioned as unit commander, 101, 146, 262
Lincoln, MA; Committee of Correspondence of, 2, 3, 6, 230, 237, 383, 461; depositions taken in, 55, *56*, 283, 284; draft letter of Dec. 1773, 2; grave of British soldiers at, 54, *166*, 431; historic markers at, 166–167, *168*; Minute Men, modern company of, 167–169, *168*; minute men and militia on April 19th, 8–9, 12–13, 45–46; residence locations of, *10-11*; roster of, 473–474; mentioned as members of original militia company of 1757, 195, 208, 211, 224, 239, 242, 276, 291, 320, 337, 368, 392, 416, 418, 444, 451; prisoner of war in, 55, *56*, 283, 284, 285; Town Meeting in, xii, xiii, 3, 5, 9, 38, 48, 71, 74, 75, 166, 167, 184, 298. *See also* April 19, 1775; Battle Road; Bloody Angles; Lexington & Concord, Second battle of
Lincoln, ME, 255
Lincoln, Amos (Capt.), 502, 503; mentioned as unit commander, 444
Lincoln County, ME, 235, 255
Liskeard, Cornwall, England, 450
Lisle, NY, 393, 529
Litchfield, CT, 436
Little, Moses (Col.), 479; mentioned as unit commander, 307
Littlefield, Noah Moulton (Capt.), 477; mentioned as unit commander, 253
Littleton, MA, 46, 154, 280, 288, 304, 359, 360, 388, 389, 413; minute men and militia on April 19th, 46

Livermore, ME, 176, 206, 345, 349, 368, 445, 528
Livermore Falls, ME, 175, 176, 418, 446, 528
Livermore, Tabitha. *See* Gove, Tabitha (Livermore)
Locke, Abigail. *See* Meriam, Abigail (Locke)
Locker, Isaac (Capt.), 474; mentioned as unit commander, 397
LONDON, EDEN, xii, 112, 119, **323–324**, 507, 510, 517, 520, 521, 528; unit listings for, 476, 486, 488, 490, 491, 495, 497
Long Island, NY, 451; Battle of, 19, 76, 100, 248, 326, 398; evacuation of, 77. *See also* Brooklyn, NY, evacuation of
Loring, Abigail. *See* Munroe, Abigail (Loring)
Loring, Mary. *See* Whelor, Mary (Loring)
Loring, Sarah. *See* Bowman, Sarah (Loring)
Lorraine, NY, 436, 529
Lot (slave of Deacon John Gove), 296, 463
LOUCKIN, STEPHEN. *SEE* LUFKIN, STEPHEN
Lovejoy, Sarah. *See* Whitney, Sarah (Lovejoy)
Lovell, Anna (Inglesbee), 325
Lovell, Jonathan, 325
Lovell, Joseph (Capt.), 483; mentioned as unit commander, 324
LOVELL, NATHANIEL, **324**, 508, 511, 516, 520, 531; unit listings for, 474, 476, 483, 485, 492, 493, 498, 505
Lovell, Rachel, 325
Lovell, Solomon (Brig. Gen.); mentioned as brigade commander, 180, 217, 238, 266, 321, 331, 336, 341, 385, 394
Lovill, David, 324
Lovill, Hannah, 324
Loyalist militias, 15, 137, 142, 428, 449, 450, 451, 453, 470. *See also* Associators, 2nd Company of; Massachusetts Company of Volunteers
Loyalists, 16, 59, 100, 115, 323, 428, 449, 455, 464, 470
LUFKIN, STEPHEN, 116, 119, 309, **325**, 508, 511, 516, 520, 531; unit listings for, 486, 487, 490, 491, 494, 497
Lunenburg, MA, 255, 307, 405
Lunt, Elisabeth, 325
Lunt, Elkanah, 325
LUNT, JOHN, **325**, 508, 511, 516, 520, 531; family relationships of, unit listings for, 505
Lyon, Mary. *See* Parker, Mary (Lyon)

M

Machias, ME, 203, 204, 212, 254
Magna Carta, 5; detail from, 5
Malcom, Colonel, 494; mentioned as unit commander, 327, 330, 344
Malden, MA, 379
Malone. *See* Meloney
Manhattan, NY, 76, 77, 78, 81, 83, 88, 92, 100, 126, 185, 187, 248, 481
Manley, John (Capt.), 504; mentioned as unit commander, 444

MANN, CHRISTOPHER, **325**, 326, 508, 511, 515, 520, 531; unit listings for, 496, 501
Mann, Lucy, 325, 326
Mann, Oliver, 325, 326
Mann, Sabin (Capt.), 324
Manpower demand. *See* Troop calls
Marett, Philip (Capt.), 263, 344, 384, 385, 386, 414, 425, 483
Marine service. *See* Naval service
Marlborough, MA, 233, 255, 299, 332, 390, 393, 429
Marlborough, NH, 271, 292, 528
Marshall, Thomas (Col.), 486, 488, 490, 491, 495, 497, 499; mentioned as unit commander, 119, 323, 338, 396
Mason, David (Lt. Col.), 497; mentioned as unit commander, 390
MASON, ELIJAH, **11**, 76, 91, 92, 128, 132, **326–327**, 329, 465, 506, 509, 513, 516, 519, 524, 529; family relationships of, 26, 328, 331; house site of, 466; unit listings for, 473, 475, 481, 482, 494, 497
Mason, Elizabeth (Brooks), 27, 328
Mason, Grace (Bond), 26, 327, 328, 331
Mason, Hannah. *See* Peirce, Hannah (Mason)
MASON, JONAS, 11, **327–328**, 332, 507, 510, 512, 515, 519, 528; family relationships of, 27, 327, 331; gravestone of, 328; house site of, 466; unit listings for, 473, 475, 478
Mason, Joseph (Sr.), 465; family relationships of, 26, 327, 328, 331; house site of, 466
MASON, JOSEPH, JR., 11, 105, 128, **329–331**, 332, 391, 433, 507, 510, 512, 513, 516, 519, 524, 529; family relationships of, 26, 283, 285, 286, 306, 327, 328, 331; house site of, 466; unit listings for, 473, 475, 478, 485, 489, 494, 496
Mason, Lucy (Flint), 26, 331
Mason, NH, 174, 179, 183, 200, 320, 339, 340; minute men and militia on April 19th, 13, 181, 189, 475
Mason, Susanna (Foster), 27, 328
Massachusetts Charter; of 1629, 5, 6; of 1691, 5, 6
Massachusetts Company of Volunteers, 449. *See also* Loyalist militias
Massachusetts Constitutional Convention, 230
Massachusetts General Court, 4, 6, 34, 35, 177, 231, 238, 299, 402, 461
Massachusetts Provincial Army, xi; formation of, 18, 38, 49, 54; mentioned as enlisting in, 176, 178, 187, 199, 201, 258, 280, 286, 289, 290, 318, 326, 327, 329, 358, 366, 370, 373, 374, 384, 387, 399, 403, 411, 413, 427, 428, 429, 434, 442, 445, 459, 472
Massachusetts Provincial Congress, 43, 56, 163, 184, 230, 383, 403, 452
Mathais. *See* Mathis
Mather. *See* Mathis
Mathews. *See* Mathis
Mathies. *See* Mathis
MATHIS, ABNER, 16, 22, 77, 84, 94, 121, 126, **331–332**, 506, 509, 515, 524, 525,

527; family relationships of, 27, 259, 345, 346, 347, 349; unit listings for, 481, 483, 485, 492
Mathis, Anna (Munroe), 27, 332
Mathis, Barnabas, 27, 332
Mathis, Lydia (Smith), 332, 525
Mathis, Molley. *See* Child, Molley (Mathis)
Mattanawcook, ME, 255
Matthes. *See* Mathis
Matthews. *See* Mathis
Matthis. *See* Mathis
Mattoon, Ebenezer (Lt.), 201
Maxwell, William (Gen.), 94, 234
May, Lemuel (Capt.), 493; mentioned as unit commander, 348
Mayflower Compact, 4; Gov. William Bradford transcription of, 4
Maynard, Jonathan (Capt.) 501, 503, 504; mentioned as unit commander, 415, 447
Maynard, Mary. *See* Sherman, Mary (Maynard)
McCarthy, Hannah Soley. *See* Adams, Hannah Soley (McCarthy)
McCarty, Hannah Soley. *See* Adams, Hannah Soley (McCarthy)
McCobb, Samuel (Col.), 488; mentioned as unit commander, 254
McDougall, Alexander (Gen.), 84, 87
McFarland, Walter (Capt.), 498; mentioned as unit commander, 374, 422
McIntosh, William (Col.), 126, 483, 492, 493; mentioned as unit commander, 180, 217, 238, 265, 266, 321, 331, 336, 341, 348, 385, 394, 422
McLellan, Alexander (Capt.), 495; mentioned as unit commander, 426
McRae, Jane, 97
MEAD, ABIJAH, 11, 36, 178, 205, 246, 328, **332–334**, 333, 507, 510, 512, 515, 519, 524, 527; family relationships of, 24, 335, 336; unit listings for, 473, 477, 478, 480
Mead, David, 24, 33, 36, 252, 333, 334, 335, 336; fine and refund, 333
Mead, Eunice. *See* Bowman, Eunice (Mead)
Mead, Hepsibah (Graves), 334
MEAD, JONATHAN, 36, 136, **335**, 506, 509, 516, 519, 522, 527; family relationships of, 24, 334, 336; payment for service of, 335; unit listings for, 493, 500, 501
Mead, Lydia (Hutchinson), 335, 336
Mead, Mary (Bond), 24, 334, 335, 336
MEAD, TILLY, 19, 36, 60, 71, 73, 121, 126, **336**, 506, 509, 516, 519, 523, 524, 527; family relationships of, 24, 333, 334, 335; unit listings for, 474, 476, 479, 492
Medfield, MA, 324, 474; minute men and militia on April 19th, 13
Medford, MA, 405
Mellen, Thomas (Capt.), 498; mentioned as unit commander, 372
MELONEY, CORNELIUS, **337**, 352, 508, 510, 514, 519, 531; family relationships of, 27, 337, 368, 370, 434; unit listing for, 500
Meloney, Elizabeth (Parks), 27, 337

Meloney, Joseph, 132, **337**, 506, 509, 516, 519, 531; family relationships of, 27, 337, 368, 370, 434; unit listings for, 498, 500
Meloney, Love (Farrar), 337
Melonia. *See* Meloney
Melony. *See* Meloney
Mendon, MA, 188, 217, 341, 414
Menotomy, MA, 4, 13, 52, 53, 54, 165; British retreat through, *472*
Meriam. *See also* Merriam
Meriam, Abigail (Locke), *22*, 340
Meriam, Abraham (brother of Ezra), 338
Meriam, Abraham (father of Ezra), *22*, 339
Meriam, Dinah (Hudson), 341
Meriam, Ezra, 32, 41, 76, 91, 92, 132, 134, 136, 156, **338–339**, 348, 506, 509, 517, 520, 524, 525, 528; family relationships of, *22*, 174, 340; unit listings for, 481, 482, 495, 498, 499, 500, 501, 503, 504
Meriam, James, 91, 120, 126, **339–340**, 508, 510, 515, 519, 527; family relationships of, *22*, 339; unit listings for, 481, 492
Meriam, John, 134, 136, **340–341**, 506, 509, 515, 520, 524, 527; unit listing for, 500
Meriam, John (father of John), 340
Meriam, Jonas, *22*, 340
Meriam, Mary (Bancroft), 340
Meriam, Mary (Cutler), *22*, 340
Meriam, Polly. *See* Abbot, Polly (Meriam)
Meriam, Sarah (Simonds), *22*, 339
Meriam, Silas, 338
Meriam, Susannah (Elliot), 339, 525
Meriam's Corner. *See* Concord, MA, Meriam's Corner
Merriam. *See also* Meriam
Merriam, Esther. *See* Bond, Esther (Merriam)
Merriam, Mary. *See* Munroe, Mary (Merriam)
Merrimac, MA, 361
Methes. *See* Mathis
Middlesex, Catharine, 342
Middlesex, Salem, 15, 64, 121, 126, 219, 252, **341–342**, 508, 511, 515, 519, 521, 528; unit listings for, 478, 492, 498
Middlesex, Vilot, 341, 342
Middlesex County, MA; Continental Army enlistment from, 198, 295, 335; unit raised in, 242, 381. *See also* Barrett, James, as muster master; Middlesex County Regiments
Middlesex County (MA) regiments, 64, 77, 98, 179; officers in, 226, 227, 230, 275, 276, 283, 316, 372; mentioned in Brooks's 3rd regiment at Dorchester Heights, 175, 176, 178, 180, 181, 184, 192, 194, 197, 205, 208, 213, 216, 223, 231, 232, 238, 241, 242, 244, 245, 249, 257, 258, 260, 268, 272, 275, 283, 287, 288, 300, 301, 304, 316, 317, 322, 328, 341, 342, 344, 346, 348, 367, 370, 371, 376, 380, 384, 386, 393, 406, 408, 413, 423, 429, 432, 435, 446; mentioned in Brooks's regiment in the New York campaign, 185, 193, 201, 210, 239, 256, 282,

304, 321, 331, 371, 392, 402, 403, 409; mentioned in Bulard's regiment in the Saratoga campaign, 178, 194, 198, 201, 206, 225, 244, 249, 255, 257, 263, 270, 310, 317, 348, 371, 377, 385, 401, 419, 421, 424, 468; mentioned as detached from Brooks's 3rd regiment, 183, 191, 192, 198, 201, 205, 206, 215, 216, 225, 233, 238, 244, 252, 255, 257, 261, 264, 265, 268, 270, 275, 294, 298, 310, 314, 329, 330, 331, 348, 353, 377, 378, 379, 393, 408, 412, 425, 443; mentioned in How's regiment at Rhode Island, 209, 234, 259, 315, 341, 347, 349, 374, 422, 433–434; mentioned in Reed's regiment in the Saratoga campaign, 183, 205, 216, 238, 268, 275, 295, 314, 329, 331, 353, 378, 408, 412, 433, 443
Miles, Charles (Capt.), 12, 74, 474, 480, 484; mentioned as unit commander, 184, 214, 232, 240, 244, 269, 271, 349, 382, 407, 435
Miles, Elizabeth, 342
Miles, James, 33, **342**, 507, 510, 514, 519, 531; unit listings for, 478, 485
Miles, James (of Concord), 342
Miles, John, 342
Miles, Noah (Capt.), 475; mentioned as unit commander, 292
Milford, H.M.S. (British frigate), 18, 183, 404
Militia; alarm lists, 35, 39, 95, 99, 348; blame for fleeing from battle at White Plains, xvi, 85, 86–87, 229; degrading of officers at Cambridge, 115, 230; training bands, 35, 95, 99, 348; units active on April 19th, 13, 474–475. *See also* Middlesex County regiments; Suffolk County, regiments; Worcester County, regiments
Militias. *See* Loyalist militias; Patriot militias
Mills, William (Capt.), 503, 504; mentioned as unit commander, 418
Milo, NY, 448, 530
Minot, Elizabeth. *See* Adams, Elizabeth (Minot)
Minot, George (Capt.), 468, 478, 485; mentioned as unit commander, 37, 98, 178, 194, 198, 201, 206, 225, 255, 257, 263, 270, 310, 317, 348, 371, 377, 385, 419, 435
Minot, John (Capt.) 483; mentioned as unit commander, 36, 94, 301, 346, 384, 394, 402, 419
Minot, Thankful Sarah. *See* Dakin, Thankful Sarah (Minot)
Minott, Jonathan (Capt.), 481, 482; mentioned as unit commander, 241, 266, 477
Minott, Love. *See* Adams, Love (Minott)
Minuteman boulder. *See* Thorning, William, boulder from which he shot Redcoats
Minute Man National Historical Park, 51, 166–16, 303, 305, 308, 349, 411
Minute men; unit listings of, 473–474. *See also* listings under specific towns; profiles of individual minute men

Mitchell, Edward (Col.), 479; mentioned as unit commander, 266
Mitchell, Jonathan (Col.), 207, 495; mentioned as unit commander, 426
Mohawk Valley, 96, 98
Monmouth Court House. *See* Monmouth, NJ, Battle of
Monmouth, NJ, Battle of, 19, 115–120, *117 (map)*, *118*, 177, 180, 219, 254, 273, 282, 347, 359, 361, 397, 400, 414, 491
Monro. *See* Munroe
Monroe. *See also* Munroe
Monroe, Abijah, 478
Monroe, Benjamin (Capt.), 493; mentioned as unit commander, 279
Monroe, Deliverance, 466
Monroe, Josiah, **466–467**
Monroe, Marrett, 466
Monroe, Susanna (Fitch), 467
Monrow. *See* Munroe
Montgomery, Richard (Gen.), 67, 68, 69, 70
Monticello, VA, 144, *145 (map)*
Montreal, Canada, 19, 67, 68, 69, 73, 201, 202, 377
Moor, Catherine. *See* Farrar, Catherine (Moor)
Moor, Mary. *See* Billing, Mary (Moor)
Moore, Anna. *See* Richardson, Anna (Moore)
Moore, Boaz (Capt.), 474; mentioned as unit commander, 299
Moore, David (Capt.), 476, 498; mentioned as unit commander, 214, 267, 294
Moore, John (Capt.), 475; mentioned as unit commander, 12, 193
More, Agnice, 343
More, Daniel, 343
More, Edward, 343
More, Elizabeth, 343
More, John, 297, **343**, 421, 508, 511, 516, 520, 531; payment for service of, *343*; unit listing for, 505
More, John (of Sudbury), 343
More, Kezia, 343
More, Mary (Bruce), 343
More, Nathan, 343
Morgan, Daniel (Col.; Gen.), 116, 139, 262
Morristown, NJ, 94, 142, 177, 180, 241, 262, 273, 333, 336, 347, 361, 388, 446
Morton, James (Capt.), 493; mentioned as unit commander, 260
Moulton, Caleb (Capt.), 495; mentioned as unit commander, 423
Munn, Reuben (Capt.), 214
Munro. *See* Munroe
Munroe, Abigail. *See* Smith, Abigail (Munroe)
Munroe, Abigail (Loring), 348
Munroe, Abigail (wife of David), 346
Munroe, Abijah, xvi, 8, *11*, 16, 60, 94, 128, **344–345**, 363, 412, 507, 509, 512, 516, 519, 524, 528; family relationships of, *27*, 188, 256, 332, 345, 347, 349; unit listings for, 473, 475, 483, 494, 495
Munroe, Abraham, 346
Munroe, Anna. *See* Mathis, Anna (Munroe)

Munroe, Benjamin (father of BENJAMIN (Jr.)), 26, 345
MUNROE, BENJAMIN (Jr.), 8, 11, 16, **345–346**, 363, 388, 431, 508, 511, 514, 519, 527; deposition of, 188, 345; family relationships of, 22, 26, 256, 332, 347, 349; unit listings for, 474, 484, 493. *See also* Depositions of April 1775
Munroe, Benjamin (of Lexington), 346
Munroe, Bulah. *See* Cabot, Bulah (Munroe)
Munroe, David, 346
Munroe, Edmund (Capt.), 485, 487, 490, 491, 492, 494, 495; mentioned as unit commander, 218, 236, 359, 425, 462
Munroe, Eunice. *See* Wheeler, Eunice (Munroe)
Munroe, Grace (Bigelow), 347
MUNROE, ISAAC, 94, 95, 101, 104, **346–347**, 506, 509, 513, 517, 519, 524, 526; family relationships of, 22, 27, 256, 332, 345, 349; unit listings for, 474, 476, 478, 483, 487, 494, 496, 498, 499
Munroe, Jedediah, 348
MUNROE, JOSEPH, 32, 41, 64, 94, 100, 154, 339, **347–348**, 506, 509, 516, 520, 524, 525, 527; unit listings for, 478, 484, 485, 493, 495, 501
Munroe, Lydia. *See* Page, Lydia (Munroe)
Munroe, Lydia (mother of BENJAMIN (Jr.)), 26, 345
Munroe, Mary. *See* Brooks, Mary (Munroe); Wheeler, Mary (Munroe)
Munroe, Mary (Merriam), 26, 345, 347, 349
MUNROE, MICAH, **349**, 506, 509, 514, 519, 528; family relationships of, 27, 256, 332, 345, 347, 349; unit listing for, 498
Munroe, Rhoda (Leathe), 348, 525
Munroe, Salley (Wheeler), 345
Munroe, Sally (Hartwell), 27, 347
Munroe's Tavern (Lexington, MA), 164
Murray, Seth (Capt.), 476; mentioned as unit commander, 427
Myrick, Eunice. *See* Hartwell, Eunice (Myrick)

N

Naval service, xvi, 181, 404, 444, 449, 488, 504
Negus, Rosanna. *See* Bond, Rosanna (Negus)
Nelson, Elizabeth (Flagg), 349, 350, 352
NELSON, JOSIAH, 7, 11, 16, 74, 214, 240, **349–352**, 353, 354, 415, 463, 508, 511, 515, 519, 527; family relationships of, 308, 467; house of, *350*; purchase of a negro servant boy, 240, 351, 353, *354*; unit listings for, 480, 484
Nelson, Lydia. *See* Hastings, Lydia (Nelson)
Nelson, Lydia (wife of Thomas), 467
Nelson, Mellacent (Bond), 349
NELSON, PETER, 13, 16, 105, 128, 236, 240, 349, 351, **353–354**, 355, 396, 506, 508, 515, 519, 521, 531; family relationships of, 463; purchase by JOSIAH NELSON, *354*; unit listings for, 485, 495. *See also* BROOKS, PETER; SHARON, PETER
Nelson, Tabitha (Hobbs), 349, 467
Nelson, Thomas (brother of JOSIAH), **467**
Nelson, Thomas (father of JOSIAH), 349, 467
Nelson's Point (NY), 390
Nero (slave of Nathan Brown, Jr.), 252
Nesmith, Lucinda. *See* Parks, Lucinda (Nesmith)
New Boston (NY), 440, 454
New Brunswick, NJ, 94, 216, 234, 254, 326, 338, 528, 547
New Haven, CT, 129
New Ipswich, NH, 189, 234, 242, 279, 300, 427, 441, 462, 529; minute men and militia on April 19th, 13, 277, 278, 475
New Jersey; Washington's 1776 retreat across, 92; 1778 British march across, 115, *116 (map)*
New London, CT, 326, 377
New Milford, CT, 128
New Windsor, NY, *127 (map)*, 362, 401, 415, 418, 441, 447
New York (City), 91, 98, 105, 111, 115, 120, 133, 143, 144, 156; New York campaign, 76–79, *78 (map)*, 81–88, *83 (map)*
Newburgh, NY, 390
Newbury, MA, 325, 409
Newburyport, MA, 228, 400
Newington, SC, 269
Newport, RI, 37, 91, 111, 120–124, *125 (map)*. *See also* Rhode Island, Battle of
Newton, Lydia. *See* Bond, Lydia (Newton)
Newton, Seth (Capt.), 493; mentioned as unit commander, 267
NICHOLS, JAMES, xiii, 16, 19, 46, 57, 94, 95, 100, **355–358**, 356, 357, 508, 511, 516, 520, 522, 531; unit listings for, 474, 476, 479, 483, 486, 487, 489
Nicholson, Samuel (Capt.), 504; mentioned as unit commander, 444
Ninety-Six, SC, *138 (map)*, 144
Nixon, John (Capt.; Col.; Gen.); 358, 474, 475, 476, 477, 481, 482; in brigade command, 131, 358; as captain of Sudbury minute men, 343, 382, 341, 474; family relationships of, 358; mentioned as 4th Cont. unit commander, 76, 294, 326, 338, 346, 388, 389, 400; mentioned as 16th Mass. (5th Cont.) unit commander, 176, 178, 181, 187, 232, 239, 256, 258, 269, 272, 283, 294, 301, 318, 326, 327, 329, 332, 344, 346, 358, 384, 386, 387, 388, 398, 399, 400, 403, 411, 413, 434, 442, 445
NIXON, JOSEPH, 13, 76, 128, 131, 136, **358–359**, 506, 508, 513, 517, 520, 524, 525, 526; family relationships of, 28, 427; unit listings for, 476, 477, 481, 486, 488, 495, 497, 499, 502
Nixon, Nancy (Weston), 28, 358, 359, 525
Nixon, Thankful (Berry), 358
Nixon, Thomas (Lt. Col.; Col.); 131, 481, 482, 486, 488, 495, 497, 499, 500; succeeded to regimental command, 272, 294, 326, 358; mentioned as deranged, 358; mentioned as unit commander, 338, 358, 361, 388, 393, 398, 435
Noddles Island (Boston Harbor); 56–57, *57 (map)*, *62 (map)*, 403
Non-importation Agreement, 452
Norfolk County, MA, 194
Northborough, MA, 15, 280, 281, 290, 450, 452, 454; Committee of Correspondence of, 452
North Bridge. *See* Concord, MA, North Bridge fight; Concord, MA, North Bridge removed
North Brookfield, MA, 217
North Castle, NY, 36, 85, 88, 91, mentioned as discharge location, 91, 185, 201, 202, 305, 321, 331; mentioned as service location, 228, 239, 272, 305, 326, 338, 364, 388, 393, 398, 481, 500. *See also* White Plains, Battle of
North Kingston, RI, 244, 279, 295, 324, 398, 485, 493
North River, 38, 128, 134, 257, 353, 423, 443
Northern Army. *See* Northern Department, Continental Army
Northern Department, Continental Army, 71, 73, 74, 76, 97, 98, 99, 101, 104, 105, 108, 128; mentioned as serving in, 172, 177, 178, 183, 198, 201, 202, 203, 205, 244, 249, 255, 257, 270, 293, 310, 329, 331, 348, 353, 377, 378, 385, 408, 412, 419, 421, 427, 443. See also Canada, campaign in; Saratoga campaign; Ticonderoga
Norwalk, CT, 129

O

Old North Bridge. *See* Concord, MA, North Bridge fight; Concord, MA, North Bridge removed
Old Port Comfort, VA, 144, *145 (map)*
Oliver, Elisabeth, 360
Oliver, Lucy, 360
Oliver, Margaret, 360
Oliver, Mary, 360
OLIVER, PETER, 15, 42, 57, 108, 111, 112, 119, 120, 124, 132, 133, 134, 136, **359–360**, 506, 509, 517, 519, 521, 531; unit listings for, 476, 480, 485, 487, 490, 491, 492, 494, 495, 496, 499, 500, 502
Oliver, Peter (father of PETER), 360
Orangetown, NY, 134, 135, 388, 447. *See also* Tappan, NY
Orleans, NY, 427, 530
ORR, WILLIAM, 42, 88, 116, 120, 124, 126, **360–361**, 508, 511, 516, 517, 520, 531; payment for service of, *361*; unit listings for, 481, 482, 488, 490, 491, 492, 494, 496, 499, 503, 505
Oxford, MA, 31, 451, 452

P

PAGE, JONATHAN, 32, 115, **362–363**, 506, 509, 512, 516, 517, 519, 524, 531; unit listings for, 489, 496, 500, 502, 503, 504
Page, Lydia (Munroe), 363

Index

Paris, Treaty of. *See* Treaty of Paris
PARKER, AARON, 14, 155, 156, **363**, 367, 506, 508, 516, 519, 530; family relationships of, 364, 365; unit listings for, 501, 503, 504
Parker, Anna. *See* Smith, Anna (Parker)
Parker, Eunice (Hobbs), 363, 364, 365
Parker, Hannah. *See* Hosmer, Hannah (Parker)
Parker, Isaac, **467**
Parker, John (Capt.), 364, 365, 475; mentioned as unit commander, 174, 307
PARKER, JOSEPH, 14, 351, **364**, 506, 508, 516, 519, 528; family relationships of, 363, 365; unit listings for, 502, 503, 505
Parker, Joseph (father of AARON; JOSEPH; LEVI), 363, 364, 365
PARKER, LEVI, 42, **364–365**, 506, 509, 516, 519, 525, 529; family relationships of, 363, 364; unit listings for, 500, 502, 503, 504
Parker, Mary (Lyon), 365, 525
Parker, Obadiah (Capt.), 475; mentioned as unit commander, 181
Parker, Phineas (Capt.), 494, 496, 499; mentioned as unit commander, 347, 437
Parker, Polly (Fisk), 364
Parker, Sibbil. *See* Hosmer, Sibbil (Parker)
PARKES, NOAH. *SEE* PARKHURST, NOAH
Parkhurst, Eunice (Harrington), 366
Parkhurst, Isaac, 372
Parkhurst, Martha. *See* Hagar, Martha (Parkhurst)
Parkhurst, Nathaniel, 366
PARKHURST, NOAH, 16, 109, 114, 157, **365–366**, 506, 509, 516, 519, 527, 529; unit listings for, 474, 476, 488, 490, 500, 501, 503, 504
PARKS, AARON, *10*, 19, 68, 71, 363, **366–367**, 373, 467, 506, 509, 516, 519, 524, 525, 528; family relationships of, *27*, 337, 368, 370, 375, 379, 380, 434; unit listings for, 473, 476, 479
Parks, Abigail, *27*, 368, 369
Parks, Abigail (Garfield), *27*, 380
Parks, Abraham, **467–468**
Parks, Anna. *See* Tower, Anna (Parks)
Parks, Anna (Faugason), 372, 374
Parks, Anna (Jennison), 367
PARKS, BENJAMIN, 360, **367–368**, 508, 510, 516, 519, 528; family relationships of, *28*, 191, 337, 367, 369, 370, 371, 372, 373, 374, 375, 377, 379, 380, 415, 418, 434; unit listings for, 477, 478, 482, 488, 495
Parks, Betsey (Buckman). *See* Parks, Betsey (Bucknam)
Parks, Betsey (Bucknam), 379
Parks, Beulah (Tower), *27*, 376, 377, 525
PARKS, DAVID, **368–370**, 508, 511, 519, 529; family relationships of, *28*; 337, 367, 368, 371, 372, 373, 374, 375, 377, 379, 380, 434; house of, *369*; unit listing for, 480,
Parks, Ebenezer, **468**
PARKS, EBENEZER. *SEE* PARKS, ELEAZER

PARKS, ELEAZER, *11*, 100, 360, **370–371**, 373, 507, 509, 516, 519, 525, 528; family relationships of, *26*, 188, 368, 370, 372, 373, 374, 377, 379, 380, 468; house of, *381*; unit listings for, 473, 476, 478, 480, 485
Parks, Elizabeth. *See* Meloney, Elizabeth (Parks)
Parks, Elizabeth (Whitney), 371, 525
Parks, Ephraim, *26*, 371, 372, 374, 377, 379, 380
Parks, Eunice (Tower), *28*, 375, 377, 525
Parks, Hannah (Richardson), 379
Parks, Hannah (Wesson), *26*, 372
PARKS, ISAAC, *10*, 360, **371–372**, 467, 507, 510, 514, 519, 529; deposition of, 55, 188, 371; family relationships of, *26*, 188, 368, 370, 371, 373, 374, 377, 379, 380; house of, *381*; unit listings for, 474, 478, 482. *See* Depositions of April 1775
PARKS, JAMES (Lt.), *10*, 252, 360, **372–373**, 450, 507, 510, 512, 515, 519, 527; family relationships of, *26*, 289, 368, 370, 371, 372, 374, 377, 379, 380; unit listings for, 473, 480, 488, 489, 498
PARKS, JOHN, *10*, 108, 360, **373–374**, 507, 510, 512, 515, 516, 519, 531; family relationships of, *26*, 188, 368, 370, 371, 372, 373, 377, 379, 380; house of, *381*; unit listings for, 473, 476, 480, 486, 489, 498
PARKS, JONAS, *10*, 57, 71, 73, 153, 373, **374–375**, 507, 509, 513, 516, 519, 523, 525, 528; family relationships of, *28*; 218, 337, 367, 368, 370, 377, 379, 380, 415, 434; house of, *369*; unit listings for, 473, 476, 477, 480, 482, 486, 487, 494, 497, 501
Parks, Joseph (father of BENJAMIN; DAVID), *27*, 368, 369
Parks, Joseph, **468**. *See also* PARKS, JOSIAH
Parks, Joseph, Jr., *27*, 367
PARKS, JOSIAH, 97, **376–377**, 506, 509, 515, 519, 524, 525, 526; family relationships of, *27*, 368, 370, 371, 372, 373, 374, 379, 380, 415, 468; gravestone of, *376*; house of, *381*; unit listings for, 478, 483, 485
Parks, Josiah (father of JAMES), *26*, 372
PARKS, LEONARD, 13, 18, 59, 71, 73, 92, 93, 360, 373, **377–379**, 506, 508, 513, 516, 519, 524, 527; family relationships of, *28*; 337, 367, 368, 369, 370, 375, 380, 415, 434; house of, *369*; unit listings for, 474, 476, 480, 482, 485, 489, 494
Parks, Lois (Gibbs), 368, 369
Parks, Love. *See* Richardson, Love (Parks)
Parks, Lucinda (Nesmith), 367, 525
Parks, Lucy. *See* Peirce, Lucy (Parks)
Parks, Lucy (wife of WILLARD), 380
Parks, Lydia (wife of WILLIAM), 381
Parks, Lydia (Allen). *See* Wheeler, Lydia (Allen)
Parks, Lydia (Garfield), *27*, 367
Parks, Lydia (Wheeler), 191

Parks, Mary (Hobbs), *26*, 371, 372, 374, 377, 379, 380
Parks, Rhoda (Faugason), 372, 374
PARKS, SAMUEL, **379**, 507, 510, 512, 514, 519, 527; family relationships of, *27*, 368, 370, 371, 372, 373, 374, 377, 380; childhood home of, *381*; unit listing for, 500
Parks, Sarah. *See* Bond, Sarah (Parks)
Parks, Sarah (wife of BENJAMIN), 368
Parks, Sarah (Gibbs), *28*, 368, 369, 375, 379
Parks, Stephen, *27*, 380
Parks, Thankful (Coolidge), *26*, 372
PARKS, WILLARD, *10*, 373, **379–380**, 507, 509, 515, 519, 527; family relationships of, *27*, 218, 337, 367, 368, 370, 375, 379, 434; unit listings for, 473, 477, 478
PARKS, WILLIAM, *10*, 109, **380–381**, 508, 510, 515, 519, 531; family relationships of, *26*, 188, 368, 370, 371, 372, 373, 374, 377, 379; house of, *381*; unit listings for, 473, 485, 488
Paterson, John (Col.; Brig. Gen.), 71, 92, 480, 482; mentioned as unit commander, 246, 247, 251, 362, 374, 375, 377, 395, 405, 413, 435, 447
Patriot militias, 137, 138, 139
Patriots Day, 166, 167, 168
Pawlet, VT, 377
Peekskill, NY, 126, *127 (map)*, *129 (map)*, 134, 241, 254, 273, 327, 330, 344, 375, 415, 435, 447
Peg (slave of William Reed), 236, 353, 463
Pegasus, H.M.S. (British frigate), 449
Peirce. *See also* Pierce
Peirce, Abigail, 469
PEIRCE, ABIJAH (Capt.; Col.), *11*, **382–383**, 424, 508, 510, 512, 514, 517, 519, 526; April 19 command of, 9, 12, 54, 275, 382; civic activity of, 3, 15, 277, 383; family relationships of, 23, *24*, 223, 248, 249, 317, 385; mentioned as unit commander, 175, 176, 178, 187, 191, 196, 197, 205, 210, 213, 225, 232, 237, 240, 244, 245, 249, 258, 260, 268, 271, 275, 279, 281, 287, 289, 290, 292, 294, 297, 298, 300, 301, 304, 316, 318, 319, 326, 327, 329, 332, 344, 366, 370, 372, 373, 374, 379, 380, 383, 386, 388, 397, 399, 401, 403, 406, 410, 413, 420, 421, 429, 431, 432, 442, 445; musket from the North Bridge, *383*; unit listings for, 473, 474, 477, 505
PEIRCE, ABRAHAM, *11*, 56, 95, **383–384**, 507, 509, 513, 516, 519, 529; family relationships of, 385, 386, 469; unit listings for, 473, 475, 483, 484
Peirce, Abraham (Capt.), 474, 479, 489, 493; mentioned as unit commander, 267, 373, 385, 416, 417, 423, 426
Peirce, Anna (Gearfield), 469
Peirce, Anna (Sanderson), 386
Peirce, Esther. *See* Hoar, Esther (Peirce)
Peirce, Hannah Mason, 385
PEIRCE, ISAAC, 94, 100, 132, **384–386**, 506, 509, 513, 516, 519, 531; family

relationships of, 384, 469; unit listings for, 478, 483, 485, 489, 492, 498, 500
Peirce, Isaac (father of ABIJAH), *24*, 383
Peirce, Isaac (of Waltham), 385
Peirce, Jonas (Jr.), **468–469**; family relationships of, 384, 386
Peirce, Jonas (Sr.), 363, **468–469**; family relationships of, 384, 386
Peirce, Jonas, of Weston, 469
Peirce, Jonas (father of Jonas of Weston), 469
PEIRCE, JOSEPH, xvi, *11*, 60, 94, 95, 128, 131, 181, **386–387**, 507, 509, 512, 513, 517, 519, 524, 527; family relationships of, 384, 385, 386, 469; unit listings for, 473, 475, 478, 483, 486, 487, 494, 497, 499
Peirce, Joseph (father of Jonas (Sr.)), 469
Peirce, Joseph, Jr., **470**
Peirce, Lavina (Pool), 469
Peirce, Lois (Clark), 470
Peirce, Lucy (Parks), 386
Peirce, Mary. *See* Underwood, Mary (Peirce)
Peirce, Mary (Adams), 384, 386, 469
Peirce, Mary (Headley), 386
Peirce, Mehitable, 386
Peirce, Phebe (Towne), 384
Peirce, Polley (Headley). *See* Peirce, Mary (Headley)
Peirce, Sarah (Bridge), 469
Peirce, Susanna. *See* Hoar, Susanna (Peirce)
Peirce, Susanna (Allen), 470
Peirce, Susanna (Bemis), *24*, 383
Peirce, Thankful (Brown), *249*, 383
Pell's Point. *See* New York (City), New York campaign
Penniman, Peter (Capt.), 485; mentioned as unit commander, 241
Penobscot Expedition, 132, 207, 208, 426, 495, 523; arrival of British ships at, *207*
Penobscot, ME, 253, 254, 255
Penobscot River, 207, 253, 255, 483
Pensions, Revolutionary War, xvi–xvii, 524–525; invalid pension, 19, 336, 375
Pepperell, MA, 178, 179, 235, 256, 279, 527
Perry, Abner (Col.), 498; mentioned as unit commander, 181, 257, 372
Perry, James (Capt.), 357
Peterborough, NH, 21, 40, 466
Petersburg, VA, 144
Petersham, MA, 216, 335, 336
Phelps, NY, 427
Philadelphia (gunboat), *80*
Philadelphia, PA, 18, 68, 74, 144, 307, 405, 449; British occupation of, 104, 111, 115; defense of, 98–104, *103 (map)*, 177, 273; mutiny at, 391, 441
Phillips, Benjamin, **470**
Phillips, Eunice. *See* Thorning, Eunice (Phillips)
Phillipston, MA, 298
Phinney, Edmund (Col.), 243
Phinney, Elias, 159, 160
Pierce. *See also* Peirce

Pierce, Abigail. *See* Knowlton, Abigail (Pierce)
Pierce, Samuel (Lt. Col.; Col.), 493, 496; mentioned as unit commander, 37, 211, 274, 279, 315, 362, 419
Pilsbury, Daniel (Capt.), 499, 501; mentioned as unit commander, 447
Pitcairn, John (Maj.), 341
Plantation No. 23, ME, 254
Plimpton, Ezekiel (Capt.), 485; mentioned as unit commander, 324
Plymouth, MA, 289, 384, 484
Plymouth County, MA, 253, 255, 259, 307
Point Judith, RI, 37, 180, 199, 271, 342, 371, 376, 391, 402, 421
Pollard, Benjamin (Capt.), 487, 494; mentioned as unit commander, 347, 437, 438
Pool, Lavina. *See* Peirce, Lavina (Pool)
Poor, Salem, 403
Poor, Thomas (Col.), 495; mentioned as unit commander, 257, 353, 423, 443
Pope Pond (NJ), 340
Pops Pond. *See* Pope Pond (NJ)
Porter, Edward G. (Rev.), 166
PORTER, JOHN, xvii, 200, **387**, 508, 511, 517, 520, 531; unit listings for, 475, 505
Portsmouth, NH, 44, 48, 164, 452
Portsmouth, VA, 142, 144, *145 (map)*
Potomac River (VA), 143
Potsdam, NY, 365
Potter, Elizabeth. *See* Brooks, Elizabeth (Potter)
POTTER, JOHN. SEE PORTER, JOHN
Powder House Alarm, 43
Prescott, Ame. *See* Baker, Ame (Prescott)
Prescott, James (Col.), 474; mentioned as unit commander, 199
Prescott, Samuel (Dr.), 7, 197
Prescott, William (Col.; Gen.), 474, 476; mentioned as unit commander, 57, 267, 302, 359, 370
Presidential Inaugural Ceremonies, 167
Prichard, Thomas (Lt.; Capt.), 494, 497, 499, 501, 502, 503, 504; mentioned as unit commander, 187, 290, 386, 388, 440
Princeton, MA, 193, 281, 300, 301, 307, 364, 365, 465, 467, 527; minute men and militia on April 19th, 13, 280, 299, 465, 474
Princeton, NJ, 142, 207, 441; Battle of, 18, 19, 93, 94, 95, 192, 248, 252, 272, 273, 285, 339, 378, 388, 399, 400
Prisoners of war; British prisoner in Lincoln, 55, *56*, 283, 284, 285; British prisoners taken at Saratoga, 108, 109, 115; Lincoln soldiers taken by the enemy; xvii, 18, 19, 73, 91, 201, 202, 244–245, 247, 290, 307, 308, 400, 405, 449, 522. *See also* Convention Army
Privateer, xi, 18, 156, 183, 248, 400, 404, 405, 449, 454
Prospect Hill (Somerville, MA); escorting the prisoners to, 108, 268, 314, 330, 378; guarding the prisoners at, 109, 206, 209, 330; 1775 service at, 243, 246, 294, 355, 365, 366, 370, 373, 374, 377, 412, 413, 416, 437
Providence, RI, 37, 38, 92, 120, 398; mentioned as serving at, 177, 186, 193, 219, 233, 234, 241, 254, 273, 282, 315, 324, 326, 330, 342, 359, 376, 459, 462, 496
Provincial Army. *See* Massachusetts Provincial Army
Provincial Congress. *See* Massachusetts Provincial Congress
Putnam, CT, 529
Putnam, John (Capt.), 493; mentioned as unit commander, 224
Putnam, Rufus (Lt. Col.; Col.; Gen.), 500, 502, 503, 504; mentioned as unit commander, 63, 233, 327, 330, 340, 362, 443

Q

Quebec (City), Canada; Battle of, 68, *70*, 232, 477. *See also* Canada, Campaign to
Quincy, Elizabeth. *See* Smith, Elizabeth (Quincy)

R

Raritan, NJ, 347
Ravena, NY, 262
Read, Sally. *See* Wheeler, Sally (Read)
Reading, MA, 104, 228, 423, 424, 467; minute men and militia on April 19th, 13, *50 (map)*, 51, 52
Recruitment. *See* Troop calls
Redoubt # 9, *148 (map)*, 150. *See also* Yorktown, VA, Siege of
Redoubt # 10, *148 (map)*, 150, *151*. *See also* Yorktown, VA, Siege of
Reed, Anna (Johnson), 389
REED, ARTEMAS, 15, 33, 42, 58, 88, 91, 93, 128, 131, 134, 136, 154, 258, **388–389**, 507, 510, 517, 519, 522, 524, 530; unit listings for, 473, 475, 481, 482, 486, 487, 494, 497, 499, 502, 503
Reed, George (Lt. Col.; Col.), 503; mentioned as unit commander, 214, 309, 339
Reed, James (Col.), 476; mentioned as unit commander, 189, 214
Reed, Jonathan (Col.), 81, 100, 115, 173, 230, 480, 485, 489; mentioned as unit commander guarding the Convention, 193, 256, 264, 274, 279, 298, 314, 362, 374, 378, 385, 393, 419, 425, 433, 470; mentioned as unit commander at Saratoga, 183, 205, 216, 238, 268, 275, 295, 314, 329, 331, 353, 378, 408, 412, 433, 443; mentioned as unit commander at Ticonderoga, 74, 175, 189, 198, 214, 215, 216, 257, 271, 309, 316, 318, 319, 322, 349, 370, 373, 407, 410, 412, 435, 442
Reed, Joseph. *See* Reed, Josiah
Reed, Joseph (Col.), 402
Reed, Josiah, 330
Reed, William (Capt.), 484; mentioned as unit commander, 203, 212
Reid, George (Lt. Col.). *See* Reed, George (Lt. Col.; Col.)
Remick, Timothy (Capt.), 245

Index 569

Renown, H.M.S., 123
Residences of Lincoln minute men and militia, 1775, *10–11 (map)*
Resolves of the General Court. *See* Troop calls
Revere, Paul (Col.); alarm ride and capture of, 7, *8*, 44, 166, 167, 350, 351; capture site and monument, *166*, 287; court martial of, 133; mentioned as unit commander, 263
Rhode Island, 33, 34, 37, 38, 60, 132, 262; response to alarm of April 19th, 54; British occupation of Newport, 91, 100, 132; mentioned as marching on alarms to, 173, 179, 180, 271, 324, 345, 372, 381, 426, 483, 485; mentioned as serving stints in, 97, 153, 181, 185, 187, 193, 199, 205, 206, 209, 210, 211, 214, 218, 224, 225, 231, 234, 241, 244, 257, 259, 266, 267, 274, 279, 294, 295, 306, 313, 315, 317, 324, 325, 329, 330, 335, 341, 342, 347, 349, 362, 370, 371, 374, 376, 391, 395, 411, 412, 413, 419, 421, 422, 423, 433, 434, 435, 436, 443; unit listings for service at, 492–493, 495, 498, 501, 505. *See also* Rhode Island, Battle of
Rhode Island, Battle of, 120–126, *122–123*, *125 (map)*, 492, 505; mentioned as a participant in, 19, 177, 180, 186, 217, 218, 219, 233, 236, 238, 254, 273, 282, 300, 321, 332, 336, 339, 341, 359, 361, 385, 394, 402, 414; unit listings at, 492
Rice, Adonijah, 95, 100, **389–390**, 508, 511, 513, 515, 516, 520, 522, 531; unit listings for, 486, 487, 497
Rice, Adonijah (of Marlborough or Westborough), 390
Rice, Adonijah (of Worcester), 390
Rice, Charles, 390
Rice, Hannah (Crosby), 390
Rice, Jonathan (Capt.), 244, 249
Rice, Patty. *See* Bacon, Patty (Rice)
Rice, Persis (Gates), 390
Rice, Rachael (Wheeler), 390
Richardson, Abigail (Swan), 392
Richardson, Abijah, 391
Richardson, Abner, 42, 154, 156, **390–391**, 506, 509, 516, 519, 524, 525, 530; payment for service of, *391*; unit listings for, 501, 503, 504
Richardson, Anna (Moore), 391, 525
Richardson, Barnabas, **391–392**, 506, 508, 509, 510, 514, 520, 531; unit listing for, 485
Richardson, Barnabas, Jr., 392
Richardson, Edward (father of Barnabas), 392
Richardson, Edward (Capt.), 495; mentioned as unit commander, 257, 353, 443
Richardson, Ezra, 75, **392**, 508, 511, 519, 527; unit listings for, 480, 505
Richardson, Hannah. *See* Parks, Hannah (Richardson)
Richardson, Jerusha, 392
Richardson, John, 392
Richardson, Love (Parks), 392
Richardson, Mary, 392

Richardson, Rebecca (Tidd), 392
Richardson, Sarah (Stewart), 391
Richmond, VA, 142, 143, 144, *145 (map)*, 254, 502
Rindge, NH, 242, 384, 529
Ringwood, NJ, 142, 204
Ripley, Ezra (Rev.), 160, 284
Ritzema, Rudolphus (Col.), 87
Robbinston, ME, 216, 254, 528
Robenson, Cain, Cane, or Kane. *See* Robinson, Keen
Robinson, Achsah (Leathe), 393, 525
Robinson, Bradbury, 393; deposition of, 184. *See also* Depositions of 1775
Robinson, Eunice (Amsden), 393
Robinson, Jeremiah (Dr.), 393
Robinson, John (Capt.), xii, 191
Robinson, John (Col.), 36, 61, 478, 479; mentioned as unit commander, 187, 198, 213, 233, 279, 304, 318, 329, 332, 340, 406, 412, 420, 421, 442
Robinson, Keen, 79, **392–393**, 509, 516, 519, 524, 525, 529; family relationships of, 184; unit listings for, 481, 489, 495
Robinson, Samuel (Capt.), 463
Robinson's Farm (NY), 126, *127 (map)*
Rochambeau, Comte de (Gen.), 146, 150, *147 (map)*
Round Hill (NY). *See* Kingsbridge, NY
Round, Jerusha. *See* Cleaveland, Jerusha (Round)
Rowley, MA, 409, 527
Roxbury, MA, 36, 54, 61, *62 (map)*, 64, 65, 158, 285, 365, 407; mentioned as serving at, 94, 198, 249, 252, 267, 268, 270, 292, 332, 346, 348, 394, 402, 422, 426; unit listings for service at, 478, 479, 483, 484, 493, 496
Royal Bounty (prize ship), 404
Royal Navy, 15, 30, 80, 126, 190, 450. *See also Greenwich*, H.M.S.; *Liberty*, H.M.S.; *Milford*, H.M.S.; *Pegasus*, H.M.S.; *Renown*, H.M.S.; *Scarborough*, H.M.S.; *Tyger*, H.M.S.
Royalton, VT, 365, 529; alarm, 379, 500
Ruggles, Timothy, 451
Russell estate. *See* Codman House
Russell, Azubah. *See* Jones, Azubah (Russell)
Russell, Betsy. *See* Thorning, Betsy (Russell)
Russell, Betty. *See* Thorning, Betsy (Russell)
Russell, Charles (Dr.), xiii, 9, 15, 59, 95, 158, **454–455**, 519; portrait of, *455*
Russell, Elizabeth (Vassall), 454
Russell, Judge James, 454
Russell, Katherine (Graves), 454
Russell, Penelope, 455
Russell, Thaddeus (Capt.), 280
Rutland, MA, 106, 275, 299, 366, 496; Barracks, 365, 490

S

Salem Light Infantry Company, 401
Salem, MA, 20, 56, 400, 401, 404, 451, 454, 527; alarm, 44, 48, 164
Salem, Peter, 341

Salmon, Catherine Louisa. *See* Smith, Catherine Louisa (Salmon)
Samson, Andrew (Capt.), 484; mentioned as unit commander, 384
Sanderson, Anna. *See* Peirce, Anna (Sanderson)
Sandy Hook, NJ, 76, 120
Santford, John (Capt.), 494; mentioned as unit commander, 327, 330, 344, 412
Saratoga, NY, 391. *See also* Saratoga campaign
Saratoga campaign, 18, 37, 41, 95–98, *96 (map)*, 98, 104–110, *106–107 (maps)*, 109; draft list for, 99; draft order for, 172; militia mobilization for, 37, 97, 99–100; mentioned as serving on, 13, 15, 16, 18, 19, 33, 128, 173, 183, 194, 198, 201, 205, 206, 213, 214–215, 216, 218, 224, 225, 230–231, 232, 233, 238, 243, 244, 246, 249, 252, 255, 257, 261, 262, 263, 264, 268, 270, 273, 275–276, 293, 294–295, 299, 309, 310, 313, 314, 317, 318, 321, 323, 329–330, 331, 348, 353, 356, 358, 359, 371, 375, 376, 378, 385, 386, 388, 396, 401, 402, 408, 411, 412, 419, 422, 423, 424, 427, 433, 437; unit listings for service on, 485–486. *See also* Arnold, Benedict (Col.; Brig. Gen.; Maj. Gen.); Burgoyne, John (Gen.); Convention Army
Saratoga Convention, 108, 115. *See also* Burgoyne, John (Gen.); Convention Army; Saratoga campaign
Sargent, Hopestill. *See* Whitney, Hopestill (Sargent)
Sargent, Joseph (Capt.), 474; mentioned as unit commander, 280
Sargentville, ME, 204, 208, 528
Savage, Jube, 65, 94, 121, 126, 274, 360, **393–394**, 508, 511, 515, 519, 521, 529; payment for service of, *394*; unit listings for, 478, 483, 492
Savage, Judith, 394
Savage, Samuel Phillips, 394, 395
Savannah, GA, 137, 144, 154
Sawyer, Ephraim (Col.), 214
Scarborough, H.M.S. (British frigate), 452
Schenectady, NY, 203, 204, 212, 497
Schuyler, Philip (Gen.), 104
Schuylkill River (PA), 111, 347
Sedgewick, ME, 203, 204, 205, 212, 528
Semple, Betty (Wheat), 428–429
Semple, John, 428–429
Semple, Mary (Wheat), 428–429
Semple, Robert, 428–429
Seven Years' War. *See* French and Indian War
Sharman. *See* Sherman
Sharmon. *See* Sherman
Sharon, NH, 188
Sharon, Peter, 33, 42, 354, 355, **395–396**, 506, 509, 516, 519, 521, 527; family relationships of, 397; unit listings for, 498, 500, 502. *See also* Nelson, Peter
Sharon, Prince, 222, 395, 396, 397
Sharon, Rose, 222, 395, 396, 397
Sharon, Silas, 41, 112, 119, 120, **396–397**, 507, 510, 516, 519, 521, 523, 531;

family relationships of, 395; unit listings for, 486, 488, 490, 491
Sharon, VT, 366
Shattuck, Job (Capt.), 479; mentioned as unit commander, 304
Shaw, Elisabeth. *See* Adams, Elisabeth (Shaw)
Shays' Rebellion, 277, 292, 299, 317
Shearman. *See* Sherman
Shed, Joseph (Capt.), 497; mentioned as unit commander, 199
Shepard, William (Col.), 501, 503, 504; mentioned as unit commander, 363
Sherborn, Henry (Maj.), 202
Sherborn, MA, 470
Sherbourn (Colonel), 488, 495, 497, 500; mentioned as unit commander, 293
Sherman, Abigail (Worcester). *See* Farrar, Abigail (Worcester)
Sherman, Elizabeth (Bruce), 398
Sherman, Eunice. *See* Farrar, Eunice (Sherman)
Sherman, Jonathan, 398
Sherman, Mary (Maynard), 398
Sherman, Samuel, 280
SHERMAN, TIMOTHY, 51, 132, **397–398**, 507, 510, 514, 515, 519, 527; family relationships of, 280; unit listings for, 473, 474, 484
Sheshequin, PA, 247
"Shot heard round the world", 162
Shrewsbury, MA, 325, 469
Sidney, ME, 176, 328, 528
Simonds, Hannah. *See* Brooks, Hannah (Simonds)
Simonds, Ruth. *See* Farrar, Ruth (Simonds)
Simonds, Sarah. *See* Meriam, Sarah (Simonds)
Skenesborough, VT, 76, 332
Slavery, the denial of English charter rights as, 7, 56. *See also* African-Americans; Slaves and slavery
Slaves and slavery, xiv; bill of manumission, 311; bill of sale, 354; identified slaves, 240, 274, 310, 312, 323, 341, 353, 394, 399; gravestone for former slave, 166; names and name changes upon manumission, 219–222, 240, *273*, 355, 394–395, 396; war service by identified slaves, 240, 274, 310, 312, 323, 341, 353, 394, 399; responsibility of former slaveholders to provide for, 219–222, 240. *See also* African-Americans
Smallpox, 71, 72, 73, 214, 238, 272, 307, 378; inoculation, 71, 72, 73, 112, 254, 375, 523
Smallwood, William (Col.), 87
Smith, Abigail. *See* Adams, Abigail (Smith); Wheat, Abigail (Smith)
Smith, Abigail (Munroe), 400
Smith, Abigail (Stratton), 402
Smith, Amos, 402
Smith, Ann (Willis), 402
Smith, Anna (Parker), 402
Smith, Benjamin, Jr., 402
Smith, Braddyll (Capt.; Col.), 219, 283, 286, 341, 342, 399, 405

Smith, Calvin (Lt. Col.; Col.), 499, 501, 502, 503; mentioned as unit commander, 358, 389, 448
Smith, Catherine Louisa (Salmon), 158, 288, 405
SMITH, CATO, 58, 76, 91, 92, 93, 219, **398–399**, 403, 404, 508, 511, 516, 520, 521, 523, 531; unit listings for, 475, 481, 482
Smith, Dorcas. *See* Wood, Dorcas (Smith)
Smith, Ebenezer (Capt.), 502, 503; mentioned as unit commander, 389
Smith, Elizabeth. *See* Tidd, Elizabeth (Smith)
Smith, Elizabeth (Quincy), 405
Smith, Ephraim, 400
Smith, Francis (Lt. Col.), 45
Smith, Isaac, 403
SMITH, JESSE, *11*, 19, 88, 101, 104, 112, 113, 116, 118, **399–401**, 428, 507, 509, 513, 517, 519, 522, 524, 527; family relationships of, 427, 429; unit listings for, 473, 475, 481, 482, 487, 490, 491, 500
Smith, John (Col.), 474; mentioned as unit commander, 324
SMITH, JONATHAN, 8, 110, **401–402**, 468, 507, 510, 516, 520, 526; family relationships of, *23*, *28*, 206, 208, 210, 211; unit listings for, 473, 477, 482, 485, 489
Smith, Jonathan (of Lexington), 402
Smith, Jonathan (of Reading), 402
Smith, Jonathan (of Sudbury), 402
Smith, Joseph (Capt.), 280, 340
Smith, Lucy. *See* Gearfield, Lucy (Smith)
Smith, Lucy (Billings), *28*, 401, 402
Smith, Lydia. *See* Mathis, Lydia (Smith)
Smith, Martha, 402
Smith, Mary. *See* Wheat, Mary (Smith)
Smith, Nathan (Capt.), 493; mentioned as unit commander, 186, 300
Smith, Polly (Haynes), 402
Smith, Sallie (Grant). *See* Smith, Sarah (Grant)
Smith, Sarah (Grant), 401
Smith, Sarah (Taylor), 402
Smith, Susanna (wife of Amos), 402
Smith, Susannah. *See* Gage, Susannah (Smith)
SMITH, THOMAS, 120, 126, **402**, 506, 509, 515, 520, 527; unit listings for, 483, 485, 492
Smith, Thomas (of Lexington), 402
Smith, Thomas (of Sudbury), 402
SMITH, WILLIAM (Capt.), *11*, *17*, 18, 42, 158, **403–406**, 500, 502, 507, 510, 512, 513, 516, 520, 522, 531; Cambridge service of, 54, 55, 56, 57, 60; farm and slave holdings of, 15, 17, 192, 288, 399; house of, *17*, *404*; mentioned as unit commander, 58, 175, 176, 178, 181, 187, 196, 197, 205, 210, 213, 225, 237, 239, 244, 245, 249, 256, 258, 260, 268, 271, 275, 281, 287, 289, 290, 292, 297, 298, 300, 301, 304, 316, 318, 319, 326, 327, 329, 332, 344, 366, 370, 372, 373, 374, 379, 380, 382, 383, 384, 386, 387, 388, 398, 399, 401, 406, 410, 411, 413, 420,

421, 429, 432, 442, 445, 460; as minute man captain, 7, 12, 36, 44, 46, 49, 54; unit listings for, 473, 475, 477, 488
Smith, William (Rev.), 399, 404, 405
Smyrna, NY, 192, 530
Snakehill (NY), 254
Sodus, NY, 325
Soldier's Fortune (NY), 126, 128, 435
Somerset County, ME, 433
Sons of the American Revolution, 458
South Carolina, 15, 76, 137, 138, 139, 143, 144, 146, 153, 262, 269, 307, 451, 454
Southport, NY, 247
Spanish Inquisition, 18, 303
Sparhawk, Nathan (Col.), 474, 490; mentioned as unit commander, 280, 345, 365
Spencer, Joseph (Gen.), 84
Spencer, Sarah. *See* Blodget, Sarah (Spencer)
Spring, Samuel; deposition of, 184. *See also* Depositions of 1775
Springfield, MA, 109, 390, 497; induction camp at, 199, 204, 206, 211, 337, 338, 340, 359, 362, 388, 389, 393, 395, 413, 435, 436, 447
Springfield, NJ, 272, 273, 405
Springfield, VT, 369, 529
Sprout, Ebenezer (Col.) 500, 503, 504; mentioned as unit commander, 340, 391
Squires, Statira. *See* Bemis, Statira (Squires)
St. Clair, Arthur (Gen.), 363
St. John's, Nova Scotia (now New Brunswick), 71, 74, 80, 81, 89, 95; expedition against, 254, 488
St. Lucia, 217, 530
St. Stephen, New Brunswick, Canada, 216, 528
Stapels, Polley. *See* Bemis, Polley (Stapels)
Stark, John (Gen.), 98, 264
Stearnes, Abegail. *See* Hartwell, Abegail (Stearnes)
Stearns (Captain), 500; mentioned as unit commander, 364
Stearns, Abijah (Col.), 493; mentioned as unit commander, 267
Stearns, Hannah. *See* Hagar, Hannah (Stearns)
Sterling, MA, 256, 386, 387
Steuben, Baron von. *See* von Steuben, Baron (Gen.)
Stewart, Sarah. *See* Richardson, Sarah (Stewart)
Stillwater, NY. *See* Saratoga campaign
Stimpson, Sarah. *See* Gearfield, Sarah (Stimpson)
Stimson, Anna. *See* Jones, Anna (Stimson)
Stirling (General), 119
Stirling, Lord. *See* Stirling (General)
Stockbridge, MA, 61, 442, 445, 523
Stockbridge, VT, 257, 529
Stoddard, NH, 234, 315, 379; Committee of Correspondence and Safety, 379
Stone, Ephraim (Capt.), 500; mentioned as unit commander, 366
STONE, GREGORY (SR.), *11*, 16, 188, 363, **407–408**, 508, 510, 514, 519, 526; deposition of, 188, 407; family relationships of, *24*, 225, 226, 231, 233, 234, 236, 238,

Index

242, 407, 408, 409, 459; unit listing for, 474. *See also* Depositions of April 1775
STONE, GREGORY, JR., *11*, 16, 74, 188, **406–407**, 507, 509, 515, 519, 525, 526; family relationships of, 24, 225, 226, 232, 233, 235, 237, 238, 242, 407, 408, 409; unit listings for, 473, 478, 480, 484
Stone, Hephzibah (Brooks), 24, 407, 408, 409
STONE, JOSHUA, 91, **408**, 507, 510, 515, 519, 527; family relationships of, 24, 225, 226, 232, 233, 235, 237, 238, 242, 407, 409; unit listings for, 478, 481, 485
Stone, Lucy (Jones), 407, 525
Stone, Mary. *See* Brooks, Mary (Stone)
Stone, Moses (Capt.), 431
Stone, Persis. *See* Adams, Persis (Stone)
Stone, Sarah (Avery), 408
STONE, TIMOTHY, 132, **408–409**, 420, 506, 509, 514, 519, 527; family relationships of, 24, 225, 226, 232, 233, 235, 237, 238, 242, 407, 408; unit listings for, 478, 497
Stony Point, NY, 126, *127 (map)*, 128, *129 (map)*, 132, 134; storming of, 129–131, *130 (map)*, 131
Storey, Elizabeth. *See* Foster, Elizabeth (Storey)
Stow, MA, 223, 244, 245, 295, 371, 426, 436, 457; minute men and militia on April 19th, 46
Stow, Timothy (Capt.), 480; mentioned as unit commander, 359
Stowell, Thankful. *See* Gearfield, Thankful (Stowell)
Stratton, Abigail. *See* Smith, Abigail (Stratton)
Stratton, Jane. *See* Colburn, Jane (Stratton)
Stratton, Rebecca. *See* Adams, Rebecca (Stratton)
Stratton, Sarah. *See* Cleaveland, Sarah (Stratton)
Substitution. *See* Draft; Enlistment
Sudbury, MA, 270, 322, 398; minute men and militia on April 19th, 13, 51, 279, 280, 343, 382, 397, 431, 473–474; mentioned as residence location, 44, 179, 185, 192, 203, 204, 249, 259, 270, 280, 293, 295, 312, 321, 341, 359, 368, 369, 397, 398, 402, 427, 431, 432
Suffolk County, MA; Continental Army enlistment from, 180, 446; regiments, 199, 305, 306, 324, 390, 400, 483, 485, 498
Sullivan, John (Gen.), 120, 123, 124, 199, 329, 375
Sumner, Job (Capt.), 486, 487, 494, 497; mentioned as unit commander, 289, 375
Surrender of Burgoyne. *See* Burgoyne, John (Gen.); Saratoga campaign
Surrender of Cornwallis. *See* Cornwallis, Charles (Gen.); Yorktown, VA
Sutton, MA, 295, 379, 451, 454
Swan, Abigail. *See* Richardson, Abigail (Swan)
Swan, James (Capt.), 483; mentioned as unit commander, 263, 344, 384, 385, 386, 414, 425

Symmes, Andrew (Maj.; Lt. Col.), 484, 493; mentioned as unit commander, 263, 415

T

Tappan, NY, 136, 340, 400. *See also* Orangetown, NY
Tarbell, Elizabeth. *See* Hartwell, Elizabeth (Tarbell)
Tarbell, Nancy. *See* Adams, Nancy (Tarbell)
Tarleton, Banastre (Col.), 133, 140
Tarrytown, NY, 92, 133, 134, 234, 281
Taunton, MA, 315
Taylor, Elizabeth. *See* Baker, Elizabeth (Taylor)
Taylor, Hepzibah. *See* Baker, Hepzibah (Taylor)
Taylor, Mary. *See* Brooks, Mary (Taylor)
Taylor, Othniel (Capt.), 499; mentioned as unit commander, 338
Taylor, Rachel. *See* Brooks, Rachel (Taylor)
Taylor, Sarah. *See* Smith, Sarah (Taylor)
Taylor, Trobridge, 279
Temple, ME, 319
Temple, NH, 234, 345, 394, 529
Templeton, MA, 183, 365
Tenney, Hannah (Boynton), 409
TENNEY, MICAH. *See* TENY, MICHAEL
Tenney, Thomas, 409
Tenney, William, 409
TENY, MICHAEL, 77, 84, 87, **409**, 507, 510, 515, 520, 527; unit listings for, 481, 489
Thatcher, Samuel (Col.), 37, 92, 479, 481, 493; mentioned as unit commander, 192, 199, 208, 234, 252, 267, 285, 286, 339, 408, 414, 423, 426, 432
Thayer, Ebenezer (Col.), 500; mentioned as unit commander, 400
Thomas, John (Gen.), 71
Thomas, Nathaniel (Lt.), 384
Thomas, Phebe (Towne). *See* Peirce, Phebe (Towne)
Thomas, Samuel (Capt.), 244
Thompson (Major), 494, 497, 499; mentioned as unit commander, 290
Thompson, CT, 372
Thoreau, Henry David, 309, 310
Thorndike, Larkin (Capt.), 475; mentioned as unit commander, 247
Thorning, Betsy (Russell), 410
Thorning, Betty (Russell). *See* Thorning, Betsy (Russell)
Thorning, Eunice (Phillips), 413, 525
THORNING, JOHN, *11*, **410**, 412, 506, 509, 515, 519, 527; family relationships of, 413; unit listings for, 473, 480, 483
Thorning, John (father of JOHN; WILLIAM), 410, 413
Thorning, Sarah (Clarke), 410, 413
THORNING, WILLIAM, *11*, 52, 56, 60, 105, 128, 153, 363, **410–413**, 506, 509, 512, 513, 517, 519, 524, 525, 527; boulder from which he shot Redcoats, *411*; family relationships of, 410; unit listings for, 473, 475, 478, 480, 483, 485, 494, 495, 496, 500, 501
Thornton, NH, 442, 529

Throg's Neck. *See* New York (City), New York campaign
Ticonderoga, NY; American 1776 defense of, 36, 71, 73–76, *75 (map)*, 81, 89, 228; British 1777 capture and occupation of, *96 (map)*, 97, 99, 105, 109; Knox's 1775 expedition to, 61, 442, *443*, 477; on the route to and from Canada, 19, 68, *72 (map)*, 73, 202, 246, 258, 286, 367; mentioned as serving in 1776 defense of, 175, 178, 189, 190, 198, 205, 213, 214, 215, 216, 224, 225, 232, 234, 235, 239, 257, 271, 275, 279, 291, 298, 300, 301, 309, 314, 316, 318, 319, 322, 332–333, 349–352, 359, 368–369, 370, 372, 373, 392, 407, 410, 412, 416, 430, 431, 435, 442; unit listings at, 480
Tidd, Amos, 414
Tidd, Benjamin, deposition of, 174. *See also* Depositions of 1775
Tidd, Elizabeth (Smith), 414
Tidd, Lydia. *See* Hastings, Lydia (Tidd)
TIDD, NATHAN, 60, 101, 104, 119, 121, **413–414**, 507, 509, 512, 513, 517, 520, 523, 531; unit listings for, 473, 475, 478, 483, 487, 490, 491, 492, 494
Tidd, Oliver, 414
Tidd, Rebecca. *See* Richardson, Rebecca (Tidd)
Tisdale, James (Capt.), 499; mentioned as unit commander, 388
Titcomb, Jonathan (Gen.), 121
Titcomb, Oliver (Capt.), 409
Tiverton, RI, 262; mentioned in Battle of Rhode Island, 123, 332; mentioned as service location, 37, 121, 186, 211, 266, 274, 279, 315, 324, 347, 362, 419, 433, 463, 496, 498
Tombo (slave of Deacon John Gove), 296, 463
Tories. *See* Loyalists
Torrey, Bethia (Bass), 415
TORREY, EBENEZER, 91, **414–415**, 508, 511, 512, 514, 515, 520, 531; unit listings for, 481, 483, 493
Torrey, Ebenezer (of Boston), 415
Torrey, Samuel, Jr., 414
Torrey, Sarah (Barron), 414
Torrey, Silence, 414
Torrey, Suzannah, 414
Torrey, William, 415
Tower, Abigail (Dudley), 415
Tower, Anna (Parks), 27, 415
Tower, Beulah. *See* Parks, Beulah (Tower)
Tower, Eunice. *See* Parks, Eunice (Tower)
Tower, Eunice (Allen), 27, 191, 415
TOWER, JOHN. *See* TOWER, JONATHAN
TOWER, JONATHAN, 42, 156, 191, **415–416**, 436, 506, 509, 516, 519, 524, 527; family relationships of, 27, 209, 210, 368, 370, 375, 377, 418, 434; unit listings for, 501, 502, 503, 504
Tower, Jonathan (father of JONATHAN), 27, 415
TOWER, JONATHAN, JR.. *See* TOWER, JONATHAN
Towne, Phebe. *See* Peirce, Phebe (Towne)
Town Meeting, 5, 6, 449; in Amherst, NH, 453; in Lexington, 159; in Sud-

bury, 252, 398; in Weston, 433. *See also* Lincoln, MA, Town Meeting in
Townsend, MA, 15, 16, 190, 234, 246, 266, 267, 379, 449, 450, 527; minute men and militia on April 19th, 13, 474
Trade; Atlantic trade routes, 30
Trask, Elizabeth. *See* Brown, Elizabeth (Trask)
Treaty of Paris, xvii, 156, 441
Tree, Jupiter. *See* Free, Jupiter
Trenton, NJ, 95, 129, 142, 192, 252, 285, 307, 339; Battle of, 18, 19, 91–93, *93 (map)*, 94; mentioned as participant in Battle of, 73, 241, 246, 248, 251, 272, 273, 326, 338, 369, 375, 378, 388, 399, 400; unit listings in Battle of, 480, 482. *See also* Delaware River, Washington's Crossing of
Trescott, Lemuel (Capt.), 492, 493; mentioned as unit commander, 177, 233
Troop calls, 32, 34–36, *36–38 (table)*, 99–100, 228, 409, 420; penalties, *35 (table)*, 333–334; sampling of bounties, *34 (table)*. *See also* Draft; Enlistment
Troy, NH, 269, 270, 271, 292, 529
Tulop, Peggy, 353
Tulop, Robbin, 353
Turner, Thomas (Capt.), 487, 490, 491, 492, 494, 496, 499, 501; mentioned as unit commander, 177, 390
Turner, William (Col.), 501; mentioned as unit commander, 179, 413, 435
Turrell, Salley. *See* Winship, Salley (Turrell)
Turtle Bay, NY, 398, 481. *See also* New York (City), New York campaign
Tyger, H.M.S. (British hospital ship), 449
Tyler, Nathan (Col.), 496; mentioned as unit commander, 325, 330, 412

U

Underwood, Joseph, 416
Underwood, Mary (Peirce), 416
UNDERWOOD, MOSES, 79, 360, **416**, 508, 510, 515, 520, 527; unit listing for, 480
Underwood, Ruth. *See* Gage, Ruth (Underwood)
Underwood, Ruth (mother of Moses), 416
Uxbridge, MA, 341

V

Valcour Island, Battle of, 79–82, *81, 82 (map)*, 89
Valentine Hill (NY), 185, 228, 304. *See also* New York (City), New York campaign
Valley Forge, PA, 1777–1778 winter encampment, 111–114, *114*, 116, 128, 134; mentioned as serving at, 19, 41, 108, 177, 180, 219, 233, 246, 254, 262, 273, 282, 323, 347, 359, 361, 397, 400, 414; unit listings at, 490, 491
Van Schaicks Island, 105
Vassall, Elizabeth. *See* Russell, Elizabeth (Vassall)
Vassall, Henry (Col.), 454, 455

Verplanck's Point, NY, 126, 128, 131, 344, 390, 412
VILA, JOHN. *SEE* VILES, JOHN
Viles, Hannah (Warren), 417
VILES, JOHN, 55, **416–417**, 507, 510, 515, 520, 528; unit listings for, 474, 476, 484, 489
Viles, John (father of JOHN), 417
Viles, John (of Waltham), 417
Viles, Mary (Warren), 417
Viles, Suzanna (Bemis), 417
VILEY, JOHN. *SEE* VILES, JOHN
Vilot (slave of Nathan Brown). *See* Middlesex, Vilot
VILS, JOHN. *SEE* VILES, JOHN
von Steuben, Baron (Gen.), 113–114, 448; drilling of troops at Valley Forge, 113–114, *114*; on the importance of the Hudson Highlands, 127, 132; in Virginia, 142, 144; Manual of Arms, 113, 128; portrait of, *113*
Vose, Joseph (Col.), 100, 119, 120, 132, 142, 486, 488, 490, 491, 492, 493, 496, 498, 500, 501, 502, 503, 504; mentioned as unit commander, 245, 246, 253, 273, 335

W

Wabash (Ohio), Battle of the, 363, 530
Wade, Nathaniel (Capt.; Col.), 479, 492, 493; mentioned as unit commander, 307, 324
Walker, Joshua (Capt.), 497; mentioned as unit commander, 203, 212, 242, 280, 409, 419
Walker, William, 274
Walpole, MA, 341, 361
Walpole, NH, 234, 286, 331, 434, 529
Waltham, MA, 13, 423, 527; minute men and militia on April 19th, 13, 267, 416, 474; militia company at Dorchester Heights, 36, 64, 419, 426; mentioned as residence location 186, 217, 248, 249, 261, 267, 298, 299, 321, 358, 359, 366, 371, 377, 383, 385, 386, 417, 427, 437, 438, 440, 460
Walton, John (Capt.), 481, 484, 489; mentioned as unit commander, 79, 392, 417, 423
Ward, Jonathan (Col.; Brig. Gen.), 476; mentioned as unit commander, 178, 280
Wardsboro, VT, 469
Warned out, 16, 215, 298, 332, 346, 366
Warner, Jonathan, 178, 393
Warner, William (Capt.), 486, 488, 490, 491, 495, 497; mentioned as unit commander, 323, 396
Warren, Hannah. *See* Viles, Hannah (Warren)
Warren, Joseph (Dr.), 3
Warren, Mary. *See* Viles, Mary (Warren)
Warren County, NY, 391
Washburn, Abram (Capt.), 479; mentioned as unit commander, 266
Washburn, Jonah (Capt.), 498; mentioned as unit commander, 426
Washington, George (Gen.), 118, 233, 358, 441, 447; at the American camp in Cambridge, *61*; appeal for re-enlistment, 93, 388; commendation of Colonel Brooks's regiment, 84, 86, 88, 228, 229; difficulty maintaining a war footing after Yorktown, 153–154; Life Guard of, 19, 101, 116, 400, 401, 428, 481, 482, 487, 490, 491; problems with General Lee, 91, 116, 118, 120; rallies the troops at Monmouth, *117 (map)*, 118; retreat across New Jersey, 91, *92*. *See also* specific campaigns and battles
Washington, William (Lt. Col.; Col.), *140*, 400
Washington's Crossing of the Delaware. *See* Delaware River, Washington's Crossing of; *See also* Trenton (NJ), Battle of
Watertown, MA, 188, 217, 218, 223, 234, 336, 353, 383, 393, 464; minute men and militia on April 19th, 13, 19, 336, 417, 474
Watertown, NY, 257
Watson, Abraham (Capt.), 494, 497, 499; mentioned as unit commander, 447
Watson, Abraham (Dr.), 336
Waxhaws, SC; massacre of the Virginia militia at, 134
Wayland, MA, 280, 312, 334, 340, 341, 367, 398, 438, 527. *See also* East Sudbury, MA
Wayne, "Mad" Anthony (Gen.), 129, 130, 131
Webb, Charles (Col.), 87, 228
Webb, Joseph (Lt. Col.), 501; mentioned as unit commander, 203, 219, 226, 266, 271, 289, 325, 338, 347, 375, 422, 448
Webster, Daniel, 278, 279
Wellington. *See* Willington
Wells, David (Col.), 486; mentioned as unit commander, 427
Wells, ME, 253, 477
Wellsburg, WV, 389, 530
Wesson. *See also* Weston
Wesson, Abigail (Allen), 29, 191, 418
Wesson, Abigail (Brown), 29, 418, 420
WESSON, ABRAHAM, 110, 114, 154, 155, **417–418**, 508, 510, 516, 519, 522, 528; abatement of taxes during service of, *418*; family relationships of, 29, 191, 368, 415, 420, 434; unit listings for, 488, 503, 504
WESSON, DANIEL, xiii, 100, 132, 409, **419–420**, 506, 509, 516, 519, 525, 527; family relationships of, 22, 29, 244, 252, 421, 422, 424, 425, 426, 430; unit listings for, 483, 485, 489, 496, 497
Wesson, Hannah. *See* Parks, Hannah (Wesson)
Wesson, James (Col.), 495, 498, 500; mentioned as unit commander, 199, 215, 337, 338, 385
WESSON, JOHN, xiii, *11*, 241, **420**, 421, 507, 510, 514, 519, 526; family relationships of, 29, 418; unit listings for, 473, 478
Wesson, John (of Hopkinton), 422
WESSON, JOHN, JR., 8, *11*, 241, 419, **421–422**, 507, 509, 514, 519, 527; family relationships of, 29, 420, 422, 424,

Index   573

425, 426, 430; unit listings for, 473, 478, 485, 496
Wesson, Lydia (Billing), *28*, 425
Wesson, Lydia (Brown), *29*, 420, 525
Wesson, Mary (Hoar), *29*, 420, 421, 422, 424, 426
WESSON, NATHAN, 478. *See also* WESTON, NATHAN
WESSON, RICHARD, 94, 95, **424–425**, 426, 508, 511, 513, 516, 520, 523, 531; unit listings for, 482, 483, 487
WESSON, STEPHEN, JR., **425–426**, 506, 509, 515, 519, 528; family relationships of, *28*, 373, 420, 421, 422, 424, 426; unit listings for, 484, 489
Wesson, Stephen, Jr. (father of STEPHEN JR.), *28*, 425
Wesson, Susanna (Whitney), 426
Wesson, Timothy, *29*, 310, 418, 420
Wesson, Zechariah (father of DANIEL; JOHN, JR.; JONATHAN WESTON; NATHAN WESTON; ZECHARIAH WESTON), *29*, 420, 421, 422, 424, 426
West Hartford, CT, 215
West Indies, 245, 530
West Point, NY, *127 (map)*, 128, 143, 497, 498, 500, 501; Arnold's treason at, 134–136, 142; mentioned as serving or being discharged at, 187, 199, 204, 215, 226, 245, 254, 257, 289, 290, 298, 323, 335, 340, 347, 353, 362, 363, 365, 375, 389, 390, 391, 395, 415, 422, 440, 441, 443, 447, 448, 462; strategic importance of, 128, 129, 132
West Woodstock, CT, 327
Westborough, MA, 217, 281, 390, 451
Westford, MA, 81, 200, 214, 282, 304, 427; minute men and militia on April 19th, 13, 46, 199, 467, 474
Westminster, MA, 293, 459; minute men and militia on April 19th, 13, 292, 475
Westmoreland, NH, 234, 434, 529
Weston. *See also* Wesson
Weston, Abigail (Fox), 363, 424
Weston, Anna (Fox), 424
WESTON, JONATHAN, xiii, 153, **422–423**, 506, 509, 512, 515, 519, 531; family relationships of, *29*, 420, 421, 424, 425, 426, 430; unit listings for, 493, 495, 501
Weston, Lucy. *See* Wheeler, Lucy (Weston)
Weston, MA; ancestral relationship with Lincoln, 21, 162, 264, 265, 393, 444, 451, 453; mentioned as home militia for detachments to Saratoga, 100, 201, 298, 371, 419; militia company at Dorchester Heights, 36, 283, 419; minute men and militia on April 19th, 13, 200, 218, 286, 320, 419, 423, 438, 469, 474, 475
Weston, Mary (Fisk), *28*, 359, 427
Weston, Nancy. *See* Nixon, Nancy (Weston)
Weston, Nancy (Fox). *See* Weston, Anna (Fox)
WESTON, NATHAN, xiii, 419, **423–424**, 507, 509, 515, 519, 526; family relationships of, *29*, 420, 421, 422, 425, 426, 430; unit listings for, 475, 476. *See also* WESSON, NATHAN

WESTON, PETER, 154, 155, 156, **424**, 508, 511, 516, 520, 531; unit listings for, 503, 505
Weston, Polly (Fisk). *See* Weston, Mary (Fisk)
WESTON, ZECHARIAH, xiii, 64, 419, **426–427**, 507, 510, 516, 519, 526; family relationships of, *28*, 358, 359, 420, 421, 422, 424, 425, 430; unit listings for, 479, 484, 490, 495, 496, 498, 505
Weymouth, MA, 399, 405
Wheat, Abigail (Smith), 427, 429
WHEAT, BENJAMIN, **427**, 428–429, 507, 510, 515, 519, 530; family relationships of, 428, 429; unit listings for, 476, 486
Wheat, Betty. *See* Semple, Betty (Wheat)
Wheat, Grace (Brown), 427, 429
Wheat, John, 400, 401, 427, 428–429
WHEAT, JOSEPH, 11, 16, 399, 428, **429–430**, 507, 510, 516, 519, 531; family relationships of, 400, 427, 428; unit listings for, 477, 478, 505
Wheat, Mary. *See* Semple, Mary (Wheat)
Wheat, Mary (Smith), 400, 429
Wheat, Sarah (Wright), 427
Wheedon, George (Col.), 87
Wheeler, Abigail (Flint), 434
WHEELER, ABNER, 79, 429, **430**, 507, 510, 516, 520, 526; family relationships of, *29*, 420, 422, 424, 427; unit listings for, 477, 480
Wheeler, Adam (Capt.), 346, 481, 482, 486, 488, 495; mentioned as unit commander, 272, 294, 326, 400, 435
Wheeler, Asahel (Capt.), 36, 61, 478, 480, 485; mentioned as unit commander at Dorchester Heights, 187, 198, 213, 233, 279, 318, 329, 332, 340, 406, 412, 420, 421, 442; mentioned as unit commander at Saratoga, 295, 402; mentioned as unit commander at Ticonderoga, 74, 175, 189, 198, 215, 216, 257, 309, 316, 318, 319, 322, 370, 373, 407, 410, 412, 442
Wheeler, Benjamin, 430
Wheeler, Cate. *See* Whitney, Cate (Wheeler)
Wheeler, Catherine (Whitney), 436
WHEELER, EDMOND, 15, 54, 158, **431**, 508, 510, 515, 519, 526; family relationships of, 22, *26*, 283, 285, 286, 297, 315, 345, 346, 347, 349, 434; unit listings for, 480, 484
WHEELER, ELISHA, 51, 190, 191, **431–432**, 507, 510, 514, 516, 520, 526; family relationships of, *28*, 458; unit listings for, 474, 480, 505
Wheeler, Elizabeth (Hunt), 430
WHEELER, ENOS, 110, **432–433**, 508, 510, 515, 520, 531; unit listings for, 473, 478, 481, 489
Wheeler, Eunice. *See* Hoar, Eunice (Wheeler)
Wheeler, Eunice (Munroe), *26*, 431
WHEELER, JOHN, **433–434**, 506, 509, 515, 519, 524, 525, 529; family relationships of, *28*, 191, 206, 209, 210, 283, 285, 286, 368, 415, 418, 431; payment for service of, *434*; unit listings for, 488, 489, 498

Wheeler, John (father of JOHN), *28*, 434
Wheeler, Joseph, 433
WHEELER, LEMUEL, 42, 58, 64, 74, 128, 131, 133, 134, 136, 153, **434–436**, 506, 509, 512, 517, 519, 524, 529; unit listings for, 475, 478, 480, 486, 488, 495, 497, 500, 501
Wheeler, Lucy (Weston), *29*, 430
Wheeler, Lydia. *See* Billing, Lydia (Wheeler); Brooks, Lydia (Wheeler); Parks, Lydia (Wheeler)
Wheeler, Lydia (Allen), *28*, 191, 434
Wheeler, Mary. *See* Child, Mary (Wheeler)
Wheeler, Mary (Adams). *See* Wheeler, Polly (Adams)
Wheeler, Mary (Garfield), 433
Wheeler, Mary (Munroe), *27*, 431. *See also* Brooks, Mary (Munroe)
Wheeler, Polly (Adams), *28*, 191, 432
Wheeler, Rachael. *See* Rice, Rachael (Wheeler)
Wheeler, Rebekah (Lee), 430
Wheeler, Ruth. *See* Flint, Ruth (Wheeler)
Wheeler, Ruth (Fox), 433
Wheeler, Salley. *See* Munroe, Salley (Wheeler)
Wheeler, Sally (Read), 434, 525
Wheeler, Sarah. *See* Foster, Sarah (Wheeler); *See* Hartwell, Sarah (Wheeler)
Wheeler, Sarah (Bond), 436
Wheeler, Sarah (Goodenow), 432
Wheeler, Thomas, 431
Wheeler, Timothy, 218
Wheeler, Timothy, 3rd, 436
Wheelock, Ephraim (Col.), 480; mentioned as unit commander, 359
WHELOR, ELISHA. *SEE* WHEELER, ELISHA
Whelor, Elisha (father of ELISHA WHEELER), 432
Whelor, Mary (Loring), 432
WHITAKER, JONAS, **436–437**, 508, 511, 514, 520, 531; unit listings for, 489, 500
Whitcom, John (Col.), 475; mentioned as unit commander, 292
Whitcomb, Asa (Col.), 476; mentioned as unit commander, 179, 180, 323
White Plains, NY, 36, 91, 120, 133; Battle of, 19, 81–84, *83 (map)*, *85 (map)*, 88, 307, 522; blaming the militia, xvi, 85–88, 228–229; mentioned as participants in the Battle of, xvii, 185, 201, 202–203, 210, 228, 229, 248, 256, 272, 273, 282, 294, 304, 321, 326, 331, 338, 371, 388, 393, 398, 400, 402, 409, 423; newspaper report of, 87
White, Ebenezer (Col.), 498; mentioned as unit commander, 426
White, Haffield (Capt.), 502, 503, 504; mentioned as unit commander, 362
White, Hannah. *See* Abbot, Hannah (White)
Whitehall, VT. *See* Skenesborough, VT
Whitehead, Abigail (Harrington), 23, 299, 437, 438, 440
Whitehead, Anna (Bond), 23, 437, 438

WHITEHEAD, DANIEL, **437**, 438, 439, 506, 508, 513, 515, 520, 523, 531; family relationships of, *23*, 298, 439, 440; unit listing for, 487
WHITEHEAD, ELISHA, **437–438**, 439, 506, 508, 513, 515, 520, 523, 531; family relationships of, *23*, 298, 437, 439, 440; unit listings for, 476, 487
Whitehead, Eunice. *See* Hagar, Eunice (Whitehead)
WHITEHEAD, JOHN, 95, **438–440**, 508, 510, 512, 513, 516, 520, 528; deposition of, 55, 188; family relationships of, *23*, 298, 299, 437; unit listings for, 474, 475, 487, 494; wife's debts disavowed by, *439*. *See also* Depositions of April 1775
Whitemarsh, PA, 104, 111
Whitemore, Israel (Capt.), 474, 475; mentioned as unit commander, 423, 438
Whitney, Anna. *See* Cutler, Anna (Whitney)
Whitney, Cate (Wheeler), 441
Whitney, Catherine. *See* Wheeler, Catherine (Whitney)
Whitney, Elizabeth. *See* Parks, Elizabeth (Whitney)
Whitney, Hezekiah (Capt.), 485; mentioned as unit commander, 381
Whitney, Hopestill (Sargent), 442
Whitney, Joshua (Capt.), 218
Whitney, Josiah (Col.), 61, 479, 485, 486, 496, 502, 503, 504; mentioned as unit commander, 180, 199, 218, 271, 279, 295, 299, 317, 342, 364, 370, 376, 381, 391
WHITNEY, LEONARD, **440–441**, 506, 509, 516, 519, 524, 528; family relationships of, 188, 281, 444; unit listings for, 501, 502, 503, 504
Whitney, Lucy. *See* Adams, Lucy (Whitney)
Whitney, Martha (Fletcher), 444
Whitney, Mary (Fay), 441, 444, 445
Whitney, Sarah (Lovejoy), 442
WHITNEY, SILAS, 156, **441–442**, 506, 509, 516, 519, 524, 525, 529; family relationships of, 188, 281, 441, 444; unit listings for, 503, 504
WHITNEY, SOLOMON, 16, 33, 42, 60, 61, 94, 128, 134, 154, **442–444**, 508, 510, 513, 517, 519, 523, 531; family relationships of, 188, 281, 441; payment for care of, *443*; unit listings for, 473, 475, 477, 478, 480, 483, 485, 495, 496, 500, 502, 503, 504
Whitney, Solomon (father of SOLOMON), 444
Whitney, Susanna. *See* Wesson, Susanna (Whitney)
Whittaker, Hanah, 437
WHITTAKER, JONAS. *SEE* WHITAKER, JONAS
Whittaker, Nathaniel, 436

Whittingham, VT, 218, 529
Widow Lydia Wesson. *See* Wesson, Lydia (Billing)
Widow Rebeckah Brown, xv, 250–251, 288. *See also* Brown, Rebeckah (Farrar); Brown, Rebeckah (Adams)
Wilder, Josiah (Capt.), 490; mentioned as unit commander, 365
Wilkes (brigantine), 183, 488
Willard, Abijah (Capt.; Col.), 449, 451, 453
Williams, Abraham (Capt.), 500, 502; mentioned as unit commander, 340
Williams, John (Capt.), 500, 501; mentioned as unit commander, 335
Williams, John Foster (Capt.), 183, 488
Williams, Joseph (Capt.), 499; mentioned as unit commander, 447
Williamsburg, VA, 142, *145 (map)*, 146
WILLINGTON, ELIJAH, xvi, *11*, 60, 108, 181, 182, **445–446**, 507, 510, 512, 515, 519, 528; family relationships of, 447; gravestone of, 445; unit listings for, 473, 475, 486
WILLINGTON, ELISHA, 42, 68, 128, 131, 155, 184, **446–447**, 506, 509, 512, 517, 519, 527; family relationships of, 445; unit listings for, 478, 479, 486, 487, 494, 497, 499, 501, 502, 503, 504
Willington, Jonathan, 445, 446
Willington, Jonathan, Jr., 446, 447
Willington, Lucy (Cutter), 447
Willington, Lydia (Fisk), 446, 447
Willington, Lydia (Gove), 445
Willington, Phoebe (Brown), 445
Willis, Ann. *See* Smith, Ann (Willis)
Willson, Jonathan (Capt.), 382
Winch, Abigail. *See* Child, Abigail (Winch)
Winch, Joseph (Capt.), 421
Winchendon, MA, 324, 371, 379, 381, 426, 528
Windsor, NY. *See* New Windsor, NY
Winnsboro, SC, 137
Winship, Prudence, 448
WINSHIP, RICHARD, 32, 134, 136, **447–448**, 506, 509, 515, 520, 524, 530; unit listings for, 499, 501
Winship, Richard (father of RICHARD), 448
Winship, Salley (Turrell), 448
Winslow, John (Capt.), 262
Winslow, ME, 216
Winter Hill (Somerville, MA); mentioned as camp during Siege of Boston, 189, 269, 326, 329, 346, 366; mentioned as camp for German prisoners, 109, 206, 209, 274, 357, 409, 424, 489
Wiscasset, ME, 235, 528
Woburn, MA, 181, 214, 264, 265, 282, 348, 392, 409, 419–420; minute men and militia on April 19th, 13, *50 (map)*, 51–52,
Wood End (Woburn, MA), 181

Wood, Dorcas (Smith), 448
Wood, Elisabeth, 448
Wood, Ephraim, 407
Wood, Ezra (Col.), 485; mentioned as unit commander, 241
Wood, Isaac (Capt.), 489; mentioned as unit commander, 374
WOOD, JOHN, 154, **448**, 508, 511, 514, 520, 531; unit listing for, 501
Wood, John (father of John of Concord), 448
Wood, John (of Cambridge), 448
Wood, John (of Concord), 448
Wood, Lidia (Hosmer), 448
Wood, Samuel (Capt.), 476; mentioned as unit commander, 280
Woodbridge, Benjamin Ruggles (Col.) 476; mentioned as unit commander, 427
Woodbridge, NJ, 37, 92, 94; mentioned as stationed at, 192, 199, 208, 234, 252, 285, 286, 339, 408, 414, 432, 481
Woodstock, CT, 327, 529
Worcester, Abigail. *See* Farrar, Abigail (Worcester)
Worcester, MA, 43, 109, 184, 390, 452, 464
Worcester, NY, 293, 530
Worcester County, MA, 281; regiments, 299, 381, 398, 465, 496
Worthington, MA, expedition to, xiii, 37, 108–109, 486; mentioned as participant on, 210, 292, 298, 300, 311, 312, 373, 445
Wright, Rebecca. *See* Flint, Rebecca (Wright)
Wright, Sarah. *See* Wheat, Sarah (Wright)
Wright, Silas (Capt.) 500; mentioned as unit commander, 379
Wyman, Abijah (Capt.) 476; mentioned as unit commander, 359
Wyman, Betsey. *See* Brown, Betsey (Wyman)
Wyman, Elizabeth (Gleason). *See* Colburn, Elizabeth (Gleason)
Wyman, Jesse (Capt.) 485; mentioned as unit commander, 180, 199, 271, 317, 342, 370, 376, 391

Y

Yates County, NY, 448
York, ME, 242, 484
York, PA, 42, 115, 307
York Hutts (NY), 363
Yorktown, VA, 19, 42, 153; Siege of, *145 (map)*, 146–152, *147 (map)*, *148 (map)*; Cornwallis's surrender at, 152; weakness of enemy fortifications at, 146, 149, 150
Young, Dinah. *See* Kneeland, Dinah (Young)
Young's House, Battle of, 133, 522